MCSA Managing a Windows® 2000 Network

Exam 70-218

Robert L. Bogue, Gord Barker, Will Schmied, Larry Chambers

Training Guide

MCSA Training Guide (70-218): Managing a Windows 2000 Network

International Standard Book Number: 0-7897-2766-8

Library of Congress Catalog Card Number: 2002104977

Printed in the United States of America

First Printing: July 2002
Second Printing with corrections: November 2002

05 04 03 02 5 4 3 2

Trademarks

All terms mentioned in this book that are known to be trademarks or service marks have been appropriately capitalized. Que Certification cannot attest to the accuracy of this information. Use of a term in this book should not be regarded as affecting the validity of any trademark or service mark.

Warning and Disclaimer

Every effort has been made to make this book as complete and as accurate as possible, but no warranty or fitness is implied. The information provided is on an "as is" basis. The authors and the publisher shall have neither liability nor responsibility to any person or entity with respect to any loss or damages arising from the information contained in this book or from the use of the CD or programs accompanying it.

PUBLISHER
David Culverwell

SR. ACQUISITIONS EDITOR
Jeff Riley

DEVELOPMENT EDITOR
Ginny Bess Munroe

MANAGING EDITOR
Thomas F. Hayes

PROJECT EDITOR
Sheila Schroeder

PRODUCTION EDITOR
Megan Wade

INDEXER
John Sleeva

PROOFREADER
Jody Larsen

TECHNICAL EDITORS
Ray Marky
Thomas Moore

TEAM COORDINATOR
Rosemary Lewis

MEDIA DEVELOPER
Michael Hunter

INTERIOR DESIGNER
Louisa Klucznik

COVER DESIGNER
Charis Ann Santillie

PAGE LAYOUT
Cheryl Lynch

Contents at a Glance

PART V Configuring, Securing, and Troubleshooting Remote Access

PART VI Final Review

PART VII Appendixes

Table of Contents

PART I Creating, Configuring, Managing, Securing, and Troubleshooting File, Print, and Web Resources

PART II Configuring, Administering, and Troubleshooting Network Infrastructure

About the Authors

Robert L. Bogue has contributed to more than 100 book projects, numerous magazine articles, and reviews. His broad experience has led him to networking and integration topics as well as software development. He is currently doing strategic IT consulting. He is MCSE (NT Server 4 & Windows 2000), CNA, A+, Network+, I-Net+, Server+, e-Biz+, IT Project+, and CDIA+ certified. He's a frequent contributor to CertCities.com. When not killing trees or getting certified, he enjoys flying planes and working toward higher ratings on his pilot's license. You can find out more information about Robert by visiting `http://www.thorprojects.com/author`, or you can email him at `Rob.Bogue@ThorProjects.com`.

Gord Barker currently works as a senior consultant for Microsoft Canada Co. in Edmonton, Alberta, Canada. He has worked with Telus to complete the largest rollout of Windows 2000 prior to the product launch. He currently works with large customers to deploy Microsoft technology, including SQL Server, Active Directory domains with Windows 2000 and Windows XP desktops, Content Manager, BizTalk, and Exchange. Gord lives in Edmonton, Alberta, with his wife Christina.

Will Schmied (BSET, MCSE 2000, MCSA) is a freelance technical writer who has contributed works to several of the Internet's largest IT Web sites, including Cramsession.com, ISAServer.org, and MSExchange.org. Will also has contributed to several other projects, including works published by *MCP Magazine*, TechRepublic, and Syngress Publishing. Additionally, Will provides consulting and training on Microsoft products to small and medium-sized organizations in the Norfolk, Virginia, area.

Will holds a bachelor's degree in engineering technology from Old Dominion University and is a member of the American Society of Mechanical Engineers and the National Society of Professional Engineers. He currently resides in Newport News, Virginia, with his family, Allison, Christopher, Austin, Andrea, and Hannah. You can visit Will at `www.soitslikethat.com`.

Larry Chambers (B. Sc., MCSD, MCSE) is a freelance technical writer who has contributed technical expertise as an editor and a writer for various Training Guides. Larry works for a large financial services firm in Winnipeg, Manitoba, Canada, and previous to that worked with a large consulting firm that provided services for Fortune 100 companies throughout Canada. Larry holds a bachelor's degree in computer science and has been providing consulting and technical expertise in the computer industry for 14 years. In his spare time, Larry can be found hanging with his two beautiful children, Courtney and Dylan.

About the Technical Editors

Ray Marky has a B.S. and an M.S. in education from Florida State University. He has taught at the high school and college levels. He is currently the Director of Technology at the Center for Professional Development. Ray is an MCP + I, MCSE, MCSA, MCT, Master Oracle DBA, CCNA, Florida State University Certified Webmaster, and CTT. Ray has also coauthored a book on the Windows 2000 Server exam.

Thomas Moore, MCSE, MCSD, MCDBA, MCT, CTT, has been in the computer industry for more than 20 years. Thomas has a wide variety of expertise in all hardware environments and with most Microsoft Server products. Thomas is comfortable in any programming language environment, achieving his MCSD and MCDBA certifications from their inception. Over the past 12 years, he has been working for a variety of Microsoft partners and currently is a systems analyst for TechServices Web Development Group in Fort Wayne, Indiana, where he has lived for the past three years. Thomas enjoys staying up-to-date, though like most of us, finds it a challenge to keep up with the pace of the industry. Thomas's most recent certification achievements include being one of the first Windows 2000 MCSEs in the world and achieving the same standard as a SQL Server 2000 MCDBA.

Dedication

Rob Bogue

To the universe for keeping me entertained.

Will Schmied

For Allision, because you said I could.

Gord Barker

This book is dedicated to my wife Christina for her unwavering support during this project.

Tell Us What You Think!

As the reader of this book, *you* are our most important critic and commentator. We value your opinion and want to know what we're doing right, what we could do better, what areas you'd like to see us publish in, and any other words of wisdom you're willing to pass our way.

As a Sr. Aquistions Editor for Que Certification, I welcome your comments. You can fax, email, or write me directly to let me know what you did or didn't like about this book—as well as what we can do to make our books stronger.

Please note that I cannot help you with technical problems related to the topic of this book, and that due to the high volume of mail I receive, I might not be able to reply to every message.

When you write, please be sure to include this book's title and authors as well as your name and phone or fax number. I will carefully review your comments and share them with the authors and editors who worked on the book.

Fax: 317-581-4666

Email: `feedback@quepublishing.com`

Mail: Jeff Riley
Que Certification
201 West 103rd Street
Indianapolis, IN 46290 USA

How to Use This Book

Que Certification has made an effort in its Training Guide series to make the information as accessible as possible for the purposes of learning the certification material. Here, you have an opportunity to view the many instructional features that have been incorporated into the books to achieve that goal.

Chapter Opener

Each chapter begins with a set of features designed to allow you to maximize study time for that material.

List of Objectives: Each chapter begins with a list of the objectives as stated by Microsoft.

Objective Explanations: Immediately following each objective is an explanation of it, providing context that defines it more meaningfully in relation to the exam. Because Microsoft can sometimes be vague in its objectives list, the objective explanations are designed to clarify any vagueness by relying on the authors' test-taking experience.

OBJECTIVES

Microsoft provides the following objectives for the "Creating, Configuring, Managing, Securing, and Troubleshooting File, Print, and Web Resources" part of the Managing a Microsoft Windows 2000 Network Environment exam:

Manage data storage. Considerations include file systems, permissions, and quotas.

- **Implement NTFS and FAT file systems.**
- **Enable and configure quotas.**
- **Implement and configure Encrypting File System (EFS).**
- **Configure volumes and basic and dynamic disks.**
- **Configure file and folder permissions.**
- **Manage a domain-based Distributed File System (Dfs).**
- **Manage file and folder compression.**

▸ This objective is necessary to ensure that a person certified in the use of Windows 2000 Server technology understands methods for creating and configuring data resources and managing their use. In addition, knowledge of controlling access to those resources and troubleshooting problems that might prevent access to resources is required.

CHAPTER 1

Data Storage and File Systems

OUTLINE

STUDY STRATEGIES

- Implement the strategies in the Step By Step examples in your own test environment. Additionally, completing the exercises helps commit the ideas to memory. You will find that going through the motions helps to make the concepts in the chapter concrete.
- Configuration and management of resources is a major part of any network administrator's job. As such, you can consider it to be a big point on the exam. Be sure you are familiar with the Disk Management facilities provided in Windows 2000. The majority of functions related to configuring disk storage occurs as a result of some action taken with this tool. Be sure to work with this tool to ensure that you have a firm understanding of what is needed to accomplish the tasks in Windows 2000. This, with the underlying theory provided in this chapter, will help to ensure you are ready for the exam.
- For the previously mentioned points, be sure you go through all the configuration properties and that you understand how the configuration is done. As an example, if the configuration requires you to open the Security tab for an NT File System (NTFS) file resource then ensure you understand which settings are available and what they do so that you can have an understanding of where the configuration takes place. This will help you to visualize the answer when you are sitting for the exam.

Chapter Outline: Learning always gets a boost when you can see both the forest and the trees. To give you a visual image of how the topics in a chapter fit together, you will find a chapter outline at the beginning of each chapter. You will also be able to use this for easy reference when looking for a particular topic.

OUTLINE

Introduction to File Systems and Data Storage **15**

- File Systems 15
  - FAT File System 16
  - FAT32 File System 17
  - NTFS File System 18
- Managing Data Storage 19
  - Overview of Disk Management 19
  - Configuring Storage 22
- Managing File Systems 24
  - NTFS Folder Permissions 24
  - NTFS File Permissions 26
  - Granular NTFS Permissions 27
  - Copying Folders and Files 30
  - Moving Folders and Files 31
  - Configuring File and Folder Permissions 31
  - Enabling and Configuring Quotas 34
  - Managing File and Folder Compression 38
- Encrypting File Systems 39
  - Overview of the Encrypted File System 40
  - Encrypting Folders and Files 41
- The Distributed File System 42
  - Standalone Dfs 44
  - Domain-Based Dfs (Fault-Tolerant Dfs) 49

Chapter Summary **55**

Apply Your Knowledge **57**

STUDY STRATEGIES

- Implement the strategies in the Step By Step examples in your own test environment. Additionally, completing the exercises helps commit the ideas to memory. You will find that going through the motions helps to make the concepts in the chapter concrete.
- Configuration and management of resources is a major part of any network administrator's job. As such, you can consider it to be a big point on the exam. Be sure you are familiar with the Disk Management facilities provided in Windows 2000. The majority of functions related to configuring disk storage occurs as a result of some action taken with this tool. Be sure to work with this tool to ensure that you have a firm understanding of what is needed to accomplish the tasks in Windows 2000. This, with the underlying theory provided in this chapter, will help to ensure you are ready for the exam.
- For the previously mentioned points, be sure you go through all the configuration properties and that you understand how the configuration is done. As an example, if the configuration requires you to open the Security tab for an NT File System (NTFS) file resource then ensure you understand which settings are available and what they do so that you can have an understanding of where the configuration takes place. This will help you to visualize the answer when you are sitting for the exam.

Study Strategies: Each topic presents its own learning challenge. To support you through this, Que Certification has included strategies for how to best approach studying in order to retain the material in the chapter, particularly as it is addressed on the exam.

INSTRUCTIONAL FEATURES WITHIN THE CHAPTER

These books include a large amount and different kinds of information. The many different elements are designed to help you identify information by its purpose and importance to the exam and also to provide you with varied ways to learn the material. You will be able to determine how much attention to devote to certain elements, depending on what your goals are. By becoming familiar with the different presentations of information, you will know what information will be important to you as a test-taker and which information will be important to you as a practitioner.

EXAM TIP

Focused Studying Even though it's important to understand the basics of Active Directory, don't be too concerned about it. This exam expects more applied knowledge than theoretical knowledge out of the candidate. Practice using Active Directory, and you will be ahead of the game.

Exam Tip: Exam Tips appear in the margins to provide specific exam-related advice. Such tips may address what material is covered (or not covered) on the exam, how it is covered, mnemonic devices, or particular quirks of that exam.

Note: Notes appear in the margins and contain various kinds of useful information, such as tips on the technology or administrative practices, historical background on terms and technologies, or side commentary on industry issues.

Objective Coverage Text: In the text before an exam objective is specifically addressed, you will notice the objective is listed to help call your attention to that particular material.

Warning: In using sophisticated information technology, there is always potential for mistakes or even catastrophes that can occur through improper application of the technology. Warnings appear in the margins to alert you to such potential problems.

18 Part I CREATING, CONFIGURING, MANAGING, SECURING, AND TROUBLESHOOTING FILE, PRINT, AND WEB RESOURCES

NOTE

NTFS File Compression and File Encryption These are mutually exclusive because of the way NTFS compression is performed. You can use only one of these options at a time on a file. You activate the encryption or compression attribute by clicking Advanced on a file or folder's Properties dialog box General tab. The compress and encrypt attributes are mutually exclusive—that is, when you

WARNING

NTFS 4.0 Versus NTFS 5.0 The version of NTFS used with Windows NT (NTFS 4.0) is different from the version used with Windows 2000 (NTFS 5.0). These two versions of NTFS are not compatible with one another so you can't dual-boot a Windows NT 4.0 and Windows 2000 system unless your installation of Windows NT 4.0 is running SP 4 or higher. This is very important if you're installing Windows 2000 on a system with an existing installation of Windows NT 4.0 because the installation process automatically upgrades NTFS 4.0 partitions to NTFS 5.0.

- **FAT32 is not supported by all versions of Windows 95 and is not supported by DOS and Windows NT**—So, you need to be careful when deciding to use it. If you plan to dual-boot your system, ensure that all operating systems you are using support FAT32. If they do not, all FAT32 partitions will not be accessible.
- **FAT32 does not support compression, encryption, or disk quotas under Windows 2000.**

NTFS File System

▶ Implement NTFS and FAT file systems.

NTFS is the file system of choice on most systems running Windows 2000.

NTFS offers the following benefits:

- **Support for long filenames**—NTFS supports long filenames up to 255 characters.
- **Preservation of case**—NTFS is not case sensitive, but it does have the capability to preserve case for POSIX compliance. POSIX stands for Portable Operating System Interface Extensions. POSIX is a set of standards begun by the Institute of Electrical and Electronics Engineers (IEEE) for ensuring applications function across different Unix environments.
- **Recoverability**—NTFS is a recoverable file system. It uses transaction logging to automatically log all files and directory updates so that, in the case of a system failure, the operating system can redo failed operations.
- **Security**—NTFS provides folder- and file-level security for protecting files.
- **Compression**—NTFS supports compression of files and folders to help save disk space.
- **Encryption**—NTFS supports file-level encryption. This gives a user the ability to encrypt sensitive files so that no one else can read them.

STEP BY STEP

1.4 Modifying File or Folder Local Permissions

1. Navigate to the object for which you want to change permissions.
2. Right-click the object, and select Properties from the menu that appears.
3. In the Properties dialog box, click the Security tab at the top to see the local permissions that are applied (see Figure 1.1).
4. Click the Add button to get a list of users and groups you can add to this local ACL. After you make those choices, you're returned to this dialog box, where you can then apply the permissions desired for the specific people or groups.
5. To remove a user or group from the DACL, select the user or group in the Name list and click the Remove button.

Permissions that show up as check marks in gray boxes are being inherited from the parent container. If you want to override these settings, remove the current check by selecting the other permission (if it is currently Allow, select Deny); then change it to how you would like it. If you do

FIGURE 1.1
Several security permissions can be applied locally.

Step by Step: Step by Steps are hands-on tutorial instructions that walk you through a particular task or function relevant to the exam objectives.

Figure: To improve readability, the figures have been placed in the margins wherever possible so they do not interrupt the main flow of text.

294 Part II CONFIGURING, ADMINISTERING, AND TROUBLESHOOTING NETWORK INFRASTRUCTURE

NOTE **You Need at Least One Scope** After installing the DHCP service, you must define at least one scope on the server. Otherwise, the service will not respond to DHCP requests.

reservations for particular addresses that you want DHCP to hand out but that need to remain static, such as a server.

Understanding DHCP Superscopes

The next type of scope was introduced to the Windows NT product family with Service Pack 2 for Windows NT 4. A *superscope* allows you to support a *supernetted* or *multinetted* network with a Windows 2000 DHCP Server.

A *supernetted* network is a network that has multiple network addresses or subnets running on the same segment (normally there is only one subnet to a segment). You commonly see this configuration in network environments with more than 254 hosts on a subnet or in an environment in which certain hosts need to be isolated from the rest of the logical network for security or routing reasons.

Superscopes will support a local multinet or a multinet that is located across a router configured to use the BOOTP Forwarder service. We discuss creating a superscope later in the chapter in the "Creating a Superscope" section.

IN THE FIELD

WHEN TO USE SUPERNETTING

Visualize a large company that occupies five floors in a building. On each of these floors are 300–500 users, all crammed in a gigantic cube farm and all on the same physical network. Traditional network design would have a routed backbone running between the floors, and each floor would be its own IP network. But there's one problem: There are too many users on these floors to be handled by a single Class C subnet. What are the alternatives?

You could place a router somewhere on each of the floors to further segment the network. This is an expensive and support-intensive solution and is generally considered to be impractical.

You could address using Class B addresses. However, that is generally very wasteful of IP addresses, and you would probably have to reconfigure your address scheme to use the private Class B Network ID.

Your other option is to place multiple IP networks on the single routed segment. In other words, create a supernet. This capability

In the Field Sidebar: These more extensive discussions cover material that perhaps is not as directly relevant to the exam, but which is useful as reference material or in everyday practice. In the Field may also provide useful background or contextual information necessary for understanding the larger topic under consideration.

CASE STUDIES

Case Studies are presented throughout the book to provide you with another, more conceptual opportunity to apply the knowledge you are developing. They also reflect the "real-world" experiences of the authors in ways that prepare you not only for the exam but for actual network administration as well. In each Case Study, you will find similar elements: a description of a Scenario, the Essence of the Case, and an extended Analysis section.

CASE STUDY: IMPLEMENTING DHCP IN A COMPLEX ENVIRONMENT

ESSENCE OF THE CASE

The essence of the case is as follows:

- Your company is about to migrate to a pure Windows 2000 environment.
- Your company has three networks, two with users and one as a backbone. The Sales network has approximately 400 users; the Engineering network has 75 users.
- The three networks are connected by two routers: router A and router B.
- The Sales network has plenty of addresses because of the multinetted network. The Engineering network does not have enough addresses for its network, but the engineers are able to work because they work in shifts.

SCENARIO

You are the network administrator for NR Widgets Inc., a computer manufacturing company. NR Widgets Inc., is just about to migrate to a pure Windows 2000 environment. You have two user networks—Sales and Engineering—and a corporate backbone network. The Sales network has more than 400 users and is multinetted to provide an adequate number of addresses for everyone. The Engineering network has only 75 users, but the network also contains a number of printers, plotters, and test equipment, so only 40 addresses are available for the users. The users work three shifts in engineering, with 25 engineers working each shift.

Today, all the hosts use static addresses, which works okay for the Sales network, but it means that to avoid IP address resolution issues, the engineers have to be careful about which computers are left connected to the network.

Essence of the Case: A bulleted list of the key problems or issues that need to be addressed in the Scenario.

Scenario: A few paragraphs describing a situation that professional practitioners in the field might face. A Scenario will deal with an issue relating to the objectives covered in the chapter, and it includes the kinds of details that make a difference.

Analysis: This is a lengthy description of the best way to handle the problems listed in the Essence of the Case. In this section, you might find a table summarizing the solutions, a worded example, or both.

CASE STUDY: IMPLEMENTING DHCP IN A COMPLEX ENVIRONMENT

Yesterday your manager suggested, "While you're migrating to Windows 2000, why don't you fix the IP address problems on the network?"

Keeping in mind that the boss's "suggestions" usually mean "Have it done by the end of the week," what should you do?

ANALYSIS

This situation provides an excellent opportunity to deploy the Windows 2000 DHCP service as part of the Windows 2000 rollout. To make it work, you need to be sure you do the following:

- Allocate the server resources to support at least one DHCP server. To avoid as much traffic traversing the router as possible, you should plan on placing the server on the network that will be generating the most DHCP requests. Because 400 users are on the Sales network, at first glance you might think that is where all the requests will be coming from. Think again. Because there are plenty of addresses for the Sales network, you can configure exceptionally long lease times, so the number of requests
- After you have identified the server and placed it on the network, you will need to install and configure DHCP. After the service is installed, you must authorize the server in Active Directory.
- When you create your scopes, you should create a single scope for the Engineering network and a superscope for the Sales network. The superscope enables you to combine multiple scopes (the Sales network has three network addresses) for easier management. The lease for each of the scopes within the superscope should be at least 30 days to ensure that a limited amount of lease traffic traverses the routers. The lease for the Engineering network should be 8 hours so that addresses are available for the incoming shift as the previous shift leaves.
- Finally, you need to ensure that the BOOTP Forwarder service is running on the routers and is configured to point to the appropriate DHCP server for forwarding DHCP traffic.

326 Part II CONFIGURING, ADMINISTERING, AND TROUBLESHOOTING NETWORK INFRASTRUCTURE

CHAPTER SUMMARY

KEY TERMS

- BOOTP protocol
- Client reservation
- DHCP client
- DHCP server
- Domain Name System (DNS)
- Dynamic Host Control Protocol (DHCP)

In this chapter, we discussed the key components of using a Windows 2000 DHCP server in a Windows 2000 environment. We first discussed what DHCP was and where it came from. We covered the various types of scopes in detail and then went through the steps of installing DHCP, creating the first scope, and then authorizing the server in Active Directory. Combined, these give you a working DHCP server.

We also discussed creating superscopes and multicast scopes, integrating DNS and DHCP, and the various methods for monitoring and managing DHCP.

Key Terms: A list of key terms appears at the end of each chapter. These are terms that you should be sure you know and are comfortable defining and understanding when you go in to take the exam.

Chapter Summary: Before the Apply Your Knowledge section, you will find a chapter summary that wraps up the chapter and reviews what you should have learned.

EXTENSIVE REVIEW AND SELF-TEST OPTIONS

At the end of each chapter, along with some summary elements, you will find a section called "Apply Your Knowledge" that gives you several different methods with which to test your understanding of the material and review what you have learned.

218 Part I CREATING, CONFIGURING, MANAGING, SECURING, AND TROUBLESHOOTING FILE, PRINT, AND WEB RESOURCES

APPLY YOUR KNOWLEDGE

Exercises

3.1 Creating a New Web Site

This exercise demonstrates how to create a new Web site that will be used for the administrator only. The site will be established on a private port and will require authentication.

Estimated Time: 10 minutes

1. From the Start menu select Settings, Control Panel.
2. Double-click Administrative Tools and Internet Services Manager.
3. Click the plus sign to the left of the computer name to display a listing of Web and FTP sites.
4. Right-click the computer and select New, Web Site from the context menu.
5. Click the Next button to move past the introductory screen.
6. Enter a description for the Web site. In this case, enter **Administrators Private Web**.
7. Click the Next button to move to the IP Address and Port Settings dialog box.
8. Select the TCP port of 8081 for the Web server.
9. Click the Next button to move to the home directory step.
10. Select the path that will be the home directory for the Web site. In this case, use `C:\inetpub`.
11. Uncheck Allow Anonymous Access to This Web Site.
12. Click the Next button to select the permissions.
13. Click the Next button, and then click the Finish button to complete the wizard.
14. Close the Internet Information Services window.

Review Questions

1. What types of sites will IIS allow you to serve?
2. Why would you use a virtual server?
3. What does a virtual directory do?
4. What is a proxy server?

Exam Questions

1. You've just created a new Web site, but when you completed the wizard the site is stopped. What is the most likely cause of this?

   A. The World Wide Web service is stopped.

   B. The IIS Admin service is stopped.

   C. The site you created is not uniquely identifiable.

   D. You selected an invalid TCP port.

2. You're accessing a URL, `http://serverA/MyMusic`, from a browser. You go to the site to find that the Web server's home directory is `C:\WebHome`. No corresponding folder called `C:\WebHome\MyMusic` exists. What is the most likely cause?

   A. The server is looking at the client's `C:\WebHome` directory.

   B. A virtual directory called `MyMusic` is defined.

Exercises: These activities provide an opportunity for you to master specific hands-on tasks. Our goal is to increase your proficiency with the product or technology. You must be able to conduct these tasks in order to pass the exam.

Review Questions: These open-ended, short-answer questions allow you to quickly assess your comprehension of what you just read in the chapter. Instead of asking you to choose from a list of options, these questions require you to state the correct answers in your own words. Although you will not experience these kinds of questions on the exam, these questions will indeed test your level of comprehension of key concepts.

Exam Questions: These questions reflect the kinds of multiple-choice questions that appear on the Microsoft exams. Use them to become familiar with the exam question formats and to help you determine what you know and what you need to review or study more.

APPLY YOUR KNOWLEDGE

Exercises

3.1 Creating a New Web Site

This exercise demonstrates how to create a new Web site that will be used for the administrator only. The site will be established on a private port and will require authentication.

Estimated Time: 10 minutes

1. From the Start menu select Settings, Control Panel.
2. Double-click Administrative Tools and Internet Services Manager.
3. Click the plus sign to the left of the computer name to display a listing of Web and FTP sites.
4. Right-click the computer and select New, Web Site from the context menu.
5. Click the Next button to move past the introductory screen.
6. Enter a description for the Web site. In this case, enter `Administrators Private Web`.
7. Click the Next button to move to the IP Address and Port Settings dialog box.
8. Select the TCP port of 8081 for the Web server.
9. Click the Next button to move to the home directory step.
10. Select the path that will be the home directory for the Web site. In this case, use `C:\inetpub`.
11. Uncheck Allow Anonymous Access to This Web Site.
12. Click the Next button to select the permissions.

Answers to Review Questions

1. IIS will serve FTP and Web (HTTP) sites. You can create as many sites as you want, but all of them running at any given moment must be capable of being uniquely identified.
2. Virtual servers enable you to service multiple FTP or Web sites from one physical server. This is important and useful when you maintain several Web sites that don't require the resources of a server on their own. Virtual servers enable multiple Web or FTP sites to share the resources of one piece of hardware.
3. Virtual directories enable you to present a hierarchy on the sites being served, which doesn't exist on disk. This is useful when large amounts of information are serviced from one Web site.
4. A proxy server is a device that allows Internet connectivity by performing operations as an intermediary between the internal clients and external Internet host. Proxy servers allow a much broader range of audit and control facilities than a firewall in addition to their caching benefits. They are often used by corporations that need to control or monitor the Internet access in the organization.

Answers to Exam Questions

1. **C.** Each site requires a set of IP address, TCP port, and host header parameters to enable it to be uniquely identified when a request comes in. If another Web site has the same parameters as the Web site being created, the site is created but left in the stopped state.

Answers and Explanations: For each of the Review and Exam questions, you will find thorough explanations located at the end of the section.

Suggested Readings and Resources: The very last element in every chapter is a list of additional resources you can use if you want to go above and beyond certification-level material or if you need to spend more time on a particular subject that you are having trouble understanding.

APPLY YOUR KNOWLEDGE

Suggested Readings and Resources

1. "Default Access Control Settings" on Microsoft's Web site at `http://www.microsoft.com/windows2000/library/planning/security/secdefs.asp`.
2. *Microsoft Windows 2000 Professional Resource Kit*. Microsoft Press, 2000:
   - Chapter 7: "Introduction to Configuration and Management"
   - Chapter 13: "Security"
3. *Microsoft Windows 2000 Server Resource Kit: Microsoft Windows 2000 Server Deployment Planning Guide*. Microsoft Press, 2000:
   - Chapter 11: "Planning Distributed Security"
4. *Microsoft Windows 2000 Server Resource Kit: Microsoft Windows 2000 Server Distributed Systems Guide*. Microsoft Press, 2000:
   - Chapter 22: "Group Policy"
5. "Securing Windows 2000 Network Resources" on Microsoft's Web site at `http://www.microsoft.com/windows2000/techinfo/planning/incremental/securenetworkresources.asp`.
6. "Step-by-Step Guide to Configuring Enterprise Security Policies" on Microsoft's Web site at `http://www.microsoft.com/windows2000/techinfo/planning/security/entsecsteps.asp`.
7. *Windows 2000 Server Administrators Companion*, Microsoft Press, 2000:
   - Chapter 12, "Managing Active Directory"
   - Chapter 13, "Understanding Network Addresses"

Introduction

MCSA Training Guide (70-218): Managing a Microsoft Windows 2000 Network Environment is designed for technicians, system administrators, or other information technology professionals with the goal of certification as a Microsoft Certified System Administrator (MCSA) or Microsoft Certified Systems Engineer (MCSE). It covers the Managing a Microsoft Windows 2000 Network Environment (70-218) exam. According to Microsoft, this exam measures your ability to administer, support, and troubleshoot information systems that incorporate Microsoft Windows 2000.

This book is your one-stop shop. Everything you need to know to pass the exam is in here. You do not have to take a class in addition to buying this book to pass the exam. However, depending on your personal study habits or learning style, you might benefit from buying this book *and* taking a class.

Que Certification Training Guides are meticulously crafted to give you the best possible learning experience for the particular characteristics of the technology covered and the actual certification exam. The instructional design implemented in the Training Guides reflects the task- and experience-based nature of Microsoft certification exams. The Training Guides provide you with the factual knowledge base you need for the exams but then take it to the next level with Case Studies, Step-by-Steps, Exercises, and Exam Questions that require you to engage in the analytic thinking necessary to successfully answer the scenario-based questions found in the Microsoft exams.

Microsoft assumes that the typical candidate for this exam will have a minimum of six months experience administering and supporting Windows 2000 server and client operating systems that use Active Directory directory services.

How This Book Helps You

This book takes you on a self-guided tour of all the areas covered by the Managing a Microsoft Windows 2000 Network Environment exam and teaches you the specific skills you'll need to achieve your MCSA or MCSE certification. You'll also find helpful hints, tips, real-world examples, and exercises, as well as references to additional study materials. Specifically, this book is set up to help you in the following ways:

- **Organization**—The book is organized by individual exam objectives. Every objective you need to know for the Managing a Microsoft Windows 2000 Network Environment exam is covered in this book. We have attempted to present the objectives in an order that is as close as possible to that listed by Microsoft. However, we have not hesitated to reorganize them where needed to make the material as easy as possible for you to learn. We have also attempted to make the information accessible in the following ways:
    - The full list of exam units and objectives is included in this introduction.
    - Each chapter begins with a list of the objectives to be covered.
    - Each chapter also begins with an outline that provides you with an overview of the material and the page numbers where particular topics can be found.
    - The objectives are repeated where the material most directly relevant to it is covered (unless the whole chapter addresses a single objective).

- **Instructional features**—This book has been designed to provide you with multiple ways to learn and reinforce the exam material. Following are some of the helpful methods:
  - **Objective Explanations**—As mentioned previously, each chapter begins with a list of the objectives covered in the chapter. In addition, immediately following each objective is an explanation in a context that defines it more meaningfully.
  - **Study Strategies**—The beginning of the chapter also includes strategies for approaching the studying and retaining of the material in the chapter, particularly as it is addressed on the exam but also in ways that will benefit you on the job.
  - **Exam Tips**—Exam tips appear in the margins to provide specific exam-related advice. Such tips may address what material is covered (or not covered) on the exam, how it is covered, mnemonic devices, or particular quirks of that exam.
  - **Summaries**—Crucial information is summarized at various points in the book in lists or tables. Each chapter ends with a summary as well.
  - **Key Terms**—A list of key terms appears at the end of each chapter.
  - **Notes**—These appear in the margins and contain various types of useful or practical information, such as tips on technology or administrative practices, historical background on terms and technologies, or side commentary on industry issues.
  - **Warnings**—When using sophisticated information technology, there is always the potential for mistakes or even catastrophes that occur because of improper application of the technology. Warnings appear in the margins to alert you to such potential problems.
  - **In the Field**—These more extensive discussions cover material that might not be directly relevant to the exam but which is useful as reference material or in everyday practice. In the Field sidebars also can provide useful background or contextual information necessary for understanding the larger topic under consideration.
  - **Case Studies**—Each chapter concludes with a Case Study. The cases are meant to help you understand the practical applications of the information covered in the chapter. They also help prepare you for the task-based analysis that is required when answering the Microsoft exam questions.
  - **Step By Steps**—These are hands-on, tutorial instructions that walk you through a particular task or function relevant to the exam objectives.
  - **Exercises**—Found at the end of the chapters in the "Apply Your Knowledge" section, exercises are performance-based opportunities for you to learn and assess your knowledge.
- **Extensive practice test options**—The book provides numerous opportunities for you to assess your knowledge and practice for the exam. The practice options include the following:
  - **Review Questions**—These open-ended questions appear in the "Apply Your Knowledge" section at the end of each chapter. They allow you to quickly assess your comprehension of what you just read in the chapter. Answers to the questions are provided later in a separate section titled "Answers to Review Questions."

- **Exam Questions**—These questions also appear in the "Apply Your Knowledge" section. Use them to help you determine what you know and what you need to review or study further. Answers and explanations for these are provided in a separate section titled "Answers to Exam Questions."
- **Practice Exam**—A Practice Exam is included in the "Final Review" section. The "Final Review" section and the Practice Exam are discussed in the following bullet.
- **PrepLogic**—The special Training Guide version of the PrepLogic software included on the CD-ROM provides further practice questions.

NOTE

For a description of the *PrepLogic, Preview Edition* software, please see Appendix C, "Using the *PrepLogic, Preview Edition* Software."

- **Final Review**—This part of the book provides you with three valuable tools for preparing for the exam:
  - **Fast Facts**—This condensed version of the information contained in the book will prove extremely useful for last-minute review.
  - **Study and Exam Tips**—Read this section early on to help you develop study strategies. It also provides you with valuable exam-day tips and information on exam/question formats such as adaptive tests and case study-based questions.
  - **Practice Exam**—A practice test is included. Questions are written in styles similar to those used on the actual exam. Use it to assess your readiness for the real thing. Use the extensive answer explanations to improve your retention and understanding of the material.

The book includes several other features, such as a section titled "Suggested Readings and Resources" at the end of each chapter that directs you toward additional information that can aid you in your exam preparation or your actual work. There are valuable appendices as well, including a glossary (Appendix D), an overview of the Microsoft certification program (Appendix A), and a description of what is on the CD-ROM (Appendix B).

For more information about the exam or the certification process, in North America contact Microsoft at:

Microsoft Education: 800-636-7544

`http://www.microsoft.com/traincert/`

`MCPHelp@microsoft.com`

What the Managing a Microsoft Windows 2000 Network Environment (70-218) Exam Covers

The Managing a Microsoft Windows 2000 Network Environment (70-218) exam covers the Windows 2000 topics represented by the conceptual groupings or units of the test objectives. The objectives reflect job skills in the following areas.

- Creating, Configuring, Managing, Securing, and Troubleshooting File, Print, and Web Resources
- Configuring, Administering, and Troubleshooting the Network Infrastructure
- Managing, Securing, and Troubleshooting Servers and Client Computers

- Configuring, Managing, Securing, and Troubleshooting Active Directory Organizational Units and Group Policy
- Configuring, Securing, and Troubleshooting Remote Access

Before taking the exam, you should be proficient in the job skills represented by the following units, objectives, and subobjectives.

Creating, Configuring, Managing, Securing, and Troubleshooting File, Print, and Web Resources

Publish resources in Active Directory. Types of resources include printers and shared folders:

- Perform a search in Active Directory Users and Computers.
- Configure a printer object.

Manage data storage. Considerations include file systems, permissions, and quotas:

- Implement NTFS and FAT file systems.
- Enable and configure quotas.
- Implement and configure Encrypting File System (EFS).
- Configure volumes and basic and dynamic disks.
- Configure file and folder permissions.
- Manage a domain-based distributed file system (DFS).
- Manage file and folder compression.

Create shared resources and configure access rights. Shared resources include printers, shared folders, and Web folders:

- Share folders and enable Web sharing.
- Configure shared folder permissions.
- Create and manage shared printers.
- Configure shared printer permissions:

Configure and troubleshoot Internet Information Services (IIS).

- Configure virtual directories and virtual servers.
- Troubleshoot Internet browsing from client computers.
- Troubleshoot intranet browsing from client computers.
- Configure authentication and SSL for Web sites.
- Configure FTP services.
- Configure access permissions for intranet Web servers.

Monitor and manage network security. Actions include auditing and detecting security breaches:

- Configure user-account lockout settings.
- Configure user-account password length, history, age, and complexity.
- Configure Group Policy to run logon scripts.
- Link Group Policy objects.
- Enable and configure auditing.
- Monitor security by using the system security log file.

Configuring, Administering, and Troubleshooting the Network Infrastructure

Troubleshoot routing. Diagnostic utilities include the `tracert` command, the `ping` command, and the `ipconfig` command:

- Validate local computer configuration by using the `ipconfig`, `arp`, and `route` commands.
- Validate network connectivity by using the `tracert`, `ping`, and `pathping` commands.

Configure and troubleshoot TCP/IP on servers and client computers. Considerations include subnet masks, default gateways, network IDs, and broadcast addresses:

- Configure client computer TCP/IP properties.
- Validate client computer network configuration by using the `winipcfg`, `ipconfig`, and `arp` commands.
- Validate client computer network connectivity by using the `ping` command.

Configure, administer, and troubleshoot DHCP on servers and client computers:

- Detect unauthorized DHCP servers on a network.
- Configure authorization of DHCP servers.
- Configure client computers to use dynamic IP addressing.
- Configure DHCP server properties.
- Create and configure a DHCP scope.

Configure, administer, and troubleshoot DNS:

- Configure DNS server properties.
- Manage DNS database records such as CNAME, A, and PTR.
- Create and configure DNS zones.

Troubleshoot name resolution on client computers. Considerations include WINS, DNS, NetBIOS, the Hosts file, and the Lmhosts file:

- Configure client computer name resolution properties.
- Troubleshoot name resolution problems by using the `nbtstat`, `ipconfig`, `nslookup`, and `netdiag` commands.
- Create and configure a Hosts file for troubleshooting name resolution problems.
- Create and configure an Lmhosts file for troubleshooting name resolution problems.

Managing, Securing, and Troubleshooting Servers and Client Computers

Install and configure server and client computer hardware:

- Verify hardware compatibility by using the qualifier tools.
- Configure driver signing options.
- Verify digital signatures on existing driver files.
- Configure operating system support for legacy hardware devices.

Troubleshoot starting servers and client computers. Tools and methodologies include Safe Mode, Recovery Console, and parallel installations:

- Interpret the startup log file.
- Repair an operating system by using the Recovery Console.

- Recover data from a hard disk in the event that the operating system will not start.
- Restore an operating system and data from a backup.

Monitor and troubleshoot server health and performance. Tools include system Monitor, Event Viewer, and Task Manager:

- Monitor and interpret real-time performance by using System Monitor and Task Manager.
- Configure and manage System Monitor alerts and logging.
- Diagnose server health problems by using Event Viewer.
- Identify and disable unnecessary operating system services.

Install and manage Windows 2000 updates. Updates include service packs, hot fixes, and security hot fixes:

- Update an installation source by using slipstreaming.
- Apply and reapply service packs and hotfixes.
- Verify service pack and hotfix installation.
- Remove service packs and hotfixes.

Configuring, Managing, Securing, and Troubleshooting Active Directory Organizational Units and Group Policy

Create, manage, and troubleshoot User and Group objects in Active Directory:

- Create and configure user and computer accounts for new and existing users.
- Troubleshoot groups. Considerations include nesting, scope, and type.
- Configure a user account by using Active Directory Users and Computers. Settings include passwords and assigning groups.
- Perform a search for objects in Active Directory.
- Use templates to create user accounts.
- Reset an existing computer account.

Manage object and container permissions:

- Use the Delegation of Control Wizard to configure inherited and explicit permissions.
- Configure and troubleshoot object permissions by using object access control lists (ACLs).

Diagnose Active Directory replication problems:

- Diagnose problems related to WAN link connectivity.
- Diagnose problems involving replication latency. Problems include duplicate objects and the LostandFound container.

Deploy software using Group Policy. Types of software include user applications, antivirus software, line-of-business applications, and software updates:

- Use Windows Installer to deploy Windows Installer packages.
- Deploy updates to installed software including antivirus updates.
- Configure Group Policy to assign and publish applications.

Troubleshoot end-user Group Policy:

- Troubleshoot Group Policy problems involving precedence, inheritance, filtering, and the No Override option.
- Manually refresh Group Policy.

Implement and manage security policies by using Group Policy:

- Use security templates to implement security policies.
- Analyze the security configuration of a computer by using the `secedit` command and Security Configuration and Analysis.
- Modify domain security policy to comply with corporate standards.

Configuring, Securing, and Troubleshooting Remote Access

Configure and troubleshoot remote access and virtual private network (VPN) connections:

- Configure and troubleshoot client-to-server PPTP and L2TP connections.
- Manage existing server-to-server PPTP and L2TP connections.
- Configure and verify the security of a VPN connection.
- Configure client computer remote access properties.
- Configure remote access name resolution and IP address allocation.

Troubleshoot a remote access policy:

- Diagnose problems with remote access policy priority.
- Diagnose remote access policy problems caused by user account group membership and nested groups.
- Create and configure remote access policies and profiles.
- Select appropriate encryption and authentication protocols.

Implement and troubleshoot Terminal Services for remote access:

- Configure Terminal Services for remote administration or application server mode.
- Configure Terminal Services for local resource mapping.
- Configure Terminal Services for user properties.

Configure and troubleshoot Network Address Translation (NAT) and Internet Connection Sharing:

- Configure Routing and Remote Access to perform NAT.
- Troubleshoot Internet Connection Sharing problems by using the `ipconfig` and `ping` commands.

HARDWARE AND SOFTWARE YOU'LL NEED

As a self-paced study guide, *MCSA Training Guide (70-218): Managing a Microsoft Windows 2000 Network Environment* is meant to help you understand concepts that must be refined through hands-on experience. To make the most of your studying, you need to have as much background on and experience with Windows 2000 environments as possible. The best way to do this is to combine studying with work on Windows 2000 networks. This section gives you a description of the minimum computer requirements you need to enjoy a solid practice environment.

You will find that many of the concepts presented in this book explore the use of Windows 2000 within a Microsoft networked environment. To fully practice some of the exam objectives, you will need access to two (or more) computers networked together. You will also find that access to the Windows server products is beneficial. The following presents a detailed list of hardware and software requirements:

- Windows 2000 or Windows XP Professional
- Windows 2000 Server
- A server and a workstation computer on the Microsoft Hardware Compatibility List
- Pentium 233MHz (or better) (Pentium 300 recommended)
- A minimum 1.5GB or free disk space
- Super VGA (800×600) or higher resolution video adapter and monitor
- Mouse or equivalent pointing device
- CD-ROM or DVD drive
- Network interface card (NIC) or modem connection to the Internet
- Presence of an existing network, or use of a two-port (or more) miniport hub to create a test network
- 128MB of RAM or higher (64MB minimum)

Obtaining access to the necessary computer hardware and software is easier in a corporate business environment. However, allocating enough time within the busy workday to complete a self-study program can be difficult. Most of your study time will occur after normal working hours, away from the everyday interruptions and pressures of your regular job.

ADVICE ON TAKING THE EXAM

More extensive tips are found in the Final Review section titled "Study and Exam Prep Tips," but keep this advice in mind as you study:

- **Read all the material**—Microsoft has been known to include material not expressly specified in the objectives. This book has included additional information not reflected in the objectives in an effort to give you the best possible preparation for the examination—and for the real-world experiences to come.
- **Do the Step By Steps and complete the exercises in each chapter**—They will help you gain experience using the specified methodology or approach. As noted previously, all Microsoft exams are task- and experienced-based and require you to have experience actually performing the tasks on which you will be tested.
- **Use the questions to assess your knowledge**—Don't just read the chapter content; use the review and exam questions to find out what you know and what you don't. If you are struggling at all, study some more, review, and then assess your knowledge again.
- **Review the exam objectives**—Develop your own questions and examples for each topic listed. If you can develop and answer several questions for each topic, you should not find it difficult to pass the exam.

Remember, the primary object is not to pass the exam—it is to understand the material. After you understand the material, passing the exam should be simple. Knowledge is a pyramid; to build upward, you need a solid foundation. This book and the Microsoft Certified Professional programs are designed to ensure that you have that solid foundation.

Good luck!

NOTE

Exam-Taking Advice Although this book is designed to prepare you to take and pass the Managing a Microsoft Windows 2000 Network Environment certification exam, there are no guarantees. Read this book, work through the questions and exercises, and when you feel confident take the Practice Exam and additional exams using the *PrepLogic, Preview Edition* test software. This should tell you whether you are ready for the real thing.

When taking the actual certification exam, be sure you answer all the questions before your time limit expires. Do not spend too much time on any one question. If you are unsure, answer it as best as you can; then mark it for review when you have finished the rest of the questions. However, this advice will not apply if you are taking an adaptive exam. In that case, take your time on each question. There is no opportunity to go back to a question.

QUE CERTIFICATION PUBLISHING

The staff of Que Certification Publishing is committed to bringing you the very best in computer reference material. Each Que Certification book is the result of months of work by authors and staff who research and refine the information contained within its covers.

As part of this commitment to you, the reader, Que Certification Publishing invites your input. Please let us know if you enjoy this book, if you have trouble with the information or examples presented, or if you have a suggestion for the next edition.

Please note, however, that Que Certification Publishing staff cannot serve as a technical resource during your preparation for the Microsoft certification exams or for questions about software- or hardware-related problems. Please refer instead to the documentation that accompanies the Microsoft products or to the applications' Help systems.

If you have a question or comment about any Que Certification Publishing book, there are several ways to contact Que Certification Publishing. We will respond to as many readers as we can. Your name, address, or phone number will never become part of a mailing list or be used for any purpose other than to help us continue to bring you the best books possible. You can write to us at the following address:

Que Certification Publishing
Attn: Executive Editor
201 W. 103rd Street
Indianapolis, IN 46290

If you prefer, you can fax Que Certification Publishing at 317-817-7448.

You also can send email to Que Certification Publishing at the following Internet address:

`certification@quepublishing.com`

Que Certification Publishing is an imprint of Pearson Education. To obtain a catalog or information, contact us at `nrmedia@newriders.com`. To purchase a `certification@quepublishing.com` book, call 800-428-5331.

Thank you for selecting *MCSA Training Guide (70-218): Managing a Microsoft Windows 2000 Network Environment.*

PART I

Creating, Configuring, Managing, Securing, and Troubleshooting File, Print, and Web Resources

CHAPTER 1

Data Storage and File Systems

OBJECTIVES

Microsoft provides the following objectives for the "Creating, Configuring, Managing, Securing, and Troubleshooting File, Print, and Web Resources" part of the Managing a Microsoft Windows 2000 Network Environment exam:

Manage data storage. Considerations include file systems, permissions, and quotas.

- **Implement NTFS and FAT file systems.**
- **Enable and configure quotas.**
- **Implement and configure Encrypting File System (EFS).**
- **Configure volumes and basic and dynamic disks.**
- **Configure file and folder permissions.**
- **Manage a domain-based Distributed File System (Dfs).**
- **Manage file and folder compression.**

▶ This objective is necessary to ensure that a person certified in the use of Windows 2000 Server technology understands methods for creating and configuring data resources and managing their use. In addition, knowledge of controlling access to those resources and troubleshooting problems that might prevent access to resources is required.

OUTLINE

STUDY STRATEGIES

- Implement the strategies in the Step By Step examples in your own test environment. Additionally, completing the exercises helps commit the ideas to memory. You will find that going through the motions helps to make the concepts in the chapter concrete.
- Configuration and management of resources is a major part of any network administrator's job. As such, you can consider it to be a big point on the exam. Be sure you are familiar with the Disk Management facilities provided in Windows 2000. The majority of functions related to configuring disk storage occurs as a result of some action taken with this tool. Be sure to work with this tool to ensure that you have a firm understanding of what is needed to accomplish the tasks in Windows 2000. This, with the underlying theory provided in this chapter, will help to ensure you are ready for the exam.
- For the previously mentioned points, be sure you go through all the configuration properties and that you understand how the configuration is done. As an example, if the configuration requires you to open the Security tab for an NT File System (NTFS) file resource then ensure you understand which settings are available and what they do so that you can have an understanding of where the configuration takes place. This will help you to visualize the answer when you are sitting for the exam.

INTRODUCTION TO FILE SYSTEMS AND DATA STORAGE

A significant part of managing a Windows 2000 network environment involves the management of disk storage. It is important for the administrator to understand how to create, configure, manage, and secure disk storage systems.

Windows 2000 can use several types of file systems to store information. Each of these file systems has different capabilities that need to be understood so that relevant decisions can be made about which file system to use for specific circumstances.

After you have decided on the type of file system that best suits your needs, you need to know how to configure data storage to allow the file system to be implemented on top of it to provide services to end users. This is accomplished by using disk management utilities to configure the physical devices to accept an appropriate file system.

After a file system has been configured on the physical storage devices, the administrator must have an understanding of how to manage the security of the data in the file system and use file system facilities such as compression and disk quotas to more effectively manage the disk usage.

Finally, the administrator must understand how advanced file system functionality, such as the encrypting file system and distributed file system, can be configured, administered, and managed.

This chapter introduces the fundamentals of the various types of storage facilities available in Windows 2000 and then moves on to discuss the configuration, management, administration, and security of these data resources.

File Systems

- ▶ Manage data storage. Considerations include file systems, permissions, and quotas.

Before you install Windows 2000, you should decide which file system to use. A *file system* is the method by which information is stored, organized, and named on a hard disk.

Windows 2000 supports the NTFS file system or one of the file allocation table file systems (FAT or FAT32). The FAT32 file system is new to Windows 2000. The choice of which of these file systems to use can be made when you install Windows 2000, format an existing `volume`, or install a new hard disk.

The preferred file system to use is NTFS because of its capability to accommodate the requirements of business, such as large volume support; the capability to secure information stored within the file system; and its support of compression, encryption, and disk quotas. However, before deciding which of the file systems to use, you should have an understanding of each of the features because they each provide an effective way of storing information depending on the requirements of the situation.

FAT File System

▶ Implement NTFS and FAT file systems.

The FAT file system has been around since the days of MS-DOS. When Windows NT was first introduced, the operating system provided support for FAT to maintain backward compatibility. This support has followed through into the current release of Windows 2000.

FAT provides a valid choice for systems that are required to dual-boot between Windows 2000 and one (or more) pre-Windows 2000 operating systems.

The version of FAT supported by Windows 2000 has a number of additional features that are not supported by systems running DOS. When used under Windows 2000, the FAT file system supports the following additional features:

- Long filenames up to 255 characters
- Multiple spaces
- Multiple periods
- Filenames that are not case sensitive but do preserve case

FAT is also a logical choice for small partitions (less than 200MB) because it has very low system overhead.

For all the benefits of FAT, it has several major limitations that should make you stop and think before it becomes your file system of choice on your Windows 2000 system.

The primary limitations of FAT are as follows:

- **FAT is inefficient for larger partitions**—As files grow in size, they can become fragmented on the disk and cause slower access times. FAT also uses inefficient cluster sizes (a *cluster* is the smallest unit of storage on a partition). If the cluster size is too large, you can end up with lots of wasted space on the partition.
- **4GB**—This is the maximum size of a FAT partition.
- **No local security**—The FAT file system does not support local security, so there is no way to prevent a user from accessing a file if she can log in to the local operating system.
- **FAT does not support compression, encryption, or disk quotas under Windows 2000.**

FAT32 File System

The FAT32 file system is very similar to FAT. FAT32 was introduced in the Microsoft product line with Windows 95 OSR 2. The primary difference between FAT and FAT32 is that FAT32 supports a smaller cluster size so it does not have as much wasted space associated with larger partitions. This, along with much larger drive support, provides more efficient usage of disk storage while accommodating larger capacities with fewer disks drives.

Like FAT, FAT32 supports long filenames, multiple spaces, and multiple periods, and preserves case while not being case sensitive.

The primary limitations of FAT32 are as follows:

- **No local security**—The FAT32 file system does not support local security so there is no way to prevent a user from accessing a file if she can log in to the local operating system.
- **8TB**—This is the maximum size of a FAT32 partition (a 32GB limit is imposed by the Windows 2000 format utility if you create the partition on a Windows 2000 system).

- **FAT32 is not supported by all versions of Windows 95 and is not supported by DOS and Windows NT**—So, you need to be careful when deciding to use it. If you plan to dual-boot your system, ensure that all operating systems you are using support FAT32. If they do not, all FAT32 partitions will not be accessible.
- **FAT32 does not support compression, encryption, or disk quotas under Windows 2000.**

NTFS File System

▶ Implement NTFS and FAT file systems.

NTFS is the file system of choice on most systems running Windows 2000.

NTFS offers the following benefits:

- **Support for long filenames**—NTFS supports long filenames up to 255 characters.
- **Preservation of case**—NTFS is not case sensitive, but it does have the capability to preserve case for POSIX compliance. POSIX stands for Portable Operating System Interface Extensions. POSIX is a set of standards begun by the Institute of Electrical and Electronics Engineers (IEEE) for ensuring applications function across different Unix environments.
- **Recoverability**—NTFS is a recoverable file system. It uses transaction logging to automatically log all files and directory updates so that, in the case of a system failure, the operating system can redo failed operations.
- **Security**—NTFS provides folder- and file-level security for protecting files.
- **Compression**—NTFS supports compression of files and folders to help save disk space.
- **Encryption**—NTFS supports file-level encryption. This gives a user the ability to encrypt sensitive files so that no one else can read them.

WARNING

NTFS 4.0 Versus NTFS 5.0 The version of NTFS used with Windows NT (NTFS 4.0) is different from the version used with Windows 2000 (NTFS 5.0). These two versions of NTFS are not compatible with one another so you can't dual-boot a Windows NT 4.0 and Windows 2000 system unless your installation of Windows NT 4.0 is running SP 4 or higher. This is very important if you're installing Windows 2000 on a system with an existing installation of Windows NT 4.0 because the installation process automatically upgrades NTFS 4.0 partitions to NTFS 5.0.

- **Disk quotas**—NTFS partitions support user-level disk quotas. This gives an administrator the ability to set an upper limit on the amount of space a user can use on a partition. After the user reaches the limit, she is not allowed to store any more information on the partition.
- **Size**—NTFS partitions can support much larger partition sizes than FAT. NTFS can support partitions up to 16 exabytes in size (this is equal to 16 billion gigabytes).

The main limitations of NTFS are that other operating systems do not support it and it has high system overhead. If you need to dual-boot your system or have partitions less than 200MB in size, you should format your partitions with FAT or FAT32.

NOTE

NTFS File Compression and File Encryption These are mutually exclusive because of the way NTFS compression is performed. You can use only one of these options at a time on a file. You activate the encryption or compression attribute by clicking Advanced on a file or folder's Properties dialog box General tab. The compress and encrypt attributes are mutually exclusive—that is, when you select one attribute, the other attribute automatically clears.

Managing Data Storage

Storage devices are one of the most important resources available in a networked environment. Much of the code in Windows 2000 is dedicated to the task of managing storage devices and the information contained within them.

Prior to Windows 2000, Microsoft used classic partitions, such as those used by DOS and Windows 9x, to configure disk storage. With Windows 2000, Microsoft introduced a new method of configuring disk storage. This section of the chapter looks at the various types of disk configuration and how they can be configured using the facilities in Windows 2000.

Overview of Disk Management

► Configuring volumes and basic and dynamic disks.

Two types of disk partitions are supported in Windows 2000. These include basic disks and dynamic disks:

- **Basic disks**—This is the classic way of allocating storage on disk, this partitioning method has been around since DOS. Disk divisions on basic disks are called *partitions* and are either primary partitions or extended partitions. Basic disks are the default method used to initialize disks by Windows 2000.

- **Dynamic disks**—This is the newest method introduced by Microsoft to allocate storage on disk. This method places a Logical Disk Manager (LDM) database in a special 1MB partition at the end of the disk. All dynamic disks that share the same database are members of the same disk group. Within the group, the dynamic disk database is replicated. This makes the disk group self configuring. With the disk management in Windows 2000, you are permitted only one group. Disk divisions on a dynamic disk are called *volumes.*

Partitions on a basic volume under Windows 2000 remain, for the most part, the same as they did under Windows NT 4.0. You can create up to four partitions on the free space of a physical hard disk, and one of these partitions can be an extended partition that enables you to create one or more logical drives.

One of the nice features that has improved over previous operating systems when it comes to configuring disks is the ability to create partitions and make them immediately available for use without having to reboot for the changes to become effective. Changes made by Disk Management are implemented immediately.

Certain legacy functions are no longer available on basic disks because multiple-disk storage systems need to use dynamic disks. This means you can't use basic disk configurations to create any kind of multiple volume sets or fault-tolerant volumes such as mirroring, volume spanning, striping, or RAID 5. These are supported, but only if they existed prior to Windows 2000 being installed on the machine during an upgrade. To use fault-tolerant or mulivolume disk sets in Windows 2000, you must use dynamic disk volumes.

Unlike basic disks, dynamic disk volumes can be accessed only by Windows 2000. If you are working in a network environment that has a requirement to dual-boot computers between Windows 2000 and a previous operating system release, then these previous versions of Windows will be incapable of accessing dynamic disk volumes.

As mentioned, dynamic disks can be used only to implement multivolume or fault-tolerant disk sets. Dynamic disks have several advantages over classic NT fault-tolerant disk sets in this regard. These include

- **Disk reconfigurations do not require rebooting.**
- **Disk sets can be remotely managed.**

- **Volumes have greater flexibility, especially when configuring volume spans**—Volume spans on the same logical drive can be mirrored. This simplifies upgrading hardware. You can add a drive in an emergency to extend a volume and then come back later to add a bigger drive and mirror it to the two spanned volumes. You can then either leave the system in that configuration for increased fault tolerance or remove the small drives and leave behind the big one with a single volume. Volume spanning is much more stable under Windows 2000.
- **The LDM database is replicated to each dynamic disk**—If a volume includes multiple drives, you can remove the drives and then replace them and get them out of order. The volume will still work because the database is on the drive, not the Registry. For the same reason, the volume structure is retained even if the Registry gets corrupted.
- **You can boot from a fault-tolerant boot floppy to the secondary drive of a mirrored volume without breaking the mirror**—This was not possible in previous versions of NT using FTDISK because the Registry on the mirrored disk was locked.

For all the new features of dynamic disks that the network administrator should be aware of, there are just as many things he should be aware of when transitioning to them. You'll find a host of prerequisites and restrictions when converting basic disks to dynamic disks. These include the following:

- **You can't convert a disk with existing partitions if there is no room for the LDM database at the end of the disk.**
- **If you have a previous NT server or workstation with an existing fault-tolerant disk configuration, you can convert the disks to dynamic disks after setup to take advantage of LDM volumes**—You can't convert just one disk out of the fault-tolerant disk configuration. It's an all or nothing conversion.
- **You can't convert removable media**—Dynamic disks are not supported on removable media devices.
- **A disk can be bootable only if it is upgraded from a basic disk with an active partition**—Ordinarily, this is not a problem because all disks are basic before they are upgraded, but you can encounter difficulties when working with mirrored volumes.

WARNING

Breaking Mirrors on Bootable Volumes Be careful when breaking mirrors on bootable volumes. The dynamic disk upgrade process places an entry in the partition table pointing at the LDM partition. This entry does not make the disk bootable; only disks with basic partitions can be bootable. You can get around both problems by using the Disk Management snap-in to create a bootable partition on the second disk while it is still a basic disk. Then, you upgrade the disk to a dynamic disk, delete the volume, and mirror the drive. You can also boot using a fault-tolerant boot floppy disk.

- **After you convert a drive containing an active (bootable) partition, you can't dual-boot the machine to any operating system other than Windows 2000**—You can't boot DOS, Windows 9x, or Windows NT from a dynamic disk. If you keep the boot disk configured as a basic disk so that you can boot to an earlier OS, or if you boot from a floppy disk, you can't view any dynamic disks in the system even if they have FAT or FAT32 file systems.
- **You can't convert back to a basic disk without first removing all volumes**—If the partition table was kept intact during the dynamic disk conversion, you retain your original partitions when you convert back to a basic disk. However, you lose your data because the file systems are removed when you remove the dynamic disk volumes. You must format the partitions and restore the data from tape.
- **You can't install Windows 2000 to a dynamic disk that was not upgraded from a basic disk and then boot directly to that disk**—The partition table will not point at a classic boot sector.
- **Dynamic disks are not available on laptops**—Because laptops usually support only a single internal hard disk, they can't take advantage of the advanced volume options that dynamic disks provide.

As you can see, several factors must be considered before transitioning your disk devices from basic disks to dynamic disks. Ensure that you have a good understanding of these issues to help you prepare for the exam, as well as to provide insight into why you might not be able to convert a basic disk into a dynamic disk within your own environment.

Configuring Storage

Now that you have a good understanding of how disks can be configured using the various partitioning schemes available with Windows 2000, let's look at putting these methods into practice by using the Disk Management Snap-in to configure disk storage.

The first task for any administrator when a new disk is configured for the system is to initialize the storage. This can be accomplished using Step By Step 1.1.

STEP BY STEP

1.1 Initializing a New Disk

1. Log in as the administrator and open Computer Management.
2. In the console tree, click Disk Management.
3. Right-click the disk you want to initialize, and then click Initialize Disk.
4. In the Initialize Disk dialog box, select the disks to initialize.

As mentioned in the previous section, Windows 2000 by default initializes disks using basic partitions. To use fault-tolerant features or multivolume configurations, you must convert a basic disk partition to a dynamic disk volume. This can be done in one of two ways—using either the Disk Management utility or a command-line utility. Step By Step 1.2 outlines how to convert a disk using the Disk Management facility.

STEP BY STEP

1.2 Converting a Disk to a Dynamic Volume

1. Log in as the administrator and open Computer Management.
2. In the console tree, click Disk Management.
3. Right-click the basic disk you want to convert, and then click Convert to Dynamic Disk.

To use the command-line interface to convert a basic disk to a dynamic volume, complete Step By Step 1.3.

STEP BY STEP

1.3 Converting a Disk to a Dynamic Volume Using the Command Line

1. Log in as the administrator and open up the command line.
2. Type **`DISKPART`** at the command line.
3. At the `DISKPART` prompt, type **`list disk`**. Copy down the disk number of the disk you want to convert to dynamic.
4. At the `DISKPART` prompt, type **`select disk n`**, where *n* is the disk number you copied down from step 3.
5. At the `DISKPART` prompt, type **`convert`** `dynamic`.

As with so many other things in Windows-based operating systems, Windows 2000 provides both a visual interface and a command-line option to configure features within the operation system. This is true of converting disks to dynamic volumes through the use of computer management or the DISKPART utility.

Managing File Systems

The previous section described how disks could be apportioned or configured into fault-tolerant or multivolume configurations. This is necessary prior to implementing any file system. This section assumes that you have configured the disk, configured the NTFS file system, and are now ready to manage the data and the security of the data located in the file system.

NTFS Folder Permissions

An optimal configuration for most Windows 2000 systems includes partitions formatted with NTFS. NTFS offers many advantages over FAT and FAT32—the most significant being folder and file security.

To secure folders and files on an NTFS partition, you assign NTFS permissions for each user or group that requires it. If a user does not have any permission assigned to his user account or does not belong to a group with permissions assigned, he will not be able to access the resource. By default, all users are given access to all file system resources on Windows 2000 NTFS partitions (the Everyone group is given the Full Control permission to all resources).

NTFS permissions can be assigned at both the file and folder levels. You use NTFS folder permission to control access to a folder; you use NTFS file permissions to control access to specific files. Because of the nature of files and folders, the permissions assigned to files are different from the permissions assigned to folders. Folders are used to organize files resources and act as a container where files can be stored. Files, on the other hand, can't contain other files. Because folders contain file permissions at the folder level, they give users the ability to create new files or list the files a folder contains. File permissions generally deal with the user's ability to manage the file itself (for example, to read or modify the file).

NTFS permissions can be assigned to both users and groups. Members of the Administrators group can assign NTFS permissions to files and folders on a system. The owner of a file or folder and users with Full Control permission can also assign permissions to a file or folder.

You assign folder permissions to control the access that users have to folders and the files contained within those folders. Table 1.1 lists the standard NTFS permissions that can be assigned to a folder and the level of access each provides.

TABLE 1.1

NTFS FOLDER PERMISISONS

Permission	*Function*
Read	Allows a user to see the files and subfolders in a folder and view folder attributes, ownership, and permissions.
Write	Allows a user to create new files and subfolders with the folder, change folder attributes, and view folder ownership and permissions.

continues

TABLE 1.1 *continued*

NTFS FOLDER PERMISISONS

Permission	*Function*
List Folder Contents	Allows a user to see the names of files and subfolders in the folder.
Read and Execute	Gives a user the rights assigned through the Read permission and the List Folder Contents permission. It also gives the user the ability to traverse folders. Traverse folders rights allow a user to reach files and folders located in subdirectories even if the user does not have permission to access portions of the directory path.
Modify	Gives a user the ability to delete the folder and perform the actions permitted by the write and read/execute permissions.
Full Control	Allows a user to change permissions, take ownership, delete subfolders and files, and perform the actions granted by all other permissions.

NTFS File Permissions

You assign file permissions to control the access that users have to files. Table 1.2 lists the standard NTFS permissions that can be assigned to a file and the level of access each provides.

TABLE 1.2

NTFS FILE PERMISISONS

Permission	*Function*
Read	Allows a user to read a file and view file attributes, ownership and permissions
Write	Allows a user to overwrite a file, change file attributes, and view file ownership and permissions
Read and Execute	Gives a user the rights required to run applications and perform the actions permitted by the read permission
Modify	Gives a user the rights required to run applications and perform the actions permitted by the write and read/execute permissions
Full Control	Allows a user to change permissions, take ownership, delete subfolders and files, and perform the actions granted by all other permissions

Granular NTFS Permissions

Generally, when the network administrator applies security settings with files or folders, she deals with the basic file and folder permissions. It is only when the administrator has a more specific requirement that she works with the more granular permissions. Table 1.3 presents a listing of the most granular permissions.

TABLE 1.3

SPECIAL LOCAL (NTFS) SECURITY PERMISSIONS

Permission	*Function*
Traverse Folder/Execute File	This permission allows or denies users the ability to pass through (traverse) a folder they do not have access to in order to get to a folder or file they do have access to. This property is applicable only if the user privilege Bypass Traverse Checking is not turned on in the system policy. By default, Bypass Traverse Checking is turned on for all users. Therefore, setting this permission has no effect.
List Folder/Read Data	This permission allows a user to list the contents of a folder that it is applied to. When applied to files, it allows or denies the ability to open a file for reading.
Read Attributes	Allows or denies the ability to look at file or folder attributes (such as System, Archive, or Read Only). These attributes are defined by the file system.
Read Extended Attributes	Allows or denies the ability to look at special file or folder attributes. These are created by special software applications and vary from application to application.
Create Files/Write Data	Allows or denies the ability to create new files (when applied to a folder) or to edit files to make changes anywhere in that file (when applied to a file).
Create Folders/Append Data	Allows or denies the ability to create new folders in a folder (when applied to a folder) or to append data to a file without changing existing data in that file (when applied to a file).

continues

TABLE 1.3 *continued*

SPECIAL LOCAL (NTFS) SECURITY PERMISSIONS

Permission	*Function*
Write Attributes	Allows or denies the ability to modify file or folder attributes (such as System, Archive, or Read Only). These attributes are defined by the file system.
Write Extended Attributes	Allows or denies the ability to modify special file or folder attributes. These are created by special software applications and vary from application to application.
Delete Subfolders and Files	Allows or denies the ability to delete subfolders and files from a folder (functions only when applied to a folder). This applies even if explicit delete permission is denied to the child folders or files.
Delete	Allows or denies the ability to delete the folder or file to which it is applied. This can be overridden if the Delete Subfolders and Files permission has been granted to its parent.
Read Permissions	Allows or denies the ability to look at the permissions applied to a file or folder.
Change Permissions	Allows or denies the ability to modify the permissions applied to a file or folder.
Take Ownership	Allows or denies the ability to become the owner of a file or folder. If you have ownership of a file or folder, you can always change permissions, regardless of any other permissions on the file or folder.

Next, we'll look at the default groupings used to separate these permissions into more manageable units. These make up the basic permissions that we have previously discussed.

The basic folder permissions are Full Control, Modify, Read & Execute, List Folder Contents, Read, and Write. The basic file permissions are Full Control, Modify, Read & Execute, Read, and Write. Tables 1.4 and 1.5 list the basic local permissions that can be granted and which of the granular permissions they encompass.

TABLE 1.4

BASIC LOCAL (NTFS) SECURITY PERMISSIONS FOR FOLDERS

Special Permission	*Full Control*	*Modify*	*Read & Execute*	*List Folder Contents*	*Read*	*Write*
Traverse Folder/ Execute File	X	X	X	X		
List Folder/Read Data	X	X	X	X	X	
Read Attributes	X	X	X	X	X	
Read Extended Attributes	X	X	X	X	X	
Create Files/Write Data	X	X				X
Create Folders/ Append Data	X	X				X
Write Attributes	X	X				X
Write Extended Attributes	X	X				X
Delete Subfolders and Files	X					
Delete	X	X				
Read Permissions	X	X	X	X	X	X
Change Permissions	X					
Take Ownership	X					
Synchronize	X	X	X	X	X	X

TABLE 1.5

BASIC LOCAL (NTFS) SECURITY PERMISSIONS FOR FILES

Special Permission	*Full Control*	*Modify*	*Read & Execute*	*List Folder Contents*	*Read*	*Write*
Traverse Folder/ Execute File	X	X	X			
List Folder/Read Data	X	X	X			
Read Attributes	X	X	X	X		
Read Extended Attributes	X	X	X	X		
Create Files/Write Data	X	X			X	
Create Folders/ Append Data	X	X			X	
Write Attributes	X	X			X	
Write Extended Attributes	X	X			X	
Delete Subfolders and Files	X					
Delete	X	X				
Read Permissions	X	X	X	X	X	
Change Permissions	X					
Take Ownership	X					
Synchronize	X	X	X	X	X	

Now that you know the local file and folder permissions, the next topics show you how to apply and maintain these permissions.

Copying Folders and Files

When you copy files or folders from one folder to another folder, or from one partition to another, permissions can change. The following lists the results you can expect from various copy operations:

- When you copy a folder or file within a single NTFS partition, the copy of the folder or file inherits the permissions of the destination folder.

- When you copy a folder or file between NTFS partitions, the copy of the folder or file inherits the permissions of the destination folder.
- When you copy a folder or file to a non-NTFS partition, all permissions are lost (this is because non-NTFS partitions do not support NTFS permissions).

Moving Folders and Files

When you move files or folders from one folder to another folder, or from one partition to another, permissions can change. The following lists the results you can expect from various move operations:

- When you move a folder or file within a single NTFS partition, the folder or file retains its original permissions.
- When you move a folder or file between NTFS partitions, the folder or file inherits the permissions of the destination folder. When you move a folder or file between partitions, you are creating a new version of the resource and therefore inherit permissions.
- When you move a folder or file to a non-NTFS partition, all permissions are lost (this is because non-NTFS partitions do not support NTFS permissions).

Configuring File and Folder Permissions

▶ Configure file and folder permissions.

When you apply file or folder permissions, by default, the permissions are cascaded down to all the files and folders in the hierarchy beginning with the folder to which you are applying them. In addition, by default, when you create a new file or folder in an already existing folder, this new object also inherits the security properties of its parent container. Unless you explicitly break the connection between the parent container and a child object, you are not allowed to modify the permissions on the child; the permissions remain grayed out. If you remove the ability for a child object to inherit permissions from the parent, you are presented with a few options that let you specify the initial permissions for the child object (remembering that the child was, until that point, receiving all its permissions from its parent). You can choose to either copy or remove.

If you choose to copy the permissions from the parent, those permissions are present in the child, but you can modify them to suit the current object. If you choose to remove the permissions of the parent from the child, all that remains are permissions that were added to the child when the parent permissions were still being inherited. If no permissions were added, the Names list is empty.

It should also be noted that every file and folder on an NTFS partition has local security applied to it. By default, the Everyone group has Full Control locally. Step By Step 1.4 walks you through modifying permissions.

STEP BY STEP

1.4 Modifying File or Folder Local Permissions

1. Navigate to the object for which you want to change permissions.
2. Right-click the object, and select Properties from the menu that appears.
3. In the Properties dialog box, click the Security tab at the top to see the local permissions that are applied (see Figure 1.1).
4. Click the Add button to get a list of users and groups you can add to this local ACL. After you make those choices, you're returned to this dialog box, where you can then apply the permissions desired for the specific people or groups.
5. To remove a user or group from the DACL, select the user or group in the Name list and click the Remove button.

   Permissions that show up as check marks in gray boxes are being inherited from the parent container. If you want to override these settings, remove the current check by selecting the other permission (if it is currently Allow, select Deny); then change it to how you would like it. If you do not want future changes in the parent to affect this object, deselect the check box labeled Allow Inheritable Permissions from Parent to Propagate to This Object.

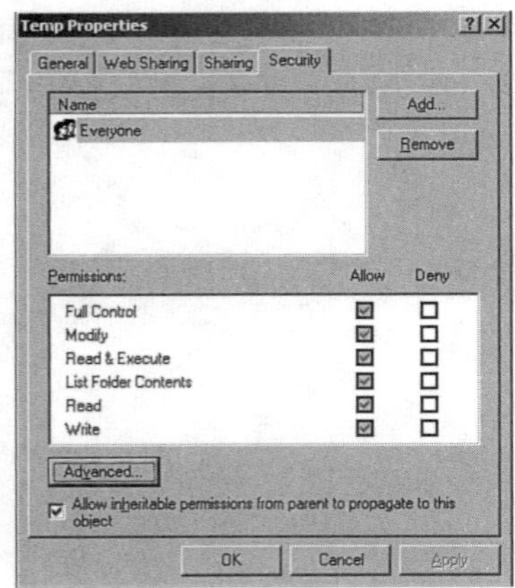

FIGURE 1.1
Several security permissions can be applied locally.

6. To set more granular permissions for a user or group, click the Advanced button. In the Access Control Settings dialog box, click the Add button (see Figure 1.2).

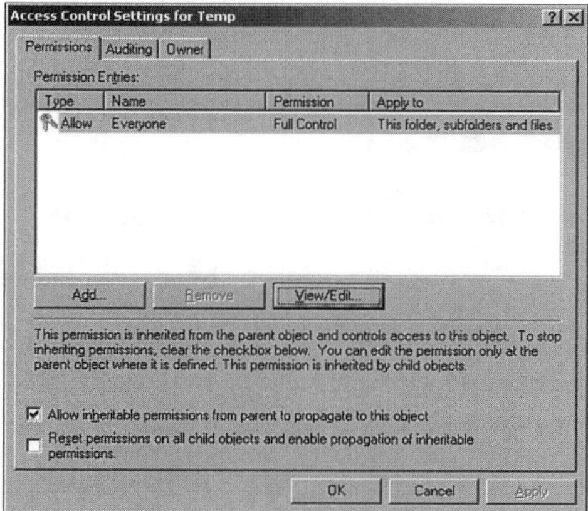

FIGURE 1.2
NTFS permissions can be assigned even more granularly than the standard permissions.

7. Having selected a user or group from the directory of your choice, you can set specific special permissions for that user or group (see Figure 1.3).

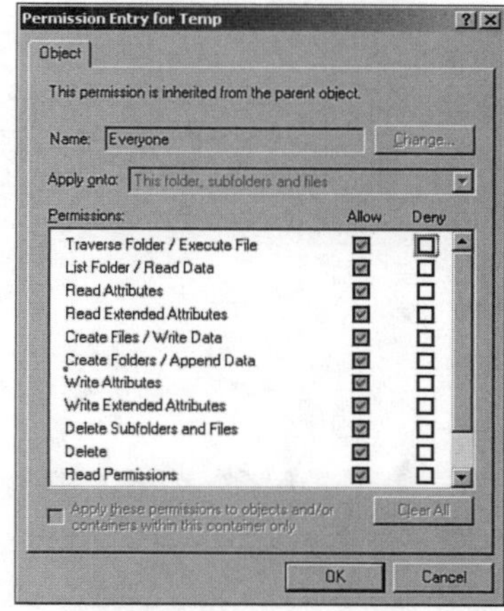

FIGURE 1.3
Any of the permissions can be granted or denied to a user.

Although local security solves several security issues, it does introduce a problem that only it can resolve. That is the problem of a file or folder being secured by its owner for only that person's access and then that person leaving the company. Because the file or folder is secured, it can be accessed only by the person who secured it, and therefore, that data is lost. One way to access the data is to change the user's password and then log on as that user. The problem is that further maintenance of that resource must be done by that user account.

Taking ownership is one way to take back the control of locally secured files. By default, an administrator has the ability to take ownership of any file or folder on his server. In addition, administrators can also give ownership to other users (a change from NT 4.0 and an ability unique to the Administrators group). For all other users, ownership can't be given to anyone. All that can be done is that the permission to take ownership can be given. Therefore, if Bob currently has ownership of a file and Sue needs it, an administrator could give Sue ownership, but Bob could not give it directly.

He would have to change the DACL to allow Sue to take ownership, and then Sue would have to take ownership of the file. At that point Sue, being the owner, could modify the DACL as she saw fit.

Step By Step 1.5 shows you how to take ownership of a file or folder.

STEP BY STEP

1.5 Taking Ownership of a File or Folder

1. Log on as someone with the ability to take ownership of the file or folder in question.
2. Right-click the object to take ownership of it, and then select Properties from the menu that appears.
3. Click the Security tab in the Properties dialog box; then click the Advanced button.
4. In the Access Control Settings dialog box, click the Owner tab.
5. On the Owner tab, select the user you want listed as the new owner, and then click OK (see Figure 1.4). If you also want to take ownership of all the folders and files inside this object, you can click the Replace Owner on Subcontainers and Objects check box.

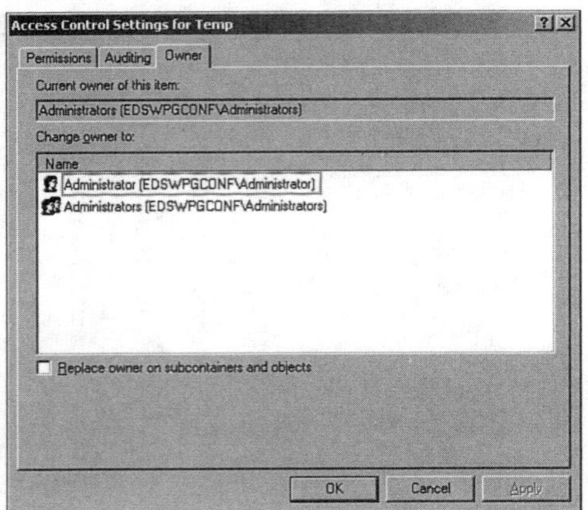

FIGURE 1.4
The ability to take ownership of a resource can be given to anyone.

Enabling and Configuring Quotas

▶ Enable and configure quotas.

One of the deficiencies of Windows NT is its lack of a mechanism to control the use of storage. After users had the ability to save information to a network server, they could save as much information as they wanted. It became the job of the network administrator to manage and control the growth of storage as users took advantage of what was essentially free disk space. Other methods to control disk storage were available to the network administrator, such as applying a charge-back scheme to the business unit for the disk space used. But this was not always a feasible way of managing disk usage effectively due to the political nature of charge back.

Realizing the absence of an effective tool to control the growth of disk use, third-party companies began to introduce quota management tools. Microsoft, realizing the need for this facility in the operating system itself finally introduced the Quota Management Service in Windows 2000.

Microsoft hasn't replaced the need for third-party quota tools. A number of limitations and requirements exist with the Windows 2000 Quota Management Service that should be understood by the network administrator. These include

- **Quotas are assigned to a volume**—You can't assign quotas to a directory. This affects the way directory space can be divided. If you assign a quota of 100MB to a volume that contains files from two departments, users who work in both departments will share the 100MB quota for the volume instead of having 100MB quotas assigned to the individual directories.
- **Quota entries are part of the file system, not the Registry**—If you move a disk from one Windows 2000 system to another, the quota settings for that volume move with the disk.
- **Quotas are not applicable to members of the Administrators group**—(This will change in the XP release.) The built-in Administrators group is exempt from quotas. Any information stored on the disk and owned by the administrator is not subject to quota restrictions.
- **Quotas are assigned to file owners**—Quotas can't be assigned to groups of users. As such, you can't grant the marketing department more space on a volume than the finance department, even though the marketing department will likely need more space than the finance department. You must assign higher quotas to individual members of the marketing department if the information they maintain is on the same volume as the data for the finance department members.
- **Quotas are based on uncompressed file size**—This means that if you compress files or use sparse files, the user can encounter a quota while still having lots of space available. It might appear as if you have plenty of quota space available, but in actuality you might have no additional space because quotas are calculated on the uncompressed file size.

To enable quotas in a network environment, the network administrator configures the volume as outlined in Step By Step 1.6. Two parameters are assigned as part of doing this: a threshold parameter and a ceiling parameter. Warnings are placed in the Event Log when users exceed either of these two parameter values. The ceiling parameter can also be used to prevent users from saving files when it is exceeded.

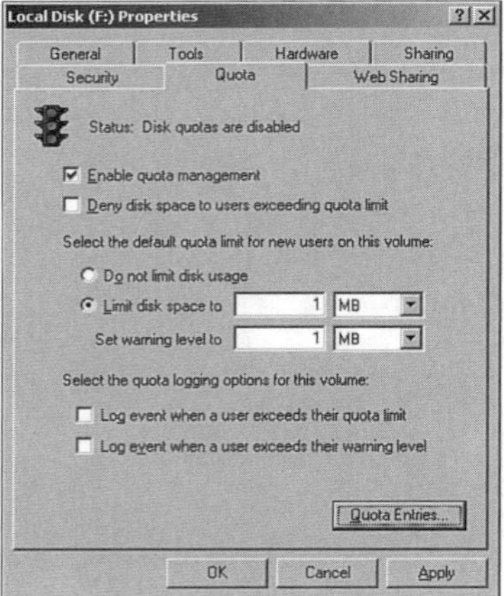

FIGURE 1.5
Quota properties for a volume.

STEP BY STEP

1.6 Assigning Quotas to a Volume

1. Log on as the Administrator and open Explorer. Right-click the disk you want to manage, and select Properties from the fly-out menu. Then, select the Quota tab, as indicated in Figure 1.5.
2. The default setting for quotas is disabled. Select Enable Quota Management to turn on quotas for the volume.
3. Select Deny Disk Space to Users Exceeding Quota Limit. It might be worthwhile to leave this option unselected for a while to gather reports about users who exceed their quotas to enable you to adjust just how much of a quota to put in place initially.
4. Select the Limit Disk Space To radio button, and enter the quota and quota thresholds you want to enforce.
5. Select both logging options. This records the quota offenders in the Application log.
6. Click Apply. The system responds with a warning that the volume will be scanned to update disk usage statistics.
7. Click OK to enable quotas on the volume. The system scans the disk to set quota bits on file records and gather ownership statistics. When complete, click the Quota Entries button to bring up the Quota Entries window, as shown in Figure 1.6.
8. If you open the Quota Entries window immediately after initializing quotas, the only name on the list is the Administrators local group. Users do not appear until they access the volume. Note that the Administrators group has no quota limits; the default limits are applied.

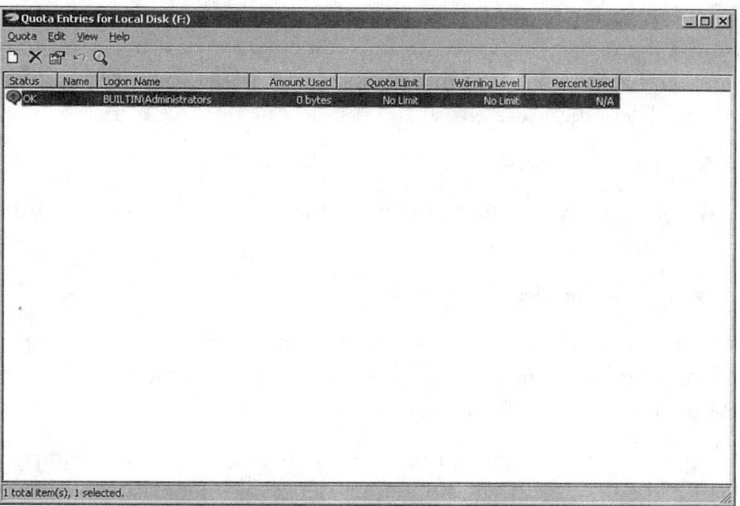

FIGURE 1.6
Quota entries for user(s).

9. If you have specific users who want higher quotas, or you want to impose lower quotas selectively, you can add specific users to the quota list or select the user from the list if she has already accessed the volume. From the menu, select Quota, New Quota Entry. This brings up the Select Users window.

10. Select the user or users to whom you want to grant individual quotas. You can select users from trusted domains anywhere in the enterprise. If you do not specify a quota for remote users, they get the default quota.

11. Click Add to put the user on the list, and then click OK to save the entries. The Add New Quota Entry window opens, as shown in Figure 1.7.

12. You can either enter special quota values for the user or choose not to impose quotas at all. Click OK to save the changes and return to the Quota Entries window. The username now appears on the list with a current status showing the new limits.

13. If you want to change quota settings for multiple users, you can select them by pressing the Ctrl key in normal Windows fashion, selecting Quota from the menu, and then selecting Properties.

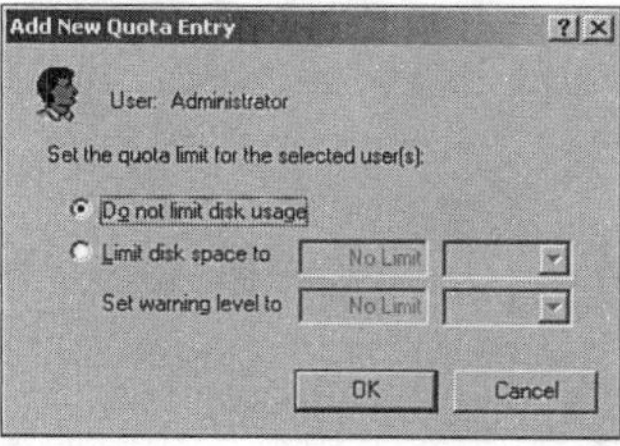

FIGURE 1.7
Adding a quota entry for a user.

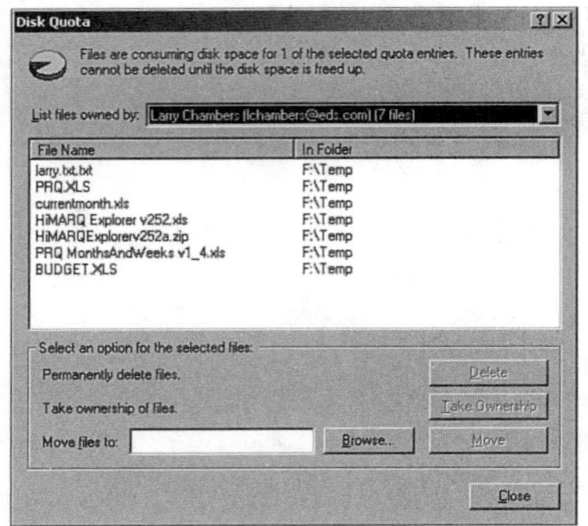

FIGURE 1.8
Files owned by the user on a quota managed volume.

After quotas are applied to a volume, you can't simply delete users from a quota list. Each user's SID is associated with files on the volume, and that association must be broken before the system enables you to delete the user's entry. You can do one of three things:

- Transfer ownership of the user's files to yourself.
- Transfer ownership of the user's files to another user's file using a third-party tool.
- Delete the files.

When you attempt to delete a user, a window opens listing all the files owned by the user on the managed volume, as shown in Figure 1.8.

Using this window, you can remove the users from the ownership list for the files. After you purge the user from responsibility for the file, you can then delete the user from the quota list.

Managing File and Folder Compression

▶ Manage file and folder compression.

NTFS compression is used to make more efficient use of the hard drive space available on your system. If you need more space on your system, you will most likely want to add an additional hard drive. In an emergency, however, you can always compress your existing folders or files to free up space. Compression is implemented at the folder or file level on NTFS formatted partitions.

To compress a file or folder in Windows 2000, complete the steps in Step By Step 1.7.

STEP BY STEP

1.7 Compressing a File or Folder

1. Right-click the file or folder you want to compress.
2. Select the Properties option from the secondary menu.
3. Click the Advanced button from the General tab.
4. Check the Compress Contents to Save Disk Space check box from the Compress or Encrypt Attributes section of the Advanced Attributes dialog box.

You also can manage the compression attributes associated with files and folders on your system from the command prompt. The Compact utility enables you to compresss files and folders as well as check the compression statistics.

The syntax for the compact utility is as follows:

```
COMPACT [/C | /U] [/S[:dir]] [/A] [/F] [/Q] [filename
[...]]
```

- `[/C]`—Compresses the specified files. Directories will be marked so that files added afterward will be compressed.
- `[/U]`—Uncompresses the specified files. Directories will be marked so those files added afterward will not be compressed.
- `[/S]`—Performs the specified operation on files in the given directory and all subdirectories. Default `dir` is the current directory.
- `[/A]`—Displays files with the hidden or system attributes. These files are omitted by default.
- `[/F]`—Forces the compress operation on all specified files, even those that are already compressed. Already compressed files are skipped by default.
- `[/Q]`—Reports only the most essential information.
- *`filename`*—Specifies a pattern, file, or directory.

It is beneficial to understand how to use the compact utility in addition to using the Property tab of the files or folders because the compact command syntax can be included in batch files.

Encrypting File Systems

▶ Implement and configure encrypting file system.

Security of information is an important part of any business these days. A good defensive security strategy not only ensures that proper access control is applied to files and folders, but it also ensures that users are provided the tools that will give them the ability to protect the information itself from unauthorized viewing. It's one thing to control access to files and folders, but if a file cabinet containined nothing but nonsense, no one would bother to break into it.

Unfortunately, people do break into files and folders all too often. One defense against that is to encrypt the contents. This provides one more level of protection that is difficult to get around. This section looks at the Encrypting File System (EFS), a facility introduced with Windows 2000 that gives users the ability to further protect their information.

Overview of the Encrypted File System

The Encrypted File System is a system service that enables the owner of a file system resource to encrypt it. The service is based on public/private key encryption technology and is managed by the Windows 2000 Public Key Infrastructure (PKI) services. Because EFS is an integrated service, it is easy to manage, difficult to break into, and transparent to the user.

A user who has ownership of a file system resource can either encrypt or decrypt the folder or file. If a user who does not own the resource attempts to access the resource, he receives an access denied message.

The technology is based on a public key-based structure. Each user has a public and a private key. The keys were created in such a way that anything encrypted using the private key can be decrypted using only the public key, and anything encrypted using the public key can be decrypted using only the private key. As the names suggest, the public key is made available to any resource that requests it, whereas the private key is kept secret and is never exposed to unauthorized resources.

When the owner of a file encrypts a file system resource, a file encryption key is generated and used to encrypt the file. The file encryption keys are based on a fast symmetric key designed for bulk encyrption. The file is encrypted in blocks with a different key for each block. All the file encryption keys are then stored with the file (as part of the header of the file), in the Data Decryption Field (DDF) and the Data Recovery Field (DRF). Before the file encryption keys are stored, they are encrypted using the public key of the owner (in the case of the DDF keys) and a recovery agent (in the case of the DRF keys). Because the keys are stored with the file, the file can be moved or renamed and it will not impact the recoverability of the file.

When a file is accessed, EFS detects the access attempt and locates the user's certificate, from the Windows 2000 PKI, and the user's associated private key. The private key is then used to decrypt the DDF to retrieve the file encryption keys used to encrypt each block of the file. The only key in existence with the capability to decrypt the information is that of the owner of the file. Access to the file is denied to anyone else because they do not hold the private key required for decrypting the file encryption keys.

If the owner's private key is not available for some reason (for example, the user account was deleted), the recovery agent can open the file. The recovery agent decrypts the DRF to unlock the list of file encryption keys. The recovery agent must be configured as part of the secrity policies of the local computer.

Encrypting Folders and Files

To enrypt a file or folder in Windows 2000, complete Step By Step 1.8.

STEP BY STEP

1.8 Encrypting a File or Folder

1. Right-click the file or folder you want to encrypt.
2. Select the Properties option from the secondary menu.
3. Click the Advanced button on the General tab.
4. Check the Encrypt Contents to Secure Data check box from the Compress or Encrypt Attributes section of the Advanced Attributes dialog box.

You can also manage the encryption attributes associated with files and folders on your system from the command prompt. The Cipher utility enables you to encyrpt files and folders as well as check the encryption statistics.

The syntax for the encryption utility is as follows:

```
CIPHER [/E | /D] [/S[:dir]] [/I] [/F] [/Q] [filename [...]]
```

- `[/E]`—Encrypts the specified files or folders. Files added to the folder afterward will be encrypted.

- `[/D]`—Decrypts the specified files or folders. Files added to the folder afterward will not be encrypted.
- `[/S]`—`dir` performs the specified operation on files in the given directory and all subdirectories. Default `dir` is the current directory.
- `[/I]`—Continues performing the specified operation even after errors have occurred. By default, Cipher stops when an error is encountered.
- `[/F]`—Forces the encryption or decryption of all specified files. By default, files that have already been encrypted or decrypted are skipped.
- `[/Q]`—Reports only the most essential information.
- *`filename`*—Specifies a pattern, file, or directory.

Using the `cipher` command provides a facility for the administrator to build batch files. Implementing encryption through Windows Explorer provides the administrator with a visual interface to managing encryption on files and folders.

The Distributed File System

▶ Manage a domain-based distributed file system (DFS).

If you have many file servers in your organization and many shares on each one, you might encounter the problem of users being confused about where to go to get what. As soon as you distribute the location of your shares, you invite problems with users locating them.

The Distributed File System started as an add-on to Windows NT 4.0 and is now an integrated part of the Windows 2000 Server operating system. Dfs enables you to collect in a virtual tree several share points. This collection makes it appear to a user browsing a server that all data is located under a certain tree structure when, in fact, the data remains scattered all over your network on different file servers. As indicated in Figure 1.9, although the shared folders are on servers 2 and 3, it appears as though they are on server 1, thanks to Dfs.

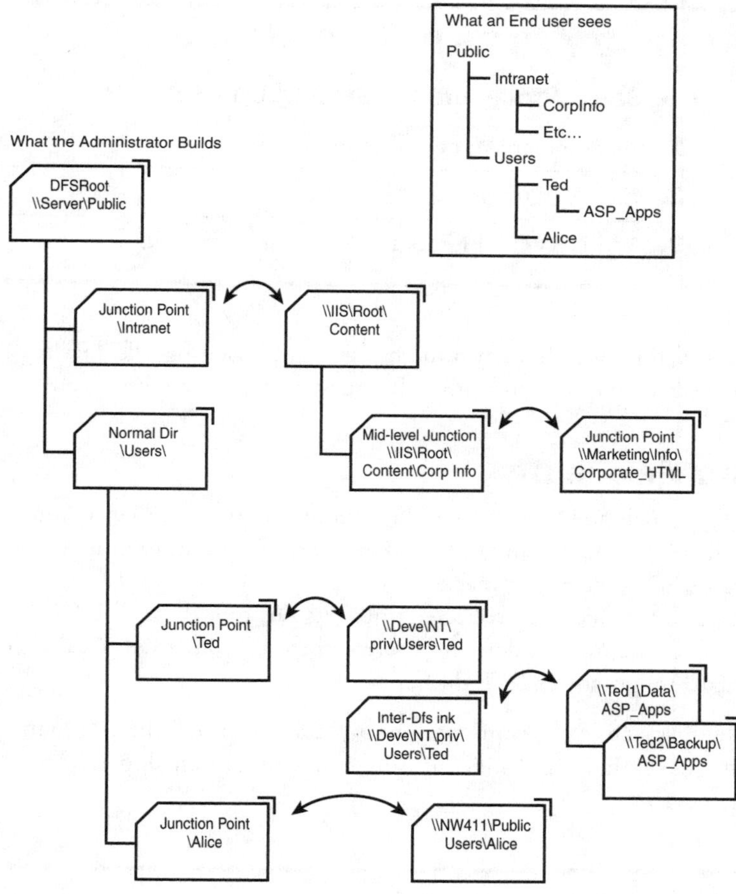

FIGURE 1.9
Dfs creates a virtual tree structure.

All characteristics of the local and share security that apply to the Dfs links apply. The Dfs root can't give out more access to a share than the local host of the share is willing to give. (In fact, no security configuration is available in Dfs; it is all controlled from the remote location.) As with any other network access point, it is recommended that you use NTFS security to provide the best, most consistent access control to your shared data.

All Dfs requires is the Dfs service installed on one or more servers, a configured Dfs root, and access to remote shares on non-Dfs servers. Step By Step 1.9 outlines the basic procedure for setting up Dfs.

NOTE

Requirement for Dfs-Aware Clients
A Dfs root can be accessed only by a client operating system that understands Dfs. Such operating systems include Windows 2000 (all versions), Windows NT 4.0 (all versions), and Windows 98. Windows 95 can be Dfs enabled by downloading the Dfs client and installing it at each client station. This client software is available on the Windows 2000 Server CD-ROM in the path `Clients\Win9x`.

STEP BY STEP

1.9 Basic Procedure for Setting Up DFS

1. Share folders on one or more servers.
2. Create a DFS root.
3. Add DFS child nodes (links) to the DFS root.

This section introduces two methods of administering Dfs: locally on a server and in a domain-wide structure in Active Directory.

Standalone Dfs

In a standalone Dfs structure, the administration of the Dfs is controlled by a server, and no redundancy is built into it; in other words, if the main Dfs machine goes down, there is no way to get to the data that has been collected under its Dfs root through DFS itself. This, however, does not prevent the user from accessing the data through normal NT shares.

The first step in the configuration process is to install the Dfs root on a server. For standalone Dfs, this is done as outlined in Step By Step 1.10.

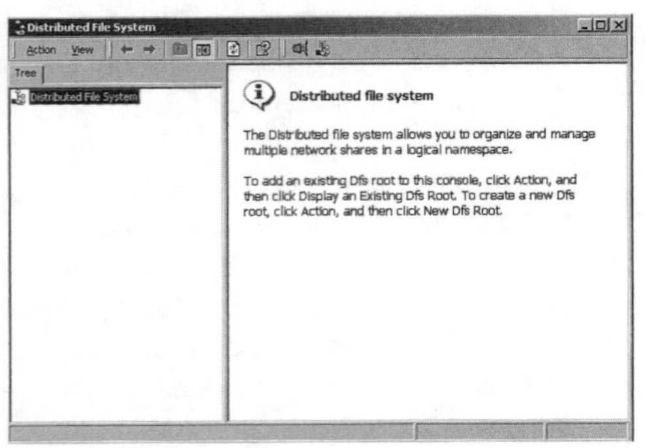

FIGURE 1.10
A Dfs server is configured in the Dfs management console.

STEP BY STEP

1.10 Installing a Standalone Dfs Root

1. From the Start menu, select Programs, Administrative Tools, Distributed File System. You should see a window similar to the one shown in Figure 1.10.
2. At the main Dfs screen, create a Dfs root by selecting New Dfs Root from the Action menu. This invokes the New Dfs Root Wizard (see Figure 1.11).

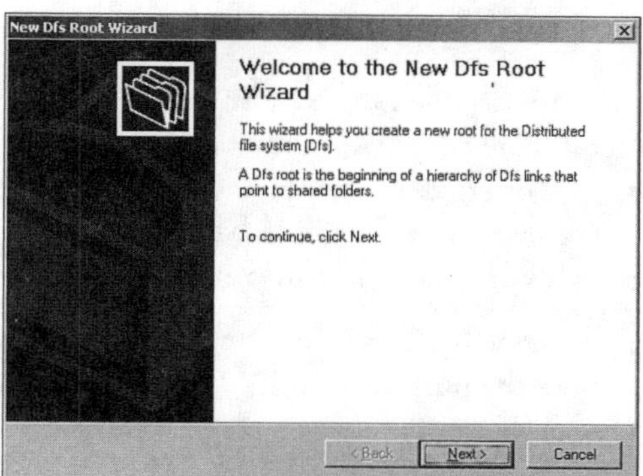

FIGURE 1.11
The Dfs Wizard enables you to create a new Dfs root.

3. At the Welcome to the New Dfs Root Wizard screen, click Next to continue.

4. At the Select the Dfs Root Type screen, select Create a Standalone Dfs Root (see Figure 1.12). Click Next to continue.

5. In the Specify the Host Server for the Dfs Root screen, type the name of the Dfs server (see Figure 1.13). (If you're configuring it on the machine that will be the root, the name of the current machine is the default.) Click Next to continue.

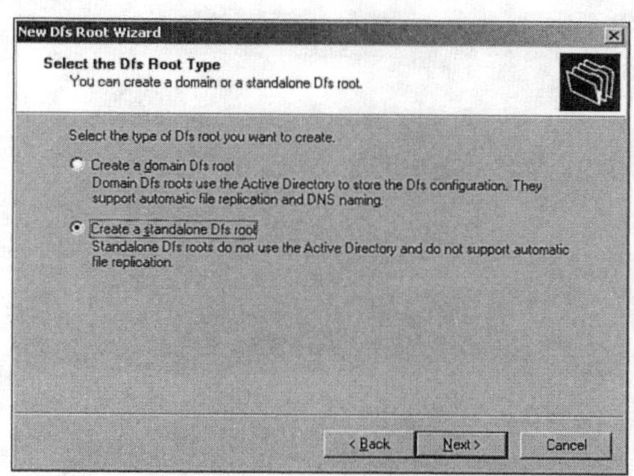

FIGURE 1.12
With the wizard, you can create a domain or standalone Dfs root.

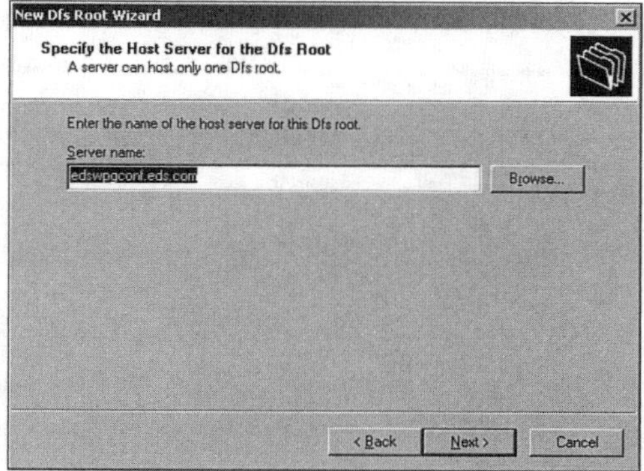

FIGURE 1.13
A Dfs root must be hosted on a machine on your LAN.

continues

continued

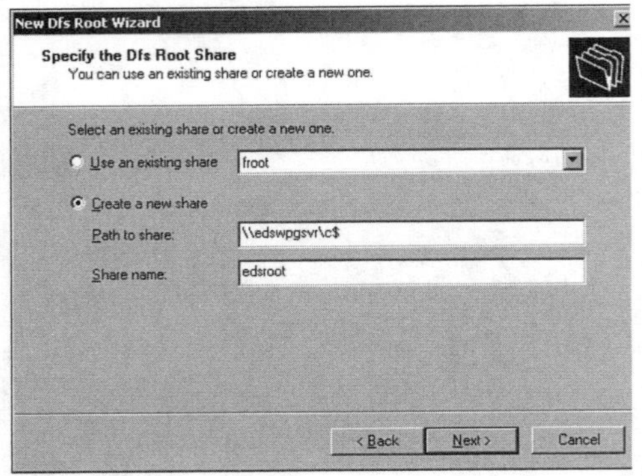

FIGURE 1.14
You can host your Dfs root from an existing share or create a new one.

6. At the Specify the Dfs Root Share screen, you can either select a share that has already been established to be the Dfs root or create a new share (see Figure 1.14). If you create a new share, the folder you are going to share must already exist. Click Next to continue.

7. In the Name the Dfs Root screen, type a comment that describes the purpose of this Dfs tree (see Figure 1.15). Then, click Next.

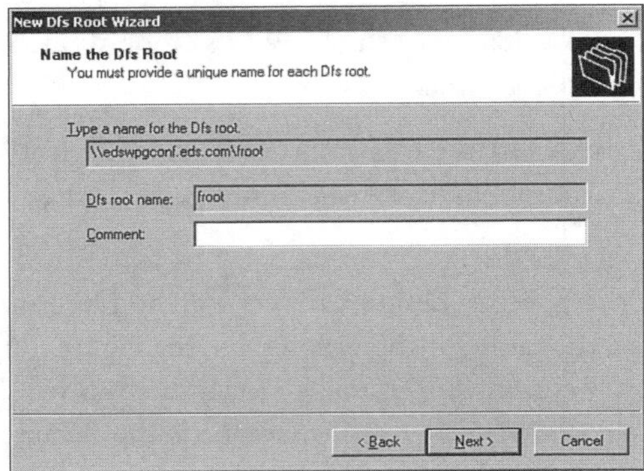

FIGURE 1.15
For administrative purposes, every Dfs root must have a unique name.

8. At the Completing the New Dfs Root Wizard screen, click Finish (see Figure 1.16).

FIGURE 1.16
The final page displays your settings and enables you to complete the task.

Now that your Dfs root has been established, you will want to maintain it. Maintenance of a standalone Dfs root consists of three tasks: adding Dfs links, removing Dfs links, and disabling Dfs links. You will add a new Dfs link when the Dfs tree needs to be expanded through the addition of a new link. Removing a node is necessary when you no longer need a node and that need is deemed to be permanent. Finally, you will disable a Dfs link when you want to temporarily prevent a certain node from being accessed in the Dfs tree. By disabling a node, you can prevent users from accessing it but ensure that it can easily be reactivated. Step By Step 1.11 walks you through adding a Dfs link to a Dfs root.

STEP BY STEP

1.11 Adding Dfs Links to a Dfs Root

1. From the Dfs Console, right-click the Dfs root under which you want to add a new link and select New Dfs Link from the menu that appears (see Figure 1.17).

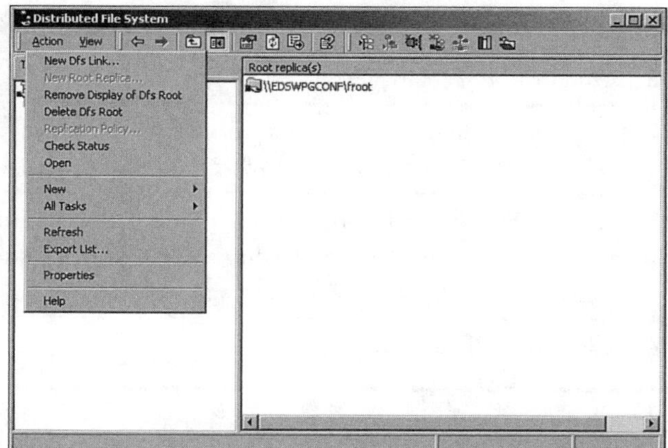

FIGURE 1.17
Select New Dfs Link from the shortcut menu to start the wizard that enables you to create a link to a virtual share.

continues

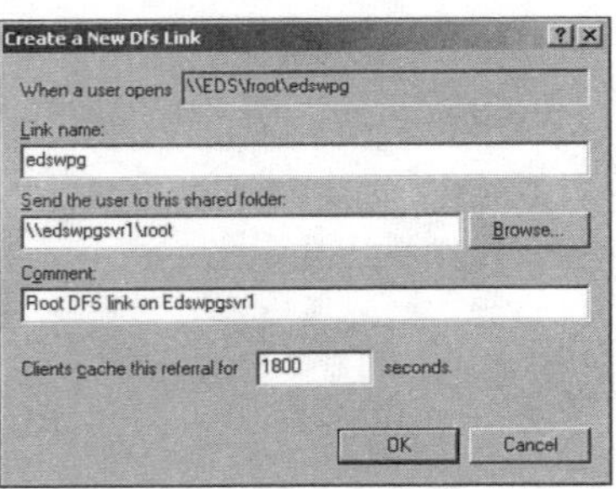

FIGURE 1.18
A Dfs link must have a name accessible by the user and a configured folder to which the name connects.

continued

2. In the Create a New Dfs Link dialog box, fill in the name of the link (that is what the user will see under the Dfs root), the share to which this link connects, a comment describing the content of the share, and a referral cache time (see Figure 1.18). The cache referral time is the length of time a Dfs client stores the location of the link to the remote machine. When this cache time expires, the client has to consult with the Dfs server to reload the location. The default for this is 1,800 seconds (30 minutes).
3. Repeat steps 1 and 2 until the Dfs tree is complete. When you finish, exit the Dfs Manager.

The second task you might need to perform is removing a Dfs link from the Dfs root. Step By Step 1.12 outlines that process.

STEP BY STEP

1.12 Removing a Dfs Link from an Existing Dfs Root

1. Open the Dfs Manager.
2. Right-click the Dfs child node you want to remove, and select Remove Dfs Link from the menu that appears.
3. A message appears informing you that deleting the link will not delete any of the files in the link. Click Yes to remove the link from your Dfs tree.
4. Close the Dfs Manager.

The final task outlined here is disabling a Dfs link. Step By Step 1.13 shows you that procedure.

STEP BY STEP

1.13 Disabling a Dfs Link in a Dfs Root

1. Open the Dfs Manager and expand the root you want to maintain.

2. In the left panel, click the Dfs link you want to enable or disable.

3. In the right panel, right-click the path to the Dfs link and select Take Replica Offline/Online from the menu that appears. If the link is currently enabled, it will be disabled and a warning icon (a yield sign with an exclamation mark in it) will be displayed on it. If the link is currently disabled, it will be enabled and an information icon (a white circle with a green check mark) will be displayed on it.

NOTE

Disabled Links Are Still Visible to Clients Even if a Dfs link is disabled, it still appears to the user when the Dfs root is opened. However, when the user tries to access it, an error message appears, informing him that the network location is inaccessible.

Troubleshooting access problems with standalone Dfs has to do primarily with configuring the Dfs properly. You must ensure that the computers and shares you are linking to are set up and are accessible to the Dfs root. In addition, the share security must be set up so that users can access the correct information. Because a standalone Dfs is not fault tolerant, ensuring that the Dfs root is always up is a major consideration in troubleshooting resource access. A more insidious problem occurs with clients that do not support Dfs. If a Windows 95 client tries to connect but does not have the proper software loaded, it will be incapable of connecting.

Domain-Based Dfs (Fault-Tolerant Dfs)

Although standalone Dfs works well in a small environment, when the number of clients you are serving increases, the need to have the Dfs root available on a consistent basis increases. Standalone Dfs has a weakness: If the Dfs root server goes down, the entire tree becomes inaccessible (unless you know on which servers the child nodes are hosted). By using the domain Active Directory to store the Dfs structure and by providing redundant locations to child nodes, you can ensure that your Dfs tree is available if your Dfs server goes down and ensure that fault tolerance exists in the child nodes as well.

As its name implies, domain-based Dfs requires that the server hosting the Dfs root be part of a Windows 2000 domain. This is required because the Dfs information is stored in Active Directory, and only a domain controller has a copy of Active Directory.

Step By Step 1.14 outlines the steps for creating a domain-based (fault-tolerant) Dfs root.

STEP BY STEP

1.14 Creating a Domain-Based Dfs Root

1. Share folders on one or more servers.
2. Create a fault-tolerant Dfs root using the Dfs Manager on a member server.
3. Add links to remote child nodes.
4. Add a second (or more) Dfs root server as a replica of the first.
5. Add replicas of the shared folders (if desired).

Creating a domain-based Dfs root is almost the same as creating a standalone version, as illustrated by Step By Step 1.15.

STEP BY STEP

1.15 Creating a Domain-Based Dfs Root

1. From the Start menu, select Programs, Administrative Tools, Distributed File System.
2. At the main Dfs screen, create a Dfs root by selecting New Dfs Root from the Action menu (this invokes the New Dfs Root Wizard).
3. At the Welcome to the New Dfs Root Wizard screen, click Next.
4. At the Select the Dfs Root Type screen, shown in Figure 1.19, select Create a Domain Dfs Root and click Next.
5. At the Select the Host Domain for the Dfs Root screen, shown in Figure 1.20, select the domain in which this Dfs will be defined. This defines which Active Directory domain will store the Dfs information. Click Next to continue.

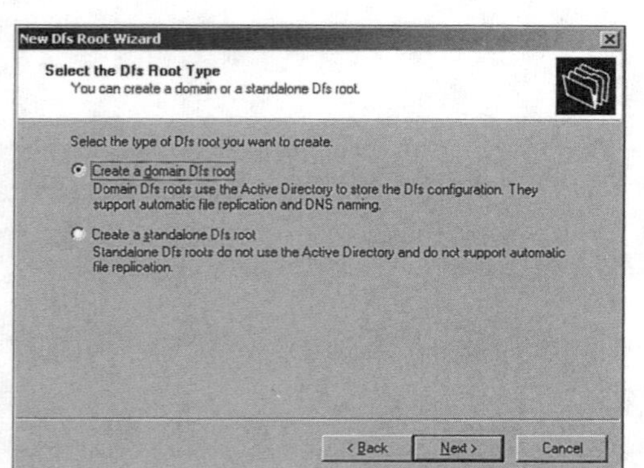

FIGURE 1.19
Begin by indicating that you want to create a domain-based Dfs root.

6. In the Select the Host Server for the Dfs Root screen, type the name of the Dfs server. (If you're configuring it on the machine that will be the root, the name of the current machine is the default.) Click Next to continue.

7. From the Specify the Dfs Root Share screen, you can either select a share that has already been established to be the Dfs root or create a new share. If you create a new share, the folder you are going to share must already exist. Click Next to continue.

8. In the Name the Dfs Root screen, type a comment that describes the purpose of this Dfs tree. Click Next to continue.

9. At the Completing the New Dfs Root Wizard screen, click Finish.

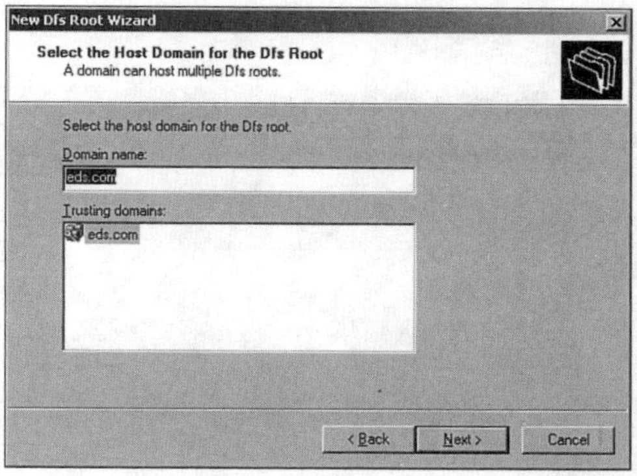

FIGURE 1.20
A domain-based Dfs must be configured to be hosted by a specific Windows 2000 Active Directory domain.

To add, remove, or disable child nodes in the domain-based Dfs structure, refer to Step By Steps 1.11, 1.12, and 1.13. Those procedures are the same whether the Dfs is domain-based or standalone.

Simply storing the Dfs root information in Active Directory does not make it fault tolerant. You must also set up replicas of the Dfs structure on one or more servers to enable failover. By setting up root replicas, you can ensure that a user trying to access the Dfs root when the Dfs root server is down will be automatically (and transparently) redirected to another location for the tree information. Step By Step 1.16 walks you through the process of setting up root replicas.

STEP BY STEP

1.16 Creating and Enabling a Dfs Root Replica

1. From the Dfs Manager, right-click the root you want to replicate and select New Root Replica from the menu that appears.

continues

continued

2. At the Specify the Host Server for the Dfs Root screen, enter the name of an additional Dfs root server for this Dfs root (see Figure 1.21). Click Next to continue.
3. At the Specify the Dfs Root Share screen, either select an existing (empty) share on the new Dfs root server or create a new share by specifying the local path to a folder and a share name (see Figure 1.22). Then, click Finish.

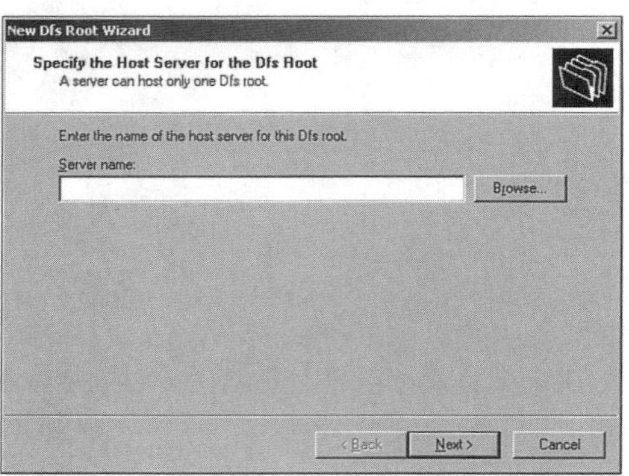

FIGURE 1.21
When you create a Dfs root replica, you must select a machine to host it.

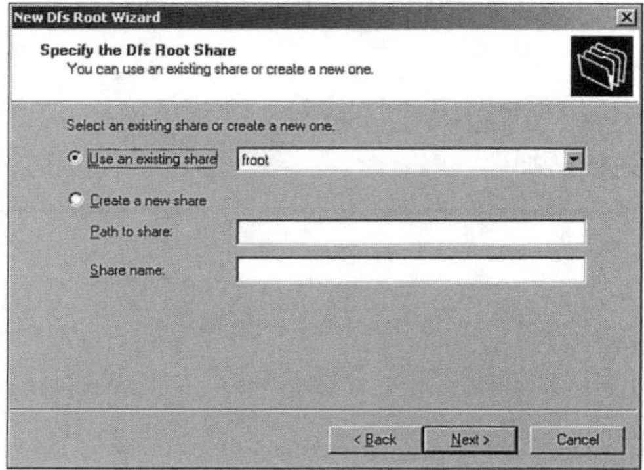

FIGURE 1.22
Similar to the original, a Dfs root replica must have a shared root.

At this point, fault tolerance has been set up, but it is not enabled. To enable it, you must configure a replication policy to define how the fault-tolerant roots get information about the main root. This is outlined in Step By Step 1.17. Note that for automatic replication to work properly, the file system on the Dfs roots must be NTFS.

STEP BY STEP

1.17 Enabling Dfs Root Replication

1. From the Dfs Manager, right-click the Dfs root you want to manage and select Replication Policy from the menu that appears.
2. In the Replication Policy dialog box, enable the folders for automatic replication by clicking the folder in the window and then clicking the Enable button (see Figure 1.23).

Then, you must define the master—that is, the primary source for Dfs root information (the first folder enabled becomes the default master). To define the master, click the folder you want to be the master and then click the Set Master button.

3. Click OK to continue.

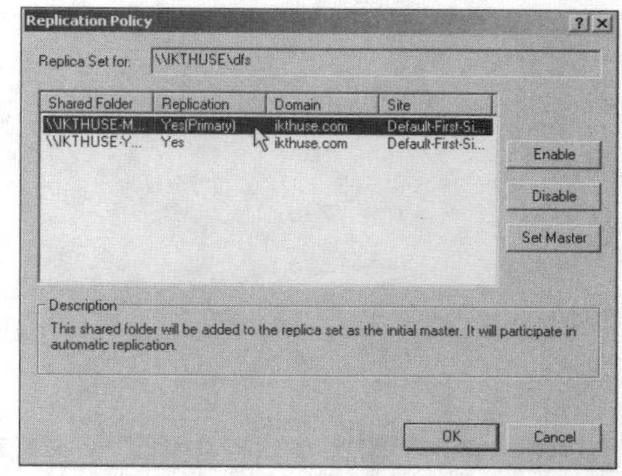

FIGURE 1.23
The replication policy governs the synchronization of Dfs information from server to server.

The Dfs Manager also enables you to configure replication of shared folders. This ensures that if a host server is not available, another replica of the same data is provided automatically to the user. Therefore, if a user clicks a folder inside the Dfs tree and the server hosting that folder is not available, Active Directory is searched, and if a replica of that folder has been configured, it is presented to the user automatically. Step By Step 1.18 walks you through configuring folder replication in a domain-based Dfs.

STEP BY STEP

1.18 Configuring Folder Replication in a Domain-Based Dfs

1. On the left side of the Dfs Manager, locate and right-click the folder you want to create a replica of. Select New Replica from the menu that appears.

2. In the Add a New Replica dialog box, enter the path to a shared folder that you want to maintain as an exact duplicate of the source folder (see Figure 1.24). Select a replication type of either manual or automatic. Automatic is preferred because replication occurs without your intervention. The underlying file systems must be NTFS for automatic replication to function.

3. When you finish, click OK.

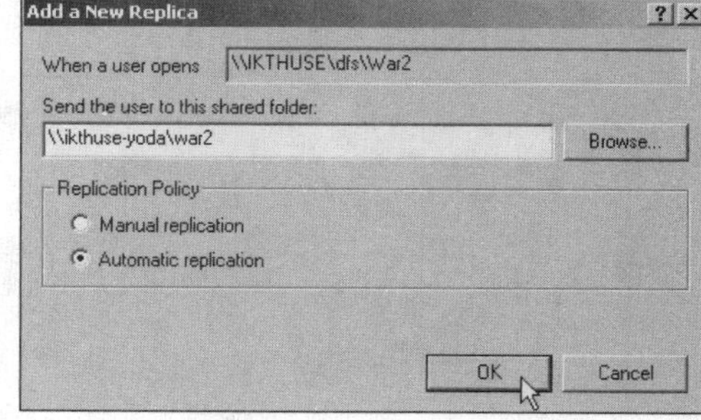

FIGURE 1.24
In addition to replicating the Dfs root structure, you can also configure replication of folder information.

With the addition of replication, a Dfs can be made completely redundant, and therefore, data is accessible to users on a continuous basis.

Troubleshooting domain-based Dfs is similar to troubleshooting standalone Dfs. You have to ensure that the links you have established are accessible by the root Dfs server. However, you must also ensure that Active Directory is accessible (that a domain controller is up and running) so Dfs information can be obtained. Some troubleshooting problems incurred with standalone Dfs can be avoided in domain-based Dfs simply by ensuring that redundancy has been configured (replication of root and folder information).

CASE STUDY: PAYROLL IS US

THE ESSENCE OF THE CASE

Here are the essential elements of the case:

- File system security
- File system conversion
- Efficient directory structures
- Shared folder permissions

SCENARIO

ABC Company is in the process of installing Windows 2000 Professional on all desktop computers in its organization. You want to ensure that you meet the following criteria with regard to the development of your file system and shared folder access plan.

- All resources must be secured.
- Only members of certain departments can gain access to department confidential data.

A large number of workstations and servers was installed six months earlier as part of the pilot rollout, and they have been in operation since then. These workstations and servers were configured with FAT32 partitions when they were installed. You need to ensure that data from these machines is not lost.

CASE STUDY: PAYROLL IS US

ANALYSIS

This case revolves around four main issues. The first is that all computers will need to be configured with NTFS. This is the case because NTFS is the only file system supported by Windows 2000 with folder- and file-level security. If security is a prime concern, NTFS is the only file system you can use to protect your equipment.

Second, for the workstations used during the pilot rollout of Windows 2000, you must convert the FAT32 partitions to NTFS. It is important that the Convert utility be used to perform the operation because it is the only utility that changes the file system and allows the data to be preserved.

The last two issues revolve around NTFS/shared folder permissions and the directory structure used. It is important that the directory structure make sense for the users of the company. To develop the structure, ABC company needs to fully define all the users that need to store information on the servers, determine who needs to access the data, and determine what level of access each user needs. The directory structure created should optimize the assignment of permissions so that permissions assigned high in the directory structure do not give too many permissions to users who do not require them.

CHAPTER SUMMARY

Summarized briefly, this chapter covered the following main points:

- **Windows 2000 file systems**—This encompassed the various types of file systems, including FAT, FAT32, and NTFS, that are available with Windows 2000 and the features and limitations of each.
- **Disk management**—This section covered the various ways in which disks could be configured or apportioned. Windows 2000 offers both dynamic disk volumes and basic partitions. The differences of each were discussed along with the limitations.
- **Securing files on a Windows 2000 server**—This included implementing security on network shares and local security using NTFS permissions.

KEY TERMS

- Encrypting file system
- Compression
- Distributed file system
- NTFS
- FAT
- FAT32
- Basic disks
- Dynamic volumes
- Quotas

CHAPTER SUMMARY

- **Compression**—The chapter discussed the ways with which compression can be applied to files and folders within Windows 2000.
- **Quotas**—This included a discussion of the features and limitations of quotas and how quotas can be applied to files and folders.
- **Encryption**—A description of how encryption works in Windows 2000 was provided, along with an explanation of how to apply it.
- **Distributed File System**—This section covered the various types of distributed file systems and how each of them can be configured in a Windows 2000 environment.

Configuring storage in your network is a very important part of an administrator's job. As a result, you can expect several questions in these areas. Because data storage is often the most critical part of what users require from their networks, this information must be well understood by any Windows 2000 administrator.

APPLY YOUR KNOWLEDGE

Exercises

1.1 Configuring a Standalone Dfs

This exercise shows you how to install and configure a standalone Dfs on a Windows 2000 server. The step-by-step procedure is based on Step By Steps 1.9 and 1.10. There you installed a Windows 2000 server and called it `WIN2000S`. If you are doing this exercise on anther machine, adjust the instructions to reflect your server's name.

Estimated Time: 20 minutes

1. Create a folder called `TestFiles` on your server, and copy some files into it. Ensure that it is shared using default properties.
2. Create another folder on your server called `DFSRoot`, and share it with default share properties. Do not put any files into it.
3. From the Start menu, select Programs, Administrative Tools, Distributed File System.
4. At the main Dfs screen, create a Dfs root by selecting New Dfs Root from the Action menu (this invokes the New Dfs Root Wizard).
5. At the Welcome to the New Dfs Root Wizard screen, click Next.
6. At the Select the Dfs Root Type screen, select Create a Standalone Dfs Root. Click Next to continue.
7. At the Select the Host Server for the Dfs Root screen, accept the default name (which will be the name of the machine on which you are configuring Dfs). Click Next to continue.
8. At the Specify the Dfs Root Share screen, select DFSRoot from the Use an Existing Share pull-down menu. Click Next to continue.
9. At the Name the Dfs Root screen, click Next to continue.
10. At the Completing the New Dfs Root Wizard screen, click Finish.
11. Right-click the name of the Dfs root you just created, and select New Dfs Link from the menu that appears.
12. In the New Link dialog box, enter **`Testing Dfs`** in the Link Name field and **`\\WIN2000S\TestFiles`** in the Send the User to This Shared Folder field. Click OK.
13. From the Start menu, select Run.
14. In the Run box, type **`\\WIN2000S\DFSRoot`**.
15. Open the Testing DFS folder that you see, and the files you copied into the folder should be present.

    You have just connected to your folder through the Dfs server.

1.2 Applying NTFS Permissions

In this exercise, you will assign permissions to a folder to test NTFS permissions. To test permissions, you will create a new folder on an NTFS partition and create a file in the folder. You will then create a new user account and assign the user account permission to the folder. You will then log on as the newly created user to test NTFS permissions.

Estimated Time: 20 minutes

APPLY YOUR KNOWLEDGE

1. Log on to your system as Administrator.
2. From the Computer Management administrative tool located under Administrative Tools, create a new user called `NTFSTest` . Remember that if you are using Active Directory then you should use the Active Directory Users and Computers application to create the new user account. Assign the user a password that you will remember.
3. Right-click the Start button (to start Explorer).
4. Scroll to an NTFS partition on your system.
5. Create a new Folder called `NTFSData` on the partition.
6. Right-click the new folder and select Properties from the secondary menu.
7. Click the Security tab. Uncheck the option Allow Inheritable Permission from Parent to Propagate to This Object, and click the Remove button when prompted.
8. Click the Add button and select the `NTFSTest` user from the Select User, Groups, Computer dialog box. Click OK.
9. Verify the default permissions of Read & Execute, List Folder Contents, and Read.
10. Click the Add button and select the Users group from the Select User, Groups, Computer dialog box.
11. Verify that the Authenticated Users group has Read permissions.
12. Create a new folder under the `NTFSData` folder called `Sub1`.
13. Verify the default permissions inherited by the `Sub1` folder when it was created. You should see the same permissions as assigned to `NTFSData`. The assignments will be grayed out to indicate that they are being inherited from the parent folders.
14. From the Security tab of the `Sub1` folder, assign the `NTFSTest` user Full Control permissions.
15. Log on as the `NTFSTest` user.
16. Use Explorer to scroll to the `NTFSData` folder. Try to create a new text file in the folder. You should be unable to complete the operation because you do not have the Write permission.
17. Try to create a new text file called `TESTDATA.TXT` in the `Sub1` folder. You should be able to create new files at this location.

1.3 Applying the Deny NTFS Permission

In this exercise you will use the Deny permission to limit the ability of a user to access a resource. In exercise 1.2, you gave a user named `NTFSTest` the ability to write to a folder named `x:\NTFSData\Sub1`. To demonstrate the Deny permission, you will assign the Users group Deny Write permission to the `Sub1` folder. This will block the `NTFSTest` user's ability to write to the `Sub1` folder.

Estimated Time: 5 minutes

1. Log on to your system as Administrator.
2. From the Security tab of the `Sub1` folder, assign the Users group the Deny Write permission.
3. Log on as `NTFSUser`.
4. Attempt to create a new file in the `Sub1` folder. You are not able to because you no longer have the Write permission. The Write permission is being denied due to your membership in the Users group.

APPLY YOUR KNOWLEDGE

Review Questions

1. What do you need to do to your servers to enable local security on files and folders?
2. What is the difference between a standalone Dfs and a domain-based Dfs?
3. How can EFS be effective when planning for the worst. How can it be used to protect information on a lost or stolen laptop?
4. What command-line utility can be used to compress files?
5. What command-line utility can be used to encrypt files?
6. What happens if the Dfs root goes down for standalone Dfs?

Exam Questions

1. As the support technician for a large company, you are called in to fix the president's PC. The president read in a magazine that Windows 2000 computers are secure only if they are configured with NTFS formatted partitions. She then proceeded to convert her hard drive from FAT to NTFS using the format utility. She is now very concerned that her PC will not boot. What should you tell her?

   A. The president should stop reading computer magazines.

   B. You will have to reinstall Windows to access the newly formatted drive to recover the data.

   C. The data is lost because the drive was formatted rather than converted.

   D. The president should have used the correct command switches with the format utilty.

2. You are working the help desk late one night when a user calls to complain that when he moves a file from one network share to another, the permissions are getting messed up. Tables 1.6 and 1.7 present the NTFS permissions on the target folder.

TABLE 1.6

SOURCE FILE NTFS PERMISSIONS

User/Group	*NTFS Permissions*
Executives	Allow Full Control (inherited from the parent folder)
Sales	Deny Full Control

TABLE 1.7

TARGET FOLDER NTFS PERMISSIONS

User/Group	*NTFS Permissions*
Sales	Allow Full Control

   When the user moves the file to the target folder, what will the effective permissions be on the file?

   A. Executives have Allow Full Control; Sales has Allow Full Control.

   B. Executives have Deny Full Control; Sales has Deny Full Control

   C. Executives have Allow Full Control; Sales has Deny Full Control.

   D. Executives have no permissions; Sales has Deny Full Control

Apply Your Knowledge

E. Executives have no permissions; Sales has Allow Full Control

F. Executives have Deny Full Control; Sales has no permissions

G. Executives have Allow Full Control; Sales has no permissions

H. Not enough information is presented to calculate permissions.

3. Alexander is a member of the Sales and the Accounting groups. You have given the Sales group Read permission and the Accounting group Change permission. Alexander is unable to access the folder. What is the most likely cause of the problem?

   A. The folder is marked as Read Only at the NTFS level.

   B. The files in the folder are marked as Read Only at the NTFS level.

   C. Alexander has not been added to the list of users with at least Read access.

   D. Alexander must have No Access assigned to his user account.

   E. The group Everyone has been removed from the list of users with access.

4. Your office is setting up several new laptop computers with Windows 2000 Professional on your network. These systems are to be provided to the VPs in the company. The CIO is concerned someone might steal a laptop and copy files to a FAT partition and read its content. How can you ensure the files are secure? (Select all that apply.)

   A. Install Windows 2000 Professional using RIS.

   B. Make sure all local drives on the laptop computers are NTFS.

   C. Make sure all local drives are configured so only owners have full access.

   D. Enable EFS on all folders you want protected.

5. You are working as a help desk operator in a large corporate environment. Sally calls to complain that she is unable to access all the data on the `\\NT4_CORP\SALES` share. You check the share permissions on the share and determine that Sally has Full Control shared folder permissions assigned to her user account. Sally is also able to ping the `\\NT4_CORP` server. What is your next course of action to help Sally?

   A. Verify Sally's membership in other groups to determine whether she is denied access to the share.

   B. Verify Sally's NTFS permissions to the file system.

   C. Verify that Sally can connect to the `\\NT4_CORP` server over the network.

   D. Verify Sally's shared folder permissions and NTFS permissions.

6. You have configured your server with FAT partitions (the D: drive) and want to convert them to FAT32. You issue the command `convert D: /fs:fat32` but find the system will not convert the drive. What is the cause of the problem? (Choose the two best answers.)

   A. The syntax for the command is `Convert d: /fs:NTFS`.

   B. You need to back up the FAT file system, reformat the drive as FAT32, and then restore from backup.

   C. You should use the `Format` command to convert the drive.

APPLY YOUR KNOWLEDGE

D. You can't convert from FAT to FAT32 in Windows 2000.

7. As the network administrator of your company, you want to create a large number of user accounts with secure home directories. What is the most efficient way to secure these directories?

    A. Create a shared folder named `Users` on a FAT or FAT32 partition and create subfolders for each user. You then share out the `Users` folders so all users can access it.

    B. Create a shared folder named `Users` on an NTFS partition and create subfolders for each user (each user directory is secured so only one user can access it).

    C. Create a folder named `Users` on an NTFS partition and create subfolders for each user. You then share each subfolder so only one user can access it.

    D. Create a shared folder named `Users` on a FAT or FAT32 partition and create subfolders for each user. You then share out each subfolder so only one user can access it.

8. You are troubleshooting a resource access issue for a user on your network. Drew is unable to access data when accessing the shared data folder over the network. If Drew logs on locally at the computer where the shared data is stored, he can access the data directly from the file system. Where should you start troubleshooting his access problems?

    A. Check the NTFS permissions assigned to Drew. He has been assigned No Access.

    B. Check the NTFS permissions assigned to Drew. They are blocking him from accessing the resource when he attaches from the network.

    C. Check the shared folder permissions assigned to Drew. He has been assigned No Access.

    D. Drew needs to be a member of the Authenticated User group to access resources from over the network.

9. You are the administrator of a small network. The manager of the accounting department approaches you because one of her staff has encrypted all his data in a shared folder. The user is sick and will not be back to work for an extended period. You are asked to decrypt the data. What is your best option?

    A. Take ownership of the files and change the permissions on them so that you own them. Then decrypt the files.

    B. Call the sick user and ask for his password. Log on as the user and decrypt the files.

    C. Log on as the administrator and decrypt the files.

    D. Log on as the recovery agent and decrypt the files.

10. As the system support specialist for the accounting department of your company, you have been asked to encrypt a large number of files and folders on several NTFS partitions on your servers. You spend an entire weekend encrypting the approximately 1,000 folders and 100,000 files. On Monday morning, users can no longer access the files they need to do their jobs. You realize that because you used your account to encrypt the files, the accounting staff will not be able to access the information unless they log on as your user account. For security reasons, you don't want regular users logged on as an administrator.

APPLY YOUR KNOWLEDGE

Your boss does not care about these technical problems and tells you to decrypt the files quickly. What is the fastest way to decrypt the files (remember that they are spread over multiple NTFS drives—it took you two days to encrypt the files using Explorer)?

A. Have everyone log on to the system as the recovery agent (Administrator) and access the files.

B. Create a batch file with the following commands and execute it at the root of all NTFS volumes containing encrypted files: `CIPHER /e /s.`

C. Create a batch file with the following commands and execute it at the root of all NTFS volumes containing encrypted files: `CIPHER /d.`

D. Create a batch file with the following commands and execute it at the root of all NTFS volumes containing encrypted files: `CIPHER /d /s /i.`

11. You are working the help desk late one night when a user calls to complain that when she copies a file from one network share to another, the permissions get messed up. Table 1.4 presents the existing NTFS permissions on the file being moved; Table 1.5 presents the NTFS permissions on the target folder.

TABLE 1.8

SOURCE FILE NTFS PERMISSIONS

User/Group	*NTFS Permissions*
Executives	Allow Full Control (inherited from the parent folder)
Sales	Deny Full Control

TABLE 1.9

TARGET FOLDER NTFS PERMISSIONS

User/Group	*NTFS Permissions*
Sales	Allow Full Control

When the user copies the file to the target folder, what will the effective permissions be on it?

A. Executives has Allow Full Control; Sales has Allow Full Control.

B. Executives has Deny Full Control; Sales has Deny Full Control.

C. Executives has Allow Full Control; Sales has Deny Full Control.

D. Executives has no permissions; Sales has Deny Full Control.

E. Executives has no permissions; Sales has Allow Full Control.

F. Executives has Deny Full Control; Sales has no permissions.

G. Executives has Allow Full Control; Sales has no permissions.

H. Not enough information is presented to determine the permissions.

12. As the network administrator for your company, you have just configured a new drive on your server to handle the additional storage requirements. The new drive is formatted with NTFS, as are the other drives in your system. You have seven compressed files in a folder named `Data` on your `C:` drive. You want to transfer these files into a directory named `Analysis` that is currently uncompressed on the newly created `D:` drive.

APPLY YOUR KNOWLEDGE

You also want to keep the other files in `Analysis` uncompressed. How would you accomplish this?

A. Move the files from the `Data` folder to the `Analysis` folder. Moving the files does not change their compression attributes.

B. Copy the files from the `Data` folder to the `Analysis` folder. Copying files does not change their compression attributes.

C. Move the files from the `Data` folder to the `Analysis` folder. Select the option Apply Changes to This Folder, Subfolders and Files.

D. Move the files from the `Data` folder to the `Analysis` folder. Manually set the compression attribute for each file so that each one is compressed.

13. You are the owner of a small training company that provides courses on network administration. A student has indicated that he has recently been asked to create a Windows 2000 server for his department by the senior network manager and he must provide a synopsis of how the system is to be configured before putting it into production. Your student is unsure of whether he should use dynamic disks or basic disks but is leaning toward dynamic disks. You indicate that some of the following can be applied to dynamic disks only and not basic disks. (Choose all that can be applied.)

    A. View volume and partition properties such as size, drive letter assignment, label, type, and file system.

    B. Create and delete simple, spanned, striped, mirrored, and RAID-5 volumes.

    C. Establish disk sharing and security arrangements for a volume or partition.

    D. Remove a mirror from a mirrored volume or split the volume into two volumes.

    E. Create and delete logical drives in an extended partition.

14. As the network administrator for a large company, you have the job of implementing Windows 2000 into your corporate network. Your current network is Windows NT 4.0 with all your servers having the latest service packs. You are in the middle of implementing an upgrade for each of these servers and have upgraded the disks on each of them from basic partitions to dynamic volumes so that you can take advantage of the fault-tolerant features of Windows 2000. During the migration, a requirement comes along from the business to extend the amount of storage that is available on one of the servers you have just converted to Windows 2000. Of the following options, which one is not feasible to perform on your system?

    A. Install an additional disk and configure it as a dynamic volume providing the additional storage you require.

    B. Create a spanned volume with an additional disk to provide the additional storage required.

    C. Revert the disk back to a basic disk and add an additional extended partition to provide the additional storage that is required.

    D. Extend the dynamic volume that was upgraded from the basic disk partition to provide the additional storage required.

15. Your network consists of several Windows 2000 domain controllers in a single domain forest.

APPLY YOUR KNOWLEDGE

These domain controllers are spread throughout various remote locations in your network. As the network administrator, you want to implement Dfs on each of these systems to take advantage of replication to remote locations. Of the following items, which one will you not be able to perform given the scenario just presented?

A. The Dfs topology will not be published in Active Directory, enabling users to locate shares across the organization.

B. You will not be able to publish a root-level Dfs share for all users to access.

C. You will not be able to publish multiple levels of Dfs links.

D. The Dfs share you have established on your domain member server that you have recently implemented will not be available for linking into the existing Dfs hierarchy.

Answers to Review Questions

1. To enable local security, you must host your folders and files on NTFS partitions and you must set the DACLs on resources to be secured. If your partitions are FAT, you can convert to NTFS without data loss by using the `convert` command. For more information, see the section "Overview of Disk Management."

2. The essential difference between a standalone Dfs and a domain-based Dfs is that the root servers in a domain-based Dfs are published to Active Directory. This enables redundant copies of the root to be configured, thus ensuring that if the root server goes down, clients are automatically directed to a functioning root when they try to connect. For more information, see the section "The Distributed File System."

3. EFS is effective when planning for the worst by ensuring that the information is encrypted and that only those who have permissions to access the information can decode it; see the section titled "Encyrpting File System."

4. The `compress` command is the utility that is used to compress files and folders at the command line.

5. The `cipher` command is the command-line equivalent needed to encrypt files and folders.

6. When the standalone Dfs root is unavailable, it is unavailable for everyone. This differs from domain-based Dfs in that the Dfs root is available through Active Directory.

Answers to Exam Questions

1. **C.** Although answer A is tempting, it is not in your best interest to get the president upset. Technically, answer C is correct and the data is lost. Answers B and D are incorrect because the format utility or reinstalling the operating system can't be used to convert a drive under any circumstances. See the section "Configuring Storage."

2. **E.** Again, recall the rules when you move files on NTFS partitions:

   - When you move a folder or file within a single NTFS partition, the folder or file retains its original permissions.

   - When you move a folder or file between NTFS partitions, the folder or file inherits the permissions of the destination folder. When you move a folder or file between partitions, you are creating a new version of the resource and therefore inherit permissions.

APPLY YOUR KNOWLEDGE

- When you move a folder or file to a non-NTFS partition, all permissions are lost (this is because non-NTFS partitions do not support NTFS permissions).

In this question you are moving a file between two different partitions, so the effective permissions on the target file are Sales Full Control. See the section "File Permissions" for details.

3. **D.** A No Access setting overrides any other permissions. The Sales and Accounting groups would give Alexander an effective permission of Change; however, No Access overrides that.

4. **B, D.** NTFS can be used to implement local permissions on files. With the help of EFS, additional encryption can be added to files so that, even if they are copied to a FAT partition, they can't be viewed by anyone but the owner.

5. **B.** Sally is able to connect to the share and access some of the data on it. Because of this, you can confirm that the shared folder is accessible. Remember that share permissions are assigned at the folder level and are then inherited from that point in the directory structure down. The only reason Sally would be unable to access all the data in the share has to do with NTFS permissions. When NTFS and share permissions are combined, the most restrictive permission applies. Answer A is incorrect because Sally can access the share. Answer C is incorrect because Sally can ping the server and access some of the data from the share. Answer D is incorrect because shared folder permissions are not the cause of Sally's difficulties.

6. **B, D.** The `convert` command enables you to convert only FAT or FAT32 to NTFS. If you want to change a FAT partition to FAT32, you need to back up your data, reformat the drive, and then restore the data. Answer A is incorrect because this command converts the drive to NTFS. Answer C is incorrect because formatting a drive is not the same as converting a drive. During a format all data is lost. Converting a drive allows the data to be retained.

7. **B.** The key to this question is understanding the limitations of FAT and FAT32 partitions. Remember that FAT and FAT32 do not support folder- and file-level security. For this reason, they are not very efficient for creating user home directories (because these directories are typically secure). Answer A is incorrect because the user folders would not be secure. Answer C is incorrect because this requires a large effort (creating all the individual user shares). The effort is not required on NTFS partitions, where we can use file and folder security to secure the resource. To simplify the creating process, you can use the `%Username%` environment variable to create user home directories and assign NTFS permissions automatically when configuring the `User` home directory property of a user account. Answer D is incorrect because this requires a large effort (creating all the individual user shares). Answer B represents the most efficient answer.

8. **C.** You must remember how shared folder and NTFS permissions are applied when a user accesses a resource over the network. In this case, Drew can access a resource if he accesses the resource while logged on locally (he is accessing the resource directly from the file system), but he can't access the same resource from over the network.

APPLY YOUR KNOWLEDGE

This situation points to a shared folder permission issue. When Drew is accessing the resource locally, shared folder permissions are not processed. You also know that Drew has NTFS permissions to the resource because he can access it locally. For these reasons, C is correct. Answer A is incorrect because Drew can access the resource if logged on locally. Answer B is incorrect because NTFS permissions can't be applied for network access versus local access. Answer D is incorrect because membership in Authenticated Users can't be changed (it is a built-in group).

9. **D.** The Encrypting File System supports a recovery agent account to assist if encrypted files need to be decrypted and the user is unavailable. Answer C is correct under the default installation of Windows 2000. The Administrator account is, by default, the recovery agent. Being the administrator, however, does not guarantee that you are also the recovery agent, if the default configuration has been changed. Answer A is incorrect because if you take ownership of the files, the encryption keys required to decrypt the file are not available to you. Answer B would work but is not an acceptable practice for network administrators.

10. **D.** This question requires that you understand how EFS works. Remember that the user who encrypts a file is the only user who can access the file (except for the recovery agent). In this scenario, you need a quick solution. The absolute fastest method available is to enable the users to log on as Administrator (in other words, the recovery agent). This solution compromises network security and is totally inappropriate (therefore, answer A is incorrect). The next best solution is to write a batch file that runs the `CIPHER` command to decrypt the files. This involves mapping a drive to the root of each NTFS drive containing encrypted files and running the file. The only trick is getting the command syntax correct. Answer B is incorrect because it uses the `/e` switch, which instructs `CIPHER` to encrypt files. Answer C is incorrect because it does not include the `/s` switch, which tells `CIPHER` to decrypt files and subfolders. Answer D is correct because `CIPHER` is configured to decrypt files (`/d`), including subfolders (`/s`), and not stop on errors (`/i`). The `/i` option is important because when the command runs, you might try to decrypt files you did not encrypt (that is, files encrypted by other users). By default, `CIPHER` stops if it encounters an error.

11. **E.** Remember the rules when you copy files on NTFS partitions:

    - When you copy a folder or file in a single NTFS partition, the copy of the folder or file inherits the permissions of the destination folder.
    - When you copy a folder or file between NTFS partitions, the copy of the folder or file inherits the permissions of the destination folder.
    - When you copy a folder or file to a non-NTFS partition, all permissions are lost (this is because non-NTFS partitions do not support NTFS permissions).

These questions will cause your mind to swim during the exam. You need to focus on each permission and determine how it will transfer. In this case, you are copying a file, so you know the file inherits the permissions of the destination folder. For this reason, the answer is Sales will receive full control (the permissions currently on the target folder).

APPLY YOUR KNOWLEDGE

12. **D.** When a file is added or copied into a compressed folder, it is compressed automatically. However, if you move a file from the same NTFS drive into a compressed folder, the file retains its original state, either compressed or uncompressed. Likewise, if you add or copy a file into an uncompressed folder, it is uncompressed automatically. If you move a file from a different NTFS drive into an uncompressed folder, it is also uncompressed. However, if you move a file from the same NTFS drive into an uncompressed folder, the file retains its original state, either compressed or uncompressed. However, in this question the files are not being moved between folders on the same drive.

    Therefore, given how compression works, if you move a file from a different NTFS drive into a compressed folder as indicated by answer A then it will be compressed as required. However, you want to leave the existing files uncompressed, and if the folder is set for compression, this will not work. This is the same for answer B. Answer C is a variation of the first two answers and still will not work. Therefore, to ensure that the files are compressed after being moved, answer D is the most appropriate way of doing it.

13. **B, D.** Both dynamic disks and basic disks enable you to view volume and partition properties. Therefore, answer A is incorrect. Dynamic disks enable you to create fault-tolerant volumes, such as RAID-5, mirrored volumes, and so on; therefore, answer B is correct. Both basic and dynamic disks enable the network administrator to share resources from them as well as arrange security, provided an appropriate file system is put in place. As such, answer C is incorrect. Removing a mirror from a mirrored volume or splitting the volume into two volumes is something that can be done only with dynamic volumes; therefore, answer D is correct. Finally, creating and deleting logical drives in extended partitions is something that can occur only with basic disks because dynamic disks do not use the concept of extended partitions. Therefore, answer E is not applicable.

14. **D.** Each of the options provided enables you to extend your existing system to provide additional storage to meet the business requirements, with the exception of answer D. Because the basic partition was upgraded to a dynamic volume during the upgrade, you will not be able to extend it. This is not an option that is available to you after upgrading.

15. **D.** With the exception of the domain member server, this is a network that consists solely of domain controllers. As such, it limits the type of Dfs you can implement on your network. Therefore, any of the answers that are inapplicable to domain-based Dfs are invalid. Of the answers provided, the only one that can't be applied in a domain-based Dfs system is answer D.

OBJECTIVES

This chapter helps you prepare for the "Creating, Configuring, Managing, Securing, and Troubleshooting File, Print, and Web Resources" section of the exam. Of the five objectives that form this section of the exam, three are presented in this chapter. The "Manage data storage" objective was covered in Chapter 1, "Data Storage and File Systems," and the "Configure and troubleshoot Internet Information Services (IIS)" objective is covered in Chapter 3, "Internet Information Services."

The following exam objectives are covered in this chapter:

Publish resources in Active Directory. Types of resources include printers and shared folders.

- **Perform a search in Active Directory Users and Computers.**
- **Configure a printer object.**

▶ One of the best parts of Active Directory is how easy it enables you to share and make available network resources. Printers and file shares are the most common types of resources you will want to make available to your network users. Knowing how to configure and manage these resources will be an important part of many administrators' daily routines.

Create shared resources and configure access rights. Shared resources include printers, shared folders, and Web folders.

- **Share folders and enable Web sharing.**
- **Configure shared folder permissions.**

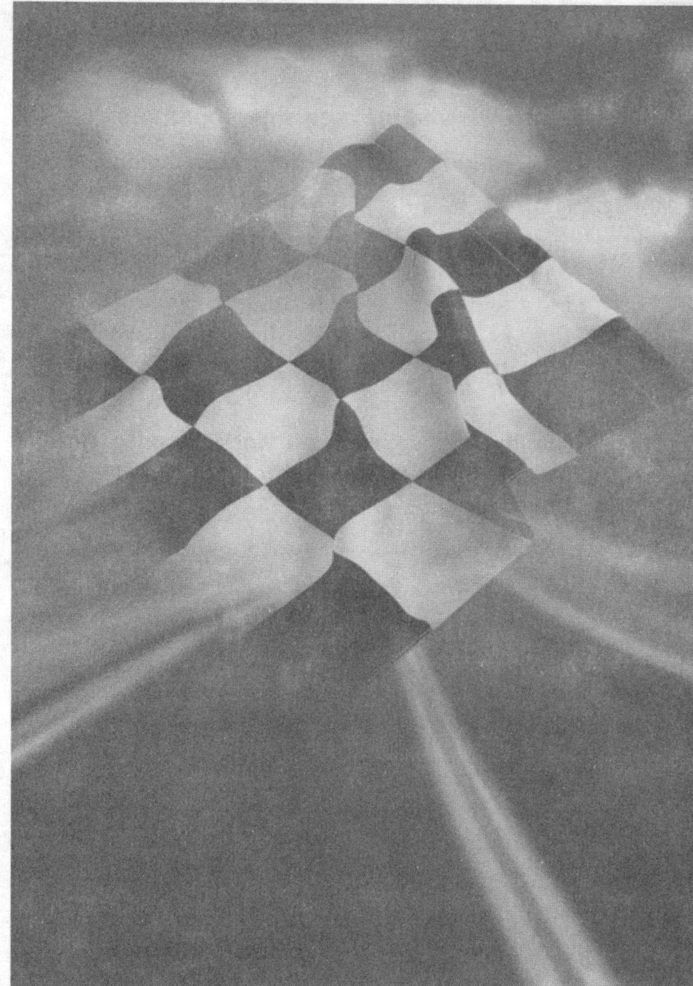

CHAPTER 2

Sharing Resources

Objectives

- **Create and manage shared printers.**
- **Configure shared printer permissions.**

▶ Configuring and sharing resources is an important and often misunderstood part of an administrator's duties. Sharing a folder is different from Web sharing a folder, and share permissions are different from NTFS permissions. All these concepts and principals will be discussed and tested in depth.

Monitor and manage network security. Actions include auditing and detecting security breaches.

- **Configure user-account lockout settings.**
- **Configure user-account password length, history, age, and complexity.**
- **Configure Group Policy to run logon scripts.**
- **Link Group Policy objects.**
- **Enable and configure auditing.**
- **Monitor security by using the system security log file.**

▶ It should go without saying that network security is of prime concern lately. It seems like every week we hear of security-related incidents at companies, both large and small. Windows 2000 provides a robust security platform from which an administrator can work when designing the perfect solution for her organization. Auditing and monitoring play important roles in this job.

Outline

OUTLINE

STUDY STRATEGIES

- The majority of this chapter focuses on sharing resources and Active Directory. A thorough understanding of Active Directory is recommended before taking this exam. You are expected to be able to use knowledge to solve problems more than being able to just spit out facts and figures.
- The physical and logical structures of Active Directory are a departure from Windows NT 4.0, although NetWare users might cite some similarities. Understanding how each part works to form the whole is key. A solid understanding of organizational units and why they are the prime means of assigning permissions is extremely important; gone are the days of resource and account domains as in Windows NT 4.0.
- A solid understanding of share and NTFS permissions is vital if you plan on providing resources across the network. Together, they determine what access each user will have when attempting to access resources. Permissions are covered in some detail in this chapter, in addition to the discussion in Chapter 1, because they are very important.
- Understanding how auditing works, its good points, and its bad points is important if you want to be able to keep an eye on what's going on with your network. Windows 2000 provides a fairly robust auditing system that is easy to implement and gives you the information you need when problems start to occur due to user actions. Ensure that you fully understand the process to enable and configure auditing, as well as the performance implications associated when auditing is in place on a network.

INTRODUCTION

This chapter tackles two fairly large areas: resource sharing and general network security. Before we can begin looking at how to configure and share resources in Active Directory, we must step back and take some time to fully understand Active Directory. The logical and physical structure of Active Directory is outlined, as is how legacy clients interact with Active Directory and the special steps involved.

After you've gained a good understanding of the design and operation of Active Directory, you will start putting it to work. Publishing resources and monitoring resource usage are examined, as are some troubleshooting techniques you might need to employ when things don't quite work right the first time around. The differences between share and NTFS permissions seems to be a source of constant problems, and they are examined in detail, including how they work together to determine the cumulative access allowed to a shared network resource.

The last thing we look at in this chapter is network security. Event auditing and the use of the Security Log are examined, and ways to implement auditing in your organization are presented.

USING ACTIVE DIRECTORY

To efficiently use any technology, especially one as powerful and complicated as Active Directory, you need to have a solid foundation of knowledge on which to base those actions. Before we get into publishing and sharing resources via Active Directory, let's take a few steps back and get a refresher on what Active Directory is, its logical and physical structures, and how your legacy clients interact with it. After you are up to speed on Active Directory's basics, you will get to work using it to make your job as an administrator easier.

Active Directory Overview

The following sections discuss the logical and physical structure of Active Directory. Understanding these structures is key to being able to use Active Directory effectively to provide resources and control usages. Also, the Active Directory client for legacy machines is examined.

> **EXAM TIP**
>
> **Focused Studying** Even though it's important to understand the basics of Active Directory, don't be too concerned about it. This exam expects more applied knowledge than theoretical knowledge out of the candidate. Practice using Active Directory, and you will be ahead of the game.

Directory Services Review

A *directory* is a listing of users, computers, groups, internal and external contacts, and various other directory objects. These users, computers, and groups are those that are allowed to connect to a system. This list further enables you to specify which users, computers, and groups are allowed to use which resources; you can set security using a username, computer name, or group name. The *directory service* is the program that runs in conjunction with the server service to establish the username. This service, in essence, provides the authentication, and the server service provides the actual access to the resource.

Although not within the scope of this exam, you can find more specific information about how Active Directory is designed and functions from the following resources:

- "Active Directory Overview" at `http://www.microsoft.com/windows2000/server/evaluation/features/dirlist.asp`
- "Active Directory Service Overview" at `http://www.microsoft.com/windows2000/server/evaluation/business/addatasheet.asp`
- "Active Directory Design" at `http://www.microsoft.com/TechNet/prodtechnol/windows2000serv/training/w2khost/w2ktad.asp`

In the next several sections, we will look at that basic security process involved in using a directory service such as Active Directory, the basic objects that populate Active Directory, and the logical and physical structure of Active Directory. So, without further ado, let's dive right in with the Active Directory objects and processes!

Objects in Active Directory

Understanding the basic objects that exist in Active Directory is an important part of being able to successfully work with Active Directory. Some objects are very obvious: users, computers, and groups. But some objects are not so obvious: organizational units and sites. The next few sections discuss each object and its use. First, however, we need to define an object as it relates to Windows 2000.

Basically everything is an object.

Obviously, this is a little on the vague side. However, it is perfectly accurate. Windows 2000 (as well as other versions of Windows) treats everything as an object primarily to simplify security. The easiest way to view an object is as a container; an *object* holds something. A *file* object holds data; a *group* object holds a list of members. Some objects, such as printers or users, hold a place rather than actually holding something tangible; such objects are known as *leaf-level* objects.

All objects have the following attached to them:

- **Methods**—All objects have some basic methods in common, such as creating the object, opening the object, and deleting the object. In addition, most objects have methods that are specific to them. Think of methods as verbs—the actions that you can perform on the object or that the object can perform.
- **Properties**—All objects have properties or attributes that distinguish them from other objects. These attributes are the things that make objects different from one another. At the very least, objects have a name and type; beyond this, the properties are type specific with a good number of common attributes between similar types.
- **Collections**—When a property or an attribute could have more than a single value (such as the ingredients in a can of soup), these values are stored as a collection—an array of values. The number of members in the collection is usually unknown.

An example of a method is performing an action on a row of a database. You might add a row, edit the information in a row, or remove a row from a table. These methods would generally be known as create, update, and delete. Notice that you can use the same verbs for everything in the operating system, including files, printers, computers, and so on. This is what makes using objects so efficient. The number of verbs (actions) the computer needs to understand is greatly reduced, and general routines can be created to handle these functions. This makes programs easier to write, but it also makes the security easier to implement because all the objects are accessed the same way.

The properties would, of course, relate to the columns in the table of a database. There are the obvious ones, such as the name of the object and the type of object. Other properties are required, such as the owner of the object. A collection actually is a multiple-value field, that is, a field in which you could enter many different values, such as "big" and "blue" to describe the sky. This isn't technically how it is implemented, but it is a good way to think of it.

A key collection that is placed on each object is the Discretionary Access Control List (DACL). This is where the security model becomes both strong and simple. Because everything in the operating system is accessed the same way and everything has a DACL, Microsoft could easily create a security reference model. For this model to work, though, we need to ensure that any process, user, service, or program that will attempt to access an object has a security context.

A security context is a group of unique characteristics that together form an identity that differentiates one object from other objects. Simply put, because of this context, the operating system knows which object (remember, users are objects) is attempting to access another object. A *process* is the general term used to describe a program that is running. A process can be a *background* process, such as a service, or a *foreground* process, such as the program a user is running. When you log on to Windows 2000, you are authenticated against the directory services, and a program called Explorer.exe is running. This is the shell that you run in; it manages your desktop; puts the taskbar on the screen; and handles the actions you take on your desktop, such as clicking the Start menu. Additionally, this very same process enables us to locate and work with files and folders via the well-known Windows Explorer.

When you are authenticated and Explorer is started for you, information about you is attached to it. The information is your unique object ID (which is your SID) and the unique object IDs for the groups to which you belong (their SIDs); together, they form the access token. When you run a program such as Word, the IDs attached to Explorer (your user process) are compared to the ACL on the Word executable (and supporting files). If you have permission, the system launches Word in another process and attaches your credentials (your object ID and those of the groups to which you belong) to the process.

Background processes also start under a given security context. They can be started using a username and password, just like you logging on, or they can start under the system account. The system account is actually the computer's local account, and it is stored in a local account's database.

By using the preceding process and treating everything like an object, Windows 2000 maintains security regardless of how a user accesses an object. Now that object access has been explained, it is appropriate to look at some of the objects with which you can work in Active Directory:

- **Computers**—The computer object is just that, a computer in the enterprise. This object is used in the background to enable the computers to be grouped together for management purposes. The account also lets the computer authenticate user logons because the computer will know which domain to use for authentication.
- **Users**—Users are obviously a big part of the network, and without them, the network would be pointless (though faster). A user object holds the user's account, and this enables the user to connect to the domain.
- **Groups**—A group object (account) contains a list of users who belong to the group. It also, in Windows 2000, can contain other groups. These objects are also used when placing permission on other objects so that, rather than adding each user account, you can work with a larger group of users in one step. Groups, therefore, are also used to gather together several user accounts into a single object.
- **Printers**—In Windows 2000, you have the option of creating a printer object in Active Directory if you share your printer. This is used primarily to enable users to search Active Directory. The printer is still an object on the local machine that acts as a print server, and that computer handles the security.

- **Shares**—Similar to printers, shares can also be published in Active Directory. This, again, is primarily to enable users to search for the share. The computer hosting the share is responsible for checking the object permissions when the share is accessed.

The Logical Structure of Active Directory

Although some of the following information has already been introduced, it is worth taking a closer look at the logical structures that make up Active Directory.

The discussion begins with a look at domains and the purpose of domains, which are the building blocks of the logical structure. Then, the discussion turns to the ways in which you can tie domains together into trees and, eventually, how trees can expand to make up a forest.

Domains

The basic unit you deal with is the domain, just like Windows NT 4.0. By breaking your enterprise into different domains, you achieve several benefits:

- Domains enable you to organize objects in a single department or a single location. Within the domain, all information about the objects is available.
- Domains act as a management boundary in that domain administrators have complete control over all the resources in the domain. Group policies can be applied at the domain level and determine how resources can be accessed, configured, and used. See the following note for the exception to this rule—you knew it was coming!
- Domain objects can be made available to other domains and be published in Active Directory.
- Domain names follow the domain name service (DNS) naming structure. This permits an infinite number of child domains.
- Domains enable you to control replication; objects stored in the domain are fully replicated only to other domain controllers in the domain.

> NOTE
>
> **The Exception to the Rule** Although beyond the scope of the exam, it is important to point out that no good rule exists without an exception of some kind. Administrators in the root of the forest can control any domain within the forest. In addition, malicious domain owners (of other domains within the same forest) can gain access to other domains in that forest. See the TechNet article "Design Considerations for Delegation of Administration in Active Directory" located at `http://www.microsoft.com/technet/prodtechnol/windows2000serv/deploy/projplan/addeladm.asp` for more information about this issue.

There are two ways to create Active Directory domains: by upgrading an existing Windows NT 4.0 domain or by installing a Windows 2000 server and then promoting it to be a domain controller.

After you have created a root domain, you can then create trees. A tree always starts with the root domain, but it then can branch out to include other domains. This provides you with the first level of hierarchies in Active Directory.

Trees and Forests

When you are controlling the domain, you are dealing with the working level of the network. Users are located in domains, and computers are located in domains. To tie the domains together, you need to organize them into a logical structure. This structure is either a domain tree or a forest.

The DNS hierarchy is used in Windows 2000 to tie the various domains together and to create the domain tree. If you start with a domain, such as `Whatsits.com`, for example, you could create a single domain that contains all the objects in your enterprise. However, this might not be practical if your organization has offices in two major geographical areas and if each area works independently from the other. In this case, you might opt to create separate domains that could be independently managed. In Figure 2.1, you will notice that a `Whatsits.com` domain, as well as an `East.Whatsits.com` domain and a `West.Whatsits.com` domain, exists. In this case, the top domain is simply a pointer to one or the other of the lower-level domains.

NOTE

DNS and the Active Directory For more information on DNS and Active Directory, see KB# Q237675 at `http://support.microsoft.com/directory/article.asp?ID=KB;EN-US;Q237675`.

If you were to break the organization down along the lines of an organizational chart, the tree might look more like Figure 2.2. This figure shows a domain for sales and marketing, a domain for logistics (production and shipping), and a domain for research and development. The administration and other support roles, in this case, would be in the top-level domain.

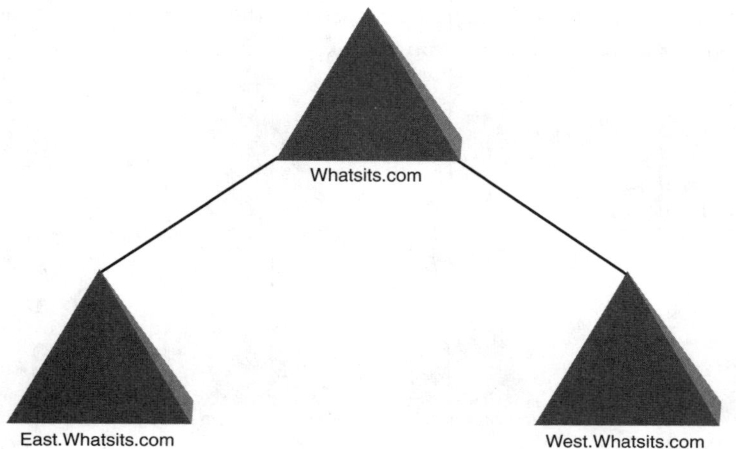

FIGURE 2.1
A sample domain tree for `Whatsits.com` broken down using geography.

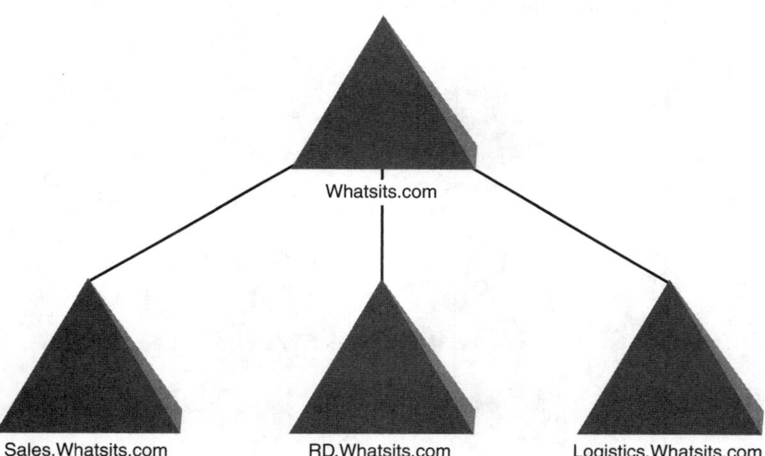

FIGURE 2.2
A sample domain tree for `Whatsits.com` broken down by function.

Throughout this enterprise, there would be a single schema, a common global catalog, and transitive two-way trust relationships. In some cases, however, a domain tree will not work. In cases in which different parts of the organization need to have separate public identities, you can't use the same structure if the internal naming is to mirror the external nature. In a case such as this, you might have more than one tree. However, it is still important to keep the three common elements: shared schema, shared configuration, and the global catalog. To do this, one of the domains becomes the root of the enterprise. The other domains are children even though their names look different. In Figure 2.3, `Things.com` has been added. Convention dictates that the line joining the new tree to the forest is drawn to the top of the root to show that it is not just a child domain.

FIGURE 2.3
A sample domain forest.

Things.com
Whatsits.com
Sales.Whatsits.com
RD.Whatsits.com
Logistics.Whatsits.com

From here, you could add children to `Things.com` (see Figure 2.4).

FIGURE 2.4
An expanded domain forest.

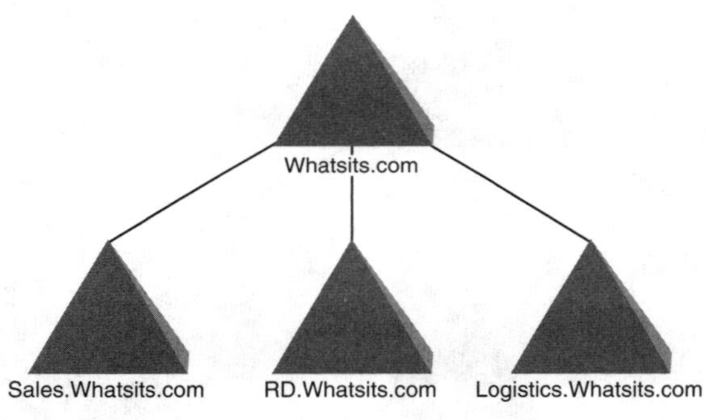

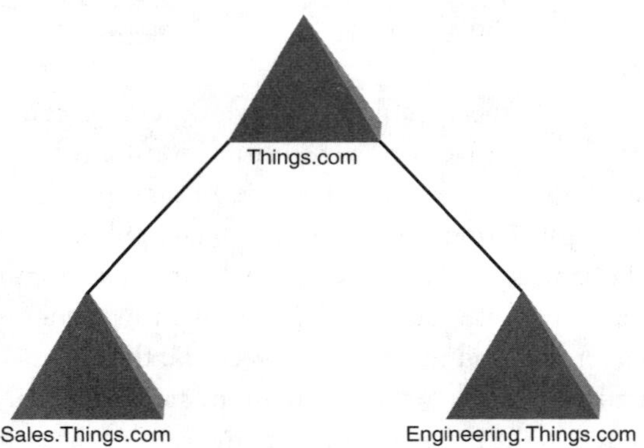

The combination of trees and forests provides you absolute flexibility in the design of your domain structure and, therefore, in the design of your Active Directory.

Now that you have knowledge of domains, which provide your first level of hierarchy, let's move on and talk about organizational units (OUs). OUs provide the secondary level of hierarchy. They let you break down a domain into logical units you can control, to a degree, independently.

Organizational Units

The capability to delegate control of part of a domain to a user or a group of users is new to Windows 2000. This is achieved through the use of organizational units. An *organizational unit* is a container in Active Directory that you create. After you create the container, you can move computers, users, and other objects into the container.

After this is accomplished, you could delegate control of those objects in the container to a set of users or groups. As a domain administrator, you still have control, but the people you delegate can also control these objects. This enables you to create workgroup administrators who can handle a limited section of your domain. You can also apply group policies to the organizational unit that are different from those policies you applied to the domain.

Figure 2.5 shows an example of how the `Whatsits.com` network could be fit into a single domain while still providing local administrators to deal with a group of users and computers.

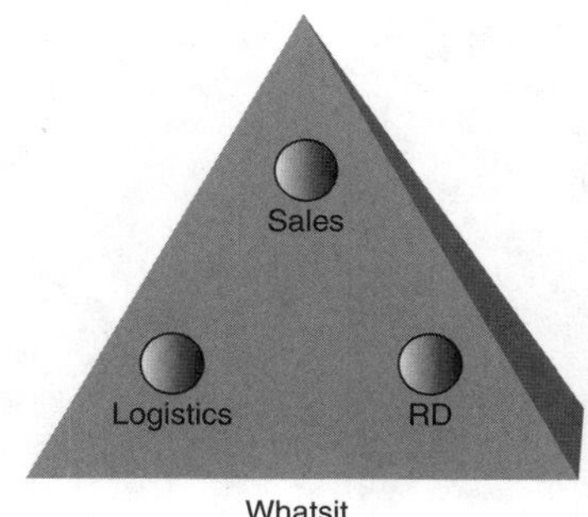

FIGURE 2.5
The `Whatsits.com` network designed using organizational units.

You can even create organizational units within another organizational unit. This enables you to create a hierarchy of organizational units in a domain.

As you can see, the logical structure of Active Directory is used to build a hierarchy that enables you to organize users in any size organization. Using domains, you can create security and replication boundaries, and then using organizational units, you can further divide domains into manageable sections.

Groups in Windows 2000

Obviously, you don't want to have to manage 70,000 users 1 at a time. You need to be able to group together users and computers so you can work with many users or computers at the same time.

As you start to learn about groups in Windows 2000, it is worth looking back over all the information you can store about users.

One of the intents of Windows 2000 is to bring together directory services from the network side and the email side. A large part of the information you can store for users is information that you normally, until now, would have stored in the email system.

This becomes even more evident as you start to look at groups because two main types of groups can be created in the Windows 2000 directory services:

- **Distribution groups**—These groups are used exclusively for email and can't be used to set security.
- **Security groups**—These groups can be used to group together users or to assign permissions to objects on the network or in Active Directory. These groups can also be used for email.

Although the distribution groups are a valid object in the Windows 2000 Active Directory, the rest of the discussion concentrates on security groups. We will examine the main functions of groups, domain modes, strategies for using groups, built-in and predefined groups, predefined global groups, special identities, and the management of groups.

Two main functions are taken on by a group in the Windows 2000 Active Directory: Groups are used to gather users accounts into a single entity to simplify the administration of users, and groups assign permissions to objects and resources. The difference is in the scope of the group:

- **Domain local**—Domain local groups are used to gather permission to perform functions in a domain. The local group in a Windows NT domain is available only on the computer on which it is created. In Windows 2000, the local group is available on all systems in the domain that run Windows 2000 and are referred to as domain local groups. Domain local groups are available in Native or Mixed mode.
- **Global**—Global groups typically are used to gather user accounts together and should normally not be given permissions. The users gain permissions from adding the global group to a local group that has permissions. Global groups can contain users from the local domain only. They are available in the domain in which they are created and in other domains in the tree or forest. Global groups are available in Native or Mixed mode.

- **Universal**—Universal groups combine the capabilities of the global and local groups. They can contain users and groups from any domain in the tree or forest and can be assigned rights to resources or objects in any domain. This group removes the boundaries of domains from management. It increases the amount of replication required between global catalog servers because global catalog servers manage these groups. Universal groups are available only in Native mode.

> NOTE
>
> **Users, Computers, and Groups** For more information on Active Directory Users, Computers, and Groups, see the white paper "Active Directory Users, Computers, and Groups," located at `http://www.microsoft.com/TechNet/prodtechnol/windows2000serv/maintain/adusers.asp`.
>
> Also see "Understanding User and Group Accounts," located at `http://www.microsoft.com/TechNet/prodtechnol/windows2000serv/evaluate/featfunc/07w2kada.asp`.

The Physical Structure of Active Directory

Now that you have a good idea of how the logical structure of Active Directory is arranged, understanding the physical structure will be an easy task.

Sites

The physical structure of Active Directory starts with sites, much the same as the logical structure starts with domains. A *site* is defined as a group of computers on one or more IP subnets that are *well connected*. Well connected has its own definition, as you might expect. Well connected means, according to Microsoft, that the systems share a network transport that provides low-cost, high-speed communications between machines. This, as you might surmise, generally refers to computers that are located in a single location (geographically or otherwise, such as a building) and are connected by a local area network (LAN).

Subnets

A *subnet* is a subnetwork—a smaller part of a network that is created to divide a larger network into smaller chunks for whatever reason. A subnet is defined as a portion of the network that operates as a separate network, without regard to what happens outside and without affecting the rest of the network.

Domain Controllers

Domain controllers have been discussed somewhat already, but not really defined. Microsoft defines a *domain controller* as a computer in a Windows domain environment running Active Directory that manages user access to a network, which includes logging on, authentication, and access to the directory and shared resources.

You must have at least one domain controller to have a Windows 2000 Active Directory domain structure. You can, however, have as many domain controllers as you like. As with most network services, more is not always better; you will need to find the right balance of domain controllers to suit your needs.

Unlike Windows NT 4.0, Windows 2000 domain controllers are created equal, with one small exception that we will explore in the next paragraph. Under NT 4.0, a single primary domain controller (PDC) and one or more backup domain controllers (BDC), as desired, existed. The PDC maintained the only writable copy of the directory database, which was then replicated to all BDCs on the network. In Windows 2000, all domain controllers contain a writable copy of the directory database, and thus, can accept and replicate changes to all other domain controllers in the domain. This way of maintaining the directory database is called a *multimaster replication system*, and it allows changes to be made at any domain controller—versus only at the PDC as in the Windows NT 4.0 *single-master replication system.*

The one exception to Windows 2000 domain controllers being absolutely equal with each other has to do with the first domain controller created. The first Windows 2000 domain controller is automatically assigned the role of global catalog server and also the five operations master roles: primary domain controller (PDC) emulator, schema master, domain naming master, relative identifier (RID) master, and infrastructure master. These five roles can be reassigned later as more domain controllers are added, but you should never assign the infrastructure master role to a domain controller that is hosting the Global Catalog. See KB# Q223346 at `http://support.microsoft.com/default.aspx?scid=kb;EN-US;q223346` for more information about locating the operations master roles.

> NOTE
>
> **Bridgehead Server Description** For more information on bridgehead servers, see KB# Q271997 at `http://support.microsoft.com/directory/article.asp?ID=KB;EN-US;Q271997`.

Bridgehead Servers

Bridgehead servers are not new in Windows 2000; the concept has been used in many products before, such as Exchange Server. In Windows 2000 Server, a *bridgehead server* serves as the point of contact when directory information must be exchanged between sites. Bridgehead servers are themselves domain controllers and have been either automatically or manually assigned the additional duty of being a bridgehead to another site.

Active Directory Client Extensions

If you need to support legacy clients on the network in your Windows 2000 Active Directory domain, Microsoft has come to the rescue with the Active Directory Client Extensions, which enable these clients to make partial use of Active Directory. The Active Directory Client Extensions are available for Windows 95, Windows 98, and Windows NT 4.0 computers.

The Windows 95 and Windows 98 versions can be found on the Windows 2000 Server CD-ROM in the `X:\CLIENTS\WIN9X` folder, where `X` is the path to your CD. The Windows NT 4.0 Workstation version can be downloaded from the Microsoft Web site, at `http://www.microsoft.com/windows2000/server/evaluation/news/bulletins/adextension.asp`.

Legacy clients connecting to a Windows 2000 Active Directory domain using the Active Directory Client Extensions will have the partial functionality (when compared with a Windows 2000 Professional client), as highlighted in Table 2.1.

TABLE 2.1

SOME OF THE ACTIVE DIRECTORY FEATURES SUPPORTED BY ACTIVE DIRECTORY CLIENT EXTENSIONS

Feature	*Description*
Site awareness	Legacy clients will have the capability to log on to the domain controller that is closest to the client in the network and the capability to change passwords on any Windows 2000-based domain controller, instead of the PDC.
Dfs fault-tolerance client	Legacy clients will be capable of using the Windows 2000 distributed file system (Dfs) fault-tolerant and fail-over file shares specified in Active Directory.
NTLM version 2 authentication	Legacy clients will be capable of taking advantage of the improved authentication features available in NTLM version 2.

Some of the Active Directory features that are not supported by the Active Directory Client Extensions are outlined in Table 2.2.

TABLE 2.2

SOME OF THE ACTIVE DIRECTORY FEATURES NOT SUPPORTED BY ACTIVE DIRECTORY CLIENT EXTENSIONS

Feature	*Description*
Kerberos	Legacy clients will be incapable of using Kerberos like Windows 2000 clients.
IntelliMirror	Legacy clients will be incapable of taking advantage of the IntelliMirror management technologies or Windows 2000 Group Policy functionality.
IPSec and L2TP support	Legacy clients will be incapable of using advanced virtual private networking (VPN) protocols, such as Internet Protocol security (IPSec) and Layer 2 Tunneling Protocol (L2TP).

The past sections covered a large amount of ground. All this work has been in preparation for the actual meat of the chapter (from an exam standpoint)—using Active Directory to publish resources to the domain and its users.

Publishing Resources in Active Directory

Publishing resources in Active Directory makes them easier to find across your organization. Because a partial replica of the database is copied to all global catalogs in the network, searching for and locating the required network resources is an easy task. Publishing resources with Active Directory makes perfect sense when you step back and think about why you have network resources in the first place: for your users to *use*. Active Directory makes this even easier than before.

Publishing Printers

- ▶ Publish resources in Active Directory. Types of resources include printers and shared folders.
    - Configure a printer object.

By default, all printers that are physically connected and installed on Windows 2000 server computers that participate in an Active Directory domain are published in the Active Directory catalog, so long as they are shared. Sharing a printer is done from the Sharing tab of the printer Properties windows, as shown in Figure 2.6.

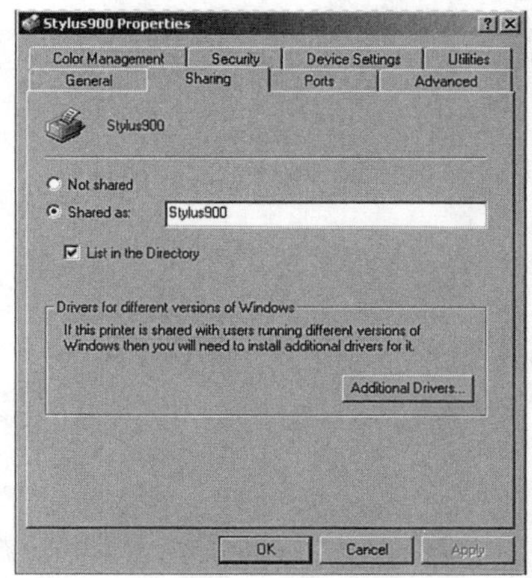

FIGURE 2.6
Publishing printers from the Properties tab.

Printer publishing is controlled by Group Policy from the following objects (see Figure 2.7):

- **Allow Printers to Be Published**—Determines whether the Add Printer Wizard automatically publishes the computer's shared printers in Active Directory
- **Automatically Publish New Printers in Active Directory**—Determines whether the computer's shared printers can be published in Active Directory

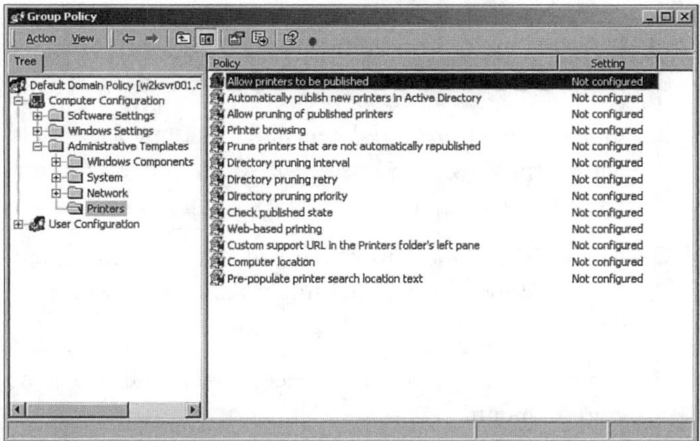

FIGURE 2.7
Configuring printer publishing behavior.

Additionally, browsing the network for printers can be configured from Group Policy with the following objects (see Figure 2.8):

- **Disable Addition of Printers**—Prevents users from using familiar methods to add local and network printers
- **Browse the Network to Find Printers**—Lets users use the Add Printer Wizard to search the network for shared printers

You can also manually publish printers in Active Directory if the printer is attached to a non-Windows 2000 machine. The process to manually publish printers is demonstrated in Step By Step 2.1.

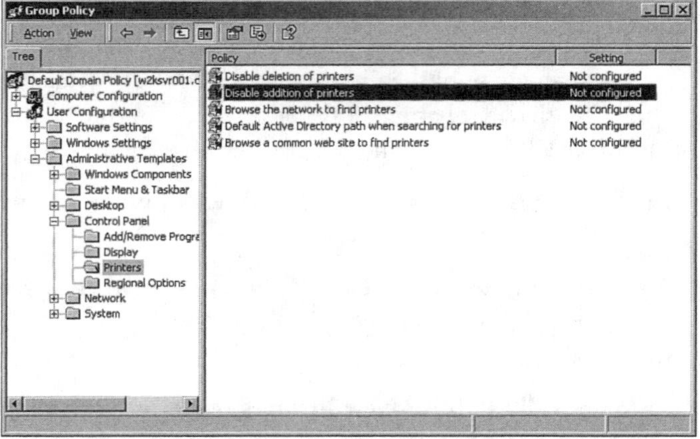

FIGURE 2.8
Configuring browsing the network for printers.

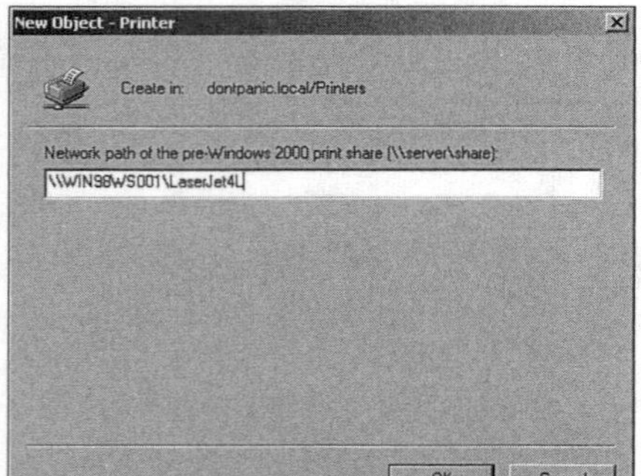

FIGURE 2.9
Manually publishing printers in Active Directory.

STEP BY STEP

2.1 Publishing a Non-Windows 2000 Printer in Active Directory

1. Open Active Directory Users and Computers by selecting Start, Programs, Administrative Tools, Active Directory Users and Computers.
2. Expand the domain in which you want to publish the share and locate the folder under which you want to publish it.
3. Right-click the folder and select New, Printer from the context menu.
4. Enter the network path for the printer (see Figure 2.9).
5. Click OK.

Publishing File Shares

- ▶ Publish resources in Active Directory. Types of resources include printers and shared folders.

By publishing a share, users can find the share in Active Directory. Publishing a share is a simple process done in Active Directory Users and Computers. This is demonstrated in Step By Step 2.2.

STEP BY STEP

2.2 Publishing a Share in Active Directory

1. Open Active Directory Users and Computers by selecting Start, Programs, Administrative Tools, Active Directory Users and Computers.
2. Expand the domain in which you want to publish the share and locate the folder under which you want to publish it.
3. Right-click the folder and select New, Shared Folder from the context menu.
4. Enter the name you want to appear in Active Directory and the name of the share it represents (see Figure 2.10).
5. Click OK.

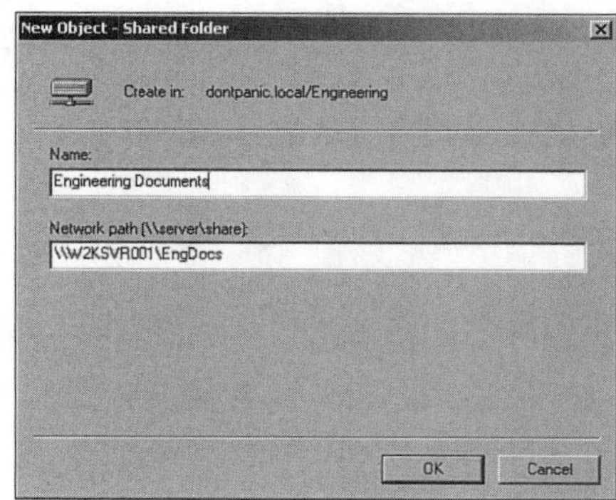

FIGURE 2.10
Publishing shared folders in Active Directory.

When you publish a shared folder in Active Directory, the folder will not be created, so ensure you have created and shared the folder before attempting to publish it.

Searching for Published Resources

- Publish resources in Active Directory. Types of resources include printers and shared folders.
  - Perform a search in Active Directory Users and Computers.

As the number of objects you store in Active Directory increases, you obviously need some method of finding the objects so you can work with them. In addition, there would be little point in configuring Active Directory to create a list of all the objects across your enterprise if the users were not able to locate the objects. In this section, you will see how to locate objects in Active Directory from both the administrative interface and the user interface.

EXAM TIP

Resources, Oh Lovely Resources
The only reason resources exist in a directory is so that they can be found and used. Being familiar with locating resources is an important part of getting ready for this exam.

Finding Objects in the Management Interface

When you are working with the users and computers that make up your network, you need to be able to find the object you want to manage. This can be done using either the Find command located in the context menu for the domain or the Find icon on the toolbar. Step By Step 2.3 walks you through using the Find command to locate an object.

STEP BY STEP

2.3 Locating an Object Using the Find Command

1. Open Active Directory Users and Computers by selecting Start, Programs, Administrative Tools, Active Directory Users and Computers.
2. On any domain, right-click and select Find from the context menu.
3. In the Find text box, select what you want to find (see Figure 2.11).

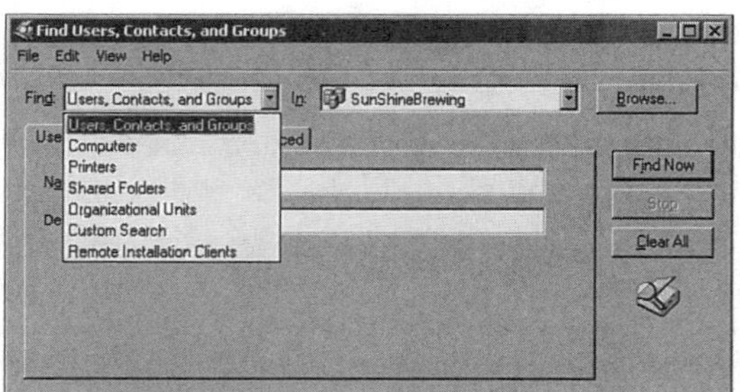

FIGURE 2.11
The Find dialog box showing what you can find.

4. In the In text box, select which domain to search or select that you want to search all of Active Directory (see Figure 2.12).

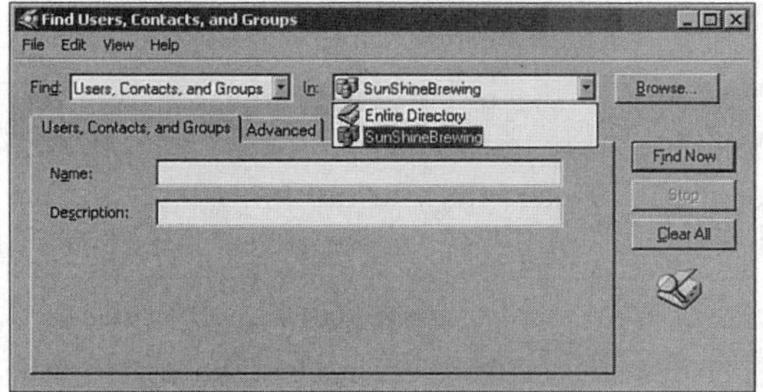

FIGURE 2.12
The Find dialog box showing you search options.

5. Depending on your selection, you can now fill in the option for which you are searching. The following is a list of the search possibilities:
   - **Users, Contacts, and Groups**—In this case, you can enter a name or description.
   - **Computers**—When searching for computers, you can enter the name of the computer, the name of the owner, or the role in the domain (domain controller or workstation/server).
   - **Printers**—For printers, you can search by printer name, location, or model.
   - **Shared Folders**—For shared folders, you have the option of searching by name or by keywords associated with the shared folder.
   - **Organizational Unit**—If you need to search for an OU, your only choice is to enter the name.
   - **Custom Search**—This option enables you to specify exactly what you want to search and to search on several criteria. The custom search main screen is the same as the Advanced option for all the other searchable items. The Advanced option is described in more detail later in this chapter in the "Advanced Searches" section.
   - **Remote Installation Clients**—This enables you to search by the globally unique identifier or the remote installation server to which it is assigned.

continues

continued

You do not have to enter the full value for a text field. Search usually finds what you are looking for using a word or two. For example, you can find all the people with the last name Smith by entering **`Smith`** in the search box.

6. If you are searching for a printer, you could click the Features tab and search for a printer based on its available features (see Figure 2.13).

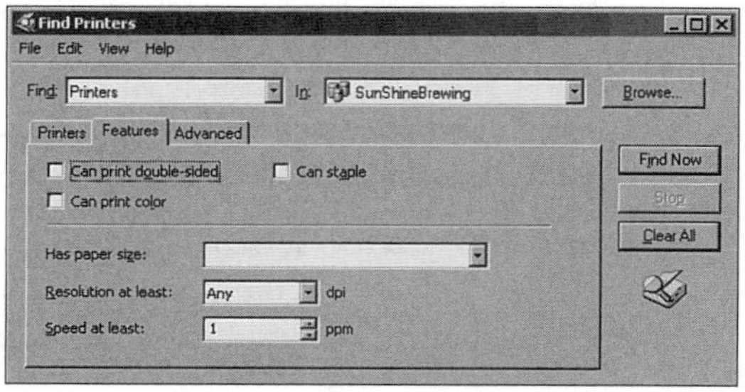

FIGURE 2.13
You can search for printers based on features.

7. Click Find Now, and the system performs the search, placing the results in a results window (see Figure 2.14).

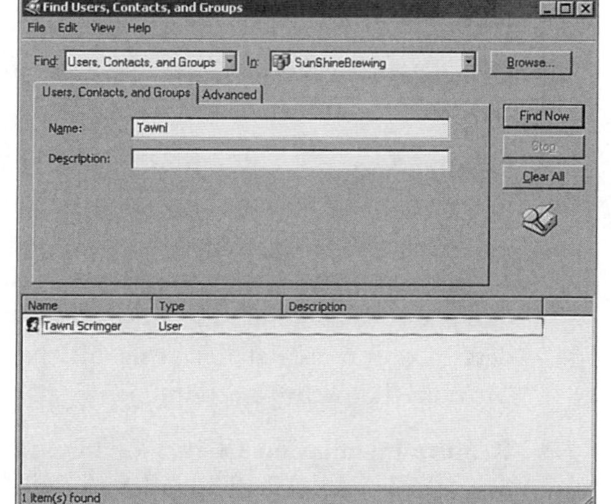

FIGURE 2.14
The results of a search.

After you have found the object or objects for which you were looking, you can select them and right-click to bring up the context menu. This gives you the same options as locating the object manually and then right-clicking.

Advanced Searches

By performing an advanced search, or using a custom search, you can be more specific about the objects you are trying to find. The objects you can search for appear along with a list of their attributes. Use Step By Step 2.4 to explore the advanced search options.

STEP BY STEP

2.4 Advanced Searches

1. In the Find dialog box, select the object to find; then, click the Advanced tab (see Figure 2.15).

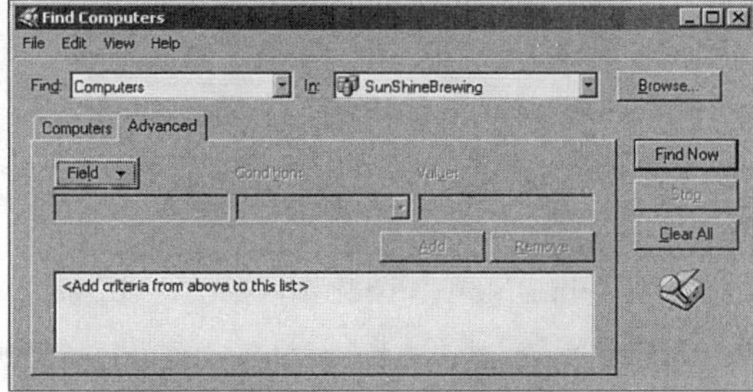

FIGURE 2.15
The Advanced search tab.

2. Click the Field button to drop down the list of fields on which you can search. Select the desired field (see Figure 2.16).

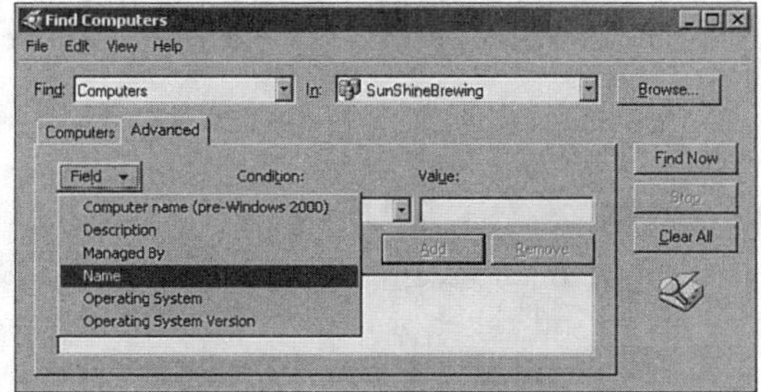

FIGURE 2.16
The options you can search for depend on the object you choose. In some cases, you have a list of objects with fields listed in a drop-down menu.

continues

continued

3. Select the type of condition from the Condition drop-down list (see Figure 2.17).

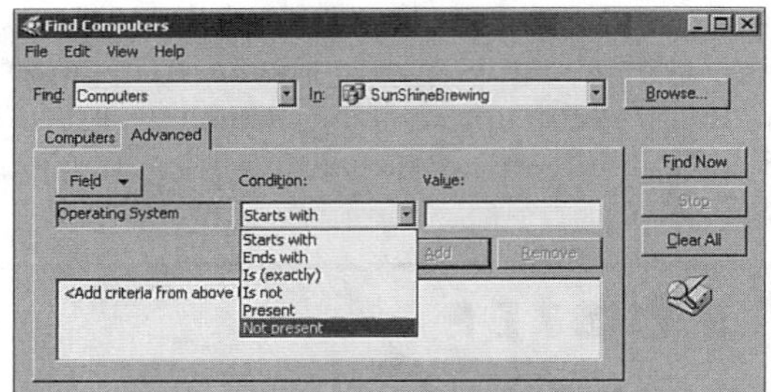

FIGURE 2.17
You can use several conditions, all of which expect a value other than Present or Not Present (which tests for the existence of the attribute).

4. If required, enter a value in the Value box.
5. Click Add to add the condition to the list. You can remove a condition by clicking the condition and then clicking Remove.
6. Repeat steps 2–5 for each additional condition for which you are searching. The conditions are treated like a logical AND.
7. Click the Find Now button to execute the search.

Using the advanced search functions enables you to find the objects you need more quickly and without having so many objects appear. The advanced search also enables you to access characteristics to find groups of objects with a common setting.

Finding objects in the administrative tools is useful for you as an administrator, but users also need to be able to find Active Directory objects.

Finding Objects As a User

Users also need to be able to search for objects in Active Directory. The users can easily find either printers or people using the Search tools on the Start menu. Step By Step 2.5 walks you through a search for a printer.

STEP BY STEP

2.5 Searching for a Printer in Active Directory

1. Select Start, Search, For Printers to bring up the dialog box shown in Figure 2.18.

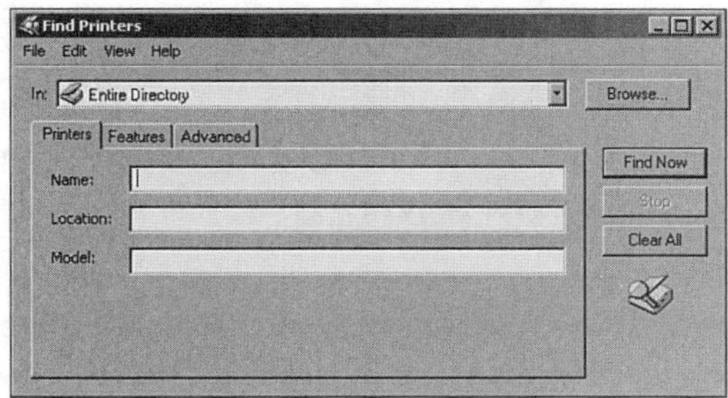

FIGURE 2.18
The interface is displayed for users to find printers.

2. Enter the search criteria as seen in Figure 2.18, or leave the Find Printers dialog box empty to find all printers.
3. Click the Find Now button.

When the user finds a printer, she can right-click the printer and select Connect to use the printer. Finding people is similar to finding printers; Step By Step 2.6 walks you through finding people with Active Directory.

STEP BY STEP

2.6 Finding People in Active Directory

1. Select Start, Search, For People to bring up the Find People dialog box.
2. In the Look In drop-down list box, select Active Directory (see Figure 2.19).
3. Enter the name or other information you are looking for, and then click Find Now (see Figure 2.20).

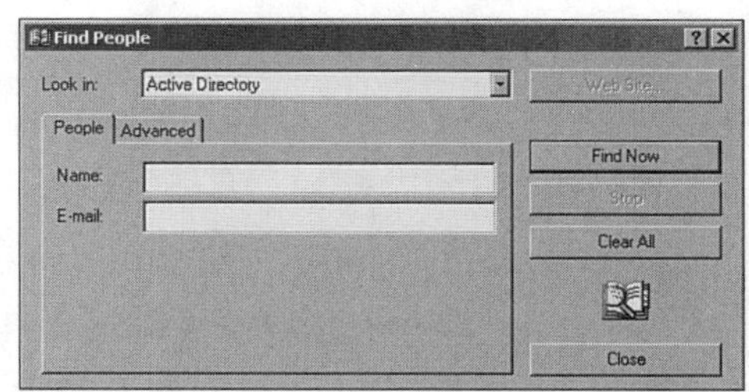

FIGURE 2.19
The Find People dialog box can search Active Directory or any other LDAP provider.

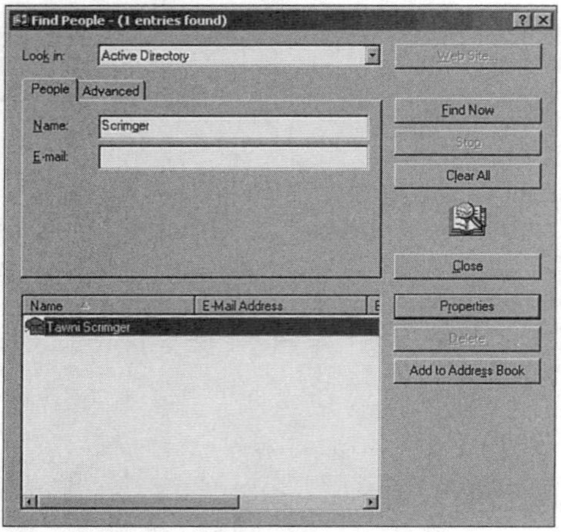

FIGURE 2.20
The results are displayed in a results pane.

Using this tool, users can find other users on the network and access information about them. They also can use this to send email to other users.

Now you should understand that you need to be able to locate objects both as an administrator and as a user.

You might be wondering about the security if just anybody can find objects on your network. This is not a concern because the objects are all protected by an access control list (ACL).

SHARING RESOURCES

To allow remote access to resources, you must make them available over the network. After resources are available on the network, users with the appropriate permissions can access resources from computers found on the network. One of the challenges facing the network administrator is how to provide access to resources and still have a secure environment. Windows 2000 enables you to control the resources you want to make available over the network.

Configuring and Managing File Shares

File shares are probably the most common type of resource shared today in the enterprise. As simple as file shares are to configure, there is still room for error. In the following sections, we look take a closer look at creating, configuring, and managing file shares effectively.

Creating Shared Folders

- ▶ Create shared resources and configure access rights. Shared resources include printers, shared folders, and Web folders.
    - Share folders and enable Web sharing.

Shared folders can be created in two different ways. This section provides detailed step-by-step instructions regarding the setup of shared folders.

Step By Step 2.7 shows how to share folders from your local hard drive. This means you have access to the local system. In Step By Step 2.7, you share a folder called `DATA` from the local `C:` partition of your system to a local group called "Account". The Account group needs Change permissions to this resource, and the local administrators group needs Full Control permissions to the share so the resource can be managed. This Step By Step assumes you have a directory called `DATA` on your local drive and a group called Account created on your local system; if you do not, you can use any folder and group of your choosing.

STEP BY STEP

2.7 Sharing Folders on Local Drives

1. From the Explorer Window, find the `DATA` directory on the `C:` partition.
2. Right-click the directory and select Properties from the context menu.
3. Click the Sharing tab.
4. Select the Share This Folder option. After this option has been selected, you can provide a share name and description and configure the share. The share name represents the name used when accessing the resource over the network. The Comment field is used to describe the resources being shared (some user interfaces show you the share description when accessing the share). For the share name, enter **`Accounting Data`** (see Figure 2.21).
5. Enter **`Test of Account Data Share`** for the Comment.
6. Leave the User Limit setting to Maximum Allowed. This setting enables you to limit the total number of users allowed to access this shared folder at any one time.
7. To set the share permissions, click the Permissions button. Figure 2.22 shows the share permissions assigned to the share.

continues

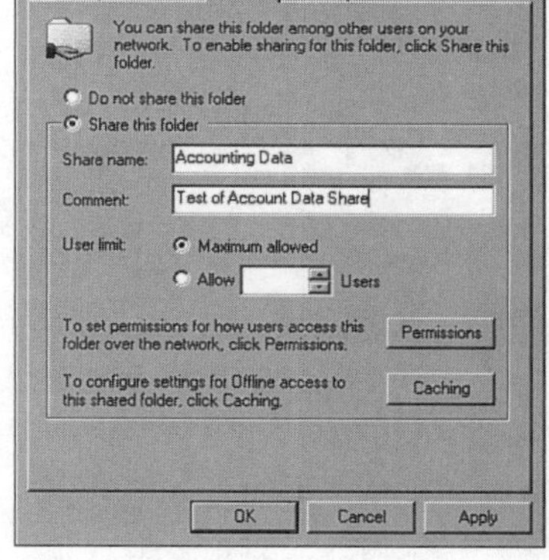

FIGURE 2.21
Creating a new share via Windows Explorer.

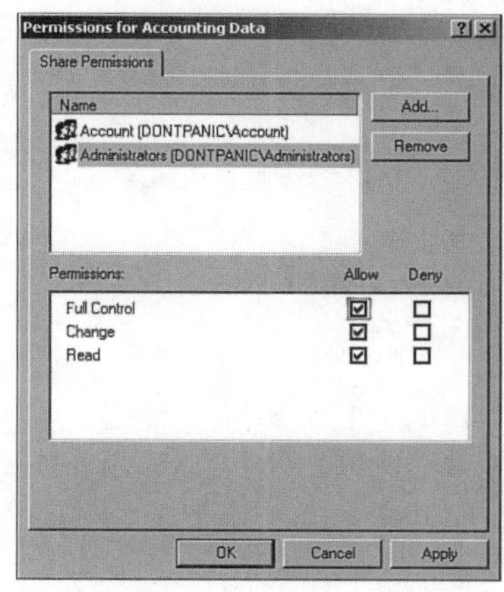

FIGURE 2.22
Windows 2000 Share Permissions property tab.

continued

8. Note the default permissions assigned to all new shares created in your environment. You should remove the default permissions of Everyone with Full Control permission by clicking the Remove button. You can now add the Account group by clicking the Add button and selecting the Account group from the Select Computer, Users, Groups dialog box. After you have found the group in the list, click the Add button; then, click OK. You can now assign share permission to the Account group. To do this, select the Account group and check the Allow box next to the Change permission. Repeat the same procedure to add the Administrator group to the list of users and groups with permission to use this share. Step By Step 2.11 has more information on working with share permissions.

9. Click OK to close the permissions window. Click Cache to open the cache window. Cache settings are explained in Table 2.3.

10. Select Allow Caching of Files in This Shared Folder, and in the Setting box, select Manual Caching for Documents (see Figure 2.23).

11. Click OK to close the cache window. Click OK to close the properties window and complete the sharing process. You should now see a small hand under the left corner of the `C:\DATA` folder to indicate that it is being shared.

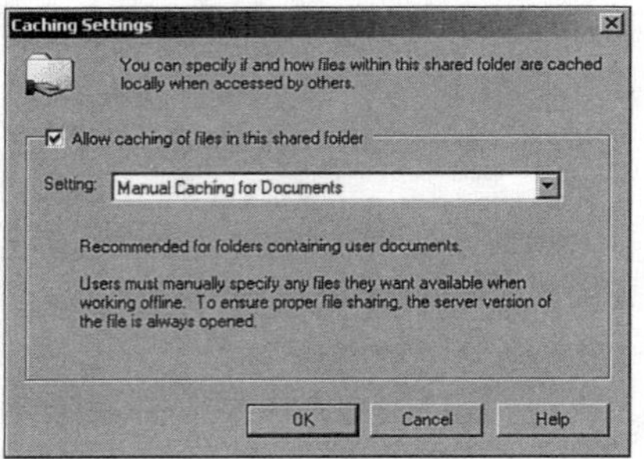

FIGURE 2.23
Setting cache properties for a share.

Offline files can be configured to store a version of them in a reserved portion of disk space on your computer called a *cache*. The computer can access this cache regardless of whether it is connected to the network. Table 2.3 presents the options available when configuring offline folders for caching.

TABLE 2.3

CACHE CONFIGURATION SETTINGS

Option	*Description*
Manual Caching for Documents	Provides offline access to only those files that someone using your shared folder specifically (or manually) identifies. This caching option is ideal for a shared network folder containing files that are to be accessed and modified by several people. This is the default option when you set up a shared folder to be used offline.
Automatic Caching for Documents	Makes every file that someone opens from your shared folder available to him offline. However, this setting does not make every file in your shared folder available to him offline—only those files that are opened. Files that are not opened are not available offline.
Automatic Caching for Programs	Provides offline access to shared folders containing files that are not to be changed. This caching option is ideal for making files available offline that are read, referenced, or run but that are not changed in the process. This option reduces network traffic because offline files are opened directly, without accessing the network versions in any way, and generally start and run faster than the network versions. When you use this option, be sure to restrict permissions on the files contained in the shared folder to read-only access.

The second method of creating shares can be performed on both local and remote computers. Step By Step 2.8 demonstrates how to create a share using the Computer Management Microsoft Management snap-in.

STEP BY STEP

2.8 Creating Shares Using the Computer Management Snap-In

1. Open Computer Manager by selecting Start, Programs, Administrative Tools, Computer Management.

2. If you want to share a folder on a remote system, click Computer Management at the root of the console. On the menu bar, click Action, Connect to Another Computer. Enter the remote computer to which you want to connect.

3. Open the Computer Management snap-in by clicking the plus sign beside the snap-in. Open the Shared Folders node of the Computer Management snap-in. From this location, you can create and manage shares on your system. Figure 2.24 shows the appropriate MMC screen.

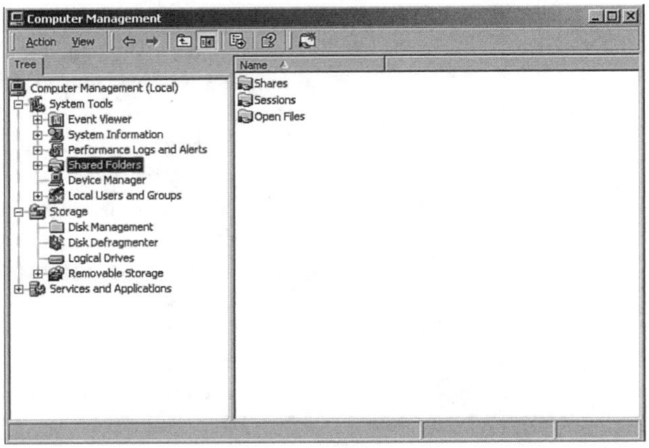

FIGURE 2.24
Computer Management snap-in with the Shared Folders node.

4. To create a new share, right-click the Shares folder in the Shared Folders node. From the context menu, select New File Share. This action launches the Create Share Folder Wizard.

5. The wizard will walk you through the process of creating the new share. At the first screen, you must indicate the physical path to the folder you want to share (a browse is provided so you can find the folder you want). For this example, enter **C:\DATA**. You also need to provide a share name and description. Click Next to continue.

6. You now must set the share permissions associated with the share. The wizard provides three common configurations and a custom option. In most cases, you need to enter a custom configuration. Entering permissions is identical to the process documented in Step By Step 2.7. Click the Finish button to create your share.

You can, alternatively, create and manage shares from the command line if you choose. This can be very useful if you plan to implement scripts to work with shares on your network. Working with shares from the command line is also useful if you take advantage of the Telnet service included in Windows 2000. Step By Step 2.9 walks you through creating a share from the command line.

STEP BY STEP

2.9 Creating a Share from the Command Line

1. Open a command prompt (Start, Programs, Accessories, Command Prompt).

2. Enter the command **NET SHARE *ShareName=Path***, such as **NET SHARE AccountingData=c:\data** where
    - *ShareName* is the name to which users to connect.
    - *Path* is the path on the disk you want to share.

3. Press Enter.

You can also get a listing of all shares, as shown in Step By Step 2.10.

STEP BY STEP

2.10 Retrieving a List of Shares at the Command Line

1. Open a command prompt (Start, Programs, Accessories, Command Prompt).
2. Enter the command **NET SHARE** and press Enter. The results will be shown as in Figure 2.25.

```
C:\WINNT\System32\cmd.exe
C:\>NET SHARE

Share name   Resource                        Remark

-------------------------------------------------------------------------------
print$       C:\WINNT\System32\spool\drivers Printer Drivers
E$           E:\                             Default share
IPC$                                         Remote IPC
D$           D:\                             Default share
C$           C:\                             Default share
ADMIN$       C:\WINNT                        Remote Admin
CD_ROM       F:\
Mac          D:\Mac
NETLOGON     C:\WINNT\SYSVOL\sysvol\dontpanic.local\SCRIPTS
                                             Logon server share
OS           C:\
Software     E:\
SYSVOL       C:\WINNT\SYSVOL\sysvol          Logon server share
Users        D:\
Webs         D:\Webs
Stylus900    LPT1:                   Spooled Stylus900
The command completed successfully.

C:\>
```

FIGURE 2.25
Using the NET SHARE command to work with shares from the command line.

> **NOTE**
> **Getting More Information** For more information on using the NET SHARE command, type **NET SHARE/?** from the command line.

Sharing a folder is a very basic operation on the network, and it is one you will do many times. Another type of sharing in Windows 2000 is called Distributed File System (Dfs). A full discussion of Dfs is outside the scope of this text; however, you should be aware of its existence for the exam.

Dfs enables you to create a single share point, such as \\server\DFS, to which users can connect. Under this share, you create Dfs child nodes, which are pointers to other shares on the network. This means a user needs to connect only to the main share, and then he could change to other shares by changing "directories." The two types of Dfs are standalone and domain. A *standalone* Dfs is similar to a regular share, and you can publish it in Active Directory. A *domain* Dfs provides you with the capability to have a child node that points at more than one server. This, in combination with the file replication system, makes the file system fault tolerant and allows for load-balancing. Domain Dfs becomes part of Active Directory and is automatically published.

However you decide to share files, you will need to set permissions.

Share Permissions

- ▶ Create shared resources and configure access rights. Shared resources include printers, shared folders, and Web folders.
    - Configure shared folder permissions.

When you create a share, the information in the share is exposed to the network. You need to set the permissions for the users who will access the share to ensure that only the users who are supposed to use the share are doing so. The effective permissions for a share are a combination of the share permissions and the NTFS permissions if, as it should be, the share is on an NTFS drive.

Normally, you set the share permissions to be more liberal than the NTFS permissions because the same share permissions are used for the shared directory and all subdirectories. The permissions through the share are compared to the NTFS permissions, and the more restrictive permissions are applied.

If a user is given control of a file through NTFS but only read permissions to the share, the read permissions win, and the user can't exercise the rights he has been given. On the other hand, if the user has control through the share and control only on the one file but nothing on the other files, he will be able to work with that one file. The permissions of the share and file combine and are equal, so the user can access the file. The control permission with no permission combines to give the user no permissions on the other files in the directory.

Table 2.4 presents a list of share permissions and the level of access associated with each.

> **EXAM TIP**
>
> **Permissions +_ Permissions = Confusion** Be sure to understand the differences between share permissions and NTFS permissions, including when and how each applies to an object.

> **NOTE**
>
> NTFS permissions are covered in Chapter 1.

TABLE 2.4

WINDOWS 2000 SHARE-LEVEL PERMISSIONS

Share Permission	*Definition*
Read	The Read permission enables the user to display files and subfolders in the shared folder. The user is also allowed to execute programs contained in the directories.

continues

WARNING

Only Assign the Required Permissions to Users You must be very careful when assigning share-level permissions. Do not give permissions to users who do not require them. After you have access to a share, the permissions can't be blocked unless you use NTFS file system permissions.

TABLE 2.4 *continued*

WINDOWS 2000 SHARE-LEVEL PERMISSIONS

Share Permission	*Definition*
Change	The Change permission gives the user all the permissions associated with the Read permission and allows him to add files or subfolders to the shared folder. The user is also allowed to append or delete the information from existing files and folders.
Full Control	The Full control permission gives the user all the permissions associated with the Change permission and allows him to change the file permissions or file system resources. The user is also allowed to take ownership of file resources (if he has the appropriate NTFS permissions).

The process for setting share permissions is quick and easy, as long as you have done your homework ahead of time and decided who is going to get what level of access. The process is outlined in Step By Step 2.11.

STEP BY STEP

2.11 Setting Shared Folder Permissions

1. Open the share properties (refer to Step By Step 2.7).
2. Click the Permissions button.
3. Click Add and add the groups or users who should have access by clicking the user and then clicking Add. If the user is in a different domain, use the Look In drop-down list to select the domain.
4. When all the users are added, select the type of access to grant; then, click OK.
5. Repeat steps 2–4 as required. If you need to remove a user, click the user and then click Remove.
6. Click OK when you are finished and close the Share Properties dialog box.

Multiple Share Permissions

Share-level permissions can be assigned to users and groups. Because of this, you might find that some users have multiple permissions assigned to them. For example, a user account named `DougH` is given the Read permission to a shared folder. The user `DougH` is a member of the group called IT_Staff, which is given Change permissions to the same shared folder. Because the user `DougH` is a member of the IT_Staff group, the effective permissions on the share are both Read (received from assignment to the user account) and Change (received from assignment to the group). This means that the user has both Read and Change access to the share. When multiple permissions are assigned, the least restrictive is the final effective permission.

The only exception to the preceding rule is if the Deny permission is applied to a user. If a user is denied permission to a share, this permission overrides all other permissions he receives and he is not given access to the resource, even if he has been granted those privileges another way or because of membership in a group that has those privileges. In addition, specific permissions can be denied. If a user is denied Full Control, the user will have no access to the share. If the user is denied Change permission, he is not able to have Full Control permissions but can still have Read Permissions.

Configuring and Managing Printer Shares

- Create shared resources and configure access rights. Shared resources include printers, shared folders, and Web folders.
  - Create and manage shared printers.

Sharing a local printer enables remote users to access it from across the network. This section describes how to share a local printer.

> **EXAM TIP**
>
> **Printer Problems** Many situations can arise that will challenge your knowledge of sharing and configuring printers. Be sure to get a thorough understanding of all printer options, and practice what you've learned!

Creating a shared printer is easy and can be accomplished in one of two ways. The first method of creating a printer share occurs during the installation of the printer. During the installation of a local printer, the Printer Setup Wizard offers to automatically create a printer share for you. The other method involves viewing the properties of an existing printer object and selecting the Sharing tab (you

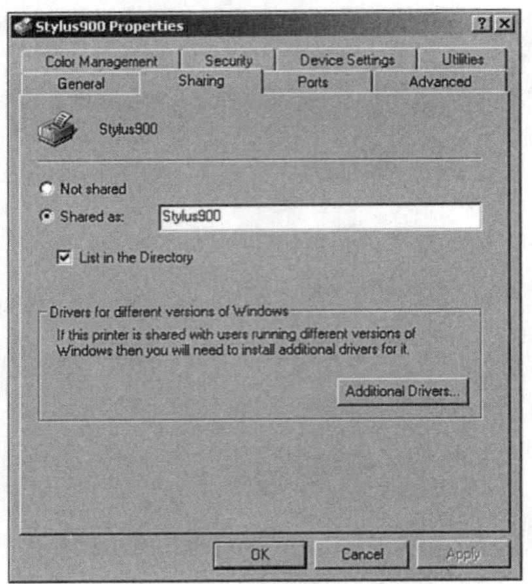

FIGURE 2.26
Sharing property tab for a local printer.

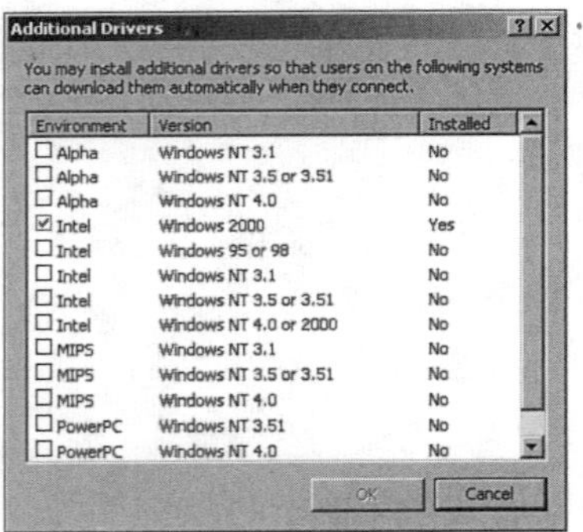

FIGURE 2.27
Additional Drivers screen of a shared printer.

can access the property tab by right-clicking the printer object and selecting Properties from the menu). Figure 2.26 shows the Sharing property tab from a local printer object.

From this tab you can configure the share name you want to use (or turn off sharing). You can also configure the print drivers associated with the printer. By clicking the Additional Drivers button, you can install additional print drivers. Figure 2.27 shows the Additional Drivers screen.

If you select additional drivers to be installed, Windows prompts you for the appropriate disk containing the drivers requested. After the drivers are installed, additional types of workstation clients can connect to the share and have the drivers made available to them without user intervention at the client side.

Printer Permissions

- ▶ Create shared resources and configure access rights. Shared resources include printers, shared folders, and Web folders.
    - Configure shared printer permissions.

In many environments, printers are managed to ensure that only certain users (or groups of users) can access specific print devices. Access to the Windows 2000 print environment is managed through printer permissions.

Similar to file system shares, printer shares enable users to access print resources over the network. Printer shares have three levels of access that can be granted, as outlined in Table 2.5. Each printer permission allows users to have a different level of access to the printer. For example, some users might have print access, which enables them to submit print jobs to the printer, whereas other users might have Manage Printers permissions that allow them to manage the print device.

Table 2.5 outlines common tasks associated with managing the print environment and explains the three levels of permissions associated with printers.

TABLE 2.5

PRINTER PERMISSIONS

Capabilities	*Print Permission*	*Manage Documents Permission*	*Manage Printer Permission*
Print documents	Yes	Yes	Yes
Pause, resume, restart, and cancel the user's own print jobs	Yes	Yes	Yes
Connect to the shared printer	Yes	Yes	Yes
Control job settings for all print jobs	No	Yes	Yes
Pause, resume, restart, and cancel all users' print jobs	No	Yes	Yes
Cancel all print jobs	No	Yes	Yes
Pause and resume a printer, and take a printer offline	No	No	Yes
Share a printer	No	No	Yes
Change printer properties	No	No	Yes
Delete a printer	No	No	Yes
Change printer permissions	No	No	Yes

You can allow or deny printer permissions. Denying permissions always takes precedence over all other permissions assigned to a user. Figure 2.28 shows the Security tab of printer properties. Right-clicking a printer object, selecting Properties from the context menu, and selecting the Security tab opens this window.

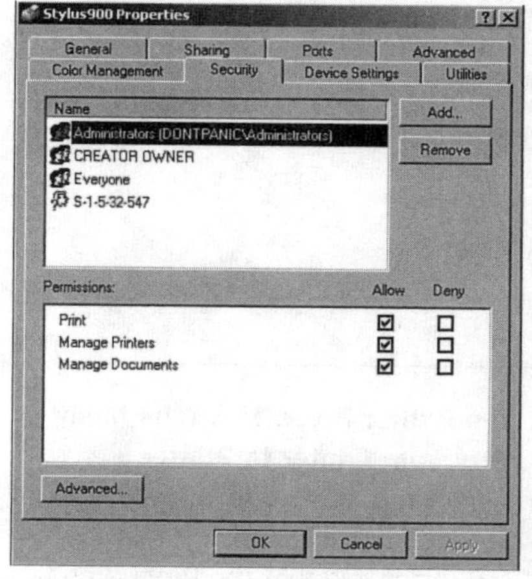

FIGURE 2.28
Printer permissions.

Connecting to a Shared Printer

Connecting to a shared printer (or a network print server) enables a user to print to a remote printer over the network. Connecting to a remote printer can be done in several ways. The following explores each of these methods:

- **Add Printer Wizard**—One of the easiest ways to connect to a remote printer is by running this wizard. You do so by double-clicking the Add Printer icon in the Printers folder of Control

Panel. After the initial welcome screen appears, you are prompted to install a local or network printer; select network printer. You then are asked to provide the universal naming convention (UNC) name for the printer you want to attach to, in the form of `\\SERVER\\PRINTER_NAME`.

- **Hypertext Transport Protocol (HTTP) request**—New in Windows 2000, you can access printers by using one of these requests. In this case, the path to the printer would be `HTTP://SERVER/PRINTER_NAME`.
- **Printers folder**—You can also connect to a printer by dragging the printer from this folder on the print server and dropping it into your Printers folder. Or, you can simply right-click the icon and then select Connect from the context menu.
- **`NET USE` command**—The last option you have for connecting to a printer involves this command. From the command prompt, you can issue the following command to map a local LTP port to a network printer:

```
Net Use LPT1 \\servername\printer name
```

After you have connected to a shared printer over the network, you can use it as if it were attached to your computer.

Managing Printers

After the print environment is set up, you must manage the printers. The Windows 2000 print environment is one of the easiest to use and manage. The following sections explore many common printer management tasks.

Assigning Forms to Paper Trays

Many printers support multiple paper trays and paper sizes. You can assign various paper types and sizes to the specific trays installed on your printer. After a form (or paper type/size) has been assigned to a specific tray, a user can select it from within her applications. When the user issues a print command, Windows 2000 automatically routes the print job to the paper tray with the correct form.

Figure 2.29 shows the device settings for an Epson Stylus Color 900 printer. From here, you can assign paper to trays. Printers that have more than one tray can have paper assigned to all their trays from here.

NOTE

The Printer Properties Tabs Might Vary from Printer to Printer

Different printers offer many different features and options. For this reason, you might find that the Properties tab for your printer is not the same as shown in this book.

Setting Separator Pages

Most printers are capable of operating in more than one mode (for example, PostScript or Printer Control Language [PCL]). Because different printers are configured to expect different print commands, you should be familiar with the various types of separator pages and how they can be specified. A *separator page* is a file that can perform one or both of the following actions:

- Identify each document that is being printed (also referred to as a banner page).
- Switch the print device between print modes (if supported by the physical printer). You could use a separator page to specify PostScript or PCL for a printer that is incapable of automatically detecting the type of print job it is processing.

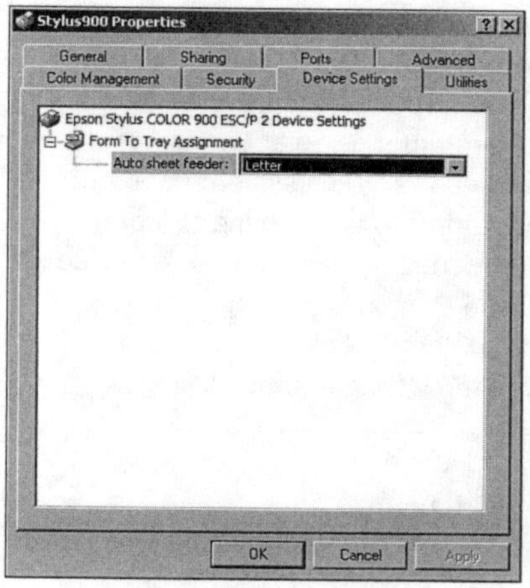

FIGURE 2.29
Device Settings tab of printer properties.

Windows 2000 ships with four separator page files. They are located in the `%systemroot%\system32` directory. Table 2.6 presents the function of each file.

TABLE 2.6

SEPARATOR PAGE FILES

Separator File	*Function*
`Pcl.sep`	Prints a page after switching the printer to PCL printing
`Sysprint.sep`	Prints a page after switching the printer to PostScript printing
`Pscript.sep`	Does not print a page after switching the printer to Postscript printing
`Sysprtj.sep`	A Japanese version of the `Sysprint.sep` file

The separator page can be changed from the Advanced tab of a printer property sheet. From the Advanced tab, you can click the Separator Page button; you will be presented with a dialog box prompting you to enter the name and path to a separator file. After the file is specified, click OK.

Pausing and Restarting Printers

As the administrator of a printer, you might encounter situations in which the printer needs to be taken out of service for a period of

NOTE

Restarting the Print Spooler Service
In some rare instances you might find that the Printer Spooler Service of your Windows 2000 system needs to be restarted to get printing to work properly. This service can be restarted from the Computer Management/ Service/Print Spooler of the MMC Computer Manager snap-in.

EXAM TIP

Their Priority Is Your Priority
Don't get confused when dealing with printer priorities. It makes sense that the lowest numerical value should get the highest priority to most people, but it doesn't work that way here. The larger the number, the higher the priority—unlike the meat counter at your local supermarket.

time. Printers can be paused (or resumed if currently paused), or all print jobs can be cancelled. This can be accomplished by double-clicking a printer object from the Printers folder (found in the Control Panel). A window opens showing all pending print jobs for the printer. From the Printer menu, you will see the Pause Printer and Cancel All Documents menu options. Alternatively, you can access these options by right-clicking a specific printer.

Pausing a printer enables users to continue submitting print jobs to the printer even though the jobs will not print. This is useful in situations in which you need to perform simple maintenance on the printer and do not want to disrupt the way users submit print jobs. After the printer is fixed, unpause the printer and print jobs will begin to print.

Canceling all documents enables you to quickly clear a print queue that has a large number of documents waiting to print.

Setting Print Priority and Printer Availability

In many environments, management of printers involves being a traffic cop regarding whose print jobs get printed first. You might, for example, want to ensure that print jobs submitted by the president and her assistant print before all other jobs. To this end, you can install two printers (the software representations of a printer) on a machine and point them to the same physical print device. You could then assign a high priority (99) to the printer used by the president and her staff and a low priority (1) to the printer used by the rest of the office staff.

Figure 2.30 shows the Advanced tab of the Printer Properties page. This is where printer priorities can be set.

Table 2.7 presents the configuration options available from this page.

TABLE 2.7

ADVANCED PRINTER SETTINGS

Option	*Description*
Availability	This option enables you to configure when this printer can be used.

Option	*Description*
Priority	Set this printer's priority relative to other printers configured to print to the same physical print device. The range is from 99 to 1 (99 being the highest priority).
Spool Print Documents so Program Finishes Printing Faster	Spooling is the process of writing the print job to the hard disk before it is sent to the physical print device. The theory is that writing to the hard disk is significantly faster than sending a job to the physical printer. After the print job is written to disk, you can continue to work with the application and the spooler takes care of submitting the job to the physical printer in the background. Two options are associated with this configuration setting. The first, Start Printing After Last Page Is Spooled, ensures that the entire print job has been completed before it is sent to the physical printer. This can require that the application participate in the print process longer because the entire job must be processed before it is printed. The second option, Start Printing Immediately, specifies that the print job be spooled and sent to the physical printer as soon as the spooler receives the job. This enables the print job to be processed more quickly.
Print Directly to the Printer	This option specifies that the print job should be sent directly to the printer and not spooled. This is a useful option if you are running low on disk space or if you have an application that requires a direct connection to the physical print device.
Hold Mismatched Documents	This option specifies that print jobs are checked to ensure the physical print device can print them (for example, the correct paper is loaded). Documents that can't be printed are left in the spooler until the configuration of the printer is adjusted to accept the job. This setting enables mismatched jobs to sit in the spooler and still allow other (nonmismatched) jobs to print.
Print Spooled Documents First	When this option is enabled, the spooler chooses documents that have completed spooling to print first. This enables spooled documents to print first regardless of print priority.
Keep Printed Documents	This option instructs the print spooler not to delete jobs that have successfully printed. This enables jobs to be resubmitted if necessary.
Enable Advanced Printing Features	This option specifies whether the advanced printer features are enabled. When enabled, metafile spooling is turned on and options such as Page Order, Booklet Printing, and Pages Per Sheet are on, as well.

continues

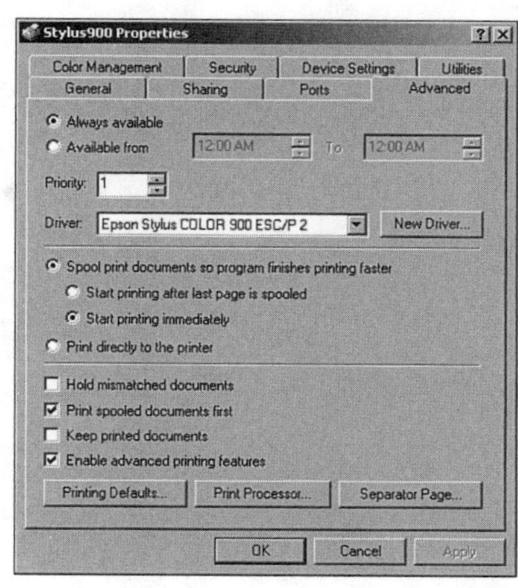

FIGURE 2.30
Printer Properties Advanced tab.

TABLE 2.7 *continued*

ADVANCED PRINTER SETTINGS

Option	*Description*
Printing Defaults	Click this button to change the default document properties for all users of the selected printer. If you share your local printer, these settings are the default document properties for each user.
Print Processor	Click this button to specify the data type used by this printer. In general, you should not need to change these settings. In some special instances, however, you might need to configure this setting for a few specialized programs.
Separator Page	As discussed previously, this option enables you to change the separator page used for this printer.

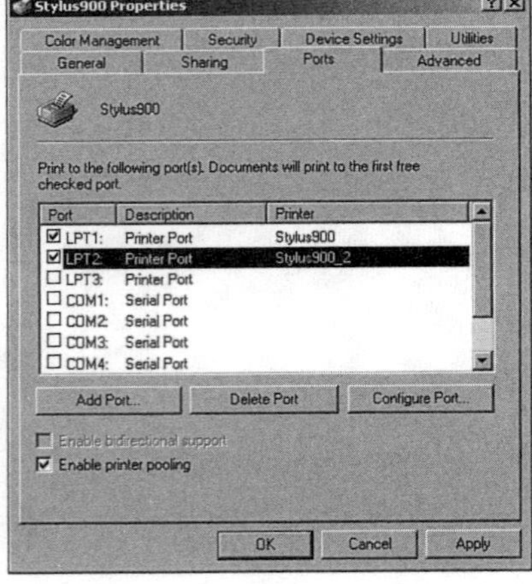

FIGURE 2.31
Printer's Properties Ports tab.

Printer Pooling

In very high-volume print environments, Windows 2000 offers a printer pooling option. Printer *pooling* enables a single printer to be directed to multiple physical printers.

Figure 2.31 shows the Ports tab of a printer's property page.

By checking the Enable Printer Pooling box on the bottom of the page, you are able to select multiple ports from the ports list shown in the figure. As shown in Figure 2.31, this printer will print to LPT1 and LPT2, depending on which printer is ready to accept a job when the spooler receives this job.

You must ensure that all physical print devices use the same printer driver (are of the same type). It is also recommended that all the printers are located in the same physical area (because users will not know which physical printer will be used to print their jobs).

Redirecting Printers

As the printer administrator in your environment, you might find it useful to redirect a printer. For example, if a printer fails and a large number of print jobs is currently spooled (and waiting to print), you can redirect the printer to another physical device so the jobs can print without needing to be resubmitted by the users who created them.

Step By Step 2.12 demonstrates the process of redirecting a printer. In this example, you will configure two local printers, pause the first printer (to simulate a printer failure), and submit a few print jobs to the printer. You will then redirect printer 1 to printer 2 and resume printing on printer 1. Through redirection, you will see the print jobs transfer from printer 1 to printer 2. In the real world, the printers would not be on the same machine, but for demonstration purposes this works well.

STEP BY STEP

2.12 Configuring Printer Redirection

1. Create two local printers based on the information in Table 2.8.

TABLE 2.8

PRINTER CONFIGURATION FOR STEP BY STEP 2.12

Configuration	*Printer 1*	*Printer 2*
Location	Local	Local
Port	LPT1	LPT2
Driver	HP LaserJet 5Si	HP LaserJet 5Si
Name	Printer1	Printer2
Share	HP1	HP2
Local/Comment	N/A	N/A

2. You should now have two printers configured on your local system. Pause Printer1 (right-click Printer1 and select Pause Printer from the context menu).
3. Set Printer1 as the Default Windows printer (right-click Printer1 and select Set As Default Printer). This step ensures that print jobs submitted are sent to Printer1.
4. Launch Notepad and submit several printer jobs. Double-click Printer1; you should see the print jobs sitting in the printer queue.

continues

continued

5. Configure Printer1 so that it redirects its print jobs to Printer2. From the Printer menu of Printer1's print queue display, select Properties. Then, select the Ports tab. Note that LPT1 is the current port for Printer1. Click the Add Port button. In the Printer Ports dialog box, click New Port; in the Port Name dialog box. enter `\\computer\HP2` (where `computer` is the name of your computer). Click OK, and then click Close.

6. Notice that the new port you just created is now the port Printer1 will print to.

7. Double-click Printer2 to display the print jobs in the print queue (it should be empty). Position the print queue windows for Printer1 and Printer2 so you can view them both onscreen.

8. Resume printing for Printer1. The jobs from Printer1 should start showing up in Printer2's print queue.

Web Folders and WebDAV

- Create shared resources and configure access rights. Shared resources include printers, shared folders, and Web folders.
  - Share folders and enable Web sharing.

Another method of sharing information with users is through the Windows 2000 Internet Information Services (IIS) and Internet Explorer (IE). You can make file resources available to users through their browsers with the click of a mouse.

Accessing Information As a Web Page

To share a file system resource through IIS, you must access the Web Sharing tab of the property page for the folder (see Figure 2.32). You can access this page by right-clicking the folder you want to share and selecting Properties from the context menu.

By selecting the Share This Folder option, you can enter the alias name you want to use to represent this folder on your Web site. For example, if you were to alias a folder as `TEST`, it would be accessible through your browser at the following URL: `http://computer_name/TEST`. This enables you to access the information from the Web folder.

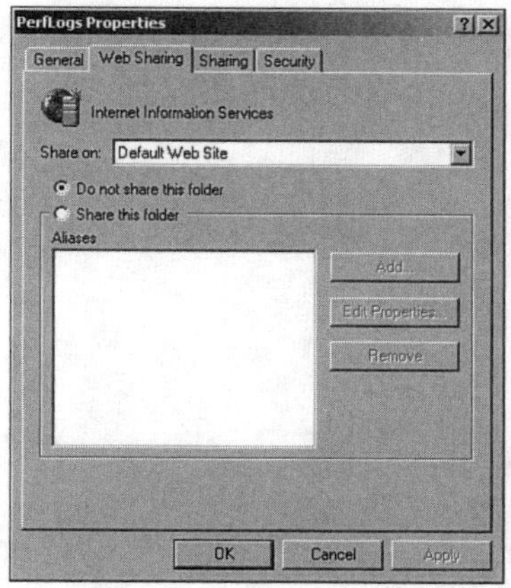

FIGURE 2.32
The Web Sharing tab.

Web Folder Functionality

Web folder behaviors available in Microsoft Internet Explorer 5 enable users to navigate to a folder view. IE 5.0 also includes support for the Distributed Authoring and Versioning (DAV) and Web Extender Client (WEC) protocols. DAV is a series of extensions to the Hypertext Transfer Protocol and defines how basic file functions, such as Copy, Move, Delete, and Create Folder, are performed across HTTP. WEC is a Microsoft FrontPage protocol that provides the same type of functionality as DAV. Both protocols define how to send and retrieve properties on HTTP resources.

The Web folder behaviors enable authors to view sites in a Web folder view, which is similar to the Microsoft Windows Explorer folder view. The DAV and WEC protocols add more capabilities to the Web folder view. For example, using the Web folder behaviors and DAV enables you to perform the equivalent of a `DIR` command on an HTTP resource and retrieve all the information necessary to fill a Windows Explorer view. Internet Explorer 5 and later supports two Web folder behaviors that allow users to browse sites in a Web folder view.

A Web folder view maintains a consistent look and feel between navigating the local file system, a networked drive, and an Internet site. Although a Web folder is a part of the file system hierarchy, it does not necessarily represent anything in the file system.

To access a Web folder, select Open on the File menu. In the Open dialog box, enter the URL (**`HTTP://computer_name/folder_name`**) and select the Open As Web Folder option. By selecting the Open As Web Folder option in IE 5.0, you access the folder and acquire the ability to manage its contents as you would any file through Windows Explorer.

NTFS Versus Share Permissions

By now, you've had a fair amount of exposure to both NTFS and share permissions. Although they are separate from each other, they work together when users are attempting to access resources across the network. Now let's spend a small amount of time looking at how they work together and how to manage them.

Shared folder permissions provide very limited security; they protect resources only if they are accessed over the network. Shared folder permissions are also limited because they provide access to the entire directory structure from the share point down into the subdirectories. For these reasons, shared folder permissions are rarely used in isolation from NTFS permissions. By combining both shared folder permissions and NTFS permissions, you have the greatest level of control and security. To effectively use shared folder and NTFS permissions together, you must understand how they interact with one another.

EXAM TIP

Permissions Confusion Be sure to understand the differences between share permissions and NTFS permissions, including when and how each applies to an object.

Combining NTFS and Shared Folder Permissions

When users gain access to a shared folder on an NTFS partition, they need shared folder permissions and the appropriate NTFS permission for each file and folder they access. This requires you to manage two sets of permissions for your environment.

Generally, you use NTFS permissions to secure the resources in your file system. NTFS offers the greatest level of control and can be assigned to resources on an individual basis. You then pick share points and create shares so users can access file resources over the network.

Users' effective permissions are a combination of both the shared folder permissions and NTFS permissions. Unlike individual shared folder and NTFS permissions, however, the effective permissions are the most restrictive permission of all permissions assigned to the user.

EXAM TIP

Permissions Remember that shared folder permissions and NTFS permissions represent two different security systems in Windows 2000.

NTFS, on its own, calculates effective permissions by adding all your permissions together (thereby granting you the least restrictive permission). Shared folder permissions are calculated the same way. You have two sets of permissions.

When the two security systems are used in combination, the most restrictive of your effective permissions (from each system) is applied.

Monitoring Share Usage

After you've created and configured shares, you need to be able to keep an eye on their usage. You might want to do this for any number of reasons, including simply monitoring usage patterns to determine whether your share resources should be moved to a dedicated server and whether you need to forcibly disconnect share users to perform maintenance on a server hosting shares.

All the information about the shares hosted by a specific computer can be obtained using the Computer Management MMC snap-in. You can open Computer Management by selecting Start, Programs, Administrative Tools, Computer Management. Open the System Tools and Shared Folders nodes, as shown previously in Figure 2.24. From here, you have three areas you can work with:

- **Shares**—Contains information about all shares located on the computer; includes information about the name, path, type, number of connections, and a comment. You can create new shares from here and choose to stop sharing an existing share. Shares are shown in Figure 2.33.

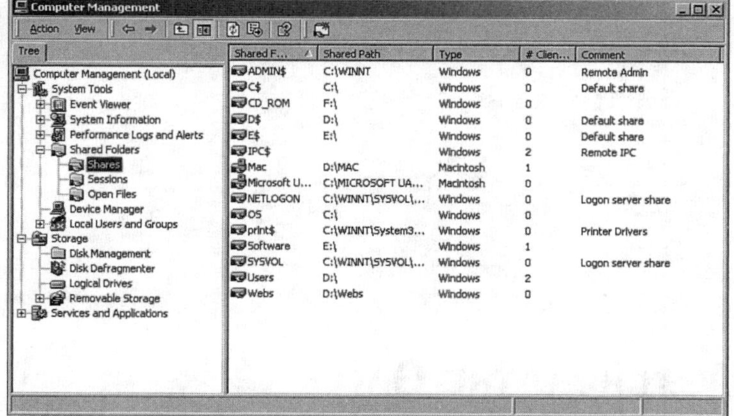

FIGURE 2.33
The Shares view.

- **Sessions**—Contains information about all users who are connected to resources on the computer; includes information about the user, computer, type, number of open files, connected time, idle time, and guest status. You can disconnect users from shares individually or force disconnection of all users from all shares. Sessions are shown in Figure 2.34.
- **Open Files**—Contains information about all open files being shared from the computer; includes information about open files, user accessing file, type, locks, and mode. You can close files individually or force disconnection of all users from all open files. Open files are shown in Figure 2.35.

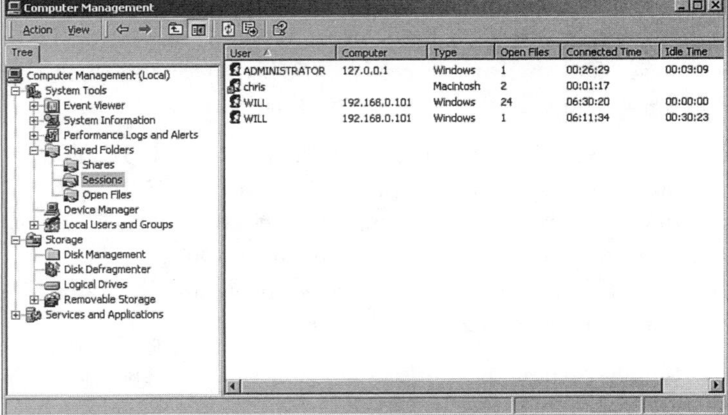

FIGURE 2.34
The Sessions view.

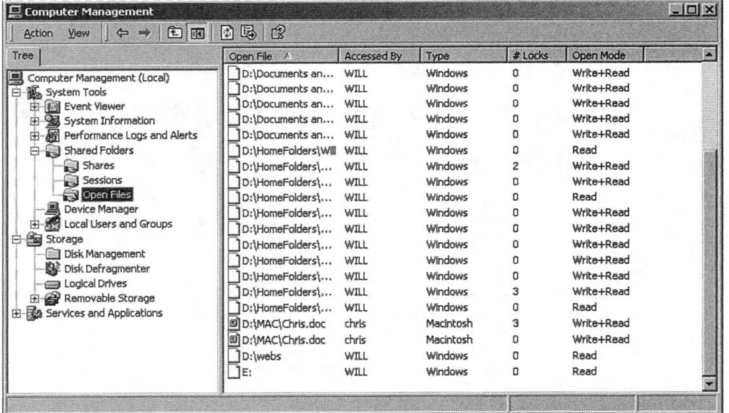

FIGURE 2.35
The Open Files view.

WATCHING THE GATES

After you've gone through all the trouble to create, configure, share, and publish resources, you might feel as if you are done. After all, that alone is a fair amount of work even on the smallest of networks. If you're working with a fairly large network, the amount of work seems to increase exponentially.

Monitoring and managing network security is just as, if not more, important than making resources available in the first place. The old saying "If you build it, they will come" still holds true today just as much as it did when it was first uttered. Configuring user account lockout and password settings will go a long way toward eliminating unauthorized users from attempting to guess their way into your networks. Configuring and implementing security policies via Group Policy will ensure that you get the desired effect. Of course, no security solution is complete without adequate monitoring and auditing to make sure things are working the way you want them to and to aid in detecting attacks, possible vulnerabilities, and permissions abuse.

Configuring User Accounts for Enhanced Security

- Monitor and manage network security. Actions include auditing and detecting security breaches.
    - Configure user-account lockout settings.
    - Configure user-account password length, history, age, and complexity.

In Windows 2000, account policy defines two separate policy areas: password policy and account lockout policy. Password policy defines how many characters passwords have to be, how long they can stay in effect until they have to be changed, and other related settings. Account lockout policies define at what point an account is locked after too many failed password attempts, how long the lockout lasts, and when the counter is reset. Because security of accounts depends on passwords being secure, these policies ensure that accounts are secure and prevents the use of an account for which security has been breached. The following sections explain how to configure user accounts for security.

Configuring Password Settings

A Windows 2000 password policy consists of six settings:

- Enforce Password History
- Maximum Password Age
- Minimum Password Age
- Minimum Password Length
- Password Must Meet Complexity Requirements
- Store Passwords Using Reversible Encryption for All Users in the Domain

This policy allows you to ensure that users adhere to the password requirements for your organization. However, a policy can't remove the disdain that users will have for you if the password policy is, in their minds, unreasonable. If, for example, you require a 14-character password that contains upper- and lowercase characters and numbers and that must be changed every three days, you will quickly have a revolt on your hands (unless people understand the need for such an extreme policy). That means the user community must be educated about the security requirements in your organization and the possibility of external vandals breaking into their systems. If the people acknowledge the need, it becomes their need and makes the requirement much easier for them to handle.

The following sections describe the six password settings and their uses.

Enforce Password History

FIGURE 2.36
Password history can be set between 0 and 24 (inclusive).

Password history is a running list of the passwords that have been set for a particular account. The setting consists of a counter that has been set between 0 and 24 (see Figure 2.36). This defines the number of passwords Windows 2000 will remember, the implication of which is that none of the remembered passwords can be used again. If, for example, the history is set to 3 and the history records passwords of *apple*, *orange*, and *banana*, those three words can't be used until they are not in the history. If the same user changes the password to *cucumber*, *apple* is forgotten and can be used again.

The reason for using a password history setting is to keep users from switching back and forth between two passwords when they are required to change them. Much manual password hacking is based on information known about a user. If a password becomes known and the user switches back to it in short order, it can be guessed again.

Maximum Password Age

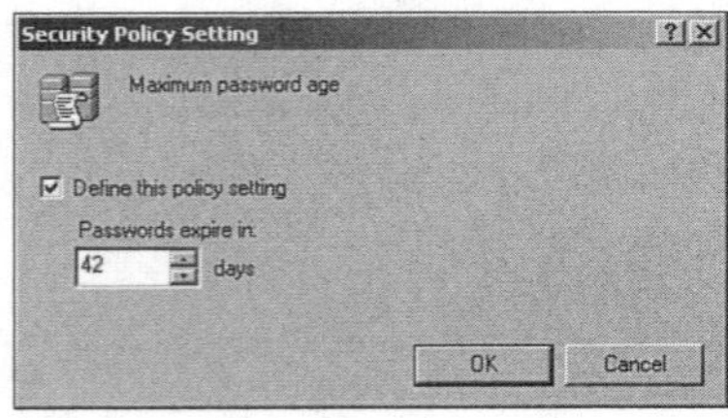

FIGURE 2.37
Maximum Password Age can be set between 0 and 999 days (inclusive).

Maximum Password Age is a numeric value between 0 and 999 days that defines how long a password can stay in effect before it must be changed (see Figure 2.37). This setting enables the administrator to exercise control over how long a user keeps the same password. Before the password expires, the user is warned; if it does expire, the user is not allowed to log on until the password is changed. If the value is set to 0, the password never expires (which is the same as selecting the account property Passwords Never Expire).

Minimum Password Age

Minimum Password Age is a numeric value between 0 and 999 days that defines the minimum length of time a password must be in place before a user can change it (see Figure 2.38). Although on the surface it looks as though this property contradicts the maximum age, they actually go together with the password history to form a complete package. Consider this scenario as an example. A password policy is set to keep five passwords in history with a maximum age of 20 days. Harold wants to keep his password of *banana* because it is easy to remember. Realizing that five passwords will be remembered, when the maximum age of 20 days is reached, he simply changes his password in quick succession as follows: *banana→apple→grape→tangerine→apricot→banana.* He has technically fulfilled the requirements of the policy: He changed his password after 20 days and did not use *banana* again until four other passwords had been used. However, he violated the spirit of the policy because he effectively keeps his password the same all the time. To prevent this, you can set the minimum password age to 15 days. That way, Harold can change his password only once every 15 days. This will ensure that Harold can't use his *banana* password again until at least 60 days have passed. If the value is set to `0`, the password can be changed immediately.

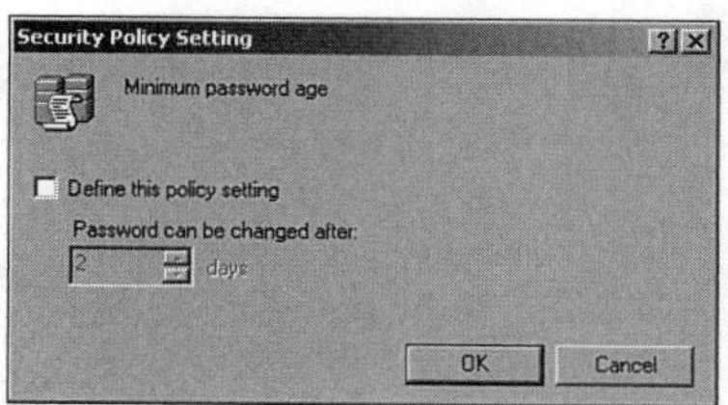

FIGURE 2.38
Minimum Password Age can be set between 0 and 999 days (inclusive).

> **NOTE**
>
> **Overcoming the Minimum Age When a Password Is Compromised** One possible problem with minimum password ages occurs when a user knows that his password has been compromised (someone knows what it is). In this case, the user wants to be able to change the password immediately to prevent the other person from using it to log into his account. This can be overcome because the administrator can still change the account password in the Computer Management console. The administrator must change the password, select the check box labeled User Must Change Password at Next Logon, and then tell the user the new password. When the user logs on the next time, he will use the new password (the one set by the administrator) and then will be forced to change that password to something new. If this procedure is followed, the minimum password age will not apply in this case. When you decide to put a minimum password age into effect, you need to be aware of this security problem and be prepared to act promptly when a user calls requesting a new password.

Minimum Password Length

Minimum Password Length is a numeric value between 0 and 14 that defines the minimum length for an account password (see Figure 2.39). If the value is 0, an account password is optional.

This value enables you to enforce passwords that are simpler than a single character or a short word. The longer the password, the more difficult it is to guess it (at least in theory). However, this setting can't require that a 14-character password be something other than a long string of the letter *a.* Windows 2000 allows password lengths of up to 127 characters and places no restrictions on the maximum password length.

Passwords Must Meet Complexity Requirements

Password complexity requirements prevent a user from creating a password that is a long string of only a single letter or that uses only the person's full name. If password complexity is enabled, as shown

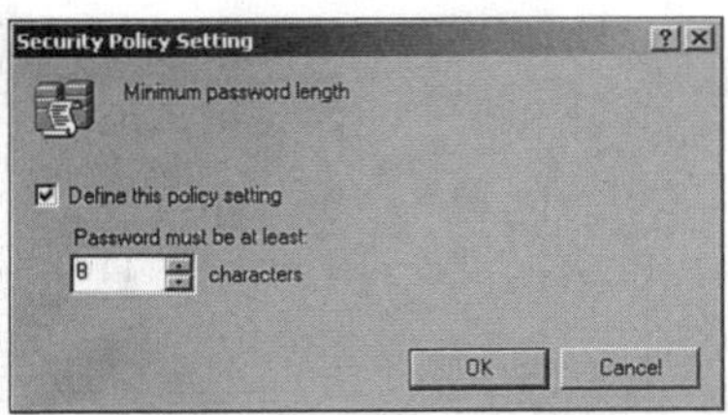

FIGURE 2.39
Minimum Password Length can be set between 0 and 14 (inclusive).

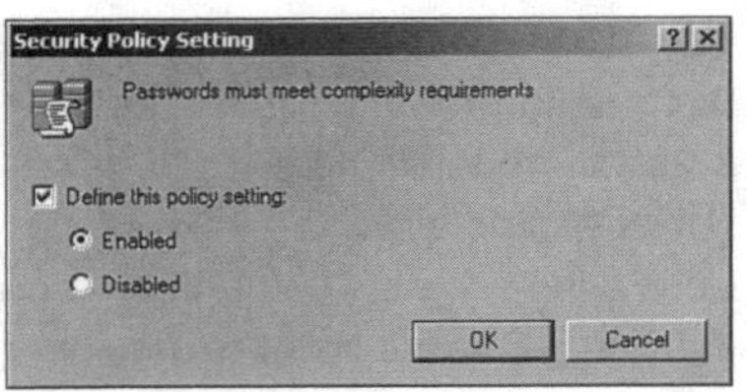

FIGURE 2.40
Complex passwords must contain at least six characters in three of the following categories: capital letters, small letters, numbers, and special characters.

in Figure 2.40, the user must adhere to the following rules when assigning or changing the password:

- Passwords must be at least six characters long, regardless of the minimum length defined in the policy.
- Passwords must contain characters from at least three of the following four character groups:
  - English uppercase characters (*A, B, C…*)
  - English lowercase characters (*a, b, c…*)
  - Westernized Arabic numerals (0, 1, 2…)
  - Nonalphanumeric symbols such as punctuation (!, @, $, and so on)
- Passwords can't contain the user's username or any single name portion of the full name.

Suppose complexity is enforced, a user's username is *Bob*, and his full name is *Bob Millar*. Table 2.9 lists some allowed and disallowed passwords.

TABLE 2.9

VALID AND INVALID PASSWORDS FOR BOB MILLAR

Valid Password	*Invalid Password*
Aardvark1	Aardvark (only two kinds of characters)
IsaacNewton?	BobMillar2 (contains parts of full name)
A1aaaa	A1aaa (too few characters)

Complexity is only part of the password checking equation. If minimum length is 10, the password must be at least 10 characters despite the fact that password complexity requires only 6.

Store Password Using Reversible Encryption

This password storage feature is required for Challenge Handshake Authentication Protocol (CHAP) authentication for non-Windows clients (see Figure 2.41). It stores the passwords using a reversible encryption scheme that can be provided during the authentication process. A common use of this in a Windows 2000 environment is non-Windows clients who must access an Exchange 2000 Server for messaging or Instant Messaging.

Step By Steps 2.13 and 2.14 show how to configure local password and domain password policies, respectively.

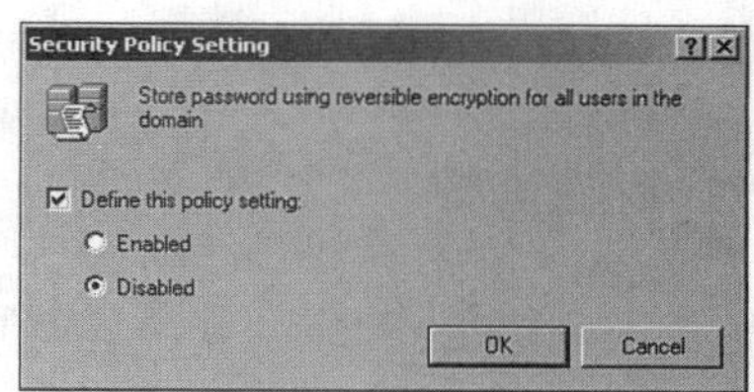

FIGURE 2.41
Enabling reversible encryption allows for CHAP authentication.

NOTE
Using Digest Authentication For more information on using reversible encryption for passwords, see KB# Q222028 at `http://support.microsoft.com/directory/article.asp?ID=KB;EN-US;Q222028`.

STEP BY STEP

2.13 Configuring Local Password Policy

1. Select Start, Programs, Administrative Tools, Local Security Policy.
2. Expand the navigation tree (on the left side) in the path Security Settings, Account Policies, Password Policy; then, click Password Policy.
3. Double-click the policy on the right that you want to set, adjust the value, and close the dialog box.

STEP BY STEP

2.14 Configuring Domain Password Policy

1. On a domain controller, select Start, Programs, Administrative Tools, Active Directory Users and Computers.
2. Right-click the domain name and select Properties from the context menu.
3. At the Domain Properties dialog box, click the Group Policy tab.
4. On the Group Policy property sheet, double-click the Default Domain Policy displayed in the Group Policy Object Links box.

continues

continued

5. From the Group Policy dialog box, expand the tree Default Domain Policy, Computer Configuration, Windows Settings, Security Settings, Account Policies, Password Policy; then, click Password Policy.
6. Double-click the policy on the right that you want to set, adjust the value, and close the dialog box.

Configuring Lockout Settings

A Windows 2000 account lockout policy consists of three settings:

- Account lockout duration
- Account lockout threshold
- Reset account lockout counter after

This policy enables you to ensure that you have control over how many times a user can enter an incorrect password and what happens when you think that an attempt to crack your network is occurring. You can control how many bad passwords can be entered before the account is locked and how long the counter tracking incorrect lockouts stays active. You can also control how long an account is locked before a user can access it again.

The following sections describe the settings and their uses.

Account Lockout Duration

Account lockout duration allows you to define the length of time an account will remain locked before it is released (see Figure 2.42). This number can be set from 0 to 99,999 minutes, where 0 represents an infinite time, which would require an administrator to manually unlock the account. The higher the security, the greater this number should be. When an account is locked, it can be unlocked from the General property sheet of the Properties dialog box for the user account.

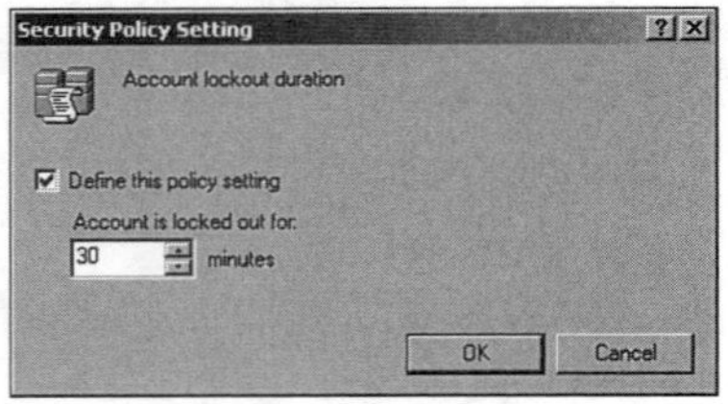

FIGURE 2.42
Lockout duration can be set between 0 and 99,999 minutes (inclusive).

Account Lockout Threshold

The Account lockout threshold enables you to define the number of incorrect password attempts that will cause the account to be unavailable to the user (see Figure 2.43). This number can be set from 0 to 999, where 0 represents an infinite number of attempts. The higher the security you want in your organization, the smaller this number should be (greater than 0, of course).

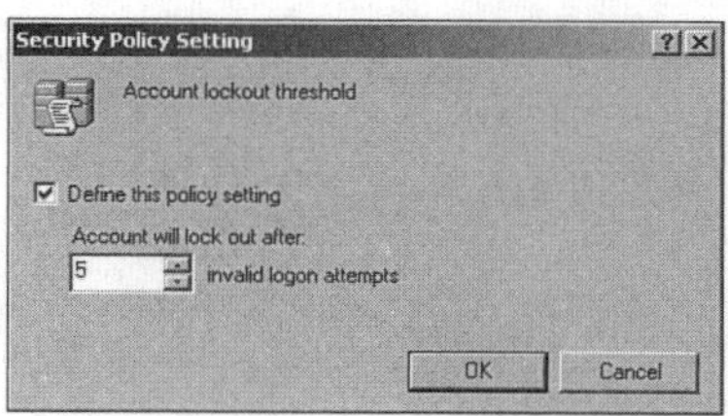

FIGURE 2.43
The Lockout threshold can be set between 0 and 999 tries (inclusive).

Reset Account Lockout Counter After

The Reset account lockout counter after parameter enables you to define the length of time Windows 2000 remembers failed logon attempts (see Figure 2.44). This number can be set from 1 to 99,999 minutes. The implication of this setting is that after a user has typed his password in incorrectly a couple of times, he can wait a predefined length of time and try again, knowing that the previous two attempts will not be held against him. Regardless of this setting, a correct logon password resets the counter back to 0.

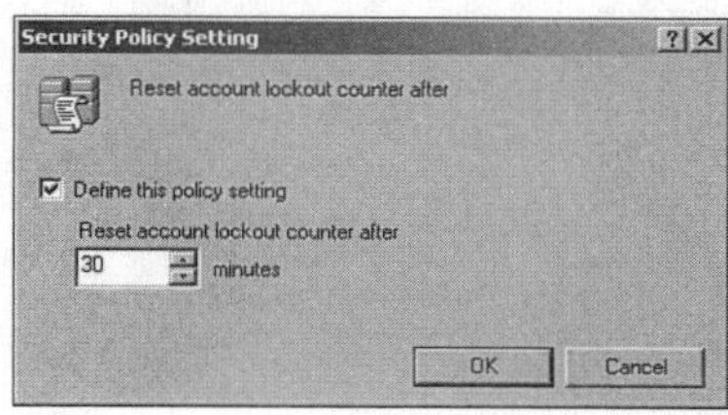

FIGURE 2.44
The Reset lockout counter can be set between 0 and 99,999 minutes (inclusive).

Step By Steps 2.15 and 2.16 demonstrate how to configure lockout policy locally and in a domain, respectively.

STEP BY STEP

2.15 Configuring Local Account Lockout Policy

1. Select Start, Programs, Administrative Tools, Local Security Policy.
2. Expand the navigation tree (on the left side) in the path Security Settings, Account Policies, Account Lockout Policy; then, click Account Lockout Policy.
3. Double-click the policy on the right that you want to set, adjust the value, and close the dialog box.
4. When you set a policy value, you might be presented with a dialog box suggesting recommended values for the other two settings. If this appears, click OK to accept the changes (you can't progress with your change unless you accept the recommendations).

STEP BY STEP

2.16 Configuring Domain Account Lockout Policy

1. On a domain controller, select Start, Programs, Administrative Tools, Active Directory Users and Computers.
2. Right-click the domain name and select Properties from the context menu.
3. At the Domain Properties dialog box, click the Group Policy tab.
4. On the Group Policy property sheet, double-click the Default Domain Policy displayed in the Group Policy Object Links box.
5. From the Group Policy dialog box, expand the tree Default Domain Policy, Computer Configuration, Windows Settings, Security Settings, Account Policies, Account Lockout Policy, and then click Account Lockout Policy.
6. Double-click the policy on the right that you want to set, adjust the value, and close the dialog box.
7. When you set a policy value, you might be presented with a dialog box suggesting recommended values for the other two settings. If this appears, click OK to accept the changes (you can't progress with your change unless you accept the recommendations).

Now that we've seen how account policies can be implemented to results in a more secure environment, we need to look at how Group Policy can be used to further enhance security by running scripts and linking Group Policy Objects to objects.

Configuring Group Policy for Enhanced Security

- Monitor and manage network security. Actions include auditing and detecting security breaches.
  - Configure Group Policy to run logon scripts.
  - Link Group Policy objects.

In this section, you learn about scripts and how they are processed on Windows 2000 computers. You then are shown how to attach a script to a GPO for the computer portion of the GPO (startup and shutdown scripts) or the user portion of the GPO (logon and logoff scripts).

Configuring and Using Scripts in Group Policy

The options available with administrative templates might not be sufficient to provide the complete environment needed by a user to perform her job. Examples of this include the automatic creation of certain shortcuts on the desktop and the establishment of printer and network shared folder connections at the time a user logs on. To have these changes take place automatically when a computer starts up or a user logs on, you can use Group Policy scripts.

Group Policy enables you to configure scripts that run when a machine starts up or shuts down. You can configure scripts that run when a user logs on or logs off to implement changes to the environment for all users or a single user. You can also configure scripts to clean up any modifications made by others before the next user logs on or the system restarts. Scripts can be batch files (BAT or CMD), executable programs (EXE), or Windows Script Host scripts (VBScript or JScript). Generally, you use scripts when you want to implement a Group Policy and when the requirement can't be met by any administrative template setting. You can set up a script to perform that task to achieve the desired result. With support for VBScript and Windows Script Host (WSH) in Windows 2000, scripts can be created to accomplish virtually any task.

Group Policy Script Processing Order

The order of execution of Group Policy scripts is quite specific, as is the application of any Group Policy setting. Similarly, if a conflict exists between different scripts, the setting found in the last script processed always prevails. This is significant because it is a slight departure from the application of administrative template settings.

When you specify an administrative template setting for both the user and the computer, the computer setting always takes precedence. Let's say in the System folder of the administrative template for the computer you configure Autoplay to be disabled, but you enable the same setting for the user. In this case, Autoplay remains disabled because the computer setting indicates it should be disabled. The reason for this result is that, when applying GPO settings, the configuration specified for the computer and the user are merged, and any conflicts are resolved before the template settings are applied. In this way, the administrator can always be sure of the end result of any changes in the template setting.

When scripts are configured, scripts can be run at computer startup, user logon, user logoff, and computer shutdown. Each of these is a very distinct event (in fact, the user logon and logoff can occur many times before the computer shutdown), and scripts are processed when the event occurs. Because scripts are simply batch files, executable files, or Windows Script Host (VBScript of JScript) scripts, they do not have any way to really check for the previous state and then determine that settings specified within the script should not be applied. The assumption is that all the settings should be applied no matter what. This blanket desire to apply all the settings specified in the script enables a setting configured in the user logon script to override one configured in the computer startup script. This is the way it is intended to work, and you, as the administrator, need to be aware of this.

The actual processing order of scripts is as follows:

1. When a user starts a computer and logs on, two scripts run: startup scripts and logon scripts. Startup scripts run in sequential order (synchronously), and each script must complete or time out before the next one starts. Scripts run in the background and are hidden (not visible) to the user. In other words, the user can't snoop and see what types of changes have been applied to the system as a result of the startup script. The

order of execution of startup scripts is specified in the Startup Properties dialog box shown in Figure 2.45. It is found under Computer Configuration, Windows Settings, Scripts, Startup in the Group Policy Editor.

Logon scripts run after the startup scripts and are run asynchronously, with the possibility of more than one script executing at the same time. If conflicting settings appear in two or more logon scripts, the last setting to execute is the one that applies. This means predicting what the end result of logon script execution will be might not always be possible if the same setting is applied in more than one script. As a general rule of thumb, do not apply the same setting in several scripts.

2. When a user logs off, logoff scripts run.
3. When a user shuts down or restarts the computer as part of the logoff process, shutdown scripts run.

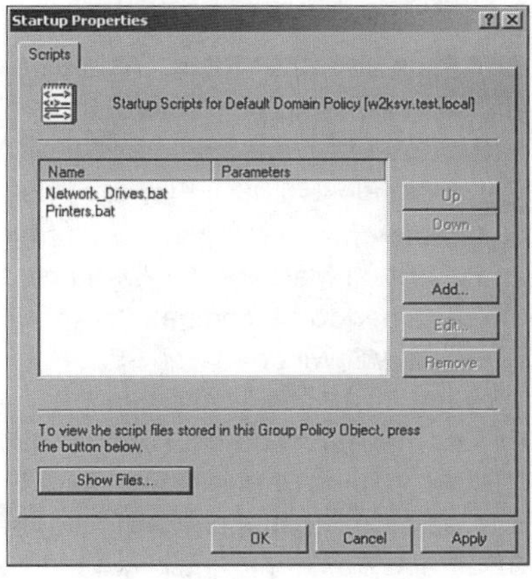

FIGURE 2.45
The startup script order of execution can be set in the Startup Properties dialog box under Windows Setting, Scripts, Startup in the Group Policy Editor.

Once again, it is important to note that startup scripts run at the time the computer starts, whereas logon scripts run when a user logs on. Similarly, logoff scripts run when a user logs off the computer, and shutdown scripts run when the computer is shut down. As previously mentioned, startup scripts run in the order specified in Group Policy, whereas logon scripts run in no particular order. If you have the same setting applied in more than one logon script, there is no way to predict the exact end result of the scripts.

> NOTE
>
> **Default Timeout Value** The default timeout value for script processing is 10 minutes. Therefore, if a script has not completed processing in 10 minutes, it is assumed to have timed out, and the next script starts. If your scripts are complex and require more than 10 minutes to run, you can change the default timeout value by modifying the setting found by selecting Computer Configuration, Administrative Templates, System, Logon, Maximum Wait Time for Group Policy Scripts. The setting applies to all scripts: startup, shutdown, logon, and logoff. This can make the process of logging on or off or starting or shutting down the machine lengthy. Setting the value too low can cause scripts to fail prematurely, not allowing the full configuration to be completed. It is generally recommended that default settings be maintained unless there is a good reason to change them.

Implementing Scripts Using Group Policy

Perhaps the hardest part of implementing scripts in Windows 2000 is their creation. This can be done using Notepad or any other editor, and it needs to take place prior to associating the script with the computer or user configuration of Group Policy. As previously mentioned, scripts can be BAT or CMD files, executable programs, or Windows Script Host files.

After you have created a script to be used to configure either a computer at startup or shutdown or a user environment at logon or logoff, you need to do two things. You must copy the file to a shared location where it can be downloaded and run. This is typically in a folder within the GPO structure located on the Sysvol shared folder on a domain controller. You must also associate the script with a GPO. Step By Step 2.17 guides you through copying the file and associating it with a GPO.

NOTE

BAT Files and CMD Files Although you can create and execute both batch (BAT) files and command (CMD) files in Windows 2000, they execute quite differently. Batch files execute in an NT Virtual Machine (NTVDM) and are designed to be compatible with DOS and MS Windows 3.x/95/98. They are inherently 16-bit, and if a BAT file hangs, it can cause the entire NTVDM to hang (if it is being shared with other applications). CMD files are 32-bit and execute in their own memory space using the CMD.EXE command interpreter. Any problem with a CMD file does not affect the execution of other programs because it is an isolated process. This distinction might be somewhat confusing because the commands you can put in a BAT file are, by and large, the same as those allowed in a CMD file.

STEP BY STEP

2.17 Implementing Scripts to be Used in Group Policy

1. Open the MMC used to administer the container at which you want to add a script to Group Policy—either Active Directory Users and Computers or Active Directory Sites and Services.
2. Right-click the container that has the GPO where you want to add the script, and select Properties.
3. In the dialog box presented, click the Group Policy tab.
4. From the list of GPOs presented, select the one to which you want to add a script and then click Edit, or simply double-click the GPO you want to edit. This starts an MMC console to edit the Group Policy.
5. To modify a startup or shutdown script, you expand Computer Configuration, Windows Settings, Scripts and are presented with a choice similar to that in Figure 2.46. For the rest of this Step By Step, you will configure a logon script. To start the process, expand User Configuration in the Group Policy Editor.

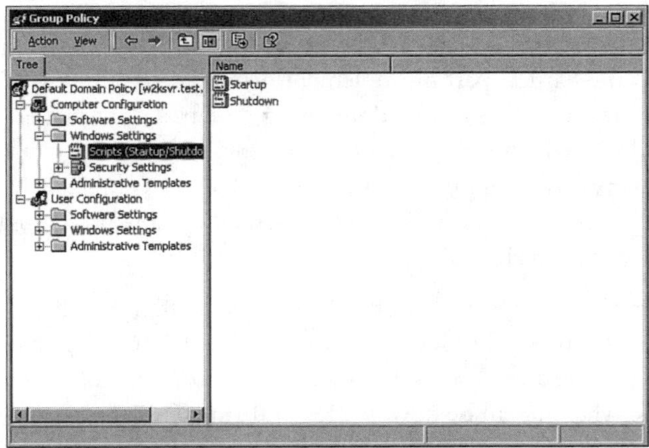

FIGURE 2.46
To create a startup or shutdown script, double-click the startup or shutdown choices presented in the Computer Configuration portion of the Group Policy Editor.

6. Expand Windows Settings. You will see a screen similar to Figure 2.47.

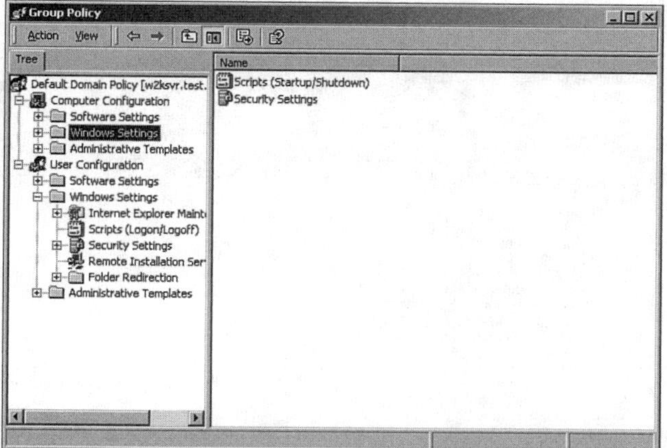

FIGURE 2.47
The Windows Settings folder of the User Configuration portion of the GPO is where logon and logoff scripts are located.

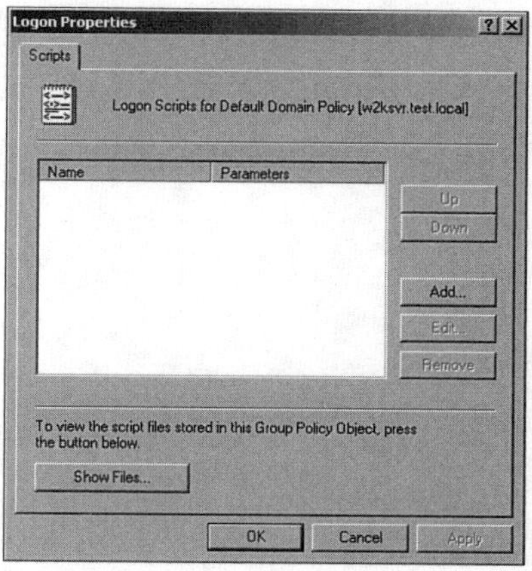

FIGURE 2.48
The Logon Properties dialog box where you can add and view the list of scripts.

7. Click Scripts and then double-click Logon or Logoff, depending on which type of script you want to create. Because you will be creating a logon script in this Step By Step, the Logon Scripts Properties dialog box, similar to the one shown in Figure 2.48, is presented.

8. At this point, you have the option to add a script. If scripts are already listed, you have the option to edit their properties or remove them. You also can click Show Files. This option shows the actual physical files on the hard drive that correspond to the scripts listed. To copy a script to the proper location for logon scripts, click Show Files to open a Windows Explorer window similar to Figure 2.49. To copy a file to the proper directory, open Windows Explorer and point to the folder where you created a logon script, click the script, and drag it to the Windows Explorer window opened by the Show Files button earlier. In Figure 2.50, you can see two scripts that have been copied to the Logon script folder.

NOTE

The Group Policy Template For a script file to be replicated to domain controllers and be run as a Group Policy script, it must be physically located in the Group Policy Template path on a domain controller. The default location of a logon script is on the domain controller's Sysvol share under the folder structure `<`*`domain name`*`>\Policies\<GPO GUID>\User\Scripts\Logon`. For a logoff script, it is in the same path except the final folder name is `Logoff` instead of `Logon`. Startup and shutdown scripts can be found in the folder structure `<`*`domain name`*`>\Policies\<GPO GUID>\Machine\Scripts\Startup` or in Shutdown folders in the Sysvol share. For scripts to run successfully, they must be copied to the preceding locations.

continued

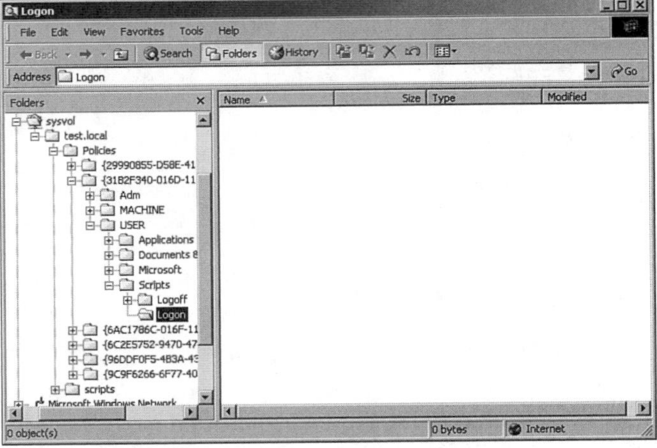

FIGURE 2.49
The Windows Explorer window shows the list of files in the Logon script folder.

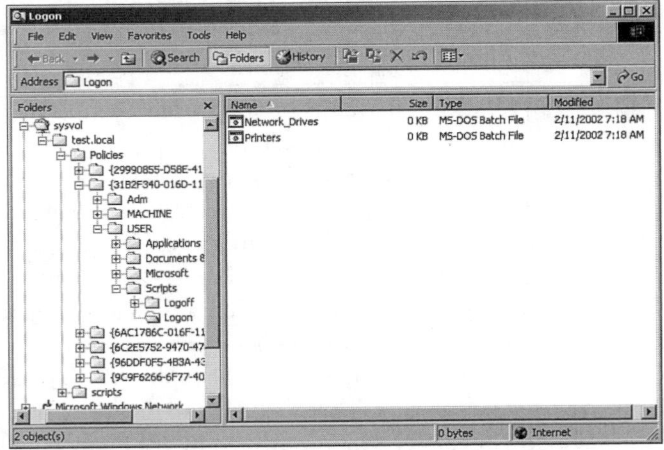

FIGURE 2.50
To copy a script from a folder on the hard drive to the appropriate folder in the GPT, just drag it from the source to the Windows Explorer opened when you clicked Show Files.

NOTE

Adding Files to the Folders for Scripts Because of the permissions automatically configured by Windows 2000 when a domain controller is set up, only members of the Administrators, Domain Admins, or Enterprise Admins group are able to add files to the folders used for scripts. This is because the GPT folder structure is one that needs to be preserved because it affects all users. If you attempt to copy a file to a script folder in the GPT and are told you do not have the proper permissions, contact your administrator.

9. To add a logon script after it has been copied to the proper folder, click Add in the Logon Properties dialog box. A dialog box similar to the one in Figure 2.51 enables you to type in the name of the script to add, specify additional parameters, or browse for the script file using the familiar Windows Explorer mechanism.

Click Browse to locate the files you created earlier and copied to the proper folder. Notice that you are automatically placed in the GPT folder for the type of script you are adding and can see the files you copied earlier. Click one of them to assign it to this GPO. Click OK when you are done. To assign more scripts, repeat the preceding process.

10. After you have added your scripts, you are returned to the Logon Properties dialog box, which should look similar to Figure 2.52 after your scripts have been added. If you click one of the scripts, notice that the Edit and Remove buttons become available. To change the parameters for script execution or the location of the script, click Edit. (Edit does not mean actually modifying the script file but rather making changes to the execution parameters.) To make a script unavailable for execution, click Remove. Remove does not delete the actual script file on disk; it only removes the link between the GPO and the script. You must manually remove the actual script file.

11. When you are satisfied that you have configured all the scripts properly, click Apply and then OK. This returns you to the Group Policy Editor.

12. To exit the Group Policy Editor MMC, close the application.

13. To exit the Properties dialog box for the Active Directory container containing the GPO, click OK.

14. You optionally can close the MMC console for Active Directory Users and Computers or Active Directory Sites and Services if you are done.

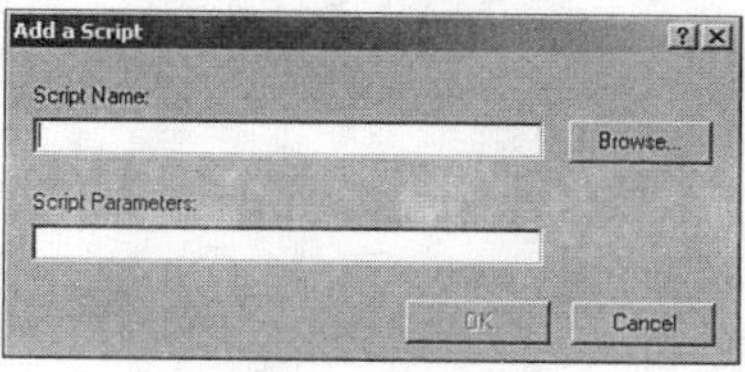

FIGURE 2.51
The Add a Script dialog box enables you to browse for the file and specify any parameters to be passed to the script when it runs.

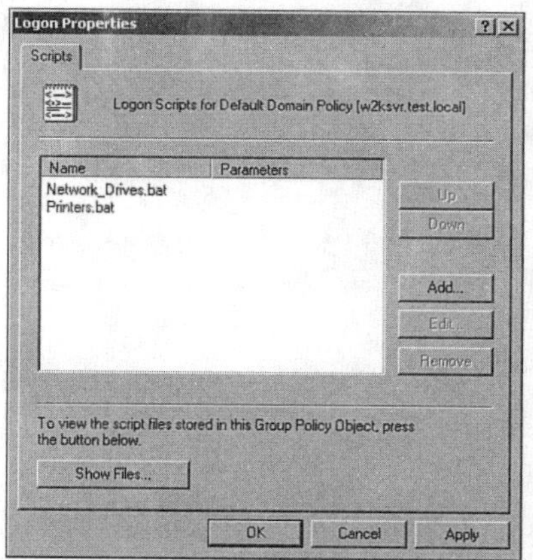

FIGURE 2.52
The Logon Properties dialog box after scripts have been added.

In terms of configuring and using scripts, the most important elements to keep in mind are that you need to determine what types of scripts are available (logon, logoff, startup, or shutdown) and why these scripts are necessary. Scripts are not shipped with Windows 2000 by default, so any you need must be created manually.

Scripts can be attached to GPOs and assigned to users and computers. Obviously, startup and shutdown scripts are assigned to computers. These scripts execute sequentially, and if settings in scripts conflict, the last setting processed is the one applied. Logon and logoff scripts apply only to users and are processed in no particular order (asynchronously), so conflicting settings might produce unpredictable behavior.

Scripts should always be stored in the Sysvol folder on a domain controller under the GUID of the GPO where they are used (as part of the Group Policy Template). They need to be copied there manually by the administrator.

In addition to scripts and administrative templates, security settings can also be configured using Group Policy. This is discussed in the next section.

Using Group Policy Objects to Apply Security Settings

As discussed previously, Group Policy is an Active Directory object that can be used to apply a large number of configuration settings to a collection of objects located in an Active Directory container, such as an OU, a domain, or a site. Just as you can use Group Policy to apply administrative template settings or software deployment to several computers in an Active Directory container at one time, the same holds true for security settings.

When applying security settings to computers using Group Policy, you still use templates. Group Policy has default templates that have no preconfigured settings and can be modified manually. It is a better approach to create a template file and then import it into Group Policy to ensure all settings that are required to conform to a corporate security policy are properly defined. This also enables the administrator to create and test security settings outside Group Policy (for example, using Security Configuration and Analysis) before rolling them out to a large number of computers on the domain, OU, or site level.

To apply security policies for an Active Directory container using Group Policy, you import one or more security templates into security settings in Group Policy. Importing a security template into a Group Policy object ensures that all members of the container automatically have the settings applied when the Group Policy propagates.

To apply security settings using Group Policy and to import a security template into a GPO, follow the steps presented in Step By Step 2.18.

STEP BY STEP

2.18 Propagating Security Template Settings Using Group Policy

1. Log on to your Windows 2000 computer as Administrator and start the MMC console where the Group Policy object whose security settings you want to modify is located (either Active Directory Users and Computers or Active Directory Sites and Services).
2. Right-click the container whose GPO will be modified to apply security settings and click Properties.
3. Click the Group Policy tab and select the GPO that will have security settings propagated to objects within its scope. Click Edit to open the Group Policy Editor.
4. Expand Computer Configuration, Windows Settings, Security Settings to show the areas that can be modified (see Figure 2.53). If you were changing user security elements, you would alternatively open the User Configuration node. You can modify the settings manually here, although they will not be saved as a security template. You can import an existing template and have its settings applied in the GPO.
5. To import a security template's settings, right-click Security Settings and select Import Policy, as shown in Figure 2.54.

continues

continued

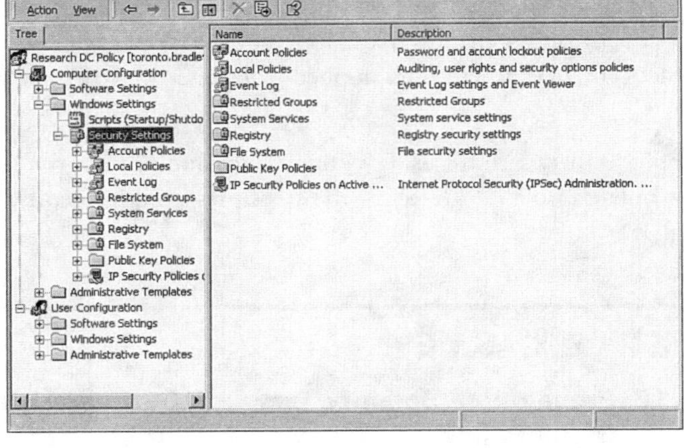

FIGURE 2.53
Expand Windows Settings and then Security Settings in the Computer Configuration container of the Group Policy Editor to see which security settings can be applied.

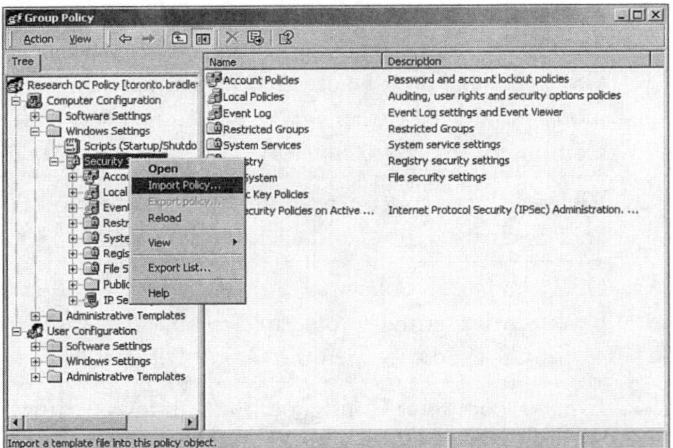

FIGURE 2.54
Right-click Security Settings and select Import Policy to import a security template into the GPO.

6. In the Import Policy From dialog box presented, locate the path and filename of the security template you want to apply; then click Open (see Figure 2.55). The security template settings will be imported, and you will be returned to the Group Policy Editor. At this point, you might want to review the settings to ensure they are as you expect and as specified in the template.

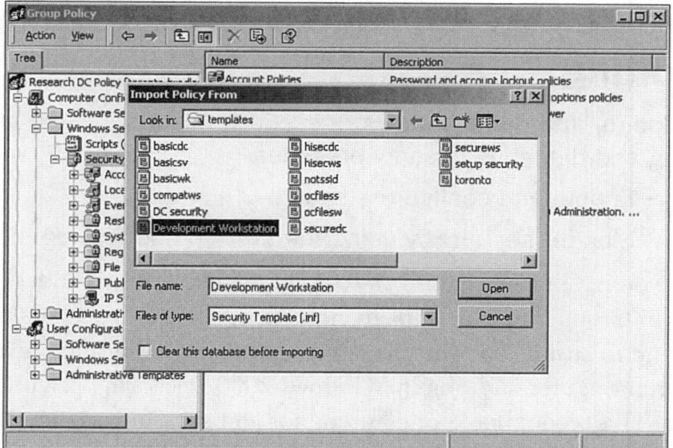

FIGURE 2.55
Locate the security template you want to import and click Open.

7. When finished, close the Group Policy Editor to save your changes.

8. Click OK to close the Active Directory Container Properties dialog box.

9. Exit Active Directory Users and Computers (or Active Directory Sites and Services) when finished.

As the discussion indicates, importing security templates and applying them in a GPO is quite straightforward. The settings included in the template are now applied to all computers and users within the scope of the GPO. You can use the Security Configuration and Analysis MMC snap-in to verify settings on individual computers.

Windows 2000 provides the administrator with a great deal of flexibility in implementing a security policy for both users and computers. As you have seen, security templates enable you to configure the settings that should be in place for a computer or user. Security Configuration and Analysis enables you to compare the currently running settings to those in a template, so you can compare the current security settings against those that should be in place (that is, those in the security template). To implement the same security settings on several computers or for a number of users, you can use Group Policy to assign those settings at the site, domain, or OU level.

NOTE

Getting More Information About Templates For more information on working with security templates, see *MCSE Training Guide: Windows 2000 Directory Services Administration,* ISBN: 0-7357-0976-9.

Configuring, Implementing, and Using Auditing

- ▶ Monitor and manage network security. Actions include auditing and detecting security breaches.
  - Enable and configure auditing.
  - Monitor security by using the system security log file.

After you have taken the time to configure user accounts and domain Group Policy to implement security settings, you should use auditing to ensure that you are achieving the desired results. Another important use for auditing in Windows 2000 is tracking privilege abuse. This section looks at planning for and subsequently implementing an audit strategy for your network as well as using the security log to monitor and interpret audit events.

Configuring Auditing

You can configure security policy using Group Policy, as discussed previously, or by using Security Configuration and Analysis. One important element that must be considered is tracking security-related events to determine whether your settings are effective and to thus prevent unauthorized access to resources.

Security auditing policy is a portion of security policy that enables you to configure which security-related events to monitor or to have the potential to monitor. By monitoring these security-related system events, you can detect attempts by intruders to compromise data on the system or to gain access to resources they should not be able to reach.

When you perform auditing, you are tracking user and operating system activities, or events, on a computer. This information is stored in the security log of Event Viewer. Each entry, or record, in the security log consists of the action performed, the user who performed the action, and whether the action was successful.

The events to be audited are configured in an audit policy, which is a component of security policy. As mentioned, an audit policy can be configured in the Security Settings of Group Policy or by using Security Configuration and Analysis to configure which events to monitor on a single computer. The events that can be monitored and be part of the audit policy are quite diverse. Table 2.10 lists the types of events. For each event, you can track the success or failure.

TABLE 2.10

AUDIT EVENTS

Audit Events	*Description*
Account logon	Account logon events take place on a domain controller and deal with the domain controller receiving a request to validate a user account. This is different from the logon event, which is discussed later in this table. This type of event takes place when a user attempts to log on to a computer and specifies a domain-level logon account. When the domain controller receives a request from the client machine to log on to the network, an account logon event is said to have occurred. It should be noted that computers as well as users can request account logon.
Account management	An account management event occurs when an administrator creates, changes, or deletes a user account or group. It is also used to track an administrator renaming, disabling, enabling, or modifying the password of a user account. Using this event, you can track changes to users and groups in the site, domain, or OU. This event can also be used to track changes in local users and groups on Windows 2000 Server and Windows 2000 Professional computers.
Directory services	This event tracks user access to a specific Active Directory object. Enabling this audit event in Windows 2000 does not automatically turn on tracking of access to all Active Directory objects. You must specify which users and groups should have access to a specific Active Directory container tracked by modifying entries in the Auditing tab of the Advanced Security settings for an Active Directory object.
Logon	The logon event is triggered when a user logs on to or logs off a local computer. It can also be used to track network access to a computer because connecting through the network to a machine requires the user to log on to establish the connection. Logon events take place on the computer where access is required, in contrast to account logon events, which always occur on domain controllers.
Object access	Object access events include a user attempting to gain access to a file or folder on an NTFS partition or to a printer. Enabling the object access event, such as directory service access, does not turn it on automatically for the computer; rather, it turns on the possibility of auditing for files and printers on the machine. To specify which files, folders, and printers will be audited, you modify the security settings of the object for which you want to track access.

continues

TABLE 2.10 *continued*

AUDIT EVENTS

Audit Events	*Description*
Policy change	The policy change event tracks success or failure on attempts to change user security options such as password policy, user rights assignment, account lockout settings, and audit policies. In other words, this series of events tracks changes to security settings on the computer or GPO, including which events to audit.
Privilege use	Privilege use events track the use of certain privileges and user rights by an individual. These include taking ownership of a file or folder, changing the system time, loading and unloading device drivers, and modifying quotas. With the exception of logon and logoff rights and events that affect the Windows 2000 security log, such as shutting down or restarting the computer, this event can be used to track almost all the user rights that can be assigned.
Process tracking	This event is used to track the execution of processes on the system. This includes invoking and stopping an application as well as which other programs an application itself opened. Generally, you would not turn on process tracking unless you were a programmer and wanted to see the flow of execution of your programs and process identification information tracked by Windows 2000.
System	This event deals with the user shutting down or restarting the computer. Other events include anything that would affect the security elements of Windows 2000, such as clearing out the security log in Event Viewer, or other security-related settings on the computer.

Looking at Table 2.10, you should now understand that you can track almost any action taken on a system, if you want to do so. Generally, however, too much auditing is not recommended. Auditing can severely impact the performance of the target system. On the other hand, although no auditing is great for performance, it provides no information on any attempts to gain access to resources by intruders. The ideal amount of auditing is the fine line between performance and security and is different for each organization. Planning is the key.

Planning an Audit Policy

When deciding whether to implement an audit policy and to what extent, planning is the most important aspect of the decision. As previously stated, too much auditing can bring systems to a crawl and can cause users to perceive the network and their machines as being too slow to perform their jobs. On the other hand, too little or no auditing can leave systems vulnerable to threats and can help rather than hinder an intruder. The general rule of thumb is to audit only those events that make sense in your environment.

When planning an audit policy, consider the following guidelines:

- **Determine which computers should have auditing configured**—Auditing can be turned on or off for individual computers; therefore, you should determine which ones should have the success or failure of user actions tracked. For example, file servers and domain controllers, which contain sensitive or critical data, are good candidates for auditing. However, users' desktop computers, except in very high-security environments such as national security agencies, the military, or certain parts of financial institutions, should probably not be audited. These computers usually do not contain sensitive or critical data. As always, exceptions can be found and should be treated as such.
- **Determine the types of events to audit for each computer**—Some computers should have certain types of events audited that might not apply to other computers. For example, domain controllers are great candidates for the auditing of account logon, account management, and directory service access events. Windows 2000 stand alone Servers are more likely to have file and folder access, as well as privilege use events, tracked. All computers can be good candidates for system (startup and shutdown) and logon events tracking. For each computer, evaluate which events make sense to be tracked on the target computer.
- **Determine whether you need to track successful access to or use of a resource, failure to do so, or both**—Obviously, tracking both provides more data, but will this data be useful information or just make it more difficult to locate attempts to bypass security settings on the computer? Success and failure together can be used for resource planning, whereas failure alone can alert you to possible breaches of security.

- **Determine for which objects and users you want to track events**—As previously outlined, some events, such as object (file, folder, and printer) access and directory service access, need to be configured for the object in question as well as the users whose access you want to monitor. Tracking success and failure by the Everyone system group includes all users but might, once again, provide too much data and not much useful information. You need to decide for which users and which objects you want to monitor access.
- **Determine whether you need to track usage trends over time**—If so, this requires that you archive security logs on a regular basis and maintain them for longer periods. This won't necessarily have an impact on what you decide to monitor; rather, it will introduce another administrative element into the equation. Factors involved include how long to keep the logs, where to keep them, whether they should be rolled up periodically to track trends, and how this should be done.
- **Review the logs frequently and regularly**—Configuring an audit policy and never looking at the security logs is about as useful as winning the lottery but failing to cash in the winning ticket. It might make you feel good to know you have the winning ticket, but it won't let you have the $10 million. In making sure everything is running as it should be, administrators need to check the logs on a regular basis (daily is good) and be on the lookout for any events that should not be there.

A lengthy planning process focusing on auditing has resulted in the agreement of management and everyone else involved. Now that you have determined what auditing needs to occur, you must implement the policy.

Setting Up an Audit Policy

In setting up an audit policy, you can use one of two tools, depending on the scope of the policy. To configure an audit policy for a single computer, you can use the Security Configuration and Analysis snap-in on the local machine where the policy is to be implemented. However, doing so only ensures that the audit policy affects that one machine and might not provide as much value as having similar settings applied to a whole range of machines.

To configure an audit policy for several machines at once, you can use Group Policy. To set an audit policy using Group Policy, follow the steps outlined in Step By Step 2.19.

STEP BY STEP

2.19 Configuring an Audit Policy Using Group Policy

1. Log on to your Windows 2000 computer as administrator and start the MMC console on which the Group Policy object you want to configure an audit policy for is located (either Active Directory Users and Computers or Active Directory Sites and Services).
2. Right-click the container whose GPO will be modified to install an audit policy and click Properties.
3. Click the Group Policy tab and select the GPO that will have security settings propagated to objects within its scope. Click Edit to open the Group Policy Editor.
4. Expand Computer Configuration, Windows Settings, Security Settings, Local Policies to show the areas of the system to which the audit policy can be applied (see Figure 2.56).

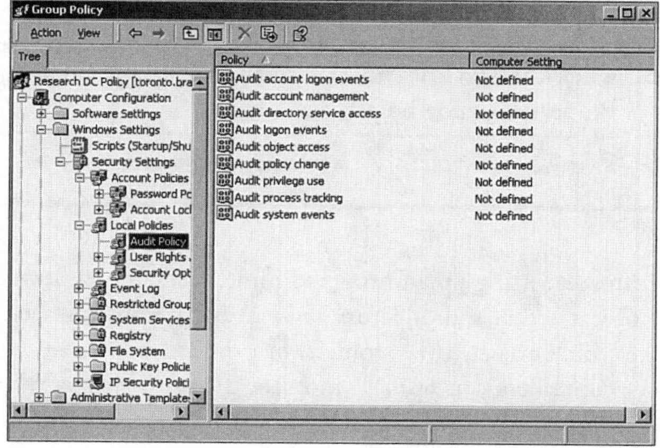

FIGURE 2.56
Configuring an audit policy.

continues

continued

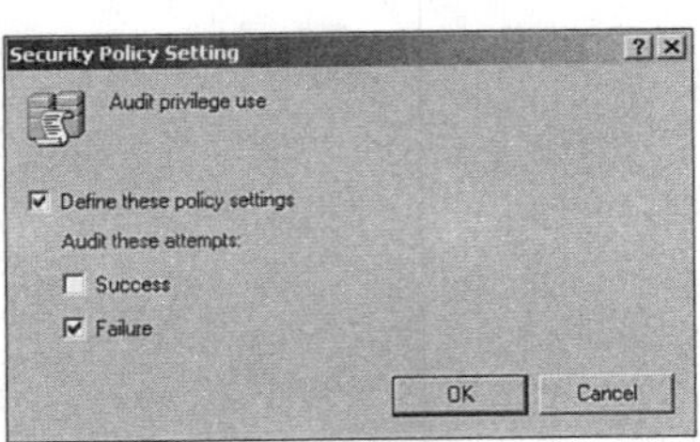

FIGURE 2.57
Configuring auditing for privilege use.

5. Select the type of event to audit and double-click to open the setting definition dialog box, as shown in Figure 2.57.
6. Click the Define These Policy Settings check box and select whether to audit Success, Failure, or both for the event by checking the appropriate check box(es). Click OK to save your changes. The Group Policy Editor will reflect your changes, as shown in Figure 2.58.

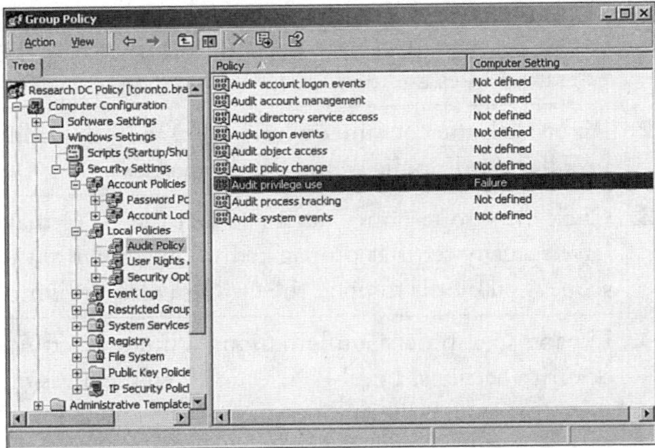

FIGURE 2.58
Changing event configuration for auditing is immediately reflected in the Group Policy Editor.

7. Repeat steps 5 and 6 for any additional events you want to audit. When finished, close the Group Policy Editor.
8. Click OK to close the Active Directory Container Properties dialog box.
9. Exit Active Directory Users and Computers.

As you can see, setting up auditing is simple. Remember, however, that for object access and directory service access, you still need to configure which objects (files, folders, or printers) or Active Directory containers you want to monitor access to and by whom.

Auditing Access to Resources

After you have configured the audit policy to audit object access or Directory Service access, you need to perform additional steps and perform more planning to ensure that events on key resources are monitored. These resources include file system objects, printer objects, and Active Directory objects.

Auditing Access to File System Objects

When you configure auditing on file system files and folders, you are doing so for files and folders on NTFS file systems only. Auditing of files on FAT or FAT32 file systems is not available; these file systems do not provide any type of security, which is required for auditing.

When you specify auditing on file system objects, keep the following in mind:

- Audit failure events for Read operations on critical or sensitive files to determine which users are attempting to gain access to files for which they have no permissions.
- Audit success and failure for Delete operations on confidential or archival files to monitor which users might be attempting malicious activities and to track which files were deleted by which users.
- Audit success and failure operations for Change Permissions and Take Ownership permission usage for confidential and personal files of users. These events might indicate that someone is trying to change security settings on files to which they do not have permission to gain access to data to which he does not currently have the rights. This also records an administrator taking ownership of a user's file or modifying permissions on a file so she can gain access. Even though administrators might be able to cover their tracks a little better than most, the event is still recorded in the log.
- Audit success and failure of all events performed by members of the Guests group. This should be done on the folders to which Guests should not have access. You can verify that no attempts by unauthorized users took place and, if they did, when they occurred so you can locate a pattern.
- Audit file and folder access (both success and failure) on all computers containing shared data that should normally be secured. This way, shared folder activities can be tracked to ensure no unwanted attempts to breach security were made.

To specify auditing on a particular file or folder on an NTFS partition, after enabling object access auditing (success and failure), perform the steps detailed in Step By Step 2.20.

STEP BY STEP

2.20 Configuring Auditing on Files and Folders

1. Log on to your Windows 2000 computer as an administrator and start Windows Explorer.
2. Locate the folder or file on an NTFS partition that you want to audit access for, right-click, and select Properties. You are presented with a dialog box similar to Figure 2.59.

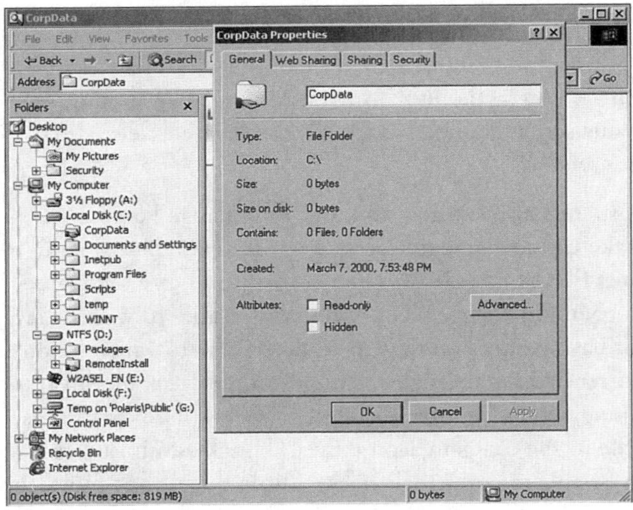

FIGURE 2.59
Selecting Properties for the NTFS folder whose access you want to audit presents this dialog box.

3. Click the Security tab to show the current permissions, as shown in Figure 2.60.
4. Click the Advanced button to go to the advanced security configuration, as shown in Figure 2.61.

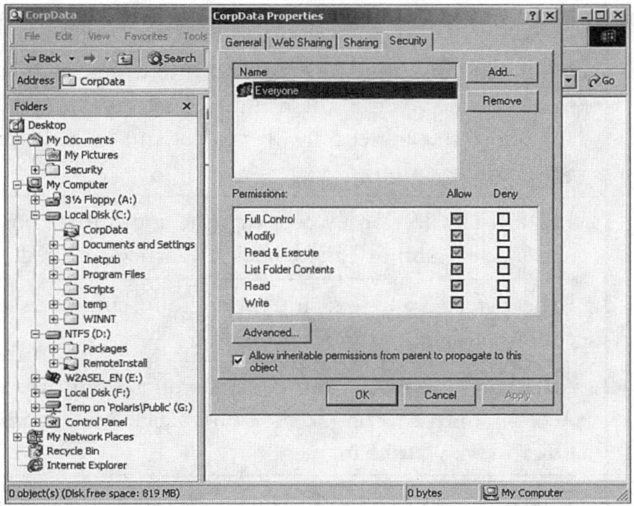

FIGURE 2.60
The Security tab of the NTFS folder shows currently assigned permissions.

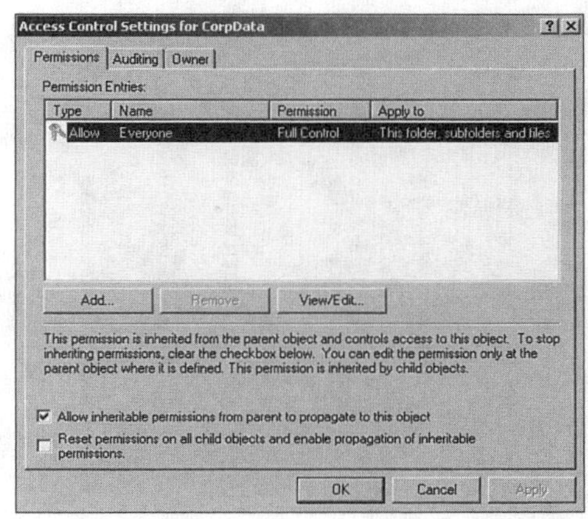

FIGURE 2.61
Clicking the Advanced button opens the Access Control Settings properties dialog box.

5. Click the Auditing tab to display the currently configured auditing settings for the folder, as shown in Figure 2.62.

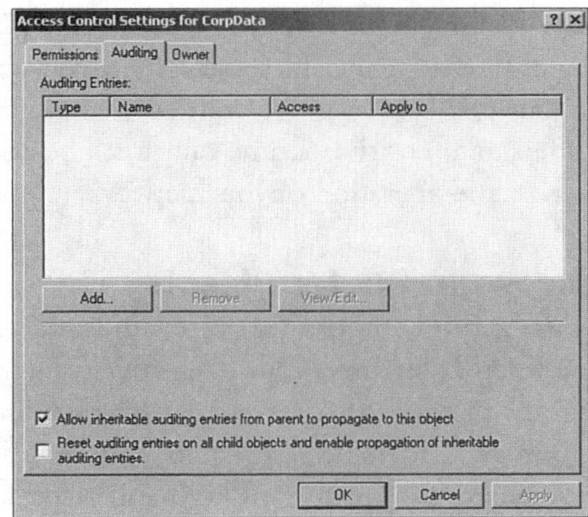

FIGURE 2.62
The Auditing tab lists the currently configured auditing options for the folder.

6. Click the Add button and select a group or user for whom you want to monitor activity to this folder. After making a selection, you are presented with a dialog box, similar to Figure 2.63, which enables you to specify for which events you want to audit successful or failed access.

continues

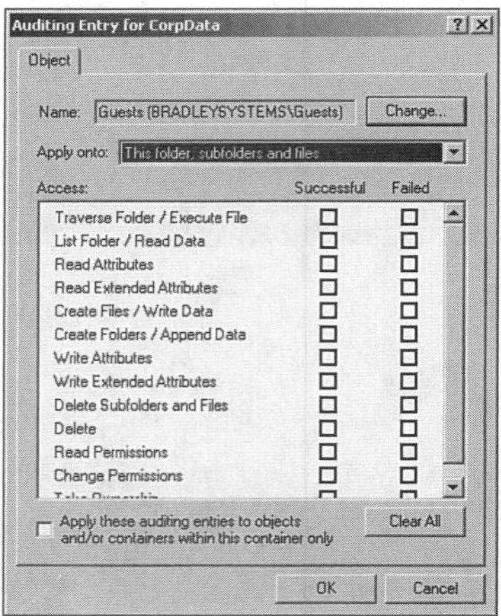

FIGURE 2.63
Selecting a group or user opens the Auditing Entry selection dialog box, enabling you to select which events for this NTFS folder to audit the success or failure of.

continued

Note that you can use the Apply Onto drop-down list box to determine whether these auditing settings should be applied to this folder only, this folder and its children, or other combinations.

7. Make your selection by checking the appropriate boxes under Successful or Failed; click OK when finished.

8. Repeat steps 6 and 7 to add more groups and users and configure their auditing settings.

9. After you have made your choices, you are returned to the Access Control Settings dialog box. Click Apply and then OK to save your changes.

10. Exit Windows Explorer if you are finished. Otherwise, repeat the preceding steps for any other folders and files for which you need to configure auditing.

As Step By Step 2.20 shows, you need to use Windows Explorer to enable auditing on the particular files and folders you want to track. This process might take some time to configure all audit settings for all files and folders of a sensitive nature, but it can be critical to ensuring proper, secure operation of your network.

Auditing Access to Printer Objects

You can configure auditing on printer objects to track usage as well as to determine whether attempts to use sensitive printers (for example, MICR printers that can be used to create checks) are taking place. Although most printers do not require auditing, those that are specialized or expensive to run, such as high-end color laser printers, might require some auditing.

When auditing printers, use these guidelines:

- Audit failure events for print operations on sensitive printers, such as those used to print or encode sensitive company documents or preprinted forms. For example, a record store using printers to create gift certificates might want to limit access to the printer that has the gift certificate stock in it.

- Audit failure and success for print operations on expensive printers so you can track usage and possibly use this information to charge back costs to a department or user.
- Audit success and failure events for use of Full Control permissions on all printers to track administrative changes to the printer. This includes updating the printer driver as well as creating and removing shares.
- Audit success events on Delete permissions on commonly used printers so that purging of documents can be seen as an administrative correction rather than printer failure.
- Audit success and failure events on Change Permissions and Take Ownership permissions on sensitive printers to have a record of who was assigned or removed from the access control list for the printer. In this way, you can determine whether an administrator might have inadvertently given permissions to a user who should not have them and can track security breaches.

To specify auditing on a printer, after enabling object access auditing (success and failure), perform the steps shown in Step By Step 2.21.

STEP BY STEP

2.21 Configuring Auditing on Printers

1. Log on to your Windows 2000 computer as an administrator and select Start, Settings, Printers. You will be shown a list of printers on the machine similar to those in Figure 2.64.
2. Right-click the printer for which you want to enable auditing and select Properties. As shown in Figure 2.65, the printer Properties dialog box displays.

continues

continued

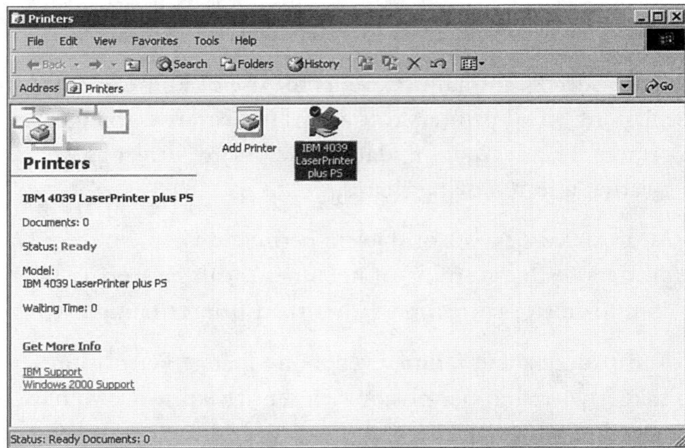

FIGURE 2.64
Selecting Printers from the Settings menu displays printers installed on the computer.

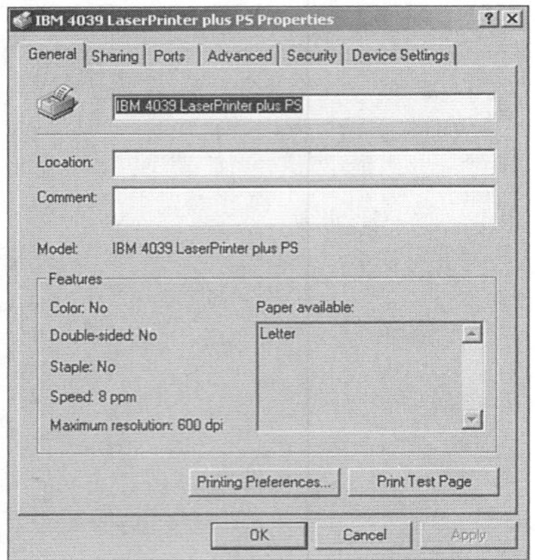

FIGURE 2.65
The printer Properties dialog box is opened by right-clicking the printer and selecting Properties.

3. Click the Security tab and then the Advanced button to bring up the Access Control Settings dialog box, as shown in Figure 2.66.

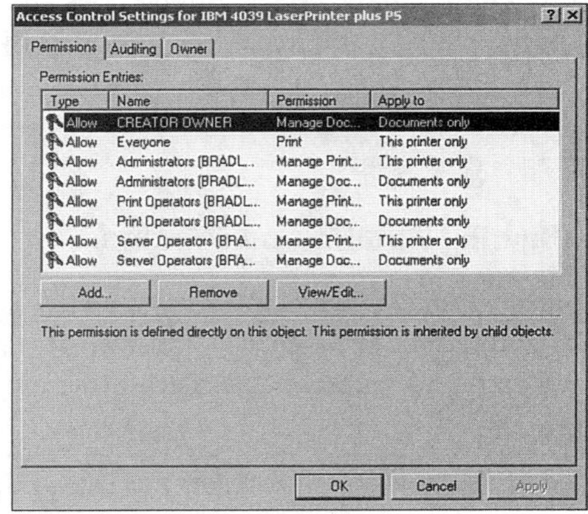

FIGURE 2.66
The Access Control Settings dialog box is opened by clicking Advanced from the Security tab in the printer Properties dialog box.

4. Click the Auditing tab of the Access Control Settings dialog box to see a list of auditing entries for the printer.

5. To add an entry, click the Add button. You will be prompted to select the user or group whose printer actions you want to audit, as shown in Figure 2.67.

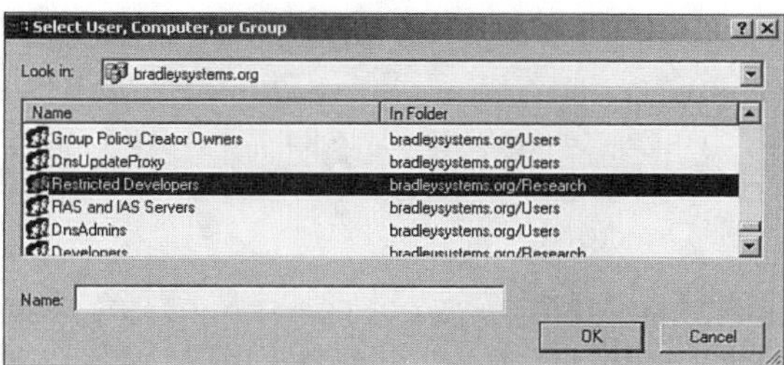

FIGURE 2.67
Clicking the Auditing tab and then Add enables you to insert additional auditing entries for the printer.

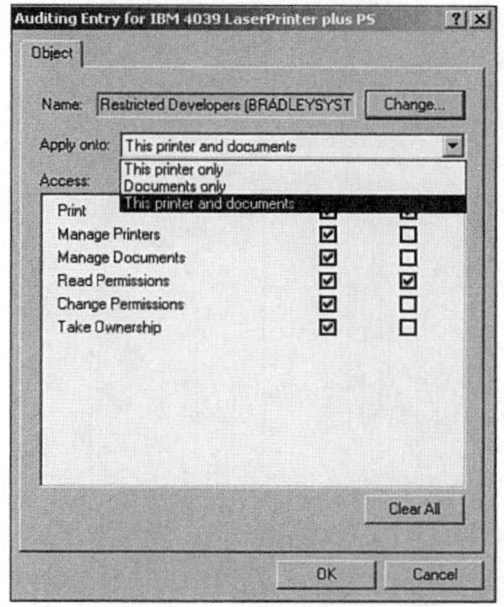

FIGURE 2.68
Selecting Printers from the Settings menu displays printers installed on the computer.

6. After selecting the user or group whose actions you want to audit, the Auditing Entry dialog box is presented (see Figure 2.68). Select the actions you want to audit and click OK when finished.

   Note that you can apply your auditing actions to the printer and documents, the printer only, or documents only.

   It is also important to note that auditing the Print permission also requires auditing the Read permissions because users need to be able to locate the printer to print to it.

7. Repeat steps 5 and 6 to add more groups and users and configure their auditing settings.
8. After you have made your choices, you are returned to the Access Control Settings dialog box. Click Apply and then OK to save your changes.
9. Click OK to exit the printer Properties dialog box.
10. Close the Printers folder if you are finished. Otherwise, repeat the preceding steps for any other printers for which you need to configure auditing.

Similar to files and folders, auditing access to printers requires that you specify which actions should be audited for which users and on which printers. It is a good idea to audit access to very specific or critical printers (such as check-printing printers or expensive color printers) but not to basic printers used by everyone or those on a user's desk.

Auditing Access to Active Directory Objects

When you configure auditing on Active Directory objects, you are able to track changes, or even simply read access, to a component of Active Directory. The objects that can be tracked are virtually everything in Active Directory.

When auditing Active Directory object access, be sure to audit both the success and failure for critical objects, such as user accounts and any groups whose membership is sensitive. You should do this for all administrative users and especially for those to whom you might have delegated control of an Active Directory object. This enables you to determine whether any of the individuals entrusted with maintaining parts of your network infrastructure are attempting to gain more access than they have been assigned.

To audit Active Directory object access, set the audit policy to track directory service access and use. Enable auditing of the object by using the appropriate MMC console, such as Active Directory Users and Computers, Active Directory Sites and Services, or Active Directory Domains and Trusts. For example, to enable auditing for the Users container in Active Directory, perform the steps described in Step By Step 2.22.

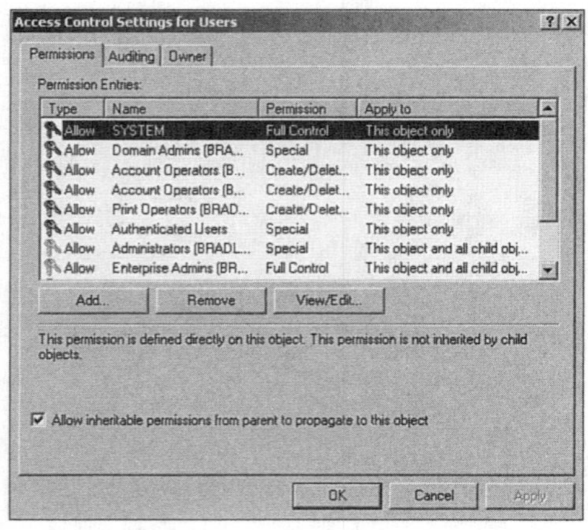

FIGURE 2.69

The Access Control Settings dialog box for the Active Directory Users container enables you to access the audit settings for the Active Directory object.

STEP BY STEP

2.22 Configuring Auditing on Active Directory Objects

1. Log on to your Windows 2000 computer as an administrator and open Active Directory Users and Computers from the Administrative Tools program group.

2. Expand your domain, right-click the container for which you want to configure auditing (such as the Users container), and select Properties.

3. From the Properties screen, click the Security tab and select Advanced. A screen similar to Figure 2.69 is displayed.

   If the Advanced option is not available, click the View menu in the MMC console and select Advanced to enable the viewing of advanced options in the console.

4. Click the Auditing tab to see a list of current auditing entries. To add a new entry, click the Add button and select a user or group to audit, as shown in Figure 2.70.

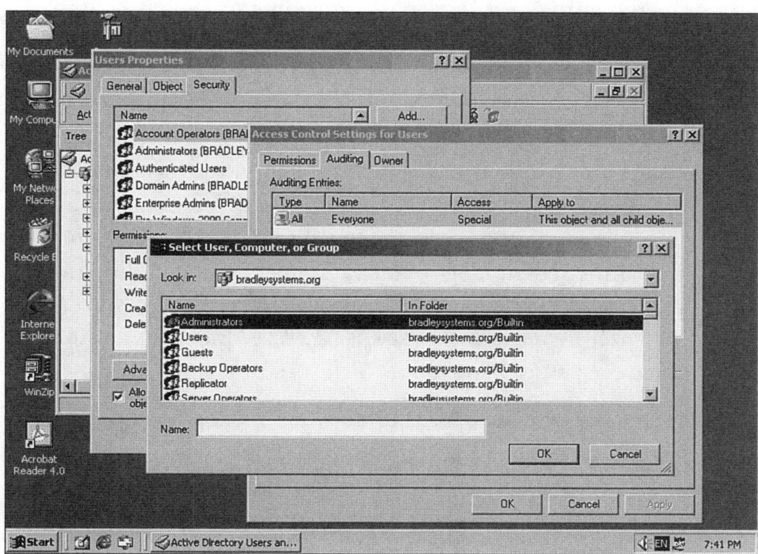

FIGURE 2.70
Clicking the Auditing tab displays a list of current auditing entries.

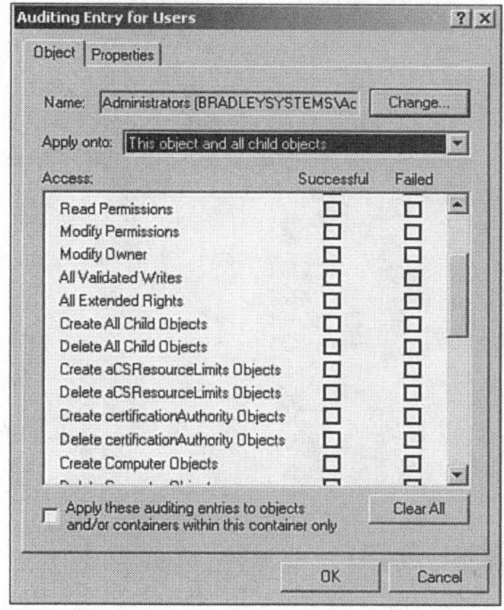

FIGURE 2.71
Adding an audit entry to an Active Directory object presents a long list of possible actions that can be tracked.

5. From the dialog box presented, select the action you want to audit, Successful or Failed, and the scope to apply the auditing to, as shown in Figure 2.71. Click OK when you're finished to save your changes.

   Note that Active Directory objects have many permissions that can be audited, such as Create Computer Objects or Delete Contact Objects. Active Directory objects can have more permissions than you have seen in either files and folders or printers.

6. If you have completed configuring audit settings for the object, click Apply and then OK to close the Access Control Settings dialog box. If not, add the necessary entries and then exit the dialog box.

7. Click OK to close the Properties dialog box.

8. If you want to audit additional objects, repeat steps 2–7 for those containers or objects. When finished, exit Active Directory Users and Computers.

NOTE

Focus Auditing at Precise Levels Be careful when applying auditing to all objects and children. This might create auditing entries for a great many objects if set at a very high container in Active Directory. It is usually a good idea to focus auditing of Active Directory objects only at the precise levels required and not allow it to propagate throughout the whole structure.

One of the wonderful features of Windows 2000 for administrators is the flexibility and control provided by Active Directory. However, ensuring that only those individuals who need it have access to a particular part of Active Directory is critical to ensuring that it operates properly. In the next section, we are going to look at how to interpret the audit logs and look for problem areas.

Auditing and the Security Log

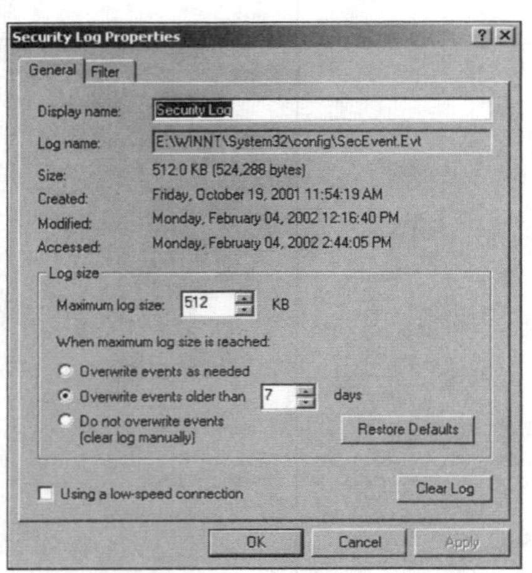

FIGURE 2.72
In the Security Log Properties dialog box, you can adjust the log size and what will happen when that size is reached.

Audit events are written into the security log on the local machine. This security log can be accessed from the Event Viewer, which is a part of the administrative tools. You need to be aware of certain properties of the security log if you are implementing auditing in your organization (see Figure 2.72). First, it is configured with a maximum size (by default, that size is 512KB), and you can store about three events per kilobyte.

Second, you can configure what to do when the log fills up. Your choices are to overwrite old events, overwrite old events only if they are beyond a certain age, or never overwrite old events. In a high-security environment, you don't want events to ever be overwritten; instead, you must manually archive logs when they reach capacity. In fact, if security is a big enough issue, you might want to enable the security policy item that shuts down the server when the security log is full (this prevents anyone from accessing anything if it can't be tracked).

Finally, you can archive log entries at any time so you can have a permanent record of all log entries made throughout history.

Step By Steps 2.23 and 2.24 show how to configure the security log properties and how to archive log entries, respectively.

STEP BY STEP

2.23 Configuring Security Log Properties

1. Select Start, Programs, Administrative Tools, Event Viewer.
2. At the Event Viewer console, right-click Security Log and select Properties from the menu that appears.

3. In the Security Log Properties dialog box, adjust the settings as desired and click OK.

STEP BY STEP

2.24 Archiving Log Entries

1. Select Start, Programs, Administrative Tools, Event Viewer.
2. At the Event Viewer console, right-click Security Log and select Save Log File As from the context menu.
3. In the Save Security Log As dialog box, enter a name and location for your log file and click OK.
4. Right-click Security Log and select Clear All Events from the menu that appears. This removes the archived events from the active log.

The security log tracks all events produced by auditing and records them as either success audit or failure audit. When you open the security log, you might be presented with a daunting list of events to sift through. To save time and effort, you can use filters to go through the events. You can select to see only certain event types; in the case of security, you can see either successes or failures. You can also choose to filter out events that fall outside a particular time range. Step By Step 2.25 shows you how to view and filter events in the log.

STEP BY STEP

2.25 Viewing and Filtering Security Log Entries

1. Select Start, Programs, Administrative Tools, Event Viewer.

continues

continued

2. At the Event Viewer console, click Security Log (see Figure 2.73).

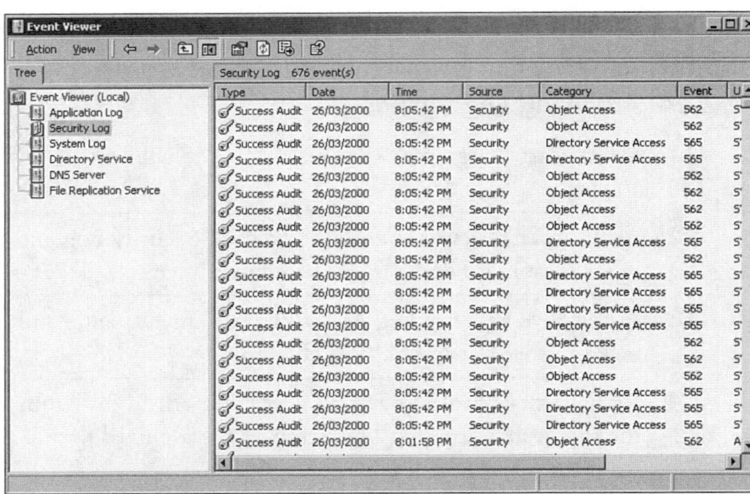

FIGURE 2.73
The security log.

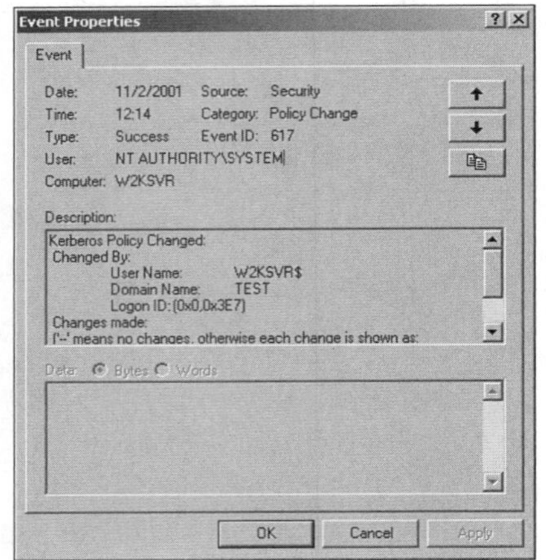

FIGURE 2.74
An audit event selected for viewing.

3. On the right side, you can see the security log with either Failure Audit or Success Audit in the Type column. Double-click an event to see its detail (see Figure 2.74). Then, click OK to continue.

4. Filter the events as desired. Right-click Security Log and select Properties from the context menu.

5. In the Security Log Properties dialog box, click the Filter tab.

6. On the Filter property sheet, configure the filter to show only the items you want to see (see Figure 2.75). Click OK to continue.

7. When you want to see all the events again, remove the filter by opening the Filter property sheet and clicking the Restore Defaults button.

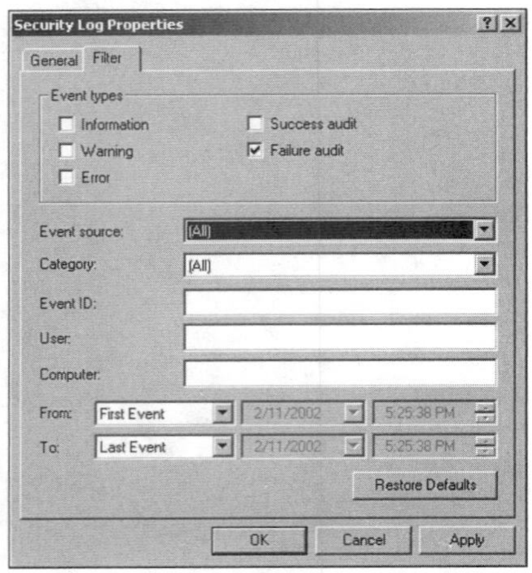

FIGURE 2.75
Configure the filter to show only what you want to see. This filter eliminates everything but the failure events.

Troubleshooting Auditing

Problems with auditing usually occur for one of three reasons:

- You are collecting too much data.
- You are collecting too little data.
- You are not collecting the right data.

To get auditing configured correctly, you have to begin with a goal. The goal should never be to collect information; information gathering is only a tool that helps you reach your goal. If, for example, your goal is to investigate how many attempts are made to hack into your server at night, you should audit failed logon attempts and then filter the results to show only those that occurred during certain hours.

The point is, when you know what the purpose is, you will be in a better position to determine what audit policy you should use to get the type of information you need to fulfill your goal. Troubleshooting auditing always comes down to understanding what the policies are and then applying what you know about them to the goal you want auditing to help you reach.

CHAPTER SUMMARY

This chapter has covered a lot of ground on two of the bigger areas associated with administering a Windows 2000 network: sharing of resources and basic network security. Some of the things covered in this chapter include

- **Active Directory basics**—Active Directory is a database that contains multiple tables, one for each class or type of object. The tables contain a unique ID and various attributes (properties) about the objects listed. From each of these tables, key fields are copied to the global catalog, which is replicated between all the domains in the enterprise. The structure of the database is common throughout the enterprise and is maintained on the schema master. Domains are used in Windows 2000 for administrative and replication boundaries. The domains are linked together in a hierarchy based on the DNS system.

KEY TERMS

- Account lockout
- Active Directory
- Audit policy
- Auditing
- Bridgehead server
- Computer
- Domain
- Domain controller
- Local password policy

CHAPTER SUMMARY

- Object
- Organizational unit
- Password age
- Password history
- Security log
- Share permissions
- Shares
- Site
- System policy
- User
- User rights

- **Resource sharing**—The sharing and publishing of resources across a network is a vital part of network services. Without the resources to share, there would be little need for the network itself. All share resources have share permissions that can be configured to determine how the shared resource can be accessed and managed across the network. Share permissions work together cumulatively with NTFS file permissions when it comes to object access.

- **Basic network security**—You can take some basic steps toward securing your network by customizing the settings in the password and account lockout sections of Group Policy. You can further increase security by implementing the included security templates. To implement uniform security measures across your entire network, you can link Group Policy objects to organizational units, domains, or sites. The security log in Event Viewer is your one-stop location for all events regarding auditing of events; however, you will have to enable and configure auditing before trying to view events.

APPLY YOUR KNOWLEDGE

Exercises

2.1 Creating and Testing a Local Account Policy

This exercise shows you how to create a local account policy and then how this policy affects users who log on to your server. You might need to create additional user accounts to complete this exercise; if so, see Chapter 10, "Fundamentals of Active Directory," for additional guidance on creating new user accounts. The account name `TestUser` refers to an account used for testing purposes.

To ensure that settings configured in the following exercises are not influenced by domain policy, if your server is a member of a domain, be sure you follow step 1 to remove the computer from the domain. Normally, you would not do this; however, to avoid having to discuss and deal with Active Directory policy issues, this step is necessary for lab purposes.

Estimated Time: 30 minutes

1. Make sure that the server is not a member of a domain. (Do this step only if your Windows 2000 server is currently a member of a domain.) Here's how:
    1. From the desktop, right-click the My Computer icon and select Properties from the menu that appears.
    2. From the System Properties dialog box, select the Network Identification tab and click the Properties button.
    3. In the Identification Changes dialog box, click the Workgroup radio button (in the Member Of section) and enter **`Workgroup`** as the workgroup name. Click OK to continue.
    4. After a pause, you should be welcomed to the Workgroup workgroup and prompted to restart your computer. Do so and log on as administrator.
2. Adjust the password policy to remember two passwords and require a minimum length of five characters. Do the following:
    1. From the Start menu, select Programs, Administrative Tools, Local Security Policy.
    2. On the Local Security Settings console, expand the Account Policies section to reveal the Password Policy. Select the Password Policy.
    3. On the right, the current password policies are displayed (the column labeled Effective Setting does not apply here because no domain policy is in effect). Double-click Enforce Password History Policy.
    4. In the Local Security Policy Setting dialog box, change the value in the Enforce Password History box to **`2`**. Click OK to continue.
    5. Change the Minimum Password Length policy to **`5`**.
    6. Close the Local Security Settings console and log off the administrator account.
3. Log on as `TestUser` and change from password to `test policy`. Follow these steps:
    1. Log on as `TestUser`.
    2. Change your password to **`1234`**. You will be told that this violates the policy. Change it to **`12345`** instead.

APPLY YOUR KNOWLEDGE

3. Upon successful logon, press Ctrl+Alt+Del to invoke the Windows Security dialog box, and then click the Change Password button.
4. In the Change Password dialog box, type in the old password (`12345`) and type the previously configured password as the new password. Click OK to continue.
5. When the Change Password Error message appears, click OK to continue. You can't change your password back to the most recent one because the password history setting prevents it.
6. When the Change Password dialog box appears again, change the password from `12345` to `54321`. You will be informed that your password has changed. Click OK to clear the informational dialog box and return to the Windows Security dialog box.
7. Click the Change Password button again and change your password from 54321 back to the original password. This time you will be successful.
8. In the Windows Security dialog box, click the Cancel button to return to the desktop.

4. Log off as `TestUser` and log on as administrator.

2.2 Configuring and Testing a Local Account Lockout Policy

This exercise shows how you can configure a local account lockout policy to prevent more than three incorrect password attempts. It also shows how to unlock an account that's locked and how to reset a user account password.

It is expected that you have already completed Exercise 2.1 and have a test account to work with.

Estimated Time: 30 minutes

1. Open the Local Security Policy console on your server.
2. Expand the Account Policies section and select the Account Lockout Policy.
3. On the right, change the Account Lockout Threshold to **`3`**. Windows 2000 will then automatically set the other two lockout policies.
4. Close the Local Security Policy console and log off as administrator.
5. Lock out the `TestUser` account by entering an incorrect password. Do the following:
    1. In the Log On to Windows dialog box, type **`TestUser`** as the username, and then enter three incorrect passwords in a row. Although you can't tell yet, the `TestUser` account becomes locked out.
    2. On the fourth attempt, correctly type in the password. You will be told that the account is locked out.
6. Log in as administrator.
7. Open the Computer Management console, expand the Local Users and Groups section, and select Users.
8. Double-click the `TestUser` account.
9. Clear the check box labeled Account Is Locked Out. Select the check box labeled User Must Change Password at Next Logon (this enables `TestUser` to change her password to a known value). Click OK to continue.

APPLY YOUR KNOWLEDGE

10. In the Computer Management console, right-click the `TestUser` account and select Set Password from the context menu that appears.
11. In the Set Password dialog box, type **`password`** into both fields. Click OK.
12. Close the Computer Management console and log off the administrator account.
13. Log on as `TestUser` using the password `password`. When prompted, change your password.
14. When finished changing your password, log off the `TestUser` account.

2.3 Configuring and Testing Local System Policy

This exercise shows how you can modify local system policy. In this case, you will modify user rights for `TestUser` to prevent her from logging in to the server locally, and when that user is able to log in, she will be prevented from shutting down the server.

Estimated Time: 20 minutes

1. Log on to the computer using the administrator account and create and configure a system policy by following these steps:
    1. Open the Local Security Policy console.
    2. In the console, expand the Local Policies section and select User Rights Assignments.
    3. Locate the Deny Logon Locally policy, double-click it, and add `TestUser` to the list. This will override the Log On Locally policy setting.
    4. Locate the Shut Down the System policy and verify that neither `TestUser` nor the group of which `TestUser` is a part has the right to shut down the system.
    5. Close the Local Security Policy console and log off the administrator account.
2. Attempt to log on as `TestUser`.
    1. In the Log On to Windows dialog box, attempt to log in as `TestUser`.
    2. When logon fails, log on as administrator.
3. Open the Local Security Policy console and adjust the user rights to allow `TestUser` to log on to the server locally. To do so, clear the check box in the policy.
4. Log on to the server as `TestUser`.
5. Attempt to shut down the server. Do the following:
    1. From the Start menu, select Shut Down. Note that all you can do is log off this account.
    2. In the Shut Down Windows dialog box, click Cancel.
    3. Press Ctrl+Alt+Del to bring up the Windows Security dialog box.
    4. In the Windows Security dialog box, click the Shut Down button. Note that the Shut Down Windows dialog box appears, and you do not have the option to shut down the system.
    5. In the Shut Down Windows dialog box, click Cancel.
    6. In the Windows Security dialog box, click Cancel to return to the desktop.
6. Log on as administrator.

APPLY YOUR KNOWLEDGE

2.4 Enabling and Examining the Effects of File Auditing

This exercise shows how you can enable auditing on a file and examine the security log to determine what access has been made to that file. This exercise requires an NTFS partition.

Estimated Time: 15 minutes

1. On your `C:` drive, create a folder called `AuditMe` and create (or copy) a text file in this folder called `WatchThis.txt`.
2. Configure audit policy to audit logon events and object access. Do the following:
    1. Open the Local Security Policy console, expand the Local Policies, and select the Audit Policy.
    2. Double-click Audit Logon Events. Then, in the Local Security Policy Settings dialog box, select the Success check box and click OK.
    3. Double-click Audit Object Access. Then, in the Local Security Policy Settings dialog box, select both the Success check box and the Failure check box. Click OK.
    4. Close the Local Security Policy console.
3. Configure the `WatchThis.txt` file for object auditing by doing the following:
    1. Navigate to the `WatchThis.txt` file in the `AuditMe` folder.
    2. Right-click the `WatchThis.txt` file and select Properties from the context menu that appears.
    3. Select the Security tab, click the Add button, and add **`Administrator`** to the Name list.
    4. Give the Administrator full control access by selecting the Administrator in the Name list and then selecting the check box next to the Full Control permission in the Allow column.
    5. Adjust the permissions of the Everyone group to allow only Read permission of the file. Because the current permissions for Everyone are inherited from the parent folder, you must first deselect the check box labeled Allow Inheritable Permissions from Parent to Propagate to This Object (when the dialog box appears, click Copy). Then, select the Everyone group in the Name list and deselect all the check boxes in the Allow column except the one labeled Read.
    6. Click the Advanced button at the bottom of the dialog box.
    7. In the Access Control Settings for WatchThis.txt dialog box, select the Auditing tab.
    8. On the Auditing tab, click the Add button and add the Everyone group to the list.
    9. In the Auditing Entry for WatchThis.txt dialog box, select the check boxes for Successful and Failed next to the Create Files/Write Data access type. Click OK to continue.
    10. Click OK to exit the Access Control Settings for WatchThis.txt dialog box.
    11. In the WatchThis.txt Properties dialog box, click OK.

APPLY YOUR KNOWLEDGE

4. Log on as `TestUser` and try to write to the `WatchThis.txt` file by doing the following:
    1. Log on as `TestUser`.
    2. Navigate to the `WatchThis.txt` file and double-click it to open it in Notepad.
    3. In the WatchThis.txt – Notepad dialog box, type **`Anything you can do I can do better`** and select File, Save.
    4. When the Save As dialog box appears, click Cancel. (Note that the reason the Save As dialog box appears is because the user account does not permissions to save the file.)
    5. Exit Notepad, discarding any changes you tried to make to the file.
5. Log off `TestUser` and log on as administrator.
6. Open the Event Viewer and examine the security log for audit entries.
    1. From the Start menu, select Programs, Administrative Tools, Event Viewer.
    2. In the Event Viewer console, select Security Log.
    3. Because you are auditing both logon/logoff events and access failures, you will see events of both types. Double-click an entry that is of type Failure Audit; this should be the entry that was generated when you tried to save changes to a file you had only Read access to.
    4. Close the Event Properties dialog box and close the Event Viewer console.

2.4 Finding a User

In this exercise, you use the Search tool to find a user account. You must have an Active Directory domain to complete this exercise.

Estimated Time: 5 minutes

1. Select Start, Search, For People to bring up the Find People dialog box.
2. In the Look In drop-down list box, select Active Directory.
3. Enter the name `TestUser` and click Find Now.
4. Verify that the information for the test user appears.

2.5 Publishing a Share

In this exercise, you publish a share in Active Directory. You must have an Active Directory domain to complete this exercise.

Estimated Time: 5 minutes

1. Open Explorer by right-clicking My Computer and selecting Explore.
2. Click the C: drive and, in the right pane, right-click in a blank area.
3. From the context menu, select New, Folder. Enter the name **`PubTest`** for the folder and press Enter.
4. Right-click the `PubTest` directory and select Sharing.
5. In the Properties dialog box, click Share This Folder and then click OK to accept the defaults.
6. Open Active Directory Users and Computers.

APPLY YOUR KNOWLEDGE

7. Expand your domain and then select an OU.
8. Right-click the OU and select New, Shared Folder.
9. Enter **`SalesFiles`** as the name you want to appear in Active Directory and **`\\`*`servername`*`\PubTest`** as the share name (where *`servername`* is the name of your server).
10. Click OK.
11. Verify that the folder appears in the chosen OU. If it does not, try right-clicking the OU and selecting Refresh from the context menu.

Review Questions

1. What do you need to do to publish a printer in Active Directory that is attached to a Windows 2000 Server computer?
2. What does the Advanced tab on the Search screen let you do?
3. What criteria apply to an account password when complexity rules are enforced?
4. To audit access to a specific file on a Windows 2000 server, what three administrative tasks must first be done?
5. If you have share-level permissions enabled on a folder and NTFS permissions enabled on the same folder, what are the effective permissions to the folder over the network? What are the effective local permissions?
6. If you want to enable Web sharing of a folder, what must be present on the computer you are doing this on?
7. What is the definition of a site?
8. What is difference between a forest and a tree?
9. What type of server is used to replicate the schema for an enterprise?
10. You suspect that co-op students hired by the software development department have been trying to gain access to the `CORPSECURE` server from the network. How can you determine whether this is the case?
11. Your company has just installed a new $35,000 color printer whose use should be limited to only the graphic arts department. You want to track any attempts to use this printer by others as well as which users in the graphic arts department make the greatest use of the printer. How would you accomplish this?

Exam Questions

1. Mark is the administrator for a small board games manufacturer. Many of his 20 users are new to computers and have a difficult time understanding the need for security. Mark wants to set up an account policy to ensure that the users must change their passwords once a month and that they can't reuse a password more than once a year. Which of the following will allow him to do that?

   A. Set the password history to 12 and set the maximum password age to 30.

   B. Set the password history to 12 and set the minimum password age to 30.

APPLY YOUR KNOWLEDGE

C. Set the maximum password age to 30 and the minimum password age to 28.

D. Set the password history to 12, the minimum password age to 28, and the maximum password age to 30.

2. Luke is the network administrator for a pharmaceutical company. He has set the account policy to require complex passwords and to require passwords of at least five characters. Using the default Windows 2000 definition of a complex password, which of the following passwords is permissible? (Select all that apply.)

   A. Kumquat

   B. Tiger359

   C. Pt109

   D. 33b!!bb

3. Felix is the network administrator for the British royal family. He wants to audit access to all files on the central file server by members of the HouseKeeping group. Which of the following are required to configure auditing? (Select all that apply.)

   A. Use NTFS partitions.

   B. Enable object auditing.

   C. Enable auditing for at least Read events on all files.

   D. Enable auditing for the Everyone group on all files.

   E. All of the above.

4. Timothy is the network administrator for Gulliver's Travels, a small travel company working primarily in the Mediterranean. He has configured auditing on his servers to monitor failed logon access. Which of the following logs will he need to archive regularly to ensure that he can keep an accurate historical record of logon failure?

   A. Application log

   B. System log

   C. Access log

   D. Security log

5. You have two groups of users who need to print to the same printer. However, one group's print jobs must have priority over the other group's print jobs. What's the best way to accomplish this arrangement?

   A. You must install two separate printing devices and assign each group to print to one of the printing devices.

   B. Make the users who need the higher printing priority printer operators so they can adjust the order of print jobs in the print queue.

   C. Set up a printing pool with multiple printers.

   D. Install two printers that are connected to the same printing device. Assign different priorities and groups to each printer.

6. Marvin is the administrator of a Windows 2000-based LAN. The folder named `Secret` is secured as described here:

NTFS	*Share*
Susan – Read and Execute	Susan – Full Control
Managers – Modify	Managers – Change
Bill – Full Control	Bill – No Access

APPLY YOUR KNOWLEDGE

Susan is a member of the Managers group. What effective level of access does Susan get over the network and locally, respectively?

A. Network = Full Control, Locally = Full Control

B. Network = No Access, Locally = Full Control

C. Network = Full Control, Locally = Modify

D. Network = Modify, Locally = Modify

7. Marvin is the administrator of a Windows 2000-based LAN. The folder named `Secret` is secured as described here:

NTFS	*Share*
Susan – Read and Execute	Susan – Full Control
Managers – Modify	Managers – Change
Bill – Full Control	Bill – No Access

Bill is not a member of the Managers group. What effective level of access does Bill get over the network and locally, respectively?

A. Network = No Access, Locally = Full Control

B. Network = No Access, Locally = No Access

C. Network = Full Control, Locally = Full Control

D. Network = No Access, Locally = No Access

8. Sally is trying to publish a printer in Active Directory. The printing device is attached to a Windows 95 computer. What must she do to create the printer in Active Directory?

A. She needs to share the printer from the Windows 95 computer.

B. She needs to update the drivers for the printer.

C. She needs to add a file share on the Windows 95 computer.

D. She needs to manually add the printer to Active Directory.

9. Tom is troubleshooting a permissions problem for Danielle. Danielle has a file she needs to upload to a server once a week. The file is then read by all the executive-level users in the organization. Danielle currently has to go to the server, log on to the server, and then copy the file to the server from a floppy. She wants to be able to connect to the share the executives use to read the file to upload the file to the server weekly. What should Tom check?

A. The NTFS permissions

B. The permissions on the Everyone group

C. The share permissions

D. The permissions on the file object in Active Directory

10. The human resources department has come to you with a problem. It has a shared directory with the HR updates, but it seems no one can find them because no one seems to have read them. The department wants to ensure that users can locate the documents. What can you do to ensure they can locate the documents?

A. Create a new group and put the documents there.

B. Create a mailing list and have HR mail the document to all users.

C. Publish the HR share in Active Directory.

D. Locate the directory in a new Dfs root.

APPLY YOUR KNOWLEDGE

11. Sally is attempting to share a directory. Which tool should she use?

    A. Explorer

    B. Active Directory Sites and Services

    C. Active Directory Users and Computers

    D. Server Manager

12. You need to track attempts to access files on a network share called SOURCECODE on the ENGINEERING member server in your domain. Which of the following tasks must you perform to accomplish your goals? (Select all correct answers.)

    A. Audit logon activity on ENGINEERING.

    B. Audit file and folder access on SOURCECODE.

    C. Audit object access on ENGINEERING.

    D. Audit directory access on ENGINEERING.

    E. Audit file and folder access on ENGINEERING.

    F. Audit object access on SOURCECODE.

13. Which of the following audit policy settings, when enabled, will by default not result in any audit entries in the security event log? (Select two correct answers.)

    A. Audit object access

    B. Audit logon events

    C. Audit system events

    D. Audit directory service access

    E. Audit account logon events

    F. Audit file and print access

14. You want to keep track of the amount of time users spend logged on to the network. Which of the following audit events should you enable? (Select the best answer.)

    A. Audit account logon events – Success

    B. Audit account management – Success

    C. Audit account logon events – Failure

    D. Audit logon events – Success

    E. Audit logon events – Failure

    F. Audit account management - Failure

15. The management of conciliar.com has decided that password policy maintenance should be determined by each area of the company. The only corporate requirement is that all users must have a password of at least five characters.

    The Active Directory structure of conciliar.com includes a top-level domain called `conciliar.com` and four additional subdomains called `namerica.conciliar.com`, `europe.conciliar.com`, `samerica.conciliar.com`, and `specific.conciliar.com` that have been created for administrative purposes. Because the migration to Windows 2000 has just recently been completed, no new Group Policy objects have been created yet.

    How would you configure Group Policy to enforce the corporate password policy setting while allowing all other elements of password management to be controlled locally? (Select all correct answers.)

    A. Modify the default domain policy at the `conciliar.com` domain with the password settings.

    B. Create a GPO called Password Policy Settings in each domain with the password policy settings.

APPLY YOUR KNOWLEDGE

C. Create a GPO at the `conciliar.com` domain called Password Policy Settings with the password policy settings.

D. Link the Password Policy Settings GPO from the `conciliar.com` domain to each subdomain.

E. Configure Block Policy Inheritance for the Password Policy Settings GPO.

F. Move all users in the subdomains to the Users container of the `conciliar.com` domain.

G. Configure No Override for the Password Policy Settings GPO.

H. Configure No Override for the Default Domain Policy GPO at the `conciliar.com domain`.

16. You decide to implement an audit policy to satisfy the following requirements:

    - All user attempts to log on to the network must be audited.
    - Users failing to log on locally to the `FINDATA` file server should be tracked.
    - Actions by administrators to add, delete, and modify users in the default Users container should be tracked.
    - Any access to the Information Services OU in Active Directory should be tracked.
    - Any attempts by any member of the SalesPersons security group to access the `Commissions` folder on the `SALESDATA` file server should be tracked.

    To satisfy these requirements, you decide to perform the following tasks:

    - Create a GPO Default Domain Audit Policy at the domain level.
    - Assign the Apply Group Policy permission to Authenticated Users and leave all other permissions at their default settings for the Default Domain Audit Policy.
    - Configure the Default Domain Audit Policy to audit the success and failure of account logon events.
    - Configure the Default Domain Audit Policy to audit the success and failure of account management events.
    - Configure the Default Domain Audit Policy to audit the success of object access.
    - Configure the Default Domain Audit Policy to audit the success and failure of directory service access.

    Which of the outlined requirements are satisfied by your solution? (Select all correct answers.)

    A. All user attempts to log on to the network must be audited.

    B. Users failing to log on locally to the `FINDATA` file server should be tracked.

    C. Actions by administrators to add, delete, and modify users in the default Users container should be tracked.

    D. Any access to the Information Services OU in Active Directory should be tracked.

    E. Any attempts by any member of the SalesPersons security group to access the `Commissions` folder on the `SALESDATA` file server should be tracked.

APPLY YOUR KNOWLEDGE

Answers to Review Questions

1. If the printer is on a Windows 2000 Server computer, all you need to do is share the printer and check the List in Directory box. This is checked by default.

2. The Advanced tab enables you to specify, in detail, what you are looking for by giving you a list of the objects for which you can search and the attributes that are available to search.

3. Enforcing complexity rules ensures that passwords must conform to three of the following four criteria: lowercase characters, uppercase characters, numbers, and symbolic characters. In addition, these passwords must be at least six characters long and can't contain any parts of the user's name.

4. To audit access to file resources, three things must be done. First, the partition on which the files are located must be (or must be converted to) NTFS. Second, local (or domain) policy must be set to enable auditing of object access. Third, each file resource must have its audit settings configured for the type of access to be audited.

5. When both share-level and local permissions are applied to a folder, the effective permissions when accessing over the network are the more restrictive of the two sets of permissions. When accessing locally, the NTFS permissions are all that apply.

6. To enable Web sharing of a folder, you must have a way to publish it to the Web. This requires that IIS be installed on the machine you want to Web share on, and directory browsing must be enabled in the IIS configuration. See Chapter 3, "Internet Information Services," for more information on IIS configuration and management.

7. A site is best defined as one or more IP subnets interconnected using a high-speed (above T1) network.

8. A tree is a structure that starts at a root domain containing only direct descendants. All the domains share a common namespace. A forest enables you to create the same type of structure; however, more than one namespace exists.

9. Whereas the domain controllers for a domain are responsible for the replication of objects that belong to the domain, the global catalog servers replicate the information about the enterprise including a list of all objects, the schema, and configuration information.

10. To determine whether co-op students are attempting to gain access to the `CORPSECURE` server, create an audit policy configured to audit privilege use for the Everyone group (because it could be some other users) and failure to use the privilege in question (Access This Computer from the Network).

11. Enable object access auditing on the Windows 2000 computer where the printer is defined. Assign appropriate permissions to the shared printer to ensure that only members of the graphic arts department have access. Configure auditing on the printer for Failure to Print and Read the Printer for the Everyone group and Success and Failure for members of the graphic arts department. The former enables you to track unauthorized attempts to access the printer; the latter tracks printer usage in the graphic arts department.

APPLY YOUR KNOWLEDGE

Answers to Exam Questions

1. **D.** To produce the result required, Mark must implement minimum age, maximum age, and history. Maximum age ensures that passwords are changed at regular intervals. Minimum age ensures that passwords are not changed and then immediately changed back. Finally, history ensures that passwords are not used more than once every 12 cycles (in this case, no more than once a year). For more information, see the "Configuring User Accounts for Enhanced Security" section in this chapter.

2. **B, D.** Complex passwords must be at least six characters long and be a combination of three of the following: uppercase characters, lowercase characters, numbers, and symbols. Kumquat does not contain enough variety of characters, and Pt109 does not contain enough characters. For more information, see the "Configuring User Accounts for Enhanced Security" section in this chapter.

3. **A, B, C.** To enable auditing, the file resources must be on NTFS partitions, and auditing on objects must be enabled. Finally, at least Read access must be audited for each file resource. Because we want to configure auditing for the HouseKeeping group, neither answer D nor answer E applies. For more information, see the "Configuring, Implementing, and Using Auditing" section in this chapter.

4. **D.** Auditing creates entries in the security log. To keep an ongoing record of audit results, this log must be archived regularly. For more information, see the "Configuring, Implementing, and Using Auditing" section in this chapter.

5. **D.** You can install more than one printer that is configured to print to the same print device. These printers can then be configured with different print priorities and groups, and the users who need to be able to access each printer can be created and assigned Print permissions to only their printers. Documents sent to the printer with the highest printing priority always take precedence over waiting jobs that come from the lower-priority printer. For more information, see the "Setting Print Priority and Printer Availability" section in this chapter.

6. **D.** Local access is determined by combining Susan's NTFS permission and share permissions. Because she is a member of the Managers group, she gets Modify access (the greater of Read and Execute and Modify). Her network permission is Full Control, but her effective permission over the network is the lesser of her share permissions and NTFS permissions. Because she has only Modify permission locally, she can't have any more than Change permission when accessing the folder over the network. For more information, see the "NTFS Versus Share Permissions" section in this chapter.

7. **A.** Bill's local access is Full Control, but his network access is No Access. Therefore, when accessing the folder locally, he has Full Control, but his effective permission when he accesses over the network is No Access (the more restrictive of his share and NTFS permissions). For more information, see the "NTFS Versus Share Permissions" section in this chapter.

8. **D.** Because the printer is attached to a Windows 95 computer, it must be manually added (published) in Active Directory before it can be used by other domain users. Sharing the printer from

APPLY YOUR KNOWLEDGE

the Windows 95 computer will not result in it being published in Active Directory; neither will updating the printer device drivers. Therefore, answers A and B are wrong. Printer shares have nothing to do with file shares, so answer C is wrong. For more information, see the "Publishing Resources in Active Directory" section in this chapter.

9. **C.** In this case, you can rule out NTFS permissions because the user is able to perform the operation locally. Therefore, answer A is incorrect. The Everyone group doesn't have permissions, which is good because this is executive information, so answer B is wrong. File objects are not part of Active Directory; therefore, answer D is wrong. This leaves share permissions, which is correct. Remember that share and NTFS permissions are combined, and the lower permission is used. Because Danielle has the NTFS permissions, she can do it locally. We can therefore assume the share permissions are wrong. For more information, see the "NTFS Versus Share Permissions" section in this chapter.

10. **C.** Although a new group could be used, this would not make the HR documents easy to find because the user would need to check the news server and look at the newsgroups. The mailing list could also work but would greatly increase the load on the mail server and the network. Locating the directory in a new Dfs root would make it easier to get to but not easier to find. This leaves C as the correct answer, which makes sense because the capability to publish a share is included to make it easier to find. For more information, see the "Publishing Resources in Active Directory" section in this chapter.

11. **A.** There are three utilities Sally can use: the `NET` command, Explorer, and Computer Management snap-in. Of these, the only one listed is Explorer. Sites and Services is used to control sites in Active Directory and some services; Users and Computers is used to manage Active Directory objects and can be used to open the Computer Management snap-in for a computer. The Server Manager could do this in NT 4; however, this is Windows 2000. For more information, see the "Configuring and Managing File Shares" section in this chapter.

12. **B, C.** To determine who is trying to gain unauthorized access to the `SOURCECODE` share on the server called `ENGINEERING`, you need to enable auditing of object access on the computer (`ENGINEERING`) and then enable auditing of files and folders on the `SOURCECODE` share. Logon activity auditing will tell you who is trying to log on to the computer but not for what purpose. It might help but is not the ideal solution. You can't audit file and folder access on the machine or object access on the share. Auditing directory access will have no effect here. For more information, see the "Configuring, Implementing, and Using Auditing" section in this chapter.

13. **A, D.** When enabling auditing of object access and directory services access, no events appear in the Windows 2000 security event log. This is because you need to further specify which objects (such as files, folders, and printers) or Active Directory elements (OUs, users, groups, and so on) you want audited and by whom. This is accomplished using Windows Explorer in the case of files, folders, and printers; Control Panel in the case of printers; and Active Directory Users and Computer or Active Directory Sites and

APPLY YOUR KNOWLEDGE

Services in the case of Active Directory. For more information, see the "Configuring, Implementing, and Using Auditing" section in this chapter.

14. **A.** To track the amount of time users spend logged on to the network, you must enable audit the success of account logon events. Account logon events deal with a user logging on to a workstation and requesting a logon to the domain. This is different from a logon event in which the user is requesting access to a resource on a member server or is logging on locally to a computer. The requirement was to track users' time on the network, which requires a domain-level logon. Auditing success of account logon events would place an entry in the security event log on a domain controller when a user logs on to the network and another when she logs off. This would enable you to track the time spent online. For more information, see the "Configuring, Implementing, and Using Auditing" section in this chapter.

15. **C, D, G.** This question is a bit tricky because it tests your knowledge of Group Policy more than anything else. The issue here is how to you enforce a corporate policy in a structure in which subdomains exist. As you learned in Chapter 6, "Host Name Resolution/DNS," domains are an administrative barrier, and GPOs do not cross domain boundaries unless configured at the site level. Sites are not mentioned here, so it won't help much. Therefore, the best way to satisfy the requirements is to create the Password Policy Settings GPO at the `concilar.com` domain level with the appropriate settings. You would then link it to each subdomain so it is available there. Finally, you would configure No Override to ensure that these minimum settings are applied throughout the company. For more information, see the "Using Group Policy Objects to Apply Security Settings" section in this chapter.

16. **A, C.** The only requirements satisfied by your solution would be the tracking of all logon attempts on the network and administrator modification of user accounts in the default Users container. In fact, the policy you implemented would track any account management activity by any user because the GPO was applied to the Authenticated Users group, which includes all users. Even though the configuration you decided on will have other things occur, the two requirements that will definitely be satisfied are answers A and C. Note that Microsoft might also provide you with answers on an exam that do more than is required, but as long as they accomplish the stated goal, they can be the correct answer. For more information, see the "Configuring, Implementing, and Using Auditing" section in this chapter.

APPLY YOUR KNOWLEDGE

Suggested Readings and Resources

1. "Default Access Control Settings" on Microsoft's Web site at `http://www.microsoft.com/windows2000/library/planning/security/secdefs.asp`.
2. *Microsoft Windows 2000 Professional Resource Kit.* Microsoft Press, 2000:
   - Chapter 7: "Introduction to Configuration and Management"
   - Chapter 13: "Security"
3. *Microsoft Windows 2000 Server Resource Kit: Microsoft Windows 2000 Server Deployment Planning Guide.* Microsoft Press, 2000:
   - Chapter 11: "Planning Distributed Security"
4. *Microsoft Windows 2000 Server Resource Kit: Microsoft Windows 2000 Server Distributed Systems Guide.* Microsoft Press, 2000:
   - Chapter 22: "Group Policy"
5. "Securing Windows 2000 Network Resources" on Microsoft's Web site at `http://www.microsoft.com/windows2000/techinfo/planning/incremental/securenetworkresources.asp`.
6. "Step-by-Step Guide to Configuring Enterprise Security Policies" on Microsoft's Web site at `http://www.microsoft.com/windows2000/techinfo/planning/security/entsecsteps.asp`.
7. *Windows 2000 Server Administrators Companion,* Microsoft Press, 2000:
   - Chapter 12, "Managing Active Directory"
   - Chapter 13, "Understanding Network Addresses"

OBJECTIVES

This chapter addresses the information you're expected to know about Internet Information Services, formerly Internet Information Server. The information you need to know about Internet Information Services (IIS) is considered a part of the "Creating, Configuring, Managing, Securing, and Troubleshooting File, Print, and Web Resources" objective. The subobjective that this chapter addresses is "Configure and Troubleshoot Internet Information Services (IIS)." Specifically, we'll cover the following sub-objectives:

Configure virtual directories and virtual servers.

- IIS can serve multiple Web sites from a single server. Successfully administering a server includes the need to understand how to create and administer virtual servers.

- Normally IIS serves a directory tree via Web or FTP protocols. However, sometimes it's desirable to serve non-contiguous directories. In other words, directories that are in different locations or directories.

Troubleshoot Internet browsing from client computers.

- One of the important functions in today's network is Internet browsing. It's important that you understand how to troubleshoot problems and identify whether they are caused by configuration or server problems.

Configure authentication and SSL for Web sites.

- Secure Socket Layer (SSL) is required to encrypt Web traffic. Encrypting Web traffic over the Internet is an important component of a security policy and necessary to ensure that private information remains private.

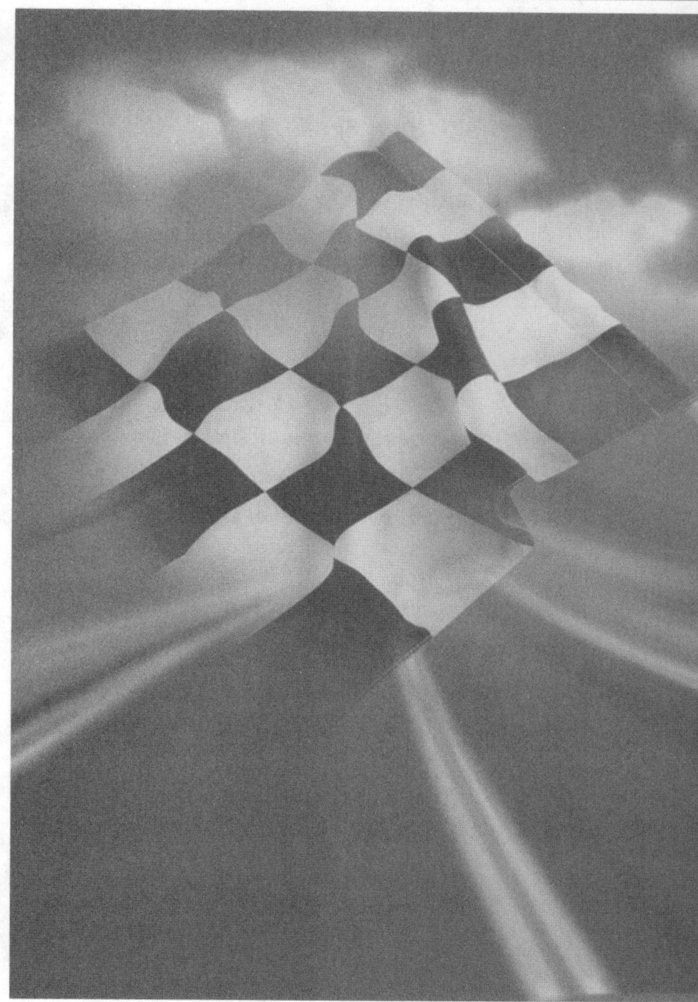

CHAPTER 3

Internet Information Services

OBJECTIVES

Configure FTP services.

- Although most of the traffic that happens on the Internet today is HTTP (Web) traffic, the File Transfer Protocol (FTP) is the real workhorse of moving files. It is still important when the goal is to transfer larger files or when you want to provide a low maintenance way for clients to gain access to files.

Configure access permissions for intranet Web servers.

- In development environments and in many intranet configurations multiple Web servers are configured within one physical server. Because of this, it is important to know how to configure permissions on individual Web sites within IIS.

OUTLINE

Outline

Study Strategies

- The best way to understand IIS is to create a new Web site or use an existing site and play with IIS. Thus, you should consider doing this when studying this chapter. This is particularly useful if the machine you use for testing purposes isn't a production Web server. Using a nonproduction server enables you to play with settings without worrying about disrupting future use of the server as a Web server.
- Another strategy you should employ is to think from the perspective of how IIS would display something. Servers, virtual directories, and documents are displayed with a set of rules. After you learn those rules, determining how to configure IIS or identifying a misconfiguration is simply a process of determining which configuration rule was neglected or must be applied.

INTRODUCTION TO INTERNET INFORMATION SERVICES

Although most people are aware that Internet Information Services (IIS) enables you to service Web pages from a Windows 2000 server, they don't realize that IIS can be used to serve files and folders via the Web. With the ability to create virtual FTP servers and Web servers with directory browsing, you can extend the reach of your server by providing file support to a broader audience—larger than machines capable of Windows file and printer sharing.

Web Services

Windows 2000 introduced a simple way of sharing folders via the Web in addition to the traditional Microsoft networking that had been available in previous revisions of the operating system. The process of setting up and configuring is not difficult at all.

Setting Up IIS for Web Sharing

Web sharing requires two things. First, you must be running IIS. Second, you must have Administrator or Power User access to your server. The default installation of Windows 2000 Server includes IIS, so it probably is installed on your server. If it is not, you must install it. Step By Step 3.1 outlines the installation process for IIS.

STEP BY STEP

3.1 Installing IIS on a Windows 2000 Server

1. From the Start menu, select Settings, Control Panel. Double-click the Add/Remove Programs icon.
2. In the Add/Remove Programs dialog box, click Add/Remove Windows Components.
3. In the Windows Components Wizard dialog box, select Internet Information Services (IIS) and then click the Details button (see Figure 3.1).

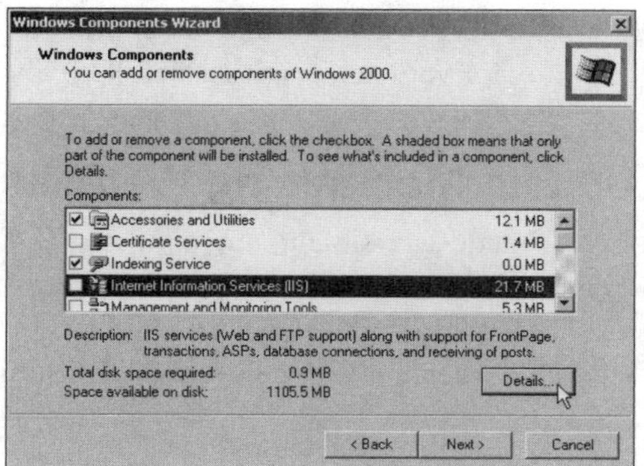

FIGURE 3.1
IIS is installed through the Windows Components Wizard.

4. From the Internet Information Services (IIS) dialog box, select the following components: Common Files, File Transfer Protocol (FTP) Server, Internet Information Services Snap-In, and World Wide Web Server (see Figure 3.2). Optionally, you also can select Documentation and Internet Services Manager (HTML). The Internet Services Manager (HTML) allows you to administrate most aspects of your IIS server from a browser. When you finish, click OK. Then, click Next in the Windows Components dialog box.

5. At this point, configuration begins. When you're asked for the CD-ROM, insert it into the drive to complete the installation. When installation is complete, exit the components wizard and the Add/Remove Programs dialog box.

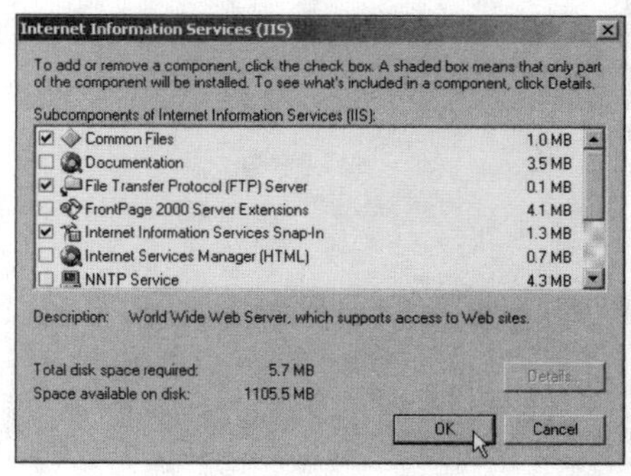

FIGURE 3.2
The IIS components are small; you might want to install them all. Note the options you can choose.

This installation process modifies your server in two ways. First, it creates a folder called Inetpub on your hard drive (on the Boot partition). Second, it creates two local user accounts, one called `IUSR_`*`servername`* (for granting anonymous access to browser clients) and another called `IWAM_`*`servername`* (the account IIS uses internally to start out-of-process applications). The anonymous user account (`IUSR_`*`servername`*) is especially useful because, when you need to control anonymous access to published resources, you will need to refer to this account. Any user who connects to your Web server who is not authenticated will use the user account `IUSR_`*`servername`* and will have whatever access has been given to that account. This account is a member of the local group Guests.

After IIS has been installed, an additional tab appears in the Properties dialog box for your folders; it's called Web Sharing.

Setting Up and Maintaining Web Sharing

Web folders can be made accessible to any or all of the Web sites you have configured on your server; you are not restricted to only the default site. These folders appear as virtual folders on your Web site and are accessible when a user types in addresses similar in format to the following:

```
http://servername/webfolderalias
```

Of course, you (or your Web developers) will be able to create HTML links to the folders as well.

Step By Step 3.2 describes the mechanics of sharing a folder via IIS. You must be a member of the Power Users or Administrators group to be able to complete Step By Step 3.2.

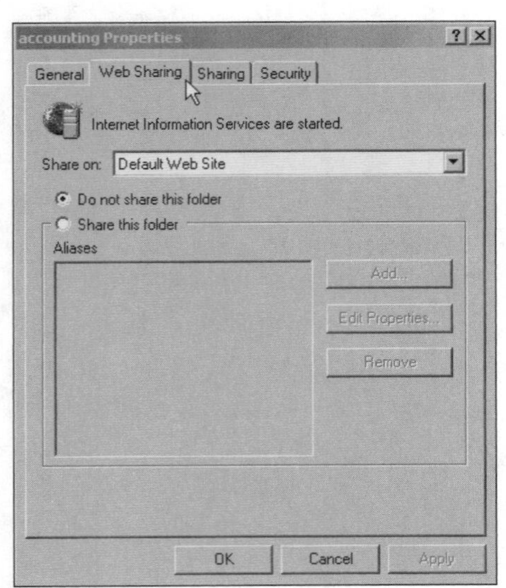

FIGURE 3.3
Web Sharing is separated from other types of network folder sharing.

STEP BY STEP

3.2 Sharing a Folder via Web Services (IIS)

1. Right-click the folder you want to share and select Sharing from the menu that appears.
2. In the Folder Properties dialog box, select the Web Sharing tab (see Figure 3.3).
3. In the Share On field, select the site on which you want to share this folder. All the virtual sites you have configured on your Web server will appear in the pull-down list. (You'll learn about virtual servers later in the chapter.)
4. Select the radio button labeled Share This Folder.
5. When the Edit Alias dialog box appears, fill in an alias name—the name by which a Web user will be able to reference this Web share (see Figure 3.4). It does not have to be the same as the folder's real name. Then, select one or more access permissions from the four security levels. Read means users will be able to look at content, whereas Write means users will be able to upload into the folder.

Script Source Access means users will be able to view the source of script files in the folder, and Directory Browsing means users will be able to browse the folder's contents and its subfolders. Generally, only Read access is given to publicly accessed folders.

6. Select an application permission. None means no scripts or applications present in the folder can be run by a browser client; Scripts means script files can be executed. Execute means all programs in the folder can be run by browser clients. If you select the Write Access and Scripts application permissions, a dialog box appears, indicating that you are allowing users to upload scripts they can then run (a potentially dangerous situation). You will be asked to confirm that you really intended to allow that. When you finish configuring these settings, click OK.

7. If the folder you are sharing resides on a FAT partition, you are done; you can click OK to complete Web sharing. If the folder is on an NTFS partition, however, you need to set NTFS permissions. Click the Security tab at the top of the Properties dialog box.

8. From the Security tab, add local permissions for all the users you want to allow to access this folder over the Web by clicking the Add button and adding them from the directory of your choice (see Figure 3.5). You can add users and groups as you normally would. However, to allow anonymous users to access the data, you must either explicitly add the IIS anonymous users or implicitly add these users by adding the local group Guests. You must set as much NTFS permissions for any user as you have given out access in step 4. If you gave out Read and Write access, you must also give out Read and Write NTFS permission; otherwise, the lesser of the access levels will prevail for your Web users. Click OK when you are done.

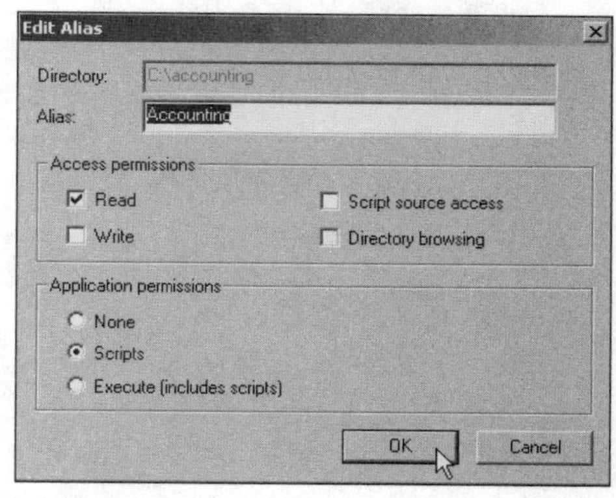

FIGURE 3.4
The alias is the name a Web user will use to access the data.

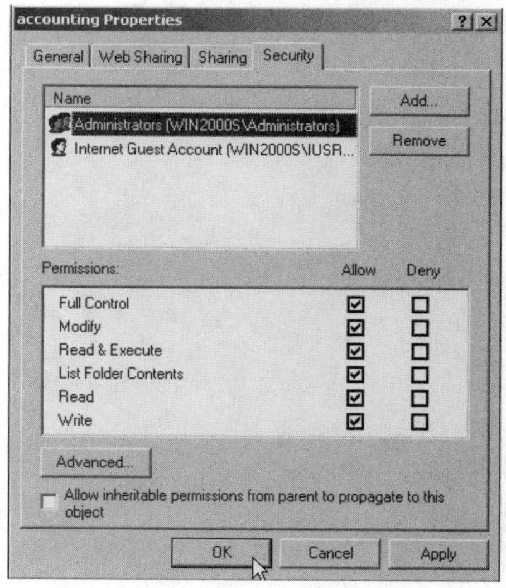

FIGURE 3.5
NTFS permissions are typically used to restrict access to a Web-shared folder.

To modify Web sharing or to stop Web sharing, you can return to the properties for the folder and add a new alias, remove an existing alias, or stop sharing altogether. If you stop sharing, all the aliases for the folder will be removed, and you will have to re-create them if you change your mind.

Web Sharing and Security

Web sharing does not happen in a vacuum. You have to realize that the shared permissions you assign are going to interact with both the local NTFS security you have applied to the shared data as well as the security you have set up for the Web site the folder is shared under.

Similar to shared folder permissions, Web sharing interacts with local security. If Web sharing is configured for a folder on an NTFS partition, the more restrictive of the two permissions will be effective for a Web browser client connecting to the folder. For example, if the anonymous Web user account (`IUSR_servername`) hasbeen given Read access through NTFS permissions and the folder has been given Web Sharing permissions of Read and Write, a Web browser client connecting to the share will get only Read access (the logical `and` of the two permissions). If the Guests group is given Full Control through NTFS permissions (thus giving the anonymous Web account Full Control) but you have established only Read access to the Web share, all clients will get only Read access to the data.

In addition to NTFS security, you also need to know what the security is on the whole Web site under which you are sharing. Any browser client trying to get to a Web share must pass through the Web site security before it gets to that share. If the site is secured so that only Read access is allowed—even if Write access is given to the Web share—that access will not be effective for the browser client trying to access the data.

Troubleshooting Web Sharing

A number of things can go wrong with Web sharing. The first major problem is a lack of an IIS server. Without a local IIS server, you will not be able to find the Web Sharing tab on the Properties dialog box for your folder. To solve this, install IIS on your Windows 2000 Server.

After an IIS server has been configured, the next problem might be your permissions to share a folder. You must have Power User or Administrator access to be able to Web share a folder. If your user account is not a member of one of those two groups, you need to gain membership or have someone with the proper rights create the

Web shares for you. This shouldn't be a problem because you won't generally be able to log on to the server locally without this level of permissions.

If the folders have been shared, the next problems might be those of access. The major problems are going to be with server access (is the server up, and is the Web service running?) and permissions.

Lack of server access can result from several things. The server itself might not be running. If it is, the Web service might not be running, the Web site in which the folder is being shared might not be enabled, or the TCP port it is running on might not be the default (port 80). Any or all of these things can prevent users from accessing the Web folder you have configured.

Problems related to the server being down (that is, the operating system is not running) are beyond the scope of this particular discussion. The bottom line is that the server must be running to provide access to your Web folders.

If the Web service itself is not running, you can start it by following Step By Step 3.3.

STEP BY STEP

3.3 Starting the World Wide Web Publishing Service

1. From the Start menu, select Programs, Administrative Tools, Services.
2. Scroll down the Services list until you find World Wide Web Publishing Services. Right-click it and select Start from the menu that appears.
3. Close the Services console.

If the Web service is running, the problem might be that the Web site is not running. To start it, you need to open the IIS Services Manager Console. Step By Step 3.4 leads you through the process of starting a Web site.

STEP BY STEP

3.4 Starting a Web Site

1. From the Start menu, select Programs, Administrative Tools, Internet Services Manager.
2. In the IIS Console window, you can locate your Web sites by expanding the Console Root, Internet Information Services, and your server. When you see your Web site in the tree under the name of your server, right-click it and select Start from the menu presented.
3. Close the IIS Console.

Finally, even if the Web site is up, if the administrator of the site has configured access on a TCP port other than the default (80), Web users will not be able to get to the Web site without specifying the new port in the URL. For the purposes of this discussion, a TCP port can be thought of like a TV channel. You might have your TV on, but if it is not tuned to the right station, you will not be able to get to the program you want. All browsers are configured to access Web sites on port 80. If the Web server is not "listening" on port 80, either the server needs to be changed or the browser has to be told which port to connect on. If the port is not 80 and you want Web users to connect, you can give them the port number. Then, they will be able to connect using the following syntax:

`http://`*`servername`*`:`*`portnumber`*`/`*`foldername`*

For example, to connect to the folder Accounting on a server called Win2000S using the port 8080, you would use the following syntax:

```
http://Win2000S:8080/Accounting
```

To find out what the port is or to change it, follow Step By Step 3.5.

STEP BY STEP

3.5 Discovering and Changing a Web Server's TCP Port

1. From the Start menu, select Programs, Administrative Tools, Internet Services Manager.

2. In the IIS Console window, you can locate your Web site by expanding the Console Root, Internet Information Services, and your server. When you see your Web site in the tree under the name of your server, right-click it and select Properties.

3. In the Web Site Properties dialog box, the Web Site tab contains a field called TCP Port (see Figure 3.6). That number is your TCP port number. If you change that, all browsers (and HTML links coded into pages) will have to explicitly use that TCP port number. Therefore, it is not a good idea to change it without first consulting your Webmaster to discuss the implications.

4. Click OK to update the Web site's properties.

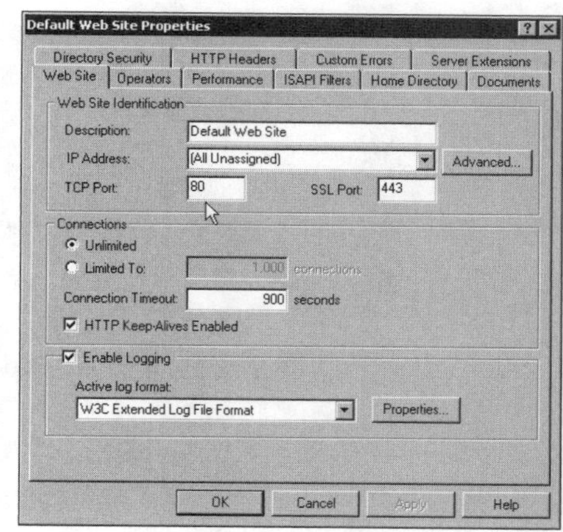

FIGURE 3.6
The TCP port number can be used to effectively hide a Web site from those who do not know the number.

When a user is able to connect to your Web site, the issue of permissions might still come up. Remember from the discussion in the last section that all the levels of permissions interact to form an effective permission. As a result, you must check permission levels at the NTFS level, the Web folder level, and the Web site level. Thus far, the only one of these three that has not been discussed is the Web site level.

File Transfer Protocol Services

In addition to Web services, IIS also enables you to serve files via the File Transfer Protocol (FTP). FTP predates the HTTP protocol the Web uses and is an efficient way to send files between two systems. In fact, FTP was designed specifically for file transfer. It's still frequently used to distribute software and updates. Although the HTTP (Web) protocol is now being used more than FTP, FTP is still the real workhorse for transferring files.

From a practical perspective, there are only a few things you need to know about FTP servers in comparison to Web servers:

- FTP servers originally were accessed via command-line utilities, like the FTP utility included in Windows NT/2000. Although all modern Web browsers support FTP, you can continue to use dedicated FTP utilities.

- FTP has far fewer configuration options than a Web server because the server provides a much simpler, more focused utility.
- FTP servers can't use any encryption. Because of this, they are sometimes configured for anonymous access only.
- FTP servers generally use TCP port 21—not TCP port 80 like Web servers do. This means a different set of rules on the firewall to allow FTP traffic.

FTP servers are definitely not as glamorous as Web servers, but they get the job done.

Virtual Servers

Although some Web sites, such as `www.microsoft.com`, can't be adequately serviced by one server, most Web sites are not accessed so frequently that one server can't address all their needs. In most cases Web sites get so little traffic that devoting an entire server to the Web site is a mistake. For most organizations that maintain multiple Web sites, using virtual servers is a way to maintain cost control.

Virtual servers work by having IIS determine which Web or FTP server is being referenced when the request comes in. This determination can be made by IP address (if the server has multiple IP addresses assigned to it), via TCP port, or in the case of Web servers by the hostname passed with the request.

The host header option that can be used with Web servers is unique because it enables you to use a single IP address and change the information returned by the name of the server the user specified in his Web browser. This is useful because prior to the introduction of the host header option, every Web site had to be on a separate IP address. The capability to use host headers has helped reduce the amount of IP addresses that must be allocated.

The way the HTTP (Web) protocol works is that the client sends a small packet of information to the Web server, which includes the capabilities of the browser and also the page the user requested that caused the request to be sent to the Web server.

The option to look at host headers to determine which Web site a user was referring to is a powerful thing. It enables multiple virtual Web servers to share the same IP address and TCP port; however, this comes at the cost of performance. Reading the HTTP header information the browser passes takes much more time than looking at the IP address or port. As a result, host headers should be used only when the traffic is very light and the additional overhead of looking into the host header won't over burden the server.

The best way to use virtual servers is to assign each one an IP address. This enables a single server to service multiple Web sites without concern for the user having to make any changes on his end and without the possibility that one site will return the information for another, as sometimes happens when using host headers.

Assigning Multiple IP Addresses

If you want to use separate IP addresses for each virtual site, the first step is to assign multiple IP addresses to the server. Step By Step 3.6 shows how to add additional IP addresses to a server.

STEP BY STEP

3.6 Specifying Additional IP Addresses

1. From the Start menu, select Settings, Network and Dial Up Connections.
2. Double-click the Local Area Network connection.
3. Select Properties from the Local Area Network Status dialog box.
4. Double-click Internet Protocol (TCP/IP).
5. Click the Advanced button. The Advanced TCP/IP Settings dialog box, as shown in Figure 3.7, is displayed.
6. Click the Add button.
7. Enter an appropriate IP address and associated subnet mask.

continues

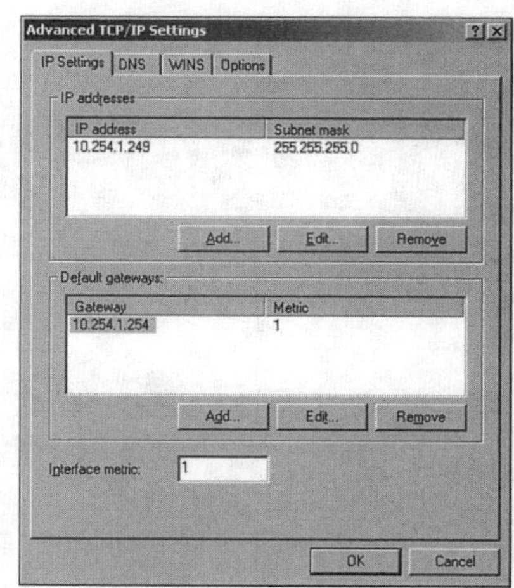

FIGURE 3.7
Additional IP addresses are added from the Advanced TCP/IP Settings dialog box.

continued

8. Click the Add button when completed.
9. Click the OK button to close the Advanced TCP/IP Settings dialog box.
10. Click the OK button to close the Internet Protocol (TCP/IP) Properties dialog box.
11. Click the OK button to close the Local Area Connection Properties dialog box.

> NOTE
>
> **Don't Use DHCP** You can't assign multiple IP addresses to a computer via DHCP—and it's a bad idea to use DHCP for a Web server anyway. You should allocate specific addresses for servers and manually assign an appropriate number to the server.

Now that you have multiple IP addresses assigned to your server, you can create Web sites that respond to different IP addresses.

Creating Virtual Web Servers

The process of creating a virtual Web server is as simple as following a few steps in a wizard. Step By Step 3.7 shows you how to create a new Web site.

STEP BY STEP

3.7 Adding a New Web Site

1. From the Start menu, select Settings, Control Panel.
2. Double-click Administrative tools and Internet Services Manager.
3. Click the plus sign to the left of the computer name to display a listing of Web and FTP sites, as shown in Figure 3.8.
4. Right-click the computer and select New, Web Site from the context menu.
5. Click the Next button to move past the introductory screen.
6. Enter a description for the Web site. For instance, if your Web site is to test Pocket Internet Explorer (pIE), you would enter **`pIE`** in the description.

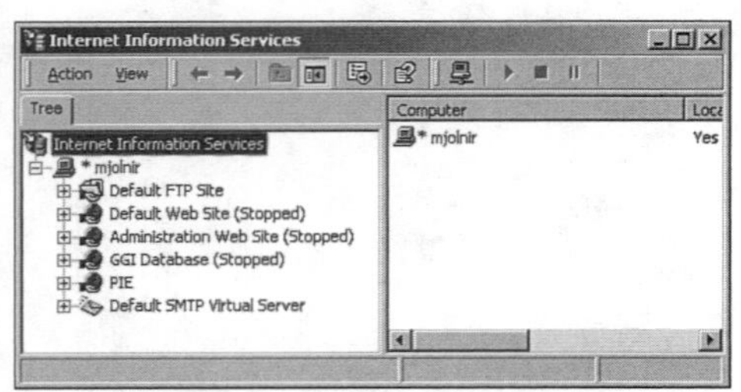

FIGURE 3.8
A listing of Web and FTP sites.

7. Click the Next button to move to the IP Address and Port Settings dialog box, as shown in Figure 3.9.

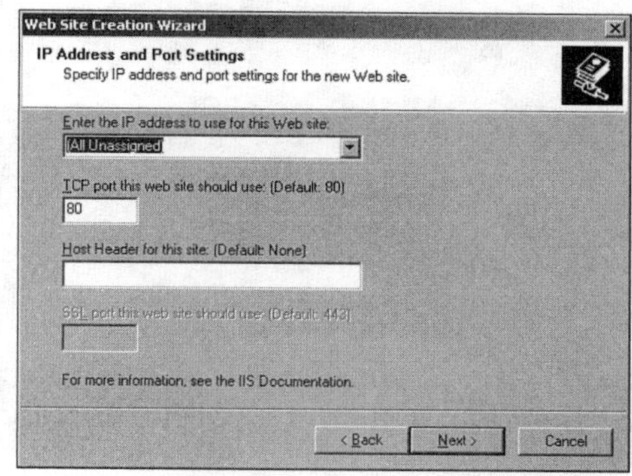

FIGURE 3.9
Select the IP address, ports, and header.

8. Select the IP Address you want the Web site to respond to. By selecting the (All Unassigned) option, the Web site will respond to Web queries on any IP addresses that are not serviced by another Web site.

9. Select the TCP port for the Web server. The default is port 80. If you choose a port other than port 80, the user must manually specify the port when referring to the Web site. Using an alternative port number is often done for administrative Web sites. Ports are discussed in detail in the next section.

10. Select the host header, if any. This setting should be used only if you're going to service multiple Web sites on the same IP address and port. In that case, the host header needs to contain the name the user will use to refer to the site, such as `www.thorprojects.com`.

11. If you have an SSL certificate installed, you will be able to specify the SSL port for the Web site. The default is 423. As with the TCP port for normal traffic, if this is changed, the users will have to manually specify the port.

12. Click the Next button to move to the home directory step.

13. Select the path that will be the home directory for the Web site. Remember that all files located in this directory and below will be available via the Web.

14. Confirm that you want to allow anonymous access to this Web site. For most Web sites, except intranet and potentially extranet sites, this setting is appropriate.

15. Click the Next button to select the permissions.

16. Confirm that you want to allow read access to the Web site. In most cases, you will. This enables the Web server to return "static" HTML files and other types of files that are not processed on the server.

continues

continued

17. Confirm that you want to allow run scripts access to the Web site. This enables the Web site to run script-based programs. In practical terms, this means Active Server Pages (ASP).
18. Confirm that you do not want to allow execute access to the Web site; in most cases you will not want to allow execute access. Execute access is necessary only for ISAPI DLLs or CGIBIN applications. It is best to turn on this option for specific directories in a Web site rather than for the whole site, as is done here.
19. Confirm that you do not want to allow write access to the Web site. This option enables users to upload Web pages, scripts, and programs to the Web site. This is not recommended and is dangerous when run script or execute permission is also specified because it enables a user to upload and run code on the Web server.
20. Confirm that you do not want to allow browse access to the Web site. This option enables users to see a directory listing of a directory when no default document (HTML file, ASP script, or executable application) is found in the directory. This is useful for some subdirectories containing only files that you want the user to be able to read; however, it generally should not be set for an entire Web site.
21. Click the Next button and then the Finish button to complete the wizard.
22. Close the Internet Information Services window.

NOTE

Use Unique Settings If you specified settings for the Web site that put it in conflict with an already running Web site then the new Web site will be created but will initially be stopped. You must change the settings of the conflicting Web site or the one you just created to be able to start it. IIS creates default Web and FTP servers that you might need to stop to install your own virtual server.

The greatest challenge with creating new, virtual Web sites is ensuring that you specify unique criteria so IIS can determine which Web site is being referred to. If you do this through IP addresses, things are relatively straightforward. However, when done with host headers, it can sometimes be confusing as to which Web site will appear and which site will appear when no host header is specified. Older Web browsers might not provide a host header.

Creating Virtual FTP Servers

The process of creating virtual FTP servers is simpler than the process of creating virtual Web servers because FTP clients don't send host headers. Also, because of this, you have only two options you can choose to differentiate FTP servers: IP Address and Port. Step By Step 3.8 shows you how to create a new virtual FTP server.

STEP BY STEP

3.8 Adding a New FTP Site

1. From the Start menu select Settings, Control Panel.
2. Double-click Administrative Tools and Internet Services Manager.
3. Click the plus sign to the left of the computer name to display a listing of Web and FTP sites (refer to Figure 3.8).
4. Right-click the computer and select New, FTP Site from the context menu.
5. Click the Next button to move past the introductory screen.
6. Enter a description for the FTP site—for instance, `Thor Projects FTP Site`.
7. Click the Next button to continue.
8. Select the IP address. As with Web sites, this should be how you differentiate one site from another. Selecting (All Unassigned) causes the site to respond to any IP address not assigned to another running FTP site using the same TCP port.
9. Enter the TCP port. This is the port on which requests will be received. The default is port 21. Note that FTP servers use a separate port for data transfers. This port can't be assigned because the client wouldn't understand receiving the data on a different port.

continues

continued

10. Click the Next button to continue.
11. Enter the path for the FTP site. As with Web sites, all files in the specified directory or any directory beneath it will be available from the FTP site.
12. Confirm read access. This is generally the access you want for an FTP site. You want to allow users to read (download) files from the server.
13. Confirm no write access. Generally, you don't want to allow users to upload to the FTP site.
14. Click the Next button, and then click Finish to complete the wizard.
15. Close the Internet Information Services window.

Creating a virtual FTP site is easier than creating a virtual Web site.

Virtual Directories

In general, the idea of an FTP or Web site is a hierarchy of pages leading down to deeper directories. Most of the time those directories are all located underneath the same directory tree, but with IIS, that doesn't necessarily need to be the case.

If you have a particularly large FTP site, you could keep some files—such as the latest service packs for your programs—on one hard drive and the latest trial versions on another, different, hard drive. This would allow you to have a single FTP site that spans multiple hard drives.

Additional reasons exist for why you might not want your hard drive space to mirror the representation on the Web. Step By Step 3.9 shows you how to create a virtual directory on a Web site. The process is almost identical for creating a virtual directory for an FTP site.

STEP BY STEP

3.9 Adding a New Virtual Directory to a Web Site

1. From the Start menu select Settings, Control Panel.
2. Double-click Administrative Tools and Internet Services Manager.
3. Clickthe plus sign to the left of the computer name to display a listing of Web and FTP sites (refer to Figure 3.8).
4. Click the Web site to add the virtual directory to.
5. Right-click the computer and select New, Virtual Directory from the context menu.
6. Click the Next button to move past the welcome step.
7. Enter the alias name for the virtual directory. This is the name that will be used to reference the virtual directory from the Web browser.
8. Click the Next button to display the directory step.
9. Select a path to which the virtual directory will refer.
10. Click the Next button to select the permissions the directory will have.
11. Select the permissions that are appropriate for the directory. (Refer to Step By Step 3.7, steps 16–20, for an explanation of what each option does.)
12. Click the Next button; then click the Finish button to close the New Virtual Directory Wizard.
13. Close the Internet Information Services window.

The process forcreating a virtual FTP directory is the same except for the permissions step, in which you are presented with the option for read and write permissions—just like when you create an FTP server.

WEB SITE SECURITY

Web sites are made available through the Web service component of Internet Information Services. Because these Web sites contain data, they need to be secured at one level or another (even if that security is to leave everything unsecured).

The following list outlines ways in which you can control access to your Web sites:

- Changing the TCP port
- Changing access permissions
- Changing execute permissions for scripts and programs
- Changing authentication methods (including enabling and disabling anonymous access)
- Adding IP address and domain name restrictions
- Adding server certificates for Secure Socket Layer (SSL) transmissions
- Authenticating users with client certificates

These topics are discussed in the following sections.

Controlling Web Site Access Through the TCP Port Number

Most common TCP/IP protocols have specific TCP ports associated with them, and the software that enables you to use these expects the ports to conform to the standard defaults. However, similar to a TV channel, these ports can be changed. If a certain set of data is being broadcast on a certain port, and that port is not the default port for that utility (such as port 80 for HTTP traffic), the port must be determined to access the data. This might sound trivial, but because more than 65,000 TCP ports are available to choose from, you can hide your site from most casual users by choosing any TCP port other than 80.

Of course, this is not very robust security because if someone knows which port you are running on, that person will be able to return to your site. In addition, if you have a port sniffer or security scanner, you could easily determine the port that a particular Web server is running on. However, it is a good way to hide information from people who do not know what they are looking for.

If you change the TCP port for your Web site (to 8080, for example), any browser client who wants to access your site will have to manually type in the TCP port number along with the address of your site. For example, if your site was `www.mydata.com` and you were using TCP port 8080, a browser client would access your site with the following URL:

```
http://www.mydata.com:8080
```

Step By Step 3.5 showed you how to determine and change a Web site's TCP port.

Controlling Web Site Access Through Access Permissions

One of the most common ways to secure a Web site is to change the global settings for what all users can do. By making a Web site read-only, for example, you ensure that no one will be able to accidentally or purposefully make changes to the content of your site.

As you can see in Figure 3.10, four access rights can be controlled for the entire site: Script Source Access, Read, Write, and Directory Browsing.

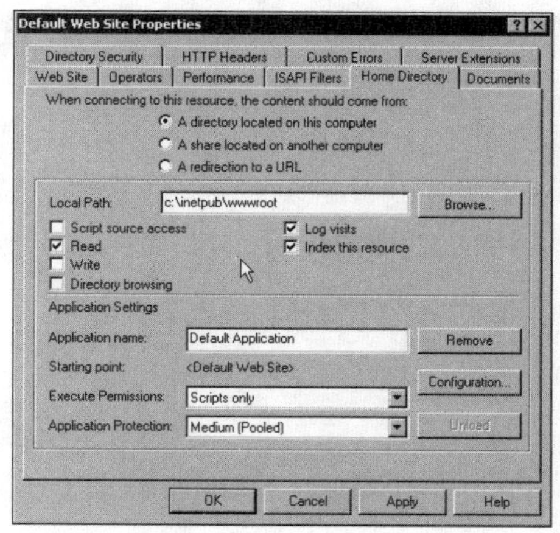

FIGURE 3.10
Web access rights can be used to restrict the file-level permissions of the files on a site.

Enabling script source access allows users to see the source code behind the Active Server Page they are currently viewing. This would enable users to access JavaScript and VBScript source code. That source code might contain sensitive information, such as the location of the database server or passwords that would be inappropriate for anyone other than the development team to have.

Read access allows users to look at the content of the Web page and download files. If read access is not enabled, no users will be able to access the content on the site.

Write access enables users to upload content to the site. This includes being able to modify the HTML or script content as well as placing new files into the site folder on your server.

WARNING

Don't Let Others Supply the Code You Run It's a bad idea to allow both execute access and write access to a directory. This enables a person to upload and execute potentially destructive programs.

Directory browsing allows users to see a file listing in your Web site's main folder. This would allow a user to know what the names of your files are and to navigate through your file path to subfolders in your Web site. If this is not enabled, users must connect through the HTML pages you have set up on your Web site. If no default HTML page has been configured, browser clients will not be able to navigate your Web site at all.

You will need to make choices about which of these rights you want to enable for your user community. Remember that these rights are global across all users of your Web site; they will not discriminate. If you want to allow some users to upload files and not others, you must give Web site rights to write and then control access using NTFS permissions on the local files or folders themselves.

You will notice in Figure 3.10 that a logging setting is also available. This setting, which is usually enabled, allows you to log all user interaction with this site. This log enables you to monitor who is connecting to your site and what she is doing. The logging options (including the location of the log file) can be configured on the Web Site tab of the Web site's Properties dialog box.

Step By Step 3.10 shows you how to adjust the site access permissions.

STEP BY STEP

3.10 Changing Site Access Permissions

1. From the Start menu, select Settings, Control Panel, Administrative Tools, Internet Services Manager.
2. In the IIS Console window, you can locate your Web site by expanding Console Root, Internet Information Services, and Your Server. When you see your Web site in the tree under the name of your server, right-click it and select Properties from the menu that appears.
3. In the Web Site Properties window, click the Home Directory tab. There you see check boxes under the Local Path field that you can use to set site access permissions. Select or deselect the appropriate rights.
4. Click OK to update the Web site's properties.

Controlling Web Site Access Through Execute Permissions

Another way to control site access is through execute permissions. Execute permissions (shown at the bottom of Figure 3.10) define what type of scripts or executables a browser client can invoke on your site. The execute permissions include None, Scripts Only, and Scripts and Executables.

If you select None, no scripts will run on this Web site. This is obviously problematic because it means that Active Server Page scripts will not run.

If you select Scripts Only, Active Server Page scripts will run on this Web site. However, executables—including ASAPI DLLs and CGIBIN applications—can't be invoked.

If you select Scripts and Executables, a user will be able to invoke any script or executable she can get at. Although this provides a lot of functionality to the user, it is the most dangerous option in terms of security.

Step By Step 3.11 demonstrates how to change a site's execute permissions.

STEP BY STEP

3.11 Changing Site Execute Permissions

1. From the Start menu, select Settings, Control Panel, Administrative Tools, Internet Services Manager.
2. In the IIS Console window, you can locate your Web site by expanding Console Root, Internet Information Services, and Your Server. When you see your Web site in the tree under the name of your server, right-click it and select Properties from the menu that appears.
3. In the Web Site Properties window, click the Home Directory tab. Click the Execute Permissions drop-down arrow to see the list of permissions (see Figure 3.11). Select the level of script execute privileges you want to give out for your site.
4. Click OK to update the Web site's properties.

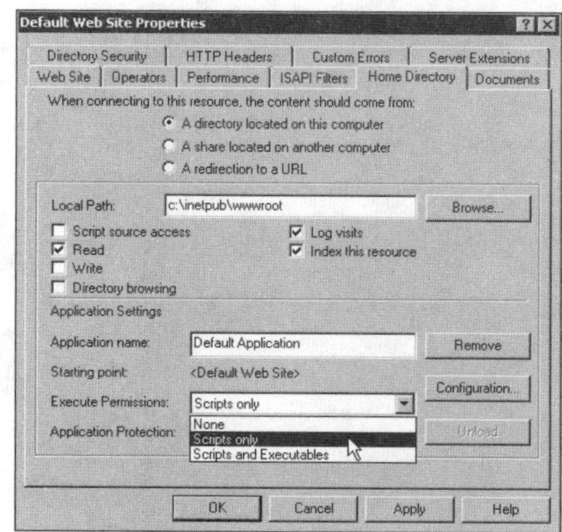

FIGURE 3.11
Execute permissions control the execution of programs and scripts on your Web server.

Controlling Web Site Access Through Authentication Methods

One of the strengths of using IIS as a Web server on a Windows 2000 Server is the capability to integrate Windows 2000 computer or domain security into Web access. Essentially, you have the ability to force users to provide names and passwords from the local machine accounts or from Active Directory to access Web sites. This eliminates the need to create your own security model.

Web authentication occurs at two levels: anonymous and authenticated. *Anonymous* access is the first method attempted when a user tries to connect to any Web site. If anonymous access is disabled, or if a Web user tries to access a function that can't be performed by an anonymous user, authenticated access is attempted. Anonymous access does not require a password. However, *authenticated* access always requires confirmation of identity, which can be in the form of a password challenge. But security information can be passed transparently (such as integrated Windows access or with client certificates, both of which are covered later).

Under IIS, anonymous access is mapped to a user account. Therefore, any attempt to access a Web site anonymously treats the user as though he were logged in as the anonymous IIS account. By default, the name of this account is `IUSR_`*`servername`*. That means that if your server were called `Green`, the anonymous user account would be called `IUSR_Green` unless you changed it to something else.

One way of securing your Web site is to disable anonymous access to the whole site. Then, for any attempted access, the browser client is prompted for a name and password to access the site. Another way to secure your site is to put NTFS security locally on some or all of your Web site. If you do this, for any attempted access of files or folders that do not allow anonymous access, a name and password is required (whether the user is prompted for it depends on the type of authentication you require and his other authentication information to the Web server).

If you do require that a user log on to your site (or some portion thereof), you can set the type of authenticated access you want to require. Three levels exist: basic authentication, digest authentication for Windows domain servers, and integrated Windows authentication.

Basic authentication is the least secure but most accessible across a variety of browsers. This type of authentication sends all login information in clear text. Unfortunately, if someone is watching your logon using a packet sniffer or other network analysis tool (Windows 2000 or NT Network Monitor, for example), she might be able to capture your username and password as you log on. Basic authentication is supported by all Web browsers, including non-Microsoft browsers. Although sending passwords in clear text is a security risk, this can be overcome by using server certificates and SSL (covered later).

When a user logs in using basic authentication, the user's combined name and password are checked against the directory IIS has been told to use (either local or an Active Directory for the domain). If the name and password pass authentication, local security is checked on the files the user is trying to access, and if the username has appropriate access in the ACL, access continues. If the name and password do not pass authentication, however, the user is prompted repeatedly until he cancels the login operation. If the username is not authorized to access the resource it is trying to access, it will pass authentication but be given an `Access denied` message.

> NOTE
>
> **Make the Message Meaningful** The exact message that is returned to the client can be controlled by setting custom errors for the Web site.

A second—and more secure—type of authentication is digest authentication. It is similar to basic authentication; however, it uses a hashing algorithm to encrypt data sent between the browser and server. This hashing algorithm is classed as one-way in that it can be used to encrypt but not decrypt the data. This type of authentication works only on browsers that support the HTTP 1.1 standard and can respond to the requests the IIS server is making. At this point, only IE4.x and greater support this authentication method. Although this method has some advantages over basic authentication, it has a major security flaw in that the password must be stored in clear text on the domain controller for the reverse encryption to be processed and compared. As a result, it is rarely used.

> NOTE
>
> **Configuration for Digest Authentication** Two things are required for this type of authentication to work. First, the IIS server must be a member of a domain. Second, each user who needs to authenticate through a browser must have her account to store the password using reversible encryption. To do this, that setting must be enabled in the properties for the user (Account tab), and then the password for the user must be reset.

If digest authentication is configured and either the user's browser is not capable of using this type of authentication or the user's account has not been configured properly (as described in the Note titled "Configuration for Digest Authentication"), the authentication will fail.

The final authentication method is integrated Windows authentication (formerly called NTLM or Windows NT Challenge/Response authentication). This method uses special encryption protocols to secure the authentication process. Unlike the other two authentication methods, IWA does not necessarily prompt for a username and password. Instead, it checks the Windows logon currently in force on the client's machine. If this can be determined and authenticated, the user might never know that any restrictions are in place on the site. If the user does not authenticate or a Windows logon name can't be determined, the browser displays a logon dialog box.

The benefit of this authentication method is its security. The disadvantages are that it works only on Internet Explorer 2.x or later (no Netscape support exists). This type of authentication is best used in an intranet environment where the browser type can be controlled.

Step By Step 3.12 demonstrates changing the type of user authentication required by your Web server.

STEP BY STEP

3.12 Changing Site Authentication Methods

1. From the Start menu, select Settings, Control Panel, Administrative Tools, Internet Services Manager.
2. In the IIS Console window, you can locate your Web site by expanding Console Root, Internet Information Services, and Your Server. When you see your Web site in the tree under the name of your server, right-click it and select Properties from the menu that appears.
3. In the Web Site Properties window, on the Directory Security tab, click the Edit button in the section labeled Anonymous Access and Authentication Control (see Figure 3.12).
4. From the Authentication Methods dialog box, select whether you want anonymous access to be configured (see Figure 3.13). If you do, you can choose to modify the account used for anonymous access or its password. To do that, click the Edit button and type in a new account name and password.

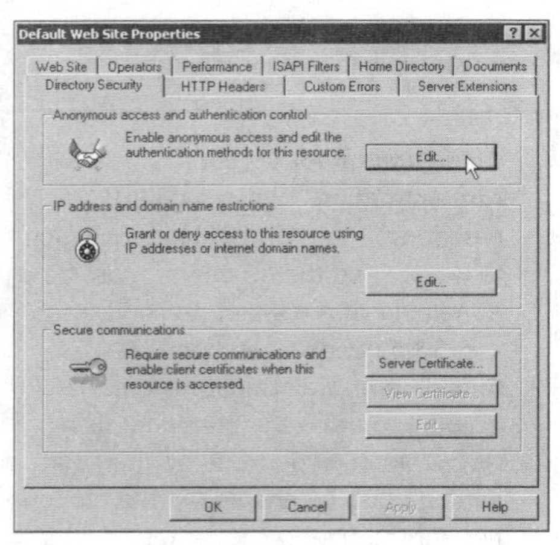

FIGURE 3.12
You can configure access authentication from the Directory Security tab of the Properties dialog box.

5. If you want to enable basic authentication, select the appropriate check box. When the Internet Service Manager warning comes up about the nature of basic authentication, click Yes to continue. Click Edit to define the location of the accounts used to authenticate Web users. If you leave it at the default, the local accounts for the server will be used. However, you can also enter a domain name to access Active Directory to use for authentication; both can't be used.
6. If you want to enable digest authentication or integrated Windows authentication, select the appropriate check box.
7. Click OK to update the Web site's properties.

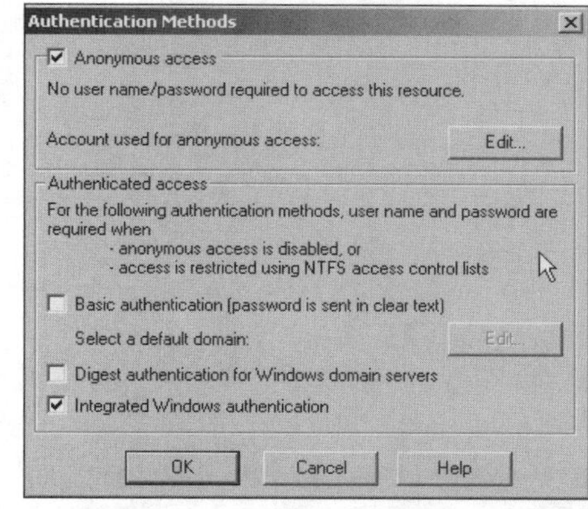

FIGURE 3.13
You can configure anonymous access and any of three authentication methods.

NOTE **Multiple Authentication Methods** If you select more than one authentication method, after attempting anonymous access, IIS attempts to authenticate using the most secure method (integrated Windows) first. Then, it tries less secure methods until all avenues of authentication have been exhausted.

Controlling Web Site Access Through IP Address and Domain Name Restrictions

You can control the access people have to your Web site to include only people with certain IP addresses (from within your company, for example) or to exclude people with certain addresses. By using IP address and domain name restrictions, you can ensure that even if someone obtains a username and password that is valid, that person can still be prevented from accessing data. This could enable company employees to access the intranet when they are at their desks (with known TCP/IP addresses) but prevent them from accessing the intranet from home (where they have unknown or unauthorized TCP/IP addresses).

When you restrict based on IP addresses or domain names, you can configure single IP addresses, multiple addresses based on a network ID and subnet mask, or addresses falling into a certain domain. If you choose to restrict based on domain (for example, to exclude all users whose IP addresses are registered to BADGUYS.com), your IIS server must do a reverse lookup on each IP address that traffic comes from. This is always very time and resource intensive and might not yield accurate results. Caution should be exercised when choosing this method.

In case you missed it, just because you can restrict access based on the client's domain affiliation doesn't mean that you should. The additional overhead of performing a reverse name lookup on an IP address is generally not justifiable.

Disallowing accesses using this method has precedence over all other access a user might have been given to the Web site.

This method for changing site address and name restrictions is covered in Step By Step 3.13.

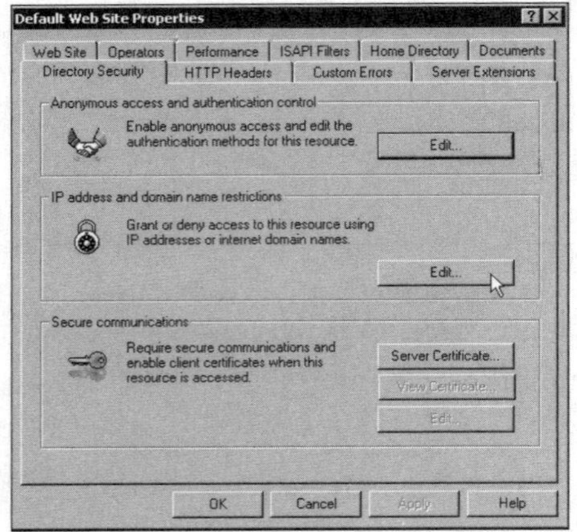

FIGURE 3.14
You can configure IP address and domain name restrictions from the Directory Services tab of the Web site's Properties dialog box page.

STEP BY STEP

3.13 Changing Site IP Address and Domain Name Restrictions

1. From the Start menu, select Settings, Control Panel, Administrative Tools, Internet Services Manager.
2. In the IIS Console window, you can locate your Web site by expanding Console Root, Internet Information Services, and Your Server. When you see your Web site in the tree under the name of your server, right-click it and select Properties from the menu that appears.
3. In the Web Site Properties window, on the Directory Security tab, click the Edit button in the section labeled IP Address and Domain Name Restrictions (see Figure 3.14).
4. In the IP Address and Domain Name Restrictions dialog box, select whether you want to implicitly grant access except to listed addresses or to implicitly deny access except to listed addresses (see Figure 3.15). Then click the Add button.

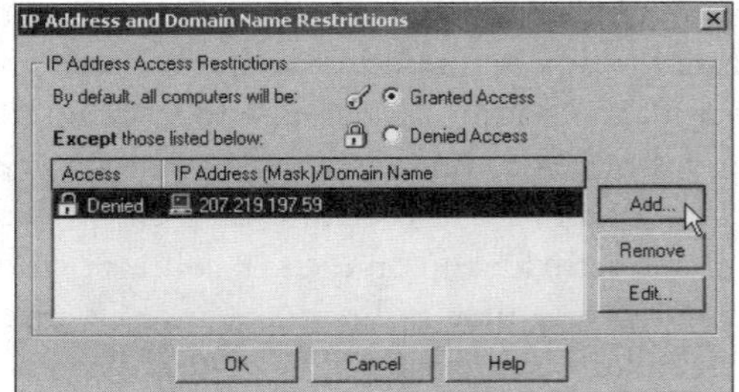

FIGURE 3.15
You can explicitly grant or explicitly deny access by IP address or domain name.

5. From the Deny Access On or Allow Access On dialog box, as shown in Figure 3.16, select Single Computer and enter the IP address, select Group of Computers and enter the network address and subnet mask, or select Domain Name and enter the domain name. Then click OK to exit.

6. Click OK until you exit back to the IIS Console.

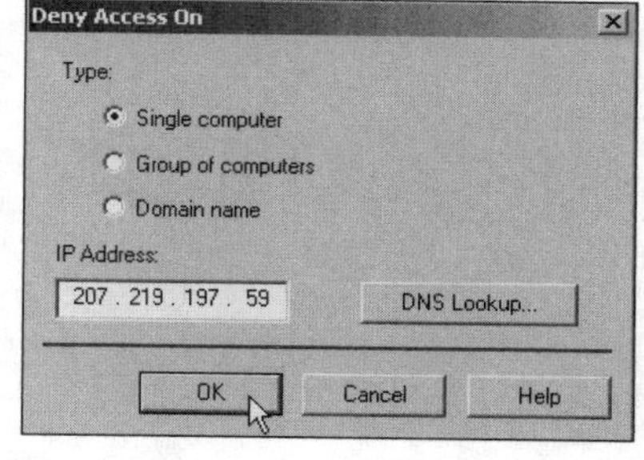

FIGURE 3.16
You can deny access by a specific IP address.

Securing Web Access Using Certificates

Certificates are a final way of securing Web access and authenticating users. In Windows 2000, the use of certificates is pervasive, as much of the security uses certificates in one way or another. As a result, the discussion of certificates here will be restricted to their use in Web transactions.

The idea of the certificate as it applies to Web transactions is that an entity (server or client) proves its identity to another using a piece of identification—the certificate. The passport provides an excellent example of how certificates work. As an American citizen, I have been issued an United States passport that verifies that I am a certain person and that I am a citizen of the United States. When I cross the border into Canada, I can show my passport to the Customs official as proof of my identification and citizenship. This passport is deemed to be valid only if two conditions are met: The passport must be authenticated by the United States government (which is done through special security coding on the passport documents), and the Customs official must recognize the United States government as being trusted to make assertions about me. If the passport is deemed to lack authenticity or if the Customs official does not recognize the United States government as a trusted authority in passport issues, my passport is not acceptable for the purposes of identification.

Computer certificates work in much the same way a passport does. A server certificate issued to a user, computer, or Web server identifies that server as being a particular entity. This certificate must be authenticated by a third party (not me and not the server itself). This authenticating party is referred to as the Certificate Authority (CA). An example of a CA that is commonly used is VeriSign.

The authentication is only half of the requirement to create a trusted environment; my Web browser must trust VeriSign to make assertions about servers. Fortunately, all current browsers are configured to trust certain so-called *root* CAs, of which VeriSign is one. After my browser and the Web server have verified that the server is who it says it is, a security negotiation can take place, thus enabling encrypted transmissions to occur.

Client certificates, on the other hand, are used to verify the identity of a person using a Web browser. Just as a server (computer) certificate allows a server to be identified, a client certificate allows a browser client to be identified. As with a server certificate, a client certificate must be authenticated by a third party, and that third party must be trusted by the server. If that is the case, the identity of a browser client can be established without sending a password over the Internet; all that is sent is the certificate information that identifies the particular user. This identification is made possible by incorporating the client certificate into the Web browser and then exporting the certificate to the IIS server. The certificate is then mapped to an account recognized by the IIS server and, when the certificate is seen in the future, it is recognized as being verification of a specific user. From that point, all permissions that apply to the user are applied to the holder of the certificate. Either certificates can be mapped on a one-to-one basis with each being mapped to a unique user account, or a group of certificates can be mapped to a single account that has access to a Web site or set of data.

The use of server certificates enables encryption of Web transmissions by way of Secure Sockets Layer (SSL). The use of client certificates enables password-free authentication of browser clients. These two certificate uses can be independently utilized, or they can be utilized together.

Certificates can be purchased from a third party or created by the Windows 2000 Certificate Services (a product that is a part of Windows 2000). For Internet applications, third-party certificates are most often used because all browsers trust a default set of third-party certificate vendors and, therefore, no browser configuration is required to trust the certificates. For intranet applications, you can use the Windows 2000 CA, but all your browsers must be configured to trust your root certifier.

Requesting an SSL Certificate

The most difficult process of getting an SSL certificate installed on your Web server is getting the certificate in the first place. There are several reasons for this difficulty:

- **Establishing identity**—In most cases you must have an outside party actually provide the SSL certificate so browsers will trust it. This means establishing your identity in a "positive" way to the certification authority.
- **Delay**—Because a third party is involved there is a delay. Most professionals are used to being able to complete activities without the involvement of third parties, and the delay they cause can be frustrating.
- **Multiple standards**—A few standards are used to make certificate requests. Each certificate authority might require different request formats.

Despite these challenges, requesting and receiving a certificate is not particularly difficult. Step By Step 3.14 shows you how to generate the request.

STEP BY STEP

3.14 Generating a Certificate Request

1. From the Start menu, select Settings, Control Panel, Administrative Tools, Internet Services Manager.
2. Click the plus sign to the left of the computer name.
3. Right-click one of the Web sites. (It doesn't matter which one.)
4. Click the Directory Security tab.
5. Click the Server Certificate button.
6. Click the Next button in the IIS Certificate Wizard to bypass the Welcome screen.
7. Click the Next button again to accept the default and create a new certificate.

continues

continued

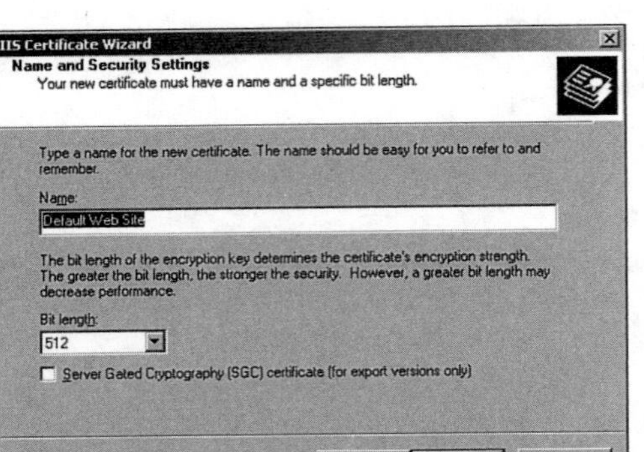

FIGURE 3.17
The longer the key, the harder it is to break.

8. Select the option to Prepare the Request Now, but Send It Later. You can select Send the Request Immediately to an Online Certification Authority if you're willing to send your request to one of the Microsoft-selected certification authorities.
9. Click the Next button to move to the next step, as shown in Figure 3.17.
10. Enter the name for the certificate. The default will be the name of the Web site. You should make this an externally meaningful name. It will appear in the certificate.
11. Set the bit length of the key. The more sensitive the information that will be transmitted, the longer the key length should be.
12. Click the Next button to move on to the next step.
13. Enter the organization and organizational unit information. This information will be encoded in the certificate and available to any user who wants to review the certificate. Be sure this information is externally meaningful. For instance, XYZ Group probably won't be helpful to a consumer reading the certificate.
14. Click the Next button.
15. Enter the site's DNS name, called a common name in the wizard. Note that any difference between what you enter here and how the browser refers to the site will be flagged to the user. Therefore, if you enter **`www.thorprojects.com`** and the user enters `thorprojects.com` in her browser, she will receive a warning message.
16. Click the Next button.
17. Enter the country, state, and city. This information is also visible to the browser. You might want to use the location information of the nearest large city rather than the name of the suburb that you are actually in.
18. Click the Next button.

19. Enter the name of the certificate request. You can specify any name you want—as long as you remember what it is.
20. Click the Next button twice to generate the file.
21. Click the Finish button to complete the wizard.
22. Click the OK button to close the site properties.
23. Close the Internet Information Services window.

Now that you have the request file, it's time to send it off to a certification authority. In the next section you'll learn how to issue your own certificate if you have certificate services loaded. This will enable you to learn how to issue certificates. Normally, you'll want to send your request off to one of the public root certificate authorities.

Issuing Your Own SSL Certificate

If you install certificate services on a server within your enterprise, you will be able to issue your own certificate. Although your certificate won't be trusted by Web browsers, by default you can use it to test SSL in your own environment.

The process for submitting a certificate request is shown in Step By Step 3.15. If you have the appropriate administrative authority and the certificate authority your referring to is a part of Active Directory, you'll be assigned the certificate immediately.

STEP BY STEP

3.15 Submitting a Certificate Request to a Windows 2000 Certificate Authority

1. Log on with an administrative account.
2. Open Internet Explorer.
3. Enter `http://servername/certsrv` in the address bar.
4. Confirm that the Request a Certificate option is selected, and then click the Next button.

continues

continued

5. Select Advanced Request.
6. Click the Next button.
7. Select Submit a Certificate Request Using a Base64 Encoded PKCS#10 File or a Renewal Request Using a Base64 Encoded PKCS#7 File. This is the file you created in the previous section.
8. Click the Next button.
9. Open the certificate request file in Notepad.
10. Select all of the text and copy it to the Clipboard.
11. Close Notepad.
12. Paste the contents of the request file into the Saved Request box.
13. Change the Certificate Template to Web Server.
14. Click the Submit button.
15. If you have administrative privileges, you'll be issued a certificate immediately. Click Download CA Certificate, and save the resulting file. If the certificate isn't automatically authorized, you must refer to the Microsoft documentation on how to approve pending certificate requests.

Now you have a file that contains the certificate. The next step is installing it on your Web server.

Implementing an SSL Certificate

The process of implementing the SSL certificate is comparatively much more straightforward than requesting the certificate in the first place. Step By Step 3.16 shows you how to implement the certificate you requested.

STEP BY STEP

3.16 Installing a Certificate

1. From the Start Menu, select Settings, Control Panel, Administrative Tools, Internet Services Manager.
2. Click the plus sign to the left of the computer name to expand the list of Web and FTP sites.
3. Right-click the Web site you want to install the certificate to, and select Properties from the context menu.
4. Click the Directory Security tab.
5. Click the Server Certificate button.
6. Click the Next button to move past the welcome step.
7. Click the Next button to confirm that you want to process the pending request and install the certificate.
8. Enter the name of the file in the Path and Filename box. You can browse to the certificate file if you don't remember the name of the file.
9. Click the Next button to continue to the confirmation step.
10. Click the Next button to confirm that the certificate is correct.
11. Click the Finish button to complete the wizard and install the certificate.
12. Click the OK button to close the Web site properties.
13. Close the Internet Information Services window.

The process of installing the server certificate might involve more than a few clicks, but most of those are just confirming that the certificate is correct. When you installed the certificate, Windows 2000 automatically enabled SSL for the Web site and set the SSL port to the default SSL port of 443.

Enabling Client Authentication Using Client Certificates

Client certificates are an alternative form of authentication to the ones described in the previous sections. What sets this form of authentication apart from the others is that no passwords are required by the client when a browser connects to a site requiring authenticated access. Instead, the browser sends certificate information the Web server has mapped to a certain user account. Using this method, any browser can be used to connect to a site requiring authentication, without having to allow clear-text passwords and without requiring the user to actually log on using a username and password.

The steps for configuring authentication using client certificates are straightforward. First, the server must have a certificate installed issued by the same CA that the clients' certificates are coming from. This enables you to set the configuration to allow for client certificates for authentication.

Next, your clients must have certificates installed on their browsers. Similar to server certificates, these certificates need to be authenticated by a trusted source. If the browsers are connecting to an intranet, you could use the certificate services to generate a root certifier and client certificates. If the connection is to an Internet site, the clients will most likely use a third-party certificate vendor, such as VeriSign.

Finally, after the clients have certificates installed, these must be exported to the Web server and mapped to user accounts. After the mapping has occurred, the server can authenticate the client as being a particular user simply by being shown the client certificate. When the user is authenticated, access to resources is the same as that of any other authenticated user.

Step By Step 3.17 shows how to enable client certificates for authentication.

STEP BY STEP

3.17 Configuring a Web Server to Accept Client Certificates for Authentication

1. Install a server certificate on your Web server (see Step By Step 3.16).

2. From the properties of the Web site for which you want to enable client certificate authentication, click the Directory Security tab.
3. On the Directory Security tab, click Edit in the Secure Communications section.
4. In the Secure Communications dialog box, you can select Accept Client Certificates or (if SSL has been enabled) Require Client Certificates. Accept Client Certificates allows but does not require a browser to attempt to authenticate with this Web server using a client certificate. Require Client Certificates forces a browser to attempt to authenticate with this Web server using a client certificate; failure or lack of a certificate causes authentication to fail.
5. In the Secure Communications dialog box, select the check box labeled Enable Client Certificate Mapping, and then click the Edit button next to it. You can then add mappings between exported client certificates (provided by the clients) and user accounts (one-to-one mapping), or you can add a mapping between a root certifier and a user account (many-to-one mapping). A mapping between a root certifier and a user account ensures that anyone authenticating with a certificate from a specific root certifier will be given the same access on the Web site.
6. In the Secure Communications dialog box, you can also enable a Certificate Trust List (CTL). A CTL is a list of certifiers you trust. If a client tries to authenticate with a certifier not in the CTL, that certificate is rejected.
7. When configuration is complete, click OK to exit.

Troubleshooting Web Site Access

Web site access is about two things: access to a running server and security.

Lack of access because of security issues revolves around all the topics that have been covered in this section. Look for TCP port incompatibilities and fix them if they are discovered.

If a user is getting `Access denied` messages, check for authentication methods and underlying NTFS permissions. In addition, check for client certificates and see whether they are required. IP address restrictions also can cause these types of messages, so check for these, too.

If a user can get to your site but can't do what is desired (such as upload files or execute scripts), check for those permissions and adjust them if necessary.

CONFIGURING WEB CLIENTS

Internet Information Services is only half of the equation when it comes to browsing the Web. It ensures that there is something to browse, but it doesn't provide the actual browsing interface to the user. In the Microsoft world, that job is taken by Internet Explorer (IE). It's IE's job to ensure that the user can reach the content on the Web servers inside the company and on the Internet.

Proxy Servers

> NOTE
>
> **Only Developers Can Prevent Caching** Controlling the caching of the proxy server and preventing it from caching inappropriate content is the responsibility of the Web developer. That being said, proxy servers generally don't cache content that contains passed parameters or where the user is logged into a site.

One of the techniques frequently used in corporate environments to protect individual user's computers from outside attack is a device called a *proxy server*. The proxy server acts as the middle man between all transactions from internal Web browsing clients and the outside world. In addition to being an intermediary, most proxy servers provide a caching feature that enables them to request a page the first time a client requests it but not when the same client or another client accesses the same page.

Proxy servers are used instead of or in conjunction with firewalls because of this caching service and because proxy servers allow tighter control of the content that can get into the network. This enables system administrators to prevent employees from going to sexually explicit sites or sites that might not be appropriate. Finally, proxy servers provide a logging feature that enables the administrator to monitor the Web sites being visited by employees.

With all these features, it's no wonder that many organizations are implementing proxy servers to help control Internet access.

However, when proxy servers are implemented it means that the browser (IE) must be told how to communicate with the proxy server to be capable of communicating with the Internet.

Recent versions of IE have a feature called automatic proxy detection. This eliminates the need for you to manually configure proxy settings on each machine. However, for the test you'll have to know how to configure a proxy server in Internet Explorer. Step By Step 3.18 shows you how to configure a proxy server in Internet Explorer.

STEP BY STEP

3.18 Configuring a Web Server to Accept Client Certificates for Authentication

1. Start Internet Explorer.
2. From the menu select Tools, Internet Options.
3. Click the Connections tab.
4. Click the LAN Settings button. A dialog box similar to Figure 3.18 appears.
5. Click the option Use a Proxy Server for Your LAN.
6. Enter the address and port for the proxy server into the Address and Port text boxes. If you need to enter separate addresses and ports by service, you can do this by clicking the Advanced button and entering the addresses into the dialog box that appears (see Figure 3.19).

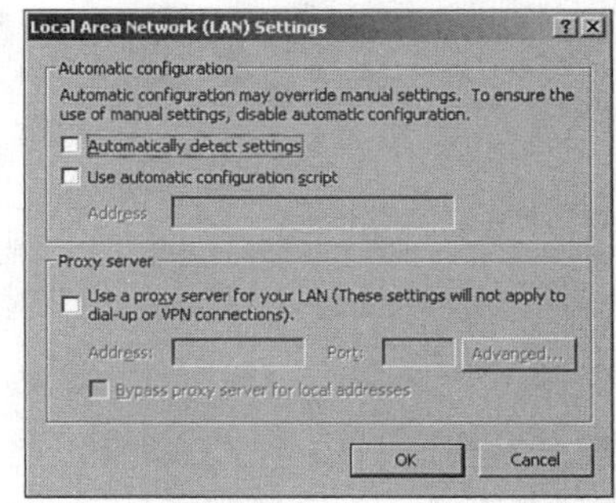

FIGURE 3.18
LAN settings are really proxy settings.

> **NOTE**
> **Possible Proxy** By selecting Automatically Detect Settings, IE will attempt to automatically find a proxy server. By selecting the Use Automatic Configuration Script option, you specify that you want IE to configure itself based on the file you point to on the intranet.

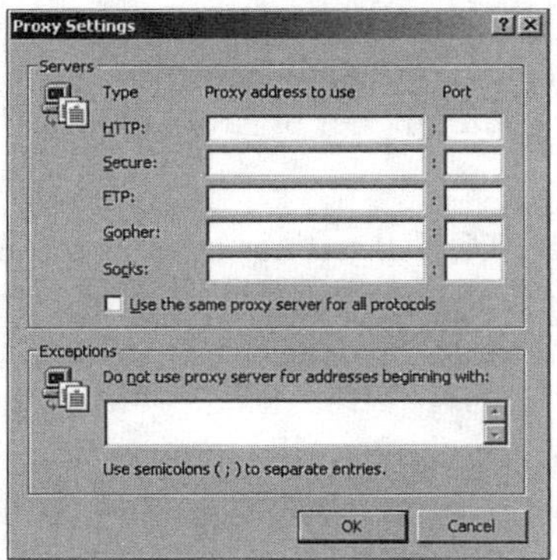

FIGURE 3.19
Advanced settings enable you to select addresses by protocol.

continues

continued

7. Click the OK button to close the LAN Settings dialog box.
8. Click the OK button to close the Internet properties.

As soon as you've entered the proxy settings, IE starts using them. In other words, as soon as they are entered, you should be able to start surfing the Internet from IE.

Troubleshooting Access

If you're having problems browsing the Web, there's a relatively short set of problems that can be the cause. In the next few sections we go through the potential problems one by one.

Network Connectivity

One of the most frequently overlooked causes of problems is that the computer has lost network connectivity all together. One of the first things to check is that the machine can communicate with other servers and machines on the local network.

Problems in cabling, a port failure on a hub, or a network card failure can all lead to a complete loss of networking. This is the first check that should be performed.

TCP/IP Settings

The next potential problem is that the computer's TCP/IP settings have become corrupted. Although this is less of an issue with DHCP being used by a large number of organizations, it is still a possibility to be explored.

> **WARNING**
>
> **No Settings for DHCP** DHCP settings are overridden by an entry in the TCP/IP settings of Windows 95/98/Me. Because of this, you should ensure that the TCP/IP settings are blank in a Windows 95/98/Me machine that should be getting all its information from DHCP.

The best way to test TCP/IP settings is to try to ping the default gateway. This is done by doing an `IPCONFIG/ALL` command from the command line to retrieve the default gateway and then a `PING` *`dftgateway`*, where *`dftgateway`* is the default gateway returned by IPCONFIG. `PING` should return the number of milliseconds it took to reach the default gateway, which is typically less than 10 milliseconds. If this test is successful then it is very likely that the TCP/IP settings are okay.

Name Resolution Settings

The next possible problem is that the name being entered in the browser isn't being resolved into the IP address the browser must contact to receive the information. This translation process is handled by DNS (and sometimes by local host files for intranet sites).

The easiest way to test whether name resolution is working properly is to open a command prompt and run the `PING` command—for instance, `PING www.microsoft.com`. Note that many Web sites will not return ping responses. However, if `PING` starts the process rather than returning a message saying you've entered a bad address then name resolution is working.

Proxy Settings

The next potential problem is that the proxy settings are missing from IE when a proxy server is required for access to the Internet—or where proxy server settings are present and there is no proxy server.

If you're using a proxy server and have just selected automatic proxy server detection, you should try to manually set up the proxy server settings. This will help eliminate the possibility of an automatic discovery failure. Similarly, it might be a good idea to manually configure the proxy settings if you normally use an automatic configuration script.

Conversely, if no proxy server exists in your environment and there are still proxy server settings in IE, you won't be able to access the Internet either.

> NOTE
>
> **Be a Proxy User** Consultants who travel frequently have problems where some clients have proxy servers and others do not. One way to help mitigate the effort of reconfiguring all the time is to use separate user profiles for each customer. IE settings are based on the user—and thus the customer if you use a separate logon to your notebook for each customer.

Server Problems

If the previous troubleshooting steps don't resolve the issue then server problems might be preventing access to the Internet. It's important at this point to check other machines to see whether they are having the same problem and check from servers to see whether they appear to be running correctly.

CASE STUDY: JOE'S BASS MAGNETS

ESSENCE OF THE CASE

Using Microsoft Internet Information Services allows Joe's Bass Magnets to gain access to a broader audience than it can by having its shop in Little Rock.

SCENARIO

Joe's Bass Magnets has built a local following in the Little Rock, Arkansas, area by providing some innovative ways to catch bass. Its lures have developed a following in the bass fishing community, and the company is ready to expand.

Armed with Front Page and its new Windows 2000 server, the company creates a simple Web site that shows customers what its lures look like along with some testimonials, including a video clip from former president Bill Clinton.

It configures a section on the Web site for users to place orders, using SSL encryption to keep the credit card numbers of its customers safe during transmission. Because it's a small outfit, the company doesn't have automated order processing yet—all the orders are routed to e-mail where they are processed manually later.

ANALYSIS

In addition to the Windows 2000 server, Joe's Bass Magnets needs to order its SSL certificate from one of the trusted root certification authorities.

CHAPTER SUMMARY

KEY TERMS

- File Transfer Protocol (FTP)
- Hypertext Transfer Protocol (HTTP)
- Internet Information Services (IIS)

In this chapter you learned what Internet Information Services is and how to set up virtual FTP and Web sites. You learned how to allow multiple FTP sites and Web sites to run on one server—and the difficulties with doing this. You also learned how to create virtual directories, which allows you to pull information from multiple locations on the server into one hierarchy.

CHAPTER SUMMARY

Next, you learned about security and how to secure a Web site, including how to require different types of authentication and how to set up an SSL certificate for a Web site. SSL, short for Secure Socket Layer, is the encryption mechanism that allows normal, unencrypted Web traffic to be encrypted in both directions. This enables even a plain-text password (or basic if you prefer) to be encrypted.

Finally, you learned how to manually set up Internet Explorer to use a proxy server and how to troubleshoot problems with Internet Explorer accessing the Internet.

KEY TERMS

- proxy server
- Secure Socket Layer (SSL)
- virtual directory
- virtual server

APPLY YOUR KNOWLEDGE

Exercises

3.1 Creating a New Web Site

This exercise demonstrates how to create a new Web site that will be used for the administrator only. The site will be established on a private port and will require authentication.

Estimated Time: 10 minutes

1. From the Start menu select Settings, Control Panel.
2. Double-click Administrative Tools and Internet Services Manager.
3. Click the plus sign to the left of the computer name to display a listing of Web and FTP sites.
4. Right-click the computer and select New, Web Site from the context menu.
5. Click the Next button to move past the introductory screen.
6. Enter a description for the Web site. In this case, enter **`Administrators Private Web`**.
7. Click the Next button to move to the IP Address and Port Settings dialog box.
8. Select the TCP port of 8081 for the Web server.
9. Click the Next button to move to the home directory step.
10. Select the path that will be the home directory for the Web site. In this case, use `C:\inetpub`.
11. Uncheck Allow Anonymous Access to This Web Site.
12. Click the Next button to select the permissions.
13. Click the Next button, and then click the Finish button to complete the wizard.
14. Close the Internet Information Services window.

Review Questions

1. What types of sites will IIS allow you to serve?
2. Why would you use a virtual server?
3. What does a virtual directory do?
4. What is a proxy server?

Exam Questions

1. You've just created a new Web site, but when you completed the wizard the site is stopped. What is the most likely cause of this?

   A. The World Wide Web service is stopped.

   B. The IIS Admin service is stopped.

   C. The site you created is not uniquely identifiable.

   D. You selected an invalid TCP port.

2. You're accessing a URL, `http://serverA/MyMusic`, from a browser. You go to the site to find that the Web server's home directory is `C:\WebHome`. No corresponding folder called `C:\WebHome\MyMusic` exists. What is the most likely cause?

   A. The server is looking at the client's `C:\WebHome` directory.

   B. A virtual directory called `MyMusic` is defined.

APPLY YOUR KNOWLEDGE

C. A virtual directory pointing to `C:\MyMusic` is defined.

D. A virtual Web site, `/MyMusic`, is defined on the server.

3. While surfing your Web site, you are suddenly prompted for a password. When you refuse to provide one, you receive an access denied message. The message includes the keyword *ACL*. Why were you prompted for a password?

A. You disabled anonymous access on the Web site.

B. You disabled anonymous access on the directory.

C. You removed the `IWAM_`*`SERVER`* user from the access control list on the directory or file.

D. You removed the `IUSR_`*`SERVER`* user from the access control list on the directory or file.

4. You've created a Web site on a server named ServerA. You created the Web site on port 80. What is the correct URL to reference the directory XYZ?

A. `http://serverA/XYZ`

B. `http://serverA:80/XYZ`

C. `http://ServerA/XYZ:80`

D. `http:80//serverA/XYZ`

5. What is the best way of ensuring that passwords are never sent via clear text to a Web server?

A. Disable anonymous access. Enable integrated Windows authentication.

B. Obtain and implement an SSL certificate. Turn on basic authentication.

C. Turn on integrated Windows authentication. Turn off basic authentication.

D. Turn off anonymous access. Turn off basic authentication. Turn on integrated Windows authentication.

6. You've set up a Web server for the accounting group, and because of security concerns you've limited the IP addresses that can access the server to the subnet used by the accounting group. The CFO connects via the VPN server and wants to know why he's unable to connect to the accounting Web server. What do you tell him?

A. Web connections are not supported across a VPN.

B. You didn't enable VPN support on the Web server. You'll make the change shortly.

C. He needs to set his IP address to one of the accounting group IP addresses.

D. Because his IP address isn't one of the authorized accounting group IP addresses, he will not be able to access the Web site.

7. The Web developers in your company have just turned over a Web site that you have to install on a Windows 2000 server. You create the Web site and then try to test the Web site. You receive an error when trying to access `MYAPP.DLL`. What is the most likely cause of the problem?

A. You do not have read permission to the file or directory.

B. You don't have script access to the file or directory.

C. You don't have execute permission to the file or directory.

D. The default document type is set wrong.

APPLY YOUR KNOWLEDGE

8. You've been called in to fix a problem with Internet Explorer. IE can't connect to any server on the network or on the Internet. You've tried referring to the servers by their IP addresses. What are the likely causes? (Choose all that apply.)

   A. Network connection failure.

   B. TCP/IP default gateway is misconfigured.

   C. The proxy server is down.

   D. The proxy settings are incorrect.

9. You've been called in because a user is complaining that he can't reach `www.playboy.com`. All other Web sites he is trying seem to work. As it turns out, this employee needs to download an article from the Playboy Web site. What is the most likely cause of the problem?

   A. Network connection failure.

   B. The proxy server has `www.playboy.com` blocked.

   C. The proxy settings in Internet Explorer are wrong.

   D. There is a name resolution failure.

10. Two weeks ago you created a virtual Web site in anticipation of a new Web site that the company wants to launch. It was working fine when you created it, loaded the content, and stopped it—to prevent people from getting access to it too soon. However, now when you try to start the Web site you receive an error message and the site refuses to start. What is the most likely cause?

    A. Another Web site has been created and started since the site was created. The new Web site has the same parameters as the Web site created two weeks ago.

    B. The Web site was created before a service pack was applied. After service packs are applied, all Web sites need to be deleted and re-created.

    C. Another machine on the network has started using the IP address assigned to the Web site so the site can't start.

    D. You can start and stop a Web site only once per reboot. You must reboot the server.

11. Some consultants are trying to use Netscape 4.7 to access one of the company Web sites and are reporting problems. What is the most likely cause?

    A. Internet Information Services is not compatible with Netscape browsers.

    B. The proxy settings in Netscape are incorrect.

    C. The proxy server is down.

    D. Basic authentication is turned off, and anonymous access is turned off.

12. Which users or groups can be used to specify anonymous access to files and directories accessed via a Web server? (Select all that apply.)

    A. Everyone

    B. Users

    C. `IUSR_`*`SERVER`*

    D. `IWAM_`*`SERVER`*

13. Joe has been able to use a Web server for the past two years. He has just moved to a new building on campus and is having trouble using one of the Web servers. He's not having trouble with any other network services. What is the most likely cause?

APPLY YOUR KNOWLEDGE

A. Joe's proxy settings are wrong.

B. Joe's TCP/IP configuration is wrong.

C. Joe's name resolution settings are wrong.

D. The Web server has IP address restrictions in effect.

14. You just renamed a server from `DAPDev` to `DapProd`, and users are now reporting that they are receiving a dialog box when they try to access the Web site on the machine. What is the most likely reason?

    A. The Web sites must be re-created after renaming the server.

    B. The SSL certificate has the wrong common name.

    C. The DNS information for the server needs to be updated.

    D. The DHCP server has to be updated to reflect the name change.

15. A user is trying to upload a file to an FTP site. She's receiving an error. What are the most likely causes? (Pick two.)

    A. The user does not have write permission to the directory.

    B. The FTP site is not enabled for write access.

    C. The FTP server does not support the `PUT` command.

    D. You can't upload files to FTP servers.

Answers to Review Questions

1. IIS will serve FTP and Web (HTTP) sites. You can create as many sites as you want, but all of them running at any given moment must be capable of being uniquely identified.
2. Virtual servers enable you to service multiple FTP or Web sites from one physical server. This is important and useful when you maintain several Web sites that don't require the resources of a server on their own. Virtual servers enable multiple Web or FTP sites to share the resources of one piece of hardware.
3. Virtual directories enable you to present a hierarchy on the sites being served, which doesn't exist on disk. This is useful when large amounts of information are serviced from one Web site.
4. A proxy server is a device that allows Internet connectivity by performing operations as an intermediary between the internal clients and external Internet host. Proxy servers allow a much broader range of audit and control facilities than a firewall in addition to their caching benefits. They are often used by corporations that need to control or monitor the Internet access in the organization.

Answers to Exam Questions

1. **C.** Each site requires a set of IP address, TCP port, and host header parameters to enable it to be uniquely identified when a request comes in. If another Web site has the same parameters as the Web site being created, the site is created but left in the stopped state.

APPLY YOUR KNOWLEDGE

2. **B.** Virtual directories enable you to create Web sites that are not mirrored in the directory structure on the server. A is incorrect because a Web server never gets content from a client. C is incorrect because where the virtual directory is pointing is immaterial to how it will be referenced from the site. D is incorrect because Web sites are defined at the root of the server. You can't define a server that starts in the `/MyMusic` directory.

3. **D.** If you remove the `IUSR_`*`SERVER`* user from the access control list on a file or directory, IIS is forced to try to get other authentication information—even if anonymous access is enabled. A and B are incorrect because an error message indicating that there is a problem due to an ACL on resource indicates that it is an ACL issue. Option C is incorrect because it is the `IUSR_`*`SERVER`* account that is used by anonymous users, not `IWAM_`*`SERVER`* account.

4. **A.** TCP port 80 is the default for HTTP traffic, and because of that it doesn't need to be specified. The correct syntax of a URL with a port number defined is shown in option B. The other syntaxes showing where the port number is provided are incorrect.

5. **B.** The only way to ensure that a client Web browser never submits a clear password is to use SSL. Even if you turn off basic authentication, some browsers will attempt basic authentication if they can't perform integrated Windows authentication. A is also incorrect because you should not change anonymous access settings. Anonymous access might be required for error pages or other special purpose pages. C and D are incorrect because they won't prevent a browser from trying basic authentication.

6. **D.** When limiting a Web site to access by a certain number of IP addresses, it's important to realize that ONLY those IP addresses will work. A is incorrect—VPN connections support all types of traffic. B is incorrect because no special settings are needed to enable VPN access to a Web server. C is incorrect because the CFO can't change his VPN server assigned IP address—or his home computer's IP address—without causing the VPN to fail.

7. **C.** To execute ISAPI DLLs or CGI executables, you must have execute access to the Web site. If you didn't have read permission to the file, as suggested in A, you would receive a security warning message and you wouldn't receive it just on the DLL. Because a DLL is not considered a script, B is inappropriate. D is incorrect because, if the default document was incorrect, nothing would have loaded and the error would have been `directory listing denied`.

8. **A, D.** If the entire network connection is down or the proxy settings are incorrect, you can see the inability to browse Web sites in IE. B is incorrect because a default gateway problem wouldn't explain the incapability to reach local servers. Because local network machines are also affected by the problem, TCP/IP configuration problems are unlikely.

9. **B.** Proxy servers are used, in part, for their capability to selectively block Web sites based on content. Because other servers are working, none of the other options are appropriate. They would cause failures for every site, not just one.

10. **A.** The most common reason a Web site won't start is because another Web site is running on the same machine with the same parameters.

APPLY YOUR KNOWLEDGE

This site either was not started when the site was created or was created after the site created two weeks ago. B is incorrect—you do not need to re-create Web sites after the installation of a service pack. C is incorrect because this would cause a pop-up message on the console; it wouldn't prevent the site from starting. D is incorrect—you can stop and restart a Web server as many times as is necessary.

11. **D.** Netscape browsers do not support Windows integrated authentication. They must have digest authentication or basic authentication turned on. (Digest authentication requires passwords encrypted with two-way encryption, which is not available by default.) B and C are incorrect because internal access to internal servers would bypass proxy servers. A is incorrect because IIS is compatible with Netscape.

12. **A, C.** The Everyone special group includes everyone—users, guests, and so on. Because of that, it will include the `IUSR_`*`SERVER`* account. The `IUSR_`*`SERVER`* account is the account IIS uses for anonymous access. B is incorrect because `IUSR_`*`SERVER`* is not a member of the users group. D is incorrect because `IWAM_`*`SERVER`* is the process account IIS uses when it runs processes in their own protected memory. It has nothing to do with anonymous logons.

13. **D.** Joe's IP address probably changed because of the new building. (It's rare that multiple buildings are on one subnet.) It's possible that the Web site has a limited range of IP addresses from which it would accept requests. A is incorrect because a local Web server would normally bypass the proxy server. B and C are incorrect because they would impact all network services, not just a single Web site.

14. **B.** When an SSL certificate is issued, it is issued to a specific common name, or in other words, a specific DNS name. When that name changes the certificate warns the client that the name doesn't match the name in the certificate any longer. This is to protect the user. A is incorrect—Web servers do not need to be re-created after a server is renamed. C is incorrect because it appears that the clients were connected with the server and thus name resolution worked. D is incorrect—DHCP is not involved with the renaming of a server.

15. **A, B.** The two most common causes for not being able to write to an FTP directory are that the user who logged in to the FTP server does not have write access to the directory she is are trying to upload into and that the FTP server does not have write access enabled. The `PUT` command is the standard command for uploading a file and is supported by IIS, so C is incorrect. D is incorrect because FTP sites are designed to download and upload files.

PART

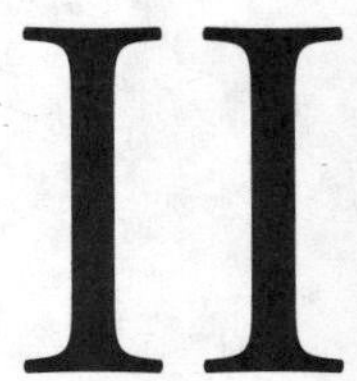

Configuring, Administering, and Troubleshooting Network Infrastructure

OBJECTIVES

This chapter starts Part II, "Configuring, Administering, and Troubleshooting Network Infrastructure." This chapter helps you prepare for the MCSE Managing a Microsoft Windows 2000 Network Environment exam by covering the following objectives:

Troubleshoot routing. Diagnostic utilities include the `tracert` command, the `ping` command, and the `ipconfig` command.

- **Validate local computer configuration by using the `ipconfig`, `arp`, and `route` commands.**
- **Validate network connectivity by using the `tracert`, `ping`, and `pathping` commands.**

▶ Windows 2000 contains some excellent diagnostic tools to help you monitor, manage, and troubleshoot your network infrastructure. We'll examine how these tools can be used to diagnose overall network connectivity problems and increase the reliability of your Windows 2000 network.

Configure and troubleshoot TCP/IP on servers and client computers. Considerations include subnet masks, default gateways, network IDs, and broadcast addresses.

- **Configure client computer TCP/IP properties.**
- **Validate client computer network configuration by using the winipcfg, ipconfig, and arp commands.**
- **Validate client computer network connectivity by using the ping command**
- **Validate client computer network configuration by using the winipcfg, ipconfig and arp commands.**
- **Validate client computer network connectivity by using the ping command.**

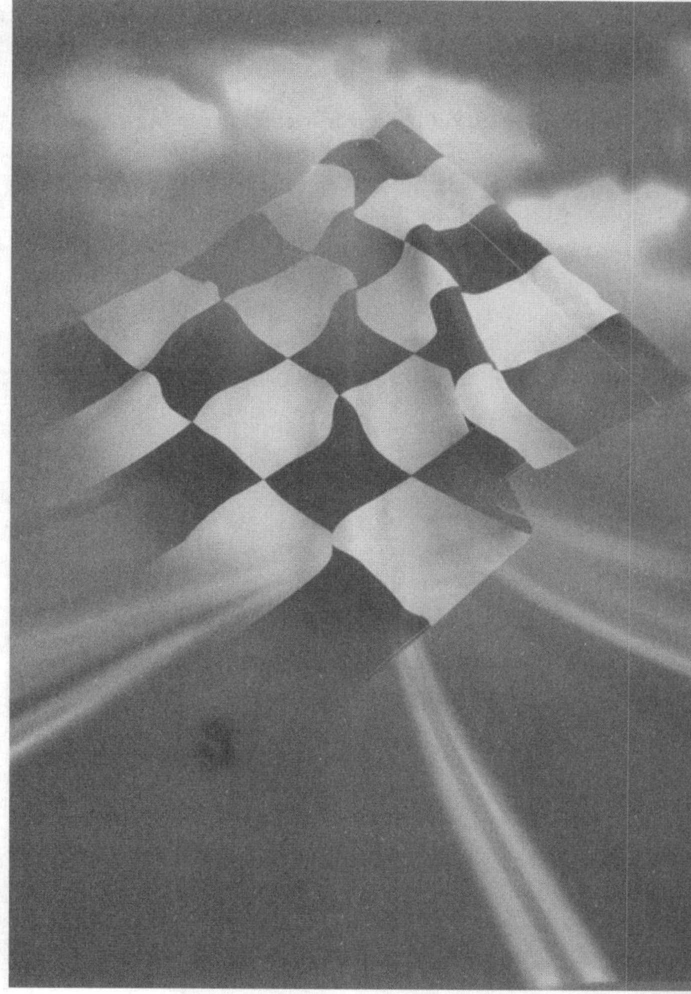

CHAPTER 4

TCP/IP Fundamentals

OBJECTIVES

- Windows 2000 networks can host many types of clients. We'll examine the setup of the different Windows clients that can use TCP/IP and interact on a Windows 2000 network. You'll also need a complete understanding of Transmission Control Protocol/Internet Protocol (TCP/IP) for this exam.

OUTLINE

OUTLINE

STUDY STRATEGIES

- Windows 2000 networking is very reliant on TCP/IP. This exam will no doubt focus heavily on the more complex issues of TCP/IP and require you to demonstrate a solid understanding of its configuration and use to solve problems. Take some time to review the basics of IP and build from there.
- Work with the step-by-steps. These exercises are placed throughout the book and provide directions on how to accomplish everyday tasks. They are included to give you an opportunity to become familiar with the configuration and use of TCP/IP in a Windows 2000 environment. Try to go beyond these examples to create some of your own. Experiment to see where each option could be used in your own network.

INTRODUCTION

A *local area network (LAN)* is a collection of computers in a specific area that are connected by a communications network. It sounds simple enough, but because a TCP/IP network can consist of literally millions of computers, the network structure can get complicated.

In fact, it can get complicated with just a few computers. The largest structure in a TCP/IP network (below the Internet) is a wide area network (WAN). This can be thought of as network connections between LANs. A LAN has a structure as well; it's made up of a collection of one or more subnets, all with a common addressing scheme but segmented to help manage traffic flow and the challenges of keeping client computer configurations straight.

Your computer connects to the network in a subnet. It will have an IP address (your place within the network structure) and a Media Access Control (MAC) address (identifying your physical network adapter card). If you want to access some other resource that's not connected to your subnet, some mechanism is needed to get your data from point A to point B.

IP is the mechanism that allows data to travel from one computer to another either on a local network or through a router to a remote network. How does this work?

A SIMPLE ROUTING SITUATION

If you have eight computers in Chicago connected on the same Ethernet network, you have a LAN (with one subnet). There's no routing and no need for it. In such an Ethernet network, each computer receives every packet, regardless of whether the packet is intended for it. The physical MAC address of the network card determines whether the packet is to be accepted or discarded.

If ComputerA needs to send a packet to ComputerB, the first thing it must do is decide whether the destination is on the same subnet. If the IP address is local (on the same subnet), Address Resolution Protocol (ARP) is used to identify the destination MAC address. This information is placed in the IP header and the packet is sent out. Because, on an Ethernet network, every machine receives every packet, ComputerB is sure to see the information ComputerA is sending. It will compare its MAC address to the MAC address in the packet from the network and accept it. Every other computer will ignore the packet.

What happens when ComputerA needs to send a packet to ComputerZ in Atlanta? In this situation, the destination computer is not on the same segment (subnet) as ComputerA. Figure 4.1 shows a computer in Chicago accessing a computer in Atlanta. To deliver the packet, a router must be used.

FIGURE 4.1
Routing information between two LANs.

A *router* is a device that routes packets from a subnet to other routers on other subnets until the destination computer is found. In Windows 2000, the address of the router that connects your subnet to all other addresses is called the *default gateway.*

If the path to the destination computer is not known up front, the routers go through a discovery mechanism that creates entries in their routing tables. The first router then forwards the packet, based on its routing table, to the next router, and onward until eventually the packet ends up at the final network and onto the target computer.

TROUBLESHOOTING ROUTING

▶ Troubleshoot routing. Diagnostic utilities include the `tracert` command, the `ping` command, and the `ipconfig` command.

Windows 2000 relies on network connectivity for many things, including domain account credentials and access to printers, file shares, databases, and application programs. Laptop computers usually connect to a network on a regular basis (whenever you are back in the office) and refresh locally cached information (offline folders, user ID credentials, and so on) at that time. A computer that is always disconnected from the network (that is, a standalone computer) is more the exception than the rule.

So, if your Windows 2000 computer can't connect to a remote computer and you suspect you have networking problems, there are a number of steps you can take to determine what and where the problem is. Your system could use DHCP to acquire its IP address and other configuration information, or it could be manually configured. In either case, the first thing you should do is confirm that the machines network configuration is correct. To confirm that your computer is configured correctly, you need to obtain information on your current configuration using commands such as IPCONFIG, TRACERT, and PING and then validate your network connectivity using commands such as TRACERT, ROUTE, and PATHPING.

Using IPCONFIG

The IPCONFIG command is used to report on the current network configuration of your computer. This includes the IP addresses and subnet mask assigned to your computer, the default gateway, and the WINS and DNS addresses (if those are configured for your network connection).

The IPCONFIG /ALL command produces a report similar to the following:

```
Windows IP Configuration

   Host Name . . . . . . . . . . . . : gordb3
   Primary Dns Suffix  . . . . . . . : barknet.ads
   Node Type . . . . . . . . . . . . : Mixed
   IP Routing Enabled. . . . . . . . : No
   WINS Proxy Enabled. . . . . . . . : No
   DNS Suffix Search List. . . . . . : barknet.ads
Ethernet adapter Local Area Connection:
   Media State . . . . . . . . . . . : Media disconnected
    Description . . . . . . . . . . . : Intel(R)PRO/100+
                                         MiniPCI
    Physical Address. . . . . . . . . :00-D0-59-10-FC-F4
Ethernet adapter Wireless Network Connection:
  Connection-specific DNS Suffix  . : Barknet.ads
  Description . . . . . . . . . . . : ORiNOCO Wireless
                                      LAN PC Card (5 volt)
  Physical Address. . . . . . . . . : 00-02-2D-1D-4C-6B
  Dhcp Enabled. . . . . . . . . . . : Yes
  Autoconfiguration Enabled . . . . : Yes
  IP Address. . . . . . . . . . . . : 192.168.0.6
  Subnet Mask . . . . . . . . . . . : 255.255.255.0
  Default Gateway . . . . . . . . . : 192.168.0.1
  DHCP Server . . . . . . . . . . . : 192.168.0.1
  DNS Servers . . . . . . . . . . . : 192.168.0.1
  Lease Obtained. . . . . . . . . . : Wednesday, December
                                      26, 2001 9:17:36 PM
  Lease Expires . . . . . . . . . . : Thursday, January 03,
                                      2002 9:17:36 PM
```

This output shows that the host name is gordb3, which is connected to a Windows 2000 domain called barknet.ads. The computer is connected by a Wireless LAN card (an ORiNOCO PC Card), and this network configuration was obtained from a DHCP server. The IP address is 192.168.0.6, and the default gateway is 192.168.0.1. The subnet mask indicates that the default gateway is on the same network segment as this computer (this is covered later in this chapter). The address was obtained on December 26 and is assigned to this computer until January 3.

If your computer is configured correctly, the next thing to look at is basic connectivity.

Using `PING`

`PING` is a tool that helps to verify connectivity at the IP level. The `PING` command sends out an ICMP echo request to the target host name or IP address. This does not always work because some servers do not respond to echo requests as a security measure. However, you will find that most workstations automatically enable it.

The first interface to check is the loopback address. The following command verifies that TCP/IP is installed correctly:

```
PING 127.0.0.1
```

If this fails, the TCP/IP drivers are corrupted, the network adapter is not working, or some other service is interfering with TCP/IP.

Next, ping the IP address of the local computer using the following command:

```
PING <ip address of local host>
```

If the routing table is correct, this is simply forwarded to the loopback address.

Next, ping the default gateway:

```
PING <ip address of gateway>
```

This command determines that the default gateway is functioning and that you can communicate with the near side of the router.

Next, ping a remote host to verify that you can access a remote network through a router:

```
PING <IP address of remote host>
```

NOTE

DNS, WINS, and Browsing Although the Windows 2000 operating system uses DNS primarily, WINS is still used to map network shares and other NetBIOS-related tasks. Browsing is still supported for the benefit of down-level clients that use this mechanism to locate other computers. In Windows 2000, one of the domain controllers assumes the role of master browser to maintain the list of computer names.

NOTE

Use an IP Address In the previous `PING` examples, the address to `PING` is always expressed as an IP address. If you use a fully qualified domain name (FQDN), you might be confusing a network connectivity problem with a DNS or namespace problem. Always begin by checking with the most basic addressing schemes first.

The `PING` command produces output similar to the following:

```
Pinging 157.55.254.208 with 32 bytes of data:
Reply from 157.55.254.208: bytes=32 time=32ms TTL=57
Reply from 157.55.254.208: bytes=32 time=33ms TTL=57
Reply from 157.55.254.208: bytes=32 time=32ms TTL=57
Reply from 157.55.254.208: bytes=32 time=31ms TTL=57
Ping statistics for 157.55.254.208:
    Packets: Sent = 4, Received = 4, Lost = 0 (0% loss),
Approximate round trip times in milli-seconds:
    Minimum = 31ms, Maximum = 33ms, Average = 32ms
```

This output shows that the computer at the IP address 157.55.254.208 can be reached and responds in just over 30ms.

`PING` uses host name resolution (via DNS, WINS, or the static name configuration files). If you can access a remote system using its IP address but not its host name, the problem is in name resolution, not network connectivity.

Using ARP

Windows 2000 TCP/IP communicates with remote computers over a network using an IP address, a NetBIOS name, or a host name. Regardless of which naming convention is used, eventually the address must be resolved to a MAC address (for shared access media such as Ethernet and token ring). ARP is used to map the physical MAC addresses on computers to the assigned IP address.

The second function ARP supports is answering requests from other machines. In this way, ARP also provides physical MAC addresses that match the assigned IP address for an adapter.

ARP maintains a cache of the known physical-to-IP address mappings. This information is not typically considered permanent because machines can be rebooted, the hardware can be upgraded, or the computer could be given different IP addresses by DHCP. The information in the ARP cache therefore expires and must be refreshed regularly.

This regular refreshing makes troubleshooting the ARP cache one of the more difficult tasks because the problems are often intermittent.

For example, if two computers are using the same IP address on a network, you might see an intermittent problem in accessing the correct one because the most recent ARP table entry is always the one from the host that responded more quickly to any ARP request.

IP addresses assigned by DHCP do not cause duplicate IP conflicts (unless of course, DHCP is configured with overlapping ranges), so most conflicts are due to static IP addresses. Examining a list of static IP addresses and their corresponding MAC addresses will help you track down the problem.

If you do not have a record of all the IP and MAC address pairs on your network, you can still get some information from the manufacturer bytes of the MAC addresses for inconsistencies. These 3-byte numbers are called *organizationally unique identifiers (OUIs)* and are assigned by the Institute of Electrical and Electronics Engineers (IEEE). The first 3 bytes of each MAC address identify the card's manufacturer. Knowing what equipment you installed and comparing that with the values returned by ARP can help you to determine which static address was entered in error.

The following is an example of the ARP `-a` command that is used to display the current cache of IP addresses and the MAC addresses associated with them:

```
ARP -a
Interface: 157.57.18.16 on Interface 0x1000003
   Internet Address      Physical Address      Type
   157.57.18.1           00-d0-ba-09-9c-d6     dynamic
   157.57.18.26          00-a0-c9-96-03-7f     dynamic
```

This output indicates that the current IP address is 157.57.18.16 and that two addresses have been recently used: 157.57.18.1 and 157.57.18.26. Check the output of the `IPCONFIG` command to see whether either or both of the addresses are part of the IP configuration (such as the default gateway), or use `TRACERT` *`<ip address>`* to resolve the name.

Determining Whether the Address Is Local

If an address is not on your subnet, your computer forwards all packets destined to that address to your default gateway. The default gateway is a router whose purpose in life is to find routes to remote addresses. Eventually, what is returned is the physical MAC address of the remote machine with the router recording the path to the address in its memory.

If the address is local to your subnet, you still need a way to find the physical MAC address of the computer to which you are trying to connect. Your machine can broadcast an ARP request (remember broadcasts are not normally forwarded by routers so it stays local to your subnet), and the remote machine replies with its physical address.

To determine whether an address is local to your subnet, your computer compares your address with your subnet mask against the remote address with your subnet mask. The network portion of the masked address must be the same for the remote address to be on your subnet. This is covered more completely in the section "Subnets and Subnet Masks," later in this chapter.

Problems at this point are usually related to an invalid ARP cache (such as a duplicate address) or an invalid subnet mask. The utilities `ARP` and `IPCONFIG` can be used to solve local address resolution problems.

Determining the Correct Gateway

If the IP address is remote from the local subnet, the gateway used to reach the remote address must be determined. If the network has a single router, this problem is straightforward. In a network with more than one router connected, however, additional steps must be taken.

> NOTE
>
> **Check Server Services** Sometimes a system configured as a remote gateway or router is not functioning as a router. To confirm that the remote computer you want to contact is set up to forward packets, you can either examine it with a remote administration tool (assuming that it is a computer you administer) or attempt to contact the person who maintains the computer.

To solve this problem, the system uses a routing table. The entries in the routing table enable IP to determine through which gateway to send outgoing traffic. The routing table has many entries for individual routes, each one consisting of a destination, network mask, gateway interface, and hop count (metric).

The Route utility can be used to diagnose problems with accessing the gateway. The Route utility is discussed in the following section.

Using Route

The Route program is a utility that is called from the command line to manipulate network routing tables. Most of the routing information your system uses is maintained automatically by Windows 2000.

However, in the event that you need to add a static route from your system to a remote network, the key to remember is to route to the network you can't see by using the nearest gateway that you can see. Because that gateway is also a router (by definition), it will be capable of accessing networks to which you have no direct access.

The structure of the command line is as follows:

```
ROUTE [-F] [-P] [COMMAND [destination] [MASK subnetmask]
                         [gateway] [METRIC costmetric]]
```

The `-F` parameter clears the routing tables of all gateway entries. If this is used in conjunction with one of the commands, the tables are cleared prior to running the command.

The `-P` parameter, when used with the `add` command, makes a route persistent across boots of the system. By default, routes are not preserved when the system is restarted. When used with the `print` command, `-P` displays the list of registered persistent routes. It is ignored for all other commands, which always affect the appropriate persistent routes.

The following defines the command-line arguments for `ROUTE`:

- `COMMAND`—Specifies one of the following commands:
    - `PRINT`—Prints a route
    - `ADD`—Adds a route
    - `DELETE`—Deletes a route
    - `CHANGE`—Modifies an existing route
- `destination`—Specifies the computer to send to.
- `MASK subnet-mask`—Specifies a subnet mask to be associated with this route entry. If it's not specified, 255.255.255.255 is used.
- `gateway`—Specifies gateway.
- `METRIC cost-metric`—Assigns an integer cost metric (ranging from 1 to 9999) to be used in calculating the fastest, most reliable, or least expensive routes.

The following is an example of the output derived from the `print` command in the Route utility.

```
===========================================================================
Interface List
0x1 ........................... MS TCP Loopback interface
0x1000003 00 80 c7 ba df 9e Xircom Ethernet 10/100 PC Card
===========================================================================
Active Routes:
    Destination      Netmask       Gateway     Interface Metric
        0.0.0.0          0.0.0.0  157.57.18.1 157.57.18.16 1
      127.0.0.0        255.0.0.0    127.0.0.1    127.0.0.1 1
    157.57.18.0  255.255.255.192 157.57.18.16 157.57.18.16 1
   157.57.18.16  255.255.255.255    127.0.0.1    127.0.0.1 1
 157.57.255.255  255.255.255.255 157.57.18.16 157.57.18.16 1
      224.0.0.0        224.0.0.0 157.57.18.16 157.57.18.16 1
255.255.255.255  255.255.255.255 157.57.18.16 157.57.18.16 1
Default Gateway:        157.57.18.1
===========================================================================
Persistent Routes:
  None
```

The IP routing table for this Windows 2000 computer contains the following routes:

- **Default route**—The route with the network destination of 0.0.0.0 and the netmask of 0.0.0.0 is the default route. Any destination IP address ANDed with 0.0.0.0 results in 0.0.0.0. Therefore, for any IP address, the default route produces a match. If the default route is chosen because no better routes are found, the IP datagram is forwarded to the IP address in the `Gateway` column using the interface corresponding to the IP address in the `Interface` column.

- **Loopback network**—The route with the network destination of 127.0.0.0 and the netmask of 255.0.0.0 is a route designed to take any IP address of the form 127.x.y.z and forward it to the special loopback address of 127.0.0.1.

- **Directly attached network**—The route with the network destination of 157.57.18.0 and the netmask of 255.255.255.192 is a route for the directly attached network. IP packets destined for the directly attached network are not forwarded to a router but are sent directly to the destination. Note that the gateway address and interface are the IP addresses of the node. This indicates that the packet is sent from the network adapter corresponding to the node's IP address.

- **Local host**—The route with the network destination of 157.57.18.16 and the netmask of 255.255.255.255 is a host route corresponding to the IP address of the host. All IP datagrams to the IP address of the host are forwarded to the loopback address.

- **All-subnets directed broadcast**—The route with the network destination of 157.57.255.255 and the netmask of 255.255.255.255 is a host route for the all-subnets directed broadcast address for the Class B network ID 157.57.0.0. The all-subnets directed broadcast address is designed to reach all subnets of class-based network ID. Packets addressed to the all-subnets directed broadcast are sent out of the network adapter corresponding to the node's IP address. A host route for the all-subnets directed broadcast is present only for network IDs that are subnets of a class-based network ID.
- **Multicast address**—The route with the network destination of 224.0.0.0 and the netmask of 240.0.0.0 is a route for all Class D multicast addresses. An IP datagram matching this route is sent from the network adapter corresponding to the node's IP address.
- **Limited broadcast**—The route with the network destination of 255.255.255.255 and the netmask of 255.255.255.255 is a host route for the limited broadcast address. Packets addressed to the limited broadcast are sent out of the network adapter corresponding to the node's IP address.

For example, when the Windows 2000 computer sends traffic to 157.57.18.60, the route determination process matches two routes: the default route and the directly attached network route. The directly attached network route is the closest matching route. Because the gateway address and interface address for the directly attached network route are the same, the forwarding IP address is set to the destination address 157.57.18.60. The interface on which to forward the IP datagram is identified by the IP address in the `Interface` column. In this case, the interface is the Xircom Ethernet 10/100 PC Card, which is assigned the IP address 157.57.18.16.

When the Windows 2000 computer sends traffic to 204.71.200.68, the route determination process matches the default route (the default route will always match with the destination IP address). Because the gateway address and the interface address for the directly attached network route are different, the forwarding IP address is set to the IP address in the `Gateway` column (157.57.18.1). The interface on which to forward the IP datagram is identified by the IP address in the `Interface` column. In this case, the interface is the Xircom Ethernet 10/100 PC Card, which is assigned the IP address 157.57.18.16.

Using TRACERT

The `TRACERT` diagnostic utility determines the route taken to a destination by sending Internet Control Message Protocol (ICMP) echo packets with varying IP time-to-live (TTL) values to the destination. Each router along the path is required to decrement the TTL on a packet by at least 1 before forwarding it. When the TTL on a packet reaches 0, the router should send an `ICMP Time Exceeded` message back to the source computer.

`TRACERT` determines the route by sending the first echo packet with a TTL of 1 and incrementing the TTL by 1 on each subsequent transmission until the target responds or the maximum TTL is reached. The route is determined by examining the `ICMP Time Exceeded` messages sent back by intermediate routers. Some routers silently drop packets with expired TTLs and are invisible to the `TRACERT` utility.

`TRACERT` can't record the path the packet takes in returning. However, it will show whether the destination was reachable. If this is not the case, the remote computer might be off the network, behind a firewall, or behind a router that filters ICMP packets.

The `TRACERT` command has the following command structure:

```
TRACERT [switches] Target-name
```

Table 4.1 lists the switches available in `TRACERT`.

TABLE 4.1

TRACERT SWITCHES

Switch	*Name*	*Description*
`-d`		Will not resolve addresses to host names
`-j`	Host-list	Specifies loose source route along the host list
`-m`	Maximum hops	Specifies the maximum hops to take to the target
`-w`	Timeout	Waits the number of milliseconds for each reply

The following is typical output of the TRACERT command:

```
Tracing route to www.yahoo.akadns.net [64.58.76.228]
over a maximum of 30 hops:

  0  gordb3.Barknet.ads [192.168.0.3]
  1  192.168.0.1
  2  24.79.156.1
  3  rc1ar-ge5-0.ed.shawcable.net [24.64.127.7]
  4  ibr01-p1-1.ekgv01.exodus.net [204.209.212.46]
  5  dcr04-g9-0.stng01.exodus.net [216.33.96.146]
  6  w7.dcx.yahoo.com [64.58.76.228]
```

Using PATHPING

The PATHPING utility traces the route that a packet takes to a destination by sending ICMP echo packets. PATHPING combines features of the PING and TRACERT commands with additional information that neither of those tools provides. The PATHPING command sends packets to each router on the way to a final destination over a period of time and then computes results based on the packets returned from each hop. Because the command shows the degree of packet loss at any given router or link, you can easily determine which routers or links might be causing network problems.

Table 4.2 shows the command-line switches that are available.

TABLE 4.2

PATHPING SWITCHES

Switch	*Name*	*Description*
-n	Hostnames	Does not resolve addresses to host names.
-h	Maximum hops	Maximum number of hops to search for target.
-g	Host-list	Loose source route along host list.
-p	Period	Number of milliseconds to wait between pings.
-q	Num-queries	Number of queries per hop.
-w	Timeout	Waits this many milliseconds for each reply.

continues

TABLE 4.2 *continued*

PATHPING SWITCHES

Switch	*Name*	*Description*
`-T`	Layer Two tag	Attaches a Layer Two priority tag (for example, for IEEE 802.1p) to the packets and sends it to each of the network devices in the path. This helps in identifying the network devices that do not have Layer Two priority configured properly. The `-T` switch is used to test for quality of service (QoS) connectivity.
`-R`	RSVP test	Checks to determine whether each router in the path supports the Resource Reservation Protocol (RSVP), which allows the host computer to reserve a certain amount of bandwidth for a data stream.

The default number of hops is 30, and the default wait time before a time-out is 3 seconds. The default period is 250 milliseconds, and the default number of queries to each router along the path is 100.

The following is typical output from a `PATHPING` command. The compiled statistics that follow the hop list indicate packet loss at each individual router:

```
Tracing route to www.yahoo.akadns.net [64.58.76.228]
over a maximum of 30 hops:

  0  gordb3.Barknet.ads [192.168.0.3]
  1  192.168.0.1
  2  24.79.156.1
  3  rc1ar-ge5-0.ed.shawcable.net [24.64.127.7]
  4  ibr01-p1-1.ekgv01.exodus.net [204.209.212.46]
  5  dcr04-g9-0.stng01.exodus.net [216.33.96.146]
  6  w7.dcx.yahoo.com [64.58.76.228]


Computing statistics for 425 seconds...
            Source to Here   This Node/Link
Hop  RTT    Lost/Sent = Pct  Lost/Sent = Pct  Address
  0                                 gordb3 [192.168.0.3]
                               14/ 100 = 14%   |
  1    2ms     15/ 100 = 15%   1/ 100 =  1%  192.168.0.1
                                0/ 100 =  0%   |
  2  109ms     16/ 100 = 16%   2/ 100 =  2%  24.79.156.1
                                0/ 100 =  0%   |
  3   81ms     14/ 100 = 14%   0/ 100 =  0%  [24.64.127.7]
                                0/ 100 =  0%   |
```

```
  4  143ms    15/ 100 = 15%  0/ 100 =  0%  [204.209.212.46]
                             0/ 100 =  0%   |
  5  185ms    16/ 100 = 16%  0/ 100 =  0%  [216.33.96.146]
                             0/ 100 =  0%   |
  6  195ms    16/ 100 = 16%  0/ 100 =  0%  [64.58.76.228]

Trace complete.
```

This output shows the path a packet will take from the source to the remote machine, as well as the packet loss statistics. In this example, the first hop (0) lost 14% of the packets it sent to the default gateway, which also lost an additional 1% of the packets. The third hop (2) lost an additional 2% of the packets. The rest of the route did not lose any additional packets.

When a packet is lost, it must be re-sent. The extra traffic on your network could cause some delays. In any event, the network adapter, the source machine, and the default gateway should be examined for problems.

Using NETDIAG

`NETDIAG` is a network diagnostic tool to help you in assessing the state of your computer system. It performs a series of tests and provides status information indicating whether the network client is functional.

`NETDIAG` is normally used without any switches to provide the maximum information on all communication systems.

The following is an example of the `NETDIAG` report:

```
C:\NETDIAG

....................................

  Computer Name: W2K3
  DNS Host Name: w2k3
  System info : Windows 2000 Server (Build 2195)
  Processor : x86 Family 5 Model 6 Stepping 2, AuthenticAMD
  List of installed hotfixes :
      Q147222
      Q252795
      Q276471
      Q285156
      Q285851
      Q292435
      Q299553
      Q299796
```

```
        Q301625
        Q302755

Netcard queries test . . . . . . . : Passed

Per interface results:
    Adapter : Barknet
        Netcard queries test . . . : Passed
        Host Name. . . . . . . . . : w2k3.Barknet.ads
        IP Address . . . . . . . . : 192.168.0.40
        Subnet Mask. . . . . . . . : 255.255.255.0
        Default Gateway. . . . . . : 192.168.0.1
        Dns Servers. . . . . . . . : 192.168.0.1

        AutoConfiguration results. . . . . . : Passed
        Default gateway test . . . : Passed
        NetBT name test. . . . . . : Passed
        WINS service test. . . . . : Skipped

There are no WINS servers configured for this interface.
Global results:

Domain membership test . . . . . . : Passed
NetBT transports test. . . . . . . : Passed
    List of NetBt transports currently configured:
        NetBT_Tcpip_{F0D7C573-13AB-4E0D-BC06-89189460CFDD}
    1 NetBt transport currently configured.
Autonet address test . . . . . . . : Passed
IP loopback ping test. . . . . . . : Passed
Default gateway test . . . . . . . : Passed
NetBT name test. . . . . . . . . . : Passed
Winsock test . . . . . . . . . . . : Passed
DNS test . . . . . . . . . . . . . : Passed
Redir and Browser test . . . . . . : Passed
    List of NetBt transports currently bound to the Redir
        NetBT_Tcpip_{F0D7C573-13AB-4E0D-BC06-89189460CFDD}
    The redir is bound to 1 NetBt transport.
    List of NetBt transports currently bound to the browser
        NetBT_Tcpip_{F0D7C573-13AB-4E0D-BC06-89189460CFDD}
    The browser is bound to 1 NetBt transport.
DC discovery test. . . . . . . . . : Passed
DC list test . . . . . . . . . . . : Passed
Trust relationship test. . . . . . : Passed
    Secure channel for domain 'BARKNET' is to
                                   '\\w2k1.barknet.ads'.
Kerberos test. . . . . . . . . . . : Failed
        [FATAL] Kerberos does not have a ticket for W2K3$.
LDAP test. . . . . . . . . . . . . : Failed
    [WARNING] The default SPN registration for
       'HOST/w2k3' is missing on DC 'w2k1.barknet.ads'.
    [WARNING] The default SPN registration for
       'HOST/W2K3' is missing on DC 'w2k1.barknet.ads'.
    [FATAL] The default SPNs are not properly
                                  registered on any DCs.
Bindings test. . . . . . . . . . . : Passed
WAN configuration test . . . . . . : Skipped
```

```
    No active remote access connections.
Modem diagnostics test . . . . . . . : Passed
IP Security test . . . . . . . . . . : Passed
 IPSec policy service is active, but no policy is assigned.

The command completed successfully
```

Using NETSTAT

NETSTAT is a command-line utility that displays the active TCP connections, ports listened to, routing table, and IP statistics. Without any switches, NETSTAT displays only the current TCP connections.

The NETSTAT command is in the following form:

```
NETSTAT [switches] Interval
```

Table 4.3 describes the switches available in NETSTAT.

TABLE 4.3

NETSTAT SWITCHES

Switch	*Name*	*Function*
-a	Active	Displays all the active TCP connections and the ports the computer is listening on
-e	Ethernet	Displays the Ethernet statistics (bytes/packets sent and received)
-n		Displays the active TCP connections but without attempting name resolution
-o		Displays the process PID for each active TCP connection
-p protocol	Protocol	Shows connection for the protocol specified
-s		Displays the contents of the routing table

The *Interval* argument causes NETSTAT to redisplay the statistics every "interval" seconds. A single Ctrl+C halts the process.

The following is an example of the Ethernet statistics that NETSTAT provides:

```
NETSTAT -e
Interface Statistics
```

```
                                    Received            Sent

Bytes                               17890409         2234177
Unicast packets                        20305           15604
Non-unicast packets                      751             227
Discards                                   0               0
Errors                                     0              10
Unknown protocols                          0
```

This output shows the amount of data sent and received, the number of broadcasts (non-unicast)packets received, and the number of errors encountered.

Using NSLOOKUP

As you learned earlier in the chapter, the process for two computers to communicate using TCP/IP involves four distinct steps:

- Resolve the host name or NetBIOS name to an IP address.
- Use the IP address and the routing table to determine the interface to use and the forwarding IP address.
- Use ARP to resolve the forwarding IP address to a MAC address.
- Use the MAC address as the destination address for the IP datagram.

If the computer to be reached is a host name or a NetBIOS name, the name must be resolved to an IP address before any data can be sent. Host names and NetBIOS names are resolved in different ways. Each of these is discussed in the following sections.

Resolving a Host or Domain Name to an IP Address

Host names are resolved by using the `HOSTS` file or by querying a DNS server. Problems in the `HOSTS` file usually involve spelling errors and duplicate entries.

The NSLOOKUP utility or the NETDIAG resource kit utility can be used to diagnose host name resolution problems.

`NSLOOKUP.exe` is a command-line administrative tool for testing and troubleshooting DNS servers, and it can be run in both interactive and noninteractive modes. Noninteractive mode is useful when only a single piece of data needs to be returned. The syntax for noninteractive mode is as follows:

```
NSLOOKUP [-option] [hostname] [server]
```

To start `NSLOOKUP.exe` in interactive mode, simply type **`NSLOOKUP`** at the command prompt:

```
C:\> NSLOOKUP
Default Server:  nameserver1.domain.com
Address:  10.0.0.1
>
```

Typing **`help`** or **`?`** at the command prompt generates a list of available commands. Anything typed at the command prompt that is not recognized as a valid command is assumed to be a host name, and an attempt is made to resolve it using the default server. To interrupt interactive commands, press Ctrl+C. To exit interactive mode and return to the command prompt, type **`exit`** at the command prompt.

What follows is the help output. It contains the complete list of options; the general syntax is given first:

```
Commands (identifiers are shown in uppercase,
                           [] means optional):
NAME            - print info about the host/domain NAME
                  using default server
NAME1 NAME2     - as above, but use NAME2 as server
help or ?       - print info on common commands
set OPTION      - set an option
    all                 - print options, current server
                          and host
    [no]debug           - print debugging information
    [no]d2              - print exhaustive debugging
                          information
    [no]defname         - append domain name to each query
    [no]recurse         - ask for recursive answer to query
    [no]search          - use domain search list
    [no]vc              - always use a virtual circuit
    domain=NAME         - set default domain name to NAME
    srchlist=N1[/N2/.../N6] - set domain to N1 and search
                              list to N1,N2, etc.
    root=NAME           - set root server to NAME
    retry=X             - set number of retries to X
    timeout=X           - set initial time-out interval
                          to X seconds
    type=X              - set query type
                        (ex. A,ANY,CNAME,MX,NS,PTR,SOA,SRV)
    querytype=X         - same as type
    class=X             - set query class
                        (ex. IN (Internet), ANY)
    [no]msxfr           - use MS fast zone transfer
```

```
    ixfrver=X           - current version to use in
                          IXFR transfer request
server NAME       - set default server to NAME, using current
                    default server
lserver NAME      - set default server to NAME, using initial
                    server
finger [USER]     - finger the optional NAME at the current
                    default host
root              - set current default server to the root
ls [opt] DOMAIN [> FILE] - list addresses in DOMAIN
                    (optional: output to FILE)
    -a            -  list canonical names and aliases
    -d            -  list all records
    -t TYPE       -  list records of the given type
                    (e.g. A,CNAME,MX,NS,PTR etc.)
view FILE         - sort an 'ls' output file and view
                    it with pg
exit              - exit the program
```

Configuring and Troubleshooting TCP/IP on Servers and Client Computers

- Configure and troubleshoot TCP/IP on servers and client computers. Considerations include subnet masks, default gateways, network IDs, and broadcast addresses.

Windows 2000 uses TCP/IP as its default networking protocol. This is the common means of internetworking computer systems together, both locally in LANs and worldwide through the Internet. In your own organization, TCP/IP is probably used to connect computers running different Windows operating systems.

Configuring the TCP/IP Protocol

TCP/IP is the default protocol for Windows 2000 and is supported by most common operating systems. TCP/IP is a suite of protocols used to provide connectivity within a LAN in addition to providing connectivity to the Internet. When you manually configure a computer with a TCP/IP network adapter, you must enter the appropriate settings for connectivity with your network. The TCP/IP settings you must understand include IP addresses, subnetting, and subnet masks.

IP Addressing

Before delving into IP addressing schemes, it is appropriate to review binary-to-decimal conversions. IP addresses are 32-bit integers that are usually depicted as four 8-bit numbers. This can be thought of as a series of 1s or 0s, with eight taken together to be a number. Each position in the 8 bits (from right to left) is twice the value of the field before it (in decimal notation, the same rule would state that each column is worth 10 times the value of the previous column—100s versus 10s versus 1s). The smallest integer number that can be represented with 8 bits then is 0 0 0 0 0 0 0 0 (2^0–1), or 0. The largest integer that can be represented by 8 bits is 1 1 1 1 1 1 1 1 (2^8–1), or 255. Because of this, you will always see IP addresses as four numbers ranging from 0 to 255.

Each TCP/IP connection must be identified by an address. The address is a 32-bit number that is used to uniquely identify a host on a network. The TCP/IP address has no dependence on the Data-Link layer address such as the MAC address of a network adapter.

Network addresses and subnet masks are used to identify network IDs and host addresses. To do that, you must interpret the number in binary form. The next section discusses breaking down IP addresses and subnet masks into their individual components.

Binary-to-Decimal Translation

Although the IP address is 32 bits, it is customary to break it into four 8-bit numbers expressed in decimal and separated by dots. This can be referred to in dotted decimal format and is expressed as *w.x.y.z.* The value to breaking down this address into four 8-bit values can be seen in the following example. Suppose you have an address that is 192.168.8.4.

You would have to remember that, as a binary 32-bit number, it would be 11000000101010000000100000000100 or, converted to a decimal number, would be the sum of $2^{32}+2^{31}+2^{24}+2^{22}+2^{20}+2^{12}+2^{3}$. This calculation is shown in Table 4.4.

TABLE 4.4

CALCULATING DECIMAL FROM A BINARY ADDRESS

Bit Number	*Decimal Equivalent*
2^3	8
2^{12}	4,096
2^{20}	1,048,576
2^{22}	4,194,304
2^{24}	16,777,216
2^{31}	2,147,483,648
2^{32}	4,294,967,296
Totals	6,464,475,144

192.168.8.4 is definitely easier to remember.

This addressing scheme is again broken down into two segments: a network ID (also known as the network address) and the host ID (also known as the host address). The network ID must be unique in the Internet or intranet, and the host ID must be unique to the network ID. The network portion of the w.x.y.z notation is separated from the host through the use of the subnet mask. See the section titled "Subnets and Subnet Masks," later in this chapter.

Decimal-to-Binary Translation

You can convert a dotted decimal address to its binary representation using a very simple technique. The decimal value is reduced by the highest binary number not exceeding the decimal value. The total of the binary numbers equals the binary equivalent to the decimal value. Fortunately, because IP addresses are broken down into four 8-bit numbers, this is a simple task. Table 4.5 shows the decimal equivalents to the binary values. The following is an example of converting a decimal number to its binary equivalent.

TABLE 4.5

DECIMAL-TO-BINARY CONVERSION

Binary Value	*Decimal Value*
2^0	1
2^1	2
2^2	4
2^3	8
2^4	16
2^5	32
2^6	64
2^7	128

To convert a number like 197 to binary, you would perform the following calculations:

- Find the largest binary number not exceeding 197. That is 2^7, or 128.
- Subtract 128 from 197, giving a remainder of 69.
- Find the largest binary number not exceeding 69. That is 2^6, or 64.
- Subtract 64 from 69, giving a remainder of 5.
- Find the largest binary number not exceeding 5. That is 2^2, or 4.
- Subtract 4 from 5, giving 1.
- Find the largest binary number not exceeding 1. That is 2^0, or 1.

The total of our calculation is $2^7 + 2^6 + 2^2 + 2^0$, or 11000101. This is the binary representation of 197.

Now that you can convert binary to decimal and back again, you can use this to help you understand the role subnets and subnet masks play in configuring TCP/IP.

Subnets and Subnet Masks

If we assume that an IP address identifies your computer, it's fair to say that a subnet identifies where your computer is in the network. The component of an IP address that determines whether packets are to be sent locally or through a router is the network ID, which is distinguished from the host ID by using the subnet mask. The network ID tells the protocol whether the local host and the destination host are on the same subnet.

Basically, when the network ID bits match, the source host and destination host are on the same subnet and no routing is necessary. When the network ID bits don't match, the destination host is on a remote network and the packets are sent to the router.

A subnet mask (also known as an *address* mask) is defined as a 32-bit value that is used to distinguish the network ID from the host ID in an IP address. The bits of the subnet mask are defined as follows:

- All bits that correspond to the network ID are set to 1.
- All bits that correspond to the host ID are set to 0.

NOTE

Hosts Need Subnet Masks Each host on a TCP/IP network requires a subnet mask even if it is on a single-segment network. Although the subnet mask is expressed in dotted decimal notation, a subnet mask is not an IP address.

The subnet mask is broken down into four 8-bit octets in the same fashion as the class addresses.

Table 4.6 lists the default subnet masks using dotted decimal notation. The Internet community was originally divided into five address classes. Microsoft TCP/IP supports classes A, B, and C of addresses assigned to hosts as well as classless networks.

TABLE 4.6

DEFAULT SUBNET MASKS

Class	*Bits for Default Subnet Mask*	*Subnet Mask*
A	11111111 00000000 00000000 00000000	255.0.0.0
B	11111111 11111111 00000000 00000000	255.255.0.0
C	11111111 11111111 11111111 00000000	255.255.255.0

Network ID and Broadcast Addresses

Two special addresses are used in TCP/IP networks. The first is the network ID. As mentioned previously, the network ID is used to identify systems on the same network segment. Systems that have the same network ID can communicate without using routing. The network ID address can be thought of as a network address in which the host part is all 0s.

The second address is the broadcast address. This special address is used when you want to send a message to every system on the subnet. Network adapters are designed to accept only their own packets plus any broadcast packets.

The broadcast address is useful in finding a service for which you don't know the address. For example, during the boot procedure in Windows 2000, there comes a point when the computer needs its IP address(es). If this is managed through DHCP, the computer must access the DHCP server and request its configuration package. It would just be blind luck if the DHCP server was actually on the same subnet as your computer—more likely it is somewhere else on the network. Your computer then sends out a broadcast packet with a DHCP request in it.

Normally, routers do not pass broadcast messages (I'll leave it up to the reader to imagine what would happen if broadcasts were propagated through a large network), but DHCP requests are recognized as a special case and routers have a configuration option called BOOTP Forwarding that must be enabled to allow DHCP to function. The DHCP request gets sent from router to router until the DHCP server is found. It responds to your broadcast request with your IP addressing information, and your boot process can continue.

Subnet Class Addresses

The class of address defines which bits are used for the network ID and which bits are used for the host ID. It also defines the possible number of networks and the number of hosts per network. Here is a rundown of the five classes:

- **Class A**—The high-order bit is always binary 0, and the next seven bits complete the network ID. The next three octets define the host ID. This represents 126 networks with 16,777,214 hosts per network.
- **Class B**—The top two bits in a Class B address are always set to binary 1 0. The next 14 bits complete the network ID, and the remaining two octets define the host ID. This represents 16,384 networks with 65,534 hosts per network.
- **Class C**—The top three bits in a Class C address are always set to binary 1 1 0. The next 21 bits define the network ID, and the remaining octet defines the host ID. This represents 2,097,152 networks with 254 hosts per network.
- **Class D**—Class D addresses are used for multicasting to a number of hosts. Packets are passed to a selected subset of hosts on a network. Only those hosts registered for the multicast address accept the packet. The four high-order bits in a Class D address are always set to binary 1 1 1 0. The remaining bits are for the address that interested hosts will recognize.
- **Class E**—Class E is an experimental address that is reserved for future use. The high-order bits in a Class E address are set to 1 1 1 1.

Table 4.7 indicates how the three classes supported by Microsoft TCP/IP divide up network IDs and host IDs.

TABLE 4.7

CLASS ADDRESS RANGES

Class	*Network ID*	*Network Portion*	*Host Portion*	*Number of Networks*	*Number of Hosts*
A	1–126	w.	x.y.z	126	16,777,214
B	128–191	w.x	y.z	16,384	65,534
C	192–223	w.x.y	z	2,097,152	254

After an IP address from a particular class has been decided upon, you can divide it into smaller segments to better utilize the addresses available. Each segment is bounded by an IP router and assigned a new subnetted network ID that is a subset of the original class-based network ID.

EXAM TIP

Assumed Knowledge The exam will not ask you specific questions about network IDs and subnet masks; however, you will be expected to use this knowledge to understand situations presented and recommend solutions to problems.

Variable Length Subnet Masks

When you're working with TCP/IP, one of the most difficult topics to understand is the concept of variable length subnet masks. As the use of TCP/IP has grown more widespread, it has become obvious that sometimes assigning even a full Class C address with 254 available hosts is a waste of address space—in a branch office with five employees, a file server, and a printer, for example. An IP address range must be broken into smaller pieces to allow for more efficient use of the address space. Variable length subnet masks (also known as *subnet addressing*) is the method for "borrowing" bits from the host ID portion of an IP address and applying them to the network ID. You need to borrow enough bits from the host ID portion to allow you to make the number of additional subnets that you require (refer to Table 4.5 for the binary-to-decimal conversions). In this case, you need to choose a binary number larger than the number of the subnet to be created. If you wanted to create four additional subnets, you would need 2^3, or 3, bits to create up to eight subnets.

Suppose that you have been assigned the Class B address 172.18.0.0. You need to create four separate networks from your one IP address range. The technique is to borrow three bits from the host ID field. These three bits let you configure six separate subnets. If you do the math, it should be eight subnets, as discussed later in this chapter.

To see how subnet addressing works, let's first convert the IP address 172.18.0.0 to binary form:

```
10101100 00010010 00000000 00000000
```

Remember, in a Class B address, the first 16 bits are the network ID and the last 16 bits are the host ID.

To indicate that bits are being borrowed from the host ID, you use a subnet mask, which is also a 32-bit binary number. To make the purpose of the subnet mask clear, you need to examine it beside the binary IP address, like this:

```
10101100 00010010 00000000 00000000
11111111 11111111 11100000 00000000
```

In dotted decimal, this is 255.255.224.0 for the subnet mask. The rules of subnet masking are simple:

- A 1 in the network mask indicates that a bit in the IP address is part of the network ID.
- 0 in the network mask indicates that a bit in the IP address is part of the host ID.

This example has 19 bits in the network mask, so within the network ID are 19 bits for addressing. This subnet mask allows the following subnetworks (subnet IDs) to be used within the Class B address range:

```
10101100 00010010 00100000 00000000
10101100 00010010 01000000 00000000
10101100 00010010 01100000 00000000
10101100 00010010 10000000 00000000
10101100 00010010 10100000 00000000
10101100 00010010 11000000 00000000
```

Why only six subnets? You have to avoid two "forbidden" subnets (000 and 111), which are not available because of TCP/IP conventions. A subnet ID can't consist entirely of 1s because all-1s addresses are used to address broadcast messages. Notice that the last range of addresses includes 255 in the network range and is not addressable.

A second restriction is that the subnet ID should not be entirely made up of 0s. This is less clear because there are no addressing restrictions regarding the use of decimal 0 in a network ID. Windows 2000 will allow you to use the 0 network, although by convention, it should be excluded.

If you do the math to convert the binary addresses to decimals, you find that the subnet mask 255.255.224.0 lets you construct six valid subnets and two "illegal" subnets, with the following address ranges:

- 172.18.0.1–172.18.31.254
- 172.18.32.1–172.18.63.254
- 172.18.64.1–172.18.95.254

- 172.18.96.1–172.18.127.254
- 172.18.128.1–172.18.159.254
- 172.18.160.1–172.18.191.254
- 172.18.192.1–172.18.223.254
- 172.18.224.1–172.18.255.254

The subnet mask actually becomes part of the configuration of each host on the network, enabling the hosts to discriminate network ID, subnet ID, and host ID.

Supernetting and Classless Interdomain Routing

The rapid growth of the Internet has created problems in assigning IP addresses. It became clear that the number of Class B addresses would soon be totally allocated. For many organizations, a Class C network does not contain enough host IDs and a Class B address does not have enough bits to provide a flexible subnetting scheme.

A new schema of assigning network IDs, called *supernetting,* was developed. Rather than assigning a Class B network ID to an organization, several Class Cs are assigned as a block. For example, if an organization needed about 2,000 hosts IDs, a block of 8 Class C addresses would be allocated (providing address space for 2,032 host IDs).

This technique creates a new problem for routers, though. Using conventional techniques, routers should have to have 8 Class C network ID entries in their routing tables to accommodate the previous supernetted example. To prevent the Internet routers from becoming overwhelmed by these new routes, a new technique called *classless interdomain routing (CIDR)* is used to collapse multiple network entries into a single entry corresponding to all the Class C network IDs allocated to that organization.

CIDR creates a single routing entry with the starting Class C address and the number of Class Cs allocated in the block.

NOTE

Network Address Syntax A shorthand method of describing a network address and subnet mask is often used in routers. Microsoft uses this syntax in its exams, so you should understand it. The first part of the network address is the network ID (all the host bits are 0), and number following the slash is the number of bits for the subnet mask. So, 10.0.0.0/8 is the network ID of 10.0.0.0 with a subnet mask of 255.0.0.0.

Private Networks

For private TCP/IP networks that are not directly or indirectly connected to the Internet, you can use any range of valid IP addresses from Class A, B, or C.

For private TCP/IP networks connected to the Internet by a network address translation service (NAT) or by proxy, three private IP address ranges are reserved for your use:

- **10.0.0.0/8**—The 10.0.0.0/8 private network is a Class A network ID that allows the following range of valid IP addresses: 10.0.0.1–10.255.255.254. The 10.0.0.0/8 private network has 24 host bits that can be used for any subnetting scheme within the private organization.
- **172.16.0.0/12**—The 172.16.0.0/12 private network can be interpreted either as a block of 16 Class B network IDs or as a 20-bit assignable address space (20 host bits) that can be used for any subnetting scheme within the private organization. The 172.16.0.0/12 private network allows the following range of valid IP addresses: 172.16.0.1–172.31.255.254.
- **192.168.0.0/16**—The 192.168.0.0/16 private network can be interpreted either as a block of 256 Class C network IDs or as a 16-bit assignable address space (16 host bits) that can be used for any subnetting scheme within the private organization. The 192.168.0.0/16 private network allows the following range of valid IP addresses: 192.168.0.1–192.168.255.254.

Table 4.8 shows the ranges of the private addresses available.

TABLE 4.8

PRIVATE NETWORK ADDRESS RANGES

Private Network ID	*Subnet Mask*	*Range of IP Addresses*
10.0.0.0	255.0.0.0	10.0.0.1–10.255.255.254
172.16.0.0	255.240.0.0	172.16.0.1–172.31.255.254
192.168.0.0	255.255.0.0	192.168.0.1–192.168.255.254

Addresses in these ranges are not used on the Internet and will not be passed by routers.

> **NOTE**
>
> **Limit Your Internet Connections**
> Usually, for security reasons, you should not connect more than a few TCP/IP systems within your network directly to the Internet. For any host systems on your network that connect to the Internet, you must obtain the use of registered IP addresses from your Internet service provider (ISP).

Default Gateway (Router) Address

The default gateway address setting is the IP address of the router for this subnet segment. Each subnet segment is bounded by a router that directs packets destined for segments outside the local one to the correct segment or to another router that can complete the connection. Routers, therefore, have connections to more than one network segment, and this address points to the router's network adapter on the same segment as your computer. If this address is left blank, this computer will be capable of communicating only with other computers on the same network segment.

Figure 4.2 shows a hypothetical network that is using a subnet mask of 255.255.224.0. This provides for a maximum of six subnets of 8,190 hosts each; however, in this example, only three connections are being shown. The hosts on the subnet 192.168.32.0 would each have the default gateway address set to the address of the router port connecting that subnet: 192.168.32.1. The IP address of each router connection is local to the subnet it serves, allowing the hosts on that subnet to communicate with it directly.

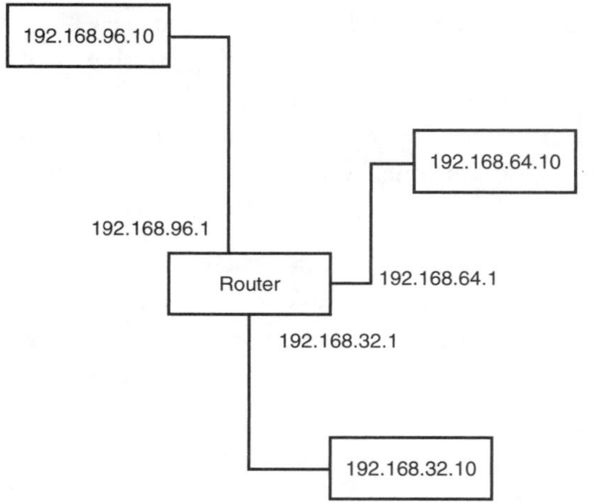

FIGURE 4.2
Default gateways on a subnetted network.

TROUBLESHOOTING TCP/IP CONNECTIONS

Several network troubleshooting tools are available for TCP/IP and the Windows 2000 platform. Some of these are included in the Windows 2000 release, and some are part of the resource kits; a network monitor is available in the Microsoft product System Management Server (SMS). However, the best approach for troubleshooting network connections is to work from the bottom up, eliminating configuration issues first before checking basic connectivity and then advancing to higher functions and services.

Checking Configuration Errors with `IPCONFIG`

Earlier in this chapter, we looked at `IPCONFIG` as a way of checking the configuration of your computer. `IPCONFIG` can also help you identify problems in your configuration and network connectivity.

Typical problems found in the configuration are duplicate IP addresses with other computers on the network or a subnet mask of 0.0.0.0.

If your local address is returned as 169.254.y.z, you have been assigned an IP address by the Automatic Private IP Addressing (APIPA) feature of Windows 2000. This means that the local DHCP server is not configured properly, can't be reached from your computer, or did not respond in time. Windows 2000 assigned an IP address automatically with a subnet mask of 255.255.0.0.

If your local address is returned as 0.0.0.0, the Microsoft MediaSense software detects that the network adapter is not connected to a network. If the connection is solid and the problem persists, you might have to update the network adapter drivers to the latest revision.

Checking Connectivity

If your computer system is configured properly and you can't establish a connection with a remote computer on your network, a number of utilities can be used to investigate the problem.

Several diagnostic utilities are included with Windows 2000 Professional. Table 4.9 shows some utilities that are useful in identifying and resolving TCP/IP networking problems. Some of these tools were discussed earlier in this chapter. They are listed here for completeness.

You should note, however, that some sites block ICMP (ping) requests and have firewalls that restrict access to specific ports, which can reduce the effectiveness of these tools.

TABLE 4.9

TCP/IP DIAGNOSTIC UTILITIES

Utility	*Function*
ARP	Views the ARP cache on the interface of the local computer to detect invalid entries
HOSTNAME	Displays the host name of the computer
IPCONFIG	Displays current TCP/IP network configuration values; updates or releases DHCP allocated leases; and displays, registers, or flushes DNS names
NBTSTAT	Checks the state of current NetBIOS over TCP/IP connections, updates the NetBIOS name cache, and determines the registered names and scope ID
NETSTAT	Displays statistics for current TCP/IP connections
NETDIAG	Checks all aspects of the network connection
NSLOOKUP	Checks records, domain host aliases, domain host services, and operating system information by querying Internet domain name servers
PATHPING	Traces a path to a remote system and reports packet losses at each router along the way
PING	Sends ICMP echo requests to verify that TCP/IP is configured correctly and that a remote TCP/IP system is available
ROUTE	Displays the IP routing table and adds or deletes IP routes
TRACERT	Traces a path to a remote system

When checking the connectivity to servers, you should also verify that a server has a static IP address and not a dynamic one assigned by DHCP. If a server is given a dynamic IP address by DHCP, it can suddenly seem to disappear if the address is changed but the information cached on your computer has not been updated. For this reason, a number of servers are usually configured with static IP address. These include Web servers, mail servers, file servers, printers, and domain controllers.

Working with TCP/IP Packet Filtering

Windows 2000 enables you to control the type of TCP/IP information that is sent to your computer. You can configure a universal rule for the type of data that reaches all network cards in your server, or you can configure each card individually.

TCP provides guaranteed packet delivery. Table 4.10 lists the common TCP ports to which you can allow or deny access.

TABLE 4.10

COMMON TCP PORT NUMBERS

TCP Port Number	*Description*
20	FTP server data channel
21	FTP server control channel
23	Telnet
80	Web server—specifically HTTP
139	NetBIOS session service

UDP does not provide guaranteed packet delivery; rather, it makes a best-effort attempt for delivery. Table 4.11 lists common UDP ports to which you can allow or deny access.

TABLE 4.11

COMMON UDP PORT NUMBERS

UDP Port Number	*Description*
69	Trivial File Transfer Protocol (TFTP)
137	NetBIOS Name Server (NBNS)
161	SNMP
520	Routing Information Protocol (RIP)

A complete list of the well-known port numbers and their meanings can be found at `http://www.iana.org/assignments/port-numbers\`.

IP is composed of different protocols. Table 4.12 lists common IP protocol numbers to which you can allow or deny access.

TABLE 4.12

COMMON IP PROTOCOL NUMBERS

Protocol Number	*Protocol*
1	Internet Control Message Protocol (ICMP)
2	Internet Group Management Protocol (IGMP)
3	Gateway-to-Gateway Protocol (GGP)
4	IP in IP (encapsulation)
5	ST stream
6	Transmission Control Protocol (TCP)
7	CBT
8	Exterior Gateway Protocol (EGP)

TCP/IP packet filtering enables you to determine the type of TCP ports that can be accessed, the UDP ports that are accessed, and (more directly) which IP protocols can access this computer. For example, you can filter port 80, which is used by the HTTP protocol. By filtering this port, you deny access to all Web servers.

To create a TCP/IP packet filter, assign the appropriate port or IP protocol number in the advanced properties of TCP/IP. Step By Step 4.1 guides you through the process of creating an IP packet filter.

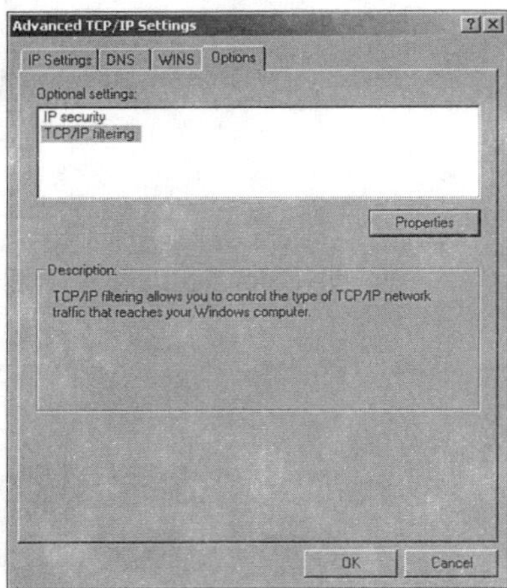

FIGURE 4.3
Further configuration options for TCP/IP.

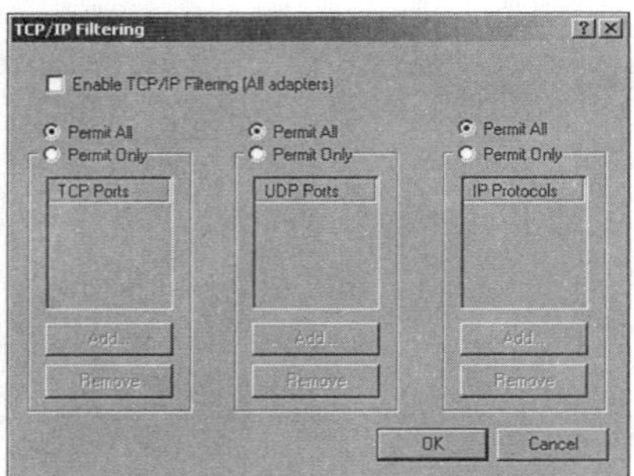

FIGURE 4.4
TCP/IP filtering can be set on all adapter cards or on one card at a time.

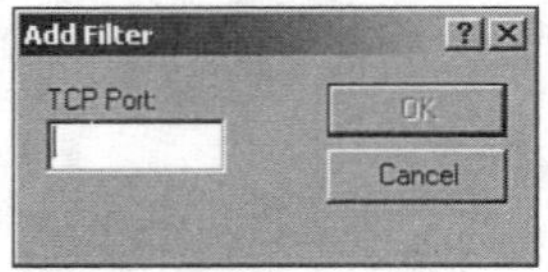

FIGURE 4.5
Enter the TCP/IP port number to which you want to permit access.

STEP BY STEP

4.1 Establishing IP Filtering

1. Open Control Panel, and then open the Network and Dial-up Connections dialog box.
2. Right-click the connection you want to configure, and then select Properties. The Local Area Connection Status dialog box opens. Click the Properties button to open the connection properties.
3. From the General tab, select Internet Protocol, and then click Properties.
4. From this General tab of IP Properties, click the Advanced button. The Advanced TCP/IP Settings dialog box pops up, which is shown in Figure 4.3.
5. In the Advanced TCP/IP Settings, click the Options tab, select TCP/IP Filtering, and then click Properties. The TCP/IP Filtering window pops up, which is shown in Figure 4.4.
6. Make sure that the Enable TCP/IP Filtering (All Adapters) option is unchecked for now.
7. Above TCP Ports, select the Permit Only option and then click the Add button. The Add Filter dialog box shown in Figure 4.5 pops up.
8. Specify Port Number 23 for Telnet sessions, and then click OK.
9. Click Add again and enter `Port Number 80` for Web Access; then click OK.
10. Select the Permit Only option for UDP Ports, and then click the Add button.
11. Enter `Port Number 69` for TFTP sessions, and then click OK.
12. Click Add again and enter `Port Number 161` for SNMP; then click OK.

13. Click OK to approve these settings. These settings allow only TCP ports 23 and 80 and UDP ports 69 and 161 to be accessed on the server.

Configuring TCP/IP on Client Computers

TCP/IP has gone from being one of many protocols in use to the dominant internetworking protocol in the last seven years. The methods for configuring Windows clients during this time have changed greatly. This section examines how to configure TCP/IP on the many Windows clients that you might have in your organization.

> NOTE
>
> **Additional Protocols and Services** When you are configuring TCP/IP on your Windows 2000 Professional or Windows 2000 Server computer, you should install only those services and protocols that are required. Adding additional protocols does nothing to increase the performance of your computer and requires additional resources to manage. Plus, adding services such as DCHP can cause problems on your network if duplicate addresses are accidentally leased to clients.

Windows 95

Step By Step 4.2 can be used to install and configure TCP/IP on Windows 95 computers.

STEP BY STEP

4.2 Configuring TCP/IP on Windows 95

1. Click Start, select Settings, and click Control Panel.
2. Double-click the Network icon.
3. If TCP/IP is not installed on your computer, click Add, select Protocol in the Select Network Component Type window, and click Add. Select Microsoft as the manufacturer and TCP/IP as the network protocol. Click OK to start the install.
4. Select TCP/IP, and click the Properties button.
5. Select the IP Address tab and complete the configuration. See Figure 4.6 for an example of this configuration.

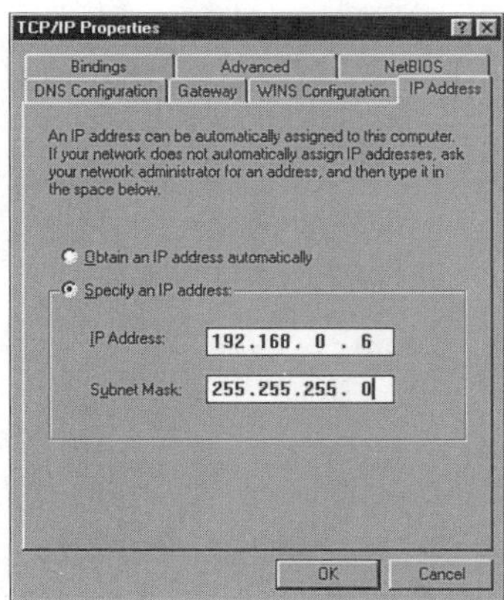

FIGURE 4.6
Configuring IP addresses.

continues

continued

6. Select the Gateway tab and complete the configuration. See Figure 4.7 for an example of this configuration.

7. Select the DNS Configuration tab and complete the configuration. See Figure 4.8 for an example of this configuration.

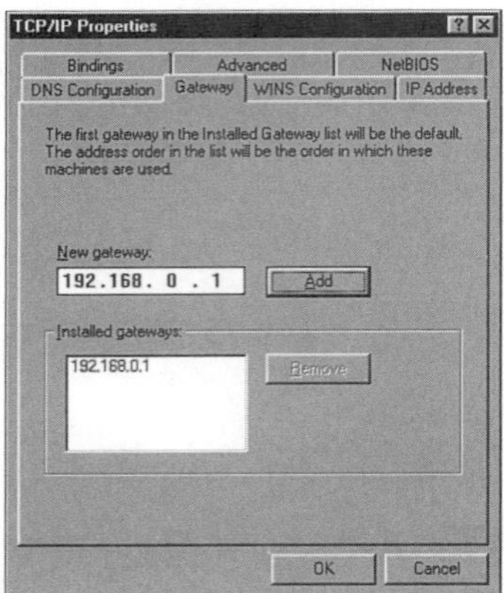

FIGURE 4.7
Configuring the TCP/IP gateway.

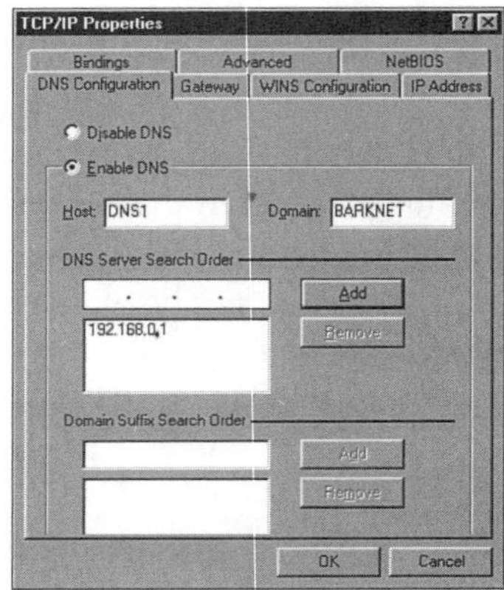

FIGURE 4.8
Configuring the DNS information.

8. Click OK to complete the configuration.

Windows 98/Windows Me

Step By Step 4.3 can be used to install and configure TCP/IP on Windows 98 or Windows Me computers.

STEP BY STEP

4.3 Configuring TCP/IP on Windows 98 or Windows Me

1. Click Start, select Settings, and click Control Panel.

2. Double-click the Network icon.

3. If TCP/IP is not installed on your computer, click Add, select Protocol in the Select Network Component Type window, and click Add. Select Microsoft as the manufacturer and TCP/IP as the network protocol. Click OK to start the install.
4. Select TCP/IP, and click the Properties button.
5. Select the IP Address tab and complete the configuration. See Figure 4.9 for an example of this configuration.
6. Select the Gateway tab and complete the configuration. See Figure 4.10 for an example of this configuration.

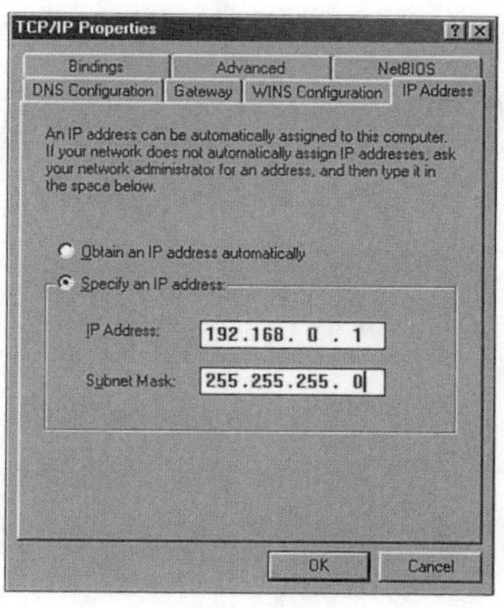

FIGURE 4.9
Configuring IP addresses.

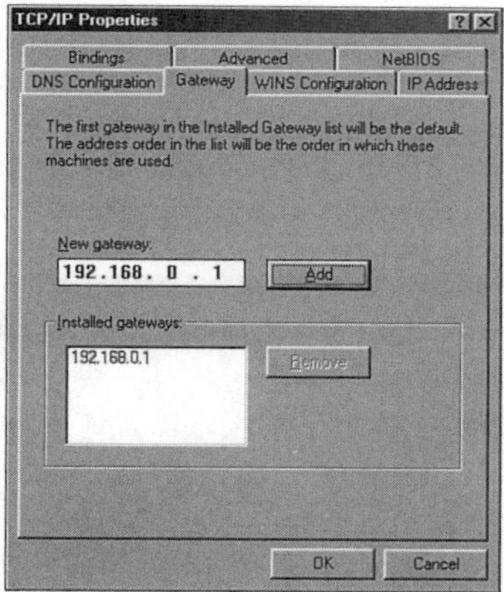

FIGURE 4.10
Configuring the TCP/IP gateway.

7. Select the DNS Configuration tab and complete the configuration. See Figure 4.11 for an example of this configuration.
8. Click OK to complete the configuration.

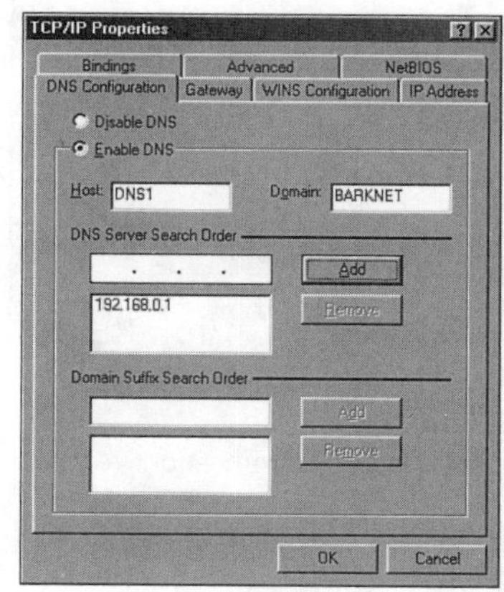

FIGURE 4.11
Configuring the DNS information.

Windows NT 4.0

Step By Step 4.4 can be used to install and configure TCP/IP on Windows NT 4.0 Workstation computers.

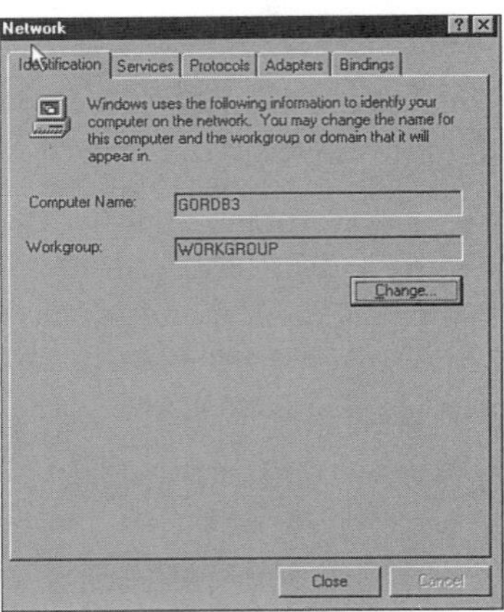

FIGURE 4.12
Network properties in Windows NT 4.0 Workstation.

STEP BY STEP

4.4 Configuring TCP/IP on Windows NT 4.0 Workstation

1. Click Start, select Settings, and click Control Panel.
2. Double-click the Network icon. The network properties in Windows NT 4.0 have a different look from earlier versions, as seen in Figure 4.12.
3. Select the Protocols tab. If the TCP/IP Protocol is not present, click the Add button, select TCP/IP Protocol, and click OK to install.
4. Select TCP/IP Protocol and click the Properties button.
5. Select the IP Address tab and complete the configuration. See Figure 4.13 for an example of this configuration.

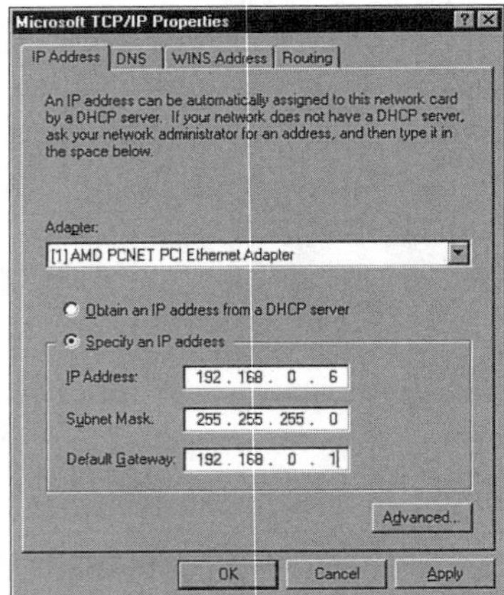

FIGURE 4.13
Configuring IP addresses.

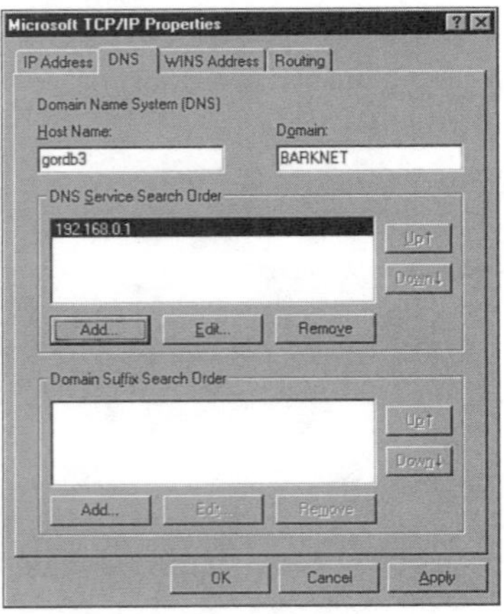

FIGURE 4.14
Configuring the DNS information.

6. Select the DNS tab and complete the configuration. See Figure 4.14 for an example of this configuration.
7. If you have more than one protocol installed on your computer, select the Bindings tab and expand the services listed. Move the protocol you want your computer to use first to the top of each list. See Figure 4.15 for an example of this configuration.

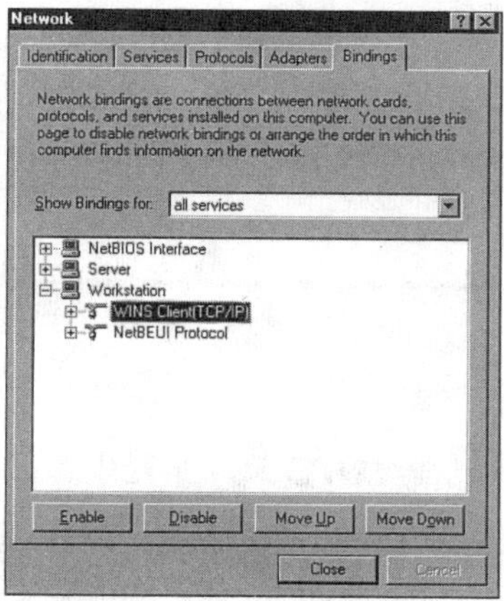

FIGURE 4.15
Setting the protocol binding order.

8. Click Close to complete the configuration.

Windows 2000 Server and Professional

Step By Step 4.5 can be used to install and configure TCP/IP on Windows 2000 Server or Windows 2000 Professional computers.

STEP BY STEP

4.5 Configuring TCP/IP on Windows Server or Windows 2000 Professional

1. Click Start, select Settings, and click the Control Panel.

2. Double-click the Network icon. Windows 2000 Professional will automatically install TCP/IP and create a local network connection. Because TCP/IP is configured by connection, right-click the connection you want to configure and select Properties from the menu. Complete the configuration as seen in Figure 4.16.

continues

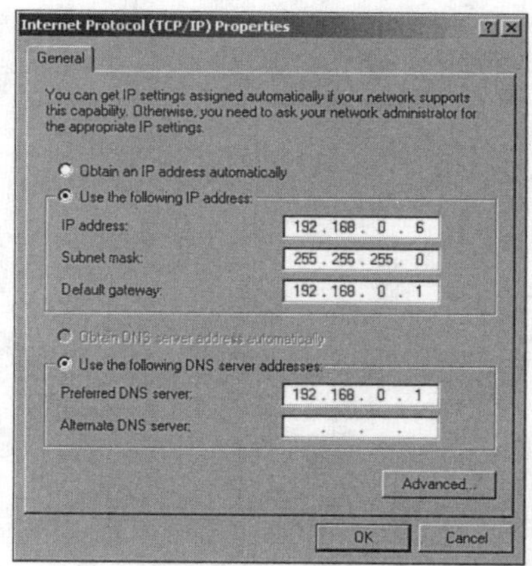

FIGURE 4.16
Configuring TCP/IP in a Windows 2000 Professional computer.

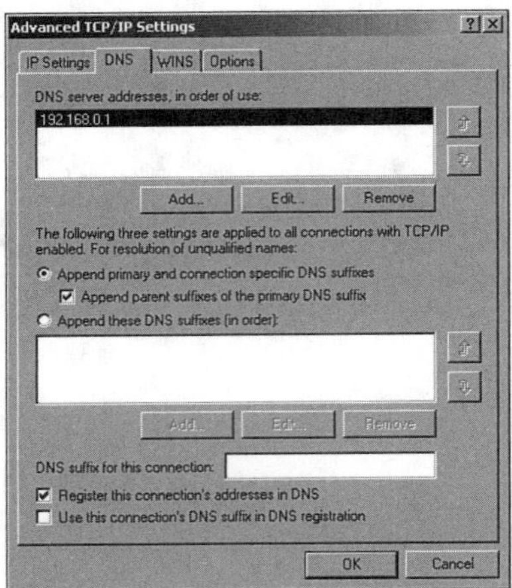

FIGURE 4.17
Configuring DNS properties in a Windows 2000 Professional computer.

continued

3. Click the Advanced button and select the DNS tab. Complete the configuration as shown in Figure 4.17.
4. Click OK to complete the configuration.

Windows XP Professional

The latest version of Windows supports TCP/IP as its default protocol. Windows XP introduces additional configuration parameters in the areas of authentication (smart cards, certificates, or MD-5 challenge) and security with the addition of a personal firewall along with Internet Connection Sharing (ICS). ICS enables you to configure your Windows XP Professional computer or Windows 2000 Server computer to act as a gateway from your local intranet to the Intenet. For example, if your Windows XP Professional computer had two network adapter cards, one would be connected to your ISP (such as a cable modem or an xDSL service) and the other adapter would be connected to your local intranet. ICS installs a single-scope DHCP server, installs a DNS proxy (forwarding requests to your ISP), and acts as your default gateway. It uses the reserved address 192.168.0.x and assigns the address 192.168.0.1 to itself.

Windows XP can also have more than one manually entered TCP/IP address configuration. Now an alternative TCP/IP configuration is available if the system exists on more than one network.

Step By Step 4.6 can be used to configure TCP/IP on a Windows XP Professional computer.

STEP BY STEP

4.6 Configuring TCP/IP in Windows XP

1. Select Start, Control Panel, Network Connections.
2. Select the network connection you want to configure and select Change Settings of This Connection in the Network Tasks pane.

3. Select Internet Protocol (TCP/IP) and click Properties.

4. Select Obtain an IP Address Automatically and Obtain DNS Server Address Automatically if your organization uses DHCP to configure IP.

5. Enter your IP, subnet mask, gateway address, and DNS addresses manually if your organization requires TCP/IP to be configured manually.

6. Select the Alternate Configuration tab, shown in Figure 4.19.

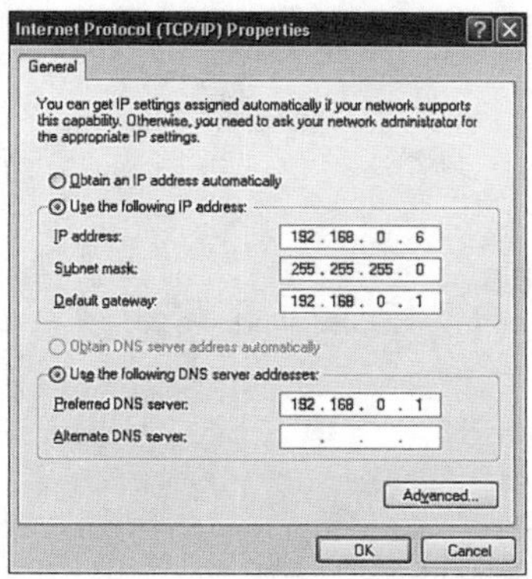

FIGURE 4.18
Configuring TCP/IP on Windows XP.

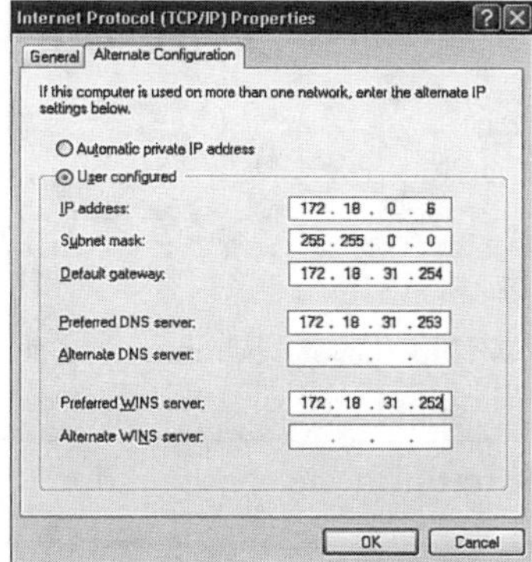

FIGURE 4.19
Entering the alternate configuration for TCP/IP on Windows XP.

7. Select Automatic Private IP Address if you want Windows XP to generate a private IP address in the absence of DHCP.

8. Complete the IP Address, Subnet Mask, Default Gateway, Preferred DNS Server, Alternate DNS Server, Preferred WINS Server, and Alternate WINS Server fields if they are to be manually configured.

9. Select the General tab, click the Advanced button, and select the DNS tab. The DNS configuration pane is shown in Figure 4.20.

10. Add additional DNS server addresses and DNS suffixes to complement any legacy DNS zones still maintained by your organization.

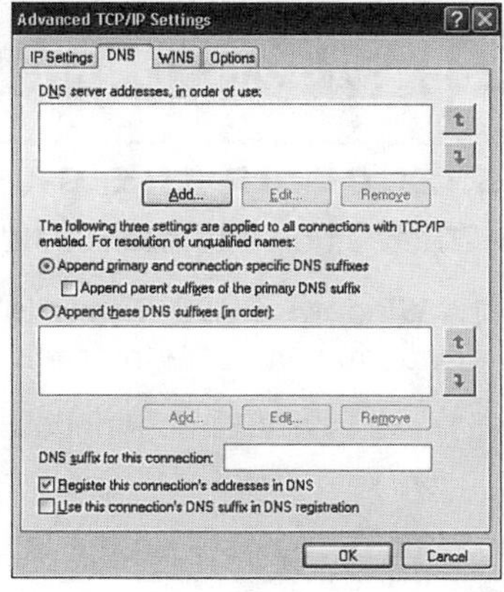

FIGURE 4.20
Configuring DNS on Windows XP.

continues

continued

11. Select the WINS tab. The WINS configuration pane is shown in Figure 4.21.

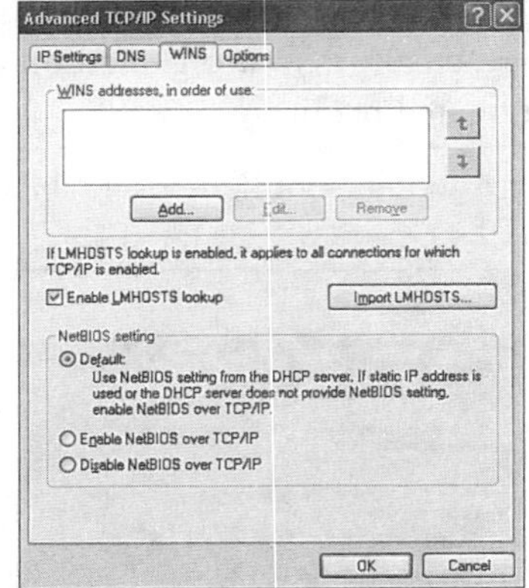

FIGURE 4.21
Configuring WINS on Windows XP.

12. Add any WINS server addresses and select whether NetBIOS is supported on your network.

13. Click OK to finish the configuration.

CASE STUDY: HOME OFFICE

ESSENCE OF THE CASE

- There is an internal TCP/IP network.
- A Windows 2000 Server is sharing a connection with the Internet.
- There is a VPN connection to a corporate server.
- Access to hosts on the Internet is failing.

SCENARIO

Like everyone else, you work too much and have set up an office in your home. A TCP/IP network internal to your house connects all the PCs and laptops you have together as one network. You are running Windows 2000 Server on one of the systems that acts as a gateway, and it is sharing a connection to the Internet through a local cable company. Your laptop is running Windows 2000 Professional with TCP/IP configured by DHCP. You normally connect to your company VPN server via the cable modem and from there, the Internet in

CASE STUDY: HOME OFFICE

general. Today you find that you can't access your favorite search engine Web page.

ANALYSIS

Several network interfaces are being used in this case study. The first is the TCP/IP configuration of the Windows 2000 Professional computer that is trying to access the search engine's home page. The TCP/IP configuration for this computer will be DHCP enabled and point to the internal domain hosted by the Windows 2000 Server system. The `IPCONFIG /ALL` command display should show a DHCP-enabled connection with the IP address in the range 192.168.0.x (the default address assigned by the server) with a gateway address that points to the Windows 2000 Server computer. In addition, the domain name should be the domain that was set up when the Windows 2000 Server was installed. If any of these values are missing or incorrect, the following command will refresh the configuration:

```
Ipconfig /release
Ipconfig /renew
```

The second network interface is on the Windows 2000 Server. This system will have two network adapters: one on the inside network and one on the outside. When this system was installed, that distinction was made and connection-sharing was enabled on the outside connection. The `IPCONFIG /ALL` display should show two connections: an inside connection that has a static IP address (usually 192.168.0.1) and an outside address that is usually configured as DHCP supplied. The local cable company would normally supply the outside address when the cable modem became active on its network. As with the Windows 2000 Professional system, the following commands will refresh the configuration provided by the cable company:

```
Ipconfig /release
Ipconfig /renew
```

The third network interface is the VPN connection between the Windows 2000 Professional computer and the VPN server in your corporation. That connection is established on the Windows 2000 Professional machine through the gateway server (the gateway server does not need a connection itself). This will appear as a new network entry on your Windows 2000 Professional computer with an IP address from your corporate network. In addition, DNS and WINS entries will be assigned from your corporate network, and they should be displayed by the `IPCONFIG /ALL` command.

The first thing to try after reviewing all the configurations is to ping the loopback address (127.0.0.1), then your own IP address, and then your gateway address. From the Windows 2000 Professional computer, that would be the Windows 2000 Server system. If that works, try to ping an outside host (such as your search engine's home page) from the Windows 2000 Server. If that works, but it does not work from the Windows 2000 Professional computer, the problem is in the connection sharing setup. Unconfiguring it and reinstalling it on the server will correct any problem.

The next thing to try is to trace the route that packets take to a known outside host (the search engine's home page again). From the Windows 2000 Professional computer, enter the following command, where *<host name>* is the search engine host name:

```
Tracert <host name>
```

continues

CASE STUDY: HOME OFFICE

continued

The TRACERT command traces the hops (routers) that a packet must take to get to the destination. If it gets to the destination, your problems are solved. If it can't display a router name and shows only IP addresses, the problem is in the DNS servers provided by your cable company. If you get to your corporate network routers (as identified by the IP address ranges) but you don't get from there to the destination, the problem is in your corporate DNS servers or gateway, or the configuration provided when you logged in to the VPN server. Logging out and logging back in will refresh this configuration and might solve the problem. If the problem persists, the error is likely on your corporate network and a call to tech support is in order.

CHAPTER SUMMARY

KEY TERMS

- APIPA
- Default gateway
- DHCP
- DNS
- Ethernet
- ICMP
- LAN
- MAC
- TCP/IP
- WINS

This chapter discussed the main topics in troubleshooting routing issues on a Windows 2000 network and the features of TCP/IP.

The essence of these topics is to understand the components of networking with emphasis on TCP/IP and the role that each component plays in successfully connecting to a network.

APPLY YOUR KNOWLEDGE

Exercises

4.1 Testing TCP/IP

This exercise guides you through the process of retrieving IP address information. Then, you use a few command-line entries to test the configuration and connectivity of the IP address. This exercise can be performed with any of the Windows 2000 series operating systems.

Estimated Time: 5 minutes

1. Select Start, Run; enter **CMD**; and then press Enter.
2. At the command prompt, enter the command **IPCONFIG** and press Enter.
3. What is your IP address?
4. What is your subnet mask?
5. Can you see the IP address of the DNS server?
6. Enter **IPCONFIG /ALL**. What additional information can you now see?
7. Enter **PING 127.0.0.1/**. This is the special loopback test that tells you whether your modem is dead, just playing sick, or (hopefully) just fine.
8. Enter **PING XX**, where *XX* is your favorite Web site.
9. If you have another computer on this network, ping the IP address of that computer.
10. Finally, ping the name of the computer.

4.2 Changing the TCP/IP Properties to Use DHCP

This exercise shows you how to change the properties of the TCP/IP protocol from a static IP to that of a DHCP client. This exercise can be performed with any of the Windows 2000 series operating systems.

Estimated Time: 10 Minutes

1. Double-click the Network Connections applet in the Control Panel.
2. Right-click the connection you want to modify TCP/IP for and select Properties.
3. Select Obtain an IP Address Automatically and click OK.
4. Click OK to close the Properties page.
5. Open a command window and enter the command **IPCONFIG /RELEASE**; then enter **IPCONFIG /RENEW**.
6. To verify that DHCP is supplying your computer with configuration information, enter the command **IPCONFIG /ALL**.
7. If you don't see a valid IP address with lease information, verify that the DHCP server is functioning and reboot your computer.

4.3 Creating a TCP/IP Packet Filter

This exercise walks you through the process of creating a TCP/IP filter on your computer. This exercise can be performed with any of the Windows 2000 series operating systems.

Estimated Time: 20 minutes

1. Open Control Panel, and then open the Network and Dial-up Connections dialog box.
2. Right-click the Local Area Connection and select Properties.
3. Click Internet Protocol and click Properties.
4. Select the Advanced tab.
5. In the Advanced TCP/IP Settings, select the Options tab.

APPLY YOUR KNOWLEDGE

6. Select TCP/IP Filtering and then click Properties.
7. Click the option button next to Permit Only for TCP Ports, and then click the Add button.
8. Enter `port 23` for Telnet and `port 80` for Web Server.
9. Click the option button next to Permit Only for UDP Ports, and then click the Add button.
10. Enter `port 53` for DNS and `port 161` for SNMP.
11. Click the option button next to Permit Only for IP Protocols, and then click the Add button.
12. Enter `2` for IGMP and click OK.
13. Click OK throughout the dialog boxes to approve your changes. You'll need to restart your computer to test the changes.
14. After your computer has restarted, go to another computer on the network. Open a command prompt and ping the IP address of the server that has the IP filtering configured.
15. Were you able to ping the computer?
16. Open TCP/IP Filtering on the original computer again. In the Permit Only IP Protocol section, add `1` for ICMP. Approve these settings and restart.
17. Go to another computer on the network. Are you able to ping the computer now?
18. Return once more to the original computer and remove all the IP packet filters. Approve your changes, reboot, and test the `PING` command now.

Review Questions

1. You are working at home dialed up to the office and have a problem with your machine. You call the corporate help desk, but they say they can't ping your machine. What is blocking the ping?
2. You have manually configured a TCP/IP connection with a subnet mask of 255.255.252.0 but find that you can't connect to any other computers on your network. What is the problem?
3. You have a machine that requests its network configuration via DHCP. You find that everything appears correct, but you can't access any servers on your network. What is the most probable cause of this difficulty?
4. You have your servers all obtain their network addresses through DHCP. When one is rebooted for routine maintenance, users complain that they can no longer see it. What should you tell them to do to fix this problem?
5. What are three requirements for a valid IP address in a Windows 2000 environment?
6. How does TCP/IP know whether the packets are local to this network or need to be forwarded to another network?
7. Why should a company choose to use DHCP over manually assigning IP addresses?
8. Why is it important to have a DNS server's IP address for a client computer in a Windows 2000 network?

APPLY YOUR KNOWLEDGE

Exam Questions

1. You are the network administrator for a small but rapidly growing company. When first installed, your network consisted of only 10 computers running Windows NT Workstation 4 and 1 computer running Windows NT Server 4. Since then, the number of computers on your network has grown considerably, and your old method of using manually assigned IP numbers is becoming clumsy. You wonder whether there is a better way to do this.

   What plan should you implement on your network?

   A. Create a common `HOSTS` file and copy it to each computer.

   B. Configure each machine to use DHCP but allow them to find their own addresses using APIPA.

   C. Configure a DHCP server and have it distribute network IP addresses.

   D. Continue using fixed addresses because that is the most efficient mechanism possible.

2. You have set up a home office that connects to a cable modem. You want the other computers in your household to be capable of accessing the Internet through this single connection.

   You add a new network card to your gateway computer and attach it to your home network. On the external connection, you enable ICS.

   One computer can't find any Web sites on the Internet. You examine its network settings and find the following when you look at `IPCONFIG`:

```
Ethernet adapter Wireless Network Connection:
        Connection-specific DNS Suffix  . :
Barknet.ads
        IP Address. . . . . . . . . . . . :
192.168.1.6
        Subnet Mask . . . . . . . . . . . :
255.255.224.0
        Default Gateway . . . . . . . . . :
192.168.1.10
```

   What should you do to fix the problem and allow the computer access to the Internet?

   A. Disable ICF from the connection that attaches to the Internet.

   B. Disable all TCP/IP filters in the Options part of the ICS gateway network configuration.

   C. Set the computer up for DHCP because it is does not have the correct subnet mask and does not point to the ICS gateway.

   D. Reset the subnet mask to 255.255.255.0.

3. Murray works on the help desk for the transportation department of the city. The building in which he works occupies three floors, with one subnet for each floor. For the network layout, see Figure 4.22.

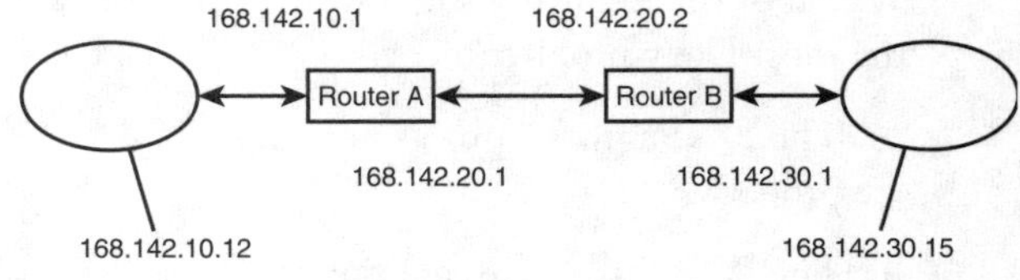

FIGURE 4.22
Transportation department network layout.

   A user who is on a Windows XP Professional workstation with an IP address of 168.142.10.12 reports that she can't reach a server that Murray identifies as having an IP address of 168.142.30.15. She also reports that she is

APPLY YOUR KNOWLEDGE

having no problem assigning a drive letter to a server that Murray identifies as being on the same subnet as she is.

Murray has tried to ping the server directly, but he receives a time out error from `PING`.

What address should he attempt to reach next?

A. 127.0.0.1

B. 168.142.20.2

C. 168.142.20.1

D. 168.142.30.1

4. Darrell is a member of the network group at a large company. The network uses TCP/IP exclusively and is made up of several subnets, each of which has servers used by the users in that subnet. He receives a report from a user who says she can't reach any servers in her local group. Using the NetMon utility, Darrell notices that every time the user tries to connect to a server, her workstation sends out an ARP request for the address of the local gateway.

   Which of the following should Darrel identify as the most likely problem?

   A. The DNS information is not configured properly.

   B. The WINS addresses are missing.

   C. The subnet mask is incorrect.

   D. The IP address is a duplicate of one on the local subnet.

5. Kevin is part of the networking group at a large metropolitan utility. He has been part of a project that involves moving several computers from one subnet to another. The next day a user complains that he can connect to local servers but can't connect to any remote server. Other users on the same subnet do not have this problem. The `IPCONFIG` output from the user's computer contains the following information:

   IP address: 168.142.66.31

   Subnet mask: 255.255.224.0

   Default gateway: 168.142.32.1

   What should Kevin identify as the most likely cause of the problem?

   A. The IP address is incorrect.

   B. The subnet mask is incorrect.

   C. The default gateway address is incorrect.

   D. There is a problem in the user's network connection.

6. You are the manager of a network that is made up of several subnets. You have a mixture of computers running Windows NT 4.0 and Windows 2000 Server in your pool of domain controllers. A user whose computer is running Windows NT Workstation on one subnet reports that she can browse servers on her local network but nothing remote. You try to map a drive to the server and are successful.

   What is most likely the problem?

   A. The default gateway on the client's computer is incorrect.

   B. The DNS server is not available.

   C. The router for this subnet is not functioning.

   D. The domain controller is unavailable.

APPLY YOUR KNOWLEDGE

7. Mary is a LAN administrator at a manufacturing company and is planning her network configuration for a Windows 2000 domain she will be implementing. The domain will consist of 8 locations, 16 Windows 2000 servers (10 of which will be domain controllers), and 862 Windows 2000 Professional Workstations. She will be using TCP/IP in this routed environment and has decided to use four DHCP servers for fault tolerance across the network. Her supervisor, Paul, is upset that Mary wants to use DHCP. He insists that it's too hard to configure, causes downtime, and won't allow an administrator to know who has what IP address the way that a simple spreadsheet of computer names and IP addresses would. What are some arguments Mary could offer to convince Paul otherwise? (Choose all that apply.)

   A. DHCP can show you which computer is assigned a given IP address.

   B. DHCP actually saves time as computers move from segment to segment.

   C. DHCP is complex and somewhat hard to configure.

   D. In Mary's plan, downtime would be at a minimum because she has distributed the available scopes across 4 DHCP servers.

8. You are a LAN administrator for your company. Your task is to configure the IP addresses of your network. You decide to implement DHCP to automate the process and ensure less downtime. You have decided, however, to manually enter the IP address of certain hosts in your network. Of the following, which would be good candidates to enter the IP address of a computer manually? (Choose all that apply.)

   A. A laptop that moves from segment to segment through the week

   B. A DNS server

   C. An Exchange server

   D. A print server located on the largest subnet

9. Janice, a user from the accounting department, calls you, the LAN administrator, to report that she's having a tough time connecting to resources on your Windows 2000 domain. You ask for more information, and Janice reveals that she is trying to connect to a server in Washington. Other users can connect to the server, but she can't. She can ping the IP address of other hosts on her segment, her default gateway, and even the IP address of the server in Washington, but when she uses the server's host name to enter the name of the server, she can't connect. What is the problem with Janice's computer?

   A. Janice has a blank or invalid DNS server IP address.

   B. Janice has a blank or invalid subnet mask.

   C. Janice has a faulty network adapter card.

   D. Janice needs to renew her IP address by running the command `IPCONFIG /RELEASE` and then `IPCONFIG /RENEW`.

10. You are a consultant for XMSGuys International. Its Windows 2000 domain consists of 4 domain controllers, 872 Windows 2000 Professional workstations, and a few Macintosh client computers that connect to one server occasionally. The company has hired you to inspect its TCP/IP network to improve performance. Upon inspecting the network, you discover they've added these protocols or services to each server: services for Macintosh, NWLink, GSNW, DHCP services (although only two are functional), NetBEUI, and TCP/IP. Of the following

APPLY YOUR KNOWLEDGE

recommendations, which would be the best solution for improving network performance?

A. Arrange the bindings to use the network providers from Microsoft Network and then Novell. Arrange the protocols on each component to be TCP/IP, NWLink, and then NetBEUI. Unbind NWLink and NetBEUI from the DHCP service.

B. Remove the GSNW and NWLink from all servers. Arrange the bindings for each component to use TCP/IP first and then NetBEUI.

C. Remove the following from all servers: GSNW, NWLink, and NetBEUI. Remove Services for Macintosh from all servers except for the server to which the Macs actually connect.

D. Remove the following from all servers: GSNW, NWLink, and NetBEUI. Remove Services for Macintosh from all servers except for the server to which the Macs actually connect. Remove the DHCP Server service from the two servers that are not currently functioning as DHCP servers.

Answers to Review Questions

1. Two common situations will cause this. If you have a laptop that moves from the corporate LAN to a dial-up network connection, you might find that ICF is configured to run when you are not on the corporate LAN. If that is the case, you must manually configure it to allow echo message in the ICMP filter of ICF. This is not on by default.
2. The subnet specified has only two nodes on it. With such a restricted subnet, every address other than the one remaining address on your subnet would be considered remote. The other local address must therefore be a router if you are to communicate with any remote systems at all. This configuration is typically used for router connections; however, it is not very useful when connecting computers.
3. The DHCP server did not respond to your request because it was busy or offline. Your machine then selects an IP address from the Automatic IP Private Addressing (APIPA) subnet with addresses in the 169.254.*.* range. You need to investigate why the DHCP server did not respond in time and reattempt the configurations by issuing an `IPCONFIG /RENEW` command.
4. When your server returned to the network, it received a different DHCP address than it had originally. The information kept in the users' Windows XP Professional computers would still be pointing to the old address. They would have to issue an `IPCONFIG /FLUSHDNS` command to delete all their cached DNS entries. When they access the server again, DNS will retrieve the latest addresses assigned by DHCP.
5. IP address, subnet mask, and default gateway
6. The subnet mask defines the network ID portion of the IP address. If the destination of the packet has a different network ID, it is forwarded to the gateway.
7. DHCP allows the dynamic assignment of IP addresses and provides greater flexibility in address management. For example, a client computer using DHCP does not have a hard-coded

APPLY YOUR KNOWLEDGE

IP address and so can be moved to another network without having to modify the TCP/IP configuration.

8. A DNS server provides the capability of resolving host names to IP addresses. Without a DNS server, you would need to know the actual IP address of the target computer. Also, with Windows 2000 Active Directory and DHCP, DNS can be dynamically updated.

Answers to Exam Questions

1. **C.** The correct answer is to set up a DHCP service on an existing server and use it to automatically manage and distribute IP addresses to computers on your network. You could create a common `HOSTS` file and distribute it to each machine; however, that does not make your system any easier to maintain. Allowing the APIPA mechanism doesn't provide a mechanism for you to see which machine is at which address because there is not central database of mappings. Continuing with your current mechanisms of fixed addresses might be slightly faster at bootup, but it is not the most efficient way to manage a large network address space because it requires manual reconfiguring whenever a change in the network topology is made. See "Using `IPCONFIG`."

2. **C.** The computer is not using DHCP. The IP addresses leased by the DHCP service set up as part of ICS range from 192.168.0.2 to 192.168.0.254 with a subnet mask of 255.255.255.0. The default gateway address will always be 192.168.0.1 on any connection configured as an ICS gateway. ICF never blocks outgoing Web traffic, and the IP filters are used to enable certain TCP or UDP protocols from reaching your system (you would have to enable everything but port 80 for your system to function correctly on you network). Just setting the subnet mask to the correct value will not provide access to the Internet due to the incorrect gateway address. See "Windows XP Professional."

3. **B.** The problem with using `PING` as a diagnostic tool is that the problem in reaching an IP address could be caused at any node along the way. The problem is to determine by the most direct method where on the network the problem occurs. The first addresses to check are 127.0.0.1 (the loop back address) and then your IP address. A reply from both of these tests indicates that the network adapter is working and configured correctly. The next step is to ping the far side of the server acting as Router A. The next step is to ping the near side of the server acting as Router B and then the far side of the same system. See "Using `PING`."

4. **C.** IP must first resolve the MAC address of the destination IP. At this point, WINS, DNS, and any static files (`HOSTS` and `LMHOSTS`) are not used. IP compares its IP address with its subnet mask and then inspects the destination address. If the destination address is remote (on a different subnet), IP uses the local gateway to help determine the destination MAC address. If the address is local (on the same subnet as defined by the IP current address and subnet mask), IP uses ARP to return the MAC address directly. If the subnet mask is incorrect, local addresses could look remote and remote addresses could look like they are local. If the IP address is duplicated, TCP/IP notifies the user with a dialog box repeatedly, until the problem is fixed. See "Using ARP."

Apply Your Knowledge

5. **C.** The default gateway for a computer must be in the same subnet. The gateway is used by IP on the local computer to help determine the MAC address of the destination IP address. If the default gateway is already remote, it can't be used to locate remote addresses. The Class B address 168.142.0.0 with a subnet mask of 255.255.224.0 divides into six usable subnets with the following addresses:

168.142.32.1	168.142.63.254
168.142.64.1	168.142.95.254
168.142.96.1	168.142.127.254
168.142.128.1	168.142.159.254
168.142.160.1	168.142.191.254
168.142.192.1	168.142.223.254

   Note that the first and last subnets are not included because they have illegal addresses.

   The IP of the computer is on the second subnet; however, the gateway address is on the first subnet and therefore can't be reached to help resolve remote addresses. If the host address was incorrect and the gateway address was correct then no local addresses would be reachable. See "Default Gateway (Router) Address."

6. **D.** In a Windows 2000 environment, browsing is still available for those clients who are using Windows 95/98 or Window NT. Browsing is concerned with keeping a list of named computers and not name-to-IP address resolution. In the case where you are mapping a drive to a computer on a remote subnet and are successful, the router, default gateway address, and name resolution service must all be working correctly. Browsing across subnets relies on the Master Browser, which is one of the domain controllers. The Master Browser merges all the computer lists from the browsers on each subnet to produce one global list. Local browsers rely on this list when looking for remote machines. If this list is not available (meaning that you can't browse) but you can map to a specific share on a named system, the Master Browser service or domain controller is not available. See "Using `PING`."

7. **A, B, D.** DHCP can reveal what IP address any computer has been assigned. DHCP does save time as computers move from segment to segment. Downtime will be minimal if a DHCP server goes down because Mary's plan has the scopes distributed across four servers. For more information, see the section "Configuring TCP/IP."

8. **B, C, D.** DNS servers require static IP addresses; typically, mail servers require static IP addresses. For more information, see the section "Checking Connectivity."

9. **A.** If Janice can successfully ping local and remote hosts, including the server she is trying to connect to, most likely she has either a missing DNS IP address or a DNS IP address that has been configured incorrectly. For more information, see the section "Configuring the TCP/IP Protocol."

APPLY YOUR KNOWLEDGE

10. **D.** You should remove GSNW, NWLINK, and NetBEUI from all servers and remove Services for Macintosh from all servers except for the server where it's actually being used. Also, remove DHCP from the two servers that are not actually being used as DHCP. Just by removing these extra configurations from the servers, network performance will increase because fewer network services and resources are contending for network time. For more information, see the section "Configuring TCP/IP on Client Computers."

Suggested Readings and Resources

1. Bott, Ed, and Carl Siechert. *Microsoft Windows XP Inside Out.* Microsoft Press, 2001.
2. Lee, Thomas, and Joseph Davies. *Microsoft Windows 2000 TCP/IP Protocol and Services.* Microsoft Press, 2000.
3. Mueller, John Paul, and Irfan Chaudhry. *Microsoft Windows 2000 Performance Tuning Technical Reference.* Microsoft Press, 2000.
4. Stanek, William R. Microsoft Windows 2000 Administrator's Pocket Consultant. Microsoft Press, 2000.

OBJECTIVES

This chapter helps you prepare for the MCSE Managing a Microsoft Windows 2000 Network Environment exam by covering the following objectives:

Configure, administer, and troubleshoot DHCP on servers and client computers.

- **Detect unauthorized DHCP servers on a network.**
- **Configure authorization of DHCP servers.**
- **Configure client computers to use dynamic IP addressing.**
- **Configure DHCP server properties.**
- **Create and configure a DHCP scope.**

► One of the first tasks when getting ready to deploy a production Windows 2000 network environment is to ensure that DHCP is installed and configured correctly. DHCP is tightly integrated with Dynamic DNS and Active Directory Services. This objective expects you to be able to install DHCP and configure it for use in an Active Directory Services network.

CHAPTER 5

Dynamic Host Configuration Protocol (DHCP)

Outline

Study Strategies

- DHCP is a service that has been used in TCP/IP-based networks for quite a while. Microsoft has extended the functionality of DHCP as part of its Windows 2000 operating system. Be sure you understand where DHCP came from, how it works, and what enhancements Microsoft's Windows 2000 DHCP Server service brings to the protocol.
- DHCP not only is used to dynamically allocate IP addresses and to configure many other options, but also plays a critical part in registering hosts in the Microsoft Active Directory. Be sure you understand the role DHCP plays in a Windows 2000 network.
- Microsoft's Windows 2000 DHCP Server service supports several types of scopes. Be sure you understand the types, how each works, and when you would use each in a production environment.

INTRODUCTION

If you've ever surfed the World Wide Web, you have almost certainly seen IP addresses, numbers like 192.168.144.77. As you administer TCP/IP on your network, a considerable part of your time will be devoted to IP address assignment because IP addresses don't just happen. They have to be entered manually into the configuration of each TCP/IP computer on your network or applied through other automated techniques. When a computer is added to your network, it needs an IP address. When it moves, it probably needs a different IP address. If you are just starting out with managing a large TCP/IP network, you might find the notion of managing all those addresses a bit daunting. Move a DNS server, and you have to reconfigure every client computer. Move a client computer to a new subnet, and you have to update its IP address. This can be a real problem if you have a significant number of employees who travel between offices (usually this includes executives). If you manually manage your IP addresses, almost any change to the network requires a visit to one or more computers to update the TCP/IP configuration—not an efficient use of your time. Fortunately, the people who brought us DNS to replace the HOSTS file also came up with a solution to this dilemma.

The Dynamic Host Configuration Protocol (DHCP) was the Internet community's answer to dynamically distributing IP addresses. DHCP is open and standards based, as defined by the Internet Engineering Task Force (IETF) Requests for Comments (RFCs) 2131 and 2132. (The IETF is the main standards organization for the Internet.)

Typically, IP addresses are registered with the Internet Assigned Numbers Authority (IANA) so that it can keep track of IP addresses used on the Internet. In some cases, a network is not connected to the Internet and does not need to use registered addresses. In other cases, the network is connected to the Internet with special hardware and software that can be configured to enable the network to use unregistered addresses in conjunction with address translations. Windows 2000 includes this capability.

Quite often, network administrators use unregistered addresses on their internal networks to ensure that addresses are available for all users. This model works great as long as the network is never tied directly to the Internet. A small percentage of networks use small pools of registered addresses to service larger numbers of DHCP clients—the idea being that not every client computer would need access simultaneously. These environments require aggressive leasing policies to ensure that everyone can get an address.

In addition to IP addresses, DHCP can also provide gateway addresses, DNS server addresses, and WINS server addresses—in essence, everything the client computer needs to participate in the network. This lets all available IP addresses be stored in a central database along with associated configuration information, such as the subnet mask, gateways, and addresses of DNS servers. You even get the Media Access Control (MAC) addresses of the client computers. The MAC address is specific to the network adapter card and is designed to be unique. This is one of the addresses that machines use to communicate.

EXAM TIP

Don't Sweat the RFCs for DHCP
Although Microsoft has been known to be very detailed in its exam questions, it will not expect you to be able to recite the RFCs for each of the protocols or services in Windows 2000.

NOTE

RFCs Are Notes About the Internet
Request For Comment documents are used to make notes about the Internet and Internet technologies. If an RFC can garner enough interest, it might eventually become a standard. Topics of RFCs range from the File Transfer Protocol (originally RFC 0114 but updated by RFC0141, RFC0172, and RFC0171) to the *Hitchhikers Guide to the Internet* (RFC1118). The first RFC was posted in 1969 by Steve Crocker, and the topic was host software. You can find listings of all the RFCs at several sites throughout the Internet. One place is `http://www.rfc-editor.org/`.

The DHCP Protocol

It's great to say that DHCP provides the mechanism for dynamically distributing IP addresses on a network, but there is a bit more to it than that. Here's how a client computer gets an address:

1. The client computer broadcasts a `DHCPDiscover` message that is forwarded to the DHCP server(s) on the network. The address of the DHCP server(s) is configured on the router, if necessary. Forwarding is done using a process called a BOOTP Forwarder. This is discussed in more detail in the next section, "The BOOTP Protocol."

2. Each DHCP server that receives the discover message responds with a `DHCPOffer` message that includes an IP address that is appropriate for the subnet where the client computer is attached. The DHCP server determines the appropriate address by looking at the source subnet for the broadcast `DHCPDiscover` message.

3. The client computer considers the offer message and selects one (usually the first offer it receives). It broadcases a `DHCPRequest` indicating the DHCP server selected (and implicitly declining the offer from other DHCP servers). If multiple DHCP servers exist, great care needs to be taken in their configuration. You can easily inadvertently configure the servers so

that they conflict. It is very important if you have multiple DHCP servers on your network that they do not have the capability to offer duplicate IP addresses. Because the DHCP servers do not communicate, they have no way of telling whether an address has already been issued by another DHCP server.

4. The DHCP server acknowledges with a `DHCPAck` message the request and grants the client computer a lease to use the address.
5. The client computer uses the IP address to bind to the network. If the IP address is associated with any configuration parameters, the parameters are incorporated into the client computer's TCP/IP configuration.

The first step of this process indicates that DHCP clients request their addresses using broadcast messages. If you are familiar with routing, particularly TCP/IP routing, you are probably familiar with the fact that one of the benefits of routing is that the router segregates network segments. One of the types of packets that routers do not forward are broadcasts. But this doesn't mean that DHCP works only on the local subnet of its server. Routers have a configuration option called a BOOTP Forwarder that forwards DHCP requests. BOOTP is the precursor to DHCP and was the first protocol used to assign IP addresses dynamically. The protocol was specially designed to pass across a router, and it continues to be used to enable DHCP broadcasts to propagate across routers. Thanks to BOOTP, a DHCP server can service clients on any number of subnets.

The BOOTP Protocol

Before we get into installing the DHCP service in Windows 2000, a brief discussion about the BOOTP protocol is a good idea. A number of DHCP's features had their beginnings in BOOTP. The BOOTP (Bootstrap Protocol) protocol was originally designed in 1985 by Bill Croft and John Gilmore to automate the configuration of network devices. To use BOOTP, the network administrator must create a table with a list of client computers, their IP addresses, and network configurations. When a client computer comes onto the network, it broadcasts a request that the BOOTP server receives. The BOOTP server looks up the client computer in the table and responds with the configuration information stored in the table, allowing the client computer to communicate on the network.

The BOOTP protocol works pretty well and was used extensively in the early 1990s in conjunction with diskless workstations. A BOOTP chip was a common option on a network interface card, and many networks thrived on BOOTP. The downside of BOOTP is that it provides only the configuration information entered in the table. The administrator still needs to configure the table. The limitations of BOOTP effectively prevented any automation of these tasks, so it was eventually replaced with DHCP. BOOTP and DHCP packets look virtually identical, and DHCP even takes advantage of the BOOTP Forwarder functionality of many routers and switches. DHCP added the automation features BOOTP was lacking.

CONFIGURING DHCP ON SERVERS

▶ Configure, administer, and troubleshoot DHCP on servers and client computers.

One of the features that makes Windows 2000 very popular with system administrators is its extensive use of configuration wizards. Most of the server configuration tasks have been bundled into the Configure Your Server application, enabling you to start a wizard for the most common configuration activities. We will try to highlight this new feature of Windows 2000 as much as possible because it is a major enhancement to the operating system and could prove to be fertile ground for exam questions.

When you install Windows 2000 Server, you have the ability to install DHCP as one of the optional services. For the purposes of the exam, we will look at installing DHCP on a server that already has the operating system installed but does not have DHCP loaded.

DHCP is installed as a Windows 2000 Server networking service. To install the DHCP Server service, follow Step By Step 5.1.

NOTE

A DHCP Server Cannot Also Be a DHCP Client If you currently have your server configured as a DHCP client, the DHCP installation will prompt you to enter a static IP address for your server.

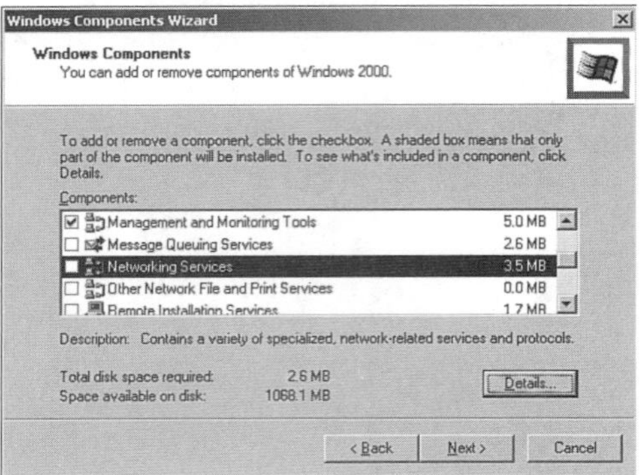

FIGURE 5.1
The Networking Services entry includes networking components such as DHCP, DNS, and WINS, among others.

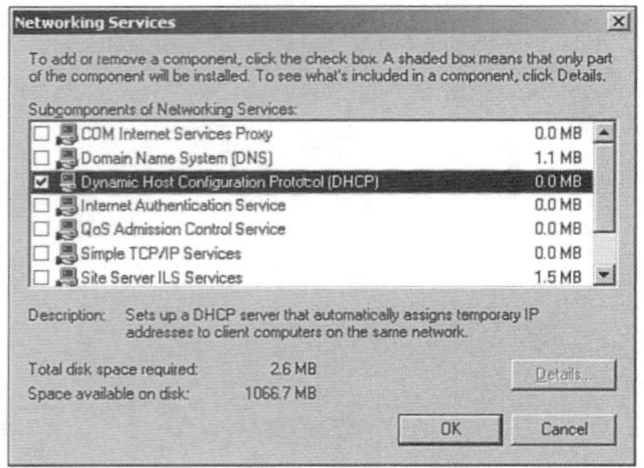

FIGURE 5.2
Selecting the Dynamic Host Control Protocol (DHCP) starts the install process.

EXAM TIP

Windows 2000 Offers Many Ways to Complete Common Tasks
Having multiple ways to complete common configuration tasks should make administering a Windows 2000 network much easier for system administrators, but it will undoubtedly make the exams more challenging because you will likely need to know the various methods of completing common tasks.

STEP BY STEP

5.1 Installing DHCP by Adding a Windows Component

1. Click the Start the Windows Component Wizard hyperlink.
2. In the Windows Component Wizard, scroll down to Networking Services, shown in Figure 5.1, and select it.
3. Click the Details button to open the list of Networking Services. From the list of Networking Services, check the box next to Dynamic Host Configuration Protocol (DHCP), shown in Figure 5.2.
4. Click the OK button to return to the Windows Components screen, and click Next to install DHCP. If you selected or deselected any other services, they will be installed or removed at this time as well.
5. Click the Finish button to exit the wizard.

As we discussed, there is more than one way to install the DHCP service. DHCP can also be installed by following Step By Step 5.2.

STEP BY STEP

5.2 Using the Network and Dial-up Connections to Install DHCP

1. Select Start, Settings, and click Control Panel.
2. Double-click the Network and Dial-up Connections icon.
3. Click the Add Network Components hyperlink at the lower left of the window to open the Windows Optional Networking Components Wizard dialog box, which contains a subset of components that can be installed. Unlike the list of available components in the previous installation method, this list is limited to networking components only. Figure 5.3 shows the networking components available to install.

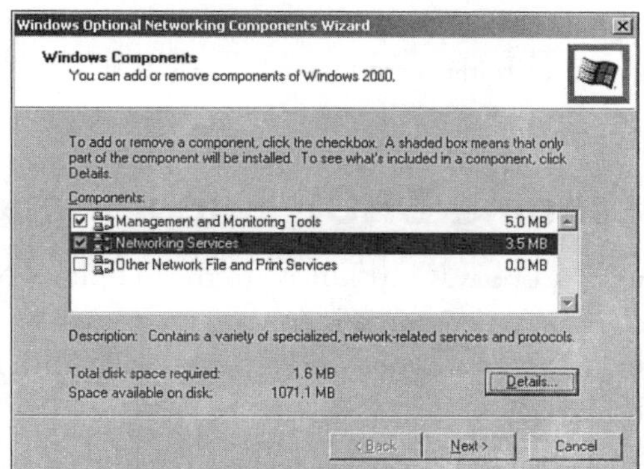

FIGURE 5.3
The Windows Optional Networking Components Wizard dialog box presents the network components available for installation.

4. Select Networking Services and then click the Details button. From this point, the installation continues exactly as the previous installation method, starting at step 4.

Now that you have seen two of the methods for installing DHCP, let's discuss how to configure DHCP. One of the important things you need to understand before you delve into the configuration of your newly installed DHCP server is the concept of scopes, including scopes, superscopes, and multicast scopes.

Creating and Configuring a Scope

A *scope* is a range of IP addresses that are available for dynamic assignment to hosts on a given subnet. The scope for a particular subnet is determined by the network address of the broadcast DHCP request. In addition to address information, a scope can include a set of configuration parameters to be assigned to client computers when the address is assigned. This list includes DNS servers, WINS server(s), gateway and subnet mask, NetBIOS scope ID, IP routing, and WINS Proxy information. To find this information, select Start, Run and type **WINIPCFG**. This shows you all the DHCP information for your Windows 98 client computer. Under Windows NT or Windows 2000, go to the command prompt, type **IPCONFIG /ALL**, and press Enter.

You should make the scope as large as you can. Later in the scope-creation process, you can exclude addresses, and you can also define

NOTE

You Need at Least One Scope After installing the DHCP service, you must define at least one scope on the server. Otherwise, the service will not respond to DHCP requests.

reservations for particular addresses that you want DHCP to hand out but that need to remain static, such as a server.

Understanding DHCP Superscopes

The next type of scope was introduced to the Windows NT product family with Service Pack 2 for Windows NT 4. A *superscope* allows you to support a *supernetted* or *multinetted* network with a Windows 2000 DHCP Server.

A *supernetted* network is a network that has multiple network addresses or subnets running on the same segment (normally there is only one subnet to a segment). You commonly see this configuration in network environments with more than 254 hosts on a subnet or in an environment in which certain hosts need to be isolated from the rest of the logical network for security or routing reasons.

Superscopes will support a local multinet or a multinet that is located across a router configured to use the BOOTP Forwarder service. We discuss creating a superscope later in the chapter in the "Creating a Superscope" section.

IN THE FIELD

WHEN TO USE SUPERNETTING

Visualize a large company that occupies five floors in a building. On each of these floors are 300–500 users, all crammed in a gigantic cube farm and all on the same physical network. Traditional network design would have a routed backbone running between the floors, and each floor would be its own IP network. But there's one problem: There are too many users on these floors to be handled by a single Class C subnet. What are the alternatives?

You could place a router somewhere on each of the floors to further segment the network. This is an expensive and support-intensive solution and is generally considered to be impractical.

You could address using Class B addresses. However, that is generally very wasteful of IP addresses, and you would probably have to reconfigure your address scheme to use the private Class B Network ID.

Your other option is to place multiple IP networks on the single routed segment. In other words, create a supernet. This capability is supported by any of the routers on the market today, including the OS-based routing services in Windows 2000, Novell NetWare, and any of the Unix flavors. So, when you think about a supernet, think about a floor in a building with too many users for 254 IP addresses.

Understanding Multicasting and Multicast Scopes

Before we discuss the multicast scopes, we need to look at what multicasting is. *Multicasting* is the act of transmitting a message to a select group of recipients. This is in contrast to the concept of a *broadcast*, in which traffic is sent to every host on the network, or a *unicast*, in which the connection is a one-to-one relationship and one recipient of the data exists.

If you send an email message to your manager, that is an example of a unicast message. If you send an email message to every user on the system, that is a broadcast. Send an email message to a mailing list, and you have sent a multicast message, which falls between the previous two. Teleconferencing and videoconferencing use the concept of multicasting, as does broadcast audio, in which the connection is between one source and a selected group of listeners. At this time, only a few applications take advantage of this feature, but with the growing popularity of multicast applications, you might see more multicast applications in the future.

We should discuss a few terms before examining the Windows 2000 multicast capabilities:

- **Multicast DHCP (MDHCP)**—An extension to the DHCP protocol standard that supports dynamic assignment and configuration of IP multicast addresses on TCP/IP-based networks.
- **Multicast forwarding table**—The table used by an IP router to forward IP multicast traffic. An entry in the IP multicast forwarding table consists of the multicast group address, the source IP address, a list of interfaces to which the traffic is forwarded (next hop interfaces), and the single interface on which the traffic must be received to be forwarded (the previous hop interface).

- **Multicast group**—A group of member TCP/IP hosts configured to listen and receive datagrams sent to a specified destination IP address. The destination address for the group is a shared IP address in the Class D address range (224.0.0.0–239.255.255.255).
- **Multicast scope**—A range of IP multicast addresses in the range of 239.0.0.0–239.254.255.255. Multicast addresses in this range can be prevented from propagating in either direction (send or receive) through the use of scope-based multicast boundaries.

A new feature of Windows 2000's DHCP service is the concept of a *multicast scope*. The Microsoft DHCP server has been extended to allow the assignment of multicast addresses in addition to unicast (single computer) addresses. A proposed IETF standard (RFC 2730, Multicast Address Dynamic Client Allocation Protocol [MADCAP]) defines multicast address allocation. The proposed standard would allow administrators to dynamically allocate multicast addresses to be assigned in the same fashion as unicast addresses. The Windows 2000 DHCP multicasting capability also supports dynamic membership. Dynamic membership enables individual computers to join or leave the multicast group at any time. This is similar to registering to receive a radio broadcast over the Internet or joining and leaving an email mailing list. Group membership is not limited by size, and computers are not restricted to membership in any single group.

Now the question is, "How do client computers join and leave a multicast group?" The answer is the Multicast Address Dynamic Client Allocation Protocol (MADCAP, but it used to be called MDHCP) protocol and the MADCAP API. Client computers using MADCAP must be configured to use the MADCAP API. MADCAP assists in simplifying and automating configuration of multicast groups on your network, but it is not required for the operation of multicast groups or for the DHCP service. Multicast scopes provide only address configuration and do not support or use other DHCP-assignable options. MADCAP address configuration for client computers should be done independently of how the client computers are configured to receive their primary IP addresses. Computers that use either static or dynamic configuration through a DHCP server can also be MADCAP clients.

EXAM TIP

Use Class D IP Addresses for the Multicast Scope Remember that, along with your primary IP address, you receive your multicast address. Also, it is for multicasts only and uses the Class D IP addresses specified in the multicast scope. It is not used for regular network traffic, such as Web traffic, or other IP-based applications.

Creating a Scope on Your DHCP Server

Now that you are familiar with the various types of scopes, let's look at creating one. To create a DHCP scope, follow Step By Step 5.3.

STEP BY STEP

5.3 Creating a DHCP Scope

1. Click Start, select Programs, click Administrative Tools, and click DHCP. Figure 5.4 shows the DHCP management console.

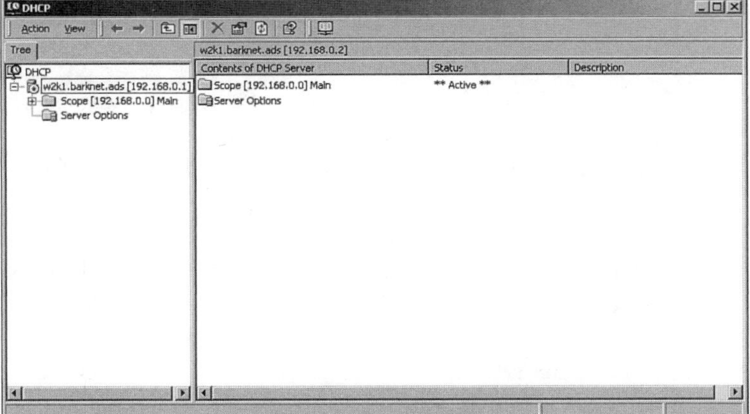

FIGURE 5.4
The DHCP management console is used for configuring all the parameters for your DHCP server.

2. Select the DHCP server listed on the left in the DHCP window; then, select Action, New Scope. Click Next, and the Scope Name dialog box opens.

3. Type a name and a description for your scope. It's a good idea to choose something descriptive for the name, so that when you need to go back after creating 35 scopes, you can tell why you created this one. Figure 5.5 shows the Scope Name dialog box. Click Next to continue.

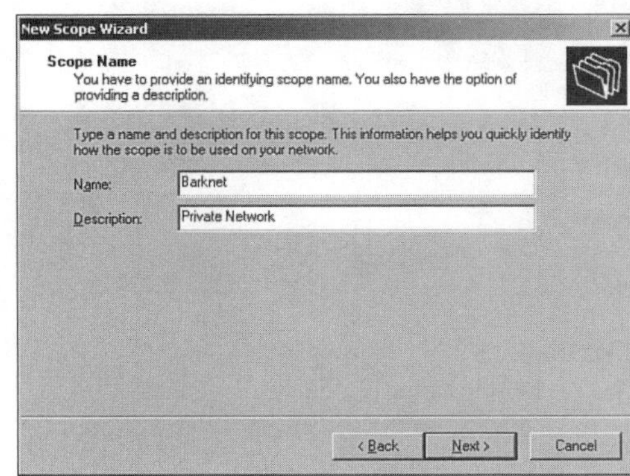

FIGURE 5.5
When you set up each scope, choose a descriptive name and a clear description to assist in identifying the scope in the future.

continues

continued

4. Define the IP address range that your server will use to assign addresses. Figure 5.6 shows the IP Address Range page.

5. Define the subnet mask using the standard octet method (in other words, 255.255.255.248) or using the more router-centric mask length field of /27. (This field enables you to specify the number of binary bits used to specify the subnet mask.) Click Next to continue.

6. Select a range of addresses that will not be leased to client computers. These are typically addresses assigned to servers, routers, printers, or other infrastructure equipment that requires static addresses. You can have multiple excluded IP addresses or ranges for each scope. Figure 5.7 shows the Address Exclusions screen. Click Next to continue.

7. Set the DHCP lease, the amount of time that must elapse before an IP address is automatically returned to the DHCP pool. This setting is particularly important when you have more hosts on a network than you have addresses. In that case, you should set a very short lease. If you have more addresses than hosts, you can make the lease as high as 999 days. By default, the lease is set to 8 days. This is usually sufficient for most networks. Figure 5.8 shows the DHCP Lease Duration screen. Click Next to continue.

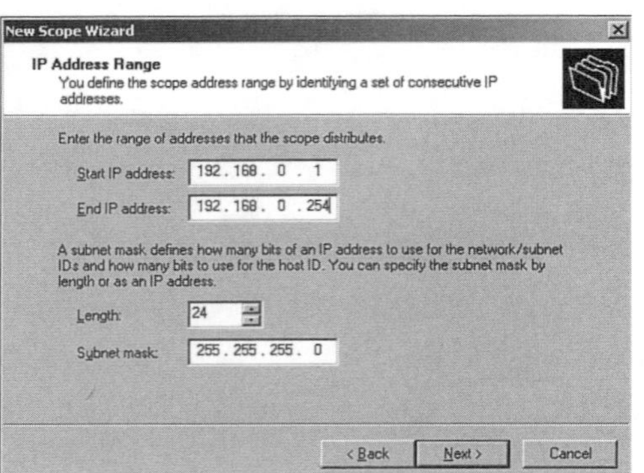

FIGURE 5.6
Be sure you select a unique range of addresses. If these addresses have already been assigned or another DHCP server is servicing this subnet, you can create problems.

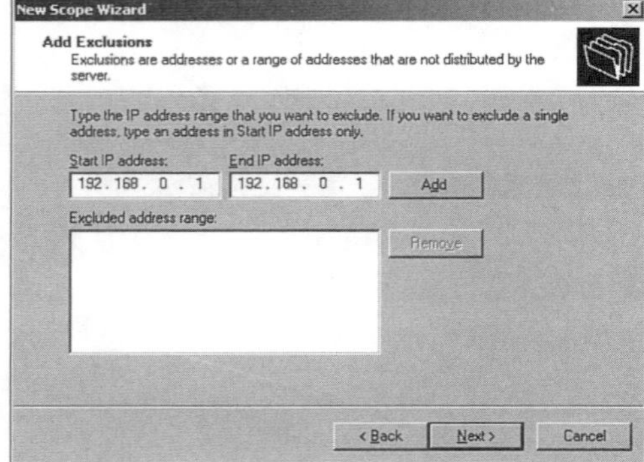

FIGURE 5.7
The Add Exclusions dialog box enables you to exclude addresses from inclusion in the pool of addresses leased to DHCP clients.

FIGURE 5.8
Be sure to set the lease duration to a length of time that matches your network environment. When in doubt, use a shorter lease and work toward a longer lease.

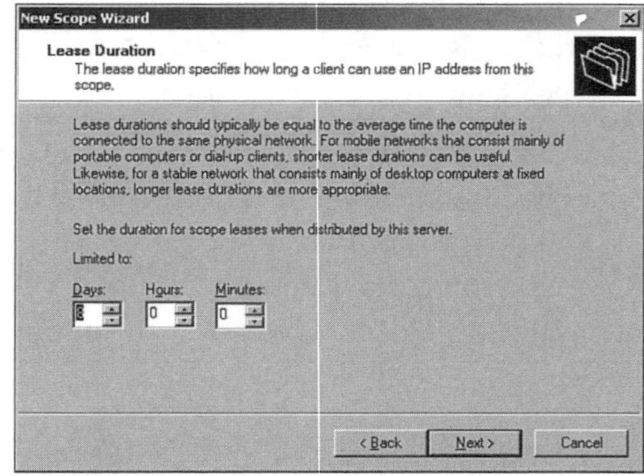

8. Configure any additional TCP/IP settings that you need to assign to DHCP clients when they request an address.

9. Configure the router, or default gateway, or specify multiple gateways. You can configure an unlimited number of gateways. Figure 5.9 shows the Router (Default Gateway) screen. Click Next to continue.

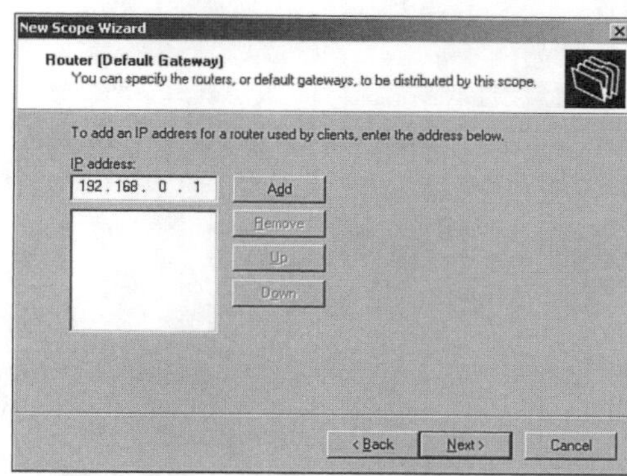

FIGURE 5.9
When you configure multiple default gateways, be sure to enter them in order of priority. The client computers will try them in the order they are issued.

10. The DNS and domain name servers enable you to specify as many DNS server addresses as necessary. You can enter only one parent domain, however. You can also use the Resolve button to get the IP address for a server by entering its name. Specify the DNS server(s) and parent domain for your environment. Figure 5.10 shows the Domain Name and DNS Servers screen. Click Next to continue.

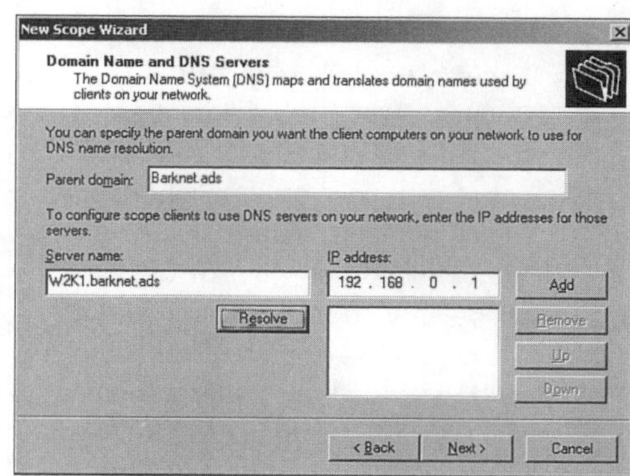

FIGURE 5.10
Configuring DNS configuration options for DHCP.

11. Provide a WINS server name and address only if you have legacy DHCP clients that still need WINS services. As in the last dialog box, the Resolve button can be used to resolve a host name to an address. Windows 2000 is heavily reliant on DNS for name resolution, and if you are working in a pure Windows 2000 environment, a WINS server is not necessary. See Figure 5.11 for the WINS Servers screen. Click Next to complete the scope creation.

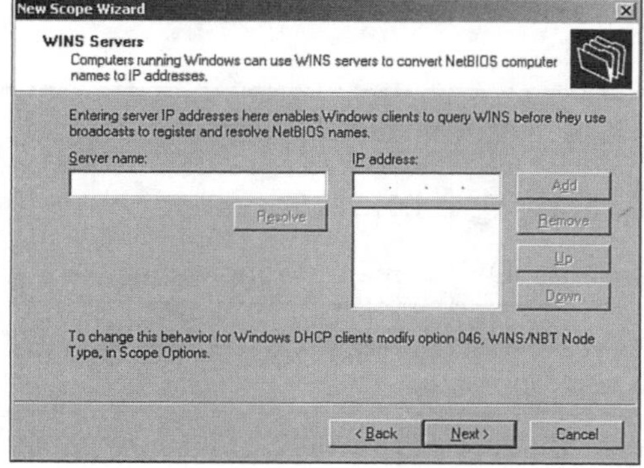

FIGURE 5.11
WINS is necessary only if you are supporting legacy systems. A pure Windows 2000 network should not need a WINS server.

continues

continued

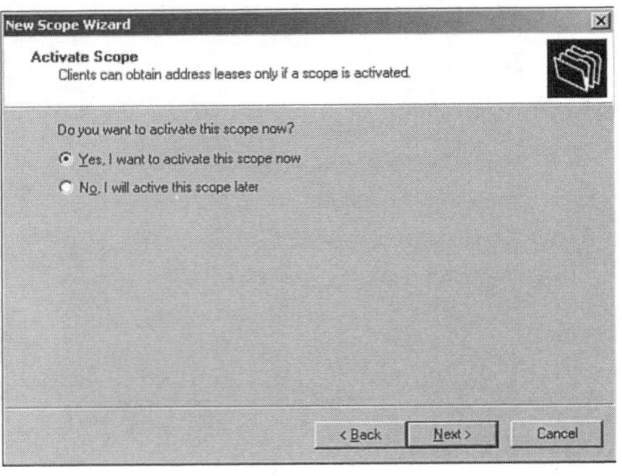

FIGURE 5.12
To make the range of addresses available to DHCP clients, the scope must be activated.

12. Specify whether to activate the scope at this time. The default on the Activate Scope dialog box is Yes, I Want to Activate This Scope Now (see Figure 5.12). If you want your client computers to have immediate access to this scope, leave the default selected. If you want to activate this scope at another time, select No, I Will Activate This Scope Later.
13. Click Next, and then click Finish to complete the creation of the scope.

You have successfully created a scope for your DHCP server. For it to go into production, it needs to be authorized in Active Directory.

WARNING

Exclude Routers from DHCP Scopes When you are configuring the gateway address for your DHCP scope, you have an excellent opportunity to ensure that your routers are excluded from your DHCP scope. You do not want to find out the hard way—when a client computer is issued the router's address and all traffic off the network stops abruptly because of an address conflict.

EXAM TIP

When to Use the New Multicast Scope Option The Actions menu creates a new scope and a new multicast scope as two different tasks. If you get a question on the exam regarding the procedure for creating a multicast scope, remember that you need to select New Multicast Scope.

Configuring Authorization of a DHCP Server

▶ Configure authorization of DHCP servers.

For the reasons mentioned previously, a new DHCP server must be authorized in Active Directory before it can assign IP addresses. To authorize a DHCP server in Active Directory, perform Step By Step 5.4.

STEP BY STEP

5.4 Authorizing a DHCP Server

1. Open the DHCP manager application.
2. Select the DHCP server you want to authorize and click the Action menu.
3. Select the Authorize action. This starts the authorize process, which can take a few minutes to complete. When the process is complete, your scope appears in the Contents of DHCP Server (the right pane) with an Active status.Your server is now ready to issue addresses when it receives a DHCP request.

Detecting Unauthorized DHCP Servers on a Network

The Microsoft DHCP server for Windows 2000 is designed to prevent unauthorized Windows 2000 DHCP servers from creating address assignment conflicts. If a user unintentionally creates a DHCP scope that begins leasing addresses that are not appropriate for your network, machines obtaining an inappropriate address will become unavailable to machines on your network.

The DHCP server for Windows 2000 has management features to prevent unauthorized deployments and detect existing unauthorized DHCP servers. In the past, anyone could bring up a DHCP server on a network. Today, though, an authorization step is required. These authorized personnel are usually the administrator of the domain to which the Windows 2000 Server platform belongs or someone to whom they have delegated the task of managing the DHCP servers.

Active Directory is now used to store records of authorized DHCP servers. When a DHCP server comes up, the directory is queried to verify the status of that server. If that server is unauthorized, no response is returned to DHCP requests and the new DHCP server will not issue any IP leases. A network manager must authorize the DHCP server before it will begin to lease addresses.

The list of authorized DHCP servers is maintained using the DHCP console. When it first comes up, the DHCP server tries to find out whether it is part of the directory domain. If it is, it tries to contact the directory to see whether it is in the list of authorized servers. If it succeeds, it sends out `DHCPINFORM` to find out whether other directory services are running and ensures that it is valid in others. If the DHCP server can't connect the directory, it assumes that it is not authorized and does not respond to client requests. Likewise, if it does reach the directory but does not find itself in the authorized list, it does not respond to clients. If it does find itself in the authorized list, it starts to service client requests.

Not all DHCP servers will be part of a Windows 2000 domain structure. The following section deals with DHCP servers that are part of workgroups.

> EXAM TIP
>
> **DHCP Clients Automatically Attempt to Extend Leases** For the exam, you should be aware of how DHCP leases work. Any DHCP client that had been assigned an address will automatically try to extend the lease when half the time of the lease has passed. If it is incapable of doing so, it will continue to try to do so for the duration of the lease.

DHCP Servers in Workgroups

When a DHCP server that is not a member server of the domain (such as a member of a workgroup) comes up, the following happens: The server broadcasts a `DHCPINFORM` message on the network; then, any other server that receives this message responds with a `DHCPACK` message and provides the name of the directory domain it is part of.

If a workgroup DHCP server detects another member DHCP server of a domain on the network, the workgroup DHCP server assumes that it is unauthorized on that network and does not service requests.

If the workgroup DHCP server detects the presence of another workgroup server, it ignores it; this means that there can be multiple workgroup servers active at the same time, as long as there is no directory service.

Even when a workgroup server comes up and finds itself allowed to run (because no other domain member server or workgroup server is on the network), it continues to probe `DHCPINFORM` every 5 minutes. If an authorized domain member DHCP server comes up later, the workgroup server becomes unauthorized and stops servicing.

Creating a Superscope

We've discussed how to create your first scope and how to authorize your DHCP server in Active Directory. Now we need to look at creating a superscope. Remember that a superscope is a grouping of scopes that are used to support multinetted IP subnets on the same physical network. To create a superscope, you must create more than one scope on your DHCP server. If you need to review how to do this, refer to the section, "Creating a Scope on Your DHCP Server." When you have multiple scopes on the DHCP server, you can create a superscope by following the steps in Step By Step 5.5.

The best reason to use superscopes is to make the scopes in a multinetted environment easier to support. If you have an environment with a lot of multinetting, identifying which scope goes with which network can get confusing. However, if you create a superscope named something like `4thFloor`, and you add all the multinetted addresses on the fourth floor to it, you'll know where to go when you need to modify or add a scope or when issues arise. You can also get statistics for all the scopes within the superscope from the superscope statistics.

You can use the process outlined in Step By Step 5.5 to create a superscope.

WARNING

All Scopes in Superscopes Must Be Active You can select only active scopes for the superscope, so be sure that all the scopes you want to include are active before you begin setting up the superscope.

STEP BY STEP

5.5 Creating a Superscope

1. Open the DHCP manager application.
2. Select the DHCP server in which you want to create the superscope and select Action, New Superscope. (You can also open the Action menu by right-clicking the DHCP server.) The New Superscope Wizard starts. Click Next; the Superscope Name dialog box shown in Figure 5.13 opens. Type a descriptive name for the superscope and click Next to continue.
3. The Select Scopes dialog box that appears enables you to select the active scopes to be included in the superscope (see Figure 5.14).
4. Select the scopes you want to include in the superscope, and click Next to continue. The Completing the New Superscope Wizard dialog box that appears gives you a summary of the selections you made throughout the wizard so that you can verify their accuracy.
5. If your selections are not correct, click Back to make changes or click Cancel to exit. When everything is correct and you are ready to create the superscope, click Finish.

You have now created a superscope, which will enable you to manage multiple scopes on the same physical network.

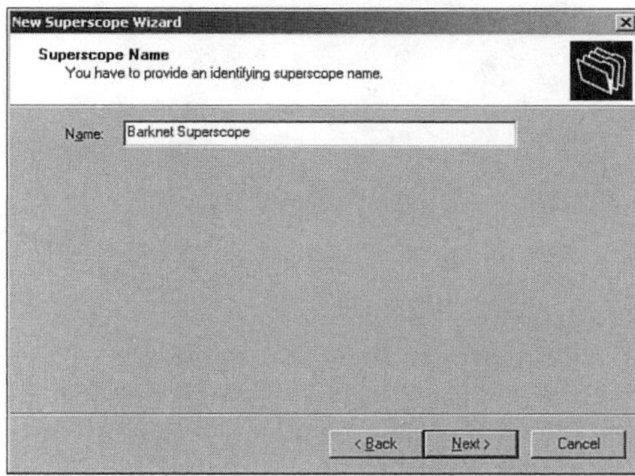

FIGURE 5.13
Using a descriptive superscope name enables you to more easily identify, manage, and troubleshoot the superscope in the future.

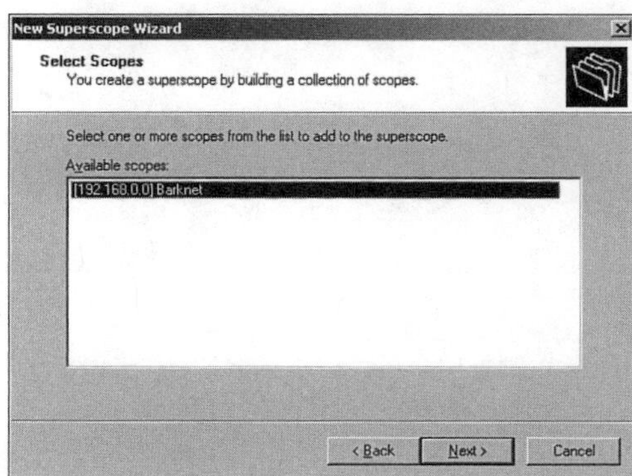

FIGURE 5.14
Select the active scopes you want included in the superscope.

Creating a Multicast Scope

Now let's discuss creating a multicast scope. To create a multicast scope, follow Step By Step 5.6.

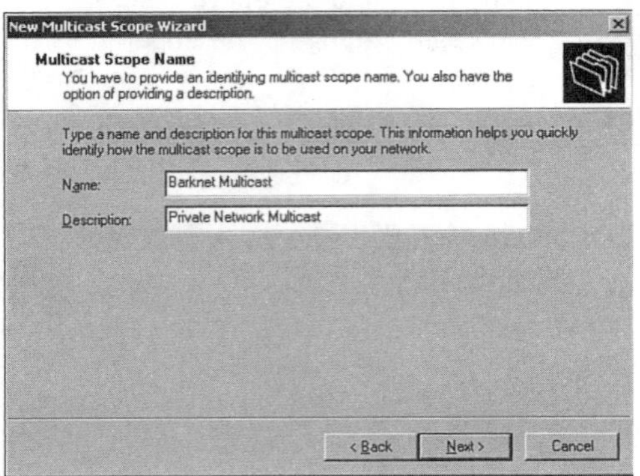

FIGURE 5.15
Using a descriptive multicast scope name enables you to more easily identify, manage, and troubleshoot the scope in the future.

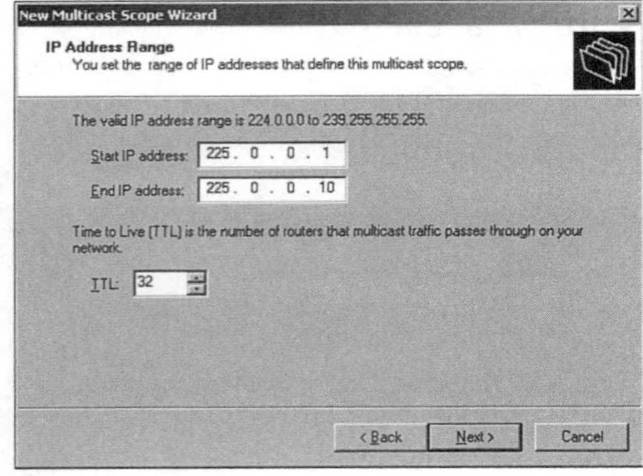

FIGURE 5.16
Enter the IP address range and TTL (time to live) for the scope.

STEP BY STEP

5.6 Creating a Multicast Scope

1. Open the DHCP manager application.
2. Select the DHCP server on which you want to create the multicast scope and select Action, New Multicast Scope. (You can also open the Action menu by right-clicking the DHCP server.) The New Multicast Scope Wizard starts. Click Next, and the Multicast Scope Name dialog box shown in Figure 5.15 opens. Type a descriptive name for the multicast scope and click Next to continue.
3. Select the range of addresses for the scope. They can range from 224.0.0.0 to 239.255.255.255. Enter the Time To Live amount. This is the number of routers the multicast packets can traverse before being discarded. Figure 5.16 shows the IP Address Range screen. Click Next to continue.
4. Add any addresses or ranges that need to be excluded from this scope. Figure 5.17 shows the Add Exclusions screen. Click Next to continue.

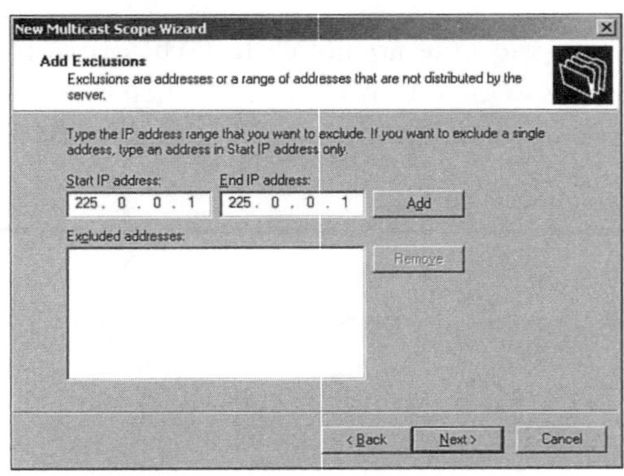

FIGURE 5.17
Enter the IP address range to exclude from the scope.

5. Set the length of the lease for the multicast address. Because these addresses are shared between multiple computers, this lease is generally longer than leases for other types of scopes. Set the lease to the amount of time you expect the multicasting to continue. Figure 5.18 shows the Lease Duration screen.

6. Click Next, and then click Finish to complete the creation of a multicast scope.

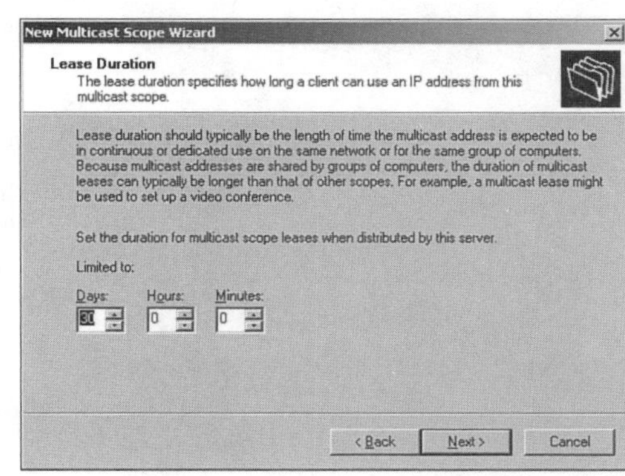

FIGURE 5.18
Multicast scopes typically have longer lease times than other types of scopes.

Now let's look at integrating DHCP into DNS.

Configuring DHCP for DNS Integration

One of the keys to effectively implementing an Active Directory environment is the capability for Windows 2000 workstations using DHCP to be automatically registered in DNS. Three settings can be set for DNS integration:

- **Automatically Update DHCP Client Information in DNS**—This is enabled by default and, if selected, the DHCP server registers the DHCP client for both forward (A-type records) and reverse lookups (PTR-type records) in DNS only when requested to by the client computer. These settings are usually adequate for a pure Windows 2000 environment because a Windows 2000 client computer updates DNS directly. If you have older Microsoft or non-Microsoft client computers on your network, you might want to change this to Always Update DNS. If the Always Update DNS option is selected, the DHCP server always registers the DHCP client for both the forward (A-type records) and reverse lookups (PTR-type records) with DNS.
- **Discard Forward (Name-to-Address) Lookups When Lease Expires**—This is also enabled by default and means that after the lease for an IP address expires (it is no longer in use by the client computer), DNS discards any resolution requests.

- **Enable Updates for DNS Clients That Do Not Support Dynamic Update**—This is another parameter you might want to enable if you are using Active Directory in a mixed client computer environment.

The DHCP server automatically updates any DNS server configured as part of the server's TCP/IP network properties. It is important to ensure that your primary DNS server is configured as one of the DNS servers because any updates sent to it will be propagated to the rest of the DNS servers for that domain.

The DNS server in question must support Dynamic DNS.

To configure the DHCP server to have the capability to automatically update your Dynamic DNS, follow Step By Step 5.7.

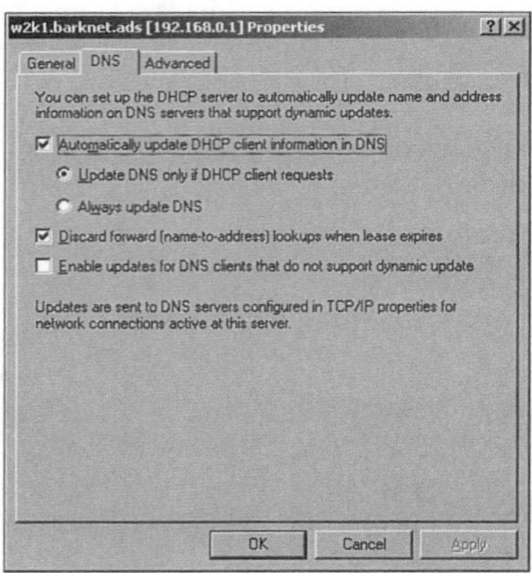

FIGURE 5.19
The DNS tab enables you to configure how the DHCP server will interact with the DNS server(s).

STEP BY STEP

5.7 Configuring DHCP for DNS Integration

1. Open the DHCP manager application.
2. Select the DHCP server you want to configure for DNS integration, and click the Action button. (You can also open the Action menu by right-clicking the DHCP server.)
3. Select Properties and then select the DNS tab (see Figure 5.19). You can configure three parameters in this dialog box. For this exercise, leave the settings at their defaults.

DHCP and DNS It is important to remember that Windows 2000 client computers can update the A records in DNS without any assistance from the DHCP server. The only client computers that DHCP updates DNS for are non-Windows 2000 client computers.

That takes care of the mechanics of integrating DHCP into your DNS environment. We should also discuss how the DHCP server actually makes the updates to DNS. A DHCP server can register and update pointer (PTR) and address (A) resource records on behalf of its DHCP-enabled clients.

The capability to register both A and PTR type records lets a DHCP server register non-Windows 2000 client computers in DNS, as you just learned. The DHCP server can differentiate between Windows 2000 Professional and other client computers.

Configuring Scope Options

In addition to supplying IP addresses and updating the Windows 2000 Dynamic DNS entries, DHCP can also configure your computer with several options. These are configured on a scope-by-scope basis.

To configure scope options, open the DHCP management screen and expand a previously created scope. This displays a folder named Server Options. Right-click the Scope Options folder and select Configure Options from the menu to display the Server Options pane. Checking the box next to an option displays the data entry pane and shows the options available to configure this scope. Figure 5.20 shows the data entry screen for a typical scope option.

NOTE

Levels of Options Options can be managed at levels for each managed DHCP server:

- **Server options**—These options are applied for all scopes defined at a DHCP server.
- **Scope options**—These options are applied specifically to all clients that obtain a lease within a particular scope.
- **Class options**—These options are applied only to clients that are identified as members of a specified user or vendor class when obtaining a lease.
- **Client options**—These options apply only for a single reserved client computer and require a reservation to be used in an active scope.

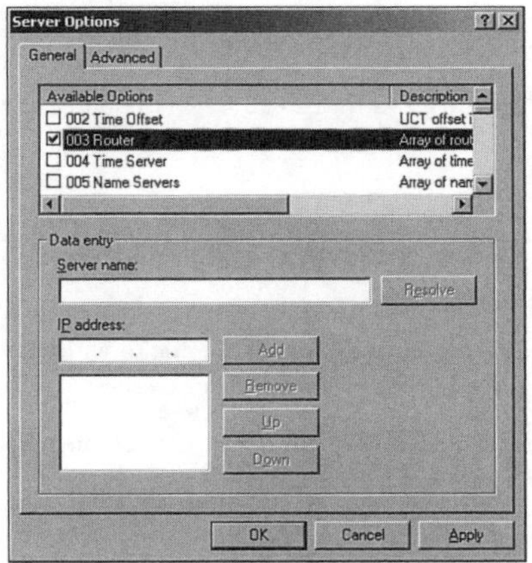

FIGURE 5.20
Defining scope options.

Table 5.1 describes the standard options available.

TABLE 5.1

DHCP SCOPE OPTIONS

Code	*Option Name*	*Description*
2	Time Offset	The time offset field specifies the offset of the client's subnet in seconds from Coordinated Universal Time (UTC).
3	Router Option	The router option specifies a list of IP addresses for routers on the client's subnet.
4	Time Server Option	The time server option specifies a list of RFC 868 [6] time servers available to the client.

continues

TABLE 5.1 *continued*

DHCP Scope Options

Code	*Option Name*	*Description*
5	Name Server Option	The name server option specifies a list of name servers available to the client.
6	Domain Name Server Option	The domain name server option specifies a list of DNS name servers available to the client.
7	Log Server Option	The log server option specifies a list of MIT-LCS UDP log servers available to the client.
8	Cookie Server Option	The cookie server option specifies a list of cookie servers available to the client.
9	LPR Server Option	The LPR server option specifies a list of RFC 1179 [10] line printer servers available to the client.
10	Impress Server Option	The Impress server option specifies a list of Imagen Impress servers available to the client.
11	Resource Location Server Option	This option specifies a list of RFC 887 [11] resource location servers available to the client.
12	Host Name Option	This option specifies the name of the client.
13	Boot File Size Option	This option specifies the length in 512-octet blocks of the default boot image for the client.
14	Merit Dump File	This option specifies the path name of a file to which the client's core image should be dumped in the event the client crashes.
15	Domain Name	This option specifies the domain name that the client should use when resolving host names via the DNS.
16	Swap Server	This specifies the IP address of the client's swap server.
17	Root Path	This option specifies the path name that contains the client's root disk.
18	Extensions Path	A string to specify a file, retrievable via TFTP, which contains information that can be interpreted in the same way as the 64-octet vendor-extension field within the BOOTP response.
19	IP Forwarding Enable/Disable Option	This option specifies whether the client should configure its IP layer for packet forwarding.
20	Non-Local Source Routing Enable/ Disable Option	This option specifies whether the client should configure its IP layer to allow forwarding of datagrams with nonlocal source routes.
21	Policy Filter Option	This option specifies policy filters for nonlocal source routing.
22	Maximum Datagram Reassembly Size	This option specifies the maximum size datagram that the client should be prepared to reassemble.
23	Default IP Time To Live	This option specifies the default TTL that the client should use on outgoing datagrams.

Code	*Option Name*	*Description*
24	Path MTU Aging Timeout Option	This option specifies the timeout (in seconds) to use when aging Path MTU values discovered by the mechanism defined in RFC 1191.
25	Path MTU Plateau Table Option	This option specifies a table of MTU sizes to use when performing Path MTU Discovery as defined in RFC 1191.
26	Interface MTU Option	This option specifies the MTU to use on this interface.
27	All Subnets Are Local Option	This option specifies whether the client can assume that all subnets of the IP network to which the client is connected use the same MTU as the subnet of the network to which the client is directly connected.
28	Broadcast Address Option	This option specifies the broadcast address in use on the client's subnet.
29	Perform Mask Discovery Option	This option specifies whether the client should perform subnet mask discovery using ICMP.
30	Mask Supplier Option	This option specifies whether the client should respond to subnet mask requests using ICMP.
31	Perform Router Discovery Option	This option specifies whether the client should solicit routers using the Router Discovery mechanism defined in RFC 1256.
32	Router Solicitation Address Option	This option specifies the address to which the client should transmit router solicitation requests.
33	Static Route Option	This option specifies a list of static routes that the client should install in its routing cache.
34	Trailer Encapsulation Option	This option specifies whether the client should negotiate the use of trailers (RFC 893) when using the ARP protocol.
35	ARP Cache Timeout Option	This option specifies the timeout in seconds for ARP cache entries. The time is specified as a 32-bit unsigned integer.
36	Ethernet Encapsulation Option	This option specifies whether the client should use Ethernet Version 2 (RFC 894 [15]) or IEEE 802.3 (RFC 1042 [16]) encapsulation if the interface is an Ethernet.
37	TCP Default TTL Option	This option specifies the default TTL the client should use when sending TCP segments.
38	TCP Keepalive Interval Option	This option specifies the interval (in seconds) the client TCP should wait before sending a keepalive message on a TCP connection.
39	TCP Keepalive Garbage Option	This option specifies the whether the client should send TCP keepalive messages with an octet of garbage for compatibility with older implementations.
40	Network Information Service Domain Option	This option specifies the name of the client's NIS domain.
41	Network Information Servers Option	This option specifies a list of IP addresses indicating NIS servers available to the client.
42	Network Time Protocol Servers Option	This option specifies a list of IP addresses indicating NTP servers available to the client.

continues

TABLE 5.1 *continued*

DHCP Scope Options

Code	*Option Name*	*Description*
43	Vendor Specific Information	This option is used by clients and servers to exchange vendor-specific information.
44	NetBIOS over TCP/IP Name Server Option	The NetBIOS name server (NBNS) option specifies a list of RFC 1001/1002 NBNS name servers listed in order of preference.
45	NetBIOS over TCP/IP Datagram Distribution Server Option	The NetBIOS datagram distribution server (NBDD) option specifies a list of RFC 1001/1002 NBDD servers listed in order of preference.
46	NetBIOS over TCP/IP Node Type Option	The NetBIOS node type option determines what methods NetBT will use to register and resolve names.
47	NetBIOS over TCP/IP Scope Option	The NetBIOS scope option specifies the NetBIOS over TCP/IP scope parameter for the client as specified in RFC 1001/1002.
48	X Window System Font Server Option	This option specifies a list of X Window System Font servers available to the client.
49	X Window System Display Manager Option	This option specifies a list of IP addresses of systems that are running the X Window System Display Manager and are available to the client.
50	Requested IP Address	This option is used in a client request (`DHCPDiscover`) to allow the client to request that a particular IP address be assigned.
51	IP Address Lease Time	This option is used in a client request (`DHCPDiscover` or `DHCPRequest`) to allow the client to request a lease time for the IP address. In a server reply (`DHCPOffer`), a DHCP server uses this option to specify the lease time it is willing to offer.
52	Option Overload	This option is used to indicate that the DHCP `sname` or `file` fields are being overloaded by using them to carry DHCP options. A DHCP server inserts this option if the returned parameters will exceed the usual space allotted for options.
66	TFTP Server Name	This option is used to identify a TFTP server when the `sname` field in the DHCP header has been used for DHCP options.
67	Bootfile Name	This option is used to identify a bootfile when the `file` field in the DHCP header has been used for DHCP options.
53	DHCP Message Type	This option is used to convey the type of the DHCP message. The code for this option is 53, and its length is 1. Legal values for this option are listed in Table 5.2.
54	Server Identifier	This option is used in `DHCPOffer` and `DHCPRequest` messages and can optionally be included in the `DHCPACK` and `DHCPNAK` messages.
55	Parameter Request List	This option is used by a DHCP client to request values for specified configuration parameters.

Code	*Option Name*	*Description*
56	Message	This option is used by a DHCP server to provide an error message to a DHCP client in a `DHCPNAK` message in the event of a failure.
57	Maximum DHCP Message Size	This option specifies the maximum length DHCP message it is willing to accept.
58	Renewal (T1) Time Value	This option specifies the time interval from address assignment until the client transitions to the `RENEWING` state.
59	Rebinding (T2) Time Value	This option specifies the time interval from address assignment until the client transitions to the `REBINDING` state.
60	Vendor Class Identifier	This option is used by DHCP clients to optionally identify the vendor type and configuration of a DHCP client.
61	Client-identifier	This option is used by DHCP clients to specify their unique identifiers. DHCP servers use this value to index their databases of address bindings.
64	Network Information Service+ Domain Option	This option specifies the name of the client's NIS+ domain.
65	Network Information Service+ Servers Option	This option specifies a list of IP addresses indicating NIS+ servers available to the client.
68	Mobile IP Home Agent Option	This option specifies a list of IP addresses indicating mobile IP home agents available to the client.
69	Simple Mail Transport Protocol (SMTP) Server Option	The SMTP server option specifies a list of SMTP servers available to the client.
70	Post Office Protocol (POP3) Server Option	The POP3 server option specifies a list of POP3 servers available to the client.
71	Network News Transport Protocol (NNTP) Server Option	The NNTP server option specifies a list of NNTP servers available to the client.
72	Default World Wide Web (WWW) Server Option	The WWW server option specifies a list of WWW servers available to the client.
73	Default Finger Server Option	The Finger server option specifies a list of Finger servers available to the client.
74	Default Internet Relay Chat (IRC) Server Option	The IRC server option specifies a list of IRC servers available to the client.
75	StreetTalk Server Option	The StreetTalk server option specifies a list of StreetTalk servers available to the client.
76	StreetTalk Directory Assistance (STDA) Server Option	The StreetTalk Directory Assistance (STDA) server option specifies a list of STDA servers available to the client.

Table 5.2 lists the values for the DHCP Message Type option.

TABLE 5.2

DHCP MESSAGE TYPE OPTION VALUES

Value	*Message Type*
1	DHCPDiscover
2	DHCPOffer
3	DHCPRequest
4	DHCPDECLINE
5	DHCPACK
6	DHCPNAK
7	DHCPRELEASE
8	DHCPINFORM

There is also a provision in DHCP for manufacturer-specific DHCP options to be configured. These options can be selected by opening the DHCP management console and selecting the scope to configure options, as described earlier. Selecting the Advanced tab enables you to select Microsoft Windows 2000 from the drop-down list in the Vendor Class window.

Table 5.3 shows the manufacturer options defined by Microsoft.

TABLE 5.3

MICROSOFT-SPECIFIC DHCP OPTIONS

Code	*Option Name*	*Description*
1	Disable NetBIOS over TCP/IP (NetBT)	This option can be used to selectively enable or disable NetBT for DHCP-enabled computers running Windows.
2	Release DHCP Lease on Shutdown	This option can be used to control whether DHCP-enabled computers running Windows send a release for their current DHCP leases to the DHCP server when shutdown occurs.
3	Default Router Metric Base	This value is a specified router metric base to be used for all default gateway routes.

Reserving IP Addresses for Client Computers

Some DHCP clients should not receive random IP addresses within the scope they belong to. Some clients should always obtain the same IP address. These types of clients can be Unix servers that could require a fixed address, Windows 2000 servers that are used for Web services, or file servers; also, they can often be known by their IP address as well as their DNS or NetBIOS names.

DHCP has a way of always leasing a fixed IP address to a server; it's called the *client reservation.* Client reservations are made based on the MAC address of the network adapter of the client computer. This is the only identifying information available when the machine is booting (typically when DHCP requests are made).

Step By Step 5.8 can be used to configure a new client reservation within a scope of addresses.

STEP BY STEP

5.8 Creating a Client Reservation

1. Open the DHCP manager application.
2. Select the DHCP server and expand the scope on which you want to create the reservation.
3. Right-click the Reservations icon and click New Reservations. Figure 5.21 shows the New Reservation screen.
4. Provide a reservation name, complete the IP address for the reservation, and add the MAC address of the remote computer (in hexadecimal with no spaces or dashes).
5. Click Add to add the reservation to the scope.
6. If the address is currently in use have the user of that computer issue an `IPCONFIG /RELEASE` command and an `IPCONFIG /RENEW` command.
7. On the client the reservation is for, issue the same two commands (`IPCONFIG /RELEASE` and `IPCONFIG /RENEW`).
8. Verify that DHCP has now assigned your client the IP address you have reserved for it.

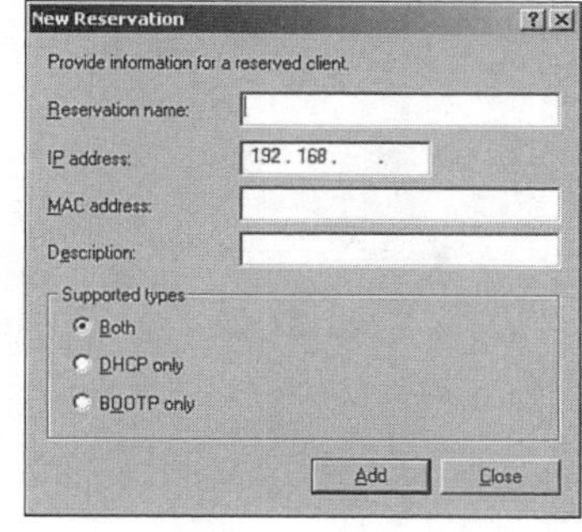

FIGURE 5.21
Use a descriptive name when completing the client reservation screen.

NOTE

DHCP Options Reserved clients can have DHCP options configured specifically for their use. When options are configured for a reserved client, these values override any option-type parameters distributed via server-based, scope-based, or class-based options assignment.

DHCP in a Routed Network

In a network that uses subnets to divide segments and uses routers to manage traffic, some specific requirements must be met for any DHCP service to function correctly. These are as follows:

- One DHCP server must be located on at least one subnet in the routed network.
- For a DHCP server to support clients on other remote subnets separated by routers, a router needs to support BOOTP forwarding or a computer on the other side of the router from the DHCP server must be configured as a DHCP relay agent to support forwarding of DHCP traffic between subnets.

Planning Your DHCP Server Deployment

When you are planning to deploy DHCP on your routed network, you have to consider the locations of routers and whether you want a DHCP server on each subnet. You will need to configure your routers to provide the BOOTP Forwarder service. You also might have to configure superscopes as well.

The speed of your network is an important factor. If you extend a DHCP server across a WAN or dial-up link, you might find that a DHCP server on both sides provides better response.

There is no fixed limit to the maximum number of clients a single DHCP server can serve. However, your network can have practical constraints based on the IP address class selected for use and other server configuration details.

There are some considerations in choosing the DHCP server hardware, as listed in the following:

- **Disk speed**—The primary contributing factor to improved DHCP server performance is disk I/O capacity (more so than CPU or memory).
- **Number of scopes**—As a general rule, each DHCP server should not support more than 1,000 scopes.
- **Number of clients**—As a general rule, each DHCP server should not support more than 10,000 clients.

So far, we have looked at DHCP services that provide a centrally managed pool of IP addresses and TCP/IP configuration information. This usually requires the routers in your network to forward BOOTP packets to accomplish this. For those networks that can't provide this, there is an alternative way of providing DHCP services in a routed network, which is discussed in the next section.

An Alternative Plan for Providing DHCP Services

If, for some reason, your network routers can't provide the BOOTP Forwarder service, you can use the following solutions for each subnet:

- **A computer running either Windows 2000 Server or Windows NT Server 4.0 configured to use the DHCP Relay Agent component**—This computer simply forwards messages back and forth between clients on the local subnet and a remote DHCP server using the IP address of the remote server. The DHCP Relay Agent service is available only on computers running Windows 2000 Server or Windows NT Server 4.0.
- **A computer running Windows 2000 Server configured as a DHCP server for the local subnet**—This server computer must contain and manage scope and other address-configurable information for the local subnet it serves.

Each of these solutions provides DHCP services for those routed networks that can't supply the BOOTP Forwarder service.

DHCP Relay Agent

If you are using the DHCP relay agent on your routers, you need to know how the agent works to distribute DHCP requests and configuration information around the network.

Figure 5.22 shows a simple network that uses a DHCP server (on Subnet 2) with a router that has the DHCP relay agent configured.

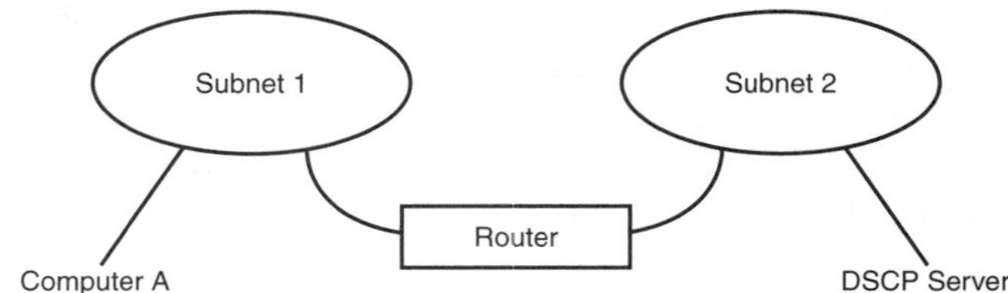

FIGURE 5.22
A simple network with a DHCP server on one subnet.

The following are the steps involved in ComputerA obtaining a DHCP leased address:

1. ComputerA broadcasts a DHCP/BOOTP discover message (`DHCPDiscover`) on Subnet 1, as a UDP datagram on port 67.
2. The relay agent in the router examines the gateway IP address field in the DHCP/BOOTP message header. If the field has an IP address of 0.0.0.0, the agent fills it with the relay agent or router's IP address and forwards the message to the remote Subnet 2, where the DHCP server is located.
3. When the DHCP server on remote Subnet 2 receives the message, it examines the gateway IP address field for a DHCP scope on which it can lease addresses.
4. When the DHCP server receives the `DHCPDiscover` message, it processes and sends an IP address lease offer (`DHCPOffer`) directly to the relay agent identified in the gateway IP address (`GIADDR`) field.
5. The router then relays the address lease offer (`DHCPOffer`) to the DHCP client.

In this section we have discussed how DHCP works in typical network situations. In the next section we will discuss how to troubleshoot your DHCP deployment and measure its activity using PerfMon.

MONITORING AND TROUBLESHOOTING DHCP

We have looked at installing and configuring the Windows 2000 DHCP service. The final piece of the DHCP puzzle is managing and monitoring the server after it is installed and configured. The Windows 2000 DHCP Server bundles enhanced monitoring and statistical reporting for precisely that purpose.

DHCP Statistics

The DHCP manager has several additional features that are found on the Action menu. The Display Statistics command opens the Server Statistics window shown in Figure 5.23. This screen displays the following statistics:

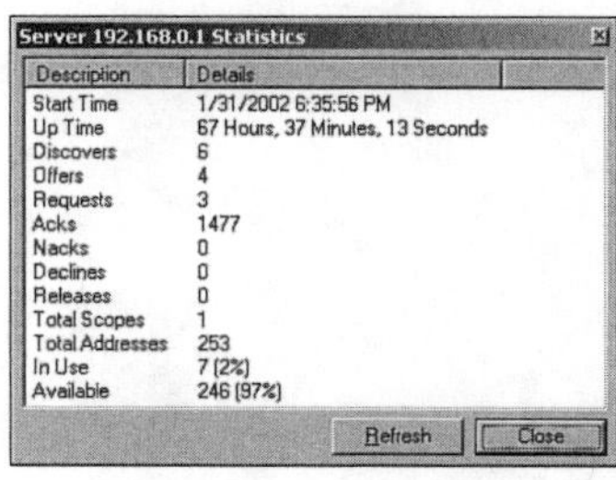

FIGURE 5.23
The Server Statistics screen gives you an excellent snapshot of the server's activities.

- **Start Time**—The date and time the service was started.
- **Up Time**—The total up time for the DHCP service. If you restart the service, this number resets to 0, even if the Windows 2000 server has not been restarted.
- **Discovers**—The number of `DHCPDiscover` packets the server has received.
- **Offers**—The number of `DHCPOffer` packets the server has sent.
- **Requests**—The number of `DHCPRequest` packets the server has received.
- **Acks**—The number of DHCP acknowledgement packets the server has sent.
- **Nacks**—The number of DHCP negative acknowledgement packets the server has sent.
- **Declines**—The number of `DHCPDecline` packets the server has received.
- **Releases**—The number of `DHCPRelease` messages the server has received.
- **Total Scopes**—The total number of scopes active on the server.
- **Total Addresses**—The total number of addresses available. This includes the number of addresses for the active scopes on the server.
- **In Use**—The number of addresses presently leased to DHCP client computers.
- **Available**—The number of addresses available for lease for the Total Address pool.

Reconciling Scopes

The Reconcile All Scopes command enables you to compare the information contained in the DHCP database with the information stored in the Registry. Use this option only when you are having issues with the DHCP server and need to verify the configured addresses. Clicking the Verify button checks the consistency of the database and returns any errors it finds.

Removing a DHCP Service

The Unauthorize command removes the DHCP server from the list of authorized DHCP servers in the Active Directory. You will be warned before the removal occurs.

The Define User Classes, Define Vendor Classes, and Set Predefined options are not typically used in a standard DHCP installation, but you should be aware of what user classes and vendor classes are for the exam:

- **User classes**—User classes are generally created for administrative purposes, similar to user groups. They can be used to identify all the DHCP clients in a specific department or location. User classes are used to assign DHCP options to groups of DHCP clients.
- **Vendor classes**—Vendor classes are generally used to provide vendor-specific DHCP enhancements. For example, the Windows 2000 DHCP Service has the capability to disable NetBIOS over TCP/IP on its DHCP clients.

Statistics and the Event Log

The Properties menu for a DHCP server has three options (in the General tab) that are useful:

- **Automatically Update Statistics Every**—This option enables you to set the automatic refresh of the statistics, as well as the interval at which they are refreshed.

- **Enable DHCP Audit Logging**—This option enables you to log all the DHCP activity to a file, which can be viewed in the System Log using Event Viewer. This is an excellent option to select if you are troubleshooting a DHCP issue and want to see what activity is taking place on the server. Figure 5.24 shows a sample of the System Log with DHCP messages in it. You can also see these messages in the Audit Log, located at `\<%system_root%>\System32\dhcp`.

```
Microsoft DHCP Service Activity Log

Event ID Meaning
00       The log was started.
01       The log was stopped.
02       The log was temporarily paused due to low disk space.
10       A new IP address was leased to a client.
11       A lease was renewed by a client.
12       A lease was released by a client.
13       An IP address was found to be in use on the network.
14       A lease request could not be satisfied because the scope's
         address pool was exhausted.
15       A lease was denied.
16       A lease was deleted.
17       A lease was expired.
20       A BOOTP address was leased to a client.
21       A dynamic BOOTP address was leased to a client.
22       ABOOTP request cold not be satisfied because the scope's
         address pool for BOOTP was exhausted.
23       A BOOTP IP address was deleted after checking to see it was
         not in use.
50+      Codes above 50 are used for Rogue Server Detection information.
51,02/01/02,21:32:45,Authorization succeeded,,barknet.ads,
63,02/01/02,22:39:06,Restarting rogue detection,,,
51,02/01/02,22:40:07,Authorization succeeded,,barknet.ads,
11,02/01/02,23:12:24,Renew,192.168.0.2,gordb3.barknet.ads,0010B555433F
63,02/01/02,23:46:27,Restarting rogue detection,,,
51,02/01/02,23:47:28,Authorization succeeded,,barknet.ads,
```

FIGURE 5.24
The System Log can be viewed using the Event Viewer. Every DHCP action is logged in the System Log when the Enable DHCP Audit Logging option is selected.

- **Show the BOOTP Table Folder**—This option deals with BOOTP backward compatibility and enables you to view the table where the BOOTP configuration entries are contained. This table appears in the Tree window of the DHCP manager and enables you to configure a BOOTP image file, which can be loaded to a BOOTP client from either a full server path or a TFTP file server.

The DNS tab of the Properties dialog box was discussed in detail in the "Configuring DHCP for DNS Integration" section earlier in the

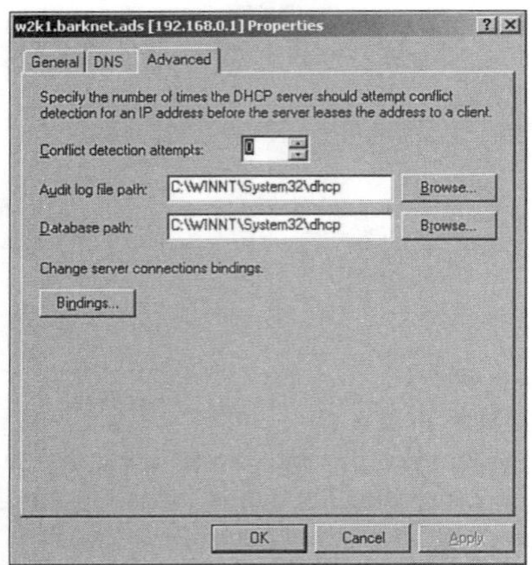

FIGURE 5.25
The Advanced options shouldn't be modified without a thorough understanding of the options and the ramifications of the change.

chapter. Use the Advanced tab (shown in Figure 5.25) for the following configuration options:

- **Conflict Detection Attempts**—This option causes the DHCP server to check for conflicting IP addresses on the network before issuing an address. Although this sounds like a great way to ensure there are no address conflicts, this can add significant overhead to the server and should be used only while troubleshooting address conflict issues. By default, this is set to 0.
- **Audit Log File Path**—If Audit Logging is enabled, the log file is located in the \<%system_root%>\System32\dhcp directory. You can modify the default from this tab.
- **Database Path**—This option enables you to specify the location of the DHCP database. By default, it is in \<%system_root%>\System32\dhcp.
- **Change Server Connections Bindings**—This option enables you to view the connections through which the DHCP server is providing addresses. If you have multiple connections to your DHCP server, you might want to configure DHCP for only selected interfaces. Click the Bindings button to view this screen.

> **EXAM TIP**
>
> **Know the Types of DHCP Statistics** Although you don't need to memorize these counters for the exam, you should at least be familiar with the types of statistics that can be gathered for DHCP.

Now that you have looked at the options for managing the DHCP server, let's take a look at some of the ways to monitor the service. First, you need to be familiar with the counters that can be measured for DHCP:

- **Packets Received/Sec**—The number of message packets received per second by the DHCP server. A large number indicates a large amount of DHCP message traffic to the server. These can be requests for addresses, renewal requests, or releases. This does not necessarily indicate just a large number of requests.
- **Duplicates Dropped/Sec**—The number of duplicate packets per second dropped by the DHCP server. Duplicate packets on a network are never a good sign, and in this case, it indicates DHCP clients are timing out before the server can respond. This can be caused by client computers timing out too quickly or the server not responding quickly enough.

- **Packets Expired/Sec**—The number of packets per second that expire and are dropped by the DHCP server. This is caused by a packet remaining in the server's internal message queue for too long. A large number here indicates that the server is taking too long to process some packets, the server is causing other packets to wait in queue, or the traffic on the network is too high for the DHCP server to handle. It is important to note that high numbers here can indicate pure network traffic issues and not necessarily DHCP-related problems.
- **Milliseconds Per Packet (Avg)**—The average time, in milliseconds, the DHCP server takes to process each packet it receives. This is a very subjective number because of the server configuration; therefore, a baseline for this number is a good idea. A sudden increase in this counter could indicate a disk issue or an increased load on the server.
- **Active Queue Length**—The current length of the internal message queue of the DHCP server. This number represents the number of unprocessed messages received by the server. A large number here could indicate an unusually high amount of network traffic or a high load on the server.
- **Conflict Check Queue Length**—The current length of the conflict check queue for the DHCP server. Before a Windows 2000 DHCP Server issues an address, it checks to see whether any IP address conflicts exist. This queue holds the messages held in queue while the DHCP server performs address conflict detection. A large value here could indicate heavy lease traffic at the server. You also should check the Conflict Detection Attempts parameter, which could be set too high.
- **Discovers/Sec**—The number of `DHCPDiscover` messages received per second by the server. The `DHCPDiscover` message is the initial request a client computer sends when it first enters the network and is looking for a DHCP server to issue an address. A sudden increase in this counter could indicate that a large number of client computers are attempting to initialize and obtain an IP address lease from the server at the same time. You might see this first thing in the morning, when users power on their PCs, or after a power failure, when all your PCs might be powered on at about the same time.

- **Offers/Sec**—The number of `DHCPOffer` messages sent per second by the DHCP server to client computers. A `DHCPOffer` message is the message the server returns to the client computer after the client computer sends a `DHCPDiscover` message, and it indicates the server is offering to issue an address to that client computer. A sudden increase in this value could indicate heavy traffic or a heavy load on the server.
- **Requests/Sec**—The number of `DHCPRequest` messages received per second by the DHCP server from client computers. This is the request the client computer sends to request an IP address after it has found a server that can issue addresses. An increase in this number indicates that a large number of client computers are probably trying to renew their leases with the DHCP server. This could be because of a short lease time configuration, or several new computers could be entering the network.
- **Informs/Sec**—The number of `DHCPInform` messages received per second by the DHCP server. `DHCPInform` messages are used when the DHCP server queries the directory service for the enterprise root and when dynamic updates are being done on behalf of client computers by the DNS server. This is part of the Dynamic DNS integration, and an unusual increase in this number could indicate a large number of addresses being issued.
- **Acks/Sec**—The number of `DHCPAck` messages sent per second by the DHCP server to client computers. The `DHCPAck` message is used by the DHCP server to acknowledge requests for an address. An increase in this number indicates that a large number of client computers are probably trying to renew their leases with the DHCP server. This could be because of a short lease time configuration, or several new computers could be entering the network.
- **Nacks/Sec**—The number of DHCP negative acknowledgment messages sent per second by the DHCP server to client computers. This indicates the server is incapable of fulfilling the DHCP request. A very high value for this counter could indicate a network issue or misconfiguration of client computers or the server. Keep an eye out for a deactivated scope as a possible culprit.

- **Declines/Sec**—The number of `DHCPDecline` messages received per second by the DHCP server from client computers. This counter indicates that the DHCP client computer has declined the IP address issued by the server. You will see this number rise when client computers start having address conflict issues. This could indicate a network issue, computers with static addresses that are also part of a scope, or potentially a "rogue" DHCP server on the network.
- **Releases/Sec**—The number of `DHCPRelease` messages received per second by the DHCP server from client computers. A `DHCPRelease` message is sent only when the client computer manually releases an address, such as when the `IPCONFIG /RELEASE` command or the Release All button in the winipcfg utility is used at the client computer. Because most users do not manually release their addresses, this number should be low in all but the most unusual network environments.

To configure DHCP Performance monitoring, follow Step By Step 5.9.

> **EXAM TIP**
>
> **What Can You Do to Resolve Conflict Issues?** When you start seeing a high number of declines per second, you might want to enable conflict detection on the DHCP server. This causes the server to look for conflicts before issuing an address, and it should take care of the conflict issues until you can find the problem. This should be used only until the issue is addressed. Forcing the DHCP server to detect conflicts every time it issues an address adds a lot of overhead to the server and the DHCP service and should be avoided on a long-term basis. After you have resolved the issue, be sure to turn off this feature.

STEP BY STEP

5.9 Monitoring DHCP Performance

1. Select Start, Programs, Administrative Tools, Performance to open the Performance application.
2. In the Performance console, highlight the System Monitor in the left frame.
3. To create an entry in System Monitor, click the Add (+) icon.
4. Select the DHCP performance object. You will see the list of counters displayed as available for DHCP (see Figure 5.26). If you need to know what a counter means, select the counter and click the Explain button.

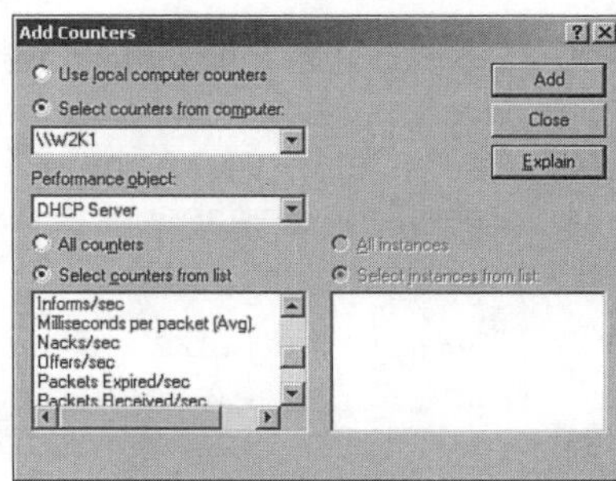

FIGURE 5.26
The counters associated with DHCP enable you to comprehensively examine the DHCP server's activities.

continues

continued

5. When you have decided on the counter you want to monitor, click Add. You can add multiple counters either by selecting each counter and clicking Add or by using the standard Windows multiple item select method of holding down the Ctrl key while you select all the counters you want to monitor and then clicking Add. Click Close when you are finished.

At this point, you should have a good understanding of the Windows 2000 DHCP service. Next, you'll see how to apply it in a practical situation.

CASE STUDY: IMPLEMENTING DHCP IN A COMPLEX ENVIRONMENT

ESSENCE OF THE CASE

The essence of the case is as follows:

- Your company is about to migrate to a pure Windows 2000 environment.
- Your company has three networks, two with users and one as a backbone. The Sales network has approximately 400 users; the Engineering network has 75 users.
- The three networks are connected by two routers: router A and router B.
- The Sales network has plenty of addresses because of the multinetted network. The Engineering network does not have enough addresses for its network, but the engineers are able to work because they work in shifts.

SCENARIO

You are the network administrator for NR Widgets Inc., a computer manufacturing company. NR Widgets Inc., is just about to migrate to a pure Windows 2000 environment. You have two user networks—Sales and Engineering—and a corporate backbone network. The Sales network has more than 400 users and is multinetted to provide an adequate number of addresses for everyone. The Engineering network has only 75 users, but the network also contains a number of printers, plotters, and test equipment, so only 40 addresses are available for the users. The users work three shifts in engineering, with 25 engineers working each shift.

Today, all the hosts use static addresses, which works okay for the Sales network, but it means that to avoid IP address resolution issues, the engineers have to be careful about which computers are left connected to the network.

CASE STUDY: IMPLEMENTING DHCP IN A COMPLEX ENVIRONMENT

Yesterday your manager suggested, "While you're migrating to Windows 2000, why don't you fix the IP address problems on the network?"

Keeping in mind that the boss's "suggestions" usually mean "Have it done by the end of the week," what should you do?

ANALYSIS

This situation provides an excellent opportunity to deploy the Windows 2000 DHCP service as part of the Windows 2000 rollout. To make it work, you need to be sure you do the following:

- Allocate the server resources to support at least one DHCP server. To avoid as much traffic traversing the router as possible, you should plan on placing the server on the network that will be generating the most DHCP requests. Because 400 users are on the Sales network, at first glance you might think that is where all the requests will be coming from. Think again. Because there are plenty of addresses for the Sales network, you can configure exceptionally long lease times, so the number of requests after the initial lease will be pretty low. On the Engineering network, however, each user will be requesting a new address every time she powers up the computer because of the limited number of addresses.
- After you have identified the server and placed it on the network, you will need to install and configure DHCP. After the service is installed, you must authorize the server in Active Directory.
- When you create your scopes, you should create a single scope for the Engineering network and a superscope for the Sales network. The superscope enables you to combine multiple scopes (the Sales network has three network addresses) for easier management. The lease for each of the scopes within the superscope should be at least 30 days to ensure that a limited amount of lease traffic traverses the routers. The lease for the Engineering network should be 8 hours so that addresses are available for the incoming shift as the previous shift leaves.
- Finally, you need to ensure that the BOOTP Forwarder service is running on the routers and is configured to point to the appropriate DHCP server for forwarding DHCP traffic.

After the DHCP server is set up and running, you also should set up some of the monitoring discussed earlier in this chapter in the section "Statistics and the Event Log."

CHAPTER SUMMARY

In this chapter, we discussed the key components of using a Windows 2000 DHCP server in a Windows 2000 environment. We first discussed what DHCP was and where it came from. We covered the various types of scopes in detail and then went through the steps of installing DHCP, creating the first scope, and then authorizing the server in Active Directory. Combined, these give you a working DHCP server.

We also discussed creating superscopes and multicast scopes, integrating DNS and DHCP, and the various methods for monitoring and managing DHCP.

KEY TERMS

- BOOTP protocol
- Client reservation
- DHCP client
- DHCP server
- Domain Name System (DNS)
- Dynamic Host Control Protocol (DHCP)
- Exclusion
- Lease
- Multicast scope
- Registered IP address
- Scope
- Supernetted network
- Superscope
- Unicast addresses

APPLY YOUR KNOWLEDGE

Exercises

5.1 Creating a DHCP Scope

In this exercise you will go through the steps required to create a scope.

Estimated Time: 30 minutes

1. Click Start, select Programs, Administrative Tools, and click DHCP.
2. Select the DHCP server listed in the DHCP window (the one on the right), and select Action, New Scope to start the New Scope Wizard. Click Next to start defining your scope. This opens the Scope Name dialog box.
3. Type the name `Exercise1` and a description in the fields provided, and then click Next. This opens the IP Address Range window.
4. Enter the appropriate address range and subnet mask. For this exercise, use 10.0.0.1–10.0.0.100, with a subnet mask of 255.255.255.0. Click Next, and the Add Exclusions dialog box opens.
5. Add addresses to be excluded, as necessary. For this exercise, you don't need to exclude any addresses. Click Next to open the Lease Duration dialog box.
6. For this exercise, leave the default lease duration. Click Next; the Configure DHCP Options dialog box opens.
7. Configure the router, or default gateway. In this exercise, use 10.0.0.254. Click Next, and the Domain Name and DNS Servers dialog box opens.
8. Specify the DNS server(s), as necessary. For this exercise, use 10.0.1.1 and 10.0.2.1. Click Next; the WINS Servers dialog box opens.
9. Define a WINS server if you have legacy DHCP client computers that still need WINS services. For this exercise, use 10.0.1.2 and 10.0.2.2.
10. Click Next, and then click Finish to complete the scope creation.

5.2 Creating a Superscope

This exercise shows you how to manage multiple scopes by creating a superscope. You will need to have completed Exercise 2.1 for this to work.

Estimated Time: 10 minutes

1. Open the DHCP manager application.
2. Select the DHCP server on which you want to create the superscope and click the Action button. You can also open this menu by right-clicking the DHCP server.
3. Select New Superscope. Click Next to continue.
4. The Superscope Name dialog box opens. Enter a name and click Next to continue. For this exercise, enter the name **`SuperExercise1`**.
5. In the Select Scopes dialog box, select the scopes you want to include in the superscope and click Next to continue. You should select the `Exercise1` scope created in the last exercise.
6. The Completing the New Superscope Wizard dialog box gives you a summary of the selections you made throughout the wizard. To create the superscope, click Finish.
7. Open the DHCP manager again and note where the superscope is in comparison to the scope created in Exercise 5.1.

APPLY YOUR KNOWLEDGE

5.3 Monitoring DHCP Server Performance Using the Performance Application

This exercise walks you through adding a counter to the Performance utility so you can baseline or troubleshoot your DHCP server.

Estimated Time: 15 minutes

1. Open the Performance application by selecting Programs, Administrative Tools, Performance.
2. In the Performance console, highlight System Monitor in the left frame.
3. To create an entry in System Monitor, click the Add (+) icon. The Add Counters windows opens. Notice that by default it opens to the Processor performance object.
4. Select the DHCP performance object.
5. Select the counter you want to monitor and click Add. You can add multiple counters either by selecting each counter and clicking Add or by using the standard Windows multiple item select method of holding down the Ctrl key while you select all the counters you want to monitor and then clicking Add. For this exercise, select the Offers/Sec, Requests/Sec, and Releases/Sec counters. Click Close when you are done.
6. Observe the results in the monitoring window. If you have multiple workstations available, make some DHCP requests to see the effect on the counters.

Review Questions

1. You are the network administrator for Exponent Mathematicians, and you have been asked to implement DHCP on a multinetted network segment. Which DHCP scope option should you implement?
2. You are the administrator of the Get Bux pawnshop chain DHCP server. You are getting complaints from your users that they keep getting address conflict messages when they turn on their computers. Which DHCP counter might help you identify the issue?
3. You are the Windows 2000 administrator for Fly Away Travel. When administering Fly Away's DHCP server, you notice that the number of DHCP requests is very high for the number of users on the network. Where is the first place you should look for a server-related issue?
4. You're the administrator of Little Faith Enterprise's Windows 2000 DHCP server at its Drive-in Acupuncture shop. You notice that the DHCP server is running sluggishly during peak hours. Checking the Performance utility, you notice the DHCP Conflict Check Queue Length is very high. What could be causing this issue?
5. You're the administrator of Little Faith Enterprise's Windows 2000 DHCP server at its other venture, Whale Away Deep Sea Tours, and you have just installed the DHCP service and created your first scope using the Scope Wizard. You are trying to provide DHCP addresses to a group of users who are two router hops away. What do you still need to do?

Exam Questions

1. You are the network administrator for Wild West Widgets of Calgary Inc. You are training a new

APPLY YOUR KNOWLEDGE

employee on the use of the DHCP service in Windows 2000 Server. She asks you how the client computer requests and receives an address from the server. What is the sequence that you should explain to the new employee?

A. The client computer broadcasts a `DHCPDiscover` message. The DHCP server offers an IP address. The client computer accepts the address and uses it to communicate on the network.

B. The client computer broadcasts a `DHCPDiscover` message. The DHCP server offers an IP address. The client computer accepts the address and sends a request to use that address back to the DHCP server. The client computer uses the address to communicate on the network.

C. The client computer broadcasts a `DHCPDiscover` message. The DHCP server offers an IP address. The client computer accepts the address and sends a request to use that address back to the DHCP server. The DHCP server acknowledges the request and grants the client computer a lease to use the address. The client computer uses the address to connect to the network.

D. The client computer broadcasts a `DHCPDiscover` message. The DHCP server offers an IP address. The client computer accepts the address and sends a request to use that address back to the DHCP server. The DHCP server acknowledges the request and grants the client computer a lease to use the address. The client computer responds with an acknowledgement of the lease and uses the address to connect to the network.

2. You are the system administrator for a chain called Come in and Get Gas, a combination gas station and restaurant. As part of the network, you maintain a Windows 2000 DHCP server to dynamically assign addresses. You have three superscopes set up, and within each superscope are four scopes. Suddenly, you start experiencing issues with one of the scopes issuing bad addresses. You check the server and suspect that a database issue exists. How can you verify that the database is intact?

   A. Open DHCP manager. Select the scope in question and click the Action menu. Then, select Reconcile Scope.

   B. Open DHCP manager. Select the superscope containing the scope in question and click the Action menu. Then, select Reconcile All Scopes.

   C. Open DHCP manager. Select the DHCP server containing the scope in question and click the Action menu. Then, select Reconcile All Scopes.

   D. Open DHCP manager. Select the DHCP server containing the scope in question and click the Action menu. Then, select Reconcile DHCP Database.

3. You are the LAN administrator for Get Stuffed, the local taxidermy run by Scotty McTavish. You are responsible for maintaining the company's Windows 2000 DHCP Server. While doing your daily system checks, you notice that the number of `DHCPDiscover` packets spiked at 9 a.m. today. What could cause this counter to spike at 9 a.m.?

   A. A network issue

   B. The DHCP service being restarted

APPLY YOUR KNOWLEDGE

C. A large number of computers entering the network at approximately the same time

D. A "rogue" DHCP server issuing duplicate addresses

4. You are the LAN administrator for the Road Kill Cafè, also run by the local taxidermist, Scotty McTavish. You are responsible for maintaining the company's Windows 2000 DHCP server. While doing your daily system checks, you notice that the number of `DHCPDiscover` packets spiked at 9 a.m. today. How would you go about monitoring the `DHCPDiscover` packets?

   A. Open PerfMon. Click the Add Counter icon. Select the DHCP Server object, and then select the DHCPDiscover Packets/Sec counter. Click Add to add the counter and monitor the packets.

   B. Open the Performance from the Control Panel. Click the Add Counter icon. Select the DHCP Server object, and then select the DHCPDiscover Packets/Sec counter. Click Add to add the counter and monitor the packets.

   C. Open Performance from the Control Panel. Click the Add Counter icon. Select the DHCP Server object, and then select the Discovers/Sec counter. Click Add to add the counter and monitor the packets.

   D. Open DHCP manager. Select the DHCP server you want to monitor. Right-click the server and select Display Statistics from the context menu. Observe the Discovers statistic.

5. You are the lead engineer for Little Faith Enterprises' West Edmonton Mall Casino division, and a customer has asked you to install the DHCP service on her Windows 2000 Server, configure one scope, and issue addresses. What minimum steps do you need to take to accomplish this?

   A. Select Network and Dial-up Connections in the Control Panel, and select Add Network Components to install the service. After the service is installed, authorize it in Active Directory. Next, create the scope. Finally, configure the DNS integration.

   B. Select Network and Dial-up Connections in the Control Panel, and select Add Network Components to install the service. After the service is installed, create the scope and configure the DNS integration.

   C. Select Network and Dial-up Conn-ections in the Control Panel, and select Add Network Components to install the service. After the service is installed, create the scope. Create a superscope and add the scope to it. Authorize the server in Active Directory.

   D. Select Network and Dial-up Connections in the Control Panel, and select Add Network Components to install the service. After the service is installed, create the scope. Authorize the server in Active Directory.

6. You are the network administrator for the Stretch 'N Snap latex glove corporation. The corporation is running a routed network with a centrally located Windows 2000 DHCP server. The server is capable of issuing addresses to users on the local segment but can't issue addresses to any of the sites that are across a router. What is the most probable cause of this problem?

   A. The DHCP Forwarder service is not enabled on the DHCP server.

APPLY YOUR KNOWLEDGE

B. The BOOTP Forwarder service is not enabled on the DHCP server.

C. The DHCP Forwarder service is not enabled on the routers.

D. The BOOTP Forwarder service is not enabled on the routers.

7. You manage the Windows 2000 DHCP servers for Al's House of Nails. You are running in a pure Windows 2000 environment, and you need to ensure that workstations are registered properly in DNS for Active Directory integration. How should you configure DNS integration?

   A. Set DNS Integration to automatically update DHCP client information in DNS.

   B. Set DNS Integration to discard forward (name-to-address) lookups when the lease expires.

   C. Set DNS Integration to enable updates for DNS clients that do not support dynamic update.

   D. Set DNS Integration to enable DNS keep-alives.

8. You are the LAN administrator for Write Up Our Alley publishing, a bookseller. Your Windows 2000 DHCP server issues a block of 40 addresses to 120 salespeople on the Sales network. These users are frequently in and out of the office, so no more than 40 users are ever on the network at one time. What do you need to do to ensure that users get addresses when necessary?

   A. Set the DHCP lease to 60 minutes.

   B. Set the DHCP lease to 5 days.

   C. Configure reservations for each user.

   D. Configure an exclusion for each user.

9. You are the distributed computing administrator for ISeeU Tele-Videophone. Your company has Windows 2000 installed with the DHCP service running. Mixed in with your DHCP client computers, you still have some old workstations on the network with BOOTP chips on their Ethernet cards. You need to add support for BOOTP for these computers. How do you ensure that support?

   A. Add the BOOTP service to the server.

   B. In the Advanced tab of the scope properties, configure the server to issue addresses to BOOTP clients.

   C. In the Advanced tab of the server properties, configure the server to issue addresses to both DHCP and BOOTP clients.

   D. In the Advanced tab of the scope properties, configure the server to issue addresses to both DHCP and BOOTP clients.

10. You are the network administrator for BT Editing Unlimited. You have a 50-host network and are running a Windows 2000 DHCP server used to assign IP addresses. You also have five IP-based printers with static IP addresses. Your assistant administrator has been working on the DHCP server and made some changes. Suddenly, your users can't print to one of the printers. What is most likely the problem?

    A. The scope from which the printers were receiving their IP addresses has been deleted.

    B. The existing scope has been modified so that it overlaps the addresses reserved for the printers.

APPLY YOUR KNOWLEDGE

C. The existing scope has been modified so that it overlaps the addresses reserved for the printers, and a workstation has been assigned the same address as one of the printers.

D. The DHCP service was inadvertently stopped.

11. You are the systems administrator for Little Faith's WindBag Music Store. You are responsible for maintaining the company's Windows 2000 DHCP server. The company recently added a new router and routed a segment to the network. Now that segment must be added to the DHCP server. The address of the router port is 10.10.25.1, and it is subnetted with a Class C subnet mask. You need to provide 20 addresses, starting at 10.10.25.20. What needs to occur for you to get DHCP working on that segment?

    A. You must install and configure an additional DHCP server on that segment to provide DHCP services.

    B. You must add a scope to the DHCP server containing the addresses from 10.10.25.20 through 10.10.25.39. The scope will need a subnet mask of 255.255.255.0. You also must configure the BOOTP Forwarder for the new segment's router using the address of the DHCP server. You then need to activate the scope.

    C. You must add a scope to the DHCP server containing the addresses from 10.10.25.20 through 10.10.25.40. The scope will need a subnet mask of 255.255.255.0. You must configure the BOOTP Forwarder for the new segment's router using the address of the DHCP server and then activate the scope.

    D. You must add a scope to the DHCP server containing the addresses from 10.10.25.20 through 10.10.25.40. The scope will need a subnet mask of 255.255.255.0. You must configure the BOOTP Forwarder for the new segment's router using the address of the DHCP server. You will not need to activate the scope because it happens automatically when the scope is created.

12. You are the network manager for IntCo Manufacturing. You are running in a mixed Windows 2000 environment, and you are using a Windows 2000 DHCP Service to support a single network segment. Your client computers consist of Windows 2000 Professional, Windows NT Workstation, and Windows 98 SE workstations. What do you need to do to ensure that all your client computers can receive DHCP addresses?

    A. Configure a scope for the network segment; configure each client computer to receive IP addresses dynamically; and configure the DHCP service for backward compatibility.

    B. Configure a scope for the network segment. Configure each client computer to receive IP addresses dynamically. For the Windows NT Workstation client computers, ensure that the DHCP update from Service Pack 6 has been installed.

    C. Configure a scope for the network segment; configure each client computer to receive IP addresses dynamically; and configure the DHCP service for mixed mode.

    D. Configure a scope for the network segment, and configure each client computer to receive IP addresses dynamically.

13. You are a consultant from Little Faith Enterprises' consulting arm, XMS. You have been asked to configure DHCP for your customer. The client is not very familiar with DHCP and wants to know what information can be assigned via DHCP.

    Which of the following parameters can DHCP assign? (Select all that apply.)

    A. IP address

    B. BOOTP Forwarder

    C. Gateway address

    D. WINS server addresses

    E. Active Directory domain controller addresses

14. You are a consultant from Little Faith Enterprises' consulting arm, XMS. You have been asked to configure DHCP for your customer. The client is not very familiar with DHCP and wants to know what information is provided to the DHCP server.

    Which of the following information is provided to the DHCP server? (Select all that apply.)

    A. IP address

    B. MAC address

    C. Host name

    D. NetBIOS name

    E. Username

15. You are the network administrator for Block and Tackle Publishing (which publishes magazines about fishing), and you are running a pure Windows 2000 network, using Active Directory and the Windows 2000 DHCP service. A user in another department has installed a DHCP server on a Unix server. How do you prevent your client computers from receiving DHCP addresses from this server?

    A. Disable the unauthorized server in Active Directory.

    B. Make sure all your users are running Windows 2000.

    C. Reconfigure BOOTP on the router.

    D. Go to each client computer and enter the address of the production DHCP server in the TCP/IP Properties.

Answers to Review Questions

1. To successfully implement DHCP in a multinetted environment, you should consider using a superscope to ease the management of the scopes for each of the multinetted networks. For more information, see the section "Understanding Multicasting and Multicast Scopes."

2. In the Performance utility, check the Declines/Sec counter for the DHCP object. The number of `DHCPDecline` messages received per second by the DHCP server from client computers can be used to see whether the DHCP client computer has declined the IP address issued by the server. You will see this number rise when client computers start having address conflict issues. This could indicate a network issue, computers with static addresses that are also part of a scope, or potentially a rogue DHCP server on the network. For more information, see the section "Monitoring and Troubleshooting DHCP."

3. Check the length of the DHCP lease. If the lease has been set to a very short duration, client computers would need to request addresses frequently.

APPLY YOUR KNOWLEDGE

For more information, see the section "Understanding Multicasting and Multicast Scopes."

4. Either a lot of DHCP requests are occurring during peak hours or the Conflict Detection Attempts parameter is set too high. If this is enabled, Windows 2000 DHCP Server issues an address and checks to see whether any IP address conflicts exist. This can put a lot of additional overhead on the server and drive up the DHCP Conflict Check Queue Length. For more information, see the section "Monitoring and Troubleshooting DHCP."

5. First, you need to activate the DHCP server in Active Directory. It will not be capable of providing addresses until that occurs. You also need to configure the BOOTP Forwarder on any routers between the DHCP server and the client workstations so that the routers know where to forward DHCP messages. For more information, see the section "Configuring Authorization of a DHCP Server."

Answers to Exam Questions

1. **C.** The client computer can't use the address until the DHCP server grants the lease. After the DHCP server acknowledges the DHCP request and grants the lease, the client computer is free to use the address. No additional step is required in the process. In Answer A, the client does not send any acceptance packet back to the DHCP server. Answer B send an acceptance package to the DHCP server but does not wait for an acknowledgement. Answer D includes a superfluous acknowledgement for the IP Address lease. For more information, see the section "The DHCP Protocol."

2. **C.** You need to reconcile all the scopes on the server. Answer A is almost correct because you can reconcile a single scope, but the correct command is Reconcile, not Reconcile Scope. You can't reconcile scopes at the Superscope level, as referenced in answer B. The command in answer D does not exist. For more information, see the section "Monitoring and Troubleshooting DHCP."

3. **C.** The `DHCPDiscover` packet is sent when a computer first requests an address. The most likely reason for this to spike would be a large number of concurrent requests, which could occur when many client workstations request addresses at the same time. A network issue (answer A) would have the opposite effect because no `DHCPDiscover` packets would reach the server. The DHCP service restart (answer B) or a rogue DHCP server (answer D) couldn't impact the number of `DHCPDiscover` packets because they are generated by client PCs. For more information, see the section "Monitoring and Troubleshooting DHCP."

4. **C.** The correct answer is to open Performance from the Control Panel and add the Discovers/sec counter for DHCP. Answer A refers to PerfMon, which is the Windows NT 4.0 Performance Monitoring console. Answer B refers to DHCP Discovers/sec, which is not the correct counter. The DHCP server statistics show you only the total number of discover packets and is unable to show any spikes. For more information, see the section "Monitoring and Troubleshooting DHCP."

APPLY YOUR KNOWLEDGE

5. **D.** The task is to install the DHCP service and get it issuing addresses. Answer A includes the step of configuring DNS integration, which is not required. Answer B failst to authorize the server in Active Directory. Answer C includes the creation of a superscope. Even though you created a superscope in this chapter, you do not need a superscope for the server to function. For more information, see the section "Configuring DHCP on Servers."

6. **D.** To issue addresses using DHCP across a router, the router needs to have the BOOTP Forwarder service enabled and configured. Answer A incorrectly specifies the forwarding service as DHCP Forwarder. Answer B correctly names the service as BOOTP Forwarder but places it on the DHCP server. Answer C correctly places the forwarding service on the router but incorrectly calls it DHCP Forwarder. For more information, see the section "Configuring DHCP on Servers."

7. **A.** In a pure environment, you need to configure DHCP to automatically update DNS to ensure that the client computers appear on the network correctly. Answer B sets the DNS integration to discard lookups after a lease expires also works with a pure Windows 2000 network, but it has nothing to do with the computers registering properly. Answer C is incorrect because the environment is pure Windows 2000. The DNS keepalive values (answer D) also have nothing to do with configuring IP addresses. For more information, see the section "Configuring DHCP for DNS Integration."

8. **A.** To ensure that addresses are available, the DHCP lease needs to be set to a short interval. Answer B might also work but there are 120 staff members and only 40 IP addresses, so a shorter time is the correct answer. Setting reservations (answer C) or exclusion addresses (answer D) will not solve the problem of too few addresses for the number of clients. For more information, see the section "Understanding Multicasting and Multicast Scopes."

9. **D.** You need to configure the scope to issue addresses to both DHCP and BOOTP clients. There is no separate BOOTP service to start (answer A), and there is no server property to add DHCP and BOOTP capability to (answer C). Answer B includes only the BOOTP capability to the scope option. For more information, see the section "Understanding Multicasting and Multicast Scopes."

10. **C.** The address from the printer has probably been issued to another computer. Because the printers use static addresses, the only change to the DHCP server that could have impacted printing would be another host with the same address. Answer B is close, but just creating an overlapping scope is not a problem until the overlapping addresses are assigned. The DCHP service halting will not affect addresses already leased (answer D), as would the scope being deleted (answer A). For more information, see the section "Configuring DHCP on Servers."

11. **B.** A single DHCP server can serve multiple segments, so you will not need an additional server as stated in answer A. To get 20 addresses, the range must be from 10.10.25.20 to 10.10.25.39 because it is an inclusive range and not 10.10.25.40 (answer C). Also, the last step of the Scope Wizard is authorizing the new scope; you must do this to use the scope. The scope will not be authorized when it is created (answer D). For

APPLY YOUR KNOWLEDGE

more information, see the section "Understanding Multicasting and Multicast Scopes."

12. **D.** You do not need to make any special configurations to the DHCP service. It can communicate with non-Windows 2000 client computers without issue, and there is no compatibility mode to set (answer A) or mixed mode to enable (answer D). You also do not need to update any of the client computers. Windows NT and Windows 98 are capable of using DHCP without needing updates applied (answer B). Just configure the appropriate scope, and configure the client computers to use that scope. For more information, see the section "Understanding Multicasting and Multicast Scopes."

13. **A, C, D.** These can all be assigned using DHCP. BOOTP Forwarder is a router configuration and can't be set by DHCP (answer B). The domain controller addresses are obtained dynamically at login time from the Dynamic DNS used by Active Directory and can't be set by DHCP (answer E). The list of parameters assignable includes IP addresses, gateway addresses, DNS server addresses, and WINS server addresses. For more information, see the section "The DHCP Protocol."

14. **B, C, D.** The MAC address, host name, and NetBIOS name are all provided to the DHCP server by default. The username (answer E) is not available to send to the DHCP (the user has not logged in yet), and the IP address (answer A) is what the DHCP will be sending the client (and not sent from the client to the server). For more information, see the section "The DHCP Protocol."

15. **B.** Because a Unix server can't be enabled in Active Directory, Windows 2000 client computers will not accept DHCP addresses from the server. Answer A is not correct because you can't put a Unix server in Active Directory at this time. Changing the BOOTP configuration on the router (answer C) might prevent remote users from receiving addresses, but local users would still be vulnerable. In answer D, there is nowhere to enter the address of the DHCP server. For more information, see the section "Configuring Authorization of a DHCP Server."

Suggested Readings and Resources

1. *The DHCP Handbook.* Indianapolis, IN: Macmillan Technical Publishing, 1999.
2. Lee, Thomas, and Joseph Davies. *Microsoft Windows 2000 TCP/IP Protocol and Services.* Microsoft Press, 2000.
3. Mueller, John Paul, and Irfan Chaudhry. *Microsoft Windows 2000 Performance Tuning Technical Reference.* Microsoft Press, 2000.
4. Stanek, William R. *Microsoft Windows 2000 Administrator's Pocket Consultant.* Microsoft Press, 2000.

OBJECTIVES

This chapter helps you prepare for the MCSE Managing a Microsoft Windows 2000 Network Environment exam by covering the following objectives:

Configure, administer, and troubleshoot DNS.

- **Configure DNS server properties.**
- **Manage DNS database records such as CNAME, A, and PTR.**
- **Create and configure DNS zones.**

▶ One of your first tasks when getting ready to deploy a production Windows 2000 network environment is to ensure that DNS is installed and configured correctly. DNS is the foundation that Active Directory relies on, and you need to have a thorough understanding not only of the Windows 2000 DNS Server service, but also of how DNS itself functions. This objective expects you to be able to install DNS, configure it for use in an Active Directory Services network, and test it to make sure it is working.

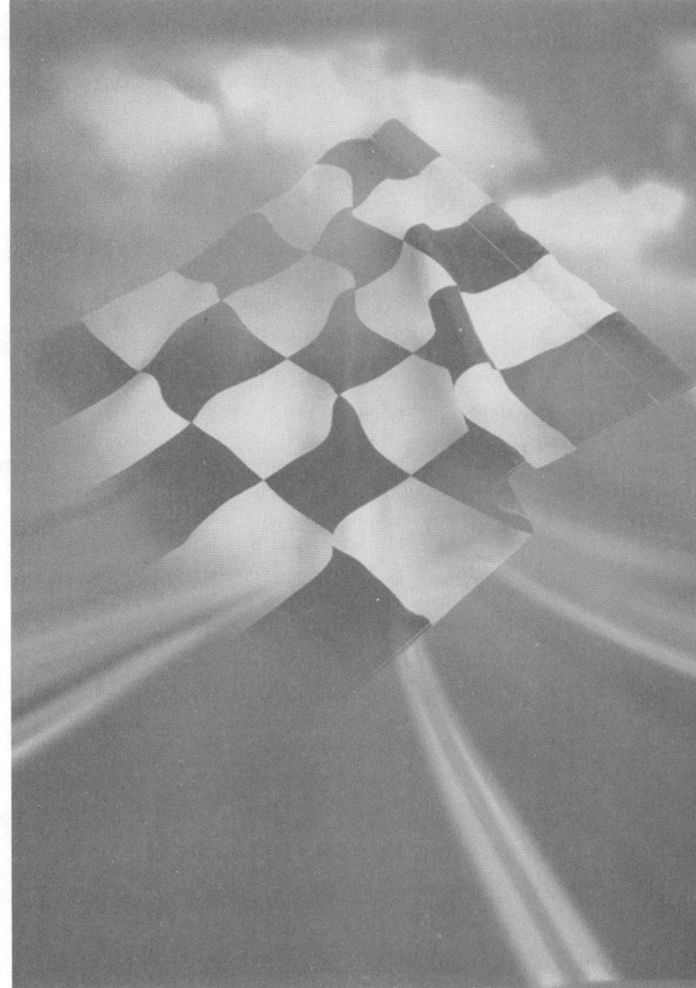

CHAPTER 6

Configuring, Administering, and Troubleshooting DNS

Outline

Study Strategies

- DNS provides the name resolution backbone for the Internet today. With the introduction of Active Directory, it is now also the backbone of Microsoft's name resolution. It is very important that you understand where DNS came from, how it works, and what enhancements Microsoft made to DNS for Active Directory.
- Part of the power of the Microsoft DNS service is its integration with DHCP through Dynamic DNS. Make sure you understand the relationship between the two and how Dynamic DNS works.
- Microsoft's Windows 2000 DNS service supports a variety of zone types and DNS server types. Be sure you understand what they are, how they work, and when you might use them in a production environment.
- Because of Microsoft's emphasis on practical exam questions, be sure to closely review the Step By Steps and the exercises at the end of the chapter.

INTRODUCTION

This chapter's discussion is about network infrastructure with domain name service (DNS), the foundation on which many of the name resolution and directory services are built today. Whenever you surf the Web, you take advantage of DNS. One of the most important services in a TCP/IP infrastructure—particularly one running Active Directory Services—is DNS. This chapter examines all the facets of running the DNS Server service in a Windows 2000 network.

If you have ever connected to a Web site by name, you have used the domain name service. The domain name service is a service used on the Internet for resolving fully qualified domain names (FQDN) to their actual IP addresses. For example, if you wanted to check out Que's Web site but not use DNS to do so, the Web address you would have to enter is 165.193.123.44. If you are like most people, you'll remember that number for less than 10 seconds, and you will probably never find the Que's Web site. What DNS does is put a user-friendly face on that obscure numeric address. With DNS, you can enter the address `www.quepublishing.com`, and the DNS infrastructure of the Internet will translate the name to the correct address, 165.193.123.15. It's like a big phone book. You put in a name and it gives you the correct number. Fortunately for those of us with a limited ability to memorize strings of numbers, the Internet community recognized the benefits of a name resolution system as a critical part of the infrastructure that would make up the original Internet architecture.

> NOTE
>
> **Domain Name System or Domain Name Service** You might have heard that the acronym DNS stands for domain name system, yet it is referred to as the domain name service in the previous sections. These names are interchangeable, although Microsoft tends to use service, whereas most Internet users use system. From here on, we will use the term service for consistency.

Introduction to DNS

DNS is a hierarchical database containing names and addresses for IP networks and hosts and is used almost universally to provide name resolution. This statement is now even more accurate because Microsoft has embraced DNS as its name resolution method for Windows 2000 and relies on the Windows Internet Naming System (WINS) less and less.

Back in the early days of the Internet, when it was known as the ARPAnet (Advanced Research Products Agency Network) and the number of hosts on the network was less than 100, there used to be a master list of names and IP addresses called the HOSTS file. It was maintained by the Stanford Research Institute's Network Information Center (known as the SRI-NIC at the time), and it worked very well as long as the number of hosts was low and changes were infrequent. Everyone using the network would periodically download a copy of this file, and they would have a local table of names and addresses to connect to computers by name. Windows 2000 (and most TCP/IP stacks in general) still have this functionality, although it is seldom used in conjunction with the Internet any longer. This method of name resolution was great for a while, but as the number of computers grew, this solution ran into a few problems, including the following:

> **EXAM TIP**
>
> **Be Able to Compare DNS with HOSTS Files** Be familiar with the advantages of DNS over the flat-file method of name resolution provided by the HOSTS file.

- **Traffic**—As more and more people tried to access this file, the load on the SRI network and servers was becoming excessive.
- **Consistency**—As the number of hosts and changes grew larger and larger, propagation of the HOSTS file became nearly impossible. As the file propagated to the most distant servers, new servers would have already been added to the network, rendering the file just distributed obsolete.
- **Flat-file limitations**—Windows NT domain administrators are familiar with these limitations. Because the HOSTS file was a flat file (similar to the way domain objects are stored under Windows NT 4 domains), a requirement existed that every name be unique. No hierarchical capabilities were built into the naming structure. As a result, coming up with unique names that were also intuitive became more and more difficult.

DNS is a distributed database allowing local control of small segments of the namespace while maintaining a logical architecture to provide that local information throughout the network. Each segment of the DNS namespace resides on a server known as a *name server*. The architecture of DNS is designed so that multiple name servers can exist to provide a level of redundancy. In addition, with parts of the overall namespace placed on separate computers, the data storage and query loads are distributed throughout thousands of DNS servers on the Internet. The hierarchical nature of DNS is designed in such a way that every computer on or off the Internet can be named as part of the DNS namespace.

To effectively install, configure, and support the Windows 2000 DNS Server service, you must have some level of understanding of the underlying architecture of today's DNS. Rather than having you read the RFCs (although you are encouraged to do so to improve your further understanding of DNS), we will look at the DNS namespace architecture and how individual DNS servers support their portions of the overall namespace and then move on to the specifics of the Windows 2000 DNS Server service.

DNS Domains

As we've discussed, you probably have already used DNS, whether you were familiar with the underlying mechanism or not. Domain names are easy. Names such as `www.microsoft.com`, `www.quepublishing.com`, or even `www.mcse.com` are all easy to comprehend. However, this simplicity comes at a price. The DNS namespace is complex. DNS names are created as part of a hierarchical database that functions much like the directories in a file system. Hierarchies are powerful database structures because they can store tremendous amounts of data while making searching for specific bits of information easy. Before examining the specifics of the DNS namespace hierarchy, let's review some rules about hierarchies in general.

> NOTE
>
> **A Simple Example of Hierarchy** Microsoft's new Active Directory Service is an excellent example of a hierarchical database. This hierarchy is created on top of the existing rules for a DNS namespace so the information in the DNS hierarchy directly relates to the construction of an Active Directory.

Hierarchies

Before we get into the details of a hierarchy, we should introduce some terms:

- **Tree**—A type of data structure with each element attached to one or more elements directly beneath it. In the case of DNS, this structure is often called an *inverted tree* because it is generally drawn with the root at the top of the tree.
- **Top-level domain (TLD)**—TLD refers to the suffix attached to Internet domain names. A limited number of predefined suffixes exist, and each one represents a top-level domain. The more popular TLDs include COM, EDU, GOV, MIL, NET, and ORG.
- **Node**—A point where two or more lines in the tree intersect. In the case of DNS, a node can represent a top-level domain (TLD), a subdomain, or an actual network node (host).

- **Fully qualified domain name (FQDN)**—A domain name that includes all domains between the host and root of DNS is a fully qualified domain name (FQDN). For example, `www.microsoft.com` is an FQDN.
- **Leaf**—A leaf is an item at the very bottom of a hierarchical tree structure, and it does not contain any other objects. In DNS, these are called nodes.
- **Zone**—A DNS zone is a logical grouping of host names within DNS. For example, `quepublishing.com` is considered the forward lookup zone for Que. It is where the information about the Que's hosts is contained within DNS.

If you told typical users that they have been working with a hierarchy since the first time they turned on a computer, many would have no idea what you are talking about. However, a hierarchy was introduced as early as MS-DOS version 2 in the form of the file system.

> NOTE
> **The Missing Dot** Because the root domain is always there, the dot is often omitted. For example, "www.microsoft.com" should really be written as "www.microsoft.com.", but the last period usually is left out for brevity.

Why do computers need a hierarchical file system? Because storing files as an endless alphabetic listing is inefficient, and files can be better understood and categorized by being stored in related groups. Today the use of hierarchical file structures is commonplace.

In DNS, the containers are called *domains*. The hierarchy starts with a root container, called the *root domain*. The root domain doesn't have a name, so it is typically represented by a single period (the dot at the end of an FQDN).

Directly below the root domain are the top-level domains (TLD). These are also sometimes called `first-level domains`. Lower-level domains are second-level, third-level, and so on. Every domain name has a suffix that indicates to which TLD domain it belongs. There are only a limited number of such domains, including the following:

- **COM**—Originally, the COM domain was supposed to contain commercial entities, but COM has become the overwhelming favorite top-level domain, and everyone wants his personal subdomains to be in COM. Because COM has been overused and abused, it's nearly impossible to come up with a sensible new name for a COM subdomain. Crowding in COM is the main impetus behind the definition of new top-level domains. (Example of COM: `mcp.com`)

- **ORG**—This domain is supposed to accommodate organizations that are noncommercial in nature. Although many noncommercial organizations have registered in the COM domain, most have respected the intent of this domain. This is a good place for nonprofit organizations, professional groups, churches, and other such organizations. (Example of ORG: `npr.org`)
- **EDU**—This domain was originally supposed to embrace all types of educational institutions, but it began to fill up quickly as schools gained access to the Internet. Now it is primarily reserved for higher education institutions. Primary and secondary schools are supposed to register in their state domains, which are subdomains of their country domains. (Example of EDU: `berkeley.edu`)
- **GOV**—This domain contains agencies of the United States federal government apart from the military, which has the MIL domain. (Example of GOV: `whitehouse.gov`)
- **NET**—This domain supports Internet service providers and Internet administrative computers. (Example of NET: `ibm.net`)
- **Country**—Each country is assigned a unique top-level domain. Some more common examples include the following:
    - **CA**—Canada
    - **TH**—Thailand
    - **UK**—United Kingdom
    - **AU**—Australia
    - **TO**—Tonga
- **CC**—This new domain was created for the same purpose as the COM domain. It is intended to extend the number of names available for commercial endeavors. (Example of CC: `www.spot.cc`)

Because of a shortage of domain names at the top level, the Internet Ad Hoc Committee (IAHC) proposed six new top-level domains, which were introduced in 2000 but are being implemented at varying speeds. They are as follows:

- **AERO**—Domain names for the air transport industry.
- **WS**—This used to be the country code for Western Samoa; however, recently it was opened up to allow a Web site's Web extension to mean "Web site."
- **TV**—This used to be the country code for Tuvalu; however, recently it was opened up to allow a Web site's Web extension to mean "television."
- **BIZ**—Business interests.
- **COOP**—Cooperatives.
- **INFO**—Information services (unrestricted use).
- **NAME**—Domains registered to individuals.
- **PRO**—Domains registered to accountants, lawyers, and physicians.

The creation of these new TLDs will help to alleviate the almost gold rush-like fervor associated with "good" domain names. Unfortunately, the various groups ultimately in charge of implementing the new domains have been doing so very slowly. Everyone wants to control the process (because that's where the money is), and they have not been able to agree on whose process will ultimately be implemented.

As we have discussed, DNS is used to translate a host name to an IP address. The DNS name typically looks something like this:

```
www.widgets.mycompany.com
```

> **EXAM TIP**
>
> **Know About FQDN** For the exam, be sure that you have a good understanding of what an FQDN is and how it is represented.

This is known as the host's fully qualified domain name because it lists the host's precise location in the DNS hierarchy. The DNS name in the example represents the (Web) host `www` in the subdomain `widgets` (this is frequently a department or division in a company), which is in the subdomain `mycompany` (this is frequently the name of the company or organization that has registered the domain), which is in the TDL `com`.

When an organization wants to establish a domain name on the Internet, the domain name must be registered with one of the authorized registration authorities. One that many people are familiar with is Network Solutions, formerly the InterNIC. You can research new domain names and access registration forms at http://www.networksolutions.com. You can also contact your Internet service provider (ISP) for assistance. To register a domain, you will need at least two name servers. Two types of name servers are defined in the DNS specifications. They are the following:

- **Primary master**—This server gets the information on the zones it is authoritative over (will resolve names for) from files on the host it runs on. This is the server where you make additions, modifications, and deletions to the DNS zone. This is similar to the NT 4 primary domain controller. It is the only place modifications to the domain can be made.
- **Secondary master**—This server gets its zone information from the master name server that is authoritative for that domain; it could be from either a primary or a secondary. When a secondary server starts, it contacts the name server it updates from (the authoritative server) and gets the latest copy of the zone data.

After you have identified the two (or more) name servers, you are ready to register your domain. To register a domain name at Network Solutions, follow Step By Step 6.1.

EXAM TIP

Know the Difference Between the Primary and the Secondary Domain Servers The major difference is that a secondary domain holds a read-only version of the DNS database.

NOTE

Zones in DNS In the world of DNS, a *zone* is the complete information about some part of the domain namespace. In other words, it is a subset of a domain. The name server is considered to have authority for that zone, and it can respond to any requests for name resolution from that zone.

STEP BY STEP

6.1 Registering a DNS Domain

1. Search the Network Solutions database (www.networksolutions.com) to find a domain name that isn't already in use. This can be pretty difficult unless you are willing to use something fairly obscure. Most of the common (and even fairly uncommon) domain names have already been registered.
2. Determine the IP addresses of two domain name servers—a master and a backup (or secondary) name server that will be authoritative for your domain. If your ISP will provide your name servers, obtain the IP addresses from your ISP.

continues

continued

3. Register the domain name with Network Solutions. The Web site includes online forms for registering and changing domain names.
4. Pay the registration fee, which varies depending on the options you select. The initial registration fee is for the first two years, and then you pay an annual fee to keep the name active.

NOTE

The Role of a Domain If you ever anticipate connecting your network to the Internet, your first installation of DNS is an excellent time to do a little preparation. More important, after Active Directory has been installed, the underlying DNS domain can't be changed without removing and re-installing Active Directory and losing all your users and permissions.

After a domain name has been chosen and registered, and you have an understanding of the basic hierarchy of DNS, the next step is to examine how DNS works. In other words, after you enter the name, how does it get translated to an IP address?

The DNS name server resolves a name to an IP address using the following process:

1. The client computer makes a request to the local DNS server. This generally occurs when an application tries to make a connection using a host name, such as when you enter `www.quepublishing.com` into your Web browser.
2. The DNS server looks in a local memory cache for names it has recently resolved. If the name is found in the local cache, the name server returns the IP address the client computer requires. Most DNS servers cache both local and remote domain names in the memory, so even a DNS request for a host on your local network might be in cache.
3. The name server looks in the DNS server's host tables to see whether a static entry (or in the case of DDNS, a dynamic entry) exists for the host name to an IP address lookup. If an entry exists, the DNS server forwards the IP address to the client computer.
4. If the request has not been resolved, the name server refers the request to a root name server. Root name servers support the root of the namespace hierarchy. At present, 13 computers support the root domain.
5. The root name server refers the request to the first-level domain in the host name. In this example, that is to the server(s) maintaining the .COM domain.

6. The .COM name server refers the request to a name server for the second-level domain in the host name. In other words, if you have requested a host address for the `quepublishing.com` domain, the root name server forwards the request to the `quepublishing.com` DNS server. The second-level domain name server refers the request to a name server for the third-level domain in the host name, and so on, until a name server is encountered that can resolve the complete host name.
7. The first name server that can resolve the host name to an IP address reports the IP address to the client computer.

NOTE

How Root Servers Work When you register your domain, you are required to provide the names and addresses of two (or more) DNS servers that will be providing DNS for the domain. The root name servers have access to these names and addresses and thus know where to send the requests.

NOTE

Migrating DNS Zones—Something that is implied in the previous statement is that DNS zone information can move around. If you have an ISP that is providing your Internet service and it maintains your company's Internet access for `www.widgets.mycompany.com`, a zone is created that holds your server address information. If you move your access to a different ISP, the first provider deletes the zone and the new provider creates a new one. Part of the job of being an ISP is to update the TLD servers with the change so that your Web site can still be found. The only important thing is that the zone information is correct and can be found.

To ensure that this process works in your environment, you need to ensure two things. First, make sure that your network has at least one, and preferably more, DNS servers. These name servers can include your Windows 2000 Server DNS server, older Microsoft DNS servers, other implementations of DNS (Unix, Linux, OS/2, and so on), or even name servers provided by your ISP. Second, make sure your client computers are all configured to use these servers for DNS lookups. The rest of the process generally works; you do not need to maintain the root name servers list or the lookup process.

Reverse Lookups

We have discussed how to get the most common form of DNS lookups, also known as forward lookups. These are the DNS lookups where you enter a name and the DNS server returns the IP address. Another type of lookup exists, known as a *reverse lookup*. A reverse lookup works very much as the name implies. You query the DNS server with an IP address, and it returns (if there is an entry) the DNS name for that host. This can be useful in two situations—when you are trying to track down a host that is causing issues on the network and when you are trying to verify the identity of a host. Some FTP sites use reverse lookups to verify who is using their services, and it was a common programming practice in the not too distant past to have Unix programs check the reverse lookup as part of their authentication schemes. Microsoft uses reverse lookups for the downloading of its 128-bit software to ensure that the user attempting to download the software is in the United States or Canada. If your host doesn't have an entry in a reverse lookup table, you will not be able to download the software. We discuss the different record types in the "DNS Record Types" section of this chapter,

EXAM TIP

Understand the Function of the Reverse Lookup Table Because they are used less frequently and as a result are less understood when compared to the forward lookup table, reverse lookup tables are an excellent topic for exam questions.

but it is important to know that reverse lookup tables use PTR records to resolve IP addresses to names. A *PTR record* is a pointer to a location (an FQDN) in the DNS domain.

IN THE FIELD

SPAM EMAILS AND REVERSE LOOKUPS

You might find that you need a reverse lookup with the sending of Internet email. One of the latest weapons in the anti-spam wars is the use of reverse lookups to verify the validity of the domain from which an email originates. When the mail server receives an email, it checks to see whether it is from a valid domain and rejects it if it is not. A lot of spam used to employ fictitious domains as part of the spammers' attempts to hide their real identities.

If you have not yet experienced spam, the electronic version of telemarketing and junk mail, not only are you very fortunate, but you are also probably due for some. Spam is generally considered unsolicited email advertising for some product sent to an email address, mailing list, or newsgroup. In addition to being annoying for the user, it also eats up significant amounts of network bandwidth. Therefore, if you are setting up DNS on the Internet, be sure to include a reverse zone for your mail servers.

The naming convention for a reverse lookup zone is

```
"Reverse the Network ID octets".in-addr.arpa
```

Thus, the reverse table for the IP network 205.133.113.87 is `113.133.205.in-addr.arpa`.

It is important to be aware that the Active Directory Installation Wizard does not automatically add a reverse lookup zone or PTR resource records. You will need to do that manually. This is because another server might control the reverse lookup zone. You might want to add one if this is not the case. Although a reverse lookup zone is not necessary for Active Directory to work, it is useful for the reasons listed previously.

DNS Record Types

Before we continue our discussion of DNS, you should take a quick look at the various types of records you can create in a DNS domain. Table 6.1 lists the record types supported by the Windows 2000 DNS Server and their meanings.

TABLE 6.1

DNS RECORD TYPES

Record Type and RFC	*Value and Meaning*
AFSDB (RFC 1183)	Andrew File System database server record. Indicates the location of either an AFS volume location server or a Distributed Computing Environment (DCE) server.
CNAME (RFC 1035)	One of the original record types, a CNAME indicates an alias domain name for a name already specified as another resource type in this zone. CNAME is the acronym for canonical name.
ATMA	ATM address; it maps a DNS name to an ATM address.
A (RFC 1035)	A host address record; it maps a DNS name to an IP (version 4) address.
AAAA (RFC 1886)	Similar to the A record, the AAAA record is a host address for IPv6 hosts. It is used to map a DNS name to an IP (version 6) address.
ISDN (RFC 1183)	An Integrated Services Digital Network (ISDN) maps a DNS name to an ISDN telephone number.
MX (RFC 1035)	A mail exchanger record is used to provide message routing to a specific mail exchange host for a specific DNS name.
MG (RFC 1035)	A mail group record is used to add mailbox (MB) records as members of a domain mailing group.
MB (RFC 1035)	A mailbox record maps a specified domain mailbox name to the host that hosts the mailbox.
MINFO (RFC 1035)	Mailbox or mailing list information that specifies a domain mailbox name to contact. It can also specify a mailbox for error messages.
PTR (RFC 1035)	A pointer record points to a location in the domain. This is typically used for reverse lookups or IP address-to-DNS name lookups.
MR (RFC 1035)	A renamed mailbox record is used to specify a domain mailbox (MB) that is the proper rename of an existing mailbox (MB) record.
RP (RFC 1183)	A responsible person record specifies the domain mail-box for a responsible person for which text (TXT) records exist.
TXT (RFC 1035)	A text record is used to hold a string of characters that serve as descriptive text to be associated with a specific DNS name.

continues

EXAM TIP

Don't Memorize the Table of DNS Record Types Although you must understand the commonly used types, entries such as the Andrew File System Database server record will not be on the exam.

TABLE 6.1 *continued*

DNS RECORD TYPES

Record Type and RFC	*Value and Meaning*
RT (RFC 1183)	A route through record provides an intermediate-route-through binding for internal hosts that do not have their own direct wide area network (WAN) addresses.
SRV (RFC 2052)	A service record allows administrators to use several servers for a single DNS domain, to easily move a TCP/IP service from host to host, and to designate primary and backup services hosts. Windows 2000 uses SRV records to map the service being offered with the server supplying the service (in other words, nearest login server).
WKS (RFC 1035)	A well-known service record is used to describe well-known TCP/IP services supported by a particular protocol (that is, TCP or UDP) on a specific IP address.
X25 (RFC 1183)	An X.25 record is used to map a DNS name to a Public Switched Data Network (PSTN) address.

NOTE

Windows 2000 DNS Supports Additional Standards Microsoft has one problem with its direction of a DNS-based directory service, and it's one that has been an issue for years. NetBIOS, the legacy Microsoft naming mechanism, does not conform to the naming standards in RFC 1123. What this means is that in some environments, companies could be forced to rename all their Microsoft devices to move to a naming standard supported by Active Directory. To avoid this, Microsoft has included support for RFCs 2181 and 2044, which enable legacy NetBIOS names to be supported under DNS.

However, there's a catch to Microsoft's proposed support for RFCs 2181 and 2044. If you move to a naming convention that takes advantage of the new standards, you can run into issues with non-Windows 2000 DNS servers, including Windows NT 4.0 DNS Servers. Most servers do not support the standards Microsoft is proposing. The reason for this is that RFC 2044 calls for the support of the character encoding UTF-8. UTF-8 supports characters from a variety of foreign languages, which are not supported by non-Windows 2000 versions of DNS.

DNS Naming Conventions

Before we move on to the installation portion of this chapter, we need to quickly review the parameters for creating a DNS name. Table 6.2 shows the restrictions for creating a DNS name and an FQDN.

TABLE 6.2

DNS NAME RESTRICTIONS

Restriction	*Standard DNS (Including Windows NT 4.0)*	*DNS in Windows 2000*
Characters	Supports RFC 1123, which permits A–Z, a–z, 0–9, and the hyphen (-)	Several configurations are possible; RFC 1123 standard, as well as support for RFCs 2181 and the character set specified in RFC 2044 (UTP-8).
FQDN length	63 bytes per label and 255 bytes for an FQDN	Domain controllers are limited to 155 bytes for an FQDN.

Now let's look at installing the Windows 2000 DNS Server service.

CONFIGURING, ADMINISTERING, AND TROUBLESHOOTING DNS

▶ Configure, administer, and troubleshoot DNS.

Now that you have a general understanding of how DNS works, we can look at installing the Windows 2000 DNS Server service. One of the first questions you will be asked is, "Do we need to upgrade to Windows 2000 DNS?" The answer is yes and no. If you don't want to take advantage of all the benefits of a Windows 2000 network and Active Directory, you don't need to upgrade, as long as your DNS supports SRV records. If you are running a version of DNS that supports RFC 2136, covering Dynamic DNS, you can run your existing DNS and take advantage of Windows 2000's features. But let's assume you are not running an RFC 2136-compliant version of DNS. Why should you upgrade? The Windows 2000 DNS contains a number of significant improvements over standard DNS (including Windows NT's implementation), including the following:

- **Notification-driven zone transfers**—The standard model for DNS updates requires secondary name servers to periodically poll the master server for table updates. Under Windows 2000's DNS, the master server can notify the secondaries when an update has occurred. This immediate notification is not only more efficient than the older methods, but it also allows for much faster distribution of changes because updates are no longer dependent on polling intervals.

- **Integrated zone tables**—With the Windows 2000 DNS Server service, you can integrate DNS into Active Directory, and now resource records are stored in Active Directory and can be updated by any domain controller running DNS. This integration is a proprietary feature of the Windows 2000 DNS, but it can yield a much more secure, robust, and fault-tolerant implementation than standard DNS.

- **Incremental zone transfers**—The standard model for DNS zone transfers is to transfer the entire zone whenever an update is made. Transferring entire zones is inefficient. Windows 2000 DNS allows secondary servers to request incremental updates, which contain changes only since the last transfer.

EXAM TIP

Be Familiar with the Advantages of the Windows 2000 Dynamic DNS Over More Traditional Servers

Because Active Directory (AD) is based entirely on DNS, this is a topic that is pretty important to the success of AD, which makes it a good topic for test questions.

- **Secure DNS updates**—Windows 2000 DNS updates can be restricted to authorized secondaries.
- **DNS-DHCP Integration**—The power of Dynamic DNS is the integration of DHCP with the DNS table. Any Windows 2000 DHCP client computer will automatically be added to the DNS table at the time its IP address is issued.

Installing DNS

One of the major improvements in Windows 2000 is the capability to perform tasks—installing services, for example—in various ways. In fact, several ways to install the DNS Server service are available, such as using the Configure My Server screen to install the DNS service or adding additional network components through the Network and Dial-up Connections applet in Control Panel. We will cover the most common method, which is adding the DNS component manually. For your benefit, finding the method you are most comfortable with and sticking to it consistently is generally the best method for working with the operating system.

To install the Windows 2000 DNS Server service, follow Step By Step 6.2.

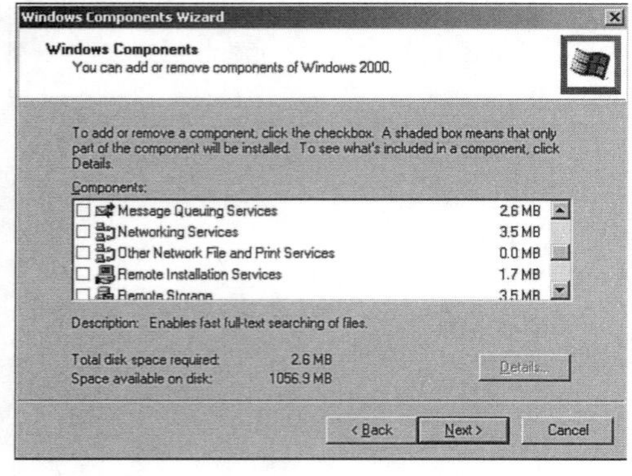

FIGURE 6.1
These component services are available under Windows 2000.

STEP BY STEP

6.2 Installing the DNS Server Service

1. Select Start, Settings, Control Panel.
2. Double-click Add/Remove Programs.
3. Click Add/Remove Windows Components. Figure 6.1 shows this display.
4. Select the Networking Services entry and click Details. This opens the Networking Services dialog box, shown in Figure 6.2. Select Domain Name System (DNS), and then click the OK button. The Windows Component Wizard will prompt you for the Windows 2000 Server CD-ROM if it needs to copy files.

5. When the wizard is finished, it displays a summary window of the changes to be made. Click OK to complete the installation.

Now that DNS is installed, let's look at configuring our first DNS zone.

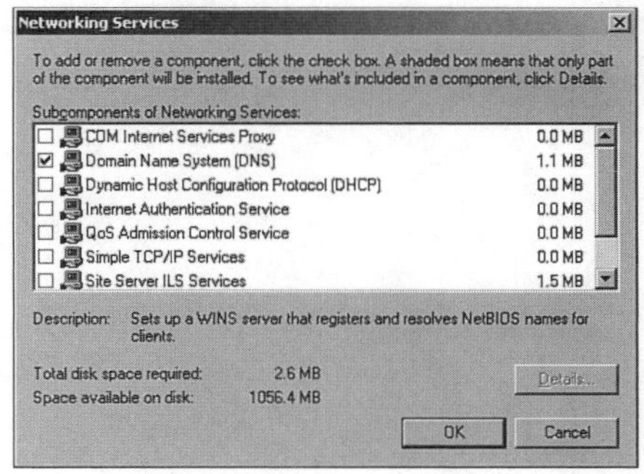

FIGURE 6.2
Selecting Domain Name System and clicking OK installs the service.

Configuring a Root Name Server

Let's discuss what Microsoft means when it asks you to configure a root name server. The root name server of a domain is the name server that is acting as the Start of Authority (SOA) for that zone. The Start of Authority record is the first record in the database, and it has the following format:

```
IN SOA <source host> <contact email> <serial number>
➥<refresh time> <retry time>
➥<expiration time> <time to live>
```

The following list defines the fields in the start of authority record:

- `source host`—The DNS server that maintains this file.
- `contact email`—The Internet email address for the person responsible for this domain's database file. See the note for important formatting information.
- `serial number`—This is important. The serial number acts as the version number for the database file. This number should increase each time the database file is changed. The file with the highest serial number takes precedence during zone transfers.
- `refresh time`—This is the elapsed time (in seconds) that a secondary server will wait between checks to its master server to see whether the database file has changed and a zone transfer should be requested. This is 15 minutes by default, but it can be increased in an environment in which DNS doesn't change often.
- `retry time`—This is the elapsed time (in seconds) that a secondary server will wait before retrying a failed zone transfer. The default for Windows 2000 is 10 minutes, and it can be increased or decreased as needed for your environment.

> NOTE
>
> **Don't Use a Standard Email Address for the SOA** One very important fact about the contact email in the SOA is that it does not use the standard Internet email format. Instead, you replace the `@` symbol in the email name with a `.`; therefore, `administrator@mycompany.com` would be `administrator.mycompany.com` in the zone file.

- `expiration time`—This is the elapsed time (in seconds) that a secondary server will keep trying to download a zone. After this time limit expires, the old zone information is discarded. This is 1 day by default. It, too, can be modified as necessary. You might want to increase this number for areas with intermittent connectivity where outages are common. DNS across a VPN is one example.
- `time to live`—This is the elapsed time (in seconds) that a DNS server is allowed to cache any resource records from this database file.

The SOA indicates the primary server for the zone. This is the root server for the domain.

Configuring Zones

DNS configuration is handled through a snap-in for the Microsoft Management Console. This can be found in the Administrative Tools program folder, under the entry DNS. It becomes available after DNS is installed. Although you can manually configure the text files that DNS creates (this is discussed in the "Manually Creating DNS Resource Records" section of the chapter), the DNS console makes managing your DNS namespace configuration much easier. When you first install your DNS server, you will need to configure your DNS server with its first zones. We'll examine how to do this with the wizard for the first zone and how to add more zones later.

Before we jump into the configuration of DNS zones, we need to take a moment to discuss the types of zone storage used in DNS:

- **Active Directory-Integrated**—This zone option stores all DNS information in Active Directory. If your entire domain infrastructure is run on a Windows 2000 platform, this is a good selection. This is the most secure option for maintaining your DNS tables because all your DNS information is stored in Active Directory, and all your updates pass as Active Directory updates. Unlike the text file method used by most DNS implementations, DNS tables stored in Active Directory can't be read by a text editor such as Notepad.

- **Standard Primary**—This zone option stores the information in a text file, like most non-Windows 2000 DNS servers, and is useful if you need to transfer information between different types of DNS servers.
- **Standard Secondary**—This option creates a read-only copy of an existing zone. The master copy (read/write version) is stored on a primary server. These are generally used to provide redundancy or load balancing of DNS on a network.

EXAM TIP

The Most Secure Implementation of DNS Is Active Directory-Integrated Active Directory is more secure than a flat file, and updates and zone transfers occur as part of AD replication activities, which are encrypted.

EXAM TIP

The DNS Console Equals MMC The DNS console is really nothing more than the Microsoft Management Console with the DNS management snap-in installed. Microsoft creates these versions of the Microsoft Management Console to make managing systems easier for new users of Windows 2000. So don't be confused if you see references to the Microsoft Management Console in the exam. That's all the DNS console is.

IN THE FIELD

USING THE MMC AND MANUALLY ADDING SNAP-INS

If you are an advanced user and would like to skip using differently configured versions of the MMC for each of the services installed on your Windows 2000 server, an easy way exists to manage everything from a single MMC configuration. Open the MMC by selecting Start, Run, MMC. This opens the MMC shell, which is empty the first time you load it. Select Console, Add/Remove Snap-in. When the Add/Remove Snap-in dialog box opens, click the Add button. In the Add Standalone Snap-in dialog box, you can select any or all of the snap-ins for Windows 2000 services.

To configure the zones on your DNS server for first time, follow Step By Step 6.3.

STEP BY STEP

6.3 Configuring Zones with Active Directory

1. Open the DNS console by selecting Administrative Tools, DNS. Right-click the DNS server and select New Zone. Click Next to continue.
2. The Zone Type dialog box is shown in Figure 6.3. Select Active Directory-Integrated and click Next to continue.
3. Figure 6.4 shows the Forward or Reverse Lookup Zone screen, which enables you choose the zone to create. Select Forward Lookup Zone and click Next to continue.

continues

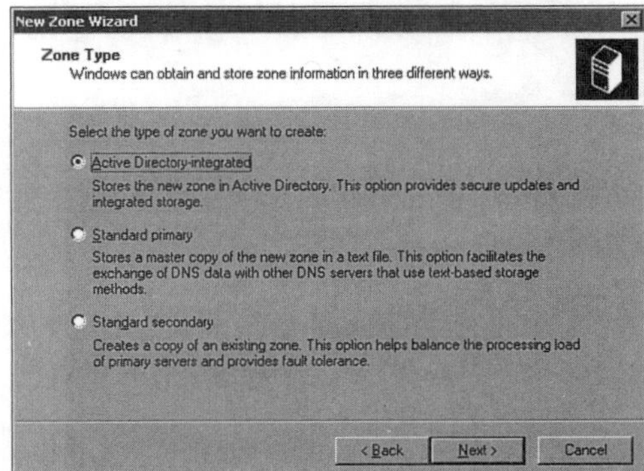

FIGURE 6.3
For the most secure implementation, store your DNS table in Active Directory.

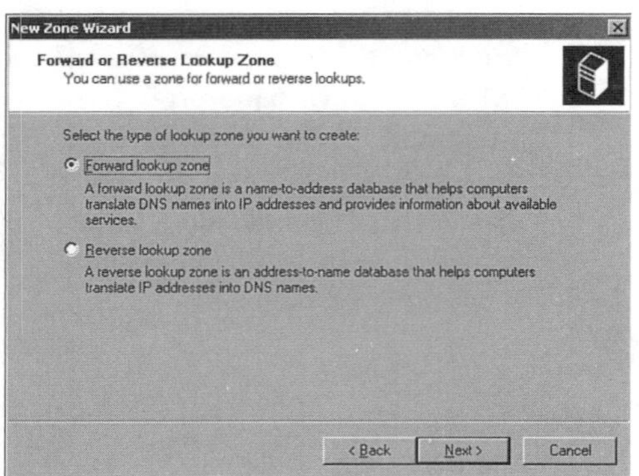

FIGURE 6.4
Selecting a forward lookup zone to create.

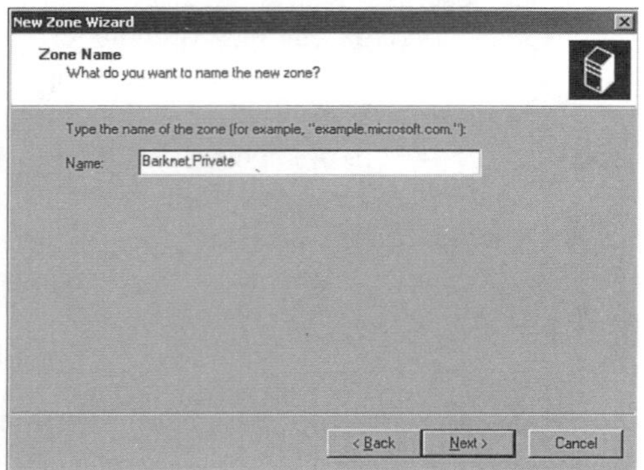

FIGURE 6.5
In general you should use a registered domain name whenever you are creating a zone.

4. The Zone Name dialog box is shown in Figure 6.5. Enter the name of the domain for which you will be resolving names into the Name field. If you are on a network that is not connected to the Internet and will not be resolving names for users outside your internal network, this name can be anything. Click Next to continue.

5. The Completion screen allows you to review the configurations you selected and either go back to correct mistakes or cancel the wizard before the changes are committed. Click Finish to complete the configuration. The new domain appears in DNS console.

6. Right-click the DNS server and select New Zone. Click Next to continue.

7. The Zone Type dialog box enables you to select whether the zone will be integrated with Active Directory or maintained in a separate database. Select Active Directory-Integrated and click Next to continue.

8. The Forward or Reverse Lookup Zone screen enables you choose the zone to create. Select Reverse Lookup Zone and click Next to continue.

9. The Reverse Lookup Zone dialog box is shown in Figure 6.6.

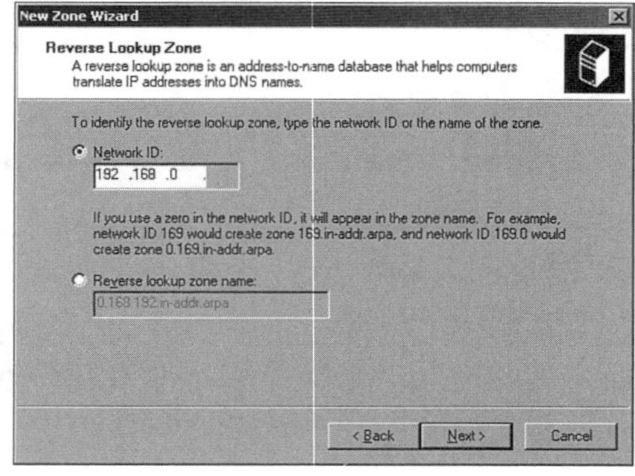

FIGURE 6.6
You can either specify a network ID or use the standard DNS naming convention to identify the reverse lookup zone.

10. Identify the reverse lookup ID by the network ID or by specifying a name. The name shown later in Figure 6.8 uses the standard naming convention, which is the network ID (in this case 10.15.100.x) in reverse order with `in-addr.arpa` appended. This results in a reverse name of `100.15.10.in-addr.arpa`. Notice the `arpa` in the name. If you guessed that this naming convention has been around since the Internet was called the ARPAnet, you're correct. As we discussed earlier in the "Reverse Lookups" section of the chapter, this is the Internet-standard naming convention, and you should try to stick with it. Click Next to continue.

11. The Completion screen enables you to review the configurations you selected and either go back to correct mistakes or cancel the wizard before the changes are committed.

12. Click Finish to complete the configuration. Notice in Figure 6.7 that the domains that were configured by the wizard now appear in the DNS console.

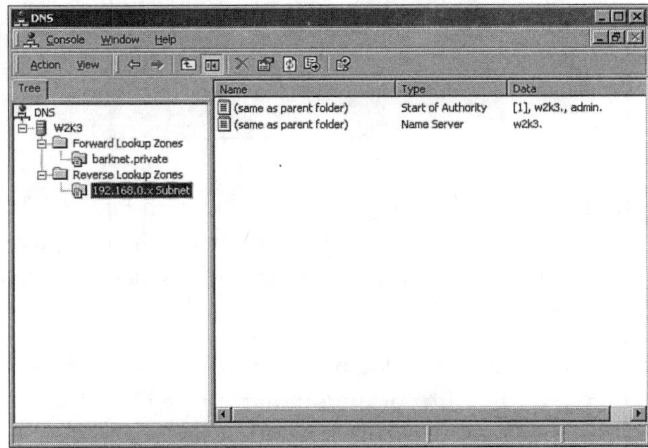

FIGURE 6.7
Your new domain(s) now appears in the DNS console application.

EXAM TIP

DNS Names Used with Active Directory Can't Be Changed In choosing a domain name to use when installing DNS, you always should register a domain name with the appropriate domain name registration agency and use that even if your internal network is isolated (not connected to the Internet) because the DNS name used with Active Directory can't be changed. That the DNS name used with Active Directory Services can't be changed would make an excellent exam question.

You have created a zone using the Configure the DNS Server Wizard. Let's now look at creating a new zone using the DNS console application.

To create a standard primary forward lookup zone on your DNS server, perform Step By Step 6.4.

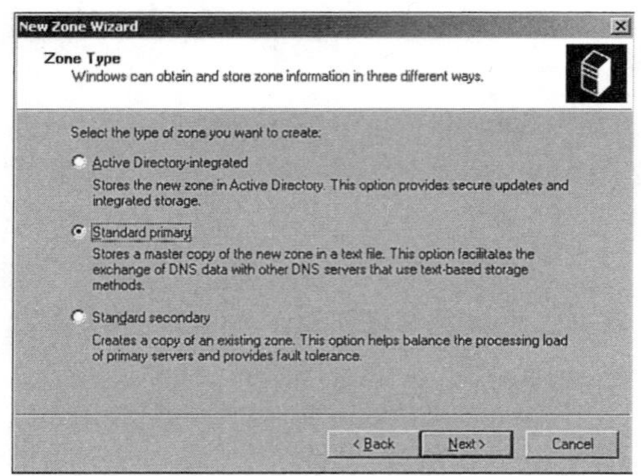

FIGURE 6.8
In this process, store your DNS table in Standard Primary, not Active Directory.

STEP BY STEP

6.4 Creating Standard Primary Zones

1. Open the DNS console by selecting Administrative Tools, DNS. Right-click the DNS server and select New Zone. Click Next to continue.
2. The Zone Type dialog box is shown in Figure 6.8. Select Standard Primary and click Next to continue.
3. The Forward or Reverse Lookup Zone dialog box is shown in Figure 6.9. Select Forward Lookup Zone and click Next to continue.

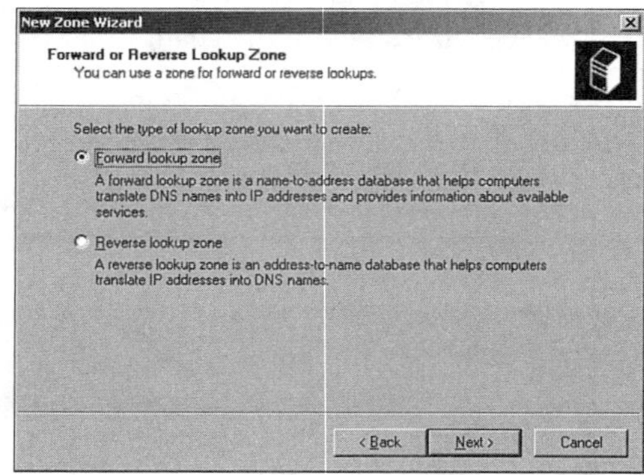

FIGURE 6.9
If you are hosting multiple domains, you typically create more forward lookup zones than reverse lookup zones.

4. The Zone Name dialog box is shown in Figure 6.10. Enter the name of the domain for which you will be resolving names into the Name field. Click Next to continue.
5. The Zone File dialog box is shown in Figure 6.11. Create a new DNS file, or import an existing DNS file. Importing is particularly useful if you are replacing a non-Windows DNS server and want to import the information. Click Next to continue.

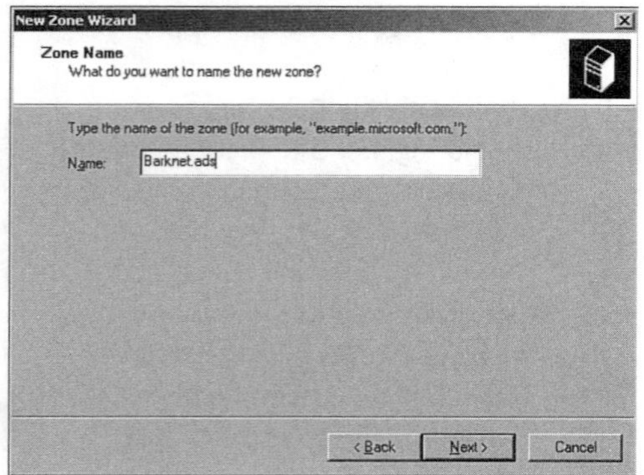

FIGURE 6.10
It is generally a good idea to use a registered domain name whenever you are creating a zone.

6. The Completion screen allows you to review the configurations you selected and either go back to correct mistakes or cancel the wizard before the changes are committed.

7. Click Finish to complete the configuration. The new domain now appears in the DNS console.

8. Right-click the DNS server and select New Zone. Click Next to continue.

9. The Zone Type dialog enables you to choose the zone to create. Select Standard Primary, and click Next to continue.

10. The Forward or Reverse Lookup Zone dialog box enables you to select the zone to create. Select Reverse and click Next to continue.

11. Figure 6.12 shows the Reverse Lookup Zone dialog box.

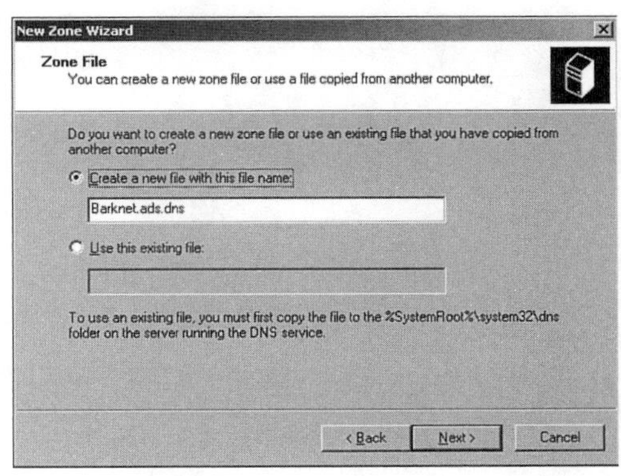

FIGURE 6.11
Using the standard naming convention for your DNS files is an excellent idea so that you can easily identify the file in the future.

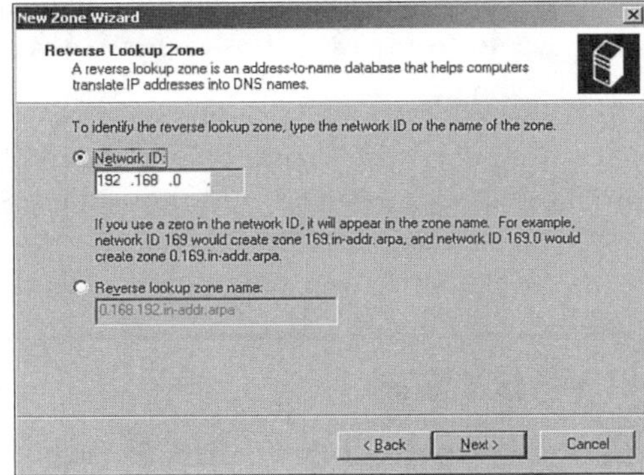

FIGURE 6.12
Specify the network address and let the wizard create the zone name.

12. Enter the IP address of the network for which you want to perform reverse lookups. If you are familiar with the naming conventions for reverse lookup zone names, you can manually specify the zone name by selecting the Reverse Lookup Zone Name option. Click Next to continue.

13. The Zone File dialog box is shown in Figure 6.13. This dialog box enables you to create a new zone file or use an already created file from another DNS server. Select the Create a New File with This Filename option. Click Next to continue.

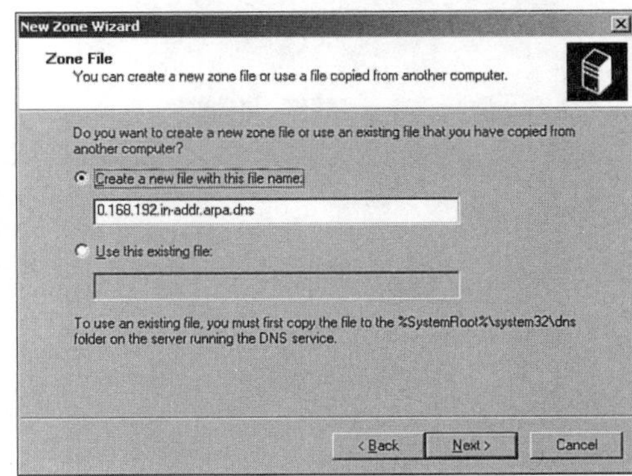

FIGURE 6.13
From the Zone File dialog box, you can create a new zone file, or you can use an existing file to populate your zone when it is created.

continues

continued

14. The Completion screen allows you to review the configurations you selected and either go back to correct mistakes or cancel the wizard before the changes are committed. Click Finish to complete the configuration. The new domain appears in the DNS console.

You should have a good understanding of how zones are created. Now let's take a look at setting up a caching-only server.

Configuring a Caching-Only Server

NOTE

Room for Cached Information All the cache entries on a caching-only server are stored in RAM. You should ensure that your caching server has plenty of RAM; otherwise, it will not be effective.

Caching-only servers are used to speed up client computer DNS queries by gathering a large number of cached records based on client computer DNS queries. A caching-only server does not have a copy of the zone table and therefore can't respond to queries against the zone unless they are already cached. A caching server is not authoritative on any zone.

To configure a caching-only server, install DNS as described previously in the installing DNS procedure, and then follow Step By Step 6.5.

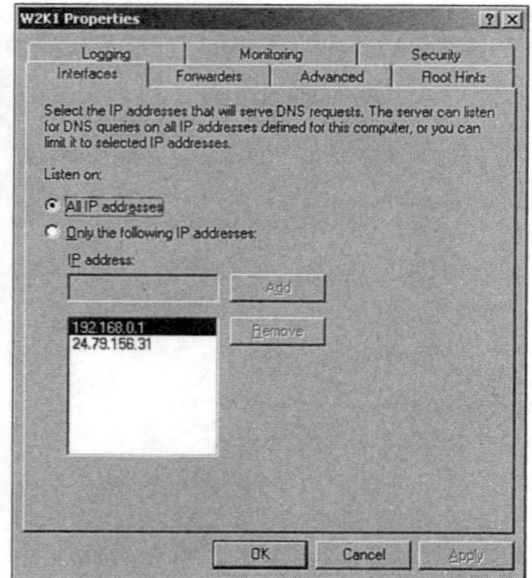

FIGURE 6.14
The DNS server Properties dialog box enables you to configure the advanced properties of the server.

STEP BY STEP

6.5 Creating a Caching-Only DNS Server

1. Open the DNS console by selecting Administrative Tools, DNS. Right-click your new server and select Properties. The DNS server Properties dialog box opens; the title bar reflects the name of your server (see Figure 6.14).

2. Click the Root Hints tab (see Figure 6.15). If any entries exist for the root servers, delete them.

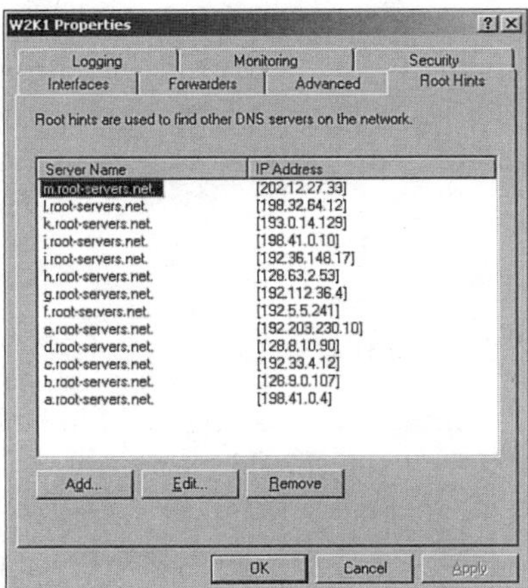

FIGURE 6.15
The root hints are used to locate other DNS servers on the network.

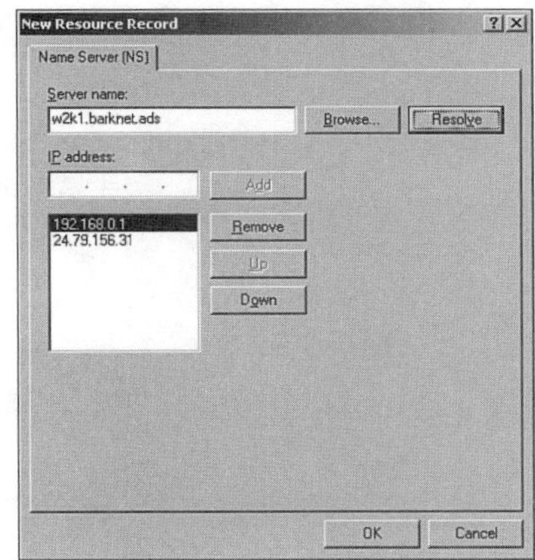

FIGURE 6.16
The New Resource Record dialog box enables you to add existing name servers to your root hints list.

3. From the Root Hints tab, click Add to open the New Resource Record dialog box, shown in Figure 6.16. Add a resource record for every DNS server you want this server to cache lookups for. These name servers must already exist in your DNS hierarchy.

4. Click OK when this is completed. Notice that the name servers appear in the Root Hints window (see Figure 6.17). Click OK to return to the DNS console.

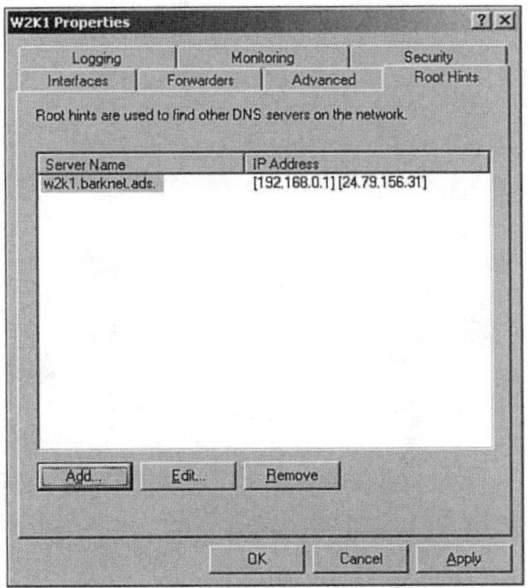

FIGURE 6.17
After you have added the name servers you will be caching, they appear in the Root Hints window.

To verify that the caching function is working, ping several hosts from a workstation configured to use that server for DNS. This builds up the cache. Then, go to another workstation also using that server for DNS and ping the same hosts. The response should be much quicker.

Configuring a DNS Client Computer

Now that you have installed and configured the DNS server portion of Windows 2000 DNS, you should take a look at how to install DNS on a Windows 2000 client computer. Step By Step 6.6 can be used to configure DNS on a Windows 2000 Professional computer.

STEP BY STEP

6.6 Configuring a DNS Client Computer

1. Select Start, Settings, Control Panel. Double-click Network and Dial-up Connections.
2. Right-click the Local Connection icon and select Properties from the context menu. The Local Area Connection Properties dialog box is shown in Figure 6.18.
3. Select the Internet Protocol (TCP/IP) entry and click the Properties button. The Internet Protocol (TCP/IP) Properties dialog box opens (see Figure 6.19).

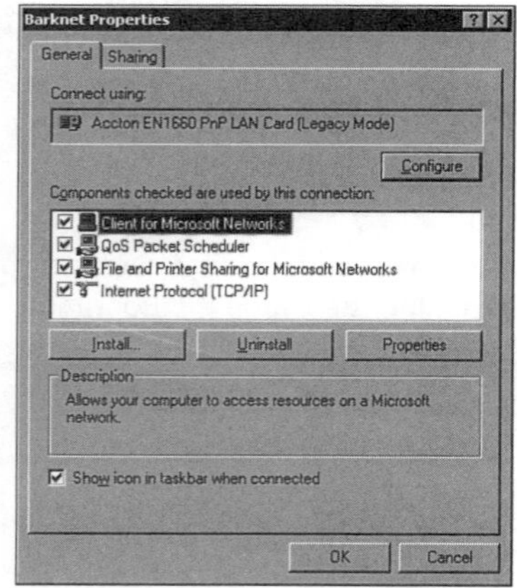

FIGURE 6.18
The Local Area Connection Properties dialog box gives you access to any of your LAN properties, including the TCP/IP settings.

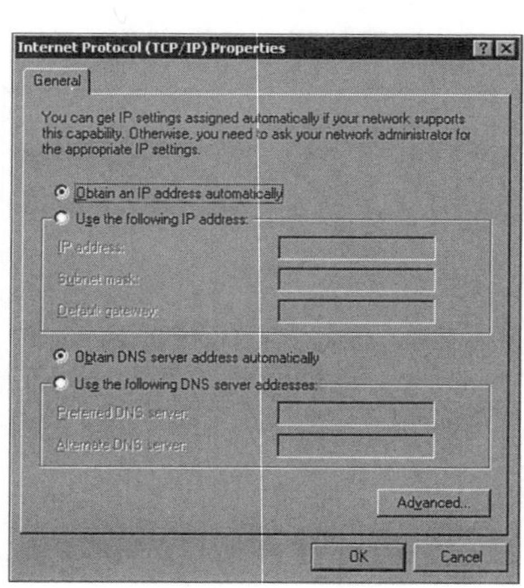

FIGURE 6.19
You can either have your DNS settings obtained automatically via DHCP or specify them manually.

4. In the DNS section of the dialog box, you can either choose to have DNS configured automatically via DHCP or specify the preferred and alternate DNS servers. Click Advanced for additional DNS options. Click the DNS tab to see the DNS options shown in Figure 6.20.

5. In the Advanced TCP/IP Settings dialog box, you can configure several DNS client computer settings. For this Step By Step, leave the default settings.

6. Click OK to return to the Internet Protocol (TCP/IP) Properties dialog box. Click OK to return to the Local Area Network Properties dialog box; then, click OK to close the Local Area Network Properties dialog box and put unapplied changes into effect.

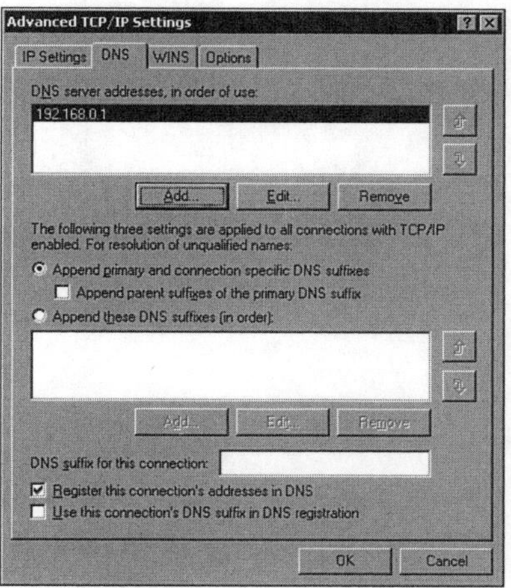

FIGURE 6.20
The Advanced TCP/IP Settings dialog box gives you additional DNS configuration options.

Several advanced TCP/IP options can be configured in conjunction with the DNS client computer. They include the following:

- DNS server addresses, in order of use.
- Parameters for resolving unqualified domain names. The options include the following:
  - **Append Primary and Connection Specific DNS Suffixes**—This option appends the domain suffixes configured in the System Properties to any unqualified domain names sent for resolution.
  - **Append Parent Suffixes of the Primary DNS Suffix**—This option adds not only the specified domain suffixes, but also the suffixes of any parent domains to any unqualified domain names sent for resolution.
  - **Append These DNS Suffixes (in order)**—This option allows you to specify certain DNS suffixes to be appended to any unqualified domain names sent for resolution.
  - **DNS Suffix for this Connection**—This option allows you to configure a specific DNS suffix for this connection in the list of Network and Dial-up Connections. You can specify different suffixes in case you have multiple LAN adapters loaded or want to use different suffixes between LAN and dial-up connections.

- **Register This Connection's Addresses in DNS**—This is how you configure the computer to take advantage of Dynamic DNS.
- **Use This Connection's DNS Suffix in DNS Registration**—This option allows you to use the DNS suffix specified with this connection as part of the information used when the host is registered with Dynamic DNS.

You have now completed configuring your Windows 2000 DNS client computer. Now let's look at configuring the zones for dynamic updates.

Configuring Zones for Dynamic Updates

One of the major advantages to running a Windows 2000 network is the capability to use Dynamic DNS. Let's look at how you configure a zone for dynamic updates.

To configure your DNS zone for dynamic updates, perform the steps in Step By Step 6.7.

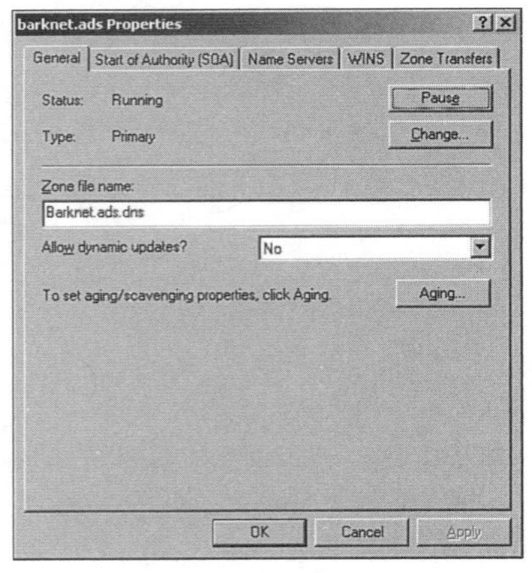

FIGURE 6.21
The zone Properties dialog box allows you to pause the DNS Server service, change the domain type, configure your DNS server to accept dynamic updates, and set the aging/scavenging options for the domain.

STEP BY STEP

6.7 Configuring Your Zone for Dynamic Updates

1. From the Administrative Tools program menu, open the DNS console.
2. Select the zone you want to configure to receive dynamic updates, and right-click. From the context menu, select Properties. This opens the Properties dialog box shown in Figure 6.21. (The title bar of the dialog box reflects the name of the zone.)
3. Set the Allow Dynamic Updates? pull-down menu to Yes. Click OK to close the dialog box and return to the DNS console. You have just configured the zone to accept dynamic updates.

Before we move on to testing the DNS Server service, we should briefly discuss what Dynamic DNS is.

Dynamic DNS (DDNS) is specified in RFC 2136——Dynamic Updates in the Domain Name System (DNS UPDATE). It is the foundation of a successful Active Directory Service implementation. As we have discussed, DNS is used to resolve a name to an IP address, or vice versa, using a defined hierarchical naming structure to ensure uniformity. Dynamic DNS takes that architecture to the next level. This section describes the Windows 2000 implementation of dynamic update.

In Windows 2000, client computers can send dynamic updates for three types of network adapters: DHCP adapters, statically configured adapters, and remote access adapters. You looked at these configurations in the "Configuring a DNS Client Computer" section earlier in the chapter.

Dynamic DNS integrates DHCP and DNS, as described in RFC 2136. When a client receives an Internet Protocol (IP) address and other related configuration information from a DHCP server, the client can register an "A" (Host) record with the DNS, or the client can allow the DHCP server to register an "A" (Host) record, a PTR (pointer) record, or both in the DNS database. The DHCP server keeps track of the PTR record for the client.

The DHCP client computer can send its FQDN back to the DHCP server with a special `DHCPRequest` packet called Option 81 (or code 81). Flags within the FQDN packet tell the DHCP server what types of records (forward lookup, reverse lookup, or both) to register with the Dynamic DNS. Optionally, the DHCP client computer can do this itself.

The DHCP server also has the capability to obtain the domain information for legacy client computers that do not support Option 81 and to update the Dynamic DNS on their behalf.

The end result is that every DHCP client computer has an entry in the DNS zones, both forward and reverse. This information can be used by other Windows 2000 computers in place of WINS for identifying the names and IP addresses of other hosts.

> NOTE
>
> **Option 81 Is FQDN** Option 81 (also known as the fully qualified domain name option) enables the client computer to send its FQDN to the DHCP server when it requests an IP address.

By default, the client computer dynamically registers its A resource records whenever any of the following events occur:

- The TCP/IP configuration is changed.
- The DHCP address is renewed, or a new lease is obtained.
- When `IPCONFIG /REGISTERDNS` is used to manually force the client name registration in the DNS.
- When the computer starts up.

By default, the client computer automatically deregisters name–to–IP address mappings whenever the DHCP lease expires.

You can force a reregistration by using the command-line tool `IPCONFIG`. For Windows 2000–based client computers, type the following at the command prompt:

```
ipconfig /registerdns
```

Now let's take a quick look at the dynamic update process and see how your Windows 2000 host gets dynamically registered with DNS. A dynamic update occurs in the following manner:

1. The DNS client computer queries its local name server to find the primary name server and the zone that is authoritative for the name it is updating. The local name server performs the standard name resolution process to discover the primary name server and returns the names of the authoritative server and zone.
2. The client computer sends a dynamic update request to the primary server. The authoritative server performs the update and replies to the client computer regarding the result of the dynamic update.

Now that DNS is installed and configured, let's examine how to test DNS.

Testing the DNS Server Service

How can you test to ensure DNS is working? Several applications allow you to perform these tests; we'll discuss them in order of complexity.

The first application for testing DNS is the PING utility. `PING` enables you to send an Internet Control Message Protocol (ICMP) to a TCP/IP host. By using the correct flag, `PING` can also perform name resolution as part of its testing procedure. The correct format for this command is the following:

```
PING -a <destination address>
```

The `-a` flag will provide host name resolution. A sample `PING` session might look like this:

```
PING -a www.yahoo.com

Pinging www.yahoo.akadns.net [216.115.102.75]
                      with 32 bytes of data:
Reply from 216.115.102.75: bytes=32 time=90ms TTL=56
Reply from 216.115.102.75: bytes=32 time=61ms TTL=56
Reply from 216.115.102.75: bytes=32 time=72ms TTL=56
Reply from 216.115.102.75: bytes=32 time=64ms TTL=56
Ping statistics for 216.115.102.75:
    Packets: Sent = 4, Received = 4, Lost = 0 (0% loss),
Approximate round-trip times in milliseconds:
    Minimum = 61ms, Maximum = 90ms, Average = 71ms
```

From this sample you can see several things. First, because your `PING` `command` returned the IP address of 216.115.102.75, you know that DNS is functional. Second, because this also returned an alternate host name of `www.yahoo.akadns.net`, you can see that `www.yahoo.com` uses a redirector (in this case Akamai's DNS system) to send your request to the nearest copy of the Web site.

> NOTE
>
> **An Alias for Another Server's FQDN** If you are familiar with the Internet's server-hosting architecture, this alias could also mean that the Web site is hosted by an ISP.

The next utility we need to look at is `NSLOOKUP`. `NSLOOKUP` is a standard command-line tool provided in most DNS server implementations, including Windows 2000. `NSLOOKUP` offers the capability to perform query testing of DNS servers and obtain detailed responses at the command prompt. This information can be useful for diagnosing and solving name resolution problems, verifying that resource records are added or updated correctly in a zone, and debugging other server-related problems. `NSLOOKUP` can be used by going to a DOS prompt, typing **`NSLOOKUP`**, and pressing Enter. `NSLOOKUP` accepts the following commands:

- `NAME`—Prints information about the host name or domain name using the default server
- `NAME1 NAME2`—Same as the preceding, but it uses `NAME2` as the server
- `help` or `?`—Prints information on common commands

- `set OPTION`—Sets an option
- The `SET` command has several options that modify the way `NSLOOKUP` works. The following is a list of additional options you can set:
  - `all`—Prints options, the current server, and the host
  - `[no]debug`—Prints debugging information
  - `[no]d2`—Prints exhaustive debugging information
  - `[no]defname`—Appends a domain name to each query
  - `[no]recurse`—Asks for a recursive answer to a query
  - `[no]search`—Uses a domain search list
  - `[no]vc`—Always uses a virtual circuit
  - `domain=NAME`—Sets the default domain name to `NAME`
  - `srchlist=N1[/N2/.../N6]`—Sets the domain to `N1` and the search list to `N1`, `N2`, and so on
  - `root=NAME`—Sets the root server to `NAME`
  - `retry=X`—Sets the number of retries to `X`
  - `timeout=X`—Sets the initial timeout interval to `X` seconds
  - `type=X`—Sets the query type (for example, `A`, `ANY`, `CNAME`, `MX`, `NS`, `PTR`, `SOA`, or `SRV`)
  - `querytype=X`—Same as the `type option`
  - `class=X`—Set the query class (for example, `IN` (Internet) or `ANY`)
  - `[no]msxfr`—Uses MS fast zone transfer
  - `ixfrver=X`—Sets the current version to use an `IXFR` transfer request
- `server NAME`—Sets the default server to `NAME`, using the current default server
- `lserver NAME`—Sets the default server to `NAME`, using the initial server
- `finger [USER]`—Fingers the optional `NAME` at the current default host

- `root`—Sets the current default server to the root
- `ls [opt] DOMAIN [> FILE]`—Lists the addresses in `DOMAIN` (optional: output to `FILE`)

The `ls` command has several options that can be applied to the output. The following is a list valid values for `[opt]`:

- `-a`—Lists canonical names and aliases
- `-d`—Lists all records
- `-t TYPE`—Lists records of the given type (for example, `A`, `CNAME`, `MX`, `NS`, `PTR`, and so on)
    - `view FILE`—Sorts an `ls` output file and views it with `pg`
    - `exit`—Exits the program

> **EXAM TIP**
>
> **Know NSLOOKUP** Because NSLOOKUP is the standard DNS tool for troubleshooting DNS, you should be familiar with its capabilities and options for the exam.

> **EXAM TIP**
>
> **Know the NSLOOKUP Modes** You should be familiar with the fact that NSLOOKUP functions in both the interactive and noninteractive modes. Noninteractive is used when you need only a single piece of information.

It is probably easier to understand what `NSLOOKUP` will do by actually trying it.

Following are a couple of examples.

The first output is from the command `nslookup www.yahoo.com`:

```
Server:  hack.ab.videon.ca
Address:  206.75.216.200

Name:    www.yahoo.akadns.net
Addresses:  216.115.102.78, 216.115.102.80, 216.115.102.76,
216.115.102.75  216.115.102.77, 216.115.102.79
Aliases:  www.yahoo.com
```

This shows that `www.yahoo.com` is `CNAME`'d to an `akamai.net` server. This server returns the appropriate list of IP addresses closest to you. If you ping `www.yahoo.com`, you will use one of these IP addresses. If you then flush the DNS cache (`IPCONFIG/FLUSHDNS`) and repeat the `ping` command, you will probably get a different IP address (but still within the list returned by `NSLOOKUP`).

The next output looks at more details from the `nslookup` program:

```
nslookup
type=any

>Server:  hack.ab.videon.ca
Address:  206.75.216.200
>www.yahoo.com
```

```
Non-authoritative answer:
www.yahoo.com    canonical name = www.yahoo.akadns.net


yahoo.com    nameserver = NS3.EUROPE.yahoo.com
yahoo.com    nameserver = NS5.DCX.yahoo.com
yahoo.com    nameserver = NS4.DAL.yahoo.com
yahoo.com    nameserver = NS2.SAN.yahoo.com
yahoo.com    nameserver = NS1.SNV.yahoo.com
NS3.EUROPE.yahoo.com    internet address = 217.12.4.71
NS5.DCX.yahoo.com    internet address = 216.32.74.10
NS4.DAL.yahoo.com    internet address = 63.250.206.50
NS2.SAN.yahoo.com    internet address = 209.132.1.29
NS1.SNV.yahoo.com    internet address = 216.115.108.33
```

In this example you can see that the information returned is actually about `akadns.net` and not `yahoo.com`. As the Internet has gone from being a local service to being a global presence, Web content that requires a large bandwidth (such as streaming media or banners, and so on) needs to be duplicated to other places in the world to allow faster access. It is common to see this type of redirection on the Internet now.

The next output results from looking up `www.quepublishing.com`:

```
Nslookup

Default Server:  hack.ab.videon.ca
Address:  206.75.216.200

>set type=CNAME
>www.quepublishing.com
>Server:  hack.ab.videon.ca
Address:  206.75.216.200

www.quepublishing.com    canonical name = quepublishing.com

quepublishing.com    nameserver = USRXDNS1.PEARSONTC.com
quepublishing.com    nameserver = OLDTXDNS1.PEARSONTC.com
USRXDNS1.PEARSONTC.com    internet address = 198.4.159.10
OLDTXDNS1.PEARSONTC.com    internet address = 63.69.110.61

>set type=A
>quepublishing.com
>Server:  hack.ab.videon.ca
Address:  206.75.216.200

Name:    quepublishing.com
Address:  165.193.123.44
Aliases:  www.quepublishing.com
```

In this example you can see that the `quepublishing.com` name is hosted by `pearsontc.com` and the Web site address is 165.193.123.15.

If the server you are looking for does not have a PTR record in a reverse lookup zone, the server name will be returned with a message that says the following:

```
***Can't find server name for address (the address
➥of the configured DNS server): Nonexistent domain
***Default servers are unavailable
```

This does not mean anything is broken. If you still get a name resolution in the `Name/Address` section of the response, your DNS server is working.

Another method for testing the DNS Server service is to use the monitoring capabilities built into the DNS console application. To set up testing and monitoring, follow Step By Step 6.8.

STEP BY STEP

6.8 Testing the DNS Service

1. Open the DNS console application.
2. Right-click the DNS server and select Properties. The DNS Server Properties dialog box opens. Select the Monitoring tab. You can configure a simple query, a recursive query, and even automatic testing of the DNS service from this tab.
3. Click Test Now to perform the selected tests.
4. Click OK to return to the DNS console application.

The test we just discussed enables you to perform two types of queries. Before we move on, we should discuss exactly what the queries are and how they work. Following are the queries:

- **Simple (iterative) query**—A simple (or *iterative*) query is one in which the name server provides the best response based on what that server knows from local zone files or caching. If a name server doesn't have any information to answer the query, it simply sends a negative response.

- **Recursive query**—A *recursive* query forces a DNS server to respond to a request with either a failure or a successful response. With a recursive query, the DNS server must contact any other DNS servers it needs to resolve the request. This is a much more resource-intensive query mechanism.

If the test fails, you will see an error message in the DNS console application and an alert icon will appear on the DNS server.

A final method for testing a DNS server is to use a Web browser such as Internet Explorer. Type the FQDN you want to reach into the URL Locator box and press Enter. If DNS is working correctly, the IP address will be displayed in the lower-left corner of the application. This occurs even if the host in question is not a Web server. The browser might not connect successfully, but you should see that resolution if DNS is configured correctly.

Implementing a Delegated Zone for DNS

The next thing we need to look at is how to create a delegated zone for your DNS. *Delegating* a domain means that DNS queries on the existing domain will be referred to the name server in the delegated domain for resolution. You can delegate only down the hierarchy, so the delegated domain must be a subdomain of the domain doing the delegation. That might be a little confusing, but the configuration procedure should make it a little clearer.

To create a delegated zone, perform Step By Step 6.9.

STEP BY STEP

6.9 Creating a Delegated Zone

1. From the Administrative Tools program group, open the DNS console application.
2. Right-click the DNS zone you want to delegate, and from the context menu select New Delegation. The New Delegation Wizard opens (see Figure 6.22). Click Next to continue.

FIGURE 6.22
As with most other administrative tasks in Windows 2000, a wizard is available for creating a new delegation for a zone.

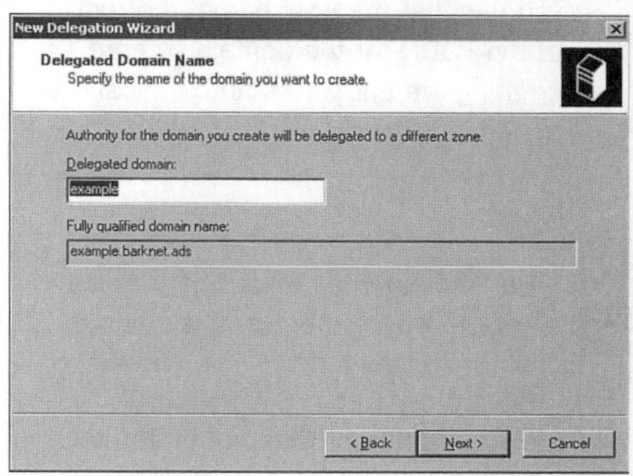

FIGURE 6.23
The Delegated Domain Name dialog box enables you to specify the domain that will respond to delegated queries.

3. The Delegated Domain Name dialog box is shown in Figure 6.23. Enter the unqualified name for the domain you want to delegate to in the Delegated Domain field, and click Next to continue. The Name Servers dialog box shown in Figure 6.24, allows you to specify the name server that will be hosting the delegated zone.

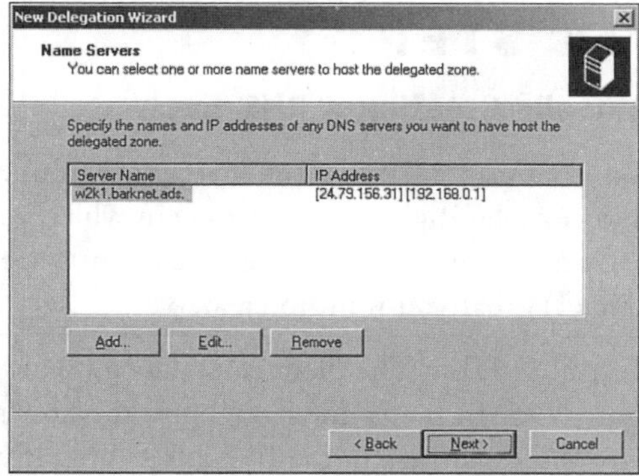

FIGURE 6.24
The Name Servers dialog box should look familiar at this point. As with the previous procedures, this dialog box is used to specify the name servers for this domain.

4. Click Add, and you can either browse to the name server or specify it by name or IP address. Click Next to complete the wizard. To create the delegation, click Finish.

Windows 2000 Professional and the Windows 2000 DHCP service can dynamically update the DNS with new information. However, for non-Windows 2000 hosts, you can manually configure DNS records on their behalf.

NOTE

Names for a Record When you create your record, you can use the FQDN name or just the host name. If you use just the host name, the rest of the FQDN for the domain you are creating the entry in is automatically appended.

EXAM TIP

Be Familiar with Table Entry Types Prior to taking the exam, you should acquaint yourself with the other table entry types. Each needs slightly different information for its entry.

Manually Creating DNS Resource Records

You can use manually created DNS entries for non-Windows 2000 hosts, table entry types that are not supported by Dynamic DNS, or hosts that you just want to configure with a static entry. When you manually create a DNS entry, you have four options of what type of entry to create:

- **New Host**—This creates an `A` record.
- **New Alias**—This creates a `CNAME` record.
- **New Mail Exchanger**—This creates an `MX` record.
- **Other New Records**—This enables you to select the other record types.

For this procedure, you will create a new host record. To manually create a DNS entry, follow Step By Step 6.10.

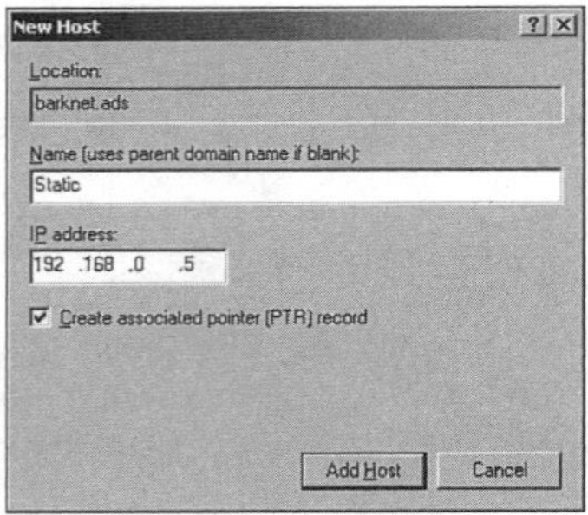

FIGURE 6.25
The New Host dialog box asks for the host name, the IP address of the host, and whether you want to create an entry in the reverse lookup zone.

STEP BY STEP

6.10 Manually Creating a DNS Entry

1. From the Administrative Tools program group, open the DNS console. Right-click the zone in which you want to add an entry, and select the type of entry (refer to Table 6.1) that you want to create.

2. Select New Host. The New Host dialog box is shown in Figure 6.25. In the Name field, enter the host name. Enter the IP address in the IP Address box. If you want to create an entry in the reverse lookup zone for that network, you can select the Create Associated Pointer (PTR) Record option. Click Add Host to create the entry.

Now you know how to install, configure, and create entries for zones. Next, we need to discuss how you manage and monitor your DNS server.

MANAGING AND MONITORING DNS

If your job is typical of most, you will spend a great deal more time managing DNS servers than you will spend installing them.

Although the DNS server doesn't include any specific monitoring capabilities, you should be aware of several additional options as you manage your DNS server over the long term. One utility that is useful for managing your DNS server is the DNS snap-in to the MMC console, which is listed as DNS in the Administrative Tools menu.

For a closer look at the capabilities of the DNS console, open the DNS console application. Select the DNS server and click the Action menu to see the available actions:

- **Set Aging/Scavenging for All Zones**—Opens the Server Aging/Scavenging Properties dialog box
- **Scavenge Stale Resource Records Manually**—Immediately starts scavenging stale resource records
- **All Tasks**—Includes starting, stopping, pausing, resuming, and restarting the DNS Server Service
- **Delete**—Deletes the DNS server
- **Refresh**—Causes all the displayed information to be refreshed with a current status
- **Export List**—Exports the information from the DNS server to a tab- or comma-delimited text or Unicode text file
- **Properties**—Opens the Properties dialog box for the selected DNS server

The following sections take a closer look at several of these actions.

Setting Aging/Scavenging for All Zones

When you select Action, Set Aging/Scavenging for All Zones, you can use the Server Aging/Scavenging Properties dialog box to set three options (see Figure 6.26).

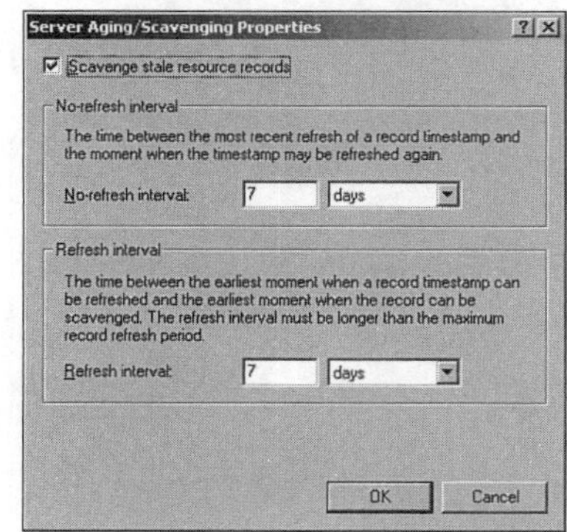

FIGURE 6.26
Setting the record scavenging parameters correctly can improve server performance and reduce problems.

The Scavenge Stale Resource Records option does exactly what its name implies. With dynamic DNS updates enabled, records are automatically added to the zone when computers come on the network. In some cases, these records are not automatically deleted. For example, if a computer is disconnected from the network, its associated resource record might not be deleted. If your network has many mobile users (and whose doesn't these days?), this can happen frequently. To keep your zone table clean of inaccurate records, you should enable this option.

The No-Refresh Interval option controls the time between the most recent refresh of a record's time stamp and when the time stamp can be refreshed again. In a very dynamic network in which computers come on and leave frequently, you might want to lower this from the default 7 days.

The Refresh Interval option sets the time between the earliest moment that a record time stamp can be refreshed and the earliest moment a record can be scavenged.

Scavenging Stale Resource Records Manually

The Scavenge Stale Resource Records Manually option also scavenges old resource records. When you select this command, the Update Server Data Files option writes any changes to the table that are in RAM to the server's hard drive. (To clear the server cache manually, right-click the DNS server and select Clear Cache from the context menu.)

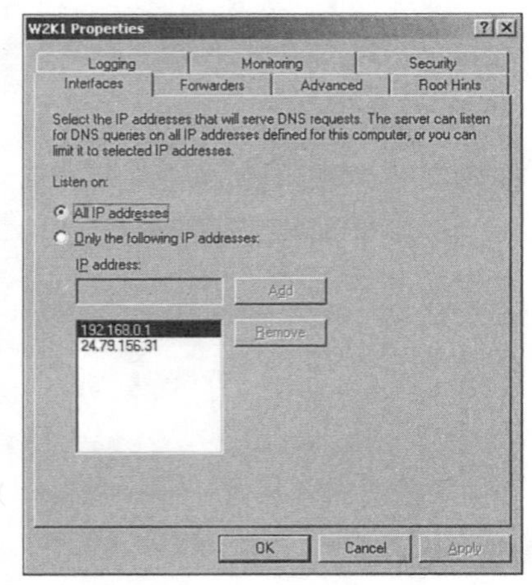

FIGURE 6.27
The Interfaces tab can be used to prevent certain IP addresses from responding to DNS requests.

Setting Zone Properties

When you select Action, Properties, the Properties dialog box opens, as (Remember that the title bar reflects the name of your server.) The Properties dialog box gives you access to the tabs shown in Figure 6.27.

The Forwarders tab enables you to configure a list of forwarders for the server to use, as shown in Figure 6.28. A *forwarder* is sort of a shortcut to domain resolution. Ordinarily, when a DNS server receives a request for a zone that it is not authoritative on, it forwards the request to the root server for the domain and then walks the tree until it either times out or receives a resolution. By using a forwarder, you are betting that the forwarder has already cached the response to the DNS request and is capable of responding much more quickly.

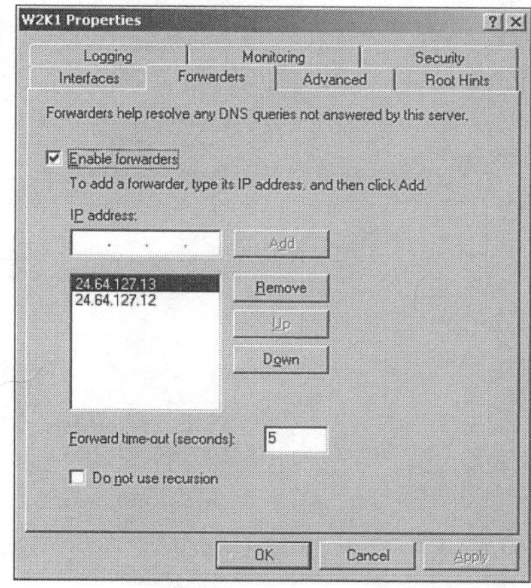

FIGURE 6.28
Forwarders can speed up domain request resolution if they are used correctly.

> **EXAM TIP**
>
> **Know When to Use Round Robin DNS** For the exam, you should be aware that round robin DNS is also known as *Poor Man's Load Balancing*. Round robin enables you to use DNS to help spread the load on a group of servers by allowing you to tie multiple IP addresses to a single DNS record. Each time a resolution is requested, DNS returns the "next" record in the list of addresses.

The Advanced tab, shown in Figure 6.29, allows you to configure the following advanced options:

- **Disable Recursion**—Allows the DNS server to make iterative queries and refer the client computer to the address of a DNS server that might have the answer. If recursion is enabled, the DNS server is forced to resolve the request itself. Iterative queries require much less overhead on the server.
- **BIND Secondaries**—Enables support for the BIND version of DNS.
- **Fail on Load if Bad Zone Data**—Prevents the server from loading if there is corrupt data in the zone file.
- **Enable Round Robin**—Allows you to pool servers in a DNS entry so that the response to a query for the host name can be any of a group of addresses.

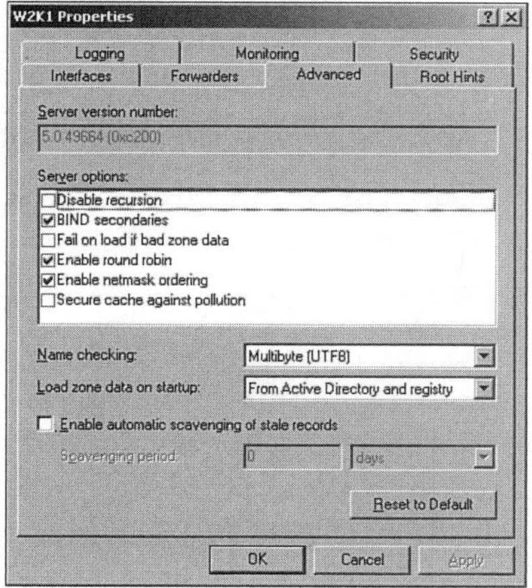

FIGURE 6.29
The Advanced page enables you to fine-tune your DNS parameters.

- **Enable Netmask Ordering**—Enabled by default, this specifies that the DNS server resolves the query with the address closest to the requesting client computer's IP address and listed first in the response. If both round robin and netmask ordering are enabled, netmask ordering is attempted first.

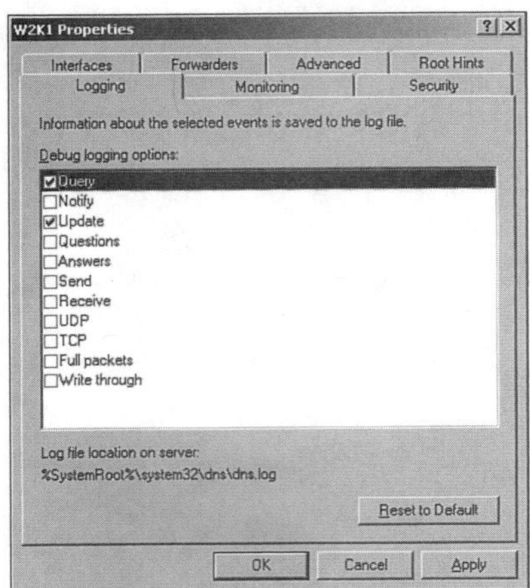

FIGURE 6.30
A number of parameters can be logged to record DNS server use.

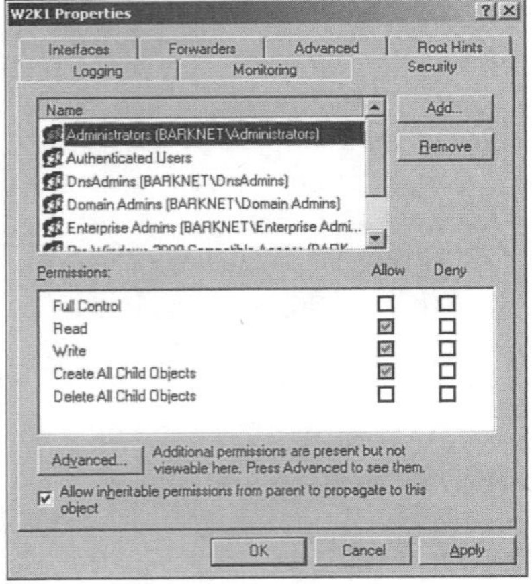

FIGURE 6.31
As with anything security related, the fewer people who have permissions on the DNS service the better.

- **Secure Cache Against Pollution**—Helps ensure that bad entries are not loaded into the server's DNS cache.
- **Name Checking**—Enables you to specify the types of names the server will accept as part of its DNS table.
- **Load Zone Data on Startup**—Enables you to specify from where DNS will load its initial table when the service starts. The most secure option is From Active Directory and Registry.
- **Enable Automatic Scavenging of Stale Records**—Gives you the capability to automate the scavenging of stale records and also to specify the scavenging period.

The Root Hints tab enables you to configure other DNS servers on the network for the forwarding of DNS requests where appropriate

The Logging tab allows you to configure server logging (see Figure 6.30). You can specify which logging options to configure by selecting the option to enable it. The log file can be found at `%SystemRoot%\system32\dns\dns.log`. `%SystemRoot%` is usually your Windows system file directory.

The Monitoring tab automates the testing of the DNS Server service, and the Security tab allows you to configure the rights to the DNS service, as shown in Figure 6.31.

Now that you have looked at the options for managing the DNS server, let's take a look at some of the ways to monitor the service.

Before we discuss how to monitor the DNS server, we should discuss what you can monitor. The Performance manager provides the following groups of counters for the DNS object. Because of the large number of counters, we will discuss the types of counters instead:

- **AXFR Counters**—These counters are associated with the full zone transfer requests received by the master DNS server. This group includes Requests Received, Requests Sent, Response Received, Success Received, and Success Sent.
- **Caching Memory**—This counter tracks the amount of memory used by the DNS server.
- **Database Node Memory**—This counter tracks the amount of database node memory used by the DNS server.

- **Dynamic Update**—These counters are associated with the dynamic updating of DNS. This group includes NoOperation, NoOperation/sec, Queued, Received, Received/sec, Rejected, Timeouts, Written to Database, and Written to Database/sec.
- **IXFR Counters**—These counters are associated with the incremental zone transfer requests received by the master DNS server. This group includes Requests Received, Requests Sent, Response Received, Success Received, Success Sent, TCP Success Received, and UDP Success Received.
- **Nbtstat Memory**—This counter tracks the amount of Nbtstat memory in use by the server.
- **Notify Received/Sent**—These counters track the notifies sent and received by the secondary DNS server.
- **Record Flow Memory**—This counter tracks the amount of record flow memory used by the DNS server.
- **Recursive**—The recursive counters are associated with the recursive queries the DNS server must make. This group includes Queries, Queries/sec, Query Failure, Query Failure/sec, Send TimeOuts, and TimeOut/sec.
- **Secure Update**—The secure update group of counters is associated with the number of secure updates sent and received. The group includes Failure, Received, and Received/sec.
- **TCP/UDP**—These counters track the respective TCP and UDP queries and responses. These groups include Message Memory, Query Received, Query Received/sec, Response Sent, and Response Sent/sec.
- **Total**—This group of counters totals the respective categories of requests and responses. This group includes Query Received, Query Received/sec, Response Sent, and Response Sent/sec.
- **WINS**—Because DNS under Windows 2000 can be used for WINS lookups, the DNS counters include the following WINS-specific counters: Lookup Received, Lookup Received/sec, Response Sent, Response Sent/sec, Reverse Lookup Received, Reverse Lookup Received/sec, Reverse Response Sent, and Reverse Response Sent/sec.

EXAM TIP

Don't Memorize All the Counters Microsoft does not expect you to memorize all these counters. You should, however, be familiar with the various types and know how to use the Performance console.

EXAM TIP

The VIP Counters Are AXFR and IXFR Two types of counters that are especially important are the AXFR and IXFR counters. Remember that AXFR counters are used in conjunction with full zone transfers, whereas IXFR counters are used in conjunction with incremental zone transfers.

NOTE

Identifying a Counter If you need to know what a counter means and have left your copy of this book at home under your pillow, fear not. Microsoft has included an option that does an excellent job of defining the counters. Select the counter you want to know more about and click the Explain button.

- **Zone Transfer**—The zone transfer counters are associated with the process of transferring copies of the DNS table between DNS servers. This group includes Failure, Request Received, SOA Request Sent, and Success.

To configure DNS performance monitoring, follow Step By Step 6.11.

STEP BY STEP

6.11 Configuring DNS Performance Monitoring

1. Select Start, Settings, Control Panel.
2. Double-click Administrative Tools and click Performance.
3. To create an entry in System Monitor, click the Add (+) icon. The Add Counters window opens. By default, it opens to the Processor performance object.
4. Select the DNS performance object. You will see the list of counters displayed as available for DNS (see Figure 6.32).
5. After you have decided on the counter you want to monitor, click Add. You can add multiple counters either by selecting each counter and clicking Add or by using the standard Windows multiple item select method of holding down the Ctrl key while you select all the counters you want to monitor and clicking Add. Click Close when you are done. You will see your counters being graphed.

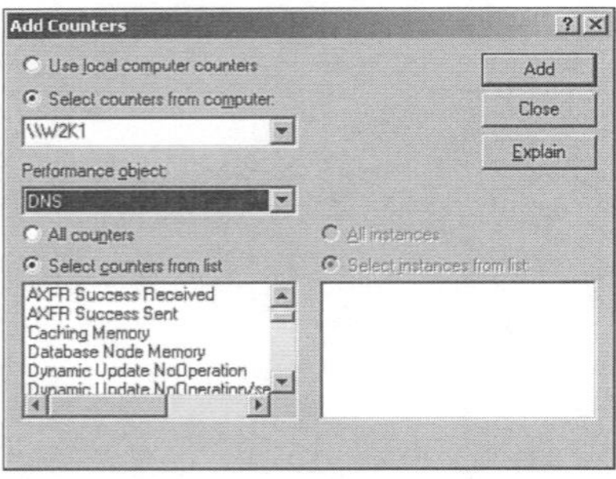

FIGURE 6.32
The counters associated with DNS allow you to comprehensively examine the DNS server's activities.

You've looked at the management options available in the DNS console application, and you've taken a look at how to monitor the performance of the various DNS counters using the Performance console. At this point, you should have a good understanding of the Windows 2000 DNS Server service and DNS in general. Now let's see how you do applying it in a practical setting.

CASE STUDY: IMPLEMENTING DNS IN A COMPLEX ENVIRONMENT

ESSENCE OF THE CASE

The essence of the case is as follows:

- Your company is about to migrate to a pure Windows 2000 environment.
- Your company is actually made up of three companies, each needing to maintain local control of its DNS.
- Users for each company need to be able to resolve addresses for other companies' hosts as quickly as possible.
- Corporate headquarters needs to resolve addresses for each of the companies but does not need to maintain a DNS domain.

SCENARIO

You are the network administrator for NR Widgets Inc., a multinational conglomerate, and you are based in the conglomerate's corporate headquarters. NR Widgets Inc., is made up of three companies: NR Manufacturing, NR Consulting, and NR Telecommunications. Each company has its own IT department and maintains its own network infrastructure. Each company also has its own DNS domain.

You have been asked to prepare the network for a complete Windows 2000 rollout, both client computers and servers, with the goal to be a pure Windows 2000 network. The first thing on your list is to implement a Windows 2000-capable DNS infrastructure. What is the best way to do this to accomplish the following:

- Each IT department keeps control of its own domain.
- Each company's users have the fastest possible resolution for other companies' hosts.
- The users in the headquarters' facility need fast DNS resolution for each of the company's hosts.
- Because the headquarters is a not a computing center, you do not need to maintain any master DNS servers.

Case Study: Implementing DNS in a Complex Environment

ANALYSIS

First, you will need to roll out Windows 2000 DNS servers. In reality, you should also have completed an Active Directory Services design, but you are concerned just with DNS services at this time. You should roll out the servers in the following manner:

- First, each company gets the primary master DNS server for its own domain. This gives it control of its DNS domain. For redundancy, each company should also have a secondary master server.
- To allow for each company to quickly resolve addresses for the other companies, each of the primary master DNS servers will also be secondary master servers for the other companies. That allows users to do local lookups.
- The corporate headquarters needs a caching-only server configured to receive cache updates from the other DNS servers on the network. An alternative is to set up a DNS server acting as a secondary master to the three company domains.
- Finally, all DNS servers should be set to accept dynamic updates. This is a requirement in a pure Windows 2000 environment.

That should have been a fairly easy case study if you read the chapter carefully. Of course, after the DNS servers are set up and running, you also should set up some of the monitoring we discussed at the end of the chapter.

Chapter Summary

KEY TERMS

- Caching
- Caching-only server
- DNS client computer
- DNS server
- Domain Name System (DNS)
- Dynamic Host Control Protocol (DHCP)
- Forward lookup

This chapter discussed all the key components of using a Windows 2000 DNS server in a Windows 2000 environment. We first covered the history and function of DNS.

We discussed reverse lookups, where an IP address can be resolved to a host name, and the various types of records. We also looked at the naming conventions for both standard DNS and the DNS service included with Windows 2000.

Next, we discussed installing and configuring the Windows 2000 DNS service. This involved all the major configuration activities from the initial installation to the manual creation of DNS records. We also covered configuring a DNS client computer and configuring a zone for dynamic updates.

CHAPTER SUMMARY

We wrapped up the chapter with a discussion of managing and monitoring the DNS service. And that wraps up the chapter summary. Let's take a look at some exercises and questions.

- Fully qualified domain name (FQDN)
- Hierarchy
- Management Information Base (MIB)
- Node
- Primary master
- Record types
- Reverse lookup
- Secondary master
- Start of Authority (SOA)
- Suffix
- Top-level domain (TLD)
- Transmission Control Protocol/Internet Protocol (TCP/IP)
- Zone

Exercises

6.1 Creating a DNS Zone

In this exercise, you will use the DNS console application to create a forward lookup zone.

Estimated Time: 10 minutes

1. Open the DNS console by selecting Administrative Tools, DNS. Right-click the DNS server and select New Zone.
2. Click Next to open the Zone Type dialog box. Select Standard Primary for the type of zone to create; then, click Next.
3. Select Forward for the zone type, and click Next.
4. In the Name field of the Zone Name dialog box, enter the name of the domain for which you will be resolving names. Click Next.
5. The Zone File dialog box opens. Accept the default to create a new zone file. Click Next.
6. The Completing the Configure DNS Server Wizard dialog box opens. Click Finish to complete the configuration. The new domain now appears in the DNS console.

6.2 Manually Creating a DNS Record

This exercise shows you how to manually create a DNS alias record.

Estimated Time: 5 minutes

1. From the Administrative Tools program group, open the DNS console. Right-click the zone you want to add an entry in and select the type of entry you want to create.
2. This procedure is to create a new alias (CNAME) record. Select New Alias, and the New Alias dialog box opens.
3. In the Alias Name field, enter the alias name. You can use the FQDN name or just the host name. If you use just the host name, the rest of the FQDN for the domain in which you are creating the entry will automatically be appended.
4. Enter the FQDN for the host you are aliasing in the Fully Qualified Name for Target Host box.
5. Click OK to create the entry.

6.3 Monitoring DNS Server Performance Using the Performance Application

This exercise will walk you through adding a counter to the Performance console so that you can baseline or troubleshoot your DNS server.

Estimated Time: 15 minutes

1. Open the Performance application by selecting Programs, Administrative Tools, Performance.
2. In the Performance management console, select System Monitor.
3. To create an entry in System Monitor, click the Add (+) icon. The Add Counters window opens. Notice that by default it opens to the Processor performance object.
4. Select the DNS performance object.
5. Select the counter you want to monitor and click Add. You can add multiple counters either by selecting each counter and clicking Add or by using the standard Windows multiple item select method of holding down the Ctrl key while you select all the counters you want to monitor and clicking Add. Click Close when you are done.

APPLY YOUR KNOWLEDGE

Review Questions

1. You are the network administrator for Exponent Mathematicians, and you have been asked to implement DNS for a pure Windows environment, taking full advantage of the benefits of Windows 2000. How should you do this and why?
2. You are the administrator of the Get Stuffed Taxidermists chain DNS server. You are getting complaints from several field locations that it takes a long time to resolve Internet addresses. All the sites complaining are across slow WAN links. What should you do?
3. You are the Windows 2000 administrator for Bug-B-Gone Exterminators. Your intranet is broken up into several DNS zones, each maintained by its respective department. You are getting complaints from several field locations that it takes a long time to resolve internal addresses. All the sites complaining are across slow WAN links. What should you do?
4. You're the administrator of Little Faith Enterprises' Windows 2000 DNS server. You have an end user who is trying to download the 128-bit version of the Windows 2000 Service Pack 1. Microsoft's Web site keeps denying him access, saying that his domain can't be resolved. What can you do to fix this?
5. You're the LAN administrator for the Pontificating Consulting Services company. You are running a Windows NT 4 domain architecture and have just implemented your first Windows 2000 client computers. You have configured the client computers to perform dynamic updates to DNS, but they are not appearing in the table. Why not, and what should you do to fix the problem?

Exam Questions

1. You are the network administrator for Wild Widgets Inc. You are training a new employee on the use of the DNS service in Windows 2000 Server. She asks you how a DNS request is resolved, assuming that the name is not cached and is for someone else's domain. What do you explain to the new employee?

   A. The client computer makes a request to the local DNS server. The DNS server looks in a local memory cache for names it has recently resolved. The name server looks in the DNS server's host tables to see whether a static entry (or in the case of DDNS, a dynamic entry) exists for the host name to an IP address lookup. The name server refers the request to a root name server, and the root name server refers the request to a name server for the first-level domain in the host name. The first-level domain name server refers the request to a name server for the second-level domain in the host name, and so on, until a name server is encountered that can resolve the complete host name.

   B. The client computer makes a request to the local DNS server. The name server looks in the DNS server's host tables to see whether a static entry (or in the case of DDNS, a dynamic entry) exists for the host name to an IP address lookup. The DNS server looks in a local memory cache for names it has recently resolved. The name server refers the request to a root name server, and the root name server refers the request to a name server for the first-level domain in the host name. The first-level domain name server refers the request to a name server for the second-level domain in the host name, and so on, until a name server is encountered that can resolve the complete host name.

C. The client computer makes a request to the local DNS server. The name server looks in the DNS server's host tables to see whether a static entry (or in the case of DDNS, a dynamic entry) exists for the host name to an IP address lookup. The name server refers the request to a root name server, and the root name server refers the request to a name server for the first-level domain in the host name. The first-level domain name server refers the request to a name server for the second-level domain in the host name, and so on, until a name server is encountered that can resolve the complete host name.

D. The client computer makes a request to the local DNS server. The DNS server looks in a local memory cache for names it has recently resolved. The name server looks in the DNS server's host tables to see whether a static entry (or in the case of DDNS, a dynamic entry) exists for the host name to an IP address lookup. The name server refers the request to a name server for the first-level domain in the host name. The first-level domain name server refers the request to a name server for the second-level domain in the host name, and so on, until a name server is encountered that can resolve the complete host name.

2. You are the system administrator for Phil's Lets Get Gas, a chain of combination gas stations and restaurants. As part of the network, you maintain a Windows 2000 DNS server to receive dynamic DNS updates. The server is installed and running but doesn't receive dynamic updates at this time. How do you set up the DNS server to receive dynamic updates?

   A. Open DNS Administrator. Select the DNS server and right-click. Then, select Receive Dynamic Updates. The Dynamic Updates Wizard will start. Follow the prompts to complete the configuration of dynamic updates.

   B. Open the DNS console. From the Administrative Tools program menu, open the DNS console. Open the properties of the zone you want to configure to receive dynamic updates. On the General tab, set the Allow Dynamic Updates pull-down menu to Yes. Click OK.

   C. Open the DNS console. From the Administrative Tools program menu, open the DNS console. Open the properties of the zone you want to configure to receive dynamic updates. From the Updates tab, set the Select to Allow Dynamic Updates option on the pull-down menu to Yes. Click OK.

   D. Open the DNS console. From the Administrative Tools program menu, open the DNS console. Open the properties of the zone you want to configure to receive dynamic updates. On the Updates tab, set the Allow Dynamic Updates pull-down menu to Yes. Click OK.

3. You are the LAN administrator for the EyeSpy detective agency. Your boss has asked you to register a DNS domain name for the company. Which of the following is not a legal second-level domain name?

   A. `eyespy.art`

   B. `eyespy.net`

APPLY YOUR KNOWLEDGE

C. `eyespy.org`

D. `eyespy.cc`

4. You are the LAN administrator for Little Faith Enterprises' Meat Packing. You run a pure Windows 2000 network, with six Windows 2000 DNS servers for your domain. One of the secondary servers doesn't seem to be getting updates. How can you check to verify that the server is receiving updates?

   A. Open Performance Manager. Click the Add Counter icon. Select the DNS Server object, and then select the Zone Transfer Success counter. Click Add to add the counter and monitor the zone transfers.

   B. Open the Performance console. Click the Add Counter icon. Select the DNS Server object, and then select the AXFR Successes counter. Click Add to add the counter and monitor the zone transfers.

   C. Open the DNS console. Select the zone you are having issues with and right-click. Select Statistics from the context menu, and verify that zone transfers are being received.

   D. Open Performance console. Click the Add Counter icon. Select the DNS Server object, and then select the Zone Transfer Success counter. Click Add to add the counter and monitor the zone transfers.

5. You are the lead engineer for Read'em and Weep Casinos, and a customer has asked you to install the DNS service on her Windows 2000 Server and get one zone configured to issue addresses. What are the minimum steps you need to take to accomplish this?

   A. Select Network and Dial-up Connections in the Control Panel and select Add Network Components to install the service. After the service is installed, authorize it in Active Directory. Then, create the zone.

   B. Open Network and Dial-up Connections in the Control Panel and select Add Network Components to install the service. After the service is installed, use the Configure Server Wizard to complete the setup and create the first zone.

   C. Open Network and Dial-up Connections in the Control Panel and select Add Network Components to install the service. After the service is installed, create the zone. Then, create a reverse lookup zone.

   D. Open Network and Dial-up Connections in the Control Panel and select Add Network Components to install the service. After the service is installed, create the zone.

6. You are the network administrator for the Hittem Boxing Glove Corporation. They are running a routed network with a centrally located Windows 2000 DNS server. You need to create a record in DNS to allow Internet mail to be sent to your domain. Which type of domain record do you need?

   A. A CNAME record

   B. An A record

   C. A PTR record

   D. An MX record

APPLY YOUR KNOWLEDGE

7. You manage the Windows 2000 DNS servers for the Sack Full of Hammers Corporation. You are running in a pure Windows 2000 environment, and you need to ensure that workstations are registered properly in DNS for Active Directory integration. How should you configure DNS integration?

   A. Configure the appropriate zones to accept dynamic updates.

   B. Configure the DNS server to accept dynamic updates.

   C. Configure the DHCP server to be sure to send dynamic updates.

   D. Install the Windows 2000 DNS client computer on the workstations.

8. You are the LAN administrator for Vanity Publishing. You are responsible for maintaining the Windows 2000 network for the company, including the Windows 2000 DNS servers. You have a remote office across a slow WAN link. What is the best way to set up DNS to resolve internal host names?

   A. Create a delegated zone for the remote office and have all the DNS client computers in that office resolve from that zone.

   B. Configure a caching-only server and have all the DNS client computers resolve from that server.

   C. Use a centralized DNS server and configure it for incremental updates.

   D. Configure the DNS client computers to autodiscover the closest DNS server.

9. You are the collaborative computing administrator for the ISeeU Tele-Videophone Company. You have a single DNS server resolving names for your internal domain, and you have an Internet connection. You need to configure DNS on the client computers to resolve Internet addresses. How do you do it?

   A. On each client computer, install the Microsoft DNS client. Configure the client computer to resolve to the DNS server. Then, configure the Root Hints on the server to point at the Internet root servers.

   B. On each client computer, configure the DNS settings under the TCP/IP Protocol properties to resolve to the DNS server. Configure the Root Hints on the server to point at the Internet root servers.

   C. Install a new DNS server to resolve Internet domain names. On each client computer, configure the DNS settings under the TCP/IP Protocol properties to resolve to the DNS server.

   D. On each client computer, configure the DNS settings under the TCP/IP Protocol properties to resolve to the DNS server.

10. Which of the following is the fully qualified domain name for the host Home in the Sales domain for the UR Write company? The company's domain is `mycompany.net`.

    A. `home`

    B. `home.sales.net`

    C. `home.mycompany.net`

    D. `home.sales.mycompany.net`

APPLY YOUR KNOWLEDGE

11. You are the LAN administrator for Pie in the Sky Airlines. Your company has a mixed Windows 2000 network, and you are still running a Windows NT 4 DNS server. You want to configure the Windows 98 computers in the sales department to use dynamic DNS updates for identification purposes. How do you do it?

    A. Upgrade your DNS server to Windows 2000. Configure it to accept dynamic updates, and then configure the Windows 98 client computers to send dynamic updates.

    B. Upgrade your DNS server to Windows 2000. Configure it to accept dynamic updates. Then, upgrade your Windows 98 computers to Windows 98 Second Edition to get the dynamic DNS capability, and configure the Windows 98 client computers to send dynamic updates.

    C. Upgrade your Windows 98 computers to Windows 2000 Professional to get the dynamic DNS capability. Configure the Windows 2000 client computers to send dynamic updates.

    D. Upgrade your DNS server to Windows 2000. Configure it to accept dynamic updates, and then upgrade your Windows 98 computers to Windows 2000 Professional to get the dynamic DNS capability. Finally, configure the Windows 2000 client computers to send dynamic updates.

12. You are the network administrator for Tall'n Skinny Clothiers. You have installed a Windows 2000 DNS server, but people are unable to resolve names. You need to test the server. How do you do it?

    A. From the command prompt of a Windows 2000 Professional host, run the `NSLOOKUP` utility to check the functionality of the DNS service.

    B. Select File, Run, and then enter **`NSLOOKUP32`**. In the DNS Server dialog box, enter the address of your DNS server and click OK to run an `NSLOOKUP` test.

    C. From the Windows 2000 DNS server, type **`PING -a`** and the address of the DNS server. Examine the results to see whether the server is working.

    D. From the Windows 2000 DNS server, type **`PING -R`** and the address of the DNS server. Examine the results to see whether the server is working.

13. You are the network administrator for Al's House of Nails, and you are running a pure Windows 2000 network. You have been having intermittent network outages for remote Windows 2000 users, and you have noticed that you are getting bad DNS entries for those workstations. What is the problem with DNS?

    A. The Dynamic DNS entry lease time is set too high.

    B. The DNS server is not configured to permit scavenging of bad DNS records.

    C. The Dynamic Update Timeout parameter is set too high.

    D. The Dynamic Update Timeout parameter is set too low.

APPLY YOUR KNOWLEDGE

14. You are the systems administrator for Over the Hill Car Parts, and you are responsible for the Windows 2000 DNS server. You are running a pure Windows 2000 network and are using dynamic updates. A new network administrator has asked you when a host dynamically updates DNS. When does an update event occur? (Select all that apply.)

    A. When the TCP/IP configuration is changed

    B. When the DHCP address is renewed or a new lease is obtained

    C. When the computer is started.

    D. When a DNS zone transfer occurs

    E. When the DNS server cache is manually flushed

15. You are the network administrator for Englebert, Verhoygen, and Snickerdoodle, the personal injury lawyers in town. You are responsible for the company's internal pure Windows 2000 network, including DNS. You have been asked to create a reverse lookup entry for each workstation on the network. How do you do it?

    A. Use the DNS console to create a reverse lookup zone. Then, manually add each workstation to the reverse lookup zone.

    B. Use the DNS console to create a reverse lookup zone, and then configure the forward lookup zone to accept dynamic updates. The reverse lookup zone will be automatically updated.

    C. Use the DNS console to create a reverse lookup zone, and then configure the DNS server to accept dynamic updates. The reverse lookup zone will be automatically updated.

    D. Use the DNS console to create a reverse lookup zone, and then configure the reverse lookup zone to accept dynamic updates.

Answers to Review Questions

1. Placement of the DNS servers is dependent on the network infrastructure of the company, but you will need a Windows 2000 DNS Service. Windows NT 4 DNS will not support the dynamic DNS, and although other DNS servers support DDNS, the requirement for a pure Windows environment leaves them out. Even though there might be benefits to some of the other platforms, a single platform solution is not uncommon in environments where the administrators are most familiar with Windows NT. See the section "Dynamic DNS."

2. Place a secondary master DNS server at each of the complaining sites. This will give them local DNS resolution and a local cache of commonly visited Internet addresses. See the section "Implementing a Delegated Zone for DNS."

3. Place a caching-only DNS server at each of the complaining sites and configure them to pull the cache information from the other DNS servers on the network. See the section "Configuring a Caching-Only Server."

4. You need to ensure he had an entry in your reverse lookup table. Microsoft's site is trying to verify his location based on your domain and needs to be capable of performing a reverse lookup. If you do not have a reverse lookup zone, you need to create one. See the section "Reverse Lookups."

APPLY YOUR KNOWLEDGE

5. Windows NT 4's DNS server will not support dynamic DNS updates. You need to upgrade to Windows 2000 DNS or migrate to a third-party DNS that supports dynamic updates. See the section "Configuring, Administering, and Troubleshooting DNS."

Answers to Exam Questions

1. **A.** The correct order is cache, local DNS server table, root server, first-level domain server, and then any additional subdomain servers. See the section "Configuring Zones."
2. **B.** Dynamic updates are set using the pull-down menu on the General tab of the zone properties. See the section "Configuring Zones for Dynamic Updates."
3. **A.** ART is a proposed top-level domain. ORG, NET, and CC are actual production top-level domains. See the section "Introduction to DNS."
4. **D.** Performance Manager was the name of the Windows NT application. In Windows 2000, the Performance console runs as part of the Microsoft Management Console. No statistics are available for the DNS server. The correct counter is Zone Transfer Success. See the section "Managing and Monitoring DNS."
5. **B.** If the task is to install it and get it resolving names, you do not need to configure a reverse lookup zone. You will need to run the Configure Server Wizard. See the section "Installing the DNS Server Service."
6. **D.** An MX (Mail Exchanger) record is used to identify the mail server(s) for a domain. A CNAME record is an alias, an A record is used for name-to-address resolution, and a PTR record is used for reverse lookups. See the section "DNS Record Types."
7. **A.** Configure the appropriate zones to accept dynamic updates. Each zone needs to be configured individually to accept dynamic updates. See the section "Configuring Zones for Dynamic Updates."
8. **B.** Configure a caching-only server and have all the remote DNS client computers resolve from that server. See the section "Configuring a Caching-Only Server."
9. **D.** You just need to configure the workstations to use the existing DNS server to resolve names. This is done under the TCP/IP Properties. The server automatically forwards any requests for unknown domains to the appropriate servers. See the section "Configuring a DNS Client."
10. **D.** `home.sales.urwrite.net` is the correct answer. `home` is the server, sales is the third level domain, `urwrite` is the second level domain, and `NET` is the top-level domain. See the section "DNS Setting Zone Properties"
11. **D.** You need a Windows 2000 DNS server and a Windows 2000 client computer to use dynamic DNS without having to reconfigure DHCP. Although it is possible, out of the offered answers, D is correct. See the section "Configuring Zones for Dynamic Updates."
12. **A.** Running `NSLOOKUP` from the command prompt is a good way to test. See the section "Testing the DNS Server Service."
13. **B.** You need to configure the DNS server to scavenge bad DNS entries. See the section "Managing and Monitoring DNS."

APPLY YOUR KNOWLEDGE

14. **A, B, C.** A host dynamically updates DNS when TCP/IP is updated, when a DHCP assignment or renewal occurs, or when there is a Plug and Play event. See the section "Configuring Zones for Dynamic Updates."

15. **D.** You must create a reverse lookup zone and configure it to accept dynamic updates. See the section "Reverse Lookups."

Suggested Readings and Resources

1. Aldous, Juliana, ed. *Windows 2000 Server Deployment Planning Guide.* Microsoft Press, 2000.
2. Comer, Douglas E. *Internetworking with TCP/IP Volume 1.* Prentice Hall, 1994.
3. Spealman, Jill. *Microsoft Windows 2000 Active Directory Services.* Microsoft Press, 2000.

OBJECTIVES

Although there has been a clear shift in Microsoft's focus on name resolution toward DNS-based name resolution, there is still a lot of NetBIOS name resolution heritage in Windows 2000. Since the introduction of networking in Microsoft Windows, NetBIOS and NetBIOS name resolution have been standard. From `LMHOSTS` files, to broadcasts, to WINS servers, Windows has always relied on NetBIOS name resolution mechanisms. It is for this reason that Microsoft still considers NetBIOS name resolution to be an important part of managing a Windows 2000 network.

This chapter addresses the subobjective in the "Configuring, Administering, and Troubleshooting Network Infrastructure" objective of the exam.

Troubleshoot name resolution on client computers. Considerations include WINS, DNS, NetBIOS, the `HOSTS` file, and LMhosts.

- **Configure Client Computer Name Resolution Properties.**
- **Troubleshoot name resolution problems by using the `nbtstat`, `ipconfig`, `nslookup`, and `netdiag` commands.**
- **Create and configure a `HOSTS` file for troubleshooting and name resolution problems.**
- **Create and configure an `LMHOSTS` file for troubleshooting and name resolution problems.**

▶ NetBIOS name resolution has become more complicated as Microsoft transitions to DNS-based name resolution. It's important to understand the tools Microsoft provides for problem resolution as well as the built-in, file-based name resolution approaches so that you can quickly diagnose and resolve name resolution problems.

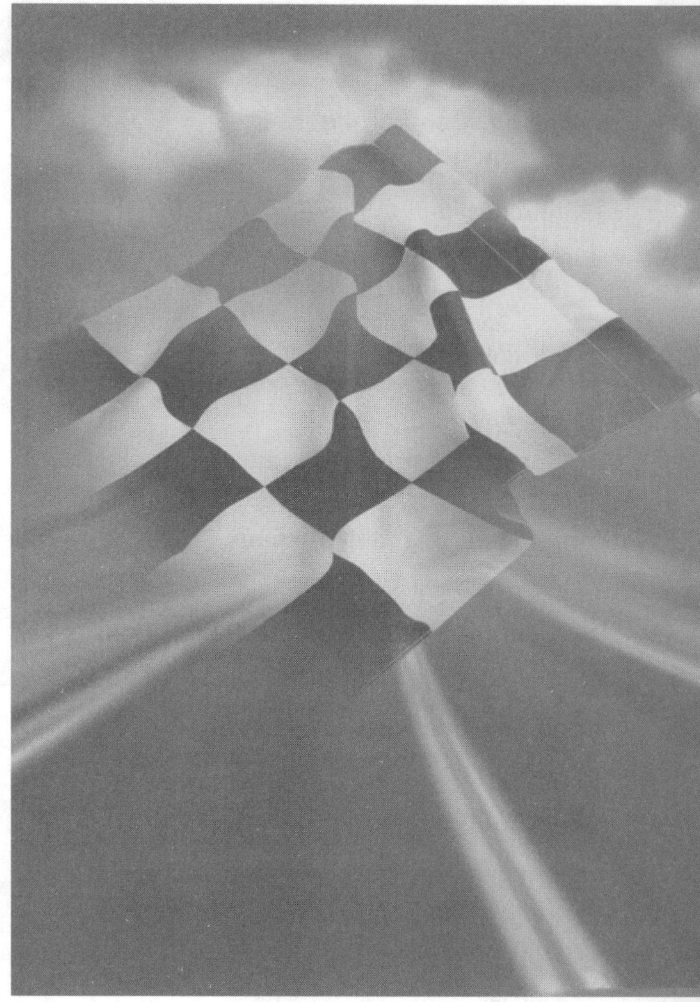

CHAPTER 7

NetBIOS Name Resolution

OUTLINE

STUDY STRATEGIES

- Be sure that you have a thorough understanding of the WINS service and NetBIOS name resolution. Although this is a legacy Microsoft name resolution mechanism, it will still be required in most environments for some time to come. Microsoft wants to be absolutely sure you understand how it works.
- Review the use of the monitoring tools and the various parameters of WINS that can be monitored. In its exams, Microsoft has focused a great deal of attention on the monitoring and troubleshooting of the various services, including the WINS service.
- Be sure to complete the exercises at the end of the chapter. As Microsoft strives to make its exams more rigorous, a familiarity with not only the theory, but also the hands-on portion of the installation, configuration, and troubleshooting, of the WINS service will be of importance.

INSTALLING, CONFIGURING, AND TROUBLESHOOTING WINS

If you are familiar with Windows NT 4 networks, you are undoubtedly familiar with the intricacies of a WINS infrastructure. You might also be wondering why Microsoft didn't get rid of WINS with Windows 2000. Well, the good news is that with Windows 2000, WINS is for backward compatibility only. Windows 2000 Server running in native mode does not need to use WINS at all. The Active Directory (AD) and Domain Name Service (DNS) are used to provide the WINS-like functionality of resolving names into IP addresses.

EXAM TIP

I Don't Need WINS That is an accurate statement only if the client computer is running DNS and no application on the network relies on NetBIOS resolution. Don't make the mistake of assuming that DNS is implied when you get WINS questions.

So, that means we don't need to talk about WINS, right? Sorry, but you don't get off that easily. Until your network is 100% Windows 2000 (or higher) and no applications on the network require NetBIOS name resolution, you will still need WINS to provide backward compatibility for legacy Windows operating systems, particularly with any NT domains. With that in mind, let's talk about what WINS is and how it works.

Introduction to WINS

In today's Internet-centric environment, the Transmission Control Protocol/Internet Protocol (TCP/IP) has become the ubiquitous networking protocol. For long-time Unix users, the reemergence of TCP/IP is a good thing. TCP/IP came out of the Unix arena and has been the native protocol for Unix systems since the late 1980s.

Microsoft, on the other hand, started with a different protocol as its LAN Manager operating system's native protocol—NetBEUI. NetBEUI was a pretty good protocol for small networks; it required no configuration and didn't require complex addressing like TCP/IP does. However, NetBEUI can't handle routing and does not perform well in large environments. Therefore, Microsoft needed to add TCP/IP support.

When Microsoft began to add TCP/IP support to its LAN server products, the company ran into a little problem. The naming system used on Microsoft networks at that time would not function on routed TCP/IP networks. Microsoft LAN Manager computers used the computer's NetBIOS names for identification. Although this makes maintaining the network very simple for an administrator because servers are automatically located on the network by name, this naming system was a problem with the TCP/IP protocol.

NetBIOS has a design limitation that shows up in routed networks because NetBIOS relies heavily on broadcast messages to locate servers. *Broadcast messages* are messages that are processed by every computer on a network segment, rather than by a specific computer. This paradigm is usable on smaller networks but can add overwhelming amounts of broadcast traffic on an enterprise network. To confine the impact of broadcast messages on a TCP/IP network, IP routers do not forward broadcast messages. Therefore, Microsoft had to find a way to make NetBIOS naming work in a standard TCP/IP network.

IN THE FIELD

BROADCASTS ARE EVIL

In most corporate networks today, Ethernet switches are in use to help route and reduce traffic. Switches work by forwarding packets to only the hardware, or MAC, addresses for which they are intended. By doing this, it effectively improves the maximum speed of the network. However, broadcast traffic isn't sent to a single address; it's sent to every address and thus must be sent to every machine connected to the Ethernet switch. The end result is that the switch can't perform its function.

The more broadcast traffic that occurs on a network, the less effective an Ethernet switch is. So, in switched environments, like most environments these days, reducing the number of broadcasts is critical.

Microsoft's first solution, introduced in its older operating system called LAN Manager server, was to use a LAN Manager HOSTS (LMHOSTS) file on each computer on the network. Similar to the HOSTS file used before DNS was available, an LMHOSTS consists of records matching NetBIOS names to IP addresses. When a computer couldn't find a particular NetBIOS computer on the local network, it would consult its LMHOSTS file to see whether the computer could be found elsewhere.

An LMHOSTS file is a text file that must be edited manually. After creating a master LMHOSTS file, an administrator must copy the file to every computer on the network. Every time a computer is installed or removed, the master LMHOSTS file must be updated and redistributed. Doesn't that sound like fun? (This might sound familiar—the architects of TCP/IP faced a similar issue with HOSTS files before the DNS specification was written.)

Microsoft also needed a dynamic name service that would maintain a list of computers on the network—a name service that could work in routed TCP/IP environments. Microsoft's answer was the Windows Internet Name Service (WINS). Four elements can be found in a WINS network:

- **WINS servers**—When WINS client computers enter the network, they contact a WINS server using a directed message. The client computer registers its name with the WINS server and uses the WINS server to resolve NetBIOS names to IP addresses.
- **WINS client computers**—WINS client computers use directed messages to communicate with WINS servers. all versions of Windows since Windows for Workgroups can be WINS client computers.
- **Non-WINS client computers**—Older Microsoft network client computers that can't use direct WINS communications can still benefit from WINS. Their broadcast messages are intercepted by WINS proxy computers that act as intermediaries between clients that must broadcast and WINS servers. MS-DOS and Windows 3.1 client computers function as non-WINS clients.
- **WINS proxies**—All versions of Windows client computers since Windows for Workgroups can function as WINS proxies. They intercept broadcasts on their local subnets and communicate with a WINS server on behalf of the broadcasting client computer.

As is discussed in the "Configuring WINS Replication" section later in this chapter, WINS servers can replicate their databases so that each WINS server can provide name resolution for the entire network. Whenever possible, it is desirable to have at least two WINS servers. This lets name resolution take place when one name server is down. It also lets administrators distribute WINS activity across multiple servers to balance the processing loads. WINS server addresses are one of the configuration settings that can be issued with DHCP.

Installing WINS

> **EXAM TIP**
>
> **Managing Windows 2000 Services** The Step By Step examples use a utility called the WINS manager. It is important to note that this manager is nothing more than the Microsoft Management Console with the WINS management snap-in installed. Microsoft creates these versions of the Microsoft Management Console to enable new users of Windows 2000 to more easily manage their systems. So, don't be confused if you see references to the Microsoft Management Console in the exam. That's all the WINS manager is.

As discussed in earlier chapters, Windows 2000 enables you to perform tasks such as installing services in a number of ways. This section covers two of the more common methods for installing WINS. Finding the method you are most comfortable with and sticking to it consistently is generally the best method for working with the operating system.

To install the Windows 2000 WINS service, follow Step By Step 7.1.

STEP BY STEP

7.1 Using the Network and Dial-Up Connections Properties to Install the Windows Internet Naming Service

1. Right-click the My Network Places icon on the desktop. From the context menu, select Properties. The Network and Dial-up Connections window opens (see Figure 7.1).

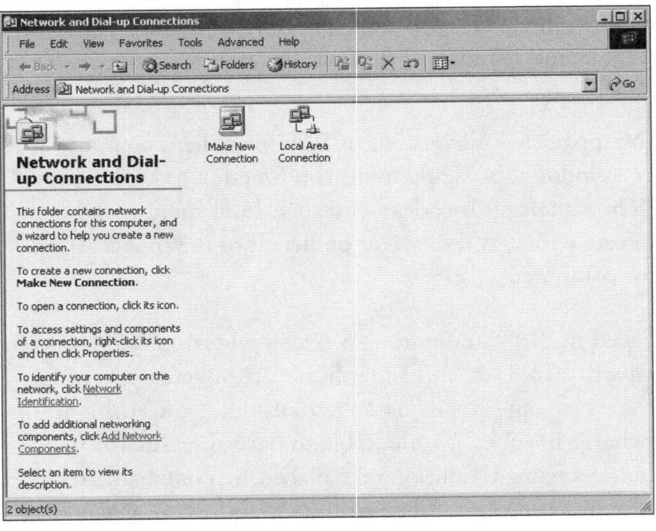

FIGURE 7.1
From here you can add, remove, or modify your network settings and services.

2. Click Add Network Components in the lower-left corner. (This icon is visible only if you are viewing the folder as a Web page, which is the system default.) This hyperlink opens the Windows Components dialog box of the Windows Optional Networking Components Wizard, shown in Figure 7.2.

3. Select the Networking Services entry and click Details. This opens the Networking Services window, as shown in Figure 7.3. Select Windows Internet Name Service (WINS).

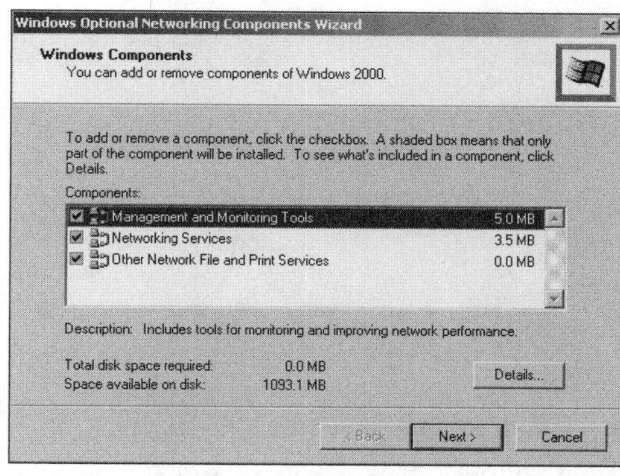

FIGURE 7.2
The Windows 2000 WINS service is part of the Networking Services components.

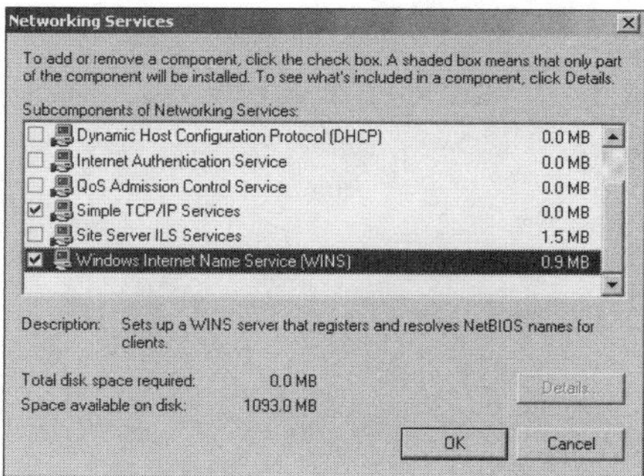

FIGURE 7.3
Selecting Windows Internet Name Service (WINS) and clicking OK installs the service.

4. Click the OK button. This returns you to the Windows Optional Networking Components Wizard dialog box. Click Next to start the installation. The Windows Component Wizard will prompt you for the Windows 2000 Server CD-ROM if it needs to copy files. When the wizard is finished, it displays a summary window of the changes to be made. Click OK to complete the installation.

Congratulations, you just installed WINS. Keep in mind that you still need to configure your client computers to use the new server, but the server portion of the install is complete. Now, let's look at Step By Step 7.2, which shows another way to do it.

NOTE

DHCP and the WINS Service If, for some reason, you have your Windows 2000 Server configured to use DHCP addressing, you will receive a message from the installation process indicating that the WINS service should be installed only on a server with a static address. The Local Area Connection Properties dialog box will open to enable you to correct the issue. Microsoft includes this message because it is actually a very bad idea to put WINS on a dynamically addressed server.

You don't want your WINS server to use a dynamic address because the address might change one day. If that occurs, all your users will lose access to the server because the addresses used to point at the WINS server are configured statically. The same is true for a DNS server.

STEP BY STEP

7.2 Using the Add/Remove Programs Applet to Install the Windows Internet Naming Service

1. Open the Control Panel and double-click the Add/Remove Programs applet (see Figure 7.4). The Add/Remove Programs dialog box opens (see Figure 7.5).

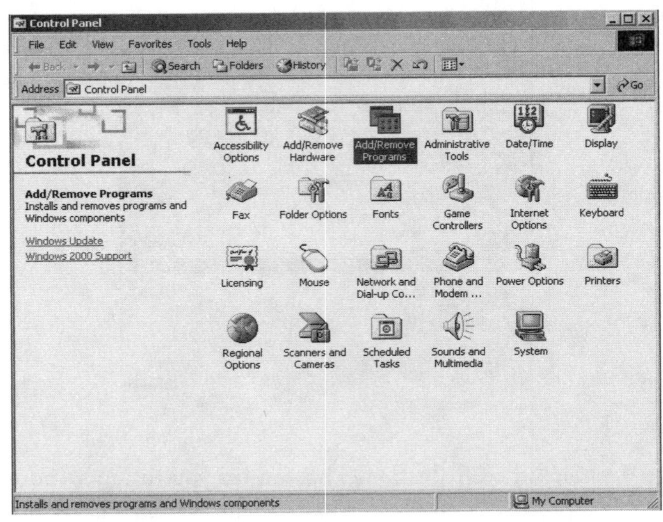

FIGURE 7.4
The Control Panel contains the system applets, including the Add/Remove Programs applet used to install WINS in this example.

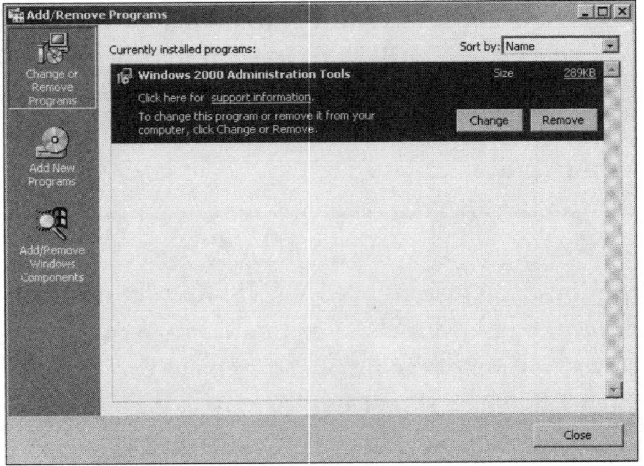

FIGURE 7.5
A major improvement over earlier versions, the Add/Remove Programs dialog box gives you more useful information about installed applications, including application size and, in some cases, the frequency of use for an installed application.

2. Select Add/Remove Windows Components. The Windows Components dialog box opens (see Figure 7.6).

3. From here, you can follow the same steps as the previous procedure (start at step 3) to complete the installation.

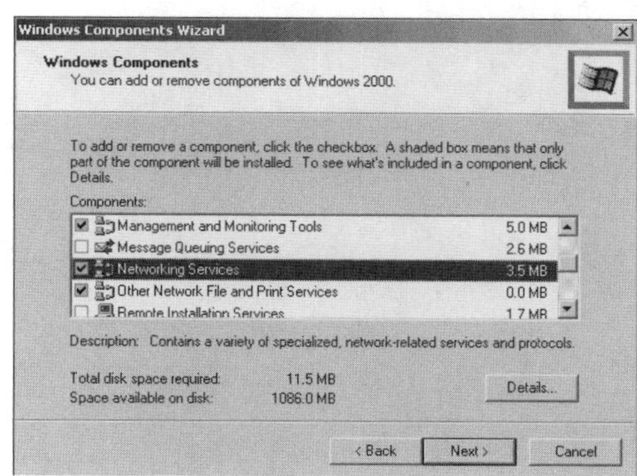

FIGURE 7.6
You can reach the same Windows Components Wizard several ways.

Now that WINS is installed, let's look at configuring it.

Configuring WINS

Several properties can be configured in the Windows Internet Naming Service. They can be accessed by opening WINS console (Start, Programs, Administrative Tools, WINS) and selecting the server you want to configure (see Figure 7.7). Right-click the server and select Properties. The sections that follow describe the property options.

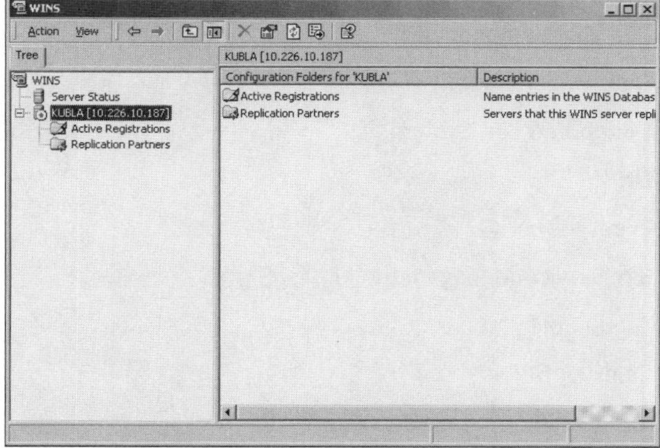

FIGURE 7.7
The WINS manager is used for all configurations for the WINS service.

IN THE FIELD

USING THE MMC AND MANUALLY ADDING SNAP-INS

If you are an advanced user and would like to skip using differently configured versions of the MMC for each of the services installed on your Windows 2000 server, Microsoft has provided an easy way to manage everything from a single MMC configuration. Open the

continues

continued

MMC by selecting Start, Run, MMC. This opens the MMC shell, which is empty the first time you load it. Select Console, Add/Remove Snap-in. After the Add/Remove Snap-in dialog box opens, click the Add button. In the Add Standalone Snap-in dialog box, you can select any or all of the snap-ins for Windows 2000 services. The list of snap-ins includes the following:

- Active Directory Domains and Trusts
- Active Directory Sites and Services
- Active Directory Users and Computers
- ActiveX Control
- Certificates
- Component Services
- Computer Management
- Device Manager
- DHCP
- Disk Defragmenter
- Disk Management
- Distributed File System
- DNS
- Event Viewer
- Fax Service Management
- Group Policy
- Indexing Service
- Internet Information Services
- IP Security Policy Management
- Local Users and Groups
- Performance Logs and Alerts
- Routing and Remote Access
- Services
- System Information
- WINS

This is not a comprehensive list. You should see several services that we have discussed already in this book and others that you will see in the following chapters. The MMC is a flexible tool, and you shouldn't limit yourself to the preconfigured Microsoft versions loaded with each service.

NOTE

To Back Up or Not to Back Up? You should configure the default database path and the automatic backup of the database on shutdown to removable media whenever possible. This configuration ensures the maximum fault tolerance for the WINS database in case the server doesn't come back up.

General Settings

The General tab, shown in Figure 7.8, is used to configure statistics and backups. You can use this tab to configure the automatic update of WINS statistics and the interval at which they update from this tab. You also can configure the default backup path for the WINS database and enable the automatic backup of the database when the server is shut down.

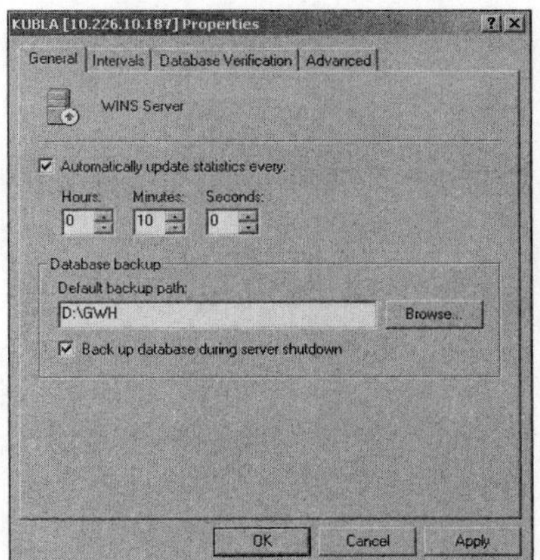

FIGURE 7.8
The General tab is used for configuring statistics and backups for the WINS database.

Intervals Settings

The Intervals tab, shown in Figure 7.9, is used to set the WINS database records renewal, deletion, and verification intervals. You can set the following intervals:

- **Renew Interval**—Determines the frequency of record renewal. The default is six days and is good for all but the most dynamic environments. If you have a very dynamic environment with computers entering and exiting the network frequently, you might want to reduce this interval.
- **Extinction Interval**—Determines the length of time before a record is considered extinct and is removed from the database. Again, in all but the most dynamic environments, the four-day default is usually adequate.
- **Extinction Timeout**—Determines the length of time a record is checked before it is declared extinct. When this occurs, the record is deleted after the Extinction Interval is met.
- **Verification Interval**—Determines the frequency at which database records are verified for accuracy.

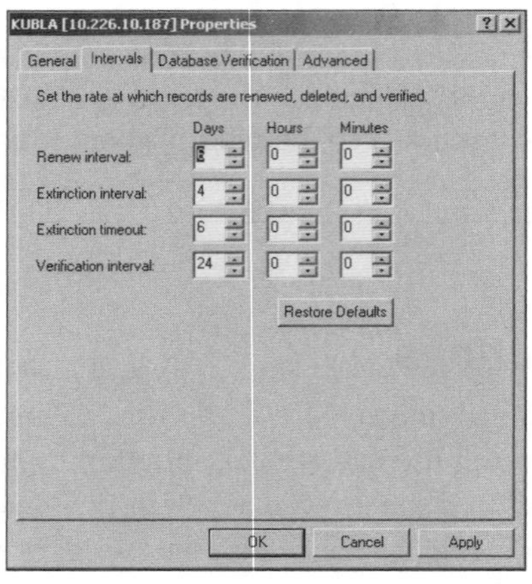

FIGURE 7.9
In most networks, the default intervals are usually adequate for a stable WINS environment.

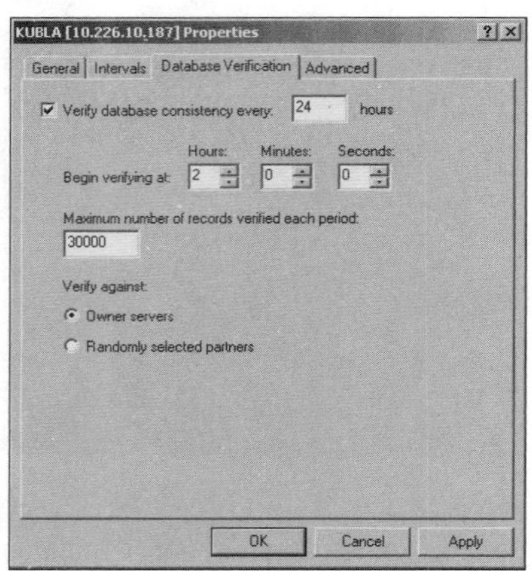

FIGURE 7.10
Ensuring the consistency of the WINS database is critical to a stable WINS environment.

Database Verification Settings

The Database Verification tab enables you to configure the parameters associated with the WINS database (see Figure 7.10). You can enable database verification for a specific interval. The default interval is 24 hours; thus, if enabled, the database consistency will be verified once a day. You also specify the time to begin the consistency check, the number of database records to check for each period, as well as the source to verify the database against. You can verify database consistency against owner servers (these are the servers from which the record being verified was replicated) or randomly selected partner servers.

Advanced Settings

The Advanced tab, shown in Figure 7.11, is used to configure the remaining WINS parameters, including the following:

- **Logging**—You can enable detailed event logging for troubleshooting WINS when there are problems.
- **Burst handling**—You can configure the load that can be put on the server by specifying the number of WINS requests the server will accept before returning a retry message. This can be set to Low, Medium, High, or Custom, which enables you to specify several connections.
- **Database path**—Path for the WINS database. If you have fault-tolerant drives in your server, be sure that the WINS database is located on one of them.

- **Database version number**—You should not need to modify this parameter, but the starting version number is used for consistency purposes. By giving each version of the database an incrementing version number, Windows 2000 is capable of comparing two WINS databases and telling which is the most recent. DNS uses a similar mechanism for synchronizing its tables.
- **LAN Manager compatibility**—You can also set WINS to use LAN Manager-compatible computer names so that any legacy LAN Manager installations can still use WINS for name resolution.

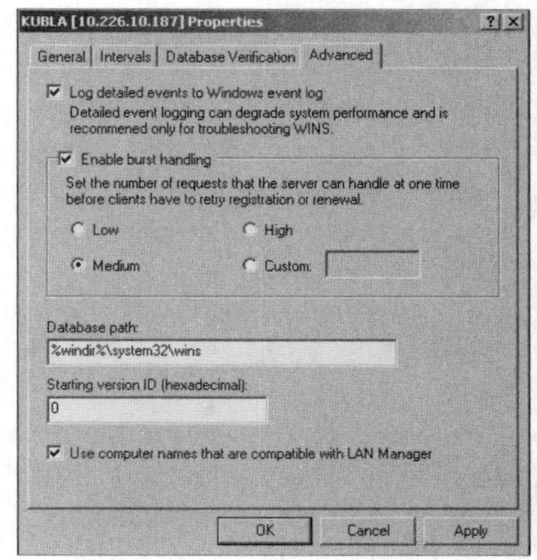

FIGURE 7.11
The Advanced tab functions as the catchall for the remaining WINS parameters and contains some important parameters for troubleshooting and load regulating.

That covers the configuration of a WINS server. Let's look at configuring WINS replication between two WINS servers.

Configuring WINS Replication

In most environments that rely on WINS for name resolution for legacy systems, it is important to ensure that more than one WINS server exists so that you provide redundancy and availability. To ensure that each server has a current copy of the database, it is important to configure replication between your WINS servers. Let's take a quick look at the types of replication you can configure for the WINS service:

- **Pull replication**—In pull replication, your server pulls the database from the replication partner. A pull replication is time based and occurs at the time you have configured. You can decide whether to establish a persistent connection for replication, and you can set the start time and interval for replication.
- **Push replication**—In push replication, your server pushes its database to the replication partner. A push replication is event driven, and the number of database updates determines when the event occurs. You can decide whether to use a persistent connection for push activities, and you can set the number of changes in version ID before replication.

EXAM TIP

WINS Replication One new feature of the Windows 2000 WINS servers is the capability to maintain a persistent connection with one or more of the replication partners, enabling real-time replication. Because this is one of the new features of the WINS service, you will probably find it on the test. Microsoft is more likely to test your familiarity with new features of the service than your understanding of the general WINS functionality because WINS has been part of the Windows server operating systems since its inception.

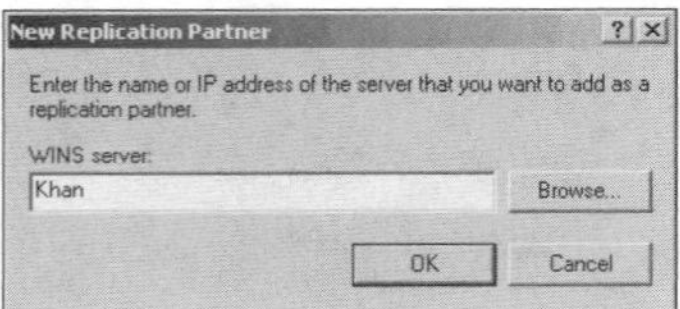

FIGURE 7.12
The replication partner can be listed by name or address.

- **Replication partner type**—The partner type can be push, pull, or push/pull, depending on your requirements. (In push/pull replication, database replication can occur using either method: push or pull.)

To configure WINS replication, follow Step By Step 7.3.

STEP BY STEP

7.3 Configuring WINS Replication

1. Open the WINS manager by selecting Start, Programs, Administrative Tools, WINS.
2. In the right pane, right-click Replication Partners and select New Replication Partner. The New Replication Partner dialog box opens and asks you to enter the address of another WINS server (see Figure 7.12). This can be either the server name or IP address. If the server name can't be resolved, you will be prompted to enter the address of the server.
3. Enter the name of the server and click OK.
4. Click Replication Partners in the left pane. You should see your new replication partner in the right pane (see Figure 7.13).

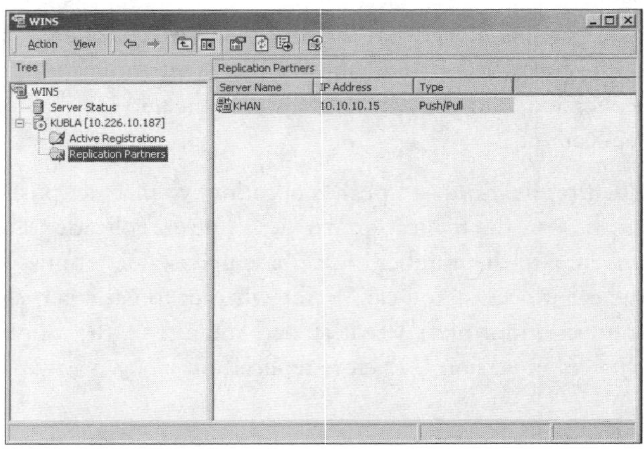

FIGURE 7.13
After the replication partner has been created, it is listed in the Replication Partners pane of WINS manager.

5. Right-click the newly created replication partner and select Properties. This opens the Replication Partner Properties dialog box, which shows only the name and address of the replication partner.

6. Click the Advanced tab (see Figure 7.14). On this tab, you can configure the replication properties for the replication partner. Select the appropriate type for your environment.

7. Click OK when the settings meet your requirements.

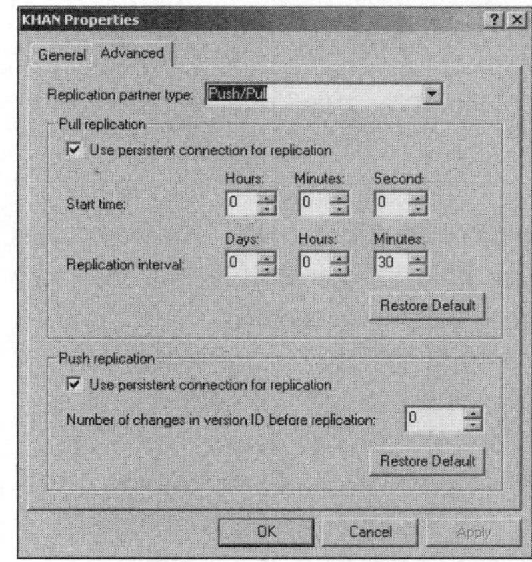

FIGURE 7.14
The Advanced tab enables you to customize the WINS replication setting to meet your network's requirements.

You have now configured replication with a WINS replication partner. Now let's look at the global replication properties. To review the global replication properties, open the WINS manager application as described in the first part of Step By Step 7.3 and select the Replication Partners folder in the left pane. Right-click and select Properties from the context menu. This opens the Replication Partners Properties dialog box to the General tab. Replication partners configurations can be set on the following tabs:

- **General**—The General tab enables you to restrict replication to replication partners as well as configure the server to enable the overwriting of static mappings on the server.
- **Push Replication**—As you can see in Figure 7.15, you can use this tab to establish whether replication will start at system startup. You also can use this tab to establish when an address changes (and you can configure the number of changes required to trigger the push replication) and whether to use persistent connections for the push replication.
- **Pull Replication**—As you can see in Figure 7.16, you can use this tab to establish whether pull replication starts at system startup, when the replication should start, the interval between replications, the number of retries, and whether to use persistent connections.

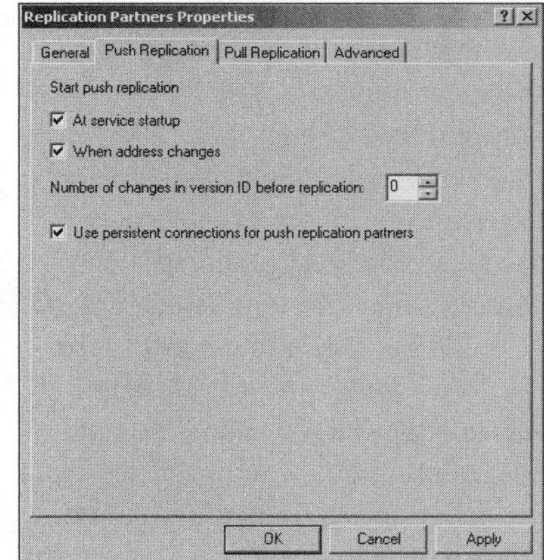

FIGURE 7.15
The Push Replication tab enables you to set the thresholds for triggering a push replication.

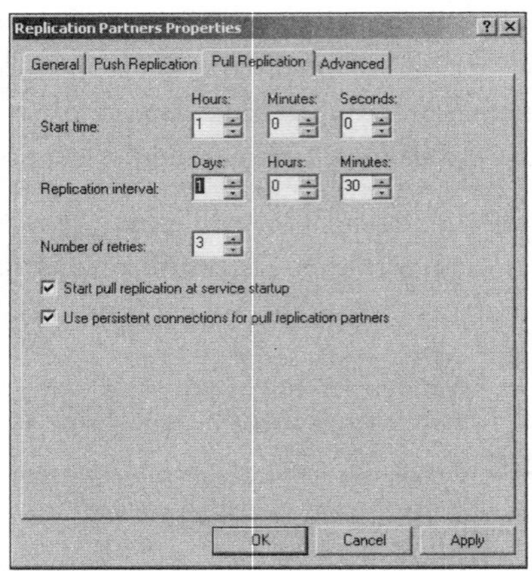

FIGURE 7.16
The Pull Replication tab enables you to configure the timing for a pull replication.

> **NOTE**
>
> **What's Multicasting?** *Multicasting* is the act of transmitting a message to a select group of recipients. This is in contrast to the concept of a *broadcast*, in which traffic is sent to every host on the network, or a *unicast*, in which the connection is a one-to-one relationship and there is only one recipient of the data. Think about sending an email message. If you send an email message to your manager, it is an example of a unicast message. If you send an email message to every user on the system, it is a broadcast. Send an email message to a mailing list and you have sent a multicast message, which falls between the previous two. Teleconferencing and videoconferencing use the concept of multicasting, as does broadcast audio, where the connection is one to a selected group. At this time, only a few applications take advantage of this feature, but with the growing popularity of multicast applications, you might see more multicast applications in the future. WINS is one that you can keep on the list, but only for small networks.

- **Advanced**—The tab shown in Figure 7.17 enables you to block servers from being capable of replicating, as well as to configure the autodiscovery and autoconfiguration of WINS partners. Because this uses multicasts (or multicasting) to find and configure the servers, enable this for small networks only.

You have now successfully configured all the possible Windows replication partner parameters. Let's take a quick look at identifying WINS issues.

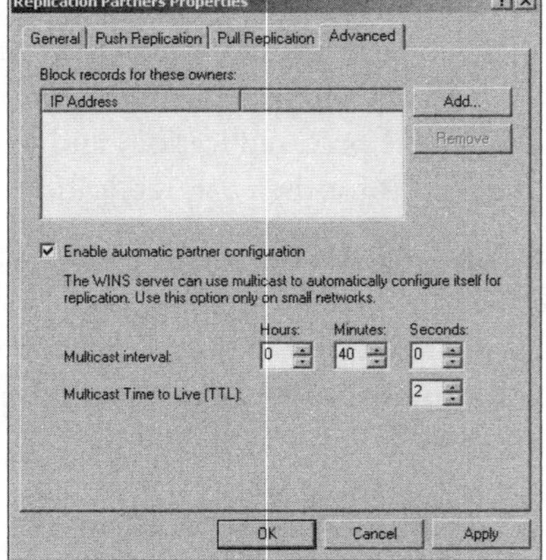

FIGURE 7.17
The Advanced tab enables you to set up your WINS server for a small network, as well as to block WINS servers from replicating.

TROUBLESHOOTING WINS ISSUES

The majority of WINS issues you encounter will be related to connectivity, so the first thing we need to examine is testing TCP/IP connectivity. The first application for testing IP connectivity is the PING.EXE utility. PING enables you to send an Internet Control Message Protocol (ICMP) to a TCP/IP host. By using the correct flag, PING can also perform name resolution as part of its testing procedure. The correct format for this command is

```
PING -a <destination address>
```

where the -a flag provides host name resolution. A sample PING session might look like this:

```
ping -a wins1.newriders.com
Pinging wins1.newriders.com [205.123.113.87] with 32 bytes
of data:
Reply from 205.123.113.87: bytes=32 time=47ms TTL=241
Reply from 205.123.113.87: bytes=32 time=60ms TTL=242
Reply from 205.123.113.87: bytes=32 time=40ms TTL=242
Reply from 205.123.113.87: bytes=32 time=37ms TTL=242
Ping statistics for 205.123.113.87:
Packets: Sent = 4, Received = 4, Lost = 0 (0% loss),
Approximate round trip times in milliseconds:
Minimum = 37ms, Maximum = 60ms, Average = 46ms
```

Because the number of sent packets equals the number of received packets, the connection between the workstation and the WINS server is good. If you do not get any packets returned, you should investigate the network issues further.

The next piece of the WINS puzzle is the client computer WINS configuration. To check whether the WINS configuration of your Windows 2000 client computers is correct, perform Step By Step 7.4.

> **EXAM TIP**
>
> **Global Replication Settings**
> Because we just finished discussing configuring replication partners, these parameters should look familiar. However, in this section the changes apply to any replication partners created after the modifications are made. They will not be applied to existing replication partners.

STEP BY STEP

7.4 Checking the WINS Settings in a Windows 2000 Client Computer

1. Open a command prompt by selecting Start, Programs, Accessories, Command Prompt.

continues

continued

2. At the command prompt, type **IPCONFIG /ALL**. You will get a result similar to the one shown in Figure 7.18.

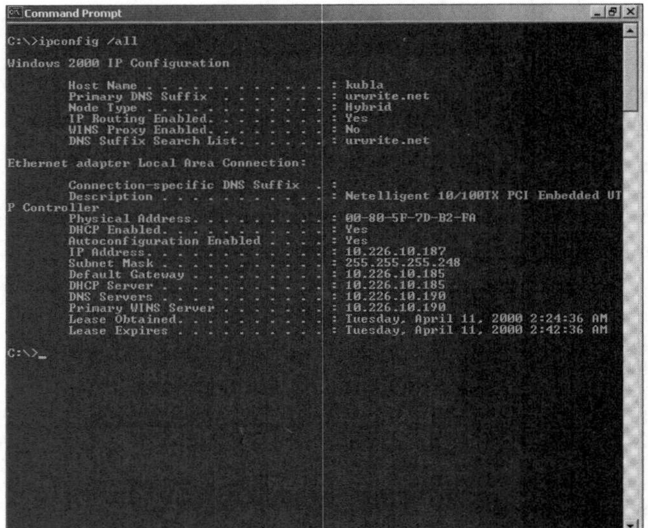

FIGURE 7.18
The IPConfig utility gives you all the information on the IP configuration of any of your adapters.

3. Check for the entry `Primary WINS Server`, toward the end of the list of parameters. Verify that a WINS server is configured and that it is the correct server. If no server exists or if the server is incorrect, you will need to set the correct server in one of two places. If you use DHCP, you must update your DHCP settings. If you are using static addresses, the WINS server can be configured by using the Network applet in the Control Panel and setting the correct server in the TCP/IP Properties.

The final piece of the WINS puzzle is verifying that the server is functioning. You should check several things, including the following:

- **Is the WINS service running?**—You can determine this by opening the Task Manager (press Ctrl+Alt+Del and select Task Manager) and, on the Processes tab, verifying that the WINS service (wins.exe) is running (see Figure 5.19). If the service is not running, you should probably reboot the server to ensure that no other issues exist.

- **Is the WINS service responding to requests?**—The best way to discover this is to check the server statistics. (You can also use the Performance console to get some of this information. That is discussed in depth in the "Managing and Monitoring WINS" section, later in this chapter.) To check the server statistics, right-click the server in the WINS Manager and select WINS Server Statistics (see Figure 7.20). If you check these statistics over a 15-minute period of time and they don't increment, you probably have a WINS issue somewhere.

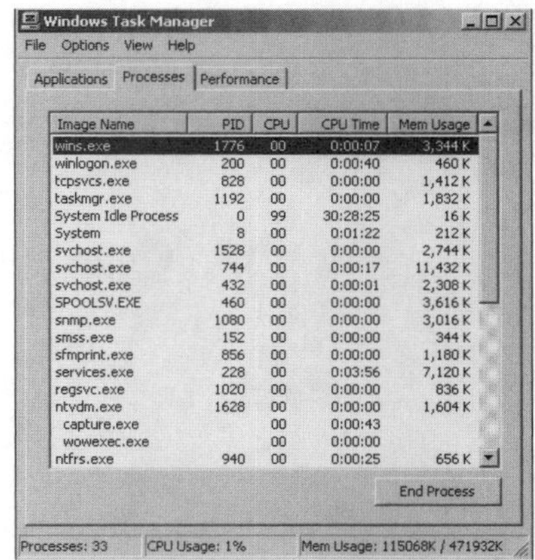

FIGURE 7.19
Task Manager is one of the fastest ways to verify that a service is running.

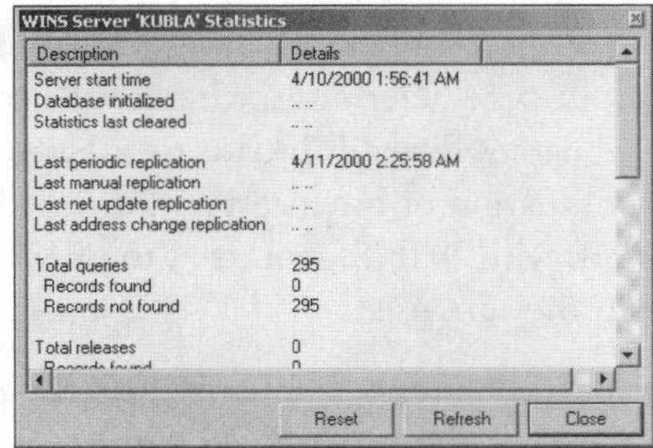

FIGURE 7.20
The WINS Server Statistics provide an excellent snapshot of the WINS service.

We have covered the basic steps in troubleshooting WINS. As with any equipment-down situation, your steps might vary. Every situation is unique and might require unique troubleshooting steps.

Configuring NetBIOS Name Resolution

Microsoft TCP/IP uses NetBIOS over TCP/IP (NetBT) as specified in RFCs 1001 and 1002 to support the NetBIOS client and server programs in the LAN and WAN environments. Before we discuss the specifics of NetBIOS name resolution, let's briefly review how computers communicate on the network. This should help in understanding how the various NetBIOS modes work and why some are preferable to others.

Computers can use two ways to communicate on a network:

- Through broadcast messages, which every computer receives
- Through directed messages, which are sent to a specific computer

Whenever possible, it is preferable to communicate through directed messages. This cuts down on the amount of network traffic and ensures that only the affected hosts receive the message. This also ensures that the messages will propagate across routers. So, Microsoft needed to ensure that WINS communicated primarily with directed messages. The company accomplished this by allowing several types of NetBIOS naming methods. These naming methods are commonly called *node types*. A *node* is simply a device on a network. Every computer running a Microsoft OS is configured to use one of four node types. The node type determines whether the computer will register and resolve names through broadcast messages, directed messages, or some combination of broadcast and directed messages. Before you can work with WINS, you need to know what the node types are and when they are used:

> **EXAM TIP**
>
> **Microsoft Does Test on Backward Compatibility** Don't be fooled. Just because WINS is a legacy technology, that doesn't mean it won't be tested on the exam. Microsoft recognizes the importance of backward compatibility, and as a result, you can expect to see questions about WINS on this exam. If you have not worked with it in a legacy environment, make sure you understand how WINS works.

- **b-node (broadcast node)**—Relies exclusively on broadcast messages and is the oldest NetBIOS name registration and resolution mode. A host needing to resolve a name request sends a message to every host within earshot, requesting the address associated with a host name. b-node has two shortcomings: broadcast traffic is undesirable and becomes a significant user of network bandwidths, and TCP/IP routers don't forward broadcast messages, which restricts b-node operation to a single network segment.
- **p-node (point-to-point node)**—Relies on WINS servers for NetBIOS name registration and resolution. Client computers register themselves with a WINS server when they come on the network. They then contact the WINS server with NetBIOS name resolution requests. WINS servers communicate using directed messages, which can cross routers, so p-node can operate on large networks. Unfortunately, if the WINS server is unavailable or if a node isn't configured to contact a WINS server, p-node name resolution fails.

- **m-node (modified node)**—A hybrid mode that first attempts to register and resolve NetBIOS names using the b-node mechanism. If that fails, an attempt is made to use p-node name resolution. m-node was the first hybrid mode put into operation, but it has the disadvantage of favoring b-node operation, which is associated with high levels of broadcast traffic.
- **h-node (hybrid node)**—A hybrid mode that favors the use of WINS for NetBIOS name registration and resolution. When a computer needs to resolve a NetBIOS name, it first attempts to use p-node resolution to resolve a name via WINS. Only if WINS resolution fails does the host resort to b-node to resolve the name via broadcasts. Because it typically results in the best network utilization, h-node is the default mode of operation for Microsoft TCP/IP client computers configured to use WINS for name resolution. Microsoft recommends leaving TCP/IP client computers in the default h-node configuration.

IN THE FIELD

THE METHOD WINS USES TO RESOLVE A NAME

The time might come when you need to understand exactly how WINS registers and resolves a name. (Because h-node is not only the default but is also the recommended configuration, we will restrict our discussion to the h-node name resolution.) When a WINS client computer configured for Hybrid mode needs to resolve a host name, it goes through the following series of steps:

1. It checks its NetBIOS name cache. If the name is found, it returns it.
2. It queries the WINS server. If the name is found, it returns it.
3. It issues a broadcast to find the host on the local network. If the name is found, it returns it.
4. It looks for the `LMHOSTS` file to check for an entry. If the name is found, it returns it.
5. It looks for the `HOSTS` file to check for an entry. If the name is found, it returns it.
6. It queries the DNS server for the entry. If the name is found, it returns it.
7. If all these methods fail, the WINS client computer issues an error message saying that it can't communicate with the host.

EXAM TIP

Registering with WINS When your Windows client computer enters the network, it registers with WINS so that other Microsoft client computers can resolve its name to an address. For the exam, you should be aware that although a WINS proxy server can be used to resolve names for hosts that have registered with WINS, it can't be used to register with WINS. You need access to the WINS server to successfully register.

Although networks can be organized using a mixture of node types, Microsoft recommends against it. b-node client computers do not receive p-node directed messages, and p-node client computers ignore b-node broadcasts. Therefore, it is conceivable that two client computers could separately be established with the same NetBIOS name.

If WINS is enabled on a Windows 2000 Professional computer, the system uses h-node by default. Without WINS, the system uses b-node by default. Non-WINS client computers can access WINS through a WINS proxy, which is a WINS-enabled computer that listens to name query broadcasts and then queries the WINS server on behalf of the requesting client computer.

To see which node type is configured on a Windows 2000 computer, follow Step By Step 7.5.

STEP BY STEP

7.5 Identifying the NetBIOS Node Type

1. Open a command prompt by selecting Start, Programs, Accessories, Command Prompt.
2. At the command prompt, type **`IPCONFIG /ALL`**. You will get a result similar to the one shown in Figure 7.21. The node type is indicated to the right of the heading Node Type. In this example, the machine is running in hybrid mode, the default for Windows 2000.

Next, let's look at the best way to manage and monitor WINS and manage your new WINS server.

```
Command Prompt

C:\>ipconfig /all

Windows 2000 IP Configuration

        Host Name . . . . . . . . . . . . : kubla
        Primary DNS Suffix  . . . . . . . : urwrite.net
        Node Type . . . . . . . . . . . . : Hybrid
        IP Routing Enabled. . . . . . . . : Yes
        WINS Proxy Enabled. . . . . . . . : No
        DNS Suffix Search List. . . . . . : urwrite.net

Ethernet adapter Local Area Connection:

        Connection-specific DNS Suffix  . :
        Description . . . . . . . . . . . : Netelligent 10/100TX PCI Embedded UT
P Controller
        Physical Address. . . . . . . . . : 00-80-5F-7D-B2-FA
        DHCP Enabled. . . . . . . . . . . : Yes
        Autoconfiguration Enabled . . . . : Yes
        IP Address. . . . . . . . . . . . : 10.226.10.187
        Subnet Mask . . . . . . . . . . . : 255.255.255.248
        Default Gateway . . . . . . . . . : 10.226.10.185
        DHCP Server . . . . . . . . . . . : 10.226.10.185
        DNS Servers . . . . . . . . . . . : 10.226.10.190
        Primary WINS Server . . . . . . . : 10.226.10.190
        Lease Obtained. . . . . . . . . . : Tuesday, April 11, 2000 2:24:36 AM
        Lease Expires . . . . . . . . . . : Tuesday, April 11, 2000 2:42:36 AM

C:\>_
```

FIGURE 7.21
The IPConfig utility gives you all the information on the IP configuration of any of your adapters, including the node type.

MANAGING AND MONITORING WINS

We have looked at installing and configuring the Windows 2000 WINS Server service. Next, we need to look at managing and monitoring the server now that it is running. If your job is typical of most, you will spend a great deal more time managing WINS servers than installing them.

Although the WINS server includes limited monitoring capabilities, you do have access to the WINS statistics referenced in the "Troubleshooting" section of the chapter. To get the server statistics, just open WINS Manager and right-click the server in question. From the context menu, select Display Server Statistics, and a snapshot of the server statistics is displayed (see Figure 7.22).

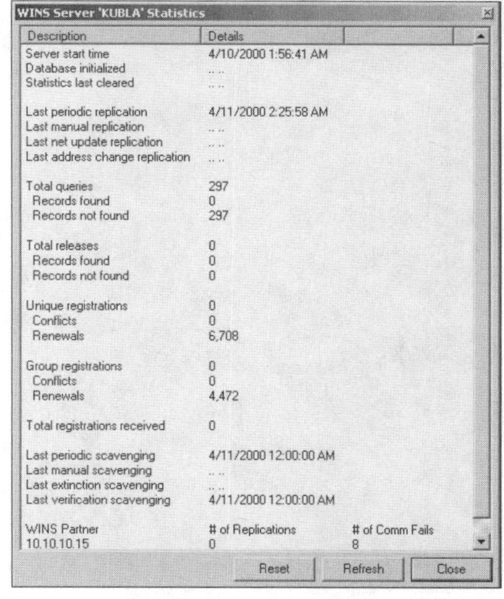

FIGURE 7.22
The WINS Server Statistics screen provides a good snapshot of WINS activity.

The WINS manager application has additional capabilities. From the open WINS manager application, you can select the WINS server and then use the Action menu to access these available actions:

- **Display Server Statistics**—This option displays statistics discussed in a preceding section.
- **Scavenge Database**—This option enables you to manually clean unused entries from the WINS database.

- **Verify Database Consistency**—This option causes the server to go out to the network hosts and verify the entries in the WINS database. This process can be very processor and network intensive, so be sure to run it after hours.
- **Verify Version ID Consistency**—This option forces the WINS server to go to all the other WINS servers on the network and has them check the database version numbers to ensure that they are consistent. This is potentially another long operation, so it should be run after hours—or at least not when everyone in the office is trying to read email.
- **Start Push Replication**—This option manually performs a push replication.
- **Start Pull Replication**—This option manually performs a pull replication.
- **Back Up Database**—This option enables you to make a backup copy of the WINS database. Always be sure you have a copy of this database, just in case. If you specify the backup directory, the server will automatically back up the database every 24 hours.
- **Restore the Database**—This option enables you to restore a backup copy of the database.
- **Tasks**—This option leads to a menu consisting of the following commands:
  - **Start**—Starts the WINS Server service. This option is available only if the service is stopped or paused.
  - **Stop**—Stops the WINS Server service. Available when the service is running or paused. This option causes the server statistics to be reset.
  - **Pause**—Pauses the WINS Server service. This option does not reset the statistics.
  - **Resume**—Resumes the WINS Server service when paused. This option is available only when the service is paused.
  - **Restart**—Restarts the WINS Server service. This option is available unless the server is stopped.

- **Delete**—This option deletes a WINS server from the WINS manager.
- **Refresh**—This option causes all the displayed information to be refreshed with a current status.
- **Export List**—This option enables you to export the information from the WINS server to a tab- or comma-delimited text or Unicode text file.
- **Properties**—This option opens the server properties, as discussed in a preceding section.

The Windows 2000 WINS service also includes some new functionality for managing the WINS database. If you open the WINS manager and click the Active Registrations, you will see a list of all the dynamically added entries in the WINS database. Although this is useful, it would be nice to be able to search for a specific entry, or even to filter on specific record types. The good news is that you can. If you right-click the Active Registration folder and select Find by Name or Find by Owner, you can search the WINS database for specific entries. Under Find by Owner, you can even filter which WINS record types should be shown. If you are working in a large environment (500 computers or greater), you will find these capabilities invaluable because computers can often enter 10–12 entries each into the WINS database. I don't know about you, but I don't relish reading through 5,000–6,000 WINS records looking for a specific machine.

Windows 2000's WINS service also enables you to delete not only static records, but also dynamic records. This is a major improvement over previous versions of WINS, in which you couldn't delete dynamic entries.

Now that we have examined the options for managing the WINS server, let's take a look at some of the ways to monitor the service. Before you get into Step By Step 7.6, you should look at which counters you can use to monitor WINS. The WINS object has the following counters associated with it:

- **Failed Queries/Sec**—Gives you the number of failed WINS queries per second. If this number is very high or suddenly spikes, you might have an issue with WINS resolution.

- **Failed Releases/Sec**—Gives you the number of failed WINS released per second. If this number is very high or suddenly spikes, you might have an issue with WINS resolution.
- **Group Conflicts/Sec**—The rate at which group registrations by the WINS server resulted in conflicts with the database.
- **Group Registrations/Sec**—The rate at which group registrations are being received.
- **Group Renewals/Sec**—The rate at which group registrations are being renewed.
- **Queries/Sec**—The rate at which queries are being received.
- **Releases/sec**—The rate at which releases are being received.
- **Successful Queries/Sec**—The number of successful queries per second. This is useful if you are trending your WINS usage.
- **Successful Releases/Sec**—The number of successful releases per second. This is useful if you are trending your WINS usage.
- **Total Number of Conflicts/Sec**—This is the sum of the unique and group conflicts per second.
- **Total Number of Registrations/Sec**—This is the sum of the unique and group registrations per second.
- **Total Number of Renewals/Sec**—This is the sum of the unique and group renewals per second.
- **Unique Conflicts/Sec**—The rate at which unique registrations and renewals caused conflicts with the database.
- **Unique Registrations/Sec**—The rate at which unique registrations are received by the server.
- **Unique Renewals/Sec**—The rate at which unique renewals are received by the server.

To configure WINS performance monitoring, follow Step By Step 7.6.

STEP BY STEP

7.6 Monitoring WINS Performance

1. Open the Performance application by selecting Programs, Administrative Tools, Performance (see Figure 7.23).

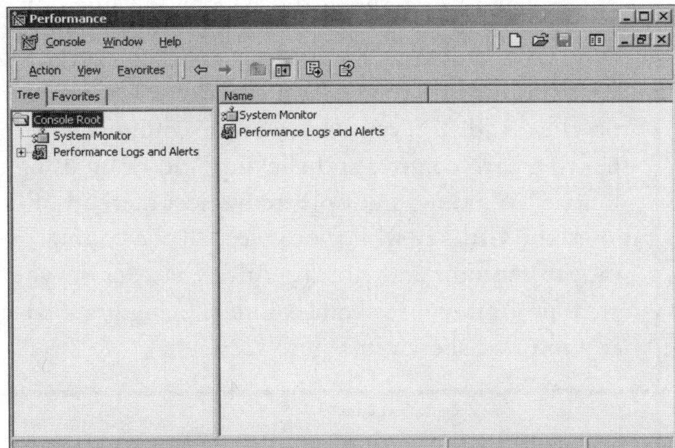

FIGURE 7.23
The Performance console enables you to monitor a variety of system and application metrics for evaluating the performance and health of the system.

2. In the Performance console, select System Monitor (see Figure 7.24).

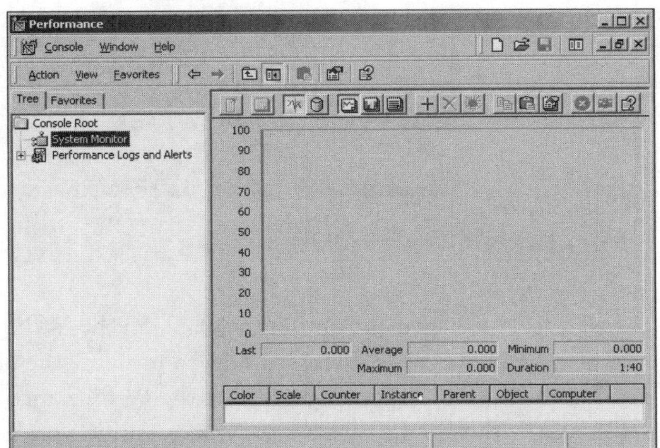

FIGURE 7.24
System Monitor enables you to monitor the performance of your server's statistics in real-time.

continues

continued

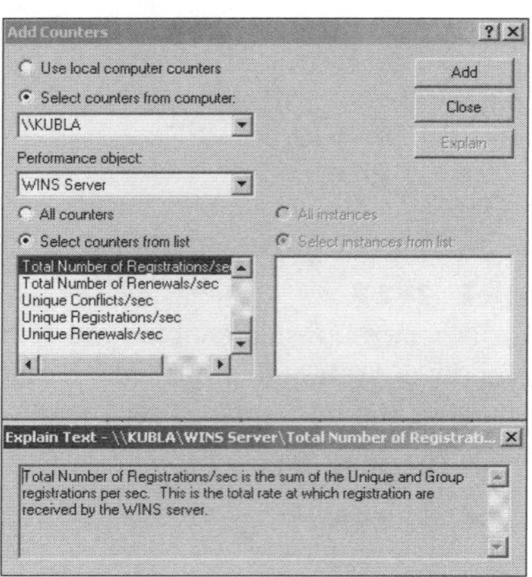

FIGURE 7.25
Clicking the Explain button.

3. To create an entry in System Monitor, click the Add (+) icon. The Add Counters windows opens. By default, it opens to the Processor performance object.
4. Select the WINS Server performance object. You will see the list of counters displayed as available for the WINS service. Figure 7.25 shows the explanation function of the Performance console.
5. After you have decided which counter you want to monitor, click Add. You can add multiple counters either by selecting each counter and clicking Add or by using the standard Windows multiple item select method of holding down the Ctrl key while you select all the counters you want to monitor and clicking Add. Click Close when you are done. You will see your counters being graphed similarly to those shown in Figure 7.26.

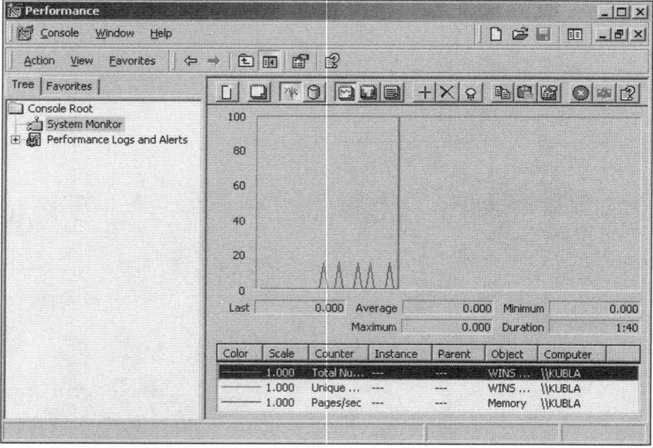

FIGURE 7.26
After the counters have been added, all that remains is successfully interpreting the data.

We've looked at the management options available in the WINS manager application, and we've discussed how to monitor the performance of the various WINS counters using the Performance console. At this point, you should have a good understanding of the Windows 2000 WINS Server service and WINS in general.

CLIENT TOOLS

A thorough understanding of WINS and server-based resolutions is great, but it won't help diagnose problems on a client. The tools discussed in the following sections—NBTStat, IPConfig, NSLookup, and NetDIAG—are all helpful in resolving name resolution problems.

NBTStat

NBT stands for NetBIOS over TCP/IP. Thus, NBTStat gives you statistics for NetBIOS over TCP/IP. The utility is used to determine which NetBIOS names the machine has cached and to which IP addresses those names resolved. You need to be aware of three basic options for using the NBTStat tool:

- `a/A`—Displays the name table of a machine given a name and an IP address, respectively. This is useful for determining to which NetBIOS names and service names a machine is responding. Figure 7.27 shows the results of an `NBTSTAT -a`.
- `c`—Displays the cache of NetBIOS names held by the local machine. This is useful for determining which names the local client has requested recently and how they were resolved. Figure 7.28 shows the results of an `NBTSTAT -c`.
- `s/S`—Displays the current NetBIOS sessions. The lowercase *s* translates the IP address of the remote machine into its machine name for the display, and the uppercase *S* displays only the IP address. Figure 7.29 shows the results of an `NBTSTAT -s`.

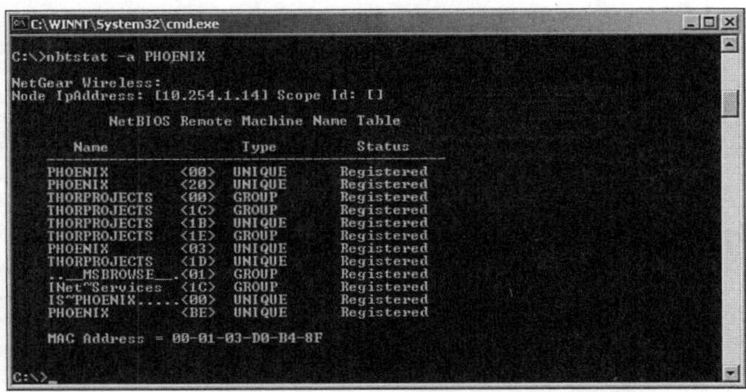

FIGURE 7.27
`NBTSTAT -a` shows the machine's NetBIOS table.

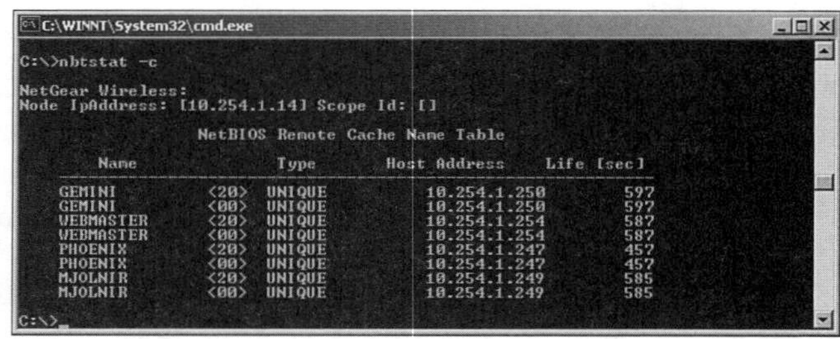

FIGURE 7.28
NBTSTAT -c shows the local NetBIOS cache.

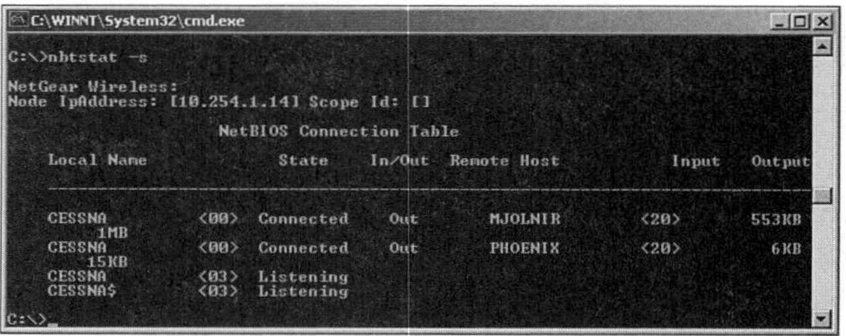

FIGURE 7.29
NBTSTAT -s shows the current NetBIOS sessions.

> **EXAM TIP**
>
> **NBTSTAT** The exam will expect you to know these three basic options (but not whether the uppercase or lowercase version is necessary). You should know how to retrieve the NetBIOS names from an IP address, retrieve the cache, and show current sessions.

IPConfig

Perhaps the most widely used TCP/IP utility is the IPConfig utility. It is the only way to display all the dynamic information retrieved from a DHCP server, as well as for providing a mechanism for updating DHCP and name resolution information. Figure 7.30 shows the results of typing **`IPCONFIG`**.

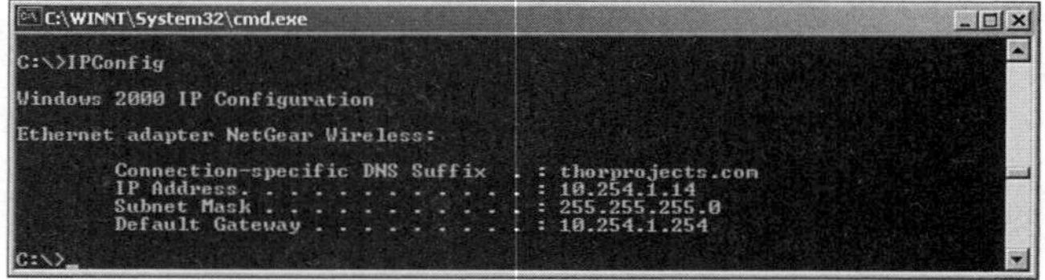

FIGURE 7.30
IPCONFIG responds with your IP address and details.

The following are some important options you can use with IPConfig:

- `/all`—Displays more detailed information about the IP configuration, including the WINS, DNS, and DHCP server addresses.
- `/release`—Causes the computer to release all DHCP addresses that have been leased. This is the nice way to let a DHCP

server know that you're done with an address, and it ensures that the computer attempts to gain an IP address from the beginning.

- `/renew`—Causes the computer to renew all DHCP leased addresses on all adapters. If some adapters have not successfully leased a DHCP address `/renew` forces the adapters to make another attempt to lease an address.
- `/flushdns`—Discards the DNS resolver cache. This removes all entries from the local cache so that the computer is forced to ask DNS to resolve the addresses again. This is necessary when the local DNS cache contains invalid information that has been corrected on the network.
- `/registerdns`—Renews all DHCP addresses and refreshes the dynamic registration of the computer name with the DNS servers. Renewing all the DHCP addresses is required in case the DHCP server is responsible for updating the DNS server.

IPConfig is the primary utility you will use when attempting to diagnose and fix IP configuration problems.

EXAM TIP

IPCONFIG Know what the options for the IPConfig utility are and, more importantly, what they do. You'll be expected to know which option to use in given a situation.

NSLookup

As you learned in Chapter 6, although you can use utilities such as PING to test whether a name can be resolved, utilities like PING are useful only for telling you that name resolution is working and that the resolution is to the correct or incorrect address. However, testing name resolution by using more generic tools does not allow you to locate the source of the incorrect information.

It's important that you understand that even though Microsoft has included the NSLookup utility under the NetBIOS objective, NSLookup's purpose is to interrogate DNS servers and resolve IP names, not NetBIOS names.

NSLookup is short for Name Server Lookup and is run by typing the name at the command prompt in Windows 2000. After a few short messages, you'll be returned to a prompt that is just a greater than sign (>). Once at this prompt, you can enter a name to have the NSLookup utility resolve that name into an address. However, the real power of NSLookup comes from the following commands that can also be entered:

- `set` *type*=—Where *type* is the type of record you want NSLookup to find. You might remember from the Chapter 6, “Host Name Resolution/DNS,” that various types of DNS records exist. Popular alternative record types are SOA and MX. To return to normal resolution, use the command `set type=A`.
- `server` <*name* or *address*>—This command changes the server that NSLookup interrogates to the name or address specified. This is used to direct the query to a particular server to enable you to test name resolution at that server.
- `set debug`—Enables you to turn on debugging so that you can see the entire path used to resolve your query. DNS, as you will remember, is a recursive process in which one server contacts another server until the answer to the query is located.

When you’re done working with NSLookup, type **`exit`** on a line by itself. This exits the NSLookup and returns you to a command prompt.

NetDIAG

Unlike the other tools discussed here, NetDIAG is not included as a part of the standard Windows 2000 installation. To install NetDIAG, you must install the Windows 2000 Support tools or download it as a separate update. The NetDIAG utility is available from the Microsoft Web site for free.

For the exam you need to know that the NetDIAG tool is used to diagnose all types of connectivity problems. It automatically runs a series of tests to tell you where your connectivity problems lie. Although there are parameters to the command, the major selling point of this utility is that you don’t need to know command-line options.

File-Based Name Resolution

One of the easiest ways to ensure that name resolution is working is to hardcode it into the local files that Windows looks to first for information. By entering the information in the local files, you can ensure that the computer does not attempt to resolve the name and will use the address you've specified. Two files are used for name resolution. The first file, the `HOSTS` file, resolves IP names into IP addresses and can be thought of as an alternative to DNS. The second file, the `LMHOSTS` file, resolves NetBIOS names into IP addresses and can be thought of as an alternative to WINS. We examine each and how you can use them to troubleshoot in the next sections.

HOSTS

In the last chapter you learned that the first name resolution on the Internet used a host file and that DNS was added later. On a Windows 2000 machine, the `HOSTS` file is located in the `%WINDIR%\System32\drivers\etc`. This is the file you must modify to change the hardcoded host resolution. Entries in the `HOSTS` file are simple; they begin with the IP address and are followed by the host name. If you open the `HOSTS` file on your system, it will already contain the special localhost name, which you can use as a template for adding new names.

After you make your changes, you do not need to reboot the system. Windows 2000 will detect the change to the file and will automatically use it, although it's never a bad idea to run a `IPCONFIG /FLUSHDNS` command after making modifications to the file.

LMHOSTS

`LMHOSTS` is short for LAN Manager Hosts. It's one of the few places with Windows 2000 truly shows its OS/2 LAN Manager heritage. The format of the `LMHOSTS` file is different, but it is located in the same `%WINDIR%\system32\drivers\etc` directory as the `HOSTS` file. Unlike the `HOSTS` file, no default `LMHOSTS` file is created when you install Windows 2000. However, Windows 2000 includes an `LMHosts.SAM` file that is a sample file you can rename to `LMHOSTS` and use as a starting point.

The LMHOSTS file is similar to the HOSTS file, except it has several additional options to be aware of:

- #PRE—Placed after an entry, it causes the entry to be preloaded. The effect of this is that the entry is permanently loaded into memory. This is a good idea for hosts that will be accessed frequently.
- #DOM:*<domain>*—Associates an entry with the domain given. Helps the computer locate a domain controller for the network.
- #INCLUDE *<filename>*—Includes the named file as if it were located in the LMHOSTS file. This is infrequently used because it incurs additional overhead to process the file.

In general, you must know that the LMHOSTS file is used for NetBIOS name resolution and that hosts is used for IP name resolution.

Case Study: Configuring Network Address Translation in a 100-User Network

ESSENCE OF THE CASE

The essence of the case is as follows:

- You have a five-site network, each site with its own IP subnet.
- You need a centralized NetBIOS name resolution service to allow users to resolve names.
- You want to deploy this to all users, and it must resolve for all Microsoft servers.

SCENARIO

You are the network administrator for LFE Incorporated, which is a lawn furniture manufacturing company. You have a five-site network, and each site has its own IP subnet. You are presently running several Windows NT workstations and servers and are in the process of upgrading to Windows 2000 servers.

You have been using LMHOSTS files for NetBIOS name resolution thus far, but you would like to move to a centralized name resolution solution as part of the Windows 2000 migration, to support legacy applications. You need to ensure that name resolution is available for all computers on all subnets and that they resolve all hosts on the network.

What do you need to do?

CASE STUDY: CONFIGURING NETWORK ADDRESS TRANSLATION IN A 100-USER NETWORK

ANALYSIS

This is an excellent example of a small Microsoft network desperately in need of a WINS infrastructure. A good WINS design requires that a WINS server be at each location for both local and remote resolution. To make it work, you need to do the following:

- Install the Windows 2000 WINS service on at least one Windows 2000 server in each location.
- Configure the WINS servers as replication partners, and make sure they replicate their databases appropriately.
- Configure each of the client computers to use WINS resolution with the local WINS server as the primary server.
- If you are using DHCP, be sure to update the DHCP setting to reflect the new WINS servers.

If you are migrating to a Windows 2000 network and do not have a WINS infrastructure for your existing Microsoft client computers, this might be a good model to deploy for interim support until you have completed your Windows 2000 migration.

CHAPTER SUMMARY

In this chapter you learned the intricacies of NetBIOS name resolution, which is heavily focused on the use of WINS servers but also uses broadcasts to resolve names when WINS servers are not available.

WINS is important because it allows for NetBIOS name resolution across router boundaries and reduces or eliminates the need for computers to broadcast to register and resolve machine names. This is, in turn, important to maintain performance on today's networks that use Ethernet switches to improve overall network performance.

Next, you learned how to configure NetBIOS name resolution, as well as how to configure WINS replication partners. Then, we discussed the various mechanisms available for managing and monitoring your WINS servers.

Next, you learned the basic troubleshooting commands and how they are used to diagnose and fix IP configuration problems. The use of the IPConfig program in particular is important to troubleshooting and resolving basic problems.

KEY TERMS

- Active Directory
- b-node
- Domain Name System (DNS)
- Dynamic Host Control Protocol (DHCP)
- h-node
- HOSTS file
- Internet Control Message Protocol (ICMP)
- LAN Manager HOSTS (LMHOSTS)
- m-node

CHAPTER SUMMARY

- NetBIOS
- p-node
- Pull replication
- Push/pull replication
- Push replication
- Replication partner
- Request for Comment (RFC) documents
- Transmission Control Protocol/Internet Protocol (TCP/IP)
- Windows Internet Naming Service (WINS)

Finally, you learned the basics of the Windows 2000 name resolution files. These files, `HOSTS` and `LMHOSTS`, resolve IP names and NetBIOS names, respectively.

APPLY YOUR KNOWLEDGE

Exercises

5.1 Installing WINS on a Windows 2000 Server

In this exercise, you will install WINS on your Windows 2000 server.

Estimated Time: 15 minutes

1. Open the Network and Dial-up Connections window.
2. Click the Add Network Components link.
3. Select the Networking Services entry and click Details.
4. Select Windows Internet Name Service (WINS).
5. Click the OK button.
6. Click Next to start the installation.
7. If you have not already done so, insert the Windows 2000 server installation media in the drive, or point the application to the appropriate directory or share for the installation files.
8. When the summary window appears, click OK to complete the installation.

5.2 Configuring a Replication Partner

In this exercise you will configure a replication partner.

Estimated Time: 10 minutes

1. Open the WINS manager by selecting Start, Programs, Administrative Tools, WINS.
2. Right-click Replication Partners and select New Replication Partner from the context menu.
3. Enter the server name `WINSTEST`. You will be prompted to enter the address of the server.
4. Enter `10.10.10.254` and click OK. You will be returned to the WINS Manager.
5. Click Replication Partners in the left pane. You should see your new replication partner in the right pane.

5.3 Performing a Manual Push Replication

In this exercise you will manually perform a push replication.

Estimated Time: 10 minutes

1. Open the WINS manager by selecting Start, Programs, Administrative Tools, WINS.
2. Right-click WINS server and select Start Push Replication.
3. Enter the server name or IP address of the other WINS server and click OK.
4. Select Start for This Partner Only as the replication method. You can select Propagate to All Partners as the other method. Click OK; you will receive a message that the replication request has been queued.
5. Check the event log for a status of the request and to see when it is completed.

5.4 Performing a Manual Pull Replication

In this exercise you will manually perform a pull replication.

Estimated Time: 10 minutes

1. Open the WINS manager by selecting Start, Programs, Administrative Tools, WINS.
2. Right-click WINS server and select Start Pull Replication.

3. Enter the server name or IP address of the other WINS server and click OK.
4. When asked to confirm the request, click Yes. You will receive a message stating that the replication request has been queued.
5. Check the event log for a status of the request and to see when it is completed.

Review Questions

1. You are the network administrator for a small company with several sites, each with host computers. You are in the process of migrating to Windows 2000, but you want to be sure that all your legacy Windows NT 4 computers can browse the network. What should you do?
2. You have successfully deployed WINS in your environment, and it is working. Your users can browse the network. How does the WINS database get populated to make this possible?
3. After the WINS is fully implemented and the database is populated, how are entries deleted from the database?
4. What is the major difference between push replication and pull replication?
5. You're the administrator of Little Faith Enterprise's Windows 2000 server, and you are considering setting up WINS. You feel you need a better understanding of how NetBIOS works and how the various node types work. What are the four NetBIOS node types, and how do they work?

Exam Questions

1. You are the WINS administrator for LFE Incorporated. You want to be sure to have a reliable backup of your WINS database available in case of problems, but you don't want to manually back up the database every day. What is the best way to automatically back up your WINS database?

   A. Purchase a third-party backup utility and schedule nightly backups of the entire server.

   B. Use the Windows scheduler service and configure a WINS Database Backup task.

   C. In the WINS manager, specify the backup directory and backup interval.

   D. In the WINS manager, specify the backup directory.

2. You are the network administrator for Lost in the Woods Guide Service. You have a Windows 2000 server running WINS in your corporate headquarters and another in a branch office. You want the server in the branch office to get a replica of the corporate server's database every two hours.

   How do you do it?

   A. Configure the branch WINS server as a push replication partner with a two-hour interval.

   B. Configure the branch WINS server as a pull replication server with a two-hour interval.

   C. Configure the corporate WINS server as a push replication partner with a two-hour interval.

   D. Configure the corporate WINS server as a pull replication server with a two-hour interval.

APPLY YOUR KNOWLEDGE

3. You are the network administrator for a five-location pet food manufacturer. You have WINS servers at all five locations, and you would like them to replicate with each other automatically.

   How do you do it?

   A. Configure each WINS server as a replication partner. In the Replication Partner Properties, select Replicate with All Partners.

   B. Configure each WINS server as a replication partner. In the Replication Partner Properties, select Replicate Only with Partners.

   C. In the Replication Partner Properties, deselect Replicate Only with Partners. The server will automatically replicate with any WINS servers.

   D. Install WINS. Any WINS servers on the network will automatically replicate.

4. You are the network administrator for LFE Inc., a novelty manufacturing company. You have a large population of Windows NT 4 Workstation client computers on your Windows 2000 network. You have a new administrator who is trying to learn how WINS works. You want to explain it. By default, which WINS server will a client computer use for resolution?

   A. The WINS server that responds to the broadcast request first

   B. The default WINS server it receives from DHCP or that is configured in TCP/IP properties

   C. The primary WINS server it receives from DHCP or that is configured in TCP/IP properties

   D. The WINS server that is the least number of network hops away

5. You are the network administrator for BT Machines, a heavy equipment manufacturing company. You have a large population of Windows NT 4 Workstation client computers on your Windows 2000 network. You are concerned that there are computers coming on the network that have the same NetBIOS name. Which WINS statistic should you check to see if this is the case?

   A. Unique Conflicts/Sec

   B. Total Number of Conflicts/Sec

   C. Group Conflicts/Sec

   D. Failed Releases/Sec

6. You are the network administrator for BT Machines, a heavy equipment manufacturing company. You have a large population of Windows NT 4 Workstation client computers on your Windows 2000 network. You want to quickly check the total number of client computers adding updates to the WINS database.

   Which parameter should you check?

   A. Unique Registrations/Sec

   B. Total Number of Registrations/Sec

   C. Total Number of Renewals/Sec

   D. Total Number of Registrations/Sec and Total Number of Renewals/Sec

7. You are the network administrator for Blue Sky Air, and you are training another administrator to assist with maintaining the network. She is having a hard time understanding the different

APPLY YOUR KNOWLEDGE

NetBIOS node types, especially which type the new Windows 2000 Professional computers use.

What is the default node type for Windows 2000?

A. h-node

B. m-node

C. p-node

D. b-node

8. Now that your new assistant understands the node type used by Windows 2000 Professional by default, she would like you to help her differentiate the node types.

   Which of the following statements about node types is accurate?

   A. h-node and m-node favor WINS servers, but m-node does not have the capability to use broadcast if the WINS server is down.

   B. h-node and b-node favor WINS servers, but b-node does not have the capability to use broadcast if the WINS server is down.

   C. b-node and m-node both favor broadcast resolution first, but b-node can resolve using a WINS server if the host is on another subnet.

   D. h-node and p-node both favor WINS servers, but h-node can use a broadcast for name resolution if the WINS server is not available.

9. You are the LAN administrator for Little Faith Enterprises, a publishing company. You have a Windows 2000 server for the corporate headquarters but have a mix of Windows 2000 and Windows NT 4 client computers on the network. You have deployed WINS for backward compatibility, but you are unsure whether WINS is working.

   What is the best way to find out?

   A. Using the Performance console, select the WINS server object and the Successful Resolutions/Sec counter. Verify that the counter value is greater than 0.

   B. Using the Performance console, select the WINS server object and the Queries/Sec counter. Verify that the counter value is greater than 0.

   C. Open the WINS manager, select the server in question, and from the Action menu select Server Statistics. Verify that the number of Total Queries is increasing. Click Refresh to update the statistics.

   D. Open the WINS manager, select the server in question, and from the Action menu select Server Statistics. Verify that the number of Records Found Under Total Queries is increasing. Click Refresh to update the statistics.

10. You are the system administrator for New Riders Harley Davidson and are installing a WINS server on your Windows 2000 server. Your end users are all using DHCP.

    What is the best way to configure the workstations to use the WINS server?

    A. Make sure the WINS server is installed on a domain controller. WINS resolution will occur automatically.

    B. Modify the DHCP scope options for the WINS server to include the address of the new WINS server.

    C. Open the Network applet and open the TCP/IP properties. On the WINS tab,

APPLY YOUR KNOWLEDGE

modify the TCP/IP properties to point at the WINS server. Repeat this for each machine.

D. Update the LMHOSTS file to include the address of the new WINS server.

11. You are the administrator for a three-location car dealership. One location is the headquarters, and the other two are dealerships. You are migrating from a workgroup-based Windows NT 4 network to a Windows 2000 network. Each site is connected to the other two using a frame relay connection and a bridge. As part of the migration, you have decided to deploy WINS for the legacy client computers. Because money is a main component of this as a temporary service for the migration only, management would like to spend as little as possible.

    What is the least expensive way to roll out WINS in this environment?

    A. Install one WINS server on the headquarters network.

    B. Install one WINS server on each network.

    C. Install a WINS server at headquarters and another for redundancy at one of the dealerships.

    D. Install one server on each dealership network and two in the headquarters network for redundancy.

12. The WINS service was created to replace what?

    A. The Domain Name Service

    B. The HOSTS file

    C. The LMHOSTS file

    D. The WINS file

13. You are the administrator for a single-site direct-marketing company. You have two network segments in your building, with servers on both networks, and a Windows 2000 server is being used to route between segments. You have a mixture of DOS, Windows 95/98, and Windows NT Workstations as client computers in this network. You install WINS on the server, and your DOS client computers are incapable of seeing the servers on the other side of the router.

    Why can't the DOS client computers see computers across the router?

    A. DOS does not use a dynamic routing protocol, so it can't see across the router.

    B. DOS can't interpret WINS names for resolution.

    C. DOS requires a WINS client computer before being capable of interfacing with the WINS server.

    D. DOS uses b-node resolution of NetBIOS names.

14. You are the manager of a small consulting company. This company has a single network segment of 225 computers and has two WINS servers installed on Windows 2000 servers. You suspect that you have two computers with the same name on the network, but you have been unable to find the culprits.

    How can you tell whether you have two computers with the same name?

    A. Open the WINS utility and, from the Action menu, select Statistics. Check to see whether the Duplicate Names statistic is incrementing.

APPLY YOUR KNOWLEDGE

B. Open the WINS utility and, from the Action menu, select Statistics. Check to see whether the Conflicts statistics are incrementing.

C. Open the Performance console and add the Duplicate Names counter for the WINS server object. Check the trend for the statistic.

D. Open the Performance console and add the Names Conflicts counter for the WINS server object. Check the trend for the statistic.

15. You are the WAN administrator for the Women's Place clothing store. You have six satellite locations all connected with low-bandwidth WAN links. Each location has its own WINS server for name resolution and will need to be replicated to.

    What is the best configuration for the WINS replication from the corporate WINS server to those in the field?

    A. Configure a pull replication from the remote servers to the central server and schedule it to occur whenever 100 entries have been added to the table.

    B. Configure a push replication from the remote servers to the central server and schedule it to occur whenever 100 entries have been added to the table.

    C. Configure a pull replication from the central server to the remote servers and schedule it to occur whenever 100 entries have been added to the table.

    D. Configure a push replication from the central server to the remote servers and schedule it to occur whenever 100 entries have been added to the table.

16. You believe that you've just resolved some IP name resolution problems but when you go to a client computer running Windows 2000, you get the old information. Which command should you run to resolve this problem?

    A. `IPCONFIG`

    B. `NetDIAG`

    C. `NBTStat`

    D. `NSLookup`

17. You have users in another building complaining that they get a response from the wrong server when they type `www.mycompany.com` in their browsers. (Your company uses the `mycompany.com` domain.) You attempt the same thing from your location, and it works fine. Which tool should you use to identify the problem?

    A. `IPCONFIG`

    B. `NetDIAG`

    C. `NBTStat`

    D. `NSLookup`

Answers to Review Questions

1. You need to deploy WINS in your environment. Depending on your environment, you might be able to deploy redundant WINS servers in your central site, or you might need to deploy WINS servers to each location. In either event, you must configure replication between the servers. For more information, see the section "Installing WINS."

APPLY YOUR KNOWLEDGE

2. The WINS database is populated by the WINS client computer. When the WINS client computer comes on the network, it registers its name and address with the WINS server automatically. After the client computer is registered, it receives a time to live for its registration. For more information, see the section "Configuring WINS."

3. There are two automated mechanisms for removing entries. When a client computer shuts down gracefully, it sends a release request to the WINS server. The entries are also removed when the time to live for that client computer's registration expires. For more information, see the section "Configuring WINS Replication."

4. The main difference between push and pull replication (besides the direction the database is replicated) is the trigger for the event. In the case of a push replication, the trigger is event based. When a specified number of changes are made to the database, the replication is triggered. A pull replication is triggered by the time configured for the replication. This is user configured. For more information, see the section "Configuring WINS Replication."

5. There are four node types, and the main differentiator between the types is the methods they use for name resolution (broadcast versus direct connection). They are

   - **b-node (broadcast node)**—Relies exclusively on broadcast messages and is the oldest NetBIOS name resolution mode. A host needing to resolve a name request sends a message to every host within earshot, requesting the address associated with a host name. b-node has two shortcomings: Broadcast traffic is undesirable and becomes a significant user of network bandwidths, and TCP/IP routers don't forward broadcast messages, which restricts b-node operation to a single network segment.
   - **p-node (point-to-point node)**—Relies on WINS servers for NetBIOS name resolution. Client computers register themselves with a WINS server when they come on the network. They then contact the WINS server with NetBIOS name resolution requests. WINS servers communicate using directed messages, which can cross routers, so p-node can operate on large networks. Unfortunately, if the WINS server is unavailable or if a node isn't configured to contact a WINS server, p-node name resolution fails.
   - **m-node (modified node)**—It's a hybrid mode that first attempts to resolve NetBIOS names using the b-node mechanism. If that fails, an attempt is made to use p-node name resolution. m-node was the first hybrid mode put into operation, but it has the disadvantage of favoring b-node operation, which is associated with high levels of broadcast traffic.
   - **h-node (hybrid node)**—It's also a hybrid mode that favors the use of WINS for NetBIOS name resolution. When a computer needs to resolve a NetBIOS name, it first attempts to use p-node resolution to resolve a name via WINS. Only if WINS resolution fails does the host resort to b-node to resolve the name via broadcasts. Because it typically results in the best network utilization, h-node is the default mode of operation for Microsoft TCP/IPs configured to use WINS for name resolution. Microsoft recommends leaving TCP/IP client computers in the default

h-node configuration. For more information, see the section "Configuring NetBIOS Name Resolution."

Answers to Exam Questions

1. **D.** If you specify the backup directory, the server will automatically back up the WINS database every 24 hours. For more information, see the section "Managing and Monitoring WINS."
2. **B.** Pull replications are triggered by a time interval. For the branch WINS server to get a replica of the corporate WINS database, it would need to be scheduled to pull the information at a two-hour interval. For more information, see the section "Configuring WINS Replication."
3. **B.** After the WINS servers have been configured as replication partners, they replicate with each other based on the replication configuration. For more information, see the section "Configuring WINS Replication."
4. **C.** Because no default WINS server exists (don't confuse it with the default gateway), the answer is C, the primary WINS server. For more information, see the section "Configuring NetBIOS Name Resolution."
5. **A.** The conflicts per second would show you whether you have computers with name conflicts. For more information, see the section "Managing and Monitoring WINS."
6. **D.** If you want to capture all the client computers that are registering with the server and not just new registrations, you need to look at the total for both the Total Number of Registrations/Sec and Total Number of Renewals/Sec. For more information, see the section "Managing and Monitoring WINS."
7. **A.** Windows 2000 Professional computers use h-node (hybrid) for NetBIOS name resolution. This node type favors the WINS server for name resolution but will attempt to resolve the name by broadcast if the WINS server is unavailable. For more information, see the section "Configuring NetBIOS Name Resolution."
8. **D.** h-node (Hybrid) is the preferred method because it relies on the WINS server before resorting to a broadcast. p-node uses a WINS server but can't use broadcasts for NetBIOS name resolution. For more information, see the section "Configuring NetBIOS Name Resolution."
9. **D.** Although answer C is almost a correct answer, the Total Queries includes records not found. If all the queries are returning a Records Not Found result, the server probably has a problem. You should make sure that the number of records found (successful queries) is increasing. For more information, see the section "Managing and Monitoring WINS."
10. **B.** Because this is a DHCP environment, just add/update the WINS option for the DHCP scope. Answer C might work, but it is much more labor intensive than the one-time scope update. For more information, see the section "Configuring WINS."
11. **A.** Because this is a bridged network, you need just a single server to provide WINS for each location. A bridged network has only one logical segment. This means that broadcasts will propagate across the WAN connections. Although this is not a typical configuration, it does still exist on

APPLY YOUR KNOWLEDGE

smaller legacy networks. For more information, see the section "Configuring WINS."

12. **C.** WINS is a dynamic replacement for the `LMHOSTS` file. For more information, see the section "Introduction to WINS."

13. **D.** DOS can't use WINS because it is limited to a b-node resolution. b-node is a broadcast-only resolution method, and the broadcasts can't cross the router. For more information, see the section "Configuring NetBIOS Name Resolution."

14. **B.** If you have frequently incrementing conflict statistics, you probably have a duplicate name. For more information, see the section "Managing and Monitoring WINS."

15. **D.** For this question, keep two components in mind: the trigger—which is when a certain number of entries are added and which is the least bandwidth-intensive mechanism—and the direction the information must travel. Answer D is the only one with the correct combination of these factors. For more information, see the section "Configuring WINS Replication."

16. **A.** `IPCONFIG` is the only command that can resolve problems. By running `IPCONFIG /FLUSHDNS`, you can remove all cached IP names and force the client to re-resolve the names the next time it needs it. `NetDIAG` can diagnose problems but not fix them. `NBTStat` shows the status of NetBIOS name resolution—not IP name resolution. `NSLookup` is used to inquire of DNS servers what the IP addresses that correspond to IP names are—it can't be used to resolve a problem with the local IP name cache. For more information, see the section "IPConfig."

17. **D.** `NSLookup` enables you to query individual name servers to determine the result. You would use `NSLookup` to identify the server that reported the incorrect information to the client at the other location. `IPCONFIG` might be valuable to inquire which DNS servers are being used but would not be the primary tool. `NetDIAG` would not be of assistance because this isn't a connectivity issue; it is an error in name resolution. `NBTStat` is used exclusively for querying NetBIOS names. For more information, see the section "NSLookup."

Suggested Readings and Resources

1. Boswell, William. *Inside Windows 2000 Server.* Indianapolis, IN: New Riders Publishing, 2000.

2. Heywood, Drew. *Networking with Microsoft TCP/IP, Third Edition.* Indianapolis, IN: New Riders Publishing, 1998.

3. Microsoft Corporation, *Microsoft Windows 2000 Server Resource Kit.* Redmond, WA: Microsoft Press, 2000.

PART 

Managing, Securing, and Troubleshooting Servers and Client Computers

OBJECTIVES

This chapter will help you prepare for the "Managing, Securing, and Troubleshooting Servers and Client Computers" section of the exam by giving you information necessary to make intelligent choices in the installation, upgrade, and management of client and server machines. Of the four topics in this section of the exam, two are covered in this chapter; the remaining two topics are covered in Chapter 9, "Managing, Securing, and Troubleshooting Server Computers."

The following exam objectives are covered in this chapter:

- **Install and configure server and client computer hardware.**
- **Verify hardware compatibility by using the qualifier tools.**
- **Configure driver signing options.**
- **Verify digital signatures on existing driver files.**
- **Configure operating system support for legacy hardware devices.**

▶ Installing and configuring hardware is an important and routine part of an administrator's job. More often than not, a bad hardware installation can be to blame for problems that suddenly appear in an otherwise healthy system. Understanding the significance of digitally signed drivers is key to keeping hardware running smoothly. Almost all new hardware conforms to the Plug and Play standards, and installation usually goes quite smoothly. Older hardware, though, might not have Plug and Play compatibility, and it is important to understand how to install and configure such hardware manually.

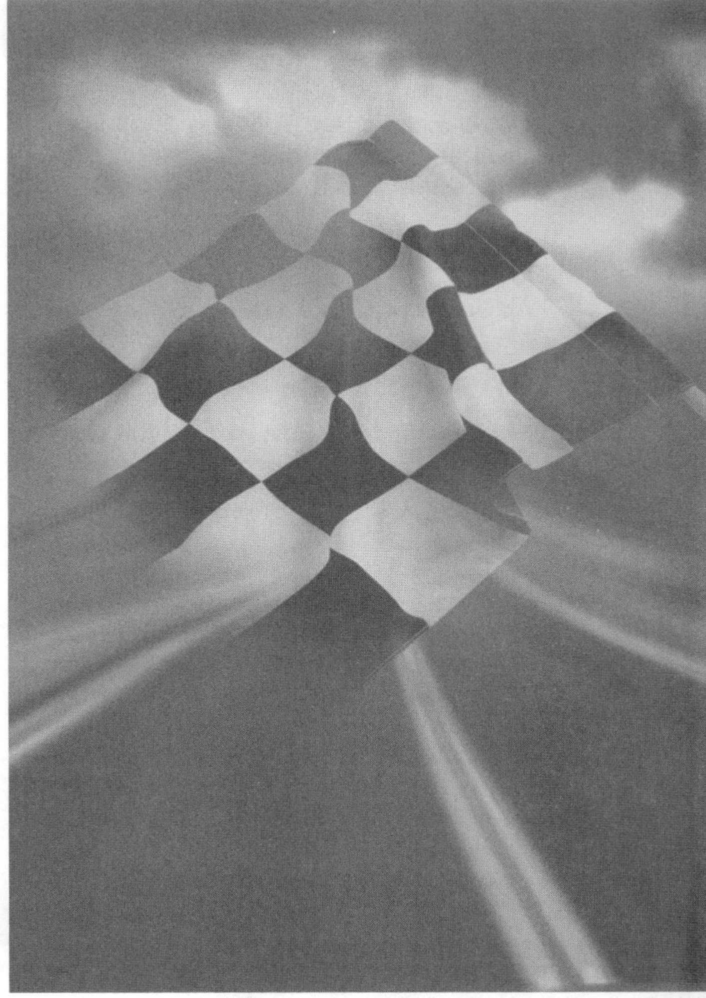

CHAPTER 8

Installing and Maintaining Clients and Servers

OBJECTIVES

- **Install and manage Windows 2000 updates. Updates include service packs, hot fixes, and security hot fixes.**
- **Update an installation source by using slip-streaming.**
- **Apply and reapply service packs and hot fixes.**
- **Verify service pack and hot fix installation.**
- **Remove service packs and hot fixes.**

▶ Software packages are constantly being updated with service packs and hot fixes to fix security flaws, update features, and streamline coding. It's a given that a fair amount of an administrator's time will be given up to researching, installing, and maintaining these service packs and hot fixes. Understanding how they are applied and removed is an important part of keeping a system's software running smoothly. Service packs under Windows 2000 have progressed a great deal from those offered under Windows NT 4.0—you can now slipstream them into existing installations and installation sources, both of which are important processes to understand and be able to perform.

OUTLINE

STUDY STRATEGIES

- Installing, configuring, and maintaining server and client computers on a network consumes much of an administrator's time, thus it makes sense to test administrators on these tasks. Installing and configuring hardware is different from installing and configuring software. With software, you have the liberty to install, format, and reinstall as often as you want. Unfortunately, hardware is not as easy. Typically, you will not deal with hardware until the time actually comes for its installation and configuration. It is for this reason that you need to understand the processes involved, so that when the time comes to install and configure a new piece of hardware, you can get the job done right the first time.
- The exam objective, however, does not end with hardware issues. After you've placed machines onto the network, you will begin the software maintenance cycle almost immediately. This cycle has four phases: preparation, deployment, maintenance, and removal. It is imperative that you, as an administrator, understand each of the phases and how hot fixes and service packs fit into the cycle.

INTRODUCTION

The ability to install and configure hardware is an important aspect of your daily duties as a system administrator. In some instances you might find that help desk or other IT department personnel will handle these installations, but in other instances they won't. Either way, you need to know what's going on and how to make your new hardware "play nice". To that end, after you have the hardware up and running, you have to maintain it and keep its software up-to-date. This chapter introduces you to the nuances of verifying, installing, and configuring hardware for your clients. Additionally, we also look at keeping your software installations up-to-date, secure, and healthy.

INSTALLING AND CONFIGURING SERVER AND CLIENT HARDWARE

▶ Install and configure server and client computer hardware.

In the "good old days," installing new hardware in a machine could actually turn out to be a major event. Plug and Play had yet to come into being, and you couldn't count on much in the way of technical support from the vendor in most cases. The Hardware Compatibility List (HCL) wasn't even a thought, and thus you oftentimes had to just hope that your hardware and software would play nice together. Sometimes you got lucky, but other times you didn't and got the pleasure of trying to figure out what went wrong and how you could fix it.

Fortunately for us, these days have all but passed. In Windows 2000, the installation and configuration of hardware devices has been simplified and improved substantially over all previous versions of Windows.

The process for installing and configuring hardware has four basic steps:

- Set driver signing restrictions.
- Select the hardware to be installed and verify its compatibility.

- Install and configure the selected hardware.
- Manage drivers over time.

Of course, there is more to this cycle than what is outlined here. You might also find it useful, and often necessary, to verify the digital signatures of existing driver files. Verifying existing drivers can help you track down problematic drivers and also aid in ensuring that drivers are digitally signed to the maximum extent practicable on your machines. The last issue you might face when working with hardware devices is providing support for legacy hardware devices that are not Plug and Play compliant. Windows 2000 makes this an easy task compared to previous versions of Windows. These items are examined in greater detail in the following sections, as are a few other things of interest in the area of hardware installation and management.

Driver Signing Restrictions

▶ Configure driver signing options.

To prevent poorly written drivers from being installed on a system, Microsoft has introduced driver signing. Driver signing, which is controlled from the System applet for standalone machines and via Group Policy for network machines, is an important piece of the pie when it comes to ensuring that your computers remain fully functional. By enforcing restrictions on the installation of unsigned drivers, you can prevent hardware conflicts and stop errors, both of which are common side effects of poorly written drivers. Poorly written drivers also tend to generate an unusually large number of CPU interrupts, thus interfering with all other operations.

Device drivers are submitted to the Windows Hardware Quality Lab (WHQL) by vendors and subsequently subjected to compatibility tests administered by the WHQL. Drivers that complete the compatibility testing process successfully are approved by Microsoft and digitally signed. Due to this rigorous compatibility testing, digitally signed drivers can be counted on to be more robust and reliable. Driver files that have been digitally signed can be found on the Windows Update Web site and also on the Windows Hardware Compatibly List. Additionally, only digitally signed drivers are found on the Windows 2000 setup CD-ROM.

> NOTE
>
> **Finding the Windows Update Web Site and the Hardware Compatibility List** The Windows Update Web site can be found at `http://windowsupdate.microsoft.com/`.
>
> The Windows Hardware Compatibility List (HCL) can be found at `http://www.microsoft.com/hcl/default.asp`.

Digitally signing a file is the process by which you can guarantee that a particular file comes from the source that it claims to. Because any file can be signed, it is necessary then to be able to handle all formats of files, including binary files. A technique called *catalog file signing* is used to provide digital signing information about files without modifying the file itself.

In catalog file signing, a CAT file is created for each driver or operating system file that is being signed. The CAT file includes a hash of the binary file. A *hash* is the result of a mathematical operation on some data (in this case, the binary file) that is sensitive to any changes made in the source data. In this way, any change to the binary file can be detected because the hash procedure produces a different value. Other information, such as filename and version number, is also added to the file. A certificate from the publisher, along with a Microsoft digital signature, is included in the catalog file to complete the signing process.

The relationship between the catalog file and the driver binary is contained in the information file (.INF) maintained by the system after the driver is installed.

The options available for configuring driver signing include the following:

- **Ignore**—Directs the system to proceed with the installation even if it includes unsigned files. You have no protection from poorly written drivers when the Ignore option is selected—as a result, it is not recommended that you configure driver signing with the Ignore option.
- **Warn**—Notifies the user that files are not digitally signed and lets the user decide whether to stop or proceed with the installation and whether to permit unsigned files to be installed. Driver signing is set to Warn by default; however, it is not recommended to keep this setting in a production environment.
- **Block**—Directs the system to refuse to install unsigned files. As a result, the installation stops, and none of the files in the driver package are installed. This is the recommended setting for a production environment, and it guarantees the highest level of protection for client machines against poorly written device drivers.

You can configure driver signing from one of two locations, depending on the configuration of your network and your preferences. Regardless of where you choose to configure driver signing from, you still have the same three choices available to choose from. The next two sections explore how the actual process of configuring driver signing is carried out.

Configuring Driver Signing via Group Policy

When dealing with a Windows 2000 Active Directory domain network, you should give consideration to setting driver signing policies via Group Policy. As with all Group Policy options, you have extremely granular control over how driver signing policies are applied in your network. For example, assume that you have the following departments in your organization:

- **Engineering**—These individuals are technically savvy and frequently need to install and configure new hardware devices. They have, however, in the past caused serious issues when installing hardware devices that shipped with poorly written device drivers. All Engineering client computers and user accounts are located in the Engineering OU.
- **Accounting**—The accountants rarely, if ever, need new hardware to be installed on their machines. In the event they need a new hardware device installed, it has been no problem in the past to send out support personnel to install and configure the hardware device properly. All Accounting client computers and user accounts are located in the Accounting OU.
- **Developers**—The development team is, coincidentally enough, responsible for all the software associated with the Civil Engineering equipment your company manufactures. They also create device drivers for this hardware. They have a need to install these device drivers on their test machines to test and troubleshoot the hardware/software combination before shipping to customers. The developers have client computers spread out in two organizational units: their standard network machines are located in the Engineering OU, whereas their testing machines are located in the Developers OU. All user accounts are located in the Developers OU.

As you can see in the examples presented here, you are faced with three very different types of clients and thus three different driver signing options you will want to configure via Group Policy for their respective OUs. In this case, you should configure driver signing as follows:

- **Configure the Warn setting for the Engineering OU**—You want the Engineers to be able to install new hardware devices as required; however, you want them to be warned before installing unsigned drivers.
- **Configure the Block setting for the Accounting OU**—The Accountants do not add new hardware very often, and thus it is safer to prevent them from being able to install any new drivers that are not signed. If they have an unsigned driver, you can address that on a case-by-case basis.
- **Configure the Ignore setting for the Developers OU**—The Developers are responsible for writing the drivers for your company's products. They have a distinct need to be able to install drivers, unsigned or not, on their computers.

> NOTE
>
> **Another Take on the Developers**
> You might decide against setting driver signing to Ignore for the Developers. Driver signing policy options are a User Group Policy item, so the key item here is the location of the user accounts. The location of the computer accounts is irrelevant in this case.

The process to configure driver signing via Group Policy is fairly simple and is outlined in Step By Step 8.1.

STEP BY STEP

8.1 Configuring Driver Signing for an Organizational Unit

1. Open the Active Directory Computers and Users snap-in by selecting Start, Programs, Administrative Tools, Active Directory Users and Computers.
2. Locate the OU for which you want to configure Group Policy and right-click it. From the context menu, select Properties. Switch to the Group Policy tab and either click New to create a new GPO or click Edit to work with an existing GPO. Because it is recommended to create GPOs for specific tasks, we will create a new GPO for this purpose by clicking New and entering the name `Driver Signing Policies`. Click Edit to open the Group Policy window, which is shown in Figure 8.1.

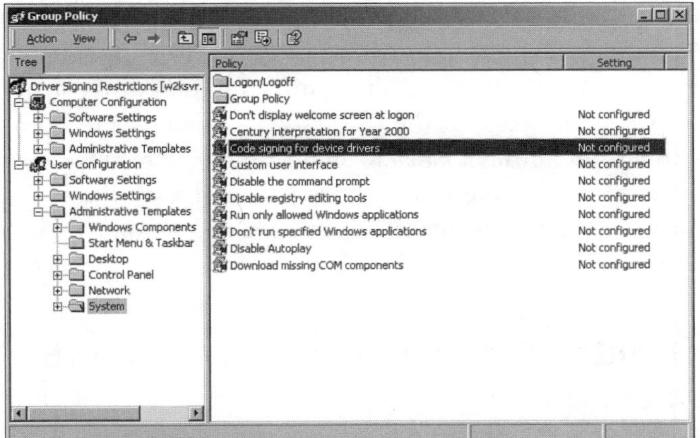

FIGURE 8.1
The Group Policy window.

3. As shown in Figure 8.1, the Group Policy option we want to work with is located in the User Configuration, Administrative Templates, System node. Double-click the Code Signing for Device Drivers option, which opens the window shown in Figure 8.2.

4. Select the Enabled radio button, and then select the appropriate behavior from the drop-down list. In this case, I have selected to Enable the Block configuration because this GPO is for the Accounting OU.

5. Close the Group Policy window by clicking OK to close out the driver signing options and then clicking the close X in the upper-right corner of the Group Policy window.

6. If you need to have the new Group Policy Object take immediate effect, you can force replication across site links from the Active Directory Sites and Services snap-in. See the Windows 2000 Server help under "To Force Replication over a Connection" for more information on forcing replication across site links. To refresh Group Policy on individual machines, the best option is to have users log off and then log back in. Alternatively, you can run the `secedit /refresh user_policy` command from the command prompt.

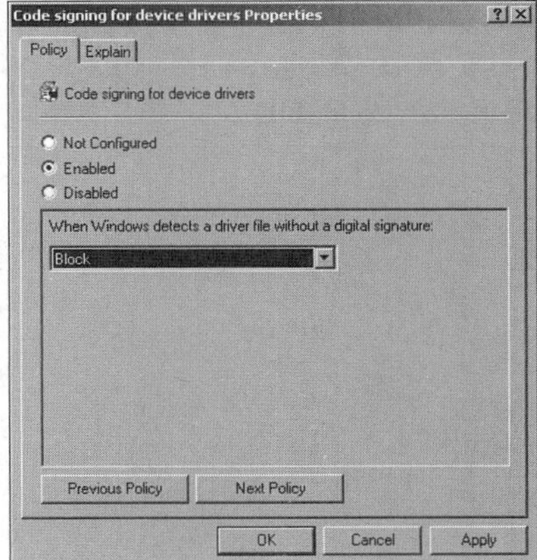

FIGURE 8.2
Configuring the driver signing options.

As soon as Group Policy has been refreshed for each user object in the Accounting OU, the users will be prevented from installing device drivers that are not digitally signed. Applying driver signing options via Group Policy is the quickest and easiest way to have them applied uniformly to a large number of users. However, if you have only a few computers to work with or need a specific computer configured in a certain manner, you can opt to configure driver signing from the Control Panel, which is discussed in the next section.

NOTE

Administrators and Driver Signing If you are logged in with local Administrative privileges, selecting Apply Settings as system default applies the configured driver signing level for all users who log on to the computer. This option is not available to users without Administrative privileges, so don't worry about your users changing the setting after the fact!

Configuring Driver Signing Locally via the Control Panel

As an alternative to Group Policy-based driver signing, you can configure it from the Control Panel locally on each machine. This is not a good approach for large networks, but it works well in small ones with few machines or peer-to-peer workgroups. The process to configure driver signing is outlined in Step By Step 8.2.

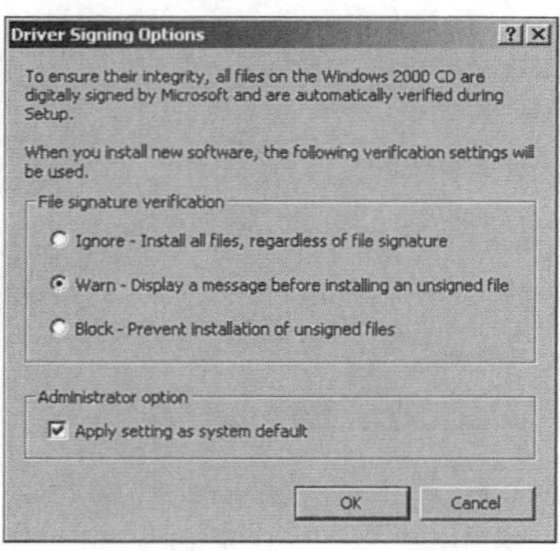

FIGURE 8.3
Configuring driver signing options from the Control Panel.

STEP BY STEP

8.2 Configuring Driver Signing for a Specific Computer.

1. Open the System applet in the Control Panel by selecting Start, Settings, Control Panel, System.
2. Switch to the Hardware tab and click Driver Signing. This opens the window shown in Figure 8.3.
3. Make your selection from the three available choices. When you are done, click OK twice to complete the process.

Thus, in three easy steps, you've configured driver signing for a specific computer.

Working with Digitally Signed Drivers

After you've set the driver signing options to your liking (and needs), you're pretty much done. Try to install an unsigned driver when you are configured for Warn, and you will get a warning dialog box similar to the one shown in Figure 8.4.

As previously mentioned, the default driver signing policy for Windows 2000 is to warn users but permit installation of unsigned drivers for the following types of hardware:

- Display
- Keyboard
- Hard-drive controllers
- Human Interface Device class devices
- Image
- Media
- Modem
- Monitor
- Mouse
- Multiport serial devices
- Net
- Printer
- SCSI adapter
- Smart Card reader

When installing drivers for any other classes, Windows 2000 ignores the installation of device drivers that are not digitally signed. This section has examined the concept of digital signatures and how you configure the driver signing options for the installation of new device drivers on your computers. You've seen how to configure driver signing quickly and easily across an entire OU (domain or site) and how to configure it on a computer-by-computer basis. The next section explores how you can ensure that your new hardware is ready for use with Windows 2000—before you install it. Later in this chapter, we will come back to driver signing when we look at working with existing drivers on your computer—not just the ones added by the installation of new hardware devices.

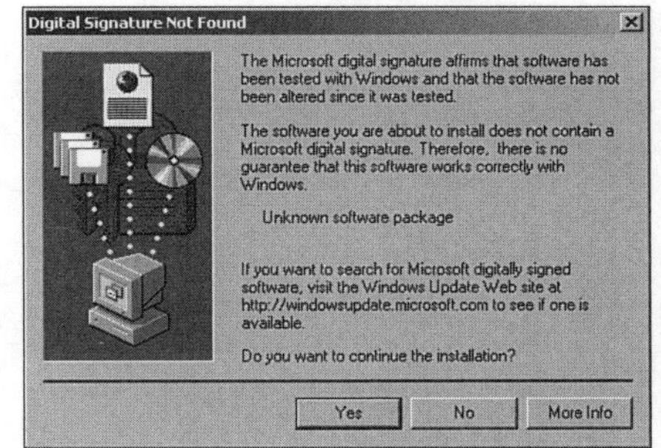

FIGURE 8.4
Warning dialog when trying to install an unsigned driver.

NOTE

Configuring Driver Signing During Unattended Setups If you are installing Windows 2000 across the network in an unattended setup, the default driver signing setting is Warn. See KB# Q236029 at `http://support.microsoft.com/default.aspx?scid=kb;EN-US;q236029` for help in changing the driver signing settings.

Verifying Hardware Compatibility

▶ Verify hardware compatibility by using the qualifier tools.

After you have your driver signing policies in place on your network, you are ready to install new hardware safely. Before you purchase new hardware (or attempt to install Windows 2000 on a new machine), you should take the time to ensure that it is compatible with Windows 2000. This can be done one of two ways:

- Check the Hardware Compatibility List (HCL). This is the preferred method because the HCL changes weekly and is updated as Microsoft certifies additional hardware items for use with Windows 2000.
- Run the Windows 2000 Readiness Analyzer.

The next two sections look at each of these methods in greater detail.

The Hardware Compatibility List

The Hardware Compatibility List (HCL) is Microsoft's published list of hardware components that have been fully tested with Windows 2000. Items that are listed in the HCL are guaranteed to function (at least at a bare minimum) with Windows 2000. If you want to ensure that all your hardware will function properly under Windows 2000, you should consult the current version of the HCL, which can be found on the Internet at `http://www.microsoft.com/hcl/`.

Note that although many products will be on the HCL (which means they have been tested and found to function with Windows 2000), not everything is. If the manufacturer has a driver available for the device that has been created for Windows 2000, the device should function. However, any problems with the driver should be addressed to the manufacturer, not Microsoft.

Once on the HCL Web site, finding your hardware is a fairly simple process. Figure 8.5 shows a query run to find Fast Ethernet cards on the HCL.

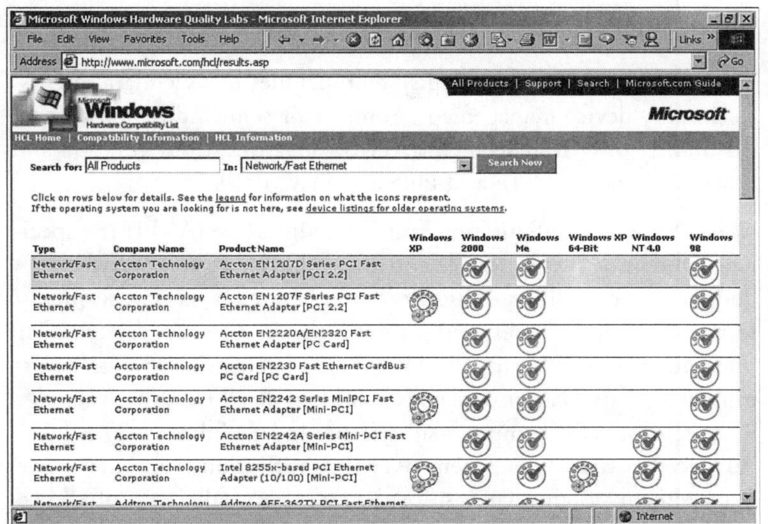

FIGURE 8.5
Using the Hardware Compatibility List to find Fast Ethernet cards.

NOTE

Windows 2000 Datacenter Server and the HCL The HCL for Windows 2000 Datacenter Server is located in a different location from the rest of the HCL. It can be found at `http://www.microsoft.com/windows2000/datacenter/hcl/`.

Windows 2000 Readiness Analyzer

The second method you have available to check the compatibility of hardware is using the Windows 2000 Readiness Analyzer, although this is usually done for new installations of the operating system. To run the Readiness Analyzer, follow Step By Step 8.3.

STEP BY STEP

8.3 Using the Windows 2000 Readiness Analyzer

1. Open a command prompt by typing **`cmd`** in the Run box (Start, Run), and then click OK.
2. From the command prompt, run the Readiness Analyzer by typing **`X:\i386\winnt32 /checkupgradeonly`** and pressing Enter, where *`X`* is the location of the Windows 2000 setup files.
3. The output window, as shown in Figure 8.6, is displayed when the Readiness Analyzer has finished. In this case, no incompatible hardware was found.
4. Should you need to, you can save the results of the Readiness Analyzer to a text file. Click Finish when you are done to close the Readiness Analyzer window.

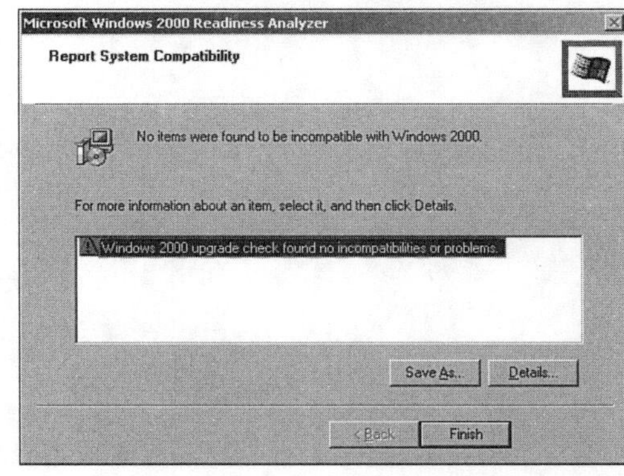

FIGURE 8.6
The Windows 2000 Readiness Analyzer.

NOTE

The Upgrade Report During Installation During the installation of Windows 2000, an Upgrade report might be presented to you. This report provides information about hardware and other items that are incompatible with Windows 2000. More information can be found in KB# Q228213 at `http://support.microsoft.com/default.aspx?scid=kb;EN-US;q228213`.

The Hardware Installation Process

The Windows 2000 operating system includes many enhancements to simplify device management. Some of these include support for Advanced Power Management (APM), Advanced Configuration and Power Interface (ACPI), and Plug and Play (PnP).

The Advanced Configuration and Power Interface (ACPI) is a specification that defines a flexible and extensible hardware. Software designers can use this specification to integrate power management features into applications and, in this case, the operating system. The integration of ACPI into Windows 2000 enables Windows to determine which applications are active and handle all the power management resources for computer subsystems and peripherals. The Advanced Power Management (APM) specification is an older power management system that has, for the most part, fallen out of popular use in newer hardware devices because ACPI offers many enhancements and improvements to the older APM standard.

Plug and Play is a combination of hardware and software that enables a computer to recognize and modify its hardware configuration changes with minimal intervention from the user. The hardware device you are installing must support the Plug and Play initiative to be automatically configured correctly. You will find that some older devices that predate Plug and Play are not recognized.

With Plug and Play, a user can add or remove a device dynamically without manual reconfiguration and without any intricate knowledge of the computer hardware. For example, you can have a laptop in a docking station that contains an Ethernet network connection and later use the same laptop connecting to the network using a built-in modem, without making any configuration changes.

With Plug and Play, you can make changes to a Windows 2000 computer's configuration with the assurance that all devices will work and the computer will reboot correctly after the changes are made.

When you install a Plug and Play device, Windows 2000 automatically configures the device to enable it to function properly with the other devices already installed on your computer. Windows 2000 assigns system resources to the device, including the following:

- Interrupt request (IRQ) number
- Direct memory access (DMA) channel

- Input/Output port address
- Memory address range

Each resource setting must be unique (that is, not applied to another device); otherwise, the device will not function properly.

When the device you are installing is not Plug and Play compatible, Windows 2000 has no way of automatically configuring the device settings. You might have to manually configure the device driver or use the manufacturer's provided installation program.

You can configure devices using the Add/Remove Hardware applet in the Control Panel or by using the Device Manager, which is located in the Computer Management icon within the Administrative Tools folder in the Control Panel.

With most Plug and Play hardware, you simply connect the device to the computer and Windows 2000 automatically configures the new settings. Plug and Play can be supported by devices and the drivers that control them. The possible combinations expand to four different support scenarios:

- Full Plug and Play support is provided when the hardware and the device driver fully support Plug and Play.
- If the hardware supports Plug and Play, but the device driver does not, Windows 2000 will not support Plug and Play and the device will be treated as a legacy NT 4.0 device.
- If the device driver supports Plug and Play, but the hardware does not, Windows 2000 can provide partial Plug and Play support. In this case, Windows 2000 will not be capable of automatically configuring the device drivers, but Plug and Play will be capable of managing resource allocations and interfacing to the power management systems.
- Windows 2000 will not provide support for Plug and Play if neither the device driver nor the hardware supports Plug and Play.

For hardware that can't be automatically identified, the Add/Remove Hardware applet provides a method of manually configuring the device resources. Occasionally, you might need to initiate automatic installation even for some Plug and Play hardware.

WARNING

Manually Adjusting Resources If you must manually configure a non-Plug and Play device, the resources assigned become fixed. This reduces the flexibility that Windows 2000 has for allocating resources to other devices. If too many resources are manually configured, Windows 2000 might not be capable of installing new Plug and Play devices.

Resource settings should be changed only if you are certain that the new settings do not conflict with any other hardware, or if the hardware manufacturer has supplied a specific set of resources settings with the device.

Using the Add/Remove Hardware Wizard

The Add/Remove Hardware Wizard started from the Control Panel is used to initiate automatic hardware installation of both Plug and Play and non-Plug and Play hardware devices. Step By Step 8.4 initiates a search for new Plug and Play hardware or, in its absence, presents you with a screen to add a new device or troubleshoot an existing device.

STEP BY STEP

8.4 Searching for New Plug and Play Hardware

1. Select Start, Settings, Control Panel.
2. Double-click the Add/Remove Hardware icon to start the wizard.
3. Click Next to close the Welcome page.
4. Select Add/Troubleshoot a Device and click Next to start the wizard.

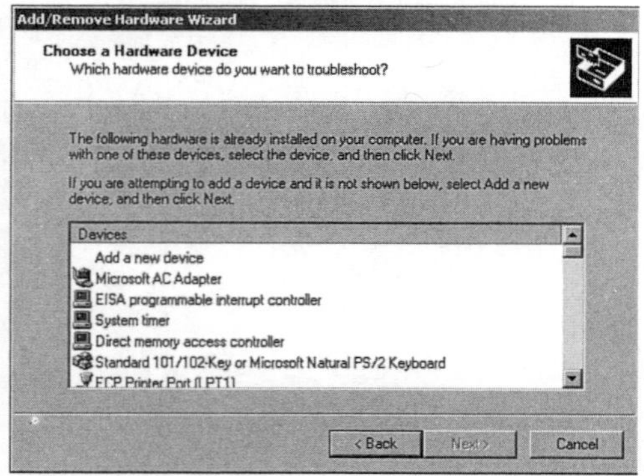

FIGURE 8.7
Installing or troubleshooting hardware.

Windows 2000 searches for any new Plug and Play hardware and installs any it finds. In the event that the wizard can't detect any new hardware, it displays a list of installed hardware from which you can choose a device for troubleshooting (see Figure 8.7). The first entry on the hardware list is Add a New Device to provide the option of installing a new device.

Confirming Hardware Installation

After you have installed new hardware, you should confirm that the device is installed and functioning properly. Use the Device Manager to do this.

To start the Device Manager, double-click the System icon in the Control Panel. Select the Hardware tab and click the Device Manager button. This displays a list of installed hardware, as shown in Figure 8.8.

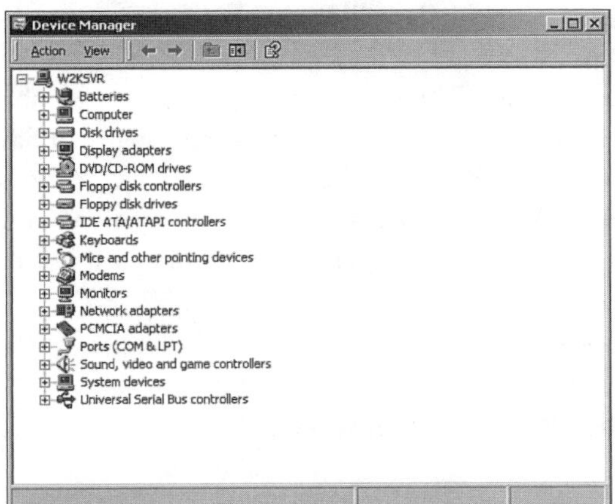

FIGURE 8.8
Installed devices listed by the Device Manager.

Expanding a device type displays all the specific devices of that type installed on the computer. The device icon indicates whether the device is functioning properly. You can use the information in Table 8.1 to determine the device's status.

> **NOTE**
>
> **Finding the Device Manager** You can access the Device Manager from a number of directions. It can be started using the Device Manager button from the Hardware tab in the System applet from the Control Panel. It can also be started from the Computer Management icon within the Administrative Tools folder in the Control Panel. Finally, it is available as a snap-in to the Microsoft Management Console.

TABLE 8.1

DEVICE MANAGER HARDWARE STATUS

Device Icon	*Device Status*
Normal icon	The device is functioning normally.
Normal icon with a red X	The device has been disabled.
Normal icon with a yellow exclamation point	Windows 2000 has disabled the hardware due to resource conflicts. To correct this, right-click the device icon, click Properties, and set the resources manually according to what is available in the system.
Yellow question mark with a red X	The device is not configured correctly, or the device drivers are missing.

Configuring Operating System Support for Legacy Hardware Devices

- Configure operating system support for legacy hardware devices.

When you are manually installing and configuring non-Plug and Play hardware, you need to understand the resources the hardware device expects to use. The manufacturer's product documentation will list the resources the device requires, and you will have to determine how to fit it into your existing system. Table 8.2 describes the resources available in a Windows 2000 computer system that hardware devices use to communicate with the operating system.

TABLE 8.2

HARDWARE DEVICE RESOURCES

Resources	*Description*
Interrupts	Hardware devices use interrupts to indicate to the processor that they need attention. The processor uses this IRQ as a way of determining which device is looking for service and what type of attention it needs. Windows 2000 provides interrupts numbered 0–15 to devices (IRQ 1 is always assigned to the keyboard).
Input/Output port	I/O ports are areas of memory the device uses to communicate with Windows 2000. When the processor sees an IRQ request, it checks the I/O port address to retrieve additional information about what the device wants.
Direct Memory Access	DMAs are channels that allow the hardware device to access memory directly. This allows a device such as a disk drive or floppy drive to write information into memory without interrupting the processor. Windows 2000 provides DMA channels 0–7.
Memory	Many hardware devices have onboard memory or can reserve system memory for their use. Any reserved memory is not available for any other device or for Windows 2000.

IN THE FIELD

SHARABLE RESOURCES

Some of the resources used by device drives are reserved for specific devices, and some can be shared between devices.

The Interrupt Request uses a Programmable Interrupt Controller (PIC) to request service for the device. When a request is seen, the current operation is suspended and control is given to the device drive associated with the IRQ number (1–15). This resource therefore can't be shared between devices.

The I/O port is a memory block used by the device to communicate the service it is requesting. This is tied to the IRQ number and therefore is dedicated to a device.

The DMA is a direct channel between the device and the computer's memory. The DMA controller supports a number of channels (usually seven), and they are shared between devices (one at a time).

A device memory block is a portion of system memory mapped to the internal memory of the device (usually). This is dedicated to the device and can't be used by any other process (including Windows 2000).

Now that you have an understanding of which system resources are available to work with, you can begin the process of installing non-Plug and Play devices. Before you actually configure resources, you must determine which resources you have available to work with. We will look at this process next.

Determining Available Resources

After you determine which resources your device requires, you can use Device Manager to display the resources available on your computer. To view the available resources list, double-click the System icon in the Control Panel and select the Hardware tab. Click the Device Manager button, and select the Resources by Connection entry in the View menu. Figure 8.9 shows the Device Manager view of resources and their availability.

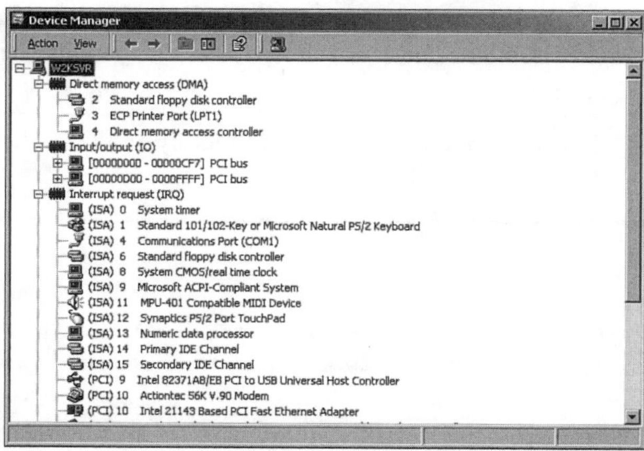

FIGURE 8.9
Hardware resources listed by connection.

The last step in the process of manually installing a non-Plug and Play device is to assign the resource settings. In some cases, you might need to change existing resource assignment settings. The next section explains this process.

Changing Resource Assignments

You might encounter two devices that request the same resources, resulting in a conflict. To change a resource setting, use the Resources tab in the device's Properties information. Step By Step 8.5 will allow you to modify a resource setting.

STEP BY STEP

8.5 Modifying a Device's Resource Configuration

1. Select Start, Settings, Control Panel.
2. Double-click the System icon and select the Hardware tab.
3. Click the Device Manager button.
4. Expand the device type you want to change.
5. Right-click the specific device you want to modify.
6. Click Properties and select the Resources tab. If the Resources tab is not present, you will not be able to modify the devices resources.
7. Select the resource setting you will be modifying.
8. Clear the Automatic Settings box if it is checked. If this box is grayed out, you will not be able to modify the device's resources.
9. Select the resource you want to modify and click the Change Setting button.

NOTE

Changing Resources for Non-Plug and Play Devices Changing the resources assigned to a non-Plug and Play device does not actually change the resources the device uses. This only instructs Windows 2000 what the device configuration is. You must consult the manufacturer's documentation on which jumpers or software switches to set on the device to conform to the resource assignment you have told Windows 2000 to expect.

At this point, you are presented with a screen that enables you to edit the value of the resource you have selected. Saving that new value changes what Windows 2000 thinks the device will be using.

Verifying Digital Signatures on Existing Drivers

▸ Verify digital signatures on existing driver files.

Even though you've taken great pains to ensure that only digitally signed drivers are being used on your network machines, you will most likely never be able to get all of them digitally signed. The real problem lies in figuring out which are digitally signed and which ones are not. Fortunately, Microsoft has provided three tools to help you identify and manage unsigned drivers on your machines. The tools available include

- File Signature Verification
- System File Checker
- Driver Verifier Manager

Each of these is discussed in the following sections.

File Signature Verification

When installing new software or device drivers on a machine, the possibility exists for system files to be overwritten by unsigned or incompatible versions of the same file. This can result in many problems, but it is usually evidenced by system instability or sluggish performance. Using File Signature Verification, you can identify unsigned files on your computer and view the following information about them:

- The file's name
- The file's location
- The file's modification date
- The file type
- The file's version number

The process to use the File Signature Verification utility to identify and manage unsigned drivers is outlined in Step By Step 8.6.

NOTE

Advanced File Signature Verification Options File Signature Verification is not just used for verifying driver files. It can search out and identify all unsigned system files, depending on the settings you configure from the Advanced tab.

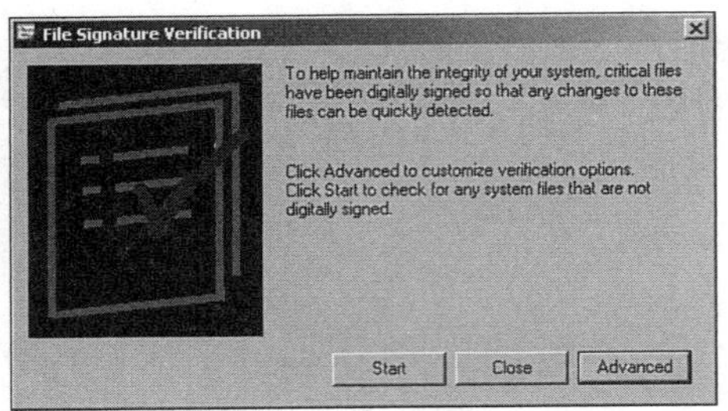

FIGURE 8.10
File Signature Verification.

Signature Verification Results

The following files have not been digitally signed:

Name	In Folder	Modified	File Type	Version
ntdetect.com	c:\	8/23/2001	MS-DOS A...	None
ntldr	c:\	8/23/2001	System file	None
syntpenh.exe	e:\program files\sy...	8/2/2001	Application	5.7.1.0
syntplpr.exe	e:\program files\sy...	8/2/2001	Application	5.7.1.0
oem3.inf	e:\winnt\inf	8/2/2000	Setup Info...	None
syntpapi.dll	e:\winnt\system32	8/2/2001	Application...	5.7.1.0
syntpfcs.dll	e:\winnt\system32	8/2/2001	Application...	5.7.1.0
es198x.sys	e:\winnt\system32...	8/2/2000	System file	5.12.1.1092

Close

Files found: 714. Signed files: 690. Unsigned files: 8. Files not scanned: 16.

FIGURE 8.11
File Signature Verification results.

STEP BY STEP

8.6 Using File Signature Verification

1. Open a command prompt by typing **`cmd`** in the Run box (or select Start, Run); then, click OK.
2. From the command prompt, run File Signature Verification by typing **`sigverif`** and pressing Enter.
3. The File Signature Verification window, as shown in Figure 8.10, is displayed. By clicking Advanced, you can change the scope of the verification (system files only or all specified files, the location to scan, and the name and location of the output text file).
4. When you are ready to begin scanning, click Start.
5. File Signature Verification will run for some time, depending on the scope of the scan. Upon its completion, you receive feedback, as shown in Figure 8.11.
6. Click Close two times to close out File Signature Verification.

File Signature Verification can also be run from the command prompt:

```
verifier [ /flags FLAGS [ /iolevel IOLEVEL ] /driver NAME
➥[NAME ...] /volatile /all /reset /query /log
➥LOG_FILE_NAME [/interval] ]
```

Table 8.3 explains the use of each switch for the `verifier` command.

TABLE 8.3

FILE SIGNATURE VERIFICATION COMMAND-LINE SWITCHES

Switch	*Function*
`/volatile /flags FLAGS`	Changes verifier flags immediately and dynamically without rebooting
`/all`	Verifies all the drivers in the system
`/reset`	Erases all current Driver Verifier settings

Switch	*Function*
/query	Dumps the current Driver Verifier status and counters to the standard output
/log LOG_FILE_NAME [/interval SECONDS]	Logs the Driver Verifier status and counters to a log file (where SECONDS is the period of time you specify)

The FLAGS and IOLEVEL values that are used with the verifier command are explained in Table 8.4.

TABLE 8.4

FLAGS AND IOLEVEL VALUES FOR FILE SIGNATURE VERIFICATION

Value	*Function*
FLAGS bit 0	Special pool checking
FLAGS bit 1	Forces IRQL checking
FLAGS bit 2	Low resources simulation
FLAGS bit 3	Pool tracking
FLAGS bit 4	I/O verification
FLAGS bit 5	Deadlock detection
FLAGS bit 6	Enhanced I/O verification
FLAGS bit 7	DMA verification
IOLEVEL 1	I/O verification level 1
IOLEVEL 2	I/O verification level 2 (more strict than level 1)

NOTE

File Signature Verification Advanced Options FLAGS is a decimal combination of bits.

The default I/O verification level is 1. The value is ignored if the I/O verification bit is not set in FLAGS.

The /volatile option can be used to change the Driver Verifier settings dynamically without restarting the system. Any new settings are lost when the system is rebooted.

NOTE

Help on the Web For more information on using File Signature Verification, see KB# Q244617, located at http://support.microsoft.com/default.aspx?scid=kb;en-us;Q244617.

System File Checker

The System File Checker is a command-line utility that scans and verifies the versions of all protected system files. If System File Checker discovers that a protected file has been overwritten or deleted, it replaces the file with the correct (digitally signed) version from the cache. The default location of the cache is %systemroot%\system32\dllcache\.

NOTE

Locating the `dllcache` The `dllcache` is a hidden, system folder that is invisible by default. You can enable the display of the `dllcache` folder from Windows Explorer by selecting Tools, Folder Options. Switch to the View tab, select the Show Hidden Files and Folders radio button, and remove the check from the Hide Protected Operating System Files (Recommended) check box to enable the display of the `dllcache` folder.

`%systemroot%` is a system variable that denotes the location of the Windows 2000 installation.

The command to start the System File Checker program is as follows:

```
sfc [/scannow] [/scanonce] [/scanboot] [/cancel] [/quiet]
➥[/enable] [/purgecache] [/cachesize=x]
```

System File Checker switches are outlined in Table 8.5.

TABLE 8.5

SYSTEM FILE CHECKER COMMAND-LINE SWITCHES

Switch	*Function*
`/scannow`	Scans all protected files immediately
`/scanonce`	Scans all protected system files once at the `next boot`
`/scanboot`	Scans all protected system files every time the computer is rebooted
`/cancel`	Cancels all pending scans
`/quiet`	Replaces all altered system files without prompting the user
`/enable`	Turns prompting back on
`/purgecache`	Purges the file cache and rescans all protected files immediately
`/cachesize=x`	Sets the cache size (in MB)

NOTE

Additional Information on the Web More detailed information on working with the System File Checker can be found in the Microsoft Knowledge Base in articles KB# Q222473 (`http://support.microsoft.com/default.aspx?scid=kb;en-us;Q222473`) and KB# Q222193 (`http://support.microsoft.com/default.aspx?scid=kb;EN-US;q222193`).

Before we move on, there are an additional few points of interest regarding the System File Checker:

- You must have administrative privileges to run the System File Checker.
- If, for some reason, the `dllcache` folder becomes corrupt or unusable, the `scannow`, `scanonce`, or `scanboot` option repairs the contents of the `dllcache` directory.
- The `dllcache` folder is a hidden folder that only the System and Administrator accounts have access to by default.

Driver Verifier Manager

The Driver Verifier Manager has been included in Windows 2000 by Microsoft in the interests of promoting stability and reliability.

The tool can be used to troubleshoot driver issues that might be causing system corruption or system failures. Although not a means to verify digital signatures of drivers, the Driver Verifier Manager is an important tool that can be used to determine whether a driver is causing system problems.

The Driver Verifier Manager is disabled by default, but it can be enabled one of two ways:

- By manually editing the Registry
- By running `VERIFIER` from the command line

To enable driver verification via the Registry, navigate to the `HKLM\SYSTEM\CurrentControlSet\Control\Session Manager\Memory Management` key and change the values of the `VerifyDriverLevel` and `VerifyDrivers` keys, as shown in Figure 8.12.

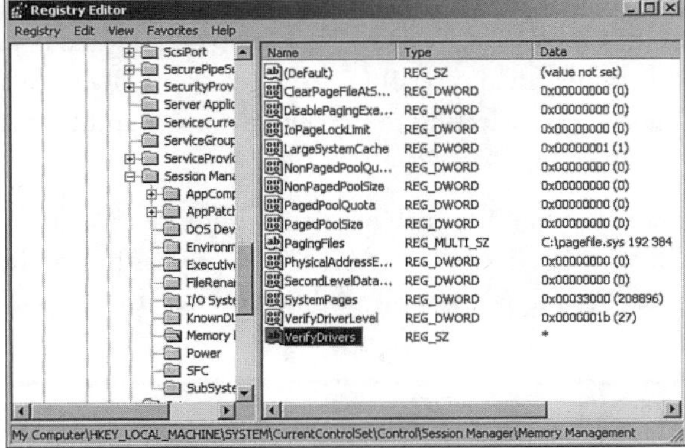

FIGURE 8.12
Enabling driver verification from the Registry.

In the `VerifyDrivers REG_SZ` key, you enter the drivers to scan, such as `ntfs.sys`, `ftdisk.sys`, or `*.sys`. In the `VerifyDriverLevel` key, you specify the level of driver verification to be performed, as provided in Table 8.6.

TABLE 8.6

BIT-FIELD VALUES FOR THE VerifyDriverLevel KEY

Value	*Function*
0x01	Attempts to satisfy all allocations from a special pool.
0x02	Applies memory pressure to this driver to validate IRQL usage in regards to accessing pageable code and data.
0x04	Randomly fails various pool allocation requests. This action is performed only after the system has started and reached a point where the problem can be treated as reasonable situations that must be handled.
0x08	Enables pool allocation tracking. Every allocation must be freed before the driver unloads or the system performs a bug check.
0x10	Enables the I/O verifier.

A default value of 3 is used if the key does not exist or if a level of driver verification has not been explicitly specified. If the Preferred settings are used (from the GUI-based Driver Verifier Manager), the value is 0x1B. Employing a value of 0xB for tracking memory leaks is useful. This value can also be obtained from the GUI-based Driver Verifier Manager by selecting the Preferred setting and then deselecting I/O Verification.

WARNING

Use Caution When Manually Editing the Registry Manually editing the Registry can cause serious problems that might require the reinstallation of the operating system to that machine. Always edit the Registry one key at a time and only after verifying what you are changing.

The preferred method for enabling and using Driver Verifier Manager is via the GUI-based version. The process to use the GUI-based Driver Verifier Manager is outlined in Step By Step 8.7.

STEP BY STEP

8.7 Using Driver Verifier Manager

1. Open a command prompt by typing **cmd** in the Run box (or selecting Start, Run), and then click OK.
2. From the command prompt, run Driver Verifier Manager by typing **verifier** and pressing Enter.
3. The Driver Verifier Manager window, as shown in Figure 8.13, is displayed.

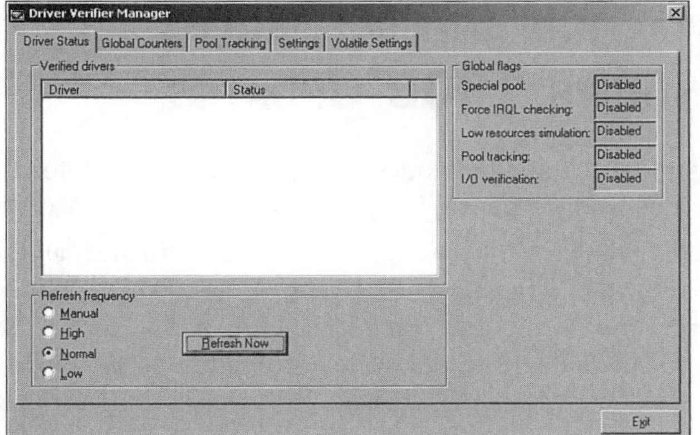

FIGURE 8.13
Driver Verifier Manager.

4. Switch to the Settings tab and make your selections as shown in Figure 8.14.

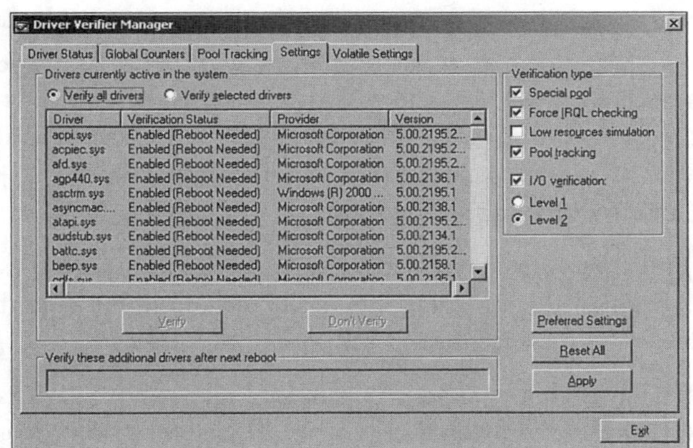

FIGURE 8.14
Configuring the Driver Verifier Manager.

5. After making your selections and exiting the Driver Verifier Manager, you will need to reboot that machine for driver verification to begin.

6. After the machine has restarted, launch Driver Verifier Manager again, and you can check the status of all the selected drivers.

INSTALLING AND MANAGING WINDOWS 2000 UPDATES

▶ Install and manage Windows 2000 updates. Updates include service packs, hot fixes, and security hot fixes.

Even after you have Windows 2000 installed, configured, and tweaked to your liking across your network, your work is not done. In fact, your work has only just begun. Without fail, you can count on an update to be issued that will have an effect on some portion of Windows 2000, whether it's IIS vulnerabilities or issues with Internet Explorer. Your job as the administrator is to keep on top of all these service packs and hot fixes, evaluating their pertinence to your network and then implementing them.

A service pack is an executable that provides for the replacement of one set of files with another. In the case of an operating system (such as NT 4.0), service packs have been a way to distribute bug fixes and fixes to security holes. However, beginning with NT 4.0's Service Pack 4, Microsoft has begun to release upgrades and additions to operating system functionality. For example, Service Pack 4 introduced the Microsoft Management Console for the purposes of providing an integrated security interface.

NOTE

Locating the Updates Although not directly covered on the exam, locating the updates you need is critical to your everyday operations.

Your starting place for hot fix information should be the Microsoft TechNet Security home page, which is located at `http://www.microsoft.com/technet/treeview/default.asp?url=/technet/security/Default.asp`.

Service pack information and status can be found at `http://support.microsoft.com/default.aspx?scid=FH;EN-US;sp&FR=0&SD=GN&LN=EN-US&`.

A *hot fix* is a very small executable that addresses one specific issue. *Service packs*, on the other hand, typically include all hot fixes that have been released since the last full service pack release.

With Windows 2000, Microsoft's plan is to release service packs on a regular schedule to fix bugs or security flaws. This plan is designed to keep the size of service packs at a manageable level.

In many regards, Windows 2000 service packs are not very different from Windows NT 4.0 service packs. When they are released, the intent is for you to install the service pack on all your Windows 2000 computers to implement fixes. However, one significant improvement has been made in the application of services packs—the concept of *slipstreaming*. Slipstreaming is discussed in more detail in the following section.

Updating an Installation Source by Using Slipstreaming

▶ Update an installation source by using slipstreaming.

Before you can understand slipstreaming, a digression into service packs on NT 4.0 is necessary. Under NT, if you install a service pack, you must ensure that if you make modifications to the operating system that involve reading files from the CD or a network share, that you subsequently reinstall the service pack. This is because the files found on the CD or in the network share are pre-service pack versions and reapplication is necessary to ensure that all components of the operating system are up to the current service pack.

Slipstreaming makes this unnecessary. With slipstreaming, changes from the service pack can be applied to the source files found on a local folder or network share (by using the `-s` switch when running `update.exe` for the service pack). This means that when you subsequently access those files, you will obtain the fixed (updated) versions of those files—not the old ones. This saves time because it means that the service packs must be applied to any machine only once and not multiple times as services (and other operating system components) are installed. In addition, this also means that new installations over the network will also automatically be up-to-date with the current service pack.

It must be noted that slipstreaming does not remove the need to install the service pack on each machine. What it does remove is the need to install the service pack on fresh Windows 2000 installations and the need to install the service pack after making operating system changes.

In the standard service pack installation, two major things happen. First, the files that are going to be replaced are copied into a backup directory so that the installation can be reversed if necessary. Although this is an optional process prompted for by the service pack installation routine, it is always recommended that you use it. Second, the service pack replaces the operating system files it finds installed on the target system with the new versions of those files.

The process to slipstream a service pack into an installation source is fairly simple and is outlined in Step By Step 8.8. The procedure assumes that you do not currently have a network installation source, and thus it will be created as part of the process.

STEP BY STEP

8.8 Slipstreaming a Service Pack

1. On a network share, create a new folder (such as `W2KSvrImage`) to hold the contents of the Windows 2000 CD-ROM. Copy the entire contents of the Windows 2000 CD-ROM to this folder.
2. On a network share, create a new folder (such as `W2Ksp2`) to hold the contents of the service pack you are slipstreaming. Extract the service pack into this folder by executing the following command at the command prompt: *`SERVICE_PACK_NAME`* `-x`, where `SERVICE_PACK_NAME` is replaced by the actual service pack file name.
3. After the service pack verifies all files, you will be asked to choose a location to extract them to, as shown in Figure 8.15. Choose the service pack folder you created earlier.
4. When the extraction is complete, click OK to close the extraction window.
5. The last step is to actually apply the service pack to the installation files (ala slipstream style). Assuming that both of your folders are located on the `D:\` volume, a sample command entered in the Run box would look like this: `D:\W2Ksp2\I386\UPDATE\UPDATE.EXE -s:D:\W2KSvrImage\`. After entering the command, a window opens and informs you of the slipstream status (see Figure 8.16).
6. When the integration is complete, click OK to close the integration window and complete the slipstream process.

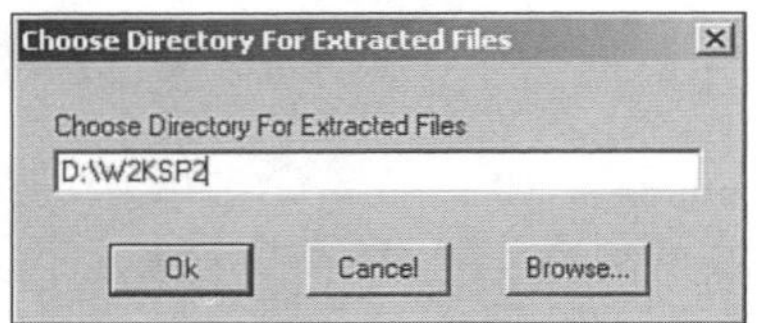

FIGURE 8.15
Choosing the location to extract service pack files to.

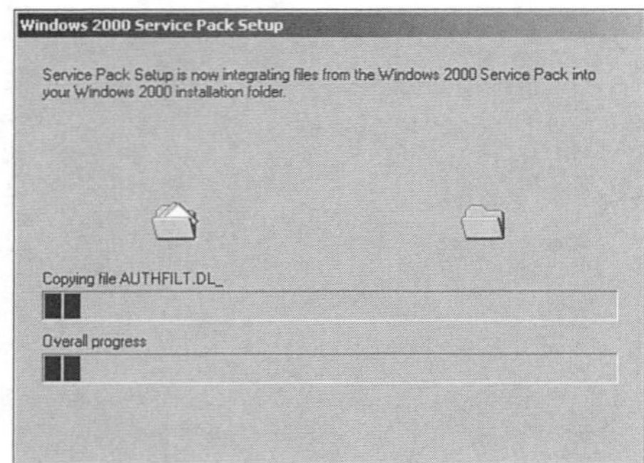

FIGURE 8.16
Slipstreaming service pack files into the installation source.

You can now use this slipstreamed installation source to install Windows 2000 on new installations. The application of service packs and hot fixes to existing installations is addressed in the following sections.

Applying Service Packs and Hot Fixes

▶ Apply and reapply service packs and hot fixes.

If you need to apply a service pack to an existing operating system, you can easily do so because the service pack is an executable file. You can simply double-click the file to run the service pack installer or, if you want, execute the service pack installer from the command line and modify its behavior by using optional switches.

Installing service packs to individual computers is a simple task that is outlined in Step By Step 8.9.

STEP BY STEP

8.9 Installing a Service Pack to Individual Computers

1. Install the service pack by running the `update.exe` file (found in the `i386\update\` folder of the extracted service pack) or by simply double-clicking the service pack executable.
2. Back up the existing files by selecting that option in the service pack installation setup program.
3. Reboot your computer to allow the changes to take effect.

The `update.exe` command includes switches that can be used to modify its behavior. These switches are explained in Table 8.7.

TABLE 8.7

`Update.exe` COMMAND-LINE SWITCHES

Switch	*Description*
`-u`	Runs the update in unattended mode
`-f`	Forces other applications to close upon computer shutdown
`-n`	Does not back up files for later service pack uninstallation
`-o`	Overwrites OEM files without prompting

continues

TABLE 8.7 *continued*

Update.exe Command-Line Switches

Switch	*Description*
`-z`	Does not reboot the computer when the service pack installation has completed
`-q`	Runs the installation in quiet mode, with no user interaction
`-s:[directory]`	Integrates the service pack files into the directory supplied

Alternatively, you can create a new Group Policy Object and use it to assign the `update.msi` file to all Windows 2000 computers within your organization. The installation and management of software via Group Policy is discussed in Chapter 11, "Fundamentals of Group Policy."

Installing hot fixes one at a time is done in much the same way as installing service packs. No command-line switches exist that you can use to modify the installation behavior of hot fixes, although several hot fixes can be "chained" together. The procedure to install a single hot fix is outlined in Step By Step 8.10.

FIGURE 8.17
Installing a single hot fix.

STEP BY STEP

8.10 Installing a Single Hot Fix

1. Double-click the downloaded hot fix. After the hot fix extracts its files, you see a progress box (see Figure 8.17).
2. Click OK after the hot fix has completed installing (see Figure 8.18). You might be required to restart the computer after the hot fix has installed.

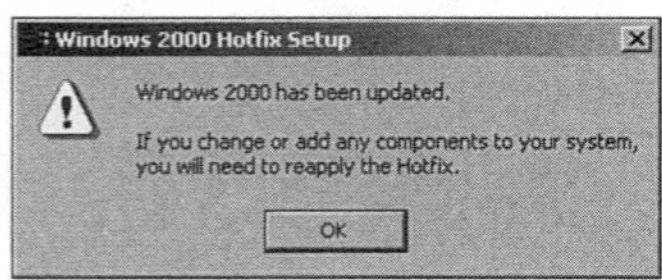

FIGURE 8.18
The hot fix installation is complete.

If you have several hot fixes you need to deploy, you can automate the process and improve reliability by chaining them together by using the `Qchain.exe` utility.

IN THE FIELD

SAFETY CHAINS

When you install hot fixes, if a file is locked or in use and can't be replaced, it is placed in the Pending File Rename queue to be replaced after the restarts. If installing more than one hot fix, you could experience a problem in this scenario: You install two hot fixes on a machine—Hot Fix 1 and Hot Fix 2—without restarting the computer between installations. Coincidentally, both hot fixes contain the same file: `QWERTY.exe`. The problem lies in the fact that Hot Fix 1 upgrades the `QWERTY.exe` file to version 3, whereas Hot Fix 2 comes with version 2 of the `QWERTY.exe` file. The current version on the machine is version 1. When each of the hot fixes is installed, they place their respective versions of `QWERTY.exe` in the Pending File Rename queue. When the computer is finally restarted (after installing both hot fixes), the hot fixes are applied in the order they were installed. The net result: version 2 of the `QWERTY.exe` file will be installed instead of the more up-to-date (and most likely required) version 3 of the file.

Using `Qchain.exe` can, in most cases, prevent this problem from occurring in your network. `Qchain` is the only safe way to install multiple hot fixes on a machine without a reboot between each installation. The bottom line is that machine up time increases because of fewer required restarts.

NOTE **Playing It Safe** Even though most hot fixes do not require you to restart the machine after installation is complete, it's always a good idea to restart the computer anyway.

NOTE **Getting Additional Information on Qchain** Because it might be on the test, you should obtain more information on using the `Qchain.exe` utility. To do so, see KB# Q296861 at `http://support.microsoft.com/default.aspx?scid=kb;EN-US;q296861`.

Verifying Service Pack and Hot Fix Installation

▶ Verify service pack and hot fix installation.

To quickly verify the service pack version on a machine, you can look at the General tab of the System applet of the Control Panel. Under the System section, you will see the operating system version, build, and service pack level, as shown in Figure 8.19.

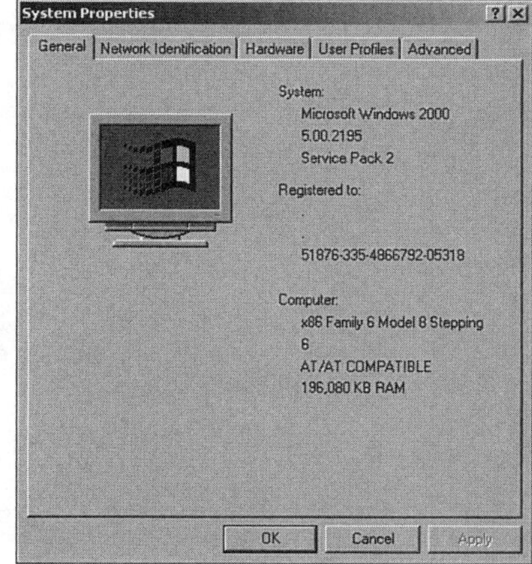

FIGURE 8.19
System properties.

Another means of verifying the service pack installed on a machine is via the System Information utility (shown in Figure 8.20). The System Information utility can provide a wealth of information above and beyond just the service pack version currently installed. Launch the System Information utility by selecting Start, Programs, Accessories, System Tools, System Information.

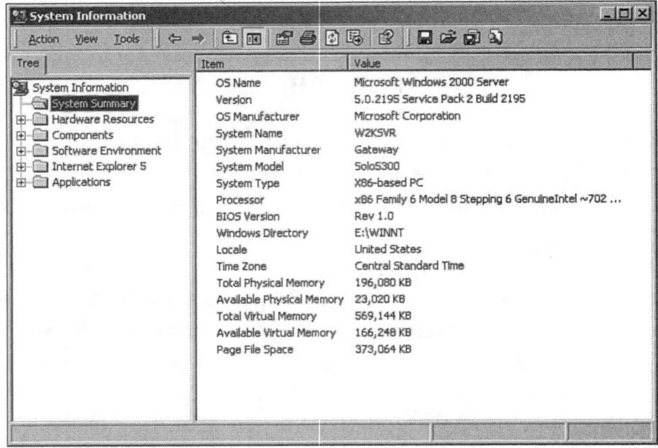

FIGURE 8.20
System Information utility.

> **NOTE** **Using the `WINVER` Command** In case you think it doesn't work anymore, you can use the `WINVER` command from the command line to display almost the same information obtained from the General tab of the System applet.

The easiest way to determine which hot fixes have been applied to a machine is via the Add/Remove Programs applet of Control Panel. Each hot fix shows up with the option to remove it (see Figure 8.21).

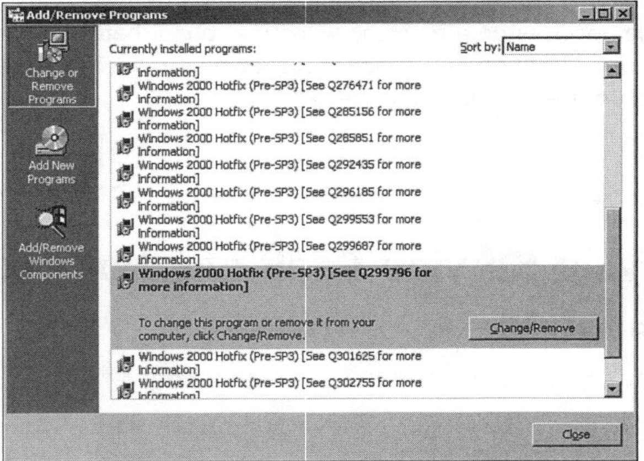

FIGURE 8.21
Listing installed hot fixes.

Alternatively, you can use the Microsoft Network Security Hotfix Checker tool. The `hfetchk.exe` utility scans selected machines for missing hot fixes and reports back to you with the ones you need to install. The default output for `hfnetchk.exe` displays only hot fixes that are necessary for your computer to be up-to-date for the currently installed operating system and service pack. Figure 8.22 shows the output from the `hfnetchk.exe` tool.

```
E:\WINNT\System32\cmd.exe
E:\hotfix>hfnetchk
Microsoft Network Security Hotfix Checker, 3.31
Copyright (C) Shavlik Technologies, 2001-2002
Developed for Microsoft by Shavlik Technologies, LLC
info@shavlik.com (www.shavlik.com)


Please use the -v switch to view details for
Patch NOT Found, Warning and Note messages


Attempting to download the CAB from:
http://download.microsoft.com/download/xml/security/1.0/NT5/EN-US/mssecure.cab

File was successfully downloaded.

Attempting to load E:\hotfix\mssecure.xml.
Using XML data version = 1.0.1.174  Last modified on 12/20/2001.

Scanning W2KSVR
..............................................................................
Done scanning W2KSVR
----------------------------------------
W2KSVR (192.168.0.150)
----------------------------------------

        * WINDOWS 2000 SERVER SP2

        Note             MS01-022          Q296441
        Patch NOT Found  MS01-041          Q298012
        Patch NOT Found  MS01-043          Q303984

        * INTERNET INFORMATION SERVICES 5.0

        Information
        All necessary hotfixes have been applied

        * INTERNET EXPLORER 5.01 SP2

        Patch NOT Found  MS01-051          Q306121


E:\hotfix>
```

FIGURE 8.22
hfnetchk.exe results.

> **NOTE**
>
> **Getting Additional Information on the Microsoft Network Security Hotfix Checker Tool** For more information at the Microsoft Network Security Hotfix Checker tool, see KB# Q305385 (`http://support.microsoft.com/default.aspx?scid=kb;EN-US;q305385`) and KB# Q303215 (`http://support.microsoft.com/default.aspx?scid=kb;en-us;Q303215`).

Removing Service Packs and Hot Fixes

▶ Remove service packs and hot fixes.

Removing service packs and hot fixes is as simple as removing any other software installed on a machine. You can remove service packs (if the option to back up existing files was selected) and hot fixes from the Add/Remove Programs applet of the Control Panel, as discussed in Step By Step 8.11.

STEP BY STEP

8.11 Removing a Service Pack or Hot Fix

1. Open the Add/Remove Programs applet of the Control Panel.
2. In the list of programs to Change or Remove, select the hot fix or service pack to uninstall.
3. Click Change/Remove and follow the screen prompts to complete the removal.
4. Restart the computer to complete the process.

CHAPTER SUMMARY

KEY TERMS

Before taking the exam, be sure you are comfortable with the definitions and concepts for all of the following key terms:

- Digital Signature
- HCL
- Plug and Play
- `Qchain.exe`
- Service pack
- Hot fix
- Slipstreaming
- System File Checker
- Windows 2000 Readiness Analyzer
- Windows File Protection
- `winnt32.exe`

Digitally signed drivers are recommended for use as often as possible to help prevent many of the problems that occurred in previous versions of Windows due to poorly written device drivers. Microsoft has included three tools to help identify unsigned drivers and manage them: File Signature Verification, System File Checker, and Driver Verifier Manager.

You can control the installation of drivers that are lacking digital signatures, and three levels of control can be set: Block, Warn, and Ignore. These settings can be applied locally one machine at a time via the Control Panel or across an organization by linking a Group Policy Object to one or more Active Directory containers (OUs, domains, and so on).

Most new hardware is Plug and Play compatible and installs with little to no effort in Windows 2000. When Plug and Play hardware is installed, Windows 2000 dynamically manages its resources. In the event that you have older, non-Plug and Play hardware, you will need to install and assign resources for the device manually. Installing devices manually can lead to system conflicts because Windows 2000 can't dynamically manage devices that have been manually installed and configured.

Windows 2000 service packs, unlike service packs in Windows NT 4.0, take advantage of a new technology known as slipstreaming. Slipstreaming enables a service pack to be applied one time per machine, regardless of what configuration changes are made after the service pack installation. Service packs can be slipstreamed into installation sources to provide integrated, up-to-date installation files.

CHAPTER SUMMARY

Hot fixes are smaller executable files that are issued by Microsoft with the intent of fixing only one specific flaw or security issue. The computer should always be restarted after applying a hot fix, and hot fixes should normally be applied only one at a time. If many hot fixes are to be installed, they should be chained together using the `Qchain.exe` utility to avoid problems with locked files.

Service packs and hot fixes can be uninstalled from the Add/Remove Programs applet of Control Panel in the same fashion as most other software packages. The ability to uninstall service packs is dependant on the options selected at the time of service pack installation. Hot fixes, on the other hand, are always available for uninstallation.

APPLY YOUR KNOWLEDGE

Exercises

8.1 Setting the Driver Signing Policy via Group Policy

In this exercise you will set the driver signing policy for an OU via Group Policy. You will be setting the behavior to Block.

To complete this exercise, you will need the following item:

- A Windows 2000 domain controller

Estimated Time: 15 minutes

1. Open the Active Directory Computers and Users snap-in by selecting Start, Programs, Administrative Tools, Active Directory Users and Computers.
2. Locate the OU for which you want to configure Group Policy and right-click it. From the context menu, select Properties. Switch to the Group Policy tab and either click New to create a new GPO or click Edit to work with an existing GPO. Because it is recommended to create GPOs for specific tasks, create a new GPO for this purpose by clicking New and entering the name `Driver Signing Policies`. Click Edit to open the Group Policy window.
3. Open the nodes as follows: User Configuration, Administrative Templates, System. Double-click the Code Signing for Device Drivers option.
4. Select the Enable radio button, and then select Block from the drop-down list.
5. Close the Group Policy window by clicking OK to close out the driver signing options and then clicking the close X in the upper-right corner of the Group Policy window.

8.2 Setting the Driver Signing Policy via Control Panel

In this exercise you will set the driver signing policy for a specific computer. You will set the behavior to Warn.

To complete this exercise, you will need the following item:

- A Windows 2000 computer

Estimated Time: 5 minutes

1. Open the System applet in the Control Panel by selecting Start, Settings, Control Panel, System.
2. Switch to the Hardware tab and click Driver Signing.
3. Select Warn; if you are logged in with administrative privileges, enable the setting for all users of the computer. When you are done, click OK twice to complete the process.

8.3 Using the Windows Readiness Analyzer

In this exercise you will use the Windows Readiness Analyzer to determine whether your computer's hardware is ready for the upgrade to Windows 2000.

To complete this exercise, you will need the following item:

- A Windows 95 or Windows 98 computer (alternatively, you can use a Windows 2000 computer if no Windows 95 or 98 computer is available).

Estimated Time: 10 minutes

1. Open a command prompt by typing `cmd` in the Run box, and then click OK.

APPLY YOUR KNOWLEDGE

2. From the command prompt, run the Readiness Analyzer by typing `X:\i386\winnt32 /checkupgradeonly` and pressing Enter, where *X* is the location of the Windows 2000 setup files.
3. From the results in the output window, determine whether your hardware is compatible with Windows 2000. If desired, save the results of the Readiness Analyzer to a text file. Click Finish when you are done to close the Readiness Analyzer window.

8.4 Installing Plug and Play Hardware

In this exercise you will use the Add/Remove Programs applet to install a new Plug and Play hardware device.

To complete this exercise, you will need the following items:

- A Windows 2000 computer
- A previously uninstalled piece of Plug and Play hardware, such as a printer or scanner.

Estimated Time: 15 minutes

1. Select Start, Settings, Control Panel.
2. Double-click the Add/Remove Hardware icon to start the wizard.
3. Click Next to close the Welcome page.
4. Select Add/Troubleshoot a Device and click Next to start the wizard.

8.5 Manually Configuring Non-Plug and Play Hardware

In this exercise you will use the Device Manager to manually configure non-Plug and Play hardware resources.

To complete this exercise, you will need the following items:

- A Windows 2000 computer.
- A non-Plug and Play hardware device.

Estimated Time: 20 minutes

1. Select Start, Settings, Control Panel.
2. Double-click the System icon and select the Hardware tab.
3. Click the Device Manager button.
4. Expand the device type you want to change.
5. Right-click the specific device you want to modify.
6. Click Properties and select the Resources tab. If the Resources tab is not present, you will not be able to modify the device's resources.
7. Select the resource setting you will be modifying.
8. Clear the Automatic Settings box if it is checked. If this box is grayed out, you will not be able to modify the device's resources.
9. Select the resource you want to modify and click the Change Setting button.

8.6 Slipstreaming a Service Pack into an Installation Source

In this exercise you will slipstream a service pack into an installation source.

To complete this exercise, you will need the following items:

- A Windows 2000 computer
- A Windows 2000 setup CD-ROM
- A Windows 2000 service pack

APPLY YOUR KNOWLEDGE

Estimated Time: 15 minutes

1. On a network share, create a new folder (such as `W2KSvrImage`) to hold the contents of the Windows 2000 CD-ROM. Copy the entire contents of the Windows 2000 CD-ROM to this folder.

2. On a network share, create a new folder (such as `W2Ksp2`) to hold the contents of the service pack you are slipstreaming. Extract the service pack into this folder by executing the *`SERVICE_PACK_NAME`* `-x` command at the command prompt, where *`SERVICE_PACK_NAME`* is replaced by the actual service pack filename.

3. After the service pack verifies all files, you will be asked to choose a location to which to extract them; choose the service pack folder you created earlier.

4. When the extraction is complete, click OK to close the extraction window.

5. The last step is to actually apply the service pack to the installation files (ala slipstream style). Assuming the both of your folders are located on the `D:\` volume, a sample command entered in the Run box would look like this: **`D:\W2Ksp2\I386\UPDATE\UPDATE.EXE -s:D:\W2KSvrImage\`**. After entering the command, a window opens and informs you of the slipstream status.

6. When the integration is complete, click OK to close the integration window and complete the slipstream process.

Review Questions

1. Which driver signing behaviors can you configure?

2. Why are digitally signed drivers so important to the effective operation of a computer?

3. Why should you avoid manually configuring resources for hardware devices?

4. What is the purpose of a service pack, and where can you get the latest one?

5. What is the largest difference between service packs in Windows 2000 and Windows NT 4.0?

6. What are hot fixes?

7. What problems are associated with installing hot fixes?

8. What does slipstreaming an installation source accomplish?

Exam Questions

1. Jack is the administrator of a medium-sized (about 500 machines) Windows 2000 network for an engineering firm. The previous administrator did a fairly good job of getting Windows 2000 rolled out in the organization, including breaking up each department into OUs. However, no matter what the administrator tried, there were one or two computers daily in the production department that ceased to operate properly. You suspect the cause might be due to the fact that the layout personnel have a tendency to experiment with new hardware. What can you do to help prevent future downtime on these computers?

APPLY YOUR KNOWLEDGE

A. On each machine, set the driver signing behavior to Block.

B. From Active Directory Users and Computers, create a GPO and link it to the production department's OU. Configure driver signing in the GPO for Ignore.

C. From Active Directory Users and Computers, create a GPO and link it to the production department's OU. Configure driver signing in the GPO to Block.

D. Remove all user accounts in the production department's OU from the Users group to the Guest group.

2. Hannah works as a help desk support technician for a large organization. Recently, she received a phone call from a user who stated that his newly installed scanner wasn't working. When instructed to look at the Device Manager, the user reported back that the icon next to the scanner was a yellow question mark with a red X. What should Hannah have the user do to correct the most likely problem with the scanner?

   A. Manually assign resources for the device because it is having a resource conflict with another device.

   B. Remove the device from the system and do not try to use it again. Devices that show this icon are incompatible with Windows 2000 and should not be used.

   C. Install the device drivers from the installation disks or from files downloaded from the manufacturer's Web site.

   D. Enable the device for use in the current hardware profile.

3. You are training a new help desk support worker. During the course of your discussions, the topic of digitally signed device drivers comes up. When asked about why digitally signed device drivers are important, what will you *not* tell your new employee?

   A. Digitally signed device drivers have passed rigorous testing by the Microsoft Hardware Quality Labs and therefore should provide a high degree of reliability.

   B. Digitally signed device drivers are protected against changes to the driver files since signing by the manufacturer.

   C. Digitally signed device drivers are the only type of driver files that are found on the Windows Update Web site or Windows 2000 CD-ROMs.

   D. Digitally signed device drivers can't be installed unless a certificate authority has been set up on your network.

4. Austin is the administrator of a large Windows 2000-based network. He oversees the maintenance of 20 Windows 2000 servers. All his servers were installed from network shares. Which of the following are benefits of the new service pack slipstreaming functionality if it is used properly? (Select all that apply.)

   A. It will ensure that he will not have to install service packs on his currently existing servers.

   B. It will ensure that he will not have to reinstall service packs on his servers after service installation.

   C. It will ensure that he will not have to install service packs on new servers after initial installation.

APPLY YOUR KNOWLEDGE

D. It will ensure that new versions of Windows will be incrementally available; he will not ever have to upgrade his servers to a new version of Windows.

5. Jose is using the Device Manager to gather information about a particular server in his company. Which of the following items will he be able to gather information on using the Device Manager? (Select all that apply.)

   A. Resource settings for a specific device

   B. A list of all interrupts currently being used on the computer

   C. The status of a particular device, such as enabled or disabled

   D. Information about specific drivers installed for a particular device

6. Chris is an Administrator for her organization. Two of her servers have hardware devices that recently have had updates issued for their drivers. Where can Chris go to install the updated device drivers?

   A. System Information

   B. Device Manager

   C. The Add/Remove Programs applet of Control Panel

   D. The Services MMC snap-in

7. Martin recently acquired a new modem for his Windows 2000 computer. The new modem is not Plug and Play compatible. How will Martin go about installing the new hardware device on his computer?

   A. Use the Device Manager to install the new hardware device.

   B. Use the Phone and Modem Options applet of the Control Panel.

   C. Install the device into the computer. Windows 2000 will detect and automatically install the device the next time it is started.

   D. Use the Add/Remove Hardware applet of the Control Panel.

8. Angela is the Windows 2000 network administrator in a school. She had been running Windows 2000 for six months when the first service pack came out. At that time, she installed the service pack on all her Windows 2000 servers, allowing the install process to back up the old configuration before proceeding with the installation. In addition, she also used slipstreaming on her network share as was recommended by Microsoft. Now she wants to install a new service on one of the machines. What steps reflect the best way to ensure that the service is covered by the service pack?

   A. She should install the service using the CD-ROM as the source and then reapply the service pack.

   B. She should install the service using the network share as the source and then reapply the service pack.

   C. She should install the service using the network share as the source (there is no need to reapply the service pack).

   D. She should uninstall the service pack, install the service using the CD-ROM as the source, and then reapply the service pack.

9. Sean is preparing to roll out 50 new Windows 2000 client machines. His organization has decided to not use any of the available network

APPLY YOUR KNOWLEDGE

installation methods available. What can Sean do to reduce the amount of time required to get the 50 new client computers operational?

A. Use System's Management Server to push the installation to the 50 new client computers.

B. Create an updated installation CD-ROM by slipstreaming the latest service pack into existing Windows 2000 installation files. Then, he should use this CD-ROM to install the 50 new client computers.

C. Install Windows 2000 on the 50 new client computers and then have a second person go behind him and install the latest service pack.

D. Use Terminal Services to deploy the clients from his desk.

10. You work as the administrator for a small defense research and development company. In the nine months that you have been employed by the company, you have not installed a service pack or a hot fix. What's more, you have no clue what the statuses of your machines are in regards to security vulnerabilities. What can you do to get your machines patched and up-to-date? (Select all that apply.)

A. Download and install all service packs that your machines are missing.

B. Use the `hfnetchk` utility to determine which hot fixes your machines need. Download all required hot fixes and install them one after another. Restart the machines.

C. Use the `hfnetchk` utility to determine which hot fixes your machines need. Download all required hot fixes and install them one after another. Run the `Qchain` utility, and restart the machines.

D. Download and install the latest service pack that each of your machines requires.

11. How you can determine which service pack has been applied to a machine? (Select all that apply.)

A. Use the System applet of the Control Panel.

B. Use the `filever` command from the command prompt.

C. Use the `ver` command from the command prompt.

D. Use the System Information utility.

12. Which of the following driver signing behaviors will not prompt the user for action when installing new device drivers and could lead to system instabilities?

A. Ignore

B. Block

C. Silent

D. Quiet

13. What is the biggest difference between Windows NT 4.0 service packs and Windows 2000 service packs?

A. Service packs under Windows NT 4.0 had to be ordered on CD-ROM directly from Microsoft.

B. Service packs under Windows 2000 can be slipstreamed into installations without ever having to reapply the service pack due to later addition or removal of operating system components.

C. Service packs under Windows NT 4.0 were actually a collection of all previously issued hot fixes, which then had to be manually installed one at a time.

D. Service packs under Windows 2000 are available only in English.

14. Andrea noticed that her tape drive backup unit stopped responding last night when she tried to use it. When she asks you for help, you instruct her to open the Device Manager and report to you the icon displayed next the tape drive unit. She tells you that a yellow question mark with a red X is next to the device. What should you do to correct the problem?

    A. Manually assign system resource settings to the tape drive because it is obviously experiencing a conflict.

    B. Attempt to reinstall the device driver because it might have become corrupted.

    C. Enable the device because someone has manually disabled it.

    D. Replace the tape drive because it has become faulty.

15. Christopher, one of your assistant administrators, has been talking with you about digitally signed device drivers. You ask him what ways are available to automatically inventory unsigned drivers on a computer. Which correct answers do you expect Christopher to provide you? (Select all that apply.)

    A. System File Checker automatically maintains all Windows 2000 system files and drivers installed with the correct version, even if they have been removed or replaced.

    B. File Signature Verification can be run to provide a listing of all unsigned drivers.

    C. System Information provides a listing of all installed drivers and their digital signature statuses.

    D. Examine the listed drivers on the Drivers tab of the Properties page for a particular piece of hardware.

Answers to Review Questions

1. When configuring driver signing, you have three options from which to choose: Ignore (directs the system to proceed with the installation even if it includes unsigned files), Warn (notifies the user that files are not digitally signed and prompts the user for action), and Block (directs the system to refuse to install unsigned files).

2. To prevent poorly written drivers from being installed on a system, Microsoft introduced driver signing. Driver signing is critical in maintaining client machines' functionality. By enforcing restrictions on the installation of unsigned drivers, you can prevent hardware conflicts and stop errors, both of which are common side effects of poorly written drivers. Poorly written drivers also tend to generate an unusually large number of CPU interrupts, thus interfering with all other operations.

3. If you must manually configure a non-Plug and Play device, the resources assigned become fixed. This reduces the flexibility that Windows 2000 has for allocating resources to other devices. If too many resources are manually configured, Windows 2000 might not be capable of installing new Plug and Play devices.

4. Service packs are designed to allow incremental upgrades to a piece of software—in this case, to the Windows 2000 operating system. Service packs distribute bug fixes and security patches and can be obtained from the Microsoft Web site

APPLY YOUR KNOWLEDGE

or from other distribution media, such as TechNet and MSDN. For more information, see the section "Installing and Managing Windows 2000 Updates."

5. In many regards, Windows 2000 service packs are not very different from Windows NT 4.0 service packs. When they are released, the intent is for you to install the service pack on all your Windows 2000 computers to implement any fixes included in them. However, one significant improvement has been made in the application of services packs: the concept of *slipstreaming*. With slipstreaming, changes from the service pack can be applied to the source files found on a local folder or network share (by using the `-s` switch when running `update.exe` for the service pack). This means that when you subsequently access those files, you will obtain the fixed versions of those files, not the old ones. This saves time because it means that the service packs will have to be applied to any machine only once and not multiple times as services (and other operating system components) are installed. In addition, this also means that new installations over the network will also automatically be up-to-date with the current service pack.

6. A hot fix is a very small executable that addresses one specific issue.

7. When you install hot fixes, if a file is locked or in use and can't be replaced, it is placed in the Pending File Rename queue to be replaced after the restarts. If not done properly, the process of applying hot fixes can cause results other than what was intended due to file version conflicts and overwriting. For more information, see the section "Applying Service Packs and Hot Fixes."

8. When you slipstream an installation source, you are applying that service pack to your installation source files. The net result is that you end up with an updated installation source that can be used to perform new operating system installations without subsequently requiring the application of the service pack. Note that installations performed with a slipstreamed installation source do not support later removal of the service pack.

Answers to Exam Questions

1. **C.** The best option in this case is to create a GPO linked to the production department's OU and configure the driver signing behavior in it for Block. You are not told how many machines are part of the production department, but in a Windows 2000 Active Directory domain, you should always strive to apply policies via Group Policy Objects instead of manually configuring them. Moving the users' accounts out of the of Users group and into the Guest group would fix the problem but would more likely than not cause additional, unnecessary problems. Configuring a GPO with the Ignore option would not be an optimal solution because all drivers (signed or not) could then be installed. When the Block behavior is set, unsigned drivers can't be installed. For more information, see the section "Driver Signing Restrictions."

2. **C.** The best course of action is to install the device drivers either from the setup disks or from files downloaded from the manufacturer's Web site. Devices that display this icon are typically not enabled due to missing or corrupted drivers. Manually assigning resources to the device will not correct the situation and is not possible

APPLY YOUR KNOWLEDGE

because the device is not currently using any resources. Devices that are experiencing a resource conflict display the normal device icon with a yellow exclamation point, and devices that are disabled show either a normal icon with a red X (disabled by the user) or a normal icon with a yellow exclamation point (disabled by Windows). In this case, the device is displaying a yellow question mark with red X icon. For more information, see the section "Confirming Hardware Installation."

3. **D.** All the other three statements are true concerning digitally signed device drivers. Because the certificate used to sign the file is traceable to a third-party certificate authority, such as Verisign, there is no need for any further certificate services to be in place. If you wanted to issue digitally signed drivers to your customers, you would need a certificate authority in place on your network, preferably with a root certificate issued by a third party. For more information, see the section "Driver Signing Restrictions."

4. **B, C.** Slipstreaming ensures that the network share containing the Windows 2000 server installation files is updated with the fixes a service pack provides. This ensures that changes made to a Windows 2000 server that require the installation files will automatically install the update versions of files, as long as they are provided from an updated network share. In addition, this also ensures that new installations will automatically end up with the fixed files installed without you having to manually install the service pack prior to operating system installation.

   Slipstreaming updates do not remove the requirement for installation of service packs on existing machines, and it is Microsoft's stated goal to provide fixes via only service packs, not operating system upgrades. For more information, see the section "Updating an Installation Source by Using Slipstreaming."

5. **A, B, C, D.** Using the Device Manager, Jose will be able to gather all this information and more. For more information, see the section "The Hardware Installation Process."

6. **B.** Chris can install the new device drivers from the Device Manager. To install the new drivers, she must right-click the device to be updated and select Properties. She then needs to switch to the Driver tab and click Update Driver. For more information, see the section "The Hardware Installation Process."

7. **D.** Non-Plug and Play hardware must be added via the Add/Remove Hardware applet of the Control Panel. All drivers to be installed should be Windows 2000 compliant. Only Plug and Play hardware can be installed physically and have Windows 2000 install and configure the device and drivers. The Phone and Modem Options applet of the Control Panel can be used to configure dialing rules and modem settings after a modem has been successfully installed. For more information, see the section "Configuring Operating System Support for Legacy Hardware Devices."

8. **C.** Because slipstreaming can be used to update the files on a network share, there is no requirement for reinstalling the service pack after installing a service. Slipstreaming ensures that the installation files have already had the service pack installed before they are used to install a new service. It is true that if Angela uses the

APPLY YOUR KNOWLEDGE

Windows 2000 Server CD-ROM as the source for her service installation, she will have to reapply the service pack. However, the question focused on the "best way," and updating using slipstreaming is the best way. For more information, see the section "Updating an Installation Source by Using Slipstreaming."

9. **B.** By slipstreaming an installation source with the latest service pack, Sean can create the most up-to-date CD-ROM to use for his installations. He can also write an answer file and use the `Qchain` utility to install hot fixes if he wants to. Using SMS to push the software installations, while the most ideal solution given to this problem, is not allowed by the instructions Sean was given to work with. Having a second person follow behind Sean installing the latest service pack will result in many more man hours used than slipstreaming an installation CD-ROM. For more information, see the section "Installing and Managing Windows 2000 Updates."

10. **C, D.** Installing multiple hot fixes without using the `Qchain` utility can be dangerous due to locked file issues. If you do not want to use the `Qchain` utility, you must restart the machine after each and every hot fix application. Service packs contain all updates issued previous to their release; this includes previous service packs and most of the commonly required hot fixes. You need to download and install only the most recent service pack required by a machine. Service packs should be installed before checking for hot fixes. For more information, see the section "Installing and Managing Windows 2000 Updates."

11. **A, D.** Although the `VER` command is a valid command, it returns only the operating system currently running. You could also use the `WINVER` command because it returns the operating system and service pack information as well. For more information, see the section "Verifying Service Pack and Hot Fix Installation."

12. **A.** The Block behavior automatically blocks all unsigned drivers and does not display or prompt for feedback to the user. Quiet and Silent are not valid driver signing behavior options. For more information, see the section "Driver Signing Restrictions."

13. **B.** Windows 2000 service packs introduced the capability to slipstream a service pack into an existing installation without ever having to reapply the service pack due to configuration changes on the machine. Under Windows NT 4.0, many administrators chose to not apply service packs because of having to reapply them after making changes to a server, such as installing a new service. For more information, see the section "Installing and Managing Windows 2000 Updates."

14. **B.** In most cases, when a yellow question mark with a red X is displayed, there is a problem with the drivers. The drivers might not be installed or might be incorrectly configured. For more information, see the section "Confirming Hardware Installation."

15. **A, B.** System File Checker runs in the background and maintains a watch on critical system files and drivers that should not be replaced with unsigned or incorrect versions. File Signature Verifier can be started from the command line and scans an entire machine for unsigned drivers. Digital signature status is not reported in System Information. Although you can get the status of a

APPLY YOUR KNOWLEDGE

digital signature from the device Properties window, this would have to be done on a one-by-one basis and is not guaranteed to get every device driver installed. Additionally, the question specifies automatic as one of the criteria. For more information, see the section "Verifying Digital Signatures on Existing Drivers."

Suggested Readings and Resources

The following are some recommended additional resources:

1. Russel, Charlie, and Sharon Crawford. *Microsoft Windows 2000 Server Administrator's Companion.* Microsoft Press, 2000.
2. Stanek, William R. *Microsoft Windows 2000 Administrator's Pocket Consultant.* Microsoft Press, 2000.
3. "Windows 2000 Deployment Guide" at `http://www.microsoft.com/windows2000/techinfo/reskit/dpg/default.asp`.
4. "Windows 2000 Resource Kits" at `http://www.microsoft.com/windows2000/techinfo/reskit/en-us/default.asp`.

OBJECTIVES

This chapter helps you prepare for the "Managing, Securing, and Troubleshooting Servers and Client Computers" section of the exam by giving you information necessary to make intelligent choices in the installation, upgrading, and management of client and server machines. Of the four topics in this section, two are covered in this chapter; the remaining two topics were previously covered in Chapter 8, "Installing and Maintaining Clients and Servers."

The following exam objectives are covered in this chapter.

Troubleshoot starting servers and client computers. Tools and methodologies include Safe Mode, Recovery Console, and parallel installations.

- **Interpret the startup log file.**
- **Repair an operating system by using various startup options.**
- **Repair an operating system by using the Recovery Console.**
- **Recover data from a hard disk in the event that the operating system will not start.**
- **Restore an operating system and data from a backup.**

▶ Troubleshooting startup problems with servers and client machines can be a problematic and troublesome evolution. The best plan of action in this situation is to have a good understanding of the various actions you can pursue in attempting to recover machines experiencing startup problems. Options available to you include Safe Mode startups, repairs from the Recovery Console, parallel installation to access data on hard drives that will not boot, and complete restorations from backup media. Each of these areas forms a part of the overall picture when it comes to dealing with startup problems and data recovery.

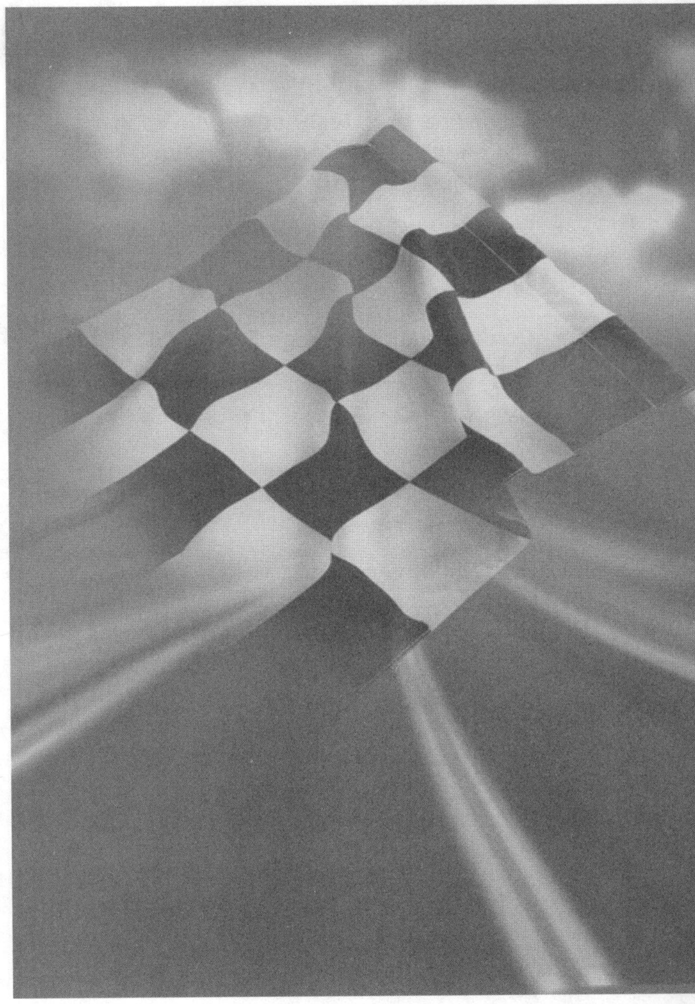

CHAPTER 9

Managing, Securing, and Troubleshooting Server Computers

OBJECTIVES

Monitor and troubleshoot server health and performance. Tools include System Monitor, Event Viewer, and Task Manager.

- **Monitor and interpret real-time performance by using System Monitor and Task Manager.**
- **Configure and manage System Monitor alerts and logging.**
- **Diagnose server health problems by using Event Viewer.**
- **Identify and disable unnecessary operating system services.**

▶ Understanding the internals of the operating system can provide an administrator with some value insight as to how and when future problems might occur. The System Monitor, Task Manager, and Event Viewer can all provide information that, if used properly, can help avoid costly downtime or performance degradation on servers and client machines.

OUTLINE

Outline

Study Strategies

- The key points to understand in this chapter revolve around the various means of disaster recovery available to you as an administrator. Additionally, it is important to have a good grasp on ways you can identify and troubleshoot performance issues that affect your computers.
- It is important to understand how the Performance Console is set up and what the component parts are. Know how to create a system monitor, create counter and trace logs, and configure alerts. Know specifically the main counters involved in the processor, memory, network, and disk (physical and logical) as outlined in this chapter. You won't likely be tested specifically on counters, but you should be aware of them anyway.
- As they pertain to system recovery, know the various mechanisms for saving system information and when each would be used. Know the limitations of Last Known Good Configuration and the Emergency Repair Disk. In addition, know how to save this information using Windows 2000 Backup because that has always been a popular question.
- As they pertain to data backup and recovery, know how Windows Backup and Restore work, how to invoke them, and how the scheduler works.
- Be comfortable performing the various Step By Steps in this chapter. They serve to give you valuable practice both for the exam and for real life.

INTRODUCTION

Troubleshooting is something we all wish we never had to do, but more often than not, we find ourselves doing it. Knowing how to properly troubleshoot and perform repairs to servers and client computers is critical for an administrator and should not be taken lightly. Knowing how to look ahead to identify problems before they occur is even more important. Unfortunately, identifying impending problems is a fine art learned over time with practice and patience.

Windows 2000 makes a big departure from Windows NT 4.0 in many areas, among them the inclusion of Safe Mode startups and the Recovery Console. The NTBACKUP utility has also gotten a face lift, gaining greater functionality and usability.

During the course of this chapter, we will look at methods to recover systems should disaster strike (despite your best efforts) and at methods for identifying and correcting problems before they occur. A good understanding of these two areas will go a long way toward making your life as an administrator a happier one.

TROUBLESHOOTING STARTUP PROBLEMS

A computer is a complicated device, much like a small child. Many things can go wrong with a computer, and you could find yourself trying to make sense of some cryptic message or error. Some of the things you might encounter are STOP errors (otherwise affectionately known as the Blue Screen of Death), error messages during or after startup, and computers that simply won't boot at all.

The next sections look at each of these areas and explore them as they relate not only to this specific exam, but also to your effectiveness on a day-by-day basis as an administrator. These sections cover various methods you can employ to restart, restore, and recover servers and clients that can't start normally. These solutions cover a broad range of possibilities, from simple repairs to complete restorations. However, before we actually get into troubleshooting and repairing startup problems, it is critical that you have an understanding of how the startup process occurs on a Windows 2000 computer—so let's examine the startup process now.

The Windows 2000 Boot Process

If you reboot your Windows 2000 computer and it fails before Windows 2000 has completely started, a problem probably exists somewhere in the boot process. The key to solving this type of problem is to understand the sequence of events that occur in the computer as it is starting up.

The boot process in Windows 2000 consists of several discreet steps, each of which is examined in the following sections.

EXAM TIP

Booting and Starting In this text, as in life, the terms *boot* and *start* (as well as *bootup* and *startup*) are used interchangeably. Don't get hung up on different terms that mean the same thing.

Power On Self Test Processing

The first stage of a computer boot process is the power on self test (POST) processing stage, which is commonly referred to as the preboot stage. This stage is handled entirely by the motherboard and its BIOS and does not actually involve Windows 2000 at all.

The computer runs a POST to determine the amount of memory and which hardware components are present. The hardware devices are enumerated and configured during preboot. The system also might display a series of messages indicating that the mouse is detected, that certain IDE or SCSI adapters are detected, responses from devices on the SCSI chain, and so forth. Failure at this stage represents a hardware concern and is not really a boot sequence error.

Initial Startup Process

If all the hardware components are present and working, the computer BIOS locates the boot device, loads the Master Boot Record (MBR) into memory, and executes it. The MBR scans the partition table to locate the active partition, loads the boot sector from the active partition into memory, and executes it.

The computer also finds and loads the file `NTLDR` from the active partition. `NTLDR` is a hidden system file located in the root folder of your system partition.

Bootstrap Loader Process

During the bootstrap loader process phase, the activity level starts to increase for the startup. NTLDR clears the screen and performs the following actions:

- Switches the processor from real mode into a 32-bit flat memory mode that NTLDR requires to complete its function.
- Starts the appropriate minifile system drivers, which are built into NTLDR to find and load Windows 2000 from different file system formats (File Allocation Table [FAT] or Windows NT File System [NTFS]).
- Displays the Boot Loader Operating System Selection menu from the boot.ini file. This provides a selection of operating systems to use. If you do not select an entry before the timer reaches 0, NTLDR loads the operating system specified by the default parameter in boot.ini. The default parameter is the more recent operating system installed.
- Allows you to start the computer normally or select an advanced startup, such as Safe Mode or Last Known Good Configuration.
- Loads and starts ntoskrnl.exe. The hardware information collected by ntdetect.com is passed off to ntoskrnl.exe.

NOTE

Dual-Boot Systems If you select another operating system, such as Microsoft Windows 98, NTLDR loads and executes bootsect.dos. This is a copy of the boot sector that was on the system partition when Windows 2000 was originally installed. Executing it begins the boot process for the selected operating system.

Selecting the Operating System

As discussed in the previous section, NTLDR displays a boot menu of the operating systems installed on the computer from which a user can choose to start the computer. If a selection is not made before the counter reaches 0, NTLDR loads the default operating system as specified in the boot.ini file.

Detecting Hardware

After NTLDR starts loading Windows 2000, it begins the hardware detection phase. ntdetect.com collects a list of the hardware components currently installed and returns this list to NTLDR for inclusion in the registry under HKEY_LOCAL_MACHINE/HARDWARE. ntdetect.com detects the following components:

- Computer ID
- Keyboard
- Communications ports
- Mouse/pointing devices
- Floating-point coprocessor
- Floppy disks
- Bus/adapter type
- Parallel ports
- Small Computer Standard Interface (SCSI) adapters
- Video adapters

You can tell when NTLDR starts to load Windows 2000 because the text Starting Windows... appears and is followed by a bar graph across the bottom of the screen. After the graph has completed, startup switches to graphical mode and the familiar Windows 2000 splash screen is displayed.

Loading and Initializing the Kernel

After you have selected a hardware profile or configuration (or NTLDR has done it for you automatically), the kernel load phase of Windows 2000 startup begins. NTLDR performs the following tasks during this phase:

- Loads the Windows 2000 kernel (ntoskrnl.exe), but does not initialize it
- Loads the hardware abstraction layer (Hal.dll) into memory, but does not initialize it
- Loads the registry key HKEY_LOCAL_MACHINE \SYSTEM from %SystemRoot%\System32\Config\System
- Selects the control set it will use to initialize the computer
- Loads device drivers that have a Start value of 0x0

NOTE

Hardware Profiles If you do not press the spacebar, or if there is only a single hardware profile, NTLDR loads Windows 2000 using the default hardware profile configuration. For more information about hardware profiles, which is beyond the scope of the exam, see MSKB# Q225810 at http://support.microsoft.com/default.aspx?scid=kb;en-us;Q225810.

NOTE

Debugging the Boot Process By entering the /SOS switch in the boot.ini file, Windows 2000 lists the drivers' names onscreen as the system starts. See the section "The Boot Log," later in this chapter, for information about editing the boot.ini file.

Logging In to Windows 2000

The last phase of the boot process involves logging in to Windows 2000. The `Winlogon.exe` is automatically started by the Windows 2000 subsystem, which in turn starts the Local Security Administration, `Lsass.exe`. At this time, the Welcome to Windows dialog box appears, even though Windows might still be initializing device drivers. You can log in at this time, which completes the boot process. After a successful login, the Last Know Good Configuration is updated.

Now that you've seen the basic process of how Windows 2000 starts, let's take a closer look at some of the things that can go wrong and what can be done to troubleshoot and repair these situations.

STOP Errors

STOP errors are the one thing that most administrators (and users) hope they never see. In times past, that was an unlikely wish because Windows 9x and Windows NT were prone to generating these cryptic error screens that users affectionately refer to as the *Blue Screen of Death*. And death it usually was for that computer and all running applications. Many STOP errors were difficult to resolve in previous versions of Windows. Even though STOP errors are less prevalent in Windows 2000, they still exist and can still ruin your day faster than a flat tire in a rain storm.

The real problem in dealing with STOP errors is that you have to be a bit of a mind reader to interpret them (well, not really, but it might help!). What you really need to interpret, understand, troubleshoot, and ultimately correct STOP errors is an understanding of what information is found in the error display and where to get more help. Of course, you will want to take the time to memorize and be able to recognize a few of the more common STOP errors, but for the most part, you will do well to create a bookmark in your Web browser to the Bug Check Codes listing at MSDN (`http://msdn.microsoft.com/library/en-us/ddtools/hh/ddtools/bcintro_3dkj.asp`).

Each STOP error contains information relating to the nature of the problem and also some specific parameters pertinent to that STOP error. If you get a STOP error upon startup (or any other time), the first thing you need to do is determine what changes have been made to the computer recently. Has a new piece of hardware been installed, or have configuration settings been modified? Keeping track of what changes are made (and by whom) goes a long way toward correcting problems that pop up after the fact. Two of the more common STOP errors you might encounter (and some basic troubleshooting tips) are as follows:

- `IRQL_NOT_LESS_OR_EQUAL (0x0000000A)`—The `0xA` error usually occurs after the installation of bug-ridden or incompatible software or drivers onto a computer. For example, when Windows 2000 first became available, installing Easy CD Creator 4.x on it would crash the system, oftentimes resulting in `0xA` errors and other strange behaviors. (This behavior was fixed by Adaptec, which is now Roxio, shortly after the release of Windows 2000.) In most cases, you can troubleshoot and repair this STOP error using the Last Known Good Configuration startup. See the section "Recovering System State with Last Known Good Configuration," later in this chapter, for more information on using the LKGC startup.
- `INACCESSIBLE_BOOT_DEVICE (0x0000007B)`—The `0x7B` error always occurs during the startup process as a result of a boot failure. In most cases, resolving this STOP error requires editing the `boot.ini` file in order to point the boot process toward the disk and partition that contain the Windows 2000 system files. However, before editing the `boot.ini` file, you should attempt to restart the computer using the Last Known Good Configuration option—especially if you have added new hardware or changed device drivers recently.

Armed with your knowledge of STOP errors, let's next examine using boot logging to help troubleshoot and repair startup problems. The good thing about finding a problem with a boot log is that the problem is usually not so severe as to completely prevent the computer from starting.

EXAM TIP

Just Become Familiar with STOP Errors Bearing in mind that developers are concerned with STOP error codes more so than network administrators, understand that Microsoft does not expect you to become an expert at working with STOP errors. The key point to get here is that you should become *familiar* with working with STOP errors and know what to do if you encounter one.

The Boot Log

▶ Interpret the startup log file.

If your computer does not start up normally, you can use the boot log to help identify which drivers have not loaded and initialized properly. By examining the boot log, you can identify the filename of the last file processed, which might be causing the problem. You can then focus your troubleshooting efforts on the suspect file and replace or update the suspect file. The procedure to enable boot logging is outlined in Step By Step 9.1.

STEP BY STEP

9.1 Enabling Boot Logging

1. Start or restart your server.
2. During the text mode of the boot process, a screen appears with the message `For troubleshooting and advanced startup options for Windows 2000, press F8.` Press F8.
3. When the Advanced Options menu appears, use the arrow keys to move to Enable Boot Logging, and then press Enter to continue.
4. The computer will continue to boot normally, only now with boot logging enabled.

Alternatively, you can edit the `boot.ini` to always create a boot log as detailed in Step By Step 9.2.

STEP BY STEP

9.2 Enabling Boot Logging on Every Startup

1. From Windows Explorer, click the Tools menu, and then select Folder Options.

2. From the View tab, select the radio button next to Show Hidden Files and Folders; then, remove the check next to Hide Protected Operating System Files.
3. Click OK to close the window.
4. Edit the `boot.ini` file (found in the `root` directory), by adding **`/bootlog`** to the end of the entry for your Windows 2000 operating system, as shown in Figure 9.1 for the Windows 2000 Professional installation. (Note that your `boot.ini` file might not look exactly like this one, but this is of no consequence as long as you edit the correct line.)
5. Save and close the `boot.ini` file.
6. Restore file and folder viewing back to normal.

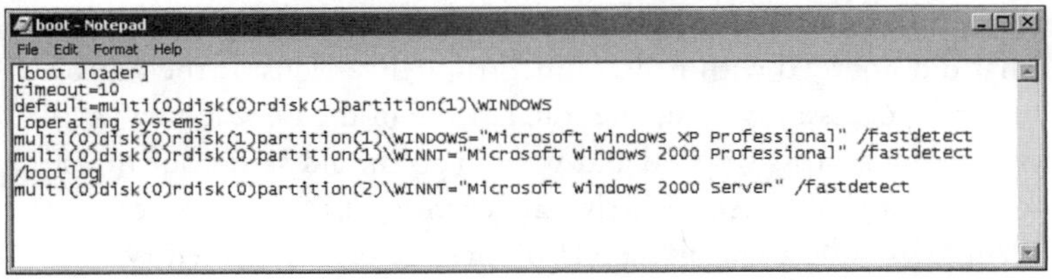

```
boot - Notepad
File Edit Format Help
[boot loader]
timeout=10
default=multi(0)disk(0)rdisk(1)partition(1)\WINDOWS
[operating systems]
multi(0)disk(0)rdisk(1)partition(1)\WINDOWS="Microsoft Windows XP Professional" /fastdetect
multi(0)disk(0)rdisk(0)partition(1)\WINNT="Microsoft Windows 2000 Professional" /fastdetect
/bootlog
multi(0)disk(0)rdisk(0)partition(2)\WINNT="Microsoft Windows 2000 Server" /fastdetect
```

FIGURE 9.1
Adding boot logging to the `boot.ini` file.

The boot log is written to a file named `ntbtlog.txt` and located in the `%windir%` directory. The contents of the file can be viewed by double-clicking it or opening it in any text editor. The log shows all the files that Windows 2000 attempted to load during startup and their statuses. The two statuses you might see are `Loaded driver` and `Did not load driver`, and they're explained here:

- `Loaded driver`—The driver or service was successfully loaded during startup by Windows 2000. The path name and filename are given.
- `Did not load driver`—The driver or service was not successfully loaded during startup by Windows 2000. The path name and filename are given.

Figure 9.2 shows a portion of a sample `ntbtlog.txt` file.

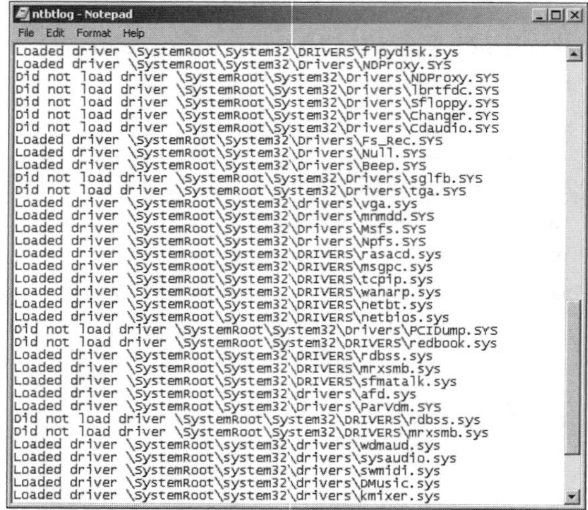

FIGURE 9.2
The boot log details the load status of services and drivers.

By examining the boot log, you can identify missing or corrupted files. If the startup completes, you have the task of replacing the files that did not load with new or uncorrupted versions. If the startup did not successfully complete, the last file in the boot log will show where the process stopped and where you should start your investigation. Critical system files that are corrupt or missing can cause Windows 2000 to display a STOP message or write an entry to the event log. Other files that are not critical do not usually generate entries in the event log. If you have files listed in the boot log as `Did not load`, you can take some or all of the following actions to correct the problem:

- Check for 0-byte files.
- Check for files with date and time stamps that do not match those of the Windows 2000 installation.
- Run the System File Checker (`Sfc.exe`) command-line tool to inspect system files. See Chapter 8 for more information on the System File Checker.
- Compare the file (using the path information given in the boot log) to the same file on the installation CD-ROM or on another Windows 2000 computer. Third-party files should be compared against verified copies obtained from the vendor or manufacturer.

If the problem your computer is experiencing is severe, you might need to attempt to repair it by using a special startup of Windows 2000. The next sections discuss this in detail.

Server, System State, and User Data Recovery

▶ Repair an operating system by using various startup options.

If you are very fortunate, you will never have to recover any lost data or restore a server after a crash. In that case, all your planning, worrying, and hard work will have paid off. However, chances are unlikely that you will be so fortunate. If nothing else, you will encounter an end-user who has accidentally deleted a file and needs you to restore it. There's a good chance that a catastrophic accident will occur while you are an administrator, and you will need to recover from it.

At that point, all the talk about saving data and restoring systems becomes practical and not simply theoretical; you had better hope that you've implemented a good strategy for dealing with the problem at hand. The following bulleted list presents the available options if you find yourself in this situation, from least effort (most preferable) to most effort (least preferable):

- **Last Known Good Configuration**—This enables you to recover from configuration changes that affect Registry settings for devices (such as installing an incorrect video driver or configuring it incorrectly). This tool has only a limited window of effectiveness; after you successfully log on locally to a Windows 2000 computer, this will no longer function.
- **Safe Mode Startup**—This enables you to troubleshoot and correct errors that might be otherwise uncorrectable. Starting in Safe Mode loads only a minimal set of drivers and is very useful in cases where device drivers are to blame for startup errors.
- **Windows 2000 Backup**—This is useful for recovering other Registry settings as well as user data. This option allows for the widest breadth of recovery but also takes the most time. Backup and restoration are discussed in the "Recovering System State and User Data with Windows 2000 Backup" section later in this chapter.

Each of these three methods is discussed at length in the following sections.

Recovering System State with Last Known Good Configuration

The Last Known Good Configuration is automatically saved whenever a user successfully logs onto the system interactively (that is, locally at the computer). This state represents the last configuration settings that were capable of supporting a successful logon. If you make a change to your system and want to reverse it, you can do so at restart by invoking the Last Known Good Configuration option.

Selecting Last Known Good Configuration provides a way to recover from problems such as a newly added driver that might be incorrect for your hardware. It does not, however, solve problems caused by corrupted or missing drivers or files. When you select Last Known Good Configuration, Windows 2000 restores information in the `HKLM\System\CurrentControlSet` Registry key only. Any changes you have made in other Registry keys remain, and all changes made since the last successful logon are lost.

The process to use the Last Known Good Configuration is outlined in Step By Step 9.3.

STEP BY STEP

9.3 Invoking Last Known Good Configuration

1. Start or restart your server.
2. During the text mode of the boot process, a screen appears with the message `For troubleshooting and advanced startup options for Windows 2000, press F8.` Press F8.
3. When the Advanced Options menu appears, use the arrow keys to move to Last Known Good Configuration, and then press Enter to continue.
4. If prompted, choose the configuration to use.
5. The computer will continue to boot normally, incorporating the Last Known Good Configuration information.

After the computer has finished starting, all should be well. If you know what the cause of the problem was, you should ensure that it has been totally corrected (in other words, that all bad drivers removed). After you log off the computer, this configuration then becomes the Last Known Good Configuration. It is for this reason that LKGC can't be used to fix problems if you have logged off and back on again before attempting to use a Last Known Good Configuration startup.

In the next section, we will look at using Safe Mode to start up the computer in a reduced capability mode that allows for troubleshooting and repair of computers experiencing startup problems.

Using Safe Mode

If your system has experienced a noncritical error during startup (in other words, you don't get a STOP error), you can perform a special type of startup known as a Safe Mode startup. Several options are available for performing Safe Mode startups, all of which are outlined in Table 9.1. Additionally, several other advanced startup options not related to Safe Mode are also presented in Table 9.1 for completeness.

TABLE 9.1

ADVANCED BOOT OPTIONS

Option	*Function*
Safe Mode	Loads only the basic devices and drivers required to start the system. This includes the mouse, keyboard, mass storage, base video, and default set of system services.
Safe Mode with Networking	This performs a Safe Load with the drivers and services necessary for networking.
Safe Mode with Command Prompt	This performs a Safe Load but launches a command prompt rather than Windows Explorer.
Enable Boot Logging	Logs the loading and initialization of drivers and services.
Enable VGA Mode	Restricts the startup to use only the base video.

continues

TABLE 9.1 *continued*

ADVANCED BOOT OPTIONS

Option	*Function*
Last Known Good Configuration	Uses the Last Known Good configuration to boot the system.
Directory Services Restore Mode	Enables the restoration of Active Directory (on domain controllers only).
Debugging Mode	Turns on debugging.

When you use one of the Safe Mode options, an environmental variable is created, `Safeboot_Option`, which is set to either Network or Minimal.

Step By Step 9.4 illustrates how to boot to Safe Mode.

STEP BY STEP

9.4 Booting to Safe Mode

1. Start or restart your server.
2. During the text mode of the boot process, a screen appears with the message `For troubleshooting and advanced startup options for Windows 2000, press F8.` Press F8.
3. When the Advanced Options menu appears, use the arrow keys to move to the Safe Mode option you want, and then press Enter to continue.
4. Log in when prompted. If you did not choose network support, you will be able to log on only with a local account. A domain controller will not be available to validate a domain login.
5. Modify the settings that are causing problems. Then, restart your computer, choosing to start normally this time.

From within Safe Mode, you can now safely and easily remove or replace drivers or other software that might be causing problems. If you are unable to correct the problem from Safe Mode, you might need to attempt repair via the Recovery Console—a new feature in Windows 2000 and the topic of the next section.

Recovering Systems with the Recovery Console

▶ Repair an operating system by using the Recovery Console.

The Recovery Console is a powerful text-based boot alternative for Windows 2000. If your system becomes so corrupt that no other repair process will help, you can boot to the Recovery Console and copy files to or from your computer. In addition, if a service you have installed causes problems with booting, you can stop and start services. The following is a list of some of the tasks you can perform from the Recovery Console:

- Start and stop services.
- Copy data from a floppy disk or CD.
- Read or write data on a local drive.
- Format a disk drive.
- Repair the boot sector or boot record.

If you get an error message when booting your computer that indicates a system file is missing, you can use the Recovery Console to start the system and copy a new version of the file from the CD to the system drive.

The Recovery Console does have some limitations, however, including the following:

- You can't copy files from the hard drive to a floppy disk by default (this must be enabled as explained later in this section).
- You can view only the `%windir%` directory (usually `C:\Winnt`) and its subdirectories.

- You need to identify yourself by logging in as the administrator. However, if the Security Accounts Manager (SAM) hive is corrupt or missing, you will not be able to use the Recovery Console.

There are two ways to boot to the Recovery Console: using the setup disks or configuring the Recovery Console as a secondary boot in the boot menu and selecting it at system startup. Step By Step 9.5 shows how to boot to this console using the Windows 2000 setup disks or setup CD-ROM.

STEP BY STEP

9.5 Booting to the Recovery Console with Setup Disks or the Windows 2000 CD-ROM

1. Place the disk labeled Windows 2000 Setup Boot Disk into the disk drive and restart your computer. Alternatively, if you can boot from the Windows 2000 CD-ROM, you can skip to step 5 of this process.
2. When prompted, insert the Windows 2000 Server Setup Disk #2 and press Enter to continue.
3. When prompted, insert the Windows 2000 Server Setup Disk #3 and press Enter to continue.
4. When prompted, insert the Windows 2000 Server Setup Disk #4 and press Enter to continue.
5. At the Welcome to Setup screen, press R to continue the repair process.
6. When the Windows Repair Options screen appears, press C to boot to the Recovery Console.
7. Select the Windows 2000 installation to which you want to log on. If you have your computer configured to multiboot more than one operating system, you might have more than one separate installation of Windows 2000 from which to choose. Press Enter to continue. The selection menu for this will look similar to the following:

```
Microsoft Windows 2000 Recovery Console.
The Recovery Console provides system repair and
```

```
recovery
functionality.
Type EXIT to quit the Recovery Console and restart
the
computer.

1. C:\WINNT

Which Windows 2000 installation would you like to
log on to
(To cancel, press ENTER)?
```

8. When prompted for the administrator password, type it in to log in.

9. When login is successful, you are taken to a command prompt. You can now use the console as though it were a command prompt, with some restricted functionality. To get help for a specific command, type the command name followed by `/?`, such as **`map /?`**. If you need to disable a service (or device) to prevent it from starting at the next reboot, type **`DISABLE servicename`**. For a list of services, type **`LISTSVC`**. If you need to copy files, all the drives (including the CD-ROM) should start as usual.

10. When you finish making repairs, type **`EXIT`** to reboot.

To make booting to the Recovery Console more convenient, you can make it a boot item. Step By Step 9.6 shows you how to install Recovery Console as a boot item.

STEP BY STEP

9.6 Installing the Recovery Console As a Boot Item

1. With Windows 2000 Server running, start a command prompt (select Start, Programs, Accessories, Command Prompt).

2. Navigate to the source of your Windows 2000 installation files (CD-ROM, network share, local folder) and change it to the `i386` folder.

continues

continued

3. From within the `i386` folder, type **`winnt32.exe /cmdcons`**.
4. When prompted to install the console, confirm by clicking Yes.
5. When prompted that the console has been installed, click OK.
6. You will see the Recovery Console as a new boot menu item on the next restart of the computer. You can now select the Recovery Console (or any other installed operating system) from the boot menu.

Table 9.2 lists the commands available when running the Windows 2000 Recovery Console.

TABLE 9.2

WINDOWS 2000 RECOVERY CONSOLE COMMANDS

Command	*Description*
`Attrib`	Changes attributes on a file or directory
`Batch`	Executes commands from a text file
`Cd`	Changes the directory or displays the name of the current directory
`Chkdsk`	Displays the current status of the disk
`Cls`	Clears the screen
`Copy`	Copies a file to another location or name
`Del`	Deletes a file(s)
`Dir`	Displays a list of file(s) or directories
`Disable`	Disables a service or driver
`Diskpart`	Manages partitions on a drive(s)
`Enable`	Starts/enables a service or driver
`Exit`	Exits the console and restarts the computer
`Expand`	Extracts a file from a compressed version
`Fixboot`	Writes a new boot sector

Command	*Description*
`Fixmbr`	Repairs the Master Boot Record
`Format`	Formats a drive/disk
`Help`	Displays lists of available commands
`Listsvc`	Lists services/drivers on this computer
`Logon`	Logs on to this system
`Map`	Displays mapped drive letters
`Md`	Creates a directory
`More`	Pauses display of text file when screen is full
`Ren`	Renames a file
`Rd`	Deletes a directory
`Set`	Shows and sets environment variables
`Systemroot`	Sets the current directory you are in to the `systemroot` directory
`Type`	Prints a file to screen

To use the SET command, you must enable its use ahead of time. The SET command can be enabled from the Group Policy snap-in or the Security Configuration and Analysis snap-in of the MMC. The procedure to do this is outlined in Step By Step 9.7.

STEP BY STEP

9.7 Enabling the SET Command

1. Select Start, Run; then type **`mmc`**. Press Enter.
2. In the Console1 dialog box, click Console, select Add/Remove Snap-in, and then click Add.
3. Select Group Policy, and then click Add.
4. In the Select Group Policy Object list box, select Local Computer, and then click Finish.
5. In the Add Standalone Snap-in dialog box, click Close.

continues

NOTE **The SET Command and Beyond** The SET command can also be enabled from the Security Configuration and Analysis snap-in. See Chapter 13 of the *Windows 2000 Server Operations Guide* for more information on the SET command and the Recovery Console at `http://www.microsoft.com/technet/prodtechnol/windows2000serv/reskit/serverop/part3/sopch13.asp`.

continued

6. In the Add/Remove Snap-in dialog box, click OK.
7. Expand Local Computer Policy, Computer Configuration, Windows Settings, Security Settings, and then Local Policies. Click Security Options.
8. Double-click the policy Recovery Console: Allow Floppy Copy and Access to All Drives and Folders.
9. In the Local Security Policy Setting dialog box, select Enabled, and then click OK.

If you have a system that can't be repaired by using either the Recovery Console or a Safe Mode startup, you might need to consider performing a restoration using Windows 2000 backup. We will look at using Windows 2000 backup in the next section.

Recovering Systems Using Windows 2000 Backup

- ▶ Recover data from a hard disk in the event that the operating system will not start.
- Restore an operating system and data from a backup.

Most Windows 2000 implementations require that data be restored from backup at some point. Assuming that you have been using good backup methods, you should be able to quickly recover from any incident, whether it is a hard drive failure or a user deletion error. Before you can get around to restoring your data, however, you must have a good understanding of how to back up your data in the first place. The next few sections discuss how backups are performed, including the various types available for use in Windows 2000; how media rotation and storage should be handled; and lastly, how to get your critical data back after all other means to repair a problem have failed.

Backup Basics

The most robust method of saving both system state and user data is to use Windows 2000 Backup. This backup utility is much improved over the version that came with Windows NT 4.0. It enables full backup of all system state information with just one check of a check box, as well as the scheduling of backup times and dates.

The importance of regular backups can't be overstated. The ability to recover from catastrophic failure or user error depends on your backups being up-to-date and secure from theft and physical damage. At some point, all computers will fail; your ability to get your system running in short order often depends on the presence of a good backup. If the possibility of a computer failing seems unlikely to you, step back and think about unscrupulous employees causing damage or perhaps the flood of the century that visits your office. In short, sometimes restoring from a backup is the only option.

What follows is a discussion of backups in general and then a discussion of backups using Windows 2000 Backup. The former covers backup processes that apply to any computerized environment in which data and system recovery are important. The second covers the backing up of information to allow the recovery of data and systems.

NOTE

System State Although the configuration can vary from computer to computer, system data encompasses the following items:

- Registry
- COM+ Class Registration database
- Boot files, including the system files
- Certificate Services database
- Active Directory directory service
- SYSVOL directory
- Cluster service information
- IIS Metadirectory
- System files that are under Windows File Protection

Of Archive Bits and Backup Types

The theory of backups, the how's and the why's, have not really changed since the need for backup was conceived. Regardless of the backup software you choose, the main features remain the same. There are essentially five backup types or five ways to determine what should be backed up and how this affects further backups. These five types are normal (or full), incremental, differential, copy, and timeframe (backups that are done on some regular interval; Windows 2000 implements this as *daily*).

On a Windows 2000 computer, each file residing on a FAT, a FAT32, or an NTFS partition has an archive bit that identifies whether that particular file has been backed up. An archive bit set to False (0) means the file has been backed up and has not been modified since it was backed up. If the file has not been modified, its archive bit will not be set. This shows that the file should now be backed up.

Windows 2000 provides the following five types of backup:

- **Normal backups**—Also called *full backups*, these save all files regardless of the state of the archive bit. While saving the files, normal backups set the archive bit to False (0) to indicate that the files have been backed up. This means that if you were to do two normal backups in a row, both would save all the data, and both would set the archive bits to False.
- **Incremental backups**—These look to see the current status of the archive bit before backing up data. If the archive bit is False (0), an incremental backup skips the file because it has been backed up. If the archive bit is True (1), an incremental backup saves the file and sets its archive bit to False. If you change a file and then run two incremental backups in a row, only the first will back up the file. The second will encounter the False archive bit set by the first incremental backup and skip the file.
- **Differential backups**—These also look at the current status of the archive bit before backing up data. As with an incremental backup, if the archive bit is False, a differential skips the file, and if the archive bit is True, the differential backup saves the file. However, it does not set the archive bit to False. Therefore, two differentials in a row will both back up the same changed file because the first backup will not set the archive bit to tell the second to skip the file.
- **Copy backups**—These are similar to normal backups in that they back up all data regardless of the state of the archive bit. However, they do not set the archive bits to true after backing up the data. They have no effect on any other backup processes. If you performed two copy backups in a row, both would back up all the information, but the archive bits would be left as they were before the backups were done.
- **Daily backups**—These are similar to copy backups. Daily backups back up all data regardless of the state of the archive bit, but they also look at the date a file was changed. As an example, daily backups (a type of timeframe backup) back up only those files modified on a specific day.

General backup theory indicates three types of ongoing backup strategies: normal only, normal/incremental, and normal/differential.

The decision to use one over the other is determined by a number of factors. The first factor is how much time you have to perform backups on any given day. If you have the time to perform a complete backup of all your systems every day, that is definitely the best option. Using a normal only strategy ensures that all your data is backed up at the end of every day. This means recovery requires that only one backup set be available and ensures that if any tape fails, you only have to go to the previous day's backup to completely recover all the information available on that tape.

The copy backup is used only to make periodic copies of the data. You can do a copy backup anytime you want for any reason without affecting any other backup processes; therefore this is an exception to the normal process of conducting backups. The copy backup is not a part of normal backup schemes, so it does not affect media rotation. Media rotation and storage issues are examined briefly in the next section before getting on to the issue at hand: working with backups and restorations.

Media Rotation and Storage Issues

Taking the time to properly conduct backups of critical information is of little use if you have not taken steps to ensure that your backup media is rotated properly and stored in a secure offsite location.

Several media rotation plans have existed as unofficial standards when it comes to dealing with backup media. You rotate backup media for two reasons: to ensure that you will have an adequate amount of backed up days available to perform a restoration and also to minimize and evenly distribute wear and tear over multiple pieces of media. Let's look at an example to help make this clearer. Say you use a tape drive to perform nightly backups of critical information on your central file server. You are using three tapes and performing a normal backup each night because the amount of information allows enough time for the normal backup. You rotate the tape each day, so that you have three days' worth of normal backups on hand at any time. This sounds like a good plan until you start to think about just how few chances you get to do it all right when disaster strikes. By using the same three tapes over and over (and over and over) again, you rapidly degrade their quality and capability to guarantee you a happy restoration. What if a disaster occurs after you've been using these tapes for a year? How likely is it that one or more of them will have errors—just like those old

8-tracks you still have lying around in the attic! What's the chance that yesterday's tape is bad and now you've lost an entire day's worth of data? These are the types of reasons you should ensure that you are rotating your media properly. This issue becomes even more important if you are using a normal/differential or normal/incremental backup strategy. Many companies exist that can provide you with a sound backup media rotation plan, as well as provide safe offsite storage of your media.

Companies exist whose sole purpose for being is to help you maintain proper backup media control. If it sounds too good to be true, just remember that you can even order pizza from the Internet now! These companies usually offer a range of services, but some of the ones you might want to consider include pickup and drop-off of media (which helps keep it rotated properly) and secure storage (which ensures it is available to you when it's needed). Your backup media is treated by these companies like your money is by the bank. Their job is to keep it safe and protected for when you need it. They also ensure that you are rotating media correctly and disposing of media when it has been used too many times. In mission-critical situations, give some thought to using a service such as these instead of just keeping your backup media in the filing cabinet in your office—the job you save might just be your own!

Performing Backups with Windows 2000 Backup

To perform a backup, you must have Read access to the files or the user right of Backup and Restore Files, which is granted by default to Administrators and Backup Operators.

Special permissions are granted the Administrators and Backup Operators groups to access all files for the purposes of doing backups. Even if members of these groups can't access the data as users, they will be able to back it up.

Using the Windows 2000 Backup utility to perform backups and restorations is a fairly easy process, although you might want to take some time out before disaster strikes to become familiar with performing restorations. In Step By Step 9.8, the process to perform a backup using the Backup Wizard is demonstrated.

> **NOTE**
>
> **Beyond Backup Basics** For more information on working with Windows 2000 Backup and configuring its options, see the Windows 2000 Resource Kit at `http://www.microsoft.com/technet/prodtechnol/windows2000serv/reskit/serverop/part3/sopch12.asp`.

STEP BY STEP

9.8 Backing Up Data Using the Backup Wizard

1. Select Start, Programs, Accessories, System Tools, Backup.
2. At the Welcome page, click the Backup Wizard icon to start the configuration process.
3. At the Welcome to the Windows 2000 Backup and Recovery Tools screen, click Next.
4. At the What to Back Up screen, select Back Up Everything on My Computer; Back Up Selected Files, Drives, or Network Data; or Only Back Up the System State Data, as shown in Figure 9.3. If you choose to back up everything, Windows will back up all the data on the local machine. The System State data was defined previously in the "Backup Basics" section. If you select either of these options, skip to step 6. If you choose to back up only selected files, you will have the option of choosing any local or remote files you want to back up. Continue to step 5.
5. At the Items to Back Up screen, you can choose which file, folders, drives, or remote data you want to back up. As you can see from Figure 9.4, you can back up mapped drives, system state data, or information from remote machines. A clear box with a blue check mark designates a drive or folder that has been chosen with all its contents, including subfolders. A clear box with a gray check mark means that there are components in the tree that have been deselected. A box that is filled in with gray means that it is not possible to save all content, and you must descend farther in the tree to select files for backup. A clear box with no check mark indicates that no files from that tree will be backed up. Select the items you want to back up, and click Next.

continues

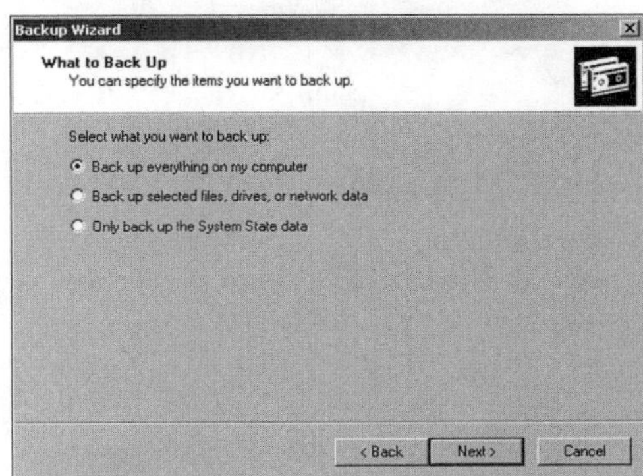

FIGURE 9.3
Choose how much of the local data you want to back up.

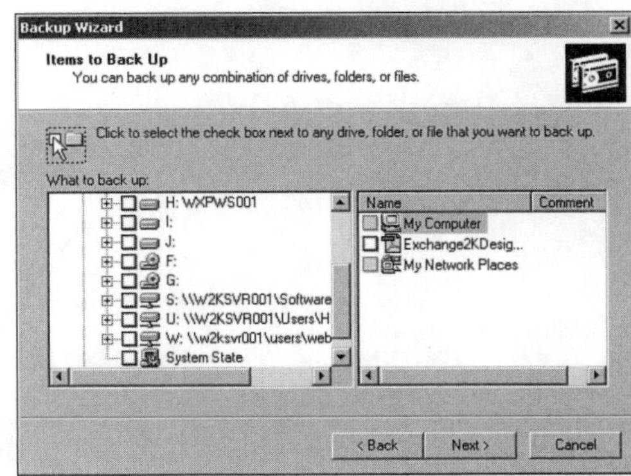

FIGURE 9.4
Select to back up remote drives, local drives, folders, and files.

continued

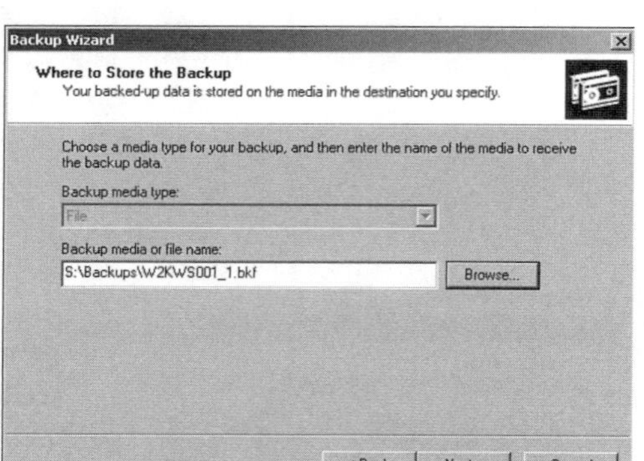

FIGURE 9.5
Choose the media type and the specific media to back up on.

6. At the Where to Store the Backup screen, choose the media type (file or tape) and the filename or media name (see Figure 9.5). If you are backing up to tape, you will notice that Backup remembers the backups that have been performed to tape. You have the option of backing up to a tape that you already created or backing up to a new tape. The assumption here is that you have specific tapes for specific purposes (which you should) and that you will always use the same media for the same backup task. If you choose a media name you have already used, you will have the option of either overwriting the previous data on the tape or appending to the data that already exists.

7. At the Completing the Backup Wizard screen, either click Finish to begin the backup immediately with the default parameters or click the Advanced button to set the parameters of your backup. These parameters are used if you want to change the current backup settings from those that are currently established as the norm. If you click Finish, the backup starts immediately.

8. At the Type of Backup screen, select the backup type from the list. In addition, you can choose to back up remote storage data. Remote storage enables you to migrate little-used data to a readily accessible archive, often centralized within your company. This is usually a tape or a group of tapes that are always mounted. When data is moved to remote storage, a pointer remains on the hard drive to allow access to the data in the future. Users do not know that the data has been archived; only Windows 2000 knows this. When you choose to back up remote storage data, the data is retrieved from the remote location and written to the backup tape or file. Select the backup type you desire, and then click Next to continue.

9. At the How to Back Up screen, choose to turn on or off data verification and hardware compression. Data verification reads back the data that was placed on your backup media to ensure that it is the same as the file from which it is copied. This option adds time to the backup but ensures that all the data went onto the tape correctly. Hardware compression takes advantage of specific tape-drive hardware that supports additional compression of files as they go onto the tape. Although hardware compression enables you to put more data on a tape, you should exercise some caution when using this. Data saved with hardware compression is readable only by using a similar tape device. Click Next to progress to the next page.

10. At the Media Options screen, you can choose either to append data to a currently existing file or tape or to overwrite the current data, if any, with the new backup data. If this is an overwrite or a new media, you also can configure access restrictions. If you select the Allow Only the Owner and the Administrator Access check box, you ensure that data on the tape can be restored only by the person who made the backup (the owner) or a member of the Administrators group. This means that even if many people have physical access to the tape, only a select group will be able to retrieve data from it. Click Next to continue.

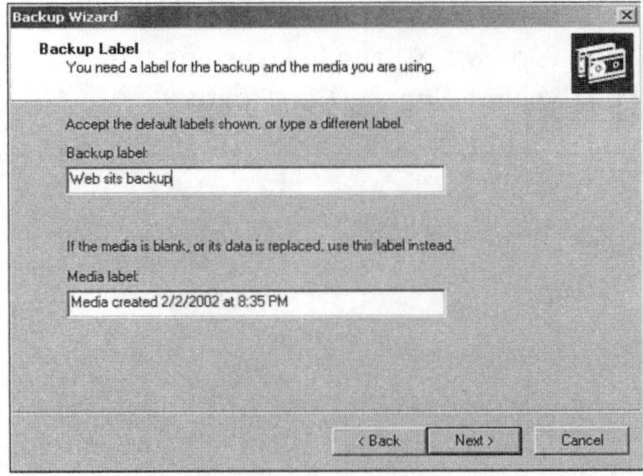

FIGURE 9.6
Enter a backup label or a media label.

11. At the Backup Label screen, you can create labels for the backup and the media (see Figure 9.6). The media label is used for the first backup set placed into a file or onto a tape. The backup label is used when two or more backups are placed into a file or onto a tape. Click Next to continue.

12. At the When to Back Up screen, you can choose to begin the backup immediately or defer it to a scheduled time (For brevity, this Step By Step assumes you are backing up immediately.) Click Next to continue.

13. When the Completing the Backup Wizard screen appears again, click Finish to begin the backup. Figure 9.7 shows the backup status.

14. When the backup completes, click Close to finish the process.

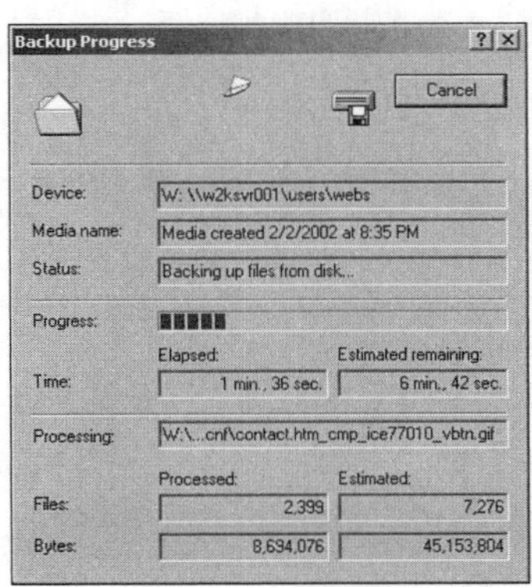

FIGURE 9.7
Backup running.

NOTE

Windows 2000 Backup Does Not Back Up Open Files Similar to many other backup programs, Windows 2000 Backup does not back up open files. This means you might have to stop some running processes to ensure that files accessed by them will be backed up. Files that are open when the backup process gets to them are skipped, and that fact is noted in the backup log (if you have logging configured).

As a side note (and off the topic here), this feature is supported under Windows XP and is known as the Volume Shadow Copy feature.

One of the strengths of Windows 2000 Backup is its capability to schedule backups for times of low system usage—typically late at night. An administrator does not need to be present during the backup as long as the correct tape or tapes are mounted.

Now that you've gotten a good review of the Windows 2000 Backup utility and how to use it, you should be ready to restore data when and if required in a disaster recovery situation.

Performing the Restoration with Windows 2000 Backup

The number of options for recovery of information are greatly reduced compared to options for saving information. In a simple recovery, you can indicate what needs to be restored and from which tape or file. Advanced options enable you to configure recovery in three ways. You can choose the location of recovered files and whether to overwrite existing files. Special options, including restoring security, restoring the removable storage database, and restoring junction points to mounted volumes, are also available.

When setting file locations, you can choose to recover data to the original location. Another option is to recover data to an alternative location with the underlying tree structure preserved. A further option is to recover data to a single folder with all the files deposited without the original structure.

When setting overwrite policy, you have three choices for recovering information. You can choose never to overwrite a file that already exists, to overwrite a file that exists if the one on the backup is newer, or to always overwrite existing files.

When using special options for recovering information, you also have three options. One of the special options enables you to define the recovery of security information: NTFS local permissions, auditing, and ownership. When restoring to an NTFS volume, you can recover NTFS permissions or leave them off. It is important to note that if you want full recovery of NTFS file properties, you must recover to an NTFS volume.

A second special option is the recovery of the removable storage database. This tracks what removable storage media were used for what purposes, including tracking where backups have been performed. This will replace the current removable storage database found in `WINNT\System32\Ntmsdata` with the one from the backup.

The final special option is the recovery of mounted volumes and their defining junction points. A *mounted volume* is essentially a pointer, or junction point, from a folder to a local drive or network location. You can choose to restore just the junction points (assuming the data is intact on the drive being pointed to) or to restore both the junction points and the information on the mounted drive.

Step By Step 9.9 shows you how to recover information stored on backup tapes or files.

NOTE

You Can Restore from GUI Only
Using the GUI program is the only way to restore data using Windows 2000 Backup. There is no command-line interface, nor can it be scheduled. If a computer experiences a total failure, you must reinstall the operating system first and then perform the restoration. This limitation might or might not apply to third-party backup solutions.

STEP BY STEP

9.9 Recovering Data from Backup Tapes or Files

1. Select Start, Programs, Accessories, System Tools, Backup.
2. At the Welcome page, click the Restore Wizard icon to start the configuration process.
3. At the Welcome to the Restore Wizard screen, click Next to continue.
4. At the What to Restore screen, choose the media type and the backup set from within that group. Finally, expand the backup set and select those files you want to restore. If your tape drive holds only a single tape, you must make sure you have the appropriate tape inserted into the drive. If you request to restore from a specific drive, it might take a minute or two to recover the folder list from the tape catalog before the tree is displayed. Click Next to continue.
5. At the Completing the Restore Wizard screen, review the settings. If they are acceptable, click Next. If not, click the Advanced button to set the advanced options.

continues

continued

6. At the Where to Restore screen, choose the location to restore to. If you select Original Location, you can click Next. Otherwise, you must fill in the location to which to restore the files in a text box that appears on this page.

7. At the How to Restore screen, specify what to do if the restore process detects a file in the restore location that is the same as a file trying to be restored (see Figure 9.8). Click Next to continue.

8. At the Advanced Restore Options screen, choose which special options you want, and then click Next (see Figure 9.9).

9. When the Completing the Restore Wizard screen appears again, click Finish to begin restoring files.

10. When the restore completes, click Close to finish the process.

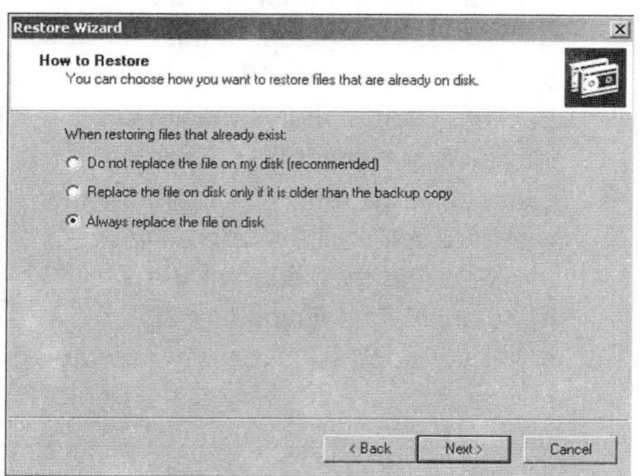

FIGURE 9.8
Define what to do if the restore process encounters a file on your hard drive that it is to restore from tape.

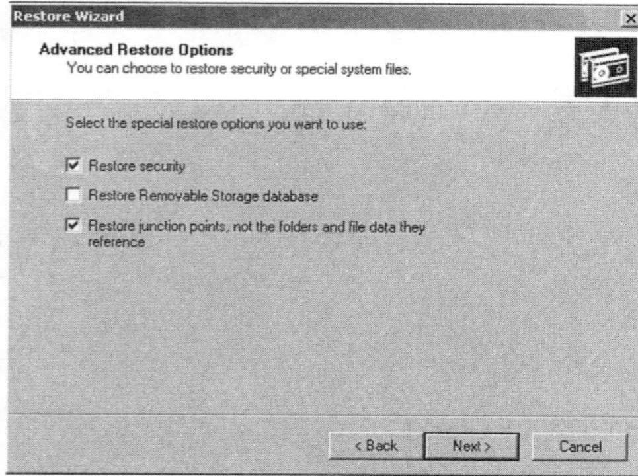

FIGURE 9.9
Define whether to restore security and what to do with removable storage and mounted drives.

> **NOTE**
> **Restoration Station** For more information on working with Windows 2000 Backup during the restoration process, see the Windows 2000 Resource Kit at `http://www.microsoft.com/technet/prodtechnol/windows2000serv/reskit/serverop/part3/sopch13.asp`.

Other Means of Recovering Data

▶ Recover data from a hard disk in the event that the operating system will not start.

If you can't get a computer started despite all your efforts, you might still be able to access the data on the machine's hard drives and even move it to a new location on the network, if you want. The easiest way to do this is via a parallel installation on that machine.

A *parallel installation* is a back door of sorts. It is a secondary installation of the operating system inside a different directory, on a different partition, or (most preferably) on a separate physical disk. Even on the most fault-tolerant installations, problems you didn't plan for can still arise and wreak havoc for you.

A parallel installation, when performed ahead of time, is the best (and safest) form of data recovery when an operating system installation is completely damaged.

A parallel installation enables you full control access to your NTFS formatted volumes in the event that disaster strikes and you need access to the files or Registry data contained on the primary installation. In this way, you can seek to repair problems yourself instead of relying on Windows recovery processes to do the work for you.

A parallel installation should include all the recovery tools (and system utilities, such as network backup software) that you would find on the primary installation, but it should not include all the services and functionality the primary installation possesses. For example, if you were to create a parallel installation on a member server that also served as a DNS/DHCP/WINS server, you wouldn't need to install those additional services because they would simply be taking up additional space. Also, you don't always need to keep your parallel installation updated with the most up-to-date service pack as long as you are comfortable with it and it can perform its duties.

NOTE

More Information on Parallel Installations Additional information on parallel installations can be found in Microsoft Knowledge Base article KB# Q266465 at `http://support.microsoft.com/default.aspx?scid=kb;EN-US;q266465` and also on the *Windows & .NET Magazine* Web site at `http://www.win2000mag.com/Articles/Index.cfm?ArticleID=7075`.

In this section we have covered a lot of ground, covering topics such as the boot process, troubleshooting STOP (Blue Screen of Death) errors, using the boot log, and methods to repair damaged operating systems ranging from the quick and easy Last Known Good Configuration to complete system restorations. In the next section, we will change gears and look at monitoring computers in an effort to tune them and keep them running to prevent disasters from occurring.

Monitoring and Troubleshooting Server Health and Performance

Administering a Windows 2000 server is not simply about making sure that people have access to it and that information is secure. The question administrators ask themselves is not just, "Is it running?" but also, "Is it running well?" Of course, "well" is relative and can't really be quantified outside your individual context.

This section covers topics related to the assessment of server performance, including a variety of monitoring and logging utilities found in the Performance Console. In addition, it discusses some tips on how to tune your server before problems occur and which devices should be monitored when they do.

Periodic monitoring of your Windows 2000 server is important to the process of optimization. Monitoring helps to overcome the feeling-based assessment of your users. For example, by comparing current network performance against a previously established baseline, you have more information than the anecdotal "The network is slow today!" to base your actions on. By gathering current information and comparing it against established norms for your systems (a baseline), you can detect bottlenecks, identify those system components that are slowing down server performance, and fix them before they become a problem to your users.

Although the actual procedure for creating a baseline is outlined later in this section, it is important to discuss the concept of a baseline here because it is the first thing you will do in practice—even if it is not the first concept that is presented here. A *baseline* is an established norm for the operation of your server as determined by normal load. This baseline can then be used as a basis of comparison for future performance to see whether repairable problems exist. As the configuration of your server changes (when, for example, a processor is added or RAM is added), new baselines are established to reflect the new expected performance.

The importance of establishing a baseline before beginning to monitor performance can't be overstated. Although there are some guidelines as to what absolute performance numbers indicate, it is as you compare current performance against past performance (the baseline) that you will really be able to evaluate how well current demand is being met and whether you require more resources on your server. In addition, it is imperative that a baseline be established before problems begin to occur. If users are already beginning to complain, "The network is slow," it is too late to establish a baseline because the statistics gathered will include whatever performance factors are contributing to the dissatisfaction.

It is important to monitor the following components of a Windows 2000 server: the hard disk(s), processor(s), memory, and network card(s). Regardless of which type of services the server is providing, these four areas interact to make your server efficient (thereby appearing fast) or inefficient. The actual speed or efficiency of each of the components varies in importance depending on the application. In some applications, memory is more important than processor speed or availability; in other applications, disk speed and availability is more important than fast network access.

Three tools are provided in Windows 2000 to aid an administrator when it comes to monitoring the status (and thus, the health) of server and client computers: the Performance Monitor, Event Viewer, and Task Manager. The next sections discuss each of these tools and how to put them to use.

Using the Performance Monitor

- ▶ Monitor and interpret real-time performance by using System Monitor and Task Manager.

Recognizing the need for administrators to be able to monitor the performance (and thus the health) of servers and client computers, Microsoft has built the Performance Monitor into Windows 2000. Whether you are looking for real-time graphical views or a log you can peruse at your convenience, the Performance Monitor can provide the type of data you need to evaluate performance and recommend system modification if necessary.

Monitoring performance begins with the collection of data. The Performance Monitor provides various methods of working with data, although all the methods use the same means of collecting data. Data collected by the Performance Monitor is broken down into objects, counters, and instances. An *object* is the software or device being monitored, such as memory or processor. A *counter* is a specific statistic for an object. Memory has a counter called `Available Bytes`, and a processor has a counter called `% Processor Time`. An *instance* is the specific occurrence of an object you are watching; in a multiprocessor server with two processors, you will have three instances: `0`, `1`, and `_Total`.

The primary difference between using the System Monitor and counter logs and trace logs is that you typically watch performance in real time in System Monitor (or play back saved logs), whereas you use counter logs and trace logs to record data for later analysis. Alerts function in real time by providing you with an alert when a user-defined threshold is exceeded. Collecting data and displaying it is discussed at length in the section "Using System Monitor," later in this chapter. Counter logs, trace logs, and alerts are discussed in the section "Configuring and Using Alerts and Logging," later in this chapter.

Using System Monitor

System Monitor enables you to view statistical data either live or from a saved log (see Figure 9.10). You can view the data in three formats: graph, histogram, or report. Graph data is displayed as a line graph; histograms are displayed as bar graphs; and reports are text-based and show the current numerical information available from the statistics.

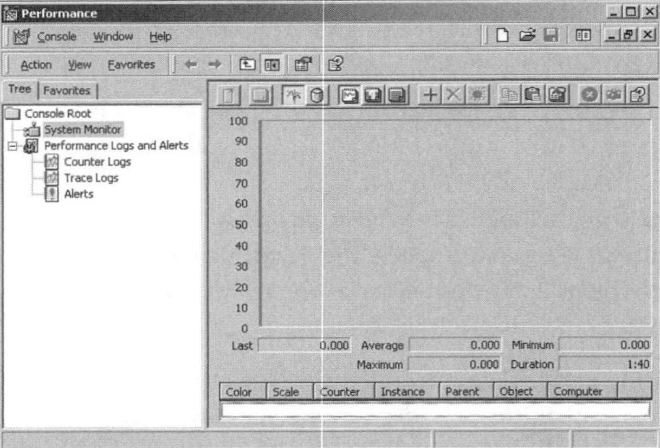

FIGURE 9.10
The System Monitor.

The basic use of the System Monitor is straightforward. You decide which object/instance/counter combinations you want to display and then configure the monitor accordingly. At that point, information begins to appear. You can also change the properties of the monitor to display information in different ways.

Figure 9.11 shows a typical Add Counters dialog box. At the top of the dialog box is a set of radio buttons with which you can obtain statistics from the local machine or a remote machine. This is useful when you want to monitor a computer in a location that is not within reasonable physical distance from you. Under the radio buttons is a pull-down list naming the performance objects that can be monitored. Which performance objects are available depends on the features (and applications) you have installed on your server. Also, some counters come with specific applications. These performance counters enable you monitor statistics relating to that application from the Performance Monitor.

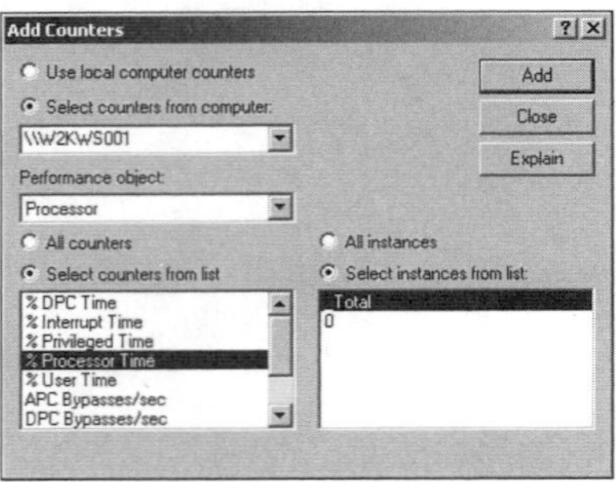

FIGURE 9.11
Adding a processor counter in the Add Counters dialog box.

When you first start the Performance Monitor, you might want to add the counters discussed later in this section from the memory, processor, hard disk, and network objects; however, you can add any combination of counters that you find helpful in tuning and monitoring your computers.

Under the performance object is a list of counters. When applied to a specific instance of an object, counters are what you are really after, and the object just narrows down your search. The counters are the actual statistical information you want to monitor. Each object has its own set of counters from which you can choose. Counters enable you to move from the abstract concept of an object to the concrete events that reflect that object's activity. For example, if you choose to monitor the processor, you can watch for the average processor time and how much time the processor spent doing non-idle activity. In addition, you can watch for %user time (time spent executing user application processes) versus %privileged time (time spent executing system processes).

To the right of the counter list is the instances list. If applicable, instances enumerate the physical objects that fall under the specific object class you have chosen. In some cases, the instances list is not applicable. For example, there is no instances list with memory. In cases where the instances list is applicable, you may see multiple instance variables. One variable represents the average of all the instances, and the rest of the variables represent the values for the first physical object (number 0, 1, and so on). For example, if you have two processors in your server, you will see (and be able to choose from) three instance variables: `_Total`, `0`, and `1`. This enables you to watch each processor individually and to watch them as a collective unit.

Step By Step 9.10 shows how to add a counter to the system monitor.

STEP BY STEP

9.10 Adding a Counter to the System Monitor

1. Select Start, Programs, Administrative Tools, Performance.
2. In the Performance Console, click System Monitor to bring up the System Monitor panel on the right side, as previously shown in Figure 9.10.

continues

continued

3. Right-click the panel on the right side and select Add Counters from the context menu. This brings up the window previously shown in Figure 9.11.

4. In the Add Counters dialog box, select the computer you want to monitor, as well as the object, counter, and instance; then click Add. If you need help understanding what a certain counter does, click the Explain button and an explanation will appear under the dialog box. As you add counters, your graph will begin to display data in real-time (see Figure 9.12).

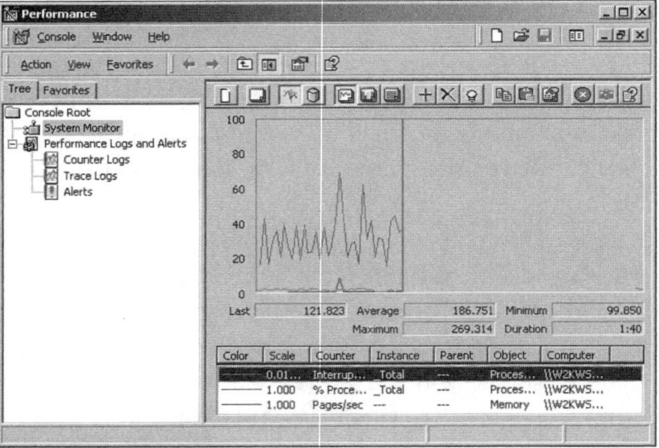

FIGURE 9.12
As you add counters in graph view, the current statistics begin to appear.

5. Repeat step 4 until you have added all the counters you want. Then, click the Close button.

You can make several modifications to the System Monitor to improve how it functions in your environment. The properties enable you to change the look, the data source, and how the data is to be displayed.

To access the properties for the System Monitor, right-click the graph and select Properties from the menu that appears. The properties window is shown in Figure 9.13.

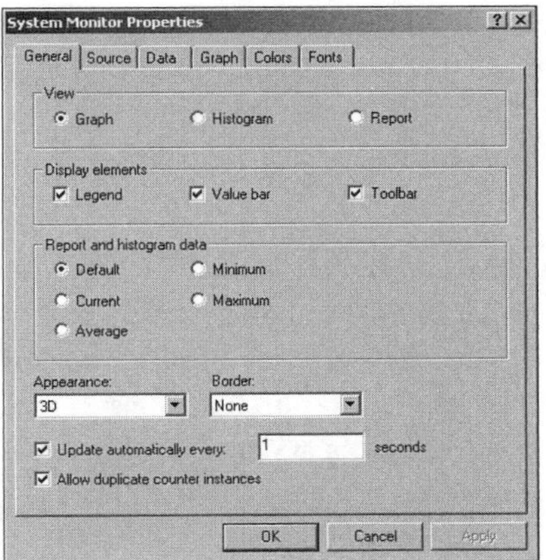

FIGURE 9.13
The General property tab for the System Monitor properties.

NOTE

Power Monitoring For more information on customizing the System Monitor (beyond the basics required for the exam), see the Windows 2000 Resource Kit at `http://www.microsoft.com/technet/prodtechnol/windows2000serv/reskit/serverop/part2/sopch05.asp`.

Using System Monitor to Discover Bottlenecks

Every chain, regardless of its strength, has its weakest link. When pulled hard enough, some point will give before all the others. Your server is similar to a chain. When it's under stress, some component will not be able to keep up with the others. This will result in a degradation of overall performance. The weak link in the server is referred to as a *bottleneck* because it's the component that slows everything else down. As an administrator responsible for ensuring efficient operation of your Windows 2000 server, you need to determine the following two things:

- Which component is causing the bottleneck?
- Is the stress on the server typical enough that action is warranted either now or in the future?

As was mentioned previously, under normal operation, only four system components affect system performance: memory, processor, disk, and network card. Therefore, you will want to monitor the counters that will tell you the most about how those four components affect system performance so you can determine the answer to the two diagnostic questions.

The biggest monitoring problem is not collecting the data, but interpreting it. Not only is it difficult to determine what a specific value for a particular counter means, it is also difficult to determine what it means in the context of other counters. The biggest difficulty is that no subsystem (disk, network, processor, or memory) exists in isolation. As a result, weaknesses in one might show up as weaknesses in another. Unless you take them all into consideration, you might end up adding another processor when all you need is more RAM.

Understanding how the subsystems interact is important to understanding the significance of the counter values that are recorded. For example, if you detect that your processor is constantly running at 90%, you might be tempted to purchase a faster processor (or another processor if you have a system board that will accommodate more than one). However, it is important to look at memory utilization and disk utilization as well because the problem could originate there instead. If you do not have enough memory, the processor must swap pages to the disk frequently. This results in high memory utilization, high disk utilization, and higher processor utilization. By purchasing more RAM, you could alleviate all those problems.

That one example illustrates how no one piece of information is enough to analyze your performance problems or your solution. You must monitor the server as a whole unit by putting together the counters from a variety of objects. Only then will you be able to see the big picture and solve problems that might arise.

The recommended method of monitoring is to use a counter log, which captures data over a period of time. This will help you eliminate questions of whether the current stress on the server is typical. If you log over a period of a week or a month and consistently see a certain component under excessive load, you can be sure the stress is typical.

The Physical Disk Counter

By default, counters are available to monitor the physical disk object. Therefore, you can watch to see just how much activity is taking place on a physical disk. Although these counters are generally sufficient for monitoring disk performance, in some rare cases you might also want to monitor the performance of logical partitions. To modify the disk counters available, you need to use the `diskperf` command. The basic syntax of `diskperf` is as follows:

```
diskperf -switch
```

A number of `diskperf` switches enable you to start and stop various counters. Table 9.3 outlines the switches and their functions.

TABLE 9.3

diskperf SWITCHES AND THEIR FUNCTIONS

Switch	*Function*
No switch	Identifies which counters are turned on (if any)
`-y`	Enables all disk counters (both logical and physical) at next restart
`-yd`	Enables physical disk counters at next restart (this is the default)
`-yv`	Enables logical disk counters at next restart
`-n`	Disables all disk counters (both logical and physical) at next restart
`-nd`	Disables physical disk counters at next restart
`-nv`	Disables logical disk counters at next restart

Up to now, we've been talking about physical disk counters and logical disk counters, but perhaps you're a bit confused about what is what. A quick review of physical versus logical disk counters is in order. *Physical* disk counters monitor a specific physical drive, whereas *logical* disk counters monitor a specific logical volume (partition). In other words, if you have two physical hard drives—each with three partitions—you can conceivably monitor two physical drives and six logical drives.

NOTE

Windows 2000 Disk Counters Differ from Those in NT 4.0 Windows NT 4.0 users are aware that no disk counters are initialized on startup. With Windows 2000, disk counters are initialized on startup for the physical counters but not the logical counters. The `-yd` switch is loaded by default, and it starts only the physical counters.

Creating Baselines

Baselines need to be established long before you encounter problems. After you have all your counters enabled, creating a baseline is the next step in the monitoring process. A baseline is a set of typical readings that define "normal" for your servers, client computers, or network under various operating conditions, such as no load, moderate load, and heavy load. Of course, what is normal is obviously open to interpretation, but one could say that normal is a server providing users with what they want in a timeframe they think is reasonable (oh no, another vague term!). By creating baselines early on, you have something that you can look back at and compare current server operating conditions to. If your system is already to the point where you are seeing system degradation, it is really too late to establish a baseline.

To establish a baseline, you pick a time (or duration of time) that represents typical user interaction with the server. Then, you create a log of important counters for the duration you have determined. Some of the more commonly used (and recommended) counters are described later in this section. The log you create should be stored in a safe place to ensure that you can refer to it in the future. Every time you perform a major hardware upgrade (such as increasing RAM or adding a processor), you should create a new set of baselines and consider deleting the old ones.

Which actual counters you want to monitor are based on the particular applications running on your server and the requirements you will have for the server. Although some recommendations are given in Table 9.4, you might want to watch other objects as well if you have specific applications installed. In addition, and as a point of clarification to the table, the second column provides an indication as to whether the counter is used to simply watch the component in question (usage) or to determine if the component is a performance bottleneck.

TABLE 9.4

COUNTERS TO MONITOR

Component	*Monitoring*	*Recommended Counters*
Disk	Usage	Physical Disk\ Disk Reads/sec Physical Disk\ Disk Writes/sec Logical Disk\% Free Space Logical Disk\% Disk Time
Disk	Bottlenecks	Physical Disk\ Current Disk Queue Length (all instances) Physical Disk\ Split IO/sec
Memory	Usage	Memory\ Available Bytes Memory\ Cache Bytes
Memory	Bottlenecks	Memory\ Pages/sec Memory\ Page reads/sec Memory\ Pool Paged Bytes Memory\ Pool Nonpaged Bytes
Network	Throughput	Network Interface\ Bytes total/sec
Processor	Usage	Processor\ % Processor Time (all instances)
Processor	Bottlenecks	System\ Processor Queue Length (all instances) Processor\ Interrupts/sec

As they pertain to Table 9.4, the following are descriptions of the counters:

- **Physical Disk\ Disk Reads/sec**—How many disk reads occur per second. This is a measure of the read activity on the disk. The transfer rate of the hard drive being used determines which values you should look for here, so check the vendor's supplied documentation. In general, Ultra Wide SCSI disks can handle about 50–70 I/O operations per second.
- **Physical Disk\ Disk Writes/sec**—How many disk writes occur per second. This is a measure of the write activity on the disk. The same guidelines apply for this counter as do for the Physical Disk\ Disk Reads/sec counter.
- **Logical Disk\ % Free Space**—The ratio of free space to total disk space on a logical drive. This is a measurement of remaining capacity on your logical drives. You generally should track this for each logical drive. To prevent excessive fragmentation, the value here should not be allowed to drop below 15%.
- **Logical Disk\ % Disk Time**—The ratio of busy time to the total elapsed time. This represents the percentage the disk is servicing read or write requests. You will generally should track this for each physical drive. If one drive is being used a lot more than another, it might be time to balance the content between the drives. The lower this number, the greater the capacity a disk has to do additional work. This value should typically not exceed 90%.
- **Physical Disk\ Current Disk Queue Length**—The average number of read and write requests that are waiting in queue. Optimally, this number should be no more than 2 because a larger number means the disk is a bottleneck; it is incapable of servicing the requests placed on it.
- **Physical Disk\ Split IO/sec**—Reports the rate at which the operating system divides I/O requests to the disk into multiple requests. A split I/O request might occur if the program requests data in a size that is too large to fit into a single request or if the disk is fragmented. Factors that influence the size of an I/O request can include application design, the file system, or drivers. A high rate of split I/O might not, in itself, represent a problem. However, on single-disk systems, a high rate for this counter tends to indicate disk fragmentation.

- **Memory\ Available Bytes**—This is the total amount of physical memory available to processes running on the computer. This number's significance varies as the amount of memory in the computer varies, but if this number is less than 4MB, you generally have a memory deficiency.
- **Memory\ Cache Bytes**—The amount of cache memory available to processes running on the computer. This counter indicates growth or shrinking of the cache. The value includes not only the size of the cache, but also the size of the paged pool and the amount of pageable driver and kernel code. Lower values indicate a problem, although there is no agreed on standard value.
- **Memory\ Pages/sec**—The number of hard page faults occurring per second. A hard page fault occurs when data or code is not in memory and must be retrieved from the hard drive. Each time this happens, disk activity is required, and process is temporarily halted (because disk access is momentarily slower than RAM access). A bottleneck in memory is likely when this number is 20 or greater.
- **Memory\ Page reads/sec**—The number of times the disk needed to be read to resolve a hard page fault. Unlike Memory\ Pages/sec, this counter is not an indicator of the quantity of data being retrieved but rather the number of times the disk had to be consulted. This counter can give a general feeling of a memory bottleneck, whereas Memory\ Pages/sec gives a more quantifiable value to the bottleneck.
- **Memory\ Pool Paged Bytes**—The number of bytes of memory taken up by system tasks that can be swapped out to disk if needed. Although this counter is not a direct indicator of a memory bottleneck, if the number of Pool Paged Bytes is large, it can indicate a lot of system processes. If this number is a significant percentage of total memory, you might need to increase RAM to allow for these tasks to remain in RAM instead of being swapped out.
- **Memory\ Pool Nonpaged Bytes**—The number of bytes of memory taken up by system tasks that can't be swapped out to disk. This figure can indicate a bottleneck in memory, especially if the figure is a significant percentage of the total amount

of RAM. Because these processes can't be swapped out, they will continue to take up RAM for as long as they are running.

- **Network Interface\ Bytes Total/sec**—This is an indication of the total throughput of the network interface. It can be used for general capacity planning and does not necessarily indicate a network bottleneck.
- **Processor\ % Processor Time**—The amount of time the processor spends executing non-idle threads. This is an indication of how busy the processor is. The processor for a single-processor system should not exceed 75% capacity for a significant period of time. The processors in a multiple-processor system should not exceed 50% for a significant period of time. High processor utilization can be an indication of processor bottlenecks, but it could also indicate lack of memory.
- **System\ Processor Queue Length**—The number of processes that are ready but waiting to be serviced by the processor(s). There is a single queue for all processors, even in a multiprocessor environment. A sustained queue of more than 2 generally indicates processor congestion.
- **Processor\ Interrupts/sec**—The number of hardware requests the processor is servicing per second. This is not necessarily an indicator of system health but, when compared against the baseline, it can help to determine hardware problems. Hardware problems are sometimes indicated by a device dramatically increasing the number of interrupts it sends.

Now that you have a basic understanding of what monitoring entails, how it's done, and which counters to look at, we need to create some baselines, logs, and alerts. These areas are examined in the next section.

NOTE

Power Performance For more information on working with Performance Monitor counters and using them to identify and troubleshoot bottlenecks, see Part 2 of the *Windows 2000 Server Operations Guide* at `http://www.microsoft.com/technet/prodtechnol/windows2000serv/reskit/serverop/w2kopgd.asp`.

EXAM TIP

Performance Counters Don't worry too much about memorizing all the different counters and their uses. This test is looking more for your ability to use the tools available to identify, troubleshoot, and correct problem situations.

Configuring and Using Alerts and Logging

▶ Configure and manage System Monitor alerts and logging.

Using the Performance Logs and Alerts section of the Performance Monitor, you can log counter and event trace data. Additionally, you can create performance triggered alerts that can notify the administrator of critical changes in monitored counters. The following three items are located in the Performance Logs and Alerts section of the Performance Monitor:

- **Counter logs**—Enable you to record data about hardware usage and the activity of system services from local or remote computers. You can configure logging to occur manually or automatically based on a predefined schedule. If you desire, continuous logging is available, but it consumes large amounts of disk space quickly. You can view the logs in System Monitor or export the data to a spreadsheet or database program, such as Microsoft Excel and Microsoft Access, respectively.
- **Trace logs**—Used to record data as certain activity, such as disk I/O or a page fault, occurs. When the event occurs, the provider sends the data to the log service.
- **Alerts**—Can be set on a specific counter defining an action to be performed when the selected counter's value exceeds, equals, or falls below the specified setting. Actions that can be set include sending a message, running a program, and starting a log.

Using Counter Logs

Although the System Monitor is useful for immediate analysis of a performance problem, it is not very useful as a real-time tool for bottleneck analysis. To get a good picture of the way resources are used on your server, you need to be able to examine data collected over a long period of time. The data collection needs to be long enough to enable you to view periodic spikes in usage in the proper context. For example, it would be a mistake to analyze the need for more system resource solely by looking at system performance between 8:30 a.m. and 9:30 a.m. This is the time when everyone is logging on, and one could expect the system to be loaded more than average at that time. Similarly, you would not want to check system performance between 12:00 p.m. and 1:00 p.m. The load might be unusually low because people are having a lunch break. To determine system performance and the need for upgrades, you should collect data over a long period of time or at several different times. This precludes using the System Monitor in real-time mode; you would have to sit in front of the console for long periods of time recording the current statistical results.

A solution to this dilemma is to use *counter logs.* A counter log takes the same information that is captured by the System Monitor and, instead of displaying it in a graph, records it in a file. You can set the log to run and then come back to it in a week (or a month) to see general trends. After the log has been created, you can use the System Monitor in a static mode to look at the data collected by the log.

When configuring a counter log, you have the same choices for monitoring as you do with the System Monitor. You can choose specific objects, as well as counters and instances associated with those objects. However, unlike System Monitor, you can use logs to log all counters and instances for a specific object. This is a good feature to use when you do not know, or do not have available, the counters you want to monitor when you set up the log. In addition, you can also choose the interval at which to poll the system for information; this is something you should experiment with to determine which interval setting gives you the best data capture with the least amount of excess data created.

One of the advantages of logging is that it can be configured to automatically start and stop itself at specific times and on specific days. If all you are interested in logging is system performance between 1:00 a.m. and 5:00 a.m., you can set the log to begin at 1:00 a.m. and then turn itself off at 5:00 a.m. Meanwhile, you're asleep at home.

You can configure as many simultaneous logs as you like. Logging does not create much system overhead, and as a result, it does not really affect the results you get from the logging process. What you do need to be careful of is how much data you collect and where you put the collected data. It is recommended that when you log, you create a partition that contains nothing but log data. In this way, if the log fills the disk, the only thing it affects is logging. It will not choke out any other applications or the operating system itself.

> NOTE
>
> **Sample Counter Log** For your convenience, a sample log configuration has been created for you, and it is installed automatically with Windows 2000 Server. You can activate it and begin logging right away, even if you do not fully understand the logging process. This sample log, named System Overview, can be found in the Counter Log node of the Performance Logs and Alerts section of Performance Monitor. To start it, simply right-click it and select Start. The icon will change from red to green after the log has been started.

When you create a log, you are presented with a dialog box with three property sheets. On these property sheets, you can configure the data to capture, the place to put the data, and the schedule by which to run the logging process.

As you can see in Figure 9.14, the General properties tab enables you to configure the log with the counters you want to track and the

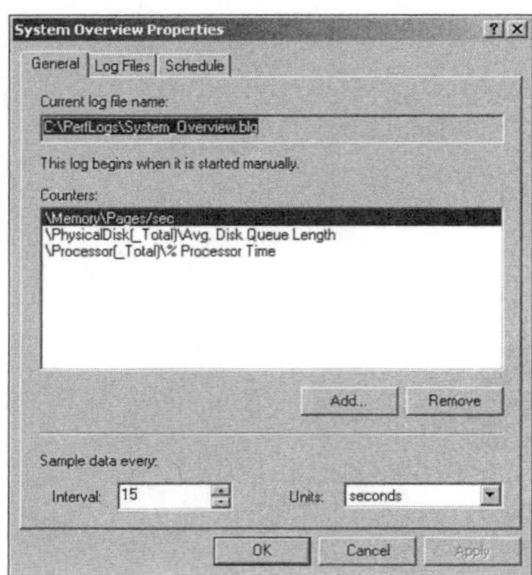

FIGURE 9.14
The General property tab.

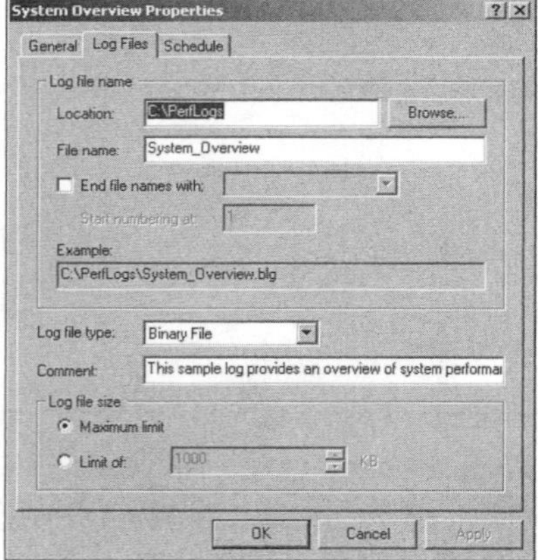

FIGURE 9.15
The Log Files property sheet.

interval at which you want to collect information. To add counters, click the Add button. The dialog box that appears is the same as what you saw when you added counters to the System Monitor (refer to Step By Step 9.10).

Besides adding counters, you can set the interval at which information is gathered. The interval can be set as high as 999,999, and the units can be set to seconds, minutes, hours, or days. Despite the large number of possible interval settings, the interval can never exceed 45 days. The rule of thumb is generally that the longer you are going to run the log, the larger the interval should be to prevent your log file from getting too large. However, sometimes you might want to log for a long time but still get finely generated data through the use of short intervals.

On the Log Files property sheet, you can specify the filename and path for the log (see Figure 9.15). You can have the logs uniquely identified using a suffix of a number (nnnnnn) or a date in any one of six formats.

The log file type defines the format of the log content. CSV and TSV are text formats you can read with the System Monitor. You can also import this data into tools such as Microsoft Excel, Microsoft Word or Microsoft Access. CSV is comma delimited, and TSV is tab delimited. Binary files can be read only by the System Monitor or a third–party tool designed to analyze binary log files. Binary circular format is a binary format in which the log file overwrites itself from the beginning when it reaches its maximum size. Cyclical logging is useful when you are concerned about data overflowing the allotted drive. With cyclical logging, when the maximum size is reached, the log is overwritten from the first data samples to the last.

The final option on this property sheet is the size of the log file. You can set the limit to no limit (Maximum Limit), which means the log file will grow until you stop it or until the disk on which it resides is full. If you set a limit, a new log file is created when the limit is reached. If you have chosen Binary Circular, the file will begin to overwrite itself.

On the Schedule property tab, you can configure the start and stop times for logging (see Figure 9.16). If both start and stop are set to manual, the log starts when you choose. It will continue logging until you manually stop it or the size limit is reached. You can also set logging to begin at a certain time and either go for a specific interval or go until a certain stop time.

When the log file is full, you can choose to begin a new log file and execute a command to do some post-logging processing.

Step By Step 9.11 shows you how to create a counter log.

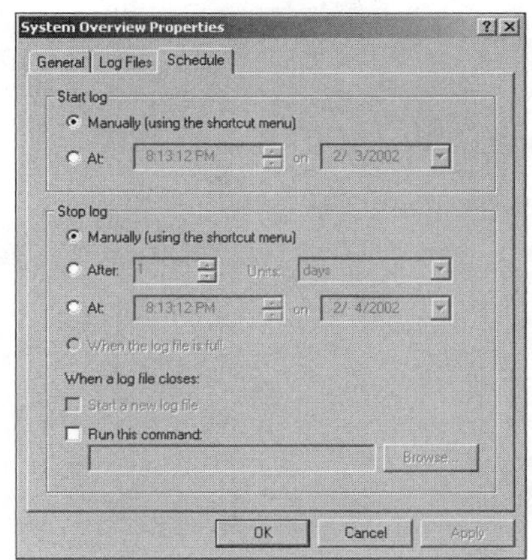

FIGURE 9.16
The Schedule property tab.

STEP BY STEP

9.11 Creating a Counter Log

1. Select Start, Programs, Administrative Tools, Performance Monitor.
2. From the Performance Console, expand the section called Performance Logs and Alerts, right-click Counter Logs, and select New Log Settings from the menu that appears.
3. When prompted, type in a name describing the purpose of this log.
4. On the General property sheet, add the counters you want to log by clicking the Add button and filling in the Select Counter dialog box.
5. On the General property sheet, select the time interval you want to log at.
6. Click the Log Files tab to move to that property sheet.
7. Type in a location, filename, and log file suffix (if desired). By default, you can use the `X:\PerfLogs` folder, where `X` is your driver letter.
8. Specify the log file type and maximum size.
9. Click the Schedule tab to move to that property sheet.
10. Define the start and stop times for logging and the When a Log File Closes parameter.
11. Click OK to save the log configuration.

If you configured your log to start manually, you will have to start it before logging will begin. A stopped log is marked with a red icon next to the log definition name. A green icon indicates that the log is active or is waiting for its scheduled time to start.

Step By Step 9.12 illustrates how to start a log manually.

STEP BY STEP

9.12 Manually Starting a Log

1. Select Start, Programs, Administrative Tools, Performance Monitor.
2. From the Performance Console, expand the section called Performance Logs and Alerts, and then click Counter Logs to view the existing logs on the right side.
3. Right-click a log definition with a red icon and select Start from the menu that appears.

Opening a binary file using the System Monitor is similar to creating a real-time graph. The exceptions in this case are that the data is static and you can't add counters to the view that are not contained in the log. With this in mind, it is better to log more information than you think you'll need in case you find you really do need it in the end.

Step By Step 9.13 describes the process for opening a log file using the System Monitor.

STEP BY STEP

9.13 Opening a Log File with System Monitor

1. Select Start, Programs, Administrative Tools, Performance Monitor.
2. In the Performance Console, click System Monitor to bring up the System Monitor panel on the right side.

3. Right-click the System Monitor window and select Properties from the menu that appears (or click the Properties icon).
4. Click the Source tab to move to that property sheet.
5. On the Source tab, type in (or browse to) the name of the log file (binary, CSV, or TSV) that you want to graph (see Figure 9.17).
6. If you want to see only a portion of the total time the log file spans, click the Time Range button. On the bar that appears below it, click and drag the blocks on the end toward the center until you reach the desired range.
7. Click the Data tab to move to that property sheet.
8. On the Data property sheet, add or remove counters as desired.
9. Click OK to return to the graph you have created.

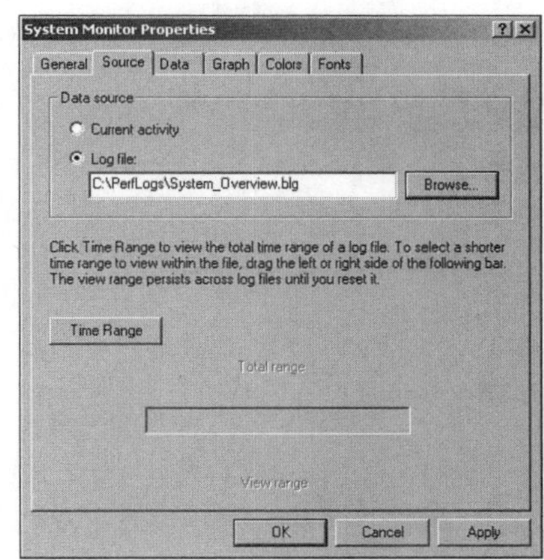

FIGURE 9.17
Choose the log file to get data from, and adjust the time if desired.

You can create a similar graph by importing a CSV text file into a spreadsheet (such as Microsoft Excel, for example). When you import, the results come in as headers with numeric data. You can then graph the results by hand. The advantage of this method over System Monitor is that these results can be pasted into word processors and very easily included in reports using OLE conventions.

Step By Step 9.14 shows you how to analyze log data in Microsoft Excel.

STEP BY STEP

9.14 Analyzing Log Data in Microsoft Excel

1. Open Microsoft Excel and open the CSV log you want to examine.
2. Select the extent of the imported data, invoke the chart wizard, and use the options of your choice (see Figure 9.18).

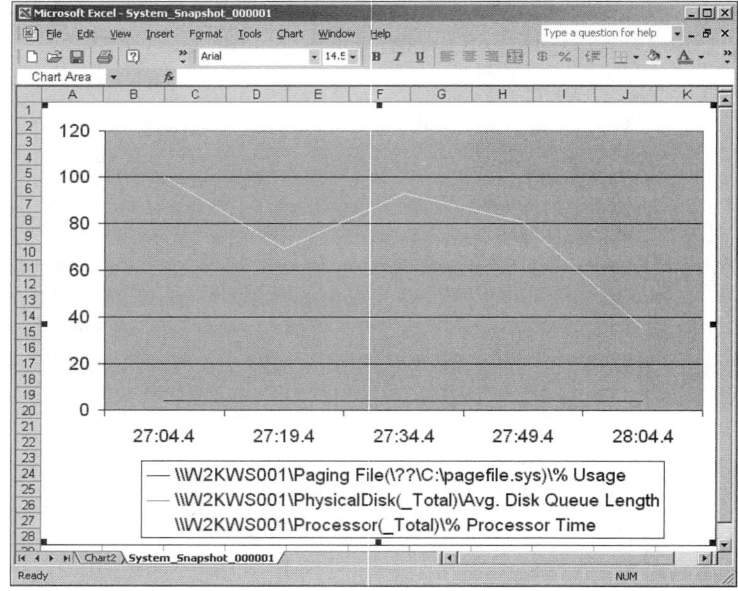

FIGURE 9.18
You can chart performance data in a spreadsheet such as Microsoft Excel.

Creating Trace Logs

The difference between a trace log and a counter log is the trigger that causes data collection. With a counter log, the trigger of data collection is a time interval. If you set the time interval to 10 seconds, you will get data every 10 seconds whether there is any change to the data from the last interval. With a trace log, the trigger of data collection is the occurrence of an event. For example, if you want to track user log in, you can set Active Directory or the Local Security Administrator (depending on whether you are tracing login in a domain or on a local server) to watch for the event. When a user log in occurs, the trace process collects the data.

The options for a trace log are similar to those for a counter log. The biggest difference is that instead of configuring the log to monitor certain counters, you configure a trace provider to monitor certain events. In addition, you can configure advanced options. Specifically, you can configure how large the memory buffer is for collecting data before data is written out to the log file.

The General property tab enables you to configure the trace provider, as well as the event types to watch for and log (see Figure 9.19).

Trace logs record performance data whenever events for their source providers occur. A source provider is an application or operating system service that has traceable events. On domain controllers you'll find two source providers—the operating system itself and Active Directory:NetLogon. On other servers, the operating system are probably the only provider available.

A *trace provider* is an application or operating system service that has traceable events (such as domain user login). The following trace providers are typically available: Active Directory: NetLogon (domain controllers only), Local Security Authority (nondomain computers), and the operating system provider. Other providers might be available depending on the services and applications running on the computer. The operating system provider enables you to watch for processes and threads being created or destroyed, disk input or output, network traffic, memory page faults, and file I/O (reads and writes). The Active Directory provider enables you to track user logon events at the domain level. The Local Security Authority (LSA) enables you to track user logon events at the local level.

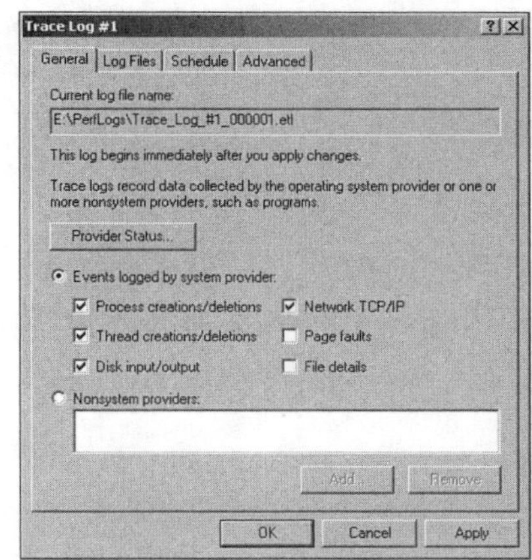

FIGURE 9.19
The General property tab.

> **EXAM TIP**
>
> **Trace Logs** Trace logs are not likely to be seen on the exam. The focus of this section is to get you acquainted with them (in a general sense) and to demonstrate how they are different from counter logs. Don't lose any sleep over not being able to get trace logs up and running on your test network!

Any trace log can track either the system provider or one or more nonsystem providers. If you need to track with more than one provider, you must create more than one trace log. One trace log must be created for the system events, and one or more trace logs must be created for the nonsystem events. The Provider Status button shows you which of the providers are enabled for logging through the creation of a trace log. This keeps track of all the trace logs, and the result is cumulative across all trace logs you create for a specific server.

The Advanced tab enables you to configure memory buffer number and size. These memory buffers are where the event data is initially captured before being written to the log file.

You can create a new trace log by right-clicking the Trace Logs header in the Performance console and selecting New Log Settings. You can then start or stop a trace log manually by right-clicking the log entry and selecting Start or Stop, depending on the current state of logging.

The Log Files page of the Trace Log configuration is nearly identical to that of the counter log. The difference between the two log files pages is that the trace log file time can be only a sequential trace file or circular trace file. This format is proprietary to the trace log. Similar to the counter log, a circular trace file begins to write over itself from the beginning after it is full. No utilities are provided with Windows 2000 for reading the .etl files created by the log; a parsing tool is required to interpret the trace log output. Developers can create such a tool using application programming interfaces (APIs) provided on the Microsoft Web site at `http://msdn.microsoft.com/`.

Creating Alerts

Over the long term, you probably do not want logging enabled all the time. However, that will necessitate that you check the system periodically to ensure that it is working efficiently and that potential problems are not sneaking up on you. Alerts are used to configure watchers, which can notify you or perform a preconfigured action when a predefined threshold has been crossed. For example, if you decide that disk utilization greater than 80% is a serious condition, you can configure an alert to watch for disk utilization crossing this threshold. When this threshold is reached, an action you configure occurs, such as sending an email notification. Email alerts, for example, are very powerful tools—especially with the advent of text-messaging-capable pagers and cell phones that can receive these email messages. You'll never be out of the loop now!

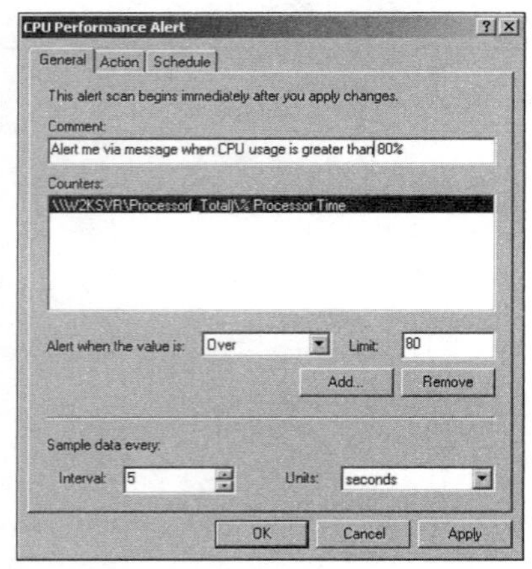

FIGURE 9.20
The General property tab.

The alert configuration dialog box consists of three pages: General, Action, and Schedule. Schedule is just like the Schedule page for counter and trace logs, so it will not be discussed further here.

The General page enables you to configure multiple counters and the thresholds for each (see Figure 9.20). In addition, you can configure the polling interval.

The Action page is used to configure what happens in response to an alert (see Figure 9.21). As you can see from Figure 9.21, there are a variety of responses. The default is to write a message to the application log (accessible from the Event Viewer console). In addition (or alternatively), you can have a message sent to a specific computer in the form of a pop-up window. You can also have the Performance Monitor begin a specific counter log (thus, making the alert a trigger for starting the collection of data about a specific set of circumstances through a log). Finally, you can also have the program of your choice run. In conjunction with the running of a program, you can send the program some arguments from the alert. These arguments can be configured in the form of pieces of text you set up in the Command Line Arguments dialog box.

The advantage of using these command-line arguments is that you do not have to reconfigure the exact information sent to a program that is executed. All you configure is the type of data; then the alert controls the specific data based on the current time or the trigger value. Receiving the data could be a Visual Basic, C++, or Java program that accepts the parameters you send to it.

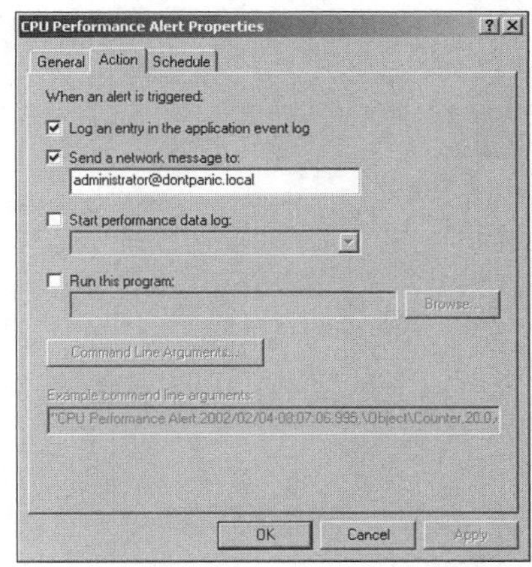

FIGURE 9.21
The Action property sheet.

Using the Event Viewer

▶ Diagnose server health problems by using Event Viewer.

Using the event logs in Event Viewer, you can gather information about hardware, software, and system problems (see Figure 9.22). Additionally, you can monitor Windows 2000 security events.

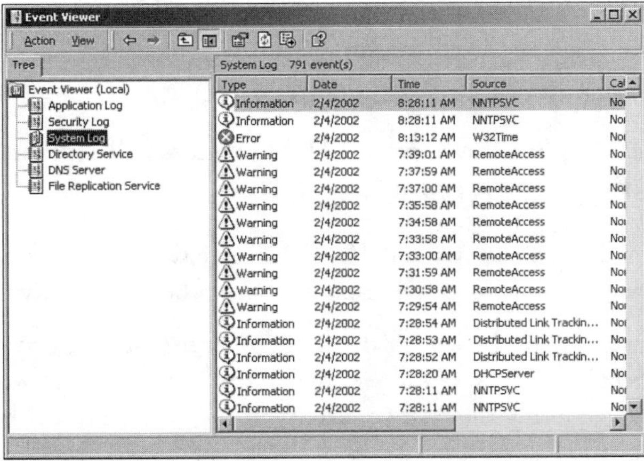

FIGURE 9.22
The Event Viewer.

> **NOTE**
>
> **Security Logging and Auditing** By default, security logging is turned off, but you can use Group Policy to enable security logging. The administrator can also set auditing policies in the Registry that cause the system to halt when the security log is full. Security logging is not covered in this section, however, because we are focusing on identifying server health problems with the Event Viewer.

The EventLog service starts automatically when you start Windows 2000. All users can view Application and System logs, but only administrators can gain access to the Security logs.

On a typical Windows 2000 machine, the following logs are created for Event Viewer (there might be others depending on which software the server is running):

- **Application log**—Contains events logged by applications or programs running on the computer. For example, a program might record a file error in the application log. The program developer decides which events to record.
- **System log**—Contains events logged by the Windows 2000 system components. For example, the failure of a driver or other system component to load during startup is recorded in the System log. The event types logged by system components are predetermined by Windows 2000 and can't be changed by developers after the fact.
- **Security log**—Records security events such as valid and invalid logon attempts as well as events related to resource use such as creating, opening, or deleting files. As the administrator, you specify which events are recorded in the Security log by enabling specific logging actions.

A domain controller has the following additional logs:

- **Directory Service**—This log records events logged by Active Directory and its related services.
- **File Replication Service**—This log records file replication activities on the system.

Additionally, a Windows 2000 DNS Server has the DNS Server log, which records DNS queries, responses, and other DNS activities.

Looking at any of the logs in the Event Viewer (with the exception of the Security log), you will see three types of events, each with its own icon denoting the relative severity of the event, as described in the following list. All three types of events can be seen in Figure 9.22:

- **Error (red circle)**—A significant problem, such as loss of data or loss of functionality. For example, if a service fails to load during startup, an error is logged.

- **Warning (yellow triangle)**—An event that is not necessarily significant but can indicate a possible future problem. For example, when disk space is low, a warning is logged.
- **Information (white bubble)**—An event that describes the successful operation of an application, a driver, or a service. For example, when a network driver loads successfully, an information event is logged.

The event logs can be used to troubleshoot problems with the server, but they require you to carefully monitor them. By taking the time to analyze the event logs, you might be able to predict and identify the sources of system problems. For example, if log warnings show that a disk driver can only read or write to a sector after several retries, the sector is likely to go bad eventually. Logs can also confirm problems with software. If a program crashes, a program event log can provide a record of activity leading up to the event. When working with event logs to troubleshoot server health issues, keep the following items in mind:

- **Archive logs in log format**—The binary data associated with an event is saved in log format (*.evt) if you archive the log, but the binary data is discarded if you archive data in text (*.txt) or comma-delimited (*.csv) format. The binary data can help a developer or technical support specialist identify the source of a problem.
- **Note event IDs**—These numbers match a text description in a message file. The numbers can be used by product support representatives to understand what occurred in the system.
- **Filter the logs**—If you suspect a specific hardware or software component is the cause of problems, you should consider filtering the log to show only those events generated by the component in question. Doing so can alleviate the difficulty associated with sifting through hundreds or thousands of event log entries, but it can also hide other developing problems because they will not be displayed in the event logs until filtering is turned off or modified.

Now let's look at the last tool available to monitor performance—and the easiest of them all to use—the Windows Task Manager.

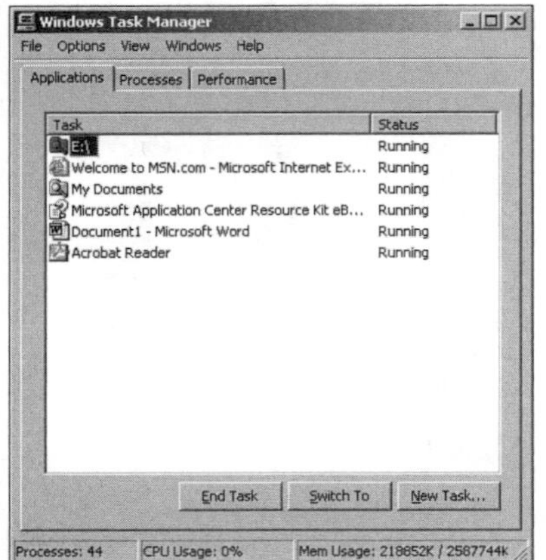

FIGURE 9.23
The Windows Task Manager Application tab.

> **NOTE**
>
> **Using the Task Manager** Task Manager is most useful when you want to look at what is happening with a system right now. It does not provide logging or long-term tracking of data. Perhaps its most famous use (and certainly the most satisfying) is to determine which program is not responding and end it forcibly.

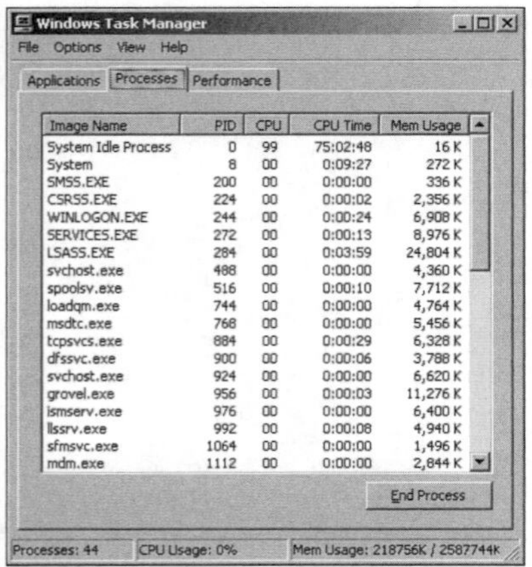

FIGURE 9.24
The Windows Task Manager Processes tab.

Using the Task Manager

► Monitor and interpret real-time performance by using System Monitor and Task Manager.

The Task Manager is a useful tool that can be used to quickly get an idea of what is going on with a specific computer. Task Manager, seen in Figure 9.23, can be accessed in several ways:

- Right-click any open area of the taskbar and select Task Manager.
- Use the Ctrl+Alt+Delete key combination and then select Task Manager from the Windows Security window.
- Type **`taskmgr`** from a command prompt or the Run dialog box.

In Windows 2000, the Task Manager has three tabs: Applications (shown in Figure 9.23), Processes, and Performance. From the Applications tab, you can quickly identify which applications are running, end a running application, switch between applications, or launch a new task.

From the Processes tab, you can get a quick look at how the running applications and services on the computer are using system resources (see Figure 9.24). You can also end a specific task or an entire task tree from the Processes tab by selecting the process, right-clicking, and selecting either End Process or End Process Tree. Additionally, you can end a process by selecting it and clicking the End Process button at the bottom of the window. If you want to see more columns with additional information, click the View menu at the top of the window and select Select Columns. This opens a new dialog box, as shown in Figure 9.25.

The Performance tab, as shown in Figure 9.26, enables you to quickly get an idea of how your computer is using memory, both physical and virtual. You can use this information to possibly help you determine the need for memory upgrades or paging file modification (in addition to using the more robust monitors found in the Performance Monitoring console).

The Performance tab at first appears to have the least amount of information on it, but in reality it has the most information available to you—if you understand it. Here's what's available:

- **CPU Usage**—A real-time graph that indicates the percentage of time the processor is being utilized. This provides a quick and easy means to get an idea of how busy the processor is, and it's usually at the high end when the computer seems to be running slowly.
- **CPU Usage History**—A moving graph that displays how busy the CPU has been over time. The sampling speed can be configured from the Update Speed option on the View menu.
- **PF Usage**—Displays the amount of paging file being used in real time. This can be used to determine whether the paging file should be resized.
- **Page File Usage History**—Displays the amount of paging file usage over time. The sampling speed can be configured from the Update Speed option on the View menu. Sustained high usage periods are indicative of a need to increase either the amount of memory (RAM) installed or the paging file size—or even both.
- **Totals**—Displays the totals for the number of handles, threads, and processes running on the computer.
- **Commit Charge (K)**—Shows the memory allocated to programs and the operating system. The value listed under Peak might exceed the maximum physical memory because of paging file usage. The value for Total is the same as the value shown in the Page File Usage History graph.
- **Physical Memory (K)**—Shows the total physical memory installed in the computer. The Available value represents the amount of free memory available for use. The System Cache value shows the current physical memory used to map pages of open files.
- **Kernel Memory (K)**—Shows the memory being used by the operating system kernel and device drivers. The Paged value represents memory that can be copied to the paging file, thereby freeing the physical memory. The physical memory can then be used by the operating system. The Nonpaged value

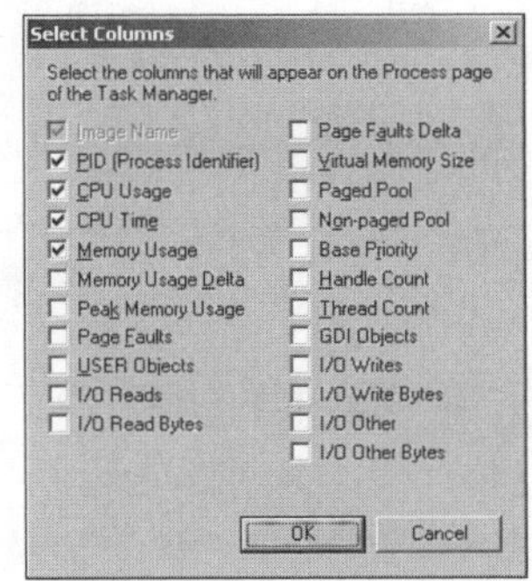

FIGURE 9.25
Selecting columns for display on the Processes tab.

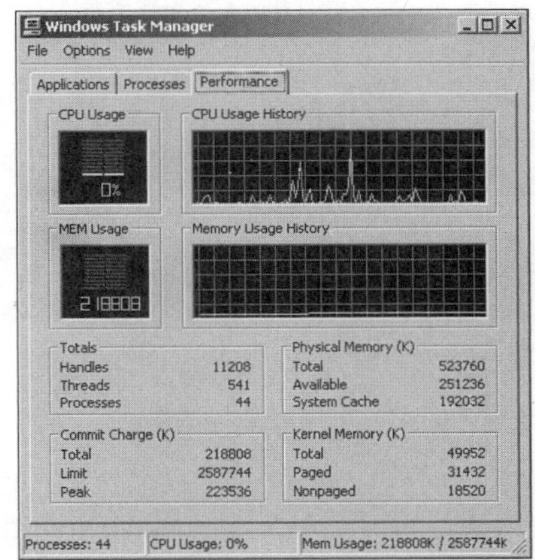

FIGURE 9.26
The Windows Task Manager Performance tab.

represents memory that remains resident in physical memory and will not be copied out to the paging file.

Using the Task Manager can give you a quick and simple real-time glimpse at what is going in with a computer and should be a part of every administrator's bag of tools. Now that we've examined the various means available for determining the health and operating status of computers, let's move on to a new topic area where you can get some ideas on how to tune your computers by removing unnecessary services and tweaking the paging file.

Tuning Your Computers

▶ Identify and disable unnecessary operating system services.

Now that you have seen how to collect statistical data, you need to understand how to use it. Your server is not a set of isolated processes and resources with which users interact. Rather, your server is a dynamically changing entity that has weaknesses in some areas. A server that appears to have a disk problem, spinning endlessly every time a user tries to read something, might, in fact, have too little RAM. Unless you have an understanding of how the major subsystems interact, you will not be able to effectively optimize your server. Furthermore, unless you know what are acceptable levels associated with the counters, all the statistics in the world will not help you troubleshoot the present or plan for the future.

Although there are dozens of objects and many times that number of counters to sift through, four primary subsystems interact to make a server operate either quickly or slowly. These subsystems are disk, memory, processor, and network. Of course, other objects are also important, but these four counters form the core of server performance monitoring. The performance of these four subsystems affects all other objects.

Even before you begin to monitor your system to increase performance, there are some things that you can do proactively. In fact, even if you do not experience a lack of performance in any area, performing some basic tasks will ensure that it will be longer until you do experience problems than if these were left undone.

We are going to cover two areas here that will help to keep servers running smoothly: removal of unnecessary components and paging file maintenance.

Removing Unnecessary Software Components

Begin attempting to improve system performance by removing unnecessary software components: devices, protocols, and services. Unnecessary components are those that were loaded for some reason in the past but that no longer have a use. Perhaps you have a device installed that you no longer use. If that device was installed manually, the driver might still load into memory when your server starts. You can use the Device Manager to ensure that the driver is no longer installed.

Network protocols are another software component that might have become unnecessary. If you used to have a NetWare server you communicated with, you might still have NWLink installed. If you no longer have that NetWare server, you should uninstall the protocol. Unused protocols not only use more system memory, but also increase the network traffic your communications generate and increase the likelihood that a security breach will occur at an unexpected entry point.

Finally, you should look at unnecessary services. The default installation of Windows 2000 Server includes IIS. If you are not using any of the Web-related services, you should uninstall IIS. You will no longer have software running in the background listening for something it will never hear.

Tuning the Size and Location of the Paging File

The paging file (`pagefile.sys`) is a hidden system file located by default in the boot partition—the place where your `WINNT` folder is. The *paging file* is the part of the disk that facilitates Windows 2000's virtual memory model. In that model, RAM is simulated through a swapping process that moves information from physical memory into virtual memory residing in a file on the hard drive. Commonly referred to as the swap file by Unix and earlier versions of Windows, the paging file acts as an extension to your computer's installed physical RAM. Together, the physical RAM and the paging file comprise the virtual memory your computer has to work with.

By default, the paging file is sized at 1.5X the amount of RAM you have installed in your computer and can expand as required. Every time the paging file expands, it takes system resources to resize the file. One recommendation is that you watch your server under typical load and then note the size of the paging file. If the paging file is larger than the minimum size, you should change the settings to ensure the paging file starts out at that size. This will use up a bit more disk space, but you will increase the efficiency of the server.

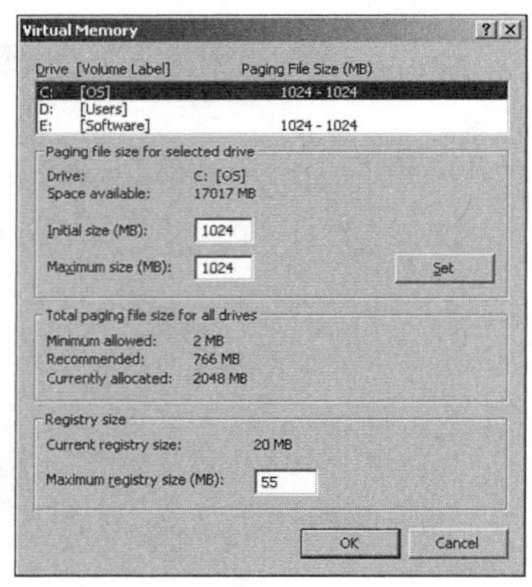

FIGURE 9.27
Configuring the Paging File.

Configuration of the paging file is done from the Advanced tab of the System applet, as shown in Figure 9.27.

You can perform three basic groups of actions from the Virtual Memory window: You can remove, relocate, or resize a paging file. All these actions are carried out in the same fashion. Select the Custom Size radio button and enter the minimum and maximum allowed paging file sizes. For best efficiency, you should make both of these sizes the same to eliminate resource utilization during the dynamic resizing of the paging file. Microsoft recommends that you make your paging file 1.5X the RAM installed, although the rule of thumb is generally 1.5X–2.5X the RAM installed. The following are some other important points to keep in mind when working paging files:

- **To enhance performance, you can move the paging file from the boot partition**—With the paging file on the boot partition, competition exists between read requests and write requests.
- **When you place a paging file on its own partition, the paging file does not become fragmented**—If a paging file resides on a partition that contains other data, it can experience fragmentation as it expands to satisfy the extra virtual memory that is required.

- **By design, Windows uses the paging file on the less frequently accessed partition over the paging file on the more heavily accessed boot partition**—An internal algorithm is used to determine which paging file to use for virtual memory management.
- **If you completely remove the paging file from the boot partition, Windows can't create a dump file (`memory.dmp`)**—This dump file is useful because Windows writes debugging information to it in the event that a kernel mode STOP error message occurs.

NOTE

Don't Remove the Paging File! You can resize and relocate the paging file, but don't completely remove it. Completely removing the paging file can render your computer incapable of booting.

Step By Step 9.15 identifies the steps for resizing a paging file.

STEP BY STEP

9.15 Resizing the Paging File

1. Right-click the My Computer icon and select Properties from the menu that appears. Alternatively, you can select Start, Settings, Control Panel, System.
2. In the System Properties dialog box, click the Advanced tab.
3. On the Advanced property sheet, click the Performance Options button.
4. On the Performance Options dialog box, click the Change button (under the heading Virtual Memory).
5. In the Virtual Memory dialog box, select the current location for the paging file (at the top), enter new initial and maximum sizes, and then click the Set button (as shown previously in Figure 9.27).
6. Click OK three times to set the paging file size and exit. (The paging file will automatically resize; you do not need to reboot.)

Step By Step 9.16 shows you how to relocate your paging file.

STEP BY STEP

9.16 Relocating the Paging File

1. Right-click the My Computer icon and select Properties from the menu that appears. Alternatively, you can select Start, Settings, Control Panel, System.
2. In the System Properties dialog box, click the Advanced tab.
3. On the Advanced property sheet, click the Performance Options button.
4. On the Performance Options dialog box, click the Change button (under the heading Virtual Memory).
5. Select the disk to which you want to move the paging file, enter the initial and maximum sizes into the fields, and click Set.
6. Select the disk from which you want to move the paging file, clear the initial and maximum sizes, and click Set. A warning appears, telling you that the paging file will not be the same size as physical RAM appears.
7. Click the OK button to complete the process. Restart the server when prompted. (Removing the paging file from the boot partition requires a restart.)

Case Study: Performance Problems with a New Process

ESSENCE OF THE CASE

The following points summarize the essence of the case study:

- The system has just had a new application installed.
- The application runs continually as a service to local and remote users.

SCENARIO

You have installed a new custom-developed program that runs as a Windows service and runs in the background continually. You and a number of remote users who are accessing data on your system use it. When you first install it, you run the Performance Monitor on your system to establish a baseline of performance during

CASE STUDY: PERFORMANCE PROBLEMS WITH A NEW PROCESS

- After several days of continual running, the system performance degrades.
- Rebooting the system temporarily solves the problem. However, it eventually returns.
- Available memory is consumed, and paging activity increases.

normal working conditions. A few days later, your system becomes sluggish and noticeably slower in all functions. You reboot your system, and it appears to be working normally again. A few days later, the same performance problems occur again. You run the Performance Monitor and discover that the amount of available memory has dropped to almost 0 and the paging file is active.

ANALYSIS

When dealing with performance problems, it is important to remember that almost everything is interrelated with everything else. Memory problems can cause disk activity, which can manifest itself as a processor bottleneck. In this case, because the problem was apparently solved when the system was restarted, the problem is likely related to consumption of a resource rather than an elevated rate of activity. When the problem occurred again days later, the Performance Monitor showed a higher than expected paging activity and almost no available memory. That combination would normally indicate a system that is under-configured in memory for the process running. Because this situation did not exist when the new application was brought online, the conclusion is that the new background service leaks memory. In this situation, memory acquired by the service during normal processing is not returned to the system. Over time, the amount of working memory assigned to the service would exceed the amount available, and the Windows 2000 operating system would begin to page to meet the needs of its normal workload. The recommendation would be to send the new service back to the developers for analysis.

CHAPTER SUMMARY

KEY TERMS

Before taking the exam, make sure you are comfortable with the definitions and concepts for each of the following key terms.

- Alert
- Baseline
- Bottleneck
- Copy backup
- Counter
- Counter log
- Daily backup
- Differential backup
- Emergency repair disk
- Incremental backup
- Last Known Good Configuration
- Normal backup
- `NTBACKUP.EXE`
- Performance Monitor
- Recovery Console
- Safe mode
- System Monitor
- Task Manager
- Trace log
- Trace provider

This chapter has covered perhaps two of the most important day-to-day activities you will be faced with as an administrator: providing disaster recovery and ensuring server performance.

This chapter also discussed disaster recovery, which encompasses a wide array of choices, including using Last Know Good Configuration, Safe Mode startups, Recovery Console repairs, and restorations using the Windows 2000 Backup utility.

Ensuring the performance and health of servers and client computers was also discussed. It entails using the Performance Monitor (System Monitor, counter logs, trace logs, and alerts), the Event Viewer, and the Task Manager. Data gathered from the System Monitor and events recorded in the Event Viewer can be used to identify, troubleshoot, and correct problem areas.

In addition, this chapter looked briefly at tuning computers by removing unused services and performing page file maintenance.

APPLY YOUR KNOWLEDGE

Exercises

9.1 Detecting a Bottleneck Using System Monitor and Counter Logs

Exercise 9.1 shows how you can use counter logs and System Monitor to detect a bottleneck on your server. To do this, you first must artificially create a memory bottleneck. Then, using a counter log and the System Monitor, you analyze the system performance during routine operation to detect the bottleneck.

Estimated Time: 60 minutes

1. Create a baseline log.
2. Create a folder called `PerfLogs` on the drive of your choice.
3. From the Start menu, select Programs, Administrative Tools, Performance.
4. Expand Performance Logs and Alerts, right-click Counter Logs, and select New Log Settings from the menu that appears.
5. When prompted, type **`BASELINE`** as the log name.
6. On the General page, click the Add button.
7. In the Add Counter dialog box, select the radio button labeled Use Local Computer Counters. Select the performance objects Processor, Memory, Paging File, and PhysicalDisk (in turn). Then, select the All Counters radio button and click Add. When you finish, click Close.
8. Click the Log Files tab, make sure the location for the log file is `C:\Perflogs` (or wherever you put your `Perflogs` folder), and make sure the Log File Type is Binary File. Then, click OK.
9. Open Notepad. Next, open Paint and spend a couple of minutes drawing. Then, open Internet Explorer and go to the Microsoft Web site. Switch back to Notepad and type a few sentences.
10. After about 3–5 minutes, switch back to the Performance Monitor, right-click the Baseline log, and select Stop from the menu that appears.
11. Close all the applications you started, including the Performance Monitor.
12. Change the `boot.ini` file, a startup file, to restrict the amount of memory your server is allowed to use by following these steps:
    1. Using My Computer or Windows Explorer, navigate to the root of the `C:` drive.
    2. From the Tools menu, select Folder Options.
    3. In the Folder Options dialog box, click the View tab.
    4. On the View property sheet, select the radio button labeled Show Hidden Files and Folders and deselect the check box labeled Hide Protected Operating System Files. When prompted, confirm that you really want to do that by clicking Yes. Click OK to continue.
    5. In the file window, locate the file named `boot.ini`, right-click it, and select Properties from the menu that appears.
    6. From the Properties dialog box, deselect Read-Only at the bottom and click OK.
    7. Double-click the `boot.ini` file to edit it in Notepad.
    8. In the `boot.ini` file, locate the line that begins `multi(0)` and move to the end of it.

APPLY YOUR KNOWLEDGE

9. At the end of the boot line, add a space and the text **/MAXMEM:24**.
10. Save and close the `boot.ini` file.

13. Restart your computer. The change to the `boot.ini` file will force your server to use only 24MB of the available RAM.
14. Repeat steps 3–11, substituting the name `MEMORYTEST` for `BASELINE`.
15. Edit the `boot.ini` file again as you did in step 12, and this time remove the memory restriction.
16. Restart your server.
17. Open the Performance Console and select System Monitor.
18. Right-click the System Monitor view (on the right) and select Properties from the menu that appears.
19. Click the Source tab, select the radio button labeled Log File, and type in the path to the `BASELINE` log file (or browse for it).
20. Click the Data tab and click the Add button at the bottom. Add the following counters: Memory\Pages/sec, Paging File\%Usage, PhysicalDisk\%Disk Time, and Processor\%Processor Time. Click Close.
21. Click OK to close the System Monitor Properties dialog box.
22. Note the condition of the graph. Although this was not a long test, you should see that the number of pages per second spiked when new applications were started (as did processor usage), but then paging dropped.
23. Right-click the graph and select Properties. On the Source tab, enter the path to the `MEMORYTEST` log and click OK.
24. Note the condition of the graph. Although the processor stays at fairly low usage, the paging is high and fairly constant. The disk usage is also high and constant. It would be tempting to see this as a disk bottleneck, what with all the disk activity as you worked.
25. Close the Performance Monitor.

9.2 Repairing Your Server Using the Recovery Console

This exercise shows how you can use the Recovery Console to repair system files and allow your server to boot. To accomplish this, you install the Recovery Console as a separate boot option and then corrupt the `boot.ini` file to prevent the server from starting. To accomplish the fix, you must have a disk and a second computer to repair the `boot.ini` file. In case you do not, an alternative course of action is given.

Estimated Time: 30 minutes

1. Install the System Console as a boot menu selection. Follow these steps:
    1. With Windows 2000 Server running, start a command prompt (select Start, Programs, Accessories, Command Prompt).
    2. Navigate to the source of your Windows 2000 installation files (CD-ROM, network share, local folder) and change to the `i386` folder.
    3. From within the `i386` folder, type **winnt32.exe /cmdcons**.

APPLY YOUR KNOWLEDGE

4. When prompted to install the console, confirm by clicking Yes.
5. When prompted that the console has been installed, click OK. If you restart your computer, you will see two choices during the text-mode section: Windows 2000 and Microsoft Windows 2000 Recovery Console.

2. Using My Computer or Windows Explorer, make a copy of the `boot.ini` file and call it `boot.old`.
3. As you did in step 12 of Exercise 9.1, modify the `boot.ini` file to restrict the maximum amount of memory available. This time use `/MAXMEM:8`.
4. Restart your server. During system startup, the server will stop and display either a blue-screen (stop) error or an error during black-screen startup telling you that it can't progress.
5. Restart your server. When you're presented with the menu that enables you to choose to boot to Windows 2000 Server or the Recovery Console, select the Recovery Console (by using your up and down arrow keys to highlight Recovery Console and pressing Enter).
6. When the Recovery Console starts and you are prompted to choose the version of Windows 2000 that you want to start, select the Windows 2000 Server installation you are working on (for most people, this will be number 1). Press Enter to continue.
7. When prompted, enter the password of the Administrator and press Enter.
8. Place a disk into the drive, type **`COPY C:\BOOT.INI A:\`**, and press Enter. If you do not have a disk or a second computer on which to edit the `boot.ini` file, type **`DEL BOOT.INI`**, press Enter, and then type **`REN BOOT.OLD BOOT.INI`**. Then, skip to step 10.
9. Remove the disk, take it to another computer, and edit the `boot.ini` file to remove the memory restriction. Place the disk back into the drive of your server.
10. At the Recovery Console, type **`DEL C:\BOOT.INI`** and press Enter; then, type **`COPY A:\BOOT.INI C:\`** and press Enter.
11. Type **`EXIT`** to restart your server. Allow it to restart normally now.

9.3 Backing Up and Restoring Files Using Windows 2000 Backup

This exercise shows how you can use Windows 2000 Backup to save and then restore a file to your server. This exercise assumes you do not have a DAT (or other tape) drive available, so the backup will be to disk. It also assumes that you have a `Perflogs` folder that contains log files. If you do not, substitute another folder as required.

Estimated Time: 20 minutes

1. Back up the `\Perflogs` folder to file. Follow these steps:
    1. From the Start menu, select Programs, Accessories, System Tools, Backup.
    2. On the Welcome page, click the Backup Wizard icon.
    3. At the Welcome to the Windows 2000 Backup and Recovery Tools screen, click Next.
    4. At the What to Back Up screen, select Back Up Selected Files, Drives, or Network Data and click Next.

APPLY YOUR KNOWLEDGE

5. At the Items to Back Up screen, locate the `Perflogs` folder on the left side and select it (a blue check mark will appear in the box). Click Next.
6. At the Where to Store the Backup screen, make sure that File is chosen as the media type, and then type **`X:\Logbackups\logback.bkf`** in the Backup Media or File Name field, where `X` is the volume on which to place the backup. Click Next.
7. At the Completing the Backup Wizard screen, click the Advanced button.
8. At the Type of Backup screen, make sure that Normal is selected and click Next.
9. At the How to Back Up screen, make sure no items are selected and click Next.
10. At the Backup Media Options screen, click Next.
11. At the Backup Label screen, type **`Performance Log Backups`** in the field labeled Media Label, and then click Next.
12. At the When to Back Up screen, make sure Now is selected and click Next.
13. At the Completing the Backup Wizard screen, click Finish.
14. When prompted to create the `\Logsbackups` folder, click Yes.

2. When the backup is complete, click Close to close the Backup Progress dialog box, and then close the backup program.
3. Delete the `\Perflogs\Baseline_000001.blg` file.
4. Recover the `\Perflogs\Baseline_000001.blg` file.
   1. From the Start menu, select Programs, Accessories, System Tools, Backup.
   2. From the Welcome page, click the Restore Wizard icon.
   3. At the Welcome to the Restore Wizard screen, click Next.
   4. At the What to Restore screen, expand File, Performance Log Backups, and `C:` (or whatever drive your `Perflogs` folder is in).
   5. When prompted for the name of the backup file to catalog, make sure `X:\Logbackups\logbackup.bkf` (`X` is the volume on which the backup resides) is in the field and click OK.
   6. Click the `Perflogs` folder on the left side and click baseline_000001.blg on the right. Then, click Next.
   7. At the Completing the Restore Wizard screen, click Finish.
   8. When prompted for the name of the backup file you want to restore, make sure `c:\logbackups\logbackup.bkf` is entered in the field, and then click OK.
5. When the restore is complete, click Close to close the Restore Progress dialog box, and then close the backup program.
6. Check to make sure that `baseline_000001.blg` has been restored.

APPLY YOUR KNOWLEDGE

Review Questions

1. What are the two types of logs available in Performance Monitor, and how can you distinguish them from one another?
2. What is the purpose of an alert, and what are three of the actions that can be taken when one occurs?
3. How does the Recovery Console differ from Safe Mode with command prompt?
4. How do you enable logical disk counters?
5. If you want to reload some files by using only two sets of backup tapes, which backup method should you use?
6. If you load a new device driver and your Windows 2000 computer will not boot, which safe boot option should you use to recover?

Exam Questions

1. Jim is the network administrator for two identical Windows 2000 servers in a high school. They both have SCSI CD-ROM drives, and all data is on NTFS partitions. He has just found one of his servers turned off. When he turns it back on, Jim gets an error that `NTOSKRNL.EXE` can't be found and will not boot. He suspects that a vandal in the school has deleted the file. He does not have the Windows 2000 Server CD-ROM, but he has disks and a CD-ROM writer. How can Jim recover his server?

   A. Boot his server to Safe mode and then copy the `NTOSKRNL.EXE` file from the other server using a floppy disk.

   B. Boot his server to the Recovery Console using the setup disk set and copy `NTOSKRNL.EXE` using a disk.

   C. Boot his server to DOS and copy the `NTOSKRNL.EXE` from the other server using a CD-ROM with the file copied from the other server.

   D. Boot his server to the Recovery Console using a secondary boot on the server and copy the `NTOSKRNL.EXE` using a CD-ROM with the file copied from the other server.

2. Pavel wants to determine whether his server is short of memory. Under light load, users get good response. However, as load increases, so does the lack of responsiveness. Which of the following counters will aid him in determining whether memory is the bottleneck in his system? (Choose two.)

   A. Memory\ pages/sec

   B. Paging File\ % Usage

   C. Processor\ Interrupts/sec

   D. Network Segment\ % Net Utilization

3. You are interviewing Chris, an applicant for the help desk technician job your company is trying to fill. While discussing Windows 2000, you ask her which of the following statements are true concerning the Recovery Console. (Select all that apply.)

   A. The Recovery Console can be accessed upon startup if you have installed it with the `winnt32 /cmdcons` command.

   B. The Recovery Console can be accessed by using the Windows 2000 Setup disks.

APPLY YOUR KNOWLEDGE

C. The Recovery Console can be accessed from the advanced startup options menu by pressing F8.

D. The Recovery Console can be accessed by using an ERD.

4. Monty is the administrator for a Windows 2000 Server. He has previously had servers fail because they have run out of disk space, so he wants to ensure the same thing will not happen in the future. How can he configure his server so that it lets him know when the amount of free disk space falls below 10%?

   A. Configure alerts in Performance Monitor to warn him when any of the instances of the counter LogicalDisk\ %Free Space fall below 10%.

   B. Configure alerts in Performance Monitor to warn him when any of the instances of the counter PhysicalDisk\ %Free Space fall below 10%.

   C. Configure System Monitor to watch PhysicalDisk\ %Free Space and check it every hour to see whether it has fallen below 10%.

   D. Configure a trace log to have the Windows 2000 Trace Provider watch the disk for %Free Space falling below 10%.

5. Andrea wants to create a baseline for her Windows 2000 server. However, when she tries to capture data for her logical disks, she finds that the counters are unavailable. What must she do to her server to enable the counters for that object?

   A. At the command line, type **`DISKPERF -yd`**.

   B. At the command line, type **`DISKPERF -yd`**. Then, restart the server.

   C. At the command line, type **`DISKPERF -nv`**. Then, restart the server.

   D. At the command line, type **`DISKPERF -y`**. Then, restart the server.

6. Christopher is doing his weekly log analysis. He notes that on Wednesday, the number of interrupts per second on his processor suddenly doubled and has remained high ever since. What does the increase in this counter likely mean?

   A. Nothing. It is normal for this counter to increase over time.

   B. It could mean that he has a potential hardware problem and that a piece of hardware is generating many more interrupts than normal.

   C. It indicates that the network card is the bottleneck in the system and should be replaced.

   D. It indicates that the CPU is the bottleneck in the system and should be replaced or upgraded.

7. Hannah calls you and says that she saw an error message pop up on one of the servers she is responsible for, but she accidentally cleared it before reading it fully. You want Hannah to be able to see what the error message was so she can troubleshoot and repair the server if required. What can you tell Hannah to do to be able to view the error message?

   A. Open the `ntbtlog.txt` file and look for service errors.

   B. Open the `boot.ini` file and make sure all entries are correct.

APPLY YOUR KNOWLEDGE

C. Check the recent logs in the Event Viewer.

D. Check the System Information display for any errors.

8. Gene wants to tune his server for optimum performance. Which of the following questions must he answer before beginning the process of server tuning?

   A. How much money is in the budget?

   B. Which tasks is the server expected to perform?

   C. What are the latest hardware breakthroughs?

   D. Which type of business is his company in?

9. Andrea is preparing a disaster recovery plan for her company. She asks you which backup option backs up only the files that have not been marked as archived and then sets the archive bit for all files that are backed up. What will you tell her?

   A. Daily backups act this way.

   B. Normal backups act this way.

   C. Copy backups act this way.

   D. Differential backups act this way.

   E. Incremental backups act this way.

10. Christopher is assisting Andrea with preparations for disaster recovery. He asks you which backup option requires only one media device for the entire backup and sets the archive bit to indicate the data has been backed up. What will you tell him?

   A. Daily backups act this way.

   B. Normal backups act this way.

   C. Copy backups act this way.

   D. Differential backups act this way.

   E. Incremental backups act this way.

11. You are a user with administrative rights on your Windows 2000 computer. You download a new driver for your video card over the Internet and update your system to include it. When you restart your computer, you find that it halts partway through the boot sequence. Which action should you take first to diagnose the problem?

   A. Reboot your computer, start the Recovery Console, and remove the new driver from your system.

   B. Use the Emergency Repair Disk feature to restore the system.

   C. Use the Recovery Console to start a restore of the system from your last backup.

   D. Reboot using the Last Known Good Configuration option and enable driver signing as soon as possible.

12. Austin wants to monitor how much of the paging file is being used. He opens the System Monitor and starts to add the counter for this, but he is unsure which one to add. Which counter will you tell him to add to monitor the paging file usage?

   A. Paging File\ Pages/sec

   B. Memory\ Pages/sec

   C. Paging File\ % Usage

   D. Memory\ % Paging File

13. Andrea is trying to determine what could be causing her disk access to slow down over time. She opens the System Monitor and starts to add counters to help her diagnose this situation, but

she is unsure what to add. Which counter will you tell her to add to help her diagnose problems with her hard drive access speed? (Select all that apply.)

A. Physical Disk\ Disk Reads/sec

B. Logical Disk\ % Free Space

C. Physical Disk\ Split IO/sec

D. Network Interface\ Bytes Total/sec

14. You suspect that one or more device drivers are not loading and initializing properly upon startup of your server, but you can't find any entries in the event log. What could you do to help troubleshoot which drivers might not be starting properly? (Select all that apply.)

    A. Start the computer in Safe mode and examine the event logs.

    B. Start the computer and enable Boot Logging from the advanced startup options menu.

    C. Edit the `boot.ini` file to enable boot logging on every startup.

    D. Start the computer using the Last Known Good Configuration because this should replace any corrupt or missing drivers with the correct versions.

Answers to Review Questions

1. The two types of logs available in Performance Monitor are counter logs and trace logs. They are distinguished by their collection triggers and how much control you have over the information you collect. The collection of data in a counter log is controlled by time interval passing, and you can finely control the type of data you collect through the application of object counters. The collection of data in a trace log is controlled by events that occur (such as user logon), and you have little control over the specific information collected outside of a general category of data.

2. The purpose of an alert is to have Performance Monitor tell you when a critical situation happens so you don't have to check for it periodically. When an alert is triggered, you can have Performance Monitor take one of the following actions: create an application log entry, send a network message, start a counter log, or run a program.

3. The Recovery Console differs from Safe mode with command prompt primarily in that it is a separate boot from the regular Windows 2000 server boot process. Safe mode requires that the server still be bootable for you to use it to effect changes. Recovery Console can be used even if your Windows 2000 server is not bootable through normal means. In addition, Recovery Console offers only a limited set of commands, whereas Safe mode provides the full set of command-line commands.

4. Typically, Windows 2000 enables physical disk counters when it starts. This can be verified by running the `DISKPERF` command, which shows the statuses of both physical and logical disk counters. To enable the logical disk counter, the command is `DISKPERF -YV`. After the system is restarted, the logical counters are available.

5. Planning your backup strategy is important and of course dependent on how you want to perform any recover actions. In this case, the choice is a normal backup at some time interval and

APPLY YOUR KNOWLEDGE

differential backups in between. The timing between normal backups will depend on how long you want to maintain those tapes and also how much the system is changing. If the number of files chosen by the differential backup becomes a significant portion of the normal backup, the differential backup becomes wasteful of both time and tape resources.

6. The best option is to reboot your computer and press F8 during the boot process to access the Last Known Good Configuration. When a change is made to the Registry to include a new driver, that change is not made permanent until after a successful reboot. If you are having problems getting past that point, you still have the last working copy of the Registry to fall back to. Rebooting with the Last Known Good option throws the changes away and reverts to a working environment.

Answers to Exam Questions

1. **D.** The only answer that works is to boot to the Recovery Console and copy the file using a CD-ROM. Safe mode does not work because you need to be able to boot to invoke Safe Mode, so answer A is incorrect. Booting to the Recovery Console and copying from a disk does not work because `ntoskrnl.exe` is too large to fit on a disk, and booting to DOS does not work because DOS will not read NTFS partitions, thus eliminating answers B and C. For more information, see the "Recovering Systems with the Recovery Console" section in this chapter.

2. **A, B.** Page/sec shows you how many times per second your server had to go to the hard drive to recover information it thought ought to be in memory but has been swapped out because of a shortage of memory. %Usage of the paging file can be an indicator of low memory because, if it constantly decreases as applications run, the amount of RAM is not sufficient to fill the demand on the server, which causes the paging file to be increased in size. Interrupts per second are generally an indication of hardware performance, and %Net Utilization is an indicator of network saturation—neither of which is a memory problem, thus making answers C and D incorrect. For more information, see the "Using System Monitor to Discover Bottlenecks" section in this chapter.

3. **A, B.** The Recovery Console can be accessed from either of these two means. You can also access the Recovery Console by booting from the Windows 2000 CD-ROM instead of using the Setup disks. The Recovery Console is not an option on the advanced startup options menu, so answer C is incorrect. The ERD disk does not start the Recovery Console, so answer D is also incorrect. For more information, see the "Recovering Systems with the Recovery Console" section in this chapter.

4. **A.** An alert is the only method that will tell Monty when something happens; System Monitor and trace logs record the occurrence, but they are both passive and have to be checked, so answers C and D are wrong. PhysicalDisk does not have a counter that monitors %Free Space, so he must use LogicalDisk, thus answer B is incorrect. For more information, see the "Using System Monitor to Discover Bottlenecks" section in this chapter.

APPLY YOUR KNOWLEDGE

5. **D.** Andrea is correct in thinking she must run `DISKPERF`. The execution of `DISKPERF` sets a start-up flag to turn on or off disk counters and must always be accompanied by a system restart. `-yd` is the default, and it starts only the physical counters, so answers A and B do are both wrong. `-nv` turns off the logical disk counters, so answer C is wrong. `-y` turns on both the physical and logical counters (`-yv` would have also worked because it turns on only logical counters). For more information, see the "The Physical Disk Counter" section in this chapter.

6. **B.** The sudden increase in interrupts generally indicates that a piece of hardware has just gone into an altered state and should be repaired or replaced. This sort of activity is not normal, so answer A is incorrect. A network card would not result in a problem such as this, so answer C is incorrect, just as a CPU would not cause this problem, so answer D is also incorrect. For more information, see the "Using System Monitor to Discover Bottlenecks" section in this chapter.

7. **C.** Errors are logged in the event logs, which can be accessed from the Event Viewer. The `ntbtlog.txt` file shows the status of all drivers and system files loaded at startup, not error messages, so answer A is incorrect. The `boot.ini` file controls how a Windows 2000 machine boots up, so answer B is incorrect. The System Information utility provides a wealth of information about a Windows 2000 system but does not help with this situation, thus answer D is also incorrect. For more information, see the "Using the Event Viewer" section in this chapter.

8. **B.** Tuning means optimizing a server for its intended task. Although you can remove certain components or modify component properties because of security or other considerations, tuning needs to be done with reference to the expected tasks the server will perform. Although the budget he has to work with is important, it's not the critical factor here, so answer A is incorrect. The latest hardware advances are really irrelevant unless the computer is out of date and requires an upgrade, so answer C is wrong. The type of business the company is in is also not the largest factor when compared to the expected function of the computer, so answer D is incorrect. For more information, see the "Tuning Your Computers" section in this chapter.

9. **E.** Incremental backups look to see the current status of the archive bit before backing up data. If the archive bit is False, an incremental backup skips the file because it has been backed up. If the archive bit it True, an incremental backup saves the file and sets its archive bit to False. If you change a file and then run two incremental backups in a row, only the first backs up the file. The second encounters the False archive bit set by the first incremental backup and skips the file. Daily backups back up only files changed that day, so answer A is incorrect. Normal backups back up all files and set the archive bit to false, regardless of the current state of the archive bit, so answer B is incorrect. Copy backups back up up all files and do not change the state of the archive bit, so answer C is wrong. Differential backups back up files with a false archive bit that have been changed since the last normal backup, so answer D is also incorrect. For more information, see the "Backup Basics" section in this chapter.

10. **B.** Normal backups (sometimes called full backups) save all files regardless of the state of the archive bit. While saving the files, normal

APPLY YOUR KNOWLEDGE

backups set the archive bit to False to indicate that the files have been backed up. This means that if you were to do two normal backups in a row, both would save all the data, and both would set the archive bits to False. Daily backups back up only files changed that day, so answer A is incorrect. Copy backups back up up all files and do not change the state of the archive bit, so answer C is wrong. Differential backups back up files with a false archive bit that have been changed since the last normal backup, so answer D is incorrect. Incremental backups back up files with a true archive bit and then set the archive bit to false, so answer E is also incorrect. For more information, see the "Backup Basics" section in this chapter.

11. **D.** The new device driver has been installed in the system, but the changes are not permanent until a successful boot has completed. No matter how many times you try to get through a boot, if it fails, the last changes made can still be rolled back. The way to recover the last working configuration is to reboot the computer and press F8 to access the Safe Boot menu; then, you select the Last Known Good Configuration option. This loads the working copy of the Registry, and the system restarts with the old video driver in place. Using the Recovery Console is primarily for repairing disk damage and file corruption and is not appropriate for reloading the system or manually configuring device drivers, so answer A is incorrect for this question. The ERD contains the configuration of the system at the point the ERD was created, and although this would work, it would also wipe out any changes made since that time, so answer B is incorrect. You can't perform a restoration from the Recovery Console, so answer C is also incorrect. For more information, see the "Recovering System State with Last Known Good Configuration" section in this chapter.

12. **C.** Paging File\ % Usage is the ratio of the amount of paging file being used to the total size of the paging file. A high number is desired here because it indicates that the paging file is sized correctly for the system. If this number is low, either the paging file has been set too large (and is, therefore, consuming more disk space than is necessary) or the paging file has been recently resized. Paging File\ Pages/sec is not a real counter, so answer A is incorrect. Memory\ Pages/sec measures the number of page faults (accesses to the paging file) per second, so answer B is incorrect. Memory\ % Paging File is not a real counter, so answer D is incorrect. For more information, see the "Using System Monitor to Discover Bottlenecks" section in this chapter.

13. **B, C.** In this case, given the counter options listed, these two are the best options. With these two counters, you can troubleshoot low disk space and fragmentation issues. Logical Disk\ % Free Space is the ratio of free space total disk space on a logical drive, which is a measurement of remaining capacity on your logical drives. You usually should track this for each logical drive. To prevent excessive fragmentation, the value here should not be allowed to drop below 10%. Physical Disk\S plit IO/sec reports the rate at which the operating system divides I/O requests to the disk into multiple requests. A split I/O request might occur if the program requests data in a size that is too large to fit into a single request or if the disk is fragmented. Factors that influence the size of an I/O request can include application design, the file system, and drivers. A

APPLY YOUR KNOWLEDGE

high rate of split I/O might not, in itself, represent a problem. However, on single-disk systems, a high rate for this counter tends to indicate disk fragmentation. Physical Disk\ Disk Reads/sec is a measure of how many reads per second are occurring on the physical disk, which does not really provide the information that Andrea requires, so answer A is incorrect. Network Interface\ Bytes Total/sec has nothing to do with her hard drive woes, so answer D is incorrect. For more information, see the "Using System Monitor to Discover Bottlenecks" section in this chapter.

14. **B, C.** Either option creates a boot log, `ntbtlog.txt`, located in the Windows directory. If you enable boot logging via the advanced startup menu, the logging will occur for only that startup. Enabling boot logging in the `boot.ini` file causes boot logging for all successive startups. Restarting the computer in Safe mode does not help determine whether a driver did not load, but it can prevent problems related to corrupt or incompatible drivers from occurring, so answer A is incorrect. Restarting in Last Known Good Configuration also does not solve this problem, so answer D is also incorrect. For more information, see the "The Boot Log" section in this chapter.

Suggested Readings and Resources

1. *Microsoft Windows 2000 Professional Resource Kit.* Microsoft Press, 2000:
   - Chapter 18, "Removable Storage and Backup"
   - Part 6 (Chapters 27–30), "Performance Monitoring"
2. *Microsoft Windows 2000 Server Resource Kit, Microsoft Windows 2000 Server Operations Guide.* Microsoft Press, 2000:
   - Part 2 (Chapters 5–10), "Performance Monitoring"
   - Part 3 (Chapters 11–13), "System Recovery"

PART 

Configuring, Managing, Securing, and Troubleshooting Active Directory Organizational Units and Group Policy

OBJECTIVES

This chapter covers the following Microsoft-specified objectives for the Configuring, Managing, Securing, and Troubleshooting Active Directory Organizational Units and Group Policy for the Managing a Microsoft Windows 2000 Network Environment exam:

Create, manage, and troubleshoot User and Group objects in Active Directory.

- **Create and configure accounts for new and existing users. Types of accounts include user and computer.**
- **Troubleshoot groups. Considerations include nesting, scope, and type.**
- **Configure a user account by using Active Directory Users and Computers. Settings include passwords and assigning groups.**
- **Perform a search for objects in Active Directory.**
- **Use templates to create user accounts.**
- **Reset an existing computer account.**

▶ The key to successfully managing a Windows 2000 Active Directory network is in managing the users and groups. One of the keys to effectively managing users is being able to create them in the appropriate organizational units. Groups are further used to simplify management and make it easier to consistently apply permissions. The nesting of groups within one another to allow the flow of security permissions is critical to effective permission management.

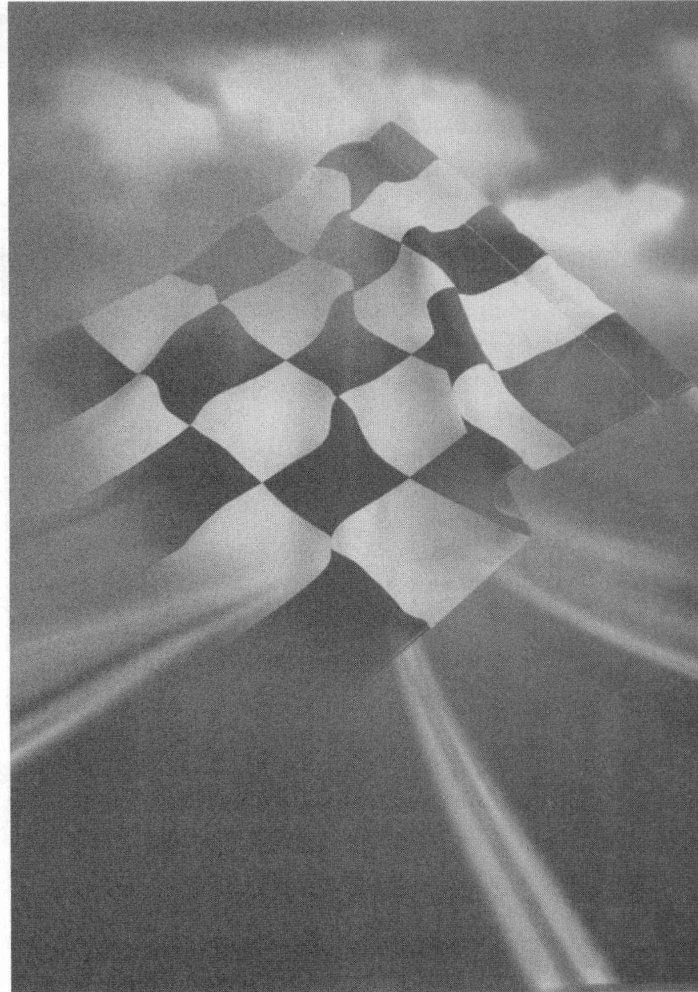

CHAPTER 10

Fundamentals of Active Directory

Objectives

Manage object and container permissions.

- **Use the Delegation of Control Wizard to configure inherited and explicit permissions.**
- **Configure and troubleshoot object permissions by using object access control lists (ACLs).**

▶ One of the exciting new features in Active Directory is the capability to delegate permissions so that administrative control can be given in granular units to only the people who need the permission.

Diagnose Active Directory replication problems.

- **Diagnose problems related to WAN link connectivity.**
- **Diagnose problems involving replication latency. Problems include duplicate objects and the LostandFound container.**

▶ Active Directory replication ensures that users are able to log on to the network from any location without the need to go out over the wide area network.

Outline

- The best way to begin studying is to create a set of organizational units, user, and computer objects. Then create a set of groups. From there you can test the impact of including groups within other groups. (You'll learn all about group nesting in this chapter.)
- A good way to ensure that you are able to remember the material in this chapter is to create your own administration scenarios from your experiences in your organization. For instance, you might want to delegate the job of resetting passwords to the manager of a group. Similarly, you might want to allow departmental liaisons the task of creating new users. Develop strategies to address the needs in your organization.

PERFORMING BASIC ADMINISTRATION

- Create, manage, and troubleshoot User and Group objects in Active Directory: Create and configure accounts for new and existing users. Types of accounts include user and computer.

Every system and user that participates on a Windows 2000 network needs to have some sort of security context, some form of identification. This means that the capability to create and manage user and computer accounts is key to making the network function correctly. A user or computer account is used to perform the following functions:

- Authenticate the identity of the user or computer
- Authorize or deny access to domain resources
- Administer other security principals
- Audit actions performed using the user or computer account

NOTE

Definition *Security principals* are directory objects that are automatically assigned security identifiers. Objects with security identifiers can log on to the network and access domain resources.

Because users need to have a computer to log on to, it makes sense to start this discussion by talking about computer accounts. The discussion that follows covers user accounts.

Computer Accounts

In Windows 2000, the management of computer accounts has been expanded so that computer accounts can be managed almost like user accounts. Any computer running Windows 2000 or Windows NT 4.0 can join the domain and therefore will be authenticated when the computer starts up.

NOTE

Windows NT The computer account features have been enhanced since Windows NT, but they are fundamentally the same. Windows NT 4.0 and Windows 2000 computers must have accounts in the active directory. Windows 95/98/Me do not.

By having the computer authenticate, the network can audit the activity from the computer and manage the computer from a central location. This is possible only for Windows 2000 and Windows NT 4.0 computers. Windows 95 and Windows 98 do not have the advanced security features of the other operating systems, and although a user can use them as a workstation, the computer cannot be managed from the centralized security database.

Managing Computers

The main tool you use to manage the computers on a network is the Active Directory Users and Computers snap-in. This tool enables you to add, delete, move, and manage the computer accounts (and other active directory objects). By default, only the group Domain Admins has permission to add and manage computers for a domain.

You can perform several actions on a computer; however, you will start by seeing how to add a computer. This can be done either from the computer itself (see Step By Step 10.1) or from the Active Directory Users and Computers snap-in.

STEP BY STEP

10.1 Joining a Computer to the Domain Without a Computer Account

1. Right-click My Computer on the desktop and select Properties from the context menu.
2. Click the Network Identification tab and click the Properties button.
3. Enter the domain you want the computer to join.
4. If required, check the Create a Computer Account in the Domain box and enter a username and password combination that has permissions to add computers to the domain. This is required if you are adding the computer without having first created the account.
5. Click OK. You should get a message welcoming you to the domain.

Using these steps, you can easily add a computer to the domain as you are installing the system.

You can also create the computer account before you install the computer. In this case, the person performing the installation does not need to be a member of the Domain Admins group because he doesn't need to create the computer account in the domain. Follow Step By Step 10.2 to add a computer account to the domain before the computer is added.

STEP BY STEP

10.2 Adding a Computer Account Before the Computer Is Added

1. Open Active Directory Users and Computers.
2. In the console tree, click Computers or click the container (organizational unit) in which you want to add the computer.
3. Right-click the container in which you want to add the computer, point to New, and then click Computer.
4. Type the computer name in the New Object - Computer dialog box and click Next (see Figure 10.1). If you want, you can change the group or user that is allowed to add the computer to the domain. You can also create an account for a Windows NT computer by checking Allow Pre-Windows 2000 Computers to Use This Account.
5. If the computer you are adding is a managed computer, you can add the globally unique identifier to Active Directory by selecting This Is a Managed Computer and entering the ID. Click Next when you have completed this screen.
6. On the next screen of the wizard, click the Finish button to add the computer account.

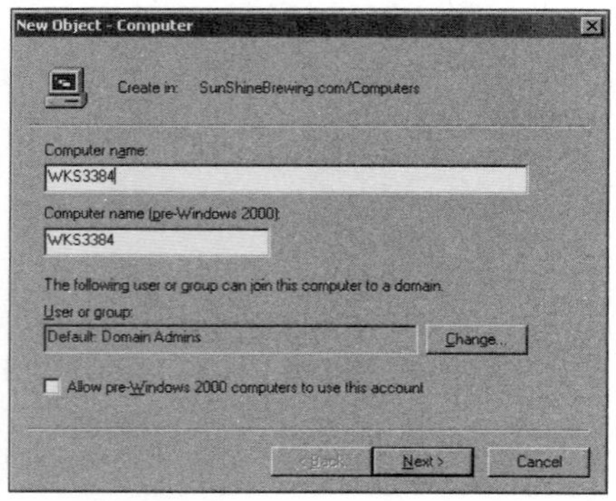

FIGURE 10.1
On this screen, enter the name of the computer to add.

After you have added the computer account to Active Directory, you can set the computer account properties. Several properties can be set, some of which are for information only. To change the properties, follow Step By Step 10.3.

STEP BY STEP

10.3 Modifying Computer Account Properties

1. Open Active Directory Users and Computers.
2. In the console tree, click the container that contains the computer whose properties you want to modify.

3. In the details pane, right-click the computer and then click Properties.
4. Set the properties as desired, and then click OK.

The first two Step By Steps showed you how to create the computer account, and this one showed you how to set the properties for the computer accounts. Many properties can be set for a computer.

The following list explains the options you can set on each of the tabs in the Properties dialog box:

- **General**—On this tab, you will see the computer name, the DNS name, and the role of the computer. You can add a description. You also can set the computer as Trust computer for delegation. This enables the local system account on the computer to request services from another system on the network.
- **Operating System**—This tab provides you with information about the operating system running on the computer, including the name, version, and service pack.
- **Member Of**—This enables you to control the group membership of the computer. Windows 2000 enables computers to be put into groups for administrative purposes and Group Policy filtering. To add a computer to a group, select Add and select the group from the list that appears. If you want to remove the computer from a group, click the group name and click Remove. The Set Primary Group option is discussed later in this chapter.
- **Location**—This enables you to enter the physical location for the computer. This is for the administrator's reference only; it is not used by Active Directory.
- **Managed By**—This screen enables you to set the user account or group account that will manage the computer. If you have entered the contact information for the user, it will appear here.
- **Object**—This is the object's full name, creation date, and update information.

- **Security**—This is where you can set the security on the object. This does not set the security on the computer but on the object in Active Directory. This is covered in detail later in this chapter.

Occasionally, you will have to remove a computer from Active Directory. You might remove a computer when it joins a different domain or if the computer is being scrapped. Follow Step By Step 10.4 to delete a computer account.

STEP BY STEP

10.4 Deleting a Computer Account

1. Open Active Directory Users and Computers.
2. In the console tree, click the folder in which the computer is located.
3. In the details pane, right-click the computer, and then click Delete.
4. Confirm the deletion by clicking Yes in the dialog box that appears.

Deleting a computer account, like deleting any other object, removes the object and the security identifier (SID) for the object. This means that deleting the object, which Windows 2000 identifies by its SID, is final. Creating a new object of the same name creates a different SID and therefore a different object.

The main reason for creating computer accounts in Active Directory is to manage the computers on your network. This includes putting them in groups and controlling their properties using group policies, but computers can be managed using the Computer Management snap-in, as shown in Step By Step 10.5.

STEP BY STEP

10.5 Managing a Computer

1. Open Active Directory Users and Computers.
2. In the console tree, click the container that contains the computer you want to manage.
3. In the details pane, right-click the computer, and then click Manage.

This enables you to manage all aspects of the computer, and it gives you critical information you will need for troubleshooting from a central location on the network.

Occasionally, computers crash. When this happens, you might have to reload or even rebuild the computer. In Windows NT, this means you must remove the computer from the domain and then add the computer back into the domain. The computer then has a new security identifier (SID), and according to the domain, it is a completely different computer.

In Windows 2000, computers can be members of groups, they can be assigned managers, and they can have group policies that apply to them. If the SID changes, all of these would need to be reset. To save you from doing this, you can reset the computer account. This breaks the computer connection with the domain and enables you to add the computer back in without losing these settings. Step By Step 10.6 walks you through resetting a computer account.

STEP BY STEP

10.6 Resetting a Computer Account

1. Open Active Directory Users and Computers.
2. In the console tree, click the container that contains the computer you want to reset.

continues

continued

3. In the details pane, right-click the computer, and then click Reset Account.
4. Click Yes to confirm that you want to reset the account.
5. Click OK to close the confirmation message.

By resetting a computer account, you can rejoin a computer to the domain. This means it still has the same name and the same SID, and it enables you to replace a computer without having to reset security information.

Along the same vein, you might also need to suspend a computer's account for a period of time. For example, you should disable the computer account if you send a computer out for service so that the computer cannot be used to break into your network. Follow Step By Step 10.7 to learn how to disable a computer account.

STEP BY STEP

10.7 Disabling a Computer Account

1. Open Active Directory Users and Computers.
2. In the console tree, click the folder that contains the computer you want to disable.
3. In the details pane, right-click the desired computer, and then click Disable Account.
4. Click Yes to confirm the resetting of the account.
5. Click OK to close the confirmation message.

The computer, once disabled, will not be capable of reconnecting to the network until the account is enabled again.

Of course, if you disable a computer account, you need to be capable of enabling the account when the computer is reconnected. Follow Step By Step 10.8 to learn how to enable a computer account.

STEP BY STEP

10.8 Enabling a Computer Account

1. Open Active Directory Users and Computers.
2. In the console tree, click the folder that contains the computer you want to enable.
3. In the details pane, right-click the desired computer, and then click Enable Account.
4. Click OK to close the confirmation message.

Now that you have seen how to manage computer accounts, you need to learn about managing users.

User Accounts

A user account enables a user to log on to computers and domains with an identity that can be authenticated and authorized for access to domain resources. Every user needs her own user account and password. User accounts also are used as service accounts for some applications, such as Microsoft SQL Server 2000 and Microsoft Exchange 2000.

Just like Windows NT before it, Windows 2000 Active Directory provides two predefined user accounts you can use to log on to a computer running Windows 2000. These predefined accounts are the Guest and Administrator accounts.

Generally, the Guest account is disabled within a domain except in cases in which security is not a concern. The Administrator account is the account you can use to create and manage all aspects of Active Directory. Typically, however, you will create additional administrator-like accounts.

Much of the management of user accounts parallels what you saw with computer accounts. A few more options are available, though, for user properties.

Managing Users

Probably the most obvious place to start looking at the management of user accounts is with the creation of user accounts. Follow Step By Step 10.9 to add a user account.

STEP BY STEP

10.9 Adding a User Account

1. Open Active Directory Users and Computers.
2. In the console tree, click the folder to which you want to add the user.
3. Right-click the folder to which you want to add the user, point to New, and then click User.
4. In the First Name box, type the user's first name.
5. In the Initials box, type the user's initials.
6. In the Last Name box, type the user's last name.
7. Modify the Full Name as desired.
8. In the User Logon Name box, type the name with which the user will log on and, from the drop-down list, select the suffix that must be appended to the user logon name. These two together make up the user principal name (UPN). This is normally the same as the user's email address.
9. If the user will use a different name to log on from down-level computers, change the user logon name as it appears in User Logon Name (Pre-Windows 2000) box to the different name.
10. Review the entries (see Figure 10.2), and then click the Next button.
11. In the Password and Confirm Password fields, type the user's password.

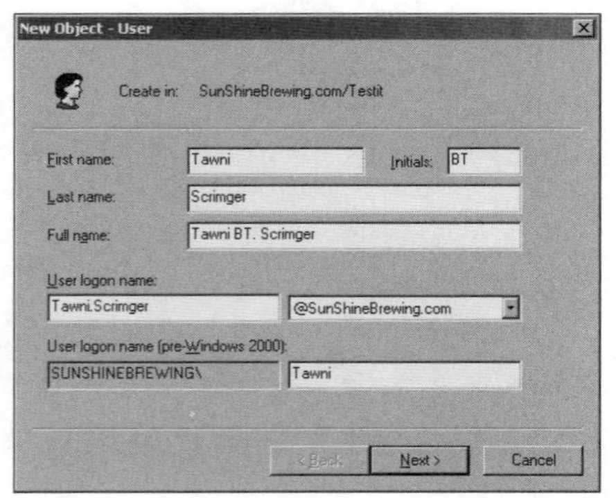

FIGURE 10.2
The first screen of the Add User Wizard is used to enter the user's identity.

12. Select the appropriate password options. The following choices are available:
    - **User Must Change Password at Next Logon**—This forces the user to change her password when she first logs on. Consider this option before using it. If the user has never worked with Microsoft networking before, changing the password during the first logon could be confusing.
    - **User Cannot Change Password**—This prevents the user from being able to change her password and forces the administrator to manage passwords for all the users on the network. This can be used on shared accounts or for other accounts you want to control.
    - **Password Never Expires**—You will probably be setting account policies on your network, including how often a user can and must change her password. This option indicates that this account is not bound by those settings. This is used mainly for service accounts.
    - **Account Is Disabled**—You can create accounts that are disabled. This is useful if the user will not actually be on the network for some time, but you are creating accounts. This is also useful for creating a template account that can be copied to create user accounts. When the account is copied, this option is cleared.
13. Review the settings (see Figure 10.3), and then click Next to continue.
14. Click Finish to create the user account.

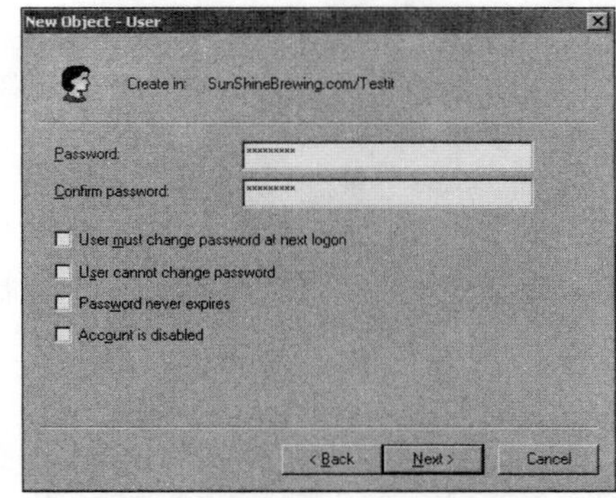

FIGURE 10.3
The second screen of the Add User Wizard is used to set the password and options.

Creating user accounts is an important part of any administrator's job. A user account is required for every user accessing the network.

As you probably guessed, the options you see here are not all the options you can set for the user. Usually, after you have created a user account, you then edit the account to set the remaining properties for the user. Step By Step 10.10 shows you how to edit the properties.

STEP BY STEP

10.10 Modifying User Account Properties

1. Open Active Directory Users and Computers.
2. In the console tree, click the folder that contains the desired user account.
3. Right-click the user account, and then click Properties.
4. Change the properties as required, and then click OK to complete the modifications.

You will want to set a number of user properties as shown in the following sections. The steps you have just seen can be used to access all of them.

Given the complexity of some of the tabs you can set for the user options, the next part of the discussion looks at each tab and the available options.

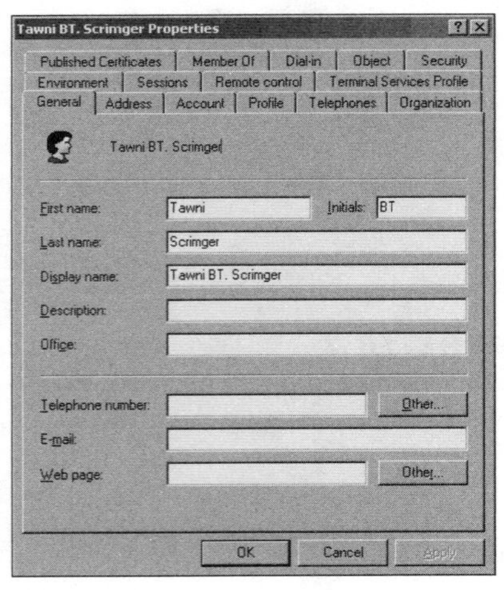

FIGURE 10.4
The General tab of the user Properties dialog box.

The General Tab

The General tab enables you to set general user properties (see Figure 10.4). A description of each of the properties is included in the following list:

- **First Name**—This is the first name of the user.
- **Initials**—This is the middle initial of the user.
- **Last Name**—This is the last name of the user.
- **Display Name**—This is the name that shows up in groups and distribution lists and when a user works with the Find command.
- **Description**—This is a description of the user. Generally, this is the user's job title.
- **Office**—This is the location of the user's office or location in the organization.
- **Telephone Number**—This is the phone number for the user. You can list other numbers using the Other button.

- **Email**—This is the user's email address. This is normally the same as the user's principal name but not always.
- **Web Page**—This is one or more Web pages that pertain to the user.

The Address Tab

The information on the Address tab provides the user's mailing address (see Figure 10.5). A description of the properties is included in the following list:

- **Street**—This is the street address for the user.
- **P.O. Box**—This is for organizations using mail drops.
- **City**—This is the city in which the user is located.
- **State/Province**—This is the state or province in which the user is located.
- **Zip/Postal Code**—This is the user's ZIP or postal code.
- **Country/Region**—This drop-down box enables you to specify the user's country or region.

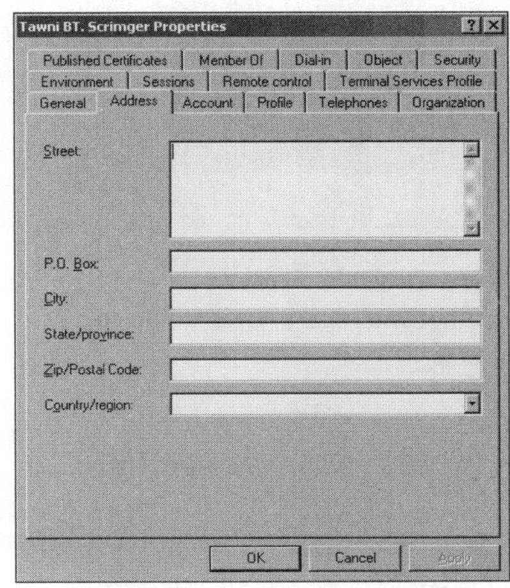

FIGURE 10.5
The Address tab of the user properties dialog box.

The Account Tab

This tab enables you to control the account settings for the user, including changing the username used to log on (see Figure 10.6). A description of the properties is included in the following list:

- **User Logon Name**—This is the name the user will use to log on to the network. You can change the logon name and the extension. Changing the extension does not move the user to a different domain.
- **User Logon Name (Pre-Windows 2000)**—This is the down-level logon name for systems not running Windows 2000.
- **Logon Hours**—This enables you to set the hours that the user is allowed to log on to the network. These should be set to the user's work hours in high-security environments (see Figure 10.7).

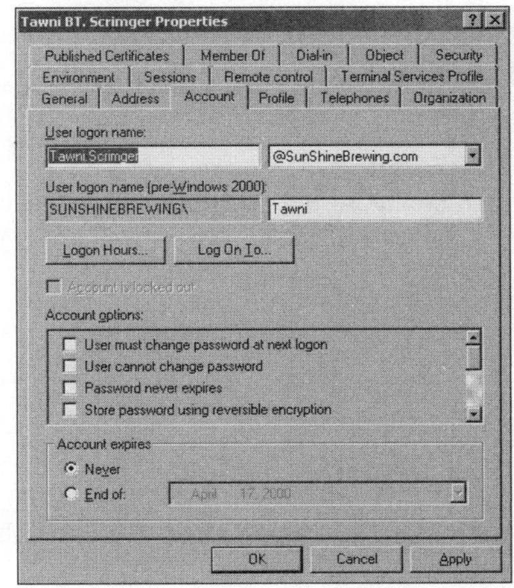

FIGURE 10.6
The Account tab of the user properties dialog box.

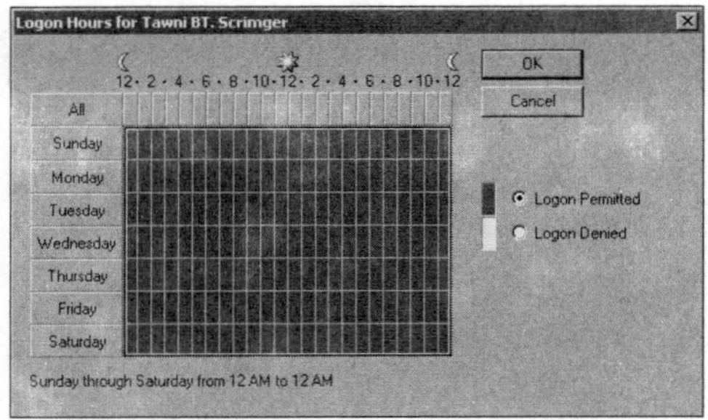

FIGURE 10.7
You can set the logon hours using this dialog box.

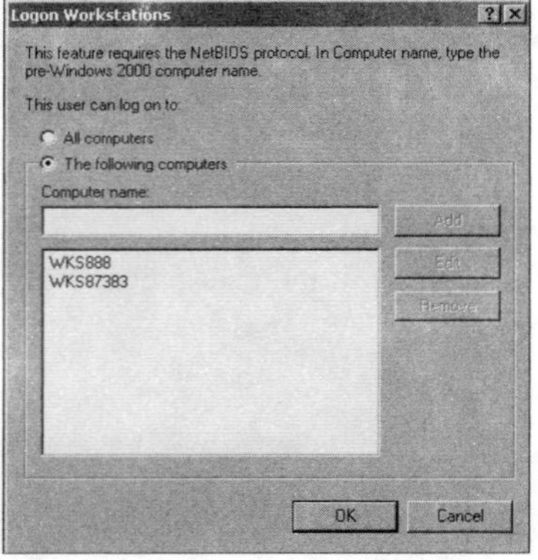

FIGURE 10.8
You can configure the computers onto which a user is allowed to log on.

- **Log On To**—This enables you to set the computers onto which the user is allowed to log on (see Figure 10.8).
- **Account Is Locked Out**—This option is available only if the account has been locked out. This happens if the user tries to guess a password more times than the effective security policy allows.
- **Account Options**—This is a series of options that can be set for the account. The following is a list of these options:
  - **User Must Change Password at Next Logon**—This forces the user to change her password when she next logs on to the domain.
  - **User Cannot Change Password**—This prevents the user from changing her password.
  - **Password Never Expires**—This sets the account so that it is exempt from the account policies such as account lock-out.
  - **Store Password Using Reversible Encryption**—This option is required to support Macintosh computers. It stores the password with encryption that can be unencrypted so that users are able to log on. Enable this for users logging on from Apple computers.
  - **Account Is Disabled**—This account cannot be used. This option can be used for a person who is going to be away from the office for an extended period or if you are creating template accounts.
  - **Smart Card Is Required for Interactive Logon**—If you are using a Smart Card system, you can set this option so that extra encryption can be used on the account information.
  - **Account Is Trusted for Delegation**—You can set this option to allow the user to delegate control of a portion of the name space to other users. This enables a user who is in charge of an organizational unit (OU) to delegate part of the responsibility to another user or group.

- **Account Is Sensitive and Cannot Be Delegated**—This prevents a user from being able to delegate control of this account.
- **Use DES Encryption Types for This Account**—By default, Active Directory uses Kerberos for security. This configures this account to use DES encryption instead.
- **Do Not Require Kerberos Preauthentication**—This option should be set if you are not using the Windows 2000 implementation of Kerberos for authentication.

◆ **Account Expires**—This sets the expiration date for the account.

The Profile Tab

The Profile tab sets the user's home directory, the logon script, and the location for the user profile (see Figure 10.9). A description of the properties is included in the following list:

◆ **Profile Path**—This is the network location for the user's profile. By entering a location using a universal naming convention name, you can configure the user to work with a roaming or mandatory user profile.

◆ **Logon Script**—This is the name of the batch file that should be run when the user logs on. This is generally for down-level clients. Only the name is required because the file will be in the Sysvol share on the domain controllers. The file can be either a BAT or CMD file. If you use BAT, Windows NT or Windows 2000 starts a DOS emulation session to run the file. A CMD file is run in 32-bit mode. The extension is not included in this box.

◆ **Home Folder**—This sets the user's home folder to a directory on the local computer or to a shared directory on the network.

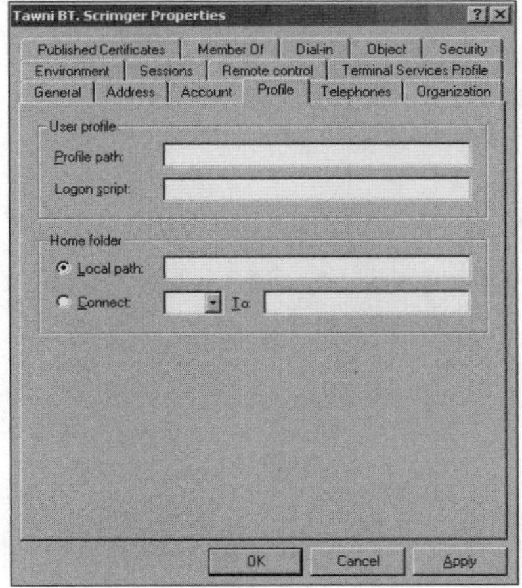

FIGURE 10.9
The Profile tab of the user properties dialog box.

> NOTE
>
> **The USERNAME Variable** The %USERNAME% variable can be used to create a directory with the same name as the user's pre-Windows 2000 logon name. This can be used for the profile path (for example, `\\server\share\%USERNAME%`) or for the home folder.

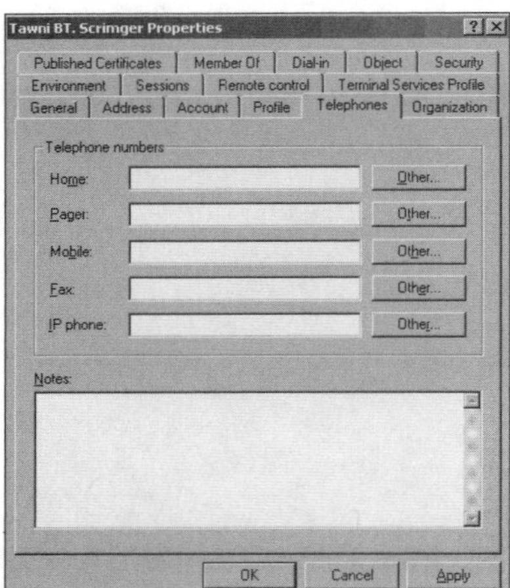

FIGURE 10.10
The Telephones tab of the user properties dialog box.

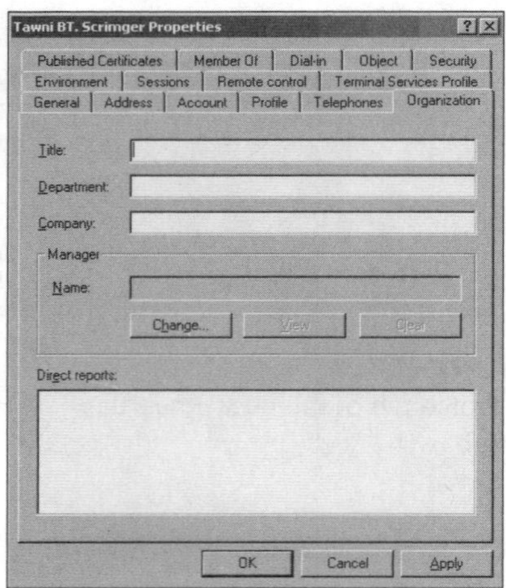

FIGURE 10.11
The Organization tab of the user properties dialog box.

The Telephones Tab

As you would expect, this tab is used to track the various phone numbers a user could have (see Figure 10.10). There are really only two sections on this tab, as shown in the following list:

- **Telephone Numbers**—This is where you can list the phone numbers you have for a person. This includes the capability to list more than one number for any of the categories.
- **Notes**—This area is set aside for your comments about the user.

The Organization Tab

The Organization tab is used to enter information about a user's role in the organization (see Figure 10.11). A description of the properties is included in the following list:

- **Title**—This is the user's title.
- **Department**—This is the department for which the user works.
- **Company**—This is the name of the company for which the user works.
- **Manager**—This is the name of the user's manager. The name is selected from the users who are already in Active Directory.
- **Direct Reports**—This is a list of the people who report to this user. This is built automatically by setting the manager field on the users who report to this person.

The Terminal Services Tabs

The next four tabs all deal with configuration settings for Terminal Services. These tabs apply only if you have Terminal Services installed.

On the Environment tab, you can set options that control the user's environment when he uses Terminal Server (see Figure 10.12). A description of the properties is included in the following list:

- **Starting Program**—This section enables you to set a program to start automatically when the user logs on.
- **Client Devices**—This enables you to control whether client drives and printers are remapped when the user starts a new session.

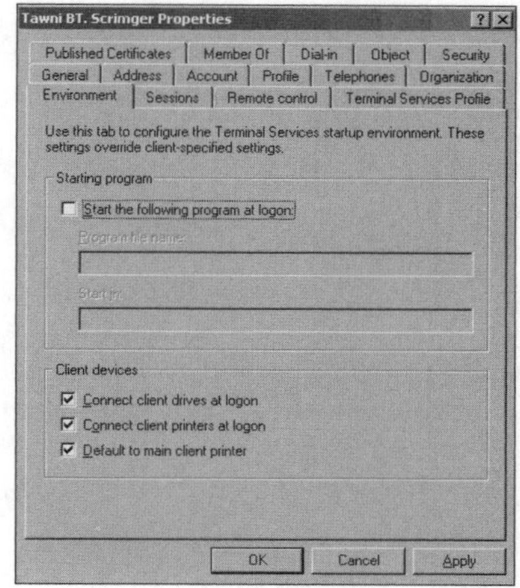

FIGURE 10.12
The Environment tab of the user properties dialog box.

The Sessions tab can be used to configure session timeout and reconnection settings (see Figure 10.13). A description of the properties is included in the following list:

- **End a Disconnected Session**—This tells the computer how long to wait before closing a session if the user is disconnected. The user can reconnect to the same session during this time.
- **Active Session Limit**—This is the maximum duration for a session on the Terminal Server for this user.
- **Idle Session Limit**—This is how long a session will be kept open without any user action.
- **When a Session Limit Is Reached or Connection Is Broken**—This tells the system what to do when one of the preceding settings is exceeded.
- **Allow Reconnection**—This enables you to set which station the user can reconnect from if the session has been disconnected.

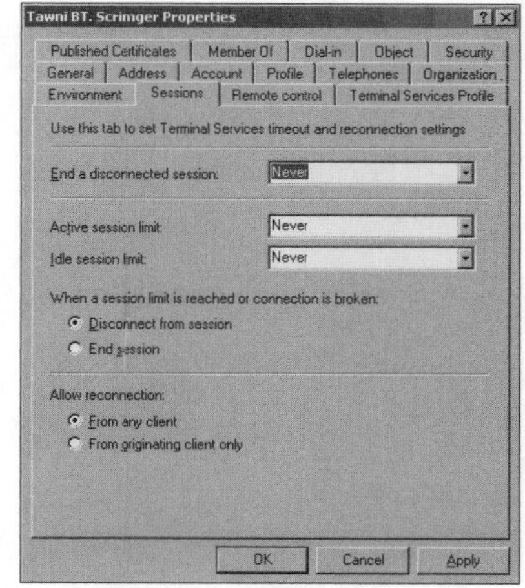

FIGURE 10.13
The Sessions tab of the user properties dialog box.

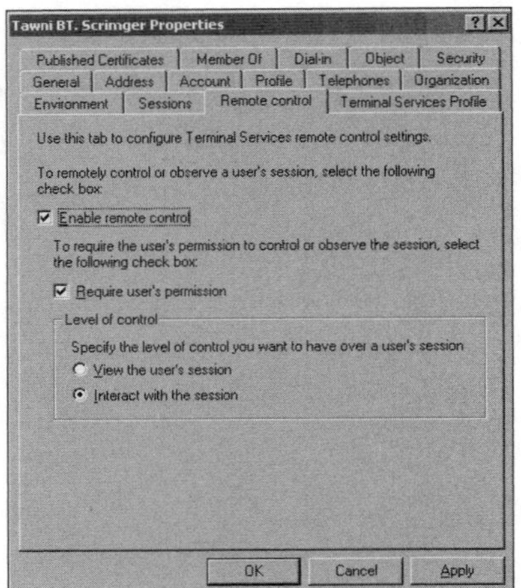

FIGURE 10.14
The Remote Control tab of the user properties dialog box.

The Remote Control tab enables you to set the options for taking control of the user session (see Figure 10.14). A description of the properties is included in the following list:

- **Enable Remote Control**—This turns on the capability to take control of a user's session.
- **Require User's Permission**—If this is set, the user will be advised when someone is taking over his session and will be asked whether to permit it.
- **Level of Control**—This sets whether you are able to simply view the session or perform actions in the session.

The last of the Terminal Services tabs is Terminal Services Profile (see Figure 10.15). This enables you to change the user's profile location and home directory when he uses a terminal server. A description of the properties is included in the following list:

- **User Profile**—This tells the server where the user's profile should be taken from and stored.
- **Terminal Services Home Directory**—This is the directory to use as a home directory when the user uses Terminal Services.
- **Allow Logon to Terminal Services**—This determines whether the user is allowed to log on to Terminal Services.

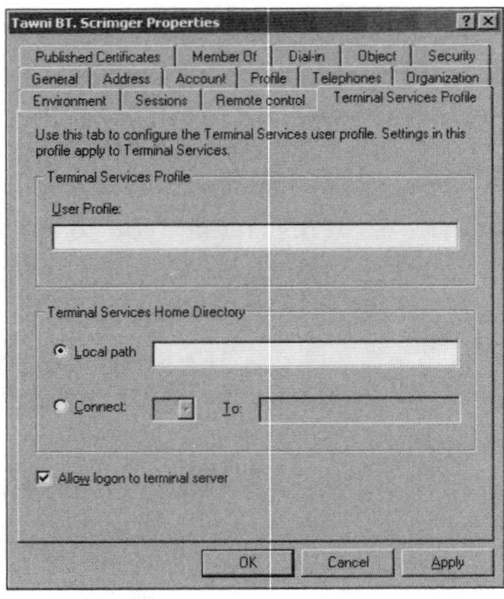

FIGURE 10.15
The Terminal Services Profile tab of the user properties dialog box.

The Published Certificates Tab

The Published Certificates tab enables you to control the certificates available for the user (see Figure 10.16).

You can add certificates from a local certificate store or from a file. These are X.509 certificates that can be used for Internet authentication, and they are also in the encrypted file system.

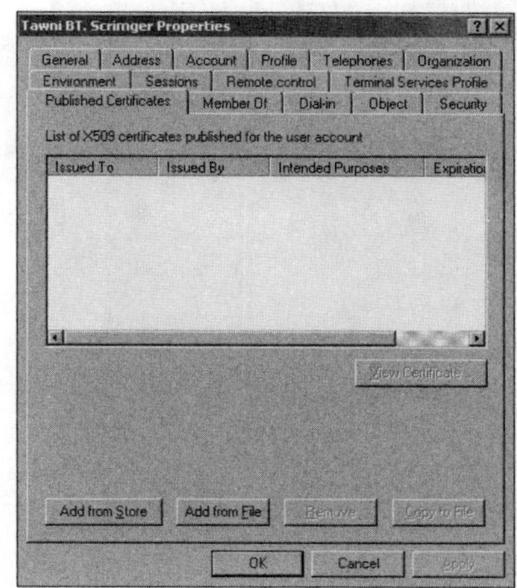

FIGURE 10.16
The Published Certificates tab of the user properties dialog box.

The Member Of Tab

The Member Of tab manages which groups a user belongs to and which group is the user's primary group (see Figure 10.17).

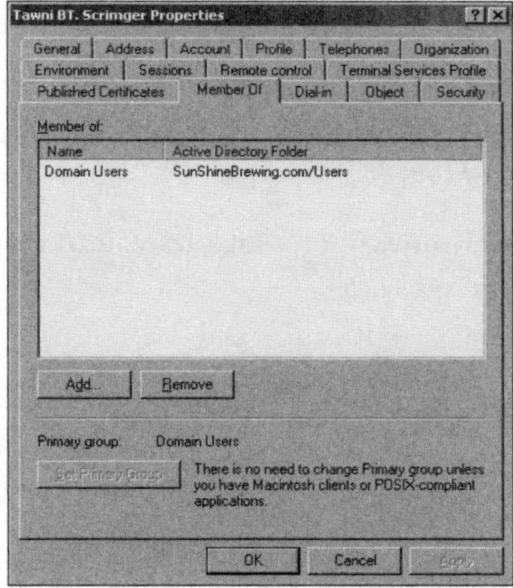

FIGURE 10.17
The Member Of tab of the user properties dialog box.

Use the Add and Remove buttons to add or remove the user from groups. The user's primary group applies only to users who log on to the network from a Macintosh or to users who run POSIX applications. Unless you are using these services, there is no need to change the primary group from Domain Users, which is the default value.

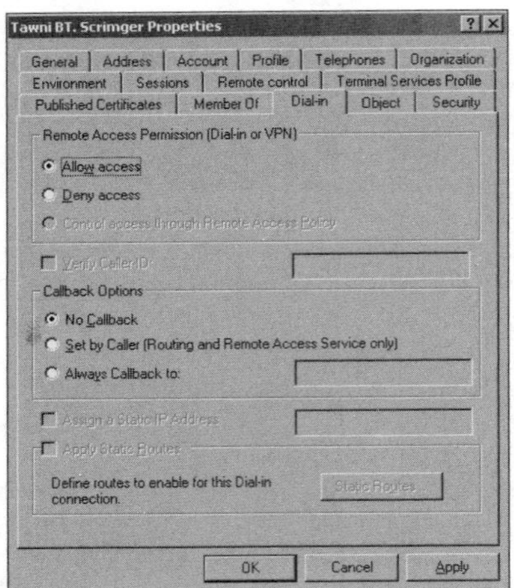

FIGURE 10.18
The Dial-In tab of the user properties dialog box.

The Dial-In Tab

On the Dial-In tab, you can set the user dial-in options (see Figure 10.18). A description of the properties is included in the following list:

- **Remote Access Permission**—Here you can choose to explicitly allow or deny the user dial-in permissions or to have permissions controlled by the Remote Access Policy.
- **Verify Caller-ID**—This information is used to set the caller ID that will be given by a RADIUS system.
- **Callback Options**—This enables you to set whether the user should be given the option of a callback, which can save long distance charges. You can also set a number to call back to, which adds security because the user must be at a preassigned number.
- **Assign a Static IP Address**—This enables you to assign the user a static IP address.
- **Apply Static Routes**—This enables you to configure routing for the remote system.

The Object and Security Tabs

The Object and Security tabs provide additional control. The Object tab is for information purposes only. It lets you know what the full name of the object is, when it was created, when it was updated, and the update sequence number.

The Security tab enables you to set security on an Active Directory object. This is covered in the "Permissions in Active Directory" section later in this chapter.

Other User Management Functions

In addition to adding an account, there are several other functions you might have to perform on user accounts. This section looks at how to perform some of these functions.

At times, you will need to delete a user account. Remember that after a user account has been deleted, all permissions and memberships associated with that user account are deleted. The SID for each account is unique; therefore, a new user account with the same name as a previously deleted user account does not automatically assume the permissions and memberships of the previously deleted account. To delete a user account, follow the steps in Step By Step 10.11.

STEP BY STEP

10.11 Deleting a User Account

1. Open Active Directory Users and Computers.
2. In the console tree, click Users or click the folder that contains the user account.
3. Right-click the user account, and then click Delete.
4. Confirm the deletion in the dialog box that appears.

Occasionally, you will need to rename a user. This often occurs when a new employee replaces an employee who has left the organization. In that case you might want to save yourself some hassle in deleting and re-creating permissions. Renaming is also sometimes appropriate when one of your users changes their name for legal reasons, such as getting married. To rename a user account, follow Step By Step 10.12.

STEP BY STEP

10.12 Renaming a User Account

1. Open Active Directory Users and Computers.
2. In the console tree, click the container that contains the desired user account.
3. In the details pane, right-click the user account, and then click Rename.
4. Type the new name or press Delete, and then press Enter to display the Rename User dialog box.
5. In the Rename User Name box, type the username.
6. In the First Name box, type the user's first name.
7. In the Last Name box, type the user's last name.
8. In the Display Name box, type the name used to identify the user.

continues

continued

9. In the User Logon Name box, type the name with which the user will log on and, from the drop-down list, select the suffix that should be appended to this name.
10. If required, change the down-level logon name.
11. Click OK.

There are obviously many reasons you might need to rename a user account, including marriage, a legal name change, or replacing a user.

Also, sometimes you will need to disable a user account. Disabling user accounts is a good practice when a user leaves the organization or is going to be gone for an extended period of time. In the case of a user who leaves, you can later rename the account if a replacement is hired.

You can also create disabled user accounts with common group memberships. Disabled user accounts can be used as account templates to simplify user account creation. Follow the steps in Step By Step 10.13 to learn how to disable a user account.

STEP BY STEP

10.13 Disabling a User Account

1. Open Active Directory Users and Computers.
2. In the console tree, click Users or click the folder that contains the desired user account.
3. In the details pane, right-click the user.
4. Click Disable Account.
5. Click OK to close the confirmation message.

If you disable an account when a user will be away for an extended period of time, you save yourself the task of re-creating the account when the user returns. This is also useful because you can create a disabled account as a template account with the settings you need. You can then copy this template account to create new users.

Obviously, you will at some point delete the account or reenable the account. Disabled accounts have an X in a red circle on their icons in Active Directory Users and Computers. Follow Step By Step 10.14 to learn how to enable a disabled user account.

STEP BY STEP

10.14 Enabling a Disabled User Account

1. Open Active Directory Users and Computers.
2. In the console tree, click Users or click the folder that contains the desired user account.
3. In the details pane, right-click the user, and then click Enable Account.
4. Click OK to close the confirmation dialog box.

Another function you will need to perform, probably more often than other functions, is resetting a user's password because he has forgotten it. Always make sure you are talking to the user who is requesting a changed password (and not an imposter). Resetting a user password is presented in Step By Step 10.15.

STEP BY STEP

10.15 Resetting a User Password

1. Open Active Directory Users and Computers.
2. In the console tree, click the folder that contains the desired user account.
3. In the details pane, right-click the user whose password you want to reset, and then click Reset Password.
4. Type and confirm the password. Passwords can be up to 128 characters in length and can contain letters, numbers, and most special characters.

continues

continued

5. If you want to require the user to change this password at the next logon process, select the User Must Change Password at Next Logon check box.
6. Click OK to reset the password, and then click OK to close the confirmation dialog box.

WARNING

Service Account Password Any services authenticated with a user account must be reset if the password for the service's user account is changed.

As you can now see, managing users is not overly complicated. However, you will likely spend a good deal of time performing these operations. Working with users and user accounts is a large part of a network administrator's job. The technique discussed in the next section, templates, can simplify the creation of new accounts by reducing the need to manually replicate settings and group memberships.

Using Templates

You can use template accounts to create a shell that can be copied to create new user accounts. This is done by creating a user account that isn't used by any user and setting the groups and other options for the account. Then, when you need another user account, you have a template. You can copy the template and then edit it to personalize the account. Copying a user account is demonstrated in Step By Step 10.16.

STEP BY STEP

10.16 Copying a User Account

1. Open Active Directory Users and Computers.
2. In the console tree, click the folder that contains the desired user account.
3. In the details pane, right-click the user account you want to copy, and then click Copy.
4. In the First Name box, type the user's first name.
5. In the Last Name box, type the user's last name.
6. Modify Full Name to add initials or reverse the order of first and last names.

7. In the User Logon Name box, type the name with which the user will log on and, from the list, select the desired suffix.
8. Set the User Logon Name (Pre-Windows 2000) as required.
9. In the Password and Confirm Password fields, type the user's password.
10. Select the appropriate password options.
11. If the user account from which the new user account was copied was disabled, click Account Is Disabled to clear the check box and enable the new account.
12. Click OK when you're done.

Using templates and copying them to create new user accounts saves you a great deal of time over creating each user account manually. The process is twofold: Create a user account with the basic information, which is disabled, and then copy it as required.

The management of users and computers is one of the most basic functions of a network administrator. In each case, you have to add, edit, and remove accounts many times over the life of a network. As you have seen, this is thankfully a simple task and is essentially the same for users and computers. There are other ways you can create and manage objects in Active Directory, though, and you should be aware of them.

Other Tools for Managing Objects

In addition to what you have already seen, there are a couple tools you need to be aware of for real-world situations. These tools include the directory exchange utilities, LDIFDE and CSVDE, and the ADSI interface. These tools and how they can be used are the focus of this section.

Directory Exchange Utilities

The two directory exchange utilities enable you to import users and other directory objects, including attributes and classes. They have been included to give you a way of handling large numbers of updates simultaneously without having to resort to a brute-force entry of the information.

Using LDIFDE

The LDAP Data Interchange Format (LDIF) Directory Exchange (LDIFDE) utility can be used to import data to or export data from Active Directory. Because the LDIF standard is an industry standard for importing or modifying LDAP directories, the LDIFDE utility can be used to perform these functions in Windows 2000. This command is run from the command line, and the operation is controlled partially by the options selected and partially by the information in the file.

The command line looks like the following:

```
LDIFDE -i -f -s -c -v -t -d -r -p -l -o -m -n -j -g -k -a
➥-b -? -u
```

Several parameters result from the flexibility of the command. These can be broken down into three main parts: common options, export options, and import options. The following list describes the options available:

- `-f` *`filename`*—This option provides the utility with the name of the file to import from or export to.
- `-u`—This option tells the command that the file you are using should be Unicode.
- `-s` *`servername`*—This tells the command on which domain controller to perform the operation. If this is not given, a domain controller from the domain the user is currently logged on to is used.
- `-c` *`distinguishedname distinguishedname`*—This tells the command to replace every occurrence of the first distinguished name with the second name listed.
- `-t` *`portnumber`*—If the LDAP server you are using is not on the standard port 389, you can enter the port number. The port number for the global catalog, for example, is 3268.

- `-v`—This tells the command to use verbose mode, which returns more information.
- `-?`—This provides you with online help.
- `-a` *`distinguishedname password`*—This tells the command what username and password to send to the LDAP server for authentication. For *`password`*, you can enter an asterisk (*) and receive a prompt for the password, which will be hidden.
- `-b` *`username domain password`*—This enables you to use the standard logon information rather than a distinguished name. For *`password`*, you can enter an asterisk (*) and receive a prompt for the password, which will be hidden.
- `-i`—This sets the command to import mode. The default is export mode, which requires no switch.
- `-k` *`action`*—This option enables you to set the action that should be taken if an error occurs.
- `-d` *`distinguishedname`*—This specifies the starting point for an export. The root of the current domain is used if this is not included.
- `-r` *`LDAPfilter`*—This option enables you to filter which records are to be exported using an LDAP property as criteria.
- `-p` *`LDAPsearchscope`*—This option enables you to specify the scope of the LDAP search. The options are base, one-level, or the entire subtree.
- `-l` *`LDAPattributelist`*—This option sets the list of LDAP attributes you want to export. The default is all attributes.
- `-o` *`attributelist`*—This option enables you to omit specific attributes from an export. This way, you can create an LDAP file that is importable to another LDAP-compliant system that does not support so many attributes.
- `-m`—This option tells the command to exclude Active Directory–specific information in the export file. This is used if you are planning to import the same list back in after making changes.
- `-n`—This option tells the command not to export binary values. By default, these values are exported.

- `-j` *`filepath`*—This option sets the path for the log file generated during an export.
- `-g`—This option turns off paged searches during an export.

As you can see, several options are available. Most of them, however, are used in the export function.

The file you will be working with is a text file, and you will be able to edit it as such. The following is a sample of the file:

```
dn: CN=Scrim,CN=Users,DC=ScrimTech, DC=com
changetype: add
cn: Scrim
description: Rob Scrimger
objectClass: user
sAMAccountName: Scrim
```

This file can be created by you, or it can be created if you export the directory by the `LDIFDE` command. In either case, you can edit the file until the information is correct, and then you would import it using the following syntax:

```
LDIFDE -i -f import.ldf
```

As you can see, the LDIFDE utility is a quick way to get a list of users from Active Directory, to import a list from another source into Active Directory, or even to export a list of attributes to modify and then reimport them afterward. The utility works exclusively with LDIF files, though, and you might have to use CSVDE if your file is a comma-separated file. A comma-separated file is a standard ASCII file that uses commas to separate fields in the record and carriage returns to separate records.

Using CSVDE

> **EXAM TIP**
>
> **CSVDE and LDIFDE** Know the differences between CSVDE and LDIFDE for the exam. You're likely to be presented with questions asking which to use to import a particular file.

The other tool available is the CSVDE, which works with comma-separated value files. This type of file is useful if you are working with programs such as Excel when you are cleaning up files that should be imported or exported.

This command is very similar to the `LDIFDE` command; the most notable difference is that it can be used only to add records to Active Directory. It cannot modify them. The file is also simpler in that it consists of a header row of attribute names and then a number of records with those attributes, one per line similar to the following list:

```
dn,cn,firstName,surname,description,objectClass,
➥sAMAccountname
"cn=Heidi Hagan,cn=Users,dc=ScrimTech,dc=com",Heidi Hagan,
➥Heidi,Hagan,VP - Research,user,HHagan
"cn=Wayne Cassidy,cn=Users,dc=ScrimTech,dc=com",Wayne
➥Cassidy,Wayne,Cassidy,Manager,user,WCassidy
```

If you look closely, you will notice there is no `changetype` included in the file. This is why you cannot perform modifications. The command line is almost identical to LDIFDE, and the options present have the same meaning as they did for LDIFDE:

```
CSVDE -i -f -s -c -v -t -d -r -p -l -o -m -n -e -j -g -k -a
➥-b -? -u
```

Although they are slightly different, both LDIFDE and CSVDE are capable of moving information into or out of Active Directory. You also will want to be able to address Active Directory programmatically. To do this, you need to use the ADSI.

Scripting Using the ADSI

As you can see, creating and importing a list of users into Active Directory is easy enough. Because the classes and attributes and their definitions are also part of Active Directory, you also can add these with the utilities you have just seen. However, sometimes you will want to work interactively with Active Directory. The best way to do this is to work with the Active Directory Service Interface (ADSI).

This interface can be used from various languages, including the Windows scripting host, to interact with Active Directory. ADSI conforms to the Component Object Model (COM) and supports standard COM features.

A full discussion of creating ADSI scripts is best left for discussions on programming, which is well outside the scope of this text. For our purposes, you should be aware that ADSI exists and works with any language, including the Windows scripting host. To give you an idea of how simple the interface is, the following example is included:

```
Dim objDomain
Dim objUser

Set objDomain=GetObject("LDAP://OU=Users,DC=ScrimTech,
➥DC=com")
Set objUser = objDomain.Create("user","cn=Dave Shapton")
objUser.Put "samAccountName","DShapton"
```

```
objUser.Put "givenName","Dave"
objUser.Put "sn","Shapton"
objUser.Put "userPrincipalName","DShapton@ScrimTech.com"
objUser.SetInfo
MsgBox "User created " & objUser.Name
Set objDomain = Nothing
MsgBox "Finished"
WScript.Quit
```

In this case, the first two lines are creating placeholders for the objects that will be created. Next, the connection is made to the LDAP server using the `LDAP://` component. A user object is then created with the new name. Next, various attributes are set; then, the information is saved. A dialog box tells you that the user was created, and the program ends.

Again, it is a simple program, but it begins to show you what is possible. For the exam, all you need to know is that ADSI exists. You do, however, need to understand groups more fully.

Groups in Windows 2000

▶ Create, manage, and troubleshoot User and Group objects in Active Directory: Troubleshoot groups. Considerations include nesting, scope, and type.

Obviously, you don't want to have to manage 70,000 users one at a time. You need to be able to group together users and computers so you can work with many users or computers at the same time.

As you start to learn about groups in Windows 2000, it is worth looking back over the information you are able to store about users. One of the intents of Windows 2000 is to bring together directory services from the network side and the email side. A large part of the information you can store for users is information that you normally, until now, would have stored in the email system.

This becomes even more evident as you start to look at groups because two main types of groups can be created in the Windows 2000 directory services. These are

- **Distribution groups**—These groups are used exclusively for email and cannot be used to set security.

- **Security groups**—These groups can be used to group together users or to assign permissions to objects on the network or in Active Directory. These groups can also be used for email.

Although the distribution groups are valid objects in Windows 2000 Active Directory, the rest of the discussion concentrates on security groups. You will examine the main functions of groups, domain modes, strategies for using groups, built-in and predefined groups, predefined global groups, special identities, and the management of groups.

A group in Windows 2000 Active Directory takes on two main functions: Groups are used to gather user accounts into a single entity to simplify the administration of users, and groups assign permissions to objects and resources. The difference is in the scope of the group. Group scope can be

- **Global**—Global groups are typically used to gather user accounts together and should normally not be given permissions. The users gain permissions from adding the global group to a local group that has permissions. Global groups can contain users from the local domain only. They are available in the domain in which they are created and in other domains in the tree or forest.
- **Local**—Local groups are used to gather permission to perform functions within a domain. The local group in a Windows NT domain is available only on the computer on which it is created. In Windows 2000, the local group is available on all systems in the domain that run Windows 2000 and is referred to as the domain local group.
- **Universal**—Universal groups combine the capabilities of the global and local groups. They can contain users and groups from any domain in the tree or forest and can be assigned rights to resources or objects in any domain. This group removes the boundaries of domains from management. It increases the amount of replication required between global catalog servers because global catalog servers manage these groups. These groups are available only in native mode.

Domain Modes

The actual use and scope of the groups depend on the mode in which you are running the domain. The two domain modes in which you can run a Windows 2000 domain are as follows:

- **Mixed mode**—In this mode, you can use both Windows NT and Windows 2000 domain controllers in the same domain. This is the default domain mode, and it provides you with the functionality needed during the upgrade process.
- **Native mode**—In this mode, you can take advantage of several group enhancements, including the capability to work with universal groups.

Windows 2000 native mode is available only for domains that have no Windows NT 4.0 domain controllers. If you have upgraded all the domain controllers that you plan to remove, and you have removed the Windows NT domain controllers, you can upgrade to native mode. Changing domain modes is addressed in Step By Step 10.17.

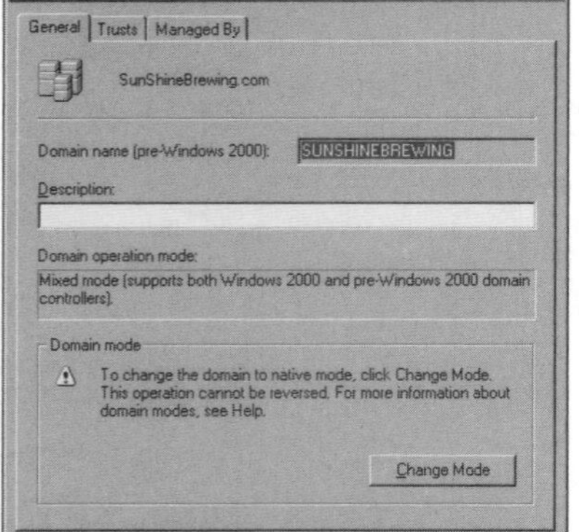

FIGURE 10.19
From the General tab, click the Change Mode button.

STEP BY STEP

10.17 Changing Domain Modes

1. Open Active Directory Domains and Trusts.
2. Right-click the domain to convert, and select Properties.
3. On the General tab, click the Change Mode button (see Figure 10.19).
4. You will receive a warning that you will not be able to return to mixed mode. Click Yes to continue.
5. Click OK to finish the operation.
6. You will receive a warning that the information could take 15 or more minutes to replicate. Click OK to close the message.

Table 10.1 summarizes the effect of domain modes on groups.

TABLE 10.1

EFFECT OF DOMAIN MODES ON GROUPS

Type of Group	*Function*	*Mixed Mode*	*Native Mode*
Universal	What can be included as members	Not available	Accounts, global groups, and universal groups from any domain
	What it can be a member of	Not available	Can be put into other groups in any domain
	What it is used for	Not available	Can be assigned permissions in any domain
	Can be converted to other types	Not available	Not available
Global	What can be included as members	Accounts from the same domain	Accounts and other global groups from the same domain
	What it can be a member of	Local groups in any domain	Can be put into other groups in any domain
	What it is used for	Can be assigned permissions in any domain	Can be assigned permissions in any domain
	Can be converted to other types	Not available	Can be converted to universal scope as long as it is not a member of any other group having global scope
Domain local	What can be included as members	Accounts and global groups	Accounts, global groups, and universal groups from any domain as well as domain local groups from the same domain
	What it can be a member of	Not available	Can be put into other domain local groups in the same domain
	What it is used for	Can be assigned permissions in the local domain	Can be assigned permissions only in the same domain
	Can be converted to other types	Not available	Can be converted to universal scope as long as it does not have as its member another group having domain local scope

You need to plan for the use of groups. The following section covers strategies for using groups.

Strategies for Using Groups

Planning how you are going to use groups before deploying Windows 2000 will save you a lot of work trying to retrofit groups into your network. The first step in planning your groups, as you might have guessed, is to determine the domain mode you will be using. Local, global, and universal groups offer the administrator varying levels of control.

Using Domain Local Groups

Normally, you use domain local groups to assign permissions. By using a domain local group to hold the permissions, you are able to use global groups and universal groups from any domain to add users to the permissions.

For example, you have a printer and allow accountants in your domain to use it. You could take a global group that has the accountants in it and add it to a local group with permissions on the printer. If you later need to add an accounting group from another domain, you can simply add the global group. Or, if you need to switch the permissions to another printer, you can just give the local group permissions on that printer.

Using local groups enables you to work with multiple global groups that need access to multiple local resources through a single entity.

Using Global Groups

Global groups should typically be used to gather users from a domain into a collective entity that can be used in the local domain or any other domain in the tree or forest. Because groups with global scope are not replicated outside their own domains, accounts in a group having global scope can be changed frequently without generating replication traffic to the global catalog.

Using Universal Groups

Use groups with universal scope to consolidate groups that span domains. To do this, add the accounts to groups with global scope and nest these groups within groups with universal scope. Using this strategy, any membership changes in the groups with global scope do not affect the groups with universal scope.

This is important because any changes to universal group membership cause the entire membership of the group to be replicated to every global catalog in the forest.

When working with groups, it is important to remember that global groups are used to gather users, and local groups are used to assign permissions. The addition of a global group to a local group is what gives the users rights. Universal groups enable you to gather global groups and add them to multiple local groups across domains.

In addition to the groups you will create, there are several built-in groups you can use to manage your network. A discussion of these follows.

Built-In and Predefined Groups

During the installation of the domain, several groups are created by default. These groups represent various roles users will take on your network, and they are included to help you set up the management of you network. The groups appear either in the Built-in folder for local groups or in the Users folder for global groups.

Built-In Local Groups

The groups placed in the Built-in folder for Active Directory Users and Computers include the following:

- Account Operators
- Administrators
- Backup Operators
- Guests
- Print Operators
- Replicator
- Server Operators
- Users
- Power Users (found on Professional and standalone servers only)

These groups have domain local scope and are used primarily to assign permissions to users who have some administrative role in that domain. Table 10.2 shows the default rights for each of these groups as well as the general rights for all users, which is a special group called Everyone.

TABLE 10.2

RIGHTS ASSIGNED TO THE BUILT-IN ADMINISTRATION GROUPS

User Right	*Allows*	*Groups Assigned This Right by Default*
Access this computer from the network	Connect to the computer over the network.	Administrators, Everyone, Power Users
Back up files and file folders	Back up files and folders regardless of file and folder permissions.	Administrators, Backup Operators
Bypass traverse checking	Move through a folder in which a user has no permissions to enable her to get a subfolder.	Everyone
Change the system time	Set the time for the computer.	Administrators, Power Users
Create a pagefile	This right has no effect.	Administrators
Debug programs	Debug various low-level objects such as threads.	Administrators
Force shutdown from a remote system	Shut down a remote computer.	Administrators
Increase scheduling priority	Increase the processing priority of a process.	Administrators, Power Users
Load and unload device drivers	Install and remove device drivers.	Administrators
Log on locally	Log on at the physical computer. Configure auditing and view and clear the security log.	Administrators, Backup Operators, Everyone, Guests, Power Users, and Users
Manage auditing and the security log	Members of the Administrators group can always view and clear the security log.	Administrators
Modify firmware environment variables	Modify system environment variables stored in nonvolatile RAM on computers that support this type of configuration.	Administrators
Profile a single process	Perform performance sampling on a process.	Administrators, Power Users
Profile system performance	Perform profiling performance sampling on the computer.	Administrators
Restore files and file folders	Restore backed-up files and folders regardless of file and folder permissions.	Administrators, Backup Operators
Shut down the system	Shut down the computer.	Administrators, Backup Operators, Everyone, Power Users, and Users
Take ownership of files or other objects	Take ownership of files, folders, printers, and other objects on (or attached to) the computer.	Administrators

In addition to the local groups that are added, several other predefined groups are global in scope.

Predefined Global Groups

The predefined groups placed in the Users folder for Active Directory Users and Computers are as follows:

- Cert Publishers
- Domain Admins
- Domain Computers
- Domain Controllers
- Domain Guests
- Domain Users
- Enterprise Admins
- Group Policy Admins
- Schema Admins

These groups enable you to collect different types of users and link them to the built-in local groups. By default, all users are members of the Domain Users groups, and all computers are added to Domain Computers. These groups can be used to manage the bulk of the users and computers on your network. By default, the Domain Users group in a domain is a member of the Users group in the same domain.

The Domain Admins group is used for the administrators of the domain and is a member of the local Administrators group. You should add users to this group only if they need to have full administrator privileges within the domain.

The built-in and predefined groups can be used to manage most of your network. These groups, in conjunction with the groups you will create, make management simple and easy.

Special Identities

There are three special groups to which users can belong. Users become members of these groups not by you adding them to the group but by the actions they take themselves. These groups are as follows:

- **Everyone**—This represents all current users of a system whether they connect across the network or log on locally.
- **Network**—This group includes any user using a resource across the network.
- **Interactive**—This group is for users physically at the computer.

Although the special identities can be assigned rights and permissions to resources, you cannot modify or view the memberships of these special identities. You do not see them when you administer groups and cannot place the special identities into groups. Group scopes do not apply to special identities. Users are automatically assigned to these special identities whenever they log on or access a particular resource.

Managing Groups

Now that you have seen some of the theory behind groups, it is time to see how administrators work with groups. This section shows you how to add, edit, and delete groups and how to add and remove members. Use Step By Step 10.18 to learn how to add a group.

STEP BY STEP

10.18 Adding a Group

1. Open Active Directory Users and Computers.
2. Right-click the folder in which you want to add the group, point to New, and then click Group.

3. Type the name of the new group. By default, the name you type is also entered as the pre-Windows 2000 name of the new group. However, you can change this if required.
4. Click the Group scope you want.
5. Click the Group type you want.
6. Verify the information (see Figure 10.20), and click OK.

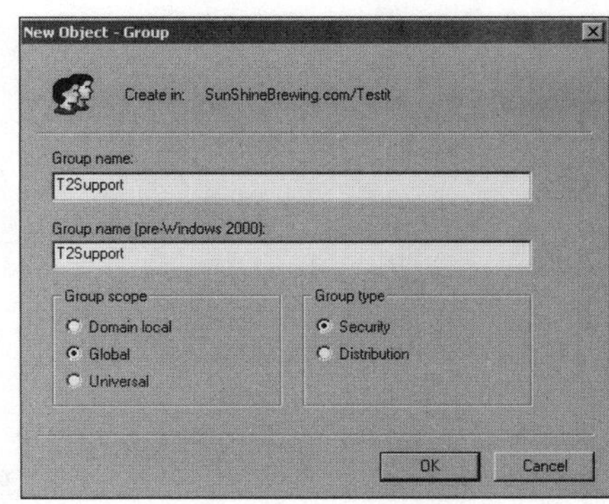

FIGURE 10.20
Verify the information and click OK.

Remember that you add global groups to gather users you want to manage as a single entity. Local groups are created to gather rights. You should always check to see whether an existing group meets your needs because this reduces the overall number of groups and in general reduces the permissions checking.

As with the user options, there are more options you can set. To edit these options, you need to edit the group properties. Use Step By Step 10.19 to learn how to modify group properties.

STEP BY STEP

10.19 Modifying Group Properties

1. Open Active Directory Users and Computers.
2. Click the folder that contains the group.
3. In the details pane, right-click the group, and then click Properties.
4. Change the properties as required, and click OK.

Although you can change all the properties of groups, you normally change the membership of groups. This enables you to add or remove users from the group. You might also change the manager of a group if the management is being delegated.

You use six tabs to configure groups. The following is a list of the tabs and what you can configure on each of them:

- **General**—This enables you to change the down-level name of the group. You can also add a description and an email address, change the scope and type of group, and add Notes.
- **Members**—This tab enables you to add or remove members. You do this by clicking Add or Remove.
- **Member Of**—Like users, groups can be members of other groups. This tab enables you to add the group to or remove the group from other groups.
- **Managed By**—This enables you to set the user who is the manager for the group. The information about that user is then displayed.
- **Object**—This tells you the name, creation date, update dates, and update sequence number for the object.
- **Security**—This enables you to set security on the object in Active Directory. This is discussed in more detail later in this chapter.

Sometimes you'll want to delete a group. Remember, though, that just like a user, a unique SID represents a group. When you delete the group, you are deleting the SID. Creating a new group with exactly the same name does not provide the rights and permissions that were assigned to the group without you assigning them again. Use Step By Step 10.20 to learn how to delete a group.

STEP BY STEP

10.20 Deleting a Group

1. Open Active Directory Users and Computers.
2. In the console tree, double-click the domain node.
3. Click the folder that contains the group.
4. In the details pane, right-click the group, and then click Delete.
5. Click Yes in the confirmation dialog box.

When you finish using a group and are sure no one else is using it, you should delete it to ensure there are no stray permissions on the group. This also removes the object from Active Directory.

Remember that you can either open the group properties to add the user or open the user properties to add the user to a group. You can also use these to see to which groups a user belongs or which users are members of a group.

As with all network operating systems, groups are a key management tool. They enable you to manage a large number of users quickly and easily. Although groups are not officially part of the exam, questions about them have appeared in some cases. Make sure you understand both the types of groups (security and distribution) and the scope of groups (global, universal, and local).

As you move into the next section, you will learn how to locate objects. This is useful when you want to create groups.

Locating Objects in Directory Services

As the number of objects you store in Active Directory increases, you obviously need some method of finding the objects so you can work with them. In addition, there would be little point in configuring Active Directory to create a list of all the objects across your enterprise if the users were unable to locate the objects. In this section, you will see how to locate objects in Active Directory from both the administrative interface and user interface.

Finding Objects in the Management Interface

When you're working with the users and computers that make up your network, you need to be able to find the object you want to manage. This can be done using either the Find command located in the context menu for the domain or the Find icon on the toolbar. Step By Step 10.21 walks you through using the Find command to locate an object.

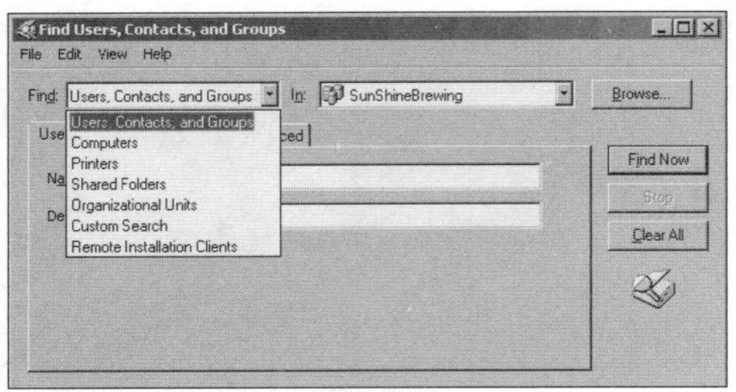

FIGURE 10.21
The Find dialog box showing what you can find.

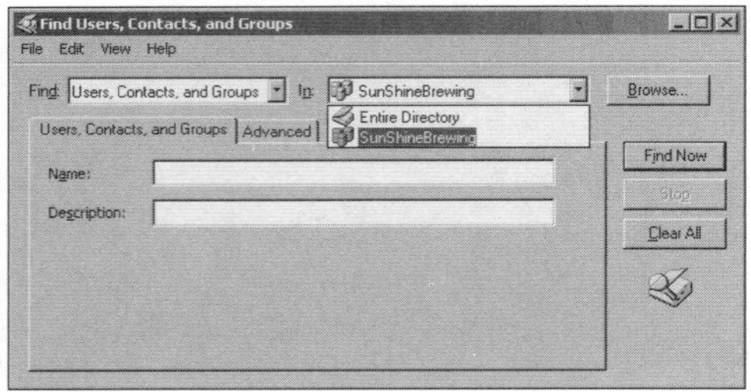

FIGURE 10.22
The Find dialog box showing you search options.

STEP BY STEP

10.21 Locating an Object Using the Find Command

1. Open Active Directory Users and Computers from the Administrative Tools menu.
2. On any domain, right-click and select Find from the context menu.
3. In the Find text box, select what you want to find (see Figure 10.21).
4. In the In text box, select which domain to search or select that you want to search all of Active Directory (see Figure 10.22).
5. Depending on your selection, you can now fill in the option for which you are searching. The following is a list of the search possibilities:
    - **Users, Contacts, and Groups**—In this case, you can enter a name or description.
    - **Computers**—When searching for computers, you can enter the name of the computer, the name of the owner, or the role in the domain (domain controller or workstation/server).
    - **Printers**—For printers, you can search by printer name, location, or model.
    - **Shared Folders**—For shared folders, you have the option of searching by name or keywords associated with the shared folder.
    - **Organizational Unit**—If you need to search for an OU, your only choice is to enter the name.
    - **Custom Search**—This option enables you to specify exactly what you want to search and to search on several criteria. The custom search main screen is the same as the Advanced option for all the other searchable items. The Advanced option is described in more detail later in this chapter.

- **Remote Installation Clients**—This enables you to search by the globally unique identifier or by the remote installation server to which it is assigned.

You do not have to enter the full value for a text field. Search usually finds what you are looking for using a word or two. For example, you can find all the people with the last name Smith by entering **`Smith`** in the search box.

6. If you are searching for a printer, you could click the Features tab and search for a printer based on its available features (see Figure 10.23).

7. Click Find Now and the system performs the search, placing the results in a results window (see Figure 10.24).

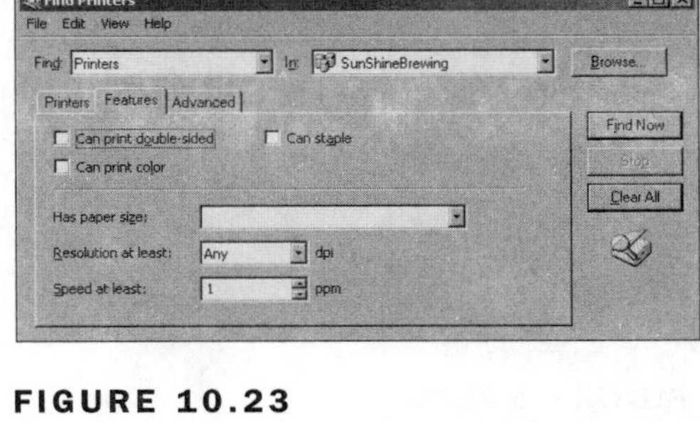

FIGURE 10.23
You can search for printers based on features.

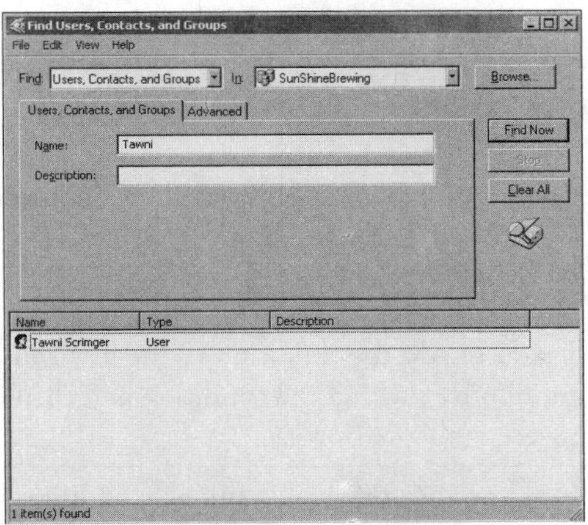

FIGURE 10.24
The results of a search.

After you have found the object or objects for which you were looking, you can select them and right-click to bring up the context menu. This gives you the same options as locating the object manually and then right-clicking.

Advanced Search

By performing an Advanced Search, or using Custom Search, you can be more specific about the objects you are trying to find. The objects you can search for appear along with a list of their attributes. Use Step By Step 10.22 to explore the Advanced Search options.

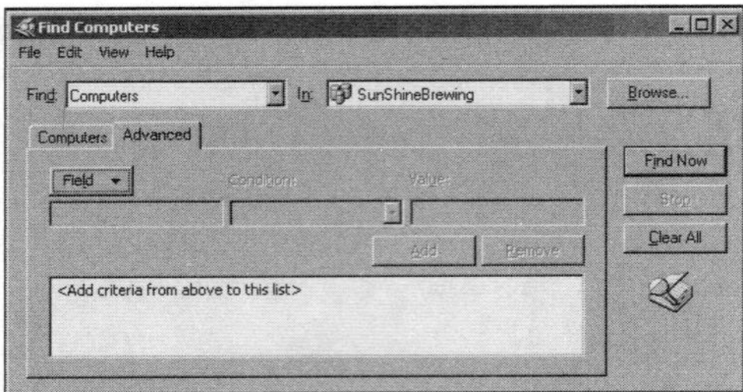

FIGURE 10.25
The Advanced Search tab.

STEP BY STEP

10.22 Advanced Searches

1. In the Find dialog box, select the object to find; then click the Advanced tab (see Figure 10.25).
2. Click the Field button to drop down the list of fields on which you can search. Click the desired field (see Figure 10.26).

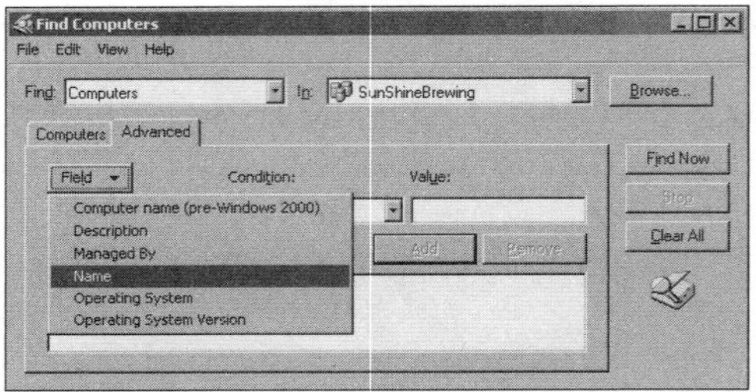

FIGURE 10.26
The options you can search for depend on the object you choose. In some cases, you have a list of objects with fields listed in a fly-out menu.

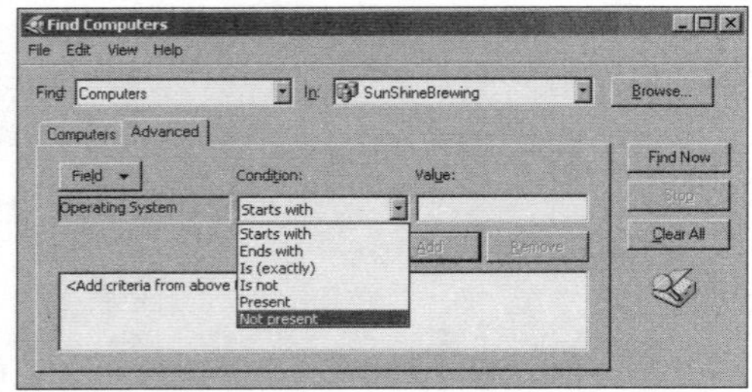

FIGURE 10.27
You can use several conditions, all of which expect a value other than Present or Not Present (which tests for the existence of the attribute).

3. Select the type of condition from the Condition drop-down list (see Figure 10.27).
4. If required, enter a value in the Value box.
5. Click Add to add the condition to the list. You can remove a condition by clicking the condition and then clicking Remove.
6. Repeat steps 2–5 for each additional condition for which you are searching. The conditions are treated like a logical AND.
7. Click the Find Now button to execute the search.

Using the Advanced Search functions enables you to find the objects you need more quickly and without having so many objects appear. The Advanced Search also enables you to access characteristics to find groups of objects with a common setting.

Finding objects in the administrative tools is useful for you as an administrator, but users also need to be able to find Active Directory objects.

Finding Objects as a User

Users also need to be able to search for objects in Active Directory. The users can easily find either printers or people using the Search tools on the Start menu. Step By Step 10.23 walks you through a search for a printer.

STEP BY STEP

10.23 Searching for a Printer as a User

1. Select Start, Search, For Printers to bring up the dialog box shown in Figure 10.28.
2. Enter the search criteria as seen in Figure 10.28, or leave the Find Printers dialog box empty to find all printers.
3. Click the Find Now dialog box.

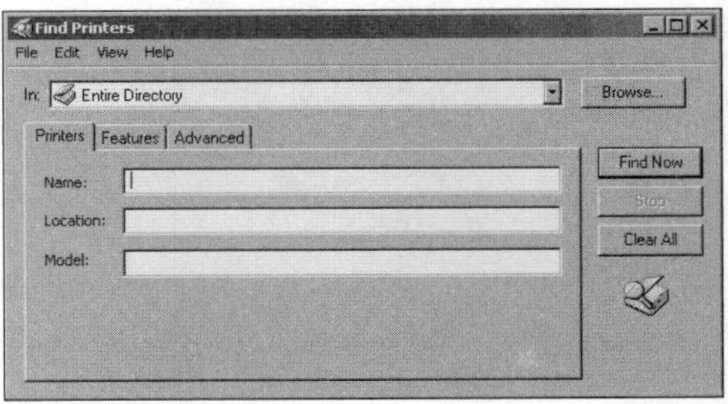

FIGURE 10.28
The interface is displayed for users to find printers.

When the user finds a printer, she can right-click the printer and select Connect to use the printer. Finding people is similar to finding printers. Step By Step 10.24 shows you how to find people with Active Directory.

STEP BY STEP

10.24 Finding People Using Active Directory

1. Select Start, Search, For People to bring up the Find People dialog box.
2. In the Look In drop-down list box, select Active Directory (see Figure 10.29).
3. Enter the name or other information you are looking for, and then click Find Now (see Figure 10.30).

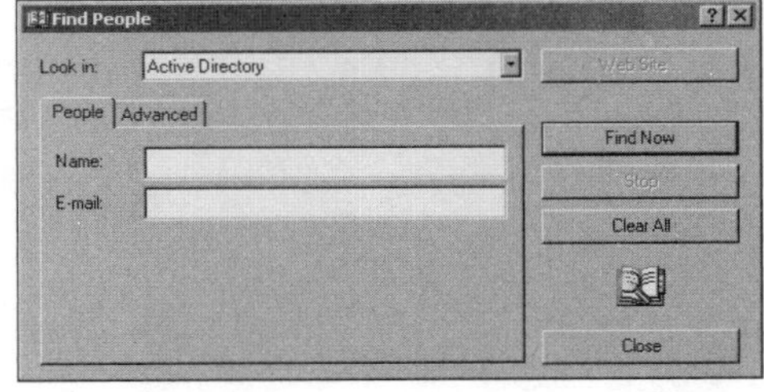

FIGURE 10.29
The Find People dialog box can search Active Directory or any other LDAP provider.

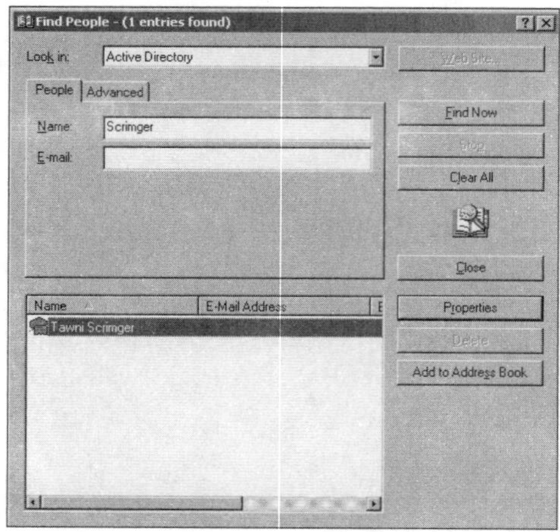

FIGURE 10.30
The results are displayed in a results pane.

Using this tool, users can find other users on the network and access information about them. They also can use this to send email to other users.

Now you should understand that you need to be able to locate objects both as an administrator and as a user.

You might be wondering about the security if just anybody can find objects on your network. This is not a concern because the objects are all protected by an access control list.

At this point, you have seen how to work with user and computer accounts and how to manage them using groups. You should also know how to find the objects in Active Directory. The next section takes you into organizational units you can use to delegate control of some of the objects to other users or groups.

PERMISSIONS IN ACTIVE DIRECTORY SERVICES

▶ Manage object and container permissions.

Every object in Active Directory has a security ID (SID), a unique number identifying the object. When a user logs on to Windows 2000, the system generates an access token, which is attached to the user's initial process (Explorer) by default. The access token is made up of the SID of the user and the SID of any group to which the user belongs, along with other information.

The access token is then attached to each process the user launches. It is used to compare object permissions to determine whether the user has access to the object. In Windows 2000, this includes access to the object in Active Directory.

Each object has a security descriptor, which includes the SID of the owner, the SID of the principal group of the owner, and a discretionary access control list (DACL) along with a system access control list (SACL). The SID of the owner is used to give the owner access to change permissions. The SID of the group is used for group access from POSIX applications and from Services for Macintosh. The SACL controls the local systems access to the object.

The DACL is filled with access control entries. An access control entry (ACE) contains a SID, the type of access the entry represents, and whether the access is granted or denied. When object access is attempted (you try to read an object's attributes, for example), the access token for your session is read, and each SID is compared with the first ACE. If this gives one of the SIDs in your access token permission, that's it—you have access. On the other hand, if this denies you the access you need, that is also it—you are denied access. Denies always are listed first. If your access is not resolved on the first ACE, the next is checked and so on until you either have the rights you require or are denied access.

By setting the permissions on objects, you can set the actions people can perform on the objects. This is how you can allow other users or groups in the network to manage parts of your organization.

Object-Level Permissions

Before you can set or even see the object-level permissions, you need to be able to see the advanced settings for the objects in Active Directory. This can be turned on under the View option in the menu. If you click View, you will see the Advanced Features option. If there is a check mark, it is turned on. Otherwise, it is off. The option acts as a toggle; if you choose it when it is off, it will turn on and vice versa.

With the advanced features turned on, you can view and set object-level permissions. You do not normally do this; rather, you create an OU and then delegate control of the OU to a user or group. Step By Step 10.25 covers the procedure.

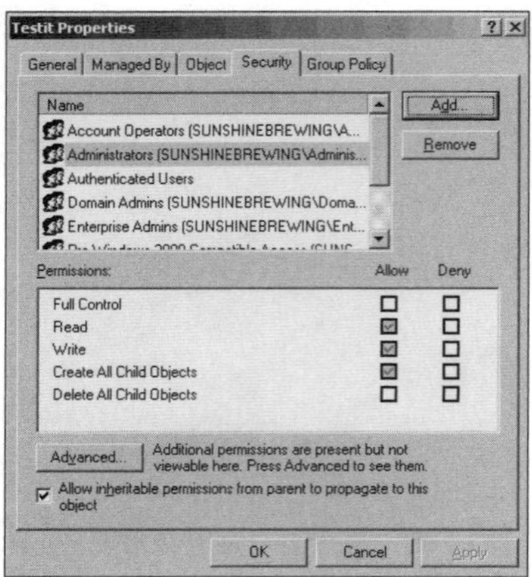

FIGURE 10.31
The Security tab for an organization unit.

> **NOTE**
> **Inherited Permission** If the permissions are grayed out, they are inherited from a higher level of Active Directory. The next section, "Permissions Inheritance," talks more about this.

STEP BY STEP

10.25 Setting Permissions on an Object

1. Open Active Directory Users and Computers.
2. Find the object for which you want to set permissions and right-click. From the context menu, select Properties.
3. Click the Security tab. If this tab does not appear, close the dialog box and verify that you have Advanced Features turned on from the View menu.
4. In the Name list, locate the user or group for which you want to review or change permissions (see Figure 10.31). If the desired user or group is not listed, click Add and select the user or group.
5. In the Permissions box, select the permissions you want to grant or deny and check those boxes. Clearing a checked box removes the permission.
6. Click OK to apply the permissions.

As you saw, five permissions can be set. The permissions are fairly straightforward. The following list reviews them:

- **Full Control**—This enables the user or group to perform any action on the object within Active Directory. Full control encompasses the permissions that follow.
- **Read**—This enables a user to read the object and the properties associated with the object. This is the default permission for everyone so that they can find the object when searching Active Directory.
- **Write**—This enables the user to change the properties of the object.
- **Create All Child Objects**—This enables a user or group with permissions to create objects. For example, you can create users and computers within container objects such as organizational units.

- **Delete All Child Objects**—This enables a user to delete the child objects from a container object, such as an OU, even if she did not create the object.

If you refer to Figure 10.31, you will notice that an Advanced button is also available. This enables you to specify permissions at a finer level of granularity, configure the auditing, and let you take ownership of the object. Step By Step 10.26 walks you through setting advanced permissions.

STEP BY STEP

10.26 Setting Advanced Permissions

1. From the Object tab of the object properties dialog box, click the Advanced button.
2. From the Permission Entries list on the Permissions tab (see Figure 10.32), select the entry to change and click View/Edit, or click Add and select a user from the list:
3. In the Permission Entry dialog box for the object, click the tab for which you want to set permissions. Select either Object, which controls the entire object, or Properties, which controls access to individual properties of the object (see Figure 10.33).

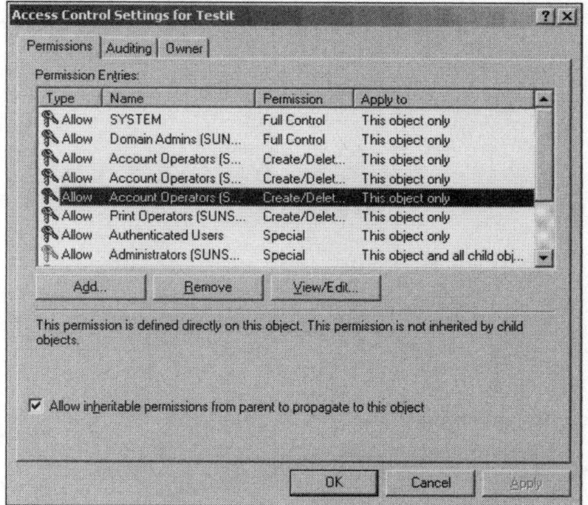

FIGURE 10.32
The Access Control Settings for objects are fine-tuned using this dialog box.

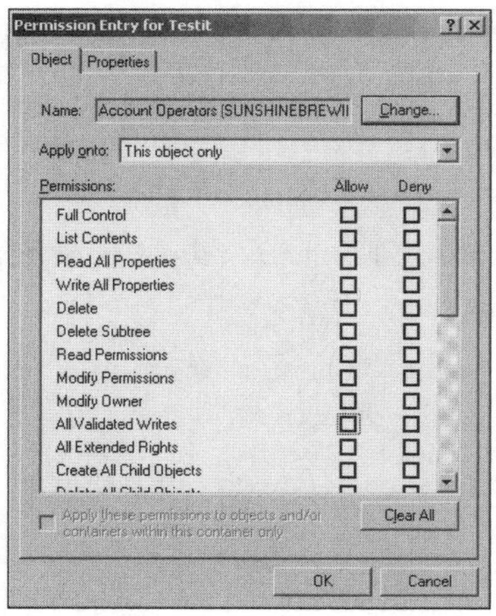

FIGURE 10.33
Advanced permissions can be set separately for the object and the properties of the object.

continues

continued

4. As you complete each tab, select the appropriate Apply setting. These affect the scope of the setting. You can click the Clear All button to clear the properties.
5. Click OK to continue.

Usually, you do not set the advanced permissions yourself. Advanced permissions are set through the Delegation of Control Wizard. You can also use these steps to check the permissions, which is more common than setting advanced permissions yourself.

A large number of permissions can be set, and these are presented in the following list. These are more for your information than for the exam itself.

Permissions you can set on the object include the following:

- **Full Control**—This gives the user or group full control of the object. It is included here so you can control the scope to which it is applied.
- **List Contents**—This enables a user or group to list the contents of a container object only.
- **Read All Properties**—This enables a user or group read all of the properties of an object.
- **Write All Properties**—This enables a user or group to write to all the properties of an object.
- **Delete**—This gives the user or group permission to delete the object.
- **Delete Subtree**—This enables the user or group to delete the object and the objects it contains.
- **Read Permissions**—The user or group is allowed to read the permissions on the object.
- **Modify Permissions**—The user or group is allowed to modify the permissions on the object.
- **Modify Owner**—If this permission is given, the user or group is allowed to change the owner (take ownership) of the object.

- **All Validated Writes**—This enables the user or group to perform any write operation on the object.
- **All Extended Rights**—This gives the user or group access to the extended rights on the object.
- **Create/Delete All Child Objects**—The user or group is able to create child objects, and with the Delete permission, it allows the user or group to delete the child objects, including those belonging to others.
- **Create/Delete *named* Objects**—This series of entries is similar to Create/Delete All Child Objects, except the rights cover only the object type named. For example, this is how you can delegate control of computers within an OU.

On the Properties tab, you can selectively give or deny a user the capability to read and write the properties of the object. Carefully consider using these settings. These settings cause Active Directory to expend more resources checking permissions.

The options for the scope break down in a manner similar to the properties. The permissions can be set to affect the current object only, the current object and its children, only the children, or a specific type of object.

Permissions you set on an object can actually affect other objects, too. This is called *inheritance*, which is discussed in the following section.

Permissions Inheritance

The objects created in a container inherit permissions set on container objects in Active Directory. This means that if you set permissions on an OU and then create another OU within it, the permissions set on the top-level OU flow down to the lower-level OU and onto the objects created within it.

Although this is the default behavior, this is not always the desired behavior. For this reason, you have the option of blocking the inheritance of permissions. This is done on the Security tab. Step By Step 10.27 explores blocking inherited permissions.

STEP BY STEP

10.27 Blocking Inherited Permissions

1. Open Active Directory Users and Computers.
2. Find the object for which you want to set permissions, and right-click. From the context menu, select Properties.
3. Click the Security tab. If this tab does not appear, close the dialog box and verify that you have Advanced Features turned on from the View menu.
4. Clear the Allow Inheritable Permissions from the Parent to Propagate to This Object check box.
5. A dialog box appears asking what you want to do with the inherited permissions already on the object (see Figure 10.34).
6. To keep the permissions, click Copy; to remove them, click Remove.

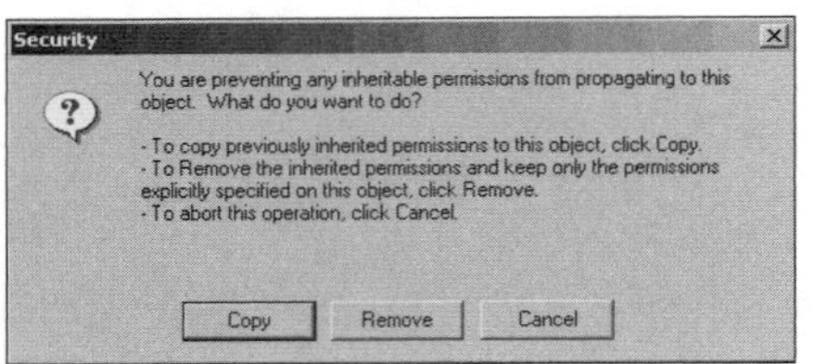

FIGURE 10.34
You have two options regarding the inheritable permissions when you clear the check box.

After you have cleared this check box, permissions are not inherited again unless you recheck the box. This is true even if you move the object to another container.

In most cases, you won't set these permissions directly; you will delegate control of an organizational unit that contains the objects.

Delegating Administrative Control

Combining the use of organizational units and permissions provides you with the capability to delegate the management of portions of Active Directory to other users. This means you can create an organizational unit and give a user or group the rights they need to manage that OU, effectively creating a workgroup or local administrator within a single domain.

Applying the required full control permissions using the Security tab can delegate control; however, you should use the Delegation of Control Wizard. This wizard enables you to completely delegate control or to delegate only partial control of an OU, as you will learn in Step By Step 10.28.

STEP BY STEP

10.28 Delegating Control with the Wizard

1. In Active Directory Users and Computers, right-click the OU for which you want to delegate control.
2. Select Delegate Control from the context menu.
3. Click Next to bypass the introductory screen.
4. On the Next screen, use the Add button to add the users and/or groups to which you will delegate control, and then click Next.
5. On the next page of the wizard, you are asked what you want to allow the user or group to do. You can select one or more common tasks from the list. You have the option of customizing what you are delegating. The common tasks include the following:
    - Create, delete, and manage user accounts.
    - Reset passwords on user accounts.
    - Read all user information.
    - Create, delete, and manage groups.
    - Modify the membership of a group.
    - Manage Group Policy links.
6. If you selected Create a Custom Task to Delegate, you are asked to specify the object or objects over which the user or group will have control.
7. You then see a list of the general permissions, as described in the preceding bulleted list. You can also see the permissions from the advanced permissions by checking the Property-Specific or Create/Deletion of Specific Child Objects check box.
8. Select the rights the user or group should have, and click Next.
9. This takes you to the finish screen. Review the information and click Finish.

The main reason for creating organization units is so you can delegate control. The delegation adds the required permissions. This can be run more than once and adds more permissions as required.

Understanding the permissions you can set on objects is important because they control the actions of the users and, in some cases, the administrators. It is permissions that make delegation of control and secure dynamic updates possible. You also need to be able to set permissions on printers and shared folders.

Working in the Physical Network

Now that you have seen how to configure the logical portion of Active Directory, it is time to look at configuring the physical side. The physical parts of Active Directory—sites and subnets—are used to control replication. By creating sites and later site links, you will be able to determine at what times replication can occur and how often during that period it will happen.

One of the key parts of using Active Directory is the TCP/IP requirement. TCP/IP is not required simply to enable Windows 2000 to use the DNS system, although that is very important. TCP/IP enables you to break your enterprise into sites and to control replication between sites. You will also be able to apply group policies to sites, enforcing certain settings for all the computers in a single location.

A site is very simply one or more IP subnets connected by high-speed links. This is perhaps a little vague. High-speed is relative to your environment. Many factors need to be examined when determining what exactly is meant by high-speed. If your domain contains 3 million objects, your password policy requires passwords to be changed every seven days, and you experience a high turnover of employees, a 10Mbps LAN might not be capable of keeping up with the replication required. On the other hand, if you have a few hundred objects in Active Directory, there are few changes in your environment, and you have only two domain controllers, you might find that a 128Kbps ISDN link is fine.

As a rule of thumb, consider anything that runs T1 (1.54Mbps) and below to be a slow link. In these cases, you want to consider the effect of replication on the link. You probably need to create two sites so you can control the replication between them.

The good news is that sites follow what most organizations already do with their networks. Also, sites are easy to create and manage in Active Directory. Normally, you already have sites defined in your network, breaking the segments into manageable sections. These sections typically are implemented to control the traffic because this is also the point of sites; the translation from the physical segments into sites is very straightforward.

Working with Sites

If you were to allow uncontrolled replication on your network, you would have many problems with available bandwidth. This is notably the case when you have a link to a remote office. In these cases, you need to remember that sites are used to control replication traffic, and to create the sites you need to control the traffic.

You must be able to create and manage sites within Active Directory. The following sections outline how to create and remove sites. Then, you will see how to add subnets to a site and move domain controllers to a site.

Adding a Site

Adding a site is a simple procedure. Step By Step 10.29 shows you the steps that are involved.

STEP BY STEP

10.29 Creating a Site

1. Start Active Directory Sites and Services.
2. Right-click the Sites folder and select New Site (see Figure 10.35).

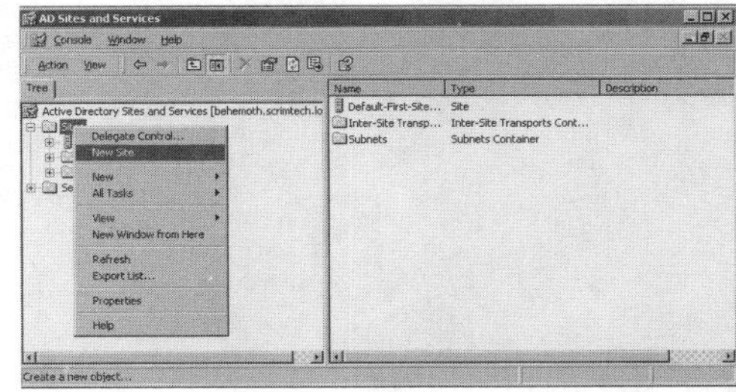

FIGURE 10.35
Select New Site from the context menu.

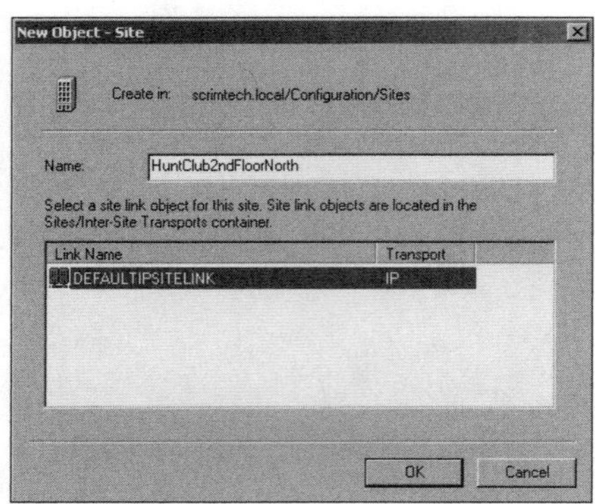

FIGURE 10.36
Enter the name of the new site.

3. In the New Object – Site dialog box, enter the name of the new site (see Figure 10.36). Letters and numbers are allowed, but spaces and special characters are not.
4. Click one of the site links, and then click OK. (Site links are covered later in this chapter.)
5. You will get a message telling you what the next steps are (see Figure 10.37). Click OK to continue.

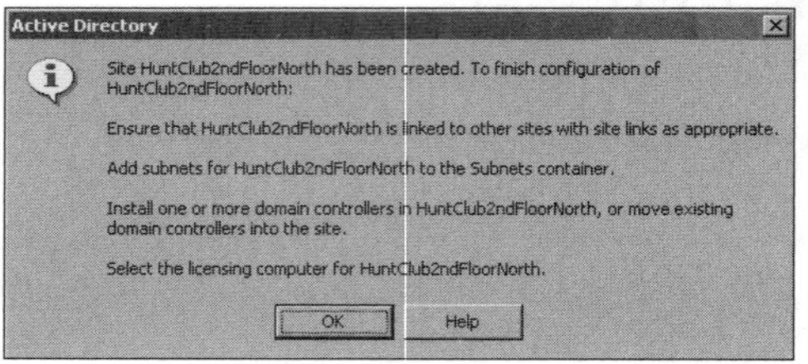

FIGURE 10.37
A message tells you what the next steps are to complete the site.

As you can see, creating a site is a simple process. You can also rename and delete sites.

Renaming a Site

Renaming a site is as simple as renaming a file. Step By Step 10.30 details all the steps you need to perform to rename a site.

STEP BY STEP

10.30 Renaming a Site

1. Open Active Directory Sites and Services.
2. Open the Sites folder, and click the site you want to rename.
3. Click once again, or right-click and select Rename.
4. Enter the new name and press Enter.

Renaming is useful when you are reorganizing your network or if a remote office changes purpose. Renaming is also useful when a site is no longer necessary.

Deleting a Site

Deleting a site is just as simple as renaming a site. You should ensure that the site is empty before you delete the site; otherwise, some objects could be lost. Step By Step 10.31 walks you through deleting a site.

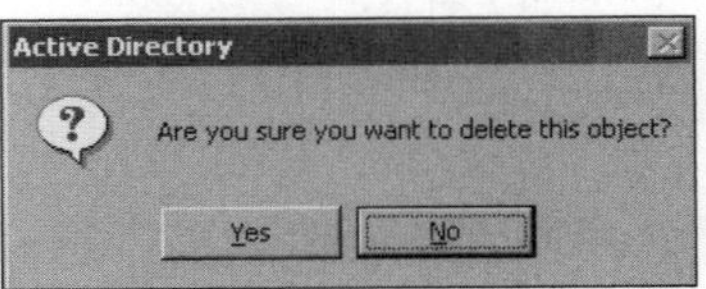

FIGURE 10.38
The confirmation dialog box.

STEP BY STEP

10.31 Deleting a Site

1. Open Active Directory Sites and Services.
2. Open the Sites folder and click the site you want to delete.
3. Press the Delete key, or right-click and select Delete. You will see a confirmation dialog box (see Figure 10.38).
4. If you're sure you want to delete the site, click Yes. You will see a warning about a site being a container object and that deleting the site will delete the other objects (see Figure 10.39).
5. Click Yes to complete the deletion.

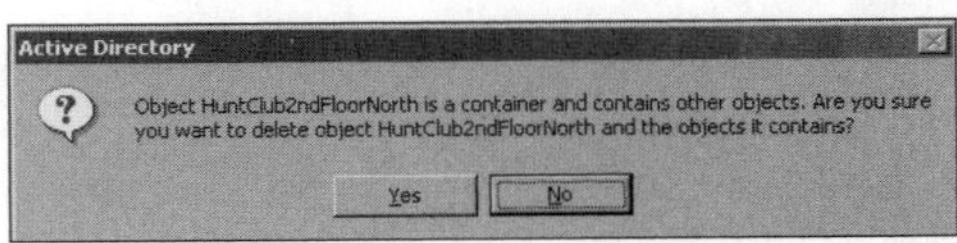

FIGURE 10.39
This diaog box is warning you that other objects could be deleted along with the site.

Again, you usually delete sites only if you are reorganizing your physical network.

In addition to creating, renaming, and deleting sites, you should be aware of and be able to set the properties of the sites in your network.

Site Properties

Some properties can be set for the sites you create in Active Directory. The following sections describe the properties that can be set for a site. To set the properties, right-click the site name and select Properties. This brings up the Properties dialog box (see Figure 10.40).

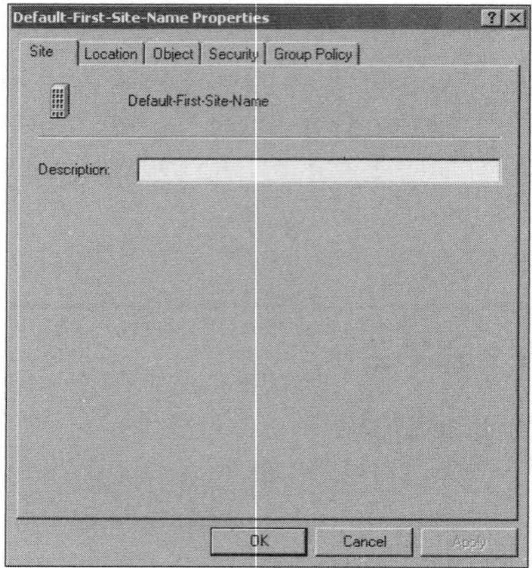

FIGURE 10.40
The site Properties dialog box.

The following are the properties you can set on each tab:

- **Site**—This enables you to enter a description for the site.
- **Location**—This enables you to enter a location for the site.
- **Object**—This enables you to see the full name of the object and other details, such as when it was created. There is nothing you can edit on this tab.
- **Security**—This enables you to set the security for the object in Active Directory. The default security enables administrators to manage the site and enables others to read the information.
- **Group Policy**—This enables you to assign group policies to the site and create and modify the policies.

Remember that a site is defined as a group of IP subnets connected using high-speed networking. This means you must be able to work with subnets as well.

Working with Subnets

Now that you can create and delete sites, you need to be able to populate the sites. This is a matter of deciding which subnets should be in a site and creating them in Active Directory. Decisions about which subnets to include depend on the network design and how you will actually control the location of objects in Active Directory.

Subnets need to be added, deleted, and moved between sites. In addition, similar to the other objects in Active Directory, you can set various properties for subnets. The next few sections show you how to perform these functions.

Adding a Subnet

Adding a subnet is very simple, as you will see in Step By Step 10.32.

STEP BY STEP

10.32 Creating a Subnet in Active Directory

1. Open Active Directory Sites and Services.
2. Right-click the Subnets folder and select New Subnet.
3. In the dialog box, enter the IP address and subnet mask for a system on that subnet.
4. The system automatically converts the information to network ID/number of bits notation (see Figure 10.41).
5. Select the site to which you want to add the subnet, and then click OK.

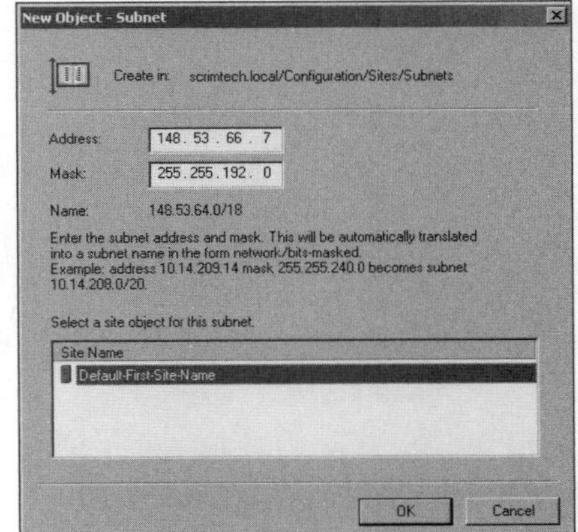

FIGURE 10.41
The dialog box used to add subnets.

Again, adding a subnet is simple, but before you click OK, you should ensure that you have entered the correct information. Sometimes you will need to delete a subnet.

Deleting a Subnet

Deleting a subnet is as simple as adding a subnet. Follow the steps in Step By Step 10.33 to learn how to delete a subnet.

STEP BY STEP

10.33 Deleting a Subnet

1. Open Active Directory Sites and Services.
2. Open the Subnets folder and click the subnet to delete.

continues

continued

3. Press the Delete key, or right-click and select Delete. You will see a confirmation dialog box.
4. Click Yes to confirm the deletion.

Although you can delete subnets, it is far more common to move a subnet to a different site. This happens as the network changes and the distribution of users and servers changes.

Moving a Subnet

Sometimes you will need to move a subnet. This can occur when the network grows or shrinks or as the bandwidth between sites is increased.

The steps for moving a subnet are, again, very simple, as shown in Step By Step 10.34.

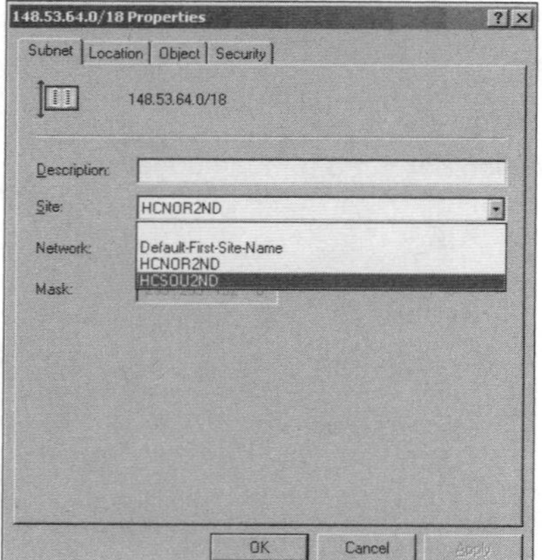

FIGURE 10.42
Moving a subnet is easy in the Properties dialog box.

STEP BY STEP

10.34 Moving a Subnet to Another Site

1. Open Active Directory Sites and Services.
2. Open the Subnets folder and click the subnet you want to move.
3. Right-click and select Properties.
4. In the Properties dialog box on the Subnet tab, use the Site drop-down list to select the site to which you want to move the subnet (see Figure 10.42).
5. Click OK to complete the move.

In most cases, even moving subnets is a rare occurrence. Moving subnets occurs only when the physical network is reorganized.

As you can see, other tabs are available in this dialog box. The following list describes the other options you can set on each tab:

- **Subnet**—This tab enables you to enter a description for the subnet and move it to another site.
- **Location**—This enables you to enter a location for the subnet.
- **Object**—This enables you to see the full name of the object and other details, such as when it was created. There is nothing you can edit on this tab.
- **Security**—This enables you to set the security for the object in Active Directory. The default security enables administrators to manage the site and enables others to read the information.

Now that you have created the sites, you need to move the domain controllers into the sites and configure the replication between the sites.

REPLICATING ACTIVE DIRECTORY INFORMATION

▶ Diagnose Active Directory replication problems.

Replication is the process of taking information from one system and copying it to another system. In Windows 2000, replication is a very important element. Changes can occur at any domain controller, not just at a primary domain controller, which is the case in Windows NT 4.0.

In addition to the multiple master replication model for the domain objects, additional information needs to be replicated throughout the organization. The following is a list of the key information that needs to be replicated.

This section looks at Active Directory replication, starting with an overview of how it works. From there, the specifics of the intrasite replication will be discussed, including a look at connections.

After that, the discussion turns to how you can control replication between sites. Finally, there will be a quick look at how you configure a Global Catalog server. Three kinds of information exist that Active Directory must replicate. They are as follows:

- **Schema information**—This is the actual structure of the database that holds information about the objects in your enterprise. You might recall that all the domains and, therefore, all the domain controllers need to use the same schema for Active Directory to work correctly. The schema must be replicated to all domain controllers.
- **Configuration information**—This is the overall design of the entire enterprise. It includes the domains, their names, and where they fit into the hierarchy. It also includes other information, such as the replication topology. This information is used by all the domain controllers and therefore is replicated to all domain controllers.
- **Domain data**—This is the information you store about the objects making up your domain. All the information is replicated within a domain by the domain controllers. The global catalog servers throughout the enterprise replicate a subset of the information.

As you can see, two levels of replication exist: the replication within a domain and the replication handled by the global catalog servers. The domain controllers primarily handle the replication within a domain. This replication is principally interested in the replication of the objects in the domain along with the attributes for each of the objects.

The global catalog servers handle the other replication. At least one global catalog server is required in the enterprise. There should also be one global catalog server for each domain and for each site in the enterprise.

The global catalog servers are responsible for replication of the following information:

- The schema information for the forest
- The configuration information for the domains in the forest
- A subset of the properties for all directory objects in the forest (replicated between global catalogs only)

- All directory objects and all their properties for the domain in which the global catalog is located

Now that you know what is replicated, we will look at how replication works.

How Replication Works

Replication is based on the Update Sequence Number (USN) in Active Directory. The USN tracks, for each domain controller, the number of changes it has made to its version of the directory. As a change is made, the current USN is assigned to the object, and the USN for the domain controller is incremented.

Each domain controller keeps track of its own USN and the USNs for its replication partners. Periodically (every 5 minutes by default), the server checks for changes on its replication partners. Requesting any changes since the last known USN for the partner accomplishes this check. The partner can then send all the changes since the USN number.

A domain controller could be offline for a period of time, and after it comes back, it can quickly get back up-to-date.

There is a danger here. Assume a domain controller receives an update. It makes the change and then updates its USN. The domain controller that originally made the change now requests the USN for the server that got the change. Its USN is updated, and therefore, the change is requested. The system that originated the change now has its own change back. If the system made the change and updated its USN, this whole cycle would repeat ad infinitum.

To avoid this scenario, Active Directory tracks the number of originating writes that have occurred for each attribute. The number of times a user changed the value, rather than the number of times it was changed using replication, is tracked. In the preceding case, the first system in which the change was made would find that it had the correct originating write value and would not make the change.

Additionally, the possibility exists that two different users could be changing the same attribute of the same object at the same time on two different controllers. When these changes both start to replicate, a conflict will be detected. Windows 2000 will choose the change with the newer timestamp (the more recent change) to resolve the conflict.

If the two changes are made at the same millisecond, the change with the higher globally unique ID will win.

Now that you have seen the theory of replication, it is time to see how the replication is configured within a site and between sites.

Replication Within a Site

Although there is little you need to do with intrasite replication, it is important for you to understand how it works and the components involved. This serves as a basis for intersite replication.

Replication within a site is handled by Active Directory. You don't need to take any action. The Knowledge Consistency Checker (KCC) evaluates the domain controllers in the site and automatically creates a replication topology. In general, the KCC configures connections so that each domain controller replicates with at least two other domain controllers.

The KCC automatically adjusts the replication topology as the network conditions change. As domain controllers are added or removed (or just moved), the KCC continues to ensure that each domain controller replicates with at least two others. Within a site, replication does not use compression, and in some cases (such as a password change), the replication is completed on an immediate basis.

Replication within a site is quite easy to work with; there is nothing to do. The KCC does most of the work for you by creating the correct connection objects to link all your servers together.

Connection Objects

Connection objects serve as the backbone for replication; they define network paths through which replication can occur. You need to know what these are and how they are defined; you should also be able to define them yourself.

The KCC essentially manages the replication within a site by creating connection objects between the various domain controllers in the site. The KCC also creates connection objects between sites where required.

A connection represents a permanent or temporary network path that can be used for replication. Typically, you will not create the connection objects within a site yourself. It is assumed that all the paths between servers are of equal speed, and therefore, the KCC should be capable of handling the creation of the connection objects.

You can create connections within a site. You can also edit the connections created by the KCC; however, you should be careful when doing this. In the case of a connection that you create, the connection is never evaluated by the KCC and is never deleted until you do so. This could cause problems if your network changes and you neglect to remove the connection you created. In cases in which you edit the connection that the KCC makes, the changes you make will be lost when the KCC next updates the connections.

The main reason you might want to create a connection object is to specify the bridgehead servers that will be used to link to sites. The bridgehead servers will be the main method of replication across a site link. To create a connection object, follow the steps in Step By Step 10.35.

STEP BY STEP

10.35 Creating a Connection Object Manually

1. Open Active Directory Sites and Services.
2. Expand the Sites folder, and then expand the site for which you want to create a link.
3. Expand the Servers folder for the site, and then expand the server that will be part of the connection.
4. On the NTDS Settings, right-click and select New Active Directory Connection.
5. In the dialog box that appears, select (or find) the server to which you want to create the link and then click OK.

Connection objects, as you have seen, provide the network paths for replication. This is true whether the connection is within a site or is used to link two sites together.

Replication Between Sites

The capability to manage intersite replication is critical for administrators on Windows 2000 networks. Without this capability, the replication would easily saturate WAN connections and make Windows 2000 Active Directory unmanageable.

While the replication within a site is not compressed, replication between sites will be compressed. Within a site, Active Directory assumes a high-speed connection and, to save processing time, does not compress the data. Between-site bandwidth is assumed to be lower. Therefore, Active Directory compresses the data being transferred between sites.

Active Directory also enables the replication between the sites to be scheduled so that it occurs only during scheduled hours. During those hours, you still have the option of changing the interval of the replication. Before you can set this up, you need to move a domain controller to another site. Then, you must create a connection between that domain controller and one in another site.

Because replication is done between domain controllers, you need to add domain controllers to the site to which they physically belong. Clients within a site also look for a domain controller in the site to log on to, and by moving a domain controller to the site, you decrease the logon times, increasing satisfaction with the network.

Moving Domain Controllers

The capability to control replication and ensure that users are able to log on within a reasonable amount of time requires that you be able to locate domain controllers near the users. This requires that you occasionally move a domain controller between sites.

The purposes of a site are to help manage the replication between domain controllers and to manage replication across slow network links. In addition to creating the site and adding subnets to that site, you need to move domain controllers into the site.

To move a domain controller, follow these simple steps.

STEP BY STEP

10.36 Moving a Domain Controller

1. Open Active Directory Sites and Services.
2. Expand the Sites folder, and then expand the site where the server is currently located.
3. In the site, expand the Servers folder.
4. Right-click the server and select Move.
5. From the dialog box, select the destination subnet and click OK (see Figure 10.43).

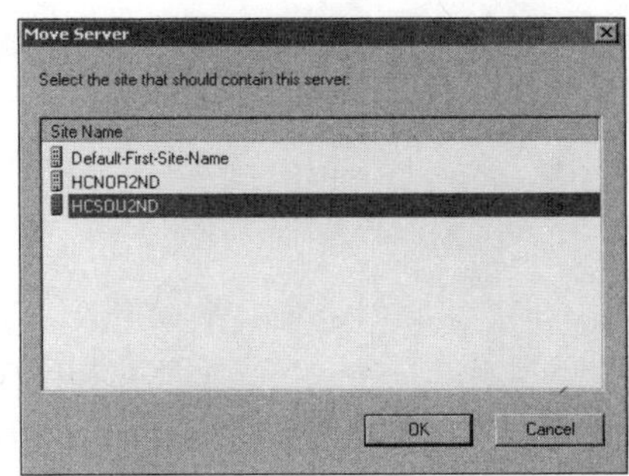

FIGURE 10.43
Select the destination subnet for the server and click OK.

Moving a domain controller to a site is part of creating and managing sites within Active Directory.

Now that you have moved the domain controllers to different sites, you need to create a site link between the sites. This provides the path through which replication to this site takes place.

Connecting Sites

The key to controlling replication is to create sites. Sites enable you to create site links that enable you to control when a link exists and how often replication can take place while the link is available. Multiple site links can be used to create different replication schedules at different times or to provide redundant links with higher costs.

Now that you have moved the domain controllers to different sites, you need to create a site link between the sites. This provides the path through which replication to this site takes place.

By creating and configuring site links, you provide the KCC with information about which connection objects to create to replicate directory data. Site links indicate where connection objects should be created. Connection objects use the network to exchange directory information.

Follow these general steps to create a site link.

STEP BY STEP

10.37 Creating a Site Link

1. Open Active Directory Sites and Services.
2. Expand the Sites folder and then the Inter-Site Transports.
3. Right-click the IP or SMTP folder, depending on the protocol you want to use (see the following discussion of the protocols), and then select New Site Link.
4. Enter a name for the site link in the Name text box. From the Sites Not in This Site Link list, select the site this will connect to and click the Add button. Click OK when you're finished.

When creating site links, you have the option of using either IP or SMTP as the transport protocol for the site link.

> NOTE
> **Creating Your own Certificate** If you don't need to authenticate with external sources, you can use the certificate server that comes with Windows 2000 to create the certificate.

- **SMTP replication**—SMTP can be used for replication only over site links. SMTP is asynchronous, meaning it typically ignores all schedules. Beware if you choose to use SMTP over site links; you must install and configure an enterprise certification authority. The certification authority (CA) signs SMTP messages exchanged between domain controllers, ensuring the authenticity of directory updates.
- **IP replication**—IP replication uses remote procedure calls (RPCs) for replication. This is the same for both intersite and intrasite replication.

After the site link is created, you can go back and set the other properties of the site link. You do this by locating the site link in the IP or SMTP folder and then bringing up the properties of the link.

The General tab on the properties sheet sets the properties for the site link. In addition, Object and Security tabs are available, which are the same as the tabs previously discussed. The items you can configure follow:

- **Description**—This is a description of the link for your information.

- **Site in This Site Link**—This area can be used to add domain controllers to and remove them from a site link.
- **Cost**—This is a relative value, and it is used by Active Directory to decide which route to use when replicating information. The cheapest available route is used based on the overall cost. This is easy to determine between two sites. When the sites are not directly connected, however, all the combinations of sites that link the two are evaluated, and the total costs through all the sites are compared.
- **Replicate Every**—This is the interval at which replication takes place over this link.
- **Change Schedule**—This button enables you to change when the site link is available for replication. Replication during the period that the link is available occurs at a frequency determined by the interval.

Site connectors provide the flexibility required to work with the physical network within a domain. In some cases, you might want to control which servers are used for replication. To do this, you need to configure a bridgehead server.

Bridgehead Servers

A bridgehead server is the main server used for intersite replication. You can configure a bridgehead server for each site you create for each of the intersite replication protocols. This enables you to control which server in a site is used to replicate information to other servers. Step By Step 10.38 walks you through the configuration of a bridgehead server.

STEP BY STEP

10.38 Configuring a Server as a Bridgehead Server

1. Open Active Directory Sites and Services and expand the Sites folder.
2. Expand the site in which you want to create a bridgehead server, and then expand the Servers folder.

continues

continued

3. Right-click the server and select Properties.
4. In the Transports Available for Intersite Transfer area, select the protocol or protocols for which this server should be a bridgehead; then, click Add.
5. Click OK to set the properties, and then close Active Directory Sites and Services.

The capability to configure a server as a bridgehead server gives you greater control over the resources used for replication between two sites or in cases such as a site link bridge between multiple sites.

Site Link Bridges

In many cases, you do not need to deal with site link bridges. By default, all site links are automatically bridged, a property known as *transitive site links.* In some cases, you will want to control through which sites data can flow. In these cases, you need to create site link bridges.

By default, all the site links you create are bridged together. This bridging enables all the sites to communicate with each other. If this is not physically possible because of the structure of your network, you must disable the automatic bridging and create the appropriate site link bridges.

For example, consider the diagram in Figure 10.44. You see three sites (1, 2, and 3) directly connected to each other. In this case, automatic bridging would work fine. However, Site 4 is connected using a low-speed connection, and therefore, you would not want it to replicate with all the other sites. In this case, you would want Site 4 to replicate only with Site 1.

To resolve this replication problem, you would turn off automatic bridging. Then, you would create a site link containing the three sites that are directly connected. Next, you would create a second site link between Site 1 and Site 4 and then create a site link bridge that gives Active Directory a way to get information from Sites 2 and 3 to Site 4 through Site 1 and vice versa.

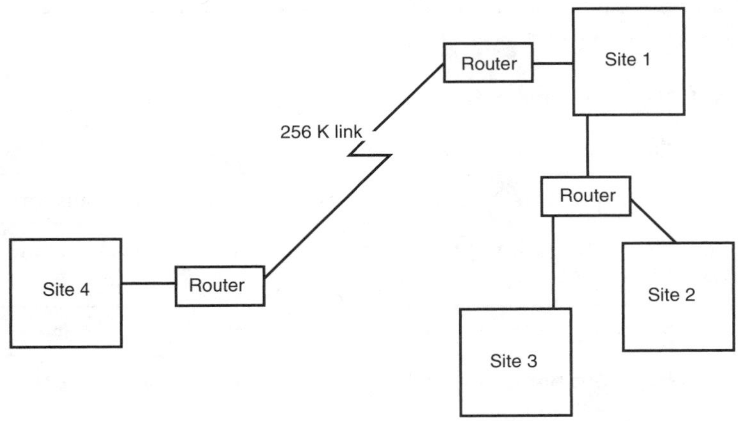

FIGURE 10.44
A network example in which automatic bridging would be problematic.

To disable the automatic bridging, follow the steps in Step By Step 10.39.

STEP BY STEP

10.39 Disabling Transitive Site Links (Automatic Bridging)

1. Open Active Directory Sites and Services.
2. Expand the Sites folder and then the Inter-Site Transports.
3. Right-click the transport for which you want to turn off the automatic bridging and select Properties (see Figure 10.45).
4. On the General tab, clear the Bridge All Site Links check box and click OK.

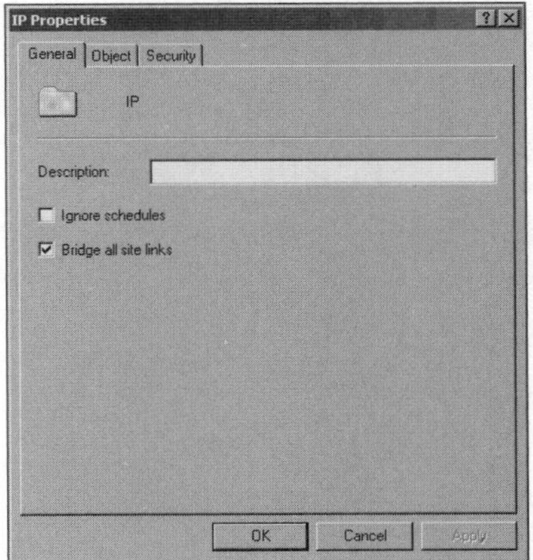

FIGURE 10.45
The IP intersite transport properties dialog box.

Notice that an option to ignore all schedules is available on the General tab. This option is used only to force changes to flow through regardless of whether replication was currently scheduled.

After you have ensured that transitive site links exist—in other words, that automatic bridging is off—you must create the site link bridge (or bridges). This process is outlined in Step By Step 10.40.

STEP BY STEP

10.40 Creating a Site Link Bridge

1. Open Active Directory Sites and Services.
2. Expand the Sites folder and then the Inter-Site Transports.
3. Right-click the transport you want to use and select New Site Link Bridge.
4. In the Name box, enter a name for the site link bridge.
5. From the list of Site Links Not in This Bridge, select the site links you want to add. Remove any extra site links in the Site Links in This Bridge box. Click OK when the correct site links are part of the bridge.

Until now, we have dealt with the replication of the domain information. You need to consider the replication of the schema and configuration partitions and of the global catalog. This is handled by global catalog servers.

Global Catalog Servers

Global catalog servers provide essential information that is used to glue together the parts of Active Directory. The global catalog server ensures that the schema and configuration information is distributed to the domains, and it also handles universal group membership. In addition, it provides a method of locating objects in Active Directory.

Previously, you were told that the global catalog servers would replicate with each other. This replication is accomplished as though the global catalog servers were all in one domain and the KCC handles the replication. Your only choice is whether a domain controller will be a global catalog server. Step By Step 10.41 outlines how to make a domain controller a global catalog server.

STEP BY STEP

10.41 Configuring a Server as a Global Catalog Server

1. Open Active Directory Sites and Services.
2. Expand the Sites folder, and expand the site where the server is located. Expand the Servers folder, and then expand the server.
3. Right-click the NTDS Setting and select Properties (see Figure 10.46).
4. If the server should be a global catalog server, make sure the Global Catalog check box is checked. Otherwise, clear the check box. Click OK, and you're finished.

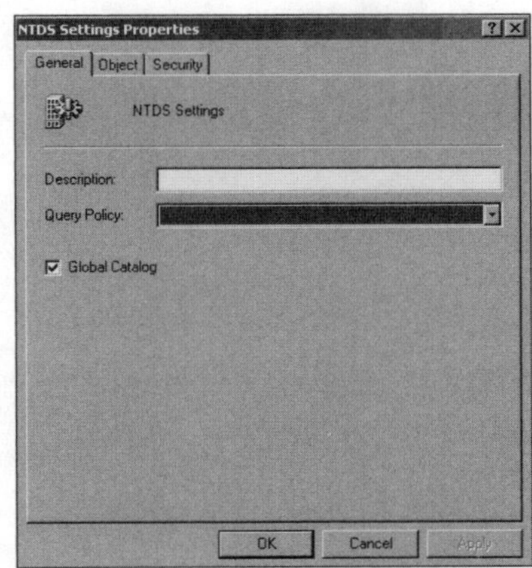

FIGURE 10.46
In the NTDS properties box, you can configure a server as a global catalog server.

One of the key jobs of an administrator is to keep the directory information up-to-date and to ensure that the domain controllers have the correct information. Replication makes this possible. You need to understand this for both the exam and real-world situations. In the real world, things don't always work as they should, and therefore you must know how to troubleshoot problems.

Troubleshooting Replication Problems

You're likely to run into two types of replication problems in real life. Not surprisingly, these two types of problems are the problems that are tested on the exam. The first type of problem occurs when connectivity between two sites fails and the domain controllers are incapable of replicating. For the most part, this kind of problem should be obvious because no data should be flowing between the two sites; however, sometimes this is missed.

The second type of problem you might encounter is objects showing up in the special LostandFound folder in Active Directory. These objects were updated on one system but deleted on another.

Let's take a look at each of these types of problems and what can be done to address them.

Troubleshooting WAN Problems

Active Directory needs the wide area network to perform replication, but the possibility exists that the WAN might be down or otherwise misconfigured for a significant length of time before it is noticed. In addition to the basic troubleshooting tools for the WAN with which you're already familiar, a diagnostic tool exists that is used specifically for testing domain controller status, including replication.

The first step in troubleshooting an Active Directory replication problem is to verify WAN connectivity. This can be done through the simple PING utility. Verifying that connectivity exists can also be done by using the TRACERT utility.

These utilities tell you only that current connectivity exists; they do not tell you that connectivity was working the last time Active Directory tried to replicate. For that, you'll need DCDIAG.

DCDIAG is a utility that can be run from the command prompt of any system, but it is typically run at the command-line prompt of the domain controller you want to test. By default, DCDIAG performs a complete health scan on the domain controller. This includes a lot of other tests, but it also specifically includes a Replication test. Table 10.3 shows you the tests DCDIAG performs.

TABLE 10.3

DCDIAG TEST OPTIONS

Connectivity	Tests that the domain controller has been registered in DNS, is pingable, and will accept both LDAP and RPC calls. It's used primarily when testing connectivity to another server.
Replications	Shows the status of recent replication attempts.
Topology	Verifies that the replication tree will fully replicate every domain controller.
CutoffServers	Identifies servers that will not receive updates because of down servers.
NCSecDesc	Verifies that the security descriptors are set appropriately to allow replication.
NetLogons	Verifies that the appropriate permissions to log on are present to allow replication to occur.

Advertising	Verifies that the domain controller is properly advertising itself as a domain controller and any other domain roles that it has been assigned through Active Directory Sites and Services.
KnowsOfRoleHolders	Checks whether the server knows which servers hold the flexible single master roles.
Intersite	Identifies problems that will prevent intersite replication.
FsmoCheck	Checks whether the domain controller knows which servers host the global master operations and whether they are responding.
RIDMaster	Checks whether the RID master is accessable.
MachineAccount	Verifies that the domain controller's machine account is set up correctly.
Services	Verifies that the appropriate DC services are running on the server.
OutboundSecureChannels	Tests whether secure channels can be established to every domain controller.
ObjectsReplicated	Checks whether the machine account and associated objects have been successfully replicated.
Frssysvol	Checks the File Replication System (FRS) SYSVOL and whether it is available.
Kccevent	Verifies that the Knowledge Consistency Checker is executing without errors. The Knowledge Consistency Checker is responsible for building the replication pattern.
Systemlog	Displays the last few entries in the system log.
DCPromo	Tests whether the DNS infrastructure will support the promotion to a domain controller. Additional options are required to indicate the type of promotion.
RegisterInDNS	Tests the capability of the domain controller to add service records to DNS.

For most cases, you can just run the DCDIAG tool without options. In this case, it will run all the tests and report only the errors. If you're concerned about not getting enough information, adding the `/v` (verbose) switch to the command line provides detailed information about the tests the command performed.

Troubleshooting LostandFound

I'm sure you've heard the statement, "He was in the wrong place at the wrong time." That is the best way to describe the objects that end up in the LostandFound folder. These are objects that were replicated after the object they belonged to had already been deleted in the forest.

In other words, an object would end up in the LostandFound folder if on one server you added a new OU underneath the Sales OU and a colleague in another location simultaneously deleted the Sales OU. When your domain controller attempted to replicate the object to your colleague's domain controller, the Sales OU would already be gone, so no container would exist for the object. These objects are put in the special lost and found folder so that your additions or changes are not lost and can be replicated if necessary.

In real life, you'll rarely encounter a situation in which one person is adding objects while another is deleting the container in which the objects are being created. It's really only important that you understand what could happen to place an object in the LostandFound folder in the off chance that it does happen.

CASE STUDY: ADMINISTERING ACTIVE DIRECTORY

ESSENCE OF THE CASE

The essence of the case is the creation of the organizational units and the placement of servers. There is little that you really need to consider as long as you keep a few basic points in mind, including the following:

- Each site requires at least one global catalog server and should have at least one domain controller from each domain.
- There are five domains based on the user's function in the organization rather than his location.

SCENARIO

SunShine Brewing company needs to set standards for different levels of security on documents. The company needs to determine the permissions and auditing requirements for these documents. Policies also need to be developed to deal with the delegation of control of organizational units and what that control will entail.

ANALYSIS

The organizational units will be somewhat numerous; however, because they exist only as objects within Active Directory, this is not a problem. For each of the domains, you will end up having a separate organizational unit for each location.

CASE STUDY: ADMINISTERING ACTIVE DIRECTORY

- The sites were created for the different locations, and the sites have been configured to replicate so that information should not be more than 3 hours out-of-date at any major location.
- There are 15 sites, 4 of which are major offices and the other 11 of which are minor offices.

Again, this is a fairly straightforward example in which you need to ensure there is a global catalog server in each site and need to create organization units.

This will enable you to manage all the users of one type at the domain level or to manage all the users of one type at the same location at the OU level. This will make the application of site-level Group Policy more difficult because you will need to define it in one domain and link to it from the other domains. This means that site-level policies should be defined in the root domain, and you will need to have at least one domain controller in each location.

As for the global catalog servers, in this case, you should configure the bridgehead servers for the site links to act as the global catalog servers.

CHAPTER SUMMARY

In this chapter you learned about the basic Active Directory objects: users, groups, and computers. These objects are the most common objects in Active Directory. In particular, you learned how to create, rename, delete, and modify users. In addition, you learned how group memberships are used to control access.

You also learned how to control access to parts of Active Directory itself. This process helps to allow granular control of administration and management duties. Even though Windows 2000 has an administration delegation wizard, Active Directory permissions can still get confusing.

We rounded the chapter out with a discussion of replication so you will understand how to troubleshoot Active Directory replication problems between sites.

KEY TERMS

- Connection objects
- Distribution group
- Domain local group
- Global group
- Inheritance
- Knowledge Consistency Checker
- Local group
- Mixed mode
- Native mode
- Object-level permissions
- Originating write
- Security group
- Security principal
- Site
- Site link bridges
- Site links
- Universal group
- Update sequence number

APPLY YOUR KNOWLEDGE

Exercises

10.1 Creating Accounts in Active Directory

In this exercise, you will use Active Directory Users and Computers to create user and computer accounts that will be used in the remaining exercises.

Estimated Time: 15 minutes

1. Open Active Directory Users and Computers.
2. Expand your domain.
3. Right-click the Users folder and then select New, User from the context menu.
4. For the First Name, enter **`Sales`**; for the Last Name, enter **`Admin`**.
5. For the User Name, enter **`SalesAdmin`**; then click Next.
6. On the password page of the wizard, clear the User Must Change Password at Next Logon option, enter **`Trojan`** as the password, and confirm the password information.
7. Click Next and then click Finish on the confirmation screen.
8. Using steps 3–7 as a guide, add the following users:

First Name	*Last Name*	*Username*	*Password*
Marylou	Scott	`Mscott`	eastern
Anne	Sheard	`Asheard`	eastern
Judy	Jamieson	`Jjamieson`	eastern
Ralph	Smith	`Rsmith`	eastern
Krista	Bailey	`Kbailey`	eastern
Dan	Harris	`Dharris`	western
Peter	Loke	`Ploke`	western
Helen	Burke	`Hburke`	western
Mark	Spence	`Mspence`	western
Jim	Xu	`Jxu`	western

9. Right-click the Computer folder and then select New, Computer from the context menu.
10. For the Computer Name, enter **`WKS5542`**.
11. Click Next and then click Finish on the confirmation screen.
12. Using steps 9–11 as a guide, add the following computers:

WKS8726
WKS8652
WKS0823
WKS0564
WKS8762
WKS7645
WKS2735
WKS0012
WKS3218

10.2 Creating Organization Units

In this exercise, you will create the Sales OU, and within the Sales OU, you will create two more OUs called Eastern and Western.

Estimated Time: 5 minutes

1. If Active Directory Users and Computers is not open, open it.
2. Right-click your domain and select New, Organizational Unit.

APPLY YOUR KNOWLEDGE

3. Enter **Sales** as the name of the OU and click OK.
4. If you need to, expand your domain and locate the OU you just created.
5. Right-click the Sales OU and select New, Organizational Unit from the context menu.
6. Enter the name **Eastern** as the new OU name and click OK.
7. Repeat steps 5 and 6 to create the Western OU.

10.3 Delegating Control of an Organizational Unit

In this exercise, you delegate control of the Sales OU to the SalesAdmin account.

Estimated Time: 10 minutes

1. If Active Directory Users and Computers is not open, open it.
2. Open the Users folder and locate the SalesAdmin account.
3. Right-click the SalesAdmin account and select Move.
4. In the list of folders, select the Sales Organizational Unit and click OK.
5. Click the Sales OU and verify that the SalesAdmin account is there.
6. Right-click the Sales OU and select Delegate Control from the context menu.
7. Click the Next button to bypass the introductory screen.
8. On the Next screen, click the Add button. Select the SalesAdmin user and click Add; then click OK. Click Next to go to the next screen.
9. On the next screen of the wizard, check the following options and then click Next:
   - Create, Delete, and Manage User Accounts
   - Reset Passwords on User Accounts
   - Read All User Information
   - Create, Delete, and Manage Groups
   - Modify the Membership of a Group
10. Review the information and click Finish.

Review Questions

1. What is the purpose of groups?
2. What is the effect of delegating control of an organizational unit?
3. If you set permissions on an organizational unit, what happens to the permissions of the object in the OU?
4. What is the difference between a site link and a site link bridge?
5. When would you create an Active Directory connection?
6. What is the definition of a site?
7. What options can you set on a site link to control replication?
8. If you create site link bridges manually, what must you do to make sure your site link bridges are used?
9. What can you do to force replication across all site links to take place?

APPLY YOUR KNOWLEDGE

Exam Questions

1. Jon is in charge of a network that has a single Windows 2000 domain. The network has 700 users at present and services the entire company.

   Jon has been dealing with the human resources department for the past few days and, after several discussions, has agreed to let them deal with their own computer accounts. What must he do to allow them to manage their own computers? (Choose two.)

   A. He needs to create a new domain.

   B. He needs to create a new OU.

   C. He needs to create a new site.

   D. He needs to set individual permissions on the computer accounts.

   E. He needs to use the Delegation of Control Wizard.

2. Sam is creating groups in a new domain in an Active Directory tree. She has a group of users in the domain who need to have access to resources in three other domains. What type of groups should she use?

   A. Global

   B. Universal

   C. Domain local

   D. Local

3. A computer running in your network recently crashed. The system was an older P233MMX with 64MB of RAM, and you'll be replacing the system with a new multiprocessor computer. Because you are changing the hardware abstraction layer from a single processor to a multiprocessor, you realize you have to reload the computer. What should you do in Active Directory to make sure you can easily add the computer to the domain?

   A. Rename the existing computer account.

   B. Move the existing computer account to the lost and found folder.

   C. Delete the computer's account.

   D. Reset the computer's account.

4. Samantha is creating groups in a new domain in an Active Directory tree. She has a resource on a Windows 2000 domain controller in the domain that will be accessed by groups from the local domain and from four other domains. What type of groups should she use?

   A. Global

   B. Universal

   C. Domain local

   D. Local

5. In an effort to reduce the number of calls handled by the help desk in your organization, you have decided to create a group of "user mentors" that will receive extra training and some extra permissions on the network. These users will be able to manage the user computers, which are grouped in a single OU in each of your six domains. They also will be able to reset the password of the users who are also grouped in an OU in each domain. The users who will be part of the program are scattered throughout the six domains. What type of group should you use to delegate the permissions they will need?

Apply Your Knowledge

A. Global

B. Universal

C. Domain local

D. Don't use a group; use an OU

6. Sally is a network administrator and is currently installing Windows 2000 with Active Directory. She has noticed that the replication between the 15 domain controllers is taking a lot of the bandwidth on her 10Mbps Ethernet network.

   The location she is working in has three floors. Sally wants to create a separate site for each floor. She has created the three sites and the site links between them, but it doesn't seem to have made a difference. What should she do next?

   A. She needs to reboot all the domain controllers.

   B. She needs to wait for the Knowledge Consistency Checker to calculate the new connections.

   C. She needs to move the domain controllers to the subnets in the Sites and Services Manager.

   D. There is nothing she can do except upgrade to 100Mbps Ethernet.

7. Marc is the administrator for a network that is part of an Active Directory tree. His network is divided into four different sites spread across two large floors in a downtown office tower.

   To work on the hardware on a domain controller, he has shut it down. Everything is going well until a user calls and tells Marc that he can't find the resources in another domain in the tree. What could be the problem?

   A. The site link between that domain and the local domain is on the domain controller on which Marc is working.

   B. The other domain has lost its primary domain controller.

   C. The replication is not scheduled until later in the day.

   D. The system Marc is working on is the global catalog server for the site.

8. Harvey has created a Windows 2000 Active Directory structure for his organization. He has set up a single domain containing the 700 users and their computers. The company is divided into two offices with a 56Kbps link between them.

   Harvey configures two sites, one for each office, and he configures a site link between them using SMTP. The replication between the sites doesn't seem to be working. What should Harvey do?

   A. He needs to create an enterprise certification authority.

   B. He needs to install Microsoft Exchange.

   C. He needs to install an SMTP-based mail system.

   D. He needs a connection faster than 56KBPS.

9. You are writing out the procedures for creating a site for a new administrator who is starting up a new office for your organization. Which of the following is the best method for creating a site?

   A. Create the site, select the site link, add the subnets, and then move in the domain controllers.

APPLY YOUR KNOWLEDGE

B. Move the domain controllers, create the site, add the subnets, and then select the site links.

C. Create a temporary site link bridge, add the domain controllers, rename the site that's created, and then add subnets.

D. Create the subnets and then create a site by grouping them. Next, create the links and then move in the domain controllers.

10. You are explaining Active Directory replication to your manager to try to convince him that you will need to upgrade your network from the current 2Mbps Arcnet. You are explaining the differences between intersite and intrasite replication. Which of the following is true only of intersite replication?

    A. Managed by the Knowledge Consistency Checker

    B. Uses Remote Procedure Calls over the Internet Protocol

    C. Sends the data in a compressed format

    D. Defined by connection objects

11. You have a single remote site on your network, and you want to make sure you use the link as little as possible for replication. You create a site link for your office, and then you create a site link between the main site and the remote site. You create a site link bridge so that data going to the remote site will all flow through the main site.

    You monitor the link, and you notice that replication is still taking place from sites other than the main site. What should you do to correct this?

    A. Check for and correct manually created link objects.

    B. Make sure the Ignore Schedule option is not selected.

    C. Make sure the Enable option is set on the site link bridge.

    D. Make sure the Bridge All Site Links option is not selected.

12. Users in the two remote sites you manage are complaining that the links to the head office where you work are slow. They report that the links have been slow for the last couple days. You check the links and find that they are, in fact, running at 100% capacity. When you investigate further, you determine the cause of the problem is Active Directory replication. When you check the site links you have created, the information is correct that the links should be checking for changes only every four hours during the day and every two hours at night. What else should you check?

    A. You should check the schedule on the site link bridges.

    B. You should check the Ignore Schedule option.

    C. You should make sure other operators are not forcing the replication for some reason.

    D. You should check how many users have been added in the previous 24 hours.

13. You are adding a remote site to your network that will be connected using a 128K ISDN line. The ISDN line is expected to be busy during the day, approximately 80% utilized, and to have only 30% utilization at night. You want to ensure that replication does not use too much bandwidth during the day but that at night it will have sufficient bandwidth to complete any synchronization.

APPLY YOUR KNOWLEDGE

The network designers have told you that you must have the capability to replicate at least once during the day. Which of the following will best deal with these requirements?

A. Create a site link that will replicate only at night and manually force the replication once a day.

B. Create a site link used during the night that has an interval of 30 minutes and one during the day with an interval of 6 hours.

C. Create a site link used during the night with a cost of 10 and a day schedule with a cost of 99.

D. Create a site link used during the night with the default cost and interval and another site link available only from noon until 1 p.m.

14. You have two sites that are linked using a fractional T1 connection. You are working to optimize the replication traffic between the sites. Each site contains one high-end domain controller that is dedicated to the global catalog. You want to ensure that replication over the site link uses these two controllers. What should you do to ensure this?

    A. Create connections objects that link these servers.

    B. Create a site link bridge that links these servers.

    C. Make sure the site link specifies these servers as the bridgehead servers.

    D. Create a separate site for each server and link these sites. Then, configure a site link between each of the servers and the other servers on their network.

15. You have configured the site links and site link bridges for your network. Replication is working, and all the sites are receiving the updates to Active Directory. You are describing the network you're working on to a colleague, and she tells you that you didn't need to configure site link bridges. Why didn't you have to create the site link bridges?

    A. The KCC will create the site link bridges for you.

    B. The sites will be automatically bridged.

    C. The domain naming master will handle this for you.

    D. The global catalog will handle this for you.

16. Your network is very stable. The users don't change much, and neither do the computers. The structure in place is working, and you rarely change anything in Active Directory. You have been working on a bandwidth problem between the main site and a remote site and have determined that some replication traffic is going across the link during the day. What can you do to remove this traffic?

    A. Create a site link that replicates only at night.

    B. Create a site link bridge that replicates only at night.

    C. Create two site links, one that replicates on a slow schedule during the day and another that replicates more frequently at night.

    D. Create two site link bridges, one that replicates on a slow schedule during the day and another that replicates more frequently at night.

APPLY YOUR KNOWLEDGE

Answers to Review Questions

1. The purpose of groups is to collect users or rights. Global groups are used to gather users into a manageable unit and to make this group available in the local domain and all the other domains. The local group typically is used to gather the rights you want to assign. Users gain the rights when you add the global group to the local group. Universal groups act as a bridge between global and local groups that can span many domains. See the section "Groups in Windows 2000."
2. When you delegate control of an organizational unit, you are really setting the permissions on the OU and the objects in the OU so that the delegate can control whatever the permissions allow. See the section "Delegating Administrative Control."
3. When you set permissions on an OU, the objects in the OU inherit the changes you make. This is the normal behavior and can be overridden by blocking inheritance. See the section "Permissions Inheritance."
4. A site link is used to describe a network path that exists directly between two sites, whereas a site link bridge describes a path between two sites that uses a third site to which both of the sites have a site link. See the section "Replication Between Sites."
5. Normally, you don't need to create Active Directory connections. The exception is a case in which the Knowledge Consistency Checker will not be capable of correctly finding the connection between two servers. Connections represent a direct network path between two servers. See the section "Connection Objects."
6. A site is best defined as one or more IP subnets interconnected using a high-speed (above T1) network. See the section "Working Within Sites."
7. The options you can set on a site link include the scheduled periods during which the site link is available and the interval (frequency) at which the controllers check for updates. See the section "Replication Between Sites."
8. By default, all site links are bridged. This means that all the sites can be reached through any combination of site links. If you are going to manage this manually, you need to disable the automatic site link bridging in the IP or SMTP properties. See the section "Replication Between Sites."
9. Site links are available only during scheduled times. If you need to force them all to be available, you need to select the Ignore All Schedules option in the IP or SMTP properties. See the section "Replication Between Sites."

Answers to Exam Questions

1. **B, E.** The best choice here is to create an OU and then use the Delegation of Control Wizard to give control to the HR users. You could create a domain (A), but this would add a layer of complication to the network that is not required. Although Jon could set the permissions on each individual computer (D), this is more work than necessary to accomplish the same functionality as creating an OU and delegating. Creating a site (C) does not allow for any delegation of control. See the section "Delegating Administrative Control."

APPLY YOUR KNOWLEDGE

2. **A.** Global groups are available in the domain in which they are created and in other domains within a forest. Local and domain local groups are available only in the domains in which they are created and therefore will not work in this case, so answers C and D are wrong. A universal group is used if you have users from multiple domains that all need access to resources in multiple domains, so answer B is not right. See the section "Strategies for Using Groups."

3. **D.** Renaming the computer account would leave a dead computer account in Active Directory that would never be used. Therefore, answer A is wrong. The lost and found directory is where the system puts orphaned objects it finds, and it is not used by users, so answer B is wrong. Deleting the account and re-creating it will lose all the group memberships and Group Policy information, so this is also wrong. Resetting the account keeps the account and enables you to add the computer to the domain again; therefore, it is the best answer in this case. See the section "Computer Accounts."

4. **C.** A local group is used on standalone servers and Windows 2000 Professional, so answer D is incorrect. Global groups are used to make the users in a domain available to other domains, so answer A is incorrect because this is a resource. Universal groups, answer B, are used to take users from many domains and give them rights in many domains. This leaves a domain local group, answer C, which is correct. The global group from the local domain and the other four domains would be added to this domain local group to give the users rights. See the section "Strategies for Using Groups."

5. **B.** In this case, you are taking users that are part of multiple domains and providing them rights in multiple domains. The correct tool to do this is a universal group. Global groups enable you to bunch users, which will be used in other domains, and local groups are used to hold the rights and normally have global groups as members. In this case, you could perform the action using a combination of global and local groups; however, the universal group does it with greater easy and is the right answer. See the section "Strategies for Using Groups."

6. **C.** Although an upgrade to 100Mbps would probably make all of Sally's users happy, this is not required and it makes answer D wrong. If you needed to reboot all the servers in your organization every time you added a site, no one would use the operating system. This means answer A is wrong. There might be a delay of a few minutes, but there wouldn't be that long of a delay in recalculating the connections. Answer B is wrong. C is the correct answer. This makes sense because the domain controllers are all still in the site and would continue to replicate at the same rate. See the section "Moving Domain Controllers."

7. **D.** In this case, answer A is wrong because site links are between sites in the same domain. Answer B is also wrong because there are no longer PDCs, only domain controllers. Replication scheduling is set on a site link, and the resources the user wants are in another domain, so answer C is also wrong. This leaves answer D, which is correct. Because the global catalog replicates the entire set of objects from the enterprise (with a few attributes) so that resources can be found, it makes sense that the users can't find the resource without the global catalog server. See the section "Global Catalog Servers."

APPLY YOUR KNOWLEDGE

8. **A.** If you are using SMTP for your site links, you need to have an enterprise certification authority. The authority will be used to sign the SMTP packets being sent. The SMTP packets are sent between servers in the sites involved in the site link and do not actually use mail servers, meaning answers B and C are incorrect. SMTP (email) can run over a modem that is as slow as 110 baud (that's what was available way back when); therefore, answer D is incorrect. See the section "Replication Between Sites."

9. **A.** In this case, the best answer is to create the site first, so answers B, C, and D are wrong. You are asked for the site link that the site will be part of during the creation of that site. This means you are selecting the site link as you create it. You can then add subnets and domain controllers (in any order). See the section "Replicating Active Directory Information."

10. **C.** In this case, the only difference listed is that it will use compression on the data. The other differences are that you can schedule the replication between sites and set the interval to check for updates. You can also have different links with different costs between two sites, and between sites you could use SMTP. After you define a site link, the KCC handles the connections for you, so answer A is incorrect. The intersite replication can use SMTP, but it also uses RPC over IP, so answer B isn't right. Answer D is incorrect because the KCC automatically establishes all required links for you. See the section "Replicating Active Directory Information."

11. **D.** In this case, you might have a problem with a manually created connection, but even a manually created connection has to follow the site link information, so answer A is incorrect. Answer B would be a problem because replication would happen continuously; however, this would not ignore the site link bridge. Answer C is not a valid option. This means that answer D must be and is correct. This option is on by default, and you need to ensure it is off if you need to create site link bridges. See the section "Replication Between Sites."

12. **B.** Site link bridges do not have schedules, so answer A is incorrect. Although other operators might be forcing replication across the link, you should probably assume they would not be continually doing this for an entire week, meaning answer C is wrong. Answer D fails for a similar reason. It should not take a week for Active Directory replication to complete unless you're using a 110-baud modem. This leaves answer B, which makes sense. This option can be used to force replication if required but should be turned off immediately so that the site link schedules are again respected. See the section "Replication Between Sites."

13. **D.** In this case, you would use two site links so that everything is automatic. The night schedule is fine with the default or could even be made more frequent. All you need to do additionally is replicate once a day, and doing that replication during lunchtime probably will cause the least interruption. See the section "Replication Between Sites."

APPLY YOUR KNOWLEDGE

14. **A.** By creating a connection, a network path, between these servers, you will have specified the path replication should take. You could also configure the server objects as the bridgehead servers for that replication protocol; however, that would cause them to be used as the main servers for all site links using that protocol. The site link does not have an option to specify the bridgehead servers, and a site link bridge is used to link sites, not servers. The last option, D, might work if you turned off the automatic site bridging. See the section "Connection Objects."

15. **B.** Although the KCC won't actually create site link bridges, it will create the required connections so that all the sites will receive the Active Directory updates. The domain naming master deals with domains, so answer C is wrong; the global catalog has nothing to do with this, meaning answer D is wrong. See the section "Site Link Bridges."

16. **A.** In this case, you can force replication if there is a problem, but after the network reaches a stable point, there is not so much need for replication. Answers B and D are wrong because they talk about site link bridges, and answer C is not the best answer because there would still be replication during the day. See the section "Replication Between Sites."

Suggested Readings and Resources

- *Windows 2000 Server Resource Kit. Deployment Planning Guide.* Microsoft, 2000.
- Archer, Scott. *MCSE Training Guide: Windows 2000 Directory Services Design.* Indianapolis: New Riders Publishing, 2000.

CHAPTER 11

Fundamentals of Group Policy

OBJECTIVES

In this chapter you'll learn the basics of group policies. Group policies are a powerful part of Active Directory. They allow you to shape and control the user experience, improve security, and even distribute software. This chapter addresses subobjectives in the "Configuring, Managing, Securing, and Troubleshooting Active Directory Organizational Units and Group Policy." objective. The objectives follow:

Deploy software by using Group Policy. Types of software include user applications, antivirus software, line-of-business applications, and software updates.

- **Use Windows Installer to deploy Windows Installer packages.**
- **Deploy updates to installed software including antivirus updates.**
- **Configure Group Policy to assign and publish applications.**

▶ One of the powerful features included with Windows 2000 (through the use of Group Policy objects) is the capability to distribute software. Previously, the only way to distribute software was through Microsoft's Systems Management Server product or through other third-party tools. It's important for the administrator of a large network to be able to quickly, easily, and reliably deploy applications via packages.

Troubleshoot end-user Group Policy.

- **Troubleshoot Group Policy problems involving precedence, inheritance, filtering, and the No Override option.**
- **Manually refresh Group Policy.**

Objectives

- With flexibility comes complexity and, ultimately, the possibility for problems. Group policies are very flexible and are therefore prone to the problems that flexibility brings? It's important for a system administrator to be able to diagnose and resolve Group policy problems.

  Implement and manage security policies by using Group Policy.

  - **Use security templates to implement security policies.**
  - **Analyze the security configuration of a computer by using the `SECEDIT` command and Security Configuration and Analysis.**
  - **Modify domain security policy to comply with corporate standards.**

- In addition to being able to deliver software, group policies can control computer settings to make them conform to corporate standards. Using Group policies is the best way to effect security changes on an entire organization quickly.

Outline

Outline

Study Strategies

- Use Windows Installer to create your own software packages and try to publish them. Then assign them instead of publishing them. Identify the differences between assigning and publishing. Consider what applications you must publish and what applicationsyou should assign.
- Create a nested OU structure so that you'll be able to test applying Group Policies at different levels to see the impact of inheritance and the No Override options. Create group policy objects with no override and associate them at the domain level. Review what happens when you apply group policies at lower levels with different settings.
- Make quick changes to group policies and then test whether those changes are always seen by computers in the network. Remember that Group Policy objects are cached and must sometimes be manually refreshed to allow for testing of policies.
- Run SECEDIT on a few different computers. Apply Group Policy objects with security policies and rerun SECEDIT. Review the results.

INTRODUCTION TO GROUP POLICY

A challenge facing any administrator of a Windows 2000 network is how to ensure users' desktops and other settings conform to corporate standards. This is especially true of large organizations with many users and even several sites in different and disparate locations. Active Directory provides a mechanism to ensure that the administration of these settings can be controlled centrally. Active Directory also provides a mechanism to ensure that the settings apply to all users who require them, regardless of the user's location. This mechanism is Group Policy.

With Group Policy, an administrator can define the state of a user's work environment once. Windows 2000 Active Directory continually enforces these settings no matter which machine the individual uses or where he might happen to be. With Group Policy, an administrator is able to do the following:

- **Enforce centralized control of user and computer settings at the site and domain level**—Optionally, you can provide the capability for local administrators to incorporate local settings at the OU level. This is useful in large organizations with many geographical locations. It enables the administrator to enforce corporate requirements while allowing for local control of other settings. For example, all users must have the corporate intranet shortcut on their desktops, but they need to still be able to control other local applications, such as Office 2000. (The version to be used in France might be French, whereas in the United Kingdom it would be English.)
- **Provide a desktop environment that enables users to perform their duties while at the same time ensuring that critical applications can't be modified or removed**—This should result in lower technical support requirements because users can't make damaging changes that result in machines becoming inoperable due to user error.
- **Control what a desktop looks like and how a computer behaves, including which software is or can be installed**—Group Policy allows control of user and computer Registry settings, the invocation of scripts to modify the computer and user environments, security settings for computers and

domains, and automatic installation (or even removal) of software. Group Policy allows control of the location of certain critical data folders such as the user's home directory and desktop working directory.

- **Ensure that corporate policies, including business rules, and security requirements are enforced**—In this way, you can ensure that user passwords are a minimum length, that users change their passwords every 90 days, and that all users have a shortcut to the corporate intranet site on their desktops at all times.

Group Policy is a technology that can be applied at the site, domain, and organizational unit level in Active Directory. Because Group Policy is an Active Directory object, it can be used to enforce the previously mentioned settings on any Windows 2000 client computer. These clients include Windows 2000 Professional, Windows 2000 Server, Windows 2000 Advanced Server, Windows 2000 Data Center Server, and Windows XP Professional.

NOTE

Group Policy on Windows NT 3.51 or Windows NT 4.0 Group Policy can't be used to enforce settings on Windows NT 3.51 or Windows NT 4.0 clients. These operating systems do not support Active Directory. For Windows NT 3.51 and later clients, you still need to use system policies available in NT to enforce user and computer settings in the NT domain structure. The same also holds true for Windows 95 and Windows 98 clients. Basically, unless the clients on the network are Windows 2000 computers, you can't use Group Policy—you must use system policies instead.

Group Policy Components

Group Policy is an object in Active Directory. It is commonly referred to as a *Group Policy object (GPO)*. The GPO includes settings that enable you to control many aspects of the computing environment. It is an object in Active Directory and can be associated with various Active Directory containers (sites, domains, and OUs). Because GPOs can be associated with different Active Directory containers, they can be used to enforce organization-wide (site and domain) or department-level (OU) rules.

Group Policy objects are actually composed of two parts: the Group Policy container (GPC) and the Group Policy Template (GPT).

The GPC is an Active Directory object that includes GPO attributes and version information (see Figure 11.1). Each GPO is represented by a Globally Unique Identifier (GUID). The GUID is a 128-bit number that uniquely identifies the GPO in the forest, domain tree, and domain. The GUID can't be changed or removed by the user and is automatically maintained by Active Directory. Version information is also attached to the GPO and is tracked in Active Directory. This information is attached to the GPC and is shared by

NOTE

Preconfigured GPOs When you install Active Directory and create the first domain controller in the first domain in the first forest, Windows 2000 Active Directory creates two Group Policy objects automatically: the Default Domain Policy and the Default Domain Controller Policy. These default policies are copied to all domain controllers in all other domains created in the forest. If you wanted to have a default set of values in GPOs for all users and computers in the domain, you would modify the Default Domain Policy. Similarly, if you wanted all domain controllers in all domains to start out with the same settings, you would modify the Default Domain Controller Policy on that first domain controller.

domain controllers. Each domain controller uses the information contained in Active Directory and the GPC to ensure it is running the most recent version of a GPO. If it does not have the most recent version, replication occurs, transferring the most recent version from another domain controller. Step By Step 11.1 shows you how.

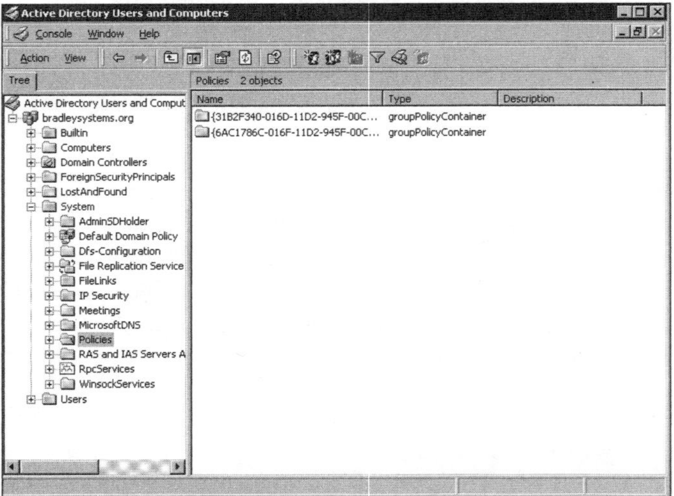

FIGURE 11.1
The Group Policy container in Active Directory Users and Computers.

STEP BY STEP

11.1 Viewing Group Policy GUIDs

1. To view the Group Policy container in Active Directory Users and Computers, click the View menu and select Advanced Features.
2. Expand the domain, System container, and Policies container to see the GUIDs representing all known GPOs in the domain.

The Group Policy Template is a set of folders and subfolders in the Sysvol share on Windows 2000 domain controllers. Each GPO created always results in the creation of a folder hierarchy, which contains the physical files and settings required by the GPO. These include administrative templates, security settings, scripts, software installation information, and folder redirection settings. Windows 2000 clients connect to the Sysvol shared folder to obtain these settings and apply what is contained within them.

Each GPT folder is named the same as the GUID of the GPO, which is also the same GUID used to identify it in the GPC. In this way, if you rename a GPO after creating it, the unique identifier used by Active Directory (the GUID) and the corresponding GPT structure, as well as the GPC, do not change. Figure 11.2 shows the structure of a sample GPT in the Sysvol share of a domain controller.

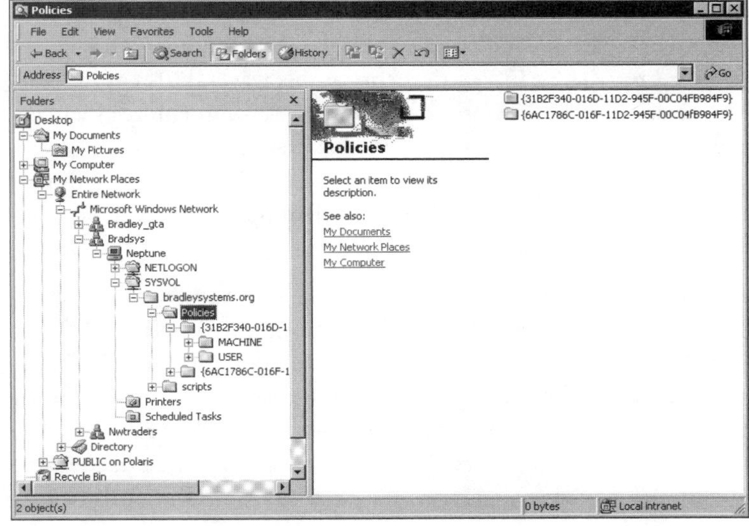

FIGURE 11.2
The Group Policy Template folder hierarchy in the Sysvol share of a Windows 2000 domain controller.

As you have seen, Group Policy can be used to enforce a number of settings for both the computer and the user. Group Policy objects are composed of two parts: a Group Policy container and a Group Policy Template. Group Policy can be used to enforce computer and user configuration items only on Windows 2000 and Windows XP machines. To enforce settings on other Microsoft operating systems (Windows NT or Windows 9x), you still need to use System Policy.

GROUP POLICY SCOPE

Group Policy has particular sets of rules it follows when applied to users and computers. One set of these rules deals with what happens at each Active Directory container where Group Policy exists (inheritance), whereas another deals with how settings from multiple GPOs are combined to provide an effective policy application. Finally, a third set of rules deals with how GPOs are processed in the same Active Directory container. All these areas are addressed here.

Each GPO can be linked to one or more containers in Active Directory because GPOs are composed of a separate Group Policy container. In other words, you can create a single Group Policy object with a predefined collection of settings to be applied (for example, specify the desktop wallpaper to be the company logo). This GPO can then be selectively linked to only the Sales and Marketing organizational units in the Corporate domain, while other organizational units such as R&D and Tech Support might not have these GPOs linked to them. In this way, GPOs ensure that only certain users and computers have these settings enforced while others do not. The benefit derived is that creating separate GPOs to enforce the same settings for several parts of your company is unnecessary. One GPO can be used for more than one organizational component in Active Directory.

Administrators can also link more than one GPO to the same Active Directory container. For example, instead of putting both user desktop settings and software installation information into one GPO, an administrator might decide to have a separate GPO for each item. In this way, any changes to the desktop, which are made through the GPO, do not cause the software installation GPO to be unnecessarily replicated. This makes administration easier and can have a beneficial impact on performance. When a user logs on or a computer is started, the appropriate GPOs are applied if configured for that container.

Group Policy Inheritance

When processing Group Policies, a clear inheritance hierarchy is followed (see Figure 11.3): site, then domain, and then OU. This means that if similar settings exist at different levels, the order in which the GPOs are applied determines which setting is the final one applied to the computer or user. In this way, an administrator at an organizational-unit level can overwrite a setting defined at the domain or site level. As you will see later in this chapter, a higher-level (domain or enterprise) administrator can also override this capability.

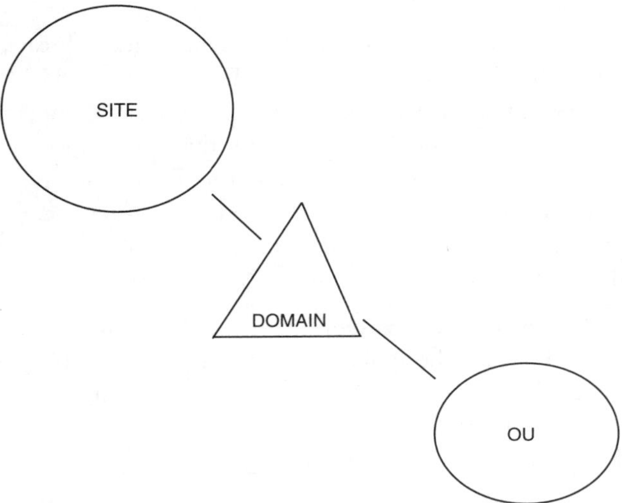

FIGURE 11.3
Group Policy inheritance during processing.

The first GPOs to be processed are those for the Active Directory site at which the user's computer is physically located. The computer and user settings for the site are processed and applied to the Registry. Because the site represents a physical location and because a single site can actually have more than one domain, it is important to start with the Group Policy that usually takes into account language and other regional differences. This is the Group Policy for the site at which the computer and user are located.

The next GPOs to be processed are those for a domain. Each user, group, and computer is always associated with a domain. Domain-wide policies affect all users and are primarily used to enforce domain-wide security restrictions or general business rules and settings that need to be in place. For enterprises that use a domain structure to differentiate between business units, this ensures that each unit enforces its set of rules without affecting the other parts of the company. As with the application of GPOs to sites, computer and user settings defined in the policy are applied to the Registry.

The last GPOs to be processed are those for the OU in which the user or computer is located in Active Directory. Active Directory enables a domain or enterprise administrator to further subdivide

NOTE

Local Group Policy Object Each computer running Windows 2000 also has a local GPO. In this way, you can configure settings that apply only to this one computer and that are not replicated to other Windows 2000 machines. When Active Directory is used, these settings can be overwritten by policies defined at the site, domain, or OU level. These settings are the least influential (that is, their settings have the lowest priority). In a non-Active Directory environment, as in a workgroup setting with no Windows 2000 domain controllers, these GPOs are the only ones that can be applied and thereby increase in importance.

NOTE

System Policy Processing In environments in which both Windows 2000 clients and Windows 9x or Windows NT 4.0 clients exist, you might still need to keep system policies around to enforce desktop and other settings. When a Windows 9x or Windows NT 4.0 client is used to log on to the network, it still processes System Policy and not Group Policy.

If Windows NT 4.0 domain controllers exist on the domain, they also supply system policy to users when they log on to the domain. This can change the configuration of a client computer, even Windows 2000 clients, based on the policy settings. It is recommended that domain controllers be upgraded to Windows 2000 as quickly as possible.

Any computer upgraded to Windows 2000 still retains the Registry changes made by Windows NT-style System Policy after the upgrade. This is because changes in the Registry as a result of System Policy are not backed out during the upgrade.

the users and computers in a domain into administrative units called OUs. This policy should apply to the smallest number of objects and should ensure that a very specific set of rules is also enforced. For example, you might have a Sales domain in your corporate structure, and within that Sales domain, you might decide to create a Telemarketing OU. The users placed in the Telemarketing OU need to have a more restrictive series of desktop settings than other salespeople in the organization. You accomplish this by associating a GPO with the Telemarketing OU and configuring the Group Policy with these settings. As with the application of GPOs to sites and domains, computer and user settings defined in the policy are applied to the Registry.

Group Policy follows a specific path of inheritance, enabling the administrator to fine-tune the application of settings to users and computers. The inheritance hierarchy is always site, domain, and then OU, ending with the OU closest to the user or computer object to whom the GPO is being applied.

Group Policy Processing

As previously mentioned, GPOs can be linked to a site, a domain, or an OU in Active Directory. More than one GPO can be linked to the same container, and they will all be processed together, depending on the security and other settings configured.

The actual steps taken by Windows 2000 in the processing of Group Policy are quite simple. First, when a Windows 2000 computer starts up, it needs to communicate with domain controllers in the domain to update DNS and other settings and to ensure the domain controllers are aware it is running. During this procedure, the GPOs that contain computer settings that need to be applied to the Windows 2000 computer are processed and applied to the Registry. At this time, any startup scripts that were created and assigned to the computer run, thereby ensuring that computer settings are as expected.

When a user logs on to a Windows 2000 computer, any GPOs that have been associated with the site, domain, or OU to which the user belongs and that have been configured to run for that user or the group of which that user is a member are applied. This means that two different users logging on to the same computer at different times might have completely different environments as a result of the policy settings applied to each. Further, after a user logs on to a computer, Windows 2000 also processes any logon scripts that have been configured to run for her or for a group of which she is a member.

Administrators can change what is contained in GPOs over time, and some of these settings might need to be applied in a very short time. This is why Windows 2000 provides for an automatic refresh of Group Policy while systems are running and users are still logged on. This ensures that Group Policy is consistently applied to all users and computers, even if the user never logs off or if the computer is never turned off. In this way, a consistent set of rules that are applied and followed throughout the enterprise or any portion thereof is possible.

Domain controllers in Windows 2000 Active Directory refresh or reapply GPOs every 5 minutes. Windows 2000 member servers, considered clients in the processing of Group Policy, refresh Group Policy every 90 minutes—plus or minus a 30-minute stagger factor. This ensures that all the domain controllers and servers to which users will be connecting have an up-to-date copy of any Group Policy. This does not, however, mean GPOs are copied between domain controllers every 5 minutes; this occurs only when the GPOs have been modified. Part of the checking that takes place is whether a GPO needs to be refreshed. Refreshing occurs if the GPO changes, which can be determined by the version number of the GPO.

Windows 2000 clients also refresh GPOs but only every 90 minutes, plus or minus 30 minutes. The refresh internal itself is staggered among Windows 2000 client computers to ensure that network bandwidth does not get saturated because of GPO refresh. For example, let's say you have 200 or more clients connecting to a small number of servers and domain controllers. Each client communicates with domain controllers at different times for a GPO refresh but always within 90 minutes of the previous refresh. The initial check is to determine whether any GPOs have changed and need to be downloaded, followed by a download of any GPOs that have been modified. During this process, any changes that have been made to the GPO are applied immediately at the client, even if the user is still logged on.

The default refresh rate for a GPO can be changed in the GPO template. This means that, if the preceding default settings are too

NOTE

Refresh Rules Software installation, offline files, and folder redirection settings, which can be configured in Group Policy, do not follow the refresh rules. These GPO settings are applied only when a computer starts up or a user logs on. For changes to the settings in a GPO to take effect, the machine needs to be restarted or the user needs to log off and then log on again. This is done to ensure that files needed by a user during a session are not directed to more than one location, thereby causing confusion.

frequent, you can reduce the frequency of GPO refresh or vice versa. Caution should be used when changing the refresh rate, though. Changing the refresh rate can result in a long lag time between a change to a GPO and its application on a client computer (if the refresh interval was made longer, such as 180 minutes instead of 90 for a client). Changing the refresh rate can cause network problems if the refresh internal is shortened because all clients need to communicate more frequently with domain controllers to see whether a refresh is required.

One of the major changes in Windows 2000 is the capability to have Group Policy settings inherited at different levels of Active Directory (site, domain, or OU). Having GPO settings automatically reapplied to all domain controllers, member servers, and Windows 2000 clients to ensure an up-to-date list of settings is a key benefit. The combination of Group Policy inheritance (the order in which GPOs are evaluated) and processing (how GPOs are processed in the same container and on the network) is a very important point of discussion and is covered next.

Combining Group Policies

NOTE

Connecting to the GPO Because site, domain, and OU policies can all be processed, the client computer might actually connect to more than one domain controller. It does this if a site GPO is to be applied and the site GPO was defined in a domain other than the one of which the computer is a member. As a rule, the client must connect to a domain controller in the domain where the GPO was created. For domain GPOs and OU GPOs, this always is the domain in which the user logging on is defined; for sites, it is the site in which the GPO was defined.

As you have seen so far, GPOs can be created at three levels: site, domain, and organization unit. You also can create more than one policy at each level with differing or similar settings. Therefore, it is important to understand exactly what happens if GPOs are combined and what the net effect of all the GPOs will be as a result. The process is a lot simpler than you might initially have thought because the rules are very straightforward.

When a computer starts up and a user logs on, the domain controller figures out which GPOs need to be applied for both the computer and the user. In doing so, the domain controller processes the GPOs for the computer first and then for the user and forwards to the client a list of GPOs to be applied. The client then connects to the Sysvol folder of the domain controller, locates the GPT of the first GPO provided by the domain controller, and applies the Group Policy settings. This process is repeated for all GPOs that the domain controller specified to the client.

The process proceeds according to the Group Policy inheritance rules previously discussed (site, then domain, and finally OU). If, at any level of this processing, multiple GPOs apply to the computer and/or user at the same level (site, domain, or OU), they are processed, bottom to top, in the order in which they appear in the Group Policy tab of the container to which they are linked. In the example shown in Figure 11.4, if both GPOs applied to the same user or computer, the Password Policy would be applied first and then the Default Domain Policy would be. If any settings in the Password Policy also existed in the Default Domain Policy, the setting in the Default Domain Policy would take precedence (see Figure 11.5 for an example of password settings).

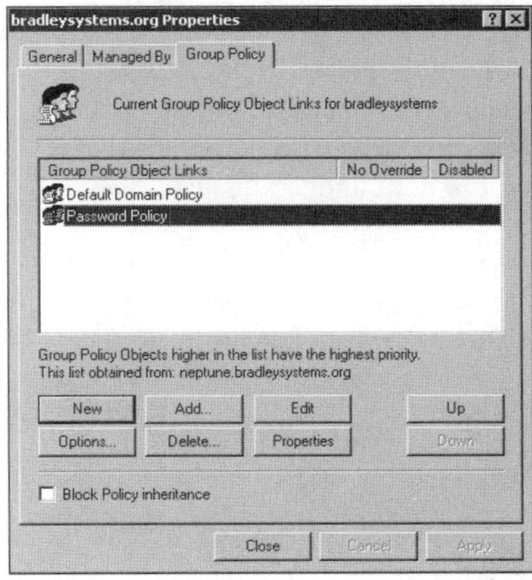

FIGURE 11.4
Multiple GPOs can be linked to the same Active Directory container. Processing is bottom to top.

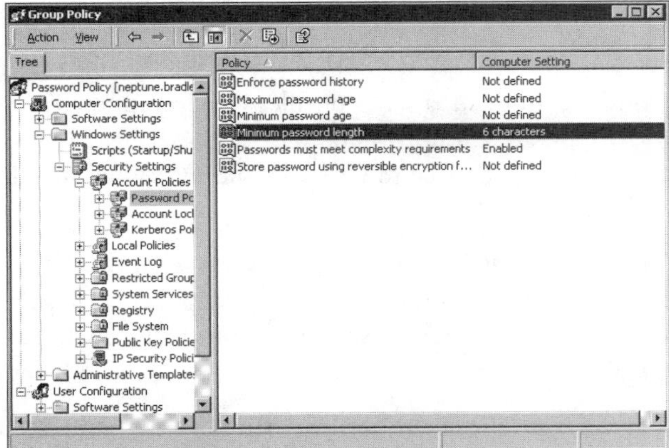

FIGURE 11.5
Password Policy settings for complexity and password length.

For example, consider the following scenario. You define a setting in the Password Policy. This policy states that passwords must be at least six characters in length and must also meet complexity requirements (that is, passwords must be a combination of uppercase letters, lowercase letters, numbers, or symbols). The Default Domain Policy also has a policy setting defined that states the password must be eight characters long, but there are no complexity requirements. In this situation, the result would be an effective policy that enforces a password of eight characters, as defined in the Default Domain Policy applied last. The policy also requires that password complexity be enforced, as specified in the Password Policy and not overridden by the Default Domain Policy because this setting was not specified (disabled) at the Default Domain Policy (see Figure 11.6).

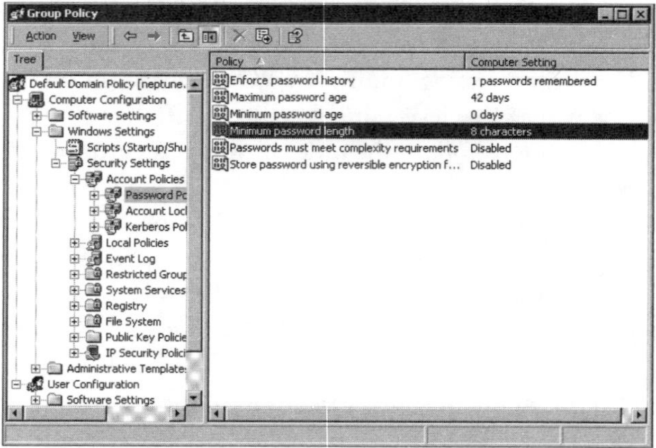

FIGURE 11.6
Default Domain Policy settings for password complexity and password length. Note that the password complexity setting is disabled, which means it is not changed at this level.

Group Policy Processing Rules

As previously mentioned, a series of rules is followed by Windows 2000 when applying Group Policy. Some of these already have been discussed, but it is beneficial to have the rules presented together. These follow:

- **All Group Policy settings apply unless a conflict is encountered**—This means the effective policy settings applied to a user or computer are the sum total of all site, domain, and OU GPOs that have been specified for the user and computer.
- **A conflict might occur and is defined as the same setting being defined at more than one level or in more than one GPO at the same level**—This is shown in the preceding example. When a conflict is encountered, the rules of policy inheritance are followed until it is resolved.
- **Policy inheritance follows the path of site, then domain, and finally OU.**
- **If more than one GPO is linked to the same Active Directory container, GPOs are processed from the bottom to the top as they are listed in the Group Policy tab for the container.**
- **The last setting processed always applies**—This means that, when settings from different GPOs in the inheritance hierarchy conflict, the one that applies is the setting specified in the last container.

- **When settings from GPOs linked to the same Active Directory container conflict, the GPO at the top of the list is the one that applies.**
- **If a setting is specified for a user as well as a computer at the same GPO level, the computer setting always applies when it conflicts with a user setting**—In other words, at the same GPO level, computer settings take precedence over user settings.

Group Policy has a clearly defined scope, inheritance, and processing order. Group Policy can be applied to the computer, the user, or both, and the computer policy always has a higher priority when it conflicts with a user setting. Now you will find out how to actually create GPOs at different levels of Active Directory.

Creating and Managing Group Policy

- Troubleshoot end-user Group Policy.
  - Troubleshoot Group Policy problems involving precedence, inheritance, filtering, and the No Override option.
  - Manually refresh Group Policy.

Creating GPOs is a relatively simple and straightforward process. As long as you have administrative rights either on the domain or in the OU in which you want to create the policy, it is quite simple. Step By Step 11.2 shows you how to create a Group Policy for the domain.

STEP BY STEP

11.2 Creating a Group Policy for the Domain

1. Click the Start button and select Programs, Administrative Tools, as shown in Figure 11.7.

continues

continued

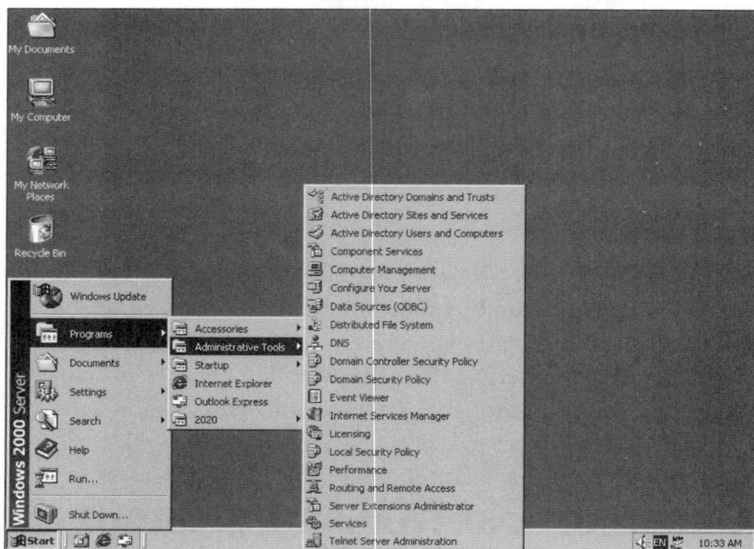

FIGURE 11.7
The Administrative Tools program group in Windows 2000.

2. Because you are creating a Group Policy for the domain, select Active Directory Users and Computers as the program to start. This choice opens a Microsoft Management Console (MMC) similar to the one in Figure 11.8.

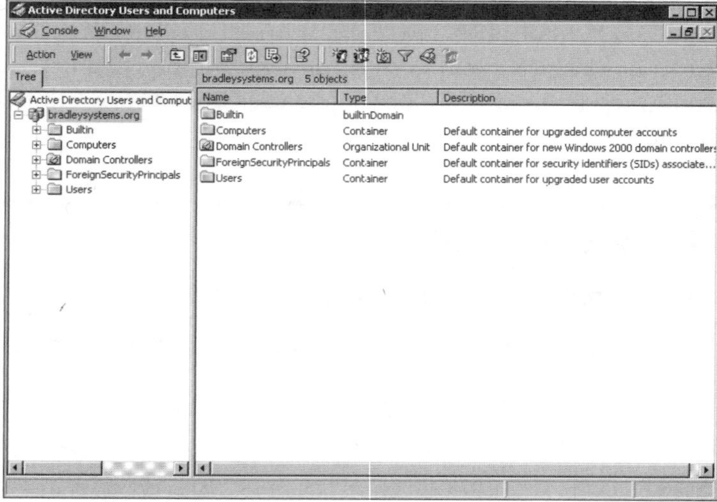

FIGURE 11.8
The Active Directory Users and Computers Microsoft Management Console snap-in main screen.

3. To create a Group Policy, right-click the Active Directory container in which you want to create the policy. In Windows 2000 Active Directory Users and Computers, you are permitted to create a GPO in the domain controller's container or at the domain itself. To create a domain-wide policy, right-click the domain name and select Properties. A screen similar to Figure 11.9 displays.

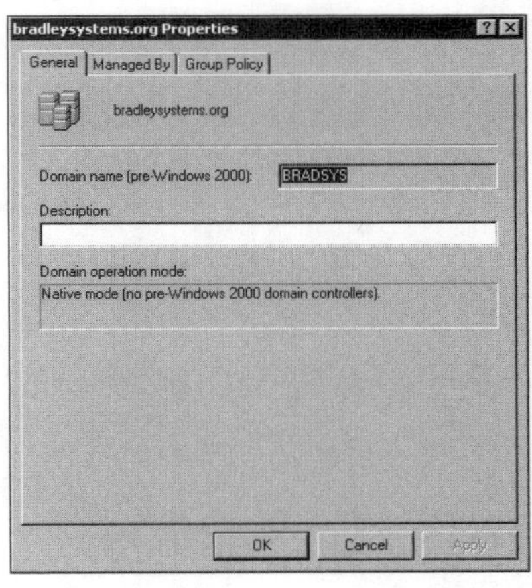

FIGURE 11.9
The Properties dialog box for the domain in Active Directory Users and Computers.

4. All containers in Active Directory that are capable of having GPOs associated with them present a dialog box similar to the one in Figure 11.9. Selecting the Group Policy tab in the dialog box presents a screen, similar to Figure 11.10, listing the currently linked GPOs for the container. If more than one GPO is linked to the container, the order in which they are applied starts from the bottom. This tab also gives you several options (by way of buttons) for creating and managing Group Policy. These options are as follows:

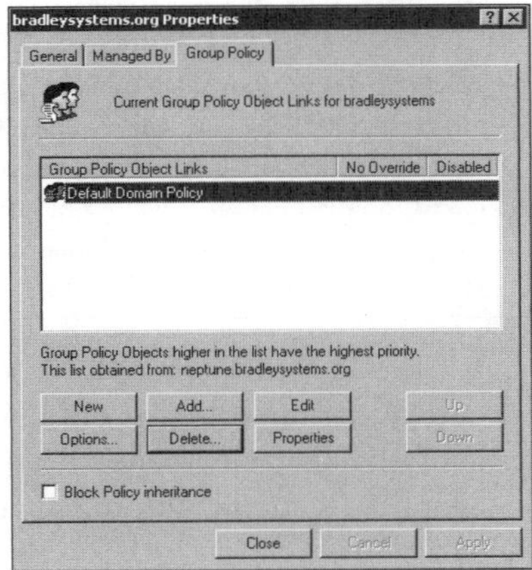

FIGURE 11.10
The Group Policy tab of an Active Directory container that supports having a GPO linked to it.

Button	*What It Does*
New	Enables you to create a new GPO at this container level and insert it at the bottom of the list of GPOs for this container. This GPO is linked automatically to this container and applies to normal users after it has been created.

continues

> **NOTE**
> **Group Policy and Default Containers** Associating a Group Policy with the default Active Directory containers Users, Computers, Built-In, or Foreign Security Principals is not possible. This is because the default domain GPO, which is created when Windows 2000 Active Directory is installed, already applies to the contents of these containers. In other words, creating a GPO in these containers would be redundant because they are the subject of any GPO created in the domain or associated with domain controllers.

continued

Button	***What It Does***
Add	Enables you to link a GPO created in another Active Directory container to this container and insert it at the bottom of the list of GPOs for this container. The GPO linked also automatically applies to normal users after it has been linked.
Edit	Enables you to modify the attributes of the GPO and enable and disable policy settings. After the editing of the GPO is completed, changes are applied to all users and computers affected by the policy using the normal refresh schedule as previously outlined.
Options	Enables you to set options for the GPO, including whether it is enabled and whether its settings can be blocked at lower levels of the inheritance hierarchy.
Delete	Enables you to remove the link to the GPO for this container and optionally delete the GPT associated with the GPO. Deleting the GPT removes the GPO completely and does not allow it to be linked to any other containers. Simply deleting the link for the GPO leaves the GPT intact and allows it to be linked to other containers.
Properties	Brings up a dialog box that enables you to configure security for the GPO, disable portions of the GPO that are not being used, and search for all containers to which the GPO is linked. This last option provides a mechanism to ensure that completely removing a GPO will not cause problems in other parts of the enterprise.

Another option that can be set by the administrator is whether to block policy inheritance. This is discussed in more detail in the "Group Policy Inheritance" section later in this chapter.

A final set of buttons enables you to set the proper order for policy application in this container if it is linked to more than one GPO. As previously discussed, GPOs are applied in the same container from bottom to top as they appear on this screen. The Up and Down buttons enable you to specify which GPO will be the first to be applied (the one closest to the bottom) and which will be the last applied, potentially overriding other GPOs settings.

5. To create a new GPO that will automatically be linked to this container, click the New button. This adds a GPO to the bottom of the list and enables you to specify the name, as shown in Figure 11.11.

6. To add, or link, an existing GPO to this Active Directory container, click the Add button. You are then presented with a dialog box containing three tabs, similar to the dialog box in Figure 11.12. Because you can link GPOs to sites, domains, and OUs, the list of GPOs that have been created at the domain or OU level is presented under the Domains/OUs tab. The list of GPOs that apply to sites is presented under the Sites tab. For an alphabetical list of all the GPOs that this domain controller recognizes, and that most likely exist in the enterprise, you can click the All tab. You are presented with a list similar to the one shown in Figure 11.13.

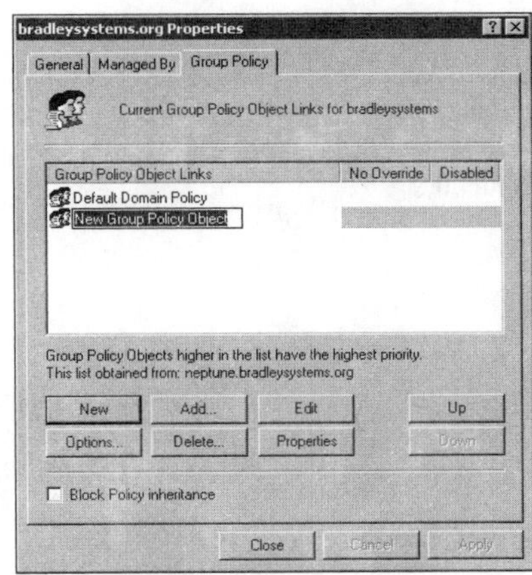

FIGURE 11.11
Creating a new GPO.

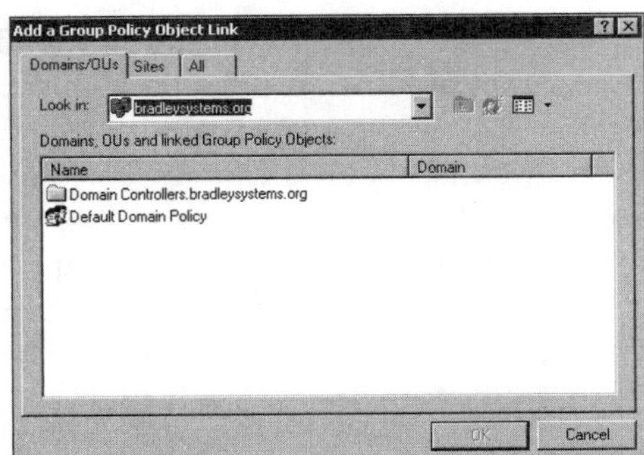

FIGURE 11.12
Adding a GPO link presents this dialog box.

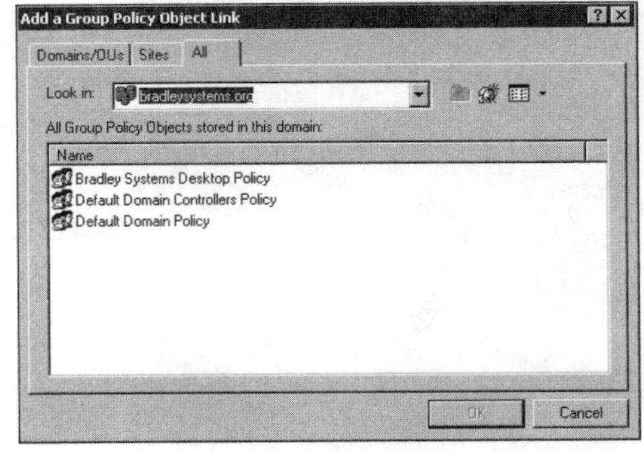

FIGURE 11.13
A list of all GPOs (in alphabetical order) in the enterprise can be found in the All tab of the Add a Group Policy Object Link dialog box.

7. Clicking the Edit button after highlighting a GPO on the list enables you to modify the settings of the GPO. If the GPO was created by another administrator at a higher level in Active Directory, you might not have the necessary permissions to perform this task, and you will be presented with an error message. If you do have the requisite permissions to change the GPO settings, you are presented with a dialog box similar to the one in Figure 11.14. As is evident in the figure, many options for both the user and the computer can be specified in Group Policy. The meaning of these settings is discussed later in this chapter.

continues

continued

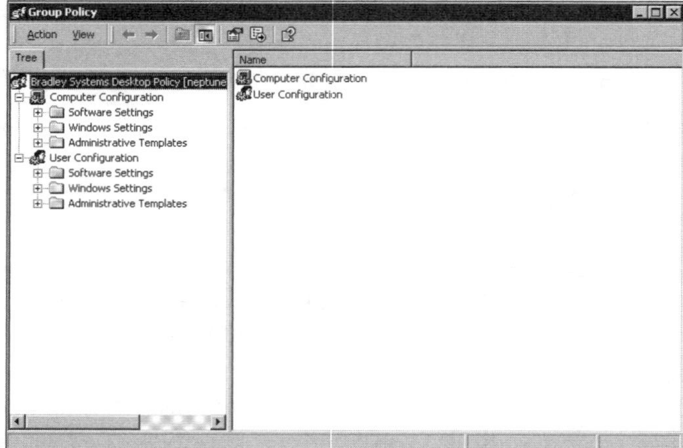

FIGURE 11.14
Group Policy settings can be modified using the MMC console. Clicking the Edit button opens it automatically.

8. Clicking the Options button presents you with a dialog box containing check boxes, as shown in Figure 11.15.

   The No Override check box enables an administrator to enforce particular GPOs settings, even if other GPOs further on in the inheritance hierarchy override the setting. The No Override option is typically used in situations in which a higher-level administrator at the domain level wants to ensure that GPO settings encompassing corporate rules are not changed by lower-level administrators at the OU level. This is a way to ensure that higher-level settings are not tampered with by other GPOs.

   The Disabled check box does exactly what it says: It does not enforce the GPO at this level. GPOs can be enabled or disabled. If you do not want a particular GPO to apply in the container, you can disable it using this option. This is also useful when you are configuring settings for a policy and do not want it to be enforced until all changes have been completed and for troubleshooting.

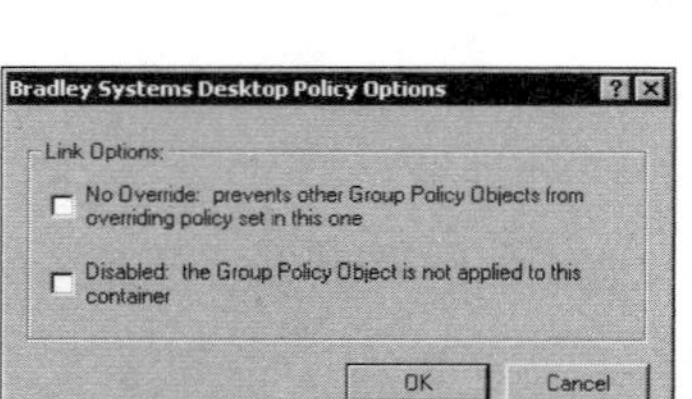

FIGURE 11.15
The Options dialog box for a GPO enables you to disable a GPO or prevent changes downstream.

9. The Delete button presents you with the dialog box shown in Figure 11.16. This option enables you to delete a link from the current Active Directory container for the GPO or to permanently remove the GPO from Active Directory. To remove the link, you must have administrative permissions for the container. To permanently remove the GPO, you must have administrative permissions in the container in which the GPO was initially created.

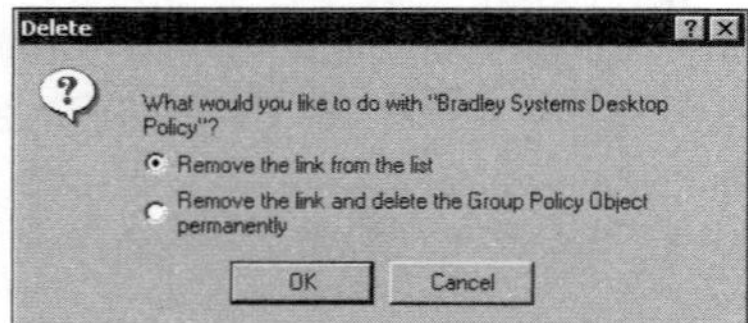

FIGURE 11.16
The Delete button presents a dialog box that enables you to remove a link for the GPO or to remove the GPO completely.

10. The dialog box presented when you click the Properties button is shown in Figure 11.17. The General tab initially shows the GUID in Active Directory for the GPO. You also are presented with the creation date and time for the GPO as well as the last change date/time and the number of revisions made to the computer and user section of the GPO. You also have the option to disable the user and computer portions of the GPO if they are not currently set, meaning they are not being used. Disabling one part or the other of the GPO makes download times quicker because not all parts of the GPT need to be downloaded and applied to the client.

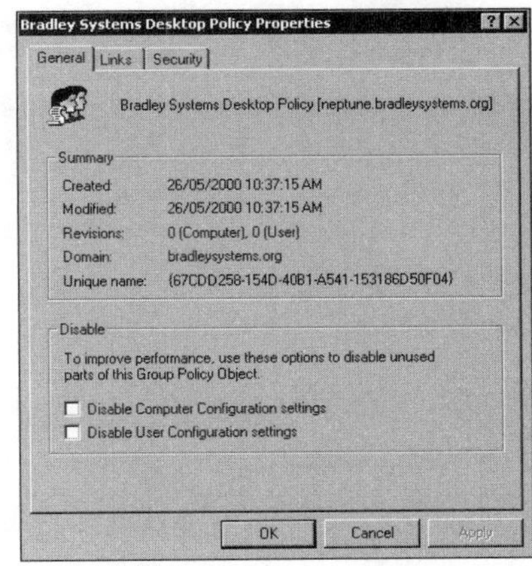

FIGURE 11.17
The main Properties dialog box for a GPO showing the GUID, creation date/time, revisions, and domain for a GPO. Computer and user settings can also be disabled for the GPO.

Clicking the Links tab of the Properties dialog box presents a screen similar to the one in Figure 11.18. Clicking the Find Now button initiates a search for links to this GPO in the scope selected. This is a useful way to ensure that any GPO you intend to permanently delete will not cause problems for other administrators relying on this GPO.

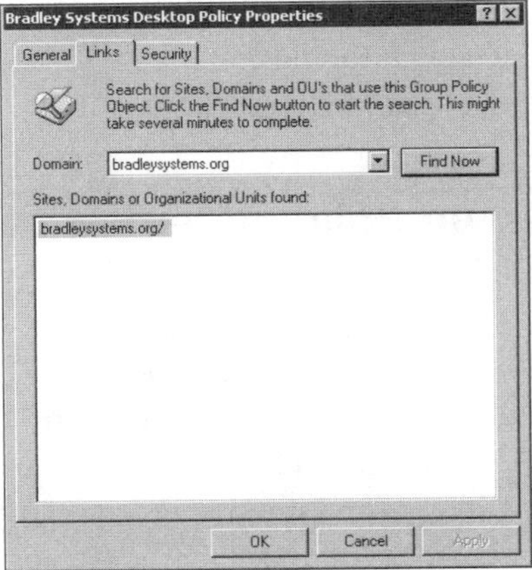

FIGURE 11.18
The Links tab enables an administrator to find out where a GPO is linked (being used).

The Security tab of the Properties dialog box enables you to grant and revoke permissions to administer this GPO. It also enables you to set permissions for those users who will have the GPO applied when they log on. This is discussed in more detail in the next section.

NOTE

Disable Computer Configuration and Disable User Configuration Settings
Selecting both the Disable Computer Configuration Settings and Disable User Configuration Settings check boxes on the General tab of the GPO Properties dialog box effectively results in no GPO settings being applied to either the user or computer. This action still forces the GPO to be processed when a user logs on. However, this is not the same as disabling the GPO in the Options dialog box because the GPO is still processed but no GPTs or scripts are downloaded. To completely disable GPO processing, use the Options dialog box.

As shown by Step By Step 11.2, creating a GPO is a very straightforward process. Managing it after the fact is quite easy, as well. The hard part is determining which settings to apply in the GPO and which users and computers should have the policy enforced.

Group Policy Inheritance

In some cases you might want to block GPOs from being applied to a part of Active Directory or force corporate standards to ensure they are adhered to by all parts of an organization. Finally, you might want to have a GPO apply only to certain users or computers and not to others. These three elements are called *blocking*, *forcing*, and *filtering* Group Policy and are discussed next.

One important element in determining how Group Policy is implemented is Group Policy inheritance. By using one or more of the methods of blocking, forcing, and filtering, you can fine-tune the application of Group Policy in your organization.

Using these same methods, you can force certain settings on all users (forcing), prevent higher-level policies from applying to a lower level such as an OU (blocking), or set permissions to ensure a policy applies only to the users it should (filtering). These methods are examined in the following sections.

Blocking Group Policy Inheritance

Group Policy can be set at the site, domain, and OU levels. An administrator at the OU or domain level, however, might not want to have higher-level GPOs apply to his specific OU. Furthermore, because Active Directory allows for a tree-type structure for domains, a lower-level domain administrator in Paris might not want the English-language-specific settings configured in a GPO at the New York headquarters to overwrite the territory-specific settings he has configured for France. Essentially, blocking is beneficial when you need a specific set of GPO settings to be applied and the inheritance of higher-level settings might be problematic because of regional differences or OU-specific characteristics. Blocking is most useful when an administrator for a container, such as an OU, needs to have total control over all characteristics of that container, including GPOs.

When deciding whether to use blocking, it is important to be aware of two rules. First, when you decide to block policy inheritance, you are doing it for all GPOs higher up in the inheritance hierarchy. You can't selectively decide which GPOs are blocked. It is an all-or-nothing proposition. Either all the GPO settings that have been configured at a higher level are blocked and any of their settings that you want applied have to be configured in your GPOs, or none of the GPO settings configured higher up are blocked. There is no middle ground; all GPOs are blocked, or none are blocked.

The second rule to consider when deciding whether to use blocking is that higher-level administrators might not want certain GPOs blocked. In this case, they might force the application of a GPO regardless of whether you decide to block inheritance. Any forced GPOs from a parent container, such as a site or domain, can't be blocked at the child. This is to ensure that vital corporate settings exist everywhere. An example in which this might be useful is a GPO that ensures the automatic installation and updating of antivirus software at the site level. You might decide to block inheritance at the OU or domain level. If the GPO containing the settings for the antivirus software is configured to be forced, the software is installed and maintained as specified in the site GPO.

To block Group Policy inheritance, perform the steps in Step By Step 11.3.

STEP BY STEP

11.3 Blocking Group Policy Inheritance

1. Open the MMC used to administer the container at which you want to block GPO inheritance—either Active Directory Users and Computers or Active Directory Sites and Services.
2. Right-click the container at which you want to block Group Policy inheritance and select Properties.
3. In the dialog box presented, click the Group Policy tab.

continues

continued

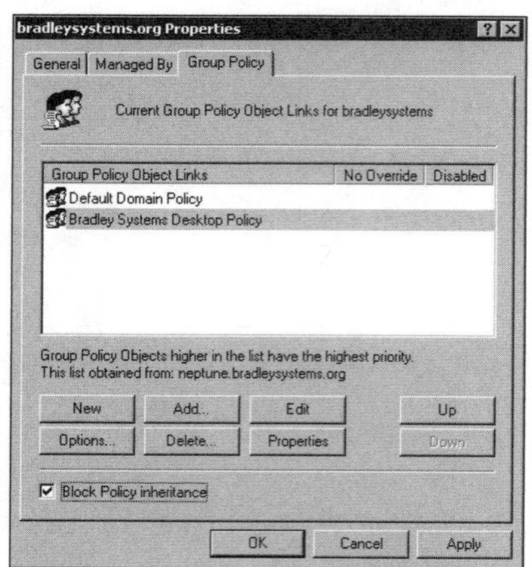

FIGURE 11.19
Block Group Policy inheritance by selecting the Block Policy Inheritance check box.

4. Click the Block Policy Inheritance check box, as shown in Figure 11.19, to block GPO settings from higher levels from being applied at this Active Directory container.
5. Click Apply, and then click OK to save your settings.

Setting a GPO to block policy inheritance is easy, but you must be aware of the consequences. After GPO settings are blocked at a particular Active Directory container, typically an OU, no higher-level settings will be applied to the container. This means that, if you want the behavior provided by the policies you just blocked, you need to create a GPO with the same settings. However, a higher-level administrator (for example, those at the domain level) might decide that certain GPOs can't be blocked. They have the option to force GPOs to apply to all lower-level Active Directory containers. You will look at this next.

Forcing Group Policy Settings

As a domain- or site-level administrator, you are responsible for a large number of users and computers in the organization. Lower-level administrators might be delegated administrative rights for their subdomains or OUs. You want to be certain that several important settings, dictated by business policies, are not modified by lower-level administrators. These business policies might specify that a corporate logo must be used as desktop wallpaper by all users or that antivirus software must be installed on all machines. You create one or more GPOs with these corporate requirements configured and now need to ensure that they are applied across the entire enterprise. Group Policy enables you to do this by forcing these GPOs and their settings to all lower levels, regardless of whether GPO inheritance has been blocked.

When deciding whether to force a GPO to lower levels, always make sure this is the best way of accomplishing your goals. For example, say you are considering forcing settings on lower-level containers in Active Directory that should apply only to the sales department. Forcing this GPO from the domain level also changes settings for users in other departments and does not produce the desired result.

When a GPO is forced, its settings override all lower-level settings whether they have been changed at the lower-level container.

When deciding whether to force GPO settings on lower levels of the hierarchy, ask yourself two questions: "Do all containers below this level HAVE TO have these settings?" and "Should lower-level administrators be able to change these settings?" If the answer to the first question is "Yes," you might want to consider forcing the GPO. If the answer to the second question is "Yes," you might want to reconsider forcing the GPO. When the answer to the first is "Yes" and the answer to the second is "No," this indicates that forcing the GPO is the best route so far.

To force GPO settings to be applied at all lower levels, perform the steps in Step By Step 11.4.

STEP BY STEP

11.4 Forcing Group Policy Inheritance

1. Open the MMC used to administer the container from which you want to force GPO settings—either Active Directory Users and Computers or Active Directory Sites and Services.
2. Right-click the container containing the GPO whose settings you want to force and select Properties.
3. In the dialog box presented, click the Group Policy tab.
4. Click the Options button to bring up the GPO Options dialog box, as presented in Figure 11.20.
5. To force GPO settings to be applied to all lower levels, check the No Override check box.
6. Click OK to save your option settings.
7. Click Apply, and then click OK in the main Properties dialog box to save your settings.

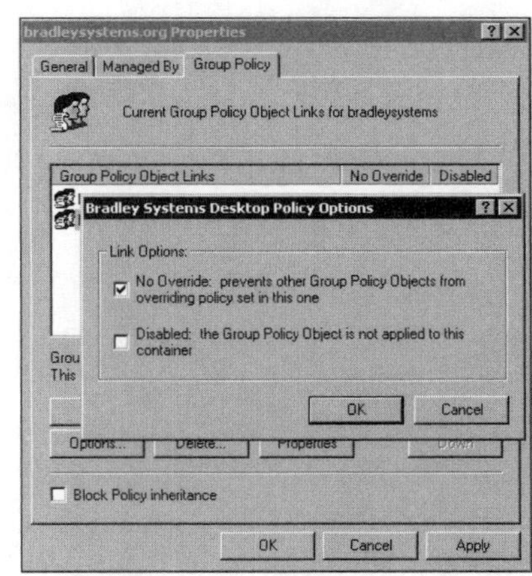

FIGURE 11.20
Force Group Policy settings to all lower-level containers by selecting the No Override option in the GPO Options dialog box.

Once again, it is important to reiterate that choosing to force GPO settings by selecting No Override in the Options dialog box forces the settings at that level to all lower-level Active Directory containers regardless of whether these same settings have been changed at the lower level. In other words, administrators who have configured the same settings at the subdomain or OU level will not have their settings applied.

Although blocking GPO settings and forcing GPO settings might provide you with much more functionality than what was available in Windows NT 4.0 System Policy, they still do not enable you to control which specific users will have the policy applied. This is done by filtering, or selectively applying permissions to, a GPO.

Filtering Group Policy

So far, you have seen how to block all GPOs from applying to a lower-level container and how to force GPO settings to all lower-level containers. However, you might want to have certain GPOs apply to some users, groups, or computers but not to others. The process used to selectively apply GPO settings is called filtering.

Filtering Group Policy means applying permissions on the GPO so it excludes certain users, security groups, or computers. In other words, filtering is really the careful management of permissions to ensure that the GPO applies only to the objects it should.

GPOs linked to Active Directory containers were discussed previously. When a GPO is linked to an Active Directory container, by default the Authenticated Users security group, which includes all users and computers, is granted the Read and Apply Group Policy permission. This means that, by default, GPO settings apply to everyone and everything unless other permissions are specified including Administrators. To filter Group Policy settings perform the steps in Step By Step 11.5.

STEP BY STEP

11.5 Filtering Group Policy

1. Open the MMC used to administer the container from which you want to filter GPO settings—either Active Directory Users and Computers or Active Directory Sites and Services.

2. Right-click the container in which the GPO settings you want to filter are located and select Properties.
3. In the dialog box presented, click the Group Policy tab.
4. Click the Properties button to open the GPO Properties dialog box.
5. Click the Security tab to see a list of users, groups, and computers that have been assigned permissions on the GPO.
6. If the user, group, or computer for whom you would like to filter the policy is not listed, click the Add button. You are then presented with a list of users, groups, and computers. Select the objects for which you want to filter the Group Policy settings and click Add; then click OK.
7. As shown in Figure 11.21, to filter the application of GPO settings, clear the Read and Apply Group Policy check boxes under the Allow column in the Security tab. This ensures that the GPO settings do not apply to the user, computer, or security group for which you have cleared these permissions. Also clear the Allow column for Apply Group Policy for the Authenticated Users group, or remove the Authenticated Users group.

   An alternative way of filtering the policy is to check Deny for Apply Group Policy for the user, group, or computer to which you do not want the policy to apply. Deny always wins over Allow and is useful when you want to apply the GPO settings to most users with a few exceptions, such as Administrators.
8. Click Apply, and then click OK to save your security settings.
9. Click Apply, and click OK on the main Properties dialog box to save your settings.

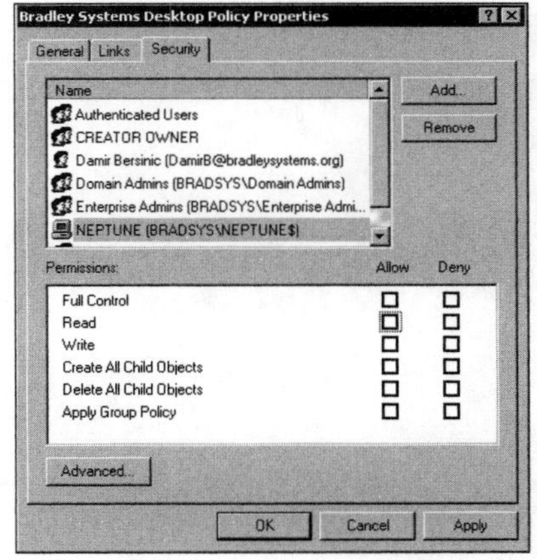

FIGURE 11.21
Clearing the Read and Apply Group Policy permissions for a user, security group, or computer filters the GPO and ensures that it does not apply to that object.

As you have learned, Group Policy inheritance can be blocked, forced, and filtered. Blocking policy inheritance means that GPO settings from higher-level Active Directory containers (sites and domains, typically) are not be applied to lower-level Active

Directory containers (OUs). Forcing GPO settings is the opposite of blocking—ensuring that settings in a GPO created at a higher-level Active Directory container apply to all lower-level Active Directory containers, regardless of whether GPO inheritance has been blocked. Filtering is the careful application of permissions to ensure that GPO settings apply only to the users and computers to which the Apply Group Policy permission has been granted.

THE SOFTWARE DISTRIBUTION LIFE CYCLE

When deploying software in an enterprise or a central location as can be done with Group Policy, you typically go through four stages: preparation, deployment, maintenance, and removal. Each of these stages is characterized by a distinct series of steps that need to take place before the next deployment phase commences. As you already have seen in Chapter 10, "Fundamentals of Active Directory," Group Policy is a powerful tool for the administrator; the fact that it also assists in the deployment of software just makes it that much better.

The stages of the software distribution life cycle are

- **Preparation**—The preparation stage deals with all the elements that need to be put in place prior to the software deployment ever taking place. These elements include the creation of a Windows Installer Package for deployment, the creation of a network share folder to hold the software to be installed, and copying the files for the software application to be deployed to the network shared folder. In some cases, software might not come in a format that can be used by the Windows Installer component of Windows 2000. You might need to use a third-party tool to create the package or, as an alternative, to create a ZAP file to install the software application. All these elements are dealt with in the "Preparing Software for Deployment Using Group Policy" section, later in this chapter.

> NOTE
>
> **ZAP Files** A ZAP file is a special file that enables you to package non-Microsoft Installer applications. These files have special limitations you must be aware of for the test. They are discussed in more detail shortly.

- **Deployment**—The deployment stage is when you actually get the software out to the user and computer. At this stage, you create a GPO automating the installation of the software and linking it to the appropriate Active Directory container (site, domain, or OU). You also decide whether the software is to be published or assigned. A decision also needs to be made concerning whether software should be deployed for the computer or the user. You also must determine how much interaction the user will have during the installation process. This, in many ways, is the easiest part of software deployment. The hard work was done in the preparation stage. If software has been properly configured, this process will run well. The various ways to deploy software and the creation of a GPO are covered in the "Software Deployment Using Group Policy" section, later in this chapter.
- **Maintenance**—As you are probably already well aware, nothing stays static in this industry. Software is no exception. Would you be reading this book if Microsoft didn't upgrade NT 4 to Windows 2000? Over time, you might need to configure and deploy an upgrade to some of the software on users' machines. Other times, software that has been deployed might need to be redeployed; patches or a service pack might need to be applied to bring software up to the most current incarnation or to repair any deficiencies (bugs or anomalies—undocumented features) that might exist. The "Maintaining Software Packages Using Group Policy" section, later in this chapter, discusses how to upgrade software in the field and the upgrade options available.
- **Removal**—Sometimes, software loses its usefulness and needs to be removed. How many of your users still need Microsoft Word 2.0 on their machines? The "Removing a Package" section, later in this chapter, deals with the issues surrounding the removal of software, forced or not, from users' desktops.

Microsoft Windows 2000 Group Policy enables an administrator to automate the deployment, removal, and maintenance of software packages on users' desktops. Let's start by looking at preparing software for deployment.

PREPARING SOFTWARE FOR DEPLOYMENT USING GROUP POLICY

Before you can use the features of Group Policy that make deploying software such an easy task, preparation must take place to ensure that the software to be deployed is in a format that can be used by Windows 2000 Group Policy. Next, a software distribution share must be created on a server from which the software will be installed, and the necessary files must be copied to that location. You are then ready to create the GPO to deploy the software. This section looks at the technologies involved in deploying software using Windows 2000 Group Policy: Windows Installer Packages (MSI) files and ZAP files. It then briefly discusses the process of creating a Windows Installer Package for legacy applications or those software packages that do not come in a format that can be used by Windows Installer.

Packaging Software for Deployment

As previously mentioned, the first step in deploying software using Group Policy is to package the software in a format that Windows Installer can use to automate the distribution process. If the software you are deploying is a newer application that has been certified to work with Windows 2000 (for example, Microsoft Office 2000), you might not have that much work to do. Newer applications most likely come in a format that can be used by Windows Installer. However, if your application is older (such as Microsoft Office 97), you might need to perform some additional tasks to ensure that the automated installation proceeds as it should. You might need to repackage the application in a format compatible with Windows Installer or create a text file (that is, a ZAP file) to tell Windows Installer how to install the application.

NOTE

Windows 2000 Certified Applications Microsoft has a process to certify applications as running correctly on Windows 2000 as well as Windows 98. More information on requirements to certify an application for Windows 2000 can be found on Microsoft's Web site at `http://msdn.microsoft.com/certification/default.asp`, including what the process involves; the various stages, certified or compliant; and some of the tools available to test a package. A list of packages that have been either certified for Windows 2000 (the highest level) or deemed compliant by the vendor can be found at `http://www.microsoft.com/windows2000/upgrade/compat/search/software.asp` on Microsoft's Web site. These are both good resources for determining whether the software you plan to deploy will work properly on Windows 2000.

Windows Installer Technology

First introduced on a large scale with Microsoft Office 2000, Windows Installer is the technology that enables Group Policy to deploy and manage software. It consists of two main components:

- Windows Installer Service
- Windows Installer Package

The Windows Installer Service is a service that is installed and runs on all Windows 2000 machines. This service facilitates the automated installation and deployment of software. It also provides the capability to automatically repair or modify existing applications when files are overwritten or removed. In this way, it ensures that the software both is properly installed and stays in working order. You can use the Windows Installer Service to install an application directly from a CD-ROM or other distribution media or through Group Policy.

The Windows Installer Package contains all the necessary information the Windows Installer Service needs to install or remove an application. This includes the files required by the software as well as Registry and INI file changes that need to be made. It also includes any additional support files that are required, summary information on the package and the application that can be shown to the user, and a reference to the location of the product files (that is, where to install the software from). The majority of this information is contained in a single file with an .MSI extension, which is the package file itself. As previously mentioned, the full package to be installed can also include other supplementary files. (For example, MS Office 2000 includes an MSI but also has many files in folders that the Windows Installer copies to the hard drive.)

Windows Installer provides the administrator, as well as the end user, with the following three major benefits over what has existed previously:

- **Resilient software**—With the Windows Installer Service, should a critical file for an application be accidentally deleted or modified in any way (for example, a virus on the system), the Windows Installer Service connects to the software distribution share and replaces the file with a known good copy. This ensures that software applications are always available to the user and are in fact self-repairing.
- **Clean removal**—One of the many problems that exists with past Windows software is that removing one piece of software can actually remove a file needed by another piece. You probably have seen a prompt from a package uninstall asking whether you want to remove some shared files. You have no way of knowing whether you should say yes or no. Will saying yes cause another program to fail? Will saying no leave a

NOTE

Windows Installer on NT 4.0

Windows Installer is also installed on Windows NT 4.0 when you install Microsoft Office 2000 or any application that uses it. It can be incorporated into the Setup program of an application by the developer and is installed on the target machine when the Setup program is launched, if it is not found. Just because the Windows Installer Service is installed on Windows NT 4.0, it does not mean you can deploy software onto Windows NT 4.0 desktops. You can't.

Windows NT 4.0 does not support Windows 2000 Group Policy and, as such, can't use the software deployment features of Group Policy. Both support of Group Policy and support of the Windows Installer Service are required on the target desktop to use Group Policy to automate software deployment.

bunch of orphaned files on your hard drive? Windows Installer runs as a service on each Windows 2000 computer and keeps track of which files are needed by which applications. This ensures that any shared critical files are not removed and that files no longer needed are removed. It does this for all applications in which it was used to perform the installation.

- **Elevated security**—In many situations, software applications require that the user performing the installation have administrative rights and permissions on the machine where the application is being installed. As an administrator, you do not want your users to have administrative permissions on their machines, enabling them to perform tasks that might make the computer inoperable. Automating the installation of these packages presented a challenge prior to Windows Installer. Because Windows Installer runs as a service under the LocalSystem account by default, it already has elevated privileges on the system. Applications that require the capability to make changes to the machine component of Windows 2000 can do so during the installation process while still not allowing the user to have administrative privileges. In this way, applications can be deployed that make changes to critical operating system settings (for example, registering DLLs and COM objects or changing the HKEY_LOCAL_MACHINE Registry hive) without giving the end user the same capability.

Windows Installer is a component that can provide many benefits to the administrator in automating software deployment. The Windows Installer Service is required to perform automated installation, upgrades, and removal of software using Group Policy. Windows Installer Package files are the preferred method of having software prepared for automated deployment.

What if you do not have a package for the software to be deployed? In Windows 2000, you can still configure software to be deployed even if you do not have a ready-made Windows Installer Package file. There are two ways to do this: You can create a ZAP file to tell Windows Installer how to install the application, or you can create a Windows Installer Package using a third-party tool. Let's look at both of these methods, starting with the ZAP file.

Creating a ZAP File to Deploy Software with Group Policy

In some cases, you might need to deploy software on Windows 2000 computers that have been around for a while. The computers might have been developed in-house or simply might not follow the Windows Installer conventions Microsoft has outlined. More applications do not use the Windows Installer Package format than do not, Microsoft has provided a way to deploy these software packages as well: the ZAP file format.

The ZAP file is a plain-text file created with any text editor (Notepad will work) that specifies a number of things about the software to be installed. The ZAP file can contain the application name, the name of the setup program, and any parameters to be used for setup as well as any file extensions to be associated with the application and tech support Web site. Not all of this information needs to be included in the ZAP file—only the application name (`FriendlyName`) and setup executable filename (`SetupCommand`). The sample ZAP file in the following code block shows a simple set of tags that can be used:

```
[Application]
FriendlyName = Microsoft Office 97
SetupCommand = setup.exe /unattend
DisplayVersion = 8.0
Publisher = Microsoft Corporation
URL = http://www.microsoft.com/office

[Ext]
DOC=
DOT=
XLS=
PPT=
RTF=
```

ZAP File Sections

The ZAP file is made up of two sections, as shown in the preceding code block: the `Application` section and the `Ext`, or extensions, section. The `Application` section outlines information about the software package and how to install it. The `Ext` section specifies which file extensions should be associated with the application in Active Directory.

The `Application` section has several tags that can be applied. They are described in Table 11.1.

TABLE 11.1

APPLICATION TAGS

Tag	*Description*	*Required or Optional*
`FriendlyName`	This is the name visible to the user and administrator when the application is installed. It also appears in Add/Remove Programs in Control Panel if the application is published or the user wants to remove the application. This is a name describing the application and should not be the name of an executable file. In other words, use something such as `Microsoft Word97` as a `FriendlyName` instead of `WINWORD.EXE`. The name should be friendly to the user.	Required
`SetupCommand`	This is the name of the executable program used to install the application. This could be an EXE file or a BAT or CMD file, as long as it performs the necessary steps to install the application. The filename specified should be relative to the physical location of the ZAP file containing it. In other words, if both the ZAP file and the setup program are in the same folder, do not precede the filename with the name of the folder. If the program is in a different folder than the ZAP file, you can use a relative pathname from the location of the ZAP file as the `SetupCommand`. For example, the ZAP file and the `SETUP.EXE` are both in a folder called `Office97` on the network distribution share. You only need to configure the tag to read `SetupCommand=setup.exe /unattend` with no pathname preceding the filename. If, on the other hand, the ZAP file is in the software distribution shared folder and the setup program is in a subfolder called `Office97`, the tag should include the pathname, as in `SetupCommand=Office97\setup.exe /unattend`.	Required
`DisplayVersion`	This is the version number of the application. This number appears in Add/Remove Programs and in the Software Installation portion of Group Policy. This is used to identify the different versions of an application that might have similar names. For example, Office97 is version 8.0; Office 2000 is version 9.0.	Optional
`Publisher`	This is the name of the company or individual that publishes the software application. The publisher of the application also appears in Add/Remove Programs and in the Software Installation portion of Group Policy.	Optional
`URL`	This is the URL containing additional information about the application and technical support details. The URL also appears in Add/Remove Programs and the Software Installation portion of Group Policy.	Optional

A ZAP file needs to contain only the `Application` section and the `FriendlyName` and `SetupCommand` tags. All other portions, including the `Ext` section, are optional. Specifying the `Ext` section might be a good idea, however.

The `Ext`, or extensions, section of the ZAP file is used to associate the application with a file extension in Windows 2000 Active Directory. Windows 2000 uses the `Ext` section to determine which application should be installed when a user decides to open, or double-click, an operating system file. If the extension of the file does not match a list of applications on the computer that can be used to open the file, the setup program for the application that defined a particular extension as belonging to or being supported by itself is called and the application is installed, enabling the user to view the file.

For example, say you use Windows Explorer to browse files on a CD-ROM sent to you by Microsoft. Browsing through the files in a folder on the CD-ROM, you locate the ZAP file `Explained.RTF` and decide you want to view its contents. You double-click the file, and the setup program from Word97 starts up. After you complete the installation of Word 97, the RTF document is displayed on the screen for you. The fact that the RTF extension was included in the `Ext` section of the ZAP file enabled it to be published in Active Directory and to automatically invoke the Word 97 Setup program, which enabled you to see the contents of the file.

To add the `Ext` section to the ZAP file, simply type the `Ext` heading on a line by itself. On lines below it, specify the extensions to be associated with the application without the leading period. See the following code block for an example:

```
[Application]
FriendlyName = Microsoft Office 97
SetupCommand = setup.exe /unattend
DisplayVersion = 8.0
Publisher = Microsoft Corporation
URL = http://www.microsoft.com/office

[Ext]
DOC=
DOT=
XLS=
PPT=
RTF=
```

ZAP File Limitations

ZAP files do have some limitations. It should be noted that the preferred method of installing any piece of software is to create a Windows Installer Package using a third-party tool. With packages, all options are available. Applications deployed using ZAP files have the following limitations:

- **ZAP files can't be assigned to users, only published**—As you will see later in this chapter, there are two ways to deploy applications using Group Policy: assign them to a user or computer, or publish them. Assignment is a mandatory installation of a software package, whereas publishing is voluntary (that is, the user might decide not to install the application after all). The fact that you can publish only applications with a ZAP file limits the flexibility of the administrator in ensuring that all users have the required software on their machines.

- **ZAP files are not self-repairing**—With applications installed using a Windows Installer Package, a critical application file that is deleted or becomes corrupt automatically is replaced with a known good copy. This behavior is not available to applications deployed using a ZAP file; Windows Installer recognizes one file for the application: the setup program. Windows Installer does not track what was installed by the application's setup program and, hence, can't tell whether the application is damaged.
- **ZAP files usually require user intervention to be installed**—The ZAP file simply invokes the install program for the application. Unless the software package has a fully unattended mode and this mode has been properly configured, the user has to provide some information for the install to complete. This might be okay in environments in which users are somewhat technically savvy, but it might prove difficult and create additional support headaches in environments in which users do not have a lot of computer experience.
- **ZAP files can't be installed using elevated privileges**—As previously mentioned, Windows Installer enables you to deploy applications to users even if they do not necessarily have full privileges to install software on their computers. This can be done because, during the installation of Windows Installer Packages, the process runs in the context of Windows Installer. Windows Installer is the one doing the install, not the user. Because Windows Installer is a service that typically has administrative privileges on the computer, any piece of software can be installed, including those requiring administrative rights during installation.

  With ZAP files, the program used to install a particular piece of software is invoked by the user and runs within the security context of the user. If the user does not have sufficient permissions to install the program, the installation fails and the application is not installed. This also can cause more support calls and not be the desired result.

So, after all of this, you're probably asking yourself, "Self, when would I decide to use a ZAP file?" The answer you're most likely to receive is, "Hardly ever." ZAP files are a perfectly acceptable way to publish software that is not required to be installed on a machine. It is a method that can be used to deploy optional software, such as utilities, in an enterprise. Examples of applications that can be safely deployed using ZAP files include WinZip32 or file decompressors, Adobe Acrobat Reader, and others. These applications are useful, though not required, on a user's machine; the user has the choice of whether to install the product.

ZAP files should not be used to deploy a critical line of business applications or any pieces of software that all users require and that need to be maintained at a consistent level for all users at all times. If an application you need to deploy fits into one of these categories but does not have a Windows Installer Package available, you can create a Windows Installer Package for the application using a third-party tool.

Creating a Windows Installer Package Using Third-Party Tools

In some cases, you might need to repackage an application so it can be deployed using Windows Installer. As previously shown, it is often easier to create a Windows Installer Package to deploy an application than to use a ZAP file to perform the same task. Packages offer more flexibility for deployment and are also self-repairing—a feature you will find to be almost the best thing since sliced bread.

The process of repacking an application and creating a Windows Installer Package to be used to deploy a piece of software involves several steps and, preferably, two computers. It is performed using WinINSTALL LE, which is shipped with Windows 2000, or any other third-party program that supports the creation of packages such as InstallShield and others. Using WinINSTALL LE is assumed for the rest of this section.

> NOTE
>
> **Location of WinINSTALL LE**
> Microsoft, on the Windows 2000 installation CD-ROM, provides a third-party application called WinINSTALL LE by Veritas Software to repackage an application. The program can be found in the `VALUEADD\3RDPARTY\MGMT\WINSTLE` folder on any of the Windows 2000 versions (Professional, Server, and Advanced Server) and is, itself, a Microsoft Windows Installer Package file.

The steps involved in repackaging an application include preparing a reference computer, preparing a network installation shared folder, installing Veritas WinINSTALL LE, and taking a before image of the system configuration. Several step-by-step tutorials walk you through the process of repackaging an application.

Prepare a Windows 2000 computer to be a reference computer. To repackage an application to be used to deploy software using Group Policy, you need to install the application on a computer as part of the repacking process. You typically use a Windows 2000 Professional computer, although Windows 2000 Server, or any variant, should also work. Use the version of the operating system that will be used by clients receiving the deployed package.

The first step required to be able to install the application to be repackaged is the preparation of a machine to be the computer on which to install the application. The reference computer should have only Windows 2000 on it and no other software. Other software installed on the machine can cause parts of the application to be repackaged to not install (for example, if the files already exist on the hard drive), which can provide incorrect information to WinINSTALL LE during the repackaging process.

Prepare a network installation shared folder to store the Windows Installer Packages and their supporting files. Users will connect to this shared folder to install the application. The shared folder name also is specified in the Group Policy Software Installation section so that Windows Installer knows where to find it when Group Policy assigns or publishes the application to the user or computer.

The next step is to install Veritas WinINSTALL LE on a second Windows 2000 machine. You should not install WinINSTALL LE on the same machine you are using as a reference computer because this can contaminate the clean environment you have configured. Always install WinINSTALL LE on a second Windows 2000 machine.

To install WinINSTALL LE on the second computer, follow Step by Step 11.6.

STEP BY STEP

11.6 Installing and Configuring WinINSTALL LE

1. Insert the Windows 2000 CD-ROM in the machine's CD-ROM drive and select Browse This CD when the Windows 2000 splash screen appears.
2. Double-click the folders presented in sequence starting with VALUEADD, then 3RDPARTY, then MGMT, and finally, WINSTLE.
3. In the WINSTLE folder, right-click SWIADMLE and select Install, or double-click the file. This starts the installation of WinINSTALL LE, and a screen similar to Figure 11.22 is presented.
4. WinINSTALL LE installs itself into two folders on the volume where you installed Windows 2000. These folders are located from the root under Program Files\VERITAS Software and include the WINSTALL folder and the WINCONSOLE folder. You need to share the WINSTALL folder by right-clicking it in Windows Explorer and selecting Sharing. Click Share This Folder and leave the configured permissions and the share name as required for your enterprise. In the example, the share is called WINSTALL.
5. You have successfully installed WinINSTALL LE and have prepared it to be used to repackage an application.

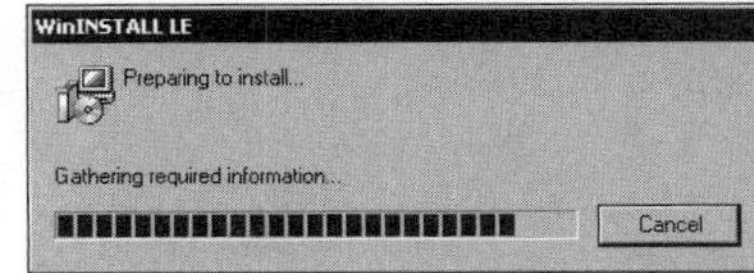

FIGURE 11.22
The WinINSTALL LE initial screen.

After installing WinINSTALL LE and sharing the WINSTALL folder, you are ready for the first major step in repackaging an application. You are ready to take the before image of the reference computer.

Taking the before image involves using the WinINSTALL Discover program to take a snapshot of the system configuration of your reference computer before the software is installed. To take the before snapshot, perform the steps shown in Step By Step 11.7.

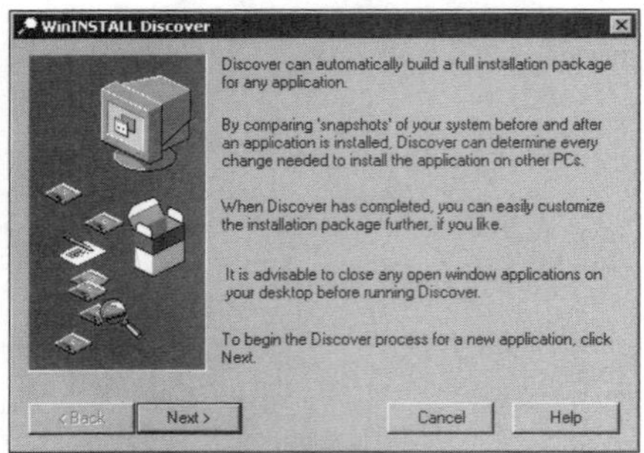

FIGURE 11.23
The WinINSTALL Discover startup dialog box.

FIGURE 11.24
The WinINSTALL Discover package specification screen.

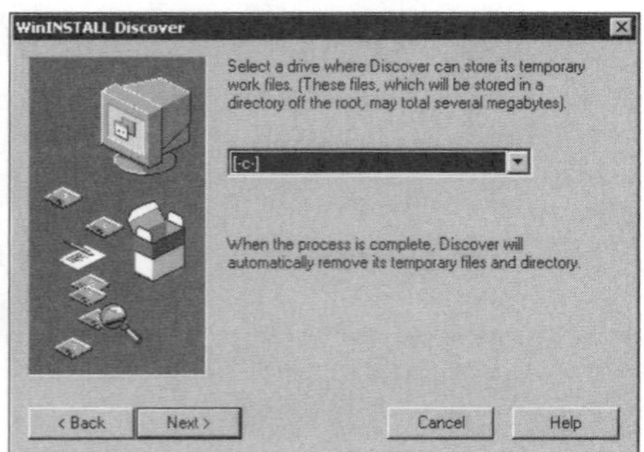

FIGURE 11.25
The WinINSTALL temporary drive selection screen.

STEP BY STEP

11.7 Taking a Before Image of the Reference Computer

1. From the reference computer, connect to the WINSTALL share of the machine where you installed WinINSTALL LE. Execute `DISCOZ.EXE` to start WinINSTALL Discover. A dialog box similar to Figure 11.23 is presented.

2. Click Next to continue creating the snapshot. You will be presented with a dialog box asking you to specify the name of the package you are creating, the location and name of the file to be created, and the language in which messages will be presented to the user, as shown in Figure 11.24.

   In the name box, type the name of the application you are repackaging. In the path and filename box, type the name of the file to create. The Windows Installer (that is, MSI) file to be created should reside on a network drive in the shared installation folder you created earlier. At this point, you might want to specify a different folder in which to store the file and move the MSI file to the final destination folder later. This is so you can test to make sure the resulting MSI file works correctly before it is placed in a location that can be accessible to users. Click Next to continue.

3. On the following screen, shown in Figure 11.25, select the drive where the Discover Wizard can store its temporary files. This should not be the same drive where you are installing the software. Click Next to continue.

4. Figure 11.26 shows the next screen. Select the drives to be included in the before image. The list of drives you select should include the drive where Windows 2000 is installed as well as the drive where you intend to install the software. Both need to be tracked because many software applications also install files on the Windows 2000 system drive (in addition to the drive where you decide to install them). After making your selection, click Next.

5. On the screen that follows, you are presented with a choice of specifying which files to exclude from the before image scan (see Figure 11.27). The preselected list includes the Windows 2000 page file, Index Server catalog files, and most temporary files. If you know of other files to be added to the list, specify them here and click Next when done; if you are not sure, do not add any additional files.

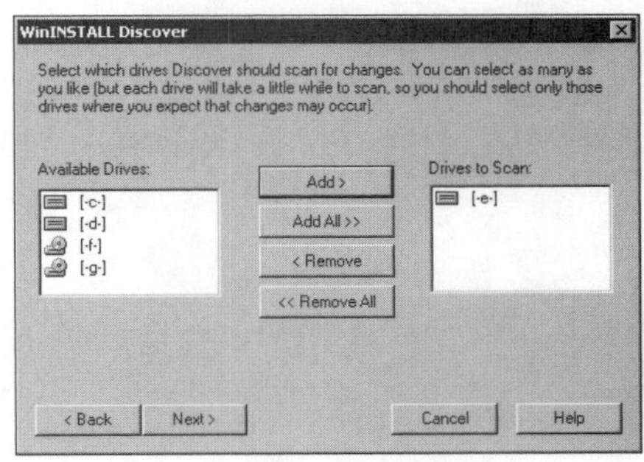

FIGURE 11.26
The WinINSTALL Discover drive scan selection screen.

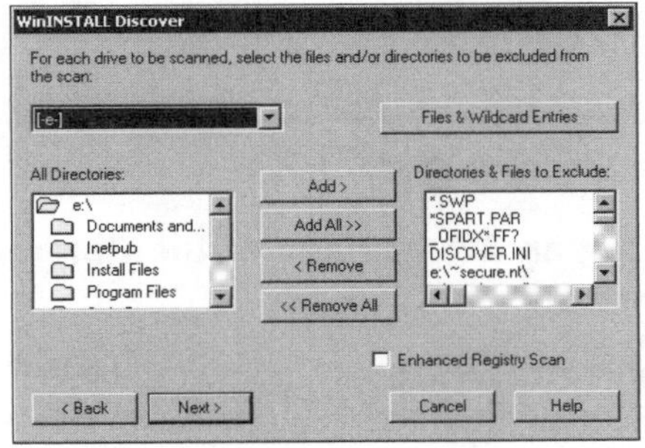

FIGURE 11.27
WinINSTALL Discover Wizard file exclusion screen.

6. The WinINSTALL LE Discover Wizard starts to scan the hard drives you specified and creates the before image. Figure 11.28 shows the dialog box shown as the scan proceeds.

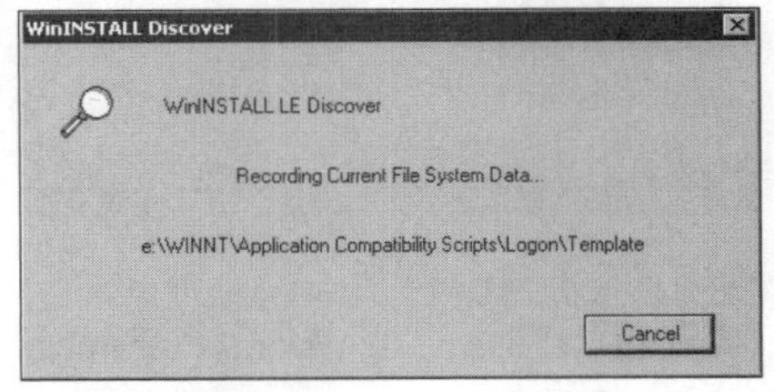

FIGURE 11.28
The WinINSTALL Discover Wizard scanning progress dialog box.

7. After the before snapshot is created, as shown in Figure 11.29, the Discover Wizard prompts you for the name and location of the setup program of the application you want to install and then launches it.

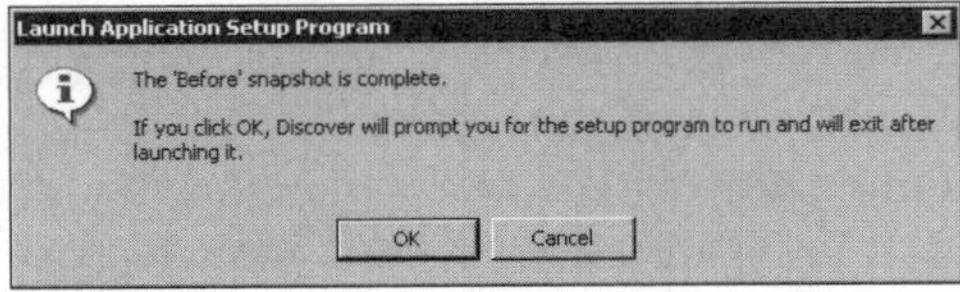

FIGURE 11.29
The WinINSTALL Discover before snapshot completion dialog box.

Now that you have taken the before image of the reference computer and the setup program has been launched for the application you want to repackage, you simply go through the normal application configuration as if you were installing it on any machine. You should choose the settings that make sense for all users who should have this package installed. If this requires you to create additional desktop icons as shortcuts, do this as well. If the install program calls for reboots, perform them. In other words, go through the same process you would use to set up the application.

After the application has been configured, you need to take an after image of the reference computer. This is scanned for differences, and the Discover Wizard determines the necessary contents of the package. Connect the reference computer to the WINSTALL share and launch the Discover Wizard again to start the process of creating an after image. Step By Step 11.8 guides you through the process.

STEP BY STEP

11.8 Taking an After Image of the Reference Computer

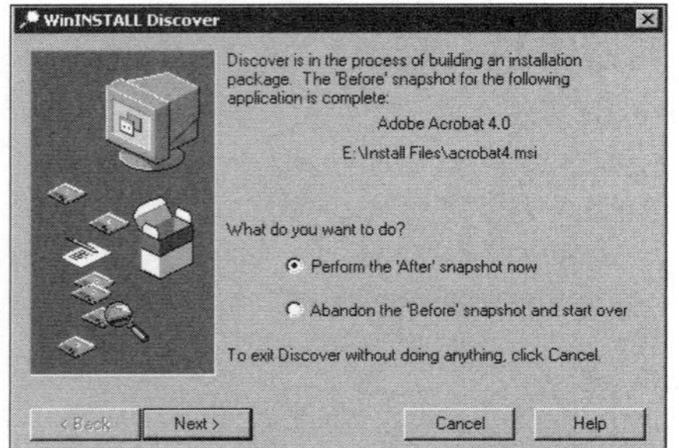

FIGURE 11.30
The WinINSTALL Discover Wizard after image selection dialog box.

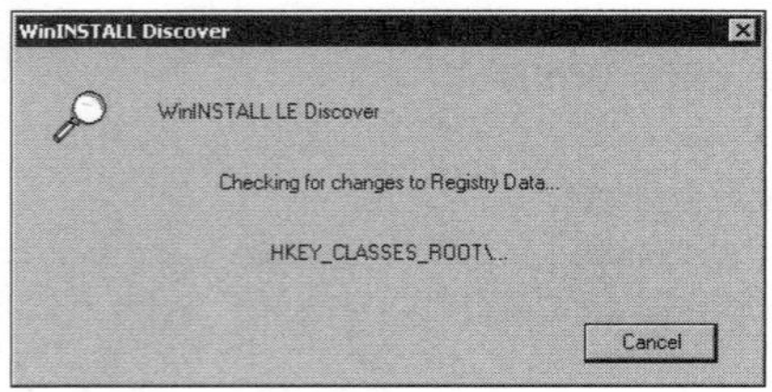

FIGURE 11.31
The WinINSTALL Discover Wizard after image progress dialog box.

1. Connect the reference computer to the WINSTALL share of the machine where you installed WinINSTALL LE. Execute `DISCOZ.EXE` to start WinINSTALL Discover. A dialog box similar to Figure 11.30 is presented.

2. At this point, you need to determine whether you would like to create the after image or abandon the old before image for the application you are repackaging. The name of the application you specified earlier is also shown as a guide (for example, Adobe Acrobat 4.0 for the Adobe Acrobat 4.0 Reader being repackaged in the figure). Select Perform the 'After' Snapshot Now radio button, and click Next to continue.

3. The WinINSTALL LE Discover Wizard starts scanning the hard drive and Registry to determine which changes took place during the application installation. During this scanning process, you are presented with a status screen, as shown in Figure 11.31. When complete, you are presented with any errors or warnings encountered, as shown in Figure 11.32. Make a note of the warnings or errors and click OK to continue.

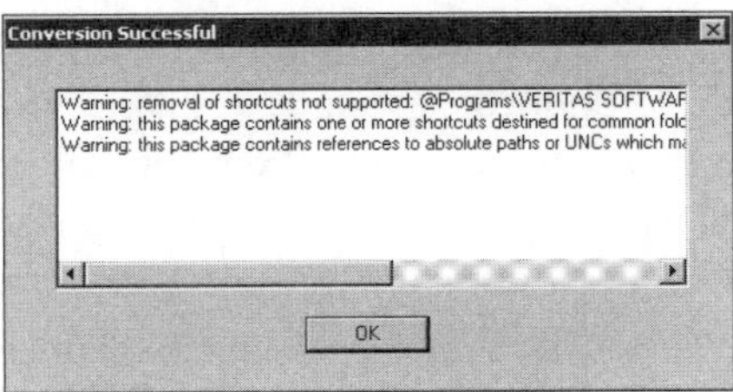

FIGURE 11.32
The WinINSTALL Discover Wizard after image warning and errors dialog box.

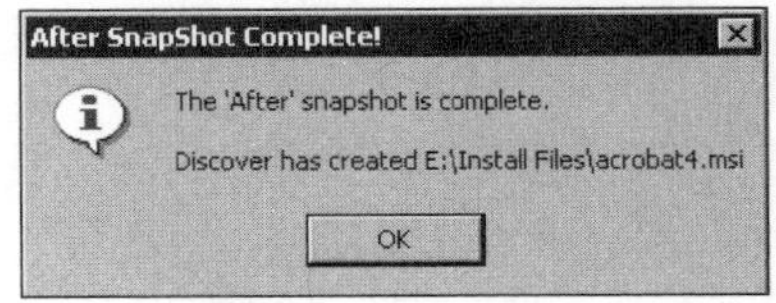

FIGURE 11.33
The WinINSTALL Discover Wizard after image completion dialog box.

4. The after snapshot is now complete, as the next dialog box shows (see Figure 11.33). You also are told where the package file was created. Click OK to complete the creation of the after image and exit the Discover Wizard.

You have now successfully repackaged an application. You should, at this point, copy the package file to the software distribution share you created earlier so it can be made available for installation.

When copying packages to the software distribution point, keep the following in mind:

- **Create individual folders for each package on the software distribution share**—In other words, put each package and all its associated files in a separate folder on the software distribution share. This enables you to easily maintain the packages and reduces any potential problems associated with figuring out which files belong with which package.
- **Make the software distribution share a hidden share so users won't be able to see it when browsing the network or searching Active Directory**—This ensures that software can still be deployed and that users won't be installing the package just because they found it on the network. Any file with an MSI extension can be installed using Windows Installer, so hiding the share from users enables you to control through Group Policy which packages are installed by which users. Hidden shares are created by appending a $ after their names.
- **Use Distributed File System (DFS) to provide a single logical share point for all applications, even if the files are physically located on a different machine**—Using DFS also enables you to configure replicas of shared folders on multiple machines, thereby ensuring that software can be installed even if a single machine is down.

If you want to make further modifications to the package, you might want to do so prior to copying it to the software distribution share. This ensures that no users install the application before it is ready. You can make these modifications later if the application will only be installed using Group Policy.

Modifying a Windows Installer Package File Using Third-Party Tools

After you have created a package for the software you will be deploying to users and computers using Group Policy, you might want to modify the contents of the package. This can be done using a third-party tool such as Veritas WinINSTALL LE, found on the Windows 2000 CD-ROM. Modifying a package can include adding desktop shortcuts to start the application, providing technical support Web site addresses and names, adding more files to the package, or removing some that might not be required. Many options are available.

To modify a package, start the Veritas Software Console for WinINSTALL LE and open the package to make the necessary changes as outlined in Step By Step 11.9.

STEP BY STEP

11.9 Modifying an Application Package Using WinINSTALL LE Software Console

1. On the machine on which you installed WinINSTALL LE, select Start, Programs, Veritas Software, Veritas Software Console. This launches the Software Console, as shown in Figure 11.34. Note that the Software Console is also subtitled the Windows Installer Package Editor.
2. To open the package file you created, select Open on the File menu and, in the Browse dialog box, locate the MSI file created by the Discover Wizard. After you have done this, click Open to load the MSI file into the editor.

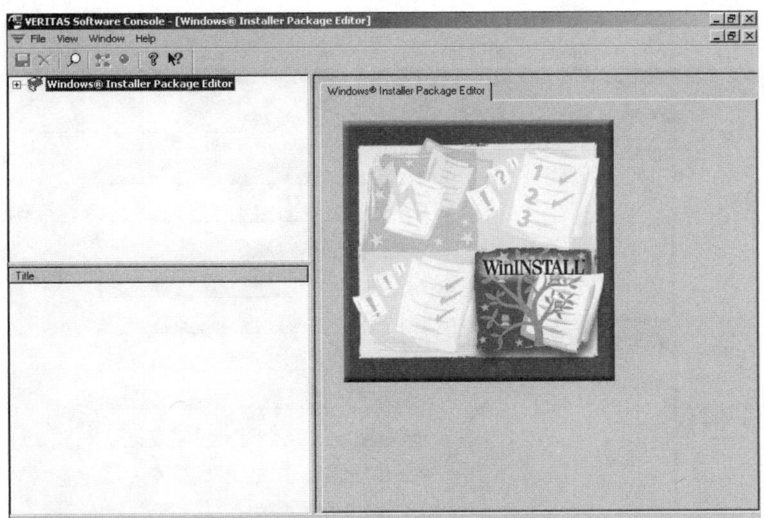

FIGURE 11.34
The Veritas Software Console main screen.

3. Figure 11.35 shows the Summary tab in the details pane after you have opened your package. As is evident, opening a package populates three panes on the Software Console:

   - The details pane on the right side of the screen shows detailed information based on the selections made in the two panes on the left side of the screen.
   - The package components listing pane in the upper-left corner shows the package. As you expand the package itself, each of the components that make up the package—such as the files installed and their GUIDs—is also shown.
   - The component properties pane is in the bottom left of the screen. This pane is used to determine the focus of the details pane. For example, if you click the GUID of a component of the package in the upper-left pane and then select Registry in the bottom left, the details pane shows Registry changes made for that component.

continues

continued

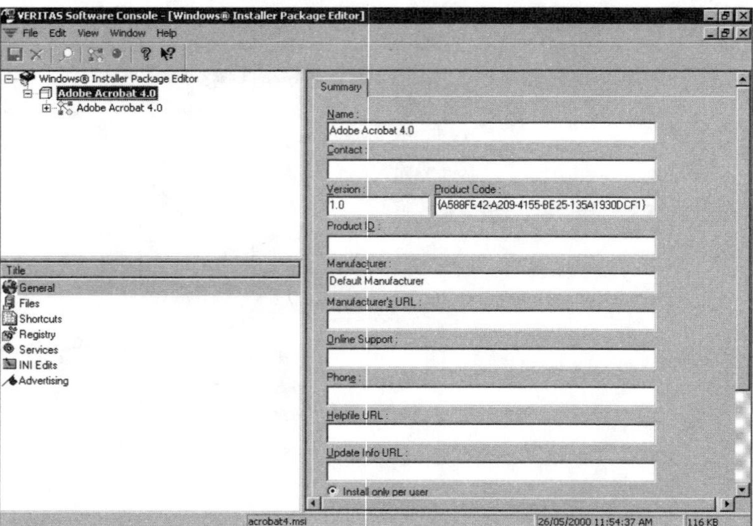

FIGURE 11.35
The Veritas Software Console summary properties screen for the package.

4. To provide additional information about the software included in the package, click the package name in the upper-left pane. Select General in the bottom-left pane. A screen similar to Figure 11.36 displays. If you want to specify a contact for the package, the URL of the vendor, version information, the online support site URL, and other factors, you can do so here. Make changes on the screen that will assist users if they have problems with the software package.

   Certain options available on this screen have special significance. The Version field can be used by Group Policy to help determine whether a software application should be updated. You can also use this option to tell Group Policy which application should be replaced by a newer version.

   The three radio buttons, close to the bottom of the details pane, determine how the package can be installed using Group Policy. Selecting Install Only per User does not allow a package to be assigned to a machine but requires the user to install it. Selecting Install Only per Machine has the opposite meaning. Attempt per Machine, if Fails, per User tries to assign an application to a machine first.

If this fails, because the application requires some user settings to be configured in install, it has the application installed per user. Further discussion of the per-user and per-machine installation options follows in the next section.

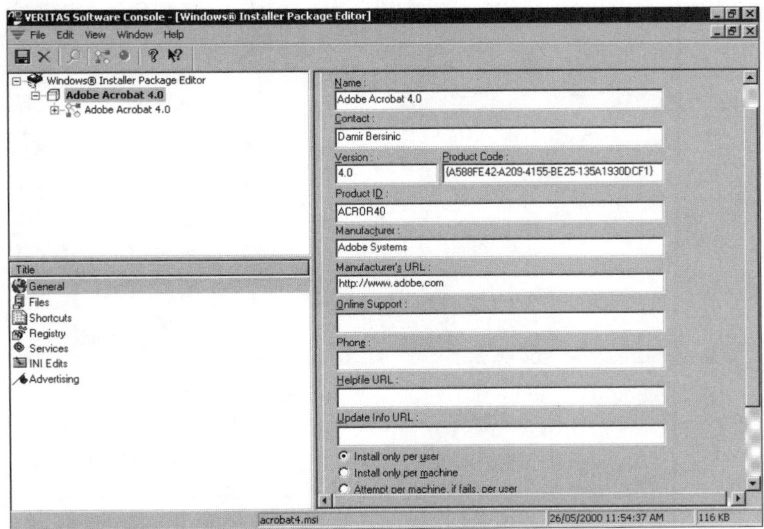

FIGURE 11.36
The Veritas Software Console package general summary information.

5. If you want to see a list of files included in the package, select the package name in the upper-left pane and the files in the bottom left. At this point, the details pane provides a total list of files for the package as well as where they will be installed, as shown in Figure 11.37. Note the three tabs in the details pane. The Add, Remove, and Fonts tabs show you which files need to be added and are required by the package, enable you to specify which files to remove during the installation, and specify fonts to add to the system if they do not already exist.

continues

continued

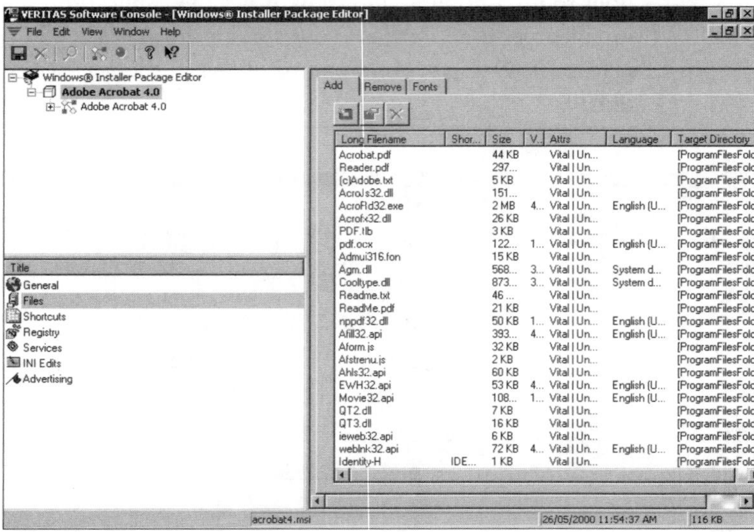

FIGURE 11.37
The Veritas Software Console package files listing.

6. To review which shortcuts will be added or to add a shortcut for the application, click Shortcuts in the bottom-left pane. The details pane will resemble Figure 11.38. For detailed information about a shortcut, double-click the shortcut about which you want to have more information. At this point, a dialog box similar to the one shown in Figure 11.39 displays. To add a shortcut, click the icon in the upper-left corner of the list of shortcuts in the details pane.

7. If you want to make other changes, explore the Veritas Software Console for WinINSTALL LE to see what choices are available. Help is available from the Help menu, explaining the choices available.

8. When you have completed your changes, save them by clicking the disk icon below the File menu. You can also save your changes by exiting Veritas Software Console and responding in the affirmative when asked whether you want to save your changes.

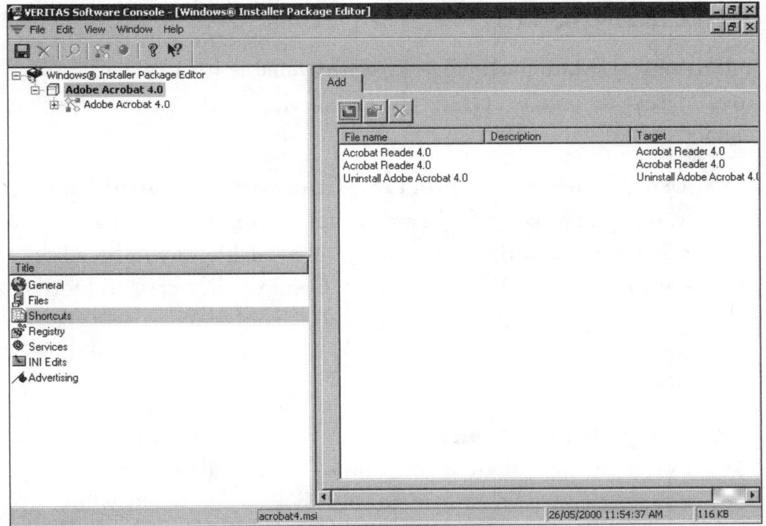

FIGURE 11.38
The Veritas Software Console package shortcuts information.

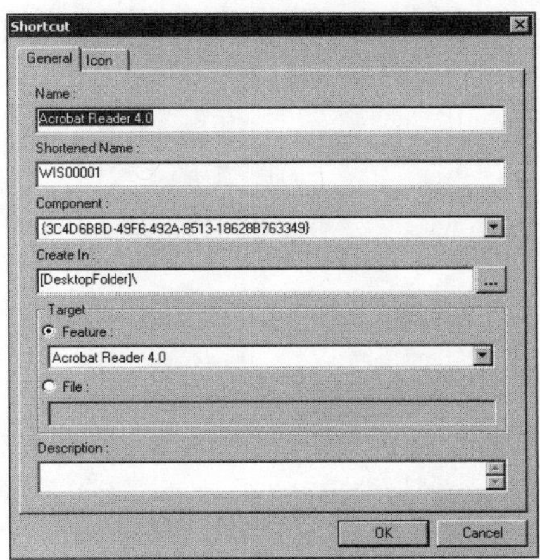

FIGURE 11.39
The Veritas Software Console application shortcut details dialog box.

Preparing software to be deployed is an important task that should be performed to ensure that what gets installed on a user's computer looks and behaves the way you want it to. Repackaging applications into an MSI file and the associated files to be installed using Windows Installer is the best way to ensure that software works as needed. Placing the completed packages on a Windows 2000 computer, sharing the folder, and applying the required permissions to the folder ensures that software can be deployed using Group Policy and be accessible to users and computers.

Software Deployment Using Group Policy

- Deploy software by using Group Policy. Types of software include user applications, antivirus software, line-of-business applications, and software updates.

Now that you've repackaged the software to be deployed and created software distribution share points, you are ready to configure Group Policy to deploy the software. In doing so, you have the option to assign a package to a user or computer or to publish a package to a user.

Publishing Software

Publishing software makes the software available for installation for users. Users are able to initiate the installation of the software package in one of two ways:

- **Using Add/Remove Programs from within Control Panel**—When you select Add/Remove Programs in Control Panel, you are presented with a list of software available to you based on your group membership and the Group Policy created by the administrator and in effect for you. You then can select the software you want to install, and Windows Installer will install the application for you.
- **Using file or document activation**—File or document activation is the automatic invocation of the installation of a software package when a user double-clicks a document whose file extension matches the file extensions configured for the application. By double-clicking the file and not having the software application already installed on the hard disk, you have signaled to Windows Installer that you want to install the program configured to read and interpret a file whose extension matches the one on which you have double-clicked. For example, you double-click a file called `GroupPolicy.PDF` on a CD-ROM in your CD-ROM drive. If you did not have Adobe Acrobat Reader installed on your computer, Windows 2000 would check to see whether a published application is configured to read PDF files. It would find that Adobe Acrobat Reader is configured to read PDF files. Windows 2000 would then invoke the Windows Installer to install Adobe Acrobat Reader so you can read the file. Automatically, the installation of the program (Adobe Acrobat Reader) was invoked by the document you double-clicked (`GroupPolicy.PDF`). This happened because the extension (PDF) of the file did not have a reader installed. The extension was published in Active Directory and was mapped to the software package.

Publishing of software is useful when you want to give the user a choice of which software products to install. Publishing is also useful when you want to ensure that users can view documents, but not all users need to have support to view all document types. Publishing software enables you to give the user more choice and is, therefore, really useful only for noncritical applications. Software that all users should have installed on their machines or that is critical to certain users performing their designated tasks in the enterprise should not be published but should be assigned.

Assigning Software to Users and Computers

Software can be assigned to either users or computers. Assigning software to either users or computers ensures that the software is always available.

Assigning software to users enables the software to be advertised on the users' desktops. This means icons for the application will be available even though the application is not currently installed. Double-clicking the software icon, or a file extension associated with the software applications, causes the installation to take place automatically. If the user never double-clicks the software icon or a file with the software extension associated with the package, the software is not installed, thus saving disk space, network bandwidth, and administrative load.

Assigning software to computers ensures that the software is installed when the computer is turned on and connects to the network. The next time the computer processes its Group Policy settings, it finds that software has been assigned to it, and the software is automatically installed. Any software assigned to a computer is available to all users on the computer.

Any software that must be installed in all cases should be assigned to a computer. Software needed by all users that is not required to be on the machine initially can be assigned to the user or group and be installed when required. Either method ensures that the software is available when required.

Deploying Software Using Group Policy

To publish or assign software, use Group Policy. Determining which method should be used to deploy the software occurs when the software application is associated with the GPO.

To deploy software using Group Policy, follow Step By Step 11.10.

STEP BY STEP

11.10 Deploying Software Using Group Policy

1. Start Active Directory Users and Computers or Active Directory Sites and Services (depending on which container you want to configure the GPO for software deployment), and expand the folder list until you reach the container for which you want to configure software deployment. (The figures in this section show Active Directory Users and Computers.)

2. Right-click the container (domain, OU, or site) for which you want to configure the GPO and select Properties.

3. Click the Group Policy tab, and select an existing GPO to be used for software deployment; click New to create a new GPO; or click Add to link an existing GPO to this container.

4. Click the GPO you will use to deploy software, and then click Edit to open the Group Policy Editor MMC, as shown in Figure 11.40.

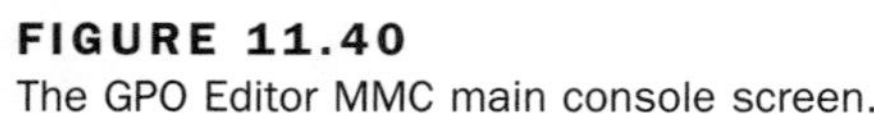

FIGURE 11.40
The GPO Editor MMC main console screen.

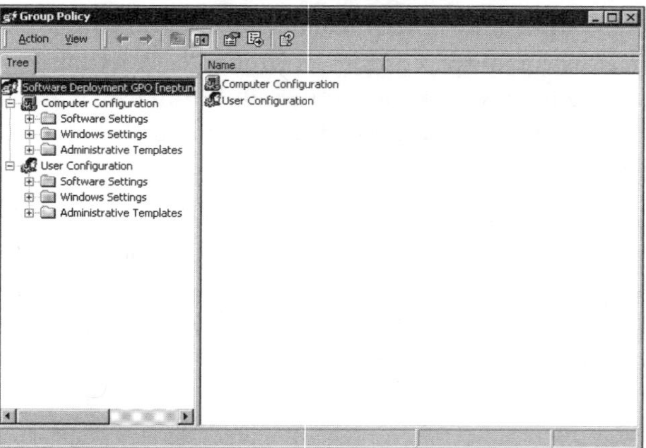

5. To configure software deployment for the computer, expand the Software Settings folder under the Computer Configuration folder in Group Policy. To configure software deployment for the user or group, expand the Software Settings folder under User Configuration, as shown in Figure 11.41.

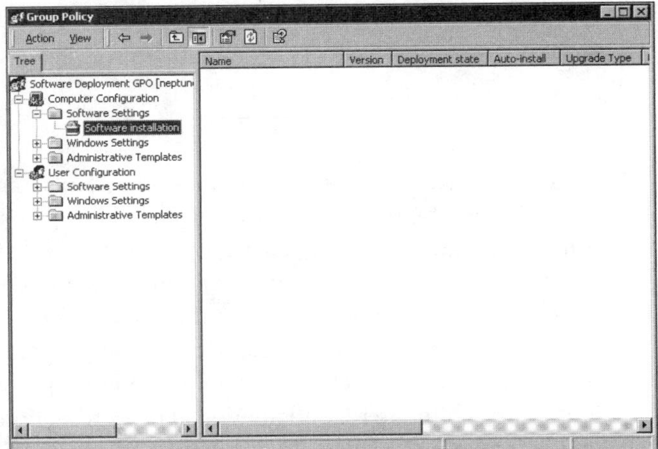

FIGURE 11.41
Software deployment can be configured for the computer or the user portion of Group Policy.

6. To configure a package for deployment, right-click the Software Installation icon and select New, Package. You are presented with a browse box. Browse the network to locate the software distribution shared folder you created earlier. The path to the package is stored in the Group Policy as the point from which to install the software package and should be a network share point.

   Do not choose a local drive because users can't connect to a local path on your machine. You will be presented with a dialog box, similar to Figure 11.42, stating that you are choosing a local path.

   Figure 11.43 shows a network share location used to locate the package file. After you have located the package you want to install, click it.

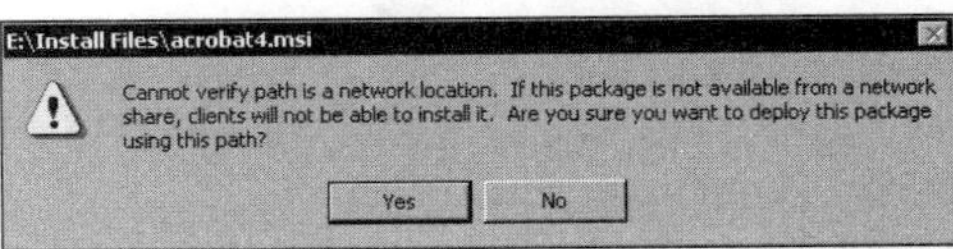

FIGURE 11.42
You receive a warning if the path to the package you have chosen is not a shared folder.

continues

continued

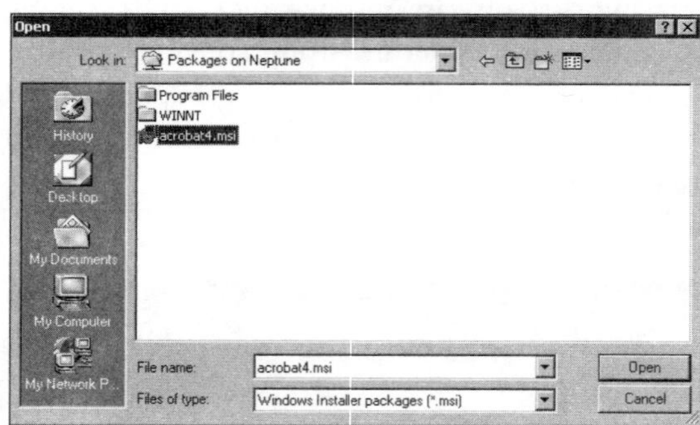

FIGURE 11.43
Selecting a package using a network share path.

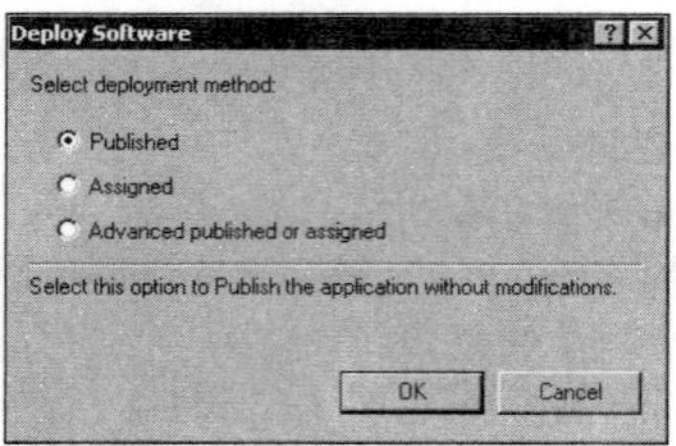

FIGURE 11.44
Package options when attaching to the user configuration in Group Policy.

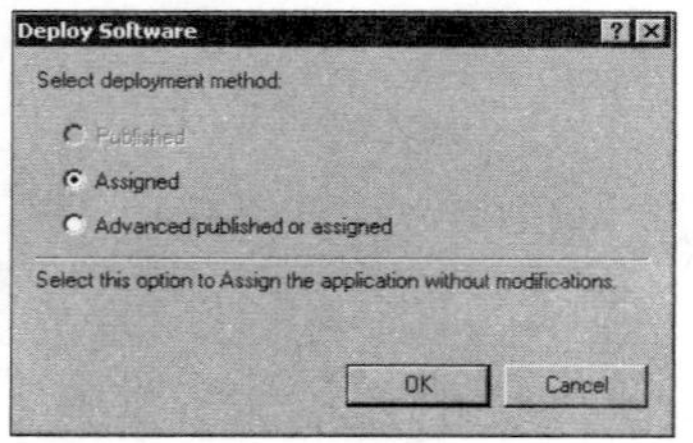

FIGURE 11.45
Package options when attaching to the computer configuration in Group Policy.

7. If you have decided to attach the software package to the user portion of Group Policy, you will see a dialog box similar to Figure 11.44. If you are attaching the package to the computer configuration portion of the GPO object, you will see a dialog box similar to the one in Figure 11.45. As previously mentioned, packages can't be published to computers; hence, the Publish option is grayed-out on the Computer Configuration. The third option presented simply enables you to configure further options (that is, modify the package) when you decide to assign or publish it. This option is discussed in more detail in the next section.

   Make your selection to publish or assign and click OK.

8. You have now published or assigned your software package to users or computers. The Group Policy Editor is similar to Figure 11.46 and shows you some information about the package you have deployed. Information presented for each package includes the name of the package and its version number, as specified in the package file. The deployment state (published or assigned) and whether the package should be automatically installed using file extension (that is, document) activation is summarized here. You can also determine the upgrade or installation type (optional or required) and whether the package is an upgrade for another, existing package. You can configure these yourself and modify the package information.

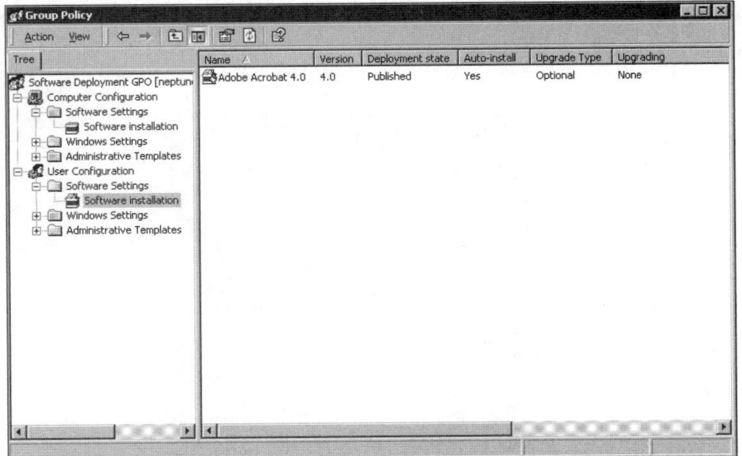

FIGURE 11.46
Clicking Software Installation presents general information for packages currently configured to be deployed using Group Policy.

9. Close the Group Policy Editor and click OK to close the Group Policy Container Properties dialog box. Exit the MMC console you were using to complete the configuration.

Package Deployment Options

After you have deployed a package, you can configure some options for the package that change its behavior and enable you to set additional options. You do this by right-clicking the Software Installation object in the Software Settings folder of the Group Policy where you configured the package.

The Software Installation Properties dialog box, as shown in Figure 11.47, enables you to configure general settings for all packages in the scope of that container. These settings include the default installation location for packages (that is, the network share where packages can be found in case the package location is not available) and the default type of installation for new packages (Display the Deploy Software Dialog Box, Publish, Assign, or Advanced Published or Assigned). You can determine the amount of user interaction possible during package installation (Basic interaction, which is not much, or Maximum). In addition, you have the option to specify whether a package is uninstalled if it falls outside the scope of the

GPO. You can also configure file extension preferences and software categories, which are discussed later.

NOTE

Advanced Published or Assigned
The Advanced Published or Assigned option shown when you add a package is not a special type of option for the package. Stating that you want to use this option simply means that the properties for the package are displayed to you, thereby enabling you to configure other options on the package. It is the same as right-clicking the package after assigning or publishing it and selecting Properties.

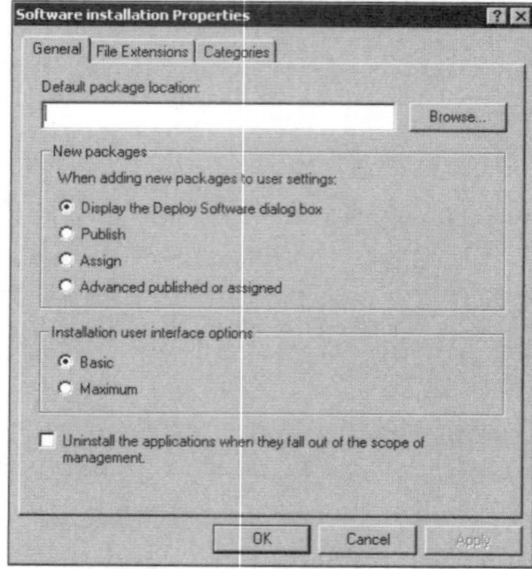

FIGURE 11.47
The Software Installation Properties dialog box in Group Policy Editor.

If you right-click a package and select Properties, you are presented with a dialog box similar to the one in Figure 11.48. The General tab of the package's Properties dialog box provides general information about the package, including the manufacturer, platform, support URL, and contact information.

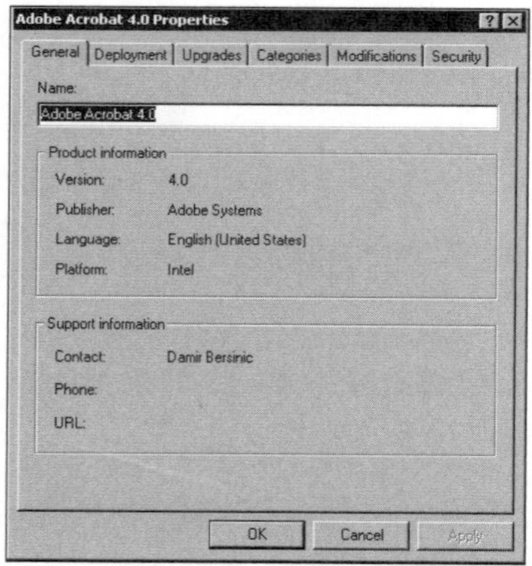

FIGURE 11.48
The package's general Properties dialog box in Group Policy.

The Deployment tab enables you to change the deployment information for this package (see Figure 11.49). You can change the Deployment Type from Published to Assigned and vice versa. This changes how the package is deployed to users or computers (for example, assigned to users or computers or published to users).

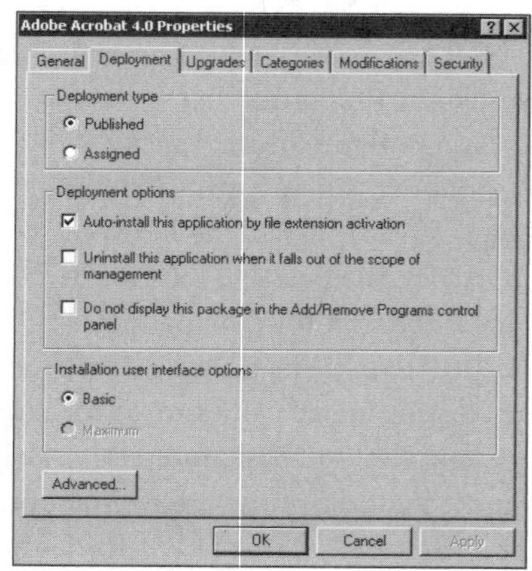

FIGURE 11.49
The package's Deployment tab in the Properties dialog box in Group Policy.

The Deployment options portion of this tab determines what happens when deployment takes place, including auto-installing the application when activated through file extension (that is, document invocation). If you uncheck this box, the file extensions associated with this package are not published, and document invocation will not take place. You can also uninstall the application if the GPO no longer applies to the user (that is, she moved to another OU in the Active Directory hierarchy). You also have the option to no \t advertise the package in Add/Remove Programs so that a user will not know whether the package exists to install it.

> NOTE
>
> **Conflicting Options** It is not a good idea to uncheck both the Auto-Install This Application by File Extension Activation and the Do Not Display This Package in the Add/Remove Programs Control Panel boxes at the same time. Doing so prevents installation of the software when a matching document is invoked; it does not allow the package to be advertised in Add/Remove Programs. The package is configured to be available to the user, but the user never knows to install it or invoke the installation program. The package takes up disk space and causes additional processing for the GPO, but it never is installed. The only time this is useful is prior to a software release. You might want to keep the package unavailable until you are ready to flip the switch.

The Installation user interface options enable you to specify how much user interaction is available to the user during installation. The default setting of Basic simply lets the user watch as the application is installed with default configuration settings. The Maximum setting prompts the user to enter values during installation. The Upgrades, Categories, Modifications, and Security tabs are discussed later in this chapter.

You have now added the package to a Group Policy so it can be deployed to users or computers. You have configured the package's deployment options and have outlined how it will be presented to the user. You have also determined whether the package needs to be installed on all computers, in which case you configured the package in the Computer Configuration portion of Group Policy, or whether it will be assigned or published to users. Over time, however, you might need to modify these options or even upgrade packages. The issue of maintaining software packages is presented next.

Maintaining Software Packages Using Group Policy

As you know by now, the only constant in this industry is change. Invariably, at some point after deploying your package using Group Policy, you most likely will have to provide an update to keep the software applications on user machines current. This section shows you how to configure an upgrade for a package using Group Policy and how to provide both mandatory and optional upgrades. Finally, you will learn how to remove software that is no longer needed by the organization or whose licenses have expired.

Upgrading a Package

In Microsoft Windows 2000 Group Policy, upgrades to existing packages can be one of two types: mandatory or optional.

Mandatory upgrades are those that must be installed where the previous version of the software exists. For example, say you repackaged Microsoft Office 97 and then received notification that the version on users' desktops is not the most recent one. You decide to upgrade all users to the most recent version of Office 97 to correct any deficiencies in the software. To do so, you configure the upgrade to be mandatory. The upgrade package is automatically installed on users' machines the next time the users log on (if the package was assigned to the users or was published) or the machines are restarted (if the software was assigned to the computers). Mandatory upgrades are an ideal way to ensure all users have the most recent version of critical business applications installed.

Optional upgrades enable the user to continue to use the older version of the software or, optionally, to upgrade to the most recent version. Optional upgrades provide users with a message indicating that a newer version is available and asking whether they want to upgrade now. If the user agrees to the upgrade, the new version of the software is installed and the old version is replaced. If the user does not agree to the upgrade, he will continue to work with the older version of the software. The user will also continue to be prompted to install the new version. You can also configure a "drop-dead date" by which users must install the upgrade, or it will be installed on their machines whether they like it or not (a kind of optional upgrade with a mandatory ending).

To perform either type of upgrade, follow Step By Step 11.11.

STEP BY STEP

11.11 Upgrading Software Using Group Policy

1. Repackage the upgraded version of the software, or acquire a Windows Installer Package with the upgraded software. To upgrade an existing package to a newer version, the newer version must also be in the form of a Windows Installer Package (or ZAP file). The first step in upgrading software is to either repackage the upgraded version, as previously shown, or acquire a Windows Installer Package.

2. Place the upgrade package in the shared folder to which users will connect and install the upgraded application.

3. Edit or create a GPO that will hold the new package. You can add the package to the same container in the GPO in which the earlier version was created. This is shown in Figure 11.50 for the sample Adobe Acrobat software package.

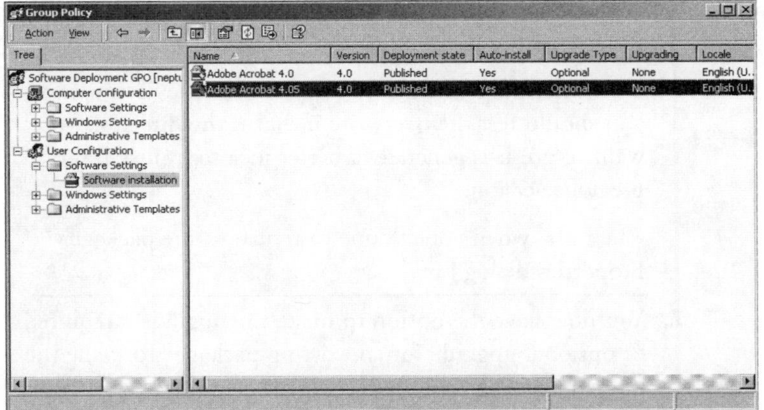

FIGURE 11.50
Adding a package to the GPO is required for the package to upgrade another package.

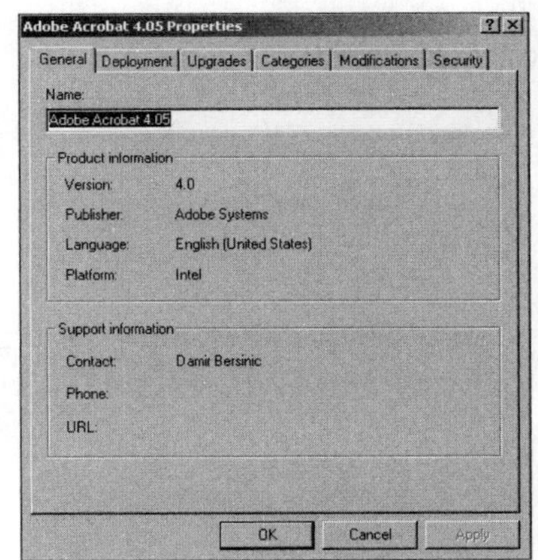

FIGURE 11.51
The package's Properties dialog box.

4. Modify the package to indicate that it will be used to upgrade an existing one. To do this, right-click the new package and select Properties. You are presented with the Properties dialog box for the package, as shown in Figure 11.51.

5. Click the Upgrades tab to show a list of other packages that this package will update, as shown in Figure 11.52.

continues

continued

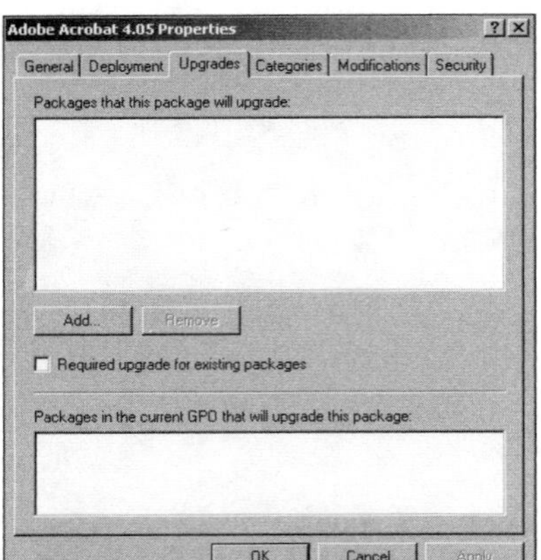

FIGURE 11.52
The Upgrades tab of the package's Properties dialog box in Group Policy.

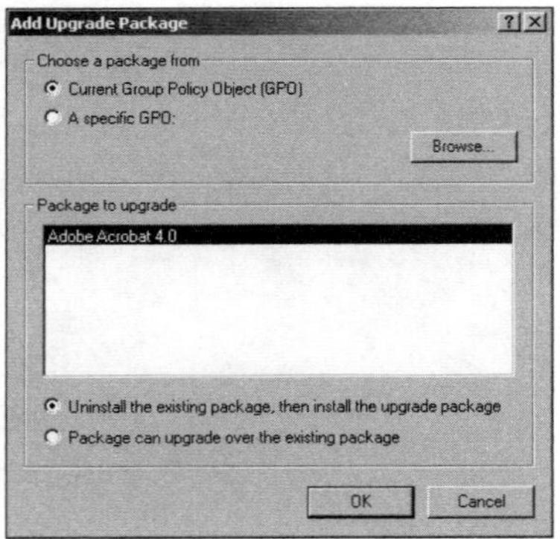

FIGURE 11.53
Specifying a package to be used to upgrade an existing package.

6. Click Add to add a package to the list of what can be used to upgrade the initial package. You are presented with a screen similar to Figure 11.53. This provides you with several choices including where to look for the upgrade package: in the current GPO or another GPO. You can then browse for a package to be used for the upgrade among the other GPOs available in the company. You also have the capability to specify how the upgrade will take place: by uninstalling the existing package and then installing the upgrade or by leaving the old software package intact and simply installing the upgrade over it.

   Care should be taken in setting the appropriate options to ensure the software works correctly after the upgrade. When deciding whether to uninstall the previous version, you should test the overwrite if that is the direction you want to go. It is generally a better idea to uninstall the previous version.

   Click OK when you're done to return to the package's Properties dialog box.

7. You now have the option to make the upgrade a required or optional upgrade for an existing package. To make the upgrade package required, click the Required Upgrade for Existing Packages check box, as shown in Figure 11.54. This causes the package to be installed automatically when a user logs on or a computer starts, based on how the initial package was deployed. When you have made your decision, click OK to close the Properties dialog box and save your changes.

8. As shown in Figure 11.55, you now have two packages in the Group Policy software packages details pane. The most recent package installed is designated as a required upgrade for the previous one in our example. Any new user installing the software gets the most recent package; existing users have their software upgraded automatically because the upgrade is marked as required. Close the Group Policy Editor MMC to have the GPO settings take effect.

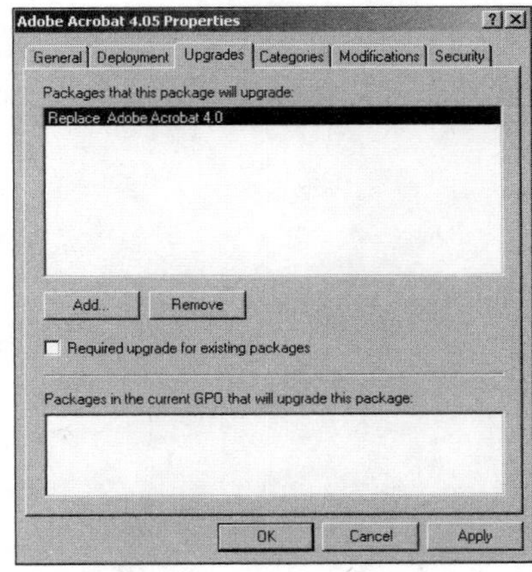

FIGURE 11.54
Package replacement information in the Upgrades tab of the package's Properties dialog box in Group Policy.

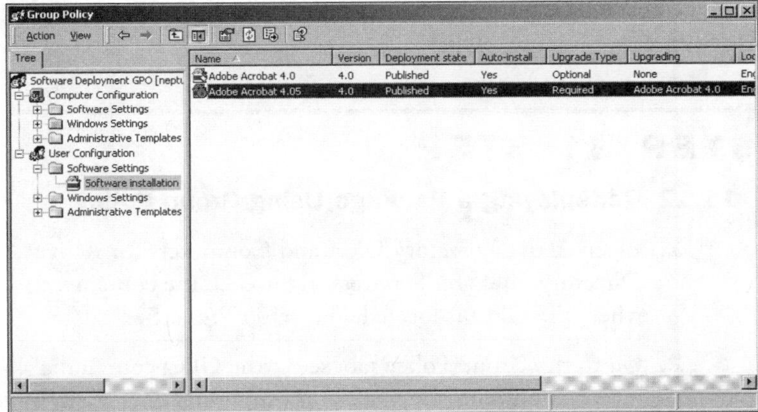

FIGURE 11.55
The Software package screen in Group Policy.

Configuring upgrades to packages is simple except for ensuring the upgrade is in the proper format (that is, an MSI file). You can configure the upgrade to be mandatory or optional. Mandatory upgrades force the user to replace the previous package with the new one. New users always receive the most recent version. However, what if you need to replace only certain files in a package, and not upgrade it?

Redeploying Software

In some situations, instead of upgrading a package, you might simply want to reinstall it on all users' machines. This method is known as *redeploying*—the reinstallation of an existing package. This method is preferable if you modified a package without changing its name (for example, you added or removed files from the package, which would include a patch to the software), added shortcuts, changed Registry settings, or in any other way changed an existing package. To ensure that all users have the updated software, you might want to redeploy the package.

You also can create a new package (MSI) file with the exact same name as the existing package and put it in the same location as the original package. Using this method, you can incorporate more widespread changes to the software than simply by modifying an existing package. As long as the version and package name are identical, it is considered to be the same software. You then can redeploy the package as necessary.

To redeploy a package, after making your modification, perform the steps shown in Step By Step 11.12.

STEP BY STEP

11.12 Redeploying a Package Using Group Policy

1. Open Active Directory Users and Computers (or Active Directory Sites and Services), right-click the container where the GPO is located, and select Properties.
2. Go to the Group Policy tab, select the GPO containing information on deploying the package, and click Edit. This opens the Group Policy Editor.
3. Expand the container in the Software Installation folder where the original package was specified and locate the package you want to redeploy, as shown in Figure 11.56.

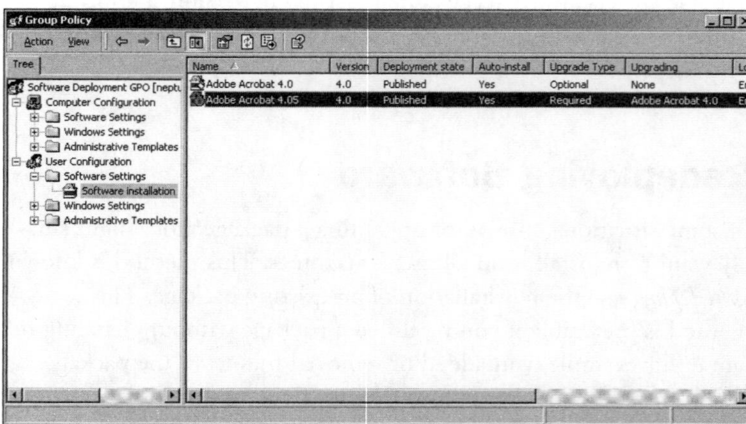

FIGURE 11.56
The package list in the Software installation folder of the Group Policy Editor.

4. To redeploy a package, right-click the package, select All Tasks, and then click Redeploy Application. Figure 11.57 shows the dialog box that asks you to confirm that you want to redeploy the application. Click Yes to do so.
5. Close the Group Policy Editor to commit to your changes.
6. Click OK to close the container Properties dialog box and then exit Active Directory Users and Computers.

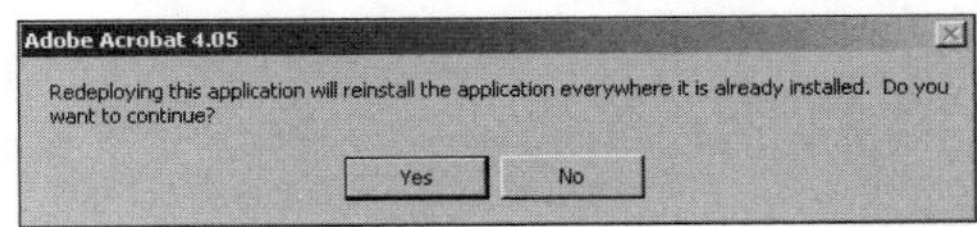

FIGURE 11.57
The redeployment confirmation Dialog box in Group Policy.

As you have seen, redeployment is simple in cases in which certain files for an application have been updated but the rest of the package stays largely intact. You should remember, however, that redeploying a package causes it to be reinstalled on all client machines, which can use up large amounts of network bandwidth.

Removing a Package

After you have deployed software using Group Policy, you also have the option to have Group Policy automate the removal of the software for you. In this way, applications that are no longer needed, or software that is out-of-date, can be removed from users' computers without a great deal of intervention on your part. This simplifies the administration of software deployment and the amount of manual effort that needs to be expended.

The removal options available in Group Policy can also be used in the case of an optional upgrade. In this situation, users have some time to upgrade to a new version. After a reasonable amount of time has lapsed, you can decide to remove the old version of the application from their machines.

Removal of software has two options:

- **Mandatory or forced removal**—The software is removed from the user's computer whether he still requires it. This is selected by specifying the Immediately Uninstall Software from Users and Computers option when configuring removal of a package for the GPO. The software is removed prior to the user's desktop being presented and is transparent to the user, if it was assigned to the user. If the package was assigned to the computer, it is removed the next time the computer restarts. If an upgrade of the software exists, the user can install the upgraded version to continue to have the functionality of the software; if not, the software becomes unavailable.

- **Optional removal**—Enables the user to continue to use the software. This option is selected when you specify the Allow Users to Continue to Use the Software But Prevent New Installations option when configuring removal. The software does not appear in the list of applications under Add/Remove Programs in Control Panel but does remain installed. After the user manually removes the software through Add/Remove Programs on his computer, he no longer can install it. This is considered the nice method of removing software, but it can be problematic if you want to maintain standard corporate software applications.

To configure removal of a package, perform the steps shown in Step By Step 11.13.

STEP BY STEP

11.13 Removing a Package Using Group Policy

1. Open Active Directory Users and Computers (or Active Directory Sites and Services), right-click the container where the GPO is located, and select Properties.
2. Go to the Group Policy tab, select the GPO containing information on the package you want to configure the removal of, and click Edit. This opens the Group Policy Editor.
3. Expand the container in the Software Installation folder where the original package was specified, and locate the package you want to remove.

4. To remove a package, right-click the package, select All Tasks, and then click Remove. Figure 11.58 shows the dialog box that asks you choose the type of removal (forced or optional). Select the method of removal and click OK to save your choice. You are then returned to the Group Policy Editor. Note that the package no longer appears on the list.

5. Close the Group Policy Editor to commit to your changes.

6. Click OK to close the container Properties dialog box and then exit Active Directory Users and Computers.

FIGURE 11.58
The package removal options selection dialog box in Group Policy.

Removing software using Group Policy is relatively simple. Keep in mind that, after you choose whether you want to use an optional removal or a forced removal, you can't change your mind. The package is removed from the GPO and is also removed from the user's machine, either forcibly or by the user agreeing to have it removed. If the user chooses to leave the package on the machine, you can't force its removal later; the package is no longer in the GPO.

MANAGING SOFTWARE DEPLOYMENT

The process of deploying software in large organizations might require that additional tasks be performed to make the deployment process more friendly by recognizing geographic and language differences. Deployment can be designed to help users select which software to install by creating software categories for similar packages. It also can be designed to automatically initiate the installation of software when a particular file is invoked by the user. The deployment process itself can encounter problems, and the administrator needs to be aware of how to correct some of the common problems encountered in software deployment. Repackaging applications can also present problems during deployment, and an administrator should be familiar these issues as well.

Managing software deployment basically has two aspects to it: configuring package modifications and creating software categories. These two aspects are discussed in the following two sections.

Configuring Package Modifications

Windows 2000 Group Policy enables the use of software modification, or transform files, to deploy several configurations of the same application. Transform files have an MST extension and are associated with an existing package. In combination with several GPOs, transform files are used to change the behavior of a package when it is deployed in different regions.

NOTE

Transform (MST) Files A transform file modifies what is installed on a user's computer based on the GPO used to deploy the software. After the software has been installed on a user's machine, it can't be modified using an MST file. Only prior to the installation taking place on a computer will the transform file have any effect. For example, 20 users have already installed application X, and you decide to specify a modification using a transform file of application X. Any users who already have application X installed can't have the modification deployed to them. Only users who do not have application X installed get the software modification specified in the MST file. To apply an MST file to all users (old and new), you also need to redeploy the package.

For example, say your organization, with offices in the United States, Canada, England, and France, wants to deploy Microsoft Office 2000 worldwide. However, you want to ensure that users in Paris and Quebec receive French dictionaries, as well as English, when Office 2000 is installed. To solve this problem, you create one package file for Office 2000. To deal with the different dictionaries that need to be supported, you create transform (MST) files for each dictionary. You then create a separate GPO for the Parisian site to include the Office 2000 package as well as the French dictionary MST file. For Quebec, you could use the same or another GPO to also roll out the French dictionary. For Canada, the United States, and England, you might create one or more GPOs that would include the English dictionary transform file.

To add modifications to a software package, perform the steps in Step By Step 11.14.

STEP BY STEP

11.14 Modifying a Package with an MST File

1. Open Active Directory Users and Computers (or Active Directory Sites and Services), right-click the container where the GPO is located, and select Properties.
2. Go to the Group Policy tab, select the GPO containing information on the package you want to modify, and click Edit. This opens the Group Policy Editor.
3. Expand the container in the Software Installation folder where the original package was specified, and locate the package to which you want to add a transform file.

4. To add modifications, right-click the package, select Properties, and then click the Modifications tab. A screen similar to Figure 11.59 displays.
5. Click Add to add an MST file; then, in the Open dialog box, select the path and filename of the MST file to be used to modify this package and click OK.
6. You can specify more than one MST file for the same package by repeating step 5. If specifying more than one MST file for the same package, they will be processed according the order presented on the Modifications tab for the package. You can use the Move Up and Move Down buttons to specify the order of processing.
7. Click OK to close the package's Properties dialog box.
8. Close the Group Policy Editor to commit your changes.
9. Click OK to close the container's Properties dialog box and then exit Active Directory Users and Computers.

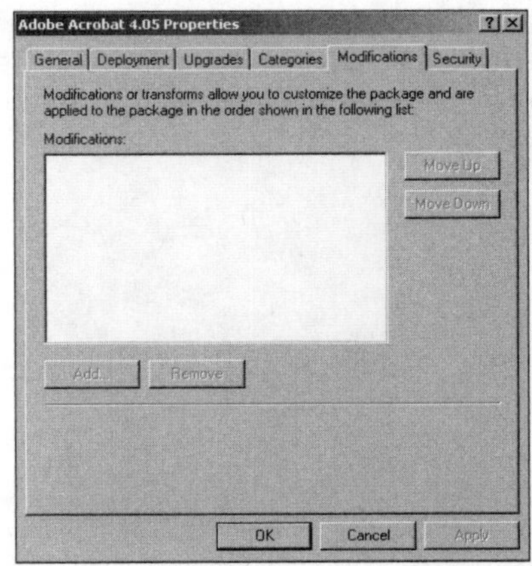

FIGURE 11.59
Modifications to a package can be added from this dialog box.

Using software modifications in the scope of software deployment in a GPO enables you to modify the settings for an application package being deployed. This is a good way to have the same package deployed to different users or computers without having to repackage the software for each specific configuration. Transform files enable you to store only the specific changes to be applied against a package and to have those deployed with a specific GPO.

Creating Software Categories

In large organizations, or even in smaller ones in which many different software applications are in use, it might be beneficial to create software categories to make enable users to more easily install the package they want. Creating software categories changes the display in Add/Remove Programs in Control Panel and enables the user to locate software of the type she needs (see Figure 11.60).

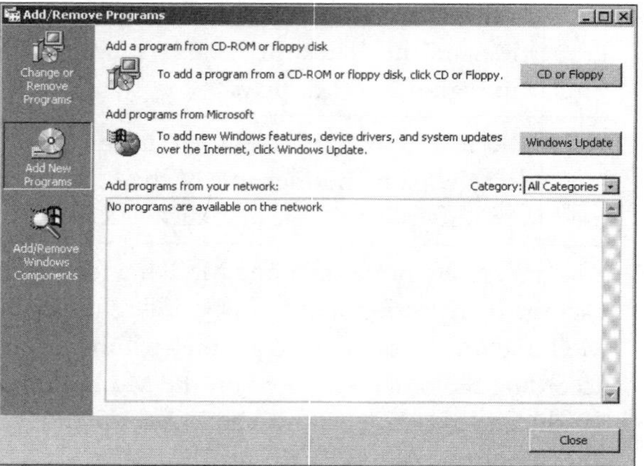

FIGURE 11.60
Add/Remove Programs in Control Panel lists packages available on the network in categories.

For example, using Group Policy, you decide to deploy many different packages including accounting applications, word processors, utilities, spreadsheets, and Internet browsers. By default, all the software available on the network is listed under a single category. If many applications are available, this requires the user to scroll down until she finds the necessary package, and it could make the process more difficult. By creating software categories, the user is able to select the category of software she wants to install from the Category drop-down list box. This display can be limited to only the software placed in the category.

A single application can appear in more than one category. For example, Microsoft Office 2000 can be placed in the Office Packages category as well as in Word Processors, Spreadsheets, and Presentation Software because it includes all these. Specifying a category for a particular package just makes finding the application easier for the user. It does not, in any way, change the behavior of the Group Policy in which the package is configured for deployment. Furthermore, if you add new categories or decide to start using categories, you can modify the software category under which a package should be listed at any time. This enables you to easily redefine and streamline categories should this be required.

One important point that needs to be conveyed is that categories configured in any GPO on the domain are available throughout the domain. This means that software categories function on a domain-wide basis. You can access the Categories tab from any GPO in any OU in the domain. Any changes made to the categories listed are reflected throughout the domain. You can't have one set of categories in the Sales OU, for example, and another set in the Development OU of the same domain. All categories in all OUs are available throughout the domain. However, you can have different sets of categories in different domains.

To create software categories, follow the steps in Step By Step 11.15.

STEP BY STEP

11.15 Creating Software Categories for the Domain

1. Open Active Directory Users and Computers (or Active Directory Sites and Services), right-click the container where the GPO is located, and select Properties.
2. Go to the Group Policy tab, select the GPO containing information on the package you want to modify, and click Edit. This opens the Group Policy Editor.
3. Expand either Computer Configuration or User Configuration, and then expand the Software Settings folder.
4. Right-click Software Installation and select Properties.
5. Click the Categories tab to see the list of categories currently configured, if any, as shown in Figure 11.61.
6. To add a category, click the Add button. A dialog box similar to Figure 11.62 is presented. Type in the name of the category you want to add and click OK to save the category.
7. You are now returned to the Software Installation Properties dialog box where the new category will be listed (see Figure 11.63). Click Add to add more categories, click Modify to change the name of an existing category, or click Remove to remove a category. When you are done, click Apply and then click OK to save your changes.

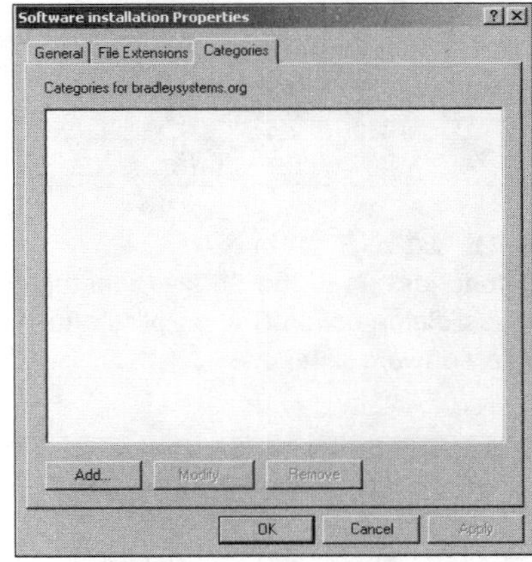

FIGURE 11.61
The Categories tab of the Software Installation Properties dialog box in Group Policy.

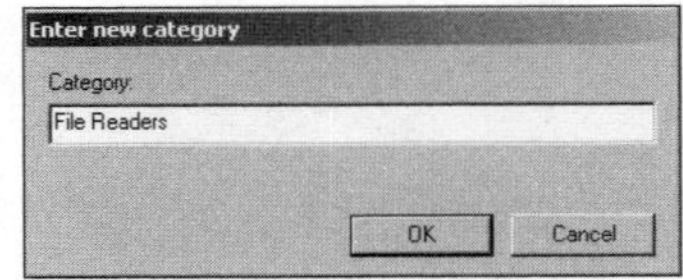

FIGURE 11.62
Clicking Add opens the Enter New Category dialog box.

continues

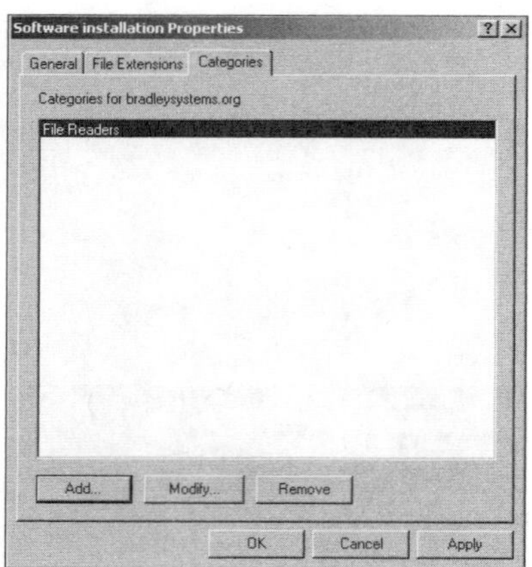

FIGURE 11.63
The Categories tab of the Software Installation Properties dialog box in Group Policy after adding a software category.

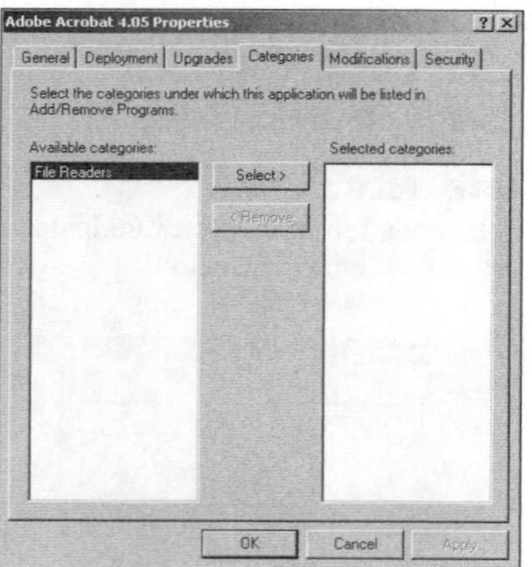

FIGURE 11.64
The Categories tab of the package shows the list of available categories and the ones selected for this package.

continued

8. Close the Group Policy Editor to commit your changes.
9. Click OK to close the container Properties dialog box and then exit Active Directory Users and Computers.

After you have created the categories, they can be used to categorize existing or new packages you have configured for deployment. To assign a software category to a package, follow the steps in Step By Step 11.16.

STEP BY STEP

11.16 Assigning a Software Package to a Category

1. Open Active Directory Users and Computers (or Active Directory Sites and Services), right-click the container where the GPO is located, and select Properties.
2. Go to the Group Policy tab, select the GPO containing information on the package you want to modify, and click Edit. This opens the Group Policy Editor.
3. Expand either Computer Configuration or User Configuration, and then expand the Software Settings folder.
4. Select the package to which you want to assign a category from the list presented when you click Software Installation. Right-click the package and select Properties.
5. Click the Categories tab to see the list of categories available and assigned to this package, as shown in Figure 11.64.
6. Click the category to which you want to assign this package under Available Categories, and then click Select to assign this package to the category. To remove this package from a category, select the category to remove under Selected Categories and click Remove. When you are done, click OK to save your changes.

7. Close the Group Policy Editor to commit your changes.

8. Click OK to close the container Properties dialog box and then exit Active Directory Users and Computers.

You have now created categories and assigned a package to one or more categories. When you go to Control Panel and select Add/Remove Programs, the list of available software that can be installed is revealed. This enables you to select the category of software you want to install and shows only the packages configured in that category.

As you have seen, creating categories for software is easy. It is of great benefit to organizations that want to publish many applications using Group Policy. It also enables users to more easily find the applications they want to install. Administrators categorize the packages available, and then users can use these categories to browse what is available. As noted, the same package can exist in multiple categories.

But what if users did not have access to Add/Remove Programs in Control Panel?

Associating File Extensions with Applications

Windows 2000 Active Directory provides new functionality when deploying software applications using Group Policy. When you obtain a package (MSI) file or after you repackage an application using third-party products such as Veritas WinINSTALL LE, you might find that the package publishes file extensions supported by the software.

For example, Adobe Acrobat 4.05 was published in the previous example, and it told Windows 2000 Active Directory that it could be used to open files with a PDF extension. This is very handy. It can provide for automatic installation of the software application on a user's machine whenever he double-clicks a PDF file to open it and the software is not yet installed on the machine. In this way, users can invoke the installation of a particular software application when they attempt to open an associated file and the software is not yet installed.

The list of file extensions and applications (packages) that support these extensions is published and tracked by Windows 2000 Active Directory. The mapping of file extension to software package is kept domain-wide, but the determination of which software package is installed when a user attempts to open a file of a particular extension can be configured at an OU or some other level. This means users in one particular branch of Active Directory (the Sales OU, for example) can install one application when they activate a document by double-clicking it, whereas users in another OU (the Development OU) can have a different application installed.

For example, say you need to support both Microsoft Word 2000 and WordPerfect 2000 in your organization for files with a DOC extension. Users in your legal department, for historical reasons, prefer to use WordPerfect 2000 to edit their documents. The WordPerfect application has templates and other useful tools to be used by the lawyers and clerks in that part of the organization. Users in other departments in the company, however, prefer to use Word 2000 because this is the corporate standard for word processing. You can configure the priority of the application to be used in the legal department when a file with the DOC extension is activated by adjusting the GPO used to deploy software in the Legal OU. All other parts of the company have Microsoft Word 2000 associated with the DOC extension at a higher priority than WordPerfect 2000 and, therefore, have that application installed when they open a DOC file.

NOTE

Windows 2000 Only File extension priority can be configured only for applications being deployed using Windows 2000 Group Policy (that is, that are configured as a Windows Installer Package). Even though another application that might be a standard component of Windows 2000 might support opening a file with a particular extension, the application can't be associated with the extension in the GPO. For example, WordPad in Windows 2000 can be used to open a file with a DOC extension, but WordPad can't be associated with the DOC extension in the GPO. This is because there is no package used to deploy WordPad through a GPO. If you want to associate WordPad with the DOC extension, you need to create a package to deploy WordPad.

The main point here is that file extension priority applies only to packages deployed using Windows 2000 Group Policy. It does not apply to software deployed using any other method.

Filename extension priorities are configured on a per-GPO basis. You configure the priority of a particular application to be installed through document activation in the GPO, and it affects only users who have the GPO applied to them. Other users are not affected by the priority established in a GPO and might, in fact, install different applications for the same file extension. For example, if you set WordPerfect 2000 as the default application for the DOC extension in the Legal GPO, only users in the Legal OU will have WordPerfect 2000 installed when they activate a DOC file.

To modify and configure filename extension priorities, perform the steps in Step By Step 11.17.

STEP BY STEP

11.17 Configuring File Extension Priority for a GPO

1. Open Active Directory Users and Computers (or Active Directory Sites and Services), right-click the container where the GPO is located, and select Properties.
2. Go to the Group Policy tab, select the GPO containing information on the package you want to modify, and click Edit. This opens the Group Policy Editor.
3. Expand either Computer Configuration or User Configuration, and then expand the Software Settings folder.
4. Right-click the Software Installation container and select Properties.
5. Click the File Extensions tab to see a list of packages and file extensions currently configured, as shown in Figure 11.65.
6. Select the extension whose application priority you want to modify by using the drop-down list box to see a list of software applications associated with that extension.
7. Use the Up and Down buttons to bring the application that should be installed by default to the top of the list. Click OK when you're done to save your changes.
8. Close the Group Policy Editor to commit your changes.
9. Click OK to close the container Properties dialog box and then exit Active Directory Users and Computers.

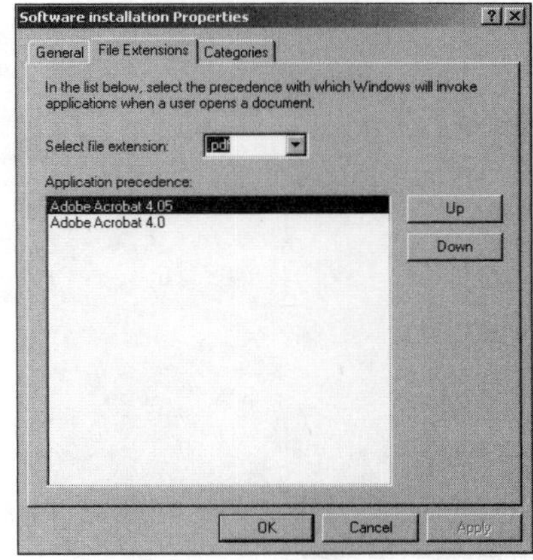

FIGURE 11.65
The File Extensions tab of the Software Installation Properties dialog box.

If you're wondering how the file extension got associated with a particular package, think back to the "Packaging Software for Deployment" section of this chapter. If you recall, when repackaging an application, you were able to specify with which file extensions that application would be associated. In the same vein, when a software developer creates a package to be used to install his software, he also associates certain file extensions with his application. In this way, users are able to use the application as intended.

Whichever way is used to associate an extension with an application, this association is published in Active Directory and is maintained on each client machine. This is so the files can be opened and the users are not left in a situation in which they have files that can't be used.

Troubleshooting Software Deployment

After you have configured software deployment—especially if you have a large organization with many GPOs used to deploy software—there might be occasions when the deployment is not working exactly as you would expect. Some of the more common problems and their causes are listed in Table 11.2.

TABLE 11.2

COMMON DEPLOYMENT PROBLEMS

Problem	*Cause and Resolution*
Application can't be installed.	The most likely cause of this problem is that the user can't reach the network share where the application package is located. Verify that the share is, in fact, available and that the user has permissions to access the package files. The permissions required are Read on the share and Read and Execute at the NTFS level on the volume where the package files are located. The NTFS permissions are required for all files and folders that make up the package.
Applications do not appear as expected on the user's desktop.	The most likely cause of this problem is in the way the application was deployed. If the application was assigned to the user, the shortcuts for the application should appear on the user's desktop. If they do not, log in as the user and check to see whether the application is listed under Add/Remove Programs in Control Panel. If it is then the application was published, not assigned. In this case, the user must install the application manually or have the installation begin through document activation.
	If the application is not listed in Add/Remove Programs and no shortcuts appear on the desktop, it might be that the application was never deployed or was deployed in another OU. It is also possible that the application was deployed in the correct OU, but the user has been filtered out of the scope of the GPO where the application deployment is defined. Check the security settings for the GPO to ensure that the user is not filtered from the GPO settings.
Deployed applications do not work properly after installation.	In some cases in which applications are repackaged using a third-party packaging program such as Veritas WinINSTALL LE, the process might not have taken place properly. If, during repackaging, the setup program of the application did not install certain files on the hard drive of the reference computer, for example, these files will not be in the package file created and will need to exist on the user's hard drive. If they are not found, the application might not work properly after it is deployed. To correct the problem, repackage the application or add the necessary files to the package.

Problem	*Cause and Resolution*
Package installation removes other files.	This is also a repackaging problem. When an application is repackaged, the period between the before and after snapshot can cause other changes to be made on the system if other programs are launched. This can cause the final package, once the after snapshot is created, to include instructions to remove files from the hard drive. If this is the case, when the package is deployed, it will cause those same files to be removed from the user's computer and might cause other software to stop functioning. To solve this problem, modify the package to remove any reference to file deletion or repackage the software to ensure it is correctly configured.
Applications are not deployed as expected or are not deployed at all.	The most likely cause of this is Group Policy conflicts. GPOs can be created at different levels of Active Directory, and these same GPOs can have application deployment configured within them. A setting in one GPO associated with an Active Directory container might conflict with a setting in another GPO in a lower-level Active Directory container. Furthermore, because software can be assigned to both computers and users, computer settings can override user settings depending on the AD level at which they are applied. For example, if a user has been assigned Microsoft Word 2000 at the domain GPO level, but this same application has been denied to him at the OU level, the application will not be installed. Furthermore, if a user has been assigned an application such as Microsoft Excel 2000 at the domain level, but Microsoft Excel 2000 has been marked for mandatory removal from his computer, Microsoft Excel 2000 will not be available to him. It is always a good idea to check the inheritance of GPOs in the Active Directory structure.

As you have read in Table 11.2, many of the common problems associated with software deployment deal with either improper repackaging or Group Policy issues. Understanding how GPOs work in general (whether you are using GPOs for software deployment) is critical. Testing software deployment on a few machines before rolling it out on a large scale reduces the chances of experiencing a large-scale problem.

SECURITY SETTINGS AVAILABLE IN WINDOWS 2000 GROUP POLICY

- Implement and manage security policies by using Group Policy.
    - Use security templates to implement security policies.
    - Analyze the security configuration of a computer by using the SECEDIT command and Security Configuration and Analysis.
    - Modify domain security policy to comply with corporate standards.

Group Policy can be used to apply both computer and group settings. This remains true for applying security policy. However, because the more important element in security is to ensure access to resources is restricted to only those individuals who should have it, Group Policy in the security context is overwhelmingly slanted toward the computer side of Group Policy.

As is evident in Figure 11.66, the number of items that can be specified in the Computer Configuration of Group Policy is quite extensive as compared to the User Configuration portion. The User Configuration portion lists only one entry: Public Key Policies. The settings that can be configured in Group Policy for the computer are outlined in the following table.

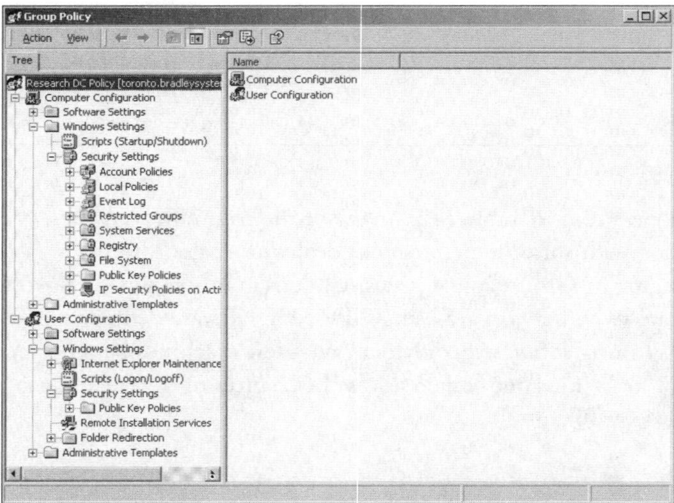

FIGURE 11.66
Group Policy security configuration options.

Setting	*Description*
Account Policies	Enables you to specify password and account lockout policy settings. Password policy settings include the password age (minimum and maximum), number of passwords that will be remembered to prevent reuse of a favorite password by users for a time (that is, until the number of remembered passwords has been reached), minimum password length, and password complexity. You also have the option to configure storing the password using reversible encryption. Account lockout policy settings include the duration of account lockout, number of incorrect login attempts before invoking lockout, and account lockout interval—the time between failed login attempts before the counter is reset.

Setting	*Description*
Local Policies	Enables you to configure local computer settings for auditing, user rights assignment (for example, Logon Locally or Logon As a Service), and specific computer security options (such as message text to present to the user prior to logon, whether the last user logon name should display when logging on, and others).
Event Log	Enables the configuration of log file sizes for the three main event logs (system, security, and application), whether logs should be overwritten after their maximum sizes are reached, and any restrictions on who is allowed to read the log files.
Restricted Groups	Enables you to manage which users can be members of certain security groups and to configure of which other groups these groups can also be members. In other words, this setting enables you to configure group membership using the security policy to ensure that users are always members of certain groups and that certain groups are members of other groups when the policy is applied.
System Services	Enables the administrator to specify how services and devices will be started on the computer. In this way, you can ensure that required services are started on the target computers, while services that can cause problems are prevented from starting.
Registry	Enables you to configure security on Registry keys. Through the security policy, you can set who is able to modify keys, read keys, and add new keys to the Registry.
File System	Through this security setting, you are able to specify file system security settings for folders and files on NTFS partitions and to ensure they will apply when the policy is in effect.
Public Key Policies	Enables you to set which users will be data recovery agents for the Encrypting File System (EFS). Recovery agents can decrypt files when the user who created them is not available or has been deleted. Here you can also import certificate files from root certification authorities that will be trusted by Windows 2000, configure trust settings for authorities and certificates they have issued, and specify automatic certificate request settings. Windows 2000 has come a long way to ensure that secure communication takes place and that only those computers and users that have valid proof of authentication, such as certificates, are allowed access. These key security functions are implemented through Group Policy.
IP Security Polices on Active Directory	Enables you to configure how clients, servers, and domain controllers communicate and what level of security is requested, required, or declined. These settings apply to TCP/IP traffic between the various types of Windows 2000 computers.

On the User Configuration side, only one area of configuration exists in Group Policy: Public key policies.

Public key policies that can be configured have only a single area: enterprise trusts. This enables the administrator to specify for the user which root certification authorities will be trusted and ensures that no other authorities are allowed by the user.

Windows 2000 enables you to configure security in many areas, including password management and account policies, local computer policies, restricted group memberships, Registry settings, and file system settings. You can also configure public key policies for the Encrypting File System, for example, and network communication through IPSec policies. These can be configured for the computer primarily, with a subset available for the user.

Implementing Security Policies

In Windows 2000, the two main ways to implement security policies are using Security Templates and using Group Policy. When evaluating security templates, you need to understand both the basics of establishing the templates and the analysis tool Microsoft provides. The difference between security templates and Group Policy is not that great. Templates make reapplying similar settings to many systems easier. A selection of settings also can be saved using a text file and then be reapplied in different areas if necessary.

Security Templates in Windows 2000

A security template is a text file with an INF extension (for example, `SECUREDC.INF`). This file includes security settings that can be applied to a single computer using the Security Configuration and Analysis MMC snap-in. These settings also can be imported into Group Policy and applied at the site, domain, or OU level. Security templates are a preconfigured list of settings and can include one or more of the sections previously described.

Microsoft Windows 2000 ships with several preconfigured security templates designed to be used in domain controllers, servers, and workstations. These templates include four levels of security that can impact the level of application functionality available. For example, if you decide to use a high level of security, some applications that use other portions of the operating system might not function correctly because the user might not have access to these secured areas of the operating system. Security templates are stored in the `WINNT\Security\Templates` folder on Windows 2000 computers. The four levels of security templates are as follows:

- **Basic**—Basic templates are the default security level of Windows 2000. They provide a high degree of application functionality but prevent basic security problems such as users configuring blank passwords or reusing the same passwords over and over again.

  As shown in Figure 11.67, Microsoft ships default basic templates for domain controllers (`basicdc`), servers (`basicsv`), and workstations (`basicwk`).

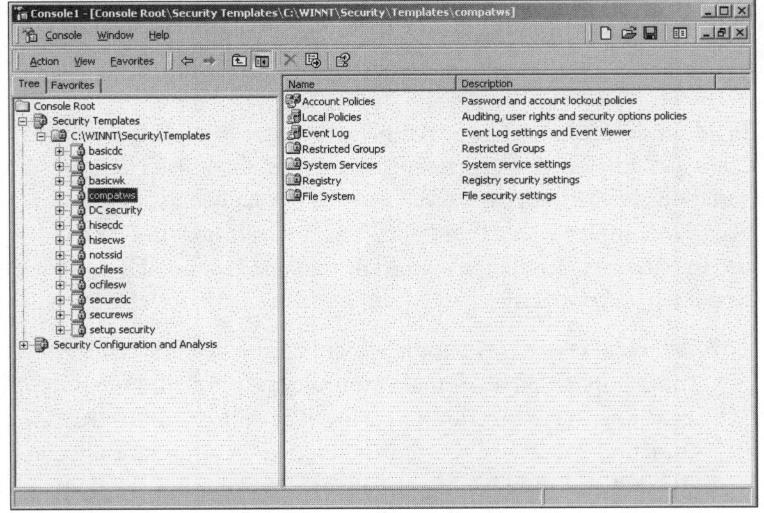

FIGURE 11.67
Preconfigured default security templates are shipped with Windows 2000.

- **Compatible**—Compatible templates provide more security, such as restricted access to certain parts of the Registry, but still ensure that business applications run as required. Windows 2000 includes only one compatible template for workstations by default (`compatws`).
- **Secure**—Secure templates begin to make security more important than business application functionality. This means that

business applications are not guaranteed to function in a secure environment because they might attempt to use portions of the operating system that have been secured. For example, business applications might put messages in the application log of Event Viewer without proper permissions. Secure templates are included for domain controllers (`securedc`) and workstations (`securews`).

- **High**—High templates enforce the maximum-security settings in Windows 2000 and do not guarantee that line-of-business applications (such as Microsoft Word 2000, accounting systems, and so on) will work. They are not normally used in a Windows 2000 environment because they might break too many applications, but they are useful in the development of high-security Windows 2000 applications. High-security templates include the signing of IP packets between server and workstation, lockout and disconnection of users, protection of Registry and file system components, and many other settings. Windows 2000 ships with high-security templates for domain controller (`hisecdc`) and workstations (`hisecws`).

In addition to the four basic template settings, Microsoft Windows 2000 also ships with other templates for specific tasks. These are all variations of the four basic levels but are not named as such in the Security Templates MMC snap-in. You find out how to open and use the Security Templates snap-in in the next section. These additional templates are

- **`DC security`**—This template includes the default security settings applied on all domain controllers. It includes file system and Registry protection to ensure that domain controllers function properly. DC security template is automatically configured and installed on all domain controllers in the domain and is part of the Default Domain Controller policy in the Domain Controller container in Active Directory.
- **`notssid`**—The `notssid` template simply removes the terminal server SID from the Windows 2000 Server computer and does not allow Terminal Services to be used on the computer. It modifies the Registry and file system to remove Terminal Services. This can be useful to prevent Terminal Services from being installed on a server that might already be busy or that might not have sufficient resources to host Terminal Services.

- **`ocfiless`**—The `ocfiless` security template is used to provide additional file security on Windows 2000 Server machines. The files included on the policy might not be installed, which can be problematic because the policy removes permissions to install the files for most users, including Administrator and System. This template should not be applied prior to installing the files protected by it (that is, install all the software first and then apply the policy). To modify the installed files, you need to remove the policy or filter it out.
- **`ocfilesw`**—This policy template is similar to `ocfiless` except it applies to Windows 2000 Professional computers. The main difference between these two templates is the files included; a number of files on Windows 2000 Server machines do not exist on Windows 2000 Professional.
- **`setup security`**—This template is the default, out-of-the-box setting applied to Windows 2000 Professional and Server computers.

Using Security Configuration and Analysis

Another tool that can be used to configure security settings on a computer is the Security Configuration and Analysis snap-in for MMC. The Security Templates snap-in was used to configure settings, which will later be imported into Group Policy. Security Configuration and Analysis is primarily designed to analyze local system security settings and apply security templates to the local computer. It can also be used to retrieve the local computer security configuration and to create a security template that will reflect the computer's settings.

In analyzing your system's security settings, Security Configuration and Analysis can be used to import a security template. This will be compared with the local machine's security configuration. The results of the analysis can be stored in a database, which enables the administrator to track changes in security settings over time. The default extension for the database file is SDB, and one SDB file is created by default when you install Windows 2000, although you can't access it directly.

In configuring system security, Security Configuration and Analysis can be used to import security template settings and then apply them directly on the local computer. Unlike Group Policy, Security Configuration and Analysis can't be used to apply the template settings to more than one computer at a time. If you need to do this, you should import a security template into Group Policy in the Active Directory container where the machines are located.

To open Microsoft Management Console (MMC) and add the Security Configuration and Analysis snap-in to the console, follow the steps presented in Step By Step 11.18.

STEP BY STEP

11.18 Configuring MMC with the Security Configuration and Analysis Snap-In

1. Log on to your Windows 2000 computer as Administrator.
2. From the Start menu, select Run. In the Run dialog box, enter `mmc`.
3. From the Console menu of the MMC console window presented, select Add/Remove Snap-in.
4. In the Add/Remove Snap-in dialog box opened, click the Add button to be shown the Add Standalone Snap-in dialog box, which enables you to choose the snap-in to add.
5. Scroll down until you find Security Configuration and Analysis, and then either double-click Security Templates or click the Add button to add the Security Configuration and Analysis snap-in to the MMC console, as shown in Figure 11.68.
6. Click Close to close the Add Standalone Snap-in dialog box.
7. Click OK to close the Add/Remove Snap-in dialog box.
8. To save your console settings, from the Console menu, select Save As and then type the filename in the Save As dialog box.
9. If you are finished, close the MMC console.

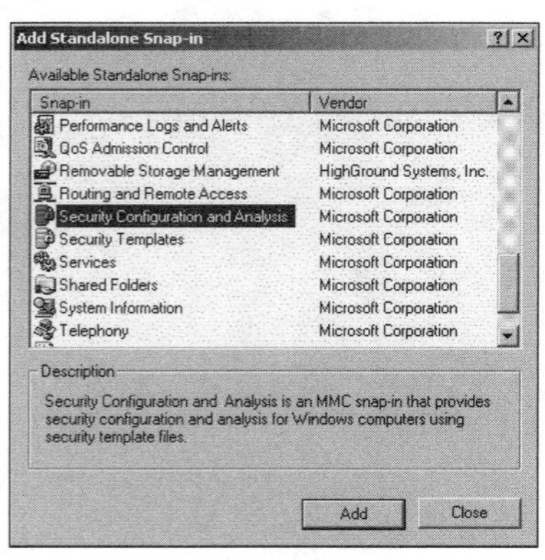

FIGURE 11.68
Click Add to add the Security Configuration and Analysis snap-in to the MMC console.

A database to hold security settings must be created when using the Security Configuration and Analysis snap-in. You can then use this database to perform analysis of your settings against a security template as well as to store your current configuration.

To create a database to be used to analyze your computer against a template, follow the steps shown in Step By Step 11.19.

STEP BY STEP

11.19 Configuring a Database for Analyzing Your Computer in Security Configuration and Analysis

1. Log on to your Windows 2000 computer as Administrator and open the Security Configuration and Analysis MMC console you created in Step By Step 11.18.
2. Click Security Configuration and Analysis to display the database requirements, as shown in Figure 11.69.

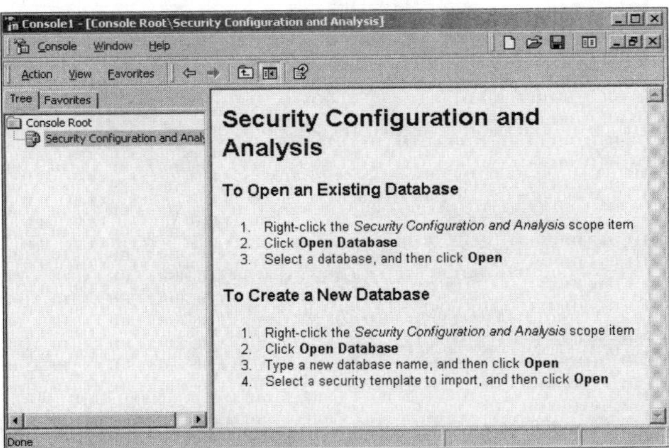

FIGURE 11.69
Security Configuration and Analysis requires a database to store security settings.

3. To create a database, follow the instructions displayed. Right-click Security Configuration and Analysis and select Open Database, as shown in Figure 11.70.

continues

continued

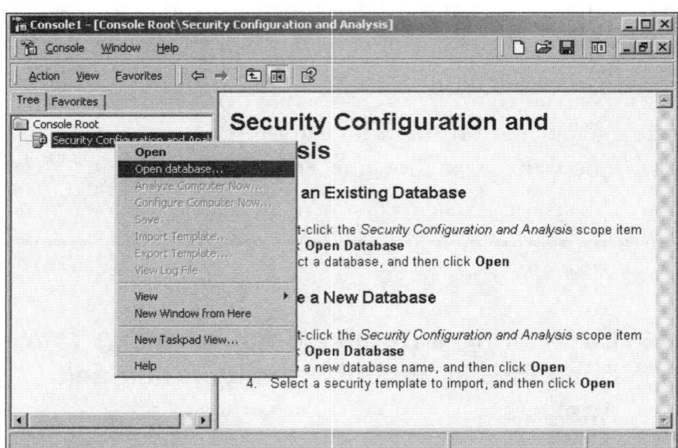

FIGURE 11.70
To create a database, select Open Database after right-clicking Security Configuration and Analysis.

4. In the File Name field of the Open Database dialog box, type the name of the database file you want to create and click Open (see Figure 11.71).

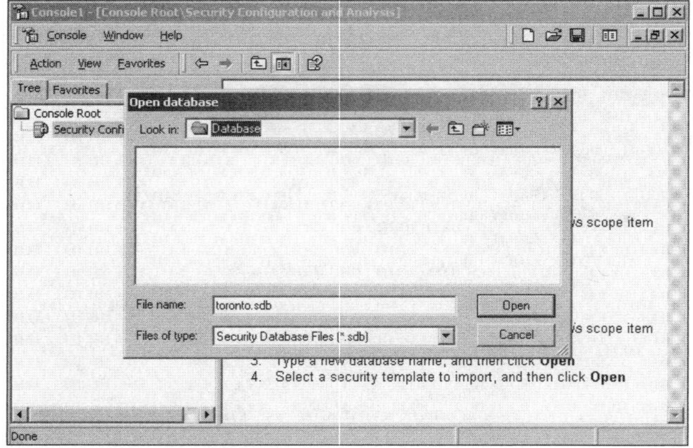

FIGURE 11.71
Select the filename and location of the Security Analysis and Configuration database.

Note that the default location of the database file being created is in your user profile in a folder called `security`. If you want to change the location of the database file, change the target folder by using the Look In drop-down list box.

5. You are next presented with a dialog box similar to Figure 11.72, in which you are asked to import a security template to be used to compare the computer's security settings against those in the template. You should select the template whose security settings are desired for the computer on which you are running Security Configuration and Analysis. For example, if you wanted to configure a domain controller with basic security settings, you would select basicdc as the security template file to import. Choose a template and click Open to load its settings.

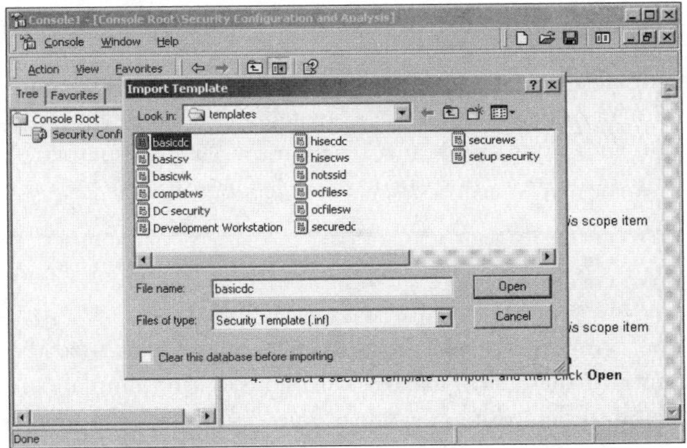

FIGURE 11.72
Click the security template whose settings should be used as the basis for analyzing the local computer, and click Open.

6. After selecting a template, Security Configuration and Analysis imports its settings and then changes the details pane of MMC to display information on how to configure your computer to use those settings or how to analyze your computer settings, as shown in Figure 11.73.

continues

continued

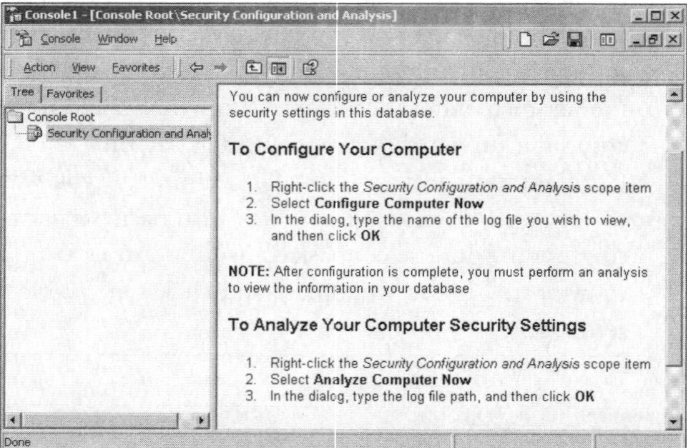

FIGURE 11.73
After importing a template, you can use it to configure your computer's security settings or to analyze your settings using the template as a point of comparison.

7. At this point, you have created a database that you can later use to analyze your computer against template settings. Close the MMC console when finished.

At this point, you have configured an MMC console with the Security Configuration and Analysis snap-in and have used that console to import the security settings from a security template. This enables you to determine how close your computer's current settings are to those in the template, as you will learn in the next section.

Analyzing Your Computer Using Security Configuration and Analysis

Analyzing a computer's security settings means comparing the current configuration of the computer to the desired configuration as stored in a security template. The tool used is the Security Configuration and Analysis MMC snap-in. You can compare security settings against a template to ensure the computer's settings are in compliance with a corporate security policy or to determine whether the settings have changed since the last time you performed the analysis.

To analyze a computer's security, perform the steps included in Step By Step 11.20.

STEP BY STEP

11.20 Analyzing a Computer's Security Configuration Using Security Configuration and Analysis

1. Log on to your Windows 2000 computer as Administrator and open the Security Configuration and Analysis MMC console you created in Step By Step 11.19.

2. Right-click Security Configuration and Analysis and select Open Database.

3. In the Open Database dialog box, locate the name of the database file you created in Step By Step 11.19, click it, and then click Open.

4. To perform an analysis of your system, you must select a security template to use as a comparison. As shown in Figure 11.74, right-click Security Configuration and Analysis and select Import Template from the list of menu choices.

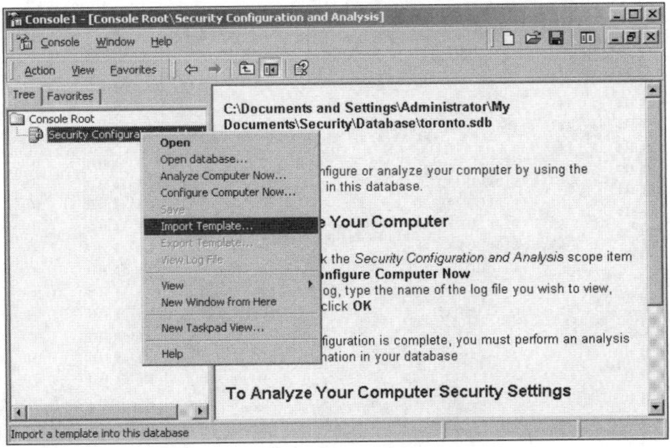

FIGURE 11.74
Right-click Security Configuration and Analysis and select Import Template to import a template to be used as the basis for analysis.

5. In the dialog box presented, select the template you want to use as the basis for analysis of your computer and click Open. As previously mentioned, select a template that closely matches the desired settings.

continues

continued

6. To perform the analysis, right-click Security Configuration and Analysis and select Analyze Computer Now, as shown in Figure 11.75.

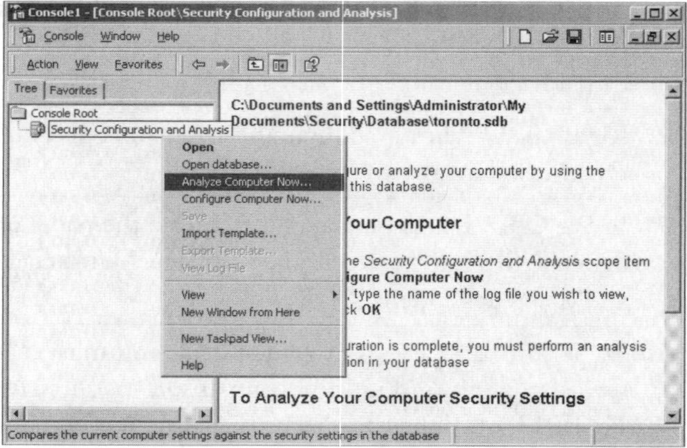

FIGURE 11.75
Right-click Security Configuration and Analysis and select Analyze Computer Now to start the analysis.

7. You are prompted to select the location of an error log file that might be generated during the analysis process (see Figure 11.76). Keep the default path, or select another one you desire; then click OK.

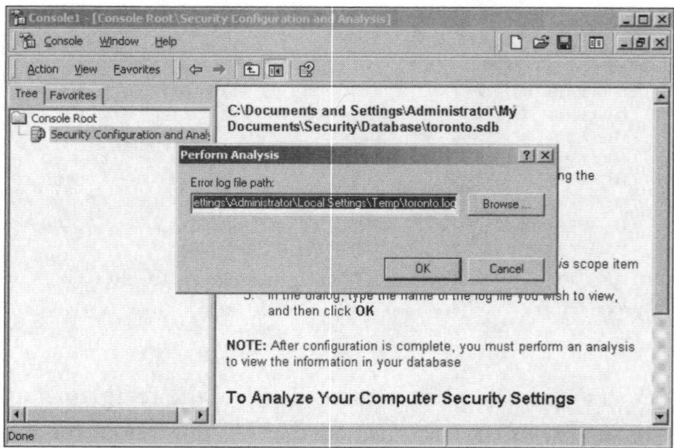

FIGURE 11.76
Choose a path and filename for the analysis error log file.

8. The analysis of the computer's security settings begins and you are presented with the Analyzing System Security progress dialog box, as shown in Figure 11.77.

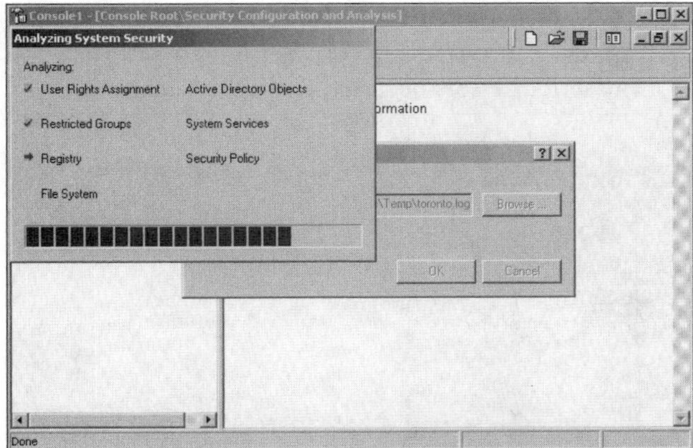

FIGURE 11.77
As the analysis proceeds, the Analyzing System Security dialog box shows status information.

9. After the analysis has completed, the console appearance changes to show all the areas that were included in the template and compared against current computer settings, as shown in Figure 11.78. You have several choices available at this point.

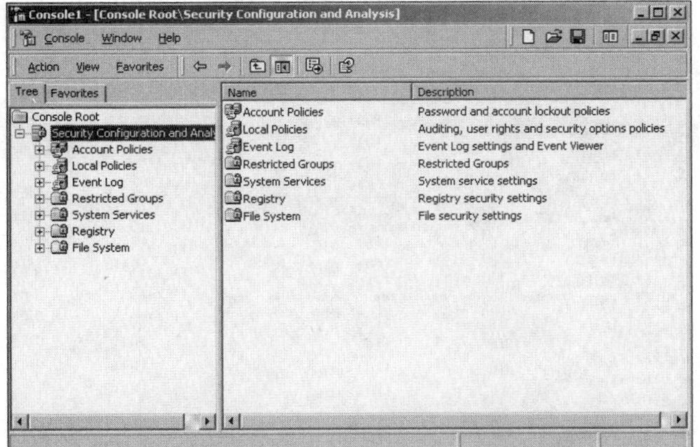

FIGURE 11.78
After the analysis is completed, all security settings in the template are visible in the MMC console.

continues

continued

10. To view the analysis log file, right-click Security Configuration and Analysis and make sure the View Log File menu option is checked. As shown in Figure 11.79, the display in the details pane now changes to show the log file. You can review the log file to determine whether any serious errors occurred during the analysis.

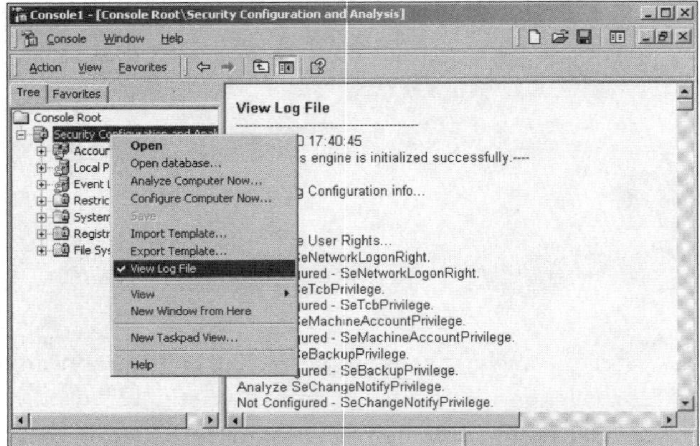

FIGURE 11.79
To view the analysis log file, right-click Security Configuration and Analysis and select View Log File.

11. To review the results of the analysis and see how the computer settings compare to the database settings, expand the area you want to compare and click it, as shown in Figure 11.80.

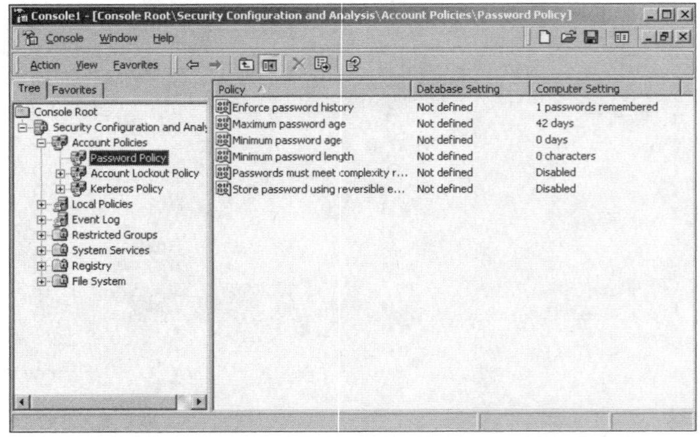

FIGURE 11.80
After analysis is complete, you can compare template settings to the actual running settings of the computer.

For example, to determine the differences between the computer's settings and those in the database (that is, the settings in the template used for comparison) for the Password Policy, you would expand Account Policies and then click Password Policy. The details pane would have three columns: Policy, for the name of the setting; Database Setting, the template setting in the database based on the template you imported; and Computer Setting, the current running configuration of the system.

12. Review the analysis to get a full picture of how closely your system resembles the template and where changes need to be made. Close the MMC console when finished.

NOTE

Analyzing Many Computers In situations in which frequent analysis of a large number of computers is required, Windows 2000 provides a command-line utility called secedit. This utility can be passed the database filename, log location, and other parameters specified in Security Configuration and Analysis. The utility performs the security analysis as you did in the MMC, but you still need to use the Security Configuration and Analysis snap-in to view the results of the analysis.

The command-line secedit.exe utility can be of value in environments in which scheduling the analysis to occur at off-peak hours is useful. In fact, it is primarily intended to be used through the Task Scheduler and not from the command prompt per se. Administrators can configure a central location for database files for many computers and then also have the results placed there. Following the overnight analysis, the administrator can review each of the database's contents using the Security Configuration and Analysis snap-in to determine whether problems exist.

Configuring a Computer with Security Settings

Using Security Configuration and Analysis, you can take the results of analysis and then determine whether the template settings are properly configured. Through Security Configuration and Analysis, you can also apply security templates settings to the local computer. To do this, perform Step By Step 11.21.

STEP BY STEP

11.21 Configuring a Computer with Security Settings Using Security Configuration and Analysis

1. Log on to your Windows 2000 computer as Administrator and open the Security Configuration and Analysis MMC console you created in Step By Step 11.19.
2. Right-click Security Configuration and Analysis and select Open Database.
3. In the Open Database dialog box, locate the name of the database file you previously created or create a new database to hold the template settings; then click Open.

continues

continued

4. To configure your computer with the template settings you have just loaded or those stored in the database, right-click Security Configuration and Analysis and select Configure Computer Now from the list of menu choices (see Figure 11.81).

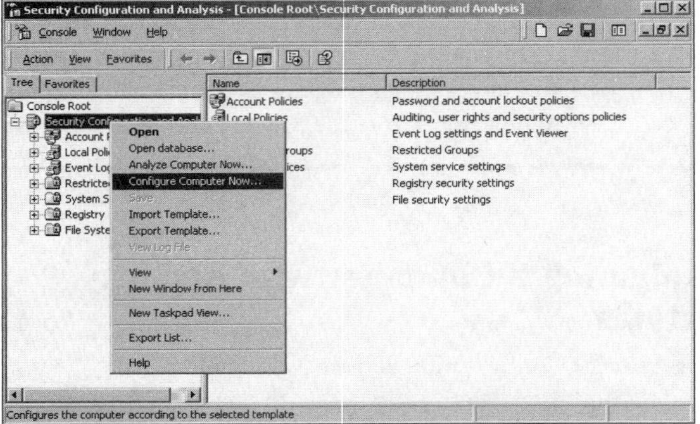

FIGURE 11.81
Right-click Security Configuration and Analysis and select Configure Computer Now to apply template settings to the computer.

5. In the dialog box presented, select the location of the error log file for the configuration and click OK, as shown in Figure 11.82.

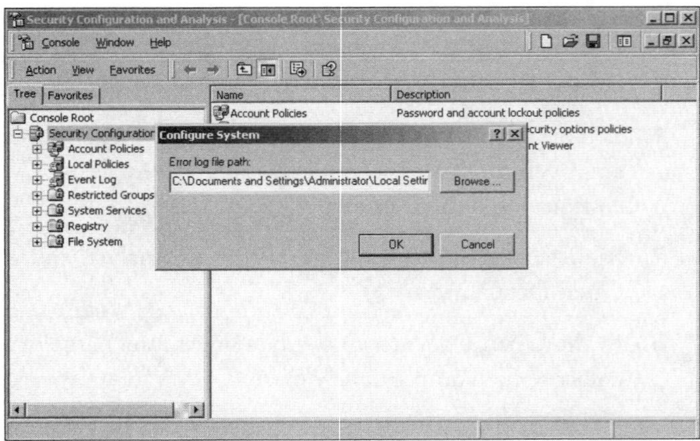

FIGURE 11.82
An error log path and filename must be specified prior to configuration of the computer commencing.

6. Just as you saw with the analysis process, configuration of the computer presents a status screen, as shown in Figure 11.83, to provide you with progress information on the application of security settings on the local computer. When finished, the Security Configuration and Analysis MMC console screen no longer has the different settings displayed.

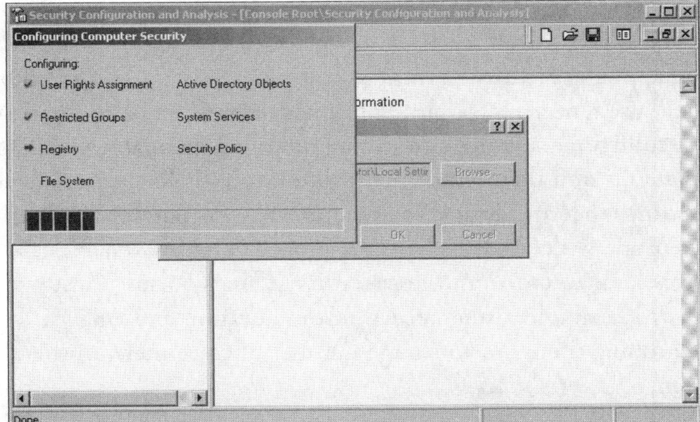

FIGURE 11.83
As configuration proceeds, a status screen shows you progress.

7. After configuration is complete, you can review the results by looking at the log file as you did for analysis (see Figure 11.84).

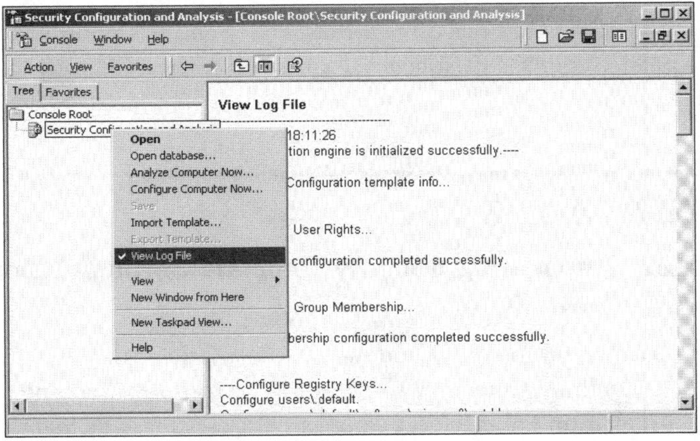

FIGURE 11.84
After configuration is complete, you can review what changed by examining the log file in Security Configuration and Analysis.

8. Close the MMC console when finished.

Using Group Policy to Apply Security Settings

Group Policy is an Active Directory object that can be used to apply a large number of configuration settings to a collection of objects located in an Active Directory container such as an OU, a domain, or a site. Just as you can use Group Policy to apply Administrative Template settings or software deployment to several computers in an Active Directory container at one time, the same holds true for security settings.

When applying security settings to computers using Group Policy, you still use templates. Group Policy has default templates that have no preconfigured settings and can be modified manually. Creating a template file and then importing it into Group Policy to ensure all the settings that are required to conform to a corporate security policy are properly defined is a better approach. This also enables the administrator to create and test security settings outside Group Policy (for example, using Security Configuration and Analysis) before rolling them out to a large number of computers on the domain, OU, or site level.

To apply security policies for an Active Directory container using Group Policy, you import one or more security templates into security settings in Group Policy. Importing a security template into a Group Policy object ensures that all members of the container automatically have the settings applied when the Group Policy propagates.

To apply security settings using Group Policy and to import a security template into a GPO, follow the steps presented in Step By Step 11.22.

STEP BY STEP

11.22 Propagating Security Template Settings Using Group Policy

1. Log on to your Windows 2000 computer as Administrator and start the MMC console where the Group Policy object whose security settings you want to modify is located (either Active Directory Users and Computer or Active Directory Sites and Services).

2. Right-click the container whose GPO will be modified to apply security settings, and click Properties.

3. Click the Group Policy tab and select the GPO that will have security settings propagated to objects within its scope. Click Edit to open the Group Policy Editor.

4. Expand Computer Configuration (or User Configuration if changing user security elements), Windows Settings, and then Security Settings to show the areas that can be modified (see Figure 11.85). You can modify the settings manually here, although they will not be saved as a security template. You can import an existing template and have its settings applied in the GPO.

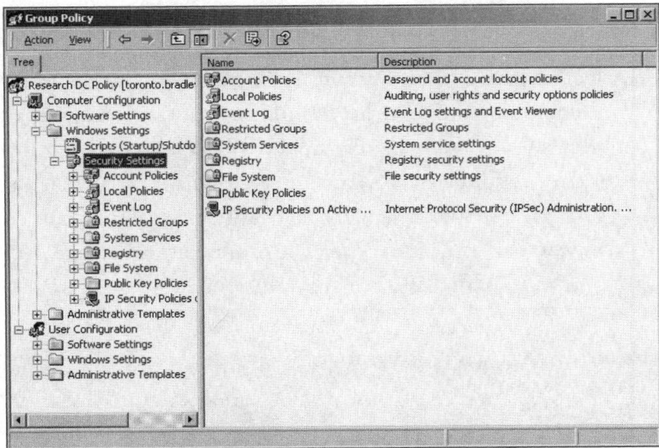

FIGURE 11.85
Expand Windows Settings and then Security Settings in the Computer Configuration container of the Group Policy Editor to see which security settings can be applied.

5. To import a security template's settings, right-click Security Settings and select Import Policy, as shown in Figure 11.86.

continues

continued

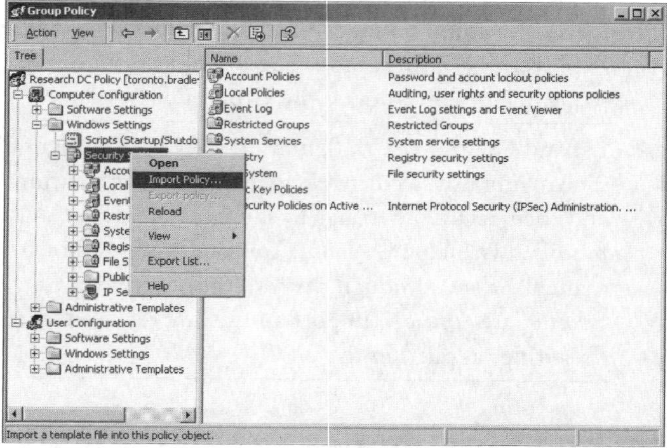

FIGURE 11.86
Right-click Security Settings and select Import Policy to import a security template into the GPO.

6. In the Import Policy From dialog box, locate the path and filename of the security template you want to apply and then click Open (see Figure 11.87). The security template settings will be imported, and you will be returned to the Group Policy Editor. At this point, you might want to review the settings to make sure they are as you expect and as specified in the template.

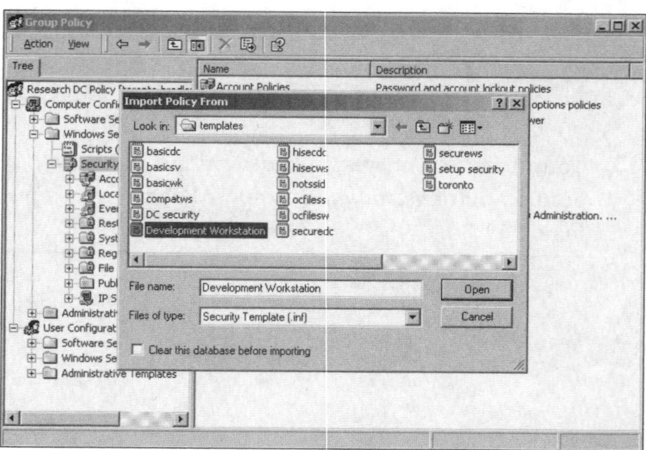

FIGURE 11.87
Locate the security template you want to import, and click Open.

7. When finished, close the Group Policy Editor to save your changes.
8. Click OK to close the Active Directory Container Properties dialog box.
9. Exit Active Directory Users and Computers (or Active Directory Sites and Services) when finished.

As the discussion indicates, importing security templates and applying them in a GPO is pretty straightforward. The settings included in the template are now applied to all computers and users in the scope of the GPO. You can use the Security Configuration and Analysis MMC snap-in to verify settings on individual computers.

Windows 2000 provides the administrator with a great deal of flexibility in implementing a security policy for both users and computers. As you have seen, security templates enable you to configure the settings that should be in place for a computer or user. Security Configuration and Analysis enables you to compare the currently running settings to those in a template, enabling you to compare the current security settings against those that should be in place (that is, those in the security template). To implement the same security settings several computers or for several users, you can use Group Policy to assign those settings at the site, domain, or OU level.

Case Study: Using Group Policy to Deploy Software Applications at SunShine Brewing

ESSENCE OF THE CASE

SunShine Brewing has purchased a new enterprise resource planning (ERP) application that needs to be deployed to all executives and administrative users. Sales people need to have the Customer Relationship Management (CRM) component of the application installed on their computers as well because they will use the intelligence of the system to process

SCENARIO

Earlier in this chapter, you were shown how Group Policy can be used to deploy software packages across the enterprise or to a specific set of users. You were also introduced to methods that can be used to upgrade packages that have been deployed, and you learned how to repackage software that does not come in a format compatible with Windows Installer. Here you

continues

CASE STUDY: USING GROUP POLICY TO DEPLOY SOFTWARE APPLICATIONS AT SUNSHINE BREWING

orders, profile customers, and check on the status of client orders and other elements. Furthermore, Microsoft Office 2000 has been purchased as the corporate office suite standard, and it needs to be installed on all users' desktops. Because the company operates in a multinational environment, specific settings for Office 2000, such as dictionary components used for spell checking, need to conform to local requirements.

It has also been decided that Windows Installer Package files for utility software, including WinZIP, Adobe Acrobat Reader, and RealAudio Player, that have been acquired from your software supplier will be available for users as an optional installation. If the users attempt to open a file of a type supported by the utility, they should be asked whether they want to install the package.

Historically, large-scale deployments of software of this nature have been handled by the IT staff with the help of co-op or summer students to perform the bulk of the grunt work. When calculating the budget for using this approach, the figure presented to the CEO was rejected, and the IT department has been told to perform the deployment using existing resources in a three-month period. As the champion of Windows 2000 in the organization, you have been told to make sure this can be done or face the consequences.

will determine how this can be used to solve a specific problem at SunShine Brewing.

ANALYSIS

Although the initial challenge presented by the scope of this software deployment might seem somewhat daunting, using Group Policy to perform the deployment easily solves this problem.

On the ERP side, you would require at least two different software configurations: one for the sales personnel who will have a subset of the ERP package (the CRM component only) and the other for all the admin users who will have the entire ERP client software installed on their desktops. Because the ERP vendor does not have the application in a Windows Installer Package format and because this would not help you with the sales requirement, you first need to create two Windows Installer Packages with the correct configuration.

To create the Windows Installer Package for the admin users, you would start with a clean Windows 2000 Professional computer and use Veritas WinInstall LE (or another third-party product) to create a before snapshot of the computer. You would then install and configure the ERP application as it should exist on all admin users' machines. During this period, you would create any shortcuts and configure any software settings as they will be required. After configuring the ERP software as needed, you would use the Discover Wizard of Veritas WinInstall LE (or the third-party tool) to create the package file with the correct configuration.

CASE STUDY: USING GROUP POLICY TO DEPLOY SOFTWARE APPLICATIONS AT SUNSHINE BREWING

After looking at the requirements, you decide to contact the ERP vendor to see whether the software has any specific installation capabilities that could assist in a deployment of this scale. The third-party vendor of the ERP application has stated that an installation program must be run on each client computer even though the end result is always the same, assuming the same components are installed. A Windows Installer Package does not exist for the ERP system, nor does the vendor plan to offer one without SunShine Brewing paying a hefty price. (They admit they have not tried it and would be starting from scratch.)

To create a Windows Installer Package file for the sales users, you would perform similar steps as for the admin package creation but include only those components of the application required by sales (CRM). At this point, you would have two Windows Installer Packages that you would place on a network share in their own separate folders. You would also place Microsoft Office 2000 on the same share point in its own folder.

To deploy the software, you would need to create three GPOs: one for the Admin OU for the ERP package, a second for the Sales OU for the CRM component of the ERP package, and a third for Microsoft Office 2000. The Microsoft Office 2000 GPO would be created at each site and would include transform (MST) files that would modify the package to include local settings.

You would have the ERP package GPO applied to Authenticated Users in the Admin OU, the CRM package applied to Authenticated Users in the Sales OU, and Microsoft Office 2000 applied to Authenticated Users at the site level with No Override to ensure all users get Microsoft Office 2000.

For the utility software, you would publish all the packages to Authenticated Users using a GPO at the domain level and would enable document activation on each package.

CHAPTER SUMMARY

KEY TERMS

- Active Directory
- Administrative templates
- Assigning software
- Auditing
- Blocking policy inheritance
- Forced (mandatory) package removal
- GPO inheritance
- GPO scope
- Group Policy Container
- Group Policy Object (GPO)
- Group Policy precedence
- GUID
- Mandatory upgrade
- No Override
- Optional removal
- Optional upgrade
- Package modifications
- Publishing software
- Registry
- Repackaging software
- Security Configuration and Analysis
- Security templates
- Software categories
- Windows Installer
- Windows Installer Service
- ZAP file

In this chapter we covered a lot of ground. Group policies are arguably one of the most flexible and useful new features of Windows 2000. Despite the length of this chapter, there are still more things that you could learn about group policies; however, the information presented here will cover your basic needs and the needs for the exam.

In this chapter you learned what group policies are and how they are connected to Active Directory. This includes all the intricacies of permissions and forcing, inheriting, and blocking group policies to and from lower objects.

You also learned how to distribute software using Microsoft's Installer technology and Group Policy objects. This includes the ability to assign—or force—applications on users and publish applications for users. You also learned how ZAP files can be used to publish applications when an installer file is not available.

Finally, you learned how to use Group Policy to implement security throughout the organization. As you learned, group policies can be used to change everything from password expiration to how audit settings are configured.

APPLY YOUR KNOWLEDGE

Exercises

All the exercises for this chapter assume you have installed Windows 2000 Server (or Advanced Server) on a computer. Your Windows 2000 Server must be configured as a domain controller of a domain for the exercises to work properly. You need to be able to log in to the domain as an administrator (that is, your user account must be a member of either the Enterprise Admins group or the Domain Admins group). If you know the password for the user Administrator, this will be sufficient.

For these exercises, you need at least two Windows Installer Package files. If you do not have these, you can use Veritas WinINSTALL LE to repackage an application of your choice and then use that application, or you can use one of the applications on the Windows 2000 CD-ROM that already come packaged in the proper format. A ready-made MSI file that can be used is the Windows 2000 Resource Kit found in the `SUPPORT\TOOLS` folder on the Windows 2000 CD-ROM.

11.1 Creating Organizational Units, Users, and Groups and Moving Your Domain Controller

In this exercise, you will create two organizational units that will be used in future exercises. You also will create a security group and some users. Finally, you will move your domain controller into one of the OUs you just created to ensure that the GPO settings you create in later exercises will be applied to your computer.

Estimated Time: 20 minutes

To create OUs, groups, and users, follow these steps:

1. Log on to the Windows 2000 Server domain controller as Administrator for your domain.
2. Select Start, Programs, Administrative Tools, Active Directory Users and Computers to open the MMC console for managing users and computers in your domain.
3. Right-click your domain and select New, Organizational Unit. In the dialog box that opens, type **`Research`**.
4. Repeat step 3 to add a Sales OU as well.
5. Right-click the Research OU and select New, Group. Enter **`Developers`** for the group name, **`Domain Local`** as the group scope, and **`Security`** as the group type.
6. Repeat step 5 to create a Domain Local Security group called Telemarketing in the Sales OU.
7. In the Sales OU, add three new users with logins of `HowardH` (Howard Ham), `PhilC` (Phillip Chambers), and `NatashaW` (Natasha Wilson). Make `PhilC` and `NatashaW` members of the Telemarketing group (but not `HowardH`). When prompted for a password, enter the word **`password`** for each user. Leave the rest of the settings at the default.
8. In the Research OU, add two new users with logins of `RalphD` (Ralph Downing) and `TimC` (Tim Clark) and make `TimC` a member of the Developers group. When prompted for a password, enter **`password`** for each user. Leave the rest of the settings at the default.

To move your domain controller to the Research OU, follow these steps:

1. If you have not already done so, start Active Directory Users and Computers and expand your domain.
2. Click Domain Controllers.

APPLY YOUR KNOWLEDGE

3. In the details pane, right-click your computer (which is also the domain controller) and select Move.
4. In the Move dialog box, expand your domain and click the Research OU; then click OK.
5. Exit Active Directory Users and Computers.

11.2 Creating a Group Policy Object for Computers

In this exercise, you create a Group Policy to enable disk quotas on the Research OU computers as well as to enforce them, and you configure a default disk quota.

Estimated Time: 20 minutes

To create the Research Computer Policy, follow these steps:

1. While logged on as a domain administrator, start Active Directory Users and Computers.
2. Expand your domain, right-click the Research OU, and select Properties.
3. On the Group Policy tab, click New, type `Research Computer Policy` as the name, and press Enter.

To edit the Research Computer Policy Administrative Template settings, follow these steps:

1. Select the Research Computer Policy you created earlier and click Edit. This starts the Group Policy Editor MMC.
2. In the Group Policy console tree, expand Computer Configuration and then expand Administrative Templates.
3. In the console tree, expand System and click Disk Quotas. In the details pane, double-click Enable Disk Quotas.
4. In the Properties dialog box, select Enabled and click OK.
5. In the details pane, double-click Default Quota Limit and Warning Level to bring up the Properties dialog box. Click Enabled and leave the default 100MB limit as is. Click OK to exit the dialog box and save your changes.
6. Double-click Enforce Disk Quota Limit in the details pane, click Enabled to select the setting, and click OK to save your changes.
7. Close the Group Policy Editor MMC console.
8. Close the Research OU Properties dialog box and exit Active Directory Users and Computers.
9. Restart your computer for the changes to take effect.

   To avoid restarting your computer, you can select Start, Programs, Accessories and click Command Prompt to start a command prompt. In the Command Prompt window, type `secedit /refreshpolicy user policy` and `secedit /refreshpolicy machine policy` to refresh the user and machine policies on the domain controller. This might take a few minutes.

11.3 Creating a Group Policy Object for Users

In this exercise, you will create a Group Policy to remove the Run command from the Start menu of all telemarketing users as well as to disable the use of Control Panel for these same users.

Estimated Time: 20 minutes

APPLY YOUR KNOWLEDGE

To create the Telemarketing Users Policy, follow these steps:

1. While logged on as a domain administrator, start Active Directory Users and Computers.
2. Expand your domain, right-click the Sales OU, and select Properties.
3. In the Group Policy tab, click New, type **`Telemarketing Users Policy`** as the name, and press Enter.

To edit the Telemarketing Users Policy Administrative Template settings, follow these steps:

1. Select the Telemarketing Users Policy you created earlier, click Properties, and then click the Security tab.
2. Select the Authenticated Users group and click Remove.
3. Click Add and, in the list of users and groups in your domain, select the Telemarketing group. Click Add, and then click OK.
4. With the Telemarketing group selected, make sure Allow Read and Allow Apply Group Policy are selected. Click OK to close the Properties dialog box.
5. Select the Telemarketing Users Policy and click Edit. This starts the Group Policy Editor MMC.
6. In the Group Policy console tree, expand User Configuration and then expand Administrative Templates.
7. In the console, click Start Menu & Taskbar; then, in the details pane, double-click Remove Run Menu from the Start menu.
8. In the Properties dialog box, select Enabled and click OK.
9. In the Group Policy Editor MMC console, click Control Panel (two folders below Start Menu & Taskbar, with which you just worked).
10. Double-click Disable Control Panel in the details pane to bring up the Properties dialog box.
11. Click Enabled and then click OK to close the Disable Control Panel Properties dialog box.
12. Close the Group Policy Editor MMC console.
13. Close the Sales OU Properties dialog box and exit Active Directory Users and Computers.
14. Restart your computer for the changes to take effect.

    To avoid restarting your computer, you can select Start, Programs, Accessories and click Command Prompt to start a command prompt. In the Command Prompt window, type **`secedit /refreshpolicy user policy`** and **`secedit /refreshpolicy machine policy`** to refresh the user and machine policies on the domain controller. This might take a few minutes.

11.4 Verifying Group Policy Administrative Template Settings

In this exercise, you will log on as `HowardH` to verify that both the computer and user policy settings you have configured are being enforced.

Estimated Time: 20 minutes

1. If you are currently logged on to your computer, log off and log on again as `HowardH` with a password of `password`.

APPLY YOUR KNOWLEDGE

2. Select Start, Programs, Accessories, Windows Explorer to launch Windows Explorer.
3. Expand My Computer and click drive C. How much free disk space is shown as available in the details pane?

   ___

4. Click another NTFS partition if available and verify the amount of free disk space available to `HowardH`. How much is available?

   ___

5. Why is this much disk space available to the user on each NTFS partition?

   ___

6. Select Start, Settings. Is Control Panel listed as one of the available settings options? Why or why not?

   ___

7. Click Start. Is the Run menu available from the Start menu? Why or why not?

   ___

8. Are the computer policy settings for the Research OU being enforced on your computer?

   ___

9. Are the user policy settings for the Sales OU being enforced on your computer?

   ___

10. Log off Windows 2000.

11.5 Verifying Group Policy Logon Script Settings

In this exercise, you will log on as `RalphD` and `HowardH` to verify that the logon script policy is being enforced.

Estimated Time: 20 minutes

1. If you are currently logged on to your computer, log off and log on again as `RalphD` with a password of `password`.
2. Select Start, Programs, Accessories, Windows Explorer to launch Windows Explorer.
3. Expand My Computer. Does a mapping to the `CORPDATA` share on your computer appear as mapped drive letter K? Why or why not?

   ___

4. Log off and log on again as `HowardH` with a password of `password`.
5. Select Start, Programs, Accessories, Windows Explorer to launch Windows Explorer.
6. Expand My Computer. Does a mapping to the `CORPDATA` share on your computer appear as mapped drive letter K? Why or why not?

   ___

7. Log off Windows 2000.

11.6 Linking an Existing GPO to an OU

In this exercise, you will link the Research Logon Script Policy to the Sales OU because Sales needs to have access to and communicate to clients the published released schedules placed in the `CORPDATA` share by the Research users.

APPLY YOUR KNOWLEDGE

Estimated Time: 20 minutes

1. Log on to the Windows 2000 Server domain controller as Administrator for your domain.
2. Select Start, Programs, Administrative Tools, Active Directory Users and Computers to open the MMC console for managing user and computers in your domain.
3. Expand your domain, and then right-click the Sales OU and select Properties.
4. In the Group Policy tab, select Add to open the Add a Group Policy Object Link dialog box.
5. Click the All tab and select Research Logon Script Policy; then, click OK.
6. In the Sales Properties dialog box, you should now see the Research Logon Script Policy added to the list.
7. Click OK to exit the Sales OU Properties dialog box, and then close Active Directory Users and Computers.
8. Log off Windows 2000.

11.7 Verifying Group Policy Link and Logon Script Settings

In this exercise, you log on as `RalphD` and `HowardH` to verify that the logon script policy is being enforced.

Estimated Time: 20 minutes

1. If you are currently logged on to your computer, log off and log on again as `RalphD` with a password of `password`.
2. Select Start, Programs, Accessories, Windows Explorer to launch Windows Explorer.
3. Expand My Computer. Does a mapping to the `CORPDATA` share on your computer appear as mapped drive letter K? Why or why not?

   ____

4. Log off and log on again as `HowardH` with a password of `password`.
5. Select Start, Programs, Accessories, Windows Explorer to launch Windows Explorer.
6. Expand My Computer. Does a mapping to the `CORPDATA` share on your computer appear as mapped drive letter K? Why or why not?

   ____

7. Log off Windows 2000.

11.8 Delegating Administrative Control of Group Policy

In this exercise, you delegate administration of the Telemarketing Users Policy to `HowardH`, who is the manager of the sales department. Because your company is quite small, its resources are scarce. Howard has taken a few Windows 2000 courses and believes he is familiar with Active Directory and Group Policy. After giving him a quick test, you feel he is able to administer this policy for his part of the company.

Estimated Time: 20 minutes

1. Log on to Windows 2000 as the administrator for your domain.
2. Start Active Directory Users and Computers and expand your domain. Right-click the Sales OU and select Properties.
3. Click the Group Policy tab, select the Telemarketing Users Policy, and select Properties.

APPLY YOUR KNOWLEDGE

4. Click the Security tab. What permissions does `HowardH` currently have for this Group Policy?

   ____

5. Click Add to be presented with a list of users and groups in your domain.
6. Scroll down the list until you find `HowardH`, highlight his name by clicking it, and then select Add. Click OK.
7. What permissions does `HowardH` now have on the Group Policy?

   ____

8. What permissions would `HowardH` need to be able to administer the GPO?

   ____

9. Grant `HowardH` the required additional permissions to administer Group Policy while still making sure the policy applies to him. Click OK to exit the Telemarketing Users Policy Properties dialog box.
10. Close Active Directory Users and Computers.
11. Log off Windows 2000.

11.9 Testing the Delegation of Administrative Control of Group Policy

In this exercise, you test to see whether `HowardH` can successfully modify the Telemarketing Users Policy.

Estimated Time: 20 minutes

1. Log on to Windows 2000 as `HowardH` with a password of `password`.
2. Start Active Directory Users and Computers and expand your domain. Right-click the Sales OU and select Properties.
3. Click the Group Policy tab and select the Telemarketing Users Policy. Which of the six options at the bottom of the dialog box are available to `HowardH`?

   ____

4. Click the Research Logon Script Policy. Is there a difference in the options available to `HowardH` for the Research Logon Script Policy and the Telemarketing Users Policy?

   ____

5. Click the Telemarketing Users Policy and click Properties. Is `HowardH` able to change permissions to this GPO? Why or why not?

   ____

6. Close the Telemarketing Users Policy Properties dialog box and click Edit. Does the Group Policy Editor MMC appear?

   ____

7. To modify the GPO as `HowardH` and to add Logoff to the Start menu, expand User Configuration, Administrative Templates, Start Menu & Programs. In the details pane, double-click Add Logoff to the Start Menu and select Enabled. Was `HowardH` able to modify the GPO setting? Why or why not?

   ____

8. Click OK to exit the Add Logoff to the Start Menu Properties dialog box, and then close the Group Policy Editor MMC.
9. Click OK to close the Sales OU Properties dialog box and close Active Directory Users and Computers.

Apply Your Knowledge

11.10 Filtering and Blocking Group Policy Inheritance

After much deliberation, it was decided that sales is a part of the company that should set its own policies for different users. Further, the Telemarketing Users Policy should apply only to users in the Telemarketing security group.

In this exercise, you will block policy inheritance for the Sales OU and filter policy inheritance to ensure the Telemarketing Users Policy is enforced only on users in the Telemarketing security group.

Estimated Time: 20 minutes

1. Log on to your computer as a domain-level administrator.
2. Start Active Directory Users and Computers, expand your domain, right-click the Sales OU, and select Properties.
3. Click the Group Policy tab. What do you need to do to ensure any higher-level policies are not enforced in this OU? Configure the setting that does not enforce higher-level GPOs on this OU.

   ____

4. Click the Telemarketing Users Policy and click the Security tab. What changes do you need to make to ensure that only the Telemarketing security group has this policy enforced? Perform the necessary changes.

   ____

5. Click OK to close the Telemarketing Users Policy Properties dialog box.
6. Click OK to close the Sales OU Properties dialog box and then close Active Directory Users and Computers.
7. Log off Windows 2000.

11.11 Testing Filtering Group Policy

In this exercise, you will log on to your computer as a member of the Telemarketing security group to test GPO filtering. You will also log on as `HowardH` and note any differences.

Estimated Time: 20 minutes

1. Log on to your computer as `NatashaW`, one of the users in the Telemarketing security group, with a password of `password`.
2. Select Start, Programs, Accessories, Windows Explorer to launch Windows Explorer.
3. Expand My Computer and click drive C. How much free disk space is shown as available in the details pane?

   ____

4. Click another NTFS partition, if available, and verify the amount of free disk space available to `NatashaW`. How much is available?

   ____

5. Why is this much disk space available to the user on each NTFS partition?

   ____

6. Select Start, Settings. Is Control Panel listed as one of the available settings options? Why or why not?

   ____

7. Click Start. Is the Run menu available from the Start menu? Why or why not?

   ____

8. Are the computer policy settings for the Research OU being enforced on your computer?

   ____

9. Are the user policy settings for the Sales OU being enforced on your computer?

 ____

10. Log off Windows 2000.
11. Log on to your computer as `HowardH` with a password of `password`.
12. Select Start, Programs, Accessories, Windows Explorer to launch Windows Explorer.
13. Expand My Computer and click drive C. How much free disk space is shown as available in the details pane?

 ____

14. Click another NTFS partition, if available, and verify the amount of free disk space available to `HowardH`. How much is available?

 ____

15. Why is this much disk space available to the user on each NTFS partition?

 ____

16. Select Start, Settings. Is Control Panel listed as one of the available settings options? Why or why not?

 ____

17. Click Start. Is the Run menu available from the Start menu? Why or why not?

 ____

18. Are the computer policy settings for the Research OU being enforced on your computer?

 ____

19. Are the user policy settings for the Sales OU being enforced on your computer?

 ____

20. Log off Windows 2000.

11.12 Using Group Policy to Deploy Software

In this exercise, you will first configure software deployment for the Research OU. Then you will test to make sure the published application is available in Add/Remove Programs in Control Panel. If the published application is available in Add/Remove Programs, you will install the package.

To add software installation components to the Research Script Policy Research OU, follow these steps:

Estimated Time: 20 minutes

1. While logged on as a domain administrator, start Active Directory Users and Computers.
2. Expand your domain, right-click the Sales OU, and select Properties.
3. Select the Research Script Policy you created in Exercise 11.1 and click Edit. This starts the Group Policy Editor MMC.
4. In the Group Policy console tree, expand User Configuration and then expand Software Settings.
5. Right-click Software Installation, select New, and then select Package. In the Open dialog box that appears, locate the package file for the software application you want to deploy and select Open. Make sure the package is located on a network share so that all users that need it can access it.

APPLY YOUR KNOWLEDGE

6. In the Deploy Software dialog box that appears, select Published as the deployment method and click OK.
7. Close the Group Policy Editor to save your changes.
8. Click OK on the Research Properties dialog box to close it.
9. Log off your computer after closing the Active Directory Users and Computers MMC.

To test software deployment using Group Policy, follow these steps:

Estimated Time: 20 minutes

1. Log on to the computer as a user in the Developers Group to whom the Group Policy applies (`TimC`).
2. From the Start menu, select Settings and then Control Panel.
3. Double-click Add/Remove Programs to start the application.
4. Click Add New Programs to see a list of available applications on the network. Does the package you configured earlier appear on the list?

   ____

5. Click the Add button to install the package on the machine. How much user interaction takes place during the installation?

   ____

6. Try to start the application and test to make sure it is working properly. Does it appear to function correctly?

   ____

7. Log off the computer when you have finished testing the application's functionality.

11.13 Configuring Software Deployment Options

In this exercise, you configure a default software installation shared folder for all applications configured for the Research OU Group Policy. You then create software categories that are available throughout the domain and will assign your package to two categories.

Estimated Time: 20 minutes

To create software categories, assign software to categories, and describe a default installation share for packages, follow these steps:

1. While logged on as a domain administrator, start Active Directory Users and Computers.
2. Expand your domain, right-click the Sales OU, and select Properties.
3. Select the Research Script Policy you created earlier and click Edit. This starts the Group Policy Editor MMC.
4. In the Group Policy console tree, expand User Configuration and then expand Software Settings.
5. Right-click Software Installation and select Properties.
6. On the General tab in the General package location field, enter your share name in the format `\\`*`SHARE`*`\`*`FOLDER`* (for example, `\\TORONTO\PACKAGES`). This configures the default location for all packages in this GPO. The actual full path to the package is retained in the package setting. Placing packages that have been moved in this folder enables them to be located during deployment.

APPLY YOUR KNOWLEDGE

7. Click the Categories tab to add software categories to this GPO and the domain.
8. Click the Add button to add a new category called Utilities, and click OK when done. Repeat this step to create two more categories called File Readers and Office Suites. If the software package you are using does not fall under these category headings, add additional categories that can be used to describe your software.
9. When done adding categories, click Apply and then OK to close the Software Installation Properties dialog box.
10. To assign your package to software categories, select the package, right-click it, and then select Properties.
11. Click the Categories tab to see into which categories the software has been placed. From the list of available categories, select File Readers and Utilities and click Select. Click OK when you have completed your category selection.
12. Close the Group Policy Editor to save your changes.
13. Click OK on the Research Properties dialog box to close it.
14. Close the Active Directory Users and Computers MMC.

To verify placement of software in categories, follow these steps:

1. Log on to the computer as a user in the Developers Group to whom the Group Policy applies (`TimC`).
2. From the Start menu, select Settings, Control Panel.
3. Double-click Add/Remove Programs to start the application.
4. Click Add New Programs to see a list of available applications on the network. Which categories are available in the Categories drop-down list box?

   ____

5. Select one of the categories in which you placed your package (Utilities or File Readers). Does your package appear in the list when the Utilities category is selected? Is it also listed in the File Readers category? (Substitute your own categories here if appropriate.)

   ____

6. Close Add/Remove Programs and then close Control Panel.
7. Log off the computer when done.

11.14 Configuring Software Upgrades

In this exercise, you will configure an upgrade to your package. You will first add another package to your GPO and then configure it as an upgrade to your existing package. You will make the upgrade required. Finally, you will test the upgrade to make sure it succeeds.

Estimated Time: 20 minutes

To add a package as an upgrade for your existing package, follow these steps:

1. While logged on as a domain administrator, start Active Directory Users and Computers.
2. Expand your domain, right-click the Sales OU, and select Properties.

APPLY YOUR KNOWLEDGE

3. Select the Research Script Policy you created earlier and click Edit. This starts the Group Policy Editor MMC.
4. In the Group Policy console tree, expand User Configuration and then expand Software Settings.
5. Right-click Software Installation and select New, Package. In the Open dialog box that appears, locate the package (MSI) file for the software application that will be used to upgrade your existing package and select Open. This must be a different file from your original application.
6. In the Deploy Software dialog box that appears, select Published as the deployment method and click OK.
7. Right-click the package you just added and select Properties.
8. Click the Categories tab and select the categories that apply to this package. These should be similar (if not identical) to the categories you selected for your original package.
9. Click the Upgrades tab and then click the Add button to add a package of which the new package will be an upgrade.
10. From the list presented, select the first application package and select either Uninstall the Existing Package, Then Install the Upgrade Package or Package Can Upgrade Over the Existing Package, as It Applies to Your Software Application. Click OK.
11. On the Upgrades tab, make sure Required Upgrade for Existing Packages is selected and click Apply; then, click OK to exit the package Properties dialog box.
12. Close the Group Policy Editor to save your changes.
13. Click OK on the Research Properties dialog box to close it.
14. Log off your computer after closing the Active Directory Users and Computers MMC.

To verify the package upgrade, follow these steps:

1. Log on to the computer as a user in the Developers Group to whom the Group Policy applies (`TimC`).
2. From the Start menu, select Settings, Control Panel.
3. Invoke your first application package by double-clicking it or by opening a file extension mapped to it. What happens?

   ____

4. Is the older version of your application still installed? Why or why not?

   ____

5. Close all programs and log off the computer when done.

11.15 Removing Deployed Packages Using Group Policy

In this exercise, you will configure the mandatory removal of the last package installed (that is, the previous upgrade). You will then test the upgrade to make sure it succeeds.

Estimated Time: 20 minutes

APPLY YOUR KNOWLEDGE

To configure the removal of a package using Group Policy, follow these steps:

1. While logged on as a domain administrator, start Active Directory Users and Computers.
2. Expand your domain, right-click the Sales OU, and select Properties.
3. Select the Research Script Policy you created earlier and click Edit. This starts the Group Policy Editor MMC.
4. In the Group Policy console tree, expand User Configuration and then expand Software Settings. Click Software Installation to display a list of packages for this GPO.
5. Right-click the older package and select All Tasks, Remove.
6. On the Remove Software dialog box, select Immediately Uninstall the Software from Users and Computers and click OK. Repeat this step for the upgrade as well. Notice that both packages are removed from the Software Installation list.
7. Close the Group Policy Editor to save your changes.
8. Click OK on the Research Properties dialog box to close it.
9. Log off your computer after closing the Active Directory Users and Computers MMC.

To verify forced package removal using Group Policy, follow these steps:

1. Log on to the computer as a user in the Developers Group to whom the Group Policy applies (`TimC`).
2. What new messages are presented to you during the logon process?

   ____

3. Do the icons or shortcuts for any of your packages appear, or are they still available? Why or why not?

   ____

4. Close all programs and log off the computer when done.

Review Questions

1. If you wanted to ensure that a GPO for a site was applied to all users and computers in the site, what would you need to do?
2. To which users and computers do GPO settings apply by default?
3. What are the benefits that Group Policy provides to administrators?
4. You want to ensure all users in the domain have the same background wallpaper on their desktops: a corporate logo. The director of sales also wants to have a quarterly promo as the background for the sales staff members who are part of the Sales security group. How would you accomplish both goals?
5. If a computer setting in a GPO disables AutoPlay and a user setting in the same GPO enables AutoPlay, will AutoPlay be disabled or enabled?
6. What does the term *forcing Group Policy* mean?
7. If all Group Policies you have configured deal with only the user portion of the GPO, how could you improve performance of GPO processing?

APPLY YOUR KNOWLEDGE

8. How must software be configured for it to be deployed using Group Policy?
9. You need to ensure that all users in your organization have Microsoft Outlook 2000 installed as their email clients. How would you accomplish this?
10. Users in your office in Germany are complaining that they do not have Microsoft Outlook 2000 prompts and other information in German. How would you correct this problem?
11. If a software application is not shipped as a Windows Installer Package file, what alternatives are available for deploying it using Group Policy?
12. If your organization has many software packages deployed, how can you enable users to more easily find the applications they want?
13. When would you assign an application to a computer rather than a user?
14. Which software deployment options are not available when using ZAP files?
15. How would you add a support telephone number and Web site location to an existing MSI file?
16. Why would a software package remove files from the user's machine when it is deployed?
17. How could you be sure that users would still be able to use an application after it has been removed from the GPO?

Exam Questions

1. You are the administrator of a large multinational organization with offices in Paris, London, Berlin, Moscow, Tokyo, and Sydney, as well as the corporate head office in New York. Your CIO has concluded negotiations with Microsoft, making Microsoft Office 2000 the corporate standard for office suites. He needs you to ensure the software gets deployed.

   The requirements for the deployment are as follows:

   - Microsoft Office 2000 must be installed on all desktops throughout the enterprise.
   - Users in each office must be able to use Microsoft Office 2000 with localized dictionaries and interfaces.
   - The corporate legal department in New York, which has its own OU in the Active Directory structure, will not have Microsoft Office 2000 installed on its desktops because all its documents rely on a third-party add-on to another office suite.
   - Travel and other costs for the deployment must be kept as low as possible.

   You conclude that the best way to satisfy the requirements is the following:

   - Use Microsoft Windows 2000 Group Policy to deploy the software.
   - Create a GPO object at the domain level (your organization consists of only one domain) that would assign the software to computers.
   - Create transform files for each localized version needed and add them to the package configured in the GPO.
   - Block policy inheritance for the legal department's OU.

APPLY YOUR KNOWLEDGE

Which of these requirements will be met by your solution? (Choose all that apply.)

A. Microsoft Office 2000 will be installed on all desktops throughout the enterprise.

B. Users in each office will be able to use Microsoft Office 2000 with localized dictionaries and interfaces.

C. The corporate legal department in New York will not have Microsoft Office 2000 installed on its desktops.

D. Travel and other costs for the deployment will be kept as low as possible.

E. The solution will not satisfy any of the outlined objectives.

2. You are the administrator of a large multinational organization with offices in Paris, London, Berlin, Moscow, Tokyo, and Sydney, as well as the corporate head office in New York. Your CIO has concluded negotiations with Microsoft, making Microsoft Office 2000 the corporate standard for office suites. He needs you to ensure the software gets deployed.

   The requirements for the deployment are as follows:

   - Microsoft Office 2000 must be installed on all desktops throughout the enterprise.
   - Users in each office must be able to use Microsoft Office 2000 with localized dictionaries and interfaces.
   - The corporate legal department in New York, which has its own OU in the Active Directory structure, will not have Microsoft Office 2000 installed on its desktops because all its documents rely on a third-party add-on to another office suite.
   - Travel and other costs for the deployment must be kept as low as possible.

   You conclude that the best way to satisfy the requirements is the following:

   - Use Microsoft Windows 2000 Group Policy to deploy the software.
   - Create GPO objects at the site level (each office is its own site) that would assign the software to computers.
   - Create transform files in each site GPO for the localized version needed at that site and add them to the package configured in the GPO.
   - At the New York site, filter the GPO to not include any computers in the legal department OU.

   Which of these requirements will be met by your solution? (Choose all that apply.)

   A. Microsoft Office 2000 will be installed on all desktops throughout the enterprise.

   B. Users in each office will be able to use Microsoft Office 2000 with localized dictionaries and interfaces.

   C. The corporate legal department in New York will not have Microsoft Office 2000 installed on its desktops.

   D. Travel and other costs for the deployment will be kept as low as possible.

   E. The solution will not satisfy any of the outlined objectives.

3. When comparing Windows Installer Package files and ZAP files, which of the following is true? (Choose the best answer.)

APPLY YOUR KNOWLEDGE

A. ZAP files can't be used to deploy software, but package files can.

B. Package files can publish extensions associated with the application, but ZAP files can't.

C. ZAP files can be installed with elevated privileges just like package files.

D. Package files include shortcuts, Registry settings, and the files required to be installed; ZAP files do not.

E. There is no difference in the functionality available in ZAP and package files.

4. You need to make a software application available to users in your sales department. The application is not provided in a Windows Installer Package file format. Users can choose to have the software installed on their computers. What is the best way to deploy this application using Group Policy? (Choose the best answer.)

   A. Repackage the application using WinINSTALL LE and assign it to the user.

   B. Repackage the application using WinINSTALL LE and publish it to the user.

   C. Create a ZAP file for the application and assign it to the user.

   D. Create a ZAP file for the application and publish it to the user.

   E. It is not possible to deploy software using Group Policy unless it is provided as a Windows Installer Package file.

5. When publishing a package to a user using Group Policy, how can the user initiate the installation of the software application in the package? (Choose two correct answers.)

   A. By opening a file whose extension is associated with the package (document activation)

   B. By starting the setup program for the package (install activation)

   C. By logging on, which starts the setup program for the application (logon activation)

   D. By using Add/Remove Programs in Control Panel (user activation)

   E. By starting his computer, which installs the application (computer activation)

6. In the GPO for the sales department OU, you have configured a package for forced removal for all users. When visiting users in the sales department, you determine that the application was removed from some users' computers but not all. What would be the reason some users in sales still have the package on their machines? (Choose the best answer.)

   A. When asked whether they want to remove the application, they said no.

   B. Their computers were filtered out of the GPO scope.

   C. They marked the package as critical on their computers, which overrode the forced removal.

   D. They are sales managers and therefore are not subject to the regular sales GPO.

   E. They reinstalled the application using Add/Remove Programs in Control after it was removed.

7. You want to deploy an upgrade to an existing application. You want to ensure that all users receive the upgrade and that the old version of

APPLY YOUR KNOWLEDGE

the software no longer is available. How should you configure the upgrade? (Choose two correct answers.)

A. Make the upgrade required.

B. Make the upgrade optional.

C. Allow users to keep the existing version.

D. Uninstall the previous version when installing the upgrade.

E. Have the upgrade overwrite the existing version.

8. What are the benefits of using Windows Installer Package files to deploy software? (Choose all that apply.)

A. You can install software on a user's computer only when the user has permission to do so.

B. Critical files can be automatically replaced if they become corrupt or deleted.

C. Shared files in use by other applications are not removed when the package is removed.

D. You can assign software to users and computers.

E. You can publish software to users and computers.

9. You are the administrator of LearnWin2K.com, an online training organization providing Windows 2000 training. You need to configure all the customer service machines so that Internet access is disabled. However, customer service supervisors need to be able to use the Internet. All customer service users are part of the CustomerService security group; customer service supervisors are also part of the CSSupervisors security group.

Which of the following do you need to perform to satisfy these goals? (Choose the best answer.)

A. Create two GPOs, one to disable Internet access and the other to enable it. Grant the CustomerService security group Read and Apply Group Policy permissions on the first GPO; grant the CSSupervisors security group Read and Apply Group Policy permissions on the second.

B. Create two GPOs, one to disable Internet access and the other to enable it. Grant the CustomerService security group Read and Apply Group Policy permissions on the first GPO; grant the CSSupervisors security group Read and Apply Group Policy permissions on the second. Grant the CSSupervisors security group Read permissions on the first.

C. Create one GPO to disable Internet access. Grant the CustomerService security group Read and Apply Group Policy permissions.

D. Create one GPO to disable Internet access. Grant the CustomerService security group Read and Apply Group Policy permissions; grant the CSSupervisors security group only Read permissions on the GPO.

10. You have linked a GPO to the domain that removes the Run command from the Start menu for all domain users. While installing a new server in the accounting department, you notice that some of the Windows 2000 Professional computers still have the Run command available. Why would this occur? (Choose two correct answers.)

A. Accountants are not domain users.

B. You did not force the GPO settings.

APPLY YOUR KNOWLEDGE

C. Group Policy is not enforced on Windows 2000 Professional computers.

D. Policy inheritance was blocked at the Accounting OU level.

E. The users are not running Windows 98 on their client computers. To disable the Run command, users must run Windows 98.

11. You are finding that administering Group Policy is becoming more time-consuming as your company grows. Departments also have been requesting more control at their own OU levels. Each department has been assigned a junior administrator to handle its requirements. What do you need to do to delegate administration of each department's GPOs to these junior administrators? (Choose the best answer.)

    A. Use the Delegation of Control Wizard to delegate control of the GPOs for their OUs to them.

    B. Grant them Full Control permissions on the GPOs linked to their OUs.

    C. Make them members of the OU Admins security group.

    D. Grant them Read and Write permissions on the GPOs linked to their OUs.

    E. Make them members of the Domain Admins security group.

    F. Grant them Read and Write permissions on their OUs.

12. You are finding that administering Group Policy is becoming more time-consuming as your company grows. Departments also have been requesting more control at their own OU levels. Each department has been assigned a junior administrator to handle its requirements. What do you need to do to allow these junior administrators to administer existing GPOs in their OUs and to create and remove GPOs if needed? (Choose all that apply.)

    A. Use the Delegation of Control Wizard to delegate control of the GPOs for their OUs to them.

    B. Grant them Full Control permissions on the GPOs linked to their OUs.

    C. Make them members of the OU Admins security group.

    D. Grant them Read and Write permissions on the GPOs linked to their OUs.

    E. Make them members of the Domain Admins security group.

    F. Grant them Read and Write permissions on their OUs.

13. What is the order of application of Group Policy? (Choose the best answer.)

    A. Computer, user, script

    B. Site, domain, OU

    C. Domain, site, OU

    D. OU, site, domain

    E. User, script, computer

14. You have configured Group Policy as follows:

    At the domain level, you have GPO1 that removes Control Panel from the Settings menu.

    At the site level, you have GPO2 that forces user passwords to be six characters long. GPO has been configured with No Override.

APPLY YOUR KNOWLEDGE

At the OU level, you have GPO3 that removes the Run command from the Start menu.

You have blocked policy inheritance at the OU level.

What is the result when a user logs on to a Windows 2000 Professional computer that is in the OU container? (Choose all that apply.)

A. Control Panel is not available.

B. Control Panel is available.

C. User passwords must be six characters long.

D. User passwords can be any length.

E. Run is available on the Start menu.

F. Run is not available on the Start menu.

15. Group Policy is enforced on computers running which of the following operating systems? (Choose all that apply.)

A. Microsoft Windows for Workgroups 3.11

B. Microsoft Windows 2000 Advanced Server

C. Microsoft Windows 95

D. Microsoft Windows NT 4.0 with Service Pack 6 or later

E. Microsoft Windows 2000 Professional

F. Red Hat Linux 6.1 with Samba installed

Answers to Review Questions

1. To make sure a GPO for a site was applied to all users and computers in the site, you would select the No Override option for the GPO. This forces the GPO settings to be applied to all subsequent levels of the hierarchy, including domains and OUs, because GPOs for a site are processed first. See "Group Policy Inheritance" and "Forcing Group Policy Settings."
2. GPO settings apply to members of the Authenticated Users group by default. At this level, all users who log on to the domain, as well as all computers that log on to the domain when started, have GPO settings applied to them. See "Implementing Security Policies."
3. Group Policy enables the administrator to set centralized and decentralized policies that provide control over computer and user environments. GPOs enable the administrator to ensure users have the application and requisite environmental settings to perform their jobs. They enable the administrator to have control over user and computer environments whether they are located in the next room or halfway around the world. Because GPO administration can be delegated to others, a corporate administrator can ensure the local requirements are incorporated into any centralized administration of desktops that is desired. Finally, GPOs enable the administrator to ensure corporate policies and business rules can be enforced throughout the enterprise. See "Introduction to Group Policy" and "Group Policy Scope."
4. To ensure all users in the domain have the corporate logo as the background wallpaper on their desktops, you would create a GPO at the domain level and configure the wallpaper settings in the User Configuration portion of the Administrative Template settings of the GPO. You would also make sure the Domain Users security group has been assigned the Read and Apply Group Policy permissions on the GPO.

APPLY YOUR KNOWLEDGE

To ensure that members of the sales department have a quarterly promo as the background wallpaper on their desktops, you would create a GPO at the domain level and configure the wallpaper settings in the User Configuration portion of the Administrative Template settings of the GPO. You would also ensure the Sales security group has been assigned the Read and Apply Group Policy permission on the GPO. To not have this GPO applied to any other users in the domain, you would also remove the Domain Users security group from the list of users and groups assigned permissions on the GPO.

Next, to ensure that the sales users would not receive the background wallpaper that all other users are getting, you would filter the domain users Group Policy, add the Sales security group to the list of groups assigned permissions on the domain users GPO, and uncheck the Apply Group Policy permission so that the policy is not enforced for the Sales security group.

Finally, to ensure that these settings are not tampered with by lower-level administrators, you would set the No Override option for both GPOs. See "Group Policy Scope."

5. AutoPlay will be disabled. Computer settings take precedence over user settings; hence, the computer setting of Disable AutoPlay wins out. See "Group Policy Scope" and "Group Policy Processing."

6. Forcing Group Policy means you have configured the No Override option for the GPO. The end result is that the settings in the GPO with the No Override option set can't be modified by lower-level GPOs even if the administrator at that lower level (domain or OU) has blocked policy inheritance. See "Blocking Group Policy Inheritance."

7. To improve performance of policy processing if only the user portion of the GPO is specified for your policy, you can check the Disable Computer Configuration settings on the General tab of the GPO Properties dialog box. This tells all computers applying the policy to download only the user configuration settings and not waste time downloading the computer portion because it is not used. See "Creating and Managing Group Policy."

8. Software must be in the form of a Windows Installer Package file, or you must create a ZAP file if you want to deploy the software using Group Policy.

   The MSI file is in native Windows Installer format and contains the files, Registry settings, and shortcuts that make up an application, as well as information on where these elements should be installed.

   A ZAP file is a text file that specifies information on the program to be invoked to install the application, including any parameters, as well as file extensions, that should be associated with the application. See the section "Preparing Software for Deployment Using Group Policy."

9. Configure a GPO at the domain level and create the Microsoft Outlook 2000 package in the Users Configuration container of the GPO. Assign, rather than publish, the application to ensure it is installed on all users' desktops. See the section "Software Deployment Using Group Policy."

10. Create a GPO at the German users' OU in Active Directory, and assign the package to it. Configure a transform (MST) file with the

APPLY YOUR KNOWLEDGE

German language characteristics required, and associate it with the package. This ensures that Microsoft Outlook 2000 is still installed (it is assigned), but the language requirements of the German users are also taken into consideration through the transform (MST) file. See the section "Managing Software Deployment."

11. You can create a ZAP file to install the application and then publish the software product in Group Policy. You also can repackage the application using a third-party repackaging tool such as Veritas WinINSTALL LE, which creates a Windows Installer Package file, providing you with greater flexibility in deployment. See the section "Preparing Software for Deployment Using Group Policy."

12. Create software categories that will be available domain-wide. Then, modify your packages in the various GPOs and assign them to one or more categories. In this way, when a user wants to install an application that has been published, she can view the list of all software or only the categories in which she is interested when going to Add/Remove Programs in Control Panel. See the section "Managing Software Deployment."

13. You would assign an application to a computer rather than a user when the application is required to be available to all users on one or more machines. In this way, users will always have critical software available. See the section "Software Deployment Using Group Policy."

14. When using ZAP files, you can't assign the package to computers or users; you can only publish them. This is because a ZAP file simply tells Windows Installer which program to invoke to start the installation process. Windows Installer has no control over what actually occurs during the application installation and, therefore, can't control it. Because of this, packages can't be assigned because this would require Windows Installer to automate the installation of a software application. See the section "Preparing Software for Deployment Using Group Policy."

15. To add a support telephone number and Web site location to an existing MSI file, you would modify the package (MSI) file using a third-party repackaging product such as Veritas WinINSTALL LE. See the section "Windows Installer Technology."

16. A software package can remove files from a user's machine when it is deployed if it was repackaged and, during the repackaging, files were removed. Because repackaging takes a before and after snapshot of the user's computer to determine what has changed during the software installation process, any files that were removed or modified by either the product's setup program or the user are incorporated in the package. If the administrator did not carefully examine the resulting package file created and correct any items that should not be passed on to users' machines, a repackaged application can make unwanted changes to a user's system. To correct this problem, either modify the package or repackage the application. See the section "Troubleshooting Software Deployment."

17. To ensure that users will still be able to use an application after it has been removed from a GPO, make the package removal optional. If the removal is optional, users can still use the application until they themselves decide to remove it, after which time the application is no longer available. See the section "Maintaining Software Packages Using Group Policy."

APPLY YOUR KNOWLEDGE

Answers to Exam Questions

1. **A, C, D.** Your solution would ensure that all computers in the domain were assigned Microsoft Office 2000 and had it installed. Any GPO defined at the domain level will apply to all containers and OUs in the domain unless blocked. Because you blocked policy inheritance at the legal department OU, the legal department will not have the software installed. The transform files you created will have no effect because they were all added in the one GPO (they will actually cause all the different language versions to be installed) and will not localize the software for each office. Costs were kept down because the deployment was handled through Group Policy and did not require anyone to really travel. See the sections "Software Deployment Using Group Policy" and "Maintaining Software Packages Using Group Policy."

2. **A, B, C, D.** By defining the GPO at the site level and creating different transform files for each site, you were able to localize the package for each location. Furthermore, by blocking policy inheritance at the legal department OU, you ensured that the legal department was exempt from this corporate policy. Finally, by doing all the work using Windows 2000 Group Policy, you kept costs down. See the sections "Software Deployment Using Group Policy" and "Maintaining Software Packages Using Group Policy."

3. **D.** Package files include shortcuts, Registry settings, and the files required to be installed; ZAP files do not. ZAP files are text files that describe the extensions associated with an application and the program to be run when installing the software application. Windows Installer can't execute ZAP files with elevated privileges because you actually need to run the setup program for the application, and this program runs in the security context of the user initiating the installation. Both ZAP and package (MSI) files can be used in software deployment with a few restrictions. See the section "Preparing Software for Deployment Using Group Policy."

4. **B.** Although both B and D would work, it is better to repackage the application and publish it to the user rather than use a ZAP file. If the user does not have permission to modify the Registry or place files in system folders, the ZAP file method might fail because the application can't be installed using elevated privileges. Windows Installer Package files, even the ones repackaged using WinINSTALL LE, can be installed using elevated privileges.

   Assigning the repackaged application to all users would install it on their computers regardless of whether they wanted the application, and you said you wanted to give them a choice. You can't assign ZAP files; you can only publish them. See the sections "Preparing Software for Deployment Using Group Policy" and "Software Deployment Using Group Policy."

5. **A, D.** When a package is published to a user, it can be installed either through document activation (the user opens a file whose extension is associated with the application) or through user activation in which the user goes to Control Panel and selects Add/Remove Programs to install the software application. The package will not be installed when the user logs on or the computer starts up because it was published and not assigned. For an automatic install to take place, you would need to assign the package to the user

APPLY YOUR KNOWLEDGE

or computer. See the section "Software Deployment Using Group Policy."

6. **B.** The most likely reason the application is still installed on their machines is that they were filtered out of the GPO scope where the forced removal was configured. Because the removal of the application was forced, they could not say no because they were never prompted. Regardless of whether they are sales managers, the Group Policy still applies to them. (Position has no priority in Group Policy.) They could not have reinstalled the package using Add/Remove Programs because it was not available any longer. It was removed. There is no way to make an application "critical" on a machine and therefore have it override GPO settings; this functionality does not exist. See the section "Software Deployment Using Group Policy."

7. **A, D.** To ensure all users have only the new version, you need to make the upgrade required and uninstall the previous version when performing the upgrade. Making the upgrade optional and enabling users to keep the old version is the same thing. Overwriting the old version might leave portions of that application still around, which is not what you said you wanted. See the section "Maintaining Software Packages Using Group Policy."

8. **B, C, D.** Windows Installer Package files enable you to assign software to users and computers. Furthermore, when removing software, the uninstall process is smart enough to know which shared files are still in use by other application because the Windows Installer service keeps track of this information. Finally, Windows Installer Packages provide for resilient software in which Windows Installer automatically replaces critical files that become damaged or corrupted. Publishing of software can be done using either ZAP files or Windows Installer Package files, so this answer is not 100% accurate when it comes to packages. Windows Installer Package files enable you to install software on users' machines even though they might not have the necessary privileges to do so because Windows Installer can perform an installation using its privileges (that is, an elevated privileges install). See the section "Preparing Software for Deployment Using Group Policy."

9. **D.** Internet access is enabled by default when you install Windows 2000. If you want to turn it off, you need to create a GPO that disables Internet access. Customer service supervisors are members of both the CustomerService security group and the CSSupervisors security group. If you grant the CustomerService group only Read and Apply Group Policy permissions, supervisors do not have Internet access. To correct this, grant the CSSupervisors only Read permissions on the GPO, thereby filtering the policy from them.

   Answer B also provides a solution that works, although creating two policies requires more administration than is actually needed with a single GPO. Because the question asked for the best answer, D is the only logical choice. See "Group Policy Scope" and "Blocking Group Policy Inheritance."

10. **B, D.** The fact that some users have the Run command still available indicates that GPO inheritance was blocked at the Accounting OU level. Other GPOs were put in place, which allowed some users to have Run on the Start menu and others to have it removed. Had you forced the GPO settings to be applied by

Apply Your Knowledge

selecting the No Override option for the GPO, this behavior would not have occurred, and the Run command would be removed from all users. Both the lack of forcing the GPO and the capability of OU administrators to block policy inheritance are the cause of the problem. See "Blocking Group Policy Inheritance" and "Group Policy Inheritance."

11. **D.** To allow the junior administrators to modify the GPOs in their OUs, you need to assign them Read and Write permissions to the GPOs in their OUs. Assigning them Full Control permissions also works, but it might give them more permissions than needed (for example, the capability to change a GPO's permissions or to specify options such as No Override). Granting them Read and Write permissions to the OU enables them to change other objects in the OU, again giving them higher permissions than necessary. You can't use the Delegation of Control Wizard to delegate control of GPOs; the Delegation of Control Wizard can only be used to delegate administrative authority to the GPO's parent container, such as OUs. Making users members of the Domain Admins group is never a good idea. See "Blocking Group Policy Inheritance," "Configuring Group Policy Security," and "Setting Permissions to Manage the Policy."

12. **D, F.** The answer to this question is similar to the preceding, except the users now need to be able to change the contents of the parent OU container. To do this, they also must have Read and Write permissions on the OU they will be controlling. In actuality, the junior administrators require only the Create groupPolicyContainer Objects permission and the Delete groupPolicyContainer Object permissions, but these were not available in the question. See "Blocking Group Policy Inheritance" and "Configuring Group Policy Security."

13. **B.** Policies are always applied starting at the site level, then the domain level, and finally the OU level. This is because site-level GPOs can be used to configure computer and user settings that might take into consideration geographic local differences; domain-level GPOs specify settings applied to all users and computers in the domain. All these settings can be overwritten and modified at the OU level, which has the smallest number of Active Directory objects to be affected—both computers and users. In each stage, you are reducing the number of Active Directory objects to be affected by a GPO. See "Group Policy Scope."

14. **B, C, F.** Policy inheritance was blocked at the OU level, which means any higher-level GPOs will not be applied at the OU, where the Run command (GPO3) was removed from the Start menu (answer F). The site-level GPO (GPO2) was configured with No Override, so the fact that the policy inheritance was blocked at the OU level has no effect. The policy still applies and states that passwords must be six characters long (answer C). Control Panel was disabled at the domain level (GPO1), but this GPO was not configured with the No Override option, so it was blocked at the OU level and was not processed. Hence, Control Panel is still available to users at the OU level (answer B). See "Blocking Group Policy Inheritance" and "Group Policy Inheritance."

APPLY YOUR KNOWLEDGE

15. **B, E.** Group Policy is enforced only on computers running any variant of Windows 2000, which includes Windows 2000 Professional and Windows 2000 Advanced Server. It also includes Windows 2000 Server and Windows 2000 Data Center Server. See "Introduction to Group Policy."

Suggested Readings and Resources

1. "Automated Deployment Options: An Overview White Paper" on Microsoft's Web site at `http://www.microsoft.com/windows2000/library/planning/client/deployops.asp`.
2. "Automating the Deployment of Windows 2000 Professional and Office 2000" on Microsoft's Web site at `http://www.microsoft.com/windows2000/library/planning/incremental/sysprep.asp`.
3. "Desktop Deployment Solutions from Third-Party Companies" on Microsoft's Web site at `http://www.microsoft.com/windows2000/guide/server/partners/DesktopSolutions.asp`.
4. *Microsoft Windows 2000 Resource Kit.* Deployment Planning Guide. Microsoft Press, 2000.
5. "Software Deployment Using Windows 2000 and Systems Management Server 2.0" on Microsoft's Web site at `http://www.microsoft.com/windows2000/library/planning/management/smsintell.asp`.
6. "Software Installation and Maintenance" on Microsoft's Web site at `http://www.microsoft.com/windows2000/library/operations/management/siamwp.asp`.
7. "Windows Installer" on Microsoft's Web site at `http://www.microsoft.com/windows2000/library/howitworks/management/installer.asp`.

PART

CONFIGURING, SECURING, AND TROUBLESHOOTING REMOTE ACCESS

OBJECTIVES

If you have ever used a modem to connect your Windows computer to another server or network, you have used remote access. With Windows 2000, Microsoft has introduced many new remote access capabilities to its operating system. This chapter covers all of the "Configuring, Securing, and Troubleshooting Remote Access" objective except for one of the sub-objectives that is deferred until the next chapter. As today's workforce becomes more and more diverse, the ability to provide reliable, secure remote access is becoming critical in every environment.

In this chapter we will cover the following subobjectives of the "Configuring, Securing, and Troubleshooting Remote Access" objective:

Configure and troubleshoot remote access and virtual private network (VPN) connections.

- **Configure and troubleshoot client-to-server PPTP and L2TP connections.**
- **Manage existing server-to-sever PPTP and L2TP connections.**
- **Configure and verify the security of a VPN connection.**
- **Configure client computer remote access properties.**
- **Configure remote access name resolution and IP address allocation.**

▶ If you want to gain access to a server or to an entire network, the previous objective covers the access mechanisms. Although the objective's emphasis is clearly on virtual private networking in its multiple forms, there is coverage of the components of any remote access scenario. The objective ensures that you are familiar with the two main types of virtual private networking and that you can set up the server to provide the appropriate information to the client.

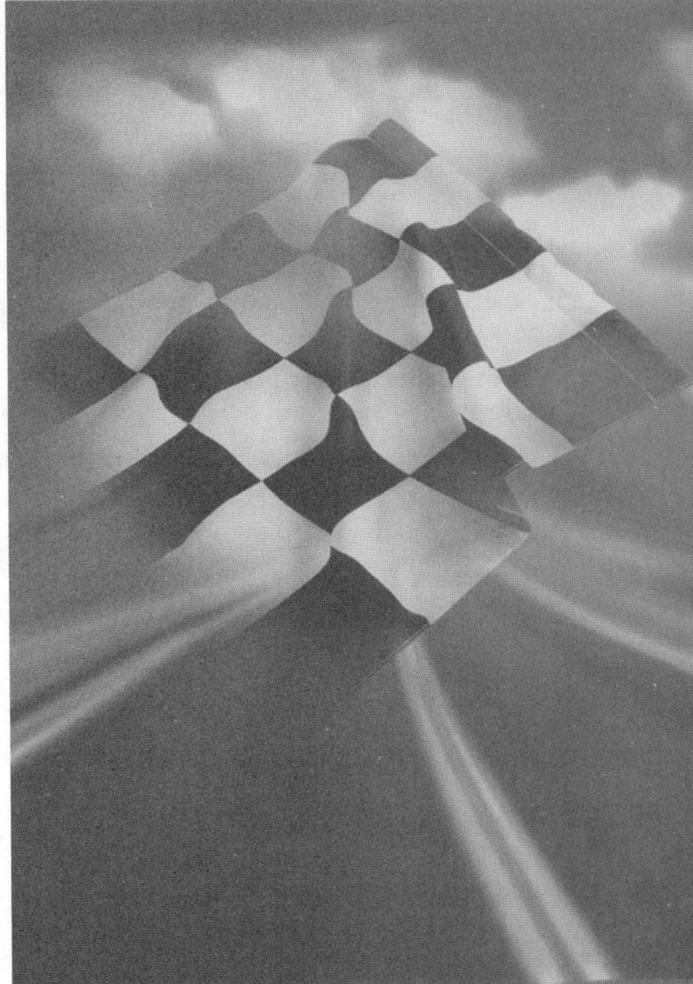

CHAPTER 12

Routing and Remote Access Service Fundamentals

OBJECTIVES

Troubleshoot Routing and Remote Access Policy.

- **Diagnose problems with remote access policy priority.**
- **Diagnose remote access policy problems caused by user account group membership and nested groups.**
- **Create and configure remote access policies and profiles.**
- **Select appropriate encryption and authentication protocols.**

▶ This objective focuses on controlling who has the ability to gain remote access to the system. Remote access is often controlled by remote access policies in large organizations. These policies, much like group policies, have specific rules for precedence. Finally, the objective also deals with identifying and using the appropriate authentication protocol given a situation.

Configure and troubleshoot Network Address Translation (NAT) and Internet Connection sharing.

- **Configure Routing and Remote Access to perform NAT.**
- **Troubleshoot Internet Connection Sharing problems by using `ipconfig` and `ping` commands.**

▶ Network Address Translation and Internet Connection Sharing (ICS) are both ways in which you can allow access from an internal network to the outside world. This doesn't provide the same feature set as the Internet Security Architecture product that Microsoft sells, but it's often enough for small offices. Internet Connection Sharing is important because for the smallest offices it offers the quickest implementation and least support.

OUTLINE

Study Strategies

- Be sure you have a thorough understanding of the security capabilities of all the remote access mechanisms. With the focus on security in the industry today, Microsoft considers security to be one of the cornerstones of Windows 2000.
- Review the various types of encryption available for authenticating and securing your information through remote access. Consider which is the most secure in a Microsoft-only network and in a heterogeneous network.
- Pay close attention to the capabilities of remote access policies. Windows 2000 includes several policy-based management capabilities, and understanding the policies associated with remote access is important for this exam.
- Be sure to complete the exercises at the end of the chapter. Microsoft is striving to make certification exams more rigorous. Familiarity not only with the theory, but also with the hands-on portion of the configuration and troubleshooting of remote access, is important for this exam.

CONFIGURING AND TROUBLESHOOTING REMOTE ACCESS

Before we discuss how to configure remote access with Windows 2000 Server, we should take a minute to review what exactly remote access is under Windows 2000. If you have worked with Windows NT 4, you are undoubtedly familiar with the Remote Access Service (RAS). RAS is an NT 4 add-on service that provides the capability for a server to receive incoming modem calls and that allows the user to optionally connect to the network. RAS also is used for the other direction: You need RAS to connect your Windows NT server or workstation to another host, either NT or a generic dial-in server.

This model has changed dramatically in Windows 2000. Not only is the Routing and Remote Access Service (the next generation of the Remote Access Service) installed automatically with the operating system, it also bundles several features that used to be distributed through other services under Windows NT. For example, not only are RAS services available with Routing and Remote Access, but the Windows 2000 VPN service, for one, is also included in Routing and Remote Access.

But before you jump into configuring the Routing and Remote Access Service, let's discuss some of the reasons for deploying remote access and some of the specifics surrounding the Windows 2000 Routing and Remote Access.

Microsoft has included remote access capabilities in all its operating systems since the introduction of Windows for Workgroups (a remote access client computer) and the Windows NT Advanced Server (a remote access server). If you have worked with earlier versions of Windows NT or Windows 9x, you are probably familiar with the term RAS, which was first used to discuss the NT Remote Access Server and later used as a generic description of most of the Windows operating system remote access applications. This changed in the midst of the Windows NT Server 4 operating system's life cycle, with the introduction of an add-on service upgrade known as the Routing and Remote Access Services, which you should note carried over to the Windows 2000 operating system. The main reason for the change was that Microsoft needed to enhance its offerings in the remote access and routing areas of networking.

The Routing and Remote Access upgrade provided the first framework for integrating all network services into a single application and introduced the following features to Windows NT networking:

- A unified service for Routing and Remote Access integrated with the operating system
- A full set of routing protocols for IP and IPX (including the noteworthy addition of OSPF)
- APIs for third-party routing protocols, user interface, and management
- Demand-dial routing
- Point-to-Point Tunneling Protocol (PPTP) server-to-server for secure virtual private networks (VPNs)
- Remote Authentication Dial-In User Service (RADIUS) client support

But that is enough history. Let's look at what the Routing and Remote Access Service included with Windows 2000 brings to the table. Routing and Remote Access includes the following capabilities:

- Full integration into the Windows 2000 operating system. This is not an add-on or a patch, but a fully integrated service built from the ground up as part of Windows 2000.
- Consistent management interface for all routing-based activities, including remote access, VPN, and IP and IPX routing.
- Additional VPN services and simplified VPN management. The two VPN interfaces, PPTP and Layer 2 Transport Protocol (L2TP), are installed and configured by default, requiring no additional configuration. There is also support for the IPSec protocol.
- Network Address Translation has been added, as has Internet Connection Sharing.
- Additional authentication mechanisms have been added to Routing and Remote Access, including MS-CHAP v2, RADIUS, and EAP (for smart card and certificate support).

EXAM TIP

Authentication Support Only Windows 2000 Server supports EAP and RADIUS for authentication.

One other key point to remember when discussing Microsoft's Routing and Remote Access Service and the remote access capabilities is that in previous incarnations, the term RAS, or Remote Access Service, was used interchangeably to refer to the dial-in connections and the service that ran the dial-up server. With the new Routing and Remote Access Service, Microsoft is striving to clarify its use of terminology. So, in Windows 2000 parlance, *Routing and Remote Access* refers only to the Routing and Remote Access application. The server is called either a *dial-in* or *dial-up server*—or in the case of VPN, a *VPN* server. The client computers are called *dial-in* or *dial-up clients.*

It is important to keep in mind that Microsoft's Routing and Remote Access Service considers all connections to be local area network (LAN) connections. What this means from a functionality perspective is that all the services that are available via LAN connection are also available via a modem connection.

Understanding Remote Access Protocols

Microsoft's Routing and Remote Access Service supports two data link control protocols for asynchronous connections:

- **Serial Line Interface Protocol (SLIP)**—The granddaddy of serial line protocols, SLIP is supported for outbound legacy applications and is almost never used.
- **Point-to-Point Protocol (PPP)**—PPP is the protocol most of us use when connecting via modem. PPP can automatically establish and reestablish connections, uses error correction, and can support multiple protocols. The Windows 2000 implementation for PPP is fully RFC 1661 "Point-to-Point Protocol" compliant.

Windows 2000 can connect to any other RFC 1661-compliant dial-up server and can accept connections from any compliant client computers. The real strength of this protocol is the support for multiple network protocols, such as IPX, IP, and AppleTalk. SLIP is restricted to IP only.

We will discuss many of the features of PPP as we move through this chapter. For now, let's take a look at the simplest use for the Routing and Remote Access Service.

Configuring Inbound Connections

If you have mobile users, it is a safe bet that you have dealt with requests for access to the network. This could be for access to mail, the company intranet, or even file shares or applications. Windows 2000 includes as part of Routing and Remote Access the capability to permit inbound connections via attached modems.

Windows 2000 uses three types of policies to control remote access:

- **Local Internet Authentication Services policies**—These local policies are derived from RADIUS and can be used to define access permissions based on several client attributes.
- **Central Internet Authentication Services policies**—A dial-up server can be configured to use a central IAS RADIUS server to provide its policies. This enables multiple Routing and Remote Access dial-up servers to use the same policies without requiring the manual replication of policies and settings.
- **Group policies**—More in line with the older versions of remote access, access can be controlled by group policies.

Now let's look at how to configure a Windows 2000 server to support an inbound connection. Step By Step 12.1 shows you how to configure remote access inbound connections.

STEP BY STEP

12.1 Configuring Remote Access Inbound Connections

1. Right-click the My Network Places icon on the desktop. From the context menu, select Properties. The Network and Dial-up Connections window opens. (You can also open this window by selecting Start, Settings, Network and Dial-up Connections.)

continues

continued

2. Double-click the Make New Connection icon; the Network Connection Wizard starts. If you have not already configured your dialing location information, you will be prompted to do so before continuing with the wizard (see Figure 12.1). Fill in the information and click OK. You will see the new location entry in the Phone and Modem Options window. Click OK to close it and return to the wizard.

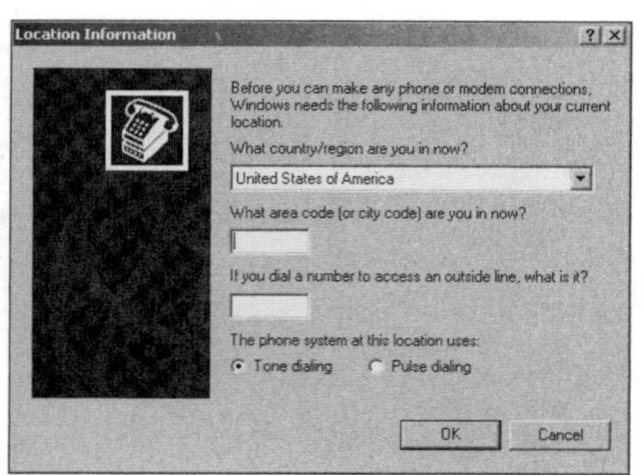

FIGURE 12.1
The location information is needed so the server knows whether a call is local or long distance. In the case of a dial-in server, this is necessary for callbacks.

3. Click Next to start the wizard process. The Network Connection Type dialog box opens (see Figure 12.2). Select the Accept Incoming Connections option and click Next. The Devices for Incoming Connections dialog box opens (see Figure 12.3).

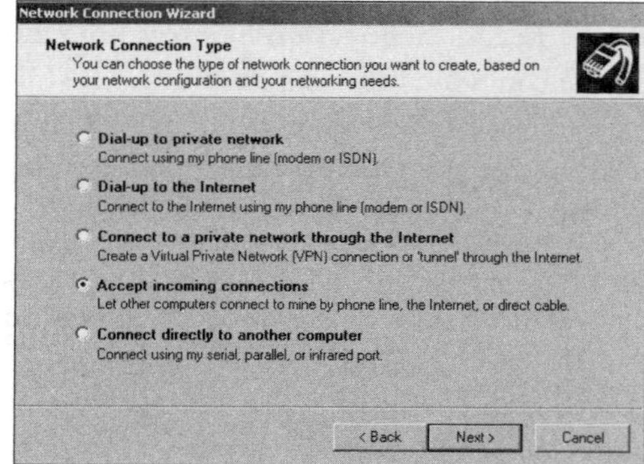

FIGURE 12.2
The Network Connection Type dialog box enables you to select from a variety of Routing and Remote Access connection options.

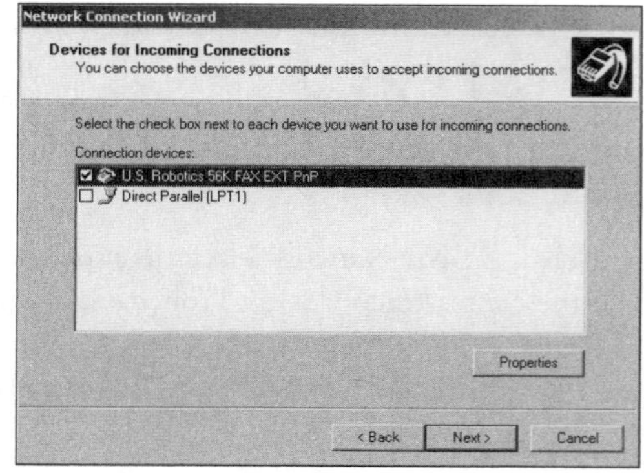

FIGURE 12.3
This dialog box allows you to selectively enable the devices that will accept incoming calls.

4. Select the device(s) you want to receive the incoming calls and click Next. The Incoming Virtual Private Connection dialog box opens (see Figure 12.4).

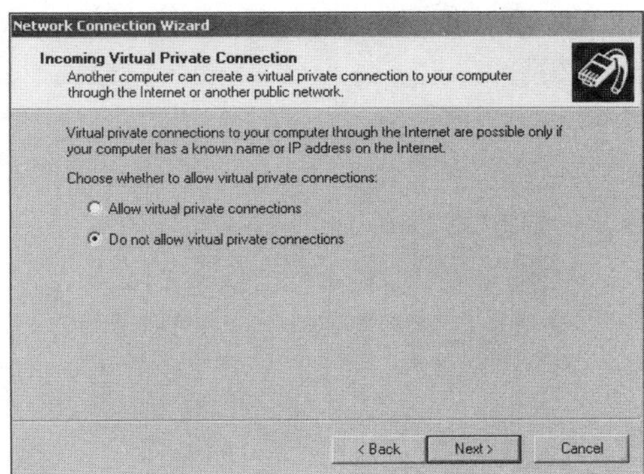

FIGURE 12.4
In addition to supporting inbound modem connections, Windows 2000 also has the capability to accept inbound virtual private connections.

5. Select Do Not Allow Virtual Private Connections and click Next. The Allowed Users dialog box opens (see Figure 12.5).

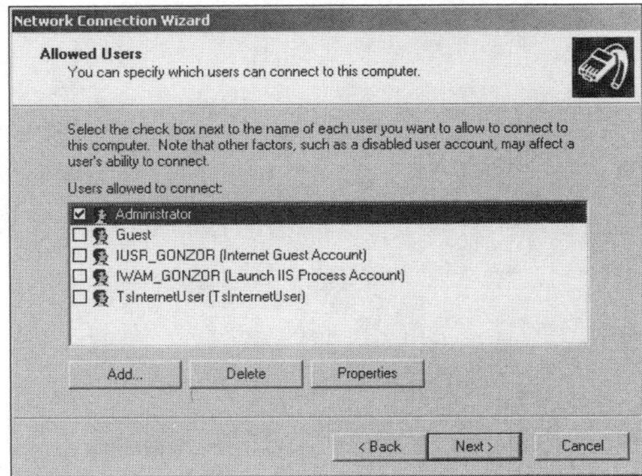

FIGURE 12.5
You can select the users who should be able to connect. However, if their accounts are disabled or locked, they will not be able to connect.

6. Select the users you want to have dial-in access. Then, click Properties to open the user properties. This enables you to configure callback, if necessary.

continues

continued

7. Click the Callback tab (see Figure 12.6). For the most secure access, select Always Use the Following Callback Number and enter the user's phone number. Click OK to return to the wizard, and click Next to continue. The Networking Components dialog box opens (see Figure 12.7).

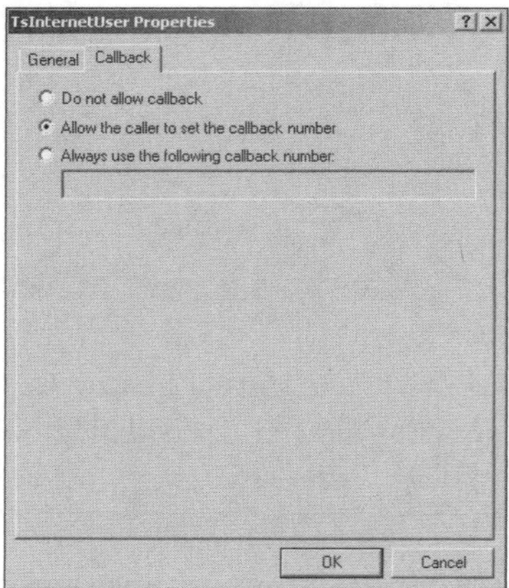

FIGURE 12.6
In a highly secure environment, use of the callback options included with Windows 2000 is a necessity.

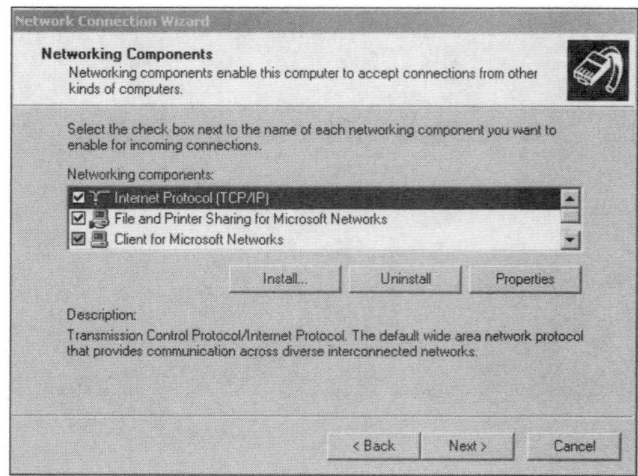

FIGURE 12.7
The Networking Connections dialog box determines which services are available to dial-in users.

8. Select the components you want the dial-in user to have access to after he connects. By default, all components are selected. Click Next to continue, and the Completing the Network Connection Wizard dialog box opens (see Figure 12.8).

9. Enter an intuitive name for the new connection and click Finish to complete the installation.

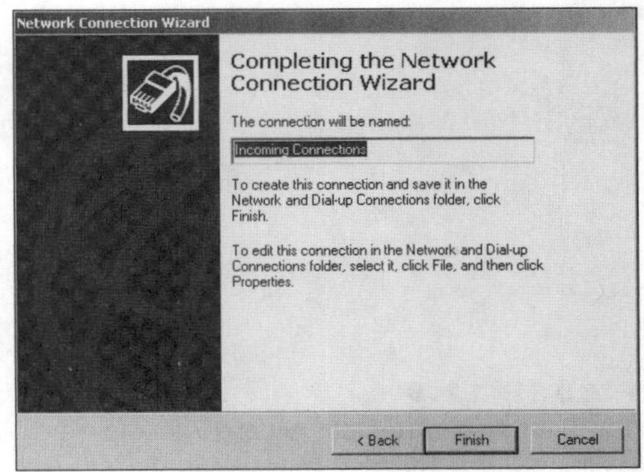

FIGURE 12.8
After the wizard is complete, you need to give it a name to identify the connection.

Now that you have a dial-up connection, let's take a look at creating a remote access policy to define what can be done with the new connections.

Creating a Remote Access Policy

▶ Troubleshoot routing and remote access policy.

- Diagnose problems with remote access policy priority.
- Diagnose remote access policy problems caused by user account group membership and nested groups.
- Create and configure remote access policies and profiles.
- Select appropriate encryption and authentication protocols.

A remote access *policy* is a set of actions that can be applied to a group of users. Any attempted access must meet a specified set of requirements. The example Microsoft uses to illustrate this point is to think about e-mail rules. In many e-mail packages, you can configure a rule that enables you to delete all messages from a specific user or group of users. A remote access policy is similar in that you can specify actions based on several criteria. Step By Step 12.2 illustrates the creation of a remote access policy.

STEP BY STEP

12.2 Creating a Remote Access Policy

1. Open the Routing and Remote Access console by selecting Start, Programs, Administrative Tools, Routing and Remote Access (see Figure 12.9).

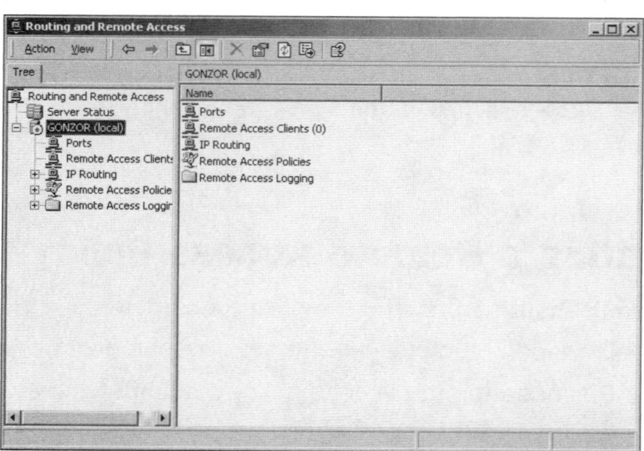

FIGURE 12.9
The Routing and Remote Access console enables you to manage your remote access server, including creating remote access policies.

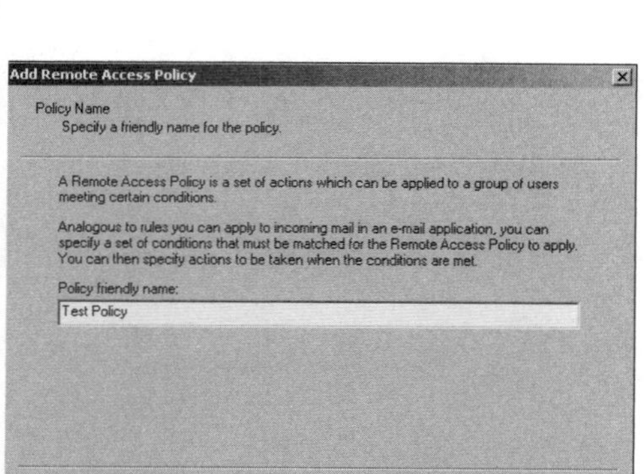

FIGURE 12.10
This dialog box enables you to give your policy a user-friendly name.

2. Expand the application tree in the left pane by double-clicking the server. Right-click Remote Access Policies and select New Remote Access Policy. The Add Remote Access Policy window opens (see Figure 12.10).

3. Enter a user-friendly name, and click Next to continue. The Add Remote Access Policy Conditions dialog box opens (see Figure 12.11).

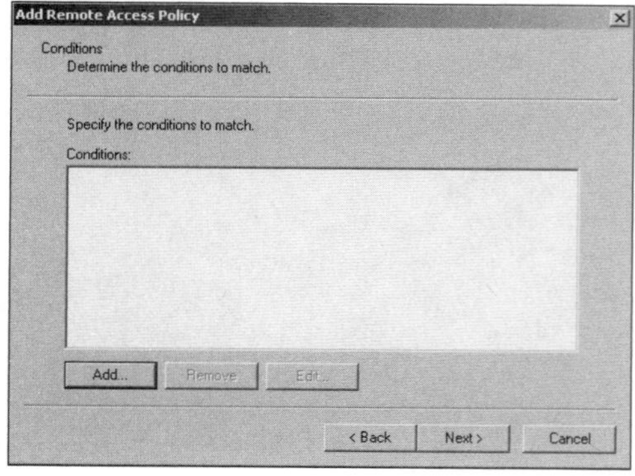

FIGURE 12.11
The first step in creating a remote access policy is to set the conditions.

4. Click Add to add a condition. Select one attribute from the list of attributes (see Figure 12.12). Each attribute creates a slightly different process, and you must configure the attribute appropriately. For this example, select Windows-Groups. Using the Windows-Groups attribute allows you to enable remote access by user groups, as defined in the Users and Groups console.

5. Click Add to go to the Groups configuration dialog box (see Figure 12.13). Then, click Add to open the Select Groups dialog box shown in Figure 12.14, and select the appropriate group(s) for the rule. Click OK to return to the Groups dialog box. Click OK to add the Windows-Groups condition to the policy. If you were to add an additional condition, users would need to meet both conditions to have the policy applied (a logical AND operation).

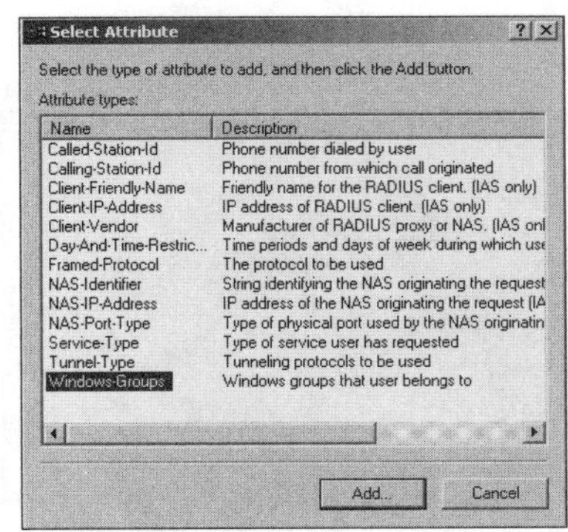

FIGURE 12.12
Select the appropriate attributes for the policy you are creating.

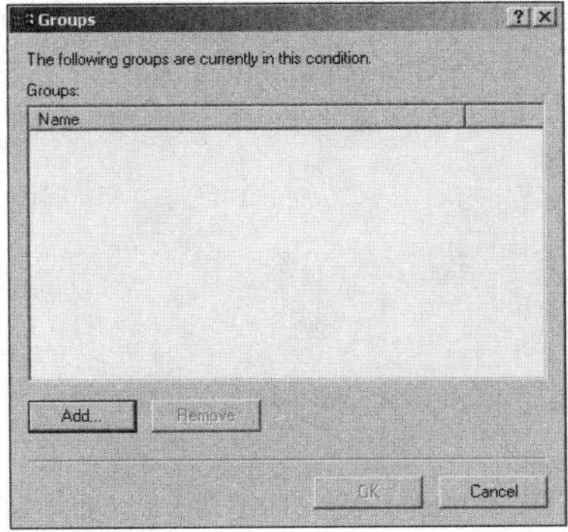

FIGURE 12.13
As a general rule, Windows-Groups is an attribute that is used frequently with remote access policies because it enables you to intuitively group users by department, function, or access rights.

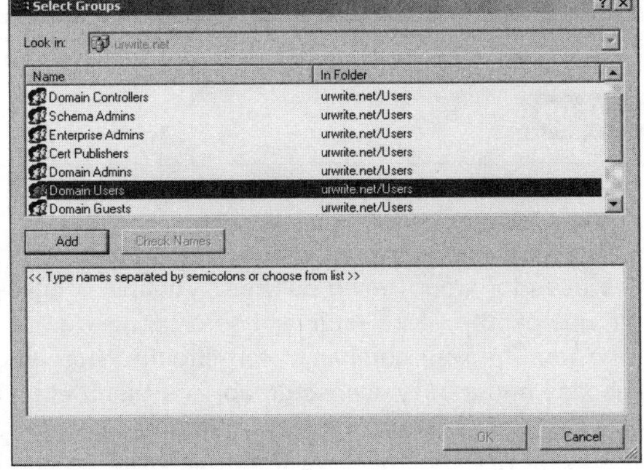

FIGURE 12.14
Select the appropriate groups for remote access permissions.

continues

continued

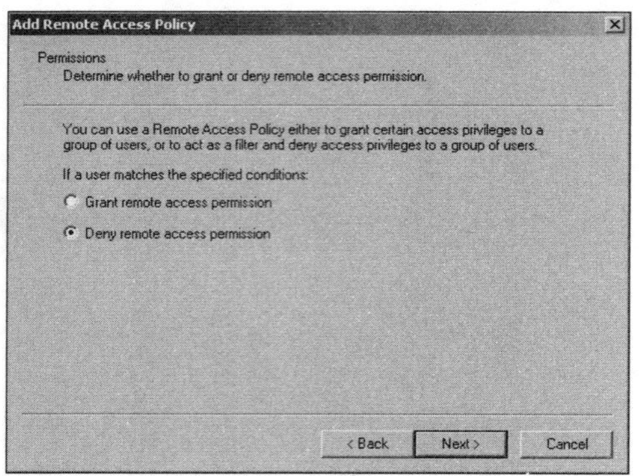

FIGURE 12.15
You can grant or deny permissions from this screen.

6. Click Next to open the Add Remote Access Policy dialog box shown in Figure 12.15. You can either grant or deny remote access permission by selecting the appropriate option. Select the Deny Remote Access Permission option and click Next. The Edit Dial-in Profile dialog box that opens enables you to access the dial-in profile for the users affected by this policy (see Figure 12.16). You can restrict a number of access parameters, which are discussed at the end of the section.

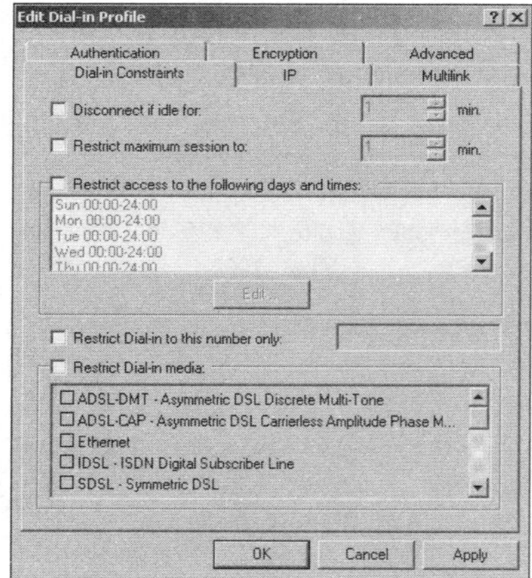

FIGURE 12.16
The Edit Dial-in Profile dialog box gives you access to the granular settings for the dial-in users.

7. Click OK to return to the User Profile screen.

8. Click Finish to complete the creation of the profile.

IN THE FIELD

DESIGN YOUR POLICIES WITH CARE

One thing you will find if you work in a large remote access environment is the uses for group-based policies. A couple of places these types of groups can be very useful include creating a group for contractors who work for your company intermittently. You can create an allow access and a deny access group, and then depending on the status of any projects, you can control their access to remote access just by moving their account from one group to another.

People on a leave of absence might be placed in an LOA group to block them from remote access until they come back on the job. The variations are endless. The trick is to really put some thought into the policy design before you start creating users. If you just start creating users with the thought of going back and organizing later, you will probably create three times as much work for yourself.

Configuring a Remote Access Profile

- Configure and troubleshoot remote access and virtual private network (VPN) connections.
    - Configure client computer remote access properties.

Now that you understand how to create a remote access policy, we need to discuss the next phase of the process—configuring a remote access profile. To configure a remote access profile, follow Step By Step 12.3.

STEP BY STEP

12.3 Configuring a Remote Access Profile

1. Open the Routing and Remote Access console by selecting Start, Programs, Administrative Tools, Routing and Remote Access.
2. Right-click the remote access policy for which you want to configure the remote access profile. Select Properties from the context menu. The Policy Properties dialog box opens (see Figure 12.17). The name in the title bar reflects the name of the policy.
3. Click the Edit Profile button; the Edit Dial-in Profile dialog box opens (refer to Figure 12.16).
4. Make any modifications necessary and click OK to return to the Properties dialog box. Click OK again to commit the changes and return to the OS.

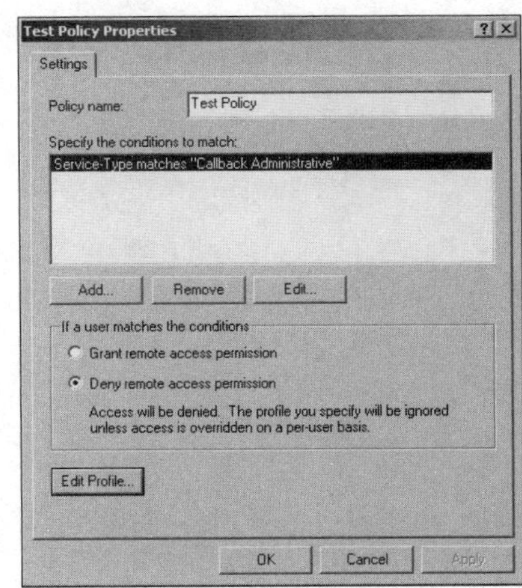

FIGURE 12.17
The Policy Properties dialog box contains all the information regarding the policy.

NOTE

What Is Dial-in Media? This is more applicable with a VPN connection than a dial-in connection, but you can disallow specific network media from connecting to the server. For example, if you didn't want DSL users to be able to connect, you could specifically deny it.

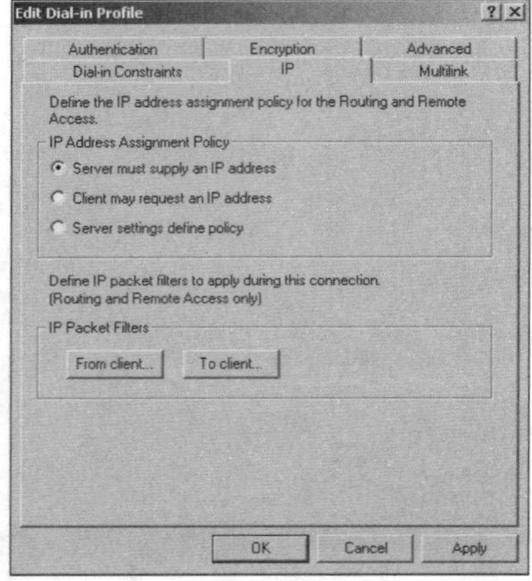

FIGURE 12.18
The IP tab can be used to set IP filters on a policy.

That's how you get to the parameters for the profile. Now let's take a look at some of the parameters you can configure before we move on to virtual private networks in the next section.

The dial-in profile contains the following settings:

- **Dial-in Constraints**—This tab enables you to configure the restrictions on the dial-in users, including the idle disconnect timer, the maximum length of the session, the time and day access is permitted, the dial-in number allowed, and the dial-in media allowed (refer to Figure 12.16).
- **IP**—This tab is used to determine the IP address assignment policy, if necessary (see Figure 12.18). The following are three possible settings for the IP Address Assignment Policy section:
    - **Server Must Supply an IP Address**—For this to work, the server must have a DHCP range configured for remote access. The client computer can't connect without requesting an address.
    - **Client May Request an IP Address**—This setting leaves the determination on whether to use a DHCP address to the client computer. If the client computer has a statically configured address, it can still connect.
    - **Server Settings Define Policy**—This setting defers the decision on IP address policy to the Routing and Remote Access Server's global policy.

  You can also apply IP packet filters from the IP tab. Packet filters can be configured for traffic sent to the client computer or traffic received from the client computer. These filters are applied by network and can be used to filter a variety of IP-based protocols, including Any, Other, ICMP, UDP, TCP, and TCP [established].
- **Multilink**—This tab enables you to configure Windows 2000's capability to aggregate multiple analog phone lines connected to multiple modems to provide greater bandwidth (see Figure 12.19). The Multilink Settings section enables you to configure the following:

- **Default to Server Settings**—Defers the configuration to the Routing and Remote Access global settings.
- **Disable Multilink (Restrict Client to Single Port)**—This setting prevents a single user from using multiple connections at the same time for aggregated bandwidth.
- **Allow Multilink**—This configuration allows a client computer to connect using multiple ports, and you can configure the number of ports it can use.

The Bandwidth Allocation Protocol (BAP) Settings can be used to configure when to drop one of the multilink lines, based on usage. If the usage drops below a configurable amount of bandwidth (50% is the default) for a specified amount of time (2 minutes is the default), one of the multilink lines is dropped. You can also enable the Require BAP for Dynamic Multilink Requests option.

◆ **Authentication**—This tab enables you to configure the authentication methods supported by Windows 2000 (see Figure 12.20). (The protocols listed in Figure 12.20 are discussed later in this chapter.)

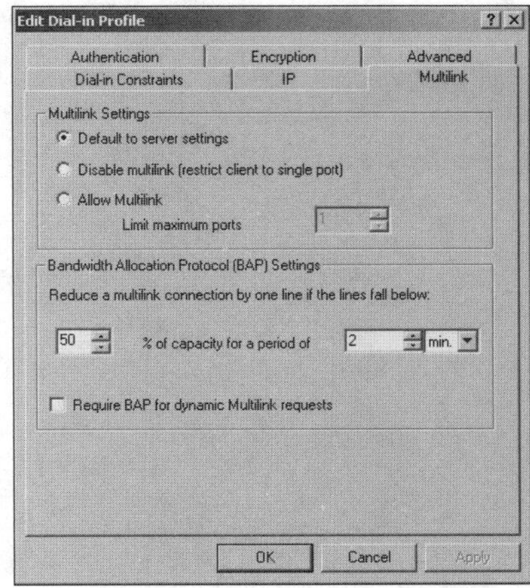

FIGURE 12.19
The multilink capabilities of Windows 2000 enable you to maximize bandwidth across multiple analog phone systems.

EXAM TIP

Both Sides Must Multilink
Multilink must be configured on both the client and server for multilink to work. If either the client or server does not allow multilink connections then a multilink connection will not be established.

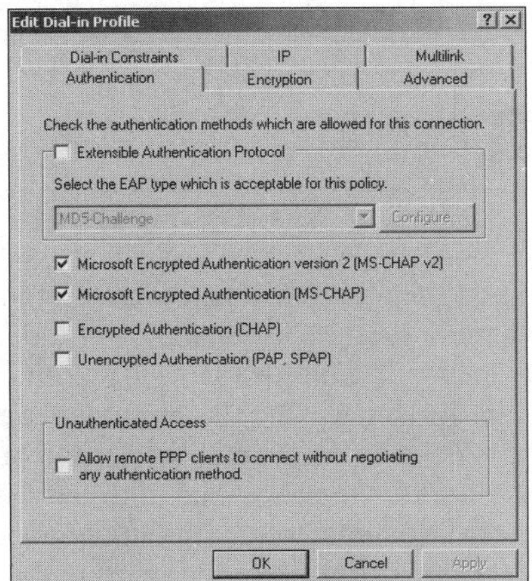

FIGURE 12.20
To take advantage of the multilink capabilities of Windows 2000, you need to enable it here for the appropriate group.

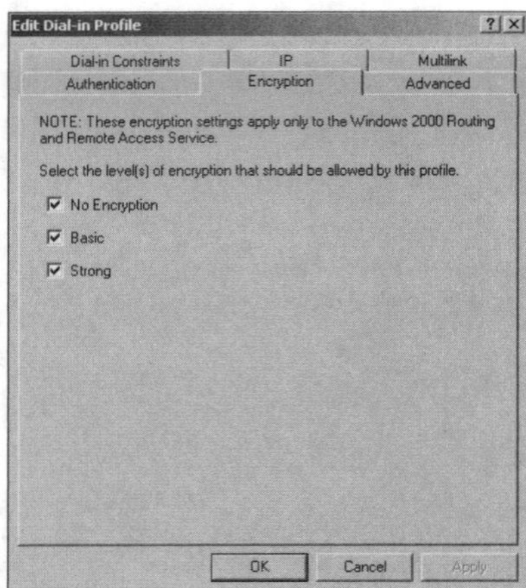

FIGURE 12.21
Routing and Remote Access supports three levels of encryption.

- **Encryption**—This tab enables you to set the level of encryption required with Routing and Remote Access authentication (see Figure 12.21). You can set it to No Encryption, Basic, or Strong, or you can allow any combination of the three.
- **Advanced**—The Advanced tab enables you to add connection attributes to be returned to the Remote Access Server (see Figure 12.22). This is usually used in conjunction with RADIUS.

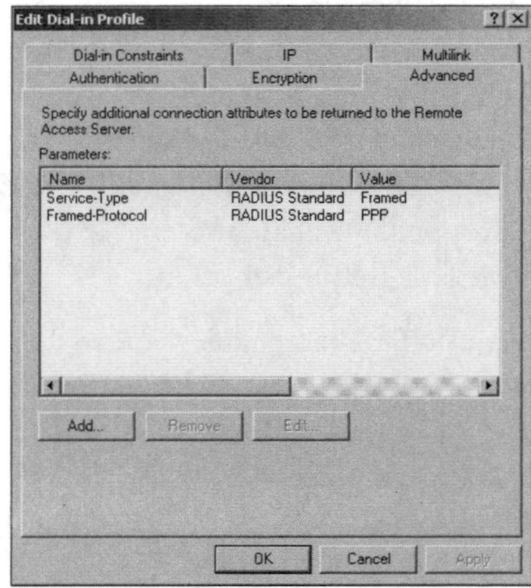

FIGURE 12.22
If you need to configure RADIUS attributes, use this tab.

IN THE FIELD

PUTTING RADIUS TO WORK

If you have worked in a large remote access environment, you might have run across RADIUS already. But for those of you who haven't, we will discuss it a bit here. RADIUS (Remote Authentication Dial-in User Service) is an authentication and accounting system used by many Internet service providers (ISPs) and enterprise networks. When you dial in to the ISP, you must enter your username and password. This information is passed to a RADIUS server, which checks that the information is correct and then authorizes access to the ISP system. Though not an official standard, the RADIUS specification is maintained by a working group of the Internet Engineering Task Force (IETF).

Another place you see RADIUS used is to leverage the account information in a Windows 2000 domain. The built-in RADIUS server can be used not only to authenticate Routing and Remote Access client computers, but it can also be used by third-party dial-in servers as an authentication method. In fact, some ISPs authenticate users for an enterprise account by passing RADIUS authentication requests to a local RADIUS server, enabling the company to control who gets access to the Internet.

Configuring a Virtual Private Network

- Configure and troubleshoot remote access and virtual private network connections.
  - Configure and troubleshoot client-to-server PPTP and L2TP connections.
  - Configure and verify the security of a VPN connection.

Before we delve into configuring the Windows 2000 Virtual Private Network, let's look at VPNs in general and some of the factors that led to the creation of them. If you have been around the industry for a while, you are probably aware that one of the most misused terms in the computer industry today is *VPN*. It seems as though every vendor has a VPN to sell you, and many times one vendor's "VPN" can seem to be the exact opposite of another's. For example, not too long ago, one of the major telecommunications vendors offered a VPN service that consisted of a private frame-relay network to which users could dial in and then, using the frame relay network, connect to the business's network. This service involved no encryption, and the only true security provided by the solution was whatever mechanism the customer provided at the frame relay's point of entry to the corporate network. Another VPN vendor might try to sell you a dedicated hardware platform designed to provide strictly VPN services. Firewall vendors try to sell you VPN in their firewall platforms, and router vendors try to convince you that the VPN services bundled with your router are the solution for you. Finally, there are the solutions that run on a network operating system, such as the VPN bundled with Windows 2000. For the sake of our discussion, a *VPN* is a private network that is constructed using a public network (such as the Internet) to connect its nodes.

The first thing you need to be aware of when discussing the Windows 2000 VPN is the encryption protocols available. Windows 2000 has two main encryption protocols that are used in the VPN:

- **Point-to-Point Tunneling Protocol (PPTP)**—PPTP is Microsoft's legacy protocol for supporting virtual private networks. Developed jointly by Microsoft Corporation, U.S. Robotics, and several remote access vendor companies (known collectively as the PPTP Forum), PPTP encountered some security issues in its original form. It has been revised by Microsoft but has never been widely accepted by the security community. Although still supported on a variety of vendors' VPN servers, PPTP is rapidly being overtaken by the more widely adopted IPSec protocol.
- **IP Security Protocol (IPSec)**—IPSec is a suite of cryptography-based protection services and security protocols that are used for the first standards-based VPN protocol. In Windows 2000, IPSec is used to provide machine-level authentication, as well as data encryption, for L2TP-based (Layer 2 Tunneling Protocol) VPN connections.

EXAM TIP

Know the Differences Between L2TP and PPTP Because Microsoft uses a custom protocol configuration for its IPSec VPN implementation, you should be sure that you understand the differences between IPSec and PPTP, as well as how Microsoft implemented its version of IPSec. Table 12.1 can help you keep them straight.

TABLE 12.1

THE DIFFERENCES BETWEEN L2TP/IPSEC AND PPTP

L2TP/IPSec	*PPTP*
Standards based	Microsoft proprietary
Windows, Linux, Macintosh, Solaris, and other platforms	Windows OS and Linux platforms
DES/3DES encryption	Microsoft-proprietary encryption
Requires only that the tunnel media provide packet-oriented point-to-point connectivity	Requires an IP-based transit internetwork
Supports header compression	No header compression

Now that you know what a VPN is and how it works, let's set up one. The good news is that installing Routing and Remote Access automatically makes a VPN connection available. What you need to understand at this point is how to configure the Virtual Private Network that is installed. To configure the VPN service, follow Step By Step 12.4.

STEP BY STEP

12.4 Configuring a Virtual Private Network

1. Open the Routing and Remote Access by selecting Start, Programs, Administrative Tools, Routing and Remote Access.

2. Click the Ports entry under the server. Notice that the sample configuration in Figure 12.23 shows five PPTP ports and five L2TP/IPSec ports. This is because the server had five user licenses configured when the Routing and Remote Access Service was installed.

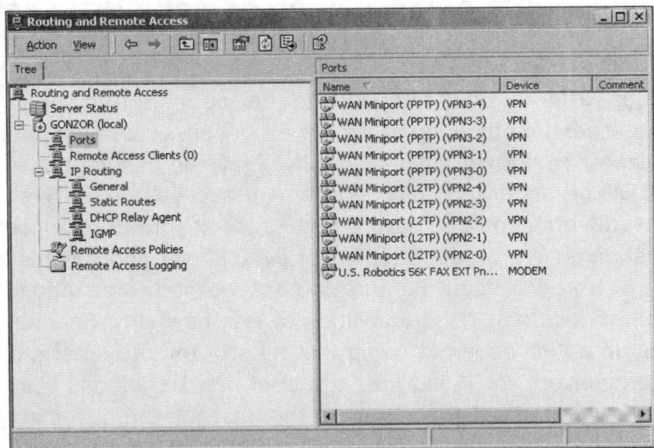

FIGURE 12.23
All the configured VPN ports are displayed in the right window.

3. To configure the ports, select Ports in the left pane and right-click. From the context menu select Properties. The Ports Properties dialog box opens (see Figure 12.24). You can see each of the protocols listed.

4. Select the protocol you want to modify and click Configure. The Configure Device dialog box opens (see Figure 12.25). This screen enables you to set the direction of the interface (Inbound Only or Inbound and Outbound) as well as the number of ports. You can also set the phone number of the device, although this is of limited use with a VPN implementation.

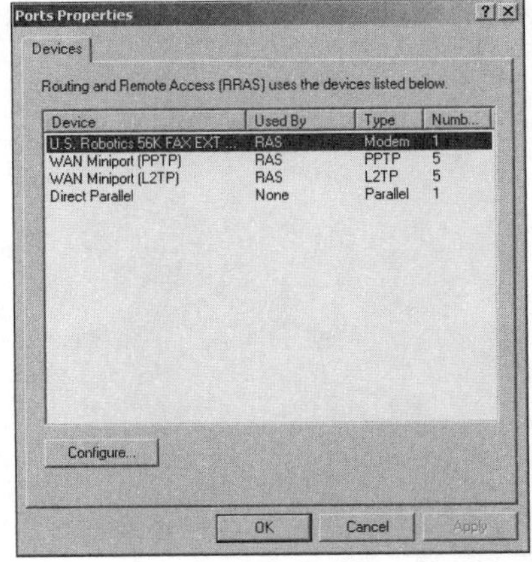

FIGURE 12.24
All the configured remote access connections appear here after they are installed.

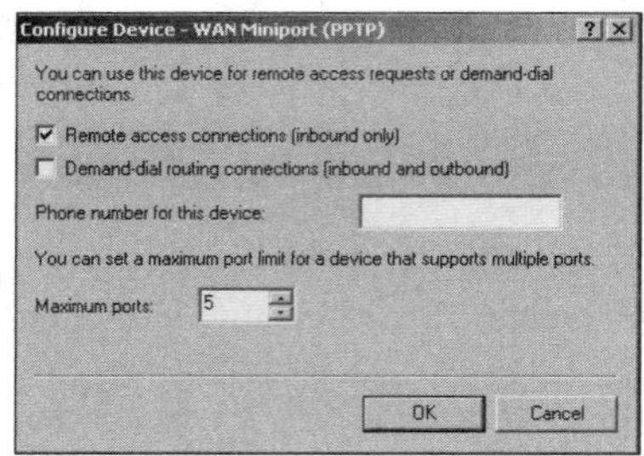

FIGURE 12.25
The Configure Device dialog box enables you to fine-tune the properties for the device, including the number of ports available.

That is all there is to configuring the VPN server bundled with Windows 2000.

IN THE FIELD

YOUR VPN IS ONLY AS GOOD AS YOUR INTERNET CONNECTION

Although VPNs are used frequently to replace more traditional remote access methods such as dial-in, people overlook a couple of things when putting together a VPN. First, the assumption is that a VPN will be faster than dialing a remote access server. This is not necessarily true. You can have a bottleneck at your ISP connection, congestion issues on the Internet, or even server capacity issues on the VPN server itself. Be sure you set realistic expectations for your users regarding the capabilities of your new VPN. Second, just putting up a VPN does not mean that all your remote access problems are solved. You'll find that a host of new issues can quickly arise. How end users get access to the Internet, the size and capacity of the VPN server, even the available Internet bandwidth can place a quick bottleneck on the performance of your VPN.

Configuring Multilink Connections

First introduced as part of Windows 98, the capability of aggregating multiple modem lines to form a single, higher-bandwidth connection to a remote access server is included in Windows 2000. This is usually an Internet service provider connection, but it could also be to another Windows 2000 server, perhaps at a different location. As part of this capability, you also can leverage the Bandwidth Allocation Protocol (BAP). BAP is a PPP control protocol that is used to dynamically add or remove additional links to a multilink connection.

To set up a multilink connection, you just need to open the Network and Dial-up Connections window, right-click the Incoming Connections icon, select Properties, and then select Enable Multilink (see Figure 12.26).

NOTE

Before You Begin Configuring Multilink If you want to configure multilink, there are a couple of prerequisites. First, you must have at least two modems installed on the system. After all, it's tough to multilink a single modem. Second, you need to have an incoming remote access connection created. Refer to Step By Step 12.1 to complete this activity.

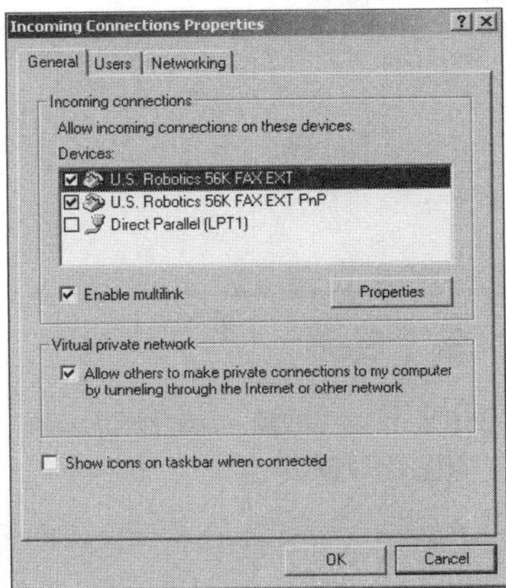

FIGURE 12.26
The Incoming Connections Properties dialog box enables you to configure all the parameters for dialing in, including the multilink configuration.

Multilink is now configured. If a user dials in with two modems, the server will now aggregate the connections and enable the user to use the additional bandwidth as needed.

EXAM TIP

Know Where Multilink Is Enabled More important, you should understand what is needed for a multilink connection and what benefits multilink provides.

Configuring Routing and Remote Access for DHCP Integration

- Configure and troubleshoot remote access and virtual private network (VPN) connections.
  - Configure remote access name resolution and IP address allocation.

If you have users who are connecting to your Routing and Remote Access server, you probably should dynamically assign them a TCP/IP address on the network. The best way to do this is with DHCP, which must be configured.

DHCP and the Routing and Remote Access Service have an important relationship that you need to understand. When the remote access server is configured to use DHCP, the Routing and Remote Access server uses the DHCP client component to obtain 10 IP addresses from a DHCP server. This could be on the network or on the same server as the Routing and Remote Access server.

EXAM TIP

Know That the Routing and Remote Access Service Requests Its DHCP Addresses 10 at a Time When it exhausts its pool, it goes back to the DHCP server for an additional 10.

The remote access server uses the first IP address obtained from DHCP for the RAS interface, and subsequent addresses are allocated to TCP/IP-based remote access client computers as they connect. IP addresses freed because of remote access client computers disconnecting are reused. When all 10 addresses have been allocated, the process starts again with the DHCP client computer requesting an additional 10 addresses.

To configure Routing and Remote Access for DHCP integration, follow Step By Step 12.5.

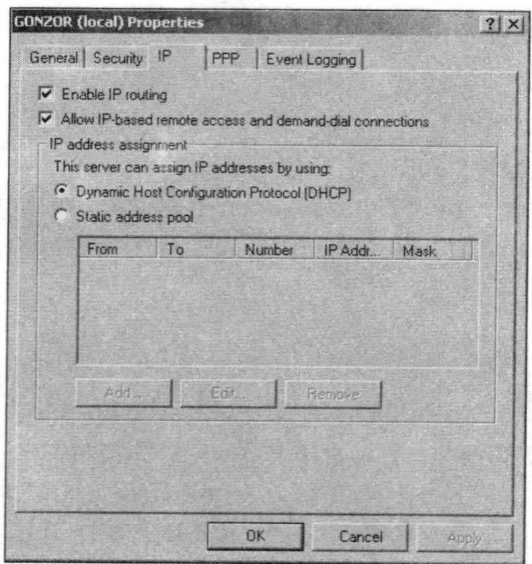

FIGURE 12.27
Configuring Routing and Remote Access to use DHCP is as easy as clicking an option.

STEP BY STEP

12.5 Configuring Routing and Remote Access for DHCP Integration

1. Open the Routing and Remote Access console by selecting Start, Programs, Administrative Tools, Routing and Remote Access.
2. From the tree, right-click the server and select Properties from the context menu. Click the IP tab (see Figure 12.27).
3. In the IP Address Assignment section, select the Dynamic Host Control Protocol (DHCP) option.

Your Routing and Remote Access will now issue DHCP addresses for users connecting via dial-in or VPN.

MANAGING AND MONITORING REMOTE ACCESS

Now you have a functional Routing and Remote Access server up and running. How do you manage and monitor it? Let's start by taking a look at what types of information the Performance console can provide. It is generally the best tool for monitoring specifics about Windows 2000 services, and it offers the following counters for the RAS object:

- **Alignment Errors**—The size of the packet received is different from the size expected.
- **Buffer Overrun Errors**—The software is incapable of handling the rate at which data is being received.
- **Bytes Received**—Total amount of bytes received by the service.
- **Bytes Received/Sec**—Number of bytes received by the service in a second.
- **Bytes Transmitted**—Total amount of bytes transmitted by the service.
- **Bytes Transmitted/Sec**—Number of bytes transmitted by the service in a second.
- **CRC Errors**—A frame received contains erroneous data, and the packet did not pass the Cyclic Redundancy Check (CRC).
- **Frames Received**—Total number of frames received by the service.
- **Frames Received/Sec**—Number of frames received by the service per second.
- **Frames Transmitted**—Total number of frames transmitted by the service.
- **Frames Transmitted/Sec**—Number of frames transmitted by the service per second.
- **Percent Compression In**—Tells how well inbound traffic is being compressed.
- **Percent Compression Out**—Tells how well outbound traffic is being compressed.
- **Errors—Serial Overrun Errors, Timeout Errors, Total Errors, and Total Errors/Sec**—These objects handle all the error information for the Routing and Remote Access Service.

Now that we have looked at the counters for the service, let's take a look at some of the ways to monitor the service.

To configure Routing and Remote Access Performance monitoring, follow Step By Step 12.6.

EXAM TIP

Don't Memorize All the Counters Be familiar with the general categories and how to use the Performance console.

NOTE

What Are We Measuring—Aggregate or Port Level? The Performance console enables you to monitor these counters on either a port–by–port or an entire server level. Select RAS Ports to look at a single port or RAS Total to see the statistics for the entire server.

STEP BY STEP

12.6 Monitoring Routing and Remote Access

1. Open the Performance console by selecting Programs, Administrative Tools, Performance (see Figure 12.28).

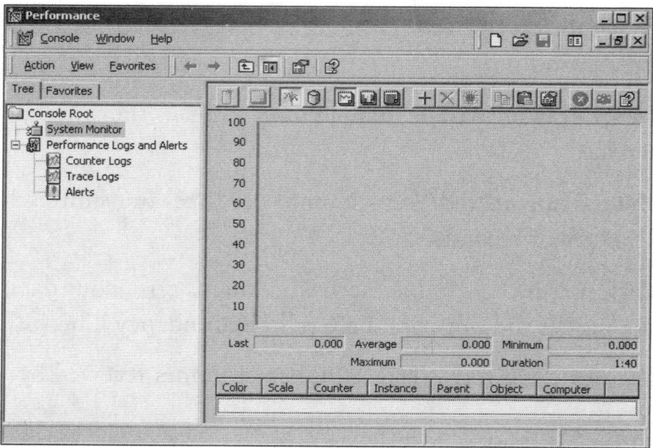

FIGURE 12.28
The Performance console enables you to monitor various system and application metrics for evaluating the performance and health of the system.

2. In the Performance console, select System Monitor.
3. To create an entry in System Monitor, click the Add (+) icon. The Add Counters window opens. By default, it opens to the Processor performance object.
4. Select the RAS Port performance object. You will see the list of counters available for RAS displayed on the left and a list of RAS devices in the right pane (see Figure 12.29).

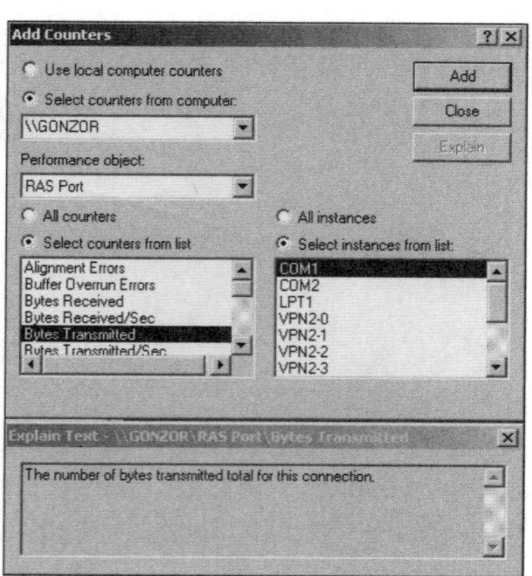

FIGURE 12.29
The counters associated with RAS are similar to the errors offered for most LAN connections, including Ethernet.

5. Select the port you want to monitor. After you have decided on the counter you want to monitor, click Add. You can add multiple counters either by selecting each counter and clicking Add or by using the standard Windows multiple-item select method of holding down the Ctrl key while you select all the counters you want to monitor and clicking Add.
6. Click Close when you are done. You will see your counters being graphed similar to those shown in Figure 12.30.

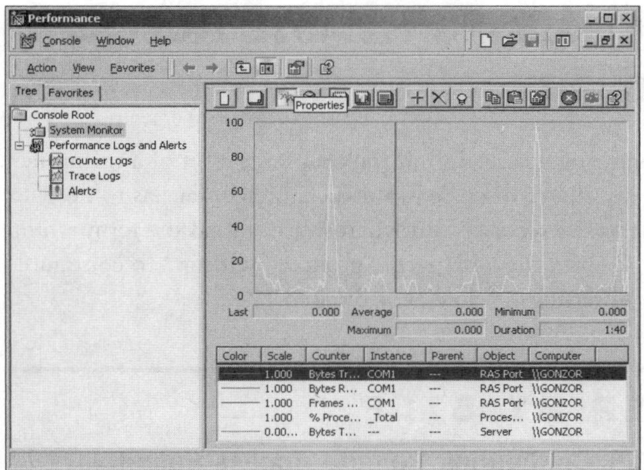

FIGURE 12.30
To find out what types of errors you might be experiencing in the field, keep an eye out for sudden jumps, either up or down. The graph in this figure shows that no RAS errors exist at this time.

If you want to see statistics on a VPN connection, follow Step By Step 12.7.

STEP BY STEP

12.7 Checking the Status of a Port

1. Open the Routing and Remote Access utility.
2. Select Ports in the left pane. A list of available ports appears in the right pane. Select the port you want to gather statistics from and right-click. From the context menu, select Status. The Port Status dialog box opens (see Figure 3.31). You can see the port condition, the line speed, the call duration, network statistics, errors, and the network protocols being used, with addresses for the port.
3. You can reset or refresh the statistics by clicking the appropriate button at the bottom of the dialog box, and in the event someone is connected to the port, you can disconnect that connection by clicking Disconnect.

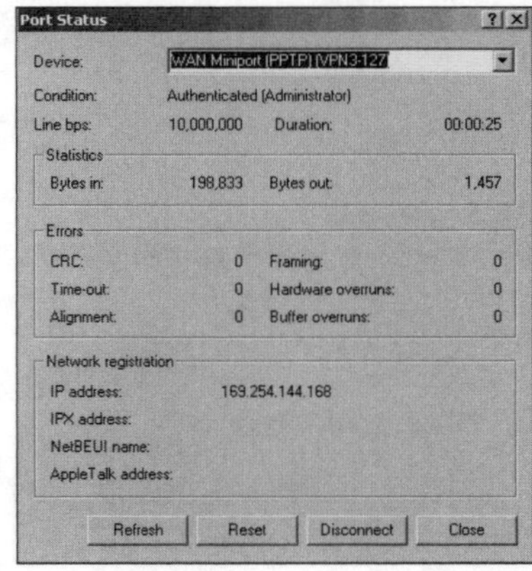

FIGURE 12.31
You can get a fairly complete port status here.

Now let's take a look at configuring remote access security.

CONFIGURING REMOTE ACCESS SECURITY

The name of this section of the chapter is a bit of a misnomer. Most of what we have discussed in this chapter so far has to do with remote access security. But Microsoft has used the term remote access security for one specific group of settings. To configure this group of settings, follow Step By Step 12.8.

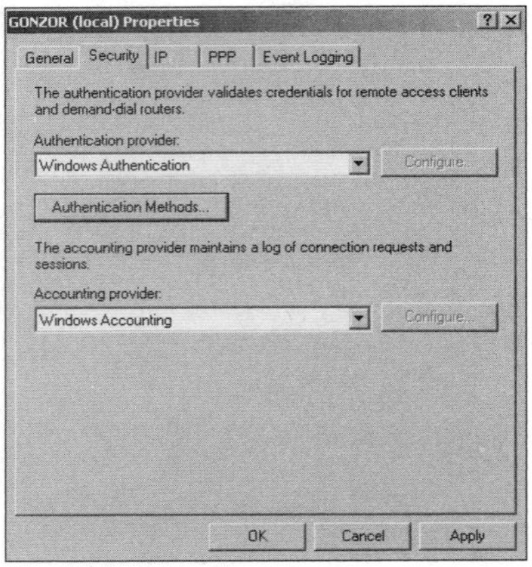

FIGURE 12.32
Remote Access security is controlled from this dialog box.

STEP BY STEP

12.8 Configuring Remote Access Security

1. Open the Routing and Remote Access console.
2. Right-click the server and select Properties. This opens the server properties.
3. Select the Security tab (see Figure 12.32). By default, the Authentication provider is Windows Authentication. You can also set it for RADIUS authentication. Select RADIUS in the pull-down menu.
4. Click Configure to configure the RADIUS server. The Edit RADIUS Server dialog box opens (see Figure 12.33). From here you can set the name and address of the RADIUS server, shared secret, timeout value, initial score, and RADIUS port. You can also require the use of digital signatures.
5. Click OK to add the RADIUS server; then, click OK to close the RADIUS authentication dialog box. You must restart Routing and Remote Access to take advantage of the RADIUS authentication. Click OK to close the window.

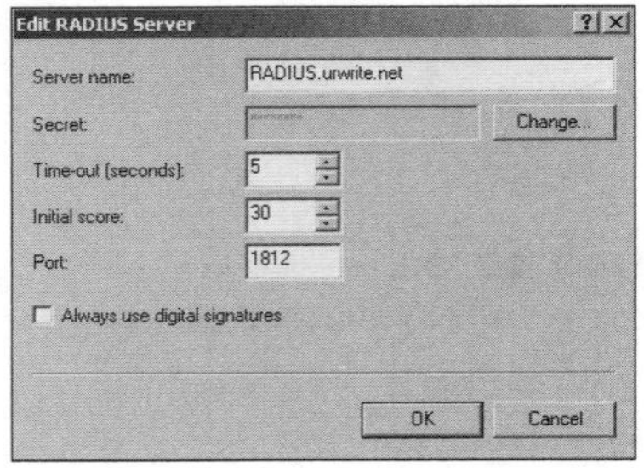

FIGURE 12.33
Adding a RADIUS server looks pretty easy, but you need to ensure that your information matches the RADIUS server configuration.

Now that you have looked at how to set up the RADIUS and Windows authentication, let's look at the authentication protocols Windows 2000 uses.

Configuring Authentication Protocols

Windows 2000 supports several authentication protocols; therefore, almost any connection configuration is supported. The protocols include the following:

- **Extensible Authentication Protocol (EAP)**—EAP-TLS is an extension to the Point-to-Point Protocol (PPP). EAP provides a standard mechanism for support of additional authentication methods within PPP, such as smart cards, one-time passwords, and certificates. EAP is critical for secure Windows 2000 VPNs because it offers stronger authentication methods (such as X.509 certificates) instead of relying on the user ID and password schemes used traditionally.
- **Challenge Handshake Authentication Protocol (CHAP)**—CHAP negotiates an encrypted authentication using MD5 (Message Digest 5), an industry-standard hashing scheme. CHAP uses challenge-response with one-way MD5 hashing on the response. This enables you to authenticate to the server without actually sending your password over the network. Because this is an industry-standard authentication method, it allows Windows 2000 to securely connect to almost all third-party PPP servers.
- **Microsoft-Created Microsoft Challenge Handshake Authentication Protocol (MS-CHAP)**—Microsoft created MS-CHAP, an extension of CHAP, to authenticate remote Windows workstations, increasing the protocol's functionality by integrating the encryption and hashing algorithms used on Windows networks. Like CHAP, MS-CHAP uses a challenge-response mechanism with one-way encryption on the response. Although MS-CHAP is consistent with standard CHAP as much as possible, the MS-CHAP response packet is in a format specifically designed for computers running a Windows operating system. A new version of the Microsoft Challenge Handshake Authentication Protocol (MS-CHAP v2) is also available. This new protocol provides mutual authentication, stronger initial data-encryption keys, and different encryption keys for sending and receiving.
- **Shiva Password Authentication Protocol (SPAP)**—SPAP is used specifically to allow Shiva client computers to connect to a Windows 2000 Server and to enable Windows 2000 client computers to connect to Shiva servers.

NOTE

MS-CHAP Versus MS-CHAP v2 Protocol When you are making a VPN connection, Windows 2000 Server attempts to authenticate using the MS-CHAP v2 protocol before offering the MS-CHAP protocol. If you are using an updated Windows client computer, you should be able to authenticate with the MS-CHAP v2 protocol. Windows NT 4.0 and Windows 98-based computers can use only MS-CHAP v2 authentication for VPN connections.

- **Password Authentication Protocol (PAP)**—PAP uses unencrypted (plain-text) passwords for authenticating users and is considered the least secure authentication protocol available. PAP typically is used as the authentication of last resort—used when a more secure form of authentication is not available. You might need to use this protocol when you are connecting to a non-Windows-based server.

To configure these protocols, follow Step By Step 12.9.

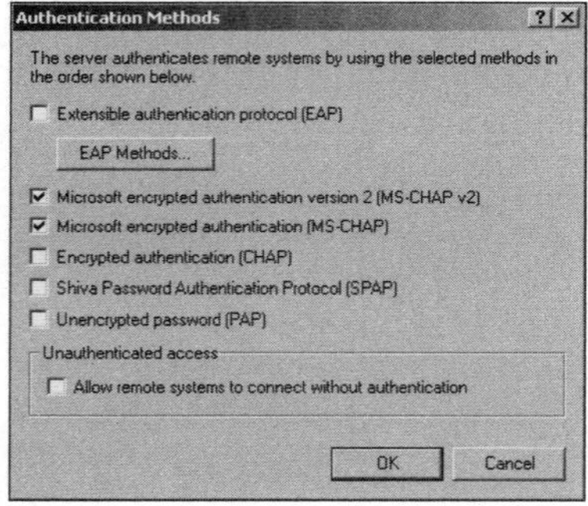

FIGURE 12.34
Remote Access security is controlled from this dialog box.

STEP BY STEP

12.9 Configuring Authentication Protocols

1. Open the Routing and Remote Access console.
2. Right-click the server and select Properties. This opens the server properties.
3. Select the Security tab and click Authentication Methods (refer to Figure 12.32). The Authentication Methods dialog box opens (see Figure 12.34). Notice that the selections look similar to what we just discussed in the last section.
4. Select the appropriate protocol for a connection and click OK. Click OK to return to the Routing and Remote Access console.

Now that you've defined authentication protocols, it's time to move on to encryption protocols.

Configuring Encryption Protocols

The first thing you need to be aware of when discussing the encryption protocols available with Windows 2000 is that two main encryption protocols are used in a Windows 2000 VPN. We discussed PPTP and IPSec earlier in the chapter, but a couple of encryption protocols are used in conjunction with IPSec that we need to cover.

Under the Microsoft model, IPSec encryption does not rely on any authentication methods for its initial encryption keys. The encryption method is determined by the IPSec Security Association (SA). An SA is a combination of a destination address, security protocol, and unique identification value, called a security parameters index (SPI). The available encryptions for IPSec include the following:

- **Data Encryption Standard (DES)**—DES uses a 56-bit encryption key. This is considered barely adequate encryption for business use, and this level of encryption has been broken using specialized hardware.
- **Triple DES (3DES)**—Similar to DES, 3DES uses a 56-bit key. But as the name implies, it encrypts the data using three 56-bit encryption keys. This is considered to be a 168-bit encryption key ($3 \times 56 = 168$) and is used in high-security environments. Until recently, the U.S. government tightly controlled the export of applications using 3DES encryption. Although these restrictions have been relaxed, exporting 3DES applications still requires government approval.

These are the encryption protocols available for remote access in Windows 2000. Windows 2000 does use other encryption, such as Kerberos, for logging on to a domain, but it is not applicable to remote access. To configure these protocols, follow Step By Step 12.10.

STEP BY STEP

12.10 Configuring Encryption Protocols

1. Open the Routing and Remote Access console and select Remote Access Policies from the tree view. In the right pane, right-click the policy you want to set the encryption level for and select Properties.
2. From the Policy Properties dialog box, click Edit Profile. The Edit Dial-in Profile dialog box opens.
3. Click the Encryption tab shown in Figure 12.35. You can set the encryption levels to No Encryption, Basic, Strong, or any combination of the three. Select the appropriate level, and then click OK twice to return to the Routing and Remote Access console.

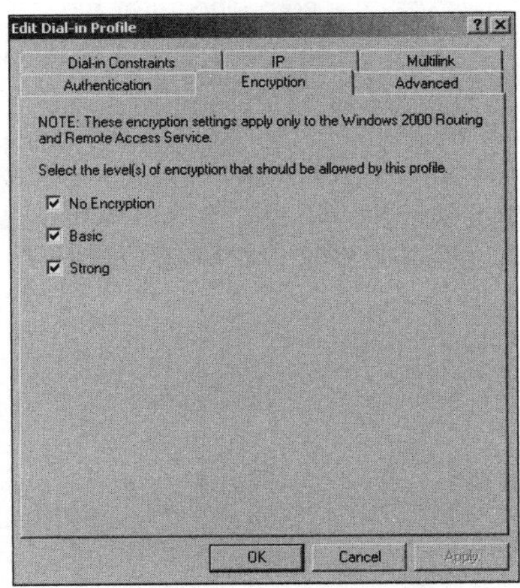

FIGURE 12.35
Windows 2000 supports three levels of encryption.

Encryption protocols are a necessary part of today's environment. Another part of today's environment, sharing an Internet connection, is the next topic we explore.

Installing Internet Connection Sharing

NOTE

Network Address Translation (NAT) NAT is a mechanism in which internal, private IP addresses are translated to external addresses. This enables multiple internal computers to share one or more public addresses, and it shields the internal machines from external attack. You'll learn more about how NAT works in the next section.

One of the services RRAS performs is to allow users from the outside world to access a network server. RRAS also enables you to control how users inside the network can gain access to the Internet. Before we cover the details of how RRAS allows access to the Internet for clients, we need to review the "consumer-friendly" way to do this. Internet Connection Sharing (ICS) enables multiple computers to share a single Internet connection—just like RRAS enables them to do. The biggest advantage to ICS is that ICS bundles many of the settings that you normally must set manually in RRAS in one simple package. The ICS services installs special "mini" versions of the following:

- Network Address Translation (NAT)
- Dynamic Host Control Protocol (DHCP)
- DNS Proxy

EXAM TIP

Know the Components and Purpose of ICS Be sure you are familiar with the components of the ICS service, and remember that it is geared to the small office. Microsoft has been known to give you a scenario (size of network, type of connection, and so on) and ask you to choose the correct application.

These services make ICS a great solution for a small office looking for a quick and easy way to connect to the Internet via dial-up.

Now you know what ICS does for you. Before you jump into installing ICS, you should learn what exactly this automated process is going to install and configure. Keep in mind that a server running ICS must have a LAN and a modem connection. Otherwise, you will be unable to install the service. ICS does the following at installation:

- **ICS sets the IP address of the LAN interface to 192.168.0.1, a private IP address**—Because you are working with the internal interface for the ICS server (that is, the internal NIC in the Windows 2000 server), it is set to a private address for security reasons. You can reset this address, although it is a good idea to use a private network address on the internal network whenever possible. Private addresses can't be routed over the Internet, so using them adds an additional layer of security.

- **The WAN interface (usually a modem) is set to be a Demand-Dial Router pointed at the ISP.**
- **A DNS Proxy service is installed to provide DNS services to the office**—This service passes client DNS requests to the DNS server configured in the ICS server's DHCP settings.
- **The AutoDHCP service is installed**—This service provides a subset of the services included with a full DHCP installation, but AutoDHCP is configured to issue addresses on the new 198.168.0.0 network.

Now let's look at the process of installing ICS, as shown in Step By Step 12.11.

> NOTE
>
> **What Is a Private IP Address?** A *private IP address* is an address that can't be routed across the Internet. Some reserved addresses are specifically set aside for private networks.

> EXAM TIP
>
> **The AutoDHCP Service Must Be the Only DHCP Server on the Network** None of the "mini" services installed by ICS can coexist with the full versions on the same server. Some services, such as the DHCP server component, must be the only DHCP server on the network. ICS requires that the internal network use the 198.168.0.0 range.

STEP BY STEP

12.11 Installing the Internet Connection Sharing Service

1. Open Network and Dial-up Connections by right-clicking the My Network Places icon on the desktop and clicking Properties. (You can also open Properties by opening the Control Panel and clicking Network and Dial-up Connections.) For the installation to continue, you need a LAN and an ISP connection (see Figure 12.36).

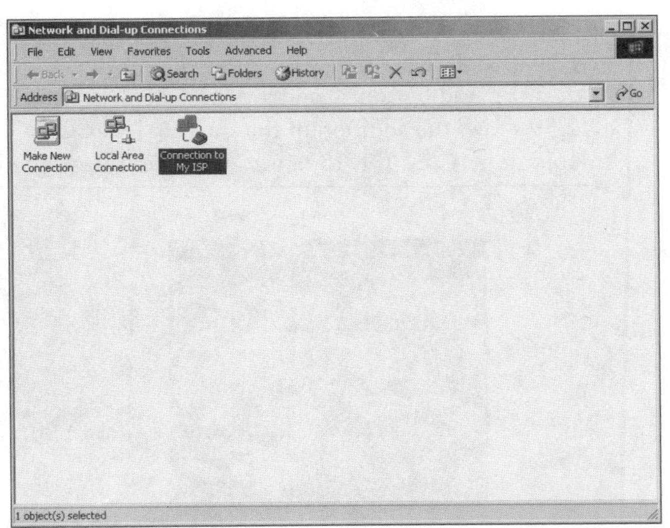

FIGURE 12.36
Network and Dial-up Connections enables you to install ICS only if you have already installed a LAN and a dial-up network connection.

continues

continued

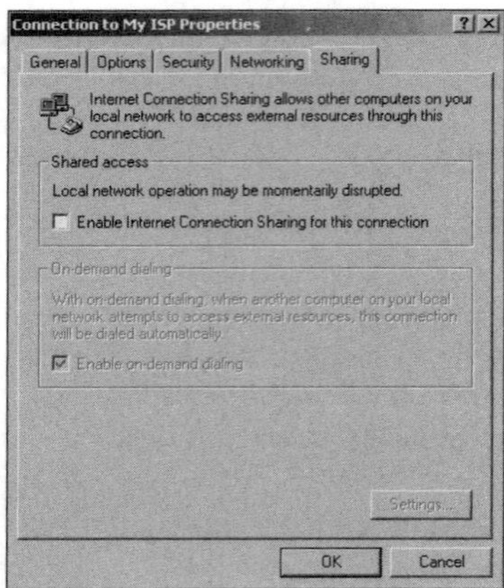

FIGURE 12.37
The Sharing tab of the Connection Properties dialog box allows you to enable Internet Connection Sharing as well as on-demand dialing.

2. Right-click the dial-up connection and select Properties from the context menu. The Connection Properties dialog box opens. Click the Sharing tab (see Figure 12.37).
3. Select the Enable Internet Connection Sharing for This Connection option. The Enable On-Demand Dialing option is enabled by default.
4. Click the Settings button to open the Internet Connection Sharing Settings dialog box (see Figure 12.38). The Applications tab enables you to configure custom applications so that you can connect across the NAT connection.

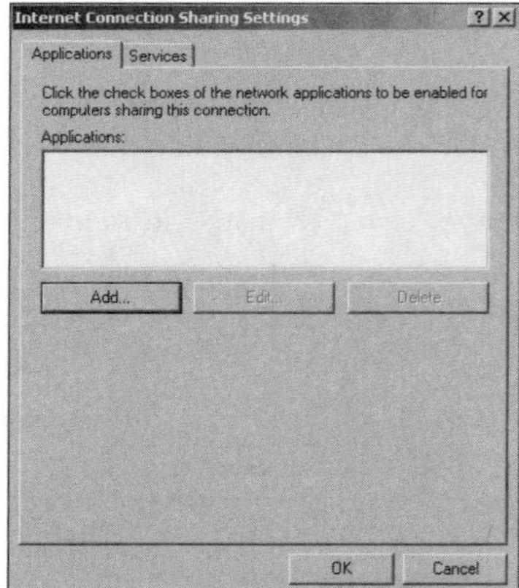

FIGURE 12.38
After you have enabled ICS, you need to configure the applications that can be used.

5. Click the Add button to add a custom application. Figure 12.39 shows the addition of the Internet Relay Chat application. Click OK to return to the Settings window.

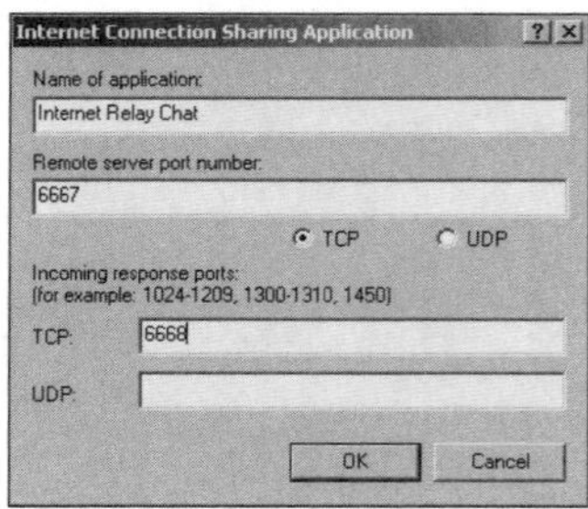

FIGURE 12.39
To add an application, you need to know which TCP/IP ports it uses.

6. Click the Services tab (see Figure 12.40). This tab enables you to configure services to be accessed from the Internet. For example, if you want to set up an FTP server on the internal network, this is where you enable it. To complete the configuration, you need to know the private address of that server. Just select the option for that application and fill in the DNS name or address of the server (see Figure 12.41). The Name of Service and Service Port Number text boxes are filled in for you and can't be changed. Click OK to return to Services.

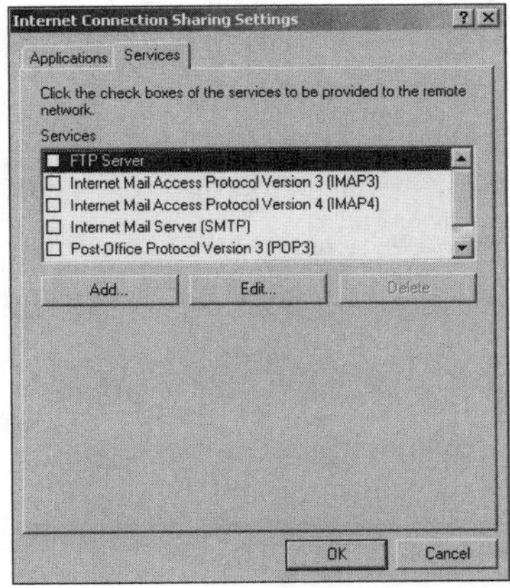

FIGURE 12.40
If you want users on the Internet to be able to access servers on your private network for activities such as Mail, FTP, or Telnet, select the Services tab to configure them.

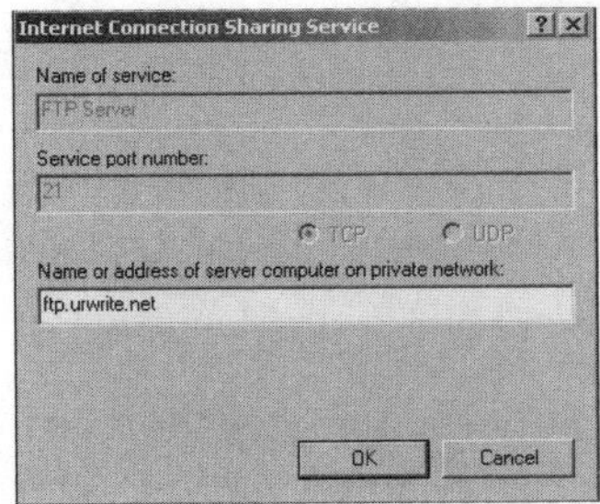

FIGURE 12.41
To make a server accessible from the Internet, you need the server address or DNS name. If you are adding a custom application, you also need the port of the application you want to use.

7. Click Add to add a custom application for inbound access. You need the name of the service, service port, and server DNS name or IP address for the new service (see Figure 12.42). Enter the information and click OK to add the service. Click OK to enable ICS.

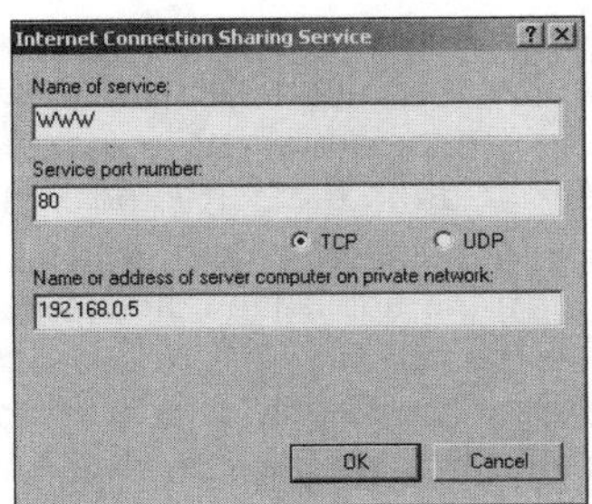

FIGURE 12.42
You can add any service for inbound access as long as you know the TCP/IP port required.

IN THE FIELD

HOW DO YOU DETERMINE THE PORT NUMBER AN APPLICATION USES?

If you are working with ICS, the ports of common applications are predefined in the application. These are shown in Table 12.2.

TABLE 12.2

PREDEFINED PORTS OF COMMON APPLICATIONS

Application	*Port*
FTP Server	21
Hypertext Transfer Protocol (HTTP)	80
Hypertext Transfer Protocol – Secure (HTTPS)	443
Internet Mail Access Protocol Version 3 (IMAP3)	220
Internet Mail Access Protocol Version 4 (IMAP4)	143
Internet Mail Server (SMTP)	25
Post Office Protocol Version 3 (POP3)	110
Telnet Server	23

This is great if you want to use one of the predefined applications. But what do you do if you have a different application you want to enable? How can you find the port you need? Four methods are generally used. First, check the product documentation and Help files. If you are using an application commonly used on the Internet, the vendor usually documents the port you need to have open to use the application. If you can't find the information in the product documentation, you can look to the Internet, or more specifically the Internet Assigned Numbers Authority (`http://www.iana.net`). This authority provides registration services for vendors who want to reserve TCP/IP ports for their applications. If you can't find your application listed, the vendor is probably using an unregistered port. The next step in tracking down the port is network analysis. You can use network analysis tools to analyze the traffic the application uses. If you are running the application on a Windows NT or Windows 2000 server, you can use the Network Monitor tool included with the operating system to provide this information. When all else fails, find a comfortable chair and a speakerphone and call the vendor. You might have to wait on hold for a while, but the vendor can almost always tell you which port its application uses.

That is about all there is to the ICS service. It is an easy, quick service perfect for a small office environment. Now, let's see what to do if you are in a larger environment or need more flexibility in your connection.

INSTALLING NAT

▶ Configure and troubleshoot Network Address Translation (NAT) and Internet Connection sharing.

- Configure routing and remote access to perform NAT.
- Troubleshoot Internet Connection Sharing problems by using the `ipconfig` and `ping` commands.

Suppose you have a larger network than the one described in the ICS section, but you still want to use Windows 2000 to connect to the Internet. You will find the Network Address Translation capabilities of Windows 2000 to be very useful. But just in case you are not familiar with NAT, take a quick look at how NAT works and what it does before you begin installing it.

Network Address Translation does pretty much what the name describes. It takes an IP address entering on one interface of the Windows 2000 Server and translates it to a different address exiting a different (usually the Internet-connected) interface. For example, suppose that your PC has an IP address of 10.10.10.10. This is an address in the reserved network of 10.0.0.0, which is not routable on the Internet. You want to be able to connect to the Internet, so you need to have an Internet-routable (registered) IP address. A server running NAT takes each packet from your workstation, strips the 10.10.10.10 address from it, and resends the packet with a registered address. The original address and the registered address are stored in a table so the server knows which translation was used. The packet is routed to the appropriate destination. If the destination responds with a packet, the NAT server looks up the address in its NAT table and reverses the original process, placing 10.10.10.10 into the destination address and resending the packet.

EXAM TIP

Know NAT For the exam, you need to understand what NAT is and how it works. The key features are the replacing of the "internal" addresses and the NAT table for maintaining the translation.

The two reasons for using NAT are as follows:

- **Security**—If you are connecting your network to the Internet, you really don't want uninvited users connecting to your private hosts. By translating the addresses of those hosts, you provide a level of security for that host.

NOTE

I Wish There Were an RFC for This
You're in luck. The RFC defining the private addresses typically used in conjunction with NAT is RFC 1597. It sets aside the address ranges 10.0.0.0–10.255.255.255, 172.16.0.0–172.31.255.255, and 192.168.0.0–192.168.255.255. RFC 1631 defines the method for Network Address Translation.

- **IP Address Conservation**—As hard as it is to believe, the Internet is running out of addresses. In the mid-1990s, some enterprising people recognized that this problem was coming and came up with NAT as a mechanism for conserving addresses. Although clearly a stop-gap mechanism until the next version of IP is widely adopted, NAT enables a company to use private addresses on its internal network and translate those addresses to a single address or multiple registered addresses. This many-to-few address-conservation mechanism has contributed in large part to the Internet's capability to continue to grow.

NAT can handle the address translation in two ways. If the translating device has only a single registered IP address available, it translates the address in the IP packet to the registered address and then sets the source port to a random port number.

For example, if the NAT device handles a request for an HTTP connection, it connects to the server on port 80 but listens for the response on the random port it assigned during the translation. It substitutes its address in the source address field and the random port number in place of the client's original port. It then uses this information to create an address mapping in the NAT table that tells it where to send the HTTP responses.

If you have multiple registered IP addresses, the NAT device performs a one-to-one translation of the address and skips any port translations.

Here's one final point before we look at the installation: Similar to the ICS service, NAT is a two-way street. You can configure NAT not only for outbound private-to-public translations, but also for public-to-private translations for inbound requests. If you wanted to put a Web server on your internal network, NAT enables you to do that.

Now that you know what NAT is, let's install it. Step By Step 12.12 shows you how.

STEP BY STEP

12.12 Installing Network Address Translation

1. Select Start, Programs, Administrative Tools, Routing and Remote Access manager. The Routing and Remote Access window opens.
2. Expand the tree under the local server icon. Under the IP Routing icon, you will find the General icon. Right-click it and select New Routing Protocol from the context menu. The New Routing Protocol window opens (see Figure 12.43).
3. Select Network Address Translation and click OK. You should see Network Address Translation show up as an additional icon under IP routing.

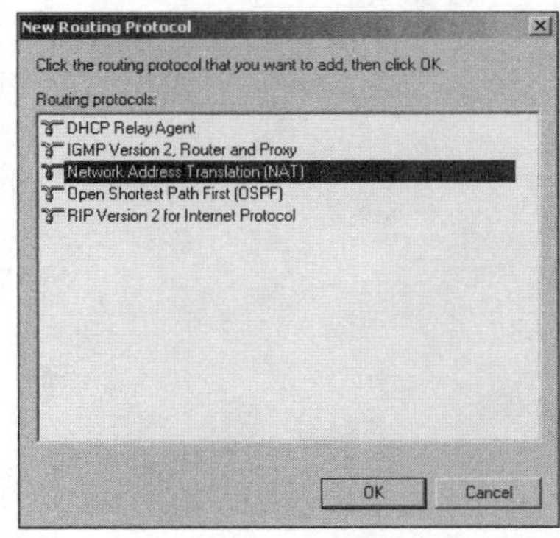

FIGURE 12.43
Network Address Translation is considered a routing protocol and is added like any other routing protocol.

Now that you have installed NAT, let's take a look at configuring it.

CONFIGURING NAT PROPERTIES

Several properties can be configured in conjunction with Network Address Translation. They can all be accessed by opening the Routing and Remote Access window (as described in Step By Step 12.12), right-clicking the Network Address Translation icon, and selecting Properties from the context menu. You will see the following tabs: General, Translation, Address Assignment, and Name Resolution.

The General tab shown in Figure 12.44 is used to configure Event Logging. Any logging enabled in this section appears in the System Event Log. You can configure Event Logging for the following levels:

- **Log Errors Only**—Logging errors is a useful setting when you want to restrict your logging to critical messages. In a busy environment, reviewing logs filled with warnings that are not in fact real issues is difficult. By keeping the logging to errors only, you increase the chances that you will see serious errors in the log.

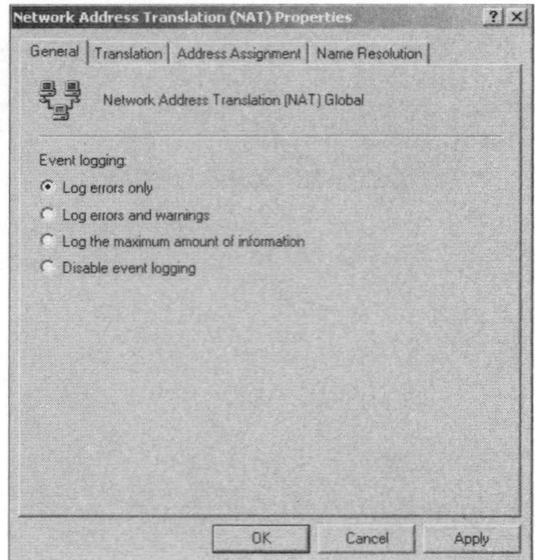

FIGURE 12.44
If you want to configure logging for the NAT protocol, do it from the General screen.

> **NOTE**
> **To Log or Not to Log?** Keep in mind that logging uses resources. If you have resources to burn (CPU, RAM, hard drive), feel free to leave the Log the Maximum Amount of Information option enabled. Otherwise, you might want to restrict your logging to the default setting, Log Errors and Warnings.

- **Log Errors and Warnings**—The default setting, logging errors and warnings, is a good idea in smaller networks. If you find that the warnings are filling the log, it might be time to log only errors.
- **Log the Maximum Amount of Information**—When you first set up your Network Address Translation, you might want to log the maximum amount of information to get a good understanding of what is going on with NAT. Keep in mind that the information logged at this level is extremely detailed and sometimes decipherable only by Microsoft support. It's great to use if you are troubleshooting an issue with Microsoft; otherwise, this is probably not a setting you will need to use.
- **Disable Event Logging**—Unless you are extremely resource bound on this server, you should never disable logging. At the very least, error logging should be used so that you can diagnose problems.

The Translation tab shown in Figure 12.45 is used to set the timeout values for the translations. You also have the capability to add inbound applications exactly the way you could in ICS. In fact, any applications configured in ICS (if you were to switch to NAT) are automatically added to the NAT translations.

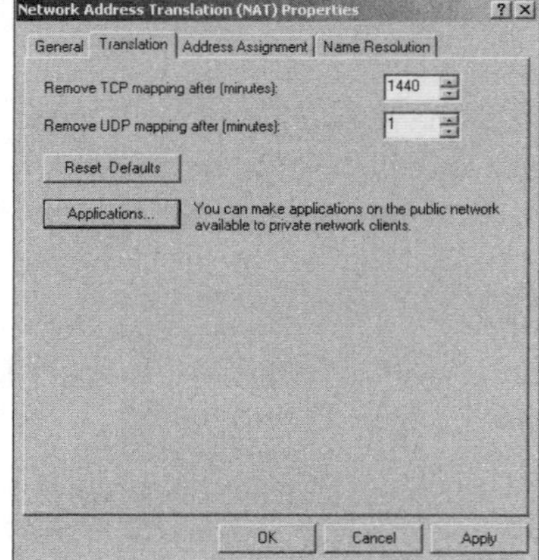

FIGURE 12.45
Use the Translation tab to set the timeouts and add inbound application translations for the NAT protocol.

IN THE FIELD

WHAT SETTINGS WORK BEST IN REAL LIFE?

As a general rule (and this is true with many Microsoft applications), the defaults will usually work for your network. Where you might want to reset these timeout values is in the case of a special application that requires higher timeouts to function. For example, if you had a UDP-based application that needed to maintain connections for a long period of time, you might want to set the UDP mapping timer to 60. However, I am not aware of any UDP-based applications that have that requirement because of the connectionless nature of UDP. In the TCP field, you might want to lower the TCP mapping timer if you have a large number of users connecting across the server for limited periods of time and if you are resource constrained. Making this parameter shorter causes resources to become available more quickly.

EXAM TIP

Use the NAT DHCP Service to Enable the Clients If you are planning to use NAT, the easiest way to enable the clients is through the NAT DHCP service. This configures the client with the correct information to use the NAT gateway when she is assigned her IP address via DHCP. If you are using the NAT DHCP, you will not need the Windows 2000 DHCP service. This is generally discouraged for large clients.

The Address Assignment tab enables you to configure the private IP addresses and the DHCP service used in conjunction with NAT (see Figure 12.46). To enable the NAT DHCP, just check the box marked Automatically Assign IP Addresses by Using DHCP. If you are using the Windows 2000 DHCP service, do not select the NAT DHCP option.

EXAM TIP

You Can Configure NAT Properties to Dial an ISP for DNS Resolution For the exam, you should be aware that you can configure NAT Properties to dial an ISP for DNS resolution if necessary. Just select the Resolve IP Addresses for Clients Using Domain Name System (DNS), and then select Connect to the Public Network When a Name Needs to Be Resolved. In the Demand-Dial Interface pull-down box, select your ISP connection. This works only if you have a dial-up ISP configured on the system.

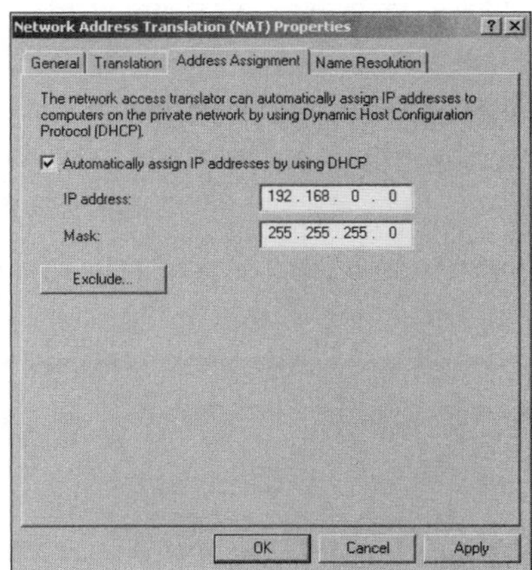

FIGURE 12.46
The Address Assignment tab enables you to configure the DHCP service for the NAT protocol.

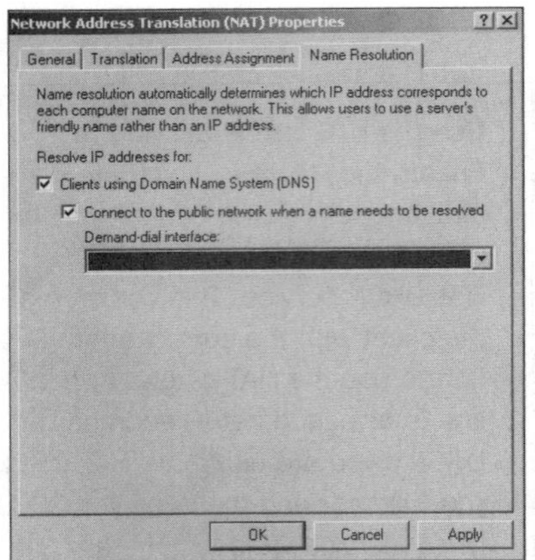

FIGURE 12.47
Use the Name Resolution tab to set the DNS resolution parameters for the NAT protocol.

The Name Resolution tab is used to configure DNS for the NAT protocol (see Figure 12.47). From this tab, you can configure who should receive DNS resolution services and how to handle resolution of nonlocal names. You can even configure the server to automatically dial the Internet if it needs to resolve a name.

You should have noticed that although ICS and NAT are different services, the capabilities are in large part the same. The configuration does differ fairly significantly, however. To recap, both ICS and the NAT service provide Network Address Translation, Dynamic Host Control Protocol, and DNS Proxy capabilities. ICS automates the installation and configuration of these services, whereas the NAT interface requires some configuration by the administrator. In addition, ICS supports features not included in NAT, such as H.323 Proxy, Lightweight Directory Access Protocol (LDAP) Proxy, and Directplay Proxy.

Configuring NAT Interfaces

So far in this chapter, you have installed NAT and configured its properties. What you haven't done yet is configure the interface NAT will run through. A NAT interface defines the connection properties for the Network Address Translation. This can be either the private interface, connected to the internal (private) network, or the public interface, connected to the Internet. Because your NAT server will most likely be bridging your private network and the Internet, you need to set up an internal and an external NAT interface.

To configure an interface for NAT, follow Step By Step 12.13.

STEP BY STEP

12.13 Configuring a NAT Interface

1. Open the Routing and Remote Access window and right-click the Network Address Translation (NAT) icon. From the context menu, select New Interface. The New Interface for Network Address Translation (NAT) window, shown in Figure 12.48, opens.

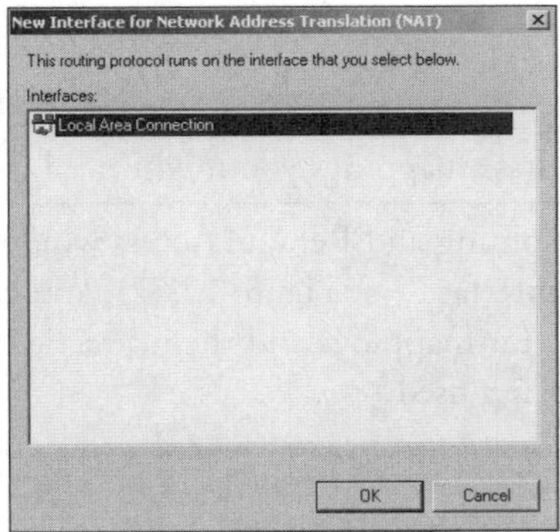

FIGURE 12.48
The New Interface for Network Address Translation (NAT) window enables you to configure the interface(s) that will be supported by NAT. You will see only LAN connections in this dialog box because WAN connections are assumed to be connected to the public network.

2. Select the LAN interface to be added and click OK. The Local Area Connection Properties dialog box for that connection opens (see Figure 12.49). This enables you to set the interface as a private (internal) or public (Internet) interface. If you have a LAN connection to the Internet, you need to configure a public and a private interface. Select the appropriate type and click OK. If you select the public interface, you must do some additional configuration.

3. Select the Address Pool tab to configure the public addresses for the server (see Figure 12.50). These are supplied by your ISP; it is these addresses that your internal addresses are translated to for routing over the Internet.

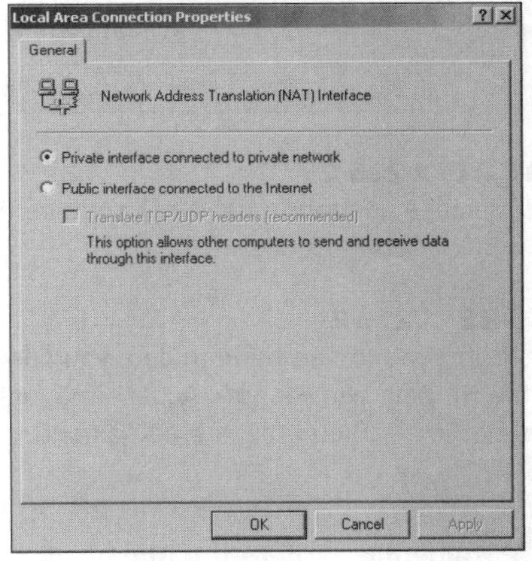

FIGURE 12.49
You must identify whether the interface is connected to a public or private network so that Windows 2000 knows how to translate the addresses.

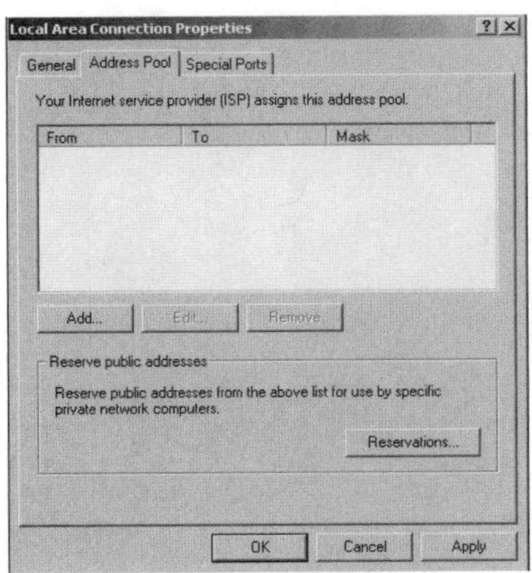

FIGURE 12.50
You need to configure registered addresses for the public interface.

continues

continued

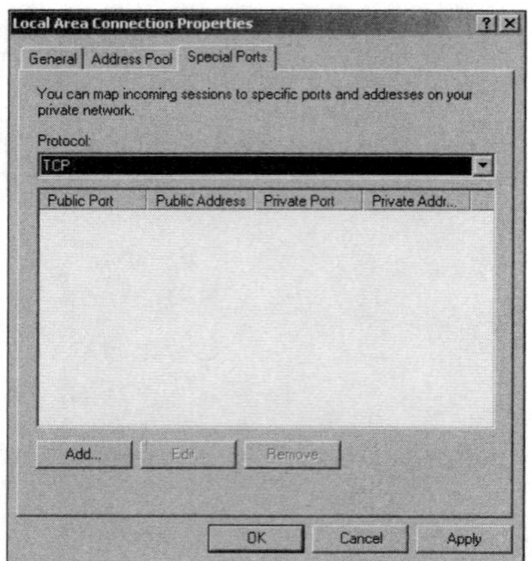

FIGURE 12.51
The Special Ports tab is used to configure custom inbound connections.

4. Select the Special Ports tab to configure any special port/address mappings you might need (see Figure 12.51).

5. In the Routing and Remote Access window, you should see the interface (see Figure 12.52). You can also see the statistics for mappings and their directions when the service is being used.

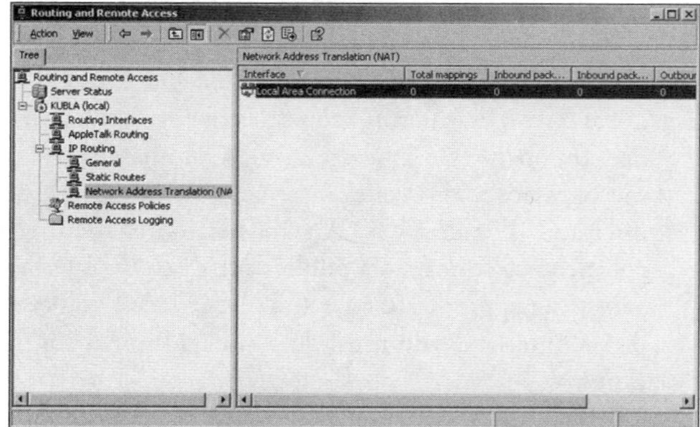

FIGURE 12.52
After the interface has been added, you can use the Routing and Remote Access manager to keep track of the mappings being used.

That completes the installation, configuration, and interfaces for the Network Address Translation protocol.

EXAM TIP

Remember Where the Mappings Are Located Because being able to monitor these mappings is one of the key components to supporting a NAT installation, you might see a question on the exam concerning the mappings.

CASE STUDY: IMPLEMENTING ROUTING AND REMOTE ACCESS IN A COMPLEX ENVIRONMENT

ESSENCE OF THE CASE

The essence of the case is as follows:

- The management of your company is reluctant to make a major investment in toll charges for a dial-based remote access solution.
- Your company has three main populations of users, each with different remote access requirements.
- Each team has the requisite level of security.

SCENARIO

You are the network administrator for NR Widgets Inc., a multinational conglomerate, and you are based in the conglomerate's corporate headquarters. NR Widgets Inc., has a mobile population of about 200 people who need access to the network for submitting expense reports.

About 100 of the users live and work within your local area code, and the rest are scattered throughout the country. Your management does not want to pay for long-distance calls for remote access.

Your mobile users consist of three groups:

- The first group is the highly technical telecommuters, who need access to everything. They are also very security conscious and want to ensure their information is as secure as possible.
- The second group is the local users who need access but are not too concerned about the security of the connection.
- The third group consists of about 35 users who work from home and have high-speed Internet connections.

What is the best way to do this so that you can accomplish the following:

- Each group has access to the network.
- Each group of users has the information security it needs.
- Long-distance or toll-free numbers are not allowed.

What should you do?

continues

CASE STUDY: IMPLEMENTING ROUTING AND REMOTE ACCESS IN A COMPLEX ENVIRONMENT

continued

ANALYSIS

As you have discovered in this chapter, you can meet these requirements by installing the Windows 2000 Routing and Remote Access Service. But by now, you probably realize that it is a bit more complicated than just running the configuration wizard. First, you need to take a close look at each population of users.

The technical telecommuters, who have access to confidential information, will need to have a configuration that leverages the robust security and encryption mechanisms of the Windows 2000 Routing and Remote Access Service. You might need to configure their profile configure dial-backsor perhaps use smart cards for authentication.

For the second group of users, you will probably need to limit their access to sensitive information on the network because they are using a less secure, more user-friendly authentication policy.

Finally, although configuring a network is easy—for example, an Internet-based VPN—you still need to make decisions. You must examine the amount of bandwidth you have to the Internet to support these users. You also must consider where the server is placed. Should it be behind a firewall or directly on the Internet? Next, you should consider which VPN protocol is best suited for your environment. You might even find that your remote users who are not in the local area code want to use a local ISP in conjunction with the VPN solution, allowing you to further save on toll charges. All this is dependent on the environment and the circumstances and requires effective planning. The following is required:

- You must install one server running Windows 2000 Server and the Routing and Remote Access Service.
- The server needs to have modems installed and configured for dial-in users.
- Users who do not have the ability to dial locally to the server need to leverage the Windows 2000 VPN service; therefore, the server needs an Internet connection.
- The server needs remote access profiles to control the session security for each group.

This should be fairly straightforward after you have read the chapter.

CHAPTER SUMMARY

This chapter covered in detail how to use the Windows 2000 Routing and Remote Access Service to provide remote access services. We started the chapter discussing how to configure Routing and Remote Access to support inbound connections, DHCP, virtual private networks, and multilink connections; we also discussed the creation and use of a remote access policy. Additionally, we examined how to use and configure a remote access profile.

We then discussed monitoring and managing the Routing and Remote Access Service. We also discussed the various security aspects of the service, including configuring remote access security, authentication protocols, and encryption.

Finally, we discussed how to use Internet Connection Sharing and the Network Address Translation protocol in RRAS and why and when you would want to use ICS versus RRAS and NAT, and vice versa.

KEY TERMS

- Authentication
- Callback
- Domain Name System (DNS)
- Dynamic Host Control Protocol (DHCP)
- Encryption
- Internet Connection Sharing (ICS)
- Internet service provider (ISP)
- Modem
- Multilink
- Network Address Translation (NAT)
- Private IP address
- Registered IP address
- Remote Access Service (RAS)
- Routing and Remote Access Server (RRAS)
- Virtual private network (VPN)

APPLY YOUR KNOWLEDGE

Exercises

12.1 Creating a Remote Access Policy

In the following exercise, you will use the Routing and Remote Access console to create a remote access policy. For this exercise, you will create a policy for users connecting with PPP.

Estimated Time: 10 minutes

1. Open the Routing and Remote Access console.
2. Expand the application tree in the left pane by double-clicking the server. Right-click Remote Access Policy and select New Remote Access Policy.
3. Enter the name `Exercise 1` and click Next to continue.
4. Click Add to add a condition. Select the Framed Protocol attribute from the list of attributes and click Add.
5. Select PPP from the list of protocols. Click Add.
6. Click OK to add the condition, and then click Next.
7. Select the Grant Remote Access Permission option; then, click Next.
8. Click Finish to complete the creation of the profile.

12.2 Configuring an Idle Timeout for Routing and Remote Access Server

This exercise walks you through modifying a profile to add an idle timeout for a remote access policy.

Estimated Time: 15 minutes

1. Open the Routing and Remote Access console.
2. Right-click the Exercise 1 remote access policy created in the last exercise. Select Properties from the context menu.
3. Click the Edit Profile button.
4. Go to the Dial-Constraints tab. Select the Disconnect if Idle option and set the timeout value to 30 minutes.
5. Click OK to commit the changes. Click OK to return to the Routing and Remote Access console.

12.3 Monitoring Routing and Remote Access Using the Performance Console

This exercise walks you through adding a counter to the Performance console so you can see how many errors the Routing and Remote Access ports are experiencing.

Estimated Time: 15 minutes

1. Open the Performance console.
2. In Performance, select System Monitor.
3. Click the Add (+) icon to add the counter.
4. Select the RAS Total Performance object.
5. Select the Total Errors counter and click Add.
6. Click Close to complete the exercise.

12.4 Installing Internet Connection Sharing

In the following exercise, you install Internet Connection Sharing to share a dial-up Internet connection.

Estimated Time: 15 minutes

APPLY YOUR KNOWLEDGE

1. Open the Network and Dial-up Connections window.
2. Right-click the dial-up connection and select Properties from the context menu. Select the Sharing tab of the Connection Properties dialog box.
3. Select the Enable Internet Connection Sharing for This Connection option.
4. Click OK to close the dialog box and enable ICS.

12.5 Adding a Custom Application

The following exercise shows you how to add the Internet Relay Chat application to a server configured to use Network Address Translation.

Estimated Time: 15 minutes

1. Open the Routing and Remote Access application.
2. Expand the tree under the local server icon. Right-click the Network Address Translation (NAT) icon and select Properties.
3. Click the Translation tab of the Network Address Translation (NAT) Properties dialog box.
4. Click Applications.
5. Click Add. In the Internet Connection Sharing Application dialog box, enter the following:
   - Name of Application: **`Internet Relay Chat`**
   - Remote Server port number: **`6667`**
   - TCP/UDP: **`TCP`**
   - Incoming Response Ports (TCP): **`6668`**
6. Click OK to add the application.
7. Click OK to close the Properties window, and click OK again to close the Routing and Remote Access Manager.

Review Questions

1. You are the network administrator for Exponent Mathematicians and have been asked to review the authentication protocols being used by your Routing and Remote Access Server. What are the available protocols, and how do they work?
2. You are the administrator of the Get Stuffed Taxidermists chain Routing and Remote Access Server. You have users who are using the Windows 2000 VPN, both with IPSec and PPTP protocols. What are those protocols, and which is the industry standard?
3. You are the Windows 2000 administrator for Bug-B-Gone Exterminators. Your users are all connecting to your network using 56K modems, and they are complaining about performance. You are using the Routing and Remote Access Service with a modem bank for providing access, and they are running Windows 2000 Professional. You have used the performance monitoring capabilities of Windows 2000 to determine that there are no issues with Routing and Remote Access, so the issue appears to be bandwidth limitations. What should you do?
4. You have just installed Routing and Remote Access for providing VPN services to 100 of your end users. You are able to get the first 5 users connected, but then the server denies access. What is the problem, and how do you fix it?

5. You're the LAN administrator for Think About IT Consulting Services company. You have just installed your first Routing and Remote Access Server, and your users are connecting without a problem. You want to see how much traffic is being added to the network by the additional users. How can you check?

6. You are the network administrator for a small company that wants to connect to the Internet for the first time. The company has 12 employees, and you don't have a lot of experience with Windows 2000 or routing. What should you do to ensure that you connect to the Internet successfully?

7. The network in the previous question has grown to 50 users, and management wants to upgrade to a DSL connection. You have configured several dozen custom applications, both inbound and outbound, as part of ICS. What should you do to accommodate the DSL connections and the applications you've configured?

8. You are the Windows 2000 administrator for Fly Away Travel. Your boss has asked you to explain the difference between the NAT protocol and the ICS services. Other than manual versus automated features, what does ICS support that NAT does not?

9. That was a good start, but now she wants to know what services are included as part of ICS.

10. You're the administrator of Little Faith Enterprise's Windows 2000 server and are considering setting up NAT. Why would you want to set up NAT?

Exam Questions

1. What portion of the Routing and Remote Access Service can be used to aggregate bandwidth across multiple modem connections?

   A. Multinet

   B Multilink

   C. X.25

   D. VPN

2. You are the system administrator for Phil's Phill-up Stations, a chain of gas stations. As part of the network, you maintain a Windows 2000 Routing and Remote Access Server to provide remote access services as part of a VPN. Which VPN protocols will the server support?

   A. PPTP

   B. IPSec

   C. PPP

   D. EAP

   E. L2TP

3. You are the LAN administrator for the OUI Find-em detective agency. You have people connecting to your Windows 2000 Routing and Remote Access from all over the country, most working from home. How can you minimize the users' toll charges using Routing and Remote Access?

   A. Configure the users' RAS client computers for Connect as Needed mode.

   B. Use IPSec to tunnel to the RAS server through the public phone network, bypassing the toll charges.

APPLY YOUR KNOWLEDGE

C. Get each user a personal 800 number to connect from.

D. Set the Routing and Remote Access Server security to use callback.

4. You are the LAN administrator for Little Faith Enterprises Meat Packing. As part of the troubleshooting of a support issue, you need to check whether a user is connected to the Routing and Remote Access Server.

   How can you check to see whether the user is logged on?

   A. Open Performance Manager. Click the Add Counter icon. Select the RAS object, and then select the Connected Users counter. Click OK and check the resulting statistic.

   B. Open the Performance console; then, click the Add Counter icon. Select the RAS object, and then select the Connected Users counter. Click OK and check the resulting statistic.

   C. Open the Routing and Remote Access console. Right-click the RAS server, and then select Connected Users. Check for the user in the Connected Users dialog box.

   D. Open the Routing and Remote Access console. Under the server in the tree view, select Remote Access Clients. Check for the user in the Remote Access Clients.

5. You need to configure strong authentication for your Windows 2000 Routing and Remote Access Server. Which protocol(s) should you use?

   A. IPSec

   B. PAP

   C. EAP

   D. CHAP

   E. MS-CHAP

6. You manage a Windows 2000 Routing and Remote Access server used for remote dial-in access. You have an end user who is trying to connect to the Routing and Remote Access Server, but he keeps getting the message that he is not an authorized user. He is able to connect to the network and log in from his office across the LAN.

   What might be causing the problem?

   A. The user is not using the correct password.

   B. The user is not using an ID that is authorized to use the dial-in server.

   C. He is trying to use his LAN account instead of his dial-in account.

   D. One of the modems on the server is probably down.

7. You manage a Windows 2000 Routing and Remote Access server used for remote dial-in access. You have an end user who is trying to connect to the Routing and Remote Access server, but keeps getting the message that he is not an authorized user. He is able to connect to the network and log in from his office across the LAN. After doing some research, you find that the user ID was not authorized for remote access. How would you fix this?

   A. Using the Routing and Remote Access console, open the user's ID and under the Remote Access tab, grant him access.

   B. Using the Routing and Remote Access console, create a remote access policy. Use the Windows-Groups criteria and add the user to an authorized group.

APPLY YOUR KNOWLEDGE

C. Using the Routing and Remote Access, create a remote access profile. Use the Windows-Groups criteria and add the user to an authorized group.

D. Using the Routing and Remote Access, create a remote access profile. Configure that profile to Grant Remote Access Permission.

8. You are the network administrator for Runaway Travel and have just installed a new Windows 2000 Routing and Remote Access Server to replace a hardware RAS server. Your users are using a third-party PPP dialer that was used for the old system.

   What is the most secure authentication protocol that can be used for this connection?

   A. PAP

   B. EAP

   C. CHAP

   D. IPSec

9. You are the network administrator for Runaway Travel and have just installed a new Windows 2000 Routing and Remote Access Server to replace a hardware RAS server. Your users are using the Windows 2000 Professional dialer.

   What is the most secure authentication protocol available?

   A. CHAP

   B. MS-CHAP

   C. PPP

   D. IPSec

10. You are the network administrator for Runaway Travel and have just installed a new Windows 2000 Routing and Remote Access Server to replace a hardware RAS server. Your users are using a variety of client computer operating systems and PPP dialers.

    What is the most secure way to ensure that all your users have access?

    A. In the dial-in profile for those users, select Microsoft Encrypted Authentication (MS-CHAP) and Microsoft Encrypted Authentication version 2 (MS-CHAP v2).

    B. In the dial-in profile for those users, select Encrypted Authentication (CHAP).

    C. Use IPSec in conjunction with RAS.

    D. Allow remote PPP client computers, as well as all the other protocols, to connect without negotiating any authentication method.

11. You are the network administrator for Go to Philly bus company and have a requirement for a Windows 2000 Routing and Remote Access Server to replace a hardware solution.

    How do you install and configure the service?

    A. Using the Networking and Dial-up Connections Wizard, install the Routing and Remote Access Service.

    B. Using the Networking and Dial-up Connections Wizard, install the Remote Access Service.

    C. Use the Routing and Remote Access Service to configure the service. Configure it with Windows 2000 Administration.

APPLY YOUR KNOWLEDGE

D. Use the Add/Remove Programs to add the Routing and Remote Access Service to the server. Configure the Routing and Remote Access service from the Control Panel.

12. You are the system administrator for Blue Cap Haberdashery, and you have a Windows 2000 Routing and Remote Access Server acting as a dial-in server. You have 15 modems on the server for users to dial in. Ten users have connected and are able to connect to the network. The eleventh user is able to connect but can't reach anything on the network.

    What could the problem be?

    A. The server is licensed for only ten dial-in users.

    B. The DHCP server was down when the eleventh user tried to connect.

    C. The user has an incompatible modem.

    D. The user's IPSec password is incorrect.

13. You are the system administrator for Blue Cap Haberdashery, and you have a Windows 2000 Routing and Remote Access Server acting as a dial-in server. You have 15 modems on the server for users to dial in. Users are able to connect without any problems, but they can't reach any systems by DNS name. They are able to connect using the IP address of the system.

    What could the problem be?

    A. The Routing and Remote Access Server is not running the DNS service.

    B. The Routing and Remote Access Server is not running the WINS service.

    C. The network DHCP server has a bad DNS configuration.

    D. The network WINS server has a bad DNS configuration.

14. You are the security administrator for Barb's House of Pancakes. You have been asked to implement smart cards for remote access authentication using the Windows 2000 Routing and Remote Access Service.

    Which protocol do you need?

    A. IPSec

    B. PPTP

    C. MS-CHAP v2

    D. EAP

15. You are the network administrator for Phil 'Em Up gas stations. You have installed a Windows 2000 Routing and Remote Access Server to provide access to the corporate network remotely. You want to see what type of utilization the server is experiencing.

    What is the easiest way to find out?

    A. Use Performance Manager to log the utilization, and check the performance logs for the information.

    B. Use the Performance console to log the utilization, and check the performance logs for the information.

    C. Go into the Registry and enable logging. Check the log file for the information.

    D. Go to the Event Logging tab in the Routing and Remote Access Server properties, and check the application log using the Event Viewer application to view the statistics.

APPLY YOUR KNOWLEDGE

16. You are the network administrator for Ye of Little Faith advertising, and you are running a Windows 2000 network made up of 6 Windows 2000 servers and 300 Windows 2000 Professional client computers. You have added 30 modems to the domain controller and need to install and configure the server for inbound connections. A secondary objective would be to install and configure VPN services.

    You do the following:

    Open the Networking and Dial-up Properties and double-click the Make New Connection icon. You follow the wizard to complete the installation, selecting Allow Virtual Private Connections to ensure that your VPN works.

    This solution:

    A. Is functional and meets the primary and secondary objectives.

    B. Is functional but meets only the primary objective.

    C. Is functional but meets only the secondary objective.

    D. Is not functional.

17. You are the system administrator for Run to the Hills Travel. You have a Windows 2000 Routing and Remote Access server configured to use multilink. You would like to configure the server to automatically drop a connection when the lines are not being used.

    Which protocol can you use to accomplish this?

    A. PPP

    B. BAP

    C. PPTP

    D. EAP

18. You are the Internet administrator and are using Windows 2000 Server as a VPN server. You need to configure additional IPSec VPN ports.

    How do you accomplish this?

    A. Run the VPN Wizard and configure the additional ports.

    B. Go to the Networking and Dial-up Connections window and double-click New Connection. When the New Connection Wizard starts, select New Inbound VPN and follow the prompts.

    C. In the Routing and Remote Access console, edit the properties of the L2TP ports and add the additional connections.

    D. In the Routing and Remote Access console, edit the properties of the IPSec ports and add the additional connections.

19. You are the security administrator for a small police force. Your network is based on Windows 2000 Server, and you have just purchased smart cards for the entire force. You would like to take advantage of these for remote access, but you are unsure how to configure Routing and Remote Access. You know you need the EAP protocol.

    Where do you configure this protocol?

    A. In the remote access policy

    B. In the modem pool properties

    C. Under the Security tab of the Routing and Remote Access Server properties

    D. In the dial-in profile for the pertinent policy

APPLY YOUR KNOWLEDGE

20. What is the strongest encryption protocol supported by Windows 2000?

    A. DES

    B. IPSec

    C. MS-CHAP v2

    D. 3DES

21. You are the security administrator for Jolly Snowmen Ice Cream. You have been asked by your manager to explain the use of encryption on your Windows 2000 Server. You know you are running DES.

    What service does DES provide to your installation?

    A. DES encrypts dial-in traffic over the phone lines.

    B. DES encrypts L2TP VPN traffic.

    C. DES provides encrypted authentication.

    D. DES provides encrypted address information in conjunction with PPTP.

22. You are the Internet administrator for Lost in the Woods Guide Service. You have a Windows 2000 server connected to the Internet and have ICS running on it. You have been asked to configure a custom outbound application. How do you do it?

    A. Open the Internet Connection Sharing manager. Select the Network Address Translation entry and right-click to open NAT Properties. On the Sharing tab, use the Add button to add the application.

    B. Open the Routing and Remote Access manager. Select the Network Address Translation entry and right-click to open NAT Properties. On the Sharing tab, use the Add button to add the application.

    C. Open the properties for the dial-up entry in the Network and Dial-up Connections window. Under the Sharing tab, add the application using the Add button.

    D. Open the properties for the dial-up entry in the Network and Dial-up Connections window. Under the Sharing tab, select Settings, and on the Applications tab add the application using the Add button.

23. You are the Internet administrator for Lost in the Woods Guide Service. You have a Windows 2000 server connected to the Internet and have Network Address Translation running on it. You have been asked to configure a custom outbound application. How do you do it?

    A. Open the Routing and Remote Access manager. Select the Network Address Translation entry and right-click to open NAT Properties. On the Sharing tab, use the Add button to add the application.

    B. Open the Routing and Remote Access manager. Select the Network Address Translation entry and right-click to open NAT Properties. On the Translation tab, use the Applications button to access the Add button to add the application.

    C. Open the properties for the dial-up entry in the Network and Dial-up Connections window. Under the Sharing tab, add the application using the Add button.

    D. Open the properties for the dial-up entry in the Network and Dial-up Connections window. Under the Sharing tab, select Settings, and on the Applications tab add the application using the Add button.

APPLY YOUR KNOWLEDGE

24. Which of the following are modifications made by Internet Connection Sharing? (Select all that apply.)

    A. Installs DNS

    B. Installs DHCP

    C. Installs Network Address Translation

    D. Sets the address of the internal interface to 198.168.0.1

    E. Sets the external interface to get its address dynamically

25. You have installed and configured NAT on your Windows 2000 server. How can you most easily monitor the usage?

    A. Open Performance Manager, and click the Add Counter icon. Then, select the NAT object.

    B. Use the Routing and Remote Access manager application and select the Network Address Translation icon. Right-click and select Statistics.

    C. Use the Routing and Remote Access manager application and select the Network Address Translation icon. The statistics will appear in the right pane of the application.

    D. Open the Routing and Remote Access manager, set logging to All Events, and use the Event Viewer to view usage.

26. You are the lead engineer for Little Faith Enterprises. You have been asked to configure Windows 2000 to connect to the Internet using a DSL connection. What should you do?

    A. Open the Routing and Remote Access manager application and install the Network Address Translation protocol. Configure the properties appropriately and add the internal interface to the protocol.

    B. Open the Routing and Remote Access manager application and install the Network Address Translation protocol. Configure the properties appropriately and add the internal interface to the protocol. Then, add the external interface to the protocol.

    C. Open the Network Connection manager and install the Network Address Translation protocol. Configure the properties appropriately and add the internal interface to the protocol. Then, add the external interface to the protocol.

    D. Install ICS and enable the demand-dial connection.

27. You are the network administrator for the Blue Sky Corporation. The corporation is running a T1 Internet connection with Network Address Translation installed. One user has just downloaded a new chat application to enable her to start chats with her friends, in German. The application doesn't work. What's the most likely reason?

    A. The English-language version of NAT was installed.

    B. You can't use chat applications with NAT; you need ICS.

    C. The application needs to be added as an outbound application.

    D. The application needs to be added as an inbound application.

APPLY YOUR KNOWLEDGE

28. The same user in question 6 just bought the latest Directplay application and wants to run it across the Internet. You have tried to add it to the outbound NAT applications, but it still doesn't work. Why not?

    A. NAT was not designed to support games.

    B. NAT can't support Directplay games.

    C. You did not add the application correctly. Most games require inbound access to the host.

    D. You added the application to the wrong interface.

29. You just upgraded your Internet connection to DSL from a dial-up connection and upgraded your Windows 2000 server from the ICS service to the NAT protocol. NetMeeting over the Internet has stopped working since the upgrade.

    Why?

    A. NetMeeting requires a dial-up connection to function.

    B. You did not add the NetMeeting application to the application list.

    C. The NAT protocol can't support NetMeeting, whereas the ICS service can.

    D. You need to reconfigure your DNS server to connect to the Internet for name resolution.

30. You are the network administrator for the LFE Construction Company. You have a Windows 2000 server running NAT for your Internet connection. You need to add an additional segment and give it access to the Internet.

    How do you add an additional segment to NAT?

    A. After the segment has been configured on the server, load the Routing and Remote Access Manager. Then, run the Add Interface Wizard to add the interface.

    B. After the segment has been configured on the server, open the Connection Properties for the new segment. Under the Sharing tab, enable NAT.

    C. After the segment has been configured on the server, load the Routing and Remote Access manager. Then, go to the Network Address Translation protocol and right-click. Select Add Interface and select the new interface.

    D. After the segment has been configured on the server, load the Routing and Remote Access Manager. Go to the Network Address Translation protocol and right-click. Then, select New Interface and select the new interface.

31. You are the network administrator for NR Publishing Unlimited. You have a 100-user network, and you just installed a Windows 2000 server to connect the network to the Internet. None of your users are able to connect to the Internet, even though the server connects fine. What is the likely problem?

    A. The users have not gotten addresses from the DHCP server installed with NAT.

    B. IP forwarding needs to be enabled.

    C. You need to add an application to NAT before anyone will be able to connect.

    D. You didn't install NAT or ICS.

APPLY YOUR KNOWLEDGE

32. You are the lead consultant for Zoom Package Delivery Services. You have configured a Windows 2000 server with Network Address Translation for your 30 users. Some of your users have complained that they have been experiencing intermittent connection issues with the Internet. You want to check the log to find out what the issue might be. Where should you look?

    A. The `<system directory>\SYSTEM32\ETC\NAT\logddmmyy.log` file

    B. The Application Event Log

    C. The System Event Log

    D. The Security Event Log

33. You are the network administrator for Gollywillikers Candy, and you are in the process of setting up your first Internet connection using Windows 2000 and the NAT protocol. Your ISP has given you a range of registered IP addresses for your Network Address Translation. Where do you configure these?

    A. In the Networking properties, under the TCP/IP protocol

    B. On a private interface for the NAT protocol

    C. On the public interface for the NAT protocol

    D. Under the Network tab of NAT Properties

34. You are the network administrator of Little Faith Enterprises, a booming retail garden center. You are trying to determine whether to use the Windows 2000 server's ICS service or NAT, but you can't decide. Your manager has asked you what the difference is. You respond that NAT doesn't support all the protocols that ICS does. Which protocol does NAT not support that ICS does?

    A. TCP/IP

    B. DNS

    C. LDAP Proxy

    D. HTTP

35. You are the system administrator for Barb's House of Cheese, a leading cheese manufacturing company. You have decided to make a Web site available on the Internet. This site resides on your internal network, and you have the Windows 2000 NAT protocol running on the server that connects you to the Internet. In the interests of security, your Web server does not use the standard port 80 for HTTP traffic, but instead uses port 333. Now you have to figure out how to configure the translation. Where do you do it?

    A. The internal NAT interface

    B. The public NAT interface

    C. The Network Applications Settings in the Network Address Translation Properties

    D. The TCP Mapping dialog box in the Network Address Translation Properties

Answers to Review Questions

1. The authentication protocols available include the following:

    - **EAP-TLS**—The Extensible Authentication Protocol (EAP) is an extension to the Point-to-Point Protocol (PPP). EAP provides a standard mechanism for support of additional authentication methods within PPP, such as smart cards, one-time passwords, and certificates. EAP is critical for secure

APPLY YOUR KNOWLEDGE

Windows 2000 VPNs because it offers stronger authentication methods (such as X.509 certificates) instead of relying on the user ID and password schemes used traditionally.

- **CHAP**—The Challenge Handshake Authentication Protocol (CHAP) negotiates an encrypted authentication using Message Digest 5 (MD5), an industry-standard hashing scheme. CHAP uses challenge-response with one-way MD5 hashing on the response. This allows you to authenticate to the server without actually sending your password over the network. Because this is an industry-standard authentication method, it enables Windows 2000 to securely connect to almost all third-party PPP servers.
- **MS-CHAP**—Microsoft created Microsoft Challenge Handshake Authentication Protocol (MS-CHAP), an extension of CHAP, to authenticate remote Windows workstations, increasing the protocol's functionality by integrating the encryption and hashing algorithms used on Windows networks. Similar to CHAP, MS-CHAP uses a challenge-response mechanism with one-way encryption on the response. Although MS-CHAP is consistent with standard CHAP as much as possible, the MS-CHAP response packet is in a format specifically designed for computers running a Windows operating system. A new version of the Microsoft Challenge Handshake Authentication Protocol (MS-CHAP v2) is also available. This new protocol provides mutual authentication, stronger initial data encryption keys, and different encryption keys for sending and receiving.
- **SPAP**—Shiva Password Authentication Protocol (SPAP) is used specifically to allow Shiva client computers to connect to a Windows 2000 server and to allow Windows 2000 client computers to connect to Shiva servers.
- **PAP**—Password Authentication Protocol (PAP) uses unencrypted (plain-text) passwords for authenticating users and is considered the least secure authentication protocol available. PAP typically is used as the authentication of last resort—when a more secure form of authentication is not available. You might need to use this protocol when you are connecting to a non-Windows-based server.

2. Understanding the differences between IPSec and PPTP is important. These points should help you distinguish between the two:

   - **IPSec (IP Security Protocol)**—IPSec is a suite of cryptography-based protection services and security protocols used to provide a secure virtual private network connection. IPSec provides machine-level authentication, as well as data encryption, for L2TP-based (Layer 2 Tunneling Protocol) VPN connections. Unlike some other IPSec-based VPNs, Microsoft's implementation uses the L2TP protocol for encrypting the usernames, passwords, and data, whereas IPSec is used to negotiate the secure connection between your computer and its remote tunnel server. All authentication under the Microsoft IPSec VPN occurs through L2TP connections. These use all standard PPP-based authentication protocols to authenticate the user after the secure IPSec communication is established.

APPLY YOUR KNOWLEDGE

- **PPTP (Point-to-Point Tunneling Protocol)**—PPTP is Microsoft's legacy protocol for supporting virtual private networks. Developed jointly by Microsoft Corporation, U.S. Robotics, and several remote access vendor companies (known collectively as the PPTP Forum), PPTP encountered some security issues in its original form. It has been revised by Microsoft, but it has never been widely accepted by the security community. Although still supported on a variety of vendors' VPN servers, PPTP is rapidly being overtaken by the more widely adopted IPSec protocol.

3. The only way to provide additional bandwidth short of a different access media is to enable multilink and have the users add an additional modem and modem line on the remote end. This enables the users to aggregate their bandwidth across two separate connections.
4. By default, Routing and Remote Access is configured with five connections for the VPN. You need to open the Routing and Remote Access application and go into the Port properties. Then, add additional ports as necessary.
5. To find out the raw numbers on bandwidth through the server, you must use the Performance console. Go to the RAS Total object and add the Total Bytes Received and Total Bytes Transmitted counters. Then, add the two counters to get the total additional traffic.
6. You should implement Internet Connection Sharing in conjunction with a dial-up ISP connection. ICS is easy to install and maintain, and it bundles the services you need to make this connection work.
7. Just migrate to the Network Address Translation protocol. This accommodates the DSL connection without a problem (although you will need to manually configure both the internal and external interfaces), and the applications you configured will still appear in the NAT list of custom applications.
8. ICS supports the following standards: H.323 Proxy, LDAP Proxy, and Directplay Proxy.
9. ICS installs a DNS and DHCP service. It also sets the IP address of the LAN interface to 192.168.0.1 and sets the WAN interface to be a demand-dial router pointed at the ISP.
10. Two reasons exist for using NAT. The first is to provide a level of security for your network when it is connected to the Internet. Not only does NAT hide your internal addresses, but it also restricts the services that can access the internal network. You will also need to conserve public IP addresses. Unless you are fortunate to have enough registered addresses for your users, you will need NAT.

Answers to Exam Questions

1. **B.** The correct term for this feature is multilink. See the section "Configuring Multilink Connections," earlier in this chapter.
2. **A, B, E.** The Windows 2000 Routing and Remote Access supports the following VPN protocols: IPSec, PPTP, and L2TP. See the section "Configuring a Virtual Private Network," earlier in this chapter.

APPLY YOUR KNOWLEDGE

3. **D.** If you configure the Routing and Remote Access server to use callback, all the toll charges following the initial connection will be on the company's bill, not the end user's. This is an old trick for reducing costs by leveraging the company's generally more favorable long distance rates. See the section "Configuring a Remote Access Profile," earlier in this chapter.

4. **D.** You can see this information in the right pane of the Routing and Remote Access console by clicking the Remote Access Clients entry. See the section "Configuring Authentication Protocols," earlier in this chapter.

5. **C, D, E.** IPSec is not an authentication protocol. PAP sends the authentication information as clear text. EAP, CHAP, and MS-CHAP are all secure authentication protocols. See the section "Creating a Remote Access Policy," earlier in this chapter.

6. **B.** The user is not using an ID that is authorized to use the dial-in server. You must be authorized in a remote access policy before you can connect via dial-in. See the section "Creating a Remote Access Policy," earlier in this chapter.

7. **B.** Using the Routing and Remote Access console, create a remote access policy. Use the Windows-Groups criteria and add the user to an authorized group. See the section "Creating a Remote Access Policy," earlier in this chapter.

8. **C.** With a third-party dialer, the best you will be able to manage for authentication is the CHAP protocol. CHAP is an industry-standard protocol supported by virtually all PPP dialers. PAP would also work, but it offers no security whatsoever. IPSec is not an authentication protocol. EAP is a protocol used for devices such as smart cards. See the section "Configuring Authentication Protocols," earlier in this chapter.

9. **B.** When you are communicating between Windows PPP client computers, MS-CHAP is the most secure protocol listed. See the section "Configuring Authentication Protocols," earlier in this chapter.

10. **D.** The trick here is to understand that the "connect without negotiating any authentication method" configuration is the lowest common denominator for connections. That's the only way to ensure that all your users can get to the network using your RAS solution. Users can still connect using greater security. See the section "Configuring Authentication Protocols," earlier in this chapter.

11. **C.** The Routing and Remote Access Service is installed with the operating system. You will need the Routing and Remote Access console to ensure everything is configured correctly. See the section "Configuring Inbound Connections," earlier in this chapter.

12. **B.** The Routing and Remote Access Service requests 10 addresses from the network DHCP server when it starts. When those 10 have been issued, RRAS requests an additional 10 addresses. If the DHCP server has gone down since the original 10 addresses were issued, the user would be able to connect but would not be able to get on the network because the Routing and Remote Access Service couldn't get additional IP addresses from the DHCP server. See the section "Configuring Routing and Remote Access for DHCP Integration," earlier in this chapter.

13. **C.** Because the Routing and Remote Access server gets its DHCP information from the network DHCP server, a bad DNS configuration on the DHCP server could cause the issue described. See the section "Configuring Routing and Remote Access for DHCP Integration," earlier in this chapter.

APPLY YOUR KNOWLEDGE

14. **D.** EAP is the protocol needed to support smart cards. See the section "Configuring Authentication Protocols," earlier in this chapter.

15. **D.** In the latest version of Routing and Remote Access, logging is enabled in the server properties. The results of the logging can be found in the Event Viewer. See the section "Managing and Monitoring Remote Access," earlier in this chapter.

16. **D.** This solution will not work because you must use the Routing and Remote Access console to configure remote access on a domain controller. See the section "Configuring Inbound Connections," earlier in this chapter.

17. **B.** BAP (Bandwidth Access Protocol) is used to accomplish this function in conjunction with multilink. See the section "Configuring Multilink Connections," earlier in this chapter.

18. **C.** You can just edit the properties of the L2TP ports, which are installed and configured when Routing and Remote Access is installed. Because by default IPSec used L2TP as a transport under Windows 2000, the ports are L2TP ports, not IPSec ports. See the section "Configuring a Virtual Private Network," earlier in this chapter.

19. **D.** The authentication protocols are configured in the dial-in profile. Although A is almost right, this is not configured as part of the policy, but is instead part of the profile. See the section "Configuring a Remote Access Profile," earlier in this chapter.

20. **D.** 3DES or Triple DES is the strongest encryption protocol used by Windows 2000. See the section "Configuring Encryption Protocols," earlier in this chapter.

21. **B.** DES is used in conjunction with IPSec. Because IPSec is used with L2TP, B is the correct answer. See the section "Configuring Encryption Protocols," earlier in this chapter.

22. **D.** All ICS settings are configured through the dial-up connection properties. To set up or modify the applications, you must get into the Sharing Settings and add them on the Applications tab. For more information see the section "Installing Internet Connection Sharing."

23. **B.** To add an application through NAT, you must use the Routing and Remote Access Manager. The Translation tab is where the applications are configured for outbound use. For more information see the section "Installing NAT."

24. **A, B, D.** The Internet Connection Sharing service does install versions of DNS and DHCP, but it does not install Network Address Translation. It provides that functionality as part of its services but does not install the actual protocol. Although it does set the address of the internal interface, the external interface is configured as part of the dial-up configuration. For more information, see the section "Installing Internet Connection Sharing."

25. **C.** The usage statistics automatically appear next to the appropriate interface in the right pane of the application. For more information, see the section "Installing NAT."

26. **B.** Because DSL connects as a LAN interface, you must use the NAT protocol for this connection. You also need to be sure to add both interfaces. For more information, see the section "Installing NAT."

APPLY YOUR KNOWLEDGE

27. **C.** For a new application to communicate across the NAT server, it must be added to the list of outbound applications. For more information, see the section "Installing NAT."

28. **B.** NAT can't support Directplay applications at this time. For more information, see the section "Installing NAT."

29. **C.** NetMeeting is one of the applications ICS supports but NAT does not. For more information, see the section "Installing NAT."

30. **D.** You need to use the Routing and Remote Access Manager to add the new interface. The correct command is New Interface, not Add Interface. For more information, see the section "Installing NAT."

31. **D.** You need to install NAT for the connection to work. For more information, see the section "Installing NAT."

32. **C.** All NAT logging is done to the System Event Log and can be viewed with the Event Viewer. For more information, see the section "Installing NAT."

33. **C.** You must configure the registered IP addresses on the NAT public interface. So that the packets are routed correctly, they need to be translated from private addresses to registered addresses. The registered addresses must be configured on the public interface for this routing to occur. For more information, see the section "Installing NAT."

34. **C.** ICS supports LDAP Proxy; NAT does not. For more information, see the section "Installing Internet Connection Sharing."

35. **B.** This type of custom port mapping is done on the public interface of the Network Address Translation interfaces. For more information, see the section "Installing NAT."

Suggested Readings and Resources

1. Boswell, William. *Inside Windows 2000 Server.* Indianapolis, IN: New Riders Publishing, 2000.

2. Siyan, Karanjit S. *Windows NT TCP/IP.* Indianapolis, IN: New Riders Publishing, 1998.

Objectives

This chapter finishes off the objectives for the exam by discussing the last subobjective of the "Configuring, Securing, and Troubleshooting Remote Access" unit of the exam.

We address only a single subobjective in this chapter:

Implement and Troubleshoot Terminal Services for Remote Access.

- **Configure Terminal Services for remote administration or application server mode.**
- **Configure Terminal Services for local resource mapping.**
- **Configure Terminal Services user properties.**

▶ Although Terminal Services is a product in its own right, the focus of the exam is how to use Terminal Services, in Remote Administration mode, to administer a server remotely. Effective use of Terminal Server can greatly reduce the support costs for nonlocal servers.

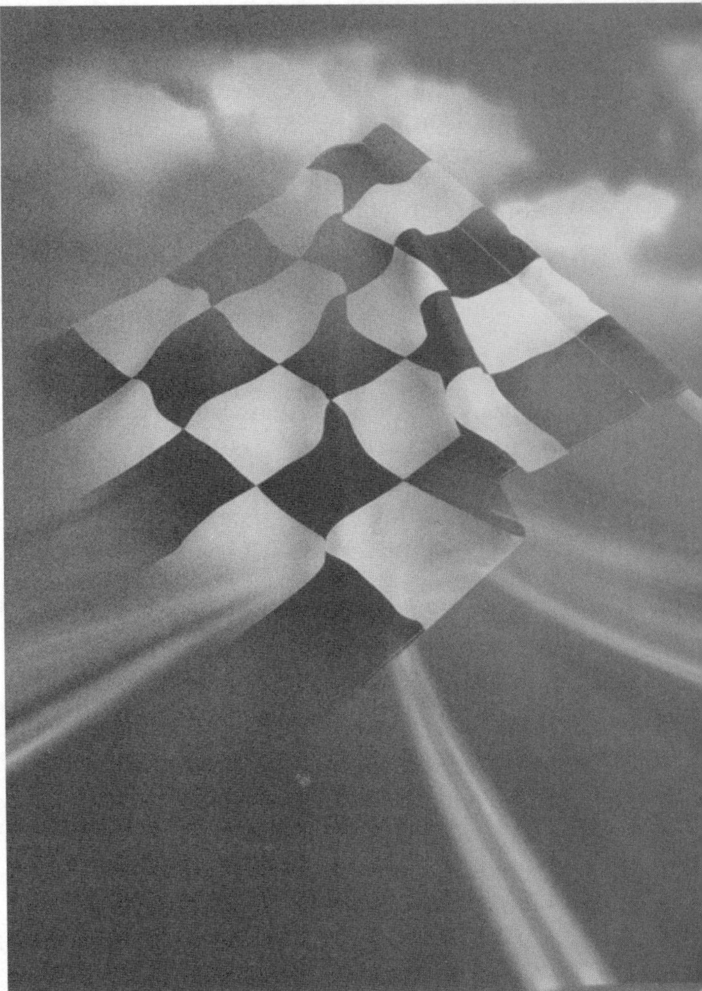

CHAPTER 13

Terminal Services Fundamentals

OUTLINE

STUDY STRATEGIES

- The best way to learn about Terminal Services is to use it. Install Terminal Services in Remote Administration mode and use it to access your server.

INSTALLING, CONFIGURING, AND TROUBLESHOOTING TERMINAL SERVICES

▶ Implement and troubleshoot Terminal Services for remote access.

Terminal services is a session hosting service that enables a Windows 2000 server to provide environment resources (memory, processor, hard drive) so that a client needs to provide only minimal memory and processor resources. The end result is that both thin clients (such as Windows CE machines and dumb terminals) and fat clients (any PC running the Terminal Services client) can use a Windows 2000 environment with little loss of performance over a Pentium machine with 64MB of RAM running the same applications.

This capability has obvious benefits. Legacy hardware can continue to be used, reducing the amount spent on hardware upgrades for old machines. Also, legacy operating systems can continue to be used while, at the same time, taking advantage of 32-bit Windows 2000 applications. In addition, because all settings are hosted on a remote machine, control can be exercised over what software can be installed by clients and what applications can be run. Finally, through the Terminal Services administrator, you can take remote control of client sessions, which will make help desk functions much easier.

In addition to the regular client options, tools also exist for configuring remote administration on the server. Therefore, Terminal Services clients can be configured to remotely administer servers by providing live sessions on the server itself. This is similar to the types of functionality that are provided by third-party products such as *Remotely Possible*. Unlike the traditional approach to remote administration, in which tools are installed on an administrator's machine, these sessions give local access to the server itself. That means processes can be terminated, software can be installed, services can be started and stopped, and so on.

The disadvantage of using the Terminal Services is that it uses server memory and sometimes increases network traffic. Because all the processing is happening on the server side, all that happens on the client is input from the keyboard and mouse and display of screen information.

So, all keyboard and mouse commands have to be sent over the network to the server, and all display information must be sent to the client over the network. With some file-based database applications, network utilization can actually be reduced, and some of the network load implications can be overcome by creative subnetting. However, network bandwidth utilization should be monitored. In addition, memory needs to be increased in any server running the Terminal Services (slightly for simple administration hosting, much more for multiple-application user sessions) to allow for multiple sessions.

Terminal Services Hardware and Software

A terminal server implementation consists of two environments: the server environment and the client environment. The server environment is where the client session is hosted, and it must be robust enough to provide services to as many concurrent users as is permitted without loss of performance in other areas on the server. As a result, hardware requirements need to be carefully considered, and hardware might need to be upgraded before and during your terminal server implementation.

The Terminal Services Server

Terminal server requires a Windows 2000 server to host it. It is recommended that the server be a member server in a domain rather than a domain controller (a server that authenticates domain logons) because Terminal Services can degrade the server's functions in other areas. Furthermore, if your implementation is large, you might need several terminal servers to service all your clients.

The primary hardware components to be managed in a terminal server environment are memory and processor power. Of course, the minimum memory requirements for Windows 2000 must be met (64MB), but on top of that, Microsoft recommends 4MB–8MB of RAM for every anticipated concurrent user. Failure to adhere to these guidelines will, at best, result in poor performance from the client's perspective and, at worst, render the clients unable to connect to the server at all (the client might get failure messages indicating that the server is too busy for the connection).

Similar to memory, processor requirements scale linearly as the number of users increases. As a result, it is recommended that when you first implement terminal server, you use a server that is capable of being expanded to multiple processors in case additional processing power is required down the line.

> NOTE
>
> **Memory** In the real world, you'll probably need more than just the 4MB–8MB Microsoft recommends. On my system even Internet Explorer 6 takes up more than 11MB of RAM when it starts.

Microsoft divides users into three categories:

- **Task-based**—Those users who run a single data entry application.
- **Typical**—Those users who run one or two simultaneous applications but whose data entry requirements are low; they might run a word processor and a browser.
- **Advanced**—Those users whose requirements are heavy, running three or more simultaneous applications and doing large queries on databases.

The number of users that can be supported on any given server depends on the types of users being supported.

Based on data published by Microsoft, Table 13.1 provides a sample of terminal server users supported on given server hardware platforms.

TABLE 13.1

AVERAGE NUMBER OF USERS SUPPORTED ON SELECT SERVER PLATFORMS

Server Configuration	*Task-Based*	*Typical*	*Advanced*
Single processor, Pentium Pro, 200MHz, 128MB RAM	25	15	8
Dual processor, Pentium Pro, 200MHz, 256MB RAM	50	30	15
Quad processor, Pentium Pro, 200MHz, 512MB RAM	100	60	30

In addition to memory and processor power, fast hard drives (preferably SCSI) are recommended, as is a network infrastructure tuned for maximum throughput (multiple network adapters are recommended and third-party NIC load-balancing software really helps).

> NOTE
>
> **Hardware Updates** As you can see, these numbers are older. You can get current numbers from the Microsoft Web site at `http://www.microsoft.com/windows2000/docs/tscaling.doc`.

The Terminal Services Client

Because Terminal Services run almost exclusively on the server, the client can be much less powerful than would be necessary if the client were hosting applications itself. That fact is one of the benefits of using Terminal Services. In fact, Terminal Services enables a wide variety of clients to support Windows 2000 applications, as shown in the following list:

- Windows 2000 (all types)
- Windows NT (all types and versions running on Intel or Alpha processors)
- Windows 9x
- Windows for Workgroups (3.11)
- Windows CE clients (appropriately configured)
- Windows-based terminals (thin clients)

To operate, all that is required is that certain minimum hardware specifications be met and that the Terminal Services client be installed on the computer. After that, when a session is opened, the user will be executing in a Windows 2000 window and will be able to work within that window as though his local operating system were Windows 2000.

Table 13.2 lists the Windows operating systems on which Terminal Services clients operate and their minimum hardware requirements.

NOTE

Pocket PCs Microsoft Windows CE-based Pocket PC devices did not support a terminal server client until Pocket PC 2002. Windows CE support was limited to handheld PC devices and Windows Terminal devices.

TABLE 13.2

MINIMUM HARDWARE REQUIREMENTS BY OPERATING SYSTEM

Operating System	*RAM*	*Processor*	*Video Card*
Windows 2000	32MB	Pentium	VGA
Windows NT	16MB	486	VGA
Windows 98	16MB	486	VGA
Windows 95	16MB	386	VGA
Windows 3.11	16MB	386	VGA
Windows CE	any	any	any

One more hardware requirement needs to be mentioned. Certain applications that are hosted from the terminal server can require special input devices (such as bar-code readers) to function properly. Because all input comes from the client, two criteria must be met. First, the device must be installed on the client computer. Second, the device must operate as a keyboard-input device for its data to be recognized by the Terminal Services server.

Hosted Terminal Services Applications

As has been mentioned already, the environment Terminal Services provides is Windows 2000. Therefore, any applications that are to be run by the Terminal Services client must be Windows 2000 compliant. If an application will not run under Windows 2000, it will not run hosted by a Terminal Services server. Although it is theoretically possible to run DOS, Windows 16-bit, and Windows 32-bit applications under Terminal Services, for best performance, Windows 32-bit applications are recommended.

Installing Terminal Services Server

When you install Terminal Services, you have three options in terms of the software to be installed. Of course, the Terminal Services server must be installed. In addition, you can install the Terminal Services client creator, used for creating client installation disks (not required if you are going to install the client software over the network). Finally, you can install the Terminal Services License Manager. You are required to install this software once for each enterprise in which applications are to run from Terminal Services clients.

During the installation process, you will be prompted for the type of application your Terminal Services installation will have. You have two choices: remote administration and application server. Remote administration is used when the purpose for installing Terminal Services is to be able to open server consoles from remote machines to administrate the server. In installations such as this, typically only one user will be connected at a time—you or another administrator (two simultaneous connections).

Application server mode is used when the primary reason for installing Terminal Services is to host client sessions executing applications (this mode includes the capability to perform remote administration of the server). In this case, the hardware requirements will be greater, but so will the administration. In addition to installing the applications for execution by the clients, you will also have to administer licensing of the clients.

Terminal Services licensing is not part of the license you buy with the operating system your clients are running. As a result, you are required to install the Terminal Services License Manager on at least one computer in your company. When a client connects to a terminal server for the first time, it obtains and stores locally a license from the License Manager. On subsequent occasions, the local license is presented to the terminal server for validation. A terminal server will allow unlicensed clients to connect for 90 days, at which time it requires a License Manager with valid licenses to function. These licenses must be obtained from Microsoft.

NOTE

Licensing Licensing of Terminal Services clients doesn't exactly work perfectly out of the box. It's recommended that you get and install the Terminal Services Licensing hot fix from the Microsoft Web site. The hot fix allows you to set an expiration interval for licenses.

The License Manager can be installed on a member server, but, in order to work for all the users in your domain, it must be installed on a domain controller. Therefore, it is recommended that the License Manager always be installed on a domain controller. Moreover, if you want to use the same License Manager for your entire organization and you have multiple domains, you can install the manager as an enterprise manager so it can be accessed by any Windows 2000 domain in your organization.

Step By Step 13.1 and Step By Step 13.2 show you how to install Terminal Services to facilitate remote server administration and run applications, respectively.

STEP BY STEP

13.1 Installing Terminal Services for Remote Server Administration

1. From the Control Panel, double-click the Add/Remove Programs icon.
2. At the Add/Remove Programs dialog box, click the Add/Remove Windows Components icon.

3. At the Windows Components screen, scroll down and select Terminal Services. Click Next to continue.

4. At the Terminal Services Setup screen, ensure that Remote Administration Mode is selected and click Next (see Figure 13.1).

5. At the Completing the Windows Components Wizard screen, click Finish.

6. When prompted, restart your server.

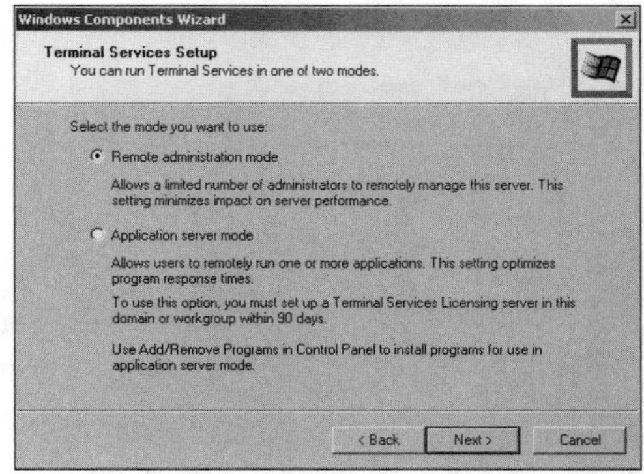

FIGURE 13.1
Remote Administration Mode enables connection to a terminal server for the purposes of administering it.

STEP BY STEP

13.2 Installing Terminal Services for Application Server Operation

1. From the Control Panel, double-click the Add/Remove Programs icon.

2. At the Add/Remove Programs dialog box, click the Add/Remove Windows Components icon.

3. At the Windows Components screen, scroll down and select Terminal Services and Terminal Services Licensing. Click Next to continue.

4. At the Terminal Services Setup screen, ensure that Application Server Mode is selected and click Next (see Figure 13.2).

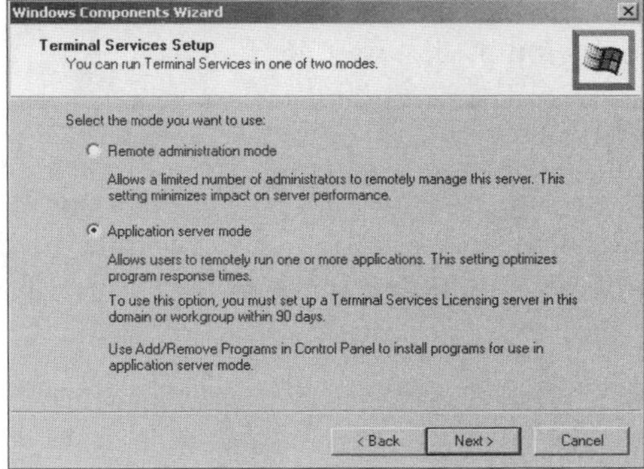

FIGURE 13.2
Application servers allow Terminal Services clients to connect and run programs. This server type requires that a License Manager be available.

continues

continued

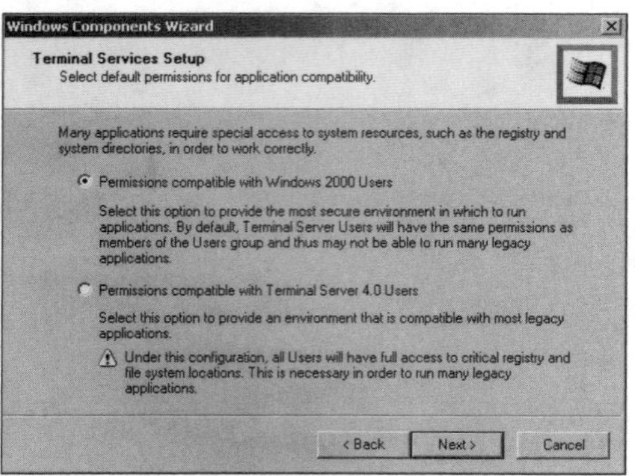

FIGURE 13.3
Choose the most restrictive permissions that will allow all your users to execute their applications.

5. At the next Terminal Services Setup screen, select the minimum permissions required to execute your applications (see Figure 13.3). If any of your applications require access to the Registry and system files to operate, you will have to select Permissions Compatible with Terminal Server 4.0 Users; otherwise, select Permissions Compatible with Windows 2000 Users. Click Next to continue.

6. At the next Terminal Services Setup screen, note any applications that are flagged as being potentially problematic. This list is compiled from your system, so yours will be different from what is shown in Figure 13.4. Applications listed might have to be reinstalled after Terminal Services is configured. Click Next to continue.

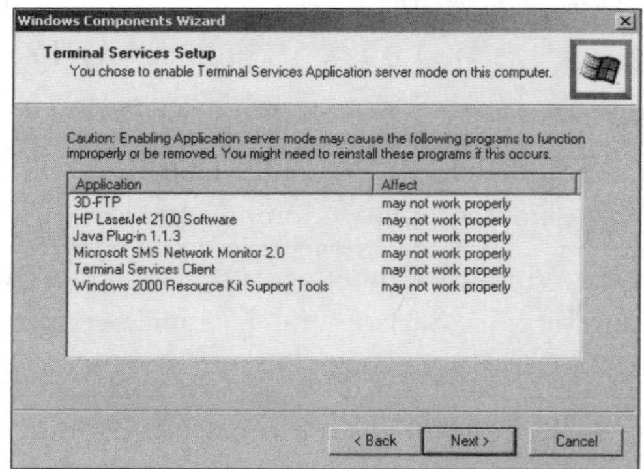

FIGURE 13.4
A list of applications with possible problems is generated.

7. At the Completing the Windows Components Wizard screen, click Finish.

8. When prompted, restart your server.

If you need to reconfigure your server from one mode to the other (from Administration to Application or vice versa), you can do so through Add/Remove Programs applet in the Control Panel. Step By Step 13.3 illustrates this process.

STEP BY STEP

13.3 Switching Between Server Modes

1. From the Control Panel, double-click the Add/Remove Programs icon.
2. At the Add/Remove Programs dialog box, click the Add/Remove Windows Components icon.
3. At the Windows Components screen, click Next to continue (there is no need to select or deselect any options at this time).
4. At the Terminal Services Setup screen, choose the mode you want to switch to and click Next. If you select Administration, the wizard completes the configuration. If you select Applications, you will continue with steps 5–8 from Step By Step 13.2.

Configuring Terminal Services Server

- Implement and troubleshoot Terminal Services for remote access.
    - Configure Terminal Services for Remote Administration or Application Server mode.
    - Configure Terminal Services for local resource mapping.
    - Configure Terminal Services user properties.

Configuration of the Terminal Services server is done in two separate areas. First, the server itself is configured. Then users are configured for Terminal Services sessions.

Terminal Services Server Configuration

Installed with the Terminal Services on the server is a Terminal Services Configuration Manager that enables you to set defaults for the operation of the terminal server. From that manager, you can configure the settings for the terminal server connection (RDP-Tcp) and the settings for the terminal server itself.

All communications between Terminal Services clients and a Windows 2000 terminal server happen using the Remote Desktop Protocol-Transmission Control Protocol (RDP-Tcp). When the Terminal Server is activated on your server, a connection is created to use this protocol. Other connections can be created, but only for other terminal server types (a topic that is beyond the scope of this book and the server exam).

When you open the properties for the RDP-Tcp connection, a dialog box with eight property sheets appears.

The General property sheet enables you to configure three things:

- A comment pertaining to the connection
- The encryption level of network data transmission
- Whether to always use Standard Windows authentication

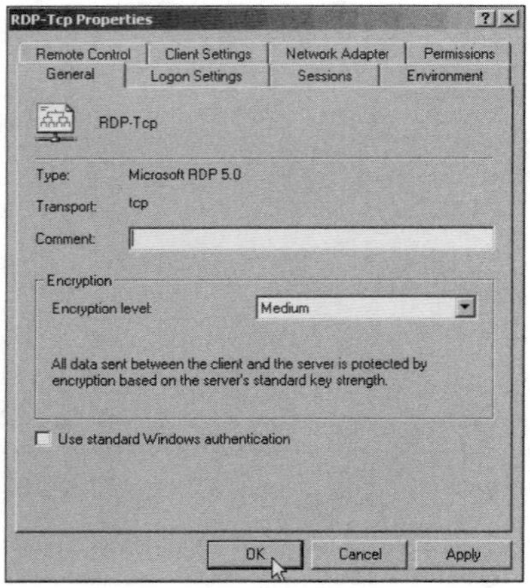

FIGURE 13.5
Client/server encryption defines the times at which encryption is applied to communication and how strong it is.

Because most of the activity that occurs during a Terminal Services client session passes over the network, some level of encryption is necessary to preserve data integrity and secrecy (see Figure 13.5). Three levels of encryption are available:

- **Low**—Only encrypt data from client to server, and not the other way around
- **Medium**—Use 40- or 56-bit encryption in both directions
- **High**—Use 128-bit encryption if the server and client are so equipped

Low encryption is used when security is not a large issue. It encrypts all data from the client to the server, ensuring that logon passwords are encrypted. Medium encryption is used when general network security is required. It encrypts data to and from the client using either 40-bit (for pre-Windows 2000 Terminal Services clients) or 56-bit (for Windows 2000 Terminal Services clients). High encryption is used when security is very important and is available in all countries except those that have state-sponsored terrorism. At time of printing, this list included Cuba, Iran, Iraq, Libya, North Korea, Syria, Sudan, and Serbia.

If Use Standard Windows Authentication is selected, Windows authentication is used even if another security provider is installed on the Windows 2000 terminal server.

The Logon Settings property sheet enables you to configure logon settings for users connecting to your server. You can have users provide their own logons (in which case, upon connection, users are prompted to log on), or you can provide a single account with which all users will connect to the server (see Figure 13.6). The check box labeled Always Prompt for Password is significant only if you also selected Always Use the Following Logon Information. In that case, you will not be able to provide a password to the logon account; the user connection will have to do that manually.

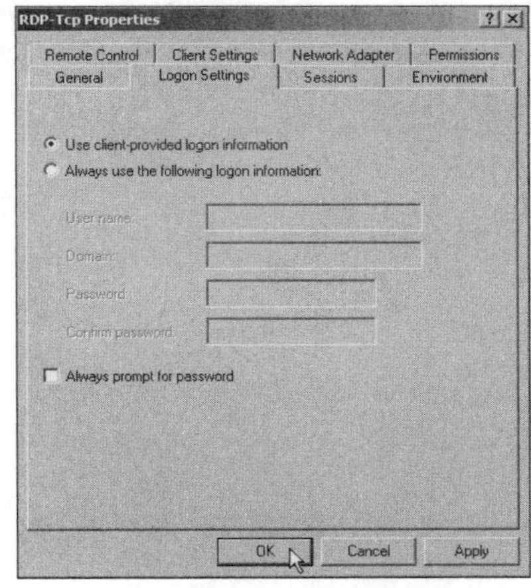

FIGURE 13.6
Configure the server to accept logon information from the client or to always use the same logon account.

The Sessions property sheet allows you to set Terminal Services timeout and reconnection settings (see Figure 13.7). The four user states for a terminal server and a client are as follows:

- Active session
- Idle session
- Disconnected session
- Terminated session

An *active* session is one in which the client is working and keyboard or mouse information is being transferred to the server, and an *idle* session is one in which no keyboard or mouse information is being transferred to the server. A *disconnected* session is one in which a user has exited the client software but has not logged off. The user can return to this session later as long as it is not terminated. A *disconnected* session takes up resources on the server and, if the number of sessions is limited, can prevent other users from connecting. Finally, *terminated* sessions are not sessions at all but are the absence of a session and the release of system resources formerly dedicated to a session.

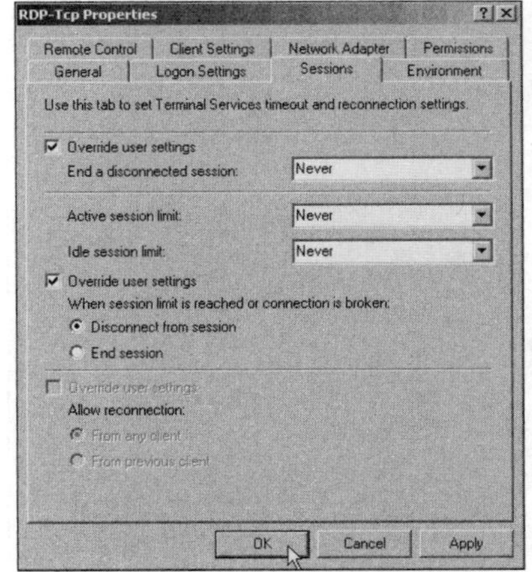

FIGURE 13.7
Set timeout settings for server sessions.

Settings for what to do with disconnected sessions, active sessions, and idle sessions can be set for individual users (as they are in the properties of a user's account). Here, these user settings can be overridden with server settings.

If you change the End a Disconnected Session setting from Never to another value, when a session is disconnected, it must be reactivated within the time you specify; otherwise, it will be terminated. You can either choose a time frame (from 1 minute to 2 days) or type in your own (using a number and the letter m for minutes, h for hours, and d for days). If you type in your own value, it can't be greater than 49 days, 17 hours.

If you change the Active Session Limit setting from Never to another value, a session can remain active only for the length of time you specify. When the limit is reached, the session is either disconnected or terminated (depending on the setting you select for When Session Limit Is Reached or Connection Is Broken). You can either select a time frame (from 1 minute to 2 days) or type in your own (using a number and the letter m for minutes, h for hours, and d for days). If you type in your own value, it can't be greater than 49 days, 17 hours.

If you change the Idle Session Limit setting from Never to another value, a session can remain idle for only the length of time you specify. When the limit is reached, the session is either be disconnected or terminated (depending on the setting you select for When Session Limit Is Reached or Connection Is Broken). You can either select a time frame (from 1 minute to 2 days) or type in your own (using a number and the letter m for minutes, h for hours, and d for days). If you type in your own value, it can't be greater than 49 days, 17 hours.

You can also choose to override the settings for what to do when a time limit on idle or active sessions has been reached (or when the network connection is broken between the client and server). You can choose to either disconnect from the session and place the session into a disconnected state or end the session and release all session resources.

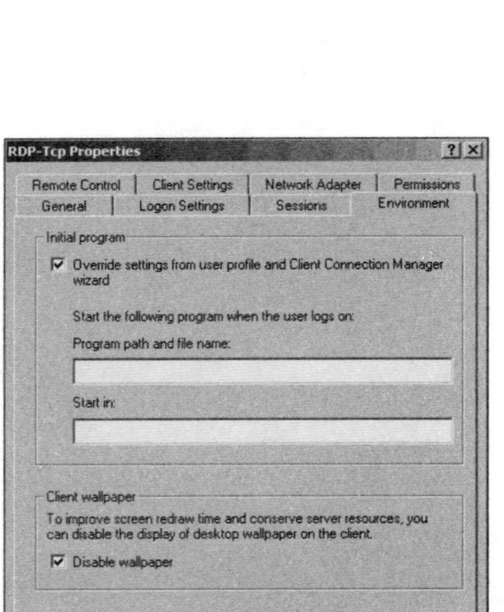

FIGURE 13.8
This property sheet enables automatic configuration of the Terminal Services client's environment after logging on.

The Allow Reconnection Override setting does not apply to Windows 2000 clients—only to Citrix ICA-based clients; with respect to Windows 2000 clients, reconnection is allowed from any client. Therefore, this option will not be discussed here.

The Environment property sheet enables you to configure the initial program to run when a client is connected and whether wallpaper should be displayed (see Figure 13.8). Both of these settings are part of the configuration for the user account. These settings override what the user account settings specify.

The Start the Following Program When the User Logs On setting defines the shell in which the user will operate (this replaces `Explorer.exe`). If, for example, you configured this to run `Notepad.exe`, when a user logged in, Notepad would be displayed. When the user exited Notepad, the session would be terminated. You can also specify where the program should start—that is, what the default data directory is.

The property sheet also enables you to configure whether to display desktop wallpaper. Because wallpaper graphics tend to be large, this eliminates network traffic that is not related to functionality. This setting is often used when connecting over a slow link or where network bandwidth is at a premium.

The Remote Control property sheet configures the capability for administrators and help desk personnel to take control of a Terminal Services client's desktop (see Figure 13.9). When activated, it allows a remote administrator to connect to an active session and transmit mouse and keyboard commands. If Use Remote Control with Default User Settings is selected, the configuration is deferred to the settings in the properties for the user account. If Do Not Allow Remote Control is set, none are available under any circumstances. If Use Remote Control with the Following Settings is selected, you will be able to use a series of check boxes to configure the remote control parameters. These parameters include requiring the user's permission before taking control (a dialog box appears on the user's screen asking for approval) and defining the level of interaction allowed (View the Session or Interact with the Session).

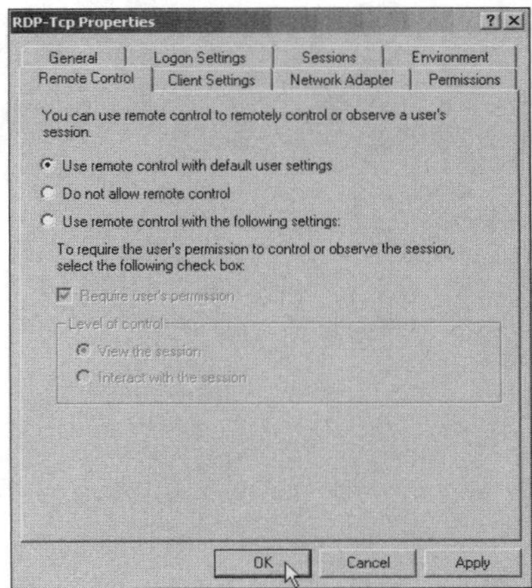

FIGURE 13.9
Configure the ability for administrators to watch or control client sessions.

The Client Settings property sheet allows configuration of persistent settings from session to session and allows you to disable certain Windows features (see Figure 13.10).

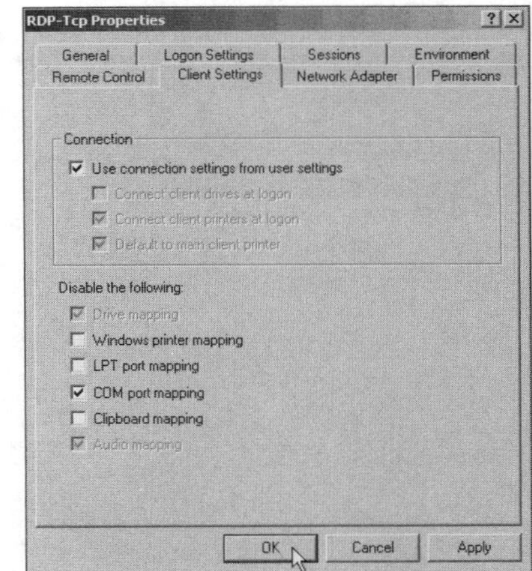

FIGURE 13.10
Configure persistent settings and hardware mappings from the client's computer.

If you deselect Use Connection Settings from User Settings, you will be able to set persistence of user-defined printer mappings (connections to network printers established manually) and default printer settings. The option to connect drives at logon is available to Citrix ICA-based clients only, so it is not discussed here.

You can choose to disable Windows printer mapping, which means users will not be able to map to network printers; this is enabled (not checked) by default. You also can choose to disable the client LPT port mapping, which means users will not be able to print to local printers on their computers; this is enabled (not checked) by default. Next, you can choose to disable the client COM port mapping, which means users will not be able to connect to devices connected to their local COM ports; this is disabled (checked) by default. You can also choose to disable Clipboard mapping, which means users will not be able to copy things to the local Clipboard on their computers.

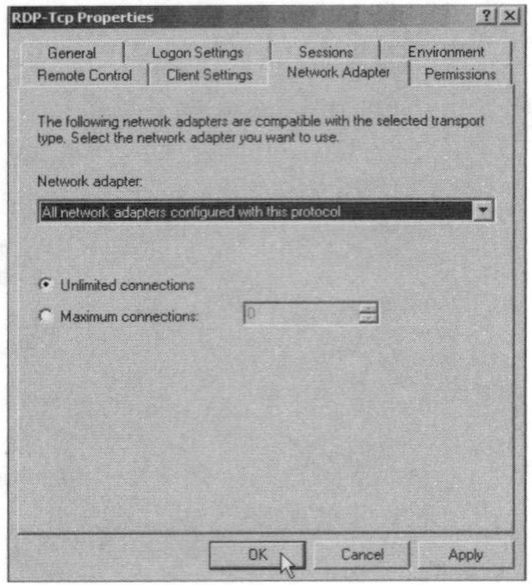

FIGURE 13.11
Configure the network adapter(s) to use for Terminal Services and the number of simultaneous client connections allowed.

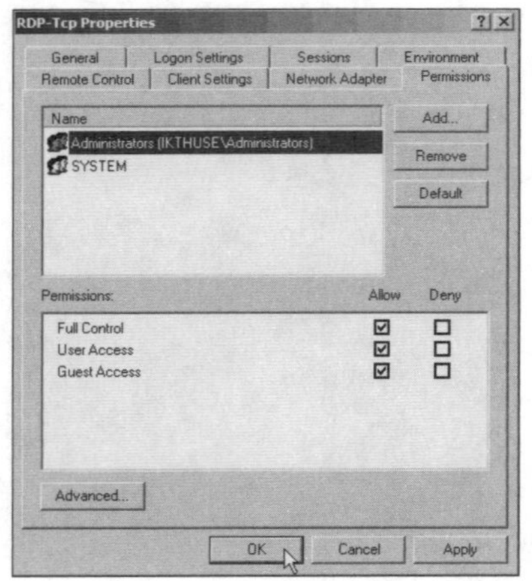

FIGURE 13.12
Configure permissions on the terminal server.

If you disable this setting, a user will not be able to copy content from the Terminal Services window to local applications running on the client operating system. This feature is enabled (not checked) by default. Of course, with true thin clients, these functions can't be made available anyway because there is no local operating system with which to interact.

Two features are disabled (checked) by default and can't be changed except on Citrix ICA-based clients. Those are drive mapping and audio mapping. As such, they are not discussed here.

The Network Adapter property sheet enables you to configure the network adapters on the server that are available for Terminal Services communication (see Figure 13.11). In addition, you can also configure the maximum number of simultaneous connections to allow. Throttling back the number of connections can be used to ensure that those clients who do connect will get satisfactory service from a terminal server that is underpowered for the total number of users trying to connect.

The Permissions property sheet enables you to configure which users or groups of users are allowed access to the terminal server and what they are allowed to do (see Figure 13.12).

Three levels of permissions are available:

- Full Control
- User Access
- Guest Access

Table 13.3 provides a breakdown of the rights given to each permission level.

TABLE 13.3

RIGHTS BY CONNECTION PERMISSION LEVEL

Right	*Full Control*	*User*	*Guest*
Query session information	X	X	
Modify connection parameters			X
Reset (end) a session			X
Remote control another session		X	

Right	*Full Control*	*User*	*Guest*
Log on to a session on the server	X	X	X
Log another user off a session	X		
Send a message to another user's session	X	X	
Connect to another session	X	X	
Disconnect a session	X		
Use virtual channels (provide access from server program to client devices)	X		

By default, the local Administrators group and the SYSTEM get full control, the local Users group gets User access, and the Guest group gets guest access. You can configure permissions for any user or group that you have access to from the terminal server.

These settings are actually from the Registry—the interface is just a little more friendly.

In addition to the Connection Properties dialog box, you can also view and configure the server from the Server Settings window. You can double-click any of the settings shown in Figure 13.13 to view the current configuration.

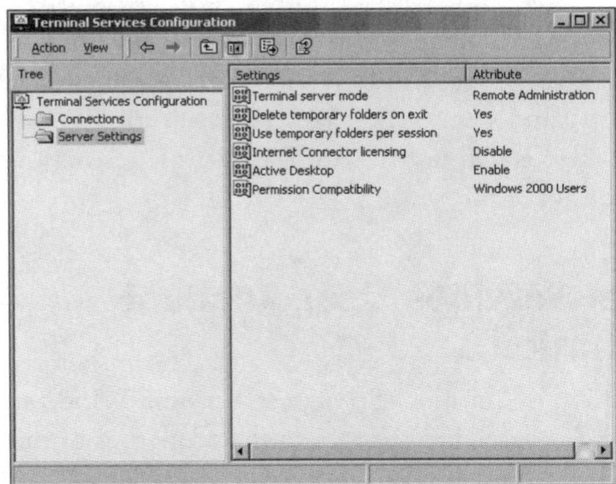

FIGURE 13.13
You view the current configuration of any of the settings by double-clicking them.

The Terminal Server Mode property indicates whether the Terminal Server is configured for Remote Administration or as an Application Server. You can't change this setting from here; the mode must be set from the Add/Remove Programs icon.

The Delete Temporary Folders on Exit property can be set to Yes or No. If it's set to Yes, all folders created to facilitate a user's session are deleted when the session is terminated.

The Use Temporary Folders per Session property can be set to Yes or No. If it's set to Yes, a separate temporary folder is created for every session established. If disk space is at a premium, you can set this to No and make all sessions share the same temporary folder.

The Internet Connector Licensing property can be set to Enabled or Disabled. When Enabled, this property allows for up to 200 nonemployees (domain authenticated users) to connect to the terminal server over the Internet. The purpose of this is to allow users to connect to an application that has not been configured for Internet (HTML, ASP, and so on) use but that needs to be accessed or demonstrated. You must purchase a separate license to legally enable this property. You can't enable this feature while the server is in Remote Administration mode.

The Active Desktop property can be enabled or disabled. By disabling this property, you eliminate the capacity for users to enable the Active Desktop on their client sessions. This reduces the network traffic between the client and server.

The Permission Compatibility property can be set to either Permissions Compatible with Windows 2000 Users or Permissions Compatible with Terminal Server 4.0 Users. If possible, you should leave the permissions as Windows 2000 because this restricts access to the Registry and system files. However, you might find that some legacy applications will not function with those restrictions, so you'll have to reconfigure this setting.

Terminal Services User Account Configuration

The installation of Terminal Services server on a Windows 2000 server makes fundamental changes to the properties of the user accounts. These changes not only extend to the local accounts, but, if the server is a member server in a domain, also extend to the properties of the domain accounts.

The extension of the user properties takes the form of four property sheets that allow configuration of Terminal Services access. The four property sheets are

- Terminal Services Profile
- Remote Control
- Sessions
- Environment

The Terminal Services Profile property sheet enables the configuration of a special profile for use when connecting to a terminal server, a home directory for use when connecting to a terminal server, and a check box that enables a user as a potential Terminal Services client (see Figure 13.14).

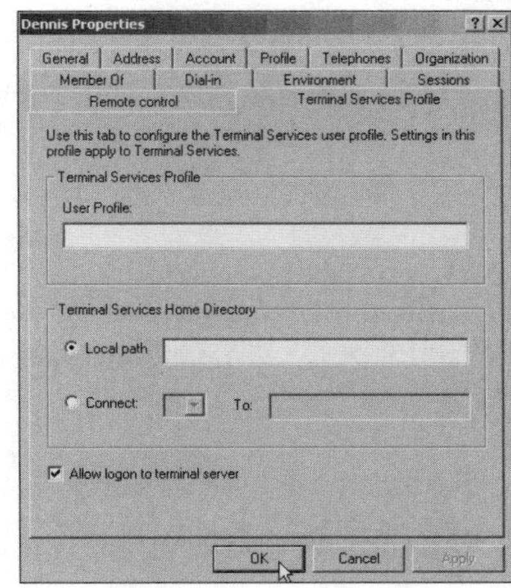

FIGURE 13.14
A separate profile can be configured for a user when she uses a Terminal Services client than when she uses local processing.

Similar to a regular user profile, a Terminal Services profile enables you to configure the desktop environment for a Terminal Services user. By pointing the profile path to a shared location with a mandatory profile in it, you can ensure that Terminal Services clients can do what they need to without being able to make extensive (network-intensive) changes to their desktop settings. Of course, the profiles do not need to be mandatory; a simple roaming profile could be created instead.

To facilitate storing data from session to session, you can create home directories for users. These directories can be the same ones the users utilize when not connecting via Terminal Services (for those users who do both), or it can be separate. If you set a local path, it will connect to a local folder on the terminal server. If you set a connect path, the drive letter of your choice will be connected to a network share. You should use the same profile and home directory for terminal and normal Windows use. This provides a consistent interface (desktop look and feel) with either connection type, lowering the learning curve and increasing the productive usage time.

Finally, on this property sheet you can configure access to Terminal Services in your environment. By selecting Allow Logon to Terminal Server, you enable a user to connect to terminal servers on your network. If this is not selected, that user will not be able to connect to any terminal servers. In conjunction with connection permissions, this setting can be used to enable a user to connect to all servers (in theory) but restrict access to only specific users (in practice).

The Remote Control property sheet enables you to set specific remote control properties for a specific user account (see Figure 13.15). If you have not configured these properties to be overridden in the connection properties for the server, these will take effect when a user connects to the terminal server.

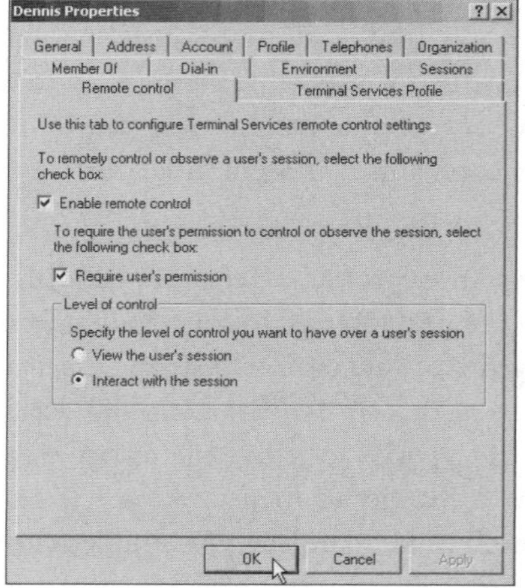

FIGURE 13.15
These remote control properties defined for the user are overridden by the server properties if those are set.

The Sessions property sheet enables you to set session-specific time and disconnection options (see Figure 13.16). If you have not configured these properties to be overridden in the connection properties for the server, these will take effect when a user connects to the terminal server.

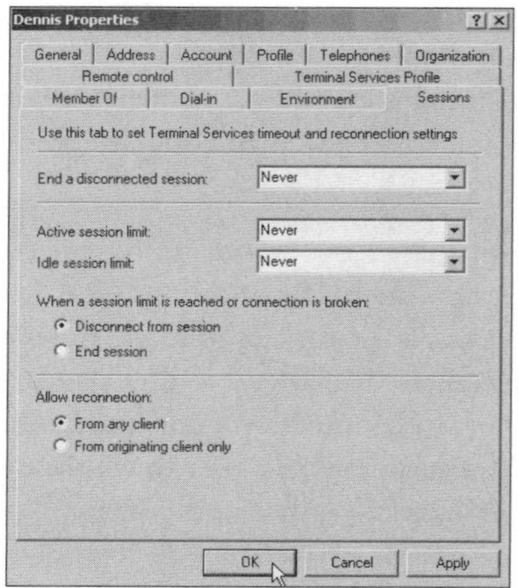

FIGURE 13.16
The user-specific session properties are overridden by the server settings if those are configured.

The Environment property sheet enables you to set the startup environment for the user (see Figure 13.17). If you have not configured these properties to be overridden in the connection properties for the server, these will take effect when a user connects to the terminal server.

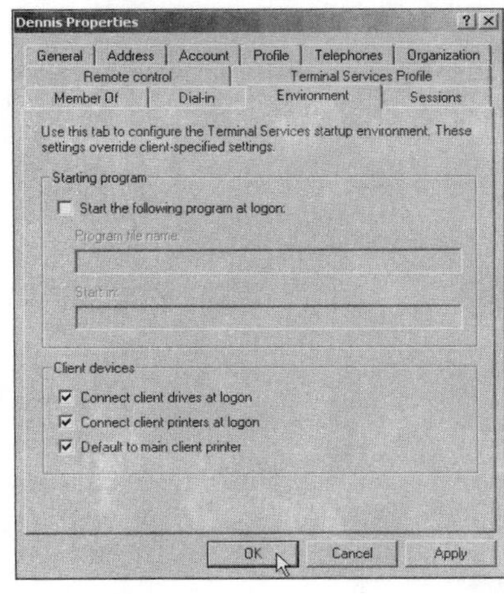

FIGURE 13.17
The user-specific environment settings are overridden by the server settings if those are configured.

Installing Terminal Services Client

To access the Terminal Services server from a user workstation, the Terminal Services client must be installed. The installation files can be distributed either on a floppy disk set (for 16-bit or 32-bit Intel) or via a network share (for any of the platforms).

When you install Terminal Services on a Windows 2000 server, a folder is installed into the system root (`WINNT`) folder that contains the installation files for 16-bit Intel, 32-bit Intel, and 32-bit Alpha clients. In addition, within the selection to install Terminal Services is the option to install the Client Creator Files that installs the program to create setup disks.

To enable installation of the Terminal Services client over the network, share the appropriate client installation files from the path `\WINNT\System32\clients\tsclient`. Also, ensure that at least read access is configured for all users who need to install the client.

Step By Step 13.4 describes how to create a client installation disk set, and Step By Step 13.5 describes how to install a Terminal Services client using that disk set.

STEP BY STEP

13.4 Creating a Client Installation Disk Set

1. From the Start menu, select Programs, Administrative Tools, Terminal Services Client Creator.
2. At the Create Installation Disks(s) dialog box, select the type of client on which you are going to install the Terminal Services client (see Figure 13.18). Select a destination drive, and if the disks are not blank, select the Format Disk(s) check box. Click OK to continue.

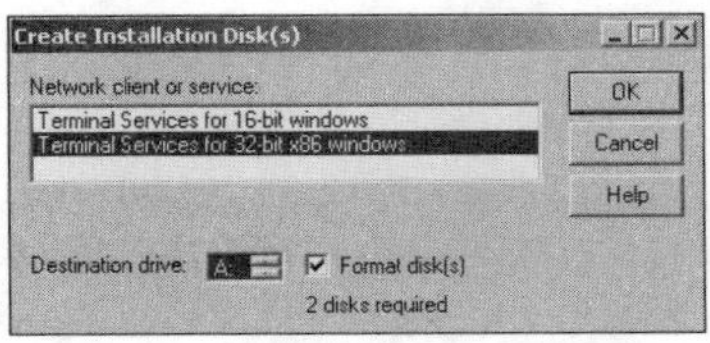

FIGURE 13.18
Installation disk sets can be created for 16-bit or 32-bit clients.

continues

continued

3. When prompted, label a disk Terminal Services for 32-bit x86 Windows DISK1 and insert it into the disk drive. Click OK to continue. If formatting, confirm the format by clicking Yes when prompted.
4. When prompted, label a disk Terminal Services for 32-bit x86 Windows DISK2 and insert it into the disk drive. Click OK to continue. If formatting, confirm the format by clicking Yes when prompted.
5. At the Network Client Administrator dialog box, click OK to confirm the creation of the installation disks.
6. Click Cancel to exit the Create Installation Disk(s) dialog box.

STEP BY STEP

13.5 Installing the Terminal Services Client

1. Either insert DISK1 of the client installation disk set or connect to the appropriate network folder for the client type on the terminal server. Run SETUP.
2. At the Welcome to the Terminal Services Client Installation Program dialog box, click Continue.
3. At the Name and Organization Information dialog box, enter your name and organization. Click OK to continue. When asked to confirm the names, click OK.
4. At the License Agreement dialog box, click I Agree to continue.
5. At the Terminal Services Client Setup dialog box, specify the location in which to install the client and click the button at the left of the dialog box.
6. At the Terminal Services Client Setup dialog box, either click Yes to install the client into the All Users profile or click No to install the client into the profile of the current user (see Figure 13.19). If you click No, you will be prompted for a location for the program group.

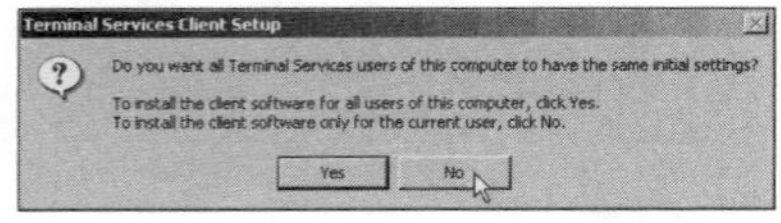

FIGURE 13.19
You can configure each user of the Terminal Services client on a machine to have the same initial settings or to be unique to the user installing the client.

7. At the Terminal Services Client Setup dialog box, click OK.

Now that you have the terminal server client installed, it's time to use it.

Connecting Using the Terminal Services Client

After the server has been configured and the client has been installed on a workstation, connecting to a terminal server is quite simple.

Step By Step 13.6 shows how to connect to a terminal server using the Terminal Services client.

STEP BY STEP

13.6 Connecting Using the Terminal Services Client

1. From the Start menu, select Programs, Terminal Services Client, Terminal Services Client.
2. At the Terminal Services Client dialog box, set the properties of your current connection (see Figure 13.20). Start by selecting the terminal server to which you want to connect. You can either type in the computer name or browse for the server.
3. Select the screen area. It can be set to anything from 640×480 to the resolution your screen is currently set to. Lower resolutions should be used for slow network links.
4. If desired, select the Enable Data Compression check box. This is used to increase performance over a slow network link.
5. If desired, select the Cache Bitmaps to Disk option. This is another network-saving feature that reduces the number of times bitmaps are sent to the client from the server.

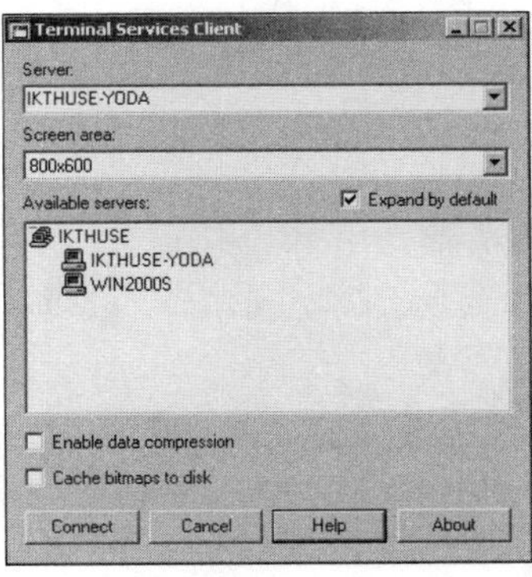

FIGURE 13.20
Set up the properties of the connection, and then attempt a connection to the server of your choice.

continues

continued

6. Click Connect to connect to the server.
7. Log in and work as usual from a Windows 2000 desktop session.

Locally Administering a Terminal Services Client

Although connecting to a terminal server is straightforward, a tool exists to make the connection process even simpler: the Client Connection Manager. Using this tool, you can preconfigure connection settings and then invoke certain connections simply by choosing a menu option.

Step By Step 13.7 shows how to create a connection using the Client Connection Manager.

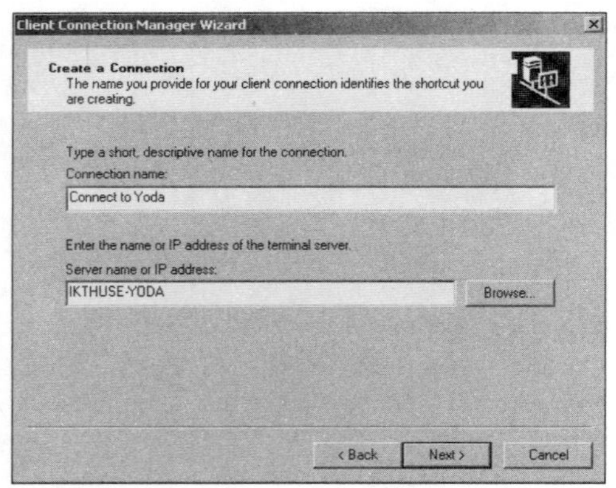

FIGURE 13.21
The connection begins with a server to connect to.

STEP BY STEP

13.7 Creating Connections Using Client Connection Manager

1. From the Start menu, select Programs, Terminal Services Client, Client Connection Manager.
2. At the Client Connection Manager dialog box, select File, New Connection.
3. At the Welcome to the Client Connection Manager Wizard dialog box, click Next to continue.
4. At the Create a Connection screen, type in a meaningful name for the connection, and then type in or browse for a server to connect to (see Figure 13.21). Click Next to continue.

5. At the Automatic Logon screen, you can select Log On Automatically with This Information and then type in the username and password you want to log in as (see Figure 13.22). If you log on as different users to the same server, you can leave this empty or create a connection for each user. If the server property Always Prompt for Password has been enabled, the automatic logon will not take effect; instead, a logon dialog box will be presented at connection time. Click Next to continue.

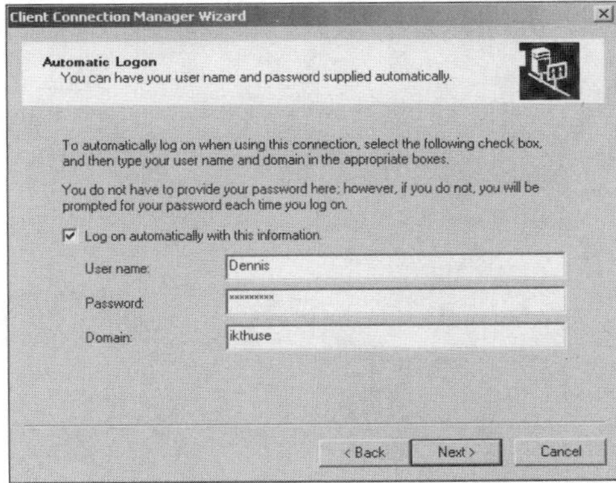

FIGURE 13.22
You can configure the client to automatically log on using a preset account and password.

6. At the Screen Options screen, select the screen area and whether you want the Terminal Services window to be initialized at full screen (see Figure 13.23). Click Next to continue.

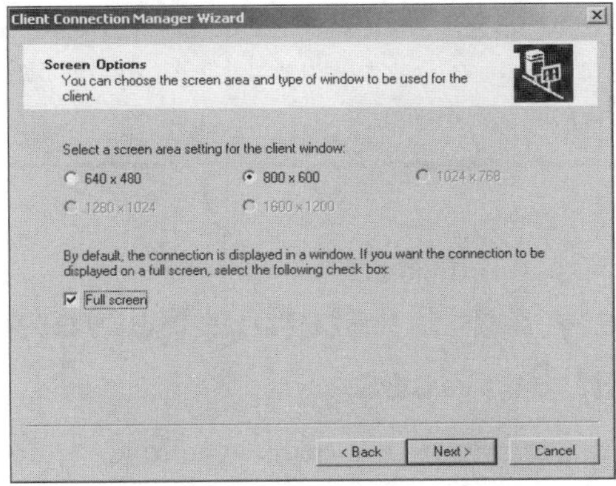

FIGURE 13.23
Configure the properties of the Terminal Services client window.

continues

continued

7. At the Connection Properties screen, select the options to Enable Data Compression and Cache Bitmaps if this connection will be used over a slow network link (see Figure 13.24). Click Next to continue.

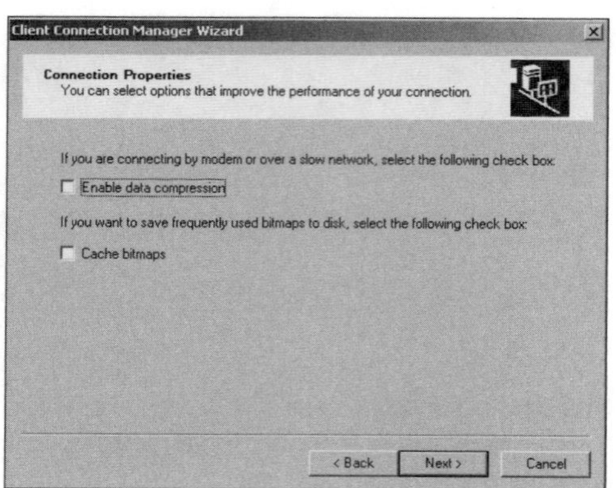

FIGURE 13.24
Configure bandwidth saving options.

8. At the Starting a Program screen, you can select the user shell to start in (see Figure 13.25). This selection is overridden by the user account setting and the server setting. Click Next to continue.

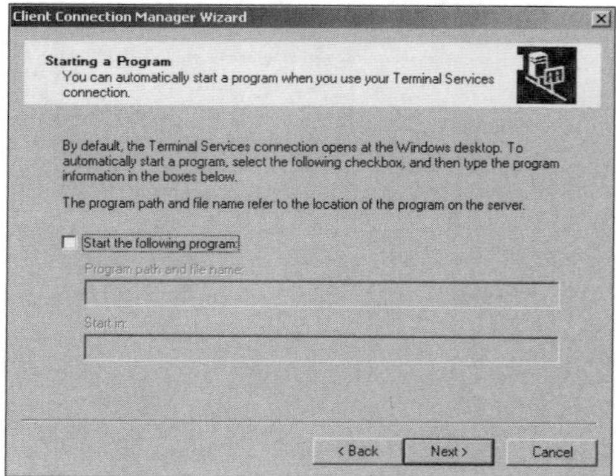

FIGURE 13.25
Configure the shell program to start on successful connection.

9. At the Icon and Program Group screen, select a new icon (if desired) and a program group location for the new connection (see Figure 13.26).

10. At the Completing the Client Connection Manager Wizard screen, click Finish to create the new connection. This connection is now available from the program group you selected in step 9.

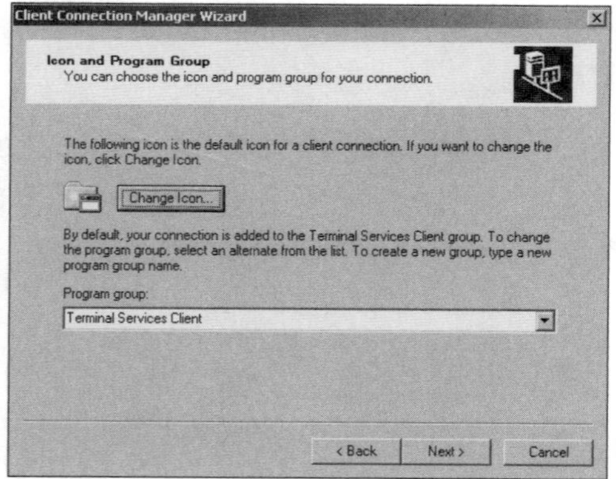

FIGURE 13.26
Configure the access location and icon for the Terminal Services client software on the local machine.

Remotely Administering Servers Using Terminal Services

Connecting to a terminal server enables you to log on to that server as though you were accessing it locally. As a result, if you log in with an administrative account, you will be able to perform any administrative tasks you could do if you had logged on locally.

If you install Terminal Services on your servers only to facilitate administration, you should implement certain performance and security optimizations. On the properties sheet of the RDP-Tcp Connection, you should change the following settings:

- **Sessions\End a Disconnected Session**—Change this to 1 minute to ensure that memory and resources are freed as soon as possible.
- **Sessions\Idle Session Limit**—Change this to 5 minutes to ensure that sessions are ended promptly and you do not attempt to exceed the maximum number of sessions (2) by leaving a session running accidentally.
- **Environment\Disable Wallpaper**—Enable this option to ensure that unnecessary network traffic is not produced.
- **General\Encryption Level**—Change this to High to ensure that maximum encryption is configured for administration.
- **Permissions**—Restrict access to only System and Administrators to reduce the possibility that unauthorized users get administrative access.
- **Network Adapter\Maximum Connections**—Set this to a low number to minimize security breaches.
- **Client Settings**—Disable Windows Printer Mapping, LPT Port Mapping, and Clipboard Mapping to reduce the possibility that confidential information is left on the client after the session is complete.

Configuring Terminal Services for Application Sharing

For a terminal server to host applications for Terminal Services clients, two things must be done. First, the terminal server must be put into Application Server Mode. Second, a License Manager must be configured in your domain or enterprise within 90 days after installation of the application server.

Step By Step 13.8 shows you how to install the Terminal Services License Manager.

STEP BY STEP

13.8 Installing Terminal Services License Manager

1. From the Control Panel, double-click the Add/Remove Programs icon.
2. At the Add/Remove Programs dialog box, click the Add/Remove Windows Components icon.
3. At the Windows Components screen, scroll down and select Terminal Services Licensing. Click Next to continue.
4. At the Terminal Services Licensing Setup screen, specify whether to install this computer as an enterprise manager or as a domain/workgroup manager (see Figure 13.27). Fill in the path to the license database and click Next to continue.
5. At the Completing the Windows Components Wizard screen, click Finish.
6. When prompted, restart your server.

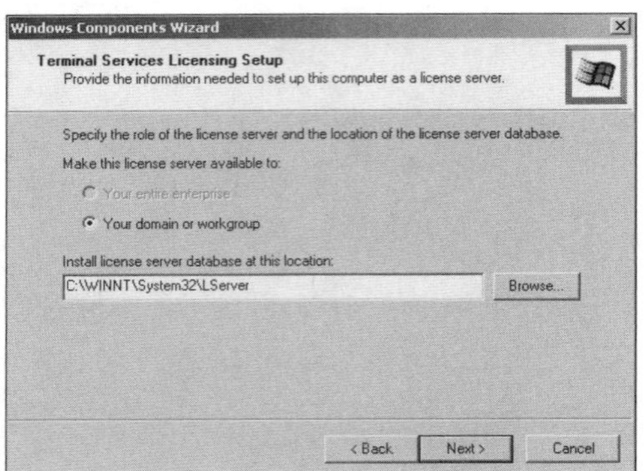

FIGURE 13.27
You can configure the scope of the License Manager and the location of the licenses.

Configuring Applications for Use with Terminal Services

Applications must be configured properly to work for all clients as though they were being executed on their local machines. You first need to ensure that they are installed using the correct method. Then, you might have to execute a script after installation to ensure that the applications have been tuned for Terminal Services execution.

Installing Applications on a Terminal Server

Any application installed on a terminal server could be available to all users on that server. You must ensure that they are available, including shortcuts in the Start menu to invoke them. In addition, you must ensure that when each new user uses the application, he starts with his own settings, which are maintained independently of everyone else's.

The tool for doing this is the `change user` command. When invoked at a command line with the `/install` switch, it puts the system into a "watch" mode that tracks the initial settings for an application and records them. If you install an application in this mode, all pertinent data can be recorded and made available to all users. To complete the process, you then must invoke the `change user /execute` command, which exits you out of the watching mode.

This might seem like a complex process to go through every time you install an application. To make the process easier, it is done automatically for you when you install applications as an administrator through a Client Services session.

Step By Step 13.9 demonstrates how to install an application through a Terminal Services client session.

STEP BY STEP

13.9 Installing Applications Through a Terminal Services Client Session

1. Establish a connection to the terminal server and log on as an administrator.
2. From the Control Panel, double-click the Add/Remove Programs icon.
3. Navigate to the Setup program and install the software.
4. The After Installation screen shown in Figure 13.28 will appear just before the Setup program begins. Leave it in the background until the installation is complete. At that time, click Next.
5. At the Finish Admin Install screen, click Finish to switch back to change user/execute mode.

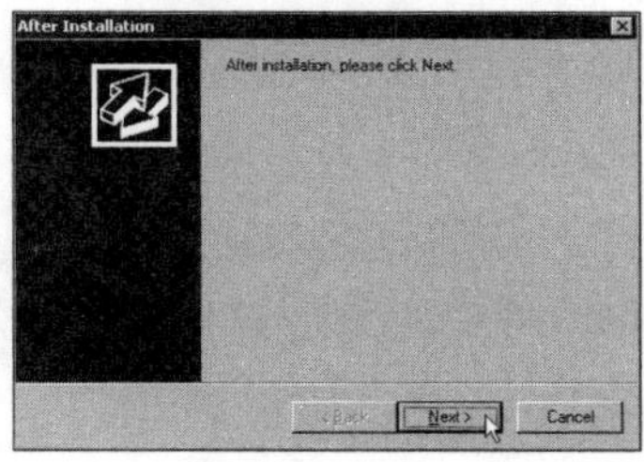

FIGURE 13.28
Do not click Next until the application is completely installed on the server.

Occasionally, an application can't be installed through Add/Remove Programs. For example, when you are browsing with Internet Explorer, you are frequently prompted to install plug-in software. To ensure that the settings are recorded properly for Terminal Services clients, before proceeding with the installation, switch to a command prompt and run `change user /install`. When the installation is complete, run `change user /execute`.

NOTE

Not All Application Scripts Are Provided Although a number of application compatibility scripts are provided by Microsoft, not all applications have scripts. Many popular Microsoft applications and some applications by other vendors are provided. At this point, for example, Office 2000 is notably absent. In fact, it will not install under a terminal server at all unless you install the Terminal Services components available in the Office 2000 Resource Kit. For more specific information on Office 2000 in a Terminal Services environment, go to `http://www.Microsoft.com/office/ork/2000/two/30t3.htm`.

Using Application Compatibility Scripts to Fine-Tune Application Execution

Microsoft has provided some application compatibility scripts for common applications to fine-tune the installations for use with Terminal Services. These scripts modify settings to ensure that applications are set for optimal execution under Terminal Services.

The application compatibility scripts are available in the path `WINNT\Application Compatibility Scripts\Install`.

Step By Step 13.10 outlines the process for running application compatibility scripts.

STEP BY STEP

13.10 Running Application Compatibility Scripts

1. Install the application.
2. In the `WINNT\Application Compatibility Scripts\Install` folder, locate the script for the application you are installing (if one is not available, check the Microsoft Web site or the Web site of the application vendor). Edit the script to modify any paths that need to be customized for your environment.
3. Open a command prompt and run the script.
4. If a logon script for the application exists in the `WINNT\Application Compatibility Scripts\Install` folder, edit it and modify the paths to suit your environment.
5. Edit the file `User.cmd` in the `WINNT\Application Compatibility Scripts\Install` folder. Add a call for each logon script you are using (there is a sample call in the existing `User.cmd` file).
6. Remove the `REM` command in front of the lines corresponding to the application you are installing.
7. Copy `User.cmd` to the `WINNT\System32` folder. (This has to be done only once on your system; subsequent installations should modify this copy of `User.cmd` rather than the one in the `Install` folder.)
8. At the command prompt, run `User.cmd`.

CASE STUDY: IN YOUR TOWN, INC.

THE ESSENCE OF THE CASE

This case requires that the following results be satisfied:

- Allow Isaiah to connect to head office servers to do administration when he is on the road.
- Secure the communications between Isaiah's laptop and servers while administration is going on.

SCENARIO

Isaiah is the network administrator for In Your Town, Inc. (IYT), a national company with 30 regional offices in the United States and Canada. Although IYT has a number of national locations, it has very few employees and a small IT staff (Isaiah and two technical assistants), which works out of the head office in New Orleans. As a result, Isaiah finds himself traveling a great deal to service servers in various locations (there is at least one Windows 2000 Server in each regional office). When he is on the road, Isaiah would like to be able to administer the Windows 2000 servers at the head office from his laptop.

Not only does Isaiah want to be able to do simple administration (such as creating new users and checking printer queues), but he also wants to be able to start and stop services, start performance monitors, observe running tasks, and restart servers that might have problems.

Because security is an issue with IYT, a firewall is configured to protect the head office servers. In addition, any communication between Isaiah's laptop and the head office servers must be done over some type of secured connection.

You have been called in to analyze this situation and make recommendations.

ANALYSIS

Windows 2000 Server has features that will allow Isaiah to satisfy both his accessibility and his security issues. First, he can install the Terminal Services component of Windows 2000 Server and configure it to operate in Administration mode.

continues

Case Study: In Your Town, Inc.

continued

This, coupled with the installation of the Terminal Services client on his laptop, will enable him to connect remotely to a local session on each server. This feature will work as long as he is inside the firewall. However, on the road, the firewall will prevent direct access to his servers from his laptop. That can be overcome by installing the RRAS services on a server inside the firewall (or by configuring a new server to be an RRAS server). Finally, for Isaiah to connect to the RRAS server, he will need to do three things: configure the RRAS server to accept VPN connections (PPTP), configure his laptop to connect to the RRAS server to establish VPN sessions, and open port 1723 in the firewall to allow the VPN traffic to pass through.

Using this configuration, Isaiah will be able to use any Internet connection to establish a VPN connection, through his firewall to his RRAS server at his head office. Having established that connection, he can then use the Terminal Services client to establish a session with any of his servers, and he will be able to perform secure administration of his servers.

The following table summarizes the solution.

OVERVIEW OF THE REQUIREMENTS AND SOLUTIONS IN THIS CASE STUDY

Requirement	Solution Provided By
Access to server sessions	Installing Terminal Services on servers in Administration mode; installing Terminal Services client on roaming laptop
Secure connection to his network	Configuring an RRAS server to accept PPTP connections via a VPN connection and placing this server inside the firewall
Allow secure connection through the firewall	Opening port 1723 in the firewall to allow PPTP traffic to pass

Chapter Summary

KEY TERMS

- Application compatibility script
- Application Server mode
- Remote Administration mode
- Remote control
- Terminal Services
- Terminal Services License Manager
- Terminal Services profile

In this chapter you learned about perhaps the “coolest” feature of Windows 2000. The capability to use Terminal Services to remotely administer a system is one of the truly useful features added to Windows 2000. It eliminates the need for, and potential compatibility issues with, third-party remote control utilities.

You learned how to configure a server to provide Terminal Services, including how to configure permissions, timeouts, and applications. You also learned how to configure clients to use Terminal Services.

APPLY YOUR KNOWLEDGE

Exercises

13.1 Installing, Configuring, and Testing Terminal Services in Administration Mode

This exercise shows how to install Terminal Services on a Windows 2000 server and configure it for Administration mode. In addition, you will also configure a Windows 2000 machine with a Terminal Services client and demonstrate administration via that connection.

To do this lab, you need one Windows 2000 Server and one Windows 2000 client (Server or Professional).

Estimated Time: 45 minutes

1. Install Terminal Services on your Windows 2000 Server. Here's how you do this:
    1. From the Start menu, select Settings, Control Panel.
    2. From the Control Panel, double-click the Add/Remove Programs icon.
    3. From the Add/Remove Programs window, click the Add/Remove Windows Components button.
    4. In the Windows Components dialog box, scroll through the Components list and select the check box labeled Terminal Services. Click Next to continue.
    5. At the Terminal Services Setup dialog box, make sure that Remote Administration Mode is selected, and then click Next. If, during installation, you are asked to insert the Windows 2000 CD-ROM, please do so.
    6. At the Completing the Windows Components Wizard dialog box, click Finish to exit.
    7. When prompted, click Yes to restart your computer.
2. Add a new user and make that user part of the local Administrators group to test Terminal Services. Follow these steps:
    1. From the Start menu, select Programs, Administrative Tools, Computer Management.
    2. In the Computer Management dialog box, expand the section labeled Local Users and Groups, right-click Users, and select New User from the menu that appears.
    3. In the New User dialog box, type **`TerminalU`** in the User Name field, type **`password`** in both password fields, clear the check box labeled User Must Change Password at Next Logon, and select the check box labeled Password Never Expires. Click Create to continue.
    4. Click Close to exit the New User dialog box.
    5. Click the Users entry on the left side of the Computer Management console (under Local Users and Groups).
    6. On the right side of the console, double-click the entry for the user `TerminalU`.
    7. In the TerminalU Properties dialog box, click the Member Of tab.
    8. On the Member Of tab, click the Add button, double-click the Administrators group, and click the OK button.

APPLY YOUR KNOWLEDGE

9. At the TerminalU Properties dialog box, click OK.
10. Close the Computer Management console.

3. Share the Terminal Server client files on the terminal server machine. Follow these steps:
    1. Navigate to the `WINNT\System32\Clients\tsclient` folder on your server.
    2. Right-click the `win32` folder and share it with default settings. Click OK to continue.
4. Configure the terminal server client (on the Windows 2000 client machine) by doing the following:
    1. From the Start menu, select Run.
    2. In the Run dialog box, type **`\\`*`servername`*`\win32\disks\disk1\setup`** (where *`servername`* is the name of your terminal server) and press Enter.
    3. In the Terminal Services Client Setup dialog box, click Continue.
    4. In the Name and Organization Information dialog box, type your name and organization (make one up if you have to) and click OK.
    5. In the Confirm Name and Organization Information dialog box, click OK.
    6. In the License Agreement dialog box, click I Agree.
    7. At the second Terminal Services Client Setup dialog box, click the button on the left side to begin installation (if you want, you can choose an alternative installation location).
    8. At the third Terminal Services Client Setup dialog box, click Yes.
    9. At the final Terminal Services Client Setup dialog box, click OK to complete the setup.
5. Use the Client Connection Manager to create a connection configuration (do this on the Terminal Services client machine) by doing the following:
    1. From the Start menu, select Programs, Terminal Services Client, Client Connection Manager.
    2. At the Client Connection Manager console, select File, New Connection.
    3. At the Welcome to the Client Connection Manager Wizard, click Next.
    4. At the Create a Connection dialog box, type **`Administrative Connection`** in the Connection name field and type the name of your server in the Server Name or IP Address field. Click Next to continue.
    5. At the Automatic Logon dialog box, select the check box labeled Log On Automatically with This Information. In the User Name field, type **`TerminalU`**; in the Password field, type **`password`**; and in the Domain field, type the name of the Terminal Services server (because you created the `TerminalU` user local to that machine). Click Next to continue.
    6. At the Screen Options dialog box, select a screen area setting and click Next.
    7. At the Connection Properties dialog box, click Next.
    8. At the Starting a Program dialog box, click Next.
    9. At the Icon and Program Group dialog box, click Next.

APPLY YOUR KNOWLEDGE

10. At the Completing the Client Connection Manager Wizard, click Finish.

11. Close the Client Connection Manager console.

6. Test the Terminal Services client by doing the following:

   1. From the Start menu, select Programs, Terminal Services client, Administrative Connection.

   2. When asked to log in as `TerminalU`, type **`password`** in the Password field and click OK.

   3. Scroll through the client window so you can see the taskbar of the Terminal Services window. Right-click that taskbar and select Task Manager from the menu that appears (be sure that you are right-clicking the Terminal Services taskbar and not the one for your client machine).

   4. In the Windows Task Manager dialog box, click the Processes tab and, at the bottom of that page, select the check box labeled Show Processes from All Users.

   5. On the Terminal Services server machine, start the Paint program from the Start menu.

   6. On the Terminal Services client machine, scroll through the Task Manager window until you see an entry for the process named `mspaint.exe`. Select that process and click the End Process button.

   7. In the Task Manager Warning dialog box, click Yes to end the process. Note that the Paint window disappears from the Terminal Services server machine.

   8. Enable a second concurrent session to the server from this client by performing steps 6.1 and 6.2 again. You can now switch back and forth between the two sessions (this would be possible to do between administrative sessions for two different machines).

   9. Disconnect each session by selecting Start, Shut Down, Log Off TerminalU. This must be done from within each session you have open with the terminal server.

Review Questions

1. What are the two modes in which Terminal Services can run on a Windows 2000 server? What are the licensing requirements of each?

2. Which Windows operating systems can support the Terminal Services client, and what is the minimum hardware required?

Exam Questions

1. Abraham is the Terminal Services administrator for a small manufacturing company. He has a number of thin network clients, and on March 23, 2000, he configured a terminal server in Application mode to host the company's applications. Initially, everything ran very smoothly. However, on June 21, 2000, all the clients received messages that there were not enough client licenses, and their applications failed to run. What should Abraham have done to prevent this problem?

   A. He should have configured his terminal server in Administration mode because there are no licensing requirements.

APPLY YOUR KNOWLEDGE

B. He should have purchased more Windows 2000 client licenses for his server running Terminal Services.

C. He should have installed Terminal Services License Manager.

D. He should have installed Terminal Services License Manager and purchased licenses for his Terminal Services clients.

2. A user named Sarah is using Windows 2000 Professional to run a Terminal Services client session. She wants to shut down her computer for lunch (as is the company policy) but does not want to end her Terminal Services session. With reference to Figure 13.29, which Shut Down option can she choose to accomplish her goal?

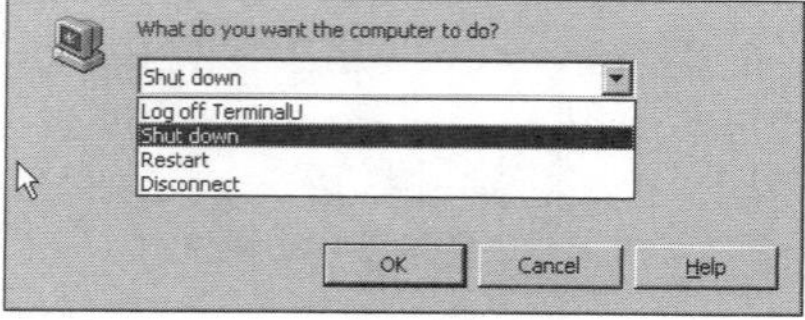

FIGURE 13.29
One of these options leaves the session running.

A. Log off

B. Shut Down

C. Restart

D. Disconnect

3. You're trying to capture an error message to give to a support professional. The error is being generated on the server. You get the error to occur on the server and use Ctrl+PrintScreen to capture the error to the Clipboard. However, you can't paste the error in the e-mail you're creating on your desk to the support professional. What's the most likely cause?

A. The Clipboard feature does not work on Terminal Server.

B. You must manually copy the Clipboard from the server to the client.

C. Transfers of the Clipboard from the server to the client are not supported.

D. You've not enabled Clipboard mapping.

4. You have a user in another building who is using Terminal Services and is having a problem you can't reproduce. You want to see the error message to figure out the next steps for diagnosis. What are the best steps to perform?

A. Ask the user to disconnect from his session. Connect to his session using an administrative account and reproduce the problem.

B. Use Terminal Services Manager to remote control the session.

C. Ask the user to disconnect from his session. Connect to his session using his username and password. Try to reproduce the problem.

D. Ask the user to call you over when the error occurs again.

5. You are a network administrator for a small organization that uses Terminal Services. While running Terminal Services Manager you notice that several sessions are in a disconnected state. What are the possible causes?

A. The user disconnected from the session manually using the Start menu.

APPLY YOUR KNOWLEDGE

B. The user closed the Terminal Services client without signing off.

C. The user signed off, and the session has not reset yet.

D. The user hasn't been active in the session with the server recently.

6. A user has asked you to show her how to create a new account in a custom application. You take remote control of her session on the terminal server but are unable to manipulate the session. What's the most likely cause?

   A. You have remote control set to view, not interact with, the session.

   B. Terminal server doesn't support interacting with a user's session via remote control. It's view only.

   C. Your keyboard isn't identical to the user's keyboard.

   D. You're running a different display resolution than the user.

7. A user is complaining that when in a Terminal Services session the desktop seems to strobe or flash. What can be done to help the user with this problem? (Choose all that apply.)

   A. Increase the refresh frequency of the monitor.

   B. Turn off the desktop wallpaper.

   C. Turn off Active Desktop.

   D. Increase the RDP-TCP packet rate.

8. Which protocol is used by Terminal Services?

   A. ICA

   B. RDP-TCP

   C. SNA

   D. DLC

9. A user reports that he can't print to his local printer from the terminal server. What is the most likely cause of this?

   A. His printer is not shared on the network.

   B. The printer was turned off when the user established the connection to the terminal server.

   C. The router doesn't allow printer traffic between the terminal server and the client.

   D. The users' local printers are not mapped to the server.

10. Memory on your terminal server is getting tight. You're looking for ways to maintain performance while the additional memory you have ordered comes in. Which is the best setting to change to maintain performance while waiting on the memory?

    A. Turn the Encryption level down to Medium or Low.

    B. Set End a Disconnected Session to 15 minutes.

    C. Set the Idle Session Limit to 15 minutes.

    D. Set session and idle limits to disconnect from the session.

APPLY YOUR KNOWLEDGE

11. The CIO of your organization wants to ensure that terminal server sessions are encrypted. What should you tell her?

    A. All communications between the client and server are always encrypted.

    B. All communications from the client to the server are encrypted.

    C. No communications are encrypted by default, but you can set encryption.

    D. No communications are encrypted by default, and encryption must be provided by an external protocol, such as IPSec.

12. You're logged into the Terminal Server console and try to take remote control of a user's session to walk her through a procedure but receive an error. Why can't you take control of her session?

    A. You can't take remote control of a session from the console.

    B. You're not authorized to see the user's session.

    C. The user didn't agree to let you see the session.

    D. You didn't configure Terminal Services to allow remote control.

13. You're noticing bandwidth problems between the client and the server. What can you do to improve performance on the server? (Choose all that apply.)

    A. Turn off wallpaper.

    B. Turn off Active Desktop.

    C. Enable data compression.

    D. End disconnected settings after 15 minutes.

14. You're noticing bandwidth problems between the client and the server. What can you do to improve performance on the client? (Choose all that apply.)

    A. Turn off wallpaper.

    B. Cache bitmaps to disk.

    C. Enable data compression.

    D. Disconnect idle sessions after 5 minutes.

15. You notice that many users have multiple sessions on the terminal server. What is the most likely cause of this?

    A. The user is being disconnecting from or is manually disconnecting from the server and is restarting a new terminal server session.

    B. They spawned a new session from the user interface.

    C. The server keeps sessions alive after the user logs off.

    D. The server is set to prevent users from reconnecting to their sessions.

Answers to Review Questions

1. Terminal Services runs in two server modes: Administration and Application. In Administration mode, a maximum of two connections can be established for the purposes of administering a server. These connections do not require client licenses. In Application mode, 90 days grace is given from the point when Terminal Services is placed into that mode. After that, licenses must be purchased from Microsoft and managed by the Terminal Services License Manager.

APPLY YOUR KNOWLEDGE

These licenses are separate from client access licenses for regular connections to a server. For more information, see the section "Configuring Terminal Services for Application Sharing."

2. The following Windows operating systems can support Terminal Services clients: Windows 3.11, Windows 95, Windows 98, Windows NT 4.0, and Windows 2000. The minimum hardware is supported under Windows 3.11. It consists of a 386 processor, 16MB of RAM, and a VGA video card. For more information, see the section "Terminal Services Hardware and Software."

Answers to Exam Questions

1. **D.** Terminal Services clients require separate licenses from regular network clients to a Windows 2000 server. There is a grace period of 90 days provided for the use of applications hosted on a Terminal Services server. If licenses have not been purchased by the end of 90 days, the clients will no longer be capable of connecting. For more information, see the section "Configuring Terminal Services for Application Sharing."

2. **D.** A Terminal Services client session will continue to be active even if the user shuts down her machine if the Disconnect option is used. If this option is used then the session is suspended, the session can be resumed upon reconnection. Of course, this puts extra load on the Terminal Services server, so this feature should be used with caution. For more information, see the section "Installing, Configuring, and Troubleshooting Terminal Services."

3. **D.** Clipboard mapping is a feature of Terminal Services, but the feature must be enabled. When enabled it allows you to paste things into local documents after you've copied them to the Clipboard on the server. For more information, see the section "Terminal Services Server Configuration."

4. **B.** Although someone can go to visit the user, it's not the best solution. Remote control allows you to take control of the user's session or view the user's session from your desk. You can't connect to a user's session with the administrative account. In general, you should never ask users for their passwords so that you can perform actions as them. For more information, see the section "Terminal Services Server Configuration."

5. **A, B.** You can become disconnected from a session in three ways. First, you can select Disconnect from the Logoff/Shutdown menu. Second, you can close the Terminal Services Client. Third, you can loose connectivity with the server. If the session hasn't reset yet, it would be shown as terminated. If the user hasn't been active in the session recently, the session would show as idle. For more information, see the section "Terminal Services Server Configuration."

6. **A.** In the settings you can control whether you can only view or interact with a Terminal Services session. The keyboard type and display resolution have no bearing on whether you can interact with a session you're remote controlling. For more information, see the section "Terminal Services Server Configuration."

APPLY YOUR KNOWLEDGE

7. **B, C.** Strobing or flickering can be caused by items on the desktop that are in motion. This can either be wallpaper that has motion in it or items on an active desktop. For more information, see the section "Terminal Services Server Configuration."

8. **B.** Terminal Services uses the RDP-TCP protocol. ICA is the Citrix-proprietary communications protocol used by Citrix WinFrame product. SNA is an IBM mainframe and midrange protocol. DLC is a printer communication protocol. For more information, see the section "Terminal Services Server Configuration."

9. **D.** Users need not share their local printers to use them on a terminal server connection. Terminal services can map local printers to the Terminal Services session. Whether the printer was on or off during the connection is not material. The router can't be the problem because the printer traffic is sent across the same data stream as the rest of the client update traffic. For more information, see the section "Terminal Services Server Configuration."

10. **B.** The best way to effectively use the memory you have is to clear disconnected sessions quickly. This is accomplished by ending disconnected sessions after 15 minutes. Changing the encryption level has almost no impact on memory performance. Changing the idle session limit would help, but only if the disconnected sessions were being ended. Because the answer doesn't specify, you can't assume that they are. Likewise, setting the active session limit wouldn't necessarily mean less memory usage. For more information, see the section "Terminal Services Server Configuration."

11. **B.** You can be sure that the user input in always encrypted but encryption from the server to the client is encrypted only when the encryption setting is Medium or High. For more information, see the section "Terminal Services Server Configuration."

12. **A.** You can take control of sessions only from Terminal Services client connections. The console is not allowed to take control of a session. For more information, see the section "Terminal Services Server Configuration."

13. **A, B.** You can reduce traffic by disabling graphics that must be transmitted repeatedly. Data compression is controlled at the client end. Because no communications is taking place on disconnected settings, ending them has no effect. For more information, see the section "Terminal Services Server Configuration"

14. **B, C.** Turning off wallpaper is a good idea, but this is done at the server. Both caching bitmaps and enabling data compression reduce network utilization. Changing the idle disconnect time is set on the server and doesn't materially change network bandwidth. For more information, see the section "The Terminal Services Client."

15. **A.** The most common cause of multiple user sessions on a server is that they are being disconnected and are creating a new session the next time they log in. It is impossible to spawn a new session from the user interface. Terminal Services does not keep sessions alive after a user has logged off. They are cleaned up as soon as possible. You can't prevent users from connecting to their own sessions. For more information, see the section "Terminal Services Server Configuration."

PART 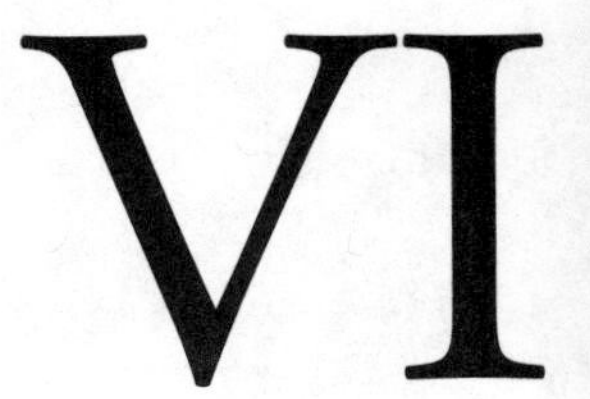

FINAL REVIEW

Now that you have finished reading this book and working through the exercises, you're ready for the exam. This final chapter is intended to be the "final cram in the parking lot."

Organized by chapter, this section is not only a summary, but also a concentrated review of the most important points. If you know and are comfortable with the content and concepts presented here, the odds are good that you are truly prepared for the certification exam.

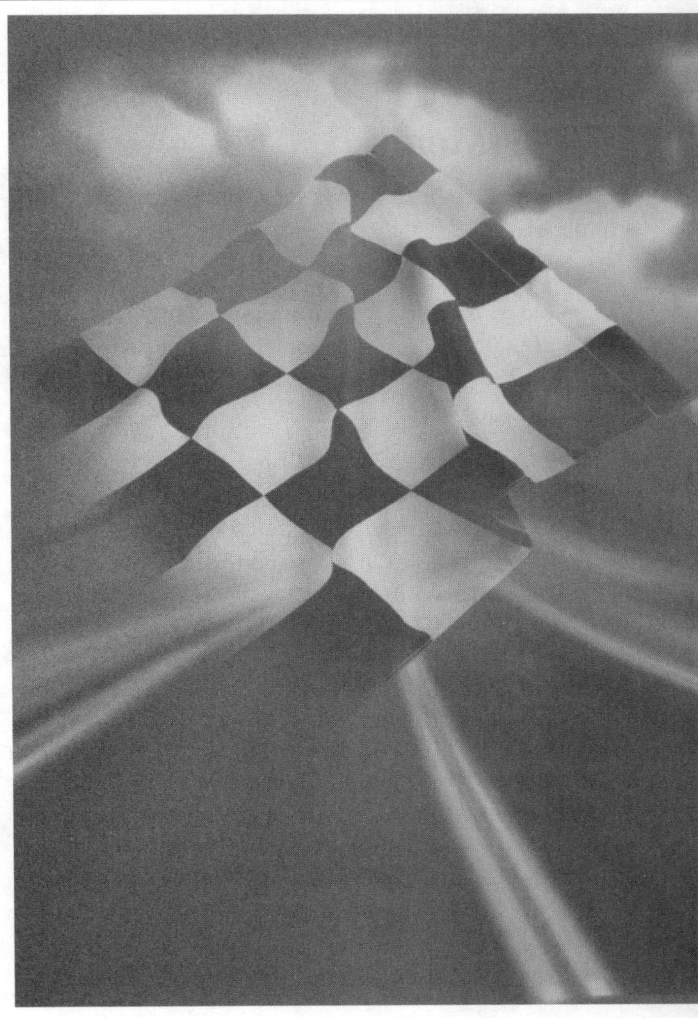

Fast Facts

Managing a Microsoft Windows 2000 Network Environment (70-218)

DATA STORAGE AND FILE SYSTEMS

The first section of the book dealt with disk storage and the file systems that are installed on that disk storage.

Managing Disk Storage

There are two types of disk partitioning schemes that you need to understand:

- **Basic**—The classic partitioning scheme used by most operating systems on the PC. Required for compatibility with other operating systems.
- **Dynamic**—An enhanced partitioning scheme that names partitions volumes, instead of partitions as was used with basic disks. Dynamic disks require a 1MB section at the end of the disk for additional partitioning information. Dynamic disks are required to take advantage of enhanced partition types, including striped volumes.

File Systems

There are three basic file systems you have to understand:

- **FAT**—The File Allocation Table format is the oldest partition format supported by Windows 2000 and is the partition type supported by most other operating systems. FAT is limited to a 2GB partition size.
- **FAT32**—FAT32 is a 32-bit extension to the FAT partition format. It is supported by Windows 95 OSR2, Windows 98, Windows Me, and Windows 2000. It is also compatible with many non-Microsoft OSes.
- **NTFS**—The preferred partition format for Windows 2000 servers, NTFS is required for encryption, compression, file and directory security, and auditing. NTFS is not compatible with other non-NT-based operating systems. When dual-booting NT and Windows 2000, NT must be at Service Pack 4 or higher to support NTFS v.5 used by Windows 2000. Windows NT uses NTFS v.4 out of the box.

Managing File Systems

NTFS permissions are applied at a file or folder level. These permissions apply to both local users on the PC and users accessing through shared directories across the network.

NTFS permissions can be applied only on NTFS partitions. You can convert other partitions to NTFS and keep data intact by using the `CONVERT` command.

Basic folder-level NTFS permissions are as follows:

- Full Control
- Modify
- Read & Execute
- List Folder Contents
- Read
- Write

Advanced permissions allow you to be more granular in your permission assignments.

Basic file-level permissions do not include List Folder Contents.

When accessing files from across the network, you will require the permission at both the Share level and the NTFS File level. For example, to read a file, you would have to be granted the Read permission at both levels.

Encrypting File Systems

The two important concepts in using encryption keys in conjunction with the Encrypting File System are

- **Removing the EFS keys**—This is done to prevent unauthorized users from accessing the data while allowing authorized users the capability to access the data if the user is unavailable.
- **Restoring EFS keys**—You must do this if you need to access the data on the system without access to the end user's account information.

The EFS is ideal for laptop users. By encrypting the data on the laptop and then removing the public and private keys, the data is secured should the computer be vandalized or stolen. To access the data, the private key is required. By removing the EFS keys from the laptop, you make it impossible for an intruder to gain access to the data simply by logging on to the laptop. The keys for the data should be stored elsewhere, such as on floppy disks.

Distributed File System

Distributed File System (Dfs) hides the physical layout of the network from users.

Windows 95 requires Dfs client software. Windows NT 4.0, Windows 2000, and Windows 98 already have a client built into the OS.

Dfs roots look like shared directories, and Dfs links point to existing shared directories on other servers.

Standalone Dfs is implemented outside of Active Directory.

Domain or Fault Tolerant Dfs can be implemented only on servers that are part of an Active Directory domain. It also provides replication of data and load-balancing of link information between specified replica servers.

Sharing Resources

Establishing files and folders on the disk is just the first step in creating a network. The next thing you must do is share those resources so they can be used across the network. This section addresses how to share and locate network resources.

Publishing Resources in Active Directory

When publishing resources in Active Directory, consider the following:

- Remember that a Distributed File System (Dfs) can be a standalone system or a fault-tolerant system. This is not published in Active Directory. Publishing takes an existing share and makes it available in Active Directory.
- Printers are published by default for Windows 2000 when they are shared. Whether they remain published depends on the List in Directory check box.
- Non–Windows 2000 printers can be published by using Active Directory Users and Computers to create the printer object.
- A non–Windows 2000 printer can also be published if you add the printer as a local printer to a Windows 2000 server and configure the port as the network address of the current share. Sharing the Windows 2000 printer now lists the printer in Active Directory by default.
- Shares are added to Active Directory using the Active Directory Users and Computers tool.

Locating Objects in Active Directory

Consider the following when locating objects in Active Directory:

- **You should know where both the administrator and users can search**—Administrators can search in the Active Directory Users and Computers console; users can search for objects in Start Search and in My Network Places.
- **You should know what the tabs do for the main objects: users, computers, printers, and groups**—Although you aren't really expected to memorize every option, you should know where to go to find an option.
- **After you have found an object or a group of objects, you should then be able to manipulate those objects as a group by selecting them from the list and then choosing an option from the context menu.**

Sharing Resources

Any user who is given the right to Create Permanent Shared Objects, either explicitly or through the groups of which she is a member, can also share directories.

Users can be granted or denied access to a share through three permission levels:

- Full Control
- Change
- Read

If a user is denied access at a specific level, she is denied that level of permission, regardless of other granted permissions. The denial of access overrides all other permissions.

Hidden shares can be created by appending a dollar sign ($) to the end of the share name. The dollar sign is treated as part of the name but prevents the viewing of the share through network browsing.

Configuring Accounts

Each user account is identified by a unique security identifier (SID).

An account can be renamed without losing permissions associated with it.

Each of the users on a system should have his own account.

Administrator and Guest are the two default system accounts; they can't be deleted but can be renamed.

Configuring an Account Policy

Account policies can be managed on a single server or through Active Directory.

Account policies enable you to set the following options:

- Password history
- Minimum age
- Maximum age
- Minimum length
- Complexity
- Reverse encryption storage
- Account lockout

Internet Information Services

Internet Information Services allows you to share your resources not only with the local network, but with the Internet as well. This section addresses the important considerations for sharing your resources via Internet technologies.

Internet Services Available

One of the key changes that was made in the move from Windows NT to Windows 2000 is that Microsoft renamed Internet Information Server to Internet Information Services to reflect the broader range of service offerings. IIS offers the following server types:

- Web (HTTP)
- File Transfer Protocol (FTP)
- News (NNTP)
- Mail (SMTP)

Only the first two are addressed on the exam.

Virtual Servers

Windows 2000 allows multiple sites to share the same server. Because of this, you need to be able to identify for which server a request is destined. This means that a unique set of criteria must exist for each site.

For both FTP and Web sites, this can be accomplished using an IP address and TCP port. The IP address is one of the IP addresses assigned to the server. The TCP port is typically set to 80 for Web traffic and 21 for FTP servers, but it can be set to other values based on your need.

Web sites can also distinguish traffic by means of an HTTP header. This is a piece of information transmitted from the Web browser indicating the site it is trying to reach. One site can be set as the default by having no host header, but all other Web sites must have a specific host header.

If you try to create a site that has the identical settings to another site so that the server would be incapable of determining for which site the traffic is destined, the site will not be started.

Virtual Directories

Typically, when a site is created a home directory is selected and all the content for the site is contained underneath the same directory tree. IIS enables you to create sites that are based off of noncontiguous file resources through the creation of virtual directories.

A *virtual directory* is a pointer stored in the site's definition that enables another area of the disk resources to appear as a directory underneath the site.

Web Security

The three components of security for the Web are TCP/IP restrictions, authentication mechanisms, and permissions.

TCP/IP Restrictions

One of the ways to restrict access to a site is to allow access to only a specific set of users based on their IP addresses or domain names. Alternatively, you can deny access to a set of users based on the same criteria. This is useful when you need to prevent a malicious set of users from attempting to compromise your Web site.

Authentication Mechanisms

Although most Web sites are available to the general public, you might want to restrict access to a group of people who can identify themselves. The following are the four authentication mechanisms in use on the Web:

- **Anonymous Access**—This is the access type that most users are familiar with. There is no access control on the content.
- **Basic Authentication**—This simple, clear-text authentication mechanism works for all platforms but requires that the user's username and password be sent across the wire without encryption and thus is not desirable.
- **Digest Authentication (NT Challenge/Response)**—Uses a simple encryption mechanism to convey the username and password. It's not compatible with non-Microsoft servers or browsers and requires at least Internet Explorer version 5.
- **Integrated Windows Authentication**—Useable only in an intranet environment, this authentication mechanism takes advantage of the Windows 2000 Kerberos infrastructure.

Permissions

In addition to the file-level permissions that can be placed on the files that make up a site, permissions can also be set on the files at the site level to allow or prevent various types of access. The most common permission that must be enabled is the Execute permission.

This permission is required for the Web server to be capable of executing code in the file.

There are two levels of Execute permission: Scripts and Scripts and Executables. With Script access, only scripts, such as Active Server Pages files, can be executed. With Scripts and Executables permission, any file can be executed on the Web server.

Execute permission is particularly dangerous in conjunction with the Write permission. This could potentially allow users to upload and then run code on your Web server—a definite security breach.

Client Configuration

Client configuration in Internet Explorer is easy with only one basic setting that must be considered—the proxy server. *Proxy servers* communicate to the Internet on behalf of their clients.

Proxy settings can be automatically detected or specified manually. If specified manually, the default option uses one port on the proxy server for all activity. Alternatively, you can specify specific ports on the proxy server (or multiple proxy servers) for access to the Internet.

Security Zones

Internet Explorer uses the concept of a security zone to control different activities that are allowed or disallowed. The four basic zones are Internet, Intranet, Trusted, and Restricted. Each zone can have its own security settings. Typically, restricted sites are not allowed to do much of anything, whereas trusted sites are allowed to do almost everything.

TCP/IP Fundamentals

TCP/IP requires a unique 32-bit address for each system on a network.

The subnet mask is used to determine whether a communication partner is local or remote.

A gateway or router is used to forward remote data. TCP/IP is a routable protocol.

TCP/IP can be configured manually or dynamically through Dynamic Host Configuration Protocol (DHCP).

Table 1 lists useful TCP/IP utilities and their uses.

TABLE 1

TCP/IP Troubleshooting Utilities

Utility	*Function*
`IPCONFIG` (IP Configuration)	Used to see the current TCP/IP configuration. It can also be used to release and renew DHCP-based addresses.
`PING` (Packet Inter-Network Grouper)	Used to test basic TCP/IP connectivity with other hosts. It can also display the first nine routers that are passed through.
`NSLOOKUP` (Name Server Lookup)	Used to troubleshoot DNS resolution problems. It can also display proper DNS names when provided an IP address, or vice versa.
`PATHPING`	A cross between `NSLOOKUP` and `PING`, it's used to determine where latency is being introduced.
`TRACERT` (Trace Route)	Used to display the full router path between your computer and a remote host. It also lets you see which routers are the busiest.
`NBTSTAT` (NetBIOS over TCP/IP Statistics)	Used to display and reset the NetBIOS name cache on your computer.

Utility	*Function*
ARP (Address Resolution Protocol)	Used to display and modify the ARP cache on your computer.

Dynamic Host Configuration Protocol (DHCP)

The Dynamic Host Configuration Protocol (DHCP) is open and standards based. It is the Internet community's answer to dynamically distributing IP addresses. In addition to IP addresses, DHCP can also provide gateway addresses, DNS server addresses, and WINS server addresses—in essence, all the TCP/IP information a client computer might need to participate in the network.

Often network administrators use unregistered addresses (not registered with IANA) on their internal networks to ensure that addresses are available for all users. This model works great as long as the network is never tied directly to the Internet.

When using DHCP, a client computer gets an address through the following steps:

1. The client computer broadcasts a `DHCPDiscover` message that is forwarded to the DHCP server(s) on the network. The address of the DHCP server(s) is configured on the router, if necessary. Forwarding is done using a process called a BOOTP Forwarder.
2. Each DHCP server that receives the discover message responds with a `DHCPOffer` message that includes an IP address appropriate for the subnet to which the client computer is attached. The DHCP server determines the appropriate address by looking at the source subnet for the broadcast `DHCPDiscover` message.
3. The client computer considers the offer message and selects one (usually the first offer it receives). It sends a `DHCPRequest` to use that address to the DHCP server that originated the offer. If multiple DHCP servers exist, great care needs to be taken in their configuration.
4. The DHCP server acknowledges the request and grants the client computer a lease to use the address.
5. The client computer uses the IP address to bind to the network. If the IP address is associated with any configuration parameters, the parameters are incorporated into the client computer's TCP/IP configuration.

Any DHCP client computer that had been assigned an address automatically tries to extend the lease when half the time of the lease has passed. If it is incapable of doing so, it continues to try to do so for the duration of the lease.

DHCP servers must be authorized in Active Directory before they will begin offering DHCP addresses. This is designed to prevent rogue DHCP servers from popping up on your network.

If you are maintaining a legacy domain and a WINS-style network, Windows 2000 can receive DHCP information from any DHCP server that Windows NT worked with. However, if you want to take advantage of the features of Active Directory Services and migrate away from the legacy WINS architecture, you will need the Windows 2000 DHCP Service.

A DHCP server can't be a DHCP client computer, too. If you currently have your server configured as a DHCP client computer, the DHCP installation will prompt you to enter a static IP address for your server.

A *scope* is a range of IP addresses that are available for dynamic assignment to client computers on a given subnet. The scope for a particular subnet is determined by the network address of the broadcast DHCP request. After installing the DHCP service, you must define at least one scope on the server. Otherwise, the service will not respond to DHCP requests.

A *superscope* enables you to support a supernetted or multinetted network with a Windows 2000 DHCP Server. A *supernetted* network is a network that has multiple network addresses or subnets running on the same segment. You can select only active scopes for inclusion in the superscope.

Multicasting is the act of transmitting a message to a select group of recipients. This is in contrast to the concepts of a *broadcast*, in which traffic is sent to every host on the network, or a *unicast*, in which the connection is a one-to-one relationship and only one recipient of the data exists. Class D IP addresses should be used for the multicast scope.

Components of Windows 2000's multicast functionality include

- Multicast DHCP (MDHCP)
- Multicast forwarding table
- Multicast group
- Multicast scope

One of the keys to effectively implementing an Active Directory environment is the capability for Windows 2000 workstations using DHCP to be automatically registered in DNS. Three settings can be set for DNS integration:

- **Automatically Update DHCP Client Computer Information in DNS**—This is enabled by default.
- **Discard Forward (Name-to-Address) Lookups When Lease Expires**—This is also enabled by default.
- **Enable Updates for DNS Client Computers That Do Not Support Dynamic Update.**

The capability to register both A- and PTR-type records lets a DHCP server register non-Windows 2000 client computers in DNS. The DHCP server can differentiate between Windows 2000 Professional and other client computers.

The DHCP console is used for managing and monitoring DHCP. It has several features on the Action menu, such as Display Statistics, that show such items as when the server started. The All Tasks selection enables you to perform the following tasks for your DHCP server:

- Start
- Stop
- Pause
- Resume
- Restart
- Delete
- Refresh
- Export List
- Properties

Host Name Resolution

The HOSTS files can do name resolution, and this was the original method employed on the predecessor to the Internet. As the number of computers grew, this solution ran into problems because it was a flat-file solution, and propagation of the file became nearly impossible.

The domain name system/service (DNS) replaced HOSTS files. DNS is a distributed, hierarchical database residing on servers known as a *name servers*. It is designed so that there can be multiple name servers for redundancy; caching of names to the local server is also supported.

DNS terminology includes the following:

- **Tree**—A data structure with each element attached to one or more elements directly beneath it. DNS is often called an *inverted tree* because it is generally drawn with the root at the top of the tree.
- **Top-level domain (TLD)**—The suffix attached to Internet domain names. A limited number of predefined suffixes exists, and each one represents a top-level domain. Examples include com, edu, org, net, and country identifiers.
- **Node**—The point at which two or more lines in the tree intersect, also known as a *leaf.*
- **Fully qualified domain name (FQDN)**—A domain name that includes all domains between the host and the root. The DNS information configured under System Properties is used as the DNS suffix for building FQDNs.
- **Zone**—A logical grouping of host names within DNS. A zone is the complete information about some part of the domain namespace.

Two types of name servers are defined within the DNS specifications:

- **Active Directory Integrated**—The DNS server provides records out of Active Directory. All the replication and updates are handled through Active Directory.
- **Primary master**—The server where you make additions, modifications, and deletions to the DNS zone.
- **Secondary master**—This server gets its zone information from another domain name server that is authoritative for that domain.

The DNS name server resolves a name to an IP address using the following process:

1. The client computer makes a request to the local DNS server.
2. The DNS server looks in a local memory cache for names it has recently resolved. If the name is found in the local cache, the name server returns the IP address the client computer requires.
3. If the name is not found in cache, the name server looks in the DNS server's host tables to see whether a static entry (or in the case of DDNS, a dynamic entry) exists for the host name to an IP address lookup. If an entry exists, the DNS server forwards the IP address to the client computer.
4. If the name is not found in the host's tables, the name server refers the request to a root name server. Root name servers support the root of the namespace hierarchy. At present, 10 computers support the root domain.
5. The root name server then refers the request to a name server for the first-level domain in the host name.
6. The first name server that can resolve the host name to an IP address reports the IP address to the client computer.

With a reverse lookup, you query the DNS server with an IP address, and it returns (if an entry exists) the DNS name for that host.

Table 2 lists the main record types supported by Windows 2000's DNS Server service, along with their meanings.

TABLE 2

DNS RECORD TYPES

Record Type	*Value and Meaning*
CNAME	One of the original record types, a CNAME indicates an alias for a host name or an A record for a name already specified as another resource type in this zone. CNAME is the acronym for canonical name.
A	One HOST address record—maps a DNS name to an IP (version 4) address.
MX	A mail exchanger record is used to provide message routing to a specific mail exchange host for a specific DNS name.
MG	A mail group record is used to add mailbox (MB) records as members of a domain mailing group.
MB	A mailbox record maps a specified domain mailbox name to the host that hosts the mailbox.
MINFO	Mailbox or mailing list information specifies a domain mailbox name to contact. Can also specify a mailbox for error messages.
PTR	A pointer record points to a location in the domain. This is typically used for reverse lookups or IP address-to-DNS name lookups.
TXT	A text record is used to hold a string of characters that serves as descriptive text to be associated with a specific DNS name.
RT	A route-through record provides an intermediate-route-through binding for internal hosts that do not have their own direct wide area network (WAN) addresses.
SRV	A service record enables administrators to use several servers for a single DNS domain to easily move a TCP/IP service from host to host and to designate primary and backup service hosts.
WKS	A well-known service record is used to describe well-known TCP/IP services supported by a particular protocol (that is, TCP or UDP) on a specific IP address.

Table 3 shows the restrictions for creating a DNS name and FQDN.

TABLE 3

DNS NAME RESTRICTIONS

Restriction	*Standard DNS (Including Windows NT 4)*	*DNS in Windows 2000*
Characters	Supports RFC 1123, which permits "A"–"Z", "a"–"z", "0"–"9", and the hyphen (-)	Several configurations are possible: RFC 1123 standard, as well as support for RFC 2181 and the character set specified in RFC 2044 (UTP-8).
FQDN length	63 bytes per label and 255 bytes for an FQDN	Domain controllers are imited to 255 bytes for an FQDN.

Windows 2000 DNS contains a number of significant improvements over standard DNS, including the following:

- **Notification-driven zone transfers**—Servers on which updates occur and notify their secondary DNS servers to fetch updates.
- **Integrated zone tables**—Active Directory can be used to manage some DNS zones.
- **Incremental zone transfers**—Only the changes to a zone need to be transferred, not the whole DNS zone.
- **Secure DNS updates**—Updates to the DNS records can be done in a way that requires authentication.
- **DNS and DHCP integration**—DHCP can provide updates to DNS on the addresses it leased to each computer.

The root name server of a domain is the name server that is acting as the start of authority for that zone. The start of authority (SOA) record is the first record in the database, and it contains the following fields:

- Source Host
- Contact Email
- Serial Number
- Refresh Time
- Retry Time
- Expiration Time
- Time to Live (TTL)

Dynamic DNS (DDNS) integrates DHCP and DNS and is necessary for Active Directory. Every time a computer requests a new address or renews its address, the computer sends its fully qualified name to the DHCP server and requests that the DHCP server register an entry in the reverse lookup DNS zone on its behalf. The DHCP client computer also requests an entry in the forward lookup zone on its own behalf.

Configuring a zone for dynamic updates enables Windows 2000 client computers to register as part of DNS. In Windows 2000, client computers can send dynamic updates for three types of network adapters: DHCP adapters, statically configured adapters, and remote access adapters. By default, the dynamic update client computer dynamically registers its A resource records whenever any of the following events occur:

- The TCP/IP configuration is changed.
- The DHCP address is renewed, or a new lease is obtained.
- A Plug and Play event occurs.
- An IP address is added or removed from the computer when the user changes or adds an IP address for a static adapter.

You can also force a reregistration by using the command `IPCONFIG /REGISTERDNS`.

To go from no DNS service to a functional DNS server, you must complete the following steps:

1. Installation can be accomplished through the use of the Configure Your Server application and is completely wizard driven. You can also install it via the Network and Dial-up Connections section of the Control Panel.
2. After the service is installed, you will need to configure it. This is done by opening the DNS console. The first thing to do in this application is to start the Configure DNS Server Wizard. This guides you through configuring the server with its first zone(s).
3. After the wizard completes the process, you are ready to resolve names.

The three types of zones supported by Windows 2000 DNS are

- Active Directory integrated
- Standard primary
- Standard secondary

For the most secure implementation, you should choose Active Directory integrated. Caching-only servers are used to speed up client DNS queries by gathering a large number of cached records based on client DNS queries. A caching-only server does not have a copy of the zone table and therefore can't respond to queries against the zone unless they are already cached. A caching server is not authoritative on any zone.

Delegating a domain means that DNS queries on the existing domain will be referred to the name server in the delegated domain for resolution. You can only delegate down the hierarchy, so the delegated domain must be a subdomain of the domain doing the delegation.

Parameters configured in the Networking Properties section are used for resolving names, whereas the System Properties parameters are used while registering the system with Active Directory.

The following are four methods of testing the DNS resolution:

- Use the `PING` utility with the `-a` flag.
- Use the `NSLOOKUP` utility.
- Use the built-in monitoring in the DNS console.
- Use a Web browser.

In managing DNS, you can configure several optional parameters, including

- **Set Aging/Scavenging for All Zones**—This controls how the server handles stale resource records.
- **Scavenge Stale Resource**—This enables you to manually scavenge the record.
- **Update Server Data Files**—This option writes any changes to the table that are in RAM to the server's hard drive.
- **Clear Cache**—This option enables you to flush the server's cache.
- **All Tasks**—This enables you to start, stop, pause, resume, or restart the service.
- **Delete**—This deletes the DNS server.
- **Properties**—This opens the Properties dialog box.

NetBIOS Name Resolution

NetBIOS name resolution can be done with `LMHOSTS` files or WINS. An `LMHOST` file is a text file that must be edited manually and copied to every computer on the network.

The Windows Internet Name Service (WINS) consists of four elements:

- **WINS servers**—When WINS client computers enter the network, they contact a WINS server using a directed message. The client computer registers its name with the WINS server and uses the WINS server to resolve NetBIOS names to IP addresses.
- **WINS client computers**—WINS clients use directed (P-node) messages to communicate with WINS servers and are typically configured to use H-node communication. Windows 2000, Windows NT, Windows 95 and 98, and Windows for Workgroups computers can be WINS client computers.
- **Non-WINS client computers**—Older Microsoft network client computers that can't use P-node can still benefit from WINS. Their broadcast messages are intercepted by WINS proxy computers that act as intermediaries between the B-node client computers and WINS servers. MS-DOS and Windows 3.1 client computers function as non-WINS client computers.
- **WINS proxies**—All Windows computers since Windows for Workgroups can function as WINS proxies. They intercept B-node broadcasts on their local subnets and communicate with a WINS server on behalf of the B-node client computer.

The WINS server should use a static (rather than a dynamic) IP address. If this is not done, all users could lose access to the server if it is issued an address different from what it had been issued by the DHCP server.

The majority of WINS troubleshooting issues relate to connectivity. Tools that can assist in troubleshooting include

- PING.exe
- Ipconfig
- Task Manager

To get the server statistics, open WINS console and right-click the server in question. From the context menu, select Display Server Statistics, and a snapshot of the server statistics will be displayed.

Node types to know for WINS and networking are

- **B-node (broadcast node)**—Relies exclusively on broadcast messages and is the oldest NetBIOS name resolution mode.
- **P-node (point-to-point node)**—Relies exclusively on WINS servers for NetBIOS name resolution. Client computers register themselves with a WINS server when they come on the network. They then contact the WINS server with NetBIOS name resolution requests.
- **M-node (modified node)**—A hybrid mode that first attempts to resolve NetBIOS names using the B-node mechanism. If that fails, an attempt is made to use P-node name resolution.
- **H-node (hybrid node)**—A hybrid mode that favors the use of WINS for NetBIOS name resolution. When a computer needs to resolve a NetBIOS name, it first attempts to use P-node resolution to resolve a name via WINS. Only if WINS resolution fails does the host resort to B-node to resolve the name via broadcasts.

Installing and Maintaining Clients and Servers

This section deals with the issues of deploying systems that stand the test of time by restricting which drivers users can install and through the management of a constant stream of updates.

Driver Signing

Microsoft has included a feature within Windows 2000 that allows you to install only Microsoft verified drivers, display a warning on non-signed drivers, or allow all drivers unencumbered.

These settings, available only to the administrator, can be found under the System applet's Hardware tab.

Deploying Service Packs

Service packs under Windows 2000 are similar to service packs under Windows NT 4.0. They are accumulated sets of fixes for the operating system published on a periodic basis. Support for the `/slip` switch enables the service pack to be applied to the installation source to allow for slipstreamed installations.

Hot Fixes

Hot fixes are updates to the operating system prior to being bundled into a service pack. They are available through Windows Update or can be found on the Microsoft TechNet home page. Hot fixes should be installed only when you can be potentially affected by the problem identified in the hot fix and should be done with caution. Hot fixes can be removed through the Add/Remove Programs applet in the Control Panel.

MANAGING, SECURING, AND TROUBLESHOOTING SERVER COMPUTERS

When booting a system, you will have the option of pressing F8 to view a Windows 95-like Boot menu. It includes options for starting the computer in the following modes:

- Safe Mode
- Safe Mode with Networking
- Safe Mode with Command Prompt
- Enable Boot Logging
- Enable VGA Mode
- Last Known Good Configuration
- Directory Service Restore Mode
- Debugging Mode

Several of these boot modes can be used to recover components of your system.

The Recovery Console enables the running of several command-line utilities that can be used to repair your system. It can be accessed from the boot menu if it was previously installed. If the Recovery Console is not installed, you can still access it by booting from the Windows 2000 CD.

Managing Processes

Applications run at one of 32 priority levels that range from 0 to 31.

Priorities of 16 and above are not normally used by applications.

Applications with the highest priority get the most processing time.

Task Manager can be used to examine and change application priorities, and Performance Monitor can be used to examine application priorities.

Table 4 contains a list of priority names and the base values for the priority levels.

TABLE 4

PRIORITY LEVELS UNDER WINDOWS 2000

Level Name	*Priority Base*
Real Time	24
High	13
Above Normal	10
Normal	8
Below Normal	6
Low	4

You can set priorities at runtime by using the `START` command (for example, `START /ABOVENORMAL WORDPAD.EXE`).

Optimizing Disk Performance

You can optimize disk performance by using some of the following options:

- Investing in a hardware RAID solution
- Implementing a Windows 2000 software RAID solution
- Organizing files that are used by the operating system and its services to reduce disk contention
- Setting up regular defragmentation of disks to enable quicker access to files

Monitoring and Optimizing

Performance Monitor supports three views:

- Chart
- Histogram
- Report

Counter logs and trace logs can be use to record performance counters so they can be viewed or analyzed later.

Counter logs can be viewed with the System Monitor snap-in or other applications, depending on the format the log is saved in:

- **Text file**—Comma-Separated Values (CSV)
- **Text file**—Tab-Separated Values (TSV)
- **Binary file**—Readable in System Monitor
- **Binary Circular file**—Same as the previous but reuses the log file as needed to keep file sizes down

Trace logs can be read by third-party applications, and logging is based on computer activity.

Alerts can be configured to monitor server performance and alert administrators.

Only physical disk performance counters are enabled by default; to enable logical disk performance counters, you must run `DISKPERF -Y` or `DISKPERF -YV` from the command prompt.

To use the Network Segment data counters, you need to install the Network Monitor Agent. This will allow you to monitor the performance of traffic going to or coming from the local network segment.

The following resources are critical to the monitor:

- Memory
- Disks
- Processor
- Network

Fundamentals of Active Directory

Although Active directory is a much broader topic than any one book can cover, you will be expected to know the basic concepts and basic management techniques for operating in an Active Directory environment.

Manage Active Directory Objects via Tools

You've already seen how to manage Active Directory objects manually; this section describes how to manage Active Directory via automated or semiautomated means.

Creating and Managing Accounts Manually or by Scripting

When creating and managing accounts manually or by scripting, consider the following:

- Know how to create an object using Active Directory Users and Computers and the other AD tools.
- You should know that the programming interface is called ADSI and that it works with a COM object called `LDAP://`. This object enables you to connect to the directory tree in different base locations and perform operations.
- Remember that LDIFDE and CSVDE can be used to copy objects into and out of Active Directory. The file can be edited outside Active Directory and then imported back in.

- You can use a Microsoft Exchange connector to connect to Exchange Server 5.5 service pack 3 and exchange users, groups, and contacts.
- You can still use the `NET USER` and `NET GROUP` commands to manage users.

Controlling Access to Active Directory Objects

Consider the following when controlling access to Active Directory objects:

- **Remember that one of the key properties stored for every object is the access control list (ACL)**—The ACL determines what users can do to the object. The access control list is made up of access control entries. Two access control lists exist in Windows 2000. The Discretionary Access Control List (DACL) maintains information on permissions, whereas the System Access Control List (SACL) is used to audit the access to a resource.
- **The objects created within container objects inherit the permissions of those container objects**—This inheritance can be turned off. If you turn off inheritance, you will be asked what you want to do with the existing permissions: keep or remove.
- **The user's credentials are attached to the user process**—When the process attempts an access, the SID from the credentials (access token) is compared to the entries in the access control list.
- **When you set permissions, you typically have the option of applying them to the object, the object and subobjects, or just the subobjects.**

Delegating Administrative Control of Objects in Active Directory

When delegating administrative control of objects in Active Directory, consider the following:

- When you delegate control, you are setting permissions on the object and subobjects.
- The Delegation of Control Wizard should be used to make the delegation simple. It sets the permissions for you, including advanced permissions.
- Delegation is normally done on organizational units. This is their main purpose.
- You should know the main permissions and on what they can be set. Remember, object permissions and properties permissions can both be set: Full Control, Write, Read, Create All Child Objects, and Delete All Child Objects.

Managing and Troubleshooting Active Directory Replication

This topic is basically a matter of knowing how the connections, site link, and site link bridges work, and the tools that can be used to monitor replication. Most of this has already been reviewed.

Managing Intersite Replication

When managing intersite replication, consider the following:

- Intersite replication is managed by the KCC. You should not create manual connections.
- KCC configures servers with two partners in a site and possibly a partner in another site.

Managing Intrasite Replication

When managing intrasite replication, consider the following:

- The key utilities are REPAdmin and REPLMon. The admin program lets you administer the replication from the command line, and the REPLMon snap-in lets you monitor replication.

FUNDAMENTALS OF GROUP POLICY

This section addresses the basics of Group Policy objects. Group Policy objects can be used to distribute software as well as control the user environment.

Managing and Troubleshooting Software by Using Group Policy

For this objective, you need to be familiar with the methods that can be used to deploy software to users and computers (publishing and assigning), how to upgrade software packages using Group Policy, how to redeploy packages to include patched files, and how to remove software using Group Policy.

Deploying Software by Using Group Policy

When deploying software by using Group Policy, consider the following:

- Software to be deployed using Group Policy must be in a format compatible with Windows Installer—that is, either a Windows Installer package (MSI) file or a ZAP file.
- Software can be delivered to users through Group Policy either by publishing it or by assigning it.
- Assigning a software package to either a computer or a user will automatically install that package (in the case of a computer) or will place icons on the desktop if the package was installed (in the case of a user).
- Publishing software makes the application available to the user but does not immediately install the software. The software will be installed either through Control Panel Add/Remove Programs or by document activation.
- Document activation involves an attempt by the user to open a file with an extension associated with a particular package and then installing the software.
- Only Windows Installer package (MSI) files can be either assigned or published to users because they contain the information necessary to install the application without user intervention.
- ZAP files can only be published, and they require the user to perform the normal install process for the software application.
- Third-party tools are available to repackage an application that is not provided in a Windows Installer package (MSI) file format. Veritas WinINSTALL LE is included on the Windows 2000 CD-ROM.
- Administrators can use transform (MST) files to deploy the same software package with different options to different OUs within the enterprise.
- Transform files (MST) modify an existing package to meet specific requirements such as language or geographic location.
- Software categories enable administrators to categorize software applications to enable users to more easily select which software to install through Add/Remove Programs in Control Panel.

Maintaining Software by Using Group Policy

Consider the following when maintaining software by using Group Policy:

- Software upgrades can be deployed using Group Policy. Upgrades can be either required or optional for an existing application.
- Required upgrades are installed without the user having a choice in this decision.
- Optional upgrades enable the user to decide whether she wants to upgrade to the most recent version.
- Software removal can also be configured through Group Policy and can be forced or optional.
- Forced removal requires that the software package be removed from the user's machine, whereas an optional removal enables the user to continue to use the application after it has been designated to be removed.

Troubleshooting Common Problems That Occur During Software Deployment

When troubleshooting common problems that occur during software deployment, consider the following:

- Most problems with deploying software using Group Policy are the result of network errors, such as not being able to reach the software distribution point, or they have to do with the application of Group Policy.
- When determining the nature of a problem, you must still adhere to all the rules governing policy inheritance, filtering, and other elements.

Implementing and Troubleshooting Group Policy

In general, you should know what Group Policy is composed of, how to create a new Group Policy, how to link an existing GPO to an Active Directory container, how to modify a GPO, how to block GPO inheritance, how to filter the application of Group Policy using permissions, and how to delegate the administration of Group Policy to lower-level administrators.

Creating a Group Policy Object

Group Policy objects are composed of two parts:

- **Group Policy Containers (GPCs)**—GPCs are Active Directory containers in which the GPO version information and globally unique identifier (GUID) are stored, such as a site, a domain, or an OU.
- **Group Policy Templates (GPTs)**—GPTs are physical files, including administrative templates and scripts, that are stored within the Policies container for the SYSVOL share on domain controllers. Each GPT is stored in a folder with the same name as the GUID of the GPO for which it is a template. The GPT is a folder structure with the following subfolders: `ADM`, `Scripts`, `USER`, `USER\Applications`, and `MACHINE`.

When creating a GPO, consider the following:

- Group Policy can be created at a site, a domain, or an OU level.
- Once created, the GPO settings are modified using the Group Policy Editor MMC snap-in.
- Only Domain Admins or those users who have been granted the Create Group Policy Object permissions can create a GPO at any level.

- Windows NT 4.0 System Policies do not migrate to Group Policy when upgrading a domain controller to Windows 2000.
- Group Policy application can be audited and the results viewed in the Event Viewer. This is a good troubleshooting tool when needed.

Linking an Existing GPO

Consider the following when linking an existing GPO:

- Linking an existing GPO to an Active Directory container enables its settings to be applied to computers and users within the OU.
- The same GPO can be linked to any number of Active Directory containers.
- The GPT contains a common collection of settings that will be applied to all Active Directory containers to which the GPO has been linked.

Delegating Administrative Control of Group Policy

When delegating administrative control of Group Policy, consider the following:

- Delegating administrative control of a GPO enables other users to modify the GPO settings.
- For a user to be delegated administrative control of a GPO, he needs to have Read and Write permissions on the GPO to modify it.
- Delegation of administrative control is done by setting appropriate permissions through the Security tab for the GPO properties.

Modifying Group Policy Inheritance

When modifying Group Policy inheritance, consider the following:

- Group Policy settings specified at a higher level, such as a domain or site, are automatically inherited by all lower-level Active Directory objects, such as subdomains and OUs.
- Group Policy is processed in the following order:
  - Site
  - Domain
  - Organizational unit
- A local administrator responsible for a subdomain or an OU can block policy inheritance from higher levels, thereby ensuring that only his GPOs will be processed.
- Higher-level administrators have the option to override the blocking of GPO application at lower levels, thereby forcing GPO settings even if they are blocked at a lower level.
- Group Policy conflict refers to the same setting being applied at different levels of Active Directory. The last GPO processed will be the one whose settings will apply unless No Override has been specified at a higher-level GPO.
- Group Policy precedence in the same container determines which conflicting settings will be applied based on the order in the Group Policy tab for the Active Directory Container. The GPO at the top of the list wins.

Filtering Group Policy Settings

To filter Group Policy settings by associating security groups to GPOs, consider the following:

- Group Policy filtering is the assignment of permissions to a GPO to ensure that it is processed only by those users for whom it was intended. In this way, you can selectively implement Group Policy for a security group, computer, or user.

- You can disable processing of the user or computer component of a GPO by selecting Properties in the Group Policy tab.
- For the GPO to be applied, the user must have the Read and Apply Group Policy permission on the GPO.
- To deny Group Policy processing and filter it so that it is not applied to the user, group, or computer, select the Deny option for the Apply Group Policy privilege for the user, group, or computer.

Modifying Group Policy

To modify Group Policy, consider the following:

- Modifying Group Policy involves changing its settings using the Group Policy Editor MMC snap-in.
- Only users with both Read and Write permissions on the GPO can modify it.
- After modifying a GPO, the new settings are replicated to domain controllers within 5 minutes and applied to users and computers within 90 minutes, although this setting can be changed using Group Policy.
- The administrator can disable processing of the unused portion of a GPO (either the user or computer portion) to speed up downloads of the GPO template to computers. Disabling both user and computer configuration disables the GPO.

Routing and Remote Access Service Fundamentals

This section covers not only the basics of the remote access features of Windows 2000's Routing and Remote Access (RRAS), but also the routing features. In particular, it covers the Network Address Translation (NAT) component of RRAS and how it differs from the Internet Connection Sharing (ICS) feature also included in Windows 2000.

Remote Access

In Windows 2000, not only is the Routing and Remote Access Service (which replaces the Remote Access Service that came with Windows NT Server 4) installed automatically with the operating system, but it also bundles features that used to be distributed through other services, such as the Windows 2000 VPN service.

A remote access policy is a set of actions that can be applied to a group of users who meet a specified set of requirements.

When creating a remote access dial-in profile, you have access to the following tabs:

- **Dial-in Constraints**—Allows you to configure the restrictions on the dial-in users, including the idle disconnect timer, the maximum length of the session, the time and day access is permitted, the dial-in number allowed, and the dial-in media allowed.
- **IP**—Used to determine the IP Address Assignment Policy; it also enables you to apply IP packet filters, if necessary.

- **Multilink**—Enables you to configure Windows 2000's capability to aggregate multiple analog phone lines connected to multiple modems to provide greater bandwidth.
- **Authentication**—Enables you to configure the authentication methods supported by Windows 2000. The protocols include EAP-TLS, CHAP, MS-CHAP, SPAP, and PAP.
- **Encryption**—Enables you to set the level of encryption required with Routing and Remote Access authentication. You can set it to No Encryption, Basic, or Strong, or allow any combination of the three.
- **Advanced**—Enables you to add connection attributes to be returned to the remote access server. This is typically used in conjunction with RADIUS.

Windows 2000 has two main encryption protocols that are used in the VPN:

- **PPTP (Point-to-Point Tunneling Protocol)**—Developed jointly by Microsoft Corporation, U.S. Robotics, and several remote access vendor companies, it has never been widely accepted by the security community.
- **IPSec (IP Security Protocol)**—A suite of cryptography-based protection services and security protocols that can provide machine-level authentication as well as data encryption for L2TP-based (Layer 2 Tunneling Protocol) VPN connections. Unlike some other IPSec-based VPNs, Microsoft's implementation uses the L2TP protocol for encrypting the usernames, passwords, and data, whereas IPSec is used to negotiate the secure connection between your computer and its remote tunnel server. Available encryptions for IPSec include Data Encryption Standard (DES) and Triple DES (3DES). These are the encryption protocols available for remote access in Windows 2000. Windows 2000 does use other encryption, such as Kerberos, for logging on to a domain, but it is not applicable to remote access.

Windows 2000 includes the capability of aggregating multiple modem lines to form a single, higher-bandwidth connection to a remote access server. This is known as *multilink* and is usually to an Internet service provider connection, but it could also be to another Windows 2000 server. Multilink is configured on the Incoming Connections Properties dialog box beneath Network and Dial-up Connections.

When the remote access server is configured to use DHCP, the Routing and Remote Access server uses the DHCP client component to obtain 10 IP addresses from a DHCP server. This could be on the network or on the same server as the Routing and Remote Access server. The remote access server uses the first IP address obtained from DHCP for the RAS interface, and subsequent addresses are allocated to TCP/IP-based remote access client computers as they connect. IP addresses freed because of remote access client computers disconnecting are reused. When all 10 addresses have been allocated, the process starts again with the DHCP client computer requesting an additional 10 addresses.

To configure Routing and Remote Access for DHCP Integration, open the Routing and Remote Access console within the Routing and Remote Access portion of Administrative Tools.

Internet Connection Sharing and Network Address Translation

The Internet Connection Sharing (ICS) service provides an automated demand-dial installation process for the following services:

- Network Address Translation
- Dynamic Host Control Protocol
- DNS Proxy

These services make ICS a quick and easy solution for a small office looking for a way to connect to the Internet via dial-up. ICS also has features that are not available in the NAT implementation:

- **H.323 Proxy**—This feature permits users to make and receive Microsoft NetMeeting calls.
- **Lightweight Directory Access Protocol (LDAP) Proxy**—The capability to proxy LDAP requests allows users to register with an Internet Locater Service (ILS) server as part of a NetMeeting directory.
- **Directplay Proxy**—This enables users to play Directplay games across the NAT router. This feature is more suited for home use than for a small office, and it is also offered in the Windows 98 version of ICS.

ICS does the following upon install:

- **ICS sets the IP address of the LAN interface to 192.168.0.1, a private IP address**—A *private* IP address is an address that can't be routed across the Internet. Reserved addresses are specifically set aside for private networks.
- **The WAN interface (usually a modem) is set to be a demand-dial router pointed at the ISP.**
- **A DNS Proxy service is installed to provide DNS services to the office**—This service passes client computer DNS requests to the DNS server configured in the ICS server's DHCP settings.
- **The AutoDHCP service is installed**—This service provides a subset of the services included with a full DHCP installation, but AutoDHCP is configured to issue addresses on the new 198.168.0.0 network.

If you have a network larger than the one ICS can support, you can use the Network Address Translation capabilities of Windows 2000. Network Address Translation takes an IP address entering on one interface of the Windows 2000 server and translates it to a different address exiting a different (usually the Internet-connected) interface. The following are two reasons for doing this:

- Security
- IP address conservation

If you are planning to use NAT, the easiest way to enable the client computers is through the NAT DHCP service. This configures the client computers with the correct information to use the NAT gateway when they are assigned their IP addresses via DHCP. If you are using the NAT DHCP, you will not need the Windows 2000 DHCP service.

A NAT interface defines the connection properties for the Network Address Translation. This can be either the private interface, connected to the internal (private) network, or the public interface, connected to the Internet.

Any logging events will be logged in the System Event Log and can be viewed with the Event Viewer.

TERMINAL SERVICES FUNDAMENTALS

The final section addresses the other type of remote access to a network—Terminal Services. Terminal Services enables a client to gain a Window's session on the server just as if she were sitting in front of the console. There are three key things to understand about Terminal Services: Terminal Server Modes, Resource Mapping, and User Configuration.

Terminal Server Modes

Terminal Server can be installed in two modes:

- **Remote Administration**—Designed for remote administration of the server. Allows two simultaneous connections and doesn't require licensing.
- **Application Server**—Designed for user access and requires a separate terminal services client license. It also requires that terminal server licensing be installed on the network within the first 90 days. If a licensing server is not installed within the first 90 days, the clients will no longer be capable of accessing the server.

Resource Mapping

Terminal Services enables you to map the following resources between the client and server:

- Client drives
- Client printers
- Printer ports
- Communications ports
- Clipboard

User Configuration

In addition to the user's standard configuration parameters that apply to all users, some separate properties override the user's default profile and home directory settings when they are attached to the terminal server. Additionally, you can individually control whether the user is allowed to log in to the terminal server.

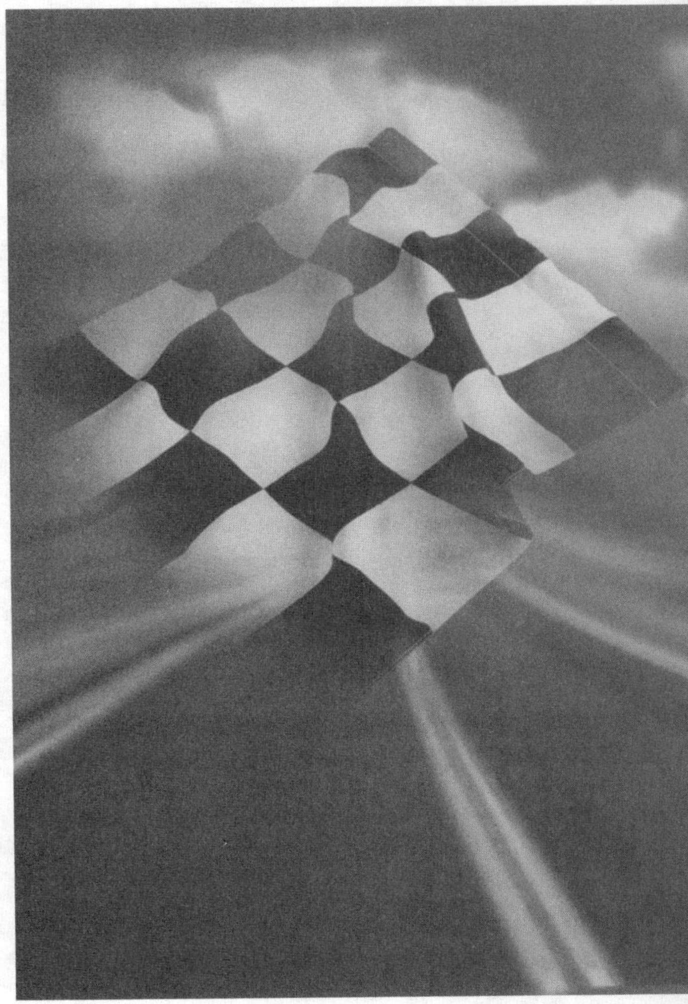

Study and Exam Prep Tips

This element of the book provides you with some general guidelines for preparing for a certification exam. It is organized into four sections. The first section addresses your learning style and how it affects your preparation for the exam. The second section covers your exam preparation activities and general study tips. This is followed by an extended look at the Microsoft Certification exams, including a number of specific tips that apply to the various Microsoft exam formats and question types. Finally, changes in Microsoft's testing policies and how these might affect you are discussed.

Learning Styles

To better understand the nature of preparation for the test, it is important to understand learning as a process. You probably are aware of how you best learn new material. You might find that outlining works best for you, or, as a visual learner, you might need to "see" things. Whatever your learning style, test preparation takes place over time. Obviously, you shouldn't start studying for these exams the night before you take them; it is very important to understand that learning is a developmental process. Understanding it as a process helps you focus on what you know and what you have yet to learn.

Thinking about how you learn should help you recognize that learning takes place when you are able to match new information to old. You have some previous experience with computers and networking. Now you are preparing for this certification exam. Using this book, software, and supplementary materials will not just add incrementally to what you know; as you study, the organization of your knowledge actually restructures as you integrate new information into your existing knowledge base. This will lead you to a more comprehensive understanding of the tasks and concepts outlined in the objectives and of computing in general.

Again, this happens as a result of a repetitive process rather than a singular event. Keep this model of learning in mind as you prepare for the exam, and you will make better decisions concerning what to study and how much more studying you need to do.

Study Tips

There are many ways to approach studying, just as there are many types of material to study. However, the tips that follow should work well for the type of material covered on the certification exams.

Study Strategies

Although individuals vary in the ways they learn information, some basic principles of learning apply to everyone. You should adopt some study strategies that take advantage of these principles. One of these principles is that learning can be broken into various depths. Recognition (of terms, for example) exemplifies a more surface level of learning in which you rely on a prompt of some sort to elicit recall. Comprehension or understanding (of the concepts behind the terms, for example) represents a deeper level of learning. The ability to analyze a concept and apply your understanding of it in a new way represents a further depth of learning.

Your learning strategy should enable you to know the material at a level or two deeper than mere recognition. This will help you perform well on the exams. You will know the material so thoroughly that you can easily handle the recognition-level types of questions used in multiple-choice testing. You will also be able to apply your knowledge to solve new problems.

Macro and Micro Study Strategies

One strategy that can lead to this deeper learning includes preparing an outline that covers all the objectives and subobjectives for the particular exam you are working on. You should delve a bit further into the material and include a level or two of detail beyond the stated objectives and subobjectives for the exam. Then, expand the outline by coming up with a statement of definition or a summary for each point in the outline.

An outline provides two approaches to studying. First, you can study the outline by focusing on the organization of the material. Work your way through the points and subpoints of your outline with the goal of learning how they relate to one another. For example, be sure you understand how each of the main objective areas is similar to and different from another. Then, do the same thing with the subobjectives; be sure you know which subobjectives pertain to each objective area and how they relate to one another.

Next, you can work through the outline, focusing on learning the details. Memorize and understand terms and their definitions, facts, rules and strategies, advantages and disadvantages, and so on. In this pass through the outline, attempt to learn detail rather than the big picture (the organizational information that you worked on in the first pass through the outline).

Research has shown that attempting to assimilate both types of information at the same time seems to interfere with the overall learning process. Separate your studying into these two approaches, and you will perform better on the exam.

Active Study Strategies

The process of writing down and defining objectives, subobjectives, terms, facts, and definitions promotes a more active learning strategy than merely reading the material does. In human information-processing terms, writing forces you to engage in more active encoding of the information. Simply reading over it exemplifies more passive processing.

Next, determine whether you can apply the information you have learned by attempting to create examples and scenarios on your own. Think about how or where you could apply the concepts you are learning. Again, write down this information to process the facts and concepts in a more active fashion.

The hands-on nature of the step-by-step tutorials and exercises at the ends of the chapters provide further active learning opportunities that will reinforce concepts as well.

Common-Sense Strategies

Finally, you should also follow common-sense practices when studying. Study when you are alert, reduce or eliminate distractions, and take breaks when you become fatigued.

Pre-Testing Yourself

Pre-testing allows you to assess how well you are learning. One of the most important aspects of learning is what has been called *meta-learning*. Meta-learning has to do with realizing when you know something well or when you need to study some more. In other words, you recognize how well or how poorly you have learned the material you are studying.

For most people, this can be difficult to assess objectively on their own. Practice tests are useful in that they reveal more objectively what you have learned and what you have not learned. You should use this information to guide review and further studying. Developmental learning takes place as you cycle through studying, assessing how well you have learned, reviewing, and then assessing again until you feel you are ready to take the exam.

You might have noticed the practice exam included in this book. Use it as part of the learning process. The ExamGear, Training Guide Edition test simulation software included on the CD also provides you with an excellent opportunity to assess your knowledge.

You should set a goal for your pre-testing. A reasonable goal would be to score consistently in the 90% range.

See Appendix C, "Using the ExamGear, Training Guide Edition Software," for more explanation of the test simulation software.

Exam Prep Tips

Having mastered the subject matter, the final preparatory step is to understand how the exam will be presented. Make no mistake: A Microsoft Certified Professional (MCP) exam will challenge both your knowledge and your test-taking skills. This section starts with the basics of exam design, reviews a new type of exam format, and concludes with hints targeted to each of the exam formats.

The MCP Exam

Every MCP exam is released in one of three basic formats. What's being called exam format here is really little more than a combination of the overall exam structure and the presentation method for exam questions.

Understanding the exam formats is key to good preparation because the format determines the number of questions presented, the difficulty of those questions, and the amount of time allowed to complete the exam.

Each exam format uses many of the same types of questions. These types or styles of questions include several types of traditional multiple-choice questions, multiple-rating (or scenario-based) questions, and simulation-based questions. Some exams include other types of questions that ask you to drag and drop objects on the screen, reorder a list, or categorize things. Still other exams ask you to answer these types of questions in response to a case study you have read. It's important that you understand the types of questions you will be asked and the actions required to properly answer them.

The rest of this section addresses the exam formats and then tackles the question types. Understanding the formats and question types will help you feel much more comfortable when you take the exam.

Exam Format

As mentioned previously, there are three basic formats for the MCP exams: the traditional fixed-form exam, adaptive-form exam, and case-study form. As its name implies, the fixed-form exam presents a fixed set of questions during the exam session. The adaptive form, however, uses only a subset of questions drawn from a larger pool during any given exam session. The case-study form includes case studies that serve as the basis for answering the various types of questions.

Fixed-Form

A fixed-form computerized exam is based on a fixed set of exam questions. The individual questions are presented in random order during a test session. If you take the same exam more than once, you won't necessarily see the exact same questions. This is because two or three final forms are typically assembled for every fixed-form exam Microsoft releases. These are usually labeled Forms A, B, and C.

The final forms of a fixed-form exam are identical in terms of content coverage, number of questions, and allotted time, but the questions are different. You might notice, however, that some of the same questions appear on, or rather are shared among, different final forms. When questions are shared among multiple final forms of an exam, the percentage of sharing is generally small. Many final forms share no questions, but some older exams might have a 10%–15% duplication of exam questions on the final exam forms.

Fixed-form exams also have a fixed time limit in which you must complete the exam. The ExamGear, Training Guide Edition software on the CD-ROM that accompanies this book provides fixed-form exams.

Finally, the score you achieve on a fixed-form exam, which is always reported for MCP exams on a scale of 0 to 1,000, is based on the number of questions you answer correctly. The passing score is the same for all final forms of a given fixed-form exam.

The typical format for a fixed-form exam is as follows:

- 50–60 questions.
- 75–90 minute testing time.
- Question review is allowed, including the opportunity to change your answers.

Adaptive-Form

An adaptive-form exam has the same appearance as a fixed-form exam, but its questions differ in quantity and process of selection. Although the statistics of adaptive testing are fairly complex, the process is concerned with determining your level of skill or ability with the exam subject matter. This ability assessment begins with the presentation of questions of varying levels of difficulty and ascertaining at what difficulty level you can reliably answer them. Finally, the ability assessment determines whether that ability level is above or below the level required to pass that exam.

Examinees at different levels of ability will see different sets of questions. Examinees who demonstrate little expertise with the subject matter continue to be presented with relatively easy questions. Examinees who demonstrate a high level of expertise are presented progressively more difficult questions. Individuals of both levels of expertise might answer the same number of questions correctly, but because the higher-expertise examinee can correctly answer more difficult questions, she receives a higher score and is more likely to pass the exam.

The typical design for the adaptive-form exam is as follows:

- 20–25 questions.
- 90 minute testing time (although this is likely to be reduced to 45–60 minutes in the near future).
- Question review is not allowed, providing no opportunity for you to change your answers.

The Adaptive-Exam Process

Your first adaptive exam will be unlike any other testing experience you have had. In fact, many examinees have difficulty accepting the adaptive testing process because they feel that they were not provided the opportunity to adequately demonstrate their full expertise.

You can take consolation in the fact that adaptive exams are painstakingly put together after months of data gathering and analysis and that adaptive exams are just as valid as fixed-form exams. The rigor introduced through the adaptive testing methodology means that there is nothing arbitrary about the exam items you'll see. It is also a more efficient means of testing, requiring less time to conduct and complete than traditional fixed-form exams.

As you can see in Figure 1, a number of statistical measures drive the adaptive examination process. The measure most immediately relevant to you is the ability estimate. Accompanying this test statistic are the standard error of measurement, the item characteristic curve, and the test information curve.

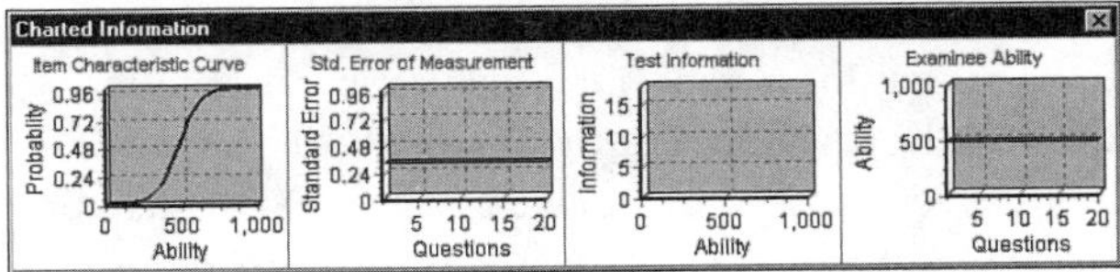

FIGURE 1
Microsoft's adaptive testing demonstration program.

The standard error, which is the key factor in determining when an adaptive exam terminates, reflects the degree of error in the exam ability estimate. The item characteristic curve reflects the probability of a correct response relative to examinee ability. Finally, the test information statistic provides a measure of the information contained in the set of questions the examinee has answered, again relative to the ability level of the individual examinee.

When you begin an adaptive exam, the standard error has already been assigned a target value below which it must drop for the exam to conclude. This target value reflects a particular level of statistical confidence in the process. The examinee ability is initially set to the mean possible exam score (500 for MCP exams).

As the adaptive exam progresses, questions of varying difficulty are presented. Based on your pattern of responses to these questions, the ability estimate is recalculated. At the same time, the standard error estimate is refined from its first estimated value of one toward the target value. When the standard error reaches its target value, the exam is terminated. Thus, the more consistently you answer questions of the same degree of difficulty, the more quickly the standard error estimate drops, and the fewer questions you will end up seeing during the exam session. This situation is depicted in Figure 2.

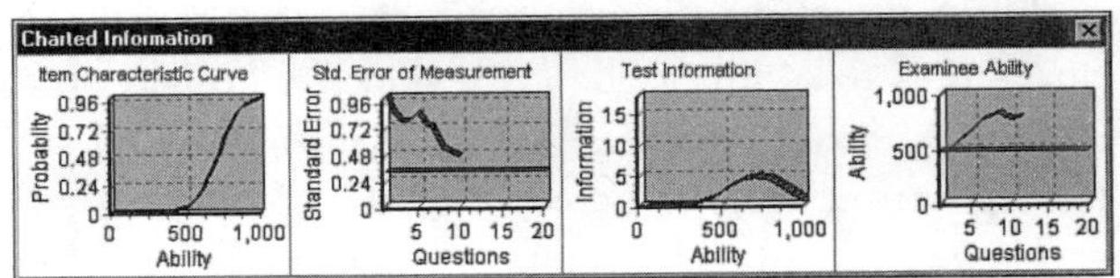

FIGURE 2
The changing statistics in an adaptive exam.

As you might suspect, one good piece of advice for taking an adaptive exam is to treat every exam question as if it were the most important. The adaptive scoring algorithm attempts to discover a pattern of responses that reflects some level of proficiency with the subject matter.

Incorrect responses almost guarantee that additional questions must be answered (unless, of course, you get every question wrong). This is because the scoring algorithm must adjust to information that is not consistent with the emerging pattern.

Case-Study Form

The case-study-based format first appeared with the advent of the 70-100 exam (Solution Architectures). The questions in the case-study format are not the independent entities that they are in the fixed and adaptive formats. Instead, questions are tied to a case study, a long scenario-like description of an information technology situation. As the test taker, your job is to extract from the case study the information that needs to be integrated with your understanding of Microsoft technology. The idea is that a case study provides you with a situation that is even more like a real-life problem situation than the other formats provide.

The case studies are presented as *testlets*. These are sections within the exam in which you read the case study and then answer 10–15 questions that apply to the case study. When you finish that section, you move on to another testlet with another case study and its associated questions. As many as five of these testlets can compose the overall exam. You are given more time to complete such an exam because reading through the cases and analyzing them takes time. You might have as much as three hours to complete the exam—and you might need all of it. The case studies are always available through a linking button while you are in a testlet. However, after you leave a testlet, you cannot come back to it.

Figure 3 provides an illustration of part of such a case study.

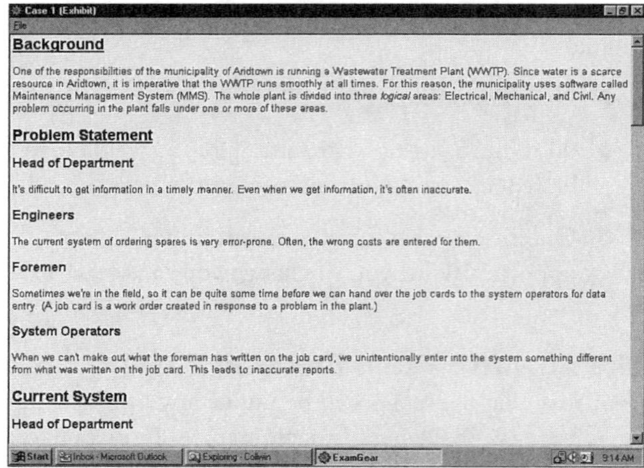

FIGURE 3
An example of a case study.

Question Types

A variety of question types can appear on MCP exams. Examples of many of the various types appear in this book and the ExamGear, Training Guide Edition software. We have attempted to cover all the types that were available at the time of this writing. Most of the question types discussed in the following sections can appear in each of the three exam formats.

The typical MCP exam question is based on the idea of measuring skills or the ability to complete tasks. Therefore, most of the questions are written so as to present you with a situation that includes a role (such as a system administrator or technician), a technology environment (for example, 100 computers running Windows 98 on a Windows 2000 Server network), and a problem to be solved (for instance, the user can connect to services on the LAN but not the intranet). The answers indicate actions you might take to solve the problem or create setups or environments that would function correctly from the start. Keep this in mind as you read the questions on the exam. You might encounter some questions that just call for you to regurgitate facts, but these will be relatively few and far between.

In the following sections we will look at the various question types.

Multiple-Choice Questions

Despite the variety of question types that now appear in various MCP exams, the multiple-choice question is still the basic building block of the exams. The multiple-choice question comes in three varieties:

- **Regular multiple-choice**—Also referred to as an *alphabetic* question, it asks you to choose one answer as correct.
- **Multiple-answer multiple-choice**—Also referred to as a *multi-alphabetic* question, this version of a multiple-choice question requires you to choose two or more answers as correct. Typically, you are told precisely the number of correct answers to choose.
- **Enhanced multiple-choice**—This is simply a regular or multiple-answer question that includes a graphic or table to which you must refer to answer the question correctly.

Examples of such questions appear at the end of each chapter.

Simulation Questions

Simulation-based questions reproduce the look and feel of key Microsoft product features for the purpose of testing. The simulation software used in MCP exams has been designed to look and act, as much as possible, just like the actual product. Consequently, answering simulation questions in an MCP exam entails completing one or more tasks just as if you were using the product itself.

The format of a typical Microsoft simulation question consists of a brief scenario or problem statement, along with one or more tasks you must complete to solve the problem. An example of a simulation question for MCP exams is shown in the following section.

A Typical Simulation Question

It sounds obvious, but your first step when you encounter a simulation question is to carefully read the question (see Figure 4). Do not go straight to the simulation application! You must assess the problem that's presented and identify the conditions that make up the problem scenario. Note the tasks that must be performed or outcomes that must be achieved to answer the question, and then review any instructions you're given on how to proceed.

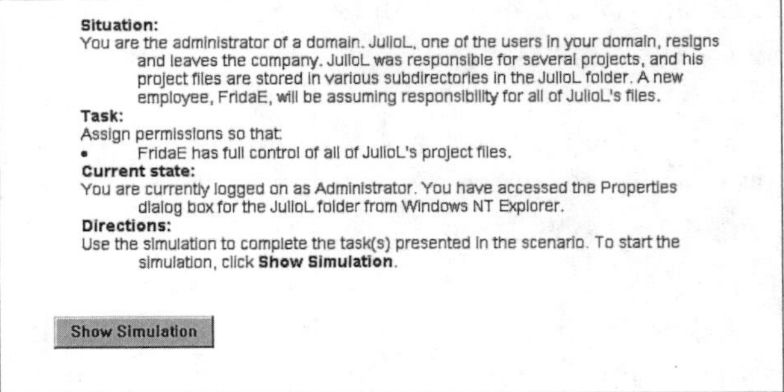

FIGURE 4
Typical MCP exam simulation question with directions.

The next step is to launch the simulator by using the button provided. After clicking the Show Simulation button, you will see a feature of the product, as shown in the dialog box in Figure 5. The simulation application will partially obscure the question text on many test center machines. Feel free to reposition the simulator and to move between the question text screen and the simulator by using hotkeys, using point-and-click navigation, or even by clicking the simulator's launch button again.

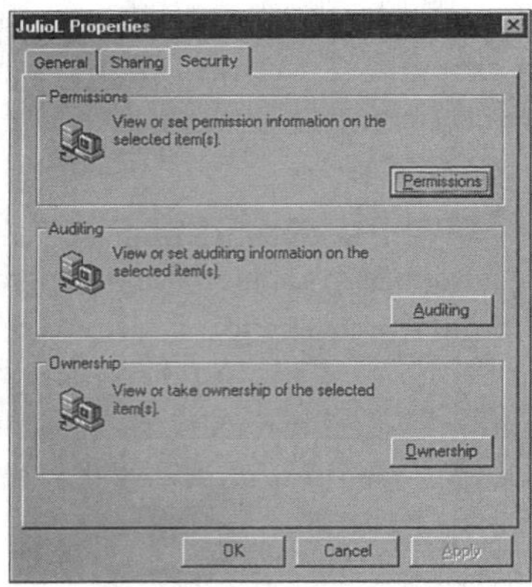

FIGURE 5
Launching the simulation application.

It is important for you to understand that your answer to the simulation question is not recorded until you move on to the next exam question. This gives you the added capability of closing and reopening the simulation application (using the launch button) on the same question without losing any partial answer you might have made.

The third step is to use the simulator as you would the actual product to solve the problem or perform the defined tasks. Again, the simulation software is designed to function—within reason—just as the product does. But don't expect the simulator to reproduce product behavior perfectly. Most importantly, do not allow yourself to become flustered if the simulator does not look or act exactly like the product.

Figure 6 shows the solution to the example simulation problem.

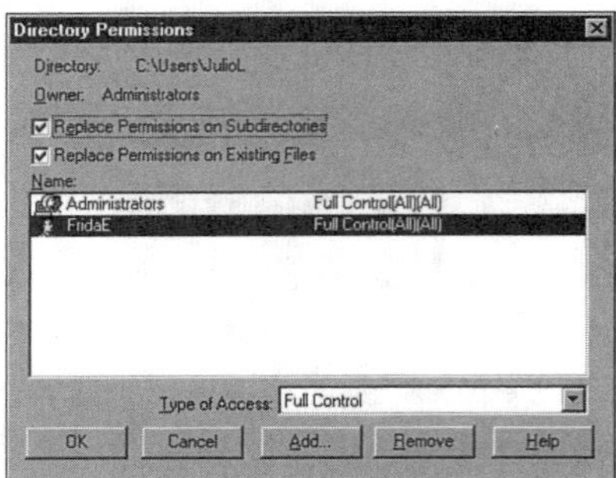

FIGURE 6
The solution to the simulation example.

Two final points will help you tackle simulation questions. First, respond only to what is being asked in the question; do not solve problems you are not asked to solve. Second, accept what is being asked of you. You might not entirely agree with conditions in the problem statement, the quality of the desired solution, or the sufficiency of defined tasks to adequately solve the problem. Always remember that you are being tested on your ability to solve the problem as it is presented.

The solution to the simulation problem shown in Figure 6 perfectly illustrates both of those points. As you'll recall from the question scenario (refer to Figure 4), you were asked to assign appropriate permissions to a new user, Frida E. You were not instructed to make any other changes in permissions. Thus, if you were to modify or remove the administrator's permissions, this item would be scored wrong on an MCP exam.

Hot Area Question

Hot area questions call for you to click a graphic or diagram to complete some task. You are asked a question that is similar to any other, but rather than clicking an option button or a check box next to an answer, you click the relevant item in a screen shot or on a part of a diagram. An example of such an item is shown in Figure 7.

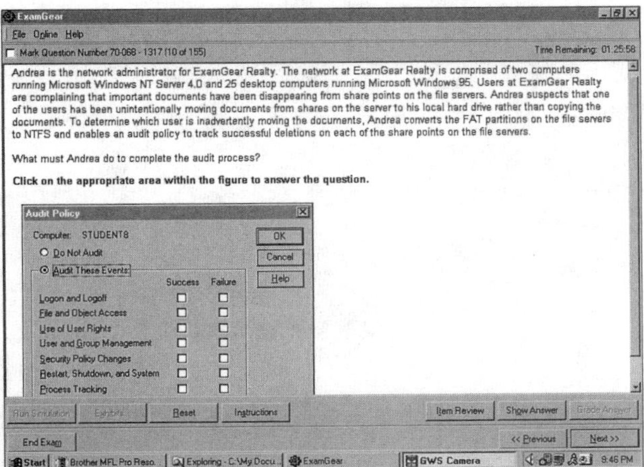

FIGURE 7
A typical hot area question.

Drag and Drop Style Questions

Microsoft has used two different types of drag-and-drop questions in exams. The first is a select-and-place question. The other is a drop-and-connect question. Both are covered in the following sections.

Select-and-Place

Select-and-place questions typically require you to drag and drop labels on images in a diagram so as to correctly label or identify some portion of a network. Figure 8 shows you the actual question portion of a select-and-place item.

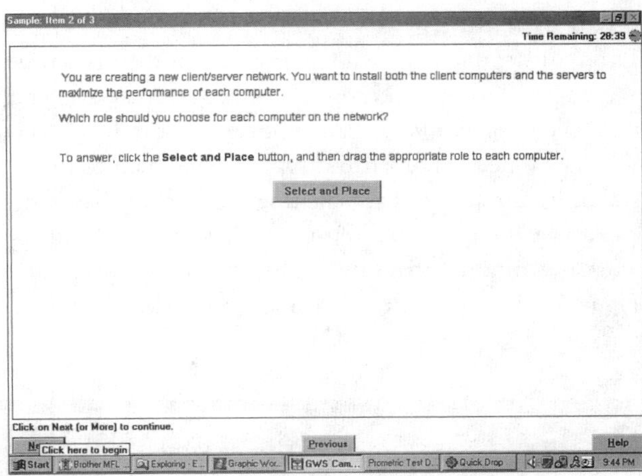

FIGURE 8
A select-and-place question.

Figure 9 shows the window you would see after you chose Select and Place. It contains the actual diagram in which you would select and drag the various server roles and match them up with the appropriate computers.

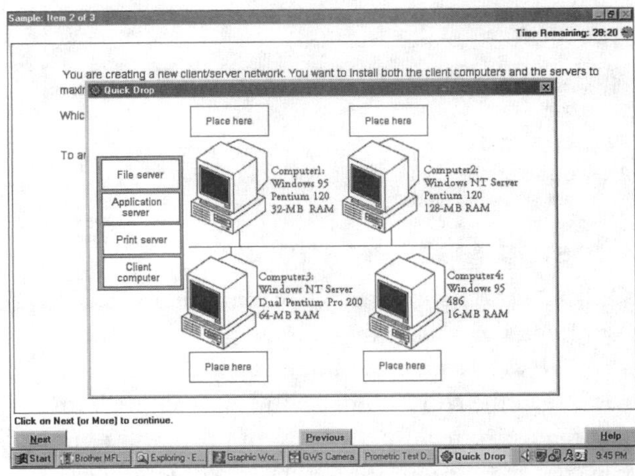

FIGURE 9
The window containing the diagram.

Drop-and-Connect

Drop-and-connect questions provide a different spin on the drag-and-drop question. The question provides you with the opportunity to create boxes you can label, as well as connectors of various types with which to link them. In essence, you are creating a model or diagram to answer the question. You might have to create a network diagram or a data model for a database system. Figure 10 illustrates the idea of a drop-and-connect question.

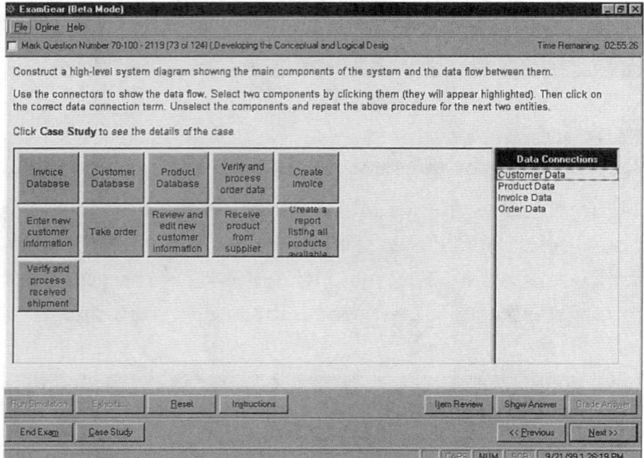

FIGURE 10
A drop-and-connect question.

Ordered List Questions

Ordered list questions simply require you to consider a list of items and place them in the proper order. You select items and then use a button to add them to a new list in the correct order. You have another button you can use to remove the items in the new list in case you change your mind and want to reorder things. Figure 11 shows an ordered list item.

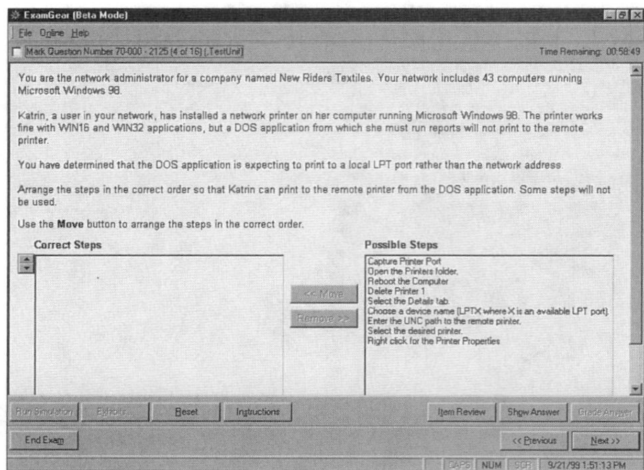

FIGURE 11
An ordered list question.

Tree Questions

Tree questions require you to think hierarchically and categorically. You are asked to place items from a list into categories that are displayed as nodes in a tree structure. Such questions might ask you to identify parent/child relationships in processes or the structure of keys in a database. You might also be required to show order within the categories much as you would in an ordered list question. Figure 12 shows a typical tree question.

As you can see, Microsoft is making an effort to use question types that go beyond asking you to simply memorize facts. These question types force you to know how to accomplish tasks and understand concepts and relationships. Study so that you can answer these types of questions rather than those that simply ask you to recall facts.

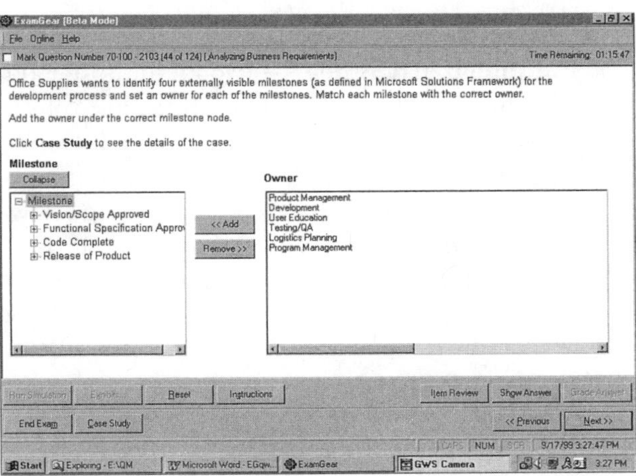

FIGURE 12
A tree question.

Putting It All Together

Given all these different pieces of information, the task now is to assemble a set of tips that will help you successfully tackle the various types of MCP exams.

More Exam Preparation Tips

Generic exam-preparation advice is always useful. Tips include the following:

- **Become familiar with the product**—Hands-on experience is one of the keys to success on any MCP exam. Review the exercises and the Step-By-Steps in the book.
- **Review the current exam-preparation guide on the Microsoft MCP Web site**—The documentation Microsoft makes available over the Web identifies the skills every exam is intended to test.
- **Memorize foundational technical detail**—But remember that MCP exams are generally heavier on problem solving and application of knowledge than on questions that require only rote memorization.
- **Take any of the available practice tests**—We recommend the one included in this book and the ones you can create using the ExamGear software on the CD-ROM. As a supplement to the material bound with this book, try the free practice tests available on the Microsoft MCP Web site.
- **Look on the Microsoft MCP Web site for samples and demonstration items**—These tend to be particularly valuable for one significant reason: They help you become familiar with new testing technologies before you encounter them on MCP exams.

During the Exam Session

The following generic exam-taking advice that you've heard for years also applies when you're taking an MCP exam:

- **Take a deep breath and try to relax when you first sit down for your exam session**—It is very important that you control the pressure you might (naturally) feel when taking exams.
- **You will be provided scratch paper**—Take a moment to write down any factual information and technical detail that you committed to short-term memory.
- **Carefully read all information and instruction screens**—These displays have been put together to give you information relevant to the exam you are taking.
- **Accept the nondisclosure agreement and preliminary survey as part of the examination process**—Complete them accurately and quickly move on.
- **Read the exam questions carefully**—Reread each question to identify all relevant detail.

- **Tackle the questions in the order in which they are presented**—Skipping around won't build your confidence; the clock is always counting down (at least in the fixed-form exams).
- **Don't rush, but also don't linger on difficult questions**—The questions vary in degree of difficulty. Don't let yourself be flustered by a particularly difficult or wordy question.
- **As for changing your answers, the general rule of thumb here is *don't***—If you read the question carefully and completely and you felt like you knew the right answer, you probably did. Don't second-guess yourself. If, as you check your answers, one clearly stands out as incorrect, however, of course you should change it. But if you are at all unsure, go with your first impression.

Fixed-Form Exams

Building from this basic preparation and test-taking advice, you also need to consider the challenges presented by the various exam designs. Because a fixed-form exam is composed of a fixed, finite set of questions, add these tips to your strategy for taking a fixed-form exam:

- **Note the time allotted and the number of questions on the exam you are taking**—Make a rough calculation of how many minutes you can spend on each question, and use this figure to pace yourself through the exam.
- **Take advantage of the fact that you can return to and review skipped or previously answered questions**—Record the questions you can't answer confidently on the scratch paper provided, noting the relative difficulty of each question. When you reach the end of the exam, return to the more difficult questions.
- **If you have session time remaining after you complete all the questions (and if you aren't too fatigued!), review your answers**—Pay particular attention to questions that seem to have a lot of detail or that require graphics.

Adaptive Exams

If you are planning to take an adaptive exam, keep these additional tips in mind:

- **Read and answer every question with great care**—When you're reading a question, identify every relevant detail, requirement, or task you must perform and double-check your answer to be sure you have addressed every one of them.
- **If you cannot answer a question, use the process of elimination to reduce the set of potential answers, and then take your best guess**—Stupid mistakes invariably mean that additional questions will be presented.
- **You cannot review questions and change answers**—When you leave a question, whether you've answered it or not, you cannot return to it. Do not skip any question, either; if you do, it's counted as incorrect.

Case-Study Exams

This new exam format calls for unique study and exam-taking strategies. When you take this type of exam, remember that you have more time than in a typical exam. Take your time and read the case study thoroughly. Use the scrap paper or whatever medium is provided to you to take notes, diagram processes, and actively seek out the important information.

Work through each testlet as if each were an independent exam. Remember, you cannot go back after you have left a testlet. Refer to the case study as often as you need to, but do not use that as a substitute for reading it carefully initially and for taking notes.

This format has appeared most often in the exams with a "Design" designation.

FINAL CONSIDERATIONS

Finally, several changes in the MCP program impact how frequently you can repeat an exam and what you will see when you do:

- **Microsoft has instituted a new exam retake policy**—The new rule is "two and two, then one and two." That is, you can attempt any exam twice with no restrictions on the time between attempts. But after the second attempt, you must wait two weeks before you can attempt that exam again. After that, you will be required to wait two weeks between subsequent attempts. Plan to pass the exam in two attempts, or plan to increase your time horizon for receiving the MCP credential.
- **New questions are always being seeded into the MCP exams**—After performance data is gathered on new questions, the examiners replace older questions on all exam forms. This means the questions appearing on exams regularly change.
- **Many of the current MCP exams might be republished in adaptive form**—The exception to this might be the case-study exams because the adaptive approach might not work with that format.

These changes mean that the brute-force strategies for passing MCP exams have lost their viability. So, if you don't pass an exam on the first or second attempt, it is likely that the exam's form could change significantly by the next time you take it. It could be updated from fixed-form to adaptive, or it could have a different set of questions or question types.

Microsoft's intention is not to make the exams more difficult by introducing unwanted change, but to create and maintain valid measures of the technical skills and knowledge associated with the various MCP credentials. Preparing for an MCP exam has always involved not only studying the subject matter, but also planning for the testing experience itself. With the continuing changes, this is now more true than ever.

This exam consists of 60 questions that reflect the material you covered in the chapters and are representative of the types of questions you should expect to see on the actual exam.

The answers to the questions appear in their own section following the exam. It is strongly suggested that when you take this exam, you treat it just as you would an actual exam at the test center. Time yourself, read carefully, and answer all the questions to the best of your ability.

Most of the questions do not simply require you to recall facts but require deduction on your part to determine the best answer. Most questions require you to identify the best course of action to take in a given situation. Many of the questions are verbose, requiring you to read them carefully and thoroughly before you attempt to answer them. Run through the exam, and for questions you miss, review any material associated with them.

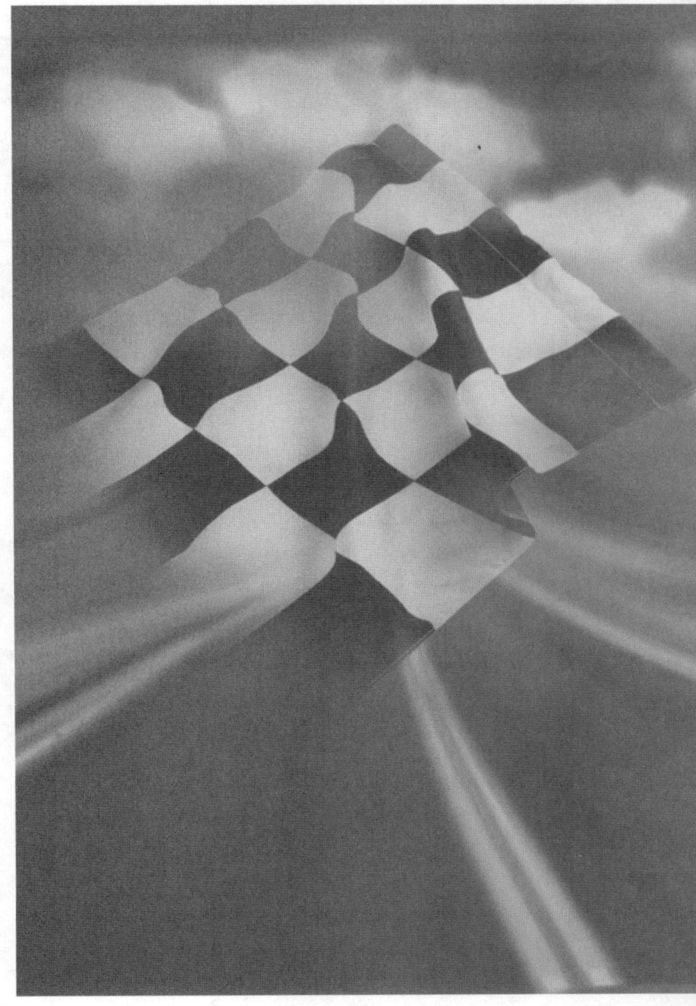

Practice Exam

EXAM QUESTIONS

1. A brand new, top-of-the-line workstation has just arrived in your office, and you are about to install Windows 2000 Professional for the first time. The system contains a new SCSI controller interface that is not on the HCL, but a driver has been provided by the manufacturer of the system. You tried to install Windows 2000 following the basic steps, but each time the system restarts, it stops. It seems the system can't access any of the SCSI drives because the driver is not installed. What should you do to load the new SCSI driver during the installation of Windows 2000?

   A. Boot from the driver disk that the manufacturer provided. Windows 2000 will recognize the SCSI devices and continue with the setup properly.

   B. During the final phase of setup, press F8 to install additional drivers for mass storage.

   C. During the first phase of setup, press F6 to load additional drivers for mass storage.

   D. Install the manufacturer's drivers on the boot disk using the makeboot.exe utility.

   E. Windows 2000 can't be installed on a system with hardware that is not on the HCL.

2. During a planning session you are asked what would be the best way to allow clients to have access to their files from any system in the network while still maintaining a secured environment. What would you propose? (Select two answers.)

   A. Set up roaming profiles.

   B. Have all users save their files in the `Mydocuments` folder.

   C. Set up a home share on an NTFS partition on the server. Allow everyone full control over the share.

   D. Configure each user with a Home directory that points to `\\server\home\%username%`, where `\\server` is a network server and `\home` is a shared folder.

   E. Set up a home share on a FAT partition. Allow everyone full control over the share.

   F. Configure each user account to use redirected folders as its home directory.

3. Alexander is a member of the Sales and the Accounting groups. You have given the Sales group Read permission and the Accounting group Change permission. Alexander is unable to access the folder. What is the most likely cause of the problem?

   A. The folder is marked as Read Only at the NTFS level.

   B. The files in the folder are marked as Read Only at the NTFS level.

   C. Alexander has not been added to the list of users with at least Read access.

   D. Alexander must have No Access assigned to his user account.

   E. The group Everyone has been removed from the list of users with access.

4. You are the network administrator for Balzac Petroleum. You are concerned that certain files are being accessed on your network without proper permissions. What can you do to prevent unauthorized users access?

   A. Change the default permission to Everyone Denied Access and add groups only as needed with the appropriate permissions.

B. Remove the default group Everyone and delete the Guest account.

C. Remove the default group Everyone and add groups only as needed with the appropriate permissions.

D. Remove the default Guest Accounts permissions on all files and add groups only as needed with the appropriate permissions.

E. Remove the default group Authenticated Users and add groups only as needed with the appropriate permissions.

5. A client would like to send you a report but tells you her email is unavailable, although she still has access to the Internet for Web browsing. You do not want her to dial in to your office. How can she send you a copy of the report without the risk of sending a virus to your servers?

A. She can connect to your Web server and upload the file.

B. She can connect to your FTP site and upload the file.

C. She can connect to your intranet site server and upload the file.

D. She can print to one of your office printers that has been shared over the Internet.

E. She can't send the report until her email has been fixed.

6. As the administrator of a small legal firm, you want to maintain certain desktop configuration standards in the organization. Which tool can you use to maintain control?

A. Group policy

B. Remote access control

C. System management

D. Intellimirror

E. Roaming profiles

7. You have decided to implement policies that will allow users to maintain a certain desktop configuration standard. You want to allow users the ability to change some personal settings, however. What do you need to do to ensure each user maintains his own settings if he shares a computer?

A. Change each user to roaming profiles.

B. Do nothing. Roaming profiles are on by default.

C. Do nothing. Local profiles will take care of each user's settings.

D. Each user must save his settings to his home folder.

E. This can't be done. All users on a system will share settings.

8. Two users are sharing a useraccount. You want to prevent the two from changing the settings that might confuse the other. What can be done?

A. Change `NTUser.dat` to `Ntuser.one`.

B. Restrict roaming profiles.

C. Disable profiles.

D. Copy `NTUser.dat` to `Ntuser.man`.

E. Rename `Ntuser.dat` to `Ntuser.man`.

9. You need to ensure that all users have the same applications ready for them to use regardless of which computer they use in the office. Which Windows 2000 Professional feature should you implement?

A. Group policy

B. Remote software installation

C. System management server installations

D. RIS (Remote Installation Server)

E. Roaming profiles

10. You are in charge of configuring TCP/IP for all the client computers and servers on your network. All clients are DHCP enabled. When you first installed the DHCP server, a Class B subnet mask was chosen. You have reconfigured the DHCP server to use a Class C subnet mask. A user calls and says she can't connect to any servers on the network. Which command would you tell the user to type to find out her IP address?

A. `NBTSTAT -c`

B. `IPCONFIG /ALL`

C. `IPCONFIG /RELEASE`

D. `PING SERVERa`

11. You are troubleshooting a connectivity problem and a Windows 2000 Professional computer. Using the `PING` command, place the following steps in the recommended order:

Ping the remote host.

Ping the address of 127.0.0.1.

Ping the local host.

Ping the gateway.

1st______________________________

2nd______________________________

3rd______________________________

4th______________________________

12. You are an administrator of a small office that has 10 Windows 2000 Professional computers. To connect to the Internet, you have shared an Internet connection. One of the users in the office can't connect to your computer to access the Internet. When you run `IPCONFIG` on his computer, you see that the address assigned to his computer is 10.1.54.232. Which of the following address ranges should his IP address fall between?

A. 1.0.0.1 and 1.255.255.254

B. 192.168.0.1 and 192.168.255.254

C. 191.191.0.1 and 191.194.0.1

D. 224.224.244.1 and 224.224.244.254

13. You are the network administrator for a network that has 50 users who dial in from home. A help desk analyst has asked you to explain the differences between SLIP and PPP. Which of the following would you tell the analyst apply only to PPP? (Select two.)

A. Supports TCP/IP, IPX, and NetBEUI.

B. Passwords are sent as clear text.

C. Usually needs scripting to complete log on.

D. Supports encryption for authentication.

E. No error detection.

F. Can be used only for dial out.

14. You are the network administrator of an office that consists of three Window 2000 Servers computers, one Novell 3.12 file server computer, and 50 Windows 2000 Professional computers. Of the Windows 2000 Professional computers, 25 are running NetBEUI and IPX/SPX. The rest of the Windows 2000 Professional computers are running TCP/IP. Users are complaining that they can't communicate with one another across your network.

You need to fix the problem.

Required Results:

All clients must be able to communicate with one another.

All clients must be able to access the Internet.

Optional Desired Results:

All clients must be able to communicate with the Novell server.

Proposed Solution:

On each client computer, install TCP/IP only.

Which results does the proposed solution produce?

A. The proposed solution produces the required results and the optional desired result.

B. The proposed solution produces one of the required results and the optional desired result.

C. The proposed solution produces the required results but not the optional desired result.

D. The proposed solution does not produce the required results nor the optional desired result.

15. You are the help desk manager. You are creating a chart that will enable the help desk analysts to understand the differences between built-in global groups and built-in local groups. Which of the following are built-in local groups? (Select all that apply.)

 A. Guests

 B. Administrators

 C. Domain Admins

 D. Power Users

 E. Everyone

 F. Domain Users

 G. Managers

16. You are an administrator of a Windows 2000 network, and you have configured a Windows 2000 server as a domain controller. You want to add several domain-level users to local groups on the server to implement a local security model, but you can't find any local groups on the server itself. Why?

 A. On a domain controller, local groups are part of the Windows 2000 domain.

 B. On a domain controller, local groups are part of Active Directory.

 C. On a domain controller, local groups are part of the domain group and, therefore, are not visible.

 D. On a domain controller, global groups are part of Active Directory.

17. As an administrator, you are responsible for creating a global management system to control all your company's print queues. You need to be able to pause and resume a printer; view, pause, resume, and cancel documents; and view the properties of your printers. What should you do to enable this functionality?

 A. Install Terminal Services on the server and then use the properties for the individual printer to pause, resume, and cancel documents and view the properties of your printers.

 B. Install a remote control package to the server and then use the properties for the individual printer to control that printer.

 C. Install Internet Information Server (IIS) on the server and use it to pause and resume a printer; view, pause, resume, and cancel documents; and view the properties of your printers.

 D. You can't enable this type of functionality with Windows 2000 Server.

18. You are an administrator of a Windows 2000 Server domain. You are told by the human resources department that an employee is being terminated today. What is the first thing you should do to keep that user from logging in to the network?

   A. Remove the check from the Account Is Disabled check box.

   B. Check the Account Is Disabled check box.

   C. Delete the user account.

   D. Rename the user account.

19. You are an administrator of a Windows 2000 domain. You need to design a remote access solution for your company. Security is very important. What are the remote access authentication methods available in Windows 2000? (Select all that apply.)

   A. EAP

   B. KERBEROS

   C. MS-CHAP V2

   D. CHAP

   E. SLIP

   F. SPAP

   G. PAP

   H. POP

20. You are an administrator of a Windows 2000 domain located in the XYZ Company. You are designing the login process for all the users at this company. You need all users to be able to log in to the Windows 2000 infrastructure from any Windows 2000-based computer. You also have several users who will never log in at any computer other than their own. Management wants to understand which options are available. You need to be able to explain all the potential options and what they do. What different kinds of user profiles are available in Windows 2000?

   A. Local, roaming, and mandatory

   B. Local, roaming, and required

   C. Local, mandatory, and secure

   D. Roaming, local, and directory-based

21. You are an administrator for a large number of Windows 2000 servers. You have been asked to set up a permission structure to protect resources available on a network. What is the recommended method for adding users to groups to protect resources?

   A. Users → global groups → domain local groups → permission to access resources

   B. Users → global groups → groups → permission to access resources

   C. Users → local groups → global groups → permission to access resources

   D. Users → groups → permission to access resources

22. You are an administrator of your company's Windows 2000 domain. Your corporate security office has decided that a RADIUS-based authentication process must be used to validate all dial-in users. What should you do?

   A. Install Dial-Up Networking and use the default settings.

   B. Install Internet Authentication Services (IAS) and configure it to use the corporate RADIUS server.

   C. Install Terminal Server and configure it to accept only remote logins to allow for access into the corporate network.

D. Install Internet Information Server and configure it for remote authentication.

23. You are an administrator of a Windows 2000 server farm that will be used for intranet access within your company. You are building a secure intranet site. During testing, you find you are having problems connecting to the test site. It appears to be an authentication problem. Which authentication type does the system attempt to use first when connecting to the site?

    A. Anonymous

    B. Authenticated

    C. Anonymous using port 8080

    D. Authenticated using the port assigned to the Administrators Web site

24. You are an administrator of a Windows 2000 server and need to limit access to the resources on that server. What does the special local NTFS security permission Transverse Folder/Execute File do?

    A. The permission allows or denies a user the ability to Read Extended Attributes on a folder to which she does not have access.

    B. The permission allows or denies a user the ability to synchronize files on a folder to which she does not have access.

    C. The permission allows or denies a user the ability to List Folder/Read Data on a folder to which she does not have access.

    D. The permission allows or denies a user the ability to pass through a folder to which she does not have access.

25. You are an administrator of a large Windows NT 4.0 server farm. Management wants to determine the advantages and disadvantages of upgrading the existing server farm to a Windows 2000 environment. In particular, they are concerned about security for several of the applications that run on member servers. Management is asking for the definition of a local user on a Windows 2000 member server. What do you tell them?

    A. A user who is logged onto the Windows 2000 member server

    B. A user who exists only on the Windows 2000 member server and does not exist in the domain's Active Directory

    C. A user account from an NT 4 domain who logs in to a Windows 2000 member server

    D. A user who exists on the Windows 2000 domain controller

26. You are an administrator of a Windows 2000 environment and are attempting to implement quotas for a Windows 2000 server. Quotas are set for individuals and not for groups. You have yet to choose your file system. What should you first install?

    A. Install HPFS.

    B. Install NTFS.

    C. Install FAT.

    D. Install FAT32.

27. An application developer has been attempting to create a share on a Windows 2000 member server but has been unable to complete the task. You check and determine that he is not in the Administrators group. What should you do to ensure the developer has the minimum necessary permission to create shares on the member server?

    A. Add the developer to the Domain Admins and Power Users groups on the local computer.

    B. Add the developer to the Administrators or Power Users group on the local computer.

C. Add the developer to the Power Users and Account Operators group on the local computer.

D. Add the developer to the Administrators and Power Users groups on the domain controller.

28. You are writing a justification document and need to explain why the Plug and Play manager is so important to the concept of reducing the cost of PC maintenance. What does the Plug and Play manager do? (Select two.)

 A. It ensures that all Plug and Play-compatible devices are automatically detected and that their drivers are installed.

 B. It delivers the capability to configure printer queues automatically.

 C. It increases the potential that Windows 2000 will locate devices that are not Plug and Play and have their drivers installed.

 D. It automates the process of installing software updates to the operating systems.

29. You have been tasked with creating a secure remote access solution for your company. You are investigating which options Windows 2000 provides. What are the tunneling protocols available under Windows 2000 Remote Access Services? (Select two.)

 A. Point to Point Tunneling Protocol

 B. Layer Two Tunneling Protocol

 C. Layer Four Tunneling Protocol

 D. VPN Tunneling Protocol

30. You are an administrator for a Windows 2000 server farm for a small company. Your boss has come to you and expressed concern about people on the Internet being able to see the IP addresses of computers on your intranet. Which feature of Windows 2000 would address her concerns?

 A. Encryption

 B. Network Address Translation

 C. Packet filtering

 D. Security authentication

31. You are an administrator for a Windows 2000 Server that is configured for dual booting. You have NT 4.0 on one partition and Windows 2000 Server on another partition, and you have enabled compression on the Windows 2000 partition. Now the Windows NT 4.0 partition can't read anything on the Windows 2000 partition. The file system versions do not appear to be compatible. What can you do to resolve the problem?

 A. Don't dual boot. This problem can't be fixed.

 B. Apply Service Pack 3 to the NT 4.0 partition to enable it to read from the Windows 2000 Server file system.

 C. Apply Service Pack 4 to the NT 4.0 partition to enable it to read from the Windows 2000 Server file system.

 D. Compatibility is problematic. Many features of the Windows 2000 file system are not supported in NT 4.0.

32. You have just completed the installation of a Windows 2000 server, and you discover that no one can access it from the network. Which tools are available to troubleshoot TCP/IP on a Windows 2000 server? (Select three.)

 A. `NETSTATE`

 B. `IPCONFIG`

 C. `PING`

 D. `TRACERT`

33. You are attempting to Web share a folder, but the Web share function is not available. You determine this is because you do not have the correct access rights to complete the function. Which level of access must you have to be able to Web share a folder?

   A. Administrator or Server Manager access

   B. Administrator or Power User access

   C. Power User, Server Manager, or Administrator access

   D. Power User, Backup Operator, or Administrator access

34. You are an administrator for several Windows 2000 servers. Purchasing has come to you and asked that you provide the hardware (memory, CPU, and disk size) requirements to support a client computer using Terminal Services for Windows 2000 Server. What are the minimum requirements for a client computer to use Terminal Services?

   A. A Windows for Workgroups (Windows 3.11) client computer with 16MB of memory, a 386 processor, and a network card

   B. A Windows 95/98 client computer with 32MB of memory, a 486 processor, and a network card

   C. A Windows NT 3.51 client computer with 24MB of memory, a Pentium Pro processor, and a network card

   D. A Windows for Workgroups (Windows 3.11) client computer with 32MB of memory, a 386 processor, and a network card

35. You have installed DNS and configured your server as a cache-only server. Where does it store the zone information?

   A. In your `%systemroot%\DNS` directory.

   B. In your `%systemroot%\system32\DNS` directory.

   C. The information is stored in Active Directory.

   D. Cache-only servers do not have any zone information.

36. You are the network administrator for JMS Technologies. You have a network with 100 computers running Windows 2000 Professional and 3 computers running Windows 2000 Server configured with Active Directory, DHCP, and DDNS. When your client computer obtains an IP address from the DHCP server, who registers the computer's host name with the DNS server?

   A. The client computer

   B. The DHCP server

   C. The WINS server

   D. Active Directory

37. You are the network administrator for Long Beach Networks. Your network consists of 100 computers running Windows 95, 125 computers running Windows 98, and 240 computers running Windows 2000 Professional. All computers are located on the same network segment. Lynne, your supervisor, has asked you to automate the process of assigning IP addresses (the addresses range is from 130.67.5.1 to 130.67.6.254). What do you need to configure?

   A. Install DHCP and configure DNS integration.

   B. Install DHCP and configure a scope.

   C. Install DHCP and configure a superscope.

   D. Install DHCP and configure BOOTP.

38. A small computer-training company has decided to install the DNS services on its network to replace the one currently supplied by its ISP. Your network currently consists of 300 Windows 2000 Professional computers.

    You are hired as a setup consultant to provide a solution for this small training company.

    Required Results:

    Provide an easy way to configure your client computers with the IP address of your DNS server.

    Provide a backup strategy to ensure that your client computers will always have a DNS server available.

    Optional Desired Results:

    Your network must be able to resolve FQDNs to IP addresses.

    Your network must be able to resolve IP addresses to host names.

    Update the client computer information in DNS automatically.

    Proposed Solution:

    Install Windows 2000 Advanced Server and configure it with DNS and Active Directory.

    You install and configure a second DNS server. This server will be configured as the secondary master to your first DNS server.

    In your MMC DNS applet, you configure a forward lookup zone.

    IN your MMC DNS applet, you configure a reverse lookup zone.

    Configure your client computers to use DHCP.

    Your DHCP server has been configured to assign an IP address with a subnet mask, a default gateway, and the IPs of your DNS server.

    Which result(s) does the proposed solution produce?

    A. The proposed solution produces all the required results and all the optional desired results.

    B. The proposed solution produces one of the required results and all the optional desired results.

    C. The proposed solution produces all the required results and one of the optional results.

    D. The proposed solution produces all the required results and two of the optional desired results.

    E. The proposed solution produces none of the required results and none of the optional desired results.

39. You are part of the team of network administrators for SunShine Networks. Your task is to segment your Class C IP address into three subnets. You have been assigned the IP address of 210.115.64.0. You must allow for the number of networks to increase. The maximum number of hosts per subnet will never surpass 14 hosts. Which subnet mask would enable you to segment your network and allow for the required growth?

    A. 255.255.255.224

    B. 255.255.255.240

    C. 255.255.255.248

    D. 255.255.255.255

40. You are the senior network administrator for JMS Technologies. Your client complains that the company lost all network connectivity after installing some new services. He also mentions that they might have misconfigured a setting. When you ask which services they installed, he

answers that they are not certain. To try to troubleshoot the server, you type **IPCONFIG /ALL** at a command prompt and receive the following. What could be the problem?

IP address	192.168.0.1
Subnet mask	255.255.0.0
Default gateway	192.168.0.1
DNS server	192.168.0.1
WINS server	192.168.0.1

A. Your IP address is the same as the default gateway.

B. They installed ICS by mistake.

C. They installed NAT by mistake.

D. Your DNS server is the same as your default gateway.

41. You are the network supervisor for CMS Networks. Your network consists of 100 computers running Windows 2000 Professional, 4 computers running Windows 2000 Server, and 2 computers running NetWare 5.1 Server. You are trying to configure ICS on your server, but you are not able to install the ICS component. What could explain why you don't have the option to install ICS?

A. Your IP address is not set to 192.168.0.1.

B. You have configured your DNS server.

C. You have not installed your DHCP server.

D. You have not installed your dial-up connection.

42. You are the network administrator for JMS Technologies and are trying to determine which settings (in addition to an IP address with your DHCP server) can be assigned to client computers running Windows 2000 Professional. (Select all that apply.)

A. The IP address of your DNS server

B. The IP address of your DHCP server

C. The IP address of your file server

D. The IP address of your default gateway

E. The IP address of your Active Directory server

43. Your supervisor has just asked you for some advice to configure the new computers that will be arriving next week. He mentions to you that you will be receiving 30 new COMPAQ computers for the sales department. You will also be receiving 25 new IBM computers for the marketing department. As the network administrator, you are aware that these two departments are on the same physical network but will require different TCP/IP configurations. Which component of Windows 2000 Server would help you in configuring the different settings?

A. DNS services

B. Active Directory

C. DHCP services

D. Active Directory with policies

44. You are the network administrator for Balzac Petroleum. You need to manually add one record to your DNS server. Which type of record do you need to add if you want to add an alias to your DNS server?

A. A record

B. MINFO record

C. CNAME record

D. PTR record

45. A small computer-training company has decided to install the DNS services on its network to replace the one currently supplied by its ISP. Its network currently consists of 300 computers running Windows 98 and 40 computers running Windows 2000 Professional.

    You are hired as a setup consultant to provide a solution for this small training company.

    Required Results:

    Provide an easy way to configure your client computers with the IP address of your DNS server.

    Provide a backup strategy to ensure that your client's computers will always have a DNS server available.

    Optional Desired Results:

    The network must be capable of resolving FQDN to IP addresses.

    The network must be capable of resolving IP addresses to host names.

    Update the client's information in DNS automatically.

    Proposed Solution:

    Install Windows 2000 Advanced Server and configure it with DNS and Active Directory.

    Install and configure a second DNS server. This server will be configured as the secondary master to the first DNS server.

    In your MMC DNS applet, you configure a forward lookup zone.

    IN your MMC DNS applet, you configure a reverse lookup zone.

    Configure your client computers with a static IP, a default gateway, and a subnet mask.

    Which result(s) does the proposed solution produce?

    A. The proposed solution produces all the required results and all the optional desired results.

    B. The proposed solution produces one of the required results and all the optional desired results.

    C. The proposed solution produces all the required results and one of the optional results.

    D. The proposed solution produces all the required results and two of the optional desired results.

    E. The proposed solution produces none of the required results and none of the optional desired results.

46. You are the network administrator for Balzac Petroleum. You have just installed and configured your DHCP server. After the installation, the wizard asked you to activate the scope; you said yes. Staff from your company are complaining, however, that they are not obtaining any IP addresses. What could be the problem?

    A. You did not activate the server.

    B. You were not authorized to activate the scope; only administrators can activate the scope.

    C. You did not authorize the server.

    D. Your scope must be misconfigured.

47. You are the network administrator for JMS Technologies. After installing and configuring DNS on your Windows 2000 Server, you set up an Active Directory-integrated zone. Where does it store the zone information?

    A. In your `%systemroot%\DNS` directory.

    B. In your `%systemrrot%\system32\DNS` directory.

C. The information is stored in Active Directory.

D. The information is stored in cache.

48. You have a network with 100 computers running Windows 2000 Professional and 3 computers running Windows 2000 Server configured with Active Directory, DHCP, and DDNS. When your client computers obtain an IP address from the DHCP server, who registers the computers' "A" name with the DNS server?

A. The client computer

B. The DHCP server

C. The WINS server

D. Active Directory

49. You are the network administrator for Mercury Technical Solutions. You are trying to explain DNS and reverse-lookup zones to your co-workers. What would you mention that reverse lookup-zone enables users to resolve?

A. An IP address to a host name

B. A host name to an IP address

C. A host name to a MAC

D. A host name to an FQDN

50. You are the LAN administrator for the OUI Find-em detective agency. You would like to be able to verify some entries on your DNS server. Which utility should you use?

A. The Properties dialog box of your DNS server in your MMC

B. `NSLOOKUP` at a command prompt

C. `IPCONFIG` at a command prompt

D. Event Viewer

51. Vincent is the senior technical instructor for a training center, and he is trying to explain to his peers over lunch where the remote access policies of RRAS are stored on the network. Where should he say they are stored?

A. Remote access policies are stored in the user properties in Active Directory.

B. Remote access policies are stored in the computer properties in Active Directory.

C. Remote access policies are stored on the root server in Active Directory.

D. Remote access policies are stored individually on every RRAS server.

52. You are the network administrator for the ShoeBox Shoe company. During the process of configuring your WINS server, you would like some information on WINS replication. Which setting of WINS server enables one server to send notification to other WINS partners when a certain amount of changes have occurred?

A. Configure for a push partner on the Advanced tab of your WINS console.

B. Configure for a pull partner on the Advanced tab of your WINS console.

C. Configure for a push partner on the Settings tab of your WINS console.

D. Configure for a pull partner on the Settings tab of your WINS console.

53. You are the network administrator for GasUp Petroleum. All your sales representatives need to dial in to access resources on your network. The problem you are having is that different users need different rights. How can you address this issue?

A. Create a different remote access policy for the different users.

B. You must configure multiple RRAS servers with different local policies and get the different groups to dial in to their respective servers.

C. Create local policies with the policy editor.

D. It can't be done. All dial-in users will have the same rights.

54. You are the administrator of a Windows 2000 network. The network is a small network with five domain controllers and 12 Windows 2000–based servers. There are 400 client computers in the network, all of which are running Windows 2000 Professional. The users are complaining that logons are taking longer than they used to and that accessing network servers is slow at times as well. You need to correct these problems, and you suspect the replication is the problem. What should you do to correct the problem?

A. Divide the network into two or more sites.

B. Divide the network into two or more domains.

C. Divide the network into two or more organizational units.

D. Reduce the number of servers by two.

55. Your network is broken down into 12 sites. Of the 12 sites, 11 are on the same network at one location, and 1 is at a remote location that uses RRAS and demand dial routing to access the main office through a VPN on the Internet. You want to ensure that the replication will work between all sites. What should you do?

A. Create connection objects between controllers in each site.

B. Create the site links and assign the correct cost and availability.

C. Create the required site links and site link bridge.

D. Create the required site links and site link bridges, and then create connections between servers at different locations.

56. You have a remote office on your network that will be connected to the main office using a 256Kbps frame relay link before you roll out Windows 2000. You are planning the connections to the office for Active Directory. Looking at the current traffic between the offices, you anticipate the traffic in the day will consume 90% of the bandwidth, and the overnight traffic (between 6 p.m. and 6 a.m.) will use 20%. You want to ensure your users get all the bandwidth they require. What should you configure?

A. Create a script that adds the connection object at night and then removes it in the morning. Use the Task Scheduler to run the script.

B. Create a site link and configure the site link with two schedules.

C. Create a site link bridge and change the site involved every morning and every evening.

D. Create two site links with different schedules.

57. You have been adding printers to a print server you recently upgraded from Windows NT 4.0 Server to Windows 2000 Server. The five new printers you just added are all working, and when you check Active Directory, you find they are all listed. You notice that the other two printers on the system are not listed. What should you do to include these printers in Active Directory?

A. In the Properties dialog box for the printers on the Active Directory tab, make sure that List in the Directory is checked.

B. In the properties dialog box for the printers on the Sharing tab, make sure that List in the Directory is selected.

C. You will need to install the printer in Active Directory User and Computers.

D. You will need to remove and then add back the printers.

58. An older Windows 98 system is running on a Pentium 133, meaning you can't upgrade the system to Windows 2000. During the upgrade process that will take several months, you want to make sure the existing users will be able to use this printer; however, you also want Windows 2000 users to be able to work with it. What action should you take?

A. Create the printer as a local printer on a Windows 2000 server and set the port to the network name of the existing printer.

B. Create the printer as a network printer on a Windows 2000 server and set the network address to the network name of the existing printer.

C. Create the printer object in the Windows 2000 Active Directory.

D. You can't share the printer from a Windows 98 system and will need to move it at least to a Windows NT server.

59. You are in the process of delegating administrative control of an OU to a user named Sandra who will be helping manage user accounts in the domain. Using the Delegation of Control Wizard, you allow Sandra to reset passwords and change the attributes of users. Later, when Sandra is trying to reset a password, she is not able to, although she could for other users. She calls to tell you this and to have you reset the password. You are able to reset the password, and you tell her you'll look into it. What should you check?

A. You should check the permissions on the OU that you delegated.

B. You should check the permissions on Sandra's account.

C. You should check the permissions on the user's account.

D. You should rerun the Delegation of Control Wizard.

60. You design a Group Policy structure with two GPOs, one at the domain level and the other at the Sales OU level.

- At the domain level, you specify a background wallpaper and assign the policy to Authenticated Users.
- At the Sales OU level, you disable Control Panel and assign the policy to the SalesPeople security group.
- At the Sales OU level, you specify a background wallpaper and assign it to the SalesPeople security group.
- At the domain level, you specify that users can use only the Add/Remove Programs and Display portions of Control Panel.
- You configure the Sales OU GPO to block policy inheritance.
- You configure the domain-level GPO with No Override.

A user in the Sales OU logs on to the network after you have saved your changes and a refresh of the GPO has taken place on all domain controllers affected. What will be the result of your

GPO settings on the user's desktop? (Select all correct answers.)

A. Control Panel will be disabled for the user.

B. Only Add/Remove Programs and Display properties will be available in Control Panel.

C. The user will have the domain-level background wallpaper.

D. The user will have the background wallpaper specified in the Sales OU GPO.

61. What are the default Group Policy refresh intervals for computers in the domain? (Select two correct answers.)

A. Group Policy is refreshed on domain controllers every 15 minutes.

B. Group Policy is refreshed on member servers and workstations every 15 minutes.

C. Group Policy is refreshed on member servers and workstations every 90 minutes.

D. Group Policy is refreshed on domain controllers every 90 minutes.

E. Group Policy is refreshed on member servers and workstations every 5 minutes.

F. Group Policy is refreshed on domain controllers every 5 minutes.

62. The management of `scriberco.com` has decided that a uniform password policy needs to exist for all users in the enterprise. The policy should enforce a minimum password length of 6 characters, a maximum password age of 30 days, a minimum password age of 1 day, and a password history of 12 passwords.

The Active Directory structure of `scriberco.com` includes four additional subdomains called `namerica.scriberco.com`, `europe.scriberco.com`, `samerica.scriberco.com`, and `specific.scriberco.com` that have been created for administrative purposes. Because the migration to Windows 2000 has just recently been completed, no new Group Policy Objects have yet been created.

What would be the easiest way to enforce the password policy settings throughout the enterprise?

A. Modify the Default Domain Policy with the password settings.

B. Create a GPO in each domain with the password policy settings.

C. Create a GPO at the `scriberco.com` domain called Password Policy Settings with the password policy settings.

D. Link the Password Policy Settings GPO from the `scriberco.com` domain to each subdomain.

E. Move all users in the subdomains to the Users container of the `scriberco.com` domain.

Answers to Exam Questions

1. **C.** There will always be new devices introduced, and Windows 2000 will be compatible with them if the manufacturer provides the appropriate drivers. In the first phase, the installation program will try to detect the SCSI interface and will fail. At this point, you can press the F6 key to install additional drivers. The boot disk created with Makeboot.exe can't be altered with any new drivers. For more information, see "Installing and Configuring Server and Client Hardware" in

Chapter 8, "Installing and Maintaining Clients and Servers."

2. **C, D.** Using an NTFS share and `%username%` creates a folder for each user with full control assigned only to them. The shared folder on the server does not need to be protected much because the local NTFS permissions are more restrictive. Roaming profiles and `Mydocuments` would allow users to access files, but this is an unsecured method and copies all files to and from the server each time the clients log on or off the system. This can be very slow. For more information, see "Configuring User Accounts for Enhanced Security" in Chapter 2, "Sharing Resources."

3. **D.** A No Access setting overrides any other permissions. The Sales and Accounting groups would give Alexander an effective permission of Change; however, No Access overrides that. For more information, see "Sharing Resources" in Chapter 2, "Sharing Resources."

4. **C.** The default permission on all shares is Everyone has Full Control; this includes the guest account as well. Remove this permission and add only groups with the appropriate permissions. For more information, see "Sharing Resources" in Chapter 2, "Sharing Resources."

5. **D.** Sending the file through the Web or FTP servers carries the risk of sending a virus. Using Internet-based printing, the report can be sent safely. For more information, see "Connecting to a Shared Printer" in Chapter 2, "Sharing Resources."

6. **A.** Group policies from Active Directory can help maintain a standard desktop and reduce administration cost. For more information, see "Introduction to Group Policy" in Chapter 11, "Fundamentals of Group Policy."

7. **C.** Local profiles are always enabled on a Windows 2000 Professional system. As long as the users do not change computers, roaming profiles are not needed. For more information, see "Performing Basic Administration" in Chapter 10, "Fundamentals of Active Directory."

8. **E.** `Ntuser.dat` can be renamed to `NTUser.man`, and it will make the profile mandatory. Users can change settings but will not be able to save them upon exiting. Unlike Windows 9x, you can't disable profiles in Windows 2000 Professional. For more information, see "Performing Basic Administration" in Chapter 10, "Fundamentals of Active Directory."

9. **A.** Group policies from Active Directory can help publish and assign applications to users. For more information, see "Software Deployment Using Group Policy" in Chapter 11, "Fundamentals of Group Policy."

10. **B.** To find out IP information on a computer that is DHCP enabled, you use the `IPCONFIG` command. The `/ALL` switch shows you all the IP information. For more information, see "Monitoring and Troubleshooting DHCP" in Chapter 5, "Dynamic Host Configuration Protocol (DHCP)."

11. The correct order is as follows:

    Ping the address of 127.0.0.1.

    Ping the local host.

    Ping the gateway.

    Ping the remote host.

    The order reflects the path information must travel through when communicating over TCP/IP: first the stack (127.0.0.1), then the card, the gateway, and the remote host. For more information, see "Using `PING`" in Chapter 4, "TCP/IP Fundamentals."

12. **B.** When you share an Internet connection on a Windows 2000 computer, it automatically assigns DHCP addresses to clients. The addresses it assigns are between 192.168.0.1 and 192.168.255.254. For more information, see "IP Addressing" in Chapter 4, "TCP/IP Fundamentals."

13. **A, D.** Only PPP supports IPX and NetBEUI as well as TCP/IP. PPP also supports encryption of logon information if configured. For more information, see "Configuring and Troubleshooting Remote Access" in Chapter 12, "Routing and Remote Access Service Fundamentals."

14. **C.** By installing only TCP/IP, the Windows 2000 client computers can't connect to the Novell server. To connect to the Novell server, you would require IPX/SPX. For more information, see "Configuring and Troubleshooting TCP/IP on Servers and Client Computers" in Chapter 4, "TCP/IP Fundamentals."

15. **A, B, D.** Answers C and F are built-in global groups. Everyone is a System group. Managers is not a built-in group; it is a group that was created by an administrator. For more information, see "Groups in Windows 2000" in Chapter 10, "Fundamentals of Active Directory."

16. **B.** Local groups are used to control access to resources on specific computers, whether those resources are data folders or printers. On a member server or a Windows 2000 Professional workstation, the local groups are a part of the local security model for the computer. On a domain controller, local groups are part of Active Directory (something that is well beyond the scope of this book). For more information, see "Groups in Windows 2000" in Chapter 10, "Fundamentals of Active Directory."

17. **C.** If you have Internet Information Server (IIS) installed on your Windows 2000 Server, you can manage the print queue of any shared printer from a browser. You can pause and resume a printer; view, pause, resume, and cancel documents; and view the properties of your printers. For more information, see "Introduction to Internet Information Services" in Chapter 3, "Internet Information Services."

18. **B.** Selecting/checking the Account Is Disabled check box makes the user account unusable. This feature is often used when a user is no longer with the company, but you want to hold onto the account in case someone else ends up with the same job and, therefore, needs the same data access. If an account is deleted, the access that user had is removed from all ACLs. This is not a good solution to use if one person is to be replaced with another. Instead of deleting the account, you should disable the account; then, when a replacement is hired, you can rename the account with the new user's name. For more information, see "User Accounts" in Chapter 10, "Fundamentals of Active Directory."

19. **A, C, D, F, G.** The available Remote Access Authentication methods are EAP, MS-CHAP v2, CHAP, SPAP, and PAP. The Extensible Authentication Method (EAP) is an authentication method that leaves open-ended the forms of authentication available. The Microsoft Challenge Handshake Authentication Protocol version 2 (MS-CHAP v2) enables challenge-response authentication based on a two-way encryption algorithm and the user name/password combination provided. The Challenge Handshake Authentication Protocol (CHAP) method enables encrypted authentication with non-Microsoft clients computers (or MS clients not capable of using MS-CHAP v2). The Shiva Password Authentication Protocol (SPAP) is an encryption

mechanism employed by Shiva. This method is more secure than sending clear-text passwords (no encryption), but it's not as secure as MS-CHAP or CHAP. The Password Authentication Protocol (PAP) is the least secure method of authentication available in dial-up access. With this method, passwords are sent plain text without any sort of encryption. This method should be left available only if authentication is required and the client computer has no way of providing encryption. POP is not an authentication protocol. For more information, see "Configuring Authentication Protocols" in Chapter 12, "Routing and Remote Access Service Fundamentals."

20. **A.** Local profiles are stored on a specific computer and are available only from that computer. Roaming profiles are stored in a central location (such as on a file server) and are accessed when a user logs in to any machine. Mandatory profiles are roaming profiles that have been designated as read-only. For more information, see "Performing Basic Administration" in Chapter 10, "Fundamentals of Active Directory."

21. **A.** This pattern (users → global groups → local groups → permission to access resources) is given the acronym "UGLP" and pronounced "uglip." For more information, see "Performing Basic Administration" in Chapter 10, "Fundamentals of Active Directory."

22. **B.** Remote Authentication Dial-In User Service (RADIUS) is an industry standard for centralized authentication and accounting in a remote access environment. These servers are generally used in large-scale, dial-up environments such as those of an Internet service provider (ISP). Windows 2000 Server has a RADIUS client computer that is capable of using the services of a RADIUS server. Windows 2000 also has the capability to function as a RADIUS server. This implementation is referred to as Internet Authentication Services (IAS) and enables the centralization of many remote access management functions in an enterprise or a multiple-enterprise environment. For more information, see "Configuring Authentication Protocols" in Chapter 12, "Routing and Remote Access Service Fundamentals."

23. **A.** Web authentication happens at two levels: anonymous and authenticated. Anonymous access is the first method attempted when you connect to any Web site. If anonymous access is disabled, or if a Web user tries to perform a function that can't be done by an anonymous user, authenticated access is attempted. Authenticated access always prompts you for a password. Whether one is required depends on whether a password has been configured for the account being used. For more information, see "Web Site Security" in Chapter 3, "Internet Information Services."

24. **D.** The Traverse Folder/Execute File permission allows or denies users the ability to pass through (traverse) a folder to which they do not have access in order to get to a folder or file to which they do have access. This property is applicable only if the user privilege Bypass Traverse Checking is not turned on in the system policy. By default, ByPass Traverse Checking is turned on for all users, so setting this permission has no effect. For more information, see "Managing File Systems" in Chapter 1, "Data Storage and File Systems."

25. **B.** A user who exists only on the Windows 2000 member server and does not exist in the domain's Active Directory is a local user. Local users are generally created only when you need to give access to resources to someone who does not log

in to your domain. For more information, see "User Accounts" in Chapter 10, "Fundamentals of Active Directory."

26. **B.** Quotas are set at the volume (or partition) level. To implement them, the volume must be formatted using the NTFS file format because FAT does not support quotas. Quotas are set for individuals and not for groups (the Administrators group being the one exception to this rule). For more information, see "Enabling and Configuring Quotas" in Chapter 1, "Data Storage and File Systems."

27. **B.** Either the Administrators or Power Users group on the local machine is correct. These two are built-in groups (that is, they are created when the operating system is installed). Because they are built-in groups, their members have certain rights on the machine. One of the rights given to each of these groups is the ability to share files. It is important to note that whether in or out of a domain context, access to resources on a member server is completely controlled by the local security model. For more information, see "Groups in Windows 2000" in Chapter 10, "Fundamentals of Active Directory."

28. **A, C.** The ability to configure Windows 2000 properly is essential to a smooth-running operating system. Windows 2000 makes the configuration of hardware devices very easy through the implementation of the Plug and Play manager. This manager ensures that all Plug and Play-compatible devices are automatically detected and their drivers installed. Windows 2000 might locate devices that are not Plug and Play and have their drivers installed. This is especially true on hot-plug buses. As a result, the amount of time you will spend manually configuring hardware IRQs will be greatly reduced. For more information, see "Installing and Configuring Server and Client Hardware" in Chapter 8, "Installing and Maintaining Clients and Servers."

29. **A, B.** Two tunneling protocols are available under Windows 2000 Remote Access Services: Point to Point Tunneling Protocol (PPTP) and Layer Two Tunneling Protocol (L2TP). For more information, see "Configuring and Troubleshooting Remote Access" in Chapter 12, "Routing and Remote Access Service Fundamentals."

30. **B.** NAT stands for Network Address Translation, the process of translating or hiding addresses on an internal network from the external network. This is useful when a limited number of network addresses are available and you might need to use the Internet reserved address groups. NAT not only maps the internal address with a destination TCP/IP address, but also assigns a port number to the transmission. When a user connects to a Web site, it uses the outgoing port 80 and the return port 1025. When this gets to the NAT server, it forwards the request to the appropriate public address, but then it changes the return port to something else (say, 5000). When the information comes back, it is destined for port 5000. The NAT server checks its map and finds out that transmissions from this server on port 5000 are really destined for port 1025 on the appropriate private address. For more information, see "Installing NAT" in Chapter 12, "Routing and Remote Access Service Fundamentals."

31. **C.** Windows NT supports NTFS version 4, and Windows 2000 is version 5; version 5 has been enhanced to provide file encryption (among other things) and is not 100% compatible with version 4. For more information, see "File Systems" in Chapter 1, "Data Storage and File Systems."

32. **B, C, D.** `IPCONFIG` is useful in troubleshooting because it not only allows you to see what your

configuration is, but also helps you determine whether you have a TCP/IP address at all. `PING` tells you whether you can communicate with other computers using TCP/IP, whereas `TRACERT` is used to determine which route is being taken from one host to another. `NETSTATE` does not exist. For more information, see "Using `IPCONFIG`" in Chapter 4, "TCP/IP Fundamentals."

33. **B.** You must have Power User or Administrator access to Web share a folder. For more information, see "Web Services" in Chapter 3, "Internet Information Services."

34. **A.** A terminal service is a session hosting service that enables a Windows 2000 server to provide environment resources (memory, processor, hard drive), whereas a client computer provides only minimal memory and processor resources. The end result is that a client computer as "thin" as a Windows for Workgroups (Windows 3.11) client computer with 16MB of memory, a 386 processor, and a network card can emulate a Windows 2000 environment with little loss of performance over a Pentium machine with 64MB of RAM running the same applications. For more information, see "Installing, Configuring, and Troubleshooting Terminal Services" in Chapter 13, "Terminal Services Fundamentals."

35. **D.** When you configure a DNS server as cache only, it does not have any zone information. For more information, see "Introduction to DNS" in Chapter 6, "Configuring, Administering, and Troubleshooting DNS."

36. **B.** Windows 2000 client computers interact directly with the DNS server to update their A resource records. The DHCP server will update the PRT record for Windows 2000 client computers and both the A record and the PTR record for non-Windows 2000 client computers. For more information, see "Introduction to DNS" in Chapter 6, "Configuring, Administering, and Troubleshooting DNS."

37. **C.** B could be a good answer but because you have 465 computers on the same segment, you will need to get two Class C addresses and configure a superscope. For more information, see "Supernetting and Classless Interdomain Routing" in Chapter 4, "TCP/IP Fundamentals."

38. **D.** It produces all the required results but only two of the optional results. It does not update the client computer information in DNS automatically. You have not enabled dynamic update. For more information, see "Introduction to DNS" in Chapter 6, "Configuring, Administering, and Troubleshooting DNS."

39. **B.** Because the question mentions that you will never exceed 14 hosts per subnet, your correct subnet mask should be 255.255.255.240. For more information, see "Subnets and Subnet Masks" in Chapter 4, "TCP/IP Fundamentals."

40. **B.** During the process of installing ICS, your server's IP address was changed to 192.168.0.1. Because your IP address was changed from its default, you have lost all connectivity. For more information, see "Installing Internet Connection Sharing" in Chapter 12, "Routing and Remote Access Service Fundamentals."

41. **D.** ICS will not install unless you have a Network and Dial-up Connection configured. For more information, see "Installing Internet Connection Sharing" in Chapter 12, "Routing and Remote Access Service Fundamentals."

42. **A, D.** The DHCP server's primary function is to assign a unique IP address to the requesting client computers. They can also be used to assign the IP address of the DNS server, the default gateway, the WINS server, and many more. For more information, see "Introduction" in Chapter 5,

"Dynamic Host Configuration Protocol (DHCP)."

43. **C.** Configuring vendor-defined classes in DHCP server enables you to configure different IP settings. For more information, see "Configuring DHCP on Servers" in Chapter 5, "Dynamic Host Configuration Protocol (DHCP)."

44. **C.** The correct record to add to your DNS server when you want to add an alias is a CNAME record. For more information, see "Configuring, Administering, and Troubleshooting DNS" in Chapter 6, "Configuring, Administering, and Troubleshooting DNS."

45. **E.** By manually configuring your client computers with static IP with no DNS configuration, you do not obtain any of the desired or optional results. For more information, see "Configuring and Troubleshooting TCP/IP on Servers and Client Computers" in Chapter 4, "TCP/IP Fundamentals."

46. **C.** Before a Windows 2000 DHCP server will issue any IP addresses, it needs to be authorized. Only members of the enterprise admin have the right to authorize a DHCP server. For more information, see "Configuring DHCP on Servers" in Chapter 5, "Dynamic Host Configuration Protocol (DHCP)."

47. **C.** When you configure an Active Directory-integrated zone, the information is stored in Active Directory. For more information, see "Configuring, Administering, and Troubleshooting DNS" in Chapter 6, "Configuring, Administering, and Troubleshooting DNS."

48. **A.** Windows 2000 client computers interact directly with the DNS server to update their A resource records. The DHCP server updates the PTR record for Windows 2000 client computers and both the A record and the PTR record for non-Windows 2000 client computers. For more information, see "Reverse Lookups" in Chapter 6, "Configuring, Administering, and Troubleshooting DNS."

49. **A.** A reverse lookup zone enables you to resolve an IP address to a host name. For more information, see "Reverse Lookups" in Chapter 6, "Configuring, Administering, and Troubleshooting DNS."

50. **B.** `NSLOOKUP` enables you to query the DNS server to verify entries. For more information, see "Using `NSLOOKUP`" in Chapter 4, "TCP/IP Fundamentals."

51. **D.** Remote access policies are stored individually on every RRAS server. For more information, see "Configuring and Troubleshooting Remote Access" in Chapter 12, "Routing and Remote Access Service Fundamentals."

52. **A.** If you want your WINS server to send notification to replication partners that a number of changes have occurred on your WINS server, you need to select the Push option on the Advanced tab of the WINS manager. For more information, see "Installing, Configuring, and Troubleshooting WINS" in Chapter 7, "NetBIOS Name Resolution."

53. **A.** You will need to create a different remote access policy for the different users. For more information, see "Configuring and Troubleshooting Remote Access" in Chapter 12, "Routing and Remote Access Service Fundamentals."

54. **A.** Sites are used to control replication traffic in Active Directory. In this case, there is no justification to use a domain model because there are not enough systems to justify it; therefore, answer B is wrong. Dividing the network into different organizational units will increase the capability to manage the network; however, this is a logical construct and does nothing in the physical world. Reducing the number of servers might help, but

obviously, if the servers are there, they are serving some purpose. Removing them just to reduce bandwidth would probably cause other problems. For more information, see "Replicating Active Directory Information" in Chapter 10, "Fundamentals of Active Directory."

55. **B.** All you need to do is create the site links, and the KCC will create the connections. The KCC will use transitive bridging (automatic bridging) to connect all the sites. You could create a site link bridge and turn off transitive bridging, but there is no stated reason to do either in the question. This means answers C and D are incorrect. Answer A is also incorrect because you want the KCC to deal with this so it can adapt the connections to network conditions. For more information, see "Replicating Active Directory Information" in Chapter 10, "Fundamentals of Active Directory."

56. **D.** The best way to deal with this is to create a site link that is active during the day with a long interval between replications. Then, create a second site link that is active at night with a short interval. Answer A could perhaps work in theory, but it is certainly not the best way to deal with this. Answer B would be okay if you could create two schedules on the same site link, but you can't. Answer C just wouldn't work because there are only two sites, and the two links between the same two sites would be automatically bridged. For more information, see "Replicating Active Directory Information" in Chapter 10, "Fundamentals of Active Directory."

57. **B.** All you need to do to list a printer from a Windows 2000 computer is select the List in the Directory option from the Sharing tab. There is no Active Directory tab in the Printers dialog box, so answer A is incorrect. The only time you need to add the printer in Active Directory User and Computers is when the printer is shared from a non-Windows 2000 computer. Because answer B is correct, you will not need to remove and re-add the printer as answer D suggests. For more information, see "Performing Basic Administration" in Chapter 10, "Fundamentals of Active Directory."

58. **C.** Although answer A is close, it does not share the printer after it is created. In the real world, you would do this and then share the printer so that the printer driver would be available to the users who want to use the printer. Answer B is wrong because it is only connecting to a network printer, and you would not be able to share the printer after connecting to it. Answer D is incorrect because you can add the printer to the Active Directory. For more information, see "Performing Basic Administration" in Chapter 10, "Fundamentals of Active Directory."

59. **C.** The specific object might have different permissions that are blocking the permissions set using the Delegation of Control Wizard. You should probably check the permissions on the OU that you delegated, but because she could reset password for other users, this wouldn't be the first choice. This means answer A isn't the best answer. Answer B isn't likely because her account is working. Rerunning the wizard might fix the problem, but it's not likely because it didn't work the first time. This means answer D is wrong. For more information, see "Permissions in Active Directory Services" in Chapter 10, "Fundamentals of Active Directory."

60. **A, C.** Because you configured the domain-level GPO with No Override, the settings that were specified at the Sales OU GPO will be ignored if they conflict with the domain-level OU settings. This means that the user will have the domain-level wallpaper because these settings directly

conflict. However, if you choose to disable the Control Panel at the Sales OU, this will also be the effective GPO setting because this is specified at the OU level, which is closest to the user logging on. However, in actuality, if the user were able to start Control Panel, her only choice would be Add/Remove Programs and Display, as configured in the domain-level GPO. Because the user is not able to start Control Panel, this is the effective setting. For more information, see "Group Policy Scope" in Chapter 11, "Fundamentals of Group Policy."

61. **C, F.** The default Group Policy refresh internal is 5 minutes on domain controllers and 90 minutes, plus or minus a 30-minute stagger interval, on member servers and workstations. For more information, see "Introduction to Group Policy" in Chapter 11, "Fundamentals of Group Policy."

62. **A.** To have the same password policy on all domains in `scriberco.com`, you must modify the Default Domain Policy at the top-level domain. Because you did not create any additional GPOs at the subdomain and because the default behavior for the Default Domain Policy is to have it copied to all subdomains in an Active Directory structure, modifying the default domain policy on `scriberco.com` accomplishes all the required goals. For more information, see "Creating and Managing Group Policy" in Chapter 11, "Fundamentals of Group Policy."

PART VII

Appendixes

APPENDIX A

Overview of the Certification Process

You must pass rigorous certification exams to become a Microsoft Certified Professional. These closed-book exams provide a valid and reliable measure of your technical proficiency and expertise. Developed in consultation with computer industry professionals who have experience with Microsoft products in the workplace, the exams are conducted by two independent organizations. Virtual University Enterprises (VUE) testing centers offer exams at more than 3,000 locations in 120 countries. Sylvan Prometric offers the exams at many Authorized Prometric Testing Centers around the world as well.

To schedule an exam, call VUE at 800-837-8734 (or register online at `http://www.vue.com/`or Sylvan Prometric Testing Centers at 800-755-EXAM (3926) (or register online at `http://www.2test.com/register`).

TYPES OF CERTIFICATION

- **Microsoft Certified Professional (MCP)**—The Microsoft Certified Professional (MCP) credential is for professionals who have the skills to successfully implement a Microsoft product or technology as part of a business solution in an organization.
- **Microsoft Certified Database Administrator (MCDBA) on Microsoft SQL Server 2000**—Qualified individuals can derive physical database designs, develop logical data models, create physical databases, create data services by using Transact-SQL, manage and maintain databases, configure and manage security, monitor and optimize databases, and install and configure Microsoft SQL Server.
- **Microsoft Certified Systems Administrator (MCSA)**—This credential certifies that the individual has the skills to successfully implement, manage, and troubleshoot the ongoing needs of Microsoft Windows 2000-based operating environments, including Windows .NET Server.

- **Microsoft Certified Systems Engineer** (MCSE) **on Microsoft Windows 2000**—These individuals are qualified to analyze the business requirements for a system architecture; design solutions; deploy, install, and configure architecture components; and troubleshoot system problems.
- **Microsoft Certified Solution Developer (MCSD)**—These individuals are qualified to design and develop custom business solutions by using Microsoft development tools, technologies, and platforms. The new track includes certification exams that test users' abilities to build Web-based, distributed, and commerce applications by using Microsoft products such as Microsoft SQL Server, Microsoft Visual Studio, and Microsoft Component Services.
- **Microsoft Certified Application Developer (MCAD)**—The Microsoft Certified Application Developer (MCAD) for Microsoft .NET credential is for professionals who use Microsoft technologies to develop and maintain department-level applications, components, Web or desktop clients, or back-end data services.
- **Microsoft Certified Trainer** (MCT)—Persons with this credential are instructionally and technically qualified by Microsoft to deliver Microsoft Education Courses at Microsoft-authorized sites. An MCT must be employed by a Microsoft Solution Provider Authorized Technical Education Center or a Microsoft Authorized Academic Training site.

NOTE

For up-to-date information about each type of certification, visit the Microsoft Training and Certification World Wide Web site at `http://www.microsoft .com/train-cert/`. You also may contact Microsoft through the following sources:

- Microsoft Certified Professional Program: 800-636-7544
- `http://register.microsoft.com/contactus/contactus.asp`

NOTE

Although most exams are no longer available for the following certifications, individuals who earned them remain certified as of Summer of 2002:

- Microsoft Certified Professional + Internet (MCP+I)
- Microsoft Certified Professional + Site Building (MCP+SB)
- Microsoft Certified Systems Engineer + Internet (MCSE+I)

CERTIFICATION REQUIREMENTS

An asterisk following an exam in any of the following lists means that it is slated for retirement.

How to Become a Microsoft Certified Professional

To become certified as an MCP, you need only to pass any Microsoft exam (with the exception of Microsoft Windows 2000 Accelerated Exam for MCPs Certified on Microsoft Windows NT 4.0, #70-240).

How to Become a Microsoft Certified Database Administrator on Microsoft SQL Server 2000

To achieve the MCDBA certification, you need to pass three core exams and one elective exam.

Core Exams

The core exams must come from three areas:

- *Administration Exams*

  Administering Microsoft SQL Server 7.0, #70-028

  OR Installing, Configuring, and Administering Microsoft SQL Server 2000, Enterprise Edition, #70-228

- *Design Exams*

  Designing and Implementing Databases with Microsoft SQL Server 7.0, #70-029

  OR Designing and Implementing Databases with Microsoft SQL Server 2000, Enterprise Edition, #70-229

- *Networking Systems Exams*

  Installing, Configuring, and Administering Microsoft Windows 2000 Server, #70-215

  OR Installing, Configuring, and Administering Microsoft .NET Enterprise Servers, #70-275

  OR Microsoft Windows 2000 Accelerated Exam for MCPs Certified on Microsoft Windows NT 4.0, #70-240 (only for those who have passed exams #70-067, #70-068, and #70-073)

Elective Exams

You also must pass one elective exam from the following list (note that #70-240 can be counted twice—as both a core and elective exam in the MCDBA track):

- Designing and Implementing Distributed Applications with Microsoft Visual C++ 6.0, #70-015
- Designing and Implementing Data Warehouses with Microsoft SQL Server 7.0 and Microsoft Decision Support Services 1.0, #70-019
- Designing and Implementing Distributed Applications with Microsoft Visual FoxPro 6.0, #70-155
- Designing and Implementing Distributed Applications with Microsoft Visual Basic 6.0, #70-175

- Implementing and Administering a Microsoft Windows 2000 Network Infrastructure, #70-216 (only for those who have *NOT* already passed #70-067*, #70-068*, and #70-073*)

  OR Implementing and Administering a Microsoft Windows .NET Server Network Infrastructure, #70-276

  OR Microsoft Windows 2000 Accelerated Exam for MCPs Certified on Microsoft Windows NT 4.0, #70-240 (only for those who have passed exams #70-067*, #70-068*, and #70-073*)

How to Become a Microsoft Certified Systems Administrator

To become certified as an MCSA, you must pass three core exams and one elective exam. The core exams must consist of one client operating system exam and two networking system exams. Exam #70-240 can count as both a core and an elective.

Core Exams

- Client Operating System Exams

  Installing, Configuring, and Administering Microsoft Windows 2000 Professional, #70-210

  OR Installing, Configuring, and Administering Microsoft Windows XP Professional, #70-270

  OR Microsoft Windows 2000 Accelerated Exam for MCPs Certified on Microsoft Windows NT 4.0, #70-240 (only for those who have passed exams #70-067*, #70-068*, and #70-073*)

- Networking System Exams

  Installing, Configuring, and Administering Microsoft Windows 2000 Server, #70-215

  OR Installing, Configuring, and Administering Microsoft Windows .NET Server, #70-275

  OR Microsoft Windows 2000 Accelerated Exam for MCPs Certified on Microsoft Windows NT 4.0, #70-240 (only for those who have passed exams #70-067*, #70-068*, and #70-073*)

  Managing a Microsoft Windows 2000 Network Environment, #70-218

  Managing a Microsoft Windows .NET Server Network Environment, #70-278

Elective Exams

- Administering Microsoft SQL Server 7.0, #70-028
- Implementing and Supporting Microsoft Exchange Server 5.5, #70-081
- Implementing and Supporting Microsoft Systems Management Server 2.0, #70-086
- Implementing and Administering a Microsoft Windows 2000 Network Infrastructure, #70-216

  OR Microsoft Windows 2000 Accelerated Exam for MCPs Certified on Microsoft Windows NT 4.0, #70-240 (only for those who have passed exams #70-067*, #70-068*, and #70-073*)
- Installing, Configuring, and Administering Microsoft Exchange 2000 Server, #70-224
- Installing, Configuring, and Administering Microsoft Internet Security and Acceleration (ISA) Server 2000, Enterprise Edition, #70-227

- Installing, Configuring, and Administering Microsoft SQL Server 2000, Enterprise Edition, #70-228
- Supporting and Maintaining a Microsoft Windows NT Server 4.0 Network, #70-244
- CompTIA A+ and CompTIA Network+

  OR CompTIA A+ and CompTIA Server+

How to Become a Microsoft Certified Systems Engineer

You must pass four core operating system exams, one core design exam, and two elective exams to become an MCSE. You must also pass two elective exams.

Core Exams

The Windows 2000 Track core requirements for MCSE certification include the following for those who have *NOT* passed #70-067,#70-068, and #70-073:

- Installing, Configuring, and Administering Microsoft Windows 2000 Professional, #70-210
- Installing, Configuring, and Administering Microsoft Windows 2000 Server, #70-215
- Implementing and Administering a Microsoft Windows 2000 Network Infrastructure, #70-216
- Implementing and Administering a Microsoft Windows 2000 Directory Services Infrastructure, #70-217

The Windows 2000 Track core requirements for MCSE certification include the following for those who have passed #70-067*, #70-068*, and #70-073*:

- Microsoft Windows 2000 Accelerated Exam for MCPs Certified on Microsoft Windows NT 4.0, #70-240

All candidates must pass one of these additional core exams:

- Designing a Microsoft Windows 2000 Directory Services Infrastructure, #70-219
- *OR* Designing Security for a Microsoft Windows 2000 Network, #70-220
- *OR* Designing a Microsoft Windows 2000 Infrastructure, #70-221
- *OR* Designing Highly Available Web Solutions with Microsoft Windows 2000 Server Technologies, #70-226

  (This exam is in development. It is expected to be released in its beta version in May 2001.)

Elective Exams

You must pass two elective exams. Exams 70-219,70-220, 70-221, and 70-226 may count as an elective exam as long as they are not already being used as an additional core exam. The elective exams are as follows:

- Implementing and Supporting Microsoft SNA Server 4.0, 70-085
- Implementing and Supporting Microsoft Systems Management Server 2.0, 70-086
- Designing and Implementing Data Warehouses with Microsoft SQL Server 7.0, 70-019
- Designing and Implementing Databases with Microsoft SQL Server 7.0, 70-029

  OR Designing and Implementing Databases with Microsoft SQL Server 2000 Enterprise Edition, 70-229

- Administering Microsoft SQL Server 7.0, 70-028

  OR Installing, Configuring, and Administering Microsoft SQL Server 2000 Enterprise Edition, 70-228
- Implementing and Supporting Web Sites Using Microsoft Site Server 3.0, 70-056
- Implementing and Supporting Microsoft Exchange Server 5.5, 70-081

  OR Installing, Configuring, and Administering Microsoft Exchange 2000 Server, 70-224
- Implementing and Supporting Microsoft Proxy Server 2.0, 70-088

  OR Installing, Configuring, and Administering Microsoft Internet Security and Acceleration (ISA) Server 2000, Enterprise Edition, 70-227
- Implementing and Supporting Microsoft Internet Explorer 5.0 by Using the Microsoft Internet Explorer, Administration Kit, 70-080
- Managing a Microsoft Windows 2000 Network Environment, 70-218
- Designing a Microsoft Windows 2000 Directory Services Infrastructure, 70-219
- Designing Security for a Microsoft Windows 2000 Network, 70-220
- Designing a Microsoft Windows 2000 Network Infrastructure, 70-221
- Migrating from Microsoft Windows NT 4.0 to Microsoft Windows 2000, 70-222
- Installing, Configuring, and Administering Microsoft Clustering Services by Using Microsoft Windows 2000 Advanced Server, 70-223
- Designing and Deploying a Messaging Infrastructure with Microsoft Exchange 2000 Server, 70-225
- Designing Highly Available Web Solutions with Microsoft Windows 2000 Server Technologies, 70-226
- Designing and Implementing Solutions with Microsoft BizTalk Server 2000, Enterprise Edition, 70-230
- Implementing and Maintaining Highly Available Web Solutions with Microsoft Windows 2000 Server Technologies and Microsoft Application Center 2000, 70-232
- Designing and Implementing Solutions with Microsoft Commerce Server 2000, 70-234
- Supporting and Maintaining a Microsoft Windows NT Server 4.0 Network, 70-244

How to Become a Microsoft Certified Solution Developer

The MCSD certification is outlined as follows. Undoubtedly, changes will come to this certification as the .NET framework continues to unfold. However, no changes had yet been announced at the time of this writing.

You must pass three core exams and one elective exam. The three core exam areas are listed as follows, as are the elective exams from which you can choose.

Core Exams

The core exams include the following:

- *Desktop Applications Development (one required)*

  Designing and Implementing Desktop Applications with Microsoft Visual C++ 6.0, #70-016

  OR Designing and Implementing Desktop Applications with Microsoft Visual FoxPro 6.0, #70-156

  OR Designing and Implementing Desktop Applications with Microsoft Visual Basic 6.0, #70-176

- *Distributed Applications Development (one required)*

  Designing and Implementing Distributed Applications with Microsoft Visual C++ 6.0, #70-015

  OR Designing and Implementing Distributed Applications with Microsoft Visual FoxPro 6.0, #70-155

  OR Designing and Implementing Distributed Applications with Microsoft Visual Basic 6.0, #70-175

- *Solution Architecture (required)*

  Analyzing Requirements and Defining Solution Architectures, #70-100

Elective Exam

You must pass one of the following elective exams:

- Designing and Implementing Distributed Applications with Microsoft Visual C++ 6.0, #70-015
- Designing and Implementing Desktop Applications with Microsoft Visual C++ 6.0, #70-016
- Designing and Implementing Data Warehouses with Microsoft SQL Server 7.0, #70-019
- Designing and Implementing Databases with Microsoft SQL Server 7.0, #70-029
- Designing and Implementing Commerce Solutions with Microsoft Site Server 3.0, Commerce Edition, #70-057
- Designing and Implementing Solutions with Microsoft Office 2000 and Microsoft Visual Basic for Applications, #70-091
- Designing and Implementing Collaborative Solutions with Microsoft Outlook 2000 and Microsoft Exchange Server 5.5, #70-105
- Designing and Implementing Web Solutions with Microsoft Visual InterDev 6.0, #70-152
- Designing and Implementing Distributed Applications with Microsoft Visual FoxPro 6.0, #70-155
- Designing and Implementing Desktop Applications with Microsoft Visual FoxPro 6.0, #70-156
- Designing and Implementing Distributed Applications with Microsoft Visual Basic 6.0, #70-175
- Designing and Implementing Desktop Applications with Microsoft Visual Basic 6.0, #70-176
- Designing and Implementing Databases with Microsoft SQL Server 2000 Enterprise Edition, #70-229

- Designing and Implementing Solutions with Microsoft BizTalk Server 2000 Enterprise Edition, #70-230
- Designing and Implementing Solutions with Microsoft Commerce Server 2000, #70-234

How to Become a Microsoft Certified Application Developer

The following bullets describe what you need to accomplish in order to achieve the MCAD certification:

- **Core Exams (2 Exams Required)**—To fulfill the core certification requirements, pass one exam focused on either Web Application Development or XML Windows Application Development in the language of your choice. Then pass one Web Services and Server Components exam.
- **Elective Exams (1 Exams Required)**—In addition to the core exam requirements, you must also pass one elective exam that provides proof of expertise with a specific Microsoft server product.

Core Exams

- **Exam 70–305***: Developing and Implementing Web Applications with Microsoft Visual Basic® .NET and Microsoft Visual Studio® .NET
- **Exam 70–306***: Developing and Implementing Windows-based Applications with Microsoft Visual Basic .NET and Microsoft Visual Studio .NET
- **Exam 70–315***: Developing and Implementing Web Applications with Microsoft Visual C#™ .NET and Microsoft Visual Studio .NET
- **Exam 70–316***: Developing and Implementing Windows-based Applications with Microsoft Visual C# .NET and Microsoft Visual Studio .NET
- **Exam 70–310***: Developing XML Web Services and Server Components with Microsoft Visual Basic .NET and the Microsoft .NET Framework
- **Exam 70–320***: Developing XML Web Services and Server Components with Microsoft Visual C# and the Microsoft .NET Framework

Elective Exams

- **Exam 70–229**: Designing and Implementing Databases with Microsoft SQL Server™ 2000 Enterprise Edition
- **Exam 70–230**: Designing and Implementing Solutions with Microsoft BizTalk Server® 2000 Enterprise Edition
- **Exam 70–234**: Designing and Implementing Solutions with Microsoft Commerce Server 2000
- **Exam 70-305*, 70-306*, 70-315*, or 70-316***

  If you use Exam 70-305 or 70-315 to satisfy the core exam requirement, you may use either Exam 70-306 or 70-316 as an elective.

  If you use Exam 70-306 or 70-316 to satisfy the core exam requirement, you may use either Exam 70-305 or 70-315 as an elective.

Becoming a Microsoft Certified Trainer

As of January 1, 2001, all MCTs must hold a premier Microsoft Certified Professional (MCP) certification (Microsoft Certified Systems Engineer, Microsoft Certified Solution Developer, or Microsoft Certified Database Administrator). To fully understand the requirements and process for becoming an MCT, you need to obtain the Microsoft Certified Trainer Guide document from `http://www.microsoft.com/trainingandservices/content/downloads/MCT_guide.doc`.

At this site, you can read the document as a Web page or display and download it as a Word file. You also can download the application form from the site. The MCT Guide explains the process for becoming an MCT. The general steps for the MCT certification are as follows:

1. Complete and mail a Microsoft Certified Trainer application to Microsoft. You must include proof of your skills for presenting instructional material. The options for doing so are described in the MCT Guide.
2. Obtain and study the Microsoft Trainer Kit for the Microsoft Official Curricula (MOC) courses for which you want to be certified. Microsoft Trainer Kits can be ordered by calling 800-688-0496 in North America. Those of you in other regions should review the MCT Guide for information on how to order a Trainer Kit.
3. Take and pass any required prerequisite MCP exam(s) to measure your current technical knowledge.
4. Prepare to teach an MOC course. Begin by attending the MOC course for the course for which you want to be certified. This is required so you understand how the course is structured, how labs are completed, and how the course flows.
5. Pass any additional exam requirement(s) to measure any additional product knowledge that pertains to the course.
6. Submit your course preparation checklist to Microsoft so that your additional accreditation may be processed and reflected on your transcript.

> WARNING
>
> **The Exact Process for Obtaining Your MCT** You should consider the preceding steps a general overview of the MCT certification process. The precise steps that you need to take are described in detail on the Web site mentioned earlier. Do not misinterpret the preceding steps as the exact process you must undergo.

If you are interested in becoming an MCT, you can obtain more information by visiting the Microsoft Certified Training WWW site at `http://www.microsoft.com/traincert/` and choosing MCT under Technical Certifications or by calling 800-688-0496.

APPENDIX **B**

What's on the CD-ROM

This appendix is a brief rundown of what you'll find on the CD-ROM that comes with this book. For a more detailed description of the PrepLogic Practice Tests, Preview Edition exam simulation software, see Appendix C, "Using the *PrepLogic, Preview Edition* Software." In addition to the *PrepLogic Practice Tests, Preview Edition,* the CD-ROM includes the electronic version of the book in Portable Document Format (PDF), several utility and application programs, and a complete listing of test objectives and where they are covered in the book.

PrepLogic Practice Tests, Preview Edition

PrepLogic is a leading provider of certification training tools. Trusted by certification students worldwide, we believe PrepLogic is the best practice exam software available. In addition to providing a means of evaluating your knowledge of the Training Guide material, *PrepLogic Practice Tests, Preview Edition* features several innovations that help you to improve your mastery of the subject matter.

For example, the practice tests allow you to check your score by exam area or domain to determine which topics you need to study more. Another feature allows you to obtain immediate feedback on your responses in the form of explanations for the correct and incorrect answers.

PrepLogic Practice Tests, Preview Edition exhibits most of the full functionality of the *Premium Edition* but offers only a fraction of the total questions. To get the complete set of practice questions and exam functionality, visit `PrepLogic.com` and order the *Premium Edition* for this and other challenging exam titles.

Again, for a more detailed description of the *PrepLogic Practice Tests, Preview Edition* features, see Appendix C.

Exclusive Electronic Version of Text

The CD-ROM also contains the electronic version of this book in Portable Document Format (PDF). The electronic version comes complete with all figures as they appear in the book. You will find that the search capabilities of the reader come in handy for study and review purposes.

APPENDIX C

Using the *PrepLogic, Preview Edition* Software

This Training Guide includes a special version of *PrepLogic Practice Tests*—a revolutionary test engine designed to give you the best in certification exam preparation. PrepLogic offers sample and practice exams for many of today's most in-demand and challenging technical certifications. This special *Preview Edition* is included with this book as a tool to use in assessing your knowledge of the Training Guide material, while also providing you with the experience of taking an electronic exam.

This appendix describes in detail what *PrepLogic Practice Tests, Preview Edition* is, how it works, and what it can do to help you prepare for the exam. Note that although the *Preview Edition* includes all the test simulation functions of the complete, retail version, it contains only a single practice test. The *Premium Edition*, available at `PrepLogic.com`, contains the complete set of challenging practice exams designed to optimize your learning experience.

Exam Simulation

One of the main functions of *PrepLogic Practice Tests, Preview Edition* is exam simulation. PrepLogic is designed to offer the most effective exam simulation available in order to prepare you to take the actual vendor certification exam.

Question Quality

The questions provided in the *PrepLogic Practice Tests, Preview Edition* are written to the highest standards of technical accuracy. The questions tap the content of the Training Guide chapters and help you to review and assess your knowledge before you take the actual exam.

Interface Design

The *PrepLogic Practice Tests, Preview Edition* exam simulation interface provides you with the experience of taking an electronic exam. This allows you to effectively prepare yourself for taking the actual exam by making the test experience a familiar one. Using this test simulation can help to eliminate the sense of surprise or anxiety you might experience in the testing center because you will already be acquainted with computerized testing.

Effective Learning Environment

The *PrepLogic Practice Tests, Preview Edition* interface provides a learning environment that not only tests you through the computer, but also teaches the material you need to know to pass the certification exam. Each question comes with a detailed explanation of the correct answer and often provides reasons the other options are incorrect. This information helps to reinforce the knowledge you already have and also provides practical information you can use on the job.

Software Requirements

PrepLogic Practice Tests requires a computer with the following:

- Microsoft Windows 98, Windows Me, Windows NT 4.0, Windows 2000, or Windows XP
- A 166 MHz or faster processor is recommended
- A minimum of 32MB of RAM
- As with any Windows application, the more memory, the better your performance
- 10MB of hard drive space

Installing *PrepLogic Practice Tests, Preview Edition*

Install *PrepLogic Practice Tests, Preview Edition* by running the setup program on the *PrepLogic Practice Tests, Preview Edition* CD. Follow these instructions to install the software on your computer.

1. Insert the CD into your CD-ROM drive. The Autorun feature of Windows should launch the software. If you have Autorun disabled, click the Start button and select Run. Go to the root directory of the CD and select setup.exe. Click Open, and then click OK.
2. The Installation Wizard copies the *PrepLogic Practice Tests, Preview Edition* files to your hard drive; adds *PrepLogic Practice Tests, Preview Edition* to your Desktop and Program menu; and installs test engine components to the appropriate system folders.

Removing *PrepLogic Practice Tests, Preview Edition* from Your Computer

If you elect to remove the *PrepLogic Practice Tests, Preview Edition* product from your computer, an uninstall process has been included to ensure that it is removed from your system safely and completely. Follow these instructions to remove *PrepLogic Practice Tests, Preview Edition* from your computer:

1. Select Start, Settings, Control Panel.
2. Double-click the Add/Remove Programs icon.
3. You are presented with a list of software currently installed on your computer. Select the appropriate *PrepLogic Practice Tests, Preview Edition* title you wish to remove. Click the Add/Remove button. The software is then removed from you computer.

Using *PrepLogic Practice Tests, Preview Edition*

PrepLogic is designed to be user friendly and intuitive. Because the software has a smooth learning curve, your time is maximized, as you will start practicing almost immediately. *PrepLogic Practice Tests, Preview Edition* has two major modes of study: Practice Test and Flash Review.

Using Practice Test mode, you can develop your test-taking abilities, as well as your knowledge through the use of the Show Answer option. While you are taking the test, you can reveal the answers along with a detailed explanation of why the given answers are right or wrong. This gives you the ability to better understand the material presented.

Flash Review is designed to reinforce exam topics rather than quiz you. In this mode, you will be shown a series of questions, but no answer choices. Instead, you will be given a button that reveals the correct answer to the question and a full explanation for that answer.

Starting a Practice Test Mode Session

Practice Test mode enables you to control the exam experience in ways that actual certification exams do not allow:

- **Enable Show Answer Button**—Activates the Show Answer button, allowing you to view the correct answer(s) and a full explanation for each question during the exam. When not enabled, you must wait until after your exam has been graded to view the correct answer(s) and explanation(s) .
- **Enable Item Review Button**—Activates the Item Review button, allowing you to view your answer choices, marked questions, and facilite navigation between questions.
- **Randomize Choices**—Randomize answer choices from one exam session to the next; makes memorizing question choices more difficult, therefore keeping questions fresh and challenging longer.

To begin studying in Practice Test mode, click the Practice Test radio button from the main exam customization screen. This will enable the options detailed above.

To your left, you are presented with the options of selecting the pre-configured Practice Test or creating your own Custom Test. The pre-configured test has a fixed time limit and number of questions. Custom Tests allow you to configure the time limit and the number of questions in your exam.

The *Preview Edition* included with this book includes a single pre-configured Practice Test. Get the compete set of challenging PrepLogic Practice Tests at `PrepLogic.com` and make certain you're ready for the big exam.

Click the Begin Exam button to begin your exam.

Starting a Flash Review Mode Session

Flash Review mode provides you with an easy way to reinforce topics covered in the practice questions. To begin studying in Flash Review mode, click the Flash Review radio button from the main exam customization screen. Select either the pre-configured Practice Test or create your own Custom Test.

Click the Best Exam button to begin your Flash Review of the exam questions.

Standard *PrepLogic Practice Tests, Preview Edition* Options

The following list describes the function of each of the buttons you see. Depending on the options, some of the buttons will be grayed out and inaccessible or missing completely. Buttons that are accessible are active. The buttons are as follows:

- **Exhibit**—This button is visible if an exhibit is provided to support the question. An exhibit is an image that provides supplemental information necessary to answer the question.
- **Item Review**—This button leaves the question window and opens the Item Review screen. From this screen you will see all questions, your answers, and your marked items. You will also see correct answers listed here when appropriate.
- **Show Answer**—This option displays the correct answer with an explanation of why it is correct. If you select this option, the current question is not scored.
- **Mark Item**—Check this box to tag a question you need to review further. You can view and navigate your Marked Items by clicking the Item Review button (if enabled). When grading your exam, you will be notified if you have marked items remaining.
- **Previous Item**—This option allows you to view the previous question.
- **Next Item**—This option allows you to view the next question.
- **Grade Exam**—When you have completed your exam, click this button to end your exam and view your detailed score report. If you have unanswered or marked items remaining you will be asked if you would like to continue taking your exam or view your exam report.

Time Remaining

If the test is timed, the time remaining is displayed on the upper right corner of the application screen. It counts down the minutes and seconds remaining to complete the test. If you run out of time, you will be asked if you want to continue taking the test or if you want to end your exam.

Your Examination Score Report

The Examination Score Report screen appears when the Practice Test mode ends—as the result of time expiration, completion of all questions, or your decision to terminate early.

This screen provides you with a graphical display of your test score with a breakdown of scores by topic domain. The graphical display at the top of the screen compares your overall score with the PrepLogic Exam Competency Score.

The PrepLogic Exam Competency Score reflects the level of subject competency required to pass this vendor's exam. While this score does not directly translate to a passing score, consistently matching or exceeding this score does suggest you possess the knowledge to pass the actual vendor exam.

Review Your Exam

From Your Score Report screen, you can review the exam that you just completed by clicking on the View Items button. Navigate through the items viewing the questions, your answers, the correct answers, and the explanations for those answers. You can return to your score report by clicking the View Items button.

Get More Exams

Each *PrepLogic Practice Tests, Preview Edition* that accompanies your Training Guide contains a single PrepLogic Practice Test. Certification students worldwide trust PrepLogic Practice Tests to help them pass their IT certification exams the first time. Purchase the *Premium Edition* of PrepLogic Practice Tests and get the entire set of all new challenging Practice Tests for this exam. PrepLogic Practice Tests—Because You Want to Pass the First Time.

Contacting PrepLogic

If you would like to contact PrepLogic for any reason, including information about our extensive line of certification practice tests, we invite you to do so. Please contact us online at `http://www.preplogic.com`.

Customer Service

If you have a damaged product and need a replacement or refund, please call the following phone number:

800-858-7674

Product Suggestions and Comments

We value your input! Please email your suggestions and comments to the following address:

`feedback@preplogic.com`

License Agreement

YOU MUST AGREE TO THE TERMS AND CONDITIONS OUTLINED IN THE END USER LICENSE AGREEMENT (“EULA”) PRESENTED TO YOU DURING THE INSTALLATION PROCESS. IF YOU DO NOT AGREE TO THESE TERMS DO NOT INSTALL THE SOFTWARE.

APPENDIX D

Glossary

%SystemRoot% A universal reference to the directory in which the Windows 2000 system files are installed. Typically, %SystemRoot% is C:\Winnt. If multiple copies of Windows 2000 are installed in a multiboot system, each copy will have its own %SystemRoot% directory.

A

access control list (ACL) An access control list is used to verify the permissions of a process to access an object. The credentials of the process are compared to the entries in the access control list to determine whether access is granted and which permissions are available if access is granted. In Windows 2000, there are two access control lists. The Discretionary Access Control List handles permissions, whereas the System Access Control List handles auditing.

account lockout policy Account lockout policies define at what point an account is locked after too many failed password attempts, how long the lockout lasts, and when the counter is reset.

Active Directory (AD) Active Directory is a hierarchical directory service used in Windows 2000. It organizes users into organizational units and domains that are all part of a common namespace.

Active Directory Services The directory services included with Windows 2000 Server. Based on the DNS hierarchy, Active Directory provides a domain-based directory service for organizing all the objects and services in a Windows 2000 network.

Active Directory—integrated zone An Active Directory-integrated zone is a type of DNS zone that uses Active Directory to store the records. The records are then replicated using Active Directory replication and have an ACL. This also enables a computer to register with any integrated domain controller.

address pool Available IP addresses within a scope for dynamic assignment by the DHCP server to DHCP clients.

address reservation An address reservation is an IP address from a scope that is reserved for a client by its MAC address.

Address Resolution Protocol (ARP) ARP is the part of the TCP/IP protocol suite that resolves an IP address to a MAC address. The ARP.EXE utility can be used to view the table of resolutions.

adjacency A term in routing referring to the record a router keeps about the state of its connectivity with a neighbor and the attributes of the neighboring router.

administrative share A hidden share, created by the Windows 2000 installation process. These shares can't be removed and are identified by a trailing $ in the name—for example, C$, D$. Any share name appended with a $ is a hidden share. Only those shares created at installation are considered administrative shares and are accessible only by administrators. The $ is part of the share name and must be referenced in all UNC paths.

administrative templates Administrative templates are a portion of Group Policy that apply Registry settings to users and computers to enforce corporate rules. Settings include which programs can be run, how offline folders are treated, desktop settings, and others.

administrator This is the principal account in a Windows 2000 domain or on a Windows 2000 standalone computer. This account has the capability to perform any action within its scope (domain or computer by virtue of being a member of the appropriate administrators group).

alert Alerts are used to configure "watchers." These watchers can be used to watch certain objects reaching or crossing predefined thresholds.

answer file An ASCII text file created by Windows Setup Manager, by the SYSPREP utility, or manually using any text editor. It specifies the installation configuration of Windows 2000 on a target computer. In RIS, answer files are used to specify how the deployment of Windows 2000 Professional will take place.

AppleShare Network client software that comes with Macintosh computers and Apple servers.

AppleTalk A network protocol developed by Apple Computer.

application compatibility script These scripts modify installation settings to ensure that applications are set for optimal execution under Terminal Services.

Application Server Mode It's used when the primary reason for installing Terminal Services is to host client sessions executing applications (this mode includes the capability to do remote administration of the server).

area In an OSPF routing environment, an area is a logical grouping of routers within the OSPF hierarchy.

ARP table The table of IP-to-MAC address translations used by a TCP/IP device to identify the physical addresses of devices on a local subnet.

assigning software packages Assigning software packages is the forced deployment of a software package to a user or computer as configured in Group Policy. Users or computers that have a package assigned to them will have it installed and can't decide not to have it installed.

attributes Attributes describe an object in the same way an adjective describes a noun (for example, the green door). In the case of an object such as a file, the file type is an attribute.

audit policy Security auditing policy is a portion of security policy that enables you to configure which security-related events to monitor or which to potentially monitor. By monitoring these security-related system events, you are able to detect attempts by intruders to compromise data on the system or to gain access to resources they should not be able to reach.

auditing Auditing is the process of tracking the execution of user rights, file access, or other security elements on a computer. Group Policy can be used to configure auditing settings for a computer.

authentication This is the process of verification that takes place when a user logs on to a computer or when a computer logs on to the domain. The authentication proves that the user or computer is the correct user or computer. This does not provide any encryption.

authoritative When a DNS name server supports the name database for a domain, it is said to be authoritative for that domain.

authoritative restore When an object is deleted, the deletion is replicated to other domain controllers with an updated USN on the object. If the object is restored from backup, the normal replication process causes it to be removed because the delete has a higher USN. To force the object back into Active Directory, you perform an authoritative restore. This increases the object USN by 10,000, which makes the update higher than the deleted USN. An authoritative restore must be preceded by a nonauthoritative restore.

authorizing a RIS server This refers to registering a RIS server within Active Directory and thereby permitting it to service client requests for a RIS image. This is performed through the DHCP MMC snap-in.

AutoDHCP AutoDHCP is the DHCP service included as part of the Windows 2000 Network Address Translation (NAT) protocol. A subset of the DHCP service, AutoDHCP is used to distribute reserved addresses to NAT users.

Automatic Private IP Addressing (APIPA) An assigned IP address of 169.254.y.z. This means that the local DHCP server is not configured properly, can't be reached from your computer, or did not respond in time. Windows 2000 assigned an IP address automatically with a subnet mask of 255.255.0.0.

B

B-node *See* Broadcast node.

background process A background process is any process, either service or user initiated, that is not currently interacting with the user. In simple terms, if the process is not capable of receiving input from the keyboard or mouse, it is a background process.

backup The process of backing up system and user files to tape or disk or any other media supported by the backup program in use.

backup browser A computer that stores a copy of the master browser database. Browse clients can browse the domain or workgroup by querying the backup browser for the browse database.

backup domain controller (BDC) This is a type of computer found in Windows NT 4.0 domains. This computer keeps a copy of the domain accounts database and can authenticate user logons. No changes can be made at a BDC, however, because the copy of the database that is kept is read-only.

backup set A collection of files, folders, or other data that have been backed up to a file or a tape or any other supported media.

Banyan VINES was one of the first PC network operating systems to provide enterprisewide directory services. In Banyan, these services were based on the Network Information System that was originally developed in the Unix world, upon which all of Banyan was based.

baseline Measurement taken on a network to provide comparison data in the event of a problem on the network. A baseline represents the "typical" state of a network at any given time. Future measurements are compared to the baseline.

basic disk A physical hard drive that uses the primary partition, extended partition, and logical drive partitioning architecture.

basic volume A logical volume that has been created on a basic disk.

binding The relationship between network adapters, drivers, and protocols in a computer's network communication configuration. For example, the TCP/IP protocol binding connects the protocol to the network interface card (NIC).

blocking policy inheritance Blocking GPO inheritance means configuring a GPO at a lower-level Active Directory container so that any policies set at a higher level of Active Directory are not applied. You would typically block policy inheritance at an OU to ensure that only OU GPO settings are applied to users and computers.

BOOTP protocol Short for Bootstrap Protocol, BOOTP is an Internet protocol that enables a diskless workstation to discover its own IP address from a BOOTP server. This protocol is still used to enable DHCP requests and responses to traverse a routed network.

Border Gateway Protocol (BGP) An IP routing protocol that enables groups of routers (organized in autonomous systems) to share routing information to create efficient routes. BGP is commonly used by Internet service providers (ISPs) as an Internet routing protocol. The protocol is defined in RFC 1771.

bottleneck The weak link in the server or network when it is under a load.

bridge A bridge works on the physical layer (or Layer 2) of the OSI model to connect two network segments. A bridge listens to traffic on both segments and builds a list of MAC addresses that reside on each. It forwards packets from one segment to the other if the destination system is known. Unlike a router, a bridge passes all broadcast traffic between segments.

bridgehead servers In Windows 2000 Server, bridgehead servers serve as the point of contact when directory information must be exchanged between sites. Bridgehead servers are themselves domain controllers and have been either automatically or manually assigned the additional duty of being a bridgehead to another site.

Broadcast node (B-node) One of the four node types that can be set for NetBIOS name resolution.

browse client A computer that doesn't store a copy of the domain or workgroup database and must browse the network by querying the browse database on a backup or master browser.

browser elections Part of the Microsoft browser system, browser elections are used to decide which system will be the master browser on a network segment. When an election is called, all systems capable of being the master browser respond after a set time. The system that responds first wins the election and becomes the master browser. It remains the master browser until circumstances require another election.

browser service In Windows NT and Windows 2000, the browser service handles your computer's role in the Microsoft browser system.

built-in groups The groups that come predefined by Windows 2000 Server. They each have special meaning to the operating system.

C

cache file In a DNS implementation, the cache file is the file that contains the address of servers higher in the DNS hierarchy. The cache file that installs as part of the Windows 2000 DNS server contains the Internet's root-level servers.

caching A high-speed access mechanism in which routes, addresses, or DNS resolutions are stored in memory to speed further requests for the information.

caching-only server A DNS server that does not have authority for any zone. It doesn't provide authoritative answers for other DNS servers but responds with the information in its cache.

caching server A caching server is a type of DNS server that caches name resolutions it retrieves. All Windows 2000 DNS servers are caching servers. If a server does not contain any zone files, however, it is considered a caching-only server.

callback A feature of the Routing and Remote Access Service. Callback allows the Routing and Remote Access Service to call a user back by initiating a new connection after the user's initial modem connection. Used mostly for security reasons, callback can also be used to minimize user long-distance charges.

Canonical name (CNAME) record A CNAME record is a DNS zone file that acts as an alias for another entry in the DNS zone. This allows a single server to be mapped to multiple names. This is often referred to as a DNS alias.

CD-based image An image of Windows 2000 stored on a CD.

certificate A credential used to authenticate the origin, identity, and purpose of the public half of a public/private key pair. A certificate ensures that the data sent and received is kept secure during transmission.

certificate authority A service that verifies that the owner of the certificate is who he says he is.

certificate services Software that provides authentication support.

Chart view One of the views in the Performance Monitor. The Chart view displays a graphical representation of either real-time or logged data.

child domain A child domain is a domain that exists as a subdomain of another domain. For example, `RD.ScrimTech.local` would be a child of `ScrimTech.local`.

class A class of objects is one type of object. For example, a file is a class of object. Different classes of objects have different extended attributes and normally have different methods that can be applied. All classes of objects have some common attributes and methods, such as `name` and `type` for attributes and `create` and `delete` for methods.

Class A network The largest of the classes of IP networks. There are 126 Class A networks, each capable of addressing up to 16,777,214 hosts.

Class B network The second largest class of IP networks. There are 16,384 Class B networks, each capable of addressing up to 65,534 hosts.

Class C network The smallest class of IP networks. There are 2,097,152 Class C networks, each capable of addressing up to 254 hosts.

client A computer that accesses resources that are shared on a network, or the software component of a computer that lets the computer access resources shared on a network.

client reservation This is when DHCP leases a fixed IP address to a client based on the client's MAC address.

cluster A technology that enables multiple servers to provide failover of services.

collection A collection is a special type of object attribute in which there could be one or more entries for the same attribute. An example of a collection is the access control list, which is a made up of one or more access control entries.

computers Within the Windows 2000 domain structure, computers are one of the object classes defined in Active Directory. This facilitates the management and location of computer objects on the network.

configuration partition This is the Active Directory partition that contains information about the domains and trusts between them. The information is replicated from the domain naming master to all domain controllers in the enterprise.

connection object A connection object represents the network path through which Active Directory replication will flow. A connection object is typically created by the Knowledge Consistency Checker.

container object This is an object in directory services, such as a group, that exists primarily to contain other Active Directory objects.

convergence Usually referred to in conjunction with the RIP, OSPF, or BGP TCP/IP routing protocols. Convergence is a state in which all the routers in a network are aware of all available routes.

copy backups These are similar to normal backups in that they back up all data regardless of the state of the archive bit. However, they do not set the archive bits to true after backing up the data.

counter A counter is a specific statistic for an object.

counter log A counter log enables you to record data about hardware usage and the activity of system services from local or remote computers.

credentials In simple terms, credentials are the information you use to connect to the remote computer. Within the Windows 2000 domain, credentials are stored in an access token and include the user information, along with a list of groups to which the user belongs. The access token can then be attached to each process the user starts, and when a process attempts to access an object, these credentials can be compared to the ACL on the object to determine whether access is allowed.

cryptography A process that defines a secure method for transmitting data using encryption algorithms.

D

daily backup These are similar to copy backups. Daily backups back up all data regardless of the state of the archive bit, but they also look at the date a file was changed. As an example, daily backups (a type of time-frame backup) back up only those files modified on a specific day.

database A database is a structure that stores data in a series of tables (lists) that have a given set of columns. Each table defines a single entity, a class in Windows 2000, with each row holding the information about one of those entities. For example, there is a user class in Windows 2000 that is a table in the Active Directory database. For each user, a row is added to the table. A single column contains a unique identifier, and all the other columns contain attributes or collections about the entity.

DCPROMO This utility is a wizard used to promote and demote computers. Promotion makes the system a domain controller, and demotion resets it to a member server or standalone server.

default gateway The configured router on a Microsoft TCP/IP-enabled system. If a packet is bound for a remote network but no route is specified, the packet is sent to this address. Also known as the default *router.*

default router Also known as the default *gateway.* When a host needs to transmit a packet to a destination not on the local network, it sends the packet to a default router, which is then responsible for routing the packet to its destination network.

DHCP *See* Dynamic Host Configuration Protocol.

DHCP client Any computer that has DHCP settings enabled and is requesting addresses from a DHCP server.

DHCP server Any computer running the Windows 2000 DHCP service.

DHCPAck An acknowledgment from a DHCP server to a DHCP client indicating that the request for a lease (or renewal) was successful.

DHCPDiscover A message sent from a DHCP client to the network broadcast address. This is the beginning of the lease process, which causes any appropriately configured DHCP server to offer a lease.

DHCPNAck A negative acknowledgment from a DHCP server to a DHCP client indicating that the request for a lease (or renewal) was not successful.

DHCPOffer A message from the DHCP server to the client that has sent a discover message indicating an address that is available.

DHCPRequest A message sent from a DHCP client to the server requesting an offer or renewing an IP address lease.

Dial-Up Networking The part of a Microsoft operating system (Windows 2000, Windows NT, Windows 9x) used to dial remote servers to gain access to a network.

differential backup A backup that back ups only files with the archive bit set to true. However, unlike an incremental backup, this does not change the archive bit after backing up the file.

digital signature An encrypted hash of the message that can be decrypted by the author's public key. This can then be compared with the hash of the message to ensure that the stated author is the real author and that the message has not been tampered with enroute.

directory In simple terms, this is a list—a simple database that contains a list of items a person might search. In Windows 2000, the directory is the collection of information about the objects that can be found on the network.

Directplay proxy A proxy service included with the Windows 2000 Internet Connection Sharing (ICS) service to allow for the use of the Directplay protocol in conjunction with NAT. Directplay is a protocol typically used in writing multiuser games.

disk drives, duplexing A configuration of mirrored disk drives in which each disk drive is serviced by a separate drive adapter. This arrangement lets one drive of the pair continue functioning if there is a failure in a disk drive adapter.

disk drives, mirroring A configuration of two disk drives in which both drives store the same data. A mirrored disk drive set can continue to function when one of the disk drives malfunctions.

disk drives, stripe set A configuration of two or more disk drives in which data is written in blocks sequentially to each drive. Stripe sets have better storage and retrieval times than single hard disks with comparable specifications, but they also are more subject to hardware failure.

disk drives, stripe set with parity A stripe set in which one record in each set contains parity data. The parity data can be used to recover data if any one drive in the stripe set fails. A stripe set with parity can continue to function despite the failure of a single disk drive.

disk quota Disk quotas are settings on an NTFS volume used to enforce the amount of disk space that can be used by each user for files she creates and owns. Disk quotas help ensure that users do not hog a disk and that enough space is available for all users.

distance vector A routing algorithm used to calculate the best path in an OSPF environment.

distinguished name A distinguished name is the full name of an object within Active Directory. This includes the domain name and the names of the organizational units to which a user belongs. For example, if a user named `BehelerS` exists in the users container of a domain called `technical.newriders.local`, the distinguished name for the user would be `cn=BehelerS, cn=users, dc=technical, dc=newriders, dc=local`. For another user in the same container, the relatively distinguished name of `cn=BehelerS` could be used because all other parts of the name are the same.

Distributed file system (Dfs) A service used to present a single directory tree of file shares that can be located on multiple machines and as multiple shares.

distribution group A distribution group is a group you create so you will be able to send it email. Distribution groups can't be assigned permissions or rights and can contain only users.

DNS *See* domain name service.

DNS client Any host that uses a DNS server for name resolution services.

DNS server A server running the Domain Name Service to provide name and address resolution services in a TCP/IP environment.

domain In terms of DNS, this is a name given to an organization on the Internet. In truth, it is only part of the namespace for the Internet. In Windows 2000, a domain is a part of the namespace, but it is also a logical division that can be used to separate a large group of users from the rest of the network, providing a security and replication boundary.

domain controller A domain controller is a computer that has a copy of the domain database. Domain controllers are capable of authenticating user logon requests. Domain controllers in Windows 2000 are also capable of modifying the domain account database.

domain local group A domain local group is typically used to assign rights or permissions to resources. Domain local groups are local to all domain controllers and member servers in native or mixed mode.

domain master browser A browser on Microsoft TCP/IP networks that collects service announcements from all servers in a domain and creates a master.

domain name service (DNS) The domain name service is the system used on the Internet and on many private networks to resolve the names of computers. DNS is made up of namespaces, name servers, and resolvers.

domain naming master The domain naming master is one of the operation master roles. This computer is responsible for ensuring that the namespace of the domain is correct; it is also responsible for the configuration of trust relationships that will be configured on the PDC emulators within the domains of the Active Directory forest. Only one domain naming master exists per forest.

domain partition The domain partition represents all the information about all the objects in a domain. The domain partition is replicated only within a domain and not between domains.

duplexing *See* disk drives, duplexing.

Dynamic DNS (DDNS) A new addition to Microsoft's DNS implementation, Dynamic DNS is a process in which a workstation's name and address are entered into the DNS table when an IP address is obtained through DHCP.

Dynamic Host Configuration Protocol (DHCP) DHCP enables computers on the network to receive an automatic TCP/IP configuration including options. DHCP servers in Windows 2000 need to be authorized in Active Directory, which is intended to stop other users from installing a DHCP server. The Windows 2000 DHCP server can update the DNS server as the addresses are assigned; however, in normal behavior, it updates only the reverse lookup information and enables the client to register its forward lookup information.

dynamic routing Provides an automatic mechanism for routers to learn available routes. This is done using a routing protocol such as RIP, OSPF, or BGP.

dynamic updates Dynamic updates are fairly new to DNS. They enable a client computer or the DHCP server to register records in the DNS. This enables a network to use DHCP, which reduces management of the network, while still being capable of updating the DNS server as the client address changes.

dynamic volume A volume that can be created, extended, or deleted without requiring a reboot of this system. This type of volume is new to Windows 2000.

E

emergency repair disk This enables you to recover from Registry settings that render your system inoperable.

Encrypting File System (EFS) The public-key-based service that provides file system encryption for Windows 2000 machines.

encryption A mechanism for securing data, encryption takes data and translates it into a secret code, which can be read only with the correct key to translate the secret code back to the original data.

enterprise A general term that describes a scope including the entire organization.

enterprise root authority The first certification authority (CA) in a branch of CAs. It is responsible for assigning certificates to intermediary CAs and other subordinate CAs.

entity An entity is the subject of a table within a database. In Windows 2000, an entity is any of the types or classes of objects stored in Active Directory.

Ethernet A network standard that uses Carrier Sense Multi-Access with Collision Detection (CSMA/CD) on a bus topology. Ethernet currently runs at 10Mbps, 100Mbps, and lGbps.

Event Viewer The Event Viewer is used to look at the system log files for various parts of the system, including system security, application, and DNS. This is the first place you should look when troubleshooting a problem.

exclusion Indicates the process during which IP addresses and address ranges are removed (excluded) from a DHCP scope.

extended partition A partition that can be configured with one or more logical drives. MS-DOS supports extended partitions as the means of configuring more than one volume on a hard disk.

extensible architecture This is a type of architecture that can be added to or extended. The Windows 2000 Active Directory is said to be extensible because the tables that make up the directory database can have columns (attributes) added to them.

Exterior Gateway Protocol (EGP) The original exterior protocol, EGP is used to exchange routing information between networks that do not share a common administration.

extinction The Windows Internet Naming Service (WINS) process used to remove released WINS database entries from the database.

F

failover A technology that monitors the "heartbeat" of a server and automatically transfers failing services to another server.

FAT (file allocation table) A list maintained by some operating systems to keep track of file storage on disk.

FAT32 An advanced implementation of FAT that uses smaller clusters.

File Transfer Protocol (FTP) A standard TCP/IP protocol and utility that uses ports 20 and 21 to transfer files between hosts. User authentication information is sent as clear text.

folder redirection Folder redirection is the selective placement of folders, of which all users will use on different volumes of local computers or on shared network volumes where they can be backed up. Folder redirection is enforced through Group Policy.

forced package removal Mandatory or forced removal is the removal (uninstallation) of a software package from the user's computer. Forced package removal can't be cancelled by the user. In a forced removal, the software package is always removed from the computer.

forcing Group Policy Forcing Group Policy is the opposite of blocking—not allowing a lower-level Active Directory container's GPO settings to overwrite a GPO setting at a higher level. You typically force Group Policy at the domain level to ensure that company rules are uniformly applied to all users, regardless of their OU settings.

foreground process The active process on a computer. The process the user is interacting with is said to be the foreground process.

forest A forest is logically any single Active Directory domain or any grouping of domains. Notably, a structure is said to be a forest if it contains one or more domain trees that don't have a contiguous namespaces.

forward lookup Forward lookups are the simplest type of resolution that is performed. In a forward lookup, the system tries to find the IP address for a computer name.

forwarder A caching-only DNS server that has been configured to send name resolution requests to another DNS server.

frame One term for a basic unit of network communication, consisting of a message and the information required for delivery. Also referred to as a *packet.*

frame type Defines the makeup of a data packet.

full backup Copying the entire contents of a computer's hard drive(s) to a media format, such as tape or CD-ROM, or to another disk.

fully qualified domain name (FQDN) The complete DNS name of a host, including the host name and all domains that connect the host to the root domain. Typically expressed without a trailing period, with the root domain assumed.

fully qualified name The name of a container or data object in a hierarchy, consisting of the object's name and the names of all containers that connect the object to the root container.

G

global catalog The global catalog in Active Directory is made up of a list of all objects within all domains along with a subset of common attributes for each of the objects. The global catalog is used to locate objects in Active Directory and is accessed using the Active Directory services interface or LDAP.

global catalog server This is the system that will contain the global catalog and will replicate with the other global catalog servers.

global group A global group is used to gather users from a domain so they can be added en mass to local groups in the domain or in other domains.

global options In the context of DHCP, global options are sent to all systems leasing an address regardless of the scope from which they lease. These include things such as the DNS and WINS server addresses.

globally unique identifier (GUID) A GUID is a 32-character string used to uniquely identify a computer for prestaging. In RIS, it is usually the identity of the PXE-enabled network card, but it can also be the MAC address of a non-PXE-compliant network card padded to 32 characters and using the proper format.

GPO inheritance Group Policy object inheritance is the set of rules by which higher-level GPO settings are applied or overwritten by lower-level GPOs in Active Directory. The default GPO inheritance hierarchy is `sitedomainOU`, which means that settings at a site level can be overwritten at a domain level, which can then be overwritten at the OU level. In this way, settings applied closest to the user or computer have precedence by default.

GPO scope GPO scope deals with which Active Directory containers a GPO is associated. Group Policy objects can be associated with a single Active Directory container (for example, an OU) or can be added to other containers at the same or a different level. The same settings are applied at all containers to which the GPO is linked.

Group Policy Used to define user and computer configurations for groups in a Windows 2000 network environment.

Group Policy container A Group Policy container is an Active Directory container that includes GPO attributes (such as the GUID) and version information.

Group Policy filtering Filtering a GPO is the assignment of permissions to a Group Policy, thereby determining to which users and computers the policy will be applied.

Group Policy object (GPO) A Group Policy object is an object within Active Directory that enables an administrator to configure software deployment settings, security settings, and administrative templates, thereby enforcing corporate rules for users and computers. Group Policy is composed of Group Policy containers and Group Policy templates.

Group Policy precedence Precedence is the order in which GPOs within the same container are processed. Because more than one GPO can be linked to the same Active Directory container, precedence determines which GPO has the final say.

Group Policy template A Group Policy template is a set of folders and subfolders in the SYSVOL share on Windows 2000 domain controllers containing the scripts, security templates, and administrative settings for Group Policy to be downloaded on client computers.

groups A group is a container-type object found in Active Directory. Groups are used primarily for collecting a consistent set of rights and permissions to be assigned to users by way of making them a member of the group.

GUID *See* globally unique identifier.

H

H-node *See* Hybrid node.

H.323 Proxy A standard used to allow videoconferencing applications to interoperate.

Hardware Compatibility List (HCL) Microsoft's published list of hardware that has passed testing on Windows 2000.

hierarchy A database structure based on the principle of categories and subcategories, typically represented in the form of an inverted tree. Each hierarchy has exactly one master category, typically called the root, and all other categories are subcategories of the root category. Categories can contain subcategories as well as data.

hive Registry data is stored in six or more sets of files, called hives. Each hive consists of two files: a data file and a log file.

hop A common metric used with routing protocols, in which one hop is counted for each network that a message traverses on a route.

host (TCP/IP) A device that is attached to a TCP/IP network.

host file A static database file used to resolve names on TCP/IP networks.

host ID The portion of an IP address that uniquely identifies a host on its local TCP/IP network.

host record The most common record in a DNS zone file (also known as an A or Alias record). It enables a host's DNS name to be resolved to an IP address.

HOSTS Hosts file. A static database file used to resolve names on TCP/IP networks.

Hybrid node (H-node) One of four node types that can be set for NetBIOS name resolution, which first uses p-node for name queries and then b-node or (broadcasts) if the WINS server is unavailable.

Hypertext Transfer Protocol (HTTP) The protocol used by the World Wide Web. It's the transport protocol for HTML files and has recently been used by many other protocols as well.

I

incremental backup These look to see the current status of the archive bit before backing up data and back up only those files set to `true`. After completion, this changes the archive bit to `false`.

infrastructure master The infrastructure master is a domain-level operations master. It is responsible for updating the group membership of the domain users across the entire enterprise.

inheritance In Active Directory, permissions are inherited from parent objects. This process is called inheritance and can be blocked if desired.

instance After selecting a counter in the Performance utility, all instances (occurrences) of the object are shown so that you can choose which one you want to monitor. For example, a server with two CPUs would show three instances—one for each processor and one called `_Total`.

Integrated Services Digital Network (ISDN) ISDN is a type of communications line that provides higher-speed access than a telephone line and modem to a digital network. Special equipment is required on both ends of the line to acquire higher speed.

Intellimirror A set of technologies included in Windows 2000 that enable a user's desktop configuration to follow that user to any machine on the network.

interface Something that connects two separate entities. These can be hardware devices, software applications, or even a user and an application.

Interior Gateway Protocol (IGP) Used to pass routing information for routing networks that are under a common network administration.

intermediate CA A CA that assigns certificates to subordinate CAs only. The subordinate CAs do not request a certificate from the root CA.

internal network number On IPX networks, each server must have an internal network number and an eight-digit hexadecimal number used to deliver data to the correct process within the server.

Internet A worldwide network used to join various corporate and public networks into a single network.

Internet Connection Sharing (ICS) A Windows 2000 service used to enable a small office to share a dial-up Internet connection easily and securely.

Internet Control Message Protocol (ICMP) A protocol in the TCP/IP suite of protocols used for testing connectivity.

Internet Explorer A browser from Microsoft that is used to view Web pages.

Internet Group Management Protocol (IGMP) One of the core protocols in the TCP/IP suite. It is a routing protocol used as part of multicasting.

Internet Information Server (IIS) Microsoft's Internet hosting software up to Version 4.

Internet Information Services (IIS) Microsoft's renamed Internet hosting software.

Internet Protocol (IP) The portion of the TCP/IP protocol suite used to provide IP packet routing.

Internet Protocol Configuration (IPCONFIG) Windows 2000/Windows NT/Windows 98/Windows Me/Windows XP utility that can be used to view the configuration details for the host's TCP/IP. IPCONFIG can also be used to release or renew an address leased from a DHCP server.

Internet Protocol Security (IPSec) The standard IP-based VPN protocol used to provide secure communications across a public network.

Internet service provider (ISP) A vendor that provides network connectivity to the Internet as well as support services such as name, news, and electronic mail.

internetwork An extended network consisting of discrete networks that communicate through routers. A "network of networks." Also called an internet.

IP address The 32-bit binary address used to identify a TCP/IP host's network and host ID.

IP address conservation The act of configuring your network in conjunction with DHCP to use the fewest number of IP addresses possible.

iterative query A DNS query sent from a DNS server to one or more DNS servers in search of the DNS server that is authoritative for the name being sought.

J, K

Kerberos An identity-based security protocol based on Internet security standards used by Windows 2000 to authenticate users.

Knowledge Consistency Checker (KCC) The KCC is responsible for creating the intrasite connections to ensure that each computer will have at least two replication partners. It also uses the site links you create to make connections between servers at different sites so that replication can take place between the sites.

L

LAN Local area network. A connection of computers via high-speed network within the same general area, typically a building.

LAN Manager A network operating system developed by IBM and Microsoft. This network was one of the first to use domain controllers to centralize the authentication of users on a network.

LAN Manager HOSTS file (LMHOSTS) The LMHOSTS file is modeled after the TCP/IP HOSTS file and is used to provide a static NetBIOS name to IP address resolution in a Windows environment. The HOST file was originally used for name resolution in a TCP/IP network environment. As the HOSTS file was replaced by DNS, the LMHOSTS file was replaced by WINS.

last known good configuration This enables you to recover from configuration changes that affect Registry settings for devices (such as installing an incorrect video driver or configuring it incorrectly). This tool has only a limited window of effectiveness; after you successfully log on to a Windows 2000 computer, this no longer functions.

Layer 2 Tunneling Protocol (L2TP) A VPN protocol created by combining the PPTP and L2F tunneling protocols. Used as the transport protocol in the Windows 2000 VPN service in conjunction with IPSec.

LDAP *See* Lightweight Directory Access Protocol.

leaf The end object in a hierarchical tree structure.

leaf-level object This is an object in directory services, such as a user object, that holds a place but does not contain other objects.

lease The process by which DHCP assigns an IP address to a client.

lease duration A DHCP lease duration is the length of time the DHCP client is authorized to use the leased address. The client starts trying to renew the address at 50% of the lease duration.

Lightweight Directory Access Protocol (LDAP) Lightweight version of the X.500 directory standard used as the primary access protocol for Active Directory.

link state Used by dynamic routing protocols to test the condition of a connection (link) between routers. OSPF is a link state protocol.

local group A local group is the same as a domain local group. It is used for rights and permissions, but it exists on standalone servers and Windows 2000 Professional computers. These are also used on member servers in mixed mode.

Local password policy The password policy that is applied to the local system, it's overridden by the password policy of a domain when the computer is a member of a domain.

Log view A view within the Performance utility that enables you to log performance data about your system to a file.

logical drive A portion of an extended partition that can be formatted as a volume.

logon/logoff scripts Logon/logoff scripts are BAT, CMD, or Windows Script Host files (VBScript or JScript) that are run at logon or logoff time by each user who has the GPO applied. Logon/logoff scripts enable the administrator to configure other settings for the user that can't be set through Group Policy.

M

M-node *See* Mixed node.

Mail Exchange (MX) A record in the DNS zone file that indicates which host in your network will receive mail.

Management Information Base (MIB) Organizes a set of manageable objects for an installed service or device. MIBs are used in conjunction with the SNMP protocol.

mandatory upgrade A mandatory upgrade is an upgrade to an existing software package deployed through Group Policy that must be installed. Mandatory upgrades can be set for the user or the computer and will remove the previous version of the package.

many-to-one mapping Many certificates mapped to one user account.

master browser A computer that collects service announcements from servers and constructs a browse list. Backup browsers periodically contact the master browser to obtain an updated copy of the master browser database.

master server A master server is the server from which a secondary DNS retrieves a copy of a zone file. The master can be a primary or secondary server.

Media Access Control (MAC) The MAC address is the physical address assigned to a network card, and it is used to identify it on the network.

Media Access Layer Part of the Data Link layer from the OSI model. The physical address of a NIC is called a MAC address.

medium The vehicle that carries data between a server and a client. Network media include copper cable, optical fiber, microwaves, and light pulses.

method A method is an action that can be performed on an object. Common methods include create and delete. Methods are important because they are used when you are programmatically accessing objects such as Active Directory.

metric A number that assigns a preference to a route within routing protocols. The route with the lowest metric is the preferred route.

Microsoft Management Console (MMC) A framework used for hosting administrative tools.

Mixed node (M-node) One of the four node types that can be set for NetBIOS name resolution.

modem (modulating/demodulating device) Hardware device used to convert digital signals to analog, and vice versa. This enables digital communications to occur over regular (analog) phone lines.

MOVETREE This utility can be used to move objects between domains. Within a domain, an object can be moved in Users and Computers using the context menu command Move.

multicast scope A range of IP multicast addresses in the range of 224.0.0.0–239.254.255.255. Multicast addresses in this range can be prevented from propagating in either direction (send or receive) through the use of scope-based multicast boundaries.

multicasting A method of sending a series of packets to a group of computers instead of to a single computer or all computers on a network. IGMP support is required to use multicasting.

multilink A capability included in Windows 2000 that allows the aggregating of multiple modem connections from a compatible host to a dial-up network.

N

name registration The act of registering a host's NetBIOS name on the network. Name registration occurs when a system starts, a service starts, or a user logs on. Registrations can be sent as a broadcast on the local network or to a WINS server, where the name and IP address are added to the database.

name release An event that occurs when a system notifies other systems (such as the master browser or a WINS server) that a system is shutting down.

name renewal A transmission sent to a WINS server requesting a renewal of the host's WINS database entry.

name resolution The process of determining the network address associated with a computer name.

name server This is a component of DNS name servers that is responsible for receiving resolution requests from other servers or from clients and processing the requests.

namespace This is an entire tree of names that starts with a root and branches from there. The namespace is similar to a directory structure on a drive. The entire Internet is controlled using a single namespace, whereas each Active Directory tree is a single namespace. In a fully qualified domain name, the namespace is the remaining part of the name after the host portion is removed.

native mode The mode in which Windows 2000 can operate after all servers are Windows 2000 computers. This mode supports the additional functionality of multimaster replication and nested groups and does not support the capability to replicate with Windows NT 4.0 domain controllers.

NetBEUI The default Application Layer protocol.

NetBIOS name The computer name for NetBIOS networking. This name can be 16 characters long: 15 provide the host name, and the 16th represents the service registering the name.

NetBIOS name cache A list of system NetBIOS names that a host has resolved or that have been preloaded from the `LMHOSTS` file.

NetBIOS node type The node type determines the order of name resolution for NetBIOS names. The four types are B-node, P-node, M-node, and H-node.

NetBIOS over TCP/IP (NBT or NetBT) The name given to the process of running NetBIOS network services over TCP/IP.

Netlogon The Netlogon or Network Logon service is the service that handles the requests for network authentication from users.

NetWare NetWare is a popular network operating system originally designed to use a separate user database on each server. Later, NetWare was improved with Novell Directory Services, which enabled it to compete more easily in the enterprise networking arena.

Network Address Translation (NAT) An Internet standard that enables a Windows 2000 server to use one set of IP addresses on the internal network and a different set of IP addresses on the external network. This can be done to hide the internal addresses or to allow unregistered addresses to be used on the internal network, whereas registered addresses are used externally.

Network Basic Input/Output System (NetBIOS) An Application Layer networking protocol that works at the Application, Presentation, and Session layers of the OSI model. Legacy Microsoft networking used NetBIOS as the default Application Layer protocol.

network binding *See* binding.

network ID The portion of an IP address that identifies the network to which a host is attached.

Network Monitor An application included with Windows 2000 that enables you to monitor the packets sent to and from your Windows 2000 host, which enables you to troubleshoot network problems.

network number On IPX networks, the network number is an eight-digit hexadecimal number that uniquely identifies each network on an internetwork.

network operating system (NOS) An operating system or extension to an operating system enables clients to use a redirector to determine whether a request is for the local machine or a remote system. The NOS can then expose the required network interface, or it can access it on behalf of the user application to pass the request to another service running, typically, on another computer connected to the network.

New Technology File System 5.0 (NTFS) Advanced file system used in Windows 2000 to offer advanced security features. It provides many benefits, including the capability to set file and folder permissions, making it a requirement for the SYSVOL share.

No Override Same as forcing Group Policy.

node A device that communicates on the network and is identified by a unique address. In hierarchies, a node is a container that contains other containers and data.

normal backup These backups save all files regardless of the state of the archive bit.

notification Master DNS servers can notify secondary servers when a change in the zone file occurs. This is done using a notification.

NTBACKUP The Microsoft provided utility for backing up a Windows NT or Windows 2000 system.

NSLOOKUP The NSLOOKUP utility can be used to query a DNS server either from the command line or by creating a session with the DNS server.

NTDSUTIL This utility is used for several functions. Notably, it is used to seize a single operations master role and perform authoritative restores.

null modem A cable that lets computers communicate through serial ports by simulating a modem connection.

NWLink Protocol written to allow Windows operating systems to communicate using the IPX protocol.

O

object An object is a general term used for any resource or other entity that exists. By using the object model, programming is simplified through the ability to use and reuse code.

object-level permissions Permission can be set on objects to control who can manage the object. This is the basis of delegating control of an OU because the permissions are inherited by child objects.

octet Commonly used to refer to groups of 8 bits in network addresses, such as IP addresses. A 32-bit IP address consists of four octets.

one-to-one mapping A single certificate mapped to a single user account.

Open Shortest Path First (OSPF) A routing protocol that enables routers to share their routing information, making them dynamic routers.

operating system An operating system is a program or set of programs that provides basic services to the user of a computer. The operating system should at least be capable of starting the computer, managing memory on the computer, interacting with the basic input/output system of the computer, and scheduling the execution of programs on the system.

optional package removal Optional removal enables the user to decide whether to remove an application from her computer or leave it installed.

optional upgrade An optional upgrade is an upgrade to a Group Policy—deployed software package that a user can decide to install on her computer but is not obliged to do so.

organization An organization is a term that refers to the company or enterprise that is implementing Active Directory. In X.400 and X.500 terms, the organization (O) is the name of the company.

organizational unit (OU) An organizational unit is a subgrouping within a domain that can be used to delegate administrative control of the objects it contains. In X.400 and X.500, an organizational unit is a subdivision of the organization.

originating write An originating write is a change to an object in Active Directory caused by a process other than replication. For example, a user changing his password is an originating write. The originating write updates the update sequence number of the object.

P

P-node *See* Point-to-Point node.

package modifications Package modifications are changes applied to a software package, and they are contained in transform (MST) files. Transform files are associated with an existing package. They, in combination with several GPOs, are used to change the behavior of a package when it is deployed in different regions.

Packet Internet Groper Utility (PING) A utility used to troubleshoot TCP/IP problems. PING sends a packet with data asking the remote system to echo the packet.

paging The process of swapping data between RAM and disk-based virtual memory.

paging file A temporary file used to support virtual memory.

parent domain The highest domain structure in a Windows 2000 server domain tree hierarchy.

partition A physical subdivision of a disk drive that can be formatted with a file system.

password age Password age is a numeric value between 0 and 999 days that defines how long a password can stay in effect before it must be changed.

password history Password history is a running list of the passwords that have been set for a particular account. The setting consists of a counter that's set between 0 and 24. This defines the number of passwords Windows 2000 will remember, the implication of which is that none of the remembered passwords can be used again.

PDC emulator This is an operations master role on the domain level. The PDC emulator handles replication with down-level domain controllers and authentication of down-level clients. It also creates the trust relationships between domains.

Performance This utility enables you to monitor and view the performance of all the parts of the system at a very low level. It can be used to troubleshoot general system problems and performance problems.

Performance Monitor The Performance Monitor enables you to watch various facets of your system, whether you are looking for real-time graphical views or a log you can peruse at your convenience.

permissions Permissions provide a user with the capability to work with an object. The permissions a user or other security principal has for an object are contained in the discretionary access control list (DACL).

Plug and Play A combination of hardware and software that enables a computer to recognize and modify its hardware configuration changes with minimal intervention from the user.

pointer record (PTR) In DNS, a pointer record is a host entry used in a reverse zone file to allow IP address-to-FQDN resolution.

Point-to-Point node (P-node) One of the four node types that can be set for NetBIOS name resolution.

Point-to-Point Protocol (PPP) A serial-line protocol that replaces the frame types found on networks when communicating over a serial line. It defines how the data is physically transmitted.

Point-to-Point Tunneling Protocol (PPTP) A protocol used by Microsoft and others to create a virtual private network.

port, hardware A hardware component that lets a computer communicate with other devices. Examples are printer ports, serial ports, and network ports.

port, TCP A software address that lets the TCP/IP protocols deliver messages to the correct process on a computer. Each process running on a TCP/IP computer must be associated with a unique combination of an IP address and a port number. The combination of an IP address and a port number is called a *socket.*

prestaging The process of creating computer accounts in Active Directory by using the GUID of the computer. Prestaging enables the administrator to configure a client computer to receive its image list from a specified Microsoft server, and it also can be used to ensure that only those computers that have been prestaged can use Microsoft.

primary DNS server The name server that contains the master copy of a zone file.

primary domain controller (PDC) In a Windows NT 4.0 network, the PDC is the main domain controller. It contains the only write-enabled version of the domain database. This system then needs to replicate that database to the backup domain controllers so that they are also capable of authenticating user logon requests.

primary master *See* Primary DNS server.

primary name server The primary name server is the server on which the zone file is created. Changes to the zone file are made on this server only and then are sent to the secondary servers. If the zone is Active Directory integrated, there will no longer be a primary server because all domain controllers with DNS installed can make modifications.

primary partition A partition that can be used to boot an operating system.

primary zone A DNS zone that contains the master copies of resource records for a domain.

print server A computer configured to share its printer through the network. Windows 2000 computers become print servers when their printers are shared.

Printers This is a class of objects in Active Directory that is used to publish or list printers in the Active Directory so that users can search for and use a printer anywhere in the enterprise if they have permissions.

private IP address An IP address range reserved for private (non-Internet-connected) networks. Private address ranges exist in the Class A, Class B, and Class C address blocks.

process A process is a combination of assigned virtual memory and at least one execution thread that is used to run an application. Services each run in a process, as do all programs that users run, including the initial user process (`Explorer.exe`). Every process has a set of credentials attached in the form of an access token, which determines the rights and permissions of the process.

profile *See* user profile.

profile, local A user profile stored on the user's workstation.

profile, mandatory A user profile that can be accessed from any workstation on a network. Users can't save changes made to a mandatory profile.

profile, roaming A personal user profile that can be accessed from any workstation on a network. Users can change settings in roaming profiles.

properties Properties describe an object in the same way an adjective describes a noun (for example, the green door). In the case of an object such as a file, the file type is a property.

protocol A standard set of rules for communicating between computers.

provider connections A provider is a component that enables you to connect to network resources. A connection is either a network connection (local or remote) or a Dial-Up Networking (DUN) connection.

proxy server Server running the proxy service.

proxy service Sits between a client application, such as a Web browser, and the destination server. It intercepts all requests to the destination to see whether it can fulfill the requests itself. If not, it forwards the request to the real server. Proxy services frequently contain caching capabilities.

public switched telephone network (PSTN) The public telephone network.

publishing software packages Publishing software packages is the capability to enable a user to optionally install a Group Policy—deployed software package by document activation through Add/Remove Programs in Control Panel.

pull replication The act of replicating a copy of the WINS database from a WINS replication partner triggered by a defined time interval.

push replication The act of replicating a copy of the WINS database to a WINS replication partner triggered by a defined number of changes to the WINS database.

Pre-boot Execution Environment (PXE) PXE is a standard by which a network card with a boot ROM complying with the standard can request a TCP/IP address from a DHCP server and the IP address of a RIS server to start the installation of a Windows 2000 Professional image.

Q, R

`Qchain.exe` A utility to help automate the process and improve reliability of deploying several hot fixes simultaneously by chaining them together.

quality of service (QoS) A set of standards used to ensure a specified quality for data transmissions across a network.

record types The various types of entries that can be created in a DNS table.

Recovery Console The Recovery Console is a powerful text-based boot alternative for Windows 2000. If your system becomes so corrupt that it will not boot and no other repair process will help, you can boot to the Recovery Console and copy files to or from your computer. In addition, you can stop and start services if a service that you have installed causes problems with booting.

recursive query A recursive query is a query between a client and the DNS server that requests the name resolution or a failure notification.

redeployment Redeployment is the reinstallation of an existing software package through Group Policy, usually to distribute a patch for an existing application.

redirector A redirector is part of the network operating system that is responsible for formulating requests that will be passed to a server service. The redirector in Windows 2000 is called the Workstation service.

registered IP address Any block of addresses registered with the Internet Assigned Numbers Authority (IANA).

Registry The Registry is a collection of settings that exists on each computer for both the computer and the users who log on to that computer. The Registry is broken down into a series of subtrees, of which `KEY_LOCAL_MACHINE` and `HKEY_USERS` are the most important because they deal with computer, COM+, and user settings. Group Policy Administrative Templates modify the Registry to enforce GPO settings at the user and computer levels.

Registry key A container for data in the Registry data hierarchy.

relative identifier (RID) master This is an operations master on the domain level. The RID master creates and distributes RIDs that are used in conjunction with domain SIDs to create the SIDs for new objects in the domains.

Remote Access Service (RAS) A feature built into Windows NT that enables users to log on to an NT-based LAN using a modem. Replaced by the Routing and Remote Access Service in Windows 2000.

Remote Administration mode Enables a connection to a terminal server for the purposes of administering it.

remote control Taking over a client's console and session.

Remote Installation Preparation (RIPrep) image RIPrep images contain the entire configuration of a source computer, including the operating system and all installed applications and shortcuts. They are deployed to target computers with the same HAL as the source using Remote Installation Services.

Remote Installation Service (RIS) This is a Windows 2000 service that facilitates the deployment of Windows 2000 Professional to computers by means of a RIS boot disk or a PXE-compliant network adapter.

remote procedure call (RPC) RPCs are one of the methods that can be used for interprocess communications. This method uses an external redirector and server that many services and clients can use at the same time. Server-to-server RPC communications should have at least 64KB of network bandwidth.

repackaging an application Repackaging an application is the creation of a Windows installer package for an application by use of a third-party repackaging tool, such as Veritas WinInstall LE.

repeater A physical device that takes a signal from one interface and retransmits it to another. This enables a network segment to be extended beyond the normal distances dictated by the limits of the topology.

replication This is the process of copying data from one location to another. Replication is important in Active Directory; Active Directory replicates schema information, configuration information, domain information, and the global catalog.

replication partner A server in a WINS architecture that sends a copy of the WINS database to another WINS server or receives a copy of the WINS database from another WINS server.

Request for Comment (RFC) Used to make notes about the Internet and Internet technologies.

reservation A permanent address lease assignment from the DHCP server to a specified client.

resolver This is a small piece of code that is built into an application or the operating system that performs the recursive query to the DNS server.

resource record A data record in a DNS zone. For example, an address resource record is the data record that describes the address-to-name relationship for a host. Many types of resource records are available.

resources Any file, folder, printer, service, or other portion of a computer that is available for use. Network resources are those that are shared to the network so that they are available to the users on the network.

restore The process of restoring files from a backup.

restricting images Restricting images is the act of assigning NTFS permissions on answer files for RIS images. Restricting images enables the administrator to specify which user or group accounts will be allowed to use a specific image through RIS.

reverse lookup A reverse lookup is the process of asking for the name of a server based on an IP address.

revocation list A published list of certificates that have been revoked.

revoked certificate A certificate that is no longer valid because the validity of the certificate was discontinued.

rights In the same way that permissions control what a user can do to a file, rights control which system actions a user can perform—for example changing the system time.

RIS boot disk A disk created by the Remote Boot Disk Generator program (`Rbfg.exe`) that emulates a PXE-based environment on a computer without a PXE-compliant network card. The RIS boot disk can be used to start the installation of a RIS image on a target computer.

RIS image An operating system image that can be deployed to computers from an Microsoft server. RIS images can be CD based or RIPrep images and are stored on a RIS server.

RIS server A Windows 2000 server that is part of an Active Directory domain and has Remote Installation Services installed.

root In a hierarchy, the container that holds all other containers.

root domain The starting point for a hierarchy. A root domain on the Internet is the starting point of the namespace for the entire Internet. In the Windows 2000 world, the root domain is the first domain that is installed, to which all other domains are joined as other branches of the namespace.

router A system or device that forwards or drops packets between networks, based on the entries in its routing table.

Routing and Remote Access (RRAS) The Windows 2000 Server Routing and Remote Access enables remote connection to the server.

Routing Information Protocol (RIP) A protocol used by dynamic routers to share their routing tables. Similar to OSPF and BGP protocols, RIP is an older, less efficient routing protocol.

routing table Each TCP/IP host maintains a routing table that describes routing decisions the host can make. Minimum entries in the routing table include routes to each local network and a default route.

Routing Table (ROUTE) utility The Windows ROUTE utility enables you to view and modify the routing table on a Windows computer.

S

Safe mode This enables you to troubleshoot and correct errors that might be otherwise uncorrectable. Starting in Safe mode loads only a minimal set of drivers and is very useful in cases in which device drivers are to blame for startup errors.

scavenging This is a process that is required on a server that performs dynamic registration. The process looks for outdated records and removes them.

schema This is the term used to describe the rows and columns that make up the tables in a database. The schema in Windows 2000 refers to the definition of classes (tables) and attributes (columns) within the directory database. Classes are templates for objects that define the attributes an object must have. Attributes are templates that define the types of values that can be contained in the attribute.

schema master This is one of the operation master roles, and it contains the only write-enabled copy of the schema of the directory database. When changes are made, this system ensures that all the other domain controllers in the enterprise are updated. There is only one schema master in an Active Directory forest, and all changes to the schema are made across the entire forest.

schema partition This is where the schema information is contained. The schema partition is replicated from the schema master to all domain controllers in the network.

scope The full, consecutive range of possible IP addresses for a network.

second-level domains In the DNS namespace, a second-level domain is a domain an organization will use. For example, the second-level domain in `www.newriders.com` is `newriders`.

secondary DNS server Provides name resolution for a zone, but it can't be used to modify the zone. It contains a read-only copy of the zone file.

secondary master *See* secondary DNS server.

secondary server This is a DNS server that can provide an authoritative answer to a client because it has a copy of the zone file. In standard mode, it can't make a change to the zone file that is copied from a master server.

secondary zone A DNS zone that obtains copies of the resource records for a domain through a zone transfer from a primary zone.

Secure Socket Layer (SSL) An add-on encryption layer for HTTP designed to make it impossible for a third party to observe the content of transactions between a Web server and a client.

Security Access Manager (SAM) The component of Windows 2000 that manages the security database and all security functions for local groups and accounts.

Security Configuration and Analysis Security Configuration and Analysis is an MMC snap-in designed primarily to analyze local system security settings and apply security templates to the local computer. It can also be used to retrieve the local computer security configuration and create a security template that reflects the computer's settings.

security context This is the user credentials under which a process is running.

security group A security group is used to set permissions. You can also use a security group for email; however, security groups are approximately 2,600 bytes larger.

security identifier (SID) This is the unique number that identifies every object in Active Directory. The SID for objects in Windows 2000 is made up of a combination of the domain SID from the domain in which they were created and a unique relative identifier.

Security Log Location within the Event Viewer where auditing details are stored.

security principal Security principal is a term applied to any object you can give permissions or rights to, such as users, computers, and groups.

security templates Security templates are text files containing the rules used to enforce security settings for users and computers. They form the basis for a security policy for users and computers.

Serial Line Internet Protocol (SLIP) A line protocol for serial communications that replaces the frames on a physical network. The SLIP protocol can transfer only TCP/IP packets and provides only limited security.

server A computer that shares resources on a network.

server mirroring Real-time replication of a server's data to another server.

service This is a background application that is started automatically when the computer starts or is started manually by an operator. Services typically do not interact with the desktop but run as background processes providing services to other processes.

service packs Updates to software packages to fix security flaws, update features, and streamline coding.

service (SRV) records The SRV record is a new type of record in DNS that enables a domain controller to register a DNS name so that users can search for a domain controller rather than a particular computer.

share A share is a class of objects that is available in Active Directory. Share objects enable share folder resources to be published to Active Directory so that users can search for them more easily.

share permissions When you create a share, the information in the share is exposed to the network. You need to set the permissions for the users that will access the share to ensure that only the users who are supposed to use the share are doing so. The effective permissions for a share are a combination of the share permissions and the NTFS permissions if, as it should be, the share is on an NTFS drive.

Simple Mail Transfer Protocol (SMTP) SMTP is a simple protocol typically used to move information from one email server to another email server. In Windows 2000, this protocol can be used for replication between sites.

Simple Network Management Protocol (SNMP) Used by a management station to read information from agents.

Single Instance Store (SIS) Service The Single Instance Store Service runs on a RIS server and is responsible for ensuring that the files required for a CD-based RIS image can be found. It also helps minimize disk space used by ensuring that multiple copies of the same file required by multiple RIS images do not exist and that a single copy of the file is instead shared.

site On an Internet server, such as a World Wide Web server, a site is a logical server. Each site must be defined by a unique combination of properties. For example, each Web site running on a given computer must be defined by a unique combination of an IP address and a TCP port.

site link A site link is a logical connection between two or more sites. A site link lets the KCC know about other sites in your network so that it can create the required links.

site link bridge This is a connection between two or more site links acting as a path for Active Directory replication between sites not directly linked. Bridges are ignored unless you turn off automatic site link bridging.

slipstreaming With slipstreaming, changes from the service pack can be applied to the source files found on a local folder or network share (by using the `s` switch when running `update.exe` for the service pack). This means that when you subsequently access those files, you obtain the fixed versions of those files, not the old ones. This saves time because the service packs must be applied to any machine only once, and not multiple times as services (and other operating system components) are installed.

snap-in A tool you can add to a Microsoft Management Console.

socket The unique combination of an IP address and a TCP port number that identifies a particular process running on a particular TCP/IP computer.

software categories Software categories are logical groupings of published software packages that enable a user to more easily browse the available software to determine which package to install. The same software package can appear in more than one category.

source computer The computer onto which Windows 2000 Professional, applications, and other settings are applied and that will be used as the source for a RIPrep image.

spanned volume A volume of disk space that resides on more than one physical disk.

special permissions Highly granular type of NTFS permissions that can be assigned to user or group objects.

split horizon The split horizon mechanism is used with the RIP protocol to prevent routing loops. Split horizon blocks information about routes from being advertised by a router or any interface from which that information originated.

split horizon with poison reverse Whereas standard split horizon blocks routes from being advertised by a router or any interface from which that information originated, split horizon with poison reverse broadcasts the routes with an infinite routing metric.

standalone certification authorities These do not require Active Directory. Standalone CAs can issue certificates for purposes such as digital signatures, secure email, and authentication to a secure Web server.

standard permissions A group of six NTFS permissions that can be assigned to user or group objects.

start of authority (SOA) In a DNS zone file, it's used to provide the zone parameters to all the DNS servers for the zone. The SOA record also provides the name of the primary server and the person in charge of the domain.

startup/shutdown scripts Startup/shutdown scripts are BAT, CMD, or Windows Script Host files (VBScript or JScript) that run at startup and shutdown time for the computers that have the GPO applied. Startup/shutdown scripts enable the administrator to configure other settings for the computer that can't be set through Group Policy.

static route An item in a routing table that is entered manually and that doesn't change based on information received from a routing protocol.

stripe set *See* disk drives, stripe set.

stripe set with parity *See* disk drives, stripe set with parity.

subdomain A DNS domain located directly beneath another DNS domain in the DNS hierarchy.

subnet A subnet is a single segment of a routed network. It is usually identified using the subnet ID followed by a slash and the number of bits in the netmask. For example, 148.53.64.0/18 would be a subnet for hosts 148.53.64.1–14.53.127.254.

subnet mask In TCP/IP, a subnet mask is a mask used to determine to which subnet an IP address belongs. The subnet mask enables a host or router to determine which portion of an IP address is the net ID and which is the host ID. The host can then use this information to determine whether to send a packet to a host on the local network or to a router.

suffix A domain suffix indicates the root domain. For example, COM is a domain suffix.

supernetted network A network that has multiple network addresses or subnets running on the same segment.

superscope A grouping of scopes that are used to support multinetted IP subnets on the same physical network.

SYSTEM account The SYSTEM account is a special account that can be used to start services that will be available on a computer. The SYSTEM account is really the computer account that has complete control of the local system.

System File Checker The System File Checker is a command-line utility that scans and verifies the versions of all protected system files. If System File Checker discovers that a protected file has been overwritten or deleted, it replaces the file with the correct (digitally signed) version from the cache.

System Monitor This enables you to view statistical data either live or from a saved log. You can view the data in three formats: graph, histogram, or report. Graph data is displayed as a line graph; histograms are displayed as bar graphs.

system policy A legacy policy based on Registry settings that have been made with the System Policy Editor, `poledit.exe`. It's used in Windows NT and Windows 95/98 environments but can be used in Windows 2000 environments. For maximum security in Windows 2000 environments, use group policies instead.

system state data The system state data is the core of the operating system and represents Active Directory, the Registry, the certificate database, and other key files. The system state data should be backed up on a schedule.

SYSVOL This is the system volume share; it is the connection point that is used to authenticate user logons and store logon scripts, group policies, and similar files.

T

table A table is a structure in a database that contains data. It is made of columns, which represent attributes or properties, and rows, which represent entities.

target computer The computer onto which RIPrep or CD-based images are installed using Remote Installation Services. The target computer must meet Windows 2000 Professional hardware requirements and must have a PXE-enabled network card or be supported by the RIS boot disk.

Task Manager This is a basic utility that can provide a quick look at the current performance of the system, including which processes are running and the overall statistics for CPU and memory. You can use this application to end a task that is not responding or change the priority of a running task.

TCP *See* Transmission Control Protocol/Internet Protocol.

TCP/IP filter Used to prevent certain addresses or protocols from traversing a router.

Terminal Emulation (Telnet) This protocol/utility is part of the TCP/IP suite and is used to provide a terminal window to another station on the network. This is generally used in conjunction with Unix hosts.

Terminal Services It's a session hosting service that enables a Windows 2000 server to provide environment resources (memory, processor, and hard drive) so that a client must provide only minimal memory and processor resources.

Terminal Services License Manager Terminal Server requires this to be installed once for each enterprise in which applications are to run from Terminal Services clients.

Terminal Services Profile The Terminal Services Profile property sheet provides the configuration of a special profile for use when connecting to a terminal server, a home directory for use when connecting to a terminal server, and a check box that enables a user as a potential Terminal Services client.

time to live (TTL) An amount of time to keep information or continue operating with a packet. In DNS it is used when a DNS server resolves an address. It caches this address for the time given in the returned information. This time is the TTL for the DNS cache entry.

token ring A networking technology comparable to Ethernet, in which a token is used to determine who can send traffic onto the network. The data circulates through the ring until the system for which it is intended receives it and marks the token with an acknowledgement. The token then circles back to the sending system, which releases the token to the other stations on the ring.

top-level domains On the Internet, top-level domains are used as the first division of the namespace. The best known is probably the `com` top-level domain.

trace log These are used to record data as a certain activity, such as disk I/O or a page fault, occurs. When the event occurs, the provider sends the data to the log service.

trace provider A piece of software that can be either provided in the operating system like the system provider is or an additional utility created to watch for certain event types.

trace router (TRACERT) utility Traces the route that packets travel between the local host and the destination host and displays it to the screen.

traffic Traffic is a general term in computing that refers to data that is traveling or must travel across the network. A great concern is that a network will have more traffic than it can handle.

transform files Same as package modifications.

Transmission Control Protocol/Internet Protocol (TCP/IP) The suite of communications protocols used to connect hosts on the Internet.

tree A root domain and all its children of a single contiguous namespace is considered a tree in Active Directory.

Trivial File Transfer Protocol (TFTP) TFTP is a protocol that runs on a RIS server and is used to transfer files to the target computer during deployment. This is not the same as the FTP protocol you might use to connect to an FTP site on the Internet. TFTP differs from FTP in that it does not require any user interaction, which is why it is used for Remote Installation Services.

trust relationships A trust relationship is a relationship between two Microsoft domains in which one of the domains trusts the other to perform authentication. The domain that trusts the other accepts logon requests for the users who exist in the other domain. The local domain controller forwards the logon requests to the trusted domain controller, which performs the authentication and returns the information to the trusting domain controller.

trusting domain A domain that assigns user permissions based on user account and group memberships in another domain it trusts.

tunneling Used to provide a secure connection to a private network across a public one. It works by encapsulating a network protocol within packets carried by the second network.

twisted pair Cable in which pairs of wires are twisted to reduce sensitivity to electronic noise.

U

unicast addresses TCP/IP addresses used for host-to-host communications. Unicast addresses are the most commonly used type of TCP/IP addresses.

universal group A universal group is a special type of group that exists in the global catalog and can span domains easily. Security groups should be used sparingly because they increase the interdomain replication. The universal group is available only in Native mode.

Universal Naming Convention (UNC) Naming convention used for defining a resource on a Windows 2000 server network.

update sequence number (USN) A number that is used on the domain controller to keep track of the number of updates the controller has made and that is on the object to keep track of the number of updates made to it. These numbers make multimaster replication possible.

user Users are obviously a big part of the network, and without them, the network would be pointless (though faster). A user object holds the user's account, and this enables the user to connect to the domain.

user (username) A user is a class of objects in the Active Directory database used to represent the people who will be able to log on and use resources from the network.

User Datagram Protocol (UDP) A connectionless protocol that is part of the TCP/IP suite. UDP is frequently used in broadcasts.

user process A user process is a process started by a user. The user's credentials are attached to the process to ensure that the process does not access information it should not access.

user profile A database that stores a user's personal computer settings so that the settings are available each time the user logs on.

user rights Privileges a user can exercise, such as the ability to log on locally, log on remotely, and shut down the computer.

User Principal Name (UPN) mapping Mapping a certificate to a user's principal name in Active Directory.

V

validity period The length of time the certificate is considered valid.

Variable Length Subnet Mask (VLSM) A subnet mask that is used either to split a large network into smaller pieces (subnetting) or to combine smaller networks into a larger one (supernetting).

virtual directory A directory visible from a Web site that does not have to be under the same directory tree as the rest of the site. It's configured separately.

virtual memory A technique for simulating RAM by swapping memory contents between RAM and disk-based files.

virtual private network (VPN) A mechanism for providing secure, private communications using a public network (such as the Internet) as the transport method. VPNs use a combination of encryption and authentication technologies to ensure data integrity and security.

virtual servers In most cases, Web sites get so little traffic that devoting an entire server to the Web site is a mistake. For most organizations that maintain multiple Web sites, using virtual servers is a way to maintain cost control.

volume A portion of one or more disk drives that can be formatted as a single storage unit. Volumes are usually identified by a drive letter from A to Z.

W

Web server A server that delivers a Web site by HTTP. Using IIS, a single computer can host multiple sites.

Web site A Web server can support multiple Web sites. Each Web site must be identified by a unique combination of an IP address and a port number.

Windows 2000 The current network operating system from Microsoft. Windows 2000 will eventually ship in four versions: Professional, Server, Advanced Server, and Data Center.

Windows 2000 Readiness Analyzer Checks the compatibility of hardware.

Windows File Protection A feature of Windows 2000 that identifies changes made to critical operating system files and enables the user to restore the original files.

Windows Installer Package The Windows Installer Package contains all the necessary information that the Windows Installer Service needs to install or remove an application. This includes the files required by the software, Registry and INI file changes that need to be made, any additional support files that are required, summary information on the package and application that can be shown to the user, and a reference to the location of the product files (that is, where to install the software from). The majority of this information is contained in a single file with an .MSI extension, which is the package file itself.

Windows Installer Service The Windows Installer Service is a service that is installed and runs on all Windows 2000 machines. This service facilitates the automated installation and deployment of software. It also provides the capability to automatically repair or modify existing applications in cases in which files are overwritten or removed.

Windows Internet Naming Service (WINS) A service that runs on a Windows 2000 server to provide NetBIOS name resolution. When you use WINS, name resolution is done using directed transmissions, resulting in a reduction in broadcast traffic and the capability to find systems on different subnets. WINS replaces the `LMHOSTS` file in a fashion similar to the way DNS replaced the `HOSTS` file.

Windows NT This is the previous version of Microsoft's network operating system. Windows NT Terminal Server Edition served as the foundation for the current Windows 2000.

winnt32.exe The setup/upgrade utility for Windows NT and Windows 2000.

WINS replication WINS servers use WINS replication to copy its database of names with other WINS servers.

workstation Workstation is the general term for a computer on a network. It is also the Windows 2000 service responsible for connecting to remote resources across the network.

X, Y

X.500 The X.500 standard is a theoretical standard that describes how to create and manage a hierarchical directory structure. Microsoft's Active Directory is loosely based on X.500.

xDSL Refers collectively to all types of digital subscriber lines (DSL). DSL technologies use sophisticated modulation schemes to pack data onto copper wires and are the main competitor to cable modems for providing high-speed Internet access to the home user.

Z

ZAP file The ZAP file is an ASCII text file created with any text editor (Notepad will work) and that specifies several things about the software to be installed, including the application name, the name of the setup, the program, any parameters to be used for setup, any file extensions to be associated with the application, the tech support Web site address, and so on. ZAP files are used to deploy software using a Group Policy for which no Windows Installer Package exists.

zone The zone, or zone file, is the group of resource records for a domain. Servers that have a copy of the zone file can service requests for authoritative answers about the system in the domain.

zone transfer This is the process of copying a zone file from a master server to a secondary server. This process is not used in Active Directory—integrated zones.

Index

Symbols

A

B

C

D

E

F

G

H

I

J-K-L

M

N

O

P

Q

R

S

T

U

V

W

X-Z